Catholic Social Thought

The Documentary Heritage

Edited by
David J. O'Brien
and
Thomas A. Shannon

Maryknoll, New York 10545

Fifth Printing, January 2016

Founded in 1970, Orbis Books endeavors to publish works that enlighten the mind, nourish the spirit, and challenge the conscience.The publishing arm of the Maryknoll Fathers and Brothers, Orbis seeks to explore the global dimensions of the Christian faith and mission, to invite dialogue with diverse cultures and religious traditions, and to serve the cause of reconciliation and peace.The books published reflect the views of their authors and do not represent the official position of the Maryknoll Society.To learn more about Maryknoll and Orbis Books, please visit our website at www.maryknollsociety.org.

Published by Orbis Books, Box 302, Maryknoll, NY 10545-0302.

2010 edition, ISBN 978-1-57075-891-1

Manufactured in the United States of America.

Library of Congress Cataloging-in-Publication Data

Catholic social thought : the documentary heritage / edited by David J. O'Brien and Thomas A. Shannon.
p. cm.
Includes index.
ISBN 0-88344-803-3 (hard)—ISBN 0-88344-787-8 (pbk.)
1. Sociology, Christian (Catholic)—Papal documents. 2. Peace—Religious aspects—Catholic Church. 3. Economics—Religious aspects—Catholic Church. 4. Catholic Church—United States—Bishops. 5. Catholic Church—Doctrines. I. O'Brien, David J. II. Shannon, Thomas A. (Thomas Anthony), 1940-
BX1753.C39 1992
261.8–dc20 92-3185
CIP

To the past and current members of the staff
of the Department of Social Development and World Peace
of the United States Catholic Conference,
and in particular to J. Bryan Hehir,
in gratitude for their untiring efforts on behalf
of the social mission of the Catholic church

Contents

Preface

Since 1978 when our previous collection of many of these documents, *Renewing the Earth* was published by Doubleday, a great deal has happened in the Roman Catholic Church. For one thing, Pope John Paul II deepened the theological and cultural foundations of Catholic social teaching. He also broadened its reach by his courage and truthfulness, commanding attention as he traveled the globe, moving among the powerful and the powerless. At the same time, the pope and his curia challenged some developments of Catholic social theology, particularly in Latin America; they even more forcefully attempted to control the application of Catholic teaching in concrete political contexts. Where once there was a more or less top down character to Catholic social teaching, as local churches and apostolic movements attempted to apply official doctrine to specific problems, there is now sharp debate, sometimes between Rome and local churches, about poverty and politics, about markets, economic growth, political pluralism, and many other issues.

Another major development since 1978 has been the vigorous development of American Catholic social thought, most notably in pastoral letters from the American bishops on such crucial subjects as racism, nuclear weapons and the economy. These pastorals make original contributions to the developing tradition, not only in their content but in their increasingly democratic method of preparation and presentation. They have won considerable attention not only within the church but in the larger society as well.

The centennial of *Rerum Novarum* in 1991 occasioned publication of a new collection of the basic documents, including the last social encyclical of Pope John Paul II, *Centesimus Annus*, and the major pastorals of the United States bishops. In this new edition, published in 2010, we have added the latest social encyclical by Pope Benedict XVI, while also rectifying the unfortunate omission from the earlier edition of the U.S. bishops' pastoral letter on racism, "Brothers and Sisters to Us."

In selecting documents we have tried to present the central elements of church teaching as well as contemporary appropriation. We have confined ourselves in this text to papal, conciliar, and North American documents, as the Latin American and other global materials are available elsewhere.

We continue to hope that these ideas will increasingly give purpose and vitality to the church in the United States. None has worked harder toward that end than the staff of the Department of Social Development and World Peace of the United States Catholic Conference, and its former, long-term director, Father J. Bryan Hehir, to whom we have dedicated this volume.

Introduction: Roman Catholic Social Teaching

The year 1991 marked the one-hundredth anniversary of the publication of Pope Leo XIII's great encyclical on social questions, *Rerum Novarum*. Leo's letter initially received only limited attention in the United States, as most educated Catholics, like other Americans, found little serious fault with the nation's economy. Later, during the progressive era of Theodore Roosevelt and Woodrow Wilson, a few Catholic reformers, led by John A. Ryan, drew on the encyclical to encourage Catholic support for social reform. This effort reached its climax with the publication, in the name of the hierarchy, of the quite radical "Bishops' Program of Social Reconstruction" in 1919.

In the 1930s, when the great depression shook popular confidence in American capitalism, a significant number of priests, religious, and lay people found support for union organizing, social action, and New Deal politics in Catholic social teaching, now supplemented by Pope Pius XI's 1931 encyclical *Quadragesimo Anno*. Influenced by Ryan, the bishops championed the cause of reform while America's largely blue-collar Catholics became solid backers of unions, moderate social welfare programs, and measured government intervention in the marketplace, what came to be called "bread and butter" liberalism.

Nevertheless, the encyclicals of Leo XIII and Pius XI were too rigid in their theology, too rooted in preindustrial and to some degree antidemocratic ideologies to be directly useful to Americans, at least without the drastic shifts provided by interpreters like Ryan. With Pope Pius XII's endorsement of democracy and human rights, and especially with publication of Pope John XXIII's *Mater et Magistra* in 1961, that began to change. The teachings of Pope John XXIII, the Second Vatican Council, Pope Paul VI, and Pope John Paul II have much in common with those of the earlier popes, but they are informed by more flexible approaches to scripture and tradition and by a more positive assessment of the modern world. Leo XIII and Pius XI were filled with charity and passion for justice, but these qualities were smothered by triumphalist ecclesiology, antidemocratic political values, and a conservative, even negative understanding of natural law. The modern documents, in contrast, communicate a vision of the church as servant to humanity, a renewed concern for the human person and human rights, an increasing emphasis on popular participation, and a more open and humble acknowledgment of the historically conditioned character of human life and consciousness. The social teachings of the modern church also reflect the ideas and perspectives of the emerging Christian communities of the Third World. Still somewhat

European-centered, the documents are nonetheless far more universal in origin, spirit, scope, and impact than ever before.

HISTORICAL BACKGROUND

Catholic social teaching, like everything else Christian, begins with the person and message of Jesus. Jesus offered no specific economic message, of course; instead, he proclaimed the advent of the kingdom of God and the redemption of people from sin. The toil and suffering that marked the lives of most people, especially the poor, was not the ultimate reality. There was another, superior reality of grace and redemption, joy and love. The life, death, and resurrection of Jesus confirmed this message and thus offered new meaning, a new vision of history and of human possibility. That good news, carried haphazardly by a remnant of quarrelling people, gave form and substance to humanity's dreams in a considerable portion of the world.

Still, the turbulent life of Christ's followers over two millennia demonstrates that his legacy was at least ambiguous. For believers, the kingdom of God had indeed arrived, yet even the most committed experienced its new life only imperfectly. The kingdom was present and the Holy Spirit continued Christ's work, yet in some sense the kingdom was not yet here but beckoned from the future. Jesus had taught his followers to pray that God's kingdom would come on earth, yet he also taught that his kingdom was not of this world but somehow apart from it. Today, as in the days following Christ's ascension to the Father, Christians live amid the mysteries of human life, knowing God as "through a glass darkly," trying to live by Christ's teachings completely, here and now, and at the same time trying to live as responsible workers and citizens. Then as now it is no simple matter.

The early Christian community expected the Lord to return quickly. As a result they practiced a heroic ethic of uncompromising love, which allowed no adjustment to the demands of worldly life. But as Christianity spread through the Mediterranean world, millennial enthusiasm waned. With more members, the church drew closer to the society around it but kept its zeal for equality and justice to itself. Christians cared for one another and for the Christian poor, practicing a charity whose purpose was not to heal social wrongs but to awaken and express a spirit of love. There was no perception that Christians could or should make a specific contribution to the larger society. Although hope for the early arrival of the kingdom had faded, its anticipation still separated Christians from the temptations and responsibilities of ordinary economic and political life.

By the time Christianity became the official religion of the empire, however, its new responsibilities had necessarily modified its earlier sectarianism. Primitive communism of property, for example, gave eloquent testimony to the equality of all believers, but such ideas could breed explosive social discontent. The subjection of property to religious authority and the denunciation of the rich, as in St. Ambrose's charge "it is greed that has engendered the rights of property," had to be toned down once Christianity assumed responsibility for social order. Private property and coercive human authority, it was argued, were required by God as a consequence of sin. Indeed, it increasingly appeared that the social order that existed had been ordained by God, so that discontent could only arise from sinful pride and selfishness. An organic social theory, strengthened by emerging ideas of natural law, provided a firm foundation for the specification by the church of rules governing social and economic activity, rules adapted to a society and economy oriented toward the efficient distribution of scarce resources.

Medieval Catholic social thought reflected this shift from a community focused on its own expression of love to one which shared responsibility for the preservation of civilization. In the work of St. Thomas Aquinas, Christianity found a synthesis that could embrace both the radical demands of the primitive gospel and the pressing responsibilities of a religious establishment. Aquinas defined society as a system of mutual exchange of services for the common good. Society and government were part of nature, operating according to laws that reflected the universal structure of creation. Before the fall, harmony existed among persons, nature, and God; no laws or government were needed. After the fall, they were needed to regulate the community and restrain evil. This understanding of society fit into a two-story model of the universe; the first story the created world, now in a state of sin, the second the supernatural order, the goal and fulfillment of the natural world.

Eternal law existed in the mind of God from all eternity. Natural law was the apprehension of eternal law by human reason, in theory capable of knowing God's will and acting on it, but in practice flawed by sin. The state was both a punishment and a remedy for sin; it provided for the common good, most notably by the repression of evil. The church, of divine origin, possesses revealed truth and directs people and institutions to their final, supernatural end.

The church is therefore superior to the state; it interprets the demands of natural law and imposes sanctions on both institutions and individuals. Some, called by God to a special vocation, practice the heroic virtues demanded by the gospel, while church and state cooperate to enforce more moderate, realistic moral demands on society at large.

The person thus stands at the center of two intersecting lines, the natural and supernatural, united through the eternal and natural law and through the church and the state. On this basis Aquinas envisioned an organically unified universe in which there were transcendent norms to assist in understanding and evaluating human experience. There was in this universe a proper ordering of all things and harmony within and among the several orders. Individuals occupied particular roles or functions within a hierarchical society. They were bound to one another and to social institutions by duties inherent in their state of life. What held society together and gave it ethical discipline and coherence was a theory of social obligation that sprang from the very nature of society and was related to a hierarchical universe presided over by God. Social obligations thus took priority over individual desires and wants.

After 1100 the economy of Western Europe entered upon a period of significant expansion, and the tension between the gospel ethic and social responsibility reappeared with renewed force. The money economy, the growing importance of trade, and vigorous competition all challenged the harmonious organic theories of the earlier era. Gradually, as conflicts sharpened, radical alternatives appeared. Exponents of primitive gospel simplicity, like Francis of Assisi, denounced the materialism of the towns and the arrogance of their merchant leaders, while religious apologists for the new classes bent gospel injunctions and ecclesiastical prescriptions in order to justify new economic activities. The later Middle Ages were thus a time of ferment occasioned by the growing chasm between Christianity and economic practice. Unfortunately the church was deeply involved in the economic developments of the era; it was an economic institution of prime importance, encouraging trade, acquiring enormous debts, engaging itself in trade, investment, and profit. Its theologians and religious leaders struggled to reconcile this vigorous economic activity with the teachings of Jesus, sometimes in creative ethical formulations, at other times in expedient compromise.

In this setting the Reformation churches arose, finding their strength in the major centers of economic modernization. It was natural for later observers to associate Protestantism with the supposedly new spirit of capitalism. Yet Protestantism's social ethic represented the reawakening of older tensions within the Christian tradition. For example, Protestantism, and especially Calvinism, rejected completely the otherworldly asceticism of Catholic religious communities. No one was to live as a hermit or monk, but everyone was to live a life of disciplined self-control and mystical piety. Theirs was a worldly asceticism, carried into the marketplace, where one was to do one's duty to God, to family, and to community, always with the inner life oriented completely toward God.

Similarly, the reformers creatively recovered and revised ancient Christian ideas of vocation, or calling, and stewardship, and they did so within an understanding of Christian society that still supposed an integration of religion and culture, church and state. Perhaps most important, one of the major consequences of the breakup of the medieval unity of civilization was the perception that individuals stood in an adversary relationship to the larger society, a perception which, together with the opportunity for choice presented by contending religious factions, fostered a deeper sense of individual autonomy and personal worth. As a result of this new perception of the individual's place in society, a new theory of the proper relationship between the individual and society was needed.

This was provided over several centuries by the elaboration of contract theories of society, the most famous associated with Hobbes and Locke. While presenting diametrically opposed pictures of human nature, both theories emphasized individual rights as claims against society, and both looked at the individual as the bearer of certain rights that society should not contravene.

This articulation of a theory of rights created a major change in social ethics. On the one hand, there was continuity with the medieval tradition in that contract theories were related to natural law understood as articulations of the demands of a permanent and universal moral order. On the other hand, there was discontinuity with medieval philosophy in that this theory of natural law based itself on inalienable rights inherent in each individual, with social and political obligations arising not from nature but from voluntary consent, even if exercised only in a mythic past. The implication of this was that forms of social organization were mutable and arbitrary, not dictated by the content of natural law. The value of the individual person was enhanced, because the individual, not society, became the locus of natural law.

In medieval formulations obligation was associated with one's state in life. In the contract framework, obligations resulted from positive law agreed upon by individuals. This gave rise to a situation in which there could be continual and inherent conflict between individuals and society. Such conflicts in fact appeared, first in churches, later in society, climaxing in the modern revolutions. For Catholics whose social thought and imagination remained grounded in premodern assumptions about individuals and institutions, the experience was one of rebellion against all authority, human and divine. Again and again the Catholic church faced a choice of adapting to new ideas of individual autonomy and popular participation, and almost always it chose to assert the need for order and hierarchy backed by a divinely constituted authority capable of announcing and enforcing the demands of nature and nature's God. This tension between modernity—in religion, culture, and politics—and the Catholic church provides the basic context for the emergence of Catholic social thought a century ago.

ON READING THE TEXTS

Introductory statements appended to the documents in this text describe how Leo XIII, faced with new challenges posed by industrial capitalism, drew on this heritage and initiated modern Catholic social teaching. As this historical review indicates, no element of the contemporary church's social teaching can be fully understood apart from the fuller body of teaching and belief on which it draws, a teaching that from the start has been torn between sectarian idealism and responsible moderation. To take but one example: Advocates of one or another of the modern church's positions on peace and human rights are often concerned primarily with the prophetic integrity of the church's witness and miss the broader "Catholic" dimensions of the teaching, its century-long effort to unify the church and enable it to exert a significant influence upon society as a whole. Critics who charge that church teaching on specific issues is too idealistic, in contrast, often miss the need for the church to preserve its prophetic integrity, to take the risk of separation from other communities in order to be faithful to its mandate to be the very presence of Christ in the midst of history.

Yet it is precisely the effort to be *both* prophetic and responsible that distinguishes Catholic social teaching and makes it so significant in the modern world. The church as a whole is trying to be both idealistic and realistic because that is what it is called to be, and it is what all persons must try to be if humanity is to overcome its apparently insurmountable problems. To put it most simply, if men and women do not believe that it is possible to live in justice and peace, they will slip ever deeper into a fatalism that only confirms the drift of events toward greater tragedy. If, on the other hand, they only dream of justice and peace and avoid the hard and ambiguous choices that people, nations, and the human community confront, they will just as surely contribute to the triumph of historical forces beyond human control.

Too often in recent years idealists and realists within the church have spent their energies combatting each other rather than confronting the problems both recognize. Familiarity with the social teaching of the church since 1891 might enable them to recognize the unity of that teaching in its foundations in Christian faith as well as the legitimate diversity it allows. Most of all, it might enable them to see that both sides need each other, that the prophet and the politician both are necessary to the full witness of the church.

The tension between the gospel and social analysis thus remains at the heart of Catholic social teaching. Even the simplest reflection on the beatitudes forces two conclusions: 1) that Christians are called to an ethic of perfection by the revelation in Christ of a God who is love; and 2) that the church and its members must respond to that vocation in the midst of a history in which real, complex human beings live. It is not a simple matter to be both a good Christian and a good citizen, any more than it is simple to be the church and to share responsibility for the problems of a pluralistic society. The documents collected in this volume reflect this ever present tension and pervasive ambiguity. So it is simply wrong to abstract any one statement or issue from the context of the overall teaching, for it is precisely that larger framework of integrity and responsibility which is the unique contribution of Catholic social teaching. If this is true, then certain conclusions follow:

1) The contemporary documents need to be examined in light of the continuing historical effort to relate Christian faith to the problems of modern society, that is, to Catholic theology broadly understood.

2) The documents need to be examined as well in the context of the overall life of the contemporary church; these teachings are one, but only one, important expression of Catholic faith and life. They can be understood and evaluated only in relation to other expressions of Catholicism, from the spiritual lives of individuals through the worship and fellowship of congregations to the ongoing development of Catholic theology.

3) The documents are best read and evaluated from the viewpoint of the laity. More than other formal documents of the church, these are located at the intersection of the church and the world, the sacred and the secular. Of their very nature they deal with the problems of living the Christian life in the midst

of ordinary human relationships. Individuals who devote their lives to the organizations of the church, of course, have something to contribute to the implementation of these teachings. But as the Second Vatican Council affirmed, social, political and economic problems are the special concern of the laity. They are uniquely qualified to describe what in fact is going on and to evaluate what should be done. In the past there has been too little effort to consult the laity in the development of these teachings, too little effort to ask lay people what they think before telling them what to do. Given the situation of the church in the modern world, and given the experience of all local churches since the Second Vatican Council, it is clear that this will no longer be acceptable, if it ever was. It is the laity who must reshape the course of history. It is they who must act and, if they are to act, they will have to be more fully enlisted in the process that determines what that action should be. Of course there are elements of faith which for Catholics evoke the unique charisma of the hierarchy; but it is not hard to determine in these documents where such matters of doctrine end and more complex matters of applied theology, including morality, begin. At that point the laity have the right, and indeed the obligation, to speak up and to act.

One final thought: Pope Paul VI argued that papal and conciliar social teaching, addressed to the universal church, was necessarily general and somewhat abstract. It remained for the local churches of the world to examine the situations of their own countries and regions, reflect on that situation in light of the gospel and the teaching of the church, and develop their own conclusions and directions for action. It is from such a process that liberation theologies have emerged, first in Latin America and now in Africa, Asia, and elsewhere. The United States pastoral letters represent an expression of that process as well. The bishops, in preparing those letters, did their best to inform themselves about the concrete problems present in the United States, to reflect on those problems in light of faith and previous teachings, and to suggest conclusions to guide the American church and to contribute to the larger public dialogue in the United States.

Students of these documents have the same obligation. Those who make these teachings their own must not only be familiar with the theological foundations of the teaching but also with the concrete realities to which they refer. The Christian, in other words, must not only be an informed Christian, familiar with church teaching, but also an informed citizen, familiar with his or her community, nation, and world. John A. Ryan, one of the greatest American Catholic social thinkers, once expressed his confidence that most priests would agree with the principles of the church's social teaching; what worried him was that too many would be unfamiliar with what was going on in political and economic life, that they would not know what they were talking about. Ryan's is a warning to all of us that sincere faith and familiarity with what popes and bishops say must always be combined with an alertness to what is going on around us and a willingness to inform ourselves about public life.

In the end, these documents are valuable to the degree they are taken seriously enough to engage the reader in dialogue about social and political responsibility. When that dialogue results in authentic commitment to building a more just and peaceful world, then the church has been the presence of Christ as it wants to be. May readers bring to these texts open minds, compassionate hearts, and critical skills.

Part I

The Classic Texts of Leo XIII and Pius XI

INTRODUCTION

Modern Catholic social thought emerged from an effort to confront transforming historical events with a reaffirmation of divine purpose and human responsibility. During the eighteenth and nineteenth centuries basic social, economic, and political changes in Western Europe undermined the whole system of Christian civilization on which traditional religious identification depended. Industrialization, nationalism, political and cultural freedom, and a bewildering variety of pluralisms were bound to influence most severely the Catholic church, which in the aftermath of the Reformation had linked its fortunes closely with the old order. In the urban, industrial society enchanted by new ideals of freedom, science, and progress, the church was perceived as essentially irrelevant. The church saw that perception as arising from a revolt against God. But, by confusing faith with the forms of a particular culture, the church had helped transform the Enlightenment's emancipation of the critical intellect into an anti-Christian secularism and the French Revolution's drive for civil freedom into a virulent anticlericalism.

The issues sharpened at the end of the eighteenth century when the church decided to become an ally of order and authority, forcing liberals to defend both their religious and social orthodoxy. The predominantly negative character of Catholic thought in the nineteenth century did not imply that Catholics were not concerned about the problems raised by the industrial and political revolutions, only that this concern was limited by ecclesiastical interest and doctrinal discipline. Catholic thinkers located the source of modern problems in secularism, particularly in the divorce of political authority from its divine foundations and the separation of economic life from moral and ethical influence. Excessive individualism had destroyed the rich group life of the Christian era and left ordinary people at the mercy of the absolute state and irresponsible capitalists. Catholic leaders differed on short-term strategies, but they almost all agreed that contemporary problems could be overcome by a restoration of organic unity and direction of modern life through the reconciliation of society and culture with the church.

In France the work of DeMaistre and Bonald provided a framework for the reactionary policies of the Restoration papacy and the Catholic monarchical party. Their clear recognition of the contrasts between the organic, hierarchical character of Catholic social philosophy and the egalitarian individualism of the revolution laid a foundation for antiliberal thought, a process in which Lamennais shared. But he and his followers emphasized with equal clarity the positive values of the revolution and pointed to a solution of the church's problems based on freedom and consent. Most disputes centered on relations between church and state; only a few individuals, like Frederic Ozanam and Charles de Coux, recognized the importance of changes in economic life. Ozanam especially anticipated much of later Catholic thought by his advocacy of a living wage and the right of workers to organize, although his major efforts were devoted to charitable activity aimed at the alleviation of misery and the easing of class hatreds.

Organized efforts by French Catholics to achieve specifically Christian reforms dated from the advent of the Third Republic. The Comte de La Tour du Pin and Comte Albert de Mun organized workers and employers in study clubs under aristocratic patronage. These "workers' circles" were designed to end class division and overcome the divorce of social and economic life from Christian principles. The objective of the founders was a restoration of the medieval economic order, with joint bodies of capital and labor eventually becoming constituents of government in a monarchical framework. A third figure in the movement, Leon Harmel, was unsympathetic with La Tour du Pin's legitimism and paternalism and instead aimed to develop working-class leadership, cooperatives, and copartnership arrangements that would give the workers a sense of responsibility and a real participation in decision-making in industrial society. But such visionary, if reactionary, reformers were few. More Catholics agreed with economist Charles Perrin that the church should accept the prevailing order, oppose labor organization and all but the most minimal forms of social legislation, and forget about any return to medieval corporatism.

In Germany the church found itself from mid-century defending itself against the nationalism that climaxed in the formation of the Prussian-dominated empire. Thereafter German Catholics, while sympathetic to revolutionary corporatism, practically adopted a more moderate reformism than was common elsewhere. The pioneer of German social Catholicism, Bishop Emmanuel von Ketteler of Mainz, believed that a revised guild organization of workers and owners, inspired by Christian principles, would restore the institutions liberalism had destroyed. He opposed state initiation of such a system both because of the consequences for state power and the necessity for a cooperative spirit and ethic as a prerequisite for the guild society. However, recognizing the impossibility of establishing a corporate social order in the near future, Ketteler, without abandoning his theoretical objective, gradually turned to state action to alleviate immediate economic abuses. Acutely aware of the responsibility of Christians to work for immediate alleviation of suffering and injustice, Ketteler eventually supported industrial legislation and trade unionism, the only methods by which the causes of poverty and insecurity could be eliminated in the reasonably near future. Not incidentally, such reforms might also attract working-class voters to the Center Party, which was the church's protector in German politics.

Rerum Novarum: The Condition of Labor (Leo XIII, 1891)

INTRODUCTION

When one considers the background out of which *Rerum Novarum* emerged, it is a wonder that the document was written at all. The nineteenth century began and ended amid hostility toward the Roman Catholic Church. Anticlerical movements fueled the fires of an already heated nationalism, leading to conflict with the church in many countries. In Italy this led to the loss of the Papal States in 1870.

There were also the struggles over the relations between the newly emerging and quite powerful states and the church. Historically, the Roman Catholic Church had been the established church of most of these countries or, after the Protestant Reformation, had had its relations with the rulers clarified by concordats. The issue now confronting the church was to understand the new reality of a secular state, in theory neutral to all religions, though such neutrality was not always practical; one thinks of the German *Kulturkampf*, for example.

In addition, the ideas of Marx and Darwin challenged the church. The thought of Marx had the more immediate and dramatic impact because of the rise of various revolutionary movements, but the impact of the concept of evolution and change was to have profound epistemological significance for both society and church.

Finally, there was the Industrial Revolution, begun in the factories of Britain, then rapidly spreading throughout Western Europe. While this revolution was most significant for the lower classes, no one escaped its effects. The shift from the land to the city caused massive social dislocation compounded by a lack of housing, and left millions unemployed. The shift from the home to the factory led to miserly wages, deplorable working conditions, particularly for children, and severe strains on families. While the social effects of this revolution were particularly keen in England, few cities in Europe or America escaped. The seeds of discontent sown by this movement found fertile ground in radical social movements, most of which regarded the church as allied with the enemy.

The world of 1891 did not seem friendly to Catholicism. With Pius IX having died a "prisoner of the Vatican," surrounded by all manner of political, economic, and social upheavals, few held high hopes for bold initiatives from his successor, Leo XIII. How much more powerful a message, then, *Rerum Novarum* is, seen against this background.

In *Rerum Novarum*, written in 1891, Leo attempted to persuade Catholics to concentrate less on politics and more on the "social question." At times his appeal sounds quite radical, reviving the earlier emphasis on the evangelical mission on behalf of the poor. But the goal was still the restoration of order and authority, and that precluded enthusiasm, class preference, or labor militancy. In his last years Leo felt constrained to issue many warnings to his subjects to show due respect for civil and ecclesiastical powers.

In the Leonine corpus, individual and social considerations blended happily together, but in the world things were quite different. In a remarkably even-handed manner the pope laid anathemas on both liberal capitalism, which released the individual from social and moral constraints, and socialism, which subordinated individual liberty to social well-being without respect for human rights or religious welfare. Economic life, like political life, should reflect the dualistic nature of the person, Leo argued, providing for bodily needs and facilitating the quest for salvation. It was a strong position from which to condemn wage slavery. Leo insisted that wages be determined not by economic considerations alone, but by taking into account the basic needs of the individual. Property, too, was subject to social and moral restraints; while all had a right to possess private property, none had the right to use that property without reference to the needs of the community. Leo insisted that the moral-law—based on a rational understanding of human nature supplemented by revelation—had to be part of every economic system and indeed of every economic transaction. The criteria given by that law were justice, demanding equity in exchange and bargaining; balance between various economic sectors; and organization of the constituent economic units. More generally, justice demanded that the common good of the community take precedence over individual gain in determining economic policy, without, however, necessarily infringing on legitimate rights. This in turn suggested a wider concept of economic organization and governance, later developed by Pius XI.

Finally, and most important, Leo initiated modern Catholic discussion of human rights in the economic order. The claim to a right to a living wage opened a bridge across which Catholics might travel to engage, perhaps even befriend, those hostile social movements. But if that journey was to take place, Leo warned, it should be guided by the church and its pastors. Catholics should dream of new things, but be cautious in bringing those dreams to life.

RERUM NOVARUM

ENCYCLICAL LETTER OF OUR HOLY FATHER
BY DIVINE PROVIDENCE
POPE LEO XIII

ON

THE CONDITION OF LABOR

To Our Venerable Brethren, All Patriarchs, Primates,
Archbishops and Bishops of the Catholic World,
In Grace and Communion with the Apostolic See,

POPE LEO XIII

Venerable Brethren,
Health and Apostolic Benediction

1. It is not surprising that the spirit of revolutionary change, which has long been predominant in the nations of the world, should have passed beyond politics and made its influence felt in the cognate field of practical economy. The elements of a conflict are unmistakable: the growth of industry, and the surprising discoveries of science; the changed relations of masters and workmen; the enormous fortunes of individuals and the poverty of the masses; the increased self-reliance and the closer mutual combination of the working population; and, finally, a general moral deterioration. The momentous seriousness of the present state of things just now fills every mind with painful apprehension; wise men discuss it; practical men propose schemes; popular meetings, legislatures, and sovereign princes, all are occupied with it—and there is nothing which has a deeper hold on public attention.

Therefore, venerable brethren, as on former occasions, when it seemed opportune to refute false teaching, we have addressed you in the interests of the Church and of the commonwealth, and have issued letters on political power, on human liberty, on the Christian constitution of the State, and on similar subjects, so now we have thought it useful to speak on.

THE CONDITION OF LABOR

It is a matter on which we have touched once or twice already. But in this letter the responsibility of the apostolic office urges us to treat the question expressly and at length, in order that there may be no mistake as to the principles which truth and justice dictate for its settlement. The discussion is not easy, nor is it free from danger. It is not easy to define the relative rights and the mutual duties of the wealthy and of the poor, of capital and of labor. And the danger lies in this, that crafty agitators constantly make use of these disputes to pervert men's judgments and to stir up the people to sedition.

2. But all agree, and there can be no question whatever, that some remedy must be found, and quickly found, for the misery and wretchedness which press so heavily at this moment on the large majority of the very poor. The ancient workmen's guilds were destroyed in the last century, and no other organization took their place. Public institutions and the laws have repudiated the ancient religion. Hence by degrees it has come to pass that workingmen have been given over, isolated and defenseless, to the callousness of employers and the greed of unrestrained competition. The evil has been increased by rapacious usury, which, although more than once condemned by the Church, is nevertheless, under a different form but with the same guilt, still practiced by avaricious and grasping men. And to this must be added the custom of working by contract, and the concentration of so many branches of trade in the hands of a few individuals, so that a small number of very rich men have been able to lay upon the masses of the poor a yoke little better than slavery itself.

3. To remedy these evils the *socialists*, working on the poor man's envy of the rich, endeavor to destroy private property, and maintain that individual possessions should become the common property of all, to be administered by the State or by municipal bodies. They hold that, by thus transferring property from private persons to the community, the present evil state of things will be set to rights, because each citizen will then have his equal share of whatever there is to enjoy. But their proposals are so clearly futile for all practical purposes, that if they were carried out the workingman himself would be among the first to suffer. Moreover they are emphatically unjust, because they would rob the lawful possessor, bring the State into a sphere that is not its own, and cause complete confusion in the community.

PRIVATE OWNERSHIP

4. It is surely undeniable that, when a man engages in remunerative labor, the very reason and motive of his work is to obtain property, and to hold it as his own private possession. If one man hires out to another his strength or his industry, he does this for the purpose of receiving in return what is necessary for food and living; he thereby expressly proposes to acquire a full and real right, not only to the remuneration, but also to the disposal of that remuneration as he pleases. Thus, if he lives sparingly, saves money, and invests his savings, for greater security, in land, the land in such a case is only his wages in another form; and, consequently, a workingman's little estate thus purchased should be as completely at his own disposal as the wages he receives for his labor. But it is precisely in this power of disposal that ownership consists,

whether the property be land or movable goods. The *socialists*, therefore, in endeavoring to transfer the possessions of individuals to the community, strike at the interests of every wage earner, for they deprive him of the liberty of disposing of his wages, and thus of all hope and possibility of increasing his stock and of bettering his condition in life.

5. What is of still greater importance, however, is that the remedy they propose is manifestly against justice. For every man has by nature the right to possess property as his own. This is one of the *chief points of distinction* between man and the animal creation. For the brute has no power of self-direction, but is governed by two chief instincts, which keep his powers alert, move him to use his strength, and determine him to action without the power of choice. These instincts are self-preservation and the propagation of the species. Both can attain their purpose by means of things which are close at hand; beyond their surroundings the brute creation cannot go, for they are moved to action by sensibility alone, and by the things which sense perceives. But with man it is different indeed. He possesses, on the one hand, the full perfection of animal nature, and therefore he enjoys, at least, as much as the rest of the animal race, the fruition of the things of the body. But animality, however perfect, is far from being the whole of humanity, and is indeed humanity's humble handmaid, made to serve and obey. It is the mind, or the reason, which is the chief thing in us who are human beings; it is this which makes a human being human, and distinguishes him essentially and completely from the brute. And on this account—namely, that man alone among animals possesses reason—it must be within his right to have things not merely for temporary and momentary use, as other living beings have them, but in stable and permanent possession; he must have not only things which perish in the using, but also those which, though used, remain for use in the future.

THE POWER OF REASON

6. This becomes still more clearly evident if we consider man's nature a little more deeply. For man, comprehending by the power of his reason, things innumerable, and joining the future with the present—being, moreover, the master of his own acts—governs himself by the foresight of his counsel, under the eternal law and the power of God, whose Providence governs all things. Wherefore it is in his power to exercise his choice not only on things which regard his present welfare, but also on those which will be for his advantage in time to come. Hence man can possess not only the fruits of the earth, but also the earth itself; for of the products of the earth he can make provision for the future. Man's needs do not die out, but recur; satisfied today, they demand new supplies tomorrow. Nature, therefore, owes to man a storehouse that shall never fail, the daily supply of his daily wants. And this he finds only in the inexhaustible fertility of the earth.

Nor must we, at this stage, have recourse to the State. Man is older than the State, and he holds the right of providing for the life of his body prior to the formation of any State.

7. And to say that God has given the earth to the use and enjoyment of the universal human race is not to deny that there can be private property. For God has granted the earth to mankind in general; not in the sense that all without distinction can deal with it as they please, but rather that no part of it has been assigned to any one in particular, and that the limits of private possession have been left to be fixed by man's own industry and the laws of individual peoples. Moreover, the earth, though divided among private owners, ceases not thereby to minister to the needs of all; for there is no one who does not live on what the land brings forth. Those who do not possess the soil, contribute their labor; so that it may be truly said that all human subsistence is derived either from labor on one's own land, or from some laborious industry which is paid either in the produce of the land itself or in that which is exchanged for what the land brings forth.

THE LAW OF NATURE

Here, again, we have another proof that private ownership is according to nature's law. For that which is required for the preservation of life and for life's well-being is produced in great abundance by the earth, but not until man has brought it into cultivation and lavished upon it his care and skill. Now, when man thus spends the industry of his mind and the strength of his body in procuring the fruits of nature by that act he makes his own that portion of nature's field which he cultivates—that portion on which he leaves, as it were, the impress of his own personality, and it cannot but be just that he should possess that portion as his own, and should have a right to keep it without molestation.

8. These arguments are so strong and convincing that it seems surprising that certain obsolete opinions should now be revived in opposition to what is here laid down. We are told that it is right for private persons to have the use of the soil and the fruits of their land, but that it is unjust for anyone to possess as owner either the land on which he has built or the estate which he has cultivated. But those who assert this do not perceive that they are robbing man of what his own labor has produced. For the soil which is tilled and cultivated with toil and skill utterly changes its condition; it was wild before, it is now fruitful; it was barren, and now it brings forth in abundance. That which has thus altered and improved it becomes so truly a part of itself as to be in a great measure indistinguishable, inseparable from it. Is it just that the fruit of a man's sweat and labor should be enjoyed by another? As effects follow their cause, so it is just and right that the results of labor should belong to him who has labored.

With reason, therefore, the common opinions of mankind, little affected by the few dissentients who have maintained the opposite view, has found in the study of nature, and in the law of nature herself, the foundations of the division of property, and has consecrated by the practice of all ages the principle of private ownership, as being preeminently in conformity with human nature, and as conducing in the most unmistakable manner to the peace and tranquillity of human life. The same principle is confirmed and enforced by the civil laws—laws which, as long as they are just, derive their binding force from the law of nature. The authority of the divine law adds its sanction, forbidding us in the gravest terms even to covet that which is another's: "Thou shalt not covet thy neighbor's wife; nor his house, nor his field, nor his man-servant, nor his maid-servant, nor his ox, nor his ass, nor anything which is his."[1]

A FAMILY RIGHT

9. The rights here spoken of belonging to each individual man are seen in a much stronger light if they are considered in relation to man's social and domestic obligations.

In choosing a state of life, it is indisputable that all are at full liberty either to follow the counsel of Jesus Christ as to virginity, or to enter into the bonds of marriage. No human law can abolish the natural and primitive right of marriage, or in any way limit the chief and principal purpose of marriage, ordained by God's authority from the beginning. "Increase and multiply."[2] Thus we have the family; the "society" of a man's own household; a society limited indeed in numbers, but a true "society," anterior to every kind of State or nation, with rights and duties of its own, totally independent of the commonwealth.

That right of property, therefore, which has been proved to belong naturally to individual persons must also belong to a man in his capacity of head of a family; nay, such a person must possess this right so much the more clearly in proportion as his position multiplies his duties.

10. For it is a most sacred law of nature that a father must provide food and all necessaries for those whom he has begotten; and, similarly, nature dictates that a man's children, who carry on, as it were, and continue his own personality, should be provided by him with all that is needful to enable them honorably to keep themselves from want and misery in the uncertainties of this mortal life. Now, in no other way can a father effect this except by the ownership of profitable property, which he can transmit to his children by inheritance. A family, no less than a State, is, as we have said, a true society, governed by a power within itself, that is to say, by the father. Wherefore, provided the limits be not transgressed which are prescribed by the very purposes for which it exists, the family has, at least, equal rights with the State in the choice and pursuit of these things which are needful to its preservation and its just liberty.

We say, at least equal rights; for since the domestic household is anterior both in idea and in fact to the gathering of men into a commonwealth, the former must necessarily have rights and duties which are prior to those of the latter, and which rest more immediately on nature. If the citizens of a State—that is to say, the families—on entering into association and fellowship, experienced at the hands of the State hindrance instead of help, and found their rights attacked instead of being protected, such associations were rather to be repudiated than sought after.

SOCIALISM REJECTED

11. The idea, then, that the civil government should, at its own discretion, penetrate and pervade the family and the household, is a great and pernicious mistake. True, if a family finds itself in great difficulty, utterly friendless, and without prospect for help, it is right that extreme necessity be met by public aid; for each family is a part of the commonwealth. In like manner, if within the walls of the household there occur grave disturbance of mutual rights, the public power must interfere to force each party to give the other what is due; for this is not to rob citizens of their rights, but justly and properly to safeguard and strengthen them. But the rulers of the State must go no further: nature bids them stop here. Paternal authority can neither be abolished by the State nor absorbed; for it has the same source as human life itself; "the child belongs to the father," and is, as it were, the continuation of the father's personality; and, to speak with strictness, the child takes its place in civil society not in its own right, but in its quality as a member of the family in which it is begotten. And it is for the very reason that "the child belongs to the father," that, as St. Thomas Aquinas says, "before it attains the use of free will, it is in the power and care of its parents."[3] The socialists, therefore, in setting aside the parent and introducing the providence of the State, *act against natural justice*, and threaten the very existence of family life.

12. And such interference is not only unjust, but is quite certain to harass and disturb all classes of citizens, and to subject them to odious and intolerable slavery. It would open the door to envy, to evil speaking, and to quarreling; the sources of wealth would themselves run dry, for no one would have any interest in exerting his talents or his industry; and that ideal equality of which so much is said would, in reality, be the leveling down of all to the same condition of misery and dishonor.

Thus it is clear *that the main tenet of socialism, the community of goods, must be utterly rejected*; for it would injure those whom it is intended to benefit, it would be contrary to the natural rights of mankind, and it would introduce confusion and disorder into the commonwealth. Our first and most fundamental principle, therefore, when we undertake to alleviate the condition of the masses, must be the inviolability of private property. This laid down, we go on to show where we must find the remedy that we seek.

THE CHURCH IS NECESSARY

13. We approach the subject with confidence, and in the exercise of the rights which belong to us. For no practical solution of this question will ever be found without the assistance of religion and the Church. It is we who are the chief guardian of religion, and the chief dispenser of what belongs to the

Church, and we must not by silence neglect the duty which lies upon us. Doubtless this most serious question demands the attention and the efforts of others besides ourselves—of the rulers of States, of employers of labor, of the wealthy, and of the working population themselves for whom we plead. But we affirm without hesitation that all the striving of men will be vain if they leave out the Church. It is the Church that proclaims from the Gospel those teachings by which the conflict can be brought to an end, or at least made far less bitter; the Church uses its efforts not only to enlighten the mind, but to direct by its precepts the life and conduct of men; the Church improves and ameliorates the condition of the workingman by numerous useful organizations; does its best to enlist the services of all ranks in discussing and endeavoring to meet, in the most practical way, the claims of the working classes; and acts on the decided view that for these purposes recourse should be had, in due measure and degree, with the help of the law and of State authority.

14. Let it be laid down, in the first place, that humanity must remain as it is. It is impossible to reduce human society to a level. The *socialists* may do their utmost, but all striving against nature is vain. There naturally exist among mankind innumerable differences of the most important kind; people differ in capability, in diligence, in health, and in strength; and unequal fortune is a necessary result of inequality in condition. Such inequality is far from being disadvantageous either to individuals or to the community; social and public life can only go on by the help of various kinds of capacity and the playing of many parts, and each man, as a rule, chooses the part which peculiarly suits his case. As regards bodily labor, even had man never fallen from the state of innocence, he would not have been wholly unoccupied; but that which would then have been his free choice, his delight, became afterwards compulsory, and the painful expiation of his sin. "Cursed be the earth in thy work, in thy labor thou shalt eat of it all the days of thy life."[4] In like manner, the other pains and hardships of life will have no end or cessation on this earth; for the consequences of sin are bitter and hard to bear, and they must be with man as long as life to suffer and to endure, therefore, is the lot of humanity, let men try as they may, no strength and no artifice will ever succeed in banishing from human life the ills and troubles which beset it. If any there are who pretend differently—who hold out to a hard-pressed people freedom from pain and trouble, undisturbed repose, and constant enjoyment—they cheat the people and impose upon them, and their lying promises will only make the evil worse than before. There is nothing more useful than to look at the world as it really is—and at the same time look elsewhere for a remedy to its troubles.

EMPLOYER AND EMPLOYEE

15. The great mistake that is made in the matter now under consideration is to possess oneself of the idea that class is naturally hostile to class; that rich and poor are intended by nature to live at war with one another. So irra-

tional and so false is this view, that the exact contrary is the truth. Just as the symmetry of the human body is the result of the disposition of the members of the body, so in a State it is ordained by nature that these two classes should exist in harmony and agreement, and should, as it were, fit into one another, so as to maintain the equilibrium of the body politic. Each requires the other; capital cannot do without labor nor labor without capital. Mutual agreement results in pleasantness and good order; perpetual conflict necessarily produces confusion and outrage. Now, in preventing such strife as this, and in making it impossible, the efficacy of Christianity is marvelous and manifold.

16. First of all, there is nothing more powerful than religion (of which the Church is the interpreter and guardian) in drawing rich and poor together, by reminding each class of its duties to the other, and especially of the duties of justice. Thus religion teaches the laboring man and the workman to carry out honestly and well all equitable agreements freely made, never to injure capital, nor to outrage the person of an employer; never to employ violence in representing his own cause, nor to engage in riot and disorder; and to have nothing to do with men of evil principles, who work upon the people with artful promises, and raise foolish hopes which usually end in disaster and in repentance when too late. Religion teaches the rich man and the employer that their work-people are not their slaves; that they must respect in every man his dignity as a man and as a Christian; that labor is nothing to be ashamed of, if we listen to right reason and to Christian philosophy, but is an honorable employment, enabling a man to sustain his life in an upright and creditable way; and that it is shameful and inhuman to treat men like chattels to make money by, or to look upon them merely as so much muscle or physical power. Thus, again, religion teaches that, as among the workmen's concerns are religion herself, and things spiritual and mental, the employer is bound to see that he has time for the duties of piety; that he be not exposed to corrupting influences and dangerous occasions; and that he be not led away to neglect his home and family or to squander his wages. Then, again, the employer must never tax his work-people beyond their strength, nor employ them in work unsuited to their sex or age.

17. His great and principal obligation is to give to every one that which is just. Doubtless before we can decide whether wages are adequate many things have to be considered; but rich men and masters should remember this—that to exercise pressure for the sake of gain, upon the indigent and destitute, and to make one's profit out of the need of another, is condemned by all laws, human and divine. To defraud any one of wages that are his due is a crime which cries to the avenging anger of heaven. "Behold, the hire of the laborers . . . which by fraud has been kept back by you, crieth, and the cry of them hath entered the ears of the Lord of Sabbath."[5] Finally the rich must religiously refrain from cutting down the workman's earnings, either by force, fraud, or by usurious dealing: and with the more reason because the poor man is weak and unprotected, and because his slender means should be sacred in proportion to their scantiness.

Were these precepts carefully obeyed and followed would not strife die out and cease?

THE GREAT TRUTH

18. But the Church, with Jesus Christ for its Master and Guide, aims higher still. It lays down precepts yet more perfect, and tries to bind class to class in friendliness and good understanding. The things of this earth cannot be understood or valued rightly without taking into consideration the life to come, the life that will last forever. Exclude the idea of futurity, and the very notion of what is good and right would perish; nay, the whole system of the universe would become a dark and unfathomable mystery. The great truth which we learn from nature herself is also the grand Christian dogma on which religion rests as on its base—that when we have done with this present life then we shall really begin to live. God has not created us for the perishable and transitory things of earth, but for things heavenly and everlasting; he has given us this world as a place of exile, and not as our true country. Money and the other things which men call good and desirable we may have them in abundance or we may want them altogether; as far as eternal happiness is concerned, it is no matter; the only thing that is important is to use them aright. Jesus Christ, when he redeemed us with plentiful redemption, took not away the pains and sorrows which in such large proportion make up the texture of our mortal life; he transformed them into motives of virtue and occasions of merit; and no man can hope for eternal reward unless he follow in the bloodstained footprints of his Saviour. "If we suffer with him, we shall also reign with him."[6] His labors and his sufferings accepted by his own free will have marvelously sweetened all suffering and all labor. And not only by his example, but by his grace and by the hope of everlasting recompense, he has made pain and grief more easy to endure; "for that which is at present momentary and light of our tribulation, worketh for us above measure exceedingly an eternal weight of glory."[7]

THE RIGHT USE OF MONEY

Therefore, those whom fortune favors are warned that freedom from sorrow and abundance of earthly riches are no guarantee of that beatitude that shall never end, but rather the contrary;[8] that the rich should tremble at the threatening of Jesus Christ—threatening so strange in the mouth of our Lord;[9] and that a most strict account must be given to the Supreme Judge for all that we possess.

19. The chief and most excellent rule for the right use of money is one which the heathen philosophers indicated, but which the Church has traced out clearly, and has not only made known to men's minds, but has impressed upon their lives. It rests on the principle that it is one thing to have a right to the

possession of money, and another to have a right to use money as one pleases. Private ownership, as we have seen, is the natural right of man; and to exercise that right, especially as members of society, is not only lawful but absolutely necessary. "It is lawful," says Thomas of Aquinas, "for a man to hold private property; and it is also necessary for the carrying on of human life."[10] But if the question be asked, How must one's possessions be used?, the Church replies without hesitation in the words of the same holy doctor: "Man should not consider his outward possessions as his own, but as common to all, so as to share them without difficulty when others are in need. Whence the Apostle saith, Command the rich of this world . . . to give with ease, to communicate."[11] True, no one is commanded to distribute to others that which is required for his own necessities and those of his household; nor even to give away what is reasonably required to keep up becomingly his condition in life; "for no one ought to live unbecomingly."[12] But when necessity has been supplied, and one's position fairly considered, it is a duty to give to the indigent out of that which is left over. "That which remaineth give aims."[13] It is a duty, not of justice (except in extreme cases), but of Christian Charity—a duty which is not enforced by human law. But the laws and judgment of men must give place to the laws and judgment of Christ, the true God; who in many ways urges on his followers the practice of almsgiving—"It is more blessed to give than to receive";[14] and who will count a kindness done or refused to the poor as done or refused to himself—"As long as you did it to one of my least brethren, you did it to me."[15] Thus to sum up what has been said: Whoever has received from the divine bounty a large share of blessings, whether they be external and corporal, or gifts of the mind, has received them for the purpose of using them for perfecting his own nature, and, at the same time, that he may employ them, as the minister of God's Providence, for the benefit of others. "He that hath a talent," says St. Gregory the Great, "let him see that he hideth not; he that hath abundance, let him arouse himself to mercy and generosity; he that hath art and skill, let him do his best to share the use and utility thereof with his neighbor."[16]

THE DIGNITY OF LABOR

20. As for those who do not possess the gifts of fortune, they are taught by the Church that, in God's sight poverty is no disgrace, and that there is nothing to be ashamed of in seeking one's bread by labor. This is strengthened by what we see in Christ himself, "Who whereas he was rich, for our sakes became poor";[17] and who, being the son of God, and God himself chose to seem and to be considered the son of a carpenter—nay, did not disdain to spend a great part of his life as a carpenter himself. "Is not this the carpenter, the son of Mary?"[18] From the contemplation of this Divine example, it is easy to understand that the true dignity and excellence of man lies in his moral qualities, that is, in virtue; that virtue is the common inheritance of all, equally

within the reach of high and low, rich and poor; and that virtue, and virtue alone, wherever found, will be followed by the rewards of everlasting happiness. Nay, God himself seems to incline more to those who suffer evil; for Jesus Christ calls the poor blessed;[19] he lovingly invites those in labor and grief to come to him for solace;[20] and he displays the tenderest charity to the lowly and oppressed. These reflections cannot fail to keep down the pride of those who are well off, and to cheer the spirit of the afflicted; to incline the former to generosity, and the latter to tranquil resignation. Thus the separation which pride would make tends to disappear, nor will it be difficult to make rich and poor join hands in friendly concord.

21. But, if Christian precepts prevail, the two classes will not only be united in the bonds of friendship, but also those of brotherly love. For they will understand and feel that all men are the children of the common Father, that is, of God; that all have the same end, which is God himself, who alone can make either men or angels absolutely and perfectly happy; that all and each are redeemed by Jesus Christ, and raised to the dignity of children of God, and are thus united in brotherly ties both with each other and with Jesus Christ, "the first born among many brethren"; that the blessings of nature and the gifts of grace belong in common to the whole human race, and that to all, except to those who are unworthy, is promised the inheritance of the kingdom of heaven. "If sons, heirs also; heirs indeed of God, and coheirs of Christ."[21]

Such is the scheme of duties and of rights which is put forth to the world by the Gospel. Would it not seem that strife must quickly cease were society penetrated with ideas like these?

THE CHURCH APPLIES THE REMEDY

22. But the Church, not content with pointing out the remedy, also applies it. For the Church does its utmost to teach and to train men, and to educate them; and by means of its bishops and clergy, it diffuses its salutary teachings far and wide. It strives to influence the mind and heart so that all may willingly yield themselves to be formed and guided by the commandments of God. It is precisely in this fundamental and principal matter, on which everything depends, that the Church has a power peculiar to itself. The agencies which it employs are given it for the very purpose of reaching the hearts of men by Jesus Christ himself, and derive their efficiency from God. They alone can touch the innermost heart and conscience, and bring men to act from a motive of duty, to resist their passions and appetites, to love God and their fellow men with love that is unique and supreme, and courageously to break down every barrier which stands in the way of a virtuous life.

On this subject we need only recall for one moment the examples written down in history. Of these things there cannot be the shadow of doubt; for instance, that civil society was renovated in every part by the teachings of Christianity; that in the strength of that renewal the human race was lifted up to better things—nay, that it was brought back from death to life, and to so excellent a life that nothing more perfect had been known before or will come to pass in the ages that are yet to be. Of this beneficent transformation, Jesus Christ was at once the first cause and the final purpose; as from him all came, so to him all was to be referred. For when, by the light of the Gospel message, the human race came to know the grand mystery of the Incarnation of the Word and the redemption of man, the life of Jesus Christ, God and Man, penetrated every race and nation, and impregnated them with his faith, his precepts, and his laws. And, if society is to be cured now, in no other way can it be cured but by a return to the Christian life and Christian institutions. When a society is perishing, the true advice to give to those who would restore it is to recall it to the principles from which it sprung; for the purpose and perfection of an association is to aim at and to attain that for which it was formed; and its operation should be put in motion and inspired by the end and object which originally gave it its being. So that to fall away from its primal constitution is disease; to go back to it is recovery. And this may be asserted with the utmost truth both of the State in general and of that body of its citizens—by far the greatest number—who sustain life by labor.

THE CHURCH AND THE POOR

23. Neither must it be supposed that the solicitude of the Church is so occupied with the spiritual concerns of its children as to neglect their interests, temporal and earthly. Its desire is that the poor, for example, should rise above poverty and wretchedness, and should better their condition in life; and for this it strives. By the very fact that it calls men to virtue and forms them to its practice, it promotes this in no slight degree. Christian morality, when it is adequately and completely practiced, conduces of itself to temporal prosperity, for it merits the blessing of that God who is the source of all blessings; it powerfully restrains the lust of possession and the lust of pleasure—twin plagues, which too often make a man without self-restraint miserable in the midst of abundance;[22] it makes men supply by economy for the want of means, teaching them to be content with frugal living, and keeping them out of the reach of those vices which eat up not merely small incomes, but large fortunes, and dissipate many a goodly inheritance.

24. Moreover, the Church intervenes directly in the interest of the poor, by setting on foot and keeping up many things which it sees to be efficacious in the relief of poverty. Here, again, it has always succeeded so well that it has even extorted the praise of its enemies. Such was the ardor of brotherly love among the earliest Christians that numbers of those who were better off deprived themselves of their possessions in order to relieve their brethren; whence "neither was there any one needy among them."[23] To the order of deacons, instituted for that very purpose, was committed by the apostles the charge of the daily distributions; and the Apostle Paul, though burdened with

the solicitude of all the churches, hesitated not to undertake laborious journeys in order to carry the alms of the faithful to the poorer Christians. Tertullian calls these contributions, given voluntarily by Christians in their assemblies, "deposits of piety," because, to cite his words, they were employed "in feeding the needy, in burying them, in the support of boys and girls destitute of means and deprived of their parents, in the care of the aged, and in the relief of the shipwrecked."[24]

Thus by degrees came into existence the patrimony which the Church has guarded with jealous care as the inheritance of the poor. Nay, to spare them the shame of begging, the common mother of the rich and poor has exerted herself to gather together funds for the support of the needy. The Church has stirred up everywhere the heroism of charity, and has established congregations of religious and many other useful institutions for help and mercy, so that there might be hardly any kind of suffering which was not visited and relieved. At the present day there are many who, like the heathen of old, blame and condemn the Church for this beautiful charity. They would substitute in its place a system of State-organized relief. But no human methods will ever supply for the devotion and self-sacrifice of Christian charity. Charity, as a virtue, belongs to the Church; for it is no virtue unless it is drawn from the Sacred Heart of Jesus Christ; and he who turns his back on the Church cannot be near to Christ.

THE STATE AND POVERTY

25. It cannot, however, be doubted that to attain the purpose of which we treat, not only the Church, but all human means must conspire. All who are concerned in the matter must be of one mind and must act together. It is in this, as in the Providence which governs the world; results do not happen save where all the causes cooperate.

Let us now, therefore, inquire what part the State should play in the work of remedy and relief.

By the State we here understand, not the particular form of government which prevails in this or that nation, but the State as rightly understood; that is to say, any government conformable in its institutions to right reason and natural law, and to those dictates of the divine wisdom which we have expounded in the encyclical on *The Christian Constitution of the State*.

26. The first duty, therefore, of the rulers of the State should be to make sure that the laws and institutions, the general character and administration of the commonwealth, shall be such as to produce of themselves public well-being and private prosperity. This is the proper office of wise statesmanship and the work of the heads of the State. Now a State chiefly prospers and flourishes by morality, well-regulated family life, by respect for religion and justice, by the moderation and equal distribution of public burdens, by the progress of the arts and of trade, by the abundant yield of the land—by everything which makes the citizens better and happier. Here, then, it is in the power

of a ruler to benefit every order of the State, and amongst the rest to promote in the highest degree the interests of the poor; and this by virtue of his office, and without being exposed to any suspicion of undue interference—for it is the province of the commonwealth to consult for the common good. And the more that is done for the working population by the general laws of the country, the less need will there be to seek for particular means to relieve them.

27. There is another and a deeper consideration which must not be lost sight of.

JUSTICE TOWARD ALL

To the State the interests of all are equal whether high or low. The poor are members of the national community equally with the rich; they are real component parts, living parts, which make up, through the family, the living body; and it need hardly be said that they are by far the majority. It would be irrational to neglect one portion of the citizens and to favor another; and therefore the public administration must duly and solicitously provide for the welfare and the comfort of the working people, or else that law of justice will be violated which ordains that each shall have his due. To cite the wise words of Thomas Aquinas: "As the part and the whole are in a certain sense identical, the part may in some sense claim what belongs to the whole."[25] Among the many and grave duties of rulers who would do their best for their people, the first and chief is to act with strict justice—with that justice which is called in the schools *distributive*—toward each and every class.

But although all citizens, without exception, can and ought to contribute to that common good in which individuals share so profitably to themselves, yet it is not to be supposed that all can contribute in the same way and to the same extent. No matter what changes may be made in forms of government, there will always be differences and inequalities of condition in the State. Society cannot exist or be conceived without them. Some there must be who dedicate themselves to the work of the commonwealth, who make the laws, who administer justice, whose advice and authority govern the nation in times of peace, and defend it in war. Such men clearly occupy the foremost place in the State, and should be held in the foremost estimation, for their work touches most nearly and effectively the general interests of the community. Those who labor at a trade or calling do not promote the general welfare in such a fashion as this; but they do in the most important way benefit the nation, though less directly. We have insisted that, since it is the end of society to make men better, the chief good that society can be possessed of is virtue. Nevertheless, in all well-constituted States it is by no means an unimportant matter to provide those bodily and external commodities, "the use of which is necessary to virtuous action."[26] And in the provision of material well-being, the labor of the poor—the exercise of their skill and the employment of their strength in the culture of the land and the workshops of trade—is most efficacious and altogether indispensable. Indeed, their co-operation in this respect is so important that it may be truly said that it is only by the labor of the workingman that States grow rich. Justice, therefore, demands that the interests of the poorer population be carefully watched over by the administration, so that they who contribute so largely to the advantage of the community may themselves share in the benefits they create—that being housed, clothed, and enabled to support life, they may find their existence less hard and more endurable. It follows that whatever shall appear to be conducive to the well-being of those who work should receive favorable consideration. Let it not be feared that solicitude of this kind will injure any interest; on the contrary it will be to the advantage of all; for it cannot but be good for the commonwealth to secure from misery those on whom it so largely depends.

THE FIRST LAW OF GOVERNMENT

28. We have said that the State must not absorb the individual or the family; both should be allowed free and untrammelled action as far as is consistent with the common good and the interests of others. Nevertheless, rulers should anxiously safeguard the community and all its parts; the community, because the conservation of the community is so emphatically the business of the supreme power, that the safety of the commonwealth is not only the first law, but is a government's whole reason of existence; and the parts, because both philosophy and the Gospel agree in laying down that the object of the administration of the State should be not the advantage of the ruler, but the benefit of those over whom he rules. The gift of authority is from God, and is, as it were, a participation of the highest of all sovereignties; and it should be exercised as the power of God is exercised—with a fatherly solicitude which not only guides the whole but reaches to details as well.

Whenever the general interest of any particular class suffers, or is threatened with, evils which can in no other way be met, the public authority must step in to meet them.

29. Now, among the interests of the public, as of private individuals, are these: that peace and good order should be maintained; that family life should be carried on in accordance with God's laws and those of nature; that religion should be reverenced and obeyed; that a high standard of morality should prevail in public and private life; that the sanctity of justice should be respected, and that no one should injure another with impunity; that the members of the commonwealth should grow up to man's estate strong and robust, and capable, if need be, of guarding and defending their country. If by a strike, or other combination of workmen, there should be imminent danger of disturbance to the public peace; or if circumstances were such that among the laboring population the ties of family life were relaxed; if religion were found to suffer through the workmen not having time and opportunity to practice it; if in workshops and factories there were danger to morals through the mixing

of the sexes or from any occasion of evil; or if employers laid burdens upon the workmen which were unjust, or degraded them with conditions that were repugnant to their dignity as human beings; finally, if health were endangered by excessive labor, or by work unsuited to sex or age—in these cases there can be no question that, within certain limits, it would be right to call in the help and authority of the law. The limits must be determined by the nature of the occasion which calls for the law's interference—the principle being this, that the law must not undertake more, nor go further, than is required for the remedy of the evil or the removal of the danger.

THE RIGHT OF PROTECTION

Rights must be religiously respected wherever they are found; and it is the duty of the public authority to prevent and punish injury, and to protect each one in the possession of his own. Still, when there is question of protecting the rights of individuals, the poor and helpless have a claim to special consideration. The richer population have many ways of protecting themselves, and stand less in need of help from the State; those who are badly off have no resources of their own to fall back upon, and must chiefly rely upon the assistance of the State. And it is for this reason that wage earners, who are, undoubtedly, among the weak and necessitous, should be specially cared for and protected by the commonwealth.

30. Here, however, it will be advisable to advert expressly to one or two of the more important details.

It must be borne in mind that the chief thing to be secured is the safeguarding, by legal enactment and policy, of private property. Most of all it is essential in these times of covetous greed, to keep the multitude within the line of duty; for if all may justly strive to better their condition, yet neither justice nor the common good allows anyone to seize that which belongs to another, or, under the pretext of futile and ridiculous equality, to lay hands on other people's fortunes. It is most true that by far the larger part of the people who work prefer to improve themselves by honest labor rather than by doing wrong to others. But there are not a few who are imbued with bad principles and are anxious for revolutionary change, and whose great purpose it is to stir up tumult and bring about a policy of violence. The authority of the State should intervene to put restraint upon these disturbers, to save the workmen from their seditious acts, and to protect lawful owners from spoliation.

THE WORKMAN'S RIGHTS

31. When work-people have recourse to a strike, it is frequently because the hours of labor are too long, or the work too hard, or because they consider their wages insufficient. The grave inconvenience of this not uncommon occurrence should be obviated by public remedial measures; for such paralysis of

labor not only affects the masters and their work-people, but is extremely injurious to trade, and to the general interests of the public; moreover, on such occasions, violence and disorder are generally not far off, and thus it frequently happens that the public peace is threatened. The laws should be made beforehand, and prevent these troubles from arising; they should lend their influence and authority to the removal in good time of the causes which lead to conflicts between masters and those whom they employ.

32. But if the owners of property must be made secure, the workman, too, has property and possessions in which he must be protected; and, first of all, there are his spiritual and mental interests. Life on earth, however good and desirable in itself, is not the final purpose for which man is created; it is only the way and the means to that attainment of truth, and that practice of goodness in which the full life of the soul consists. It is the soul which is made after the image and likeness of God; it is in the soul that sovereignty resides, in virtue of which man is commanded to rule the creatures below him, and to use all the earth and ocean for his profit and advantage. "Fill the earth and subdue it; and rule over the fishes of the sea and the fowls of the air, and all living creatures which move upon the earth."[27] In this respect all men are equal; there is no difference between rich and poor, master and servant, ruler and ruled, "for the same is Lord over all."[28] No man may outrage with impunity that human dignity which God himself treats with reverence, nor stand in the way of that higher life which is the preparation for the eternal life of heaven. Nay, more; a man has here no power over himself. To consent to any treatment which is calculated to defeat the end and purpose of his being is beyond his right; he cannot give up his soul to servitude; for it is not man's own rights which are here in question, but the rights of God, most sacred and inviolable.

From this follows the obligation of the cessation of work and labor on Sundays and certain festivals. This rest from labor is not to be understood as mere idleness; much less must it be an occasion of spending money and a vicious excess, as many would desire it to be; but it should be rest from labor consecrated by religion. Repose united with religious observance disposes man to forget for a while the business of this daily life, and to turn his thoughts to heavenly things and to the worship which he so strictly owes to the Eternal Deity. It is this, above all, which is the reason and motive for the Sunday rest; a rest sanctioned by God's great law of the ancient covenant, "Remember thou keep holy the Sabbath day,"[29] and taught to the world by his own mysterious "rest" after the creation of man, "He rested on the seventh day from all his work which he had done."[30]

HOURS OF LABOR

33. If we turn now to things exterior and corporal, the first concern of all is to save the poor workers from the cruelty of grasping speculators, who use human beings as mere instruments for making money. It is neither justice nor

humanity so to grind men down with excessive labor as to stupefy their minds and wear out their bodies. Man's powers, like his general nature, are limited, and beyond these limits he cannot go. His strength is developed and increased by use and exercise, but only on condition of due intermission and proper rest. Daily labor, therefore, must be so regulated that it may not be protracted during longer hours than strength admits. How many and how long the intervals of rest should be will depend upon the nature of the work, on circumstances of time and place, and on the health and strength of the workman. Those who labor in mines and quarries, and in work within the bowels of the earth, should have shorter hours in proportion, as their labor is more severe and more trying to health. Then, again, the season of the year must be taken in account; for not infrequently a kind of labor is easy at one time which at another is intolerable or very difficult. Finally, work which is suitable for a strong man cannot reasonably be required from a woman or a child.

CHILD LABOR

And in regard to children, great care should be taken not to place them in workshops and factories until their bodies and minds are sufficiently mature. For just as rough weather destroys the buds of spring, so too early an experience of life's hard work blights the young promise of a child's powers, and makes any real education impossible. Women, again, are not suited to certain trades; for a woman is by nature fitted for home work, and it is that which is best adapted at once to preserve her modesty, and to promote the good bringing up of children and the well-being of the family. As a general principle, it may be laid down that a workman ought to have leisure and rest in proportion to the wear and tear of his strength; for the waste of strength must be repaired by the cessation of work.

In all agreements between masters and work-people, there is always the condition, expressed or understood, that there be allowed proper rest for soul and body. To agree in any other sense would be against what is right and just; for it can never be right or just to require on the one side, or to promise on the other, the giving up of those duties which a man owes to his God and to himself.

JUST WAGES

34. We now approach a subject of very great importance and one on which, if extremes are to be avoided, right ideas are absolutely necessary. Wages, we are told, are fixed by free consent; and, therefore, the employer when he pays what was agreed upon has done his part, and is not called upon for anything further. The only way, it is said, in which injustice could happen would be if the master refused to pay the whole of the wages, or the workman would not complete the work undertaken; when this happens the State should intervene, to see that each obtains his own, but not under any other circumstances.

This mode of reasoning is by no means convincing to a fair-minded man, for there are important considerations which it leaves out of view altogether. To labor is to exert one's self for the sake of procuring what is necessary for the purposes of life, and most of all for self-preservation. "In the sweat of thy brow thou shalt eat bread."[31] Therefore, a man's labor has two notes or characters. First of all, it is *personal*; for the exertion of individual power belongs to the individual who puts it forth, employing this power for that personal profit for which it was given. Secondly, a man's labor is *necessary*; for without the results of labor a man cannot live; and self-conservation is a law of nature, which it is wrong to disobey. Now, if we were to consider labor merely so far as it is *personal*, doubtless it would be within the workman's right to accept any rate of wages whatever; for in the same way as he is free to work or not, so he is free to accept a small remuneration or even none at all. But this is a mere abstract supposition; the labor of the workingman is not only his personal attribute, but it is *necessary*; and this makes all the difference. The preservation of life is the bounden duty of each and all, and to fail therein is a crime. It follows that each one has a right to procure what is required in order to live; and the poor can procure it in no other way than by work and wages.

Let it be granted, then, that, as a rule, workman and employer should make free agreements, and in particular should freely agree as to wages; nevertheless, there is a dictate of nature more imperious and more ancient than any bargain between man and man, that the remuneration must be enough to support the wage earner in reasonable and frugal comfort. If through necessity or fear of a worse evil, the workman accepts harder conditions because an employer or contractor will give him no better, he is the victim of force and injustice. In these and similar questions, however—such as, for example, the hours of labor in different trades, the sanitary precautions to be observed in factories and workshops, etc.—in order to supersede undue interference on the part of the State, especially as circumstances, times and localities differ so widely, it is advisable that recourse be had to societies or boards such as we shall mention presently, or to some other method of safeguarding the interests of wage earners; the State to be asked for approval and protection.

BENEFITS OF PROPERTY OWNERSHIP

35. If a workman's wages be sufficient to enable him to maintain himself, his wife, and his children in reasonable comfort, he will not find it difficult, if he is a sensible man, to study economy; and he will not find it difficult, by cutting down expenses, to put by a little property: nature and reason would urge him to do this. We have seen that this great labor question cannot be solved except by assuming as a principle that private ownership must be held sacred and inviolable. The law, therefore, should favor ownership, and its policy should be to induce as many people as possible to become owners.

Many excellent results will follow from this; and first of all, property will certainly become more equitably divided. For the effect of civil change and revolution has been to divide society into two widely different castes. On the one side there is the party which holds the power because it holds the wealth; which has in its grasp all labor and all trade; which manipulates for its own benefit and its own purposes all the sources of supply; and which is powerfully represented in the councils of the State itself. On the other side there is the needy and powerless multitude, sore and suffering, always ready for disturbance. If working people can be encouraged to look forward to obtaining a share in the land, the result will be that the gulf between vast wealth and deep poverty will be bridged over, and the two orders will be brought nearer together. Another consequence will be the great abundance of the fruits of the earth. Men always work harder and more readily when they work on that which is their own; nay, they learn to love the very soil which yields in response to the labor of their hands, not only food to eat, but an abundance of the good things for themselves and those that are dear to them. It is evident how such a spirit of willing labor would add to the produce of the earth and to the wealth of the community. And a third advantage would arise from this: men would cling to the country in which they were born; for no one would exchange his country for a foreign land if his own afforded him the means of living a tolerable and happy life. These three important benefits, however, can only be expected on the condition that a man's means be not drained and exhausted by excessive taxation. The right to possess private property is from nature, not from man; and the State has only the right to regulate its use in the interests of the public good, but by no means to abolish it altogether. The State is, therefore, unjust and cruel, if, in the name of taxation, it deprives the private owner of more than is just.

WORKMEN'S ASSOCIATIONS

36. In the first place—employers and workmen may themselves effect much in the matter of which we treat, by means of those institutions and organizations which afford opportune assistance to those in need, and which draw the two orders more closely together. Among these may be enumerated: societies for mutual help; various foundations established by private persons for providing for the workman, and for his widow or his orphans, in sudden calamity, in sickness, and in the event of death; and what are called "patronage," or institutions for the care of boys and girls, for young people, and also for those of more mature age.

The most important of all are workmen's associations; for these virtually include all the rest. History attests what excellent results were effected by the artificer's guilds of a former day. They were the means not only of many advantages to the workmen, but in no small degree of the advancement of art, as numerous monuments remain to prove. Such associations should be adapted to the requirements of the age in which we live—an age of greater instruction, of different customs, and of more numerous requirements in daily life. It is gratifying to know that there are actually in existence not a few societies of this nature, consisting either of workmen alone, or of workmen and employers together; but it were greatly to be desired that they should multiply and become more effective. We have spoken of them more than once; but it will be well to explain here how much they are needed, to show that they exist by their own right, and to enter into their organization and their work.

37. The experience of his own weakness urges man to call in help from without. We read in the pages of Holy Writ: "It is better that two should be together than one; for they have the advantage of their society. If one fall he shall be supported by the other. Woe to him that is alone, for when he falleth he hath none to lift him up."[32] And further: "A brother that is helped by his brother is like a strong city."[33] It is this natural impulse which unites men in civil society; and it is this also which makes them band themselves together in associations of citizen with citizen; associations which, it is true, cannot be called societies in the complete sense of the word, but which are societies nevertheless.

These lesser societies and the society which constitutes the State differ in many things, because their immediate purpose and end is different. Civil society exists for the common good, and, therefore, is concerned with the interests of all in general, and with the individual interests in their due place and proportion. Hence, it is called *public* society, because by its means, Thomas Aquinas says, "Men communicate with one another in the setting up of a commonwealth."[34] But the societies which are formed in the bosom of the State are called *private*, and justly so, because their immediate purpose is the private advantage of the associates. "Now, a private society," says St. Thomas again, "is one which is formed for the purpose of carrying out private business; as when two or three enter into partnership with the view of trading in conjunction."[35]

38. Particular societies, then, although they exist within the State, and are each a part of the State, nevertheless cannot be prohibited by the State absolutely and as such. For to enter into a "society" of this kind is the natural right of man; and the State must protect natural rights, not destroy them; and if it forbids its citizens to form associations, it contradicts the very principle of its own existence; for both they and it exist in virtue of the same principle, viz., the natural propensity of man to live in society.

There are times, no doubt, when it is right that the law should interfere to prevent association; as when men join together for purposes which are evidently bad, unjust, or dangerous to the State. In such cases the public authority may justly forbid the formation of association, and may dissolve them when they already exist. But every precaution should be taken not to violate the rights of individuals, and not to make unreasonable regulations under the pretense of public benefit. For laws only bind when they are in accordance with right reason, and therefore with the eternal law of God.[36]

VIOLENT OPPRESSION

39. And here we are reminded of the confraternities, societies, and religious orders which have arisen by the Church's authority and the piety of the Christian people. The annals of every nation down to our own times testify to what they have done for the human race. It is indisputable on grounds of reason alone, that such associations, being perfectly blameless in their objects, have the sanction of the law of nature. On their religious side, they rightly claim to be responsible to the Church alone. The administrators of the State, therefore, have no rights over them, nor can they claim any share in their management; on the contrary, it is the State's duty to respect and cherish them, and, if necessary, to defend them from attack. It is notorious that a very different course has been followed, more especially in our own times. In many places the State has laid violent hands on these communities, and committed manifold injustice against them; it has placed them under the civil law, taken away their rights as corporate bodies, and robbed them of their property. In such property the Church had her rights, each member of the body had his or her rights, and there were also the rights of those who had founded or endowed them for a definite purpose, and of those for whose benefit and assistance they existed. Wherefore we cannot refrain from complaining of such spoliation as unjust and fraught with evil results; and with the more reason because, at the very time when the law proclaims that association is free to all, we see that Catholic societies, however peaceable and useful, are hindered in every way, whilst the utmost freedom is given to men whose objects are at once hurtful to religion and dangerous to the State.

40. Associations of every kind, and especially those of workingmen, are now far more common than formerly. In regard to many of these there is no need at present to inquire whence they spring, what are their objects or what means they use. But there is a good deal of evidence which goes to prove that many of these societies are in the hands of invisible leaders, and are managed on principles far from compatible with Christianity and the public well-being; and that they do their best to get into their hands the whole field of labor and to force workmen either to join them or to starve. Under these circumstances Christian workmen must do one of two things: either join associations in which their religion will be exposed to peril or form associations among themselves—unite their forces and courageously shake off the yoke of an unjust and intolerable oppression. No one who does not wish to expose man's chief good to extreme danger will hesitate to say that the second alternative must by all means be adopted.

PRINCIPLES OF ORGANIZATION

41. Those Catholics are worthy of all praise—and there are not a few—who, understanding what the times require, have, by various enterprises and

experiments, endeavored to better the conditions of the working people without any sacrifice of principle. They have taken up the cause of the workingman, and have striven to make both families and individuals better off; to infuse the spirit of justice into the mutual relations of employers and employed; to keep before the eyes of both classes the precepts of duty and the laws of the Gospel—that Gospel which, by inculcating self-restraint, keep men within the bounds of moderation, and tends to establish harmony among the divergent interests and various classes which compose the State. It is with such ends in view that we see men of eminence meeting together for discussion, for the promotion of united action, and for practical work. Others, again, strive to unite working people of various kinds into associations, help them with their advice and their means, and enable them to obtain honest and profitable work. The bishops, on their part, bestow their ready good will and support; and with their approval and guidance many members of the clergy, both secular and regular, labor assiduously on behalf of the spiritual and mental interests of the members of associations. And there are not wanting Catholics possessed of affluence, who have, as it were, cast their lot with the wage earners, and who have spent large sums in founding and widely spreading benefit and insurance societies, by means of which the workingman may without difficulty acquire by his labor not only many present advantages, but also the certainty of honorable support in time to come. How much this multiplied and earnest activity has benefited the community at large is too well known to require us to dwell upon it. We find in it the grounds of the most cheering hope for the future; provided that the associations we have described continue to grow and spread, and are well and wisely administered. Let the State watch over these societies of citizens united together in the exercise of their right; but let it not thrust itself into their peculiar concerns and their organization, for things move and live by the soul within them, and they may be killed by the grasp of a hand from without.

RELIGION FIRST

42. In order that an association may be carried on with a unity of purpose and harmony of action, its organization and government must be firm and wise. All such societies, being free to exist, have the further right to adopt such rules and organization as may best conduce to the attainment of their objects. We do not deem it possible to enter into definite details on the subject of organization, this must depend on national character, on practice and experience, on the nature and scope of the work to be done, on the magnitude of the various trades and employments, and on other circumstances of fact and of time—all of which must be carefully weighed. Speaking summarily, we may lay it down as a general and perpetual law, that workmen's associations should be so organized and governed as to furnish the best and most suitable means for attaining what is aimed at, that is to say, for helping each individual member

to better his condition to the utmost, in body, mind and property. It is clear that they must pay special and principal attention to piety and morality, and that their internal discipline must be directed precisely by these considerations; otherwise they entirely lose their special character, and come to be very little better than those societies which take no account of religion at all. What advantage can it be to a workman to obtain by means of a society all that he requires, and to endanger his soul for want of spiritual food? "What doth it profit a man if he gain the whole world and suffer the loss of his own soul?"[37]

This, as our Lord teaches, is the note or character that distinguishes the Christian from the heathen. "After all these things do the heathen seek. . . . Seek ye first the kingdom of God and his justice, and all these things shall be added unto you."[38] Let our associations, then, look first and before all to God; let religious instruction have therein a foremost place, each one being carefully taught what is his duty to God, what to believe, what to hope for, and how to work out his salvation; and let all be warned and fortified with especial solicitude against wrong opinions and false teaching. Let the workingman be urged and led to the worship of God, to the earnest practice of religion, and, among other things, to the sanctification of Sundays and festivals. Let him learn to reverence and love holy Church the common Mother of us all; and so to obey the precepts and frequent the sacraments of the Church, those sacraments being the means ordained by God for obtaining forgiveness of sin and for leading a holy life.

RELATION OF MEMBERS

43. The foundations of the organization being laid in religion, we next go on to determine the relations of the members, one to another, in order that they may live together in concord, and go on prosperously and successfully. The offices and charges of the society should be distributed for the good of the society itself, and in such manner that difference in degree or position should not interfere with unanimity and good will. Office-bearers should be appointed with prudence and discretion, and each one's charge should be carefully marked out; thus no member will suffer wrong. Let the common funds be administered with strictest honesty, in such a way that a member receives assistance in proportion to his necessities. The rights and duties of employers should be the subject of careful consideration as compared with the rights and duties of the employed. If it should happen that either a master or a workman deemed himself injured, nothing would be more desirable than that there should be a committee composed of honest and capable men of the association itself, whose duty it should be, by the laws of the association, to decide the dispute. Among the purposes of a society should be an effort to arrange for a continuous supply of work at all times and seasons; and to create a fund from which the members may be helped in their necessities, not only in case of accident, but also in sickness, old age, and misfortune.

Such rules and regulations, if obeyed willingly by all, will sufficiently ensure the well-being of poor people; while such mutual associations among Catholics are certain to be productive, in no small degree, of prosperity to the State. It is not rash to conjecture the future from the past. Age gives way to age, but the events of one century are wonderfully like those of another; for they are directed by the Providence of God, who overrules the course of history in accordance with his purposes in creating the race of man. We are told that it was cast as a reproach on the Christians of the early ages of the Church that the greater number of them had to live by begging or by labor. Yet, destitute as they were of wealth and influence they ended by winning over to their side the favor of the rich and the good will of the powerful. They showed themselves industrious, laborious, and peaceful, men of justice, and, above all, men of brotherly love. In the presence of such a life and such an example, prejudice disappeared, the tongue of malevolence was silenced, and the lying traditions of ancient superstition yielded little by little to Christian truth.

HONESTY

44. At this moment the condition of the working population is the question of the hour; and nothing can be of higher interest to all classes of the State than that it should be rightly and reasonably decided. But it will be easy for Christian workingmen to decide it aright if they form associations, choose wise guides, and follow the same path which with so much advantage to themselves and the commonwealth was trod by their fathers before them. Prejudice, it is true, is mighty, and so is the love of money; but if the sense of what is just and right be not destroyed by depravity of heart, their fellow citizens are sure to be won over to a kindly feeling toward men whom they see to be so industrious and so modest, who so unmistakably prefer honesty to lucre, and the sacredness of duty to all other considerations.

And another great advantage would result from the state of things we are describing; there would be so much more hope and possibility of recalling to a sense of their duty those workingmen who have either given up their faith altogether, or whose lives are at variance with its precepts. These men, in most cases, feel that they have been fooled by empty promises and deceived by false appearances. They cannot but perceive that their grasping employers too often treat them with the greatest inhumanity, and hardly care for them beyond the profit their labor brings; and if they belong to an association, it is probably one in which there exists, in place of charity and love, that internal strife which always accompanies unresigned and irreligious poverty. Broken in spirit and worn down in body, how many of them would gladly free themselves from this galling slavery! But human respect, or the dread of starvation, makes them afraid to take the step. To such as these, Catholic associations are of incalculable service, helping them out of their difficulties, inviting them to companionship, and receiving the repentant to a shelter in which they may securely trust.

CONCLUSION

45. We have now laid before you, venerable brethren, who are the persons, and what are the means, by which this most difficult question must be solved. Every one must put his hand to work which falls to his share, and that at once and immediately, lest the evil which is already so great may by delay become absolutely beyond remedy. Those who rule the State must use the law and the institutions of the country; masters and rich men must remember their duty; the poor, whose interests are at stake, must make every lawful and proper effort; since religion alone, as we said at the beginning, can destroy the evil at its root, all men must be persuaded that the primary thing needful is to return to real Christianity, in the absence of which all the plans and devices of the wisest will be of little avail.

As far as regards the Church, its assistance will never be wanting, be the time or the occasion what it may; and it will intervene with great effect in proportion as its liberty of action is the more unfettered; let this be carefully noted by those whose office it is to provide for the public welfare. Every minister of holy religion must throw into the conflict all the energy of his mind, and all the strength of his endurance; with your authority, venerable brethren, and by your example, they must never cease to urge upon all men of every class, upon the high as well as the lowly, the Gospel doctrines of Christian life; by every means in their power they must strive for the good of the people; and above all they must earnestly cherish in themselves, and try to arouse in others, charity, the mistress and queen of virtues. For the happy results we all long for must be chiefly brought about by the plenteous outpouring of charity; of that true Christian charity which is the fulfilling of the whole Gospel law, which is always ready to sacrifice itself for other's sake, and which is man's surest antidote against worldly pride and immoderate love of self; that charity whose office is described and whose Godlike features are drawn by the Apostle St. Paul in these words: "Charity is patient, is kind, . . . seeketh not her own, . . . suffereth all things, . . . endureth all things."[39]

On each of you, venerable brethren, and on your clergy and people, as an earnest of God's mercy and a mark of our affection, we lovingly in the Lord bestow the apostolic benediction.

Given at St. Peter's in Rome, the fifteenth day of May, 1891, the fourteenth year of our Pontificate.

LEO XIII

NOTES

1. Deut. 5:21.
2. Gen. 1:28.
3. Thomas Aquinas, *Summa Theologiae* 2a 2æ Q. x. art. 12.

4. Gen. 3:17.
5. James 5:4.
6. 2 Tim. 2:12.
7. 2 Cor. 4:17.
8. Matt. 19:23, 24.
9. Luke 6:24, 25.
10. Thomas Aquinas, 2a 2æ Q. lxvi. art. 2.
11. Ibid., Q. lxv. art. 2.
12. Ibid., 2a 2æ Q. xxxii. art. 6.
13. Luke 11:41.
14. Acts 20:35.
15. Matt. 25:40.
16. Gregory the Great, Hom. ix *in Evangel.* n. 7.
17. 2 Cor. 8:9.
18. Mark 6:3.
19. Matt. 5:3: "Blessed are the poor in spirit."
20. Matt. 11:28: "Come to me all you that labor and are burdened, and I will refresh you."
21. Rom. 8:17.
22. 1 Tim. 6:10: "The root of all evils is cupidity."
23. Acts 4:34.
24. Tertullian, *Apologia Secunda*, xxxix.
25. Thomas Aquinas, 2a 2æ Q. lxi. art. 1 and 2.
26. Thomas Aquinas, *De Regimine Principum*, I, cap. 15.
27. Gen. 1:28.
28. Rom. 10:12.
29. Exod. 20:8.
30. Gen. 2:2.
31. Gen. 3:1.
32. Eccles. 4:9, 10.
33. Prov. 18:19.
34. Thomas Aquinas, *Contra impugnantes Dei cultum et religionem*, Cap. II.
35. Ibid.
36. "Human law is law only in virtue of its accordance with right reason: and thus it is manifest that it flows from the eternal law. And in so far as it deviates from right reason it is called an unjust law; in such case it is not law at all, but rather a species of violence." Thomas Aquinas, *Summa Theologiae* 1a 2æ Q. xciii. art. iii.
37. Matt. 16:26.
38. Matt. 6:32, 33.
39. 1 Cor. 13:4–7.

Quadragesimo Anno: After Forty Years (Pius XI, 1931)

INTRODUCTION

When Leo XIII wrote in 1891, liberal capitalism was at the zenith of its power. Opting for reform rather than counterrevolution, Leo tried to nudge European Catholics away from an apparently hopeless alliance with monarchy and preindustrial feudal economic ideals toward a more promising strategy of political participation and social reform. In 1931 Pius XI faced a very different situation. World War I had shattered liberal confidence. Parliamentary democracy seemed almost helpless in the face of the mass movements of fascism and communism. And the economy of the Western world lay in the ruins of a worldwide depression. The church, better organized and more united than ever before, might be able to offer a credible alternative to a failed capitalism and a fearsome socialism.

Drawing on the writings of numerous Central European economists and theologians, Pius XI projected structures of economic self-government, modeled on the medieval guilds, to overcome the chaotic injustice of capitalism and the regimented injustice of socialism. These structures, vocational groups, would bring workers and managers together in joint organizations to determine policy for the industry as a whole, with a council of industry representatives determining overall national economic policy. Based on the law of justice and infused with a sense of social responsibility and Christian charity, taught and sanctioned by the church, such a system would not simply be another method of social organization but, indeed, the "Christian social order." For Pius, the Catholic social doctrine was a package and demanded acceptance in toto in the name of faith.

Pius and the Catholics to whom he spoke believed they saw a way out of the crises before them: the conflicts between political freedom and economic security; between the economic elite and the working class; between economic expansion and moral values; and between the state and the individual. If men and women would turn to God, to Christ, and to the church, if they would return to the faith they had once shared, they would experience unity on the basis of which order and authority could be restored without losing "true" freedom, which had to be grounded in divine truth, in the rightly ordered world created by God.

Backed by religious sanctions and positive law, justice would be restored, rights respected, and harmony created. A new phrase—*social justice*—appeared in *Quadragesimo Anno* to describe the type of justice that demanded due recognition of the common good, a good which included, and did not contradict, the authentic good of each and every person. Thus the church could lift up both human rights and human solidarity as the basis of its response to the extremes of both totalitarianism and capitalism. This provided the foundation for the balancing of political and civil with social and economic rights and the committed but detached advocacy of a way other than Left or Right.

On the whole, however, the project of Christianizing the modern social order had to be judged, at mid-century, a failure. The magnificent effort to construct a body of Catholic social teaching produced thinkers and documents that were insightful and powerful in perceiving and denouncing the evils of liberalism, capitalism, and democracy, but which could never transcend that critique to formulate a positive, attractive, and compelling alternative. Because they distanced the church from the worst features of the age, they could and did generate a pastoral approach that brought the church closer to the suffering poor, but they never succeeded in relating to the hopes and aspirations of the working class. For all its failings, liberalism had excited new hopes and aspirations among masses of ordinary people; the church seemed only to offer a return to a former age, which many knew instinctively had been neither secure nor happy for most people.

QUADRAGESIMO ANNO

ENCYCLICAL LETTER OF HIS HOLINESS
PIUS XI
BY DIVINE PROVIDENCE
POPE

To Our Venerable Brethren: The Patriarchs, Primates, Archbishops, Bishops and Other Local Ordinaries, in Peace and Communion with the Apostolic See, and to All the Faithful of the Catholic World: on Reconstructing the Social Order and Perfecting It Conformably to the Precepts of the Gospel, in Commemoration of the Fortieth Anniversary of the Encyclical "Rerum Novarum."

Venerable Brethren and Beloved Children,
Health and Apostolic Benediction

1. Forty years have elapsed since the admirable encyclical of Leo XIII of happy memory, *Rerum Novarum*, first saw the light. The whole Catholic world gratefully recalls the event, and prepares to celebrate it with befitting solemnity.

2. The way for this remarkable document of pastoral solicitude, it is true, had been in a measure prepared by other pronouncements of our predecessor. His letters on the foundation of human society, the family and the holy sacrament of matrimony;[1] on the origin of civil power;[2] and its proper coordination with the Church;[3] on the belief and duties of Christian citizens;[4] against the tenets of socialism;[5] and the false notions of human liberty;[6] these and others of the kind had unmistakably revealed the mind of Leo XIII. *Rerum Novarum*, however, stood out in this, that it laid down for all mankind unerring rules for the right solution of the difficult problem of human community, called the "social question," at the very time when such guidance was most opportune and necessary.

OCCASION OF *RERUM NOVARUM*

3. Toward the close of the nineteenth century, new economic methods and new developments of industry had in many nations led to a situation wherein the human community appeared more and more divided into two classes. The first, small in numbers, enjoyed practically all the comforts so plentifully supplied by modern invention. The second class, comprising the immense multitude of workingmen, was made up of those who, oppressed by dire poverty, struggled in vain to escape from the straits which encompassed them.

4. This state of things was quite satisfactory to the wealthy, who looked upon it as the consequence of inevitable and natural economic laws, and who, therefore, were content to abandon to charity alone the full care of relieving the unfortunate, as though it were the task of charity to make amends for the open violation of justice, a violation not merely tolerated, but sanctioned at times by legislators. On the other hand, the working classes, victims of these harsh conditions, submitted to them with extreme reluctance, and became more and more unwilling to bear the galling yoke. Some, carried away by heat of evil counsels, went so far as to seek the disruption of the whole social fabric. Others, whom a solid Christian training restrained from such misguided excesses, convinced themselves nevertheless that there was much in all this that needed a radical and speedy reform.

5. Such also was the opinion of many Catholics, priests and laymen who with admirable charity had long devoted themselves to relieving the undeserved misery of the laboring classes and who could not persuade themselves that so vast and unfair a distinction in the distribution of temporal goods was really in harmony with the designs of an all-wise Creator.

6. They therefore sought in all sincerity a remedy against the lamentable disorder already existing in society, and a firm barrier against worse dangers to come. But such is the infirmity of even the best minds, that these men either found themselves repelled as dangerous innovators or opposed by fellow workers in the same cause, who held views different from theirs, and thus wavering in uncertainty, they did not, under the circumstances, know which way to turn.

7. This grave conflict of opinions was accompanied by discussions not always of a peaceful nature. The eyes of all, as often in the past, turned toward the Chair of Peter, sacred repository of the fullness of truth whence words of salvation are dispensed to the whole world. To the feet of Christ's vicar on earth were seen to flock, in unprecedented numbers, specialists in social affairs, employers, the very workingmen themselves, begging with one voice that at last a safe road might be pointed out to them.

8. Long did the prudent pontiff ponder all these things before God, seeking the advice of the most experienced counselors available, and carefully considering the matter in its many aspects. At last, urged by "the responsibility of the Apostolic office"[7] and fearing lest by silence he should seem to neglect his duty,[8] he decided, in virtue of the teaching authority divinely entrusted to him, to address himself to the entire Church of Christ and indeed to the whole human race.

9. On May 15, 1891, therefore, the long-desired message was given to the world. Undaunted by the difficulty of the undertaking or by the weight of years, with awakened courage, the venerable pontiff taught mankind new methods of approach to social problems.

10. You know, venerable brethren and beloved children, you know full well the admirable teaching which has made the encyclical *Rerum Novarum*

forever memorable. In this document the supreme shepherd, grieving that so large a proportion of mankind "should be living disgracefully in a wretched and tragic situation," boldly took in his own hands "the cause of the workingmen, whom the times had delivered, isolated and helpless, to the niggardliness of employers and the greed of unrestrained competition."[9] He sought help neither from liberalism nor socialism. The former had already shown its utter impotence to find a right solution of the social question, while the latter would have exposed human society to still graver dangers by offering a remedy much more disastrous than the evil it designed to cure.

11. But the supreme pontiff, exercising his manifest rights and maintaining correctly that on him primarily devolved the care of religion and the supervision of what intimately relates to it, approached the question as one for which there would be found "no solution, not even tentative, apart from the assistance of religion and of the Church."[10] Basing his teaching only upon the unchanging principles drawn from right reason and divine revelation, he indicated and proclaimed with confidence and "as one having authority,"[11] what are "the rights and duties whereby the wealthy and the propertyless, those providing capital and those who labor, should be mutually united and restrained,"[12] and furthermore what should be the role of the Church, of the public authorities, and of the parties themselves.

12. Nor was the apostolic voice raised in vain. It was listened to with genuine admiration and greeted with profound sympathy not only by the loyal children of the Church, but by many also who had wandered far from the truth and from the unity of faith; and in addition by practically everyone who, either in study or in legislative action, was thereafter concerned about social and economic matters.

13. With particular enthusiasm was the pontifical letter welcomed by Christian workingmen, who felt themselves vindicated and defended by the highest authority on earth, and by all those devoted men whose concern it had long been to better the conditions of labor, and who heretofore had found nothing but general indifference, not to say unfriendly suspicion, or even open hostility. All these men have ever deservedly held the encyclical in the highest esteem to the extent of celebrating its memory in various ways year after year throughout the world in token of gratitude.

14. Despite this widespread agreement, however, some minds were not a little disturbed, with the result that the noble and exalted teaching of Leo XIII, quite novel to worldly ears, was looked upon with suspicion by some, even among Catholics, and gave offense to others. For it boldly attacked and overthrew the idols of liberalism, swept aside inveterate prejudices, and was so far and so unexpectedly in advance of its time, that the slow of heart ridiculed the study of the new social philosophy, and the timid feared to scale its lofty heights. Nor were there wanting those who, while professing their admiration for this message of light, regarded it as a utopian ideal, desirable rather than attainable in practice.

SCOPE OF THE PRESENT ENCYCLICAL

15. And now that the solemn commemoration of the fortieth anniversary of *Rerum Novarum* is being enthusiastically celebrated in every country, but particularly in the Holy City to which Catholic workingmen are gathering from all sides, we deem it opportune, venerable brethren and beloved children, first to recall the great benefits which this encyclical has brought to the Catholic Church and to the world at large: secondly to develop as regards certain points the teaching of so great a master on social and economic affairs after vindicating it from some doubts which have arisen: finally after arraigning the contemporary economy and listening to socialism's charges, to expose the root of the present social disorder, and to point out the only way to a salutary renewal, namely a Christian reform of morals. Such are the three topics chosen for treatment in the present letter.

I. BENEFITS DERIVING FROM *RERUM NOVARUM*

16. Beginning, then, with the topic we have mentioned first, we cannot refrain from earnestly thanking Almighty God for the benefits which have come to the Church and human society from the encyclical of Leo XIII. For we remember the counsel of St. Ambrose: "No duty is more urgent than that of returning thanks."[13] Were we to enumerate these benefits even in a cursory way, it would be necessary to recall almost the whole social history of the past forty years. We may summarize them conveniently under three heads, corresponding to the three kinds of help which our predecessor earnestly sought in accomplishing his great work of reconstruction.

1. WHAT WAS DONE BY THE CHURCH

17. In the first place, Leo himself clearly stated what could be expected from the Church. "It is the Church that proclaims from the Gospel those teachings by which the conflict can be brought to an end, or at least made far less bitter. The Church uses her efforts not only to enlighten the mind, but to direct by her precepts the life and conduct of men. The Church improves and ameliorates the condition of the workingman by numerous useful organizations."[14]

In Doctrinal Matters

18. This mighty power for good the Church did not suffer to remain unprofitably stored away, but drew upon it freely in the cause of a peace that was so universally desired. Time and again the teaching of the encyclical *Rerum Novarum* on social and economic affairs was proclaimed and emphasized in spoken and written word by Leo XIII himself and by his successors, who were ever careful to adapt it to the changing conditions of the times, and who never relaxed their paternal solicitude and pastoral constancy, particu-

larly in defense of the poor and the weak.[15] With like zeal and erudition did numerous bishops of the Catholic world interpret and comment upon this doctrine, and apply it, according to the mind and instructions of the Holy See, to the special circumstances of the various regions.[16]

19. It is not surprising, therefore, that under the leadership and guidance of the Church, many learned priests and laymen earnestly applied themselves to the study of social and economic science in accordance with the procedures of our age, being especially eager that the unchanging and unchangeable teaching of the Church might be related to the new developments.

20. Under the guidance and in the light of Leo's encyclical there thus arose a truly Catholic social teaching, which continues to be fostered and enriched daily by the tireless labors of those picked men whom we have named the auxiliaries of the Church. They do not allow it to remain hidden in learned obscurity, but bring it forth into the full view of public life, as is clearly shown by the valuable and well-frequented courses established in Catholic universities, academies and seminaries, by social congress and "weeks" held at frequent intervals and with gratifying success, by study circles, by sound and timely publications spread far and wide.

21. Nor were these the only blessings which followed from the encyclical. The teaching of *Rerum Novarum* began little by little to penetrate among those also who, being outside Catholic unity, do not recognize the authority of the Church; and thus Catholic principles on social affairs gradually became part of the heritage of the whole human race. Thus, too, we rejoice that the eternal truths, proclaimed so vigorously by our illustrious predecessor, are advanced and advocated not merely in non-Catholic books and journals, but frequently also in legislative assemblies and in courts of justice.

22. Moreover, when after the great war the rulers of the leading nations wished to restore peace by an entire reform of social conditions, and among other measures drew up principles to regulate the just rights of labor, many of their conclusions agreed so perfectly with the principles and warnings of Leo XIII as to seem expressly deduced from them. The encyclical *Rerum Novarum* has become in truth a memorable document to which may well be applied the words of Isaiah: "He shall set up a standard unto the nations."[17]

In Practical Applications

23. In the meantime, study and investigation caused Pope Leo's teaching to become widely known throughout the world, and steps were taken to apply to it practical use. In the first place in a spirit of active beneficence, every effort was made to lift up a class of men, who, owing to the expansion of modern industry, had enormously increased in numbers, but whose rightful position in society had not yet been achieved, and who in consequence experienced much neglect and contempt.

These were the workingmen. In addition, therefore, to their other heavy pastoral duties, the secular and regular clergy, under the guidance of the bishops began at once the work of popular education and culture to the immense advantage of souls.

This constant endeavor to imbue the minds of the workingmen with the Christian spirit did much to awaken in them at the same time a sense of their true dignity. By keeping clearly before their mind the rights and duties of their position, it rendered them capable of legitimate genuine progress, and of becoming leaders of their fellows.

24. From that time onward, the resources of life were provided for in larger measure and more securely. In answer to the appeal of the pontiff, works of beneficence and charity began to multiply under the direction of the Church. And frequently under the guidance of her priests, there sprang up further an ever increasing number of new institutions, by which workingmen, craftsmen, farmers, wage earners of every kind could give and receive mutual assistance and support.

2. WHAT WAS DONE BY CIVIL AUTHORITY

25. With regard to the civil power, Leo XIII boldly passed beyond the restrictions imposed by liberalism, and fearlessly proclaimed the doctrine that the civil power is more than the mere guardian of law and order, and that it must strive with all zeal "to make sure that the laws and institutions, the general character and administration of the commonwealth, should be such as of themselves to realize public well-being and private prosperity."[18] It is true, indeed, that requisite freedom of action must be left to individual citizens and families; but this should be with due regard for the common good and with no injury to anyone. It is the duty of rulers to protect the community and its various parts, but in protecting the rights of individuals they must have special regard for the infirm and needy. "For the richer class, surrounded as they are by their own resources, have less need of public protection, whereas the mass of the poor, with no resources of their own to rely on, must look to the State for protection. And hence wage earners, since they mostly belong to that class, should be the objects of special care and solicitude on the part of the commonwealth."[19]

26. We do not, of course, deny that even before the encyclical of Leo, some rulers had provided for the more urgent needs of the working classes, and had checked the more flagrant acts of injustice perpetrated against them. But after the apostolic voice had sounded from the Chair of Peter throughout the world, the leaders of the nations, at last more conscious of their obligations, set their hearts and minds to the promotion of a broader social policy.

27. In fact, the encyclical *Rerum Novarum* completely overthrew those tottering tenets of liberalism which had long hampered effective intervention by the government. It prevailed upon the peoples themselves to develop their social policy more intensely and on truer lines, and also encouraged outstanding Catholics to give such efficacious help and assistance to rulers of the State

that in legislative assemblies they were not infrequently the foremost advocates of the new policy. Furthermore, not a few recent laws dealing with social questions were originally proposed to the suffrages of the people's representatives by ecclesiastics thoroughly imbued with Leo's teaching, who afterward with watchful care promoted and fostered their execution.

28. As a result of these steady and tireless efforts, there has arisen a new branch of jurisprudence unknown to earlier times, whose aim is the energetic defense of those sacred rights of the workingman which proceed from his dignity as a man and as a Christian. These laws concern the soul, the health, the strength, the housing workshops, wages, dangerous employments, in a word all that concerns the wage earners, with particular regard to women and children. Even though these regulations do not agree always and in every detail with the recommendations of Pope Leo, it is none the less certain that much which they contain is strongly suggestive of *Rerum Novarum*, to which in large measure must be attributed the improved condition of the workingmen.

3. WHAT WAS DONE BY THE PARTIES CONCERNED

29. In the last place, the wise pontiff pointed out that employer and workmen may of themselves effect much in the matter we are treating by means of "such organizations as afford opportune aid to those who are in distress and which draw the two classes more closely together."[20] Among these he attributed prime importance to societies consisting either of workingmen alone or of workingmen and employers together. He devotes much space to describing and commending these societies and expounds with remarkable prudence their nature, reason and opportunities, their rights, duties and laws.

30. The lesson was opportune. For at that time governments of not a few nations were much given to *laissez faire*, and regarded such unions of workingmen with disfavor, if not with open hostility. While readily recognizing and protecting similar associations among other classes, with shameful hurt they denied the innate right of forming associations to those who needed them most for self-protection against oppression by the more powerful. There were even Catholics who viewed with suspicion the efforts of the laboring classes to form such unions, as if these reflected a socialistic or revolutionary spirit.

Workingmen's Unions

31. Worthy of all praise, therefore, are the directions authoritatively promulgated by Leo XIII, which served to break down this opposition and dispel these suspicions. They have a still higher distinction, however, that of encouraging Christian workingmen to form unions according to their several trades, and of teaching them how to do it. Many were thus confirmed in the path of duty, in spite of very strong attractions of socialist organizations, which claimed to be the sole defenders and champions of the lowly and the oppressed.

32. The encyclical *Rerum Novarum* declared quite opportunely that in establishing associations of this kind, they "should be so organized and directed as to furnish a very apt and suitable means for achieving what is aimed at, namely, that each member better his condition so far as possible as regards body, soul and property." Moreover, the encyclical made clear that these associations "should pay special attention to the fostering of piety and morality, and that their internal discipline should be directed precisely by these considerations." For "the foundation of social laws being thus laid in religion, it is not hard to establish the relation of members one to another, in order that they may live together in concord and achieve prosperity."[21]

33. Eager to carry out to the full the program of Leo XIII, the clergy and many of the laity devoted themselves everywhere with admirable zeal to the creation of such unions, which in turn became instrumental in building up a body of truly Christian workingmen. These happily combined the successful plying of their trade with deep religious convictions; they learned to defend their temporal rights and interests energetically and efficiently, retaining at the same time a due respect for justice and a sincere desire to collaborate with other classes. Thus they prepared the way for a Christian renewal of the whole social life.

34. These counsels of Leo XIII were reduced to practice differently in different places. In some countries one and the same association included within its scope all the ends and purposes proposed by him. In others, according as circumstances seemed to counsel or demand, a division of function developed, and various associations were founded. Some of these associations undertook the protection of the rights and legitimate interests of their members in the labor market; others had as their object the provision of mutual help in economic matters; while still others were concerned exclusively with religion and moral duties and with similar pursuits.

35. The latter method was chiefly used wherever the laws of the country, or given economic conditions, or the lamentable dissension of minds and hearts so prevalent in modern society, or the necessity of uniting forces to combat the growing ranks of revolutionaries, made it impossible for Catholics to form Catholic unions. Under such circumstances, they seem to have no choice but to enroll themselves in neutral trade unions. These, however, should always respect justice and equity, and leave to their Catholic members full freedom to follow the dictates of their conscience and to obey the precepts of the Church. It belongs to the bishops to permit Catholic workingmen to join these unions, where they judge that circumstances make it necessary and there appears no danger for religion, observing however the rules and precautions recommended by our predecessor of saintly memory, Pius X.[22]

Among these precautions the first and most important is that side by side with these trade unions, there must always be associations which aim at giving their members a thorough religious and moral training, that these in turn may impart to the labor unions to which they belong the upright spirit which should direct their entire conduct. Thus will these unions exert a beneficent influence far beyond the ranks of their own members.

36. It must be set to the credit of the encyclical that these unions of workingmen have everywhere so flourished that in our days, though unfortunately still inferior in number to the organizations of socialists and communists, they already muster an imposing body of wage earners able to maintain successfully, both in national and international assemblies, the rights and legitimate demands of Catholic laborers, and to assert the saving principle on which Christian society is based.

Organization among Other Classes

37. There is the further fact that the doctrine concerning the innate right of forming unions, which Leo XIII treated so learnedly and defended so bravely, began to find ready application to associations other than those of workingmen. It would seem, therefore, that the encyclical is in no small measure responsible for the gratifying increase and spread of associations among farmers and others of modest circumstances. These excellent organizations, with others of a similar kind, happily combine economic advantages with cultural aims.

Associations of Employers

38. Associations of employers and industrial leaders, which our predecessor so earnestly pleaded for, did not meet with the same success; they are, we regret to say, still few in number. The reason for this must not be entirely attributed to want of good will, but to other and far more serious obstacles, whose nature and gravity we know and appreciate to the full. There are, however, well-founded hopes that these obstacles also will shortly be removed. We hail even now with deep joy of soul certain experiments, far from negligible, which have been made in this regard, for the future.[23]

RERUM NOVARUM, "MAGNA CHARTA" OF SOCIAL ORDER

39. These beneficent results of Leo's encyclical, venerable brethren and beloved children, which we have here suggested rather than described, are so many and so great as to prove beyond question that this immortal document portrays more than an idealistic, though beautiful, picture of human society.

We would rather say that our illustrious predecessor drew from the Gospel as from a living and life-giving source doctrines capable, if not of settling at once, at least of considerably mitigating the fatal internal strife which rends the human family. That the good seed sown with a lavish hand forty years ago fell in part on good ground is shown by the rich harvest which by God's favor the Church of Christ and the whole human race have reaped unto salvation. It would not be rash to say that during the long years of its usefulness Leo's encyclical has proved itself the Magna Charta on which all Christian activities in social matters are ultimately based.

Nevertheless, there are some who seem to attach little importance to this encyclical and to the present anniversary celebration. These men either slander a doctrine of which they are entirely ignorant, or if not unacquainted with this teaching, they betray their failure to understand it, or else if they understand it they lay themselves open to the charge of base injustice and ingratitude.

40. In the course of these years, however, doubts have arisen concerning the correct interpretation of certain passages of the encyclical or their inferences, and these doubts have led to controversies even among Catholics, not always of a peaceful character. On the other hand, the new needs of our age and the changed conditions of society have rendered necessary a more precise application and amplification of Leo's doctrine. We, therefore, gladly take this opportunity of answering their doubts, so far as in us lies, and of satisfying the demands of the present day. This we do in virtue of our apostolic office by which we are a debtor to all.[24]

II. AUTHORITY OF THE CHURCH IN SOCIAL AND ECONOMIC AFFAIRS

41. But before proceeding to discuss these problems we lay down the principle long since clearly established by Leo XIII that it is our right and our duty to deal authoritatively with social and economic problems.[25] It is not of course for the Church to lead men to transient and perishable happiness only, but to that which is eternal. Indeed "the Church believes that it would be wrong for her to interfere without just cause in such earthly concerns";[26] but she never can relinquish her God-given task; of interposing her authority not indeed in technical matters, for which she has neither the equipment nor the mission, but in all those that have a bearing on moral conduct. For the deposit of truth entrusted to us by God, and our weighty office of propagating, interpreting, and urging in season and out of season the entire moral law, demand that both social and economic questions be brought within our supreme jurisdiction, insofar as they refer to moral issues.

42. For, though economic activity and moral discipline are guided each by its own principles in its own sphere, it is false that the two orders are so distinct and alien that the former in no way depends on the latter. The laws of economics, as they are called, derived from the nature of earthly goods and from the qualities of the human body and soul, determine what aims are unattainable or attainable in economic matters and what means are thereby necessary. But reason itself clearly deduces from the nature of things and from the individual and social character of man what is the end and object of the whole economic order assigned by God the Creator.

43. For it is the moral law alone which commands us to seek in all our conduct our supreme and final end, and to strive directly in our specific actions for those ends which nature, or rather, the Author of nature, has established for

them, duly subordinating the particular to the general. If this law be faithfully obeyed, the result will be that particular economic aims, whether of society as a body or of individuals, will be intimately linked with the universal teleological order, and as a consequence we shall be led by progressive stages to the final end of all, God himself, our highest and lasting good.

1. THE RIGHT OF PROPERTY

44. Descending now to details, we commence with ownership or the right of property. You are aware, venerable brethren and beloved children, how strenuously our predecessor of happy memory defended the right of property against the teachings of the socialists of his time, showing that the abolition of private ownership would prove to be not beneficial, but grievously harmful to the working classes. Yet, since there are some who falsely and unjustly accuse the supreme pontiff and the Church as upholding both then and now the wealthier classes against the proletariat, and since controversy has arisen among Catholics as to the true sense of Pope Leo's teaching, we have thought it well to defend from calumny the Leonine doctrine in this matter, which is also the Catholic doctrine, and to safeguard it against false interpretations.

Its Individual and Social Character

45. First, let it be made clear beyond all doubt that neither Leo XIII nor those theologians who have taught under the guidance and direction of the Church have ever denied or called in question the twofold aspect of ownership, which is individual or social accordingly as it regards individuals or concerns the common good. Their unanimous contention has always been that the right to own private property has been given to man by nature or rather by the Creator himself, not only in order that individuals may be able to provide for their own needs and those of their families, but also that by means of it, the goods which the Creator has destined for the human race may truly serve this purpose. Now these ends cannot be secured unless some definite and stable order is maintained.

46. There is, therefore, a double danger to be avoided. On the one hand, if the social and public aspect of ownership be denied or minimized, the logical consequence is "individualism," as it is called; on the other hand, the rejection or diminution of its private and individual character necessarily leads to some form of "collectivism." To disregard these dangers would be to rush headlong into the quicksands of the moral, juridical, and social modernism, which we condemned in the encyclical letter issued at the beginning of our pontificate.[27]

Let this be noted particularly by those seekers after novelties who launch against the Church the odious calumny that she has allowed a pagan concept of ownership to creep into the teachings of her theologians and that another concept must be substituted, which in their astounding ignorance they call "Christian."

Obligations Implicit in Ownership

47. That we may keep within bounds the controversies which have arisen concerning ownership and the duties attaching to it, we reassert in the first place the fundamental principle laid down by Leo XIII, that the right of property must be distinguished from its use.[28] It belongs to what is called commutative justice faithfully to respect the possessions of others, and not to invade the rights of another, by exceeding the bounds of one's own property. The putting of one's own possessions to proper use, however, does not fall under this form of justice, but under certain other virtues and therefore it is "a duty not enforced by courts of justice."[29] Hence it is false to contend that the right of ownership and its proper use are bounded by the same limits; and it is even less true that the very misuse or even the non-use of ownership destroys or forfeits the right itself.

48. Most helpful therefore and worthy of all praise are the efforts of those who, in a spirit of harmony and with due regard for the traditions of the Church, seek to determine the precise nature of these duties and to define the boundaries imposed by the requirements of social life upon the right of ownership itself or upon its use. On the contrary, they err seriously who so weaken the individual character of property that they in fact destroy it.

Authority of the State

49. It follows from the twofold character of ownership, which we have termed individual and social, that men must take into account in this matter not only their own advantage but also the common good. To define in detail these duties, when the need occurs and when the natural law does not do so, is the function of the government. Provided that the natural and divine law be observed, the public authority, in view of the common good, may specify more accurately what is licit and what is illicit for property owners in the use of their possessions. Moreover, Leo XIII had wisely taught that "the delimiting of private possession has been left by God to man's industry and to the laws of individual peoples."[30]

History proves that the right of ownership, like other elements of social life, is not absolutely rigid, and this doctrine we ourselves have given utterance to on a previous occasion in the following terms: "How varied are the forms which the right of property has assumed! First, a primitive form in use among untutored and backward peoples, which still exists in certain localities even in our own day; then, that of the patriarchal age; later came various tyrannical types (we use the word in its classical meaning); finally, the feudal and monarchic systems down to the varieties of more recent times."[31]

It is plain, however, that the State may not discharge this duty in an arbitrary manner. Man's natural right of possessing and transmitting property by inheritance must be kept intact and cannot be taken away by the State from man. "For man is older than the State."[32] Moreover, "the domestic household is antecedent, logically as well as in fact, to the civil community."[33]

The prudent pontiff had already declared it unlawful for the State to exhaust the means of individuals by crushing taxes and tributes. "The right to possess private property is derived from nature, not from man; and the State has by no means the right to abolish it, but only to control its use and bring it into harmony with the interests of the public good."[34]

However, when civil authority adjusts ownership to meet the needs of the public good it acts not as an enemy, but as the friend of private owners; for thus it effectively prevents the possession of private property, intended by nature's Author in his wisdom for the sustaining of human life, from creating intolerable burden and so rushing to its own destruction. It does not therefore abolish, but protects private ownership, and far from weakening the right of private property, it gives it new strength.

Obligations Regarding Superfluous Income

50. At the same time a man's superfluous income is not left entirely to his own discretion. We speak of that portion of his income which he does not need in order to live as becomes his station. On the contrary, the grave obligations of charity, beneficence and liberality which rest upon the wealthy are constantly insisted upon in telling words by Holy Scripture and the Fathers of the Church.

51. However, the investment of superfluous income in developing favorable opportunities for employment, provided the labor employed produces results which are really useful, is to be considered according to the teaching of the Angelic Doctor[35] an act of real liberality particularly appropriate to the needs of our time.

Titles in Acquiring Ownership

52. The original acquisition of property takes place by first occupation and by industry, or, as it is called, specification. This is the universal teaching of tradition and the doctrine of our predecessor, despite unreasonable assertions to the contrary, and no wrong is done to any man by the occupation of goods unclaimed and which belong to nobody. The only form of labor, however, which gives the workingman a title to its fruits is that which man exercises as his own master, and by which some new form or new value is produced.

2. CAPITAL AND LABOR

53. Altogether different is the labor one man hires out to another and which is expended on the property of another. To it apply oppositely the words of Leo XIII: "It is only with the labor of workingmen that States grow rich."[36] Is it not indeed apparent that the huge possessions which constitute human

wealth are begotten by and flow from the hands of the workingman, toiling either unaided or with the assistance of tools and machinery which wonderfully intensify his efficiency?

Universal experience teaches us that no nation has ever yet risen from want and poverty to a better and loftier station without the unremitting toil of all its citizens, both employers and employed. But it is no less self-evident that these ceaseless labors would have remained ineffective, indeed could never have been attempted, had not God, the Creator of all things, in his goodness bestowed in the first instance the wealth and resources of nature, its treasures and its powers. For what else is work but the application of one's forces of soul and body to these gifts of nature for the development of one's powers by this means?

Now the natural law, or rather, God's will manifested by it, demands that right order be observed in the application of natural resources to human need; and this order consists in everything having its proper owner. Hence it follows that unless a man apply his labor to his own property, an alliance must be formed between his toil and his neighbor's property, for each is helpless without the other. This was what Leo XIII had in mind when he wrote: "Capital cannot do without labor, nor labor without capital."[37] It is therefore entirely false to ascribe the results of their combined efforts to either party alone; and it is flagrantly unjust that either should deny the efficacy of the other and seize all the profits.

Unjust Claims of Capital

54. Capital, however, was long able to appropriate to itself excessive advantages. It claimed all the products and profits and left to the laborer the barest minimum necessary to repair his strength and to ensure the continuation of his class. For by an inexorable economic law, it was held, all accumulation of riches must fall to the share of the wealthy, while the workingman must remain perpetually in indigence or reduced to the minimum needed for existence. It is indeed true that the actual state of things was not always and everywhere as bad as the liberalistic tenets of the so-called Manchester School might lead us to conclude; but it cannot be denied that a steady drift of economic and social tendencies was in this direction. These false opinions and specious axioms were vehemently attacked, as was to be expected, and by others also than merely those whom such principles deprived of their innate right to better their condition.

Unjust Claims of Labor

55. The cause of the harassed workingman was espoused by the "intellectuals," as they are called, who set up in opposition to this fictitious law another equally false moral principle: that all products and profits, excepting those required to repair and replace invested capital, belong by every right to the workingman. This error, more subtle than that of the socialists who

hold that all means of production should be transferred to the State, or, as they term it, "socialized," is for that reason more dangerous and apt to deceive the unwary. It is an alluring poison, consumed with avidity by many not deceived by open socialism.

Guiding Principle of Just Distribution

56. To prevent erroneous doctrines of this kind from blocking the path of justice and peace, the advocates of these opinions should have hearkened to the wise words of our predecessor: "The earth even though apportioned among private owners ceases not thereby to minister to the needs of all."[38] This teaching we ourselves have reaffirmed above when we wrote that the division of goods which is effected by private ownership is ordained by nature itself and has for its purpose that created things may minister to man's needs in orderly and stable fashion. This principle must be constantly borne in mind if we would not wander from the path of truth.

57. Now, not every kind of distribution of wealth and property among men is such that it can satisfactorily, still less adequately, attain the end intended by God. Wealth, therefore, which is constantly being augmented by social and economic progress, must be so distributed among the various individuals and classes of society that the common good of all, of which Leo XIII spoke, be thereby promoted. In other words, the good of the whole community must be safeguarded. By these principles of social justice one class is forbidden to exclude the other from a share in the profits. This law is violated by an irresponsible wealthy class who, in their good fortune, deem it a just state of things that they should receive everything and the laborer nothing. It is violated also by the propertyless class, when, strongly aroused because justice is ignored and too prone to vindicate improperly the one right well known to them, they demand for themselves all the fruits of production. They are wrong in thus attacking and seeking the abolition of ownership and all profits deriving from sources other than labor, whatever be their nature or significance in human society, for the sole reason that they were not obtained by toil. In this connection it must be noted that the appeal made by some to the words of the Apostle: "If any man will not work, neither let him eat"[39] is as inept as it is unfounded. The Apostle is here passing judgment on those who refuse to work though they could and ought to do so: he admonishes us to use diligently our time and our powers of body and mind, and not to become burdensome to others as long as we are able to provide for ourselves. In no sense does he teach that labor is the sole title which gives a right to a living or to profits.[40]

58. Each class, then, must receive its due share, and the distribution of created goods must be brought into conformity with the demands of the common good and social justice. For every sincere observer realizes that the vast differences between the few who hold excessive wealth and the many who live in destitution constitute a grave evil in modern society.

3. UPLIFTING THE PROLETARIAT

59. This is the aim which our predecessor urged as the necessary object of our efforts: the uplifting of the proletariat. It calls for more emphatic assertion and more insistent repetition on the present occasion because these salutary injunctions of the pontiff have not infrequently been forgotten, deliberately ignored, or deemed impractical, whereas they were both feasible and imperative. They have lost none of their force or wisdom for our own age, even though the horrible "pauperism" of the days of Leo XIII is less prevalent today. The condition of the workingmen has indeed been improved and rendered more equitable in many respects, particularly in the larger and more developed States, where the laboring class can no longer be said to be universally in misery and want. But after modern machinery and modern industry had progressed with astonishing speed and become common in many newly colonized countries as well as in the ancient civilizations of the Far East, the number of the dispossessed laboring masses, whose cries mount to heaven from these lands, increased exceedingly.

Moreover, there is the immense army of hired rural laborers whose condition is depressed in the extreme, and who have no hope of ever "obtaining a share in the land."[41] These, too, unless efficacious remedies be applied, will remain permanently in a proletarian condition.

60. It is true that there is a formal difference between pauperism and proletarianism. Nevertheless, the immense number of propertyless wage earners on the one hand, and the superabundant riches of the fortunate few on the other, is an unanswerable argument that the earthly goods so abundantly produced in this age of "industrialism" are far from rightly distributed and equitably shared among the various classes of men.

Proletarian Conditions to Be Overcome by Wage Earner Ownership

61. Every effort, therefore, must be made that at least in future only a fair share of the fruits of production be permitted to accumulate in the hands of the wealthy, and that an ample sufficiency be supplied to the workingmen. The purpose is not that these become slack at their work, for man is born to labor as the bird to fly, but that by thrift they may increase their possessions and by the prudent management of the same may be enabled to bear the family burden with greater ease and security, being freed from that hand-to-mouth uncertainty which is the lot of the proletarian. Thus they will not only be in a position to support life's changing fortunes, but will also have the reassuring confidence that when their lives are ended, some little provision will remain for those whom they leave behind them.

62. These ideas were not merely suggested, but stated in frank and open terms by our predecessor. We emphasize them with renewed insistence in the present encyclical. For unless efforts are made with all energy and without delay to put them into practice, let no one persuade himself that public order

and the peace and tranquillity of human society can be defended effectively against agitators of revolution.

4. A JUST WAGE

63. This program cannot, however, be realized unless the propertyless wage earner be placed in such circumstances that by skill and thrift he can acquire a certain moderate ownership, as was already declared by us, following the footsteps of our predecessor. But how can he ever save money, except from his wages and by living sparingly, who has nothing but his labor by which to obtain food and the necessities of life? Let us turn, therefore, to the question of wages, which Leo XIII held to be "of great importance,"[42] stating and explaining where necessary its principles and precepts.

Wage Contract Not Essentially Unjust

64. And first of all, those who hold that the wage contract is essentially unjust, and that in its place must be introduced the contract of partnership, are certainly in error. They do a grave injury to our predecessor, whose encyclical not only admits this contract, but devotes much space to its determination according to the principles of justice.

65. In the present state of human society, however, we deem it advisable that the wage contract should, when possible, be modified somewhat by a contract of partnership, as is already being tried in various ways with significant advantage to both wage earners and employers. For thus the workers and executives become sharers in the ownership or management, or else participate in some way in the profits.

66. In estimating a just wage, not one consideration alone but many must be taken into account. According to the wise words of Leo XIII: "Before deciding whether wages are fair, many things have to be considered."[43]

67. In this way he refuted the irresponsible view of certain writers who declare that this momentous question can easily be solved by the application of a single principle, and that not even a true one.

68. Entirely false is the principle, widely propagated today, that the worth of labor and therefore the return to be made for it, should equal the entire value added. Thus a right to the full product of his toil is claimed for the wage earner. How erroneous this is appears from what we have written above concerning capital and labor.

Individual and Social Character of Labor

69. The obvious truth is that in labor, especially wage labor, as in ownership, there is a social as well as a personal or individual aspect to be considered. For unless human society forms a truly social and organic body; unless labor be protected in the social and juridical order; unless the various forms of human endeavor, dependent one upon the other, are united in mutual harmony and

mutual support; unless, above all, intellect, capital and labor are brought together in a common effort, man's toil cannot produce due fruit. Hence, if the social and individual character of labor be overlooked, it can be neither equitably appraised nor properly recompensed according to strict justice.

Three Things to Be Considered

70. From this double aspect growing out of the very notion of human labor, follow important conclusions for the regulation and fixing of wages.

(a) Support of the Workingman and His Family

71. In the first place, the wage paid to the workingman should be sufficient for the support of himself and of his family.[44] It is indeed proper that the rest of the family contribute according to their power toward the common maintenance, as in the rural home or in the families of many artisans and small shopkeepers. But it is wrong to abuse the tender years of children or the weakness of woman. Mothers should especially devote their energies to the home and the things connected with it. Most unfortunate, and to be remedied energetically, is the abuse whereby mothers of families, because of the insufficiency of the father's salary, are forced to engage in gainful occupations outside the domestic walls to the neglect of their own proper cares and duties, particularly the education of their children.

Every effort must therefore be made that fathers of families receive a sufficient wage adequate to meet ordinary domestic needs. If in the present state of society this is not always feasible, social justice demands that reforms be introduced without delay which will guarantee every adult workingman just such a wage. In this connection we might utter a word of praise for various systems devised and attempted in practice, by which an increased wage is paid in view of increased family burdens, and a special provision is made for special needs.

(b) The State of Business

72. The condition of any particular business and of its owner must also come into question in settling the scale of wages; for it is unjust to demand wages so high that an employer cannot pay them without ruin, and without consequent distress among the working people themselves. If the business makes smaller profit on account of bad management, want of enterprise or out-of-date methods, this is not a just reason for reducing the workingmen's wages. If, however, the business does not make enough money to pay the workman a just wage, either because it is overwhelmed with unjust burdens, or because it is compelled to sell its products at an unjustly low price, those who thus injure it are guilty of grievous wrong; for it is they who deprive the workingmen of the just wage and force them to accept lower terms.

73. Let employers, therefore, and employed join in their plans and efforts to overcome all difficulties and obstacles, and let them be aided in this wholesome endeavor by the wise measures of the public authority. In the last extreme, counsel must be taken whether the business can continue, or whether some other provision should be made for the workers. The guiding spirit in

this crucial decision should be one of mutual understanding and Christian harmony between employers and workers.

(c) Requirements of the Common Good

74. Finally, the wage level should be arrived at with the public economic welfare in mind. We have already shown how conducive it is to the common good that workers and executives enabled, by setting aside that portion of their wages remaining after necessary expenses are met, to attain to a modest fortune. Another point, however, of no less importance and especially necessary these days, is that employment opportunities be provided those able and willing to work. This depends in large measure upon the scale of wages, which multiplies opportunities for work as long as it remains within proper limits, and reduces them if allowed to pass these limits. All are aware that a scale of wages too low, no less than a scale excessively high, causes unemployment. Now unemployment, particularly if widespread and of long duration, as we have been forced to experience it during our pontificate, is a dreadful scourge; it causes misery and temptation to the laborer, ruins the prosperity of nations, and endangers public order, peace and tranquility the world over. To lower or raise wages unduly, with a view to private profit, and with no consideration for the common good, is contrary to social justice. This latter requires that by combining effort and good will to the extent possible, wages be so determined as to offer to the greatest number opportunities of employment and of securing for themselves suitable means of livelihood.

75. A reasonable relationship between different wages here enters into consideration. Intimately connected with this is a reasonable relationship between the prices obtained for the products of the various economic groups, agrarian, industrial, etc. Where such balance is preserved, man's various economic activities combine, as it were, into one single organism and become members of a common body, lending each other mutual help and service. For then only will the economic and social system be soundly established and attain its end, when it secures for all and each those goods which the wealth and resources of nature, technical achievement, and the social organization of economic affairs can give. These goods should be sufficient to supply all needs and an honest livelihood, and to uplift men to that higher level of prosperity and culture which, provided it be used with prudence, is not only no hindrance but is of singular help to virtue.[45]

5. RECONSTRUCTION OF THE SOCIAL ORDER

76. What we have written thus far regarding a right distribution of property and a just scale of wages is concerned directly with the individual, and deals only indirectly with the social order. To this latter, however, our predecessor, Leo XIII, devoted special thought and care in his efforts to reconstruct and perfect it according to the principles of sound philosophy and the sublime precepts of the Gospel.[46]

77. A happy beginning has here been made. But in order that what has been well begun may be rendered stable, that what has not yet been accomplished may now be achieved, and that still richer and brighter blessings may descend upon mankind, two things are particularly necessary: the reform of institutions and the correction of morals.

78. When we speak of the reform of institutions it is principally the State we have in mind. Not indeed that all salvation is to be hoped for from its intervention, but because on account of the evil of "individualism," as we called it, things have come to such a pass that the highly developed social life, which once flourished in a variety of prosperous and interdependent institutions, has been damaged and all but ruined, leaving virtually only individuals and the State, with no little harm to the latter. But the State, deprived of a supporting social structure, and now encumbered with all the burdens once borne by the disbanded associations, is in consequence overwhelmed and submerged by endless affairs and responsibilities.

79. It is indeed true, as history clearly shows, that owing to the change in social conditions, much that was formerly done by small bodies can nowadays be accomplished only by large organizations. Nevertheless, it is a fundamental principle of social philosophy, fixed and unchangeable, that one should not withdraw from individuals and commit to the community what they can accomplish by their own enterprise and industry. So, too, it is an injustice and at the same time a grave evil and a disturbance of right order to transfer to the larger and higher collectivity functions which can be performed and provided for by lesser and subordinate bodies. Inasmuch as every social activity should, by its very nature, prove a help to members of the body social, it should never destroy or absorb them.

80. The State authorities should leave to other bodies the care and expediting of business and activities of lesser moment, which otherwise become for it a source of great distraction. It then will perform with greater freedom, vigor and effectiveness, the tasks belonging properly to it, and which it alone can accomplish, directing, supervising, encouraging, restraining, as circumstances suggest or necessity demands. Let those in power, therefore, be convinced that the more faithfully this principle of "subsidiarity" is followed and a hierarchical order prevails among the various organizations, the more excellent will be the authority and efficiency of society, and the happier and more prosperous the condition of the commonwealth.

Harmony between Ranks in Society

81. Now this is a major and pressing duty of the State and of all good citizens: to get rid of conflict between "classes" with divergent interests, and to foster and promote harmony between the various "ranks" or groupings of society.

82. It is necessary, then, that social policy be directed toward the reestablishment of functional groups. Society today continues in a strained and hence

unstable and uncertain condition, for it relies upon "classes" with diverse interests and opposing each other and hence prone to enmity and strife.

83. Labor, indeed, as has been well said by our predecessor in his encyclical, is not a mere chattel, since the human dignity of the workingman must be recognized in it, and consequently it cannot be bought and sold like any piece of merchandise. None the less the demand and supply of labor divides men on the labor market into two classes, as into two camps, and the bargaining between these parties transforms this labor market into an arena where the two armies are engaged in combat. To this grave disorder which is leading society to ruin a remedy must evidently be applied as speedily as possible. But there cannot be question of any perfect cure, except this opposition be done away with, and well-ordered members of the social body come into being: functional "groups"; namely, binding men together not according to the position they occupy in the labor market, but according to the diverse functions which they exercise in society. For as nature induces those who dwell in close proximity to unite into municipalities, so those who practice the same trade or profession, economic or otherwise, constitute as it were fellowships or bodies. These groupings, autonomous in character, are considered by many to be, if not essential to civil society, at least a natural accompaniment thereof.

84. Order, as the Angelic Doctor well defines, is unity arising from the apt arrangement of a plurality of objects; hence, true and genuine social order demands various members of society, joined together by a common bond.[47] Such a bond of union is provided on the one hand by the common effort to employers and employees of one and the same "group" joining forces to produce goods or give service; on the other hand, by the common good which all "groups" should unite to promote, each in its own sphere, with friendly harmony. Now this union will become powerful and efficacious in proportion to the fidelity with which the individuals and the "groups" strive to discharge their professional duties and to excel in them.

85. From this it is easy to conclude that in these associations the common interest of the whole "group" must predominate: and among these interests the most important is the directing of the activities of the group to the common good. Regarding cases in which interests of employers and employees call for special care and protection against opposing interests, separate deliberation will take place in their respective assemblies and separate votes will be taken as the matter may require.

86. It is hardly necessary to note that what Leo XIII taught concerning the form of political government can, in due measure, be applied also to vocational groups. Here, too, men may choose whatever form they please, provided that both justice and the common good be taken into aceount.[48]

87. Just as the citizens of the same municipality are wont to form associations with diverse aims, which various individuals are free to join or not, similarly, those who are engaged in the same trade or profession will form free associations among themselves, for purposes connected with their occupations.

Our predecessor explained clearly and lucidly the nature of free associations. We are content, therefore, to emphasize this one point: not only is man free to institute such associations legally and functionally of private character, but he also has the right of "freely adopting such organization and such rules as are judged best for the end in view."[49] The same liberty must be claimed for the founding of associations which extend beyond the limits of a single trade. Let those free associations which already flourish and produce salutary fruits make it the goal of their endeavors, in accordance with Christian social teaching to prepare the way and to do their part toward the realization of those more ideal vocational fellowships or "groups" which we have mentioned above.

Restoration of the Guiding Principle of Economic Life

88. Another and closely related aim should be kept in view. Just as the unity of human society cannot be built upon "class" conflict, so the proper ordering of economic affairs cannot be left to the free play of rugged competition. From this source as from a polluted spring have proceeded all the errors of the "individualistic" school. This school, forgetful or ignorant of the social and moral aspect of economic activities, regarded these as completely free and immune from any intervention by public authority, for they would have in the market place and in unregulated competition a principle of self-direction more suitable for guiding them than any created intellect which might intervene. Free competition, however, though justified and quite useful within certain limits, cannot be an adequate controlling principle in economic affairs. This has been abundantly proved by the consequences that have followed from the free rein given to these dangerous individualistic ideals. It is therefore very necessary that economic affairs be once more subjected to and governed by a true and effective guiding principle. Still less can this function be exercised by the economic supremacy which within recent times has taken the place of free competition: for this is a headstrong and vehement power, which, if it is to prove beneficial to mankind, needs to be curbed strongly and ruled with prudence. It cannot, however, be curbed and governed by itself. More lofty and noble principles must therefore be sought in order to regulate this supremacy firmly and honestly: to wit, social justice and social charity.

To that end all the institutions of public and social life must be imbued with the spirit of justice, and this justice must above all be truly operative. It must build up a juridical and social order able to pervade all economic activity. Society charity should be, as it were, the soul of this order. It is the duty of the State to safeguard effectively and to vindicate promptly this order, a task it will perform the more readily if it free itself from those burdens which, as we stated above, are not properly its own.

89. Further, it would be well if the various nations in common counsel and effort strove to promote a healthy economic cooperation by prudent pacts and institutions, since in economic matters they are largely dependent one upon the other, and need one another's help.

90. If then the members of the social body be thus reformed, and if the true directive principle of social and economic activity be thus reestablished, it will be possible to say, in a sense, of this body what the Apostle said of the Mystical Body of Christ: "The whole body (being closely joined and knit together through every joint of the system according to the functioning in due measure of each single part) derives its increase to the building up of itself in love."[50]

91. Within recent times, as all are aware, a special syndical and corporative organization has been inaugurated which, in view of the subject of the present encyclical, should now be briefly outlined and commented upon.

92. The State here grants legal recognition to the syndicate or union, and thereby confers on it some of the features of a monopoly, for in virtue of this recognition, it alone can represent respectively workingmen and employers, and it alone can conclude labor contracts and labor agreements. Affiliation to the syndicate is optional for everyone; but in this sense only can the syndical organization be said to be free, since the contribution to the union and other special taxes are obligatory for all who belong to a given branch, whether workingmen or employers, and the labor contracts drawn up by the legal syndicate are likewise obligatory. True, it has been authoritatively declared that the juridically established syndicate does not preclude the existence of trade or professional associations not recognized in law.

93. The corporations are composed of representatives of the unions of workingmen and employers of the same trade or profession, and as genuine and exclusive instruments and institutions of the State they direct and coordinate the activities of the syndicates in all matters of common interest.

94. Strikes and lockouts are forbidden. If the contending parties cannot come to an agreement, public authority intervenes.

95. Little reflection is required to perceive advantages in the institution thus summarily described: peaceful collaboration of the classes, repression of socialist organizations and efforts, the moderating authority of a special ministry.

But in order to overlook nothing in a matter of such importance, and in the light of the general principles stated above, as well as that of which we are now about to formulate, we feel bound to add that to our knowledge there are some who fear that the State is substituting itself in the place of private initiative, instead of limiting itself to necessary and sufficient help and assistance. It is feared that the new syndical and corporative order possesses an excessively bureaucratic and political character, and that, notwithstanding the general advantages referred to above, it risks serving particular political aims rather than contributing to the restoration of social order and the improvement of the same.

96. We believe that to attain this last-named lofty purpose for the true and permanent advantage of the commonwealth, there is need before and above all else of the blessing of God, and, in the second place of the cooperation of all men of good will. We believe, moreover, as a necessary consequence, that the end intended will be the more certainly attained the greater the contribution

furnished by men of technical, professional and social competence, and more still, by Catholic principles and their application. We look for this contribution, not to Catholic Action, which has no intention of displaying any strictly syndical or political activities, but to our sons, whom Catholic Action imbues with these principles and trains for the apostolate under the guidance and direction of the Church. We refer to the Church, which in the above-mentioned sphere, as in all others where moral questions are discussed and regulated, cannot forget or neglect the mandate as custodian and teacher given it by God.

97. However, all that we have taught about reconstructing and perfecting the social order will be of no avail without a reform of manners. Of this, history affords the clearest evidence. At one period there existed a social order which, though by no means perfect in every respect, corresponded nevertheless in a certain measure to right reason according to the needs and conditions of the times. That this order has long since perished is not due to the fact that it was incapable of development and adaptation to changing needs and circumstances, but rather to the wrongdoing of men. Men were hardened in excessive self-love and refused to extend that order, as was their duty, to the increasing numbers of the people; or else, deceived by the attractions of false liberty and other errors, they grew impatient of every restraint and endeavored to throw off all authority.

98. It remains for us then to turn our attention to the system of economic life which prevails and to its sharpest accuser, namely socialism. On these we shall pronounce a frank and just sentence; we shall examine more closely the root of the present grave evils, and shall indicate the first and most necessary remedy, which lies in a reform of morals.

III. MANY CHANGES SINCE LEO XIII

99. Since the time of Leo XIII important changes have taken place both in the economic system and in regard to socialism.

100. In the first place, it is obvious to all that the entire economic scene has greatly changed. You are aware, venerable brethren and beloved children, that our predecessor, of happy memory, had chiefly in mind that economic system in which were provided by different people the capital and labor jointly needed for production. He described it in a happy phrase: "Capital cannot do without labor, nor labor without capital."[51]

1. CHANGING FORM OF ECONOMIC LIFE

101. Leo XIII's whole endeavor was to adjust this economic system to the norms of right order. It is clear then that the system as such is not to be condemned. Surely it is not vicious of its very nature; but it violates right order whenever capital so employs the working or wage-earning classes as to divert

business and economic activity entirely to its own arbitrary will and advantage without any regard to the human dignity of the workers, the social character of economic life, social justice, and the common good.

102. It is true that not even today does this economic system prevail exclusively. There exists another economic system which still embraces a vast and important body of men. Thus, for example, there is the whole group of farmers, to which belongs the major portion of the human race, providing for themselves honestly and honorably the means of livelihood. This system also has its problems and difficulties, as our predecessor noted a number of times in his encyclical, and we have more than once mentioned in this letter.

103. But it is the "capitalist" economic regime that, with worldwide diffusion of industry, has penetrated everywhere, particularly since the publication of Leo XIII's encyclical. It has entered and pervaded the economic and social sphere even of those who live outside its ambit, influencing them, and, as it were, intimately affecting them by its advantages, inconveniences and vices.

104. When we turn our attention, therefore, to the changes which this capitalistic economic order has undergone since the days of Leo XIII, we have regard to the interests, not of those only who live in countries where "capital" and industry prevail, but of the whole human race.

Domination Has Replaced Free Competition

105. In the first place, then, it is patent that in our days not alone is wealth accumulated, but immense power and despotic economic domination is concentrated in the hands of a few, and that those few are frequently not the owners, but only the trustees and directors of invested funds, who administer them at their good pleasure.

106. This power becomes particularly irresistible when exercised by those who, because they hold and control money, are able also to govern credit and determine its allotment, for that reason supplying, so to speak, the life-blood to the entire economic body, and grasping, as it were, in their hands the very soul of the economy, so that no one dare breathe against their will.

107. This accumulation of power, a characteristic note of the modern economic order, is a natural result of unrestrained free competition which permits the survival of those only who are the strongest. This often means those who fight most relentlessly, who pay least heed to the dictates of conscience.

108. This concentration of power has led to a threefold struggle for domination. First, there is the struggle for dictatorship in the economic sphere itself; then, the fierce battle to acquire control of the State, so that its resources and authority may be abused in the economic struggles. Finally, the clash between States themselves.

This latter arises from two causes: Because the nations apply their power and political influence, regardless of circumstances, to promote the economic advantages of their citizens; and because, vice versa, economic forces and economic domination are used to decide political controversies between peoples.

Unfortunate Consequences

109. You assuredly know, venerable brethren and beloved children, and you lament the ultimate consequences of this individualistic spirit in economic affairs. Free competition has committed suicide; economic dictatorship has replaced a free market.

Unbridled ambition for domination has succeeded the desire for gain; the whole economic life has become hard, cruel and relentless in a ghastly measure. Furthermore, the intermingling and scandalous confusing of the duties and offices of civil authority and of the economy has produced grave evils, not the least of which has been a downgrading of the majesty of the State. The State which should be the supreme arbiter, ruling in queenly fashion far above all party contention, intent only upon justice and the common good, has become instead a slave, bound over to the service of human passion and greed. As regards the relations of nations among themselves, a double stream has issued forth from this one fountainhead; on the one hand, economic "nationalism" or even economic "imperialism"; on the other, a no less noxious and detestable "internationalism" or "international imperialism" in financial affairs, which holds that where a man's fortune is, there is his country.

Remedies

110. The remedies for these great evils we have indicated in the second part of the present encyclical, where we explicitly dwelt upon their doctrinal aspect. It will, therefore, be sufficient to recall them briefly here. Since the present economic system is based mainly upon capital and labor, it follows that the principles of right reason and Christian social philosophy regarding capital, labor and their mutual cooperation must be accepted in theory and reduced to practice. In the first place, due consideration must be had for the double character, individual and social, of capital and labor, in order that the dangers of individualism and of collectivism be avoided. The mutual relations between capital and labor must be regulated according to the laws of strict justice, called commutative justice, supported however by Christian charity. Free competition, and especially economic domination, must be kept within definite and proper bounds, and must be brought under effective control of the public authority, in matters pertaining to the latter's competence. The public institutions of the nations should be such as to make all human society conform to the requirements of the common good, that is, the norm of social justice. If this is done, that very important part of social life, the economic system, will of necessity be restored to sanity and right order.

2. CHANGES IN SOCIALISM

111. No less profound than the change in the general economy has been the development occurring within socialism since the days when Leo XIII contended with this latter. At that time socialism could be termed a single

system, generally speaking, and one which defended definite and coherent doctrines. Today, indeed, it has for the most part split into two opposing and hostile camps. Neither of them, however, has abandoned socialism's fundamental principles, which do not accord with Christian belief.

(a) The More Violent Section, Communism

112. One section of socialism has gone through a change comparable to that experienced by the capitalistic economy, as we indicated above, and has degenerated into "communism." Now communism teaches and pursues a twofold aim: merciless class warfare and the complete abolition of private ownership. This it does, not in secret and by hidden methods, but openly, frankly and by every means, even the most violent. To obtain these ends, it shrinks from nothing and fears nothing, and when it comes to power, it shows itself cruel and inhuman in a manner unbelievable and monstrous. Witness to this are the tragic ruins and destruction which communism has left throughout the vast reaches of Eastern Europe and Asia. Moreover, the antagonism and open hostility it has shown Holy Church and even God himself are, alas, well proven by facts and known to all. We do not think it necessary to warn upright and faithful children of the Church against the impious and nefarious character of communism. But we cannot contemplate without sorrow the heedlessness of those who seem to make light of these imminent dangers and with stolid indifference allow the propagation far and wide of those doctrines which seek by violence and bloodshed the destruction of all society. Even more severely must be condemned the foolhardiness of those who neglect to remove or modify such conditions as exasperate the minds of the people, and so prepare the way for the overthrow and ruin of the social order.

(b) More Moderate Socialism

113. The other section, which has retained the name of "socialism," is much less radical in its views. Not only does it condemn recourse to physical force, it even mitigates and moderates to some extent class warfare and the abolition of private property. It does not reject them entirely. It would seem as if socialism were afraid of its own principles and of the conclusion drawn therefrom by the communists, and in consequence were moving toward the truth which Christian tradition has always held in respect; for it cannot be denied that its programs often strikingly approach the just demands of Christian social reformers.

A Retreat from Class War and Abolition of Property

114. Class war, provided it abstains from enmities and mutual hatred, is changing gradually to an honest discussion of differences, based upon a concern for justice. If this is by no means the blessed social peace which we all long for, it can be and must be an approach toward the mutual cooperation of "groups." The war declared against private ownership has also abated more and

more in such a way that nowadays it is not really the possession of the means of production which is attacked but that type of social authority, which, in violation of all justice, has been seized and usurped by the owners of wealth. This authority in fact belongs, not to the individual owners, but to the State.

If these changes continue, it may well come about that gradually the tenets of mitigated socialism will no longer be different from the program of those who seek to reform human society according to Christian principles.

For it is rightly contended that certain forms of property must be reserved to the State, since they carry with them an opportunity of domination too great to be left to private individuals without injury to the community at large.

115. Just demands and desires of this kind contain nothing opposed to Christian truth, nor are they in any sense peculiar to socialism. Those therefore who look for nothing else have no reason for becoming socialists.

Possibility of a Middle Course

116. It must not be imagined however that all the socialist sects or factions which are not communist have in fact or in theory uniformly returned to this reasonable position. For the most part they do not reject class warfare and the abolition of property, but merely are more moderate in regard to them. Now, when false principles are thus mitigated and in some sense waived, the question arises, or is unwarrantably proposed in certain quarters, whether the principles of Christian truth also could not be somewhat moderated and attenuated, so as to meet socialism, as it were, halfway upon common ground. Some are engaged by the empty hope of gaining in this way the socialists to our cause. But such hopes are vain. Those who wish to be apostles among the socialists should preach the Christian truth whole and entire openly and sincerely, without any connivance with error. If they wish in truth to be heralds of the Gospel, let their endeavor be to convince socialists that their demands, in so far as they are just, are defended much more cogently by the principles of Christian faith, and are promoted much more efficaciously by the power of Christian charity.

117. But what if, in questions of class war and private ownership, socialism were to become so mitigated and amended that nothing reprehensible could any longer be found in it? Would it by that very fact have laid aside its character of hostility to the Christian religion? This is a question which holds many minds in suspense; and many are the Catholics who, realizing clearly that Christian principles can never be either sacrificed or minimized, seem to be raising their eyes toward the Holy See, and earnestly beseeching us to decide whether or not this form of socialism has retracted so far its false doctrines that it can now be accepted without the loss of any Christian principle, and be baptized into the Church. In our fatherly solicitude we desire to satisfy these petitions, and we pronounce as follows: Whether socialism be considered as a doctrine, or as a historical fact, or as a "movement," if it really remain socialism, it cannot be brought into harmony with the dogmas of the

Catholic Church, even after it has yielded to truth and justice in the points we have mentioned; the reason being that it conceives human society in a way utterly alien to Christian truth.

Socialism Conceives Society and Social Character of Man Foreign to Christian Truth

118. According to Christian doctrine, man, endowed with a social nature, is placed here on earth in order that he may spend his life in society, and under an authority ordained by God; that he may develop and evolve to the full all his faculties to the praise and glory of his Creator; and that, by fulfilling faithfully the duties of his station, he may attain to temporal and eternal happiness. Socialism, on the contrary, entirely ignorant of or unconcerned about this sublime end both of individuals and of society, affirms that living in community was instituted merely for the sake of advantages which it brings to mankind.

119. Goods are produced more efficiently by a suitable distribution of labor than by the scattered efforts of individuals. Hence the socialists argue that economic production, of which they see only the material side, must necessarily be carried on collectively, and that because of this necessity men must surrender and submit themselves wholly to society with a view to the production of wealth. Indeed, the possession of the greatest possible amount of temporal goods is esteemed so highly that man's higher goods, not excepting liberty, must, they claim, be subordinated and even sacrificed to the exigencies of efficient production. They affirm that the loss of human dignity, which results from these "socialized" methods of production, will be easily compensated for by the abundance of goods produced in common and accruing to the individual who can turn them at his will to the comforts and culture of life. Society, therefore, as socialism conceives it, is, on the one hand, impossible and unthinkable without the use of compulsion of the most excessive kind; on the other it fosters a false liberty, since in such a scheme no place is found for true social authority, which is not based on temporal and material advantages, but descends from God alone, the Creator and Last End of all things.[52]

Catholic and Socialist Are Opposing Terms

120. If, like all errors, socialism contains a certain element of truth (and this the sovereign pontiffs have never denied), it is nevertheless founded upon a doctrine of human society peculiarly its own, which is opposed to true Christianity. "Religious socialism," "Christian socialism" are expressions implying a contradiction in terms. No one can be at the same time a sincere Catholic and a true socialist.

Cultural Socialism

121. All that we have thus far laid down and established by our sovereign authority bears application also to a certain new socialist phenomenon, hitherto little known, but nowadays common to many sections of socialism. Its

main aim is the formation of minds and manners. Under the appearance of friendship, it attracts little children in particular and attaches them to itself, though its activity extends to all the people, to make of them convinced socialists, upon whom to build a society modeled on socialistic principles.

122. In our encyclical letter *Divini Illius Magistri*,[53] we have expounded at length the true principles on which Christian education rests and the end which it pursues. The contradiction between these and the actions and aims of cultural socialism is so clear and evident as to require no comment. Nevertheless, the formidable dangers which this form of socialism brings in its train seem to be ignored or underestimated by those who are little concerned to resist it with strength and zeal, as the gravity of the situation demands.

It is a duty of our pastoral office to warn these men of the grave danger which threatens. Let us bear in mind that the parent of this cultural socialism was liberalism and that its offspring will be "bolshevism."

Catholic Deserters to Socialism

123. This being so, you can understand, venerable brethren and beloved children, with what grief we perceive, in certain countries particularly, not a few of our children, who, while still preserving, as we are convinced, their true faith and good will, have deserted the camp of the Church and passed over to the ranks of socialism. Some openly boast of its name and profess socialistic doctrines; others, either through indifference or even almost in spite of themselves, join associations which in theory or in fact, are socialist.

124. In our paternal solicitude, therefore, we have mediated and sought to understand what can have been the reason of their going so far astray; and we seem to hear what many of them allege in excuse: the Church and those professing attachment to the Church favor the rich and neglect workingmen and have no care for them: they were obliged therefore in their own interest to join the socialist ranks.

125. What a lamentable fact, venerable brethren and beloved children, that there have been, and that there are even now some who, while professing, the Catholic faith, are well-nigh unmindful of that sublime law of justice and charity which binds us not only to give each man his due, but to succor our brethren as Christ our Lord himself: worse still, that there are those who out of greed for gain are not ashamed to oppress the workingman. Indeed, there are some who can abuse religion itself, cloaking their own unjust imposition under its name, that they may protect themselves against the clearly just demands of their employees.

We shall never desist from gravely censuring such conduct. Such men are the cause that the Church, without deserving it, may have the appearance and be accused of taking sides with the wealthy, and of being little moved by the needs and sufferings of the disinherited. That these appearances and these accusations are undeserved and unjust, the whole history of the Church clearly shows. The very encyclical, the anniversary of which we are celebrating, affords the clearest evidences that these calumnies and contumelies have been most unfairly directed at the Church and her teaching.

An Invitation to Return

126. But we are far indeed from being exasperated by these injustices or dejected by our pastoral sorrow. We have no wish to drive away or repel our children who have been so unhappily deceived, and who are wandering so far from the paths of truth and salvation. On the contrary, we invite them with all possible solicitude to return to the maternal bosom of the Church. God grant that they listen to our voice. God grant that whence they set out, thither they may return, to their father's house: that where their true practice, their true place is, there they may remain, among the ranks of those who, zealously following the directions promulgated by Leo XIII and solemnly repeated by ourselves, unremittingly endeavor to reform society according to the mind of the Church on a firm basis of social justice and social charity. Let it be their firm persuasion that nowhere, even on earth, can they find an ampler happiness than in company with him, who being rich became poor for our sakes. That through his poverty we might become rich:[54] Who was poor and in labors from his youth:[55] Who invites to himself all who labor and are burdened that he may refresh them bounteously in the love of his heart:[56] Who, in fine, without any respect for persons, will require more of him to whom more has been given, and "will render to everyone according to his conduct."[57]

3. MORAL RENOVATION

127. However, if we examine matters diligently and thoroughly we shall perceive clearly that this longed-for social reconstruction must be preceded by a profound renewal of the Christian spirit, from which so many of those engaged in economic activity have in many places unhappily departed. Otherwise, all our endeavors will be futile, and our social edifice will be built, not upon a rock, but upon shifting sand.[58]

128. We have passed in review, venerable brethren and beloved children, the state of the modern economic world and have found it suffering from the greatest evils. We have investigated anew socialism and communism, and have found them, even in their mitigated forms, far removed from the precepts of the Gospel.

129. "And if society is to be healed now"—we use the words of our predecessor—"in no way can it be healed save by a return to Christian life and Christian institutions,"[59] for Christianity alone can apply an efficacious remedy for the excessive solicitude for transitory things, which is the origin of all vices. When men are fascinated and completely absorbed in the things of the world, it alone can draw away their attention and raise it to heaven. And who will deny that this remedy is not urgently needed by society?

Chief Disorder of the Modern World: Ruin of Souls

130. For most men are affected almost exclusively by temporal upheavals, disasters and ruins. Yet if we view things with Christian eyes, and we should, what are they all in comparison with the ruin of souls?

Nevertheless, it may be said with all truth that nowadays the conditions of social and economic life are such that vast multitudes of men can only with great difficulty pay attention to that one thing necessary, namely their eternal salvation.

131. Constituted pastor and protector of these innumerable sheep by the Prince of pastors, who redeemed them by his blood, we can scarcely restrain our tears when we reflect upon the dangers which threaten them. Our pastoral office, moreover, reminds us to search constantly, with paternal solicitude, for means of coming to their assistance, appealing to the unwearying zeal of others who are bound to this cause by justice and charity. For what will it profit men that a more prudent distribution and use of riches make it possible for them to gain even the whole world, if thereby they suffer the loss of their own souls?[60] What will it profit to teach them sound principles in economics, if they permit themselves to be so swept away by selfishness, by unbridled and sordid greed, that "hearing the commandments of the Lord, they do all things contrary"?[61]

Cause of the Loss of Souls

132. The fundamental cause of this defection from the Christian law in social and economic matters, and of the apostasy of many workingmen from the Catholic faith which has resulted from it, is the disorderly affection of the soul, a sad consequence of original sin, the source of these and of all other evils. By original sin the marvelous harmony of man's faculties has been so deranged that now he is easily led astray by low desires, and strongly tempted to prefer the transient goods of this world to the lasting goods of heaven.

Hence comes that unquenchable thirst for riches and temporal possessions, which at all times has impelled men to break the law of God and trample on the rights of their neighbors; but the condition of the economic world today lays more snares than ever for human frailty. For the uncertainty of economic life and especially of current conditions demands the keenest and most unceasing straining of energy on the part of those engaged therein; and as a result, some have become so hardened against the stings of conscience as to hold all means good which enable them to increase their profits, and to safeguard against sudden changes of fortune the wealth amassed by unremitting toil. Easy returns, which an open market offers to any one, lead many to interest themselves in trade and exchange, their one aim being to make clear profits with the least labor. By their unchecked speculation prices are raised and lowered out of mere greed for gain, making void all the most prudent calculations of producers.

The regulations legally enacted for corporations, with their divided responsibility and limited liability, have given occasion to abominable abuses. The greatly weakened accountability makes little impression, as is evident, upon the conscience. The worst injustices and frauds take place beneath the obscurity of the common name of a corporative firm. Boards of directors proceed in their unconscionable methods even to the violation of their trust in regard to those whose savings they administer. In the last place must still be mentioned the unscrupulous but well-calculated speculation of men who, without seeking to answer real needs, appeal to the lowest human passions. These are aroused in order to turn their satisfaction into gain.

133. A stern insistence on the moral law, enforced with vigor by civil authority, could have dispelled or perhaps abetted these enormous evils. This, however, was too often lamentably wanting. For at the time when the new social order was beginning, the doctrines of rationalism had already taken firm hold of large numbers, and an economic teaching alien to the true moral law had soon arisen, whence it followed that free rein was given to human avarice.

134. As a result, a much greater number than ever before, solely concerned with adding to their wealth by any means whatsoever, sought their own selfish interests above all things; they had no scruple in committing the gravest injustices against others.

Those who first entered upon this broad way which leads to destruction[62] easily found many imitators of their iniquity because of their manifest success, their extravagant display of wealth, their derision of the scruples of more delicate consciences and the crushing of more cautious competitors.

135. With the leaders of the economy abandoning the true path, it is not surprising that in every country multitudes of workingmen, too, sank in the same morass: all the more so, because very many employers treated their workmen as mere tools, without any concern for the welfare of their souls, indeed, without the slightest thought of higher interests. The mind shudders if we consider the frightful perils to which the morals of workers (of boys and young men particularly), and the virtue of girls and women are exposed in modern factories; if we recall how the present economic situation and above all the disgraceful housing conditions prove obstacles to the family tie and family life; if we remember the insuperable difficulties placed in the way of a proper observance of the holy days.

How universally has the true Christian spirit become impaired; which formerly produced such lofty sentiments even in uncultured and illiterate men! In its stead, man's one solicitude is to obtain his daily bread in any way he can. And so bodily labor, which was decreed by Providence for the good of man's body and soul even after original sin has everywhere been changed into an instrument of strange perversion: for dead matter leaves the factory ennobled and transformed, where men are corrupted and degraded.

The Remedies

(a) Christian Norms of Economic Life

136. Economic life must be inspired by Christian principles. For this pitiable ruin of souls, which if it continue, will frustrate all efforts to reform

society,[63] there can be no other remedy than a frank and sincere return to the teaching of the Gospel. Men must observe anew the precepts of him who alone has the words of eternal life, words which, even though heaven and earth be changed, shall not pass away.[64]

All those versed in social matters demand a rationalization of economic life which will restore a sound and true order. But this order, which we ourselves desire and make every effort to promote, will necessarily be quite faulty and imperfect, unless all man's activities harmoniously unite to imitate and, as far as is humanly possible, attain the marvelous unity of the divine plan. This is the perfect order which the Church preaches, with intense earnestness, and which right reason demands: which places God as the first and supreme end of all created activity, and regards all created goods as mere instruments under God, to be used only in so far as they help toward the attainment for our supreme end.

Nor is it to be imagined that remunerative occupations are thereby belittled or deemed less consonant with human dignity. On the contrary, we are taught to recognize and reference in them the manifest will of God the Creator, who placed man upon earth to work it and use it in various ways in order to supply his needs. Those who are engaged in production are not forbidden to increase their fortunes in a lawful and just manner: indeed it is just that he who renders service to society and develops its wealth should himself have his proportionate share of the increased public riches, provided always that he respects the law of God and the rights of his neighbor, and uses his property in accord with faith and right reason. If these principles be observed by all, everywhere and at all times, not merely the production and acquisition of goods, but also the use of wealth, now so often uncontrolled, will within a short time be brought back again to the standards of equity and just distribution.

Mere sordid selfishness, which is the disgrace and the great crime of the present age, will be opposed in very deed by the kindly and forceful law of Christian moderation, whereby man commanded to seek first the kingdom of God and his justice, confiding in God's liberality and definite promise that temporal goods also, so far as it is necessary, will be added unto him.[65]

(b) Role of Charity

137. Now, in effecting this reform, charity, "which is the bond of perfection,"[66] must play a leading part. How completely deceived are those inconsiderate reformers, who, zealous only for commutative justice, proudly disdain the help of charity. Charity cannot take the place of justice unfairly withheld, but, even though a state of things be pictured in which every man receives at last all that is his due, a wide field will nevertheless remain open for charity. For, justice alone, even though most faithfully observed, can remove indeed the cause of social strife, but can never bring about a union of hearts and minds. Yet this union, binding men together, is the main principle of stability in all institutions, no matter how perfect they may seem, which aim at establishing social peace and promoting mutual aid. In its absence, as repeated

experience proves, the wisest regulations come to nothing. Then only will it be possible to unite all in harmonious striving for the common good, when all sections of society have the intimate conviction that they are members of a single family and children of the same Heavenly Father, and further, that they are one body in Christ and "severally members one of another,"[67] so that "if one member suffers anything, all the members suffer with it."[68] Then the rich and others in power will change their former negligence of their poorer brethren into solicitous and effective regard; will listen with kindly feeling to their just complaints; and will readily forgive them the faults and mistakes they possibly make. Workingmen, too, will lay aside all feelings of hatred or envy, which the instigators of social strife arouse so skillfully. Not only will they cease to feel weary of the position allotted them by divine providence in human society; they will become proud of it, well aware that every man by doing his duty is working usefully and honorably for the common good, and is following in the footsteps of him, who, being in the form of God, chose to become a carpenter among men, and to be known as the son of a carpenter.

A Difficult Task

138. Because of this new diffusion throughout the world of the Gospel spirit, which is a spirit of Christian moderation and of universal charity, we confidently look forward to that complete and much desired renewal of human society, and to "the Peace of Christ in the kingdom of Christ," to which we firmly resolved at the very beginning of our pontificate to devote all our care and all our pastoral solicitude.[69] You, venerable brethren, who by ordinance of the Holy Spirit rule with us the Church of God,[70] are laboring strenuously and with admirable zeal in all parts of the world, not exclusive of the sacred missions among unbelievers, toward this same end of capital importance and necessity today. Receive your well-deserved meed of praise: and with you all those, of the clergy and laity, whom we rejoice to see daily taking part in this great work and affording valuable help; our beloved sons devoted to Catholic Action, who with extraordinary zeal aid us in the solution of social problems, in so far as the Church in virtue of her divine institution has the right and the duty to concern herself with them. With repeated insistence we exhort all these in the Lord to spare no labor and be overcome by no difficulty, but daily more to take courage and be valiant.[71]

The task we propose to them is truly difficult, for well do we know that many are the obstacles to be overcome on either side, whether among the higher classes of society or the lower. Still, let them not lose heart, nor in any way allow themselves to be diverted by any art from their purpose. To face stern combats is the part of a Christian: and to endure labor is the lot of those, who, as good soldiers of Christ,[72] follow closely in His footsteps.

139. Relying therefore solely on the assistance of him who "will have all men be saved,"[73] let us devote all our energies to helping those unhappy souls who are turned away from God; let us withdraw them from the temporal cares

in which they are too much involved, and teach them to aspire with confidence to things that are eternal. At times, indeed, this will be easier to accomplish than appears at first sight: for if in the depths of even the most abandoned hearts lurk, like sparks beneath the ashes, spiritual forces of unexpected strength—a clear testimony of a "naturally Christian soul"—how much more then must these abide in the hearts of the many who largely through ignorance and unfavorable surroundings have wandered into error!

140. For the rest, the associations of the workingmen themselves provide glad signs of coming social reconstruction. To the great joy of our heart we discern among them great numbers of young workers who listen readily to the call of divine grace and strive with splendid zeal to win their fellows to Christ. No less praise is due to those leaders of workingmen's organizations who, sacrificing their own interests, and anxious only for the good of their companions, strive with prudence to bring their just demands into harmony with the prosperity of their entire professional group, nor by any obstacle or misgiving do they permit themselves to be deterred from this noble task. Further, many young men, destined soon by reason of theft talents or their wealth to hold distinguished places in the foremost ranks of society, are studying social matters with growing earnestness. These youths encourage the fairest hopes that they will devote themselves wholly to social reforms.

The Course to Be Followed

141. Present circumstances, therefore, venerable brethren and beloved children, indicate clearly the course to be followed. Nowadays, as more than once in the history of the Church, we are confronted with a world which in large measure has almost fallen back into paganism. In order to bring back to Christ these whole classes of men who have denied him, we must gather and train from amongst their very ranks auxiliary soldiers of the Church, men who know their mentality and their aspirations, and who with kindly fraternal charity will be able to win their hearts. Undoubtedly the first and immediate apostles of the workingmen must themselves be workingmen, while the apostles of the industrial and commercial world should themselves be employers and merchants.

142. It is your chief duty, venerable brethren, and that of your clergy, to seek diligently, to select prudently, and to train fittingly these lay apostles, among workingmen and among employers. No easy task is here imposed upon the clergy, wherefore all candidates for the sacred priesthood must be adequately prepared to meet it by intense study of social matters. It is particularly necessary, however, that they whom you specially select and devote to this work show themselves endowed with a keen sense of justice ready to oppose with real manly constancy unjust claims and unjust actions; that they avoid every extreme with consummate prudence and discretion; above all, that they be thoroughly imbued with the charity of Christ, which alone has power to incline men's hearts and wills firmly and gently to the laws of equity and

justice. This course, already productive of success in the past, we must follow now with alacrity.

143. Further, we earnestly exhort in the Lord the beloved sons who are chosen for this task; to devote themselves wholeheartedly to the formation of the men entrusted to them. In the execution of this most priestly and apostolic work, let them make opportune use of the powerful resources of Christian training, by instructing youth, by founding Christian associations, by forming study circles on Christian lines.

Above all, let them hold in high esteem and employ with diligence for the benefit of their disciples the spiritual exercises, a most precious means of personal and of social reform, as we said in our encyclical *Mens Nostra.* These exercises we declared in express terms to be most useful for the laity in general and especially for workingmen, and we warmly recommend them; for in that school of the spirit not only are excellent Christians formed, but real apostles of every state of life are trained and enkindled with the fire of the heart of Christ. From that school they will go forth, as the apostles from the Cenacle in Jerusalem, strong in faith, unconquerable in steadfastness under trials, aflame with zeal, eager only for the spread in every way of the kingdom of Christ.

144. And in truth, the world has nowadays sore need of valiant soldiers of Christ, who strain every thew and sinew to preserve the human family from the dire havoc which would befall it were the teachings of the Gospel to be flouted, and a social order permitted to prevail, which spurns no less the laws of nature than those of God. For herself the Church of Christ, built upon the solid rock, has nothing to fear, for she knows that the gates of hell shall not prevail against her:[74] and the experience of centuries has taught her that storms, even the most violent, pass, leaving her stronger and triumphantly victorious. But her maternal bosom cannot but be stirred at the thought of the countless ills which tempests of the world occasion to so many thousands; at the thought, above all, of the immense spiritual evils which ensue, entailing the eternal ruin of so many souls redeemed by the blood of Christ.

145. No stone, then, must be left unturned to avert these grave misfortunes from human society.

Toward this one aim we must tend all our effort and endeavor, supported by assiduous and fervent prayers to God. For, with the assistance of divine grace, the destiny of the human family lies in our hands.

146. Let us not permit, venerable brethren and beloved children, the children of this world to seem wiser in their generation than we who by God's goodness are children of light.[75] We see these men cunningly select and train resolute disciples, who spread their false doctrines daily more widely among men of every station and of every clime.

And when it becomes a question of attacking more vehemently the Church of Christ, we see them lay aside their internal quarrels, link up harmoniously into a single battleline, and strive with united force toward this common aim.

147. No one indeed is unaware of the many and splendid works in the social and economic field, as well as in education and religion, laboriously set in motion with indefatigable zeal by Catholics. But this admirable and self-sacrificing activity not infrequently loses some of its effectiveness by being directed into too many different channels. Let, then, all men of good will stand united. Let all those who, under the pastors of the Church, wish to fight this good and peaceful fight of Christ, as far as talents, powers and station allow, strive to play their part in the Christian renewal of human society, which Leo XIII inaugurated in his immortal encyclical *Rerum Novarum*. Let them seek, not themselves and the things that are their own, but the things that are Jesus Christ's.[76] Let them not urge their own ideas with undue persistence, but be ready to abandon them, however admirable, should the greater common good seem to require it: that in all and above all Christ may reign and rule, to whom be "honor and glory and dominion forever and ever."[77]

148. That this happy result may be attained, venerable brethren and beloved children, we impart to you all members of the great Catholic family entrusted to our care, but with special affection of our heart to artisans and other workingmen engaged in manual labor, by Divine Providence committed to us in a particular manner, and to Christian employers and managers, with paternal affection, the apostolic benediction.

Given at Rome, at Saint Peter's the fifteenth day of May in the year 1931, the tenth of our pontificate.

PIUS XI

NOTES

1. Encyclical *Arcanum*, Feb. 10, 1880.
2. Encyclical *Diuturnum*, June 29, 1881.
3. Encyclical *Immortale Dei*, Nov. 1, 1885.
4. Encyclical *Sapientiae Christianae*, Jan. 10, 1890.
5. Encyclical *Quod Apostolici Muneris*, Dec. 28, 1878.
6. Encyclical *Libertas*, June 20, 1888.
7. Encyclical *Rerum Novarum*, 1.
8. Encyclical *Rerum Novarum*, 13.
9. Encyclical *Rerum Novarum*, 2.
10. Encyclical *Rerum Novarum*, 13.
11. Matt. 7:29.
12. Encyclical *Rerum Novarum*, 1.
13. Ambrose, *On the Passing of His Brother Satyrus*, Book 1, Capt. 44.
14. Encyclical *Rerum Novarum*, 13.
15. Leo XIII, *Litt. Apost. Praeclara*, June 20, 1894; Encyclical *Graves De Communi*, Jan. 18, 1901; Pius X, *Motu Proprio De Actione Populari Christiana*, Dec. 8, 1903; Benedict XV, Encyclical *Ad Beatissimi*, Nov. 1, 1914;

Pius XI, Encyclical *Ubi Arcano*, Dec. 23, 1922; Encyclical *Rite Expiatis*, Apr. 30, 1926.

16. Cf. *La Hierarchie Catholique et le Probleme Social Depuis L'Encyclique Rerum Novarum*, 1891–1931, pp. xvi, 335; *Union Internationale Etudes Sociale Fondes a Malines en 1920, Sous La Presidence du Card. Mercier*, Paris, "*Editions Spes*," 1931.

17. Isa. 11:12.

18. Encyclical *Rerum Novarum*, 26.

19. Encyclical *Rerum Novarum*, 29.

20. Encyclical *Rerum Novarum*, 36.

21. Encyclical *Rerum Novarum*, 42.

22. Encyclical *Singulari Quadam*, Sept. 24, 1912.

23. See Letter of the S. Congregation of the Council to the Bishop of Lille, June 5, 1929.

24. Rom. 1:14.

25. Encyclical *Rerum Novarum*, 1.

26. Encyclical *Rerum Novarum*, 13.

27. Encyclical *Ubi Arcano*, Dec. 23, 1922.

28. Encyclical *Rerum Novarum*, 19.

29. Encyclical *Rerum Novarum*, 19.

30. Encyclical *Rerum Novarum*, 7.

31. Allocution to the A.C.I., May 6, 1926.

32. Encyclical *Rerum Novarum*, 6.

33. Encyclical *Rerum Novarum*, 9.

34. Encyclical *Rerum Novarum*, 35.

35. Thomas Aquinas, *Summa Theologiae* 2. 2. Q. 134.

36. Encyclical *Rerum Novarum*, 27.

37. Encyclical *Rerum Novarum*, 15.

38. Encyclical *Rerum Novarum*, 7.

39. 2 Thess. 3:10.

40. 2 Thess. 3:8, 10.

41. Encyclical *Rerum Novarum*, 35.

42. Encyclical *Rerum Novarum*, 34.

43. Encyclical *Rerum Novarum*, 17.

44. Encyclical *Casti Connubii*, Dec. 31, 1930, p. 116.

45. Cf. Thomas Aquinas, *De Regimine Principum*, 1, 15; Encyclical *Rerum Novarum*, 35.

46. Encyclical *Rerum Novarum*, 13.

47. Thomas Aquinas, *Cont., Gent.*, 3, 71; Cf. *Summa Theologiae* I, Q. 65; A. 2 C.C.

48. Encyclical *Immortale Dei*, Nov. 1, 1885.

49. Encyclical *Rerum Novarum*, 42.

50. Eph. 4:16.

51. Encyclical *Rerum Novarum*, 15.

52. Encyclical *Diuturnum Illud*, June 29, 1881.
53. Encyclical *Divini Illius Magistri*, Dec. 31, 1929.
54. 2 Cor. 8:8.
55. Cf. Ps. 87:16.
56. Cf. Matt. 11:28.
57. Luke 12:48; Matt. 16:27.
58. Matt. 7:24, 27.
59. Encyclical *Rerum Novarum*, 13.
60. Cf. Matt. 16:26.
61. Cf. Judg. 2:17.
62. Cf. Matt. 7:13.
63. Cf. John 6:69.
64. Cf. Matt. 24:35.
65. Cf. Matt. 6:33.
66. Col. 3:14.
67. Rom. 12:5.
68. 1 Cor. 12:26.
69. Encyclical *Ubi Arcano*, Dec. 23, 1922.
70. Cf. Acts 20:28.
71. Cf. Deut. 31:7.
72. 2 Tim. 2:3.
73. 1 Tim. 2:4.
74. Matt. 16:18.
75. Luke 16:8.
76. Phil. 2:21.
77. Rev. 5:13.

PART II

CATHOLIC SOCIAL THOUGHT IN TRANSITION

INTRODUCTION

World War II brought another turning point in the history of the West. The church, insulated from the structures of liberalism and skillfully present to both sides of the war, emerged from that terrible experience as one of the few transnational institutions left intact. Catholic support for fascism in much of Southern, Central, and Eastern Europe was quickly forgotten, at least in Western Europe and North America. So, too, was the all but total rejection of modern understandings of civil rights and religious freedom by popes from Gregory VI through Pius IX. Before the war was over Pope Pius XII began to offer a new affirmation of democratic political structures. Catholic anticommunism now corresponded to the stance of most leaders of Western governments. As a result, the papacy experienced a new prestige, and Christian democratic governments became major vehicles for the rebuilding of Western European society. That society, once perceived as threatening to the church, seemed the only available bulwark against a Communist menace now even more dangerous as it turned viciously against the church in Eastern Europe.

Catholic social thought, under Pius XII's leadership, deemphasized the call for total reorganization of society articulated by Pius XI and returned to the reformism and moderation of Leo XIII. Trade unionism, social insurance, and the welfare state, even mixed economic arrangements of government and private enterprise, enjoyed the favor of the church and the Catholic parties. Humanistic liberals like Jacques Maritain enjoyed prominence and importance and, while radical efforts such as that of the French worker-priests were rejected, a style of positive social action and liberal reformist politics became normative. Yet even though theological pioneers and critics still labored under the suspicion that had beset them since the ultramontane triumph of Vatican I, new seeds were being planted in movements for pastoral renewal in France and theological renewal in Germany, France, and the English-speaking world. While liberal Catholics still chafed under ecclesiastical restrictions in the fifteen years following World War II, the climate had undoubtedly changed, new voices were being heard, and the church was beginning to look at itself through the lenses of new experiences.

Mater et Magistra: *Christianity and Social Progress* *(John XXIII, 1961)*

INTRODUCTION

The death of Pius XII and the election of John XXIII marked the end of an era in many ways. The image of the rotund, smiling Pope John contrasted significantly with the ascetic, gaunt Pius. John also seemed to move more easily with people, to be at home with them. But it was John's calling of Vatican Council II that defined his papacy and marked a new era in twentieth-century Catholicism.

While John's encyclicals were characterized by the use of natural law, he brought a new openness and style to that method that liberated it from static assumptions. Also John shared the liberal assumption that new wealth could be created and that the first task of justice was to generate it, not equitably to distribute what was available. He also assumed that a wider distribution of property would narrow the gap between rich and poor. In many ways John's assumptions were the assumptions of his age: an acceptance of the Western economic order, a reformist attitude to the status quo, and a wider role for the state.

Two features of his teaching are significant. First is his emphasis on socialization, an increase of the network of relations by which individuals are connected to each other. Justice takes on even more significance as we move into more complex and numerous interrelations. Second, John argued for state intervention to ensure that property would achieve its social functions. Justice requires that property be used for the common good.

John XXIII's first major encyclical on social issues was *Mater et Magistra*, issued in 1961. Several themes are present in this first major statement of John's pontificate. As noted, he highlighted the social dimension of property and related it to the need for a more effective distribution of goods in society. Then he broadened the criteria of the just wage to take into account the contribution of the individual, the economic state of the enterprise in which individuals work, the requirements of each community, and the common good. He also warned against the dangers of neocolonialism, which continued the political dominance of the poor by the rich. Finally, the pope developed a lengthy section on agriculture, in which he touched on issues such as health and crop insurance, price management, agricultural technology, and the relation between market value and the necessity of a just wage for farmers.

Mater et Magistra drew mixed reactions, ranging from William F. Buckley's celebrated "Mother, yes; teacher, no" to widespread applause from the liberal community. The encyclical did lead, however, to a greater sense of acceptance of full and personal participation in the world community and a new wave of ecumenical cooperation in social issues. It also laid a foundation for new developments in Catholic social teaching.

MATER ET MAGISTRA

ENCYCLICAL LETTER OF HIS HOLINESS, JOHN XXIII BY DIVINE PROVIDENCE POPE

To Our Venerable Brothers, the Patriarchs, Primates, Archbishops, Bishops, and Other Local Ordinaries in Peace and Communion with the Holy See, and to All the Clergy and Faithful of the Catholic World:

ON RECENT DEVELOPMENTS OF THE SOCIAL QUESTION IN THE LIGHT OF THE CHRISTIAN TEACHING

POPE JOHN XXIII

Venerable Brothers and Dear Sons, Health and Apostolic Benediction

1. The Catholic Church has been established by Jesus Christ as *Mother and Teacher* of nations, so that all who in the course of centuries come to her loving embrace, may find salvation as well as the fullness of a more excellent life. To this Church, "the pillar and mainstay of the truth,"[1] her most holy Founder has entrusted the double task of begetting sons unto herself, and of educating and governing those whom she begets, guiding with maternal providence the life both of individuals and of peoples. The lofty dignity of this life she has always held in the highest respect and guarded with watchful care.

2. For the teaching of Christ joins, as it were, earth with heaven, in that it embraces the whole man, namely, his soul and body, intellect and will, and bids him to lift up his mind from the changing conditions of human existence to that heavenly country where he will one day enjoy unending happiness and peace.

3. Hence, although Holy Church has the special task of sanctifying souls and of making them sharers of heavenly blessings, she is also solicitous for the requirements of men in their daily lives, not merely those relating to food and sustenance, but also to their comfort and advancement in various kinds of goods and in varying circumstances of time.

4. Realizing all this, Holy Church implements the commands of her founder, Christ, who refers primarily to man's eternal salvation when he says, "I am the Way, and the Truth, and the Life"[2] and elsewhere "I am the Light

of the World."[3] On other occasions, however, seeing the hungry crowd, he was moved to exclaim sorrowfully, "I have compassion on the crowd,"[4] thereby indicating that he was also concerned about the earthly needs of mankind. The divine Redeemer shows this care not only by his words but also by the actions of his life, as when, to alleviate the hunger of the crowds, he more than once miraculously multiplied bread.

5. By this bread, given for the nourishment of the body, he wished to foreshadow that heavenly food of the soul which he was to give to men on *the day before he suffered.*

6. It is no wonder, then, that the Catholic Church, instructed by Christ and fulfilling his commands, has for two thousand years, from the ministry of the early deacons to the present time, tenaciously held aloft the torch of charity not only by her teaching but also by her widespread example—that charity which, by combining in a fitting manner the precepts and the practice of mutual love, puts into effect in a wonderful way this twofold commandment of *giving*, wherein is contained the full social teaching and action of the Church.

7. By far the most notable evidence of this social teaching and action, which the Church has set forth through the centuries, undoubtedly is the very distinguished encyclical letter *Rerum Novarum*,[5] issued seventy years ago by our predecessor of immortal memory, Leo XIII. Therein he put forward teachings whereby the question of the workers' condition would be resolved in conformity with Christian principles.

8. Seldom have the admonitions of a pontiff been received with such universal approbation, as was that encyclical of Leo XIII, rivaled by few in the depth and scope of its reasoning and in the forcefulness of its expression. Indeed, the norms and recommendations contained therein were so momentous that their memory will never fall into oblivion. As a result, the action of the Catholic Church became more widely known. For its supreme pastor, making his own the problems of weak and harassed men, their complaints and aspirations had devoted himself especially to the defense and restoration of their rights.

9. Even today, in spite of the long lapse of time since the letter was published, much of its effectiveness is still evident. It is indeed evident in the documents of the popes who succeeded Leo XIII, and who, when they discussed economic and social affairs, have always borrowed something from it, either to clarify its application or to stimulate further activity on the part of Catholics. The efficacy of the document also is evident in the laws and institutions of many nations. Thus does it become abundantly clear that the solidly grounded principles, the norms of action, and the paternal admonitions found in the masterly letter of our predecessor, even today retain their original worth. Moreover, from it can be drawn new and vital criteria, whereby men may judge the nature and extent of the social question, and determine what their responsibilities are in this regard.

PART I: TEACHINGS OF THE ENCYCLICAL *RERUM NOVARUM* AND TIMELY DOCTRINAL DEVELOPMENTS DURING THE PONTIFICATES OF PIUS XI AND PIUS XII

THE PERIOD OF THE ENCYCLICAL *RERUM NOVARUM*

10. The teachings addressed to mankind by this most wise pontiff undoubtedly shone with greater brilliance because they were published when innumerable difficulties obscured the issue. On the one hand, the economic and political situation was in process of radical change; on the other, numerous clashes were flaring up and civil strife had been provoked.

11. As is generally known, in those days an opinion widely prevailed and was commonly put into practice, according to which, in economic matters, everything was to be attributed to inescapable, natural forces. Hence, it was held that no connection existed between economic and moral laws. Wherefore, those engaged in economic activity need look no further than their own gain. Consequently, mutual relations between economic agents could be left to the play of free and unregulated competition. Interest on capital, prices of goods and services, profits and wages, were to be determined purely mechanically by the laws of the marketplace. Every precaution was to be taken lest the civil authority intervene in any way in economic affairs. During the era, trade unions, according to circumstances in different countries, were sometimes forbidden, sometimes tolerated, sometimes recognized in private law.

12. Thus, at that time, not only was the proud rule of the stronger regarded as legitimate, so far as economic affairs were concerned, but it also prevailed in concrete relations between men. Accordingly, the order of economic affairs was, in general, radically disturbed.

13. While a few accumulated excessive riches, large masses of workingmen daily labored in very acute need. Indeed, wages were insufficient for the necessities of life, and sometimes were at starvation level. For the most part, workers had to find employment under conditions wherein there were dangers to health, moral integrity, and religious faith. Especially inhuman were the working conditions to which children and women were subjected. The specter of unemployment was ever present, and the family was exposed to a process of disorganization.

14. As a natural consequence, workers, indignant at their lot, decided that this state of affairs must be publicly protested. This explains why, among the working classes, extremist theories that propounded remedies worse than the evil to be cured, found widespread favor.

THE WAY TO RECONSTRUCTION

15. Such being the trend of the times, Leo XIII, in his encyclical letter *Rerum Novarum*, proclaimed a social message based on the requirements

of human nature itself and conforming to the precepts of the Gospel and reason. We recall it as a message which, despite some expected opposition, evoked response on all sides and aroused widespread enthusiasm. However, this was not the first time the Apostolic See, in regard to the affairs of this life, undertook the defense of the needy, since that same predecessor of happy memory, Leo XIII, published other documents which to some extent paved the way for the document mentioned above. But this letter so effected for the first time an organization of principles, and, as it were, set forth singlemindedly a future course of action, that we may regard it as a summary of Catholic teaching, so far as economic and social matters are concerned.

16. It can be said with considerable assurance that such proved to be the situation. For while some, confronted with the social question, unashamedly attacked the Church as if she did nothing except preach resignation to the poor and exhort the rich to generosity, Leo XIII did not hesitate to proclaim and defend quite openly the sacred rights of workers. In beginning his exposition of the principles and norms of the Church in social matters, he frankly stated: "We approach the subject with confidence and in the exercise of the rights that belong to us. For no satisfactory solution of this question will ever be found without the assistance of religion and the Church."[6]

17. Venerable brothers, you are quite familiar with those basic principles expounded both clearly and authoritatively by the illustrious pontiff, according to which human society should be renewed in so far as economic and social matters are concerned.

18. He first and foremost stated that work, inasmuch as it is an expression of the human person, can by no means be regarded as a mere commodity. For the great majority of mankind, work is the only source from which the means of livelihood are drawn. Hence, its remuneration is not to be thought of in terms of merchandise, but rather according to the laws of justice and equity. Unless this is done, justice is violated in labor agreements, even though they are entered into freely on both sides.

19. Private property, including that of productive goods, is a natural right possessed by all, which the State may by no means suppress. However, as there is from nature a social aspect to private property, he who uses his right in this regard must take into account not merely his own welfare but that of others as well.

20. The State, whose purpose is the realization of the common good in the temporal order, can by no means disregard the economic activity of its citizens. Indeed, it should be present to promote in a suitable manner the production of a sufficient supply of material goods, "the use of which is necessary for the practice of virtue."[7] Moreover, it should safeguard the rights of all citizens, but especially the weaker, such as workers, women, and children. Nor may the State ever neglect its duty to contribute actively to the betterment of the living conditions of workers.

21. In addition, the State should see to it that labor agreements are entered into according to the norms of justice and equity, and that in the environment of work the dignity of the human being is not violated either in body or spirit. On this point, Leo XIII's letter delineated the broad principles regarding a just and proper human existence. These principles, modern States have adopted in one way or another in their social legislation, and they have—as our predecessor of immortal memory, Pius XI, declared, in his encyclical letter *Quadragesimo Anno*[8]—contributed much to the establishment and promotion of that new section of legal science known as *labor law*.

22. In the same letter, moreover, there is affirmed the natural right to enter corporately into associations, whether these be composed of workers only or of workers and management; and also the right to adopt that organizational structure judged more suitable to meet their professional needs. And workers themselves have the right to act freely and on their own initiative within the abovementioned associations, without hindrance and as their needs dictate.

23. Workers and employers should regulate their mutual relations in a spirit of human solidarity and in accordance with the bond of Christian brotherhood. For the unregulated competition which so-called *liberals* espouse, or the class struggle in the *Marxist sense*, are utterly opposed to Christian teaching and also to the very nature of man.

24. These, venerable brothers, are the fundamental principles on which a healthy socioeconomic order can be built.

25. It is not surprising, therefore, that outstanding Catholic men inspired by these appeals began many activities in order to put these principles to action. Nor were there lacking other men of good will in various parts of the world who, impelled by the needs of human nature, followed a similar course.

26. For these reasons the encyclical is known even to the present day as the Magna Charta[9] for the reconstruction of the economic and social order.

THE ENCYCLICAL *QUADRAGESIMO ANNO*

27. Furthermore, after a lapse of forty years since publication of that outstanding corpus, as it were, of directives, our predecessor of happy memory, Pius XI, in his turn decided to publish the encyclical letter *Quadragesimo Anno*.[10]

28. In it the supreme pontiff first of all confirmed the right and duty of the Catholic Church to make its special contribution in resolving the more serious problems of society which call for the full cooperation of all. Then he reaffirmed those principles and directives of Leo XIII's letter related to the conditions of the times. Finally, he took this occasion not only to clarify certain points of doctrine on which even Catholics were in doubt, but he also showed how the principles and directives themselves regarding social affairs should be adapted to the changing times.

29. For at that time, some were in doubt as to what should be the judgment of Catholics regarding private property, the wage system, and more especially, a type of moderate socialism.

30. Concerning private property, our predecessor reaffirmed its natural-law character. Furthermore, he set forth clearly and emphasized the social character and function of private ownership.

31. Turning to the wage system, after having rejected the view that would declare it unjust by its very nature, the pontiff criticized the inhuman and unjust forms under which it was sometimes found. Moreover, he carefully indicated what norms and conditions were to be observed, lest the wage system stray from justice and equity.

32. In this connection, it is today advisable as our predecessor clearly pointed out, that work agreements be tempered in certain respects with partnership arrangements, so that "workers and officials become participants in ownership, or management, or share in some manner in profits."[11]

33. Of great theoretical and practical importance is the affirmation of Pius XI that "if the social and individual character of labor be overlooked, the efficiency of men can neither be justly appraised nor equitably recompensed."[12] Accordingly, in determining wages, justice definitely requires that, in addition to the needs of the individual worker and his family, regard be had on the one hand for conditions within the productive enterprises wherein the workers labor; on the other hand, for the "public economic good"[13] in general.

34. Furthermore, the supreme bishop emphasized that the views of *communists*, as they are called, and of Christians are radically opposed. Nor may Catholics, in any way, give approbation to the teachings of *socialists* who seemingly profess more moderate views. From their basic outlook it follows that, inasmuch as the order of social life is confined to time, it is directed solely to temporal welfare; that since the social relationships of men pertain merely to the production of goods, human liberty is excessively restricted and the true concept of social authority is overlooked.

35. Pius XI was not unaware that, in the forty years that had elapsed since the appearance of Leo XIII's letter, historical conditions had profoundly altered. In fact, unrestricted competition, because of its own inherent tendencies, had ended by almost destroying itself. It had caused a great accumulation of wealth and a corresponding concentration of power in the hands of a few who "are frequently not the owners, but only the trustees and directors of invested funds, who administer them at their good pleasure."[14]

36. Therefore, as the supreme pontiff noted, "economic power has been substituted for the free marketplace. Unbridled ambition for domination has replaced desire for gain; the whole economy has become harsh, cruel, and relentless in frightful measure."[15] Thus it happened that even public authorities were serving the interests of more wealthy men and that concentrations of wealth, to some extent, achieved power over all peoples.

37. In opposition to this trend, the supreme pontiff laid down the following fundamental principles: the organization of economic affairs must be con-

formable to practical morality; the interests of individuals or of societies especially must be harmonized with the requirements of the common good. This evidently requires, as the teaching of our predecessor indicated, the orderly reorganization of society with smaller professional and economic groups existing in their own right, and not prescribed by public authority. In the next place, civil authority should reassume its function and not overlook any of the community's interests. Finally, on a worldwide scale, governments should seek the economic good of all peoples.

38. The two fundamental points that especially characterize the encyclical of Pius XI are these: First, one may not take as the ultimate criteria in economic life the interests of individuals or organized groups, nor unregulated competition, nor excessive power on the part of the wealthy, nor the vain honor of the nation or its desire for domination, nor anything of this sort.

39. Rather it is necessary that economic undertakings be governed by justice and charity as the principle laws of social life.

40. The second point that we consider to be basic to the letter of Pius XI is that both within individual countries and among nations there be established a juridical order, with appropriate public and private institutions, inspired by social justice, so that those who are involved in economic activities are enabled to carry out their tasks in conformity with the common good.

RADIO BROADCAST OF PENTECOST 1941

41. In specifying social rights and obligations, our predecessor of immortal memory, Pius XII, made a significant contribution, when on the feast of Pentecost, June 1, 1941, he broadcast to the world community a message: "In order to call to the attention of the Catholic world the memory of an event worthy of being written in letters of gold on the Calendar of the Church: namely, the fiftieth anniversary of the publication of the epoch-making encyclical of Leo XIII, *Rerum Novarum*."[16] He broadcast this message, moreover, "to render special thanks to Almighty God that his Vicar on earth, in a letter such as this, gave to the Church so great a gift, and also to render praise to the eternal Spirit that through this same letter, he enkindled a fire calculated to rouse the whole human race to new and better effort."[17]

42. In the message, the great pontiff claimed for the Church "the indisputable competence" to "decide whether the bases of a given social system are in accord with the unchangeable order which God our Creator and Redeemer has fixed both in the natural law and revelation."[18] He noted that the letter of Leo XIII is of permanent value and has rich and abiding usefulness. He takes the occasion "to explain in greater detail what the Catholic Church teaches regarding the three principal issues of social life in economic affairs, which are mutually related and connected one with the other, and thus interdependent: namely, the use of material goods, labor, and the family."[19]

43. Concerning the use of material goods, our predecessor declared that the right of every man to use them for his own sustenance is prior to all other

rights in economic life, and hence is prior even to the right of private ownership. It is certain, however, as our predecessor noted, that the right of private property is from the natural law itself. Nevertheless, it is the will of God the Creator that this right to own property should in no wise obstruct the flow of "material goods created by God to meet the needs of all men, to all equitably, as justice and charity require."[20]

44. As regards labor, Pius XII, repeating what appeared in Leo XIII's letter, declared it to be both a duty and a right of every human being. Consequently, it is in the first place the responsibility of men themselves to regulate mutual labor relations. Only in the event that the interested parties are unwilling or unable to fulfill their functions, does it "devolve upon the State to intervene and to assign labor equitably, safeguarding the standards and aims that the common good properly understood demands."[21]

45. Turning to the family, the supreme pontiff stresses that private ownership of material goods helps to safeguard and develop family life. Such goods are an apt means "to secure for the father of a family the healthy liberty he needs in order to fulfill the duties assigned him by the Creator, regarding the physical, spiritual, and religious welfare of the family."[22] From this arises the right of the family to migrate. Accordingly, our predecessor reminds governments, both those permitting emigration and those accepting immigrants, that "they never permit anything whereby mutual and sincere understanding between States is diminished or destroyed."[23] If this be mutually accomplished, it will come to pass that benefits are equalized and diffused widely among peoples, as the supply of goods and the arts and crafts are increased and fostered.

FURTHER CHANGES

46. But just as contemporary circumstances seemed to Pius XII quite dissimilar from those of the earlier period, so they have changed greatly over the past twenty years. This can be seen not only in the internal situation of each individual country, but also in the mutual relations of countries.

47. In the fields of science, technology, and economics, these developments are especially worthy of note: the discovery of atomic energy, employed first for military purposes and later increasingly for peaceful ends; the almost limitless possibilities opened up by chemistry in synthetic products; the growth of automation in the sectors of industry and services; the modernization of agriculture; the nearly complete conquest, especially through radio and television, of the distance separating peoples; the greatly increased speed of all manner of transportation; the initial conquests of outer space.

48. Turning to the social field, the following contemporary trends are evident: development of systems for social insurance; the introduction of social security systems in some more affluent countries; greater awareness among workers, as members of unions, of the principal issues in economic and social life; a progressive improvement of basic education; wider diffusion among the

citizenry of the conveniences of life; increased social mobility and a resulting decline in divisions among the classes; greater interest than heretofore in world affairs on the part of those with average education. Meanwhile, if one considers the social and economic advances made in a growing number of countries, he will quickly discern increasingly pronounced imbalances: first, between agriculture on the one hand and industry and the services on the other; between the more and the less developed regions within countries; and, finally, on a worldwide scale, between countries with differing economic resources and development.

49. Turning now to political affairs, it is evident that there, too, a number of innovations have occurred. Today, in many communities, citizens from almost all social strata participate in public life. Public authorities intervene more and more in economic and social affairs. The peoples of Asia and Africa, having set aside colonial systems, now govern themselves according to their own laws and institutions. As the mutual relationships of peoples increase, they become daily more dependent one upon the other. Throughout the world, assemblies and councils have become more common, which, being supranational in character, take into account the interests of all peoples. Such bodies are concerned with economic life, or with social affairs, or with culture and education, or, finally, with the mutual relationships of peoples.

REASONS FOR THE NEW ENCYCLICAL

50. Now, reflecting on all these things, we feel it our duty to keep alive the torch lighted by our great predecessors and to exhort all to draw from their writings light and inspiration, if they wish to resolve the social question in ways more in accord with the needs of the present time. Therefore, we are issuing this present letter not merely to commemorate appropriately the encyclical letter of Leo XIII, but also, in the light of changed conditions, both to confirm and explain more fully what our predecessors taught, and to set forth the Church's teaching regarding the new and serious problems of our day.

PART II: EXPLANATION AND DEVELOPMENT OF THE TEACHINGS OF *RERUM NOVARUM*

PRIVATE INITIATIVE AND STATE INTERVENTION IN ECONOMIC LIFE

51. At the outset it should be affirmed that in economic affairs first place is to be given to the private initiative of individual men who, either working by themselves, or with others in one fashion or another, pursue their common interests.

52. But in this matter, for reasons pointed out by our predecessors, it is necessary that public authorities take active interest, the better to increase output of goods and to further social progress for the benefit of all citizens.

53. This intervention of public authorities that encourages, stimulates, regulates, supplements, and complements, is based on the *principle of subsidiarity*[24] as set forth by Pius XI in his encyclical *Quadragesimo Anno*: "It is a fundamental principle of social philosophy, fixed and unchangeable, that one should not withdraw from individuals and commit to the community what they can accomplish by their own enterprise and industry. So, too, it is an injustice and at the same time a grave evil and a disturbance of right order, to transfer to the larger and higher collectivity functions which can be performed and provided for by lesser and subordinate bodies. Inasmuch as every social activity should, by its very nature, prove a help to members of the body social, it should never destroy or absorb them."[25]

54. Indeed, as is easily perceived, recent developments of science and technology provide additional reasons why, to a greater extent than heretofore, it is within the power of public authorities to reduce imbalances, whether these be between various sectors of economic life, or between different regions of the same nation, or even between different peoples of the world as a whole. These same developments make it possible to keep fluctuations in the economy within bounds, and to provide effective measures for avoiding mass unemployment. Consequently, it is requested again and again of public authorities responsible for the common good, that they intervene in a wide variety of economic affairs, and that, in a more extensive and organized way than heretofore, they adapt institutions, tasks, means, and procedures to this end.

55. Nevertheless, it remains true that precautionary activities of public authorities in the economic field, although widespread and penetrating, should be such that they not only avoid restricting the freedom of private citizens, but also increase it, so long as the basic rights of each individual person are preserved inviolate. Included among these is the right and duty of each individual normally to provide the necessities of life for himself and his dependents. This implies that whatever be the economic system, it allow and facilitate for every individual the opportunity to engage in productive activity.

56. Furthermore, the course of events thus far makes it clear that there cannot be a prosperous and well-ordered society unless both private citizens and public authorities work together in economic affairs. Their activity should be characterized by mutual and amicable efforts, so that the roles assigned to each fit in with requirements of the common good as changing times and customs suggest.

57. Experience, in fact, shows that where private initiative of individuals is lacking, political tyranny prevails. Moreover, much stagnation occurs in various sectors of the economy, and hence all sorts of consumer goods and services, closely connected with needs of the body and more especially of the spirit, are in short supply. Beyond doubt, the attainment of such goods and services provides remarkable opportunity and stimulus for individuals to exercise initiative and industry.

58. Where, on the other hand, appropriate activity of the State is lacking or defective, commonwealths are apt to experience incurable disorders, and there

occurs exploitation of the weak by the unscrupulous strong, who flourish, unfortunately, like cockle among the wheat, in all times and places.

COMPLEXITY OF SOCIAL STRUCTURE

Direction of the Trend

59. One of the principal characteristics of our time is the multiplication of social relationships, that is, a daily more complex interdependence of citizens, introducing into their lives and activities many and varied forms of association, recognized for the most part in private and even in public law. This tendency seemingly stems from a number of factors operative in the present era, among which are technical and scientific progress, greater productive efficiency, and a higher standard of living among citizens.

60. These developments in social living are at once both a symptom and a cause of the growing intervention of public authorities in matters which, since they pertain to the more intimate aspects of personal life, are of serious moment and not without danger. Such, for example, are the care of health, the instruction and education of youth, the choice of a personal career, the ways and means of rehabilitating or assisting those handicapped mentally or physically. But this trend also indicates and in part follows from that human and natural inclination, scarcely resistible, whereby men are impelled voluntarily to enter into association in order to attain objectives which each one desires, but which exceed the capacity of single individuals. This tendency has given rise, especially in recent years, to organizations and institutes on both national and international levels which relate to economic and social goals, to cultural and recreational activities, to athletics, to various professions, and to political affairs.

Evaluation

61. Such an advance in social relationships definitely brings numerous services and advantages. It makes possible, in fact, the satisfaction of many personal rights, especially those of economic and social life; these relate, for example, to the minimum necessities of human life, to health services, to the broadening and deepening of elementary education, to a more fitting training in skills, to housing, to labor, to suitable leisure and recreation. In addition, through the ever more perfect organization of modern means for the diffusion of thought—press, cinema, radio, television—individuals are enabled to take part in human events on a worldwide scale.

62. But as these various forms of association are multiplied and daily extended, it also happens that in many areas of activity, rules and laws controlling and determining relationships of citizens are multiplied. As a consequence, opportunity for free action by individuals is restricted within narrower limits. Methods are often used, procedures are adopted, and such an atmosphere develops wherein it becomes difficult for one to make decisions independently of outside influences, to do anything on his own initiative, to carry out in a fitting way his rights and duties, and to fully develop and perfect his

personality. Will men perhaps then become automatons, and cease to be personally responsible, as these social relationships multiply more and more? It is a question which must be answered negatively.

63. Actually, increased complexity of social life by no means results from a blind drive of natural forces. Indeed, as stated above, it is the creation of free men who are so disposed to act by nature as to be responsible for what they do. They must, of course, recognize the laws of human progress and the development of economic life and take these into account. Furthermore, men are not altogether free of their milieu.

64. Accordingly, advances in social organization can and should be so brought about that maximum advantages accrue to citizens while at the same time disadvantages are averted or at least minimized.

65. That these desired objectives be more readily obtained, it is necessary that public authorities have a correct understanding of the common good. This embraces the sum total of those conditions of social living, whereby men are enabled more fully and more readily to achieve their own perfection. Hence, we regard it as necessary that the various intermediary bodies and the numerous social undertakings wherein an expanded social structure primarily finds expression, be ruled by their own laws, and as the common good itself progresses, pursue this objective in a spirit of sincere concord among themselves. Nor is it less necessary that the above-mentioned groups present the form and substance of a true community. This they will do, only if individual members are considered and treated as persons, and are encouraged to participate in the affairs of the group.

66. Accordingly, as relationships multiply between men, binding them more closely together, commonwealths will more readily and appropriately order their affairs to the extent these two factors are kept in balance: (1) the freedom of individual citizens and groups of citizens to act autonomously, while cooperating one with the other; (2) the activity of the State whereby the undertakings of private individuals and groups are suitably regulated and fostered.

67. Now if social systems are organized in accordance with the above norms and moral laws, their extension does not necessarily mean that individual citizens will be gravely discriminated against or excessively burdened. Rather, we can hope that this will enable man not only to develop and perfect his natural talents, but also will lead to an appropriate structuring of the human community. Such a structure, as our predecessor of happy memory, Pius XI, warned in his encyclical letter *Quadragesimo Anno*,[26] is absolutely necessary for the adequate fulfillment of the rights and duties of social life.

REMUNERATION FOR WORK

Standards of Justice and Equity

68. Our heart is filled with profound sadness when we observe, as it were, with our own eyes a wretched spectacle indeed—great masses of workers

who, in not a few nations, and even in whole continents, receive too small a return from their labor. Hence, they and their families must live in conditions completely out of accord with human dignity. This can be traced, for example, to the fact that in these regions, modern industrial techniques either have only recently been introduced or have made less than satisfactory progress.

69. It happens in some of these nations that, as compared with the extreme need of the majority, the wealth and conspicuous consumption of a few stand out, and are in open and bold contrast with the lot of the needy. It happens in other places that excessive burdens are placed upon men in order that the commonwealth may achieve within a brief span an increase of wealth such as can by no means be achieved without violating the laws of justice and equity. Finally, it happens elsewhere that a disproportionate share of the revenue goes toward the building up of national prestige, and that large sums of money are devoted to armaments.

70. Moreover, in the economically developed countries, it frequently happens that great, or sometimes very great, remuneration is had for the performance of some task of lesser importance or doubtful utility. Meanwhile, the diligent and profitable work that whole classes of decent and hard-working citizens perform, receives too low a payment and one insufficient for the necessities of life, or else, one that does not correspond to the contribution made to the community, or to the revenues of the undertakings in which they are engaged, or to the national income.

71. Wherefore, we judge it to be our duty to reaffirm once again that just as remuneration for work cannot be left entirely to unregulated competition, neither may it be decided arbitrarily at the will of the more powerful. Rather, in this matter, the norms of justice and equity should be strictly observed. This requires that workers receive a wage sufficient to lead a life worthy of man and to fulfill family responsibilities properly. But in determining what constitutes an appropriate wage, the following must necessarily be taken into account: first of all, the contribution of individuals to the economic effort; the economic state of the enterprises within which they work; the requirements of each community, especially as regards overall employment; finally, what concerns the common good of all peoples, namely, of the various States associated among themselves, but differing in character and extent.

72. It is clear that the standards of judgment set forth above are binding always and everywhere. However, the measure in which they are to be applied in concrete cases cannot be established unless account is taken of the resources at hand. These resources can and in fact do vary in quantity and quality among different peoples, and may even change within the same country with the passing of time.

Balancing Economic Development and Social Progress

73. Whereas in our era the economies of various countries are evolving very rapidly, more especially since the last great war, we take this opportunity

to draw the attention of all to a strict demand of social justice, which explicitly requires that, with the growth of the economy, there occur a corresponding social development. Thus, all classes of citizens will benefit equitably from an increase in national wealth. Toward this end vigilance should be exercised and effective steps taken that class differences arising from disparity of wealth not be increased, but lessened so far as possible.

74. "National wealth"—as our predecessor of happy memory, Pius XII, rightfully observed—"inasmuch as it is produced by the common efforts of the citizenry, has no other purpose than to secure without interruption those material conditions in which individuals are enabled to lead a full and perfect life. Where this is consistently the case, then such a people is to be judged truly rich. For the system whereby both the common prosperity is achieved and individuals exercise their right to use material goods, conforms fully to norms laid down by God the Creator."[27] From this it follows that the economic prosperity of any people is to be assessed not so much from the sum total of goods and wealth possessed as from the distribution of goods according to norms of justice, so that everyone in the community can develop and perfect himself. For this, after all, is the end toward which all economic activity of a community is by nature ordered.

75. We must here call attention to the fact that in many countries today, the economic system is such that large- and medium-size productive enterprises achieve rapid growth precisely because they finance replacement and plant expansion from their own revenues. Where this is the case, we believe that such companies should grant to workers some share in the enterprise, especially where they are paid no more than the minimum wage.

76. In this matter, the principle laid down by our predecessor of happy memory, Pius XI, in the encyclical letter *Quadragesimo Anno*, should be borne in mind: "It is totally false to ascribe to a single factor of production what is in fact produced by joint activity; and it is completely unjust for one factor to arrogate to itself what is produced, ignoring what has been contributed by other factors."[28]

77. The demands of justice referred to can be met in various ways, as experience shows. Not to mention other ways, it is very desirable that workers gradually acquire some share in the enterprise by such methods as seem more appropriate. For today, more than in the times of our predecessor, "every effort should be made that, at least in the future, only an equitable share of the fruits of production accumulate in the hands of the wealthy, and a sufficient and ample portion go to the workingmen."[29]

78. But we should remember that adjustments between remuneration for work and revenues are to be brought about in conformity with the requirements of the common good, both of one's own community and of the entire human family.

79. Considering the common good on the national level, the following points are relevant and should not be overlooked: to provide employment for

as many workers as possible; to take care lest privileged groups arise even among the workers themselves; to maintain a balance between wages and prices; to make accessible the goods and services for a better life to as many persons as possible; either to eliminate or to keep within bounds the inequalities that exist between different sectors of the economy—that is, between agriculture, industry and services; to balance properly any increases in output with advances in services provided to citizens, especially by public authority; to adjust, as far as possible, the means of production to the progress of science and technology; finally, to ensure the advantages of a more humane way of existence not merely subserve the present generation but have regard for future generations as well.

80. As regards the common good of human society as a whole, the following conditions should be fulfilled: that the competitive striving of peoples to increase output be free of bad faith; that harmony in economic affairs and a friendly and beneficial cooperation be fostered; and, finally, that effective aid be given in developing the economically underdeveloped nations.

81. It is evident from what has been said that these demands of the common good, on both the national and world levels, should be borne in mind, when there is question of determining the share of earnings assigned to those responsible for directing the productive enterprise, or as interest and dividends to those who have invested capital.

DEMANDS OF JUSTICE AS REGARDS PRODUCTIVE INSTITUTIONS

Institutions Conforming to the Dignity of Man

82. Justice is to be observed not merely in the distribution of wealth, but also in regard to the conditions under which men engaged in productive activity have an opportunity to assume responsibility and to perfect themselves by their efforts.

83. Consequently, if the organization and structure of economic life be such that the human dignity of workers is compromised, or their sense of responsibility is weakened, or their freedom of action is removed, then we judge such an economic order to be unjust, even though it produces a vast amount of goods whose distribution conforms to the norms of justice and equity.

Reaffirmation of a Directive

84. Nor is it possible in economic affairs to determine in one formula all the measures that are more conformable to the dignity of man, or are more suitable in developing in him a sense of responsibility. Nevertheless, our predecessor of happy memory, Pius XII, appropriately laid down certain norms of action: "Small and medium-sized holdings in agriculture, in the arts and crafts, in commerce and industry, should be safeguarded and fostered. Such enterprises should join together in mutual-aid societies in order that the services and benefits of large-scale enterprises will be available to them. So far

as these larger enterprises are concerned, work agreements should in some way be modified by partnership arrangements."[30]

Artisan Enterprises and Cooperative Associations

85. Wherefore, conformable to requirements of the common good and the state of technology, artisan and farm enterprises of family type should be safeguarded and fostered, as should also cooperatives that aim to complement and perfect such enterprises.

86. We shall return shortly to the subject of farm enterprises. Here, we think it appropriate to say something about artisan enterprises and cooperative associations.

87. Above all, it must be emphasized that enterprises and bodies of this sort, in order that they may survive and flourish, should be continuously adapted—both in their productive structure and in their operating methods—to new conditions of the times. These new conditions constantly arise from advances in science and technology, or from changing consumer needs and preferences. It is especially appropriate that all this can be done by the craftsmen themselves and by the associates in the cooperatives.

88. Hence, it is more fitting not only that both these groups be suitably formed in technical and in spiritual and intellectual matters, but also that they be joined together professionally. Nor is it less fitting that the State make special provision for them in regard to instruction, taxes, credit facilities, social security, and insurance.

89. Moreover, the measures taken by the State on behalf of the craftsmen and members of cooperatives are also justified by the fact that these two categories of citizens are producers of genuine wealth, and contribute to the advance of civilization.

90. Accordingly, we paternally exhort our beloved sons, craftsmen and members of cooperatives throughout the world, that they fully realize the dignity of their role in society, since, by their work, the sense of responsibility and spirit of mutual aid can be daily more intensified among the citizenry, and the desire to work with dedication and originality be kept alive.

Participation of Workers in Medium-Size and Large Enterprises

91. Furthermore, as did our predecessors, we regard as justifiable the desire of employees to be partners in enterprises with which they are associated and wherein they work. We do not think it possible, however, to decide with certain and explicit norms the manner and degree of such partnership, since this must be determined according to the state of the individual productive enterprises. For the situation is not everywhere the same, and, in fact, it can change suddenly within one and the same enterprise. Nevertheless, we do not doubt that employees should have an active part in the affairs of the

enterprise wherein they work, whether these be private or public. But it is of utmost importance that productive enterprises assume the character of a true human fellowship whose spirit suffuses the dealings, activities, and standing of all its members.

92. This requires that mutual relations between employers and directors on the one hand and the employees of the enterprise on the other be marked by mutual respect, esteem, and good will. It also demands that all collaborate sincerely and harmoniously in their joint undertaking, and that they perform their work not merely with the objective of deriving an income, but also of carrying out the role assigned them and of performing a service that results in benefit to others. This means that the workers may have a say in, and may make a contribution toward, the efficient running and development of the enterprise. Thus, our predecessor of happy memory, Pius XII, clearly indicated: "The economic and social functions of individuals be not wholly subjected to the will of others."[31] Beyond doubt, an enterprise truly in accord with human dignity should safeguard the necessary and efficient unity of administration. But it by no means follows that those who work daily in such an enterprise are to be considered merely as servants, whose sole function is to execute orders silently, and who are not allowed to interject their desires and interests, but must conduct themselves as idle standbys when it comes to assignment and direction of their tasks.

93. Finally, attention is drawn to the fact that the greater amount of responsibility desired today by workers in productive enterprises, not merely accords with the nature of man, but also is in conformity with historical developments in the economic, social, and political fields.

94. Unfortunately, in our day, there occur in economic and social affairs many imbalances that militate against justice and humanity. Meanwhile, throughout all of economic life, errors are spread that seriously impair its operation, purposes, organization, and the fulfillment of responsibilities. Nevertheless, it is an undeniable fact that the more recent productive systems, thanks to the impulse deriving from advances in technology and science, are becoming more modern and efficient, and are expanding at a faster rate than in the past. This demands of workers greater abilities and professional qualifications. Accordingly, workers should be provided with additional aids and time to achieve a suitable and more rounded formation, and to carry out more fittingly their duties as regards studies, morals, and religion.

95. Thus it happens that in our day youths can be allotted additional years to acquire a basic education and necessary skills.

96. Now if these things be done, a situation will emerge wherein workers are enabled to assume greater responsibilities even within their own enterprises. As regards the commonwealth as such, it is of great importance that all ranks of citizens feel themselves daily more obligated to safeguard the common good.

Participation of Workers at All Levels

97. Now, as is evident to all, in our day associations of workers have become widespread, and for the most part have been given legal status within individual countries and even across national boundaries. These bodies no longer recruit workers for purposes of strife, but rather for pursuing a common aim. And this is achieved especially by collective bargaining between associations of workers and those of management. But it should be emphasized how necessary, or at least very appropriate, it is to give workers an opportunity to exert influence outside the limits of the individual productive unit, and indeed within all ranks of the commonwealth.

98. The reason is that individual productive units, whatever their size, efficiency, or importance within the commonwealth, are closely connected with the overall economic and social situation in each country, whereon their own prosperity ultimately depends.

99. Nevertheless, to decide what is more helpful to the overall economic situation is not the prerogative of individual productive enterprises, but pertains to the public authorities and to those institutions which, established either nationally or among a number of countries, function in various sectors of economic life. From this is evident the propriety or necessity of ensuring that not only managers or agents of management are represented before such authorities and institutions, but also workers or those who have the responsibility of safeguarding the rights, needs, and aspirations of workers.

100. It is fitting, therefore, that our thoughts and paternal affection be directed toward the various professional groups and associations of workers which, in accord with principles of Christian teaching, carry on their activities on several continents. We are aware of the many and great difficulties experienced by these beloved sons of ours, as they effectively worked in the past and continue to strive, both within their national boundaries and throughout the world, to vindicate the rights of workingmen and to improve their lot and conduct.

101. Furthermore, we wish to give deserved praise to the work of these our sons. Their accomplishments are not always immediately evident, but nevertheless permeate practically the entire field of labor, spreading correct norms of action and thought, and the beneficial influence of the Christian religion.

102. And we wish also to praise paternally those dear sons of ours who, imbued with Christian principles, give their special attention to other labor associations and those groups of workingmen that follow the laws of nature and respect the religious and moral liberty of individuals.

103. Nor can we at this point neglect to congratulate and to express our esteem for the International Labor Organization—variously signified popularly by the letters O.I.L. or I.L.O. or O.I.T.—which, for many years, has done effective and valuable work in adapting the economic and social order everywhere to the norms of justice and humanity. In such an order, the legitimate rights of workers are recognized and preserved.

PRIVATE PROPERTY

Changed Conditions

104. In recent years as we are well aware, the role played by the owners of capital in very large productive enterprises has been separated more and more from the role of management. This has occasioned great difficulties for governments, whose duty it is to make certain that directors of the principal enterprises, especially those of greatest influence in the economic life of the entire country, do not depart from the requirements of the common good. These difficulties, as we know from experience, are by no means less, whether it be private citizens or public bodies that make the capital investments requisite for largescale enterprises.

105. It is also quite clear that today the number of persons is increasing who, because of recent advances in insurance programs and various systems of social security, are able to look to the future with tranquillity. This sort of tranquillity once was rooted in the ownership of property, albeit modest.

106. It sometimes happens in our day that men are more inclined to seek some professional skill than possession of goods. Moreover, such men have greater esteem for income from labor or rights arising from labor, than for that deriving from capital investment or rights associated therewith.

107. This clearly accords with the inherent characteristics of labor, inasmuch as this proceeds directly from the human person, and hence is to be thought more of than wealth in external goods. These latter, by their very nature, must be regarded as instruments. This trend indicates an advance in civilization.

108. Economic conditions of this kind have occasioned popular doubt as to whether, under present circumstances, a principle of economic and social life, firmly enunciated and defended by our predecessors, has lost its force or is to be regarded as of lesser moment; namely, the principle whereby it is established that men have from nature a right of privately owning goods, including those of a productive kind.

Confirmation of the Right of Private Property

109. Such a doubt has no foundation. For the right of private property, including that pertaining to goods devoted to productive enterprises, is permanently valid. Indeed, it is rooted in the very nature of things, whereby we learn that individual men are prior to civil society, and hence, that civil society is to be directed toward man as its end. Indeed, the right of private individuals to act freely in economic affairs is recognized in vain, unless they are at the same time given an opportunity of freely selecting and using things necessary for the exercise of this right. Moreover, experience and history testify that where political regimes do not allow to private individuals the possession also of productive goods, the exercise of human liberty is violated or completely destroyed in matters of primary importance. Thus it becomes

clear that in the right of property, the exercise of liberty finds both a safeguard and a stimulus.

110. This explains the fact that sociopolitical groups and associations which endeavor to reconcile freedom with justice within society, and which until recently did not uphold the right of private property in productive goods, have now, enlightened by the course of social events, modified their views and are disposed actually to approve this right.

111. Accordingly, we make our own the insistence of our predecessor of happy memory, Pius XII: "In defending the right of private property, the Church has in mind a very important ethical aim in social matters. She does not, of course, strive to uphold the present state of affairs as if it were an expression of the divine will. And even less does she accept the patronage of the affluent and wealthy, while neglecting the rights of the poor and needy. . . . The Church rather does intend that the institution of private property be such as is required by the plan of divine wisdom and the law of nature."[32] Private ownership should safeguard the rights of the human person, and at the same time make its necessary contribution to the establishment of right order in society.

112. While recent developments in economic life progress rapidly in a number of countries, as we have noted, and produce goods ever more efficiently, justice and equity require that remuneration for work also be increased within limits allowed by the common good. This enables workers to save more readily and hence to achieve some property status of their own. Wherefore, it is indeed surprising that some reject the natural role of private ownership. For it is a right which continually draws its force and vigor from the fruitfulness of labor, and which, accordingly, is an effective aid in safeguarding the dignity of the human person and the free exercise of responsibility in all fields of endeavor. Finally, it strengthens the stability and tranquillity of family life, thus contributing to the peace and prosperity of the commonwealth.

Effective Distribution

113. It is not enough, then, to assert that man has from nature the right of privately possessing goods as his own, including those of productive character, unless, at the same time, a continuing effort is made to spread the use of this right through all ranks of the citizenry.

114. Our predecessor of happy memory, Pius XII, clearly reminded us that on the one hand the dignity of the human person necessarily "requires the right of using external goods in order to live according to the right norm of nature. And to this right corresponds a most serious obligation, which requires that, so far as possible, there be given to all an opportunity of possessing private property."[33] On the other hand, the nobility inherent in work, besides other requirements, demands "the conservation and perfection of a social order that makes possible a secure, although modest, property to all classes of the people."[34]

115. It is especially appropriate that today, more than heretofore, widespread private ownership should prevail, since, as noted above, the number of

nations increases wherein the economic systems experience daily growth. Therefore, by prudent use of various devices already proven effective, it will not be difficult for the body politic to modify economic and social life so that the way is made easier for widespread private possession of such things as durable goods, homes, gardens, tools requisite for artisan enterprises and family-type farms, investments in enterprises of medium or large size. All of this has occurred satisfactorily in some nations with developed social and economic systems.

Public Property

116. Obviously, what we have said above does not preclude ownership of goods pertaining to production of wealth by States and public agencies, especially "if these carry with them power too great to be left in private hands, without injury to the community at large."[35]

117. It seems characteristic of our times to vest more and more ownership of goods in the State and in other public bodies. This is partially explained by the fact that the common good requires public authorities to exercise ever greater responsibilities. However, in this matter, the *principle of subsidiarity*, already mentioned above, is to be strictly observed. For it is lawful for States and public corporations to expand their domain of ownership only when manifest and genuine requirements of the common good so require, and then with safeguards, lest the possession of private citizens be diminished beyond measure, or, what is worse, destroyed.

118. Finally, we cannot pass over in silence the fact that economic enterprises undertaken by the State or by public corporations should be entrusted to citizens outstanding in skill and integrity, who will carry out their responsibilities to the commonwealth with a deep sense of devotion. Moreover, the activity of these men should be subjected to careful and continuing supervision, lest, in the administration of the State itself, there develop an economic imperialism in the hands of a few. For such a development is in conflict with the highest good of the commonwealth.

Social Function of Property

119. Our predecessors have always taught that in the right of private property there is rooted a social responsibility. Indeed, in the wisdom of God the Creator, the overall supply of goods is assigned, first of all, that all men may lead a decent life. As our predecessor of happy memory, Leo XIII, clearly reminded us in the encyclical letter *Rerum Novarum*, "This is the heart of the matter: whoever has received from the divine bounty a larger share of blessings, whether these be corporal or external or gifts of mind, has received them to use for his own perfection, and, at the same time, as the minister of God's providence, for the benefit of others. 'He who has a talent' [says St. Gregory the Great], 'let him take care that he hides it not; he who has abundance, let him arouse himself to mercy and generosity; he who has skill in managing

affairs, let him make special effort to share the use and utility thereof with his neighbor.'"[36]

120. Although in our day, the role assigned the State and public bodies has increased more and more, it by no means follows that the social function of private ownership is obsolescent, as some seem to think. For social responsibility in this matter derives its force from the very right of private property. Furthermore, it is quite clear that there always will be a wide range of difficult situations, as well as hidden and grave needs, which the manifold providence of the State leaves untouched, and of which it can in no way take account. Wherefore, there is always wide scope for humane action by private citizens and for Christian charity. Finally, it is evident that in stimulating efforts relating to spiritual welfare, the work done by individual men or by private civic groups has more value than what is done by public authorities.

121. Moreover, it is well to recall here that the right of private ownership is clearly evident in the Gospels, which reveal Jesus Christ ordering the rich to share their goods with the poor so as to turn them into spiritual possessions: "Do not lay up for yourselves treasures on earth, where rust and moth consume, and where thieves break in and steal; but lay up for yourselves treasures in heaven, where neither rust nor moth consumes nor thieves break in and steal."[37] And the divine Master states that whatever is done for the poor is done for him: "Amen I say to you, as long as you did it for one of these, the least of my brethren, you did it for me."[38]

PART III: NEW ASPECTS OF THE SOCIAL QUESTION

122. The progress of events and of time has made it increasingly evident that the relationships between workers and management in productive enterprises must be readjusted according to norms of justice and charity. But the same is also true of the systems whereby various types of economic activity and the differently endowed regions within a country ought to be linked together. Meanwhile, within the overall human community, many nations with varied endowments have not made identical progress in their economic and social affairs.

JUST REQUIREMENTS IN THE MATTER OF INTERRELATED PRODUCTIVE SECTORS

Agriculture: A Depressed Sector

123. First of all, to lay down some norms in regard to agriculture, we would note that the overall number of rural dwellers seemingly has not diminished. Beyond doubt, however, many farmers have abandoned their rural birthplace, and seek out either the more populous centers or the cities themselves. Now since this is the case in almost all countries, and since it affects large numbers of human beings, problems concerning life and dignity of citizens arise, which are indeed difficult to overcome.

124. Thus, as economic life progresses and expands, the percentage of rural dwellers diminishes, while the great number of industrial and service workers increases. Yet, we feel that those who transfer from rural activities to other productive enterprises often are motivated by reasons arising from the very evolution of economic affairs. Very often, however, they are caught up by various enticements of which the following are noteworthy: a desire to escape from a confined environment offering no prospect of a more comfortable life; the wish, so common in our age, to undertake new activities and to acquire new experiences; the attraction of quickly acquired goods and fortunes; a longing after a freer life, with the advantages that larger towns and cities usually provide. But there is no doubt about this point: rural dwellers leave the fields because nearly everywhere they see their affairs in a state of depression, both as regards labor productivity and the level of living of farm populations.

125. Accordingly, in this grave matter, about which enquiries are made in nearly all countries, we should first of all ask what is to be done to prevent so great imbalances between agriculture, industry, and the services in the matter of productive efficiency? Likewise, what can be done to minimize differences between the rural standard of living and that of city dwellers whose money income is derived from industry or some service or other? Finally, how can it be brought about that those engaged in agricultural pursuits no longer regard themselves as inferior to others? Indeed, rural dwellers should be convinced not only that they can strengthen and develop their personalities by their toil, but also that they can look forward to the future vicissitudes with confidence.

126. Accordingly, we judge it opportune in this connection to lay down some norms of permanent validity; although, as is evident, these must be adapted as various circumstances of time and place permit, or suggest, or absolutely require.

Provision for Essential Public Services

127. First, it is necessary that everyone, and especially public authorities, strive to effect improvements in rural areas as regards the principal services needed by all. Such are, for example: highway construction; transport services; marketing facilities; pure drinking water; housing; medical services; elementary, trade, and professional schools; things requisite for religion and for recreation; finally, furnishings and equipment needed in the modern farm home. Where these requirements for a dignified farm life are lacking to rural dwellers, economic and social progress does not occur at all, or else very slowly. Under such conditions, nothing can be done to keep men from deserting the fields, nor can anyone readily estimate their number.

Gradual and Orderly Development of the Economic System

128. It is desirable, moreover, that economic development of commonwealths proceed in orderly fashion, meanwhile preserving appropriate balance

between the various sectors of the economy. In particular, care must be had that within the agricultural sector innovations are introduced as regards productive technology whether these relate to productive methods, or to cultivation of the fields, or to equipment for the rural enterprise, as far as the overall economy allows or requires. And all this should be done, as far as possible, in accordance with technical advances in industry and in the various services.

129. In this way, agriculture not only absorbs a larger share of industrial output, but also demands a higher quality of services. In its turn, agriculture offers to the industrial and service sectors of the economy, as well as to the community as a whole, those products which in kind and in quantity better meet consumer needs. Thus, agriculture contributes to stability of the purchasing power of money, a very positive factor for the orderly development of the entire economic system.

130. By proceeding in this manner, the following advantages, among others, arise: first of all, it is easier to know the origins and destinations of rural dwellers displaced by modernization of agriculture. Thereupon, they can be instructed in skills needed for other types of work. Finally, economic aids and helps will not be lacking for their intellectual and cultural development, so that they can fit into new social groups.

Appropriate Economic Policy

131. To achieve orderly progress in various sectors of economic life, it is absolutely necessary that as regards agriculture, public authorities give heed and take action in the following matters: taxes and duties, credit, insurance, prices, the fostering of requisite skills, and, finally, improved equipment for rural enterprises.

Taxation

132. As regards taxation, assessment according to ability to pay is fundamental to a just and equitable system.

133. But in determining taxes for rural dwellers, the general welfare requires public authorities to bear in mind that income in a rural economy is both delayed and subject to greater risk. Moreover, there is difficulty in finding capital so as to increase returns.

Capital at Suitable Interest

134. Accordingly, those with money to invest are more inclined to invest it in enterprises other than in the rural economy. And for the same reason, rural dwellers cannot pay high rates of interest. Nor are they generally able to pay prevailing market rates for capital wherewith to carry on and expand their operations. Wherefore, the general welfare requires that public authorities not merely make special provision for agricultural financing, but also for establishment of banks that provide capital to farmers at reasonable rates of interest.

Social Insurance and Social Security

135. It also seems necessary to make provision for a twofold insurance, one covering agricultural output, the other recovering farmers and their families. Because, as experience shows, the income of individual farmers is, on the average, less than that of workers in industry and the services, it does not seem to be fully in accord with the norms of social justice and equity to provide farmers with insurance or social security benefits that are inferior to those of other classes of citizens. For those insurance plans or provisions that are established generally should not differ markedly one from the other, whatever be the economic sector wherein the citizens work or from which they derive their income.

136. Moreover, since social security and insurance can help appreciably in distributing national income among the citizens according to justice and equity, these systems can be regarded as means whereby imbalances among various classes of citizens are reduced.

Price Protection

137. Since agricultural products have special characteristics, it is fitting that their price be protected by methods worked out by economic experts. In this matter, although it is quite helpful that those whose interests are involved take steps to safeguard themselves, setting up, as it were, appropriate goals, public authorities cannot stand entirely aloof from the stabilization procedure.

138. Nor should this be overlooked, that, generally speaking, the price of rural products is more a recompense for farmers' labor than for capital investment.

139. Thus, our predecessor of happy memory, Pius XI, touching on the welfare of the human community, appropriately notes in his encyclical letter *Quadragesimo Anno*, that "a reasonable relationship between different wages here enters into consideration." But he immediately adds, "Intimately connected with this is a reasonable relationship between the prices obtained for the products of the various economic groups: agrarian, industrial, and so forth."[39]

140. Inasmuch as agricultural products are destined especially to satisfy the basic needs of men, it is necessary that their price be such that all can afford to buy them. Nevertheless, there is manifest injustice in placing a whole group of citizens, namely, the farmers, in an inferior economic and social status, with less purchasing power than required for a decent livelihood. This, indeed, is clearly contrary to the common good of the country.

Strengthening Farm Income

141. In rural areas it is fitting that industries be fostered and common services be developed that are useful in preserving, processing, and finally, in transporting farm products. There is need, moreover, to establish councils and activities relating to various sectors of economic and professional affairs. By such means, suitable opportunity is given farm families to supplement their incomes, and that within the milieu wherein they live and work.

Appropriate Organization of Farming Enterprises

142. Finally, no one person can lay down a universal rule regarding the way in which rural affairs should be definitely organized, since in these matters there exists considerable variation within each country, and the difference is even greater when we consider the various regions of the world. However, those who hold man and the family in proper esteem, whether this be based upon nature alone, or also upon Christian principles, surely look toward some form of agricultural enterprise, and particularly of the family type, which is modeled upon the community of men wherein mutual relationships of members and the organization of the enterprise itself are conformed to norms of justice and Christian teaching. And these men strive mightily that such organization of rural life be realized as far as circumstances permit.

143. The family farm will be firm and stable only when it yields money income sufficient for decent and humane family living. To bring this about, it is very necessary that farmers generally receive instruction, be kept informed of new developments, and be technically assisted by trained men. It is also necessary that farmers form among themselves mutual-aid societies; that they establish professional associations; that they function efficiently in public life, that is, in various administrative bodies and in political affairs.

RURAL WORKERS: PARTICIPANTS IN IMPROVING CONDITIONS

144. We are of the opinion that in rural affairs, the principal agents and protagonists of economic improvement, of cultural betterment, or of social advance, should be the men personally involved, namely, the farmers themselves. To them it should be quite evident that their work is most noble, because it is undertaken, as it were, in the majestic temple of creation; because it often concerns the life of plants and animals, a life inexhaustible in its expression, inflexible in its laws, rich in allusions to God, Creator and Provider. Moreover, labor in the fields not only produces various foodstuffs wherewith humankind is nourished, but also furnishes an increasing supply of raw materials for industry.

145. Furthermore, this is a work endowed with a dignity of its own, for it bears a manifold relationship to the mechanical arts, chemistry, and biology: these must be continually adapted to the requirements of emerging situations because scientific and technological advance is of great importance in rural life. Work of this kind, moreover, possesses a special nobility because it requires farmers to understand well the course of the seasons and to adapt themselves to the same; that they await patiently what the future will bring; that they appreciate the importance and seriousness of their duties; that they constantly remain alert and ready for new developments.

Solidarity and Cooperation

146. Nor may it be overlooked that in rural areas, as indeed in every productive sector, farmers should join together in fellowships, especially when the

family itself works the farm. Indeed, it is proper for rural workers to have a sense of solidarity. They should strive jointly to set up mutual-aid societies and professional associations. All these are very necessary either to keep rural dwellers abreast of scientific and technical progress, or to protect the prices of goods produced by their labor. Besides, acting in this manner, farmers are put on the same footing as other classes of workers who, for the most part, join together in such fellowships. Finally, by acting thus, farmers will achieve an importance and influence in public affairs proportionate to their own role. For today it is unquestionably true that the solitary voice speaks, as they say, to the winds.

Recognizing Demands of the Common Good

147. But when rural dwellers, just as other classes of workers, wish to make their influence and importance felt, they should never disregard moral duties or civil law. Rather they should strive to bring their rights and interests into line with the rights and needs of other classes, and to refer the same to the common good. In this connection, farmers who strive vigorously to improve the yield of their farm may rightly demand that their efforts be aided and complemented by public authorities, provided they themselves keep in mind the common needs of all and also relate their own efforts to the fulfillment of these needs.

148. Wherefore, we wish to honor appropriately those sons of ours who everywhere in the world, either by founding and fostering mutual-aid societies or some other type of association, watchfully strive that in all civic affairs farmers enjoy not merely economic prosperity but also a status in keeping with justice.

Vocation and Mission

149. Since everything that makes for man's dignity, perfection, and development seems to be invoked in agricultural labor, it is proper that man regard such work as an assignment from God with a sublime purpose. It is fitting, therefore, that man dedicate work of this kind to the most provident God who directs all events for the salvation of men. Finally, the farmer should take upon himself, in some measure, the task of educating himself and others for the advancement of civilization.

AID TO LESS DEVELOPED AREAS

150. It often happens that in one and the same country citizens enjoy different degrees of wealth and social advancement. This especially happens because they dwell in areas which, economically speaking, have grown at different rates. Where such is the case, justice and equity demand that the government make efforts either to remove or to minimize imbalances of this sort. Toward this end, efforts should be made, in areas where there has been less economic progress, to supply the principal public services, as indicated by circumstances of time and place and in accord with the general level of living.

But in bringing this about, it is necessary to have very competent administration and organization to take careful account of the following: labor supply, internal migration, wages, taxes, interest rates, and investments in industries that foster other skills and developments—all of which will further not merely the useful employment of workers and the stimulation of initiative, but also the exploitation of resources locally available.

151. But it is precisely the measures for advancement of the general welfare which civil authorities must undertake. Hence, they should take steps, having regard for the needs of the whole community, that progress in agriculture, industry, and services be made at the same time and in a balanced manner so far as possible. They should have this goal in mind, that citizens in less developed countries—in giving attention to economic and social affairs, as well as to cultural matters—feel themselves to be the ones chiefly responsible for their own progress. For a citizen has a sense of his own dignity when he contributes the major share to progress in his own affairs.

152. Hence, those also who rely on their own resources and initiative should contribute as best they can to the equitable adjustment of economic life in their own community. Nay, more, those in authority should favor and help private enterprise in accordance with the *principle of subsidiarity*, in order to allow private citizens themselves to accomplish as much as is feasible.

Imbalances between Land and Population

153. It is appropriate to recall at this point that in a number of nations there exists a discrepancy between available agricultural land and the number of rural dwellers. Some nations experience a shortage of citizens, but have rich land resources; others have many citizens but an insufficiency of agricultural land.

154. Nor are there lacking nations wherein, despite their great resource potential, farmers use such primitive and obsolete methods of cultivation that they are unable to produce what is needed for the entire population. On the other hand, in certain countries, agriculture has so adapted itself to recent advances that farmers produce surpluses which to some extent harm the economy of the entire nation.

155. It is evident that both the solidarity of the human race and the sense of brotherhood which accords with Christian principles require that some peoples lend others energetic help in many ways. Not merely would this result in a freer movement of goods, of capital, and of men, but it also would lessen imbalances between nations. We shall treat of this point in more detail below.

156. Here, however, we cannot fail to express our approval of the efforts of the Institute known as F.A.O. which concerns itself with the feeding of peoples and the improvement of agriculture. This Institute has the special goal of promoting mutual accord among peoples, of bringing it about that rural life is modernized in less developed nations, and finally, that help is brought to people experiencing food shortages.

REQUIREMENTS OF JUSTICE AS BETWEEN NATIONS DIFFERING IN ECONOMIC DEVELOPMENT

Problem of the Modern World

157. Perhaps the most pressing question of our day concerns the relationship between economically advanced commonwealths and those that are in process of development. The former enjoy the conveniences of life; the latter experience dire poverty. Yet, today men are so intimately associated in all parts of the world that they feel, as it were, as if they are members of one and the same household. Therefore, the nations that enjoy a sufficiency and abundance of everything may not overlook the plight of other nations whose citizens experience such domestic problems that they are all but overcome by poverty and hunger, and are not able to enjoy basic human rights. This is all the more so inasmuch as countries each day seem to become more dependent on each other. Consequently, it is not easy for them to keep the peace advantageously if excessive imbalances exist in their economic and social conditions.

158. Mindful of our role of universal father, we think it opportune to stress here what we have stated in another connection: "We all share responsibility for the fact that populations are undernourished."[40] "[Therefore], it is necessary to arouse a sense of responsibility in individuals and generally, especially among those more blessed with this world's goods."[41]

159. As can be readily deduced, and as the Church has always seriously warned, it is proper that the duty of helping the poor and unfortunate should especially stir Catholics, since they are members of the Mystical Body of Christ. "In this we have come to know the love of God," said John the Apostle, "that he laid down his life for us; and we likewise ought to lay down our life for the brethren. He who has the goods of this world and sees his brother in need and closes his heart to him, how does the love of God abide in him?"[42]

160. Wherefore, we note with pleasure that countries with advanced productive systems are lending aid to less privileged countries, so that these latter may the more readily improve their condition.

Emergency Assistance

161. It is clear to everyone that some nations have surpluses in foodstuffs, particularly of farm products, while elsewhere large masses of people experience want and hunger. Now justice and humanity require that these richer countries come to the aid of those in need. Accordingly, to destroy entirely or to waste goods necessary for the lives of men runs counter to our obligations in justice and humanity.

162. We are quite well aware that to produce surpluses, especially of farm products, in excess of the needs of a country, can occasion harm to various classes of citizens. Nevertheless, it does not therefore follow that nations with surpluses have no obligation to aid the poor and hungry where some particular emergency arises. Rather, diligent efforts should be made

that inconveniences arising from surplus goods be minimized and borne by every citizen on a fair basis.

Scientific, Technical, and Financial Cooperation

163. However, the underlying causes of poverty and hunger will not be removed in a number of countries by these means alone. For the most part, the causes are to be found in the primitive state of the economy. To effect a remedy, all available avenues should be explored with a view, on the one hand, to instruct citizens fully in necessary skills and in carrying out their responsibilities, and, on the other hand, to enable them to acquire the capital wherewith to promote economic growth by ways and means adapted to our times.

164. It has not escaped our attention that in recent years there has grown in many minds a deep awareness of their duty to aid poorer countries still lacking suitable economic development, in order that these may more readily make economic and social progress.

165. Toward this end, we look to councils, either of a number of nations, or within individual nations; we look to private enterprises and societies to exert daily more generous efforts on behalf of such countries, transmitting to them requisite productive skills. For the same reason help is given to as many youths as possible that they may study in the great universities of more developed countries, thus acquiring a knowledge of the arts and sciences in line with the standards of our time. Moreover, international banks, single nations, or private citizens often make loans to these countries that they may initiate various programs calculated to increase production. We gladly take this opportunity to give due praise to such generous activity. It is hoped that in the future the richer countries will make greater and greater efforts to provide developing countries with aid designed to promote sciences, technology, and economic life.

Avoidance of Past Errors

166. In this matter we consider it our duty to offer some warnings.

167. First of all, it seems only prudent for nations which thus far have made little or no progress, to weigh well the principal factor in the advance of nations that enjoy abundance.

168. Prudent foresight and common need demand that not only more goods be produced, but that this be done more efficiently. Likewise, necessity and justice require that wealth produced be distributed equitably among all citizens of the commonwealth. Accordingly, efforts should be made to ensure that improved social conditions accompany economic advancement. And it is very important that such advances occur simultaneously in the agricultural, industrial, and various service sectors.

Respect for Individual Characteristics of Countries

169. It is indeed clear to all that countries in process of development often have their own individual characteristics, and that these arise from

the nature of the locale, or from cultural tradition, or from some special trait of the citizens.

170. Now when economically developed countries assist the poorer ones, they not only should have regard for these characteristics and respect them, but also should take special care lest, in aiding these nations, they seek to impose their own way of life upon them.

Disinterested Aid

171. Moreover, economically developed countries should take particular care lest, in giving aid to poorer countries, they endeavor to turn the prevailing political situation to their own advantage, and seek to dominate them.

172. Should perchance such attempts be made, this clearly would be but another form of colonialism, which, although disguised in name, merely reflects their earlier but outdated dominion, now abandoned by many countries. When international relations are thus obstructed, the orderly progress of all peoples is endangered.

173. Genuine necessity, as well as justice, requires that whenever countries give attention to the fostering of skills or commerce, they should aid the less developed nations without thought of domination, so that these latter eventually will be in a position to progress economically and socially on their own initiative.

174. If this be done, it will help much toward shaping a community of all nations, wherein each one, aware of its rights and duties, will have regard for the prosperity of all.

Respect for a Hierarchy of Values

175. There is no doubt that when a nation makes progress in science, technology, economic life, and the prosperity of its citizens, a great contribution is made to civilization. But all should realize that these things are not the highest goods.

176. Accordingly, we note with sorrow that in some nations economic life indeed progresses, but that not a few men are there to be found who have no concern at all for the just ordering of goods. No doubt, these men either completely ignore spiritual values, or put these out of their minds, or else deny they exist. Nevertheless, while they pursue progress in science, technology, and economic life, they make so much of external benefits that for the most part they regard these as the highest goods of life. Accordingly, there are not lacking grave dangers in the help provided by more affluent nations for development of the poorer ones. For among the citizens of these latter nations, there is operative a general awareness of the higher values on which moral teachings rest—an awareness derived from ancient traditional custom which provides them with motivation.

177. Thus, those who seek to undermine in some measure the right instincts of these peoples assuredly do something immoral. Rather, those attitudes,

besides being held in honor, should be perfected and refined, since upon them true civilization depends.

CONTRIBUTION OF THE CHURCH

178. Moreover, the Church by divine right pertains to all nations. This is confirmed by the fact that she already is everywhere on earth and strives to embrace all peoples.

179. Now, those peoples whom the Church has joined to Christ have always reaped some benefits, whether in economic affairs or in social organization, as history and contemporary events clearly record. For everyone who professes Christianity promises and gives assurance that he will contribute as far as he can to the advancement of civil institutions. He must also strive with all his might not only that human dignity suffer no dishonor, but also, by the removal of every kind of obstacle, that all those forces be promoted which are conducive to moral living and contribute to it.

180. Moreover, when the Church infuses her energy into the life of a people, she neither is, nor feels herself to be, an alien institution imposed upon that people from without. This follows from the fact that wherever the Church is present, there individual men are reborn or resurrected in Christ. Those who are thus reborn or who have risen again in Christ feel themselves oppressed by no external force. Rather, realizing they have achieved perfect liberty, they freely move toward God. Hence, whatever is seen by them as good and morally right, that they approve and put into effect.

181. "The Church of Jesus Christ," as our predecessor Pius XII clearly stated, "is the faithful guardian of God's gracious wisdom. Hence, she makes no effort to discourage or belittle those characteristics and traits which are proper to particular nations, and which peoples religiously and tenaciously guard, quite justly, as a sacred heritage. She aims indeed at a unity which is profound and in conformity with that heavenly love whereby all are moved in their innermost being. She does not seek a uniformity which is merely external in its effects and calculated to weaken the fiber of the peoples concerned. And all careful rules that contribute to the wise development and growth within bounds of these capacities and forces, which indeed have their deeply rooted ethnic traits, have the Church's approval and maternal prayers, provided they are not in opposition to those duties which spring from the common origin and destiny of all mortal men."[43]

182. We note with deep satisfaction that Catholic men, citizens of the less developed nations, are for the most part second to no other citizens in furthering efforts of their countries to make progress economically and socially according to their capacity.

183. Furthermore, we note that Catholic citizens of the richer nations are making extensive efforts to ensure that aid given by their own countries to needy countries is directed increasingly toward economic and social progress. In this connection, it seems specially praiseworthy that appreciable aid in

various forms is provided increasingly each year to young people from Africa and Asia, so that they may pursue literary and professional studies in the great universities of Europe and America. The same applies to the great care that has been taken in training for every responsibility of their office men prepared to go to less developed areas, there to carry out their profession and duties.

184. To those sons of ours who, by promoting solicitously the progress of peoples and by spreading, as it were, a wholesome civilizing influence, everywhere demonstrate the perennial vitality of Holy Church and her effectiveness, we wish to express our paternal praise and gratitude.

POPULATION INCREASE AND ECONOMIC DEVELOPMENT

185. More recently, the question often is raised how economic organization and the means of subsistence can be balanced with population increase, whether in the world as a whole or within the needy nations.

Imbalance between Population and Means of Subsistence

186. As regards the world as a whole, some, consequent to statistical reasoning, observe that within a matter of decades mankind will become very numerous, whereas economic growth will proceed much more slowly. From this some conclude that unless procreation is kept within limits, there subsequently will develop an even greater imbalance between the number of inhabitants and the necessities of life.

187. It is clearly evident from statistical records of less developed countries that, because recent advances in public health and in medicine are there widely diffused, the citizens have a longer life expectancy consequent to lowered rates of infant mortality. The birth rate, where it has traditionally been high, tends to remain at such levels, at least for the immediate future. Thus the birth rate in a given year exceeds the death rate. Meanwhile the productive systems in such countries do not expand as rapidly as the number of inhabitants. Hence, in poorer countries of this sort, the standard of living does not advance and may even deteriorate. Wherefore, lest a serious crisis occur, some are of the opinion that the conception of birth of humans should be avoided or curbed by every possible means.

The Terms of the Problem

188. Now to tell the truth, the interrelationships on a global scale between the number of births and available resources are such that we can infer grave difficulties in this matter do not arise at present, nor will in the immediate future. The arguments advanced in this connection are so inconclusive and controversial that nothing certain can be drawn from them.

189. Besides, God in his goodness and wisdom has, on the one hand, provided nature with almost inexhaustible productive capacity; and, on the other hand, has endowed man with such ingenuity that, by using suitable means, he can apply nature's resources to the needs and requirements of existence.

Accordingly, that the question posed may be clearly resolved, a course of action is not indeed to be followed whereby, contrary to the moral law laid down by God, procreative function also is violated. Rather, man should, by the use of his skills and science of every kind, acquire an intimate knowledge of the forces of nature and control them ever more extensively. Moreover, the advances hitherto made in science and technology give almost limitless promise for the future in this matter.

190. When it comes to questions of this kind, we are not unaware that in certain locales and also in poorer countries, it is often argued that in such an economic and social order, difficulties arise because citizens, each year more numerous, are unable to acquire sufficient food or sustenance where they live, and peoples do not show amicable cooperation to the extent they should.

191. But whatever be the situation, we clearly affirm these problems should be posed and resolved in such a way that man does not have recourse to methods and means contrary to his dignity, which are proposed by those persons who think of man and his life solely in material terms.

192. We judge that this question can be resolved only if economic and social advances preserve and augment the genuine welfare of individual citizens and of human society as a whole. Indeed, in a matter of this kind, first place must be accorded everything that pertains to the dignity of man as such, or to the life of individual men, than which nothing can be more precious. Moreover, in this matter, international cooperation is necessary, so that, conformably with the welfare of all, information, capital, and men themselves may move about among the peoples in orderly fashion.

Respect for the Laws of Life

193. In this connection, we strongly affirm that human life is transmitted and propagated through the instrumentality of the family, which rests on marriage, one and indissoluble, and, so far as Christians are concerned, elevated to the dignity of a sacrament. Because the life of man is passed on to other men deliberately and knowingly, it therefore follows that this should be done in accord with the most sacred, permanent, inviolate prescriptions of God. Everyone without exception is bound to recognize and observe these laws. Wherefore, in this matter, no one is permitted to use methods and procedures which may indeed be permissible to check the life of plants and animals.

194. Indeed, all must regard the life of man as sacred, since, from its inception, it requires the action of God the Creator. Those who depart from this plan of God not only offend his divine majesty and dishonor themselves and the human race, but they also weaken the inner fiber of the commonwealth.

Education Toward a Sense of Responsibility

195. In these matters it is of great importance that new offspring, in addition to being very carefully educated in human culture and in religion—which indeed is the right and duty of parents—should also show themselves very

conscious of their duties in every action of life. This is especially true when it is a question of establishing a family and of procreating and educating children. Such children should be imbued not only with a firm confidence in the providence of God, but also with a strong and ready will to bear the labors and inconveniences which cannot be lawfully avoided by anyone who undertakes the worthy and serious obligation of associating his own activity with God in transmitting life and in educating offspring. In this most important matter certainly nothing is more relevant than the teachings of and supernatural aids provided by the Church. We refer to the Church whose right of freely carrying out her function must be recognized also in this connection.

Creation for Man's Benefit

196. When God, as we read in the book of Genesis, imparted human nature to our first parents, he assigned them two tasks, one of which complements the other. For he first directed: "Be fruitful and multiply,"[44] and then immediately added: "Fill the earth and subdue it."[45]

197. The second of these tasks, far from anticipating a destruction of goods, rather assigns them to the service of human life.

198. Accordingly, with great sadness we note two conflicting trends: on the one hand, the scarcity of goods is vaguely described as such that the life of men reportedly is in danger of perishing from misery and hunger; on the other hand, the recent discoveries of science, technical advances and economic productivity are transformed into means whereby the human race is led toward ruin and a horrible death.

199. Now the provident God has bestowed upon humanity sufficient goods wherewith to bear with dignity the burdens associated with procreation of children. But this task will be difficult or even impossible if men, straying from the right road and with a perverse outlook, use the means mentioned above in a manner contrary to human reason or to their social nature, and hence, contrary to the directives of God himself.

INTERNATIONAL COOPERATION

World Dimensions of Important Human Problems

200. Since the relationships between countries today are closer in every region of the world, by reason of science and technology, it is proper that peoples become more and more interdependent.

201. Accordingly, contemporary problems of moment—whether in the fields of science and technology, or of economic and social affairs, or of public administration, or of cultural advancement—these, because they may exceed the capacities of individual States, very often affect a number of nations and at times all the nations of the earth.

202. As a result, individual countries, although advanced in culture and civilization, in number and industry of citizens, in wealth, in geographical extent,

are not able by themselves to resolve satisfactorily their basic problems. Accordingly, because States must on occasion complement or perfect one another, they really consult their own interests only when they take into account at the same time the interests of others. Hence, dire necessity warns commonwealths to cooperate among themselves and provide mutual assistance.

Mutual Distrust

203. Although this becomes more and more evident each day to individuals and even to all peoples, men, and especially those with high responsibility in public life, for the most part seem unable to accomplish the two things toward which peoples aspire. This does not happen because peoples lack scientific, technical, or economic means, but rather because they distrust one another. Indeed, men, and hence States, stand in fear of one another. One country fears lest another is contemplating aggression and lest the other seize an opportunity to put such plans in effect. Accordingly, countries customarily prepare defenses for their cities and homeland, namely, armaments designed to deter other countries from aggression.

204. Consequently, the energies of man and the resources of nature are very widely directed by peoples to destruction rather than to the advantage of the human family, and both individual men and entire peoples become so deeply solicitous that they are prevented from undertaking more important works.

Failure to Acknowledge the Moral Order

205. The cause of this state of affairs seems to be that men, more especially leaders of States, have differing philosophies of life. Some even dare to assert that there exists no law of truth and right which transcends external affairs and man himself, which of necessity pertains to everyone, and, finally, which is equitable for all men. Hence, men can agree fully and surely about nothing, since one and the same law of justice is not accepted by all.

206. Although the word *justice* and the related term *demands of justice* are on everyone's lips, such verbalizations do not have the same meaning for all. Indeed, the opposite frequently is the case. Hence, when leaders invoke *justice* or the *demands of justice*, not only do they disagree as to the meaning of the words, but frequently find in them an occasion of serious contention. And so they conclude that there is no way of achieving their rights or advantages, unless they resort to force, the root of very serious evils.

God, the Foundation of the Moral Order

207. That mutual faith may develop among rulers and nations and may abide more deeply in their minds, the laws of truth and justice first must be acknowledged and preserved on all sides.

208. However, the guiding principles of morality and virtue can be based only on God; apart from him, they necessarily collapse. For man is composed not merely of body, but of soul as well, and is endowed with reason and free-

dom. Now such a composite being absolutely requires a moral law rooted in religion, which, far better than any external force or advantage, can contribute to the resolution of problems affecting the lives of individual citizens or groups of citizens, or with a bearing upon single States or all States together.

209. Yet, there are today those who assert that, in view of the flourishing state of science and technology, men can achieve the highest civilization even apart from God and by their own unaided powers. Nevertheless, it is because of this very progress in science and technology that men often find themselves involved in difficulties which affect all peoples and which can be overcome only if they duly recognize the authority of God, author and ruler of man and of all nature.

210. That this is true, the advances of science seem to indicate, opening up, as they do, almost limitless horizons. Thus, an opinion is implanted in many minds that, inasmuch as mathematical sciences are unable to discern the innermost nature of things and their changes, or express them in suitable terms, they can scarcely draw inferences about them. And when terrified men see with their own eyes that the vast forces deriving from technology and machines can be used for destruction as well as for the advantage of peoples, they rightly conclude that things pertaining to the spirit and to moral life are to be preferred to all else, so that progress in science and technology does not result in destruction of the human race, but prove useful as instruments of civilization.

211. Meanwhile it comes to pass that in more affluent countries men, less and less satisfied with external goods, put out of their minds the deceptive image of a happy life to be lived here forever. Likewise, not only do men grow daily more conscious that they are fully endowed with all the rights of the human person, but they also strive mightily that relations among themselves become more equitable and more conformed to human dignity. Consequently, men are beginning to recognize that their own capacities are limited, and they seek spiritual things more intensively than heretofore. All of which seems to give some promise that not only individuals, but even peoples may come to an understanding for extensive and extremely useful collaboration.

PART IV: RECONSTRUCTION OF SOCIAL RELATIONSHIPS IN TRUTH, JUSTICE, AND LOVE

INCOMPLETE AND ERRONEOUS PHILOSOPHIES OF LIFE

212. As in the past, so too in our day, advances in science and technology have greatly multiplied relationships between citizens; it seems necessary, therefore, that the relationships themselves, whether within a single country or between all countries, be brought into more humane balance.

213. In this connection many systems of thought have been developed and committed to writing: some of these already have been dissipated as mist by the sun; others remain basically unchanged today; still others now elicit

less and less response from men. The reason for this is that these popularized fancies neither encompass man, whole and entire, nor do they affect his inner being. Moreover, they fail to take into account the weaknesses of human nature, such as sickness and suffering: weaknesses that no economic or social system, no matter how advanced, can completely eliminate. Besides, men everywhere are moved by a profound and unconquerable sense of religion, which no force can ever destroy nor shrewdness suppress.

214. In our day, a very false opinion is popularized which holds that the sense of religion implanted in men by nature is to be regarded as something adventitious or imaginary, and hence, is to be rooted completely from the mind as altogether inconsistent with the spirit of our age and the progress of civilization. Yet, this inward proclivity of man to religion confirms the fact that man himself was created by God, and irrevocably tends to him. Thus we read in Augustine: "Thou hast made us for Thyself, O Lord, and our hearts are restless until they rest in Thee."[46]

215. Wherefore, whatever the progress in technology and economic life, there can be neither justice nor peace in the world, so long as men fail to realize how great is their dignity; for they have been created by God and are his children. We speak of God, who must be regarded as the first and final cause of all things he has created. Separated from God, man becomes monstrous to himself and others. Consequently, mutual relationships between men absolutely require a right ordering of the human conscience in relation to God, the source of all truth, justice, and love.

216. It is well-known and recognized by everyone that in a number of countries, some of ancient Christian culture, many of our very dear brothers and sons have been savagely persecuted for a number of years. Now this situation, since it reveals the great dignity of the persecuted, and the refined cruelty of their persecutors, leads many to reflect on the matter, though it has not yet healed the wounds of the persecuted.

217. However, no folly seems more characteristic of our time than the desire to establish a firm and meaningful temporal order, but without God, its necessary foundation. Likewise, some wish to proclaim the greatness of man, but with the source dried up from which such greatness flows and receives nourishment: that is, by impeding and, if it were possible, stopping the yearning of souls for God. But the turn of events in our times, whereby the hopes of many are shattered and not a few have come to grief, unquestionably confirm the words of scripture: "Unless the Lord build the house, they labor in vain who built it."[47]

THE CHURCH'S TRADITIONAL TEACHING REGARDING MAN'S SOCIAL LIFE

218. What the Catholic Church teaches and declares regarding the social life and relationships of men is beyond question for all time valid.

219. The cardinal point of this teaching is that individual men are necessarily the foundation, cause, and end of all social institutions. We are referring to human beings, insofar as they are social by nature, and raised to an order of existence that transcends and subdues nature.

220. Beginning with this very basic principle whereby the dignity of the human person is affirmed and defended, Holy Church—especially during the last century and with the assistance of learned priests and laymen, specialists in the field—has arrived at clear social teachings whereby the mutual relationships of men are ordered. Taking general norms into account, these principles are in accord with the nature of things and the changed conditions of man's social life, or with the special genius of our day. Moreover, these norms can be approved by all.

221. But today, more than ever, principles of this kind must not only be known and understood, but also applied to those systems and methods which the various situations of time or place either suggest or require. This is indeed a difficult, though lofty, task. Toward its fulfillment we exhort not only our brothers and sons everywhere, but all men of good will.

Study of Social Matters

222. Above all, we affirm that the social teaching proclaimed by the Catholic Church cannot be separated from her traditional teaching regarding man's life.

223. Wherefore, it is our earnest wish that more and more attention be given to this branch of learning. First of all, we urge that attention be given to such studies in Catholic schools on all levels, and especially in seminaries, although we are not unaware that in some of these latter institutions this is already being done admirably. Moreover, we desire that social study of this sort be included among the religious materials used to instruct and inspire the lay apostolate, either in parishes or in associations. Let this diffusion of knowledge be accomplished by every modern means: that is, in journals, whether daily or periodical; in doctrinal books, both for the learned and the general reader; and finally, by means of radio and television.

224. We judge that our sons among the laity have much to contribute through their work and effort, that this teaching of the Catholic Church regarding the social question be more and more widely diffused. This they can do, not merely by learning it themselves and governing their actions accordingly, but also by taking special care that others also come to know its relevance.

225. Let them be fully persuaded that in no better way can they show this teaching to be correct and effective than by demonstrating that present day social difficulties will yield to its application. In this way they will win minds today antagonistic to the teaching because they do not know it. Perhaps it will also happen that such men will find some enlightenment in the teaching.

APPLICATION OF SOCIAL TEACHING

226. But social norms of whatever kind are not only to be explained but also applied. This is especially true of the Church's teaching on social matters, which has truth as its guide, justice as its end, and love as its driving force.

227. We consider it, therefore, of the greatest importance that our sons, in addition to knowing these social norms, be reared according to them.

228. To be complete, the education of Christians must relate to the duties of every class. It is therefore necessary that Christians thus inspired conform their behavior in economic and social affairs to the teachings of the Church.

229. If it is indeed difficult to apply teaching of any sort to concrete situations, it is even more so when one tries to put into practice the teachings of the Catholic Church regarding social affairs. This is especially true for the following reasons: there is deeply rooted in each man an instinctive and immoderate love of his own interests; today there is widely diffused in society a materialistic philosophy of life; it is difficult at times to discern the demands of justice in a given situation.

230. Consequently, it is not enough for men to be instructed, according to the teachings of the Church, on their obligation to act in a Christian manner in economic and social affairs. They must also be shown ways in which they can properly fulfill their duty in this regard.

231. We do not regard such instructions as sufficient, unless there be added to the work of instruction that of the formation of man, and unless some action follow upon the teachings, by way of experience.

232. Just as, proverbially, no one really enjoys liberty unless he uses it, so no one really knows how to act according to Catholic teaching in the economic and social fields, unless he acts according to this teaching in the same area.

A Task for Lay Apostolate

233. Accordingly, in popular instruction of this kind, it seems proper that considerable attention be paid to groups promoting the lay apostolate, especially those whose aim is to ensure that efforts in our present concern draw their inspiration wholly from Christian law. Seeing that members of such groups can first train themselves by daily practice in these matters, they subsequently will be able the better to instruct young people in fulfilling obligations of this kind.

234. It is not inappropriate in this connection to remind all, the great no less than the lowly, that the will to preserve moderation and to bear difficulties, by God's grace, can in no wise be separated from the meaning of life handed down to us by Christian wisdom.

235. But today, unfortunately, very many souls are preoccupied with an inordinate desire for pleasure. Such persons see nothing more important in the whole of life than to seek pleasure, to quench the thirst for pleasure.

Beyond doubt, grave ills to both soul and body proceed therefrom. Now in this matter, it must be admitted that one who judges even with the aid of human nature alone concludes that it is the part of the wise and prudent man to preserve balance and moderation in everything, and to restrain the lower appetites. He who judges matter in the light of divine revelation assuredly will not overlook the fact that the Gospel of Christ and the Catholic Church, as well as the ascetical tradition handed down to us, all demand that Christians steadfastly mortify themselves and bear the inconveniences of life with singular patience. These virtues, in addition to fostering a firm and moderate rule of mind over body, also present an opportunity of satisfying the punishment due to sin, from which, except for Jesus Christ and his immaculate mother, no one is exempt.

Practical Suggestions

236. The teachings in regard to social matters for the most part are put into effect in the following three stages: first, the actual situation is examined; then, the situation is evaluated carefully in relation to these teachings; then only is it decided what can and should be done in order that the traditional norms may be adapted to circumstances of time and place. These three steps are at times expressed by the three words: *observe, judge, act.*

237. Hence, it seems particularly fitting that youth not merely reflect upon this order of procedure, but also, in the present connection, follow it to the extent feasible, lest what they have learned be regarded merely as something to be thought about but not acted upon.

238. However, when it comes to reducing these teachings to action, it sometimes happens that even sincere Catholic men have differing views. When this occurs they should take care to have and to show mutual esteem and regard, and to explore the extent to which they can work in cooperation among themselves. Thus they can in good time accomplish what necessity requires. Let them also take great care not to weaken their efforts in constant controversies. Nor should they, under pretext of seeking what they think best, meanwhile, fail to do what they can and hence should do.

239. But in the exercise of economic and social functions, Catholics often come in contact with men who do not share their view of life. On such occasions, those who profess Catholicism must take special care to be consistent and not compromise in matters wherein the integrity of religion or morals would suffer harm. Likewise, in their conduct they should weigh the opinions of others with fitting courtesy and not measure everything in the light of their own interests. They should be prepared to join sincerely in doing whatever is naturally good or conducive to good. If, indeed, it happens that in these matters sacred authorities have prescribed or decreed anything, it is evident that this judgment is to be obeyed promptly by Catholics. For it is the Church's right and duty not only to safeguard principles relating to the integrity of

religion and morals, but also to pronounce authoritatively when it is a matter of putting these principles into effect.

Manifold Action and Responsibility

240. But what we have said about the norms of instruction should indeed be put into practice. This has special relevance for those beloved sons of ours who are in the ranks of the laity, inasmuch as their activity ordinarily centers around temporal affairs and making plans for the same.

241. To carry out this noble task, it is necessary that laymen not only should be qualified, each in his own profession, and direct their energies in accordance with rules suited to the objective aimed at, but also should conform their activity to the teachings and norms of the Church in social matters. Let them put sincere trust in her wisdom; let them accept her admonitions as sons. Let them reflect that, when in the conduct of life they do not carefully observe principles and norms laid down by the Church in social matters, and which we ourselves reaffirm, then they are negligent in their duty and often injure the rights of others. At times, matters can come to a point where confidence in this teaching is diminished, as if it were indeed excellent but really lacks the force which the conduct of life requires.

A GRAVE DANGER

242. As we have already noted, in this present age men have searched widely and deeply into the laws of nature. Then they invented instruments whereby they can control the forces of nature; they have perfected and continue to perfect remarkable works worthy of deep admiration. Nevertheless, while they endeavor to master and transform the external world, they are also in danger, lest they become neglectful and weaken the powers of body and mind. This is what our predecessor of happy memory, Pius XI, noted with sorrow of spirit in his encyclical letter *Quadragesimo Anno*: "And so bodily labor, which was decreed by divine providence for the good of man's body and soul even after original sin, has too often been changed into an instrument of perversion: for dead matter leaves the factory ennobled and transformed whereas men are there corrupted and degraded."[48]

243. And our predecessor of happy memory, Pius XII, rightly asserted that our age is distinguished from others precisely by the fact that science and technology have made incalculable progress, while men themselves have departed correspondingly from a sense of dignity. It is a "monstrous masterpiece" of this age "to have transformed man, as it were, into a giant as regards the order of nature, yet in the order of the supernatural and the eternal, to have changed him into a pygmy."[49]

244. Too often in our day is verified the testimony of the Psalmist concerning worshipers of false gods, namely, human beings in their activity very

frequently neglect themselves, but admire their own works as if these were gods: "Their idols are silver and gold; the handiwork of men."[50]

Respect for the Hierarchy of Values

245. Wherefore, aroused by the pastoral zeal wherewith we embrace all men, we strongly urge our sons that, in fulfilling their duties and in pursuing their goals, they do not allow their consciousness of responsibilities to grow cool, nor neglect the order of the more important goods.

246. For it is indeed clear that the Church has always taught and continues to teach that advances in science and technology and the prosperity resulting therefrom are truly to be counted as good things and regarded as signs of the progress of civilization. But the Church likewise teaches that goods of this kind are to be judged properly in accordance with their natures: they are always to be considered as instruments for man's use, the better to achieve his highest end: that he can the more easily improve himself, in both the natural and supernatural orders.

247. Wherefore, we ardently desire that our sons should at all times heed the words of the divine Master: "For what does it profit a man, if he gain the whole world, but suffer the loss of his own soul? Or what will a man give in exchange for his soul?"[51]

Sanctification of Holy Days

248. Not unrelated to the above admonitions is the one having to do with rest to be taken on feast days.

249. In order that the Church may defend the dignity with which man is endowed, because he is created by God and because God has breathed into him a soul to His own image, she has never failed to insist that the third commandment: "Remember to keep holy the Sabbath day,"[52] be carefully observed by all. It is the right of God, and within His power, to order that man put aside a day each week for proper and due worship of the divinity. He should direct his mind to heavenly things, setting aside daily business. He should explore the depths of his conscience in order to know how necessary and inviolable are his relations with God.

250. In addition, it is right and necessary for man to cease for a time from labor, not merely to relax his body from daily hard work and likewise to refresh himself with decent recreation, but also to foster family unity, for this requires that all its members preserve a community of life and peaceful harmony.

251. Accordingly, religion, moral teaching, and care of health in turn require that relaxation be had at regular times. The Catholic Church has decreed for many centuries that Christians observe this day of rest on Sunday, and that they be present on the same day at the eucharistic sacrifice because it renews the memory of the divine redemption and at the same time imparts its fruits to the souls of men.

252. But we note with deep sorrow, and we cannot but reprove the many who, though they perhaps do not deliberately despise this holy law, yet more and more frequently disregard it. Whence it is that our very dear working-men almost necessarily suffer harm, both as to the salvation of their souls and to the health of their bodies.

253. And so, taking into account the needs of soul and body, we exhort, as it were, with the words of God himself, all men, whether public officials or representatives of management and labor, that they observe this command of God himself and of the Catholic Church, and judge in their souls that they have a responsibility to God and society in this regard.

RENEWED DEDICATION

254. From what we have briefly touched upon above, let none of our sons conclude, and especially the laity, that they act prudently if, in regard to the transitory affairs of this life, they become quite remiss in their specific Christian contributions. On the contrary, we reaffirm that they should be daily more zealous in carrying out this role.

255. Indeed, when Christ our Lord made that solemn prayer for the unity of his Church, he asked this from the Father on behalf of his disciples: "I do not pray that thou take them out of the world, but that Thou keep them from evil."[53] Let no one imagine that there is any opposition between these two things so that they cannot be properly reconciled: namely, the perfection of one's own soul and the business of this life, as if one had no chance but to abandon the activities of this world in order to strive for Christian perfection, or as if one could not attend to these pursuits without endangering his own dignity as a man and as a Christian.

256. However, it is in full accord with the designs of God's providence that men develop and perfect themselves by exercise of their daily tasks, for this is the lot of practically everyone in the affairs of this mortal life. Accordingly, the role of the Church in our day is very difficult: to reconcile a man's modern respect for progress with the norms of humanity and of the Gospel teaching. Yet, the times call the Church to this role; indeed, we may say, earnestly beseech her, not merely to pursue the higher goals, but also to safeguard her accomplishments without harm to herself. To achieve this, as we have already said, the Church especially asks the cooperation of the laity. For this reason, in their dealings with men, they are bound to exert effort in such a way that while fulfilling their duties to others, they do so in union with God through Christ, for the increase of God's glory. Thus the Apostle Paul asserts: "Whether you eat or drink, or do anything else, do all for the glory of God."[54] And elsewhere: "Whatever you do in word or in work, do all in the name of the Lord Jesus Christ, giving thanks to God the Father through Him."[55]

Greater Effectiveness in Temporal Affairs

257. As often, therefore, as human activity and institutions having to do with the affairs of this life help toward spiritual perfection and everlasting beatitude, the more they are to be regarded as an efficacious way of obtaining the immediate end to which they are directed by their very nature. Thus, valid for all times is that noteworthy sentence of the divine Master: "Seek first the kingdom of God and his justice, and all these things shall be given you besides."[56] For he who is, as it were, *a light in the Lord*,[57] and walks as a *son of light*,[58] perceives more clearly what the requirements of justice are, in the various sectors of human zeal, even in those that involve greater difficulties because of the excessive love which many have for their own interests, or those of their country, or race. It must be added that when one is motivated by Christian charity, he cannot but love others, and regard the needs, sufferings and joys of others as his own. His work, wherever it be, is constant, adaptable, humane, and has concern for the needs of others: For "charity is patient, is kind; charity does not envy, is not pretentious, is not puffed up, is not ambitious, is not self-seeking, is not provoked; thinks no evil, does not rejoice over wickedness, but rejoices with the truth; bears with all things, believes all things, hopes all things, endures all things."[59]

LIVING MEMBERS OF THE MYSTICAL BODY OF CHRIST

258. But we do not wish to bring this letter of ours to a close, venerable brothers, without recalling to your minds that most fundamental and true element of Catholic teaching, whereby we learn that we are living members of his Mystical Body, which is the Church: "For as the body is one and has many members, and all the members of the body, many as they are, form one body, so also is it with Christ."[60]

259. Wherefore, we urgently exhort all our sons in every part of the world, whether clergy or laity, that they fully understand how great is the nobility and dignity they derive from being joined to Christ, as branches to the vine, as he himself said: "I am the vine, you are the branches,"[61] and that they are sharers of His divine life. Whence it is, that if Christians are also joined in mind and heart with the most Holy Redeemer, when they apply themselves to temporal affairs, their work in a way is a continuation of the labor of Jesus Christ himself, drawing from it strength and redemptive power: "He who abides in me, and I in him, he bears much fruit."[62] Human labor of this kind is so exalted and ennobled that it leads men engaged in it to spiritual perfection, and can likewise contribute to the diffusion and propagation of the fruits of the redemption to others. So also it results in the flow of that Gospel leaven, as it were, through the veins of civil society wherein we live and work.

260. Although it must be admitted that the times in which we live are torn by increasingly serious errors, and are troubled by violent distur-

bances, yet, it happens that the Church's laborers in this age of ours have access to enormous fields of apostolic endeavor. This inspires us with uncommon hope.

261. Venerable brothers and beloved sons, beginning with that marvelous letter of Leo, we have thus far considered with you the varied and serious issues which pertain to the social conditions of our time. From them we have drawn norms and teachings, upon which we especially exhort you not merely to meditate deeply, but also to do what you can to put them into effect. If each one of you does his best courageously, it will necessarily help in no small measure to establish the kingdom of Christ on earth. This is indeed: "A kingdom of truth and of life; a kingdom of holiness and grace; a kingdom of justice, of love and of peace."[63] And this we shall some day leave to go to that heavenly beatitude, for which we were made by God, and which we ask for with most ardent prayers.

262. For it is a question here of the teaching of the Catholic and Apostolic Church, mother and teacher of all nations, whose light illumines, sets on fire, inflames. Her warning voice, filled with heavenly wisdom, reaches out to every age. Her power always provides efficacious and appropriate remedies for the growing needs of men, for the cares and solicitudes of this mortal life. With this voice, the age-old song of the Psalmist is in marvelous accord, to strengthen at all times and to uplift our souls: "I will hear what God proclaims; the Lord—for he proclaims peace to his people, and to his faithful ones, and to those who put in him their hope. Near indeed is his salvation to those who fear him, glory dwelling in our land. Kindness and truth shall meet; justice and peace shall kiss. Truth shall spring out of the earth, and justice shall look down from heaven. The Lord himself will give his benefits; our land shall yield its increase. Justice shall walk before him, and salvation, along the way of his steps."[64]

263. This is the plea, venerable brothers, we make at the close of this letter, to which we have for a considerable time directed our concern about the universal Church. We desire that the divine Redeemer of mankind, "who has become for us God-given wisdom, and justice, and sanctification, and redemption,"[65] may reign and triumph gloriously in all things and over all things, for centuries on end. We desire that, in a properly organized order of social affairs, all nations will at last enjoy prosperity, and happiness, and peace.

264. As an evidence of these wishes, and a pledge of our paternal good will, we affectionately bestow in the Lord our apostolic blessing upon you, venerable brothers, and upon all the faithful committed to your care, and especially upon those who will reply with generosity to our appeals.

265. Given at Rome, at Saint Peter's, the fifteenth day of May, in the year 1961, the third year of our Pontificate.

JOHN XXIII

NOTES

1. Cf. 1 Tim. 3:15.
2. John 14:6.
3. John 8:12.
4. Mark 8:2.
5. *Acta Leonis XIII*, XI (1891), pp. 97–144.
6. Ibid., p. 107.
7. Thomas Aquinas, *De regimine principum*, I, 15.
8. Cf. *Acta Apostolicae Sedis*, XXIII (1931), p. 185.
9. Cf. ibid., p. 189.
10. Ibid., pp. 177–228.
11. Cf. ibid., p. 190.
12. Cf. ibid., p. 200.
13. Cf. ibid., p. 201.
14. Cf. ibid., p. 210f.
15. Cf. ibid., p. 211.
16. Cf. *Acta Apostolicae Sedis*, XXXIII (1941), p. 196.
17. Cf. ibid., p. 197.
18. Cf. ibid., p. 196.
19. Cf. ibid., p. 198f.
20. Cf. ibid., p. 199.
21. Cf. ibid., p. 201.
22. Cf. ibid., p. 202.
23. Cf. ibid., p. 203.
24. *Acta Apostolicae Sedis*, XXIII (1931), p. 203.
25. Ibid., p. 203.
26. Cf. ibid., p. 222f.
27. Cf. *Acta Apostolicae Sedis*, XXXIII (1941), p. 200.
28. *Acta Apostolicae Sedis*, XXIII (1931), p. 195.
29. Ibid., p. 198.
30. Radio Broadcast, September 1, 1944; cf. AAS, XXXVI (1944), p. 254.
31. *Allocution*, October 8, 1956; cf. AAS, XLVIII (1956), pp. 799–800.
32. Radio Broadcast, September 1, 1944; cf. AAS, XXXVI (1944), p. 253.
33. Radio Broadcast, December 24, 1942; cf. AAS, XXXV (1943), p. 17.
34. Cf. ibid., p. 20.
35. Encycl. *Quadragesimo Anno*; AAS, XXIII (1931), p. 214.
36. *Acta Leonis XIII*, XI (1891), p. 114.
37. Matt. 6:19–20.
38. Matt. 25:40.
39. Cf. *Acta Apostolicae Sedis*, XXIII (1931), p. 202.
40. *Allocution*, May 3, 1960; cf. AAS, LII (1960), p. 465.
41. Cf. ibid.
42. 1 John 3:16–17.

43. Encycl. *Summi Pontificatus*; AAS, XXXI (1939), pp. 428–29.
44. Gen. 1:28.
45. Ibid.
46. Augustine, *Confessions* I, 1.
47. Ps. 126:1.
48. *Acta Apostolicae Sedis*, XXIII (1931), pp. 221f.
49. Radio Broadcast, Christmas Eve, 1953; cf. AAS, XLVI (1954), p. 10.
50. Ps. 113:4.
51. Matt. 16:26.
52. Exod. 20:8.
53. John 17:15.
54. 1 Cor. 10:31.
55. Col. 3:17.
56. Matt. 6:33.
57. Eph. 5:8.
58. Cf. ibid.
59. 1 Cor. 13:4–7.
60. 1 Cor. 12:12.
61. John 15:5.
62. Ibid.
63. *Preface of Jesus Christ the King.*
64. Ps. 84:9ff.
65. 1 Cor. 1:30.

Pacem in Terris: Peace on Earth (John XXIII, 1963)

INTRODUCTION

Issued in 1963, only a few months before John XXIII's death, *Pacem in Terris* seemed to come at an appropriate time. The Second Vatican Council had begun, and the process of the renewal of the church was underway. John's own personality touched a vital nerve in Western society, and the world seemed eager to hear what he had to say. The encyclical spoke in a language of fraternity, shared concern, and mutual responsibility. More ominously, the world had been to the nuclear brink twice, over Berlin and Cuba. Thus when for the first time in an encyclical, the pope spoke to "all men of good will," many seemed anxious to listen.

Four major themes stand out in *Pacem in Terris*: the rights proper to each individual, the relation between authority and conscience, disarmament, and the development of the common good.

The rights that the pope argues are proper to all individuals are not in themselves unique or constitutive of a major departure from traditional Catholic social thought. What is important is the encyclical's grouping of them together and listing them in such an explicit manner. In addition to traditional rights such as respect for one's person and religious freedom, John also argues for some not accepted as easily: the right to freedom in searching for the truth and in expressing one's opinions, the right to choose freely one's state of life, the right to work, the right to free initiative in economics, the right of freedom of assembly and association, and the right to emigrate and immigrate. Such a listing both sets out a social agenda and provides criteria for evaluation of social practices.

These rights form a general background for the document's teaching on the relation between conscience and authority. John begins with the traditional doctrine that authority is derived from God, but affirms that it also must derive its obligatory force from the moral order. While affirming the traditional doctrine that social positions imply social duties binding on all by natural law, he also provides a more democratic emphasis on participation. Then the pope argues that the state can oblige individuals in conscience only if its authority is intrinsically related to the moral order, that is, God. This provides the basis for individual claims against a government.

The problems of the arms race are of central concern to the encyclical. John argues that the arms race deprives individuals and nations of the economic goods necessary for social progress. It also causes individuals to live in constant fear not only of nuclear war but also of hazards from nuclear testing. The pope argues that justice, reason, and humanity demand that the arms race should cease, that nuclear weapons be banned, and that progressive disarmament begin. And, in a celebrated statement, John argues that because of the destructive force of these weapons and the terrible consequences of their use, "it is contrary to reason to hold that war is now a suitable way to restore rights which have been violated." As the restoration of violated rights was the fundamental basis for a just war, some observers concluded that in the nuclear age, a just war was no longer possible.

Finally, Pope John uses the concept of the common good as a principle of integration. Important in the pope's argument is that each political community also has a common good, which transcends the individual person's good, but which cannot be divorced from the common good of the entire human community. Such a realization of a variety of goods demands international cooperation and planning so that each individual entity—a person or a political community—can realize the goods proper to it. This finds its fulfillment in what Pope John refers to as the universal common good, the common good of the entire family.

With *Pacem in Terris* and the Second Vatican Council, Catholicism was emerging into participation in the full human community. This encyclical was a fitting climax to Pope John's reign, offering a standard of human rights and world peace against which to measure the pastoral effectiveness of the changes initiated by the council. The standard of Catholic life could never again be simply the power and strength of the church, for the church itself would now be judged by the standards of truth, justice, charity, and freedom Pope John set forth.

PACEM IN TERRIS

ENCYCLICAL LETTER ON ESTABLISHING UNIVERSAL PEACE IN TRUTH, JUSTICE, CHARITY AND LIBERTY

To Our Venerable Brothers the Patriarchs, Primates, Archbishops, Bishops and Other Local Ordinaries in Peace and Communion with the Apostolic See, to the Clergy and Faithful of the Whole World and to All Men of Good Will

POPE JOHN XXIII

Venerable Brothers and Beloved Children,
Health and Apostolic Benediction

INTRODUCTION

ORDER IN THE UNIVERSE

1. Peace on earth, which all men of every era have most eagerly yearned for, can be firmly established only if the order laid down by God be dutifully observed.

2. The progress of learning and the inventions of technology clearly show that, both in living things and in the forces of nature, an astonishing order reigns, and they also bear witness to the greatness of man, who can understand that order and create suitable instruments to harness those forces of nature and use them to his benefit.

3. But the progress of science and the inventions of technology show above all the infinite greatness of God, who created the universe and man himself. He created all things out of nothing, pouring into them the abundance of his wisdom and goodness, so that the holy psalmist praises God in these words: "O Lord our master, the majesty of thy name fills all the earth."[1] Elsewhere he says: "What diversity, Lord, in thy creatures! What wisdom has designed them all!"[2] God also created man in his own "image and likeness,"[3] endowed him with intelligence and freedom, and made him lord of creation, as the same psalmist declares in the words: "Thou hast placed him only a little below the angels, crowning him with glory and honor and bidding him rule over the works of thy hands. Thou hast put all under his dominion."[4]

ORDER IN HUMAN BEINGS

4. How strongly does the turmoil of individual men and peoples contrast with the perfect order of the universal. It is as if the relationships which bind them together could be controlled only by force.

5. But the Creator of the world has imprinted in man's heart an order which his conscience reveals to him and enjoins him to obey: "This shows that the obligations of the law are written in their hearts; their conscience utters its own testimony."[5] And how could it be otherwise? For whatever God has made shows forth his infinite wisdom, and it is manifested more clearly in the things which have greater perfection.[6]

6. But fickleness of opinion often produces this error, that many think that the relationships between men and States can be governed by the same laws as the forces and irrational elements of the universe, whereas the laws governing them are of quite a different kind and are to be sought elsewhere, namely, where the Father of all things wrote them, that is, in the nature of man.

7. By these laws men are most admirably taught, first of all how they should conduct their mutual dealings among themselves, then how the relationships between the citizens and the public authorities of each state should be regulated, then how states should deal with one another, and finally how, on the one hand individual men and states, and on the other hand the community of all peoples, should act toward each other, the establishment of such a community being urgently demanded today by the requirements of universal common good.

PART I: ORDER BETWEEN MEN

EVERY MAN IS A PERSON WITH RIGHTS AND DUTIES

8. First of all, it is necessary to speak of the order which should exist between men.

9. Any human society, if it is to be well-ordered and productive, must lay down as a foundation this principle, namely, that every human being is a person; that is, his nature is endowed with intelligence and free will. Indeed, precisely because he is a person he has rights and obligations flowing directly and simultaneously from his very nature.[7] And as these rights and obligations are universal and inviolable, so they cannot in any way be surrendered.

10. If we look upon the dignity of the human person in the light of divinely revealed truth, we cannot help but esteem it far more highly; for men are redeemed by the blood of Jesus Christ, they are by grace the children and friends of God and heirs of eternal glory.

RIGHTS

The Right to Life and a Worthy Standard of Living

11. Beginning our discussion of the rights of man, we see that every man has the right to life, to bodily integrity, and to the means which are suitable for the proper development of life; these are primarily food, clothing, shelter, rest, medical care, and finally the necessary social services. Therefore a human being also has the right to security in cases of sickness, inability to work, widowhood, old age, unemployment, or in any other case in which he is deprived of the means of subsistence through no fault of his own.[8]

Rights Pertaining to Moral and Cultural Values

12. By the natural law every human being has the right to respect for his person, to his good reputation; the right to freedom in searching for truth and in expressing and communicating his opinions, and in pursuit of art, within the limits laid down by the moral order and the common good; and he has the right to be informed truthfully about public events.

13. The natural law also gives man the right to share in the benefits of culture, and therefore the right to a basic education and to technical and professional training in keeping with the stage of educational development in the country to which he belongs. Every effort should be made to ensure that persons be enabled, on the basis of merit, to go on to higher studies, so that, as far as possible, they may occupy posts and take on responsibilities in human society in accordance with their natural gifts and the skills they have acquired.[9]

The Right to Worship God according to One's Conscience

14. This too must be listed among the rights of a human being, to honor God according to the sincere dictates of his own conscience, and therefore the right to practice his religion privately and publicly. For as Lactantius so clearly taught: "We were created for the purpose of showing to the God Who bore us the submission we owe Him, of recognizing Him alone, and of serving Him. We are obliged and bound by this duty to God; from this religion itself receives its name."[10] And on this point our predecessor of immortal memory, Leo XIII, declared: "This genuine, this honorable freedom of the sons of God, which most nobly protects the dignity of the human person, is greater than any violence or injustice; it has always been sought by the Church, and always most dear to her. This was the freedom which the apostles claimed with intrepid constancy, which the apologists defended with their writings, and which the martyrs in such numbers consecrated with their blood."[11]

The Right to Choose Freely One's State of Life

15. Human beings have the right to choose freely the state of life which they prefer, and therefore the right to set up a family, with equal rights and

duties for man and woman, and also the right to follow a vocation to the priesthood or the religious life.[12]

16. The family, grounded on marriage freely contracted, monogamous and indissoluble, is and must be considered the first and essential cell of human society. From this it follows that most careful provision must be made for the family both in economic and social matters as well as in those which are of a cultural and moral nature, all of which look to the strengthening of the family and helping it carry out its function.

17. Parents, however, have a prior right in the support and education of their children.[13]

Economic Rights

18. If we turn our attention to the economic sphere, it is clear that man has a right by the natural law not only to an opportunity to work, but also to go about his work without coercion.[14]

19. To these rights is certainly joined the right to demand working conditions in which physical health is not endangered, morals are safeguarded, and young people's normal development is not impaired. Women have the right to working conditions in accordance with their requirements and their duties as wives and mothers.[15]

20. From the dignity of the human person, there also arises the right to carry on economic activities according to the degree of responsibility of which one is capable.[16] Furthermore—and this must be specially emphasized—the worker has a right to a wage determined according to criterions of justice, and sufficient, therefore, in proportion to the available resources, to give the worker and his family a standard of living in keeping with the dignity of the human person. In this regard, our predecessor Pius XII said: "To the personal duty to work imposed by nature, there corresponds and follows the natural right of each individual to make of his work the means to provide for his own life and the lives of his children; so fundamental is the law of nature which commands man to preserve his life ."[17]

21. The right to private property, even of productive goods, also derives from the nature of man. This right, as we have elsewhere declared, "is an effective means for safeguarding the dignity of the human person and for the exercise of responsibility in all fields; it strengthens and gives serenity to family life, thereby increasing the peace and prosperity of the state."[18]

22. However, it is opportune to point out that there is a social duty essentially inherent in the right of private property.[19]

The Right of Meeting and Association

23. From the fact that human beings are by nature social, there arises the right of assembly and association. They have also the right to give the societies of which they are members the form they consider most suitable for the aim

they have in view and to act within such societies on their own initiative and on their own responsibility in order to achieve their desired objectives.[20]

24. And, as we ourselves in the encyclical *Mater et Magistra* have strongly urged, it is by all means necessary that a great variety of organizations and intermediate groups be established which are capable of achieving a goal which an individual cannot effectively attain by himself. These societies and organizations must be considered the indispensable means to safeguard the dignity of the human person and freedom while leaving intact a sense of responsibility.[21]

The Right to Emigrate and Immigrate

25. Every human being has the right to freedom of movement and of residence within the confines of his own country; and, when there are just reasons for it, the right to emigrate to other countries and take up residence there.[22] The fact that one is a citizen of a particular state does not detract in any way from his membership in the human family as a whole, nor from his citizenship in the world community.

Political Rights

26. The dignity of the human person involves the right to take an active part in public affairs and to contribute one's part to the common good of the citizens. For, as our predecessor of happy memory, Pius XII, pointed out: "The human individual, far from being an object and, as it were, a merely passive element in the social order, is in fact, must be and must continue to be, its subject, its foundation and its end."[23]

27. The human person is also entitled to a juridical protection of his rights, a protection that should be efficacious, impartial, and inspired by the true norms of justice. As our predecessor Pius XII teaches: "That perpetual privilege proper to man, by which every individual has a claim to the protection of his rights, and by which there is assigned to each a definite and particular sphere of rights, immune from all arbitrary attacks, is the logical consequence of the order of justice willed by God."[24]

DUTIES

Rights and Duties Necessarily Linked in the One Person

28. The natural rights with which we have been dealing are, however, inseparably connected, in the very person who is their subject, with just as many respective duties; and rights as well as duties find their source, their sustenance and their inviolability in the natural law which grants or enjoins them.

29. Therefore, to cite a few examples, the right of every man to life is correlative with the duty to preserve it; his right to a decent standard of living with the duty of living it becomingly; and his right to investigate the truth freely, with the duty of seeking it ever more completely and profoundly.

Reciprocity of Rights and Duties between Persons

30. Once this is admitted, it also follows that in human society to one man's right there corresponds a duty in all other persons: the duty, namely, of acknowledging and respecting the right in question. For every fundamental human right draws its indestructible moral force from the natural law, which in granting it imposes a corresponding obligation. Those, therefore, who claim their own rights, yet altogether forget or neglect to carry out their respective duties, are people who build with one hand and destroy with the other.

Mutual Collaboration

31. Since men are social by nature they are meant to live with others and to work for one another's welfare. A well-ordered human society requires that men recognize and observe their mutual rights and duties. It also demands that each contribute generously to the establishment of a civic order in which rights and duties are more sincerely and effectively acknowledged and fulfilled.

32. It is not enough, for example, to acknowledge and respect every man's right to the means of subsistence if we do not strive to the best of our ability for a sufficient supply of what is necessary for his sustenance.

33. The society of men must not only be organized but must also provide them with abundant resources. This certainly requires that they observe and recognize their mutual rights and duties; it also requires that they collaborate in the many enterprises that modern civilization either allows or encourages or even demands.

An Attitude of Responsibility

34. The dignity of the human person also requires that every man enjoy the right to act freely and responsibly. For this reason, therefore, in social relations man should exercise his rights, fulfill his obligations and, in the countless forms of collaboration with others, act chiefly on his own responsibility and initiative. This is to be done in such a way that each one acts on his own decision, of set purpose and from a consciousness of his obligation, without being moved by force or pressure brought to bear on him externally. For any human society that is established on relations of force must be regarded as inhuman, inasmuch as the personality of its members is repressed or restricted, when in fact they should be provided with appropriate incentives and means for developing and perfecting themselves.

Social Life in Truth, Justice, Charity, and Freedom

35. A civic society is to be considered well-ordered, beneficial and in keeping with human dignity if it is grounded on truth. As the Apostle Paul exhorts us: "Away with falsehood then; let everyone speak out the truth to his neighbor; membership of the body binds us to one another."[25] This will

be accomplished when each one duly recognizes both his rights and his obligations toward others. Furthermore, human society will be such as we have just described it, if the citizens, guided by justice, apply themselves seriously to respecting the rights of others and discharging their own duties; if they are moved by such fervor of charity as to make their own the needs of others and share with others their own goods; if, finally, they work for a closer fellowship in the world of spiritual values. Yet this is not sufficient; for human society is bound together by freedom, that is to say, in ways and means in keeping with the dignity of its citizens, who accept the responsibility of their actions, precisely because they are by nature rational beings.

36. Therefore, venerable brothers and beloved children, human society must primarily be considered something pertaining to the spiritual. Through it, in the bright light of truth men should share their knowledge, be able to exercise their rights and fulfill their obligations, be inspired to seek spiritual values, mutually derive genuine pleasure from the beautiful of whatever order it be, always be readily disposed to pass on to others the best of their own cultural heritage and eagerly strive to make their own the spiritual achievements of others. These benefits not only influence, but at the same time give aim and scope to all that has bearing on cultural expressions, economic and social institutions, political movements and forms, laws, and all other structures by which society is outwardly established and constantly developed.

God and the Moral Order

37. The order which prevails in society is by nature moral. Grounded as it is in truth, it must function according to the norms of justice, it should be inspired and perfected by mutual love, and finally it should be brought to an ever more refined and human balance in freedom.

38. Now an order of this kind, whose principles are universal, absolute and unchangeable, has its ultimate source in the one true God, who is personal and transcends human nature. Inasmuch as God is the first truth and the highest good, he alone is that deepest source from which human society can draw its vitality, if that society is to be well-ordered, beneficial, and in keeping with human dignity.[26] As St. Thomas Aquinas says: "Human reason is the norm of the human will, according to which its goodness is measured, because reason derives from the eternal law which is the divine reason itself. It is evident then that the goodness of the human will depends much more on the eternal law than on human reason."[27]

CHARACTERISTICS OF THE PRESENT DAY

39. Our age has three distinctive characteristics.

40. First of all, the working classes have gradually gained ground in economic and public affairs. They began by claiming their rights in the

socioeconomic sphere; they extended their action then to claims on the political level, and finally applied themselves to the acquisition of the benefits of a more refined culture. Today, therefore, workers all over the world refuse to be treated as if they were irrational objects without freedom, to be used at the arbitrary disposition of others. They insist that they be always regarded as men with a share in every sector of human society: in the social and economic sphere, in the fields of learning and culture, and in public life.

41. Secondly, it is obvious to everyone that women are now taking part in public life. This is happening more rapidly perhaps in nations of Christian civilization, and, more slowly, but broadly, among peoples who have inherited other traditions or cultures. Since women are becoming ever more conscious of their human dignity, they will not tolerate being treated as mere material instruments, but demand rights befitting a human person both in domestic and in public life.

42. Finally, in the modern world human society has taken on an entirely new appearance in the field of social and political life. For since all nations have either achieved or are on the way to achieving independence, there will soon no longer exist a world divided into nations that rule others and nations that are subject to others.

43. Men all over the world have today—or will soon have—the rank of citizens in independent nations. No one wants to feel subject to political powers located outside his own country or ethnic group. Thus in very many human beings the inferiority complex which endured for hundreds and thousands of years is disappearing, while in others there is an attenuation and gradual fading of the corresponding superiority complex which had its roots in socioeconomic privileges, sex or political standing.

44. On the contrary, the conviction that all men are equal by reason of their natural dignity has been generally accepted. Hence racial discrimination can in no way be justified, at least doctrinally or in theory. And this is of fundamental importance and significance for the formation of human society according to those principles which we have outlined above. For, if a man becomes conscious of his rights, he must become equally aware of his duties. Thus he who possesses certain rights has likewise the duty to claim those rights as marks of his dignity, while all others have the obligation to acknowledge those rights and respect them.

45. When the relations of human society are expressed in terms of rights and duties, men become conscious of spiritual values, understand the meaning and significance of truth, justice, charity and freedom, and become deeply aware that they belong to this world of values. Moreover, when moved by such concerns, they are brought to a better knowledge of the true God who is personal and transcendent, and thus they make the ties that bind them to God the solid foundation and supreme criterion of their lives, both of that life which they live interiorly in the depths of their own souls and of that in which they are united to other men in society.

PART II: RELATIONS BETWEEN INDIVIDUALS AND THE PUBLIC AUTHORITIES WITHIN A SINGLE STATE

NECESSITY AND DIVINE ORIGIN OF AUTHORITY

46. Human society can be neither well-ordered nor prosperous unless it has some people invested with legitimate authority to preserve its institutions and to devote themselves as far as is necessary to work and care for the good of all. These, however, derive their authority from God, as St. Paul teaches in the words: "Authority comes from God alone."[28] These words of St. Paul are explained thus by St. John Chrysostom: "What are you saying? Is every ruler appointed by God? I do not say that, he replies, for I am not dealing now with individual rulers, but with authority itself. What I say is, that it is the divine wisdom and not mere chance, that has ordained that there should be government, that some should command and others obey."[29] Moreover, since God made men social by nature, and since no society "can hold together unless some one be over all, directing all to strive earnestly for the common good, every civilized community must have a ruling authority, and this authority, no less than society itself, has its source in nature, and has, consequently, God for its author."[30]

47. But authority is not to be thought of as a force lacking all control. Indeed, since it is the power to command according to right reason, authority must derive its obligatory force from the moral order, which in turn has God for its first source and final end. Wherefore our predecessor of happy memory, Pius XII, said: "The absolute order of living beings and man's very destiny (we are speaking of man who is free, bound by obligations and endowed with inalienable rights, and at once the basis of society and the purpose for which it exists) also includes the state as a necessary society invested with the authority without which it could not come into being or live. . . . And since this absolute order, as we learn from sound reason, and especially from the Christian faith, can have no origin save in God who is our Creator, it follows that the dignity of the state's authority is due to its sharing to some extent in the authority of God himself."[31]

48. Wherefore, a civil authority which uses as its only or its chief means either threats and fear of punishment or promises of rewards cannot effectively move men to promote the common good of all. Even if it did so move them, this would be altogether opposed to their dignity as men, endowed with reason and free will. As authority rests chiefly on moral force, it follows that civil authority must appeal primarily to the conscience of individual citizens, that is, to each one's duty to collaborate readily for the common good of all. But since by nature all men are equal in human dignity, it follows that no one may be coerced to perform interior acts. That is in the power of God alone, Who sees and judges the hidden designs of men's hearts.

49. Those therefore who have authority in the State may oblige men in conscience only if their authority is intrinsically related with the authority of God and shares in it.[32]

50. By this principle the dignity of the citizens is protected. When, in fact, men obey their rulers, it is not at all as men that they obey them, but through their obedience it is God, the provident Creator of all things, whom they reverence, since he has decreed that men's dealings with one another should be regulated by an order which he himself has established. Moreover, in showing this due reverence to God, men not only do not debase themselves but rather perfect and ennoble themselves. "For to serve God is to rule."[33]

51. Since the right to command is required by the moral order and has its source in God, it follows that, if civil authorities pass laws or command anything opposed to the moral order and consequently contrary to the will of God, neither the laws made nor the authorizations granted can be binding on the consciences of the citizens, since "God has more right to be obeyed than men."[34] Otherwise, authority breaks down completely and results in shameful abuse. As St. Thomas Aquinas teaches: "Human law has the true nature of law only in so far as it corresponds to right reason, and in this respect it is evident that it is derived from the eternal law. In so far as it falls short of right reason, a law is said to be a wicked law; and so, lacking the true nature of law, it is rather a kind of violence."[35]

52. It must not be concluded, however, because authority comes from God, that therefore men have no right to choose those who are to rule the state, to decide the form of government, and to determine both the way in which authority is to be exercised and its limits. It is thus clear that the doctrine which we have set forth can be fully consonant with any truly democratic regime.[36]

ATTAINMENT OF THE COMMON GOOD IS THE PURPOSE OF THE PUBLIC AUTHORITY

53. Individual citizens and intermediate groups are obliged to make their specific contributions to the common welfare. One of the chief consequences of this is that they must bring their own interests into harmony with the needs of the community, and must contribute their goods and their services as civil authorities have prescribed, in accord with the norms of justice and within the limits of their competence. Clearly then those who wield power in the state must do this by such acts which not only have been justly carried out, but which also either have the common welfare primarily in view or which can lead to it.

54. Indeed since the whole reason for the existence of civil authorities is the realization of the common good, it is clearly necessary that, in pursuing this objective, they should respect its essential elements, and at the same time conform their laws to the circumstances of the day.[37]

Essentials of the Common Good

55. Assuredly, the ethnic characteristics of the various human groups are to be respected as constituent elements of the common good,[38] but these values and characteristics by no means exhaust the content of the common good. For the common good since it is intimately bound up with human nature cannot therefore exist fully and completely unless the human person is taken into consideration and the essential nature and realization of the common good be kept in mind.[39]

56. In the second place, the very nature of the common good requires that all members of the state be entitled to share in it, although in different ways according to each one's tasks, merits and circumstances. For this reason, every civil authority must take pains to promote the common good of all, without preference for any single citizen or civic group. As our predecessor of immortal memory, Leo XIII, has said: "The civil power must not serve the advantage of any one individual, or of some few persons, inasmuch as it was established for the common good of all."[40] Considerations of justice and equity, however, can at times demand that those involved in civil government give more attention to the less fortunate members of the community, since they are less able to defend their rights and to assert their legitimate claims.[41]

57. In this context, we judge that attention should be called to the fact that the common good touches the whole man, the needs both of his body and of his soul. Hence it follows that the civil authorities must undertake to effect the common goods by ways and means that are proper to them; that is, while respecting the hierarchy of values, they should promote simultaneously both the material and the spiritual welfare of the citizens.[42]

58. These principles are clearly contained in the doctrine stated in our encyclical *Mater et Magistra*, where we emphasized that the common good of all "embraces the sum total of those conditions of social living whereby men are enabled to achieve their own integral perfection more fully and more easily."[43]

59. Men, however, composed as they are of bodies and immortal souls, can never in this mortal life succeed in satisfying all their needs or in attaining perfect happiness. Therefore the common good is to be procured by such ways and means which not only are not detrimental to man's eternal salvation but which positively contribute to it.[44]

Responsibilities of the Public Authority, and Rights and Duties of Individuals

60. It is agreed that in our time the common good is chiefly guaranteed when personal rights and duties are maintained. The chief concern of civil authorities must therefore be to ensure that these rights are acknowledged, respected, coordinated with other rights, defended and promoted, so that in this way each one may more easily carry out his duties. For "to safeguard the inviolable rights of the human person, and to facilitate the fulfillment of his duties, should be the chief duty of every public authority."[45]

61. This means that, if any government does not acknowledge the rights of man or violates them, it not only fails in its duty, but its orders completely lack juridical force.[46]

Reconciliation and Protection of Rights and Duties of Individuals

62. One of the fundamental duties of civil authorities, therefore, is to coordinate social relations in such fashion that the exercise of one man's rights does not threaten others in the exercise of their own rights nor hinder them in the fulfillment of their duties. Finally, the rights of all should be effectively safeguarded and, if they have been violated, completely restored.[47]

Duty of Promoting the Rights of Individuals

63. It is also demanded by the common good that civil authorities should make earnest efforts to bring about a situation in which individual citizens can easily exercise their rights and fulfill their duties as well. For experience has taught us that, unless these authorities take suitable action with regard to economic, political and cultural matters, inequalities between the citizens tend to become more and more widespread, especially in the modern world, and as a result human rights are rendered totally ineffective and the fulfillment of duties is compromised.

64. It is therefore necessary that the administration give wholehearted and careful attention to the social as well as to the economic progress of the citizens, and to the development, in keeping with the development of the productive system, of such essential services as the building of roads, transportation, communications, water supply, housing, public health, education, facilitation of the practice of religion, and recreational facilities. It is necessary also that governments make efforts to see that insurance systems are made available to the citizens, so that, in case of misfortune or increased family responsibilities, no person will be without the necessary means to maintain a decent standard of living. The government should make similarly effective efforts to see that those who are able to work can find employment in keeping with their aptitudes, and that each worker receives a wage in keeping with the laws of justice and equity. It should be equally the concern of civil authorities to ensure that workers be allowed their proper responsibility in the work undertaken in industrial organization, and to facilitate the establishment of intermediate groups which will make social life richer and more effective. Finally, it should be possible for all the citizens to share as far as they are able in their country's cultural advantages.

Harmonious Relation between Public Authority's Two Forms of Intervention

65. The common good requires that civil authorities maintain a careful balance between coordinating and protecting the rights of the citizens, on the one hand, and promoting them, on the other. It should not happen that certain

individuals or social groups derive special advantage from the fact that their rights have received preferential protection. Nor should it happen that governments, in seeking to protect these rights, become obstacles to their full expression and free use. "For this principle must always be retained: that State activity in the economic field, no matter what its breadth or depth may be, ought not to be exercised in such a way as to curtail an individual's freedom of personal initiative. Rather it should work to expand that freedom as much as possible by the effective protection of the essential personal rights of each and every individual."[48]

66. The same principle should inspire the various steps which governments take in order to make it possible for the citizens more easily to exercise their rights and fulfill their duties in every sector of social life.

STRUCTURE AND OPERATION OF THE PUBLIC AUTHORITY

67. It is impossible to determine, in all cases, what is the most suitable form of government, or how civil authorities can most effectively fulfill their respective functions, i.e., the legislative, judicial, and executive functions of the state.

68. In determining the structure and operation of government which a state is to have, great weight has to be given to the circumstances of a given people, circumstances which will vary at different times and in different places. We consider, however, that it is in keeping with the innate demands of human nature that the state should take a form which embodies the threefold division of powers corresponding to the three principal functions of public authority. In that type of state, not only the official functions of government but also the mutual relations between citizens and public officials are set down according to law, which in itself affords protection to the citizens both in the enjoyment of their rights and in the fulfillment of their duties.

69. If, however, this political and juridical structure is to produce the advantages which may be expected of it, public officials must strive to meet the problems which arise in a way that conforms both to the complexities of the situation and the proper exercise of their function. This requires that, in constantly changing conditions, legislators never forget the norms of morality, or constitutional provisions, or the common good. Moreover, executive authorities must coordinate the activities of society with discretion, with a full knowledge of the law and after a careful consideration of circumstances, and the courts must administer justice impartially and without being influenced by favoritism or pressure. The good order of society also demands that individual citizens and intermediate organizations should be effectively protected by law whenever they have rights to be exercised or obligations to be fulfilled. This protection should be granted to citizens both in their dealings with each other and in their relations with government agencies.[49]

Law and Conscience

70. It is unquestionable that a legal structure in conformity with the moral order and corresponding to the level of development of the state is of great advantage to achievement of the common good.

71. And yet, social life in the modern world is so varied, complex and dynamic that even a juridical structure which has been prudently and thoughtfully established often seems inadequate for the needs of society.

72. It is also true that the relations of the citizens with each other, of citizens and intermediate groups with public authorities, and finally of the public authorities with one another are often so complex and so sensitive that they cannot be regulated by inflexible legal provisions. Such a situation therefore demands that the civil authorities have clear ideas about the nature and extent of their official duties if they wish to maintain the existing juridical structure in its basic elements and principles, and at the same time meet the exigencies of social life, adapting their legislation to the changing social scene and solving new problems. They must be men of great equilibrium and integrity, competent and courageous enough to see at once what the situation requires and to take necessary action quickly and effectively.[50]

Citizens' Participation in Public Life

73. It is in keeping with their dignity as persons that human beings should take an active part in government, although the manner in which they share in it will depend on the level of development of the country to which they belong.

74. Men will find new and extensive advantages in the fact that they are allowed to participate in government. In this situation, those who administer the government come into frequent contact with the citizens, and it is thus easier for them to learn what is really needed for the common good. And since public officials hold office only for a specified period of time their authority, far from withering, rather takes on a new vigor in a measure proportionate to the development of human society.[51]

CHARACTERISTICS OF THE PRESENT DAY

75. From these considerations it becomes clear that in the juridical organization of states in our times the first requisite is that a charter of fundamental human rights be drawn up in clear and precise terms and that it be incorporated in its entirety in the constitution.

76. The second requisite is that the constitution of each state be drawn up, phrased in correct juridical terminology, which prescribes the manner of designating the public officials along with their mutual relations, the spheres of their competence, the forms and systems they are obliged to follow in the performance of their office.

77. The last requisite is that the relations between the government and the governed are then set forth in terms of rights and duties; and it is clearly laid

down that the paramount task assigned to government officials is that of recognizing, respecting, reconciling, protecting and promoting the rights and duties of citizens.

78. It is of course impossible to accept the theory which professes to find the original and single source of civic rights and duties, of the binding force of the constitution, and of a government's right to command, in the mere will of human beings, individually or collectively.[52]

79. The tendencies to which we have referred, however, do clearly show that the men of our time are becoming increasingly conscious of their dignity as human persons. This awareness prompts them to claim a share in the public administration of their country, while it also accounts for the demand that their own inalienable and inviolable rights be protected by law. It also requires that government officials be chosen in conformity with constitutional procedures, and perform their specific functions within the limits of law.

PART III: RELATIONS BETWEEN STATES

SUBJECTS OF RIGHTS AND DUTIES

80. Our predecessors have constantly maintained, and we join them in reasserting, that nations are reciprocally subjects of rights and duties. This means that their relationships also must be harmonized in truth, in justice, in a working solidarity, in liberty. The same natural law, which governs relations between individual human beings, serves also to regulate the relations of nations with one another.

81. This is readily clear to anyone if he would consider that the heads of states can in no way put aside their natural dignity while they represent their country and provide for its welfare, and that they were never allowed to depart from the natural law by which they are bound and which is the norm of their conduct.

82. Moreover, it is inconceivable that men because they are heads of government are forced to put aside their human endowments. On the contrary, they occupy this place of eminence for the very reason that they have earned a reputation as outstanding members of the body politic in view of their excellent intellectual endowments and accomplishments.

83. Indeed it follows from the moral order itself that authority is necessary for civil society, for civil society is ruled by authority; and that authority cannot be used to thwart the moral order without instantly collapsing because its foundation has been destroyed. This is the warning of God himself: "A word, then, for the kings' ears to hear, kings' hearts to heed: a message for you, rulers, wherever you be! Listen well, all you that have multitudes at your command, foreign hordes to do your bidding. Power is none but comes to you from the Lord, nor any royalty but from one who is above all. He it is

that will call you to account for your doings with a scrutiny that reads your inmost thoughts."[53]

84. Lastly it is to be borne in mind that also in the regulating of relations between states, authority is to be exercised for the achievement of the common good which constitutes the reason for its existence.

85. But a fundamental factor of the common good is acknowledgment of the moral order and exact observance of its commands. "A well-established order among nations must be built upon the unshakable and unchangeable rock of the moral law, made manifest in the order of nature by the Creator himself and by him engraved on the hearts of men with letters that can never be effaced. . . . Like the rays of a gleaming beacon, its principles must guide the plans and policies of men and nations. From its signals, which give warning and point out the safe and sure course, they must get their norms and guidance if they would not see all their laborious efforts to establish a new order condemned to tempest and shipwreck."[54]

IN TRUTH

86. First among the rules governing the relations between states is that of truth. This calls, above all, for the elimination of every trace of racism, and the consequent recognition of the principle that all states are by nature equal in dignity. Each of them accordingly is vested with the right to existence, to self-development, to the means fitting to its attainment, and to be the one primarily responsible for this self-development. Add to that the right of each to its good name, and to the respect which is its due.

87. Very often, experience has taught us, individuals will be found to differ enormously, in knowledge, power, talent and wealth. From this, however, no justification is ever found for those who surpass the rest to subject others to their control in any way. Rather they have a more serious obligation which binds each and everyone to lend mutual assistance to others in their efforts for improvement.

88. Likewise it can happen that one country surpasses another in scientific progress, culture and economic development. But this superiority, far from permitting it to rule others unjustly, imposes the obligation to make a greater contribution to the general development of the people.

89. In fact, men cannot by nature be superior to others since all enjoy an equal natural dignity. From this it follows that countries too do not differ at all from one another in the dignity which they derive from nature. Individual states are like a body whose members are human beings. Furthermore, we know from experience that nations are wont to be very sensitive in all matters which in any way concern their dignity and honor, and rightly so.

90. Truth further demands that the various media of social communications made available by modern progress, which enable the nations to know each other better, be used with serene objectivity. That need not, of course,

rule out any legitimate emphasis on the positive aspects of their way of life. But methods of information which fall short of the truth, and by the same token impair the reputation of this people or that, must be discarded.[55]

IN JUSTICE

91. Relations between nations are to be further regulated by justice. This implies, over and above recognition of their mutual rights, the fulfillment of their respective duties.

92. Since nations have a right to exist, to develop themselves, to acquire a supply of the resources necessary for their development, to defend their good name and the honor due to them, it follows that they are likewise bound by the obligation of effectively guarding each of these rights and of avoiding those actions by which these rights can be jeopardized. As men in their private enterprises cannot pursue their own interests to the detriment of others, so too states cannot lawfully seek that development of their own resources which brings harm to other states and unjustly oppresses them. This statement of St. Augustine seems to be very apt in this regard: "What are kingdoms without justice but large bands of robbers."[56]

93. Not only can it happen, but it actually does happen that the advantages and conveniences which nations strive to acquire for themselves become objects of contention; nevertheless, the resulting disagreements must be settled, not by force, nor by deceit or trickery, but rather in the only manner which is worthy of the dignity of man, i.e., by a mutual assessment of the reasons on both sides of the dispute, by a mature and objective investigation of the situation, and by an equitable reconciliation of differences of opinion.

The Treatment of Minorities

94. Closely related to this point is the political trend which since the nineteenth century has gathered momentum and gained ground everywhere, namely, the striving of people of the same ethnic group to become independent and to form one nation. Since this cannot always be accomplished for various reasons, the result is that minorities often dwell within the territory of a people of another ethnic group, and this is the source of serious problems.

95. In the first place, it must be made clear that justice is seriously violated by whatever is done to limit the strength and numerical increase of these lesser peoples; the injustice is even more serious if vicious attempts of this kind are aimed at the very extinction of these groups.

96. It is especially in keeping with the principles of justice that effective measures be taken by the civil authorities to improve the lot of the citizens of an ethnic minority, particularly when that betterment concerns their language, the development of their natural gifts, their ancestral customs, and their accomplishments and endeavors in the economic order.[57]

97. It should be noted, however, that these minority groups, either because of their present situation which they are forced to endure, or because of past experiences, are often inclined to exalt beyond due measure anything proper to their own people, and to such a degree as to look down on things common to all mankind, as if the welfare of the human family must yield to the good of their own ethnic group. Reason rather demands that these very people recognize also the advantages that accrue to them from their peculiar circumstances; for instance, no small contribution is made toward the development of their particular talents and spirit by their daily dealings with people who have grown up in a different culture since from this association they can gradually make their own the excellence which belongs to the other ethnic group. But this will happen only if the minorities through association with the people who live around them make an effort to share in their customs and institutions. Such, however, will not be the case if they sow discord, which causes great damage and hinders progress.

ACTIVE SOLIDARITY

98. Since the mutual relations among nations must be regulated by the norm of truth and justice, they must also derive great advantage from an energetic union of mind, heart and resources. This can be effected at various levels by mutual cooperation in many ways, as is happening in our own time with beneficial results in the economic, social, political, educational, public health and sports spheres. We must remember that, of its very nature, civil authority exists, not to confine its people within the boundaries of their nation, but rather to protect, above all else, the common good of the entire human family.

99. So it happens that civil societies in pursuing their interests not only must not harm others, but must join their plans and forces whenever the efforts of an individual government cannot achieve its desired goals; but in the execution of such common efforts, great care must be taken lest what helps some nations should injure others.

100. Furthermore, the universal common good requires that in every nation friendly relations be fostered in all fields between the citizens and their intermediate societies. Since in many parts of the world there are groups of people of varying ethnic backgrounds, we must be on our guard against isolating one ethnic group from its fellow men. This is clearly inconsistent with modern conditions since distances which separate people from each other have been almost wiped out. Neither are we to overlook the fact that men of every ethnic group, in addition to their own characteristic endowments by which they are distinguished from the rest of men, have other important gifts of nature in common with their fellow men by which they can make more and more progress and perfect themselves, particularly in matters that pertain to the spirit. They have the right and duty therefore to live in communion with one another.

The Proper Balance between Population, Land, and Capital

101. Everyone certainly knows that in some parts of the world there is an imbalance between the amount of arable land and the size of the population, and in other parts between the fertility of the soil and available farm implements. Consequently, necessity demands a cooperative effort on the part of the people to bring about a quicker exchange of goods, or of capital, or the migration of people themselves.[58]

102. In this case we think it most opportune that as far as possible employment should seek the worker, not vice versa. For then most citizens have an opportunity to increase their holdings without being forced to leave their native environment and seek a new home with many a heartache, and adopt a new state of affairs and make new social contacts with other citizens.

The Problem of Political Refugees

103. The sentiment of universal fatherhood which the Lord has placed in our heart makes us feel profound sadness in considering the phenomenon of political refugees: a phenomenon which has assumed large proportions and which always hides numberless and acute sufferings.

104. Such expatriations show that there are some political regimes which do not guarantee for individual citizens a sufficient sphere of freedom within which their souls are allowed to breathe humanly; in fact, under those regimes even the lawful existence of such a sphere of freedom is either called into question or denied. This undoubtedly is a radical inversion of the order of human society, because the reason for the existence of public authority is to promote the common good, a fundamental element of which is the recognition of that sphere of freedom and the safeguarding of it.

105. At this point it will not be superfluous to recall that such exiles are persons, and that all their rights as persons must be recognized, since they do not lose those rights on losing the citizenship of the states of which they are former members.

106. Now among the rights of a human person there must be included that by which a man may enter a political community where he hopes he can more fittingly provide a future for himself and his dependents. Wherefore, as far as the common good rightly understood permits, it is the duty of that state to accept such immigrants and to help to integrate them into itself as new members.

107. Wherefore, on this occasion, we publicly approve and commend every undertaking, founded on the principles of human solidarity and Christian charity, which aims at making migration of persons from one country to another less painful.

108. And we will be permitted to signal for the attention and gratitude of all right-minded persons the manifold work which specialized international agencies are carrying out in this very delicate field.

Disarmament

109. On the other hand, it is with deep sorrow that we note the enormous stocks of armaments that have been and still are being made in more economically developed countries, with a vast outlay of intellectual and economic resources. And so it happens that, while the people of these countries are loaded with heavy burdens, other countries as a result are deprived of the collaboration they need in order to make economic and social progress.

110. The production of arms is allegedly justified on the grounds that in present-day conditions peace cannot be preserved without an equal balance of armaments. And so, if one country increases its armaments, others feel the need to do the same; and if one country is equipped with nuclear weapons, other countries must produce their own, equally destructive.

111. Consequently, people live in constant fear lest the storm that every moment threatens should break upon them with dreadful violence. And with good reason, for the arms of war are ready at hand. Even though it is difficult to believe that anyone would dare bring upon himself the appalling destruction and sorrow that war would bring in its train, it cannot be denied that the conflagration can be set off by some unexpected and unpremeditated act. And one must bear in mind that, even though the monstrous power of modern weapons acts as a deterrent, there is nevertheless reason to fear that the mere continuance of nuclear tests, undertaken with war in mind, can seriously jeopardize various kinds of life on earth.

112. Justice, then, right reason and consideration for human dignity and life urgently demand that the arms race should cease, that the stockpiles which exist in various countries should be reduced equally and simultaneously by the parties concerned, that nuclear weapons should be banned, and finally that all come to an agreement on a fitting program of disarmament, employing mutual and effective controls. In the words of Pius XII, our predecessor of happy memory: "The calamity of a world war, with the economic and social ruin and the moral excesses and dissolution that accompany it, must not be permitted to envelop the human race for a third time."[59]

113. All must realize that there is no hope of putting an end to the building up of armaments, nor of reducing the present stocks, nor, still less—and this is the main point—of abolishing them altogether, unless the process is complete and thorough and unless it proceeds from inner conviction: unless, that is, everyone sincerely cooperates to banish the fear and anxious expectation of war with which men are oppressed. If this is to come about, the fundamental principle on which our present peace depends must be replaced by another, which declares that the true and solid peace of nations consists not in equality of arms but in mutual trust alone. We believe that this can be brought to pass, and we consider that, since it concerns a matter not only demanded by right reason but also eminently desirable in itself, it will prove to be the source of many benefits.

114. In the first place, it is an objective demanded by reason. There can be, or at least there should be, no doubt that relations between states, as between individuals, should be regulated not by the force of arms but by the light of reason, by the rule, that is, of truth, of justice and of active and sincere cooperation.

115. Secondly, we say that it is an objective earnestly to be desired in itself. Is there anyone who does not ardently yearn to see dangers of war banished, to see peace preserved and daily more firmly established?

116. And finally, it is an objective which will be a fruitful source of many benefits, for its advantages will be felt everywhere, by individuals, by families, by nations, by the whole human family. The warning of Pius XII still rings in our ears: "Nothing is lost by peace; everything may be lost by war."[60]

117. Since this is so, we, the vicar on earth of Jesus Christ, Savior of the world and Author of peace, and as interpreter of the very profound longing of the entire human family, following the impulse of our heart, seized by anxiety for the good of all, feel it our duty to beseech men, especially those who have the responsibility of public affairs, to spare no pain or effort until world events follow a course in keeping with man's destiny and dignity.

118. In the highest and most authoritative assemblies, let men give serious thought to the problem of a peaceful adjustment of relations between political communities on a world level: an adjustment founded on mutual trust, on sincerity in negotiations, on faithful fulfillment of obligations assumed. Let them study the problem until they find that point of agreement from which it will be possible to commence to go forward toward accords that will be sincere, lasting and fruitful.

119. We, for our part, will not cease to pray God to bless these labors so that they may lead to fruitful results.

IN LIBERTY

120. It has also to be borne in mind that relations between states should be based on freedom, that is to say, that no country may unjustly oppress others or unduly meddle in their affairs. On the contrary, all should help to develop in others a sense of responsibility, a spirit of enterprise, and an earnest desire to be the first to promote their own advancement in every field.

The Evolution of Economically Underdeveloped Countries

121. Because all men are joined together by reason of their common origin, their redemption by Christ, and their supernatural destiny, and are called to form one Christian family, we appealed in the encyclical *Mater et Magistra* to economically developed nations to come to the aid of those which were in the process of development.[61]

122. We are greatly consoled to see how widely that appeal has been favorably received; and we are confident that even more so in the future it will contribute to the end that the poorer countries, in as short a time as possible, will arrive at that degree of economic development which will enable every citizen to live in conditions more in keeping with his human dignity.

123. But it is never sufficiently repeated that the cooperation to which reference has been made should be effected with the greatest respect for the liberty of the countries being developed, for these must realize that they are primarily responsible, and that they are the principal artisans in the promotion of their own economic development and social progress.

124. Our predecessor Pius XII already proclaimed that "in the field of a new order founded on moral principles, there is no room for violation of freedom, integrity and security of other nations, no matter what may be their territorial extension or their capacity for defense. It is inevitable that the powerful states, by reason of their greater potential and their power, should pave the way in the establishment of economic groups comprising not only themselves but also smaller and weaker states as well. It is nevertheless indispensable that in the interests of the common good they, as all others, should respect the rights of those smaller states to political freedom, to economic development and to the adequate protection, in the case of conflicts between nations, of that neutrality which is theirs according to the natural, as well as international, law. In this way, and in this way only, will they be able to obtain a fitting share of the common good, and assure the material and spiritual welfare of their people."[62]

125. It is vitally important, therefore, that the wealthier states, in providing varied forms of assistance to the poorer, should respect the moral values and ethnic characteristics peculiar to each, and also that they should avoid any intention of political domination. If this is done, "a precious contribution will be made towards the formation of a world community, a community in which each member, whilst conscious of its own individual rights and duties, will work in a relationship of equality towards the attainment of the universal common good."[63]

SIGNS OF THE TIME

126. Men are becoming more and more convinced that disputes which arise between States should not be resolved by recourse to arms, but rather by negotiation.

127. We grant indeed that this conviction is chiefly based on the terrible destructive force of modern weapons and a fear of the calamities and frightful destruction which such weapons would cause. Therefore, in an age such as ours which prides itself on its atomic energy it is contrary to reason to hold that war is now a suitable way to restore rights which have been violated.

128. Nevertheless, unfortunately, the law of fear still reigns among peoples, and it forces them to spend fabulous sums for armaments, not for aggression

they affirm—and there is no reason for not believing them—but to dissuade others from aggression.

129. There is reason to hope, however, that by meeting and negotiating, men may come to discover better the bonds that unite them together, deriving from the human nature which they have in common; and that they may also come to discover that one of the most profound requirements of their common nature is this: that between them and their respective peoples it is not fear which should reign but love, a love which tends to express itself in a collaboration that is loyal, manifold in form and productive of many benefits.

PART IV: RELATIONSHIP OF MEN AND OF POLITICAL COMMUNITIES WITH THE WORLD COMMUNITY

INTERDEPENDENCE BETWEEN POLITICAL COMMUNITIES

130. The recent progress of science and technology, since it has profoundly influenced human conduct, is rousing men everywhere in the world to more and more cooperation and association with one another. Today the exchange of goods and ideas, as well as travel from one country to another have greatly increased. Consequently, the close relations of individuals, families, intermediate associations belonging to different countries have become vastly more frequent and conferences between heads of states are held at shorter intervals. At the same time the interdependence of national economies has grown deeper, one becoming progressively more closely related to the other, so that they become, as it were, integral parts of the one world economy. Finally, the social progress, order, security, and peace of each country are necessarily connected with the social progress, order, security, and peace of all other countries.

131. Given these conditions, it is obvious that individual countries cannot rightly seek their own interests and develop themselves in isolation from the rest, for the prosperity and development of one country follows partly in the train of the prosperity and progress of all the rest and partly produces that prosperity and progress.

Insufficiency of Modern States to Ensure the Universal Common Good

132. No era will destroy the unity of the human family since it is made up of human beings sharing with equal right their natural dignity. For this reason, necessity, rooted in man's very nature, will always demand that the common good be sought in sufficient measure because it concerns the entire human family.

133. In times past, it seemed that the leaders of nations might be in a position to provide for the universal common good, either through normal diplomatic channels, or through top-level meetings, or through conventions or treaties, by making use of methods and instruments suggested by natural law, the law of nations, or international law.

134. In our time, however, relationships between States have changed greatly. On the one hand, the universal common good poses very serious questions which are difficult and which demand immediate solution especially because they are concerned with safeguarding the security and peace of the whole world. On the other hand, the heads of individual States, inasmuch as they are juridically equal, are not entirely successful no matter how often they meet or how hard they try to find more fitting juridical instruments. This is due not to lack of good will and initiative but to lack of adequate power to back up their authority.

135. Therefore, under the present circumstances of human society, both the structure and form of governments as well as the power which public authority wields in all the nations of the world must be considered inadequate to promote the universal common good.

Connection between the Common Good and Political Authority

136. Moreover, if we carefully consider the essential nature of the common good on the one hand, and the nature and function of public authority on the other, everyone sees that there is an intrinsic connection between the two. And, indeed, just as the moral order needs public authority to promote the common good in civil society, it likewise demands that public authority actually be able to attain it. From this it follows that the governmental institutions, on which public authority depends and through which it functions and pursues its end, should be provided with such structure and efficacy that they can lead to the common good by ways and methods which are suitably adapted to various contingencies.

137. Today the universal common good poses problems of worldwide dimensions, which cannot be adequately tackled or solved except by the efforts of public authority endowed with a wideness of powers, structure and means of the same proportions: that is, of public authority which is in a position to operate in an effective manner on a worldwide basis. The moral order itself, therefore, demands that such a form of public authority be established.

Public Authority Instituted by Common Consent and Not Imposed by Force

138. This public authority, having worldwide power and endowed with the proper means for the efficacious pursuit of its objective, which is the universal common good in concrete form, must be set up by common accord and not imposed by force. The reason is that such an authority must be in a position to operate effectively; yet, at the same time, its action must be inspired by sincere and real impartiality: it must be an action aimed at satisfying the universal common good. The difficulty is that there would be reason to fear that a supranational or worldwide public authority, imposed by force by the more powerful nations, might be an instrument of one-sided interests; and even should this not happen, it would be difficult for it to avoid all suspicion of partiality in its actions, and this would take from the force and effectiveness

of its activity. Even though there may be pronounced differences between nations as regards the degree of their economic development and their military power, they are all very sensitive as regards their juridical equality and the excellence of their way of life. For that reason, they are right in not easily yielding obedience to an authority imposed by force, or to an authority in whose creation they had no part, or to which they themselves did not decide to submit by their own free choice.

The Universal Common Good and Personal Rights

139. Like the common good of individual States, so too the universal common good cannot be determined except by having regard for the human person. Therefore, the public and universal authority, too, must have as its fundamental objective the recognition, respect, safeguarding and promotion of the rights of the human person; this can be done by direct action when required, or by creating on a world scale an environment in which leaders of the individual countries can suitably maintain their own functions.

The Principle of Subsidiarity

140. Moreover, just as it is necessary in each State that relations which the public authority has with its citizens, families, and intermediate associations be controlled and regulated by the principle of subsidiarity, it is equally necessary that the relationships which exist between the worldwide public authority and the public authorities of individual nations be governed by the same principle. This means that the worldwide public authority and the public authorities must tackle and solve problems of an economic, social, political, or cultural character which are posed by the universal common good. For, because of the vastness, complexity and urgency of those problems, the public authorities of the individual States are not in a position to tackle them with any hope of a positive solution.

141. The worldwide public authority is not intended to limit the sphere of action of the public authority of the individual state, much less to take its place. On the contrary, its purpose is to create, on a world basis, an environment in which the public authorities of each state, its citizens, and intermediate associations, can carry out their tasks, fulfill their duties and exercise their rights with greater security.[64]

Modern Developments

142. As is known, the United Nations Organization (U.N.O.) was established on June 26, 1945, and to it there were subsequently added specialized agencies consisting of members designated by the public authority of the various countries with important international tasks in the economic, social, cultural, educational, and health fields. The United Nations Organization had as its essential purpose the maintenance and consolidation of peace between peoples, fostering between them friendly relations, based on the principles of

equality, mutual respect, and varied forms of cooperation in every sector of human endeavor.

143. An act of the highest importance performed by the United Nations Organization was the Universal Declaration of Human Rights, approved in the General Assembly on December 10, 1948. In the preamble of that declaration, the recognition and respect of those rights and respective liberties is proclaimed as a goal to be achieved by all peoples and all countries.

144. We are fully aware that some objections and reservations were raised regarding certain points in the declaration, and rightly so. There is no doubt, however, that the document represents an important step on the path toward the juridical-political organization of all the peoples of the world. For in it, in most solemn form, the dignity of a human person is acknowledged to all human beings; and as a consequence there is proclaimed, as a fundamental right, the right of every man freely to investigate the truth and to follow the norms of moral good and justice, and also the right to a life worthy of man's dignity, while other rights connected with those mentioned are likewise proclaimed.

145. It is therefore our ardent desire that the United Nations Organization—in its structure and in its means—may become ever more equal to the magnitude and nobility of its tasks, and may the time come as quickly as possible when every human being will find therein an effective safeguard for the rights which derive directly from his dignity as a person, and which are therefore universal, inviolable and inalienable rights. This is all the more to be hoped for since all human beings, as they take an ever more active part in the public life of their own country, are showing an increasing interest in the affairs of all peoples, and are becoming more consciously aware that they are living members of the whole human family.

PART V: PASTORAL EXHORTATIONS

Duty of Taking Part in Public Life

146. Once again we exhort our children to take an active part in public life, and to contribute toward the attainment of the common good of the entire human family as well as to that of their own country. They should endeavor, therefore, in the light of the faith and with the strength of love, to ensure that the various institutions—whether economic, social, cultural, or political in purpose—should be such as not to create obstacles, but rather to facilitate or render less arduous man's perfecting of himself both in the natural order as well as in the supernatural.

Scientific Competence, Technical Capacity, and Professional Experience

147. Nevertheless in order to imbue civilization with right norms and Christian principles, it is not enough to be illumined with the gift of faith and enkindled with the desire of forwarding a good cause. For this end it is

necessary to take an active part in the various organizations and influence them from within.

148. And since our present age is one of outstanding scientific and technical progress and excellence, one will not be able to enter these organizations and work effectively from within unless he is scientifically competent, technically capable, and skilled in the practice of his own profession.

Apostolate of a Trained Laity

149. We desire to call attention to the fact that scientific competence, technical capacity, and professional experience, although necessary, are not of themselves sufficient to elevate the relationships of society to an order that is genuinely human: that is, to an order whose foundation is truth, whose measure and objective is justice, whose driving force is love, and whose method of attainment is freedom.

150. For this end it is certainly necessary that human beings carry on their own temporal activities in accordance with the laws governing them and following the methods corresponding to their nature. But at the same time it is also necessary that they should carry on those activities as acts within the moral order: therefore, as the exercise or vindication of a right, as the fulfillment of a duty or the performance of a service, as a positive answer to the providential design of God directed to our salvation. In other words, it is necessary that human beings, in the intimacy of their own consciences, should so live and act in their temporal lives as to create a synthesis between scientific, technical, and professional elements on the one hand, and spiritual values on the other.

Integration of Faith and Action

151. It is no less clear that today, in traditionally Christian nations, secular institutions, although demonstrating a high degree of scientific and technical perfection and efficiency in achieving their respective ends, not infrequently are but slightly affected by Christian motivation or inspiration.

152. It is beyond question that in the creation of those institutions many contributed and continue to contribute who were believed to be and who consider themselves Christians; and without doubt, in part at least, they were and are. How does one explain this? It is our opinion that the explanation is to be found in an inconsistency in their minds between religious belief and their action in the temporal sphere. It is necessary, therefore, that their interior unity be reestablished, and that in their temporal activity faith should be present as a beacon to give light, and charity as a force to give life.

Integral Education

153. It is our opinion, too, that the above-mentioned inconsistency between the religious faith in those who believe and their activities in the temporal sphere, results—in great part—from the lack of a solid Christian education. Indeed, it happens in many quarters and too often that there is no proportion

between scientific training and religious instruction: the former continues and is extended until it reaches higher degrees, while the latter remains at elementary level. It is indispensable, therefore, that in the training of youth, education should be complete and without interruption, namely, that in the minds of the young religious values should be cultivated and the moral conscience refined in a manner to keep pace with the continuous and ever more abundant assimilation of scientific and technical knowledge. And it is indispensable, too, that they be instructed regarding the proper way to carry out their actual task.[65]

Constant Endeavor

154. We deem it opportune to point out how difficult it is to understand clearly the relation between the objective requirements of justice and concrete situations, namely to define the degrees and forms in which doctrinal principles and directives ought to be applied to reality.

155. And the definition of those degrees and forms is all the more difficult in our times, which are marked by a pronounced dynamism. For this reason, the problem of bringing social reality into line with the objective requirements of justice is a problem which will never admit of a definitive solution. Meanwhile, our children must watch over themselves lest they relax and feel satisfied with objectives already achieved.

156. In fact, all human beings ought rather to reckon that what has been accomplished is but little in comparison with what remains to be done in regard to organs of production, trade unions, associations, professional organizations, insurance systems, legal systems, political regimes, institutions for cultural, health, recreational or sporting purposes. These must all be adjusted to the era of the atom and of the conquest of space: an era which the human family has already entered, wherein it has commenced its new advance toward limitless horizons.

Relations between Catholics and Non-Catholics in Social and Economic Affairs

157. The doctrinal principles outlined in this document derive from both nature itself and the natural law. In putting these principles into practice it frequently happens that Catholics in many ways cooperate either with Christians separated from this Apostolic See, or with men of no Christian faith whatever, but who are endowed with reason and adorned with a natural uprightness of conduct. "In such relations let the faithful be careful to be always consistent in their actions, so that they may never come to any compromise in matters of religion and morals. At the same time, however, let them be, and show themselves to be, animated by a spirit of understanding and detachment, and disposed to work loyally in the pursuit of objectives which are of their nature good, or conducive to good."[66]

158. However, one must never confuse error and the person who errs, not even when there is question of error or inadequate knowledge of truth in the

moral or religious field. The person who errs is always and above all a human being, and he retains in every case his dignity as a human person; and he must be always regarded and treated in accordance with that lofty dignity. Besides, in every human being, there is a need that is congenital to his nature and never becomes extinguished, compelling him to break through the web of error and open his mind to the knowledge of truth. And God will never fail to act on his interior being, with the result that a person, who at a given moment of his life lacks the clarity of faith or even adheres to erroneous doctrines, can at a future date be enlightened and believe the truth. For Catholics, if for the sake of promoting the temporal welfare they cooperate with men who either do not believe in Christ or whose belief is faulty because they are involved in error, can provide them either the occasion or the inducement to turn to truth.

159. It is, therefore, especially to the point to make a clear distinction between false philosophical teachings regarding the nature, origin, and destiny of the universe and of man, and movements which have a direct bearing either on economic and social questions, or cultural matters or on the organization of the state, even if these movements owe their origin and inspiration to these false tenets. While the teaching once it has been clearly set forth is no longer subject to change, the movements, precisely because they take place in the midst of changing conditions, are readily susceptible of change. Besides, who can deny that those movements, insofar as they conform to the dictates of right reason and are interpreters of the lawful aspirations of the human person, contain elements that are positive and deserving of approval?

160. For these reasons it can at times happen that meetings for the attainment of some practical results which previously seemed completely useless now are either actually useful or may be looked upon as profitable for the future. But to decide whether this moment has arrived, and also to lay down the ways and degrees in which work in common might be possible for the achievement of economic, social, cultural, and political ends which are honorable and useful, these are the problems which can only be solved with the virtue of prudence, which is the guiding light of the virtues that regulate the moral life, both individual and social. Therefore, as far as Catholics are concerned, this decision rests primarily with those who live and work in the specific sectors of human society in which those problems arise, always, however, in accordance with the principles of the natural law, with the social doctrine of the church, and with the directives of ecclesiastical authorities. For it must not be forgotten that the Church has the right and the duty not only to safeguard the principles of ethics and religion, but also to intervene authoritatively with her children in the temporal sphere when there is a question of judging the application of those principles to concrete cases.[67]

Little by Little

161. There are some souls, particularly endowed with generosity, who, on finding situations where the requirements of justice are not satisfied or not

satisfied in full, feel enkindled with the desire to change the state of things, as if they wished to have recourse to something like a revolution.

162. It must be borne in mind that to proceed gradually is the law of life in all its expressions; therefore in human institutions, too, it is not possible to renovate for the better except by working from within them gradually. Pius XII proclaimed: "Salvation and justice are not to be found in revolution, but in evolution through concord. Violence has always achieved only destruction, not construction; the kindling of passions, not their pacification; the accumulation of hate and ruin, not the reconciliation of the contending parties. And it has reduced men and parties to the difficult task of rebuilding, after sad experience, on the ruins of discord."[68]

An Immense Task

163. We must therefore consider this point most closely joined to the great tasks of magnanimous men, namely, to establish with truth, justice, charity, and liberty new methods of relationships in human society: the relations among individual citizens, among citizens and their own countries, among nations themselves, among individuals, families, intermediate associations, and individual states on the one hand, and with the community of all mankind on the other. This is a most exalted task, for it is the task of bringing about true peace in the order established by God.

164. These men, necessarily few in number, but deserving recognition for their contributions in the field of human relations, we publicly praise and at the same time we earnestly invite them to persevere in their work with ever greater zeal. And we are comforted by the hope that their number will increase, especially among those who believe. For it is an imperative duty; it is a requirement of Love. Every believer in this world of ours must be a spark of light, a center of love, a vivifying leaven amid his fellowmen; and he will be this all the more perfectly the more closely he lives in communion with God and in the intimacy of his own soul.

165. In fact, there can be no peace between men unless there is peace within each one of them, unless, that is, each one builds up within himself the order wished by God. Hence St. Augustine asks: "Does your soul desire to overcome your lower inclinations? Let it be subject to Him Who is on high and it will conquer the lower self: there will be peace in you; true, secure and well-ordered peace. In what does that order consist? God commands the soul; the soul commands the body; and there is nothing more orderly than this."[69]

The Prince of Peace

166. These words of ours, which we have wished to dedicate to the problems that most beset the human family today and on the just solution of which the ordered progress of society depends, are dictated by a profound aspiration which we know is shared by all men of good will: the consolidation of peace in the world.

167. As the humble and unworthy vicar of him whom the prophet announced as the *Prince of Peace*,[70] we have the duty to expend all our energies in an effort to protect and strengthen this gift. However, peace will be but an empty-sounding word unless it is founded on the order which this present document has outlined in confident hope: an order founded on truth, built according to justice, vivified, and integrated by charity, and put into practice in freedom.

168. This is such a noble and elevated task that human resources, even though inspired by the most praiseworthy good will, cannot bring it to realization alone. In order that human society may reflect as faithfully as possible the kingdom of God, help from on high is absolutely necessary.

169. For this reason, during these sacred days our supplication is raised with greater fervor towards him who by his painful passion and death overcame sin—the root of discord and the source of sorrows and inequalities—and by his Blood reconciled mankind to the eternal Father: "For he himself is our peace, he it is that hath made both one. . . . And coming he announced the good tidings of peace to you who were afar off, and of peace to those who were near."[71]

170. And in the liturgy of these days we hear the announcement: "Our Lord Jesus Christ, after his resurrection, stood in the midst of his disciples and said 'Peace be to you,' alleluia: The disciples rejoiced seeing the Lord."[72] He leaves us peace, he brings us peace: "Peace I leave with you, my peace I give to you; not as the world gives do I give to you."[73]

171. This is the peace which we implore of him with the ardent yearning of our prayer. May he banish from the hearts of men whatever might endanger peace. May he transform them into witnesses of truth, justice, and brotherly love. May he enlighten the rulers of peoples so that in addition to their solicitude for the proper welfare of their citizens, they may guarantee and defend the great gift of peace; may he enkindle the wills of all, so that they may overcome the barriers that divide, cherish the bonds of mutual charity, understand others, and pardon those who have done them wrong; by virtue of his action, may all peoples of the earth become as brothers, and may the most longed-for peace blossom forth and reign always among them.

172. As a pledge of this peace, and with the ardent wish that it may shine forth on the Christian communities entrusted to your care, especially for the benefit of those who are most lowly and in the greatest need of help and defense, We are glad to impart to you, venerable brothers, to the priests both secular and religious, to the religious men and women and to the faithful of your dioceses, particularly to those who make every effort to put these exhortations of ours into practice, our apostolic blessing. Finally, upon all men of good will, to whom this encyclical letter is also addressed, we implore from almighty God health and prosperity.

173. Given at Rome at St. Peter's, on Holy Thursday, the eleventh day of April, in the year 1963, the fifth of Our Pontificate.

JOHN XXIII

NOTES

1. Ps. 8:1.
2. Ps. 103:24.
3. Cf. Gen. 1:26.
4. Ps. 8:6–8.
5. Rom. 2:15.
6. Cf. Ps. 18:8–11.
7. Cf. Radio Message of Pius XII, Christmas Eve, 1942, AAS XXXV, 1943, pp. 9–24; and Discourse of John XXIII, Jan. 4, 1963, AAS LV, 1963, pp. 89–91.
8. Cf. Encycl. *Divini Redemptoris* of Pius XI, AAS XXIX, 1937, p. 78; and Radio Message of Pius XII, Pentecost, June 1, 1941, AAS XXXIII, 1941, pp. 195–205.
9. Cf. Radio Message of Pius XII, Christmas Eve, 1942, AAS XXXV, 1943, pp. 9–24.
10. Lactantius, *Divinae Institutiones*, Book IV, ch. 28, 2; Patrologia Latina, 6, 535.
11. Encycl. *Libertas Praestantissimum*, *Acta Leonis XIII*, VIII, 1888, pp. 237–38.
12. Cf. Radio Message of Pius XII, Christmas Eve, 1942, AAS XXXV, 1943, pp. 9–24.
13. Cf. Encycl. *Casti Connubii* of Pius XI, AAS XXII, 1930, pp. 539–592; and Radio Message of Pius XII, Christmas Eve, 1942, AAS XXXV, 1943, pp. 9–24.
14. Cf. Radio Message of Pius XII, Pentecost, June 1, 1941, AAS XXXIII, 1941, p. 201.
15. Cf. Encycl. *Rerum Novarum* of Leo XIII, *Acta Leonis XIII*, 1891, pp. 128–129.
16. Cf. Encycl. *Mater et Magistra* of John XXIII, AAS LIII, 1961, p. 422.
17. Cf. Radio Message, Pentecost, June 1, 1941, AAS XXXIII, 1941, p. 201.
18. Encycl. *Mater et Magistra*, AAS LIII, 1961, p. 428.
19. Cf. ibid., p. 430.
20. Cf. Encycl. *Rerum Novarum* of Leo XIII, *Acta Leonis XIII*, XI, 1891, pp. 134–142; Encycl. *Quadragesimo Anno* of Pius XI, AAS XXIII, 1931, pp. 199–200; Encycl. *Sertum Laetitiae* of Pius XII, AAS XXXI, 1930, pp. 635–644.
21. Cf. AAS LIII, 1961, p. 430.
22. Cf. Radio Message of Pius XII, Christmas Eve, 1952, AAS XLV, 1953, pp. 33–46.
23. Cf. Radio Message, Christmas Eve, 1944, AAS XXXVII, 1945, p. 12.
24. Cf. Radio Message, Christmas Eve, 1942, AAS XXXV, 1943, p. 21.
25. Eph. 4:25.

26. Radio Message of Pius XII, Christmas Eve, 1942, AAS XXXV, 1943, p. 14.

27. Thomas Aquinas, *Summa Theologica*, Ia-IIae, q. 19, a. 4; cf. a. 9.

28. Rom. 13:1–6.

29. John Chrysostom, *In Epist. ad Rom.* c. 13, w. 1–2, homil. XXIII; Patrologia Graeca, 6c, 615.

30. Encycl. *Immortale Dei* of Leo XIII, *Acta Leonis XIII*, V, 1885, p. 120.

31. Cf. Radio Message, Christmas Eve, 1944, AAS XXXVII, 1945, p. 15.

32. Cf. Encycl. *Diuturnum illud* of Leo XIII, *Acta Leonis XIII*, II, 1881, p. 274.

33. Cf. ibid., p. 278; and Encycl. *Immortale Dei* of Leo XIII, *Acta Leonis XIII*, V, 1885, p. 130.

34. Acts 5:29.

35. Thomas Aquinas, *Summa Theologica*, I^{a}-II^{ae}, q. 93, a. 3 ad 2um; cf. Radio Message of Pius XII, Christmas Eve, 1944, AAS XXXVII, 1945, pp. 5–23.

36. Cf. Encycl. *Diuturnum illud* of Leo XIII, *Acta Leonis XIII*, II, 1881, pp. 271–272; and Radio Message of Pius XII, Christmas Eve, 1944, AAS XXXVII, 1945, pp. 5–23.

37. Cf. Radio Message of Pius XII, Christmas Eve, 1942, AAS XXXV, 1943, p. 13; and Encycl. *Immortale Dei* of Leo XIII, *Acta Leonis XIII*, V, 1885, p. 120.

38. Cf. Encycl. *Summi Pontificatus* of Pius XII, AAS XXXI, 1939, pp. 412–453.

39. Cf. Encycl. *Mit brennender Sorge* of Pius XI, AAS XXIX, 1937, p. 159; and Encycl. *Divini Redemptoris*, AAS XXIX, 1937, pp. 65–196.

40. Encycl. *Immortale Dei, Acta Leonis XIII*, V, 1885, p. 121.

41. Cf. Encycl. *Rerum Novarum* of Leo XIII, *Acta Leonis XIII*, XI, 1891, pp. 133–134.

42. Cf. Encycl. *Summi Pontificatus* of Pius XII, AAS XXXI, 1939, p. 433.

43. AAS LIII, 1961, p. 19.

44. Cf. Encycl. *Quadragesimo Anno* of Pius XI, AAS XXIII, 1931, p. 215.

45. Cf. Radio Message of Pius XII, Pentecost, June 1, 1941, AAS XX–XIII, 1941, p. 200.

46. Cf. Encycl. *Mit brennender Sorge* of Pius XI, AAS XXIX, 1937, p. 159; and Encycl. *Divini Redemptoris*, AAS XXIX, 1937, p. 79; and Radio Message of Pius XII, Christmas Eve, 1942, AAS XXXV, 1943, pp. 9–24.

47. Cf. Encycl. *Divini Redemptoris* of Pius XI, AAS XXIX, 1937, p. 81; and Radio Message of Pius XII, Christmas Eve, 1942, AAS XXXV, 1943, pp. 9–24.

48. Encycl. *Mater et Magistra* of John XXIII, AAS LIII, 1961, p. 415.

49. Cf. Radio Message of Pius XII, Christmas Eve, 1942, AAS XXXV, 1943, p. 21.

50. Cf. Radio Message of Pius XII, Christmas Eve, 1944, AAS XXXVII, 1945, pp. 15–16.

51. Cf. Radio Message of Pius XII, Christmas Eve, 1942, AAS XXXV, 1943, p. 12.

52. Cf. Apostolic letter *Annum ingressi* of Leo XIII, *Acta Leonis XIII*, XXII, 1902–1903, pp. 52–80.

53. Wis. 6:1–4.

54. Cf. Radio Message of Pius XII, Christmas Eve, 1941, AAS XXXIV, 1942, p. 16.

55. Cf. Radio Message of Pius XII, Christmas Eve, 1940, AAS XXXIII, 1941, pp. 5–14.

56. Augustine, *De civitate Dei*, Book IV, ch. 4; Patrologia Latina, 41, 115; cf. Radio Message of Pius XII, Christmas Eve, 1939, AAS XXXII, 1940, pp. 5–13.

57. Cf. Radio Message of Pius XII, Christmas Eve, 1941, AAS XXXIV, 1942, pp. 10–21.

58. Cf. Encycl. *Mater et Magistra* of John XXIII, AAS LIII, 1961, p. 439.

59. Cf. Radio Message, Christmas Eve, 1941, AAS XXXIV, 1942, p. 17; and Exhortation of Benedict XV to the rulers of peoples at war, Aug. 1, 1917, AAS IX, 1917, p. 418.

60. Cf. Radio Message, Aug. 24, 1939, AAS XXXI, 1939, p. 334.

61. AAS LIII, 1961, pp. 440–441.

62. Cf. Radio Message, Christmas Eve, 1941, AAS XXIV, pp. 16–17.

63. Encycl. *Mater et Magistra* of John XXIII, AAS LIII, 1961, p. 443.

64. Cf. Address of Pius XII to youths of Catholic Action from the dioceses of Italy gathered in Rome, Sept. 12, 1948, AAS XL, 1948, p. 412.

65. Cf. Encycl. *Mater et Magistra* of John XXIII; AAS LIII, 1961, p. 454.

66. Ibid., p. 456.

67. Ibid., p. 456; cf. Encycl. *Immortale Dei* of Leo XIII, *Acta Leonis XIII*, V, 1885, p. 128; Encycl. *Ubi Arcano* of Pius XI, AAS XIV, 1922, p. 698; and Address of Pius XII to Delegates of the International Union of Catholic Women's Leagues gathered in Rome for a joint convention, Sept. 11, 1947, AAS XXXIX, 1947, p. 486.

68. Cf. Address to workers from the dioceses of Italy gathered in Rome, Pentecost, June 13, 1943, AAS XXXV, 1943, p. 175.

69. Augustine, *Miscellanea Augustiniana . . . Sermones post Maurinos reperti* of St. Augustine, Rome, 1930, p. 633.

70. Cf. Is. 9:5.

71. Eph. 2:14–17.

72. Responsory at Matins on the Friday after Easter.

73. Jn. 14:27.

PART III

VATICAN II AND POST-CONCILIAR CATHOLIC SOCIAL TEACHING

INTRODUCTION

In the years following Vatican II Catholic social doctrine has won wide attention in circles formerly far from interested in the church. The encyclicals of John XXIII and Pope Paul VI, the *Pastoral Constitution on the Church in the Modern World*, and *Justice in the World*, the statement of the 1971 bishops' synod, appeared to many to place the church in a whole new stance in regard to the major social and economic questions confronting the human community.

Vatican II replaced the juridical, hierarchical definition of church with more biblical and symbolic images and clearly articulated a sense of the church as taking its form and function from its relationship to the kingdom of God. A second shift marked by the Second Vatican Council resulted from the long, agonizing effort of church leaders to come to terms with liberal, democratic principles. Most evident in the conciliar statement on religious freedom, this new stress of human liberties and human rights occupied a central place with Pope John XXIII and Pope Paul VI.

Pope Paul VI continued these and other aspects of modern social teaching. In *Populorum Progressio* and *Octagesima Adveniens*, Paul focuses on the issues of social justice with which he had long been concerned. He argued for a pluralism of approaches to the problem of poverty and a greater role for the local church in identifying problems and responding to them.

These themes continued into the papacy of John Paul II. He showed much concern and compassion to the needs of the poor, spoke eloquently against war and the arms race, and addressed significant issues of international economic relations.

This section will present several of the documents shaping modern Catholic thought.

Gaudium et Spes: Pastoral Constitution on the Church in the Modern World (Second Vatican Council, 1965)

INTRODUCTION

The *Pastoral Constitution on the Church in the Modern World*, written in 1965, is an attempt to read the signs of the times so that the church can articulate its best hopes for humanity. The basic characteristic of the document is its feeling of openness to the contemporary situation. The document emphasizes that the church can learn from this world. It also emphasizes that the church must help in the process of evaluating what the world has to offer. What is critical, therefore, is that this critique must also occur from within—that is, from a positive understanding and appreciation of the values under discussion.

Five elements in particular are central to the document: personalism, the social nature of the person, the relation between the church and the world, justice, and development.

A new focus is the category of the person, which represents a major shift of emphasis from the traditional use of natural law categories. The Second Vatican Council centers on a doctrine of individual rights that focuses on the person and validates the claims of the person over and against society. As the center and crown of all things on earth, the person is the meaning and fulfillment of created reality.

Second, individuals, though centers of freedom and individual responsibility, are not solitary beings. In their inmost nature human beings are social and can neither live nor attain their full potential by themselves. Thus the interdependence characteristic of our modern age is rooted in and finds fulfillment in the very nature of the person.

Third, the Council strongly affirmed that the Christian community is "truly and internally linked with humanity and its history." It affirms that human activity which betters the world accords with God's mandate to human beings to subject to themselves the world and all that it contains and to govern the world with justice and holiness. This subjugation of all things to humans, the Council says, is a form of worship. This then is the moral norm for individuals: in accordance with the divine will, they should harmonize with the genuine good of the human race and allow persons as individuals and members of society to pursue their total vocation and to fulfill it.

Fourth, the indirect mission to society, based on its religious mission, is to help examine the values of life, defend human dignity, promote human rights and help build up the human family. Thus the church is deeply committed to the pursuit of justice by seeking more humane and just conditions of life and directing institutions to guaranteeing human dignity. Included in justice is the search for peace by safeguarding personal rights and guaranteeing respect for the person.

Finally, the *Pastoral Constitution on the Church in the Modern World* begins an initial discussion of the theme of development. Progress should be directed to the complete human fulfillment of all citizens. Wealthier nations must help less developed nations achieve this goal. This requires both the stimulation of economic growth as well as the reform of economic and social structures.

Gaudium et Spes was a powerful document, more powerful perhaps than the encyclicals because it represented the opinion of the overwhelming majority of the world's bishops. It embodied the incarnationalist theology that brought the church into the heart of human life; it spoke in humble and sincere terms to Catholics and non-Catholics alike; it offered a systematic and synthetic ethical framework for dealing with world problems; and it urged pastoral action to make its commitments real in Christian life and work. By giving strong and forceful voice to Pope John's vision of a church in service to real people in the concrete circumstances of human history, *Gaudium et Spes* represented the culmination of the changes begun with *Mater et Magistra* and set new directions for Catholic social thought.

GAUDIUM ET SPES

PASTORAL CONSTITUTION ON THE CHURCH IN THE MODERN WORLD[1]

PAUL, BISHOP,

SERVANT OF THE SERVANTS OF GOD TOGETHER WITH THE FATHERS OF THE SACRED COUNCIL, FOR EVERLASTING MEMORY

PREFACE

The Intimate Bond between the Church and Mankind

1. The joys and the hopes, the griefs and the anxieties of the men of this age, especially those who are poor or in any way afflicted, these too are the joys and hopes, the griefs and anxieties of the followers of Christ. Indeed, nothing genuinely human fails to raise an echo in their hearts. For theirs is a community composed of men. United in Christ, they are led by the Holy Spirit in their journey to the kingdom of their Father and they have welcomed the news of salvation which is meant for every man. That is why this community realizes that it is truly and intimately linked with mankind and its history.

For Whom This Message Is Intended

2. Hence this Second Vatican Council, having probed more profoundly into the mystery of the Church, now addresses itself without hesitation, not only to the sons of the Church and to all who invoke the name of Christ, but to the whole of humanity. For the Council yearns to explain to everyone how it conceives of the presence and activity of the Church in the world of today.

Therefore, the Council focuses its attention on the world of men, the whole human family along with the sum of those realities in the midst of which that family lives. It gazes upon that world which is the theater of man's history, and carries the marks of his energies, his tragedies, and his triumphs; that world which the Christian sees as created and sustained by its Maker's love, fallen indeed into the bondage of sin, yet emancipated now by Christ. He was crucified and rose again to break the stranglehold of personified Evil, so that this world might be fashioned anew according to God's design and reach its fulfillment.

The Service to Be Offered to Humanity

3. Though mankind today is struck with wonder at its own discoveries and its power, it often raises anxious questions about the current trend of the world, about the place and role of man in the universe, about the meaning of his individual and collective strivings, and about the ultimate destiny of reality and of humanity. Hence, giving witness and voice to the faith of the whole People of God gathered together by Christ, this Council can provide no more eloquent proof of its solidarity with the entire human family with which it is bound up, as well as its respect and love for that family, than by engaging with it in conversation about these various problems.

The Council brings to mankind light kindled from the gospel, and puts at its disposal those saving resources which the Church herself, under the guidance of the Holy Spirit, receives from her Founder. For the human person deserves to be preserved; human society deserves to be renewed. Hence the pivotal point of our total presentation will be man himself, whole and entire, body and soul, heart and conscience, mind and will.

Therefore, this sacred synod proclaims the highest destiny of man and champions the godlike seed which has been sown in him. It offers to mankind the honest assistance of the Church in fostering that brotherhood of all men which corresponds to this destiny of theirs. Inspired by no earthly ambition, the Church seeks but a solitary goal: to carry forward the work of Christ himself under the lead of the befriending Spirit. And Christ entered this world to give witness to the truth, to rescue and not to sit in judgment, to serve and not to be served.[2]

INTRODUCTORY STATEMENT: THE SITUATION OF MEN IN THE MODERN WORLD

Hope and Anguish

4. To carry out such a task, the Church has always had the duty of scrutinizing the signs of the times and of interpreting them in the light of the gospel. Thus, in language intelligible to each generation, she can respond to the perennial questions which men ask about this present life and the life to come, and about the relationship of the one to the other. We must therefore recognize and understand the world in which we live, its expectations, its longings, and its often dramatic characteristics. Some of the main features of the modern world can be sketched as follows:

Today, the human race is passing through a new stage of its history. Profound and rapid changes are spreading by degrees around the whole world. Triggered by the intelligence and creative energies of man, these changes recoil upon him, upon his decisions and desires, both individual and collective, and upon his manner of thinking and acting with respect to things and to people. Hence we can already speak of a true social and cultural transformation, one which has repercussions on man's religious life as well.

As happens in any crisis of growth, this transformation has brought serious difficulties in its wake. Thus while man extends his power in every direction, he does not always succeed in subjecting it to his own welfare. Striving to penetrate farther into the deeper recesses of his own mind, he frequently appears more unsure of himself. Gradually and more precisely he lays bare the laws of society, only to be paralyzed by uncertainty about the direction to give it.

Never has the human race enjoyed such an abundance of wealth, resources, and economic power. Yet a huge proportion of the world's citizens is still tormented by hunger and poverty, while countless numbers suffer from total illiteracy. Never before today has man been so keenly aware of freedom, yet at the same time, new forms of social and psychological slavery make their appearance.

Although the world of today has a very vivid sense of its unity and of how one man depends on another in needful solidarity, it is most grievously torn into opposing camps by conflicting forces. For political, social, economic, racial, and ideological disputes still continue bitterly, and with them the peril of a war which would reduce everything to ashes. True, there is a growing exchange of ideas, but the very words by which key concepts are expressed take on quite different meanings in diverse ideological systems. Finally, man painstakingly searches for a better world, without working with equal zeal for the betterment of his own spirit.

Caught up in such numerous complications, very many of our contemporaries are kept from accurately identifying permanent values and adjusting them properly to fresh discoveries. As a result, buffeted between hope and anxiety and pressing one another with questions about the present course of events, they are burdened down with uneasiness. This same course of events leads men to look for answers. Indeed, it forces them to do so.

Profoundly Changed Conditions

5. Today's spiritual agitation and the changing conditions of life are part of a broader and deeper revolution. As a result of the latter, intellectual formation is ever increasingly based on the mathematical and natural sciences and on those dealing with man himself, while in the practical order the technology which stems from these sciences takes on mounting importance.

This scientific spirit exerts a new kind of impact on the cultural sphere and on modes of thought. Technology is now transforming the face of the earth, and is already trying to master outer space. To a certain extent, the human intellect is also broadening its dominion over time: over the past by means of historical knowledge; over the future by the art of projecting and by planning.

Advances in biology, psychology, and the social sciences not only bring men hope of improved self-knowledge. In conjunction with technical methods, they are also helping men to exert direct influence on the life of social groups. At the same time, the human race is giving ever-increasing thought to forecasting and regulating its own population growth.

History itself speeds along on so rapid a course that an individual person can scarcely keep abreast of it. The destiny of the human community has become all of a piece, where once the various groups of men had a kind of private history of their own. Thus, the human race has passed from a rather static concept of reality to a more dynamic, evolutionary one. In consequence, there has arisen a new series of problems, a series as important as can be, calling for new efforts of analysis and synthesis.

Changes in the Social Order

6. By this very circumstance, the traditional local communities such as father-centered families, clans, tribes, villages, various groups and associations stemming from social contacts experience more thorough changes every day.

The industrial type of society is gradually being spread, leading some nations to economic affluence, and radically transforming ideas and social conditions established for centuries. Likewise, the practice and pursuit of city living has grown, either because of a multiplication of cities and their inhabitants, or by a transplantation of city life to rural settings.

New and more efficient media of social communication are contributing to the knowledge of events. By setting off chain reactions, they are giving the swiftest and widest possible circulation to styles of thought and feeling.

It is also noteworthy how many men are being induced to migrate on various counts, and are thereby changing their manner of life. Thus a man's ties with his fellows are constantly being multiplied. At the same time "socialization" brings further ties, without, however, always promoting appropriate personal development and truly personal relationships ("personalization").

This kind of evolution can be seen more clearly in those nations which already enjoy the conveniences of economic and technological progress, though it is also astir among peoples still striving for such progress and eager to secure for themselves the advantages of an industrialized and urbanized society. These peoples, especially those among them who are attached to older traditions, are simultaneously undergoing a movement toward more mature and personal exercise of liberty.

Psychological, Moral, and Religious Changes

7. A change in attitudes and in human structures frequently calls accepted values into question. This is especially true of young people, who have grown impatient on more than one occasion, and indeed become rebels in their distress. Aware of their own influence in the life of society, they want to assume a role in it sooner. As a result, parents and educators frequently experience greater difficulties day by day in discharging their tasks.

The institutions, laws, and modes of thinking and feeling as handed down from previous generations do not always seem to be well adapted to the contemporary state of affairs. Hence arises an upheaval in the manner and even the norms of behavior.

Finally, these new conditions have their impact on religion. On the one hand a more critical ability to distinguish religion from a magical view of the world and from the superstitions which still circulate purifies religion and exacts day by day a more personal and explicit adherence to faith. As a result many persons are achieving a more vivid sense of God.

On the other hand, growing numbers of people are abandoning religion in practice. Unlike former days, the denial of God or of religion, or the abandonment of them, is no longer unusual and individual occurrences. For today it is not rare for such decisions to be presented as requirements of scientific progress or of a certain new humanism. In numerous places these views are voiced not only in the teachings of philosophers, but on every side they influence literature, the arts, the interpretation of the humanities and of history, and civil laws themselves. As a consequence, many people are shaken.

Imbalances in the Modern World

8. Because they are coming so rapidly, and often in a disorderly fashion, all these changes beget contradictions and imbalances, or intensify them. Indeed the very fact that men are more conscious than ever of the inequalities in the world has the same effect.

Within the individual person there too often develops an imbalance between an intellect which is modern in practical matters, and a theoretical system of thought which can neither master the sum total of its ideas, nor arrange them adequately into a synthesis. Likewise, an imbalance arises between a concern for practicality and efficiency, and the demands of moral conscience; also, very often, between the conditions of collective existence and the requisites of personal thought, and even of contemplation. Specialization in any human activity can at length deprive a man of a comprehensive view of reality.

As for the family, discord results from demographic, economic, and social pressures, or from difficulties which arise between succeeding generations, or from new social relationships between men and women.

Significant differences crop up too between races and between various kinds of social orders; between wealthy nations and those which are less influential or are needy; finally, between international institutions born of the popular desire for peace, and the ambition to propagate one's own ideology, as well as collective greed existing in nations or other groups.

What results is mutual distrust, enmities, conflicts, and hardships. Of such is man at once the cause and the victim.

The Broader Desires of Mankind

9. Meanwhile, the conviction grows not only that humanity can and should increasingly consolidate its control over creation, but even more, that it devolves on humanity to establish a political, social, and economic order which will to

an ever-better extent serve man and help individuals as well as groups to affirm and develop the dignity proper to them.

As a result very many persons are quite aggressively demanding those benefits of which with vivid awareness they judge themselves to be deprived either through injustice or unequal distribution. Nations on the road to progress, like those recently made independent, desire to participate in the goods of modern civilization, not only in the political field but also economically, and to play their part freely on the world scene. Still they continually fall behind while very often their dependence on wealthier nations deepens more rapidly, even in the economic sphere.

People hounded by hunger call upon those better off. Where they have not yet won it, women claim for themselves an equity with men before the law and in fact. Laborers and farmers seek not only to provide for the necessities of life but to develop the gifts of their personality by their labors, and indeed to take part in regulating economic, social, political, and cultural life. Now, for the first time in human history, all people are convinced that the benefits of culture ought to be and actually can be extended to everyone.

Still, beneath all these demands lies a deeper and more widespread longing. Persons and societies thirst for a full and free life worthy of man—one in which they can subject to their own welfare all that the modern world can offer them so abundantly. In addition, nations try harder every day to bring about a kind of universal community.

Since all these things are so, the modern world shows itself at once powerful and weak, capable of the noblest deeds or the foulest. Before it lies the path to freedom or to slavery, to progress or retreat, to brotherhood or hatred. Moreover, man is becoming aware that it is his responsibility to guide aright the forces which he has unleashed and which can enslave him or minister to him. That is why he is putting questions to himself.

Man's Deeper Questionings

10. The truth is that the imbalances under which the modern world labors are linked with that more basic imbalance rooted in the heart of man. For in man himself many elements wrestle with one another. Thus, on the one hand, as a creature he experiences his limitations in a multitude of ways. On the other, he feels himself to be boundless in his desires and summoned to a higher life.

Pulled by manifold attractions, he is constantly forced to choose among them and to renounce some. Indeed, as a weak and sinful being, he often does what he would not, and fails to do what he would.[3] Hence he suffers from internal divisions, and from these flow so many and such great discords in society.

No doubt very many whose lives are infected with a practical materialism are blinded against any sharp insight into this kind of dramatic situation. Or else, weighed down by wretchedness, they are prevented from giving the matter any thought.

Thinking that they have found serenity in an interpretation of reality everywhere proposed these days, many look forward to a genuine and total emancipation of humanity wrought solely by human effort. They are convinced that the future rule of man over the earth will satisfy every desire of his heart.

Nor are there lacking men who despair of any meaning to life and praise the boldness of those who think that human existence is devoid of any inherent significance and who strive to confer a total meaning on it by their own ingenuity alone.

Nevertheless, in the face of the modern development of the world, an ever-increasing number of people are raising the most basic questions or recognizing them with a new sharpness: What is man? What is this sense of sorrow, of evil, of death, which continues to exist despite so much progress? What is the purpose of these victories, purchased at so high a cost? What can man offer to society, what can he expect from it? What follows this earthly life?

The Church believes that Christ, who died and was raised up for all,[4] can through his Spirit offer man the light and the strength to measure up to his supreme destiny. Nor has any other name under heaven been given to man by which it is fitting for him to be saved.[5] She likewise holds that in her most benign Lord and Master can be found the key, the focal point, and the goal of all human history.

The Church also maintains that beneath all changes there are many realities which do not change and which have their ultimate foundation in Christ, who is the same yesterday and today, yes and forever.[6] Hence in the light of Christ,[7] the image of the unseen God, the firstborn of every creature, the Council wishes to speak to all men in order to illuminate the mystery of man and to cooperate in finding the solution to the outstanding problems of our time.

PART I: THE CHURCH AND MAN'S CALLING

The Impulses of the Spirit Demand a Response

11. The People of God believes that it is led by the Spirit of the Lord who fills the earth. Motivated by this faith, it labors to decipher authentic signs of God's presence and purpose in the happenings, needs, and desires in which this People has a part along with other men of our age. For faith throws a new light on everything, manifests God's design for man's total vocation, and thus directs the mind to solutions which are fully human.

This Council, first of all, wishes to assess in this light those values which are most highly prized today, and to relate them to their divine source. For insofar as they stem from endowments conferred by God on man, these values are exceedingly good. Yet they are often wrenched from their rightful function by the taint in man's heart, and hence stand in need of purification.

What does the Church think of man? What recommendations seem needful for the upbuilding of contemporary society? What is the ultimate significance of human activity throughout the world? People are waiting for an answer to these questions. From the answers it will be increasingly clear that the People of God and the human race in whose midst it lives render service to each other. Thus the mission of the Church will show its religious, and by that very fact, its supremely human character.

Chapter 1: The Dignity of the Human Person

Man as Made in God's Image

12. According to the almost unanimous opinion of believers and unbelievers alike, all things on earth should be related to man as their center and crown.

But what is man? About himself he has expressed, and continues to express, many divergent and even contradictory opinions. In these he often exalts himself as the absolute measure of all things or debases himself to the point of despair. The result is doubt and anxiety.

The Church understands these problems. Endowed with light from God, she can offer solutions to them so that man's true situation can be portrayed and his defects explained, while at the same time his dignity and destiny are justly acknowledged.

For sacred scripture teaches that man was created "to the image of God," is capable of knowing and loving his Creator, and was appointed by him as master of all earthly creatures[8] that he might subdue them and use them to God's glory.[9] "What is man that thou art mindful of him or the son of man that thou visitest him? Thou hast made him a little less than the angels, thou hast crowned him with glory and honor: thou hast set him over the works of thy hands, thou hast subjected all things under his feet" (Ps. 8:5–6).

But God did not create man as a solitary. For from the beginning "male and female he created them" (Gen. 1:27). Their companionship produces the primary form of interpersonal communion. For by his innermost nature man is a social being, and unless he relates himself to others he can neither live nor develop his potential.

Therefore, as we read elsewhere in holy scripture, God saw "all the things that he had made, and they were very good" (Gen. 1:31).

Sin

13. Although he was made by God in a state of holiness, from the very dawn of history man abused his liberty, at the urging of personified Evil. Man set himself against God and sought to find fulfillment apart from God. Although he knew God, he did not glorify him as God, but his senseless mind was darkened and he served the creature rather than the Creator.[10]

What divine revelation makes known to us agrees with experience. Examining his heart, man finds that he has inclinations toward evil too, and is engulfed by manifold ills which cannot come from his good Creator. Often refusing to acknowledge God as his beginning, man has disrupted also his proper relationship to his own ultimate goal. At the same time he became out of harmony with himself, with others, and with all created things.

Therefore man is split within himself. As a result, all of human life, whether individual or collective, shows itself to be a dramatic struggle between good and evil, between light and darkness. Indeed, man finds that by himself he is incapable of battling the assaults of evil successfully, so that everyone feels as though he is bound by chains.

But the Lord himself came to free and strengthen man, renewing him inwardly and casting out that prince of this world (cf. John 12:31) who held him in the bondage of sin.[11] For sin has diminished man, blocking his path to fulfillment.

The call to grandeur and the depths of misery are both a part of human experience. They find their ultimate and simultaneous explanation in the light of God's revelation.

The Make-up of Man

14. Though made of body and soul, man is one. Through his bodily composition he gathers to himself the elements of the material world. Thus they reach their crown through him, and through him raise their voice in free praise of the Creator.[12]

For this reason man is not allowed to despise his bodily life. Rather, he is obliged to regard his body as good and honorable since God created it and will raise it up on the last day. Nevertheless, wounded by sin, man experiences rebellious stirrings in his body. But the very dignity of man postulates that man glorify God in his body[13] and forbid it to serve the evil inclinations of his heart.

Now, man is not wrong when he regards himself as superior to bodily concerns, and as more than a speck of nature or a nameless constituent of the city of man. For by his interior qualities he outstrips the whole sum of mere things. He finds reinforcement in this profound insight whenever he enters into his own heart. God, who probes the heart,[14] awaits him there. There he discerns his proper destiny beneath the eyes of God. Thus, when man recognizes in himself a spiritual and immortal soul, he is not being mocked by a deceptive fantasy springing from mere physical or social influences. On the contrary he is getting to the depths of the very truth of the matter.

The Dignity of the Mind; Truth; Wisdom

15. Man judges rightly that by his intellect he surpasses the material universe, for he shares in the light of the divine mind. By relentlessly employing his talents through the ages, he has indeed made progress in the practical sciences, technology, and the liberal arts. In our times he has won superlative victories, especially in his probing of the material world and in subjecting it to himself.

Still he has always searched for more penetrating truths, and finds them. For his intelligence is not confined to observable data alone. It can with genuine certitude attain to reality itself as knowable, though in consequence of sin that certitude is partly obscured and weakened.

The intellectual nature of the human person is perfected by wisdom and needs to be. For wisdom gently attracts the mind of man to a quest and a love for what is true and good. Steeped in wisdom, man passes through visible realities to those which are unseen.

Our era needs such wisdom more than bygone ages if the discoveries made by man are to be further humanized. For the future of the world stands in peril unless wiser men are forthcoming. It should also be pointed out that many nations, poorer in economic goods, are quite rich in wisdom and can offer noteworthy advantages to others.

It is, finally, through the gift of the Holy Spirit that man comes by faith to the contemplation and appreciation of the divine plan.[15]

The Dignity of the Moral Conscience

16. In the depths of his conscience, man detects a law which he does not impose upon himself, but which holds him to obedience. Always summoning him to love good and avoid evil, the voice of conscience can when necessary speak to his heart more specifically: do this, shun that. For man has in his heart a law written by God. To obey it is the very dignity of man; according to it he will be judged.[16]

Conscience is the most secret core and sanctuary of a man. There he is alone with God, whose voice echoes in his depths.[17] In a wonderful manner conscience reveals that law which is fulfilled by love of God and neighbor.[18] In fidelity to conscience, Christians are joined with the rest of men in the search for truth, and for the genuine solution to the numerous problems which arise in the life of individuals and from social relationships. Hence the more that a correct conscience holds sway, the more persons and groups turn aside from blind choice and strive to be guided by objective norms of morality.

Conscience frequently errs from invincible ignorance without losing its dignity. The same cannot be said of a man who cares but little for truth and goodness, or of a conscience which by degrees grows practically sightless as a result of habitual sin.

The Excellence of Liberty

17. Only in freedom can man direct himself toward goodness. Our contemporaries make much of this freedom and pursue it eagerly; and rightly so, to be sure. Often, however, they foster it perversely as a license for doing whatever pleases them, even if it is evil.

For its part, authentic freedom is an exceptional sign of the divine image within man. For God has willed that man be left "in the hand of his own counsel"[19] so that he can seek his Creator spontaneously, and come freely to utter and blissful perfection through loyalty to him. Hence man's dignity demands that he act according to a knowing and free choice. Such a choice is personally motivated and prompted from within. It does not result from blind internal impulse nor from mere external pressure.

Man achieves such dignity when, emancipating himself from all captivity to passion, he pursues his goal in a spontaneous choice of what is good, and procures for himself, through effective and skillful action, apt means to that end. Since man's freedom has been damaged by sin, only by the help of God's grace can he bring such a relationship with God into full flower. Before the judgment seat of God each man must render an account of his own life, whether he has done good or evil.[20]

The Mystery of Death

18. It is in the face of death that the riddle of human existence becomes most acute. Not only is man tormented by pain and by the advancing deterioration of his body, but even more by a dread of perpetual extinction. He rightly follows the intuition of his heart when he abhors and repudiates the absolute ruin and total disappearance of his own person.

Man rebels against death because he bears in himself an eternal seed which cannot be reduced to sheer matter. All the endeavors of technology, though useful in the extreme, cannot calm his anxiety. For a prolongation of biological life is unable to satisfy that desire for a higher life which is inescapably lodged in his breast.

Although the mystery of death utterly beggars the imagination, the Church has been taught by divine revelation, and herself firmly teaches, that man has been created by God for a blissful purpose beyond the reach of earthly misery. In addition, that bodily death from which man would have been immune had he not sinned[21] will be vanquished, according to the Christian faith, when man who was ruined by his own doing is restored to wholeness by an almighty and merciful Savior.

For God has called man and still calls him so that with his entire being he might be joined to him in an endless sharing of a divine life beyond all corruption. Christ won this victory when he rose to life, since by his death he freed man from death.[22] Hence to every thoughtful man a solidly established faith provides the answer to his anxiety about what the future holds for him. At the same time faith gives him the power to be united in Christ with his loved ones who have already been snatched away by death. Faith arouses the hope that they have found true life with God.

The Forms and Roots of Atheism

19. An outstanding cause of human dignity lies in man's call to communion with God. From the very circumstance of his origin, man is already invited to converse with God. For man would not exist were he not created by God's love and constantly preserved by it. And he cannot live fully according to truth unless he freely acknowledges that love and devotes himself to his Creator.

Still, many of our contemporaries have never recognized this intimate and vital link with God, or have explicitly rejected it. Thus atheism must be accounted among the most serious problems of this age, and is deserving of closer examination.

The word atheism is applied to phenomena which are quite distinct from one another. For while God is expressly denied by some, others believe that man can assert absolutely nothing about him. Still others use such a method so to scrutinize the question of God as to make it seem devoid of meaning. Many, unduly transgressing the limits of the positive sciences, contend that everything can be explained by this kind of scientific reasoning alone, or, by contrast, they altogether disallow that there is any absolute truth.

Some laud man so extravagantly that their faith in God lapses into a kind of anemia, though they seem more inclined to affirm man than to deny God. Again some form for themselves such a fallacious idea of God that when they repudiate this figment they are by no means rejecting the God of the gospel. Some never get to the point of raising questions about God, since they seem to experience no religious stirrings nor do they see why they should trouble themselves about religion.

Moreover, atheism results not rarely from a violent protest against the evil in this world, or from the absolute character with which certain human values are unduly invested, and which thereby already accords them the stature of God. Modern civilization itself often complicates the approach to God, not for any essential reason, but because it is excessively engrossed in earthly affairs.

Undeniably, those who willfully shut out God from their hearts and try to dodge religious questions are not following the dictates of their consciences. Hence they are not free of blame.

Yet believers themselves frequently bear some responsibility for this situation. For, taken as a whole, atheism is not a spontaneous development but stems from a variety of causes, including a critical reaction against religious beliefs, and in some places against the Christian religion in particular. Hence believers can have more than a little to do with the birth of atheism. To the extent that they neglect their own training in the faith, or teach erroneous doctrine, or are deficient in their religious, moral, or social life, they must be said to conceal rather than reveal the authentic face of God and religion.

Systematic Atheism

20. Modern atheism often takes on a systematic expression, which, in addition to other arguments against God, stretches the desire for human independence to such a point that it finds difficulties with any kind of dependence on God. Those who profess atheism of this sort maintain that it gives man freedom to be an end unto himself, the sole artisan and creator of his own history. They claim that this freedom cannot be reconciled with the affirmation of a Lord who is author and purpose of all things, or at least that this freedom makes such an affirmation altogether superfluous. The sense of

power which modern technical progress generates in man can give color to such a doctrine.

Not to be overlooked among the forms of modern atheism is that which anticipates the liberation of man especially through his economic and social emancipation. This form argues that by its nature religion thwarts such liberation by arousing man's hope for a deceptive future life, thereby diverting him from the constructing of the earthly city. Consequently, when the proponents of this doctrine gain governmental power they vigorously fight against religion. They promote atheism by using those means of pressure which public power has at its disposal. Such is especially the case in the work of educating the young.

The Church's Attitude toward Atheism

21. In her loyal devotion to God and men, the Church has already repudiated[23] and cannot cease repudiating, sorrowfully but as firmly as possible, those poisonous doctrines and actions which contradict reason and the common experience of humanity, and dethrone man from his native excellence.

Still, she strives to detect in the atheistic mind the hidden causes for the denial of God. Conscious of how weighty are the questions which atheism raises, and motivated by love for all men, she believes these questions ought to be examined seriously and more profoundly.

The Church holds that the recognition of God is in no way hostile to man's dignity, since this dignity is rooted and perfected in God. For man was made an intelligent and free member of society by the God who created him. Ever more importantly, man is called as a son to commune with God and to share in his happiness. She further teaches that a hope related to the end of time does not diminish the importance of intervening duties, but rather undergirds the acquittal of them with fresh incentives. By contrast, when a divine substructure and the hope of life eternal are wanting, man's dignity is most grievously lacerated, as current events often attest. The riddles of life and death, of guilt and of grief go unsolved, with the frequent result that men succumb to despair.

Meanwhile, every man remains to himself an unsolved puzzle, however obscurely he may perceive it. For on certain occasions no one can entirely escape the kind of self-questioning mentioned earlier, especially when life's major events take place. To this questioning only God fully and most certainly provides an answer as he summons man to higher knowledge and humbler probing.

The remedy which must be applied to atheism, however, is to be sought in a proper presentation of the Church's teaching as well as in the integral life of the Church and her members. For it is the function of the Church, led by the Holy Spirit who renews and purifies her ceaselessly,[24] to make God the Father and his Incarnate Son present and in a sense visible.

This result is achieved chiefly by the witness of a living and mature faith, namely, one trained to see difficulties clearly and to master them. Very many martyrs have given luminous witness to this faith and continue to do so. This faith needs to prove its fruitfulness by penetrating the believer's entire life, including its worldly dimensions, and by activating him toward justice and love, especially regarding the needy. What does the most to reveal God's presence, however, is the brotherly charity of the faithful who are united in spirit as they work together for the faith of the gospel[25] and who prove themselves a sign of unity.

While rejecting atheism, root and branch, the Church sincerely professes that all men, believers and unbelievers alike, ought to work for the rightful betterment of this world in which all alike live. Such an ideal cannot be realized, however, apart from sincere and prudent dialogue. Hence the Church protests against the distinction which some state authorities unjustly make between believers and unbelievers, thereby ignoring fundamental rights of the human person. The Church calls for the active liberty of believers to build up in this world God's temple too. She courteously invites atheists to examine the gospel of Christ with an open mind.

Above all the Church knows that her message is in harmony with the most secret desires of the human heart when she champions the dignity of the human vocation, restoring hope to those who have already despaired of anything higher than their present lot. Far from diminishing man, her message brings to his development light, life, and freedom. Apart from this message nothing will avail to fill up the heart of man: "Thou hast made us for Thyself," O Lord, "and our hearts are restless till they rest in Thee."[26]

Christ as the New Man

22. The truth is that only in the mystery of the incarnate Word does the mystery of man take on light. For Adam, the first man, was a figure of him who was to come,[27] namely, Christ the Lord. Christ, the final Adam, by the revelation of the mystery of the Father and his love, fully reveals man to man himself and makes his supreme calling clear. It is not surprising, then, that in him all the aforementioned truths find their root and attain their crown.

He who is "the image of the invisible God" (Col. 1:15),[28] is himself the perfect man. To the sons of Adam he restores the divine likeness which had been disfigured from the first sin onward. Since human nature as he assumed it was not annulled,[29] by that very fact it has been raised up to a divine dignity in our respect too. For by his incarnation the Son of God has united himself in some fashion with every man. He worked with human hands, he thought with a human mind, acted by human choice,[30] and loved with a human heart. Born of the virgin Mary, he has truly been made one of us, like us in all things except sin.[31]

As an innocent lamb he merited life for us by the free shedding of his own blood. In him God reconciled us[32] to himself and among ourselves. From bondage to the devil and sin, he delivered us, so that each of us can say with the Apostle: The Son of God "loved me and gave himself up for me"

(Gal. 2:20). By suffering for us he not only provided us with an example for our imitation.[33] He blazed a trail, and if we follow it, life and death are made holy and take on a new meaning.

The Christian man, conformed to the likeness of that Son who is the first-born of many brothers,[34] receives "the firstfruits of the Spirit" (Rom. 8:23) by which he becomes capable of discharging the new law of love.[35] Through this Spirit, who is "the pledge of our inheritance" (Eph. 1:14), the whole man is renewed from within, even to the achievement of "the redemption of the body" (Rom. 8:23): "If the Spirit of him who raised Jesus from the dead dwells in you, then he who raised Jesus Christ from the dead will also bring to life your mortal bodies because of his Spirit who dwells in you" (Rom. 8:11).[36]

Pressing upon the Christian, to be sure, are the need and the duty to battle against evil through manifold tribulations and even to suffer death. But, linked with the paschal mystery and patterned on the dying Christ, he will hasten forward to resurrection in the strength which comes from hope.[37]

All this holds true not only for Christians, but for all men of good will in whose hearts grace works in an unseen way.[38] For, since Christ died for all men,[39] and since the ultimate vocation of man is in fact one and divine, we ought to believe that the Holy Spirit in a manner known only to God offers to every man the possibility of being associated with this paschal mystery.

Such is the mystery of man, and it is a great one, as seen by believers in the light of Christian revelation. Through Christ and in Christ, the riddles of sorrow and death grow meaningful. Apart from his gospel, they overwhelm us. Christ has risen, destroying death by his death. He has lavished life upon us[40] so that, as sons in the Son, we can cry out in the Spirit: Abba, Father![41]

Chapter 2: The Community of Mankind

The Council's Intention

23. One of the salient features of the modern world is the growing interdependence of men one on the other, a development very largely promoted by modern technical advances. Nevertheless, brotherly dialogue among men does not reach its perfection on the level of technical progress, but on the deeper level of interpersonal relationships. These demand a mutual respect for the full spiritual dignity of the person. Christian revelation contributes greatly to the promotion of this communion between persons, and at the same time leads us to a deeper understanding of the laws of social life which the Creator has written into man's spiritual and moral nature.

Since rather recent documents of the Church's teaching authority have dealt at considerable length with Christian doctrine about human society,[42] this Council is merely going to call to mind some of the more basic truths, treating their foundations under the light of revelation. Then it will dwell more at length on certain of their implications having special significance for our day.

God's Plan Gives Man's Vocation a Communitarian Nature

24. God, who has fatherly concern for everyone, has willed that all men should constitute one family and treat one another in a spirit of brotherhood. For having been created in the image of God, who "from one man has created the whole human race and made them live all over the face of the earth" (Acts 17:26), all men are called to one and the same goal, namely, God himself.

For this reason, love for God and neighbor is the first and greatest commandment. Sacred scripture, however, teaches us that the love of God cannot be separated from love of neighbor: "If there is any other commandment, it is summed up in this saying, Thou shalt love thy neighbor as thyself. . . . Love therefore is the fulfillment of the Law" (Rom. 13:9–10; cf. 1 John 4:20). To men growing daily more dependent on one another, and to a world becoming more unified every day, this truth proves to be of a paramount importance.

Indeed, the Lord Jesus, when he prayed to the Father, "that all may be one . . . as we are one" (John 17:21–22) opened up vistas closed to human reason. For he implied a certain likeness between the union of the divine Persons, and in the union of God's sons in truth and charity. This likeness reveals that man, who is the only creature on earth which God willed for itself, cannot fully find himself except through a sincere gift of himself.[43]

The Interdependence of Person and Society

25. Man's social nature makes it evident that the progress of the human person and the advance of society itself hinge on each other. For the beginning, the subject, and the goal of all social institutions is and must be the human person, which for its part and by its very nature stands completely in need of social life.[44] This social life is not something added on to man. Hence, through his dealings with others, through reciprocal duties, and through fraternal dialogue he develops all his gifts and is able to rise to his destiny.

Among those social ties which man needs for his development, some, like the family and political community, relate with greater immediacy to his innermost nature. Others originate rather from his free decision. In our era, for various reasons, reciprocal ties and mutual dependencies increase day by day and give rise to a variety of associations and organizations, both public and private. This development, which is called socialization, while certainly not without its dangers, brings with it many advantages with respect to consolidating and increasing the qualities of the human person, and safeguarding his rights.[45]

But if by this social life the human person is greatly aided in responding to his destiny, even in its religious dimensions, it cannot be denied that men are often diverted from doing good and spurred toward evil by the social circumstances in which they live and are immersed from their birth. To be sure, the disturbances which so frequently occur in the social order result in part from the natural tensions of economic, political, and social forms. But at a deeper level they flow from man's pride and selfishness, which contaminate even the social sphere. When the structure of affairs is flawed by the consequences of sin, man, already born with a bent toward evil, finds there new inducements to sin, which cannot be overcome without strenuous efforts and the assistance of grace.

Promoting the Common Good

26. Every day human interdependence grows more tightly drawn and spreads by degrees over the whole world. As a result the common good, that is, the sum of those conditions of social life which allow social groups and their individual members relatively thorough and ready access to their own fulfillment, today takes on an increasingly universal complexion and consequently involves rights and duties with respect to the whole human race. Every social group must take account of the needs and legitimate aspirations of other groups, and even of the general welfare of the entire human family.[46]

At the same time, however, there is a growing awareness of the exalted dignity proper to the human person, since he stands above all things, and his rights and duties are universal and inviolable. Therefore, there must be made available to all men everything necessary for leading a life truly human, such as food, clothing, and shelter; the right to choose a state of life freely and to found a family; the right to education, to employment, to a good reputation, to respect, to appropriate information, to activity in accord with the upright norm of one's own conscience, to protection of privacy, and to rightful freedom in matters religious too.

Hence, the social order and its development must unceasingly work to the benefit of the human person if the disposition of affairs is to be subordinate to the personal realm and not contrariwise, as the Lord indicated when he said that the Sabbath was made for man, and not man for the Sabbath.[47]

This social order requires constant improvement. It must be founded on truth, built on justice, and animated by love; in freedom it should grow every day toward a more humane balance.[48] An improvement in attitudes and widespread changes in society will have to take place if these objectives are to be gained.

God's Spirit, who with a marvelous providence directs the unfolding of time and renews the face of the earth, is not absent from this development. The ferment of the gospel, too, has aroused and continues to arouse in man's heart the irresistible requirements of his dignity.

Reverence for the Human Person

27. Coming down to practical and particularly urgent consequences, the Council lays stress on reverence for man; everyone must consider his every neighbor without exception as another self, taking into account first of all his life and the means necessary to living it with dignity,[49] so as not to imitate the rich man who had no concern for the poor man Lazarus.[50]

In our times a special obligation binds us to make ourselves the neighbor of absolutely every person, and of actively helping him when he comes across our path, whether he be an old person abandoned by all, a foreign laborer unjustly looked down upon, a refugee, a child born of an unlawful union and wrongly suffering for a sin he did not commit, or a hungry person who disturbs our conscience by recalling the voice of the Lord: "As long as you did it for one of these, the least of my brethren, you did it for me" (Matt. 25:40).

Furthermore, whatever is opposed to life itself, such as any type of murder, genocide, abortion, euthanasia, or willful self-destruction, whatever violates the integrity of the human person, such as mutilation, torments inflicted on body or mind, attempts to coerce the will itself; whatever insults human dignity, such as subhuman living conditions, arbitrary imprisonment, deportation, slavery, prostitution, the selling of women and children; as well as disgraceful working conditions, where men are treated as mere tools for profit, rather than as free and responsible persons; all these things and others of their like are infamies indeed. They poison human society, but they do more harm to those who practice them than those who suffer from the injury. Moreover, they are a supreme dishonor to the Creator.

Reverence and Love for Enemies

28. Respect and love ought to be extended also to those who think or act differently than we do in social, political, and religious matters, too. In fact, the more deeply we come to understand their ways of thinking through such courtesy and love, the more easily will we be able to enter into dialogue with them.

This love and good will, to be sure, must in no way render us indifferent to truth and goodness. Indeed love itself impels the disciples of Christ to speak the saving truth to all men. But it is necessary to distinguish between error, which always merits repudiation, and the person in error, who never loses the dignity of being a person, even when he is flawed by false or inadequate religious notions.[51] God alone is the judge and searcher of hearts; for that reason he forbids us to make judgments about the internal guilt of anyone.[52]

The teaching of Christ even requires that we forgive injustices,[53] and extends the law of love to include every enemy, according to the command of the New Law: "You have heard that it was said, 'Thou shalt love thy neighbor, and shalt hate thy enemy.' But I say to you, love your enemies, do good to those who hate you, and pray for those who persecute and calumniate you" (Matt. 5:43–44).

The Essential Equality of Men; and Social Justice

29. Since all men possess a rational soul and are created in God's likeness, since they have the same nature and origin, have been redeemed by Christ, and enjoy the same divine calling and destiny, the basic equality of all must receive increasingly greater recognition.

True, all men are not alike from the point of view of varying physical power and the diversity of intellectual and moral resources. Nevertheless, with respect to the fundamental rights of the person, every type of discrimination, whether social or cultural, whether based on sex, race, color, social condition, language, or religion, is to be overcome and eradicated as contrary to God's intent. For in truth it must still be regretted that fundamental personal rights are not yet being universally honored. Such is the case of a woman who is denied the right and freedom to choose a husband, to embrace a state of life, or to acquire an education or cultural benefits equal to those recognized for men.

Moreover, although rightful differences exist between men, the equal dignity of persons demands that a more humane and just condition of life be brought about. For excessive economic and social differences between the members of the one human family or population groups cause scandal, and militate against social justice, equity, the dignity of the human person, as well as social and international peace. Human institutions, both private and public, must labor to minister to the dignity and purpose of man. At the same time let them put up a stubborn fight against any kind of slavery, whether social or political, and safeguard the basic rights of man under every political system. Indeed human institutions themselves must be accommodated by degrees to the highest of all realities, spiritual ones, even though meanwhile, a long enough time will be required before they arrive at the desired goal.

More Than an Individualistic Ethic Is Required

30. Profound and rapid changes make it particularly urgent that no one, ignoring the trend of events or drugged by laziness, content himself with a merely individualistic morality. It grows increasingly true that the obligations of justice and love are fulfilled only if each person, contributing to the common good, according to his own abilities and the needs of others, also promotes and assists the public and private in situations dedicated to bettering the conditions of human life.

Yet there are those who, while professing grand and rather noble sentiments, nevertheless in reality live always as if they cared nothing for the needs of society. Many in various places even make light of social laws and precepts, and do not hesitate to resort to various frauds and deceptions in avoiding just taxes or other debts due to society. Others think little of certain norms of social life, for example those designed for the protection of health, or laws establishing speed limits. They do not even avert to the fact that by such indifference they imperil their own life and that of others.

Let everyone consider it his sacred obligation to count social necessities among the primary duties of modern man, and to pay heed to them. For the more unified the world becomes, the more plainly do the offices of men extend beyond particular groups and spread by degrees to the whole world. But this challenge cannot be met unless individual men and their associations cultivate in themselves the moral and social virtues, and promote them in society. Thus, with the needed help of divine grace, men who are truly new and artisans of a new humanity can be forthcoming.

Responsibility and Participation

31. In order for individual men to discharge with greater exactness the obligations of their conscience toward themselves and the various groups to which they belong, they must be carefully educated to a higher degree of culture through the use of the immense resources available today to the human race. Above all the education of youth from every social background has to be undertaken, so that there can be produced not only men and women of refined talents, but those great-souled persons who are so desperately required by our times.

Now a man can scarcely arrive at the needed sense of responsibility unless his living conditions allow him to become conscious of his dignity, and to rise to his destiny by spending himself for God and for others. But human freedom is often crippled when a man falls into extreme poverty, just as it withers when he indulges in too many of life's comforts and imprisons himself in a kind of splendid isolation. Freedom acquires new strength, by contrast, when a man consents to the unavoidable requirements of social life, takes on the manifold demands of human community.

Hence, the will to play one's role in common endeavors should be everywhere encouraged. Praise is due to those national procedures which allow the largest possible number of citizens to participate in public affairs with genuine freedom. Account must be taken, to be sure, of the actual conditions of each people and the vigor required by public authority.

If every citizen is to feel inclined to take part in the activities of the various groups which make up the social body, these must offer advantages which will attract members and dispose them to serve others. We can justly consider that the future of humanity lies in the hands of those who are strong enough to provide coming generations with reasons for living and hoping.

The Incarnate Word and Human Solidarity

32. God did not create man for life in isolation, but for the formation of social unity. So also "it has pleased God to make men holy and save them not merely as individuals, without any mutual bonds, but by making them into a single people, a people which acknowledges him in truth and serves him in holiness."[54] So from the beginning of salvation history he has chosen men not just as individuals but as members of a certain community. Revealing his mind to them, God called these chosen ones "His people" (Exod. 3:7–12), and, furthermore, made a covenant with them on Sinai.[55]

This communitarian character is developed and consummated in the work of Jesus Christ. For the very Word made flesh willed to share in the human fellowship. He was present at the wedding of Cana, visited the house of

Zacchaeus, ate with publicans and sinners. He revealed the love of the Father and the sublime vocation of man in terms of the most common of social realities and by making use of the speech and the imagery of plain everyday life. Willingly obeying the laws of his country he sanctified those human ties, especially family ones, from which social relationships arise. He chose to lead the life proper to an artisan of his time and place.

In his preaching he clearly taught the sons of God to treat one another as brothers. In his prayers he pleaded that all his disciples might be "one." Indeed, as the Redeemer of all, he offered himself for all even to point of death. "Greater love than this no one has, that one lay down his life for his friends" (John 15:13). He commanded his apostles to preach to all peoples the gospel message so that the human race might become the family of God, in which the fullness of the Law would be love.

As the firstborn of many brethren and through the gift of his Spirit, he founded after his death and resurrection a new brotherly community composed of all those who receive him in faith and in love. This he did through his Body which is the Church. There everyone, as members one of the other, would render mutual service according to the different gifts bestowed on each.

This solidarity must be constantly increased until that day on which it will be brought to perfection. Then, saved by grace, men will offer flawless glory to God as a family beloved of God and of Christ their Brother.

Chapter 3: Man's Activity throughout the World

The Problem Defined

33. Through his labors and his native endowments man has ceaselessly striven to better his life. Today, however, especially with the help of science and technology, he has extended his mastery over nearly the whole of nature and continues to do so. Thanks primarily to increased opportunities for many kinds of interchange among nations, the human family is gradually recognizing that it comprises a single world community and is making itself so. Hence many benefits once looked for, especially from heavenly powers, man has now enterprisingly procured for himself.

In the face of these immense efforts which already preoccupy the whole human race, men raise numerous questions among themselves. What is the meaning and value of this feverish activity? How should all these things be used? To the achievement of what goal are the strivings of individuals and societies heading?

The Church guards the heritage of God's Word and draws from it religious and moral principles, without always having at hand the solution to particular problems. She desires thereby to add the light of revealed truth to mankind's store of experience, so that the path which humanity has taken in recent times will not be a dark one.

The Value of Human Activity

34. Throughout the course of the centuries, men have labored to better the circumstances of their lives through a monumental amount of individual and collective effort. To believers, this point is settled: considered in itself, such human activity accords with God's will. For man, created to God's image, received a mandate to subject to himself the earth and all that it contains, and to govern the world with justice and holiness,[56] a mandate to relate himself and the totality of things to him who was to be acknowledged as the Lord and Creator of all. Thus, by the subjection of all things to man, the name of God would be wonderful in all the earth.[57]

This mandate concerns even the most ordinary everyday activities. For while providing the substance of life for themselves and their families, men and women are performing their activities in a way which appropriately benefits society. They can justly consider that by their labor they are unfolding the Creator's work, consulting the advantages of their brother men, and contributing by their personal industry to the realization in history of the divine plan.[58]

Thus, far from thinking that works produced by man's own talent and energy are in opposition to God's power, and that the rational creature exists as a kind of rival to the Creator, Christians are convinced that the triumphs of the human race are a sign of God's greatness and the flowering of his own mysterious design. For the greater man's power becomes, the farther his individual and community responsibility extends. Hence it is clear that men are not deterred by the Christian message from building up the world, or impelled to neglect the welfare of their fellows. They are, rather, more stringently bound to do these very things.[59]

The Regulation of Human Activity

35. Just as human activity proceeds from man, so it is ordered toward man. For when a man works he not only alters things and society, he develops himself as well. He learns much, he cultivates his resources, he goes outside of himself and beyond himself.

Rightly understood, this kind of growth is of greater value than any external riches which can be garnered. A man is more precious for what he is than for what he has.[60] Similarly, all that men do to obtain greater justice, wider brotherhood, and a more humane ordering of social relationships has greater worth than technical advances. For these advances can supply the material for human progress, but of themselves alone they can never actually bring it about.

Hence, the norm of human activity is this: that in accord with the divine plan and will, it should harmonize with the genuine good of the human race, and allow men as individuals and as members of society to pursue their total vocation and fulfill it.

The Rightful Independence of Earthly Affairs

36. Now, many of our contemporaries seem to fear that a closer bond between human activity and religion will work against the independence of men, of societies, or of the sciences.

If by the autonomy of earthly affairs we mean that created things and societies themselves enjoy their own laws and values which must be gradually deciphered, put to use, and regulated by men, then it is entirely right to demand that autonomy. Such is not merely required by modern man, but harmonizes also with the will of the Creator. For by the very circumstance of their having been created, all things are endowed with their own stability, truth, goodness, proper laws, and order. Man must respect these as he isolates them by the appropriate methods of the individual sciences or arts.

Therefore, if methodical investigation within every branch of learning is carried out in a genuinely scientific manner and in accord with moral norms, it never truly conflicts with faith. For earthly matters and the concerns of faith derive from the same God.[61] Indeed, whoever labors to penetrate the secrets of reality with a humble and steady mind, is, even unawares, being led by the hand of God, who holds all things in existence, and gives them their identity.

Consequently, we cannot but deplore certain habits of mind, sometimes found too among Christians, which do not sufficiently attend to the rightful independence of science. The arguments and controversies which they spark lead many minds to conclude that faith and science are mutually opposed.[62]

But if the expression, the independence of temporal affairs, is taken to mean that created things do not depend on God, and that man can use them without any reference to their Creator, anyone who acknowledges God will see how false such a meaning is. For without the Creator the creature would disappear. For their part, however, all believers of whatever religion have always heard his revealing voice in the discourse of creatures. But when God is forgotten the creature itself grows unintelligible.

Human Activity as Infected by Sin

37. Sacred scripture teaches the human family what the experience of the ages confirms: that while human progress is a great advantage to man, it brings with it a strong temptation. For when the order of values is jumbled, and bad is mixed with the good, individuals and groups pay heed solely to their own interests, and not to those of others. Thus it happens that the world ceases to be a place of true brotherhood. In our own day, the magnified power of humanity threatens to destroy the race itself.

For a monumental struggle against the powers of darkness pervades the whole history of man. The battle was joined from the very origins of the world and will continue until the last day, as the Lord has attested.[63] Caught in this conflict, man is obliged to wrestle constantly if he is to cling to what is good. Nor can he achieve his own integrity without valiant efforts and the help of God's grace.

That is why Christ's Church, trusting in the design of the Creator, acknowledges that human progress can see man's true happiness. Yet she cannot help echoing the Apostle's warning "Be not conformed to this world" (Rom. 12:2). By the world is here meant that spirit of vanity and malice which transforms into an instrument of sin those human energies intended for the service of God and man.

Hence if anyone wants to know how this unhappy situation can be overcome, Christians will tell him that all human activity, constantly imperiled by man's pride and deranged self-love, must be purified and perfected by the power of Christ's cross and resurrection. For, redeemed by Christ and made a new creature in the Holy Spirit, man is able to love the things themselves created by God, and ought to do so. He can receive them from God, and respect and reverence them as flowing constantly from the hand of God.

Grateful to his Benefactor for these creatures, using and enjoying them in detachment and liberty of spirit, man is led forward into a true possession of the world, as having nothing, yet possessing all things.[64] "All are yours, and you are Christ's, and Christ is God's" (1 Cor. 3:22–23).

Human Activity Finds Perfection in the Paschal Mystery

38. For God's Word, through whom all things were made, was himself made flesh and dwelt on the earth of men.[65] Thus he entered the world's history as a perfect man, taking that history up into himself and summarizing it.[66] He himself revealed to us that "God is love" (1 John 4:8). At the same time he taught us that the new command of love was the basic law of human perfection and hence of the world's transformation.

To those, therefore, who believe in divine love, he gives assurance that the way of love lies open to all men and that the effort to establish a universal brotherhood is not a hopeless one. He cautions them at the same time that this love is not something to be reserved for important matters, but must be pursued chiefly in the ordinary circumstances of life.

Undergoing death itself for all of us sinners,[67] he taught us by example that we too must shoulder that cross which the world and the flesh inflict upon those who search after peace and justice. Appointed Lord by his resurrection and given plenary power in heaven and on earth,[68] Christ is now at work in the hearts of men through the energy of his Spirit. He arouses not only a desire for the age to come, but, by that very fact, he animates, purifies, and strengthens those noble longings too by which the human family strives to make its life more human and to render the whole earth submissive to this goal.

Now, the gifts of the Spirit are diverse. He calls some to give clear witness to the desire for a heavenly home and to keep that desire green among the human family. He summons others to dedicate themselves to the earthly service of men and to make ready the material of the celestial realm by this ministry of theirs. Yet he frees all of them so that by putting aside love of self and bringing all earthly resources into the service of human life they can devote themselves to that future when humanity itself will become an offering accepted by God.[69]

The Lord left behind a pledge of this hope and strength for life's journey in that sacrament of faith where natural elements refined by man are changed into his glorified body and blood, providing a meal of brotherly solidarity and a foretaste of the heavenly banquet.

A New Earth and a New Heaven

39. We do not know the time for the consummation of the earth and of humanity.[70] Nor do we know how all things will be transformed. As deformed by sin, the shape of this world will pass away.[71] But we are taught that God is preparing a new dwelling place and a new earth where justice will abide,[72] and whose blessedness will answer and surpass all the longings for peace which spring up in the human heart.[73]

Then, with death overcome, the sons of God will be raised up in Christ. What was sown in weakness and corruption will be clothed with incorruptibility.[74] While charity and its fruits endure,[75] all that creation[76] which God made on man's account will be unchained from the bondage of vanity.

Therefore, while we are warned that it profits a man nothing if he gain the whole world and lose himself,[77] the expectation of a new earth must not weaken but rather stimulate our concern for cultivating this one. For here grows the body of a new human family, a body which even now is able to give some kind of foreshadowing of the new age.

Earthly progress must be carefully distinguished from the growth of Christ's kingdom. Nevertheless, to the extent that the former can contribute to the better ordering of human society, it is of vital concern to the kingdom of God.[78]

For after we have obeyed the Lord, and in his Spirit nurtured on earth the values of human dignity, brotherhood, and freedom, and indeed all the good fruits of our nature and enterprise, we will find them again, but freed of stain, burnished and transfigured. This will be so when Christ hands over to the Father a kingdom eternal and universal: "a kingdom of truth and life, of holiness and grace, of justice, love and peace."[79] On this earth that kingdom is already present in mystery. When the Lord returns, it will be brought into full flower.

Chapter 4: The Role of the Church in the Modern World

The Church and the World as Mutually Related

40. Everything we have said about the dignity of the human person, and about the human community and the profound meaning of human activity, lays the foundation for the relationship between the Church and the world, and provides the basis for dialogue between them.[80] In this chapter, presupposing everything which has already been said by this Council concerning the mys-

tery of the Church, we must now consider this same Church inasmuch as she exists in the world, living and acting with it.

Coming forth from the eternal Father's love,[81] founded in time by Christ the Redeemer, and made one in the Holy Spirit,[82] the Church has a saving and an eschatological purpose which can be fully attained only in the future world. But she is already present in this world, and is composed of men, that is, of members of the earthly city who have a call to form the family of God's children during the present history of the human race, and to keep increasing it until the Lord returns.

United on behalf of heavenly values and enriched by them, this family has been "constituted and organized in the world as a society"[83] by Christ, and is equipped with "those means which befit it as a visible and social unity."[84] Thus the Church, at once a visible assembly and a spiritual community,[85] goes forward together with humanity and experiences the same earthly lot which the world does. She serves as a leaven and as a kind of soul for human society[86] as it is to be renewed in Christ and transformed into God's family.

That the earthly and the heavenly city penetrate each other is a fact accessible to faith alone. It remains a mystery of human history, which sin will keep in great disarray until the splendor of God's sons is fully revealed. Pursuing the saving purpose which is proper to her, the Church not only communicates divine life to men, but in some way casts the reflected light of that life over the entire earth.

This she does most of all by her healing and elevating impact on the dignity of the person, by the way in which she strengthens the seams of human society and imbues the everyday activity of men with a deeper meaning and importance. Thus, through her individual members and her whole community, the Church believes she can contribute greatly toward making the family of man and its history more human.

In addition, the Catholic Church gladly holds in high esteem the things which other Christian Churches or ecclesial communities have done or are doing cooperatively by way of achieving the same goal. At the same time, she is firmly convinced that she can be abundantly and variously helped by the world in the matter of preparing the ground for the gospel. This help she gains from the talents and industry of individuals and from human society as a whole. The Council now sets forth certain general principles for the proper fostering of this mutual exchange and assistance in concerns which are in some way common to the Church and the world.

The Help the Church Strives to Bring to Individuals

41. Modern man is on the road to a more thorough development of his own personality, and to a growing discovery and vindication of his own rights. Since it has been entrusted to the Church to reveal the mystery of God, who is the ultimate goal of man, she opens up to man at the same time the meaning of his own existence, that is, the innermost truth about himself. The

Church truly knows that only God, whom she serves, meets the deepest longings of the human heart, which is never fully satisfied by what this world has to offer.

She also knows that man is constantly worked upon by God's Spirit, and hence can never be altogether indifferent to the problems of religion. The experience of past ages proves this, as do numerous indications in our own times. For man will always yearn to know, at least in an obscure way, what is the meaning of his life, of his activity, of his death. The very presence of the Church recalls these problems to his mind.

But only God, who created man to his own image and ransomed him from sin, provides a fully adequate answer to these questions. This he does through what he has revealed in Christ his Son, who became man. Whoever follows after Christ, the perfect man, becomes himself more of a man.

Thanks to this belief, the Church can anchor the dignity of human nature against all tides of opinion, for example, those which undervalue the human body or idolize it. By no human law can the personal dignity and liberty of man be so aptly safeguarded as by the gospel of Christ which has been entrusted to the Church.

For this gospel announces and proclaims the freedom of the sons of God, and repudiates all the bondage which ultimately results from sin.[87] The gospel has a sacred reverence for the dignity of conscience and its freedom of choice, constantly advises that all human talents be employed in God's service and men's, and, finally, commends all to the charity of all.[88]

All this corresponds with the basic law of the Christian dispensation. For though the same God is Savior and Creator, Lord of human history as well as of salvation history, in the divine arrangement itself the rightful autonomy of the creature, and particularly of man, is not withdrawn. Rather it is reestablished in its own dignity and strengthened in it.

Therefore, by virtue of the gospel committed to her, the Church proclaims the rights of man. She acknowledges and greatly esteems the dynamic movements of today by which these rights are everywhere fostered. Yet these movements must be penetrated by the spirit of the gospel and protected against any kind of false autonomy. For we are tempted to think that our personal rights are fully ensured only when we are exempt from every requirement of divine law. But this way lies not the maintenance of the dignity of the human person, but its annihilation.

The Help the Church Strives to Give to Society

42. The union of the human family is greatly fortified and fulfilled by the unity, founded on Christ,[89] of the family of God's sons.

Christ, to be sure, gave his Church no proper mission in the political, economic, or social order. The purpose which he set before her is a religious one.[90] But out of this religious mission itself come a function, a light, and an energy which can serve to structure and consolidate the human community according to the divine law. As a matter of fact, when circumstances of time and place create the need, she can and indeed should initiate activities on behalf of all men. This is particularly true of activities designed for the needy, such as the works of mercy and similar undertakings.

The Church further recognizes that worthy elements are found in today's social movements, especially an evolution toward unity, a process of wholesome socialization and of association in civic and economic realms. For the promotion of unity belongs to the innermost nature of the Church, since she is, "by her relationship with Christ, both a sacramental sign and an instrument of intimate union with God, and of the unity of all mankind."[91]

Thus she shows the world that an authentic union, social and external, results from a union of minds and hearts, namely, from that faith and charity by which her own unity is unbreakably rooted in the Holy Spirit. For the force which the Church can inject into the modern society of man consists in that faith and charity put into vital practice, not in any external dominion exercised by merely human means.

Moreover, in virtue of her mission and nature, she is bound to no particular form of human culture, nor to any political, economic, or social system. Hence the Church by her very universality can be a very close bond between diverse human communities and nations, provided these trust her and truly acknowledge her right to true freedom in fulfilling her mission. For this reason, the Church admonishes her own sons, but also humanity as a whole, to overcome all strife between nations and races in this family spirit of God's children, and in the same way, to give internal strength to human associations which are just.

This Council, therefore, looks with great respect upon all the true, good, and just elements found in the very wide variety of institutions which the human race has established for itself and constantly continues to establish. The Council affirms, moreover, that the Church is willing to assist and promote all these institutions to the extent that such a service depends on her and can be associated with her mission. She has no fiercer desire than that, in pursuit of the welfare of all, she may be able to develop herself freely under any kind of government which grants recognition to the basic rights of person and family and to the demands of the common good.

The Help the Church Strives to Give to Human Activity through Christians

43. This Council exhorts Christians, as citizens of two cities, to strive to discharge their earthly duties conscientiously and in response to the gospel spirit. They are mistaken who, knowing that we have here no abiding city but seek one which is to come,[92] think that they may therefore shirk their earthly responsibilities. For they are forgetting that by the faith itself they are more than ever obliged to measure up to these duties, each according to his proper vocation.[93]

Nor, on the contrary, are they any less wide of the mark who think that religion consists in acts of worship alone and in the discharge of certain moral obligations, and who imagine they can plunge themselves into earthly affairs in such a way as to imply that these are altogether divorced from the religious life. This spirit between the faith which many profess and their daily lives deserves to be counted among the more serious errors of our age. Long since, the prophets of the Old Testament fought vehemently against this scandal[94] and even more so did Jesus Christ himself in the New Testament threaten it with grave punishments.[95]

Therefore, let there be no false opposition between professional and social activities on the one part, and religious life on the other. The Christian who neglects his temporal duties neglects his duties toward his neighbor and even God, and jeopardizes his eternal salvation. Christians should rather rejoice that they can follow the example of Christ, who worked as an artisan. In the exercise of all their earthly activities, they can thereby gather their humane, domestic, professional, social, and technical enterprises into one vital synthesis with religious values, under whose supreme direction all things are harmonized unto God's glory.

Secular duties and activities belong properly although not exclusively to laymen. Therefore acting as citizens of the world, whether individually or socially, they will observe the laws proper to each discipline, and labor to equip themselves with a genuine expertise in their various fields. They will gladly work with men seeking the same goals. Acknowledging the demands of faith and endowed with its force, they will unhesitatingly devise new enterprises, where they are appropriate, and put them into action.

Laymen should also know that it is generally the function of their well-formed Christian conscience to see that the divine law is inscribed in the life of the earthly city. From priests they may look for spiritual light and nourishment. Let the layman not imagine that his pastors are always such experts, that to every problem which arises, however complicated, they can readily give him a concrete solution or even that such is their mission. Rather, enlightened by Christian wisdom and giving close attention to the teaching authority of the Church,[96] let the layman take on his own distinctive role.

Often enough the Christian view of things will itself suggest some specific solution in certain circumstances. Yet it happens rather frequently, and legitimately so, that with equal sincerity some of the faithful will disagree with others on a given matter. Even against the intentions of their proponents, however, solutions proposed on one side or another may be easily confused by many people with the gospel message. Hence it is necessary for people to remember that no one is allowed in the aforementioned situations to appropriate the Church's authority for his opinion. They should always try to enlighten one another through honest discussion, preserving mutual charity and caring above all for the common good.

Since they have an active role to play in the whole life of the Church, laymen are not only bound to penetrate the world with a Christian spirit. They are also called to be witnesses to Christ in all things in the midst of human society.

Bishops, to whom is assigned the task of ruling the Church of God, should, together with their priests, so preach the message of Christ that all the earthly activities of the faithful will be bathed in the light of the gospel. All pastors should remember too that by their daily conduct and concern[97] they are revealing the face of the Church to the world. Men will judge the power and truth of the Christian message thereby. By their lives and speech, in union with religious and their faithful, may pastors demonstrate that even now the Church, by her presence alone and by all the gifts which she possesses, is an unspent fountain of those virtues which the modern world most needs.

By unremitting study they should fit themselves to do their part in establishing dialogue with the world and with men of all shades of opinion. Above all let them take to heart the words which this Council has spoken: "Because the human race today is joining more and more in civic, economic, and social unity, it is that much more necessary that priests, united in concern and effort under the leadership of the bishops and the supreme pontiff, wipe out every ground of division, so that the whole human race may be brought into the unity of the family of God."[98]

Although by the power of the Holy Spirit the Church has remained the faithful spouse of her Lord and has never ceased to be the sign of salvation on earth, still she is very well aware that among her members,[99] both clerical and lay, some have been unfaithful to the Spirit of God during the course of many centuries. In the present age, too, it does not escape the Church how great a distance lies between the message she offers and the human failings of those to whom the gospel is entrusted.

Whatever be the judgment of history on these defects, we ought to be conscious of them, and struggle against them energetically, lest they inflict harm on the spread of the gospel. The Church also realizes that in working out her relationship with the world she always has great need of the ripening which comes with the experience of the centuries. Led by the Holy Spirit, Mother Church unceasingly exhorts her sons "to purify and renew themselves so that the sign of Christ can shine more brightly on the face of the Church."[100]

The Help the Church Receives from the Modern World

44. Just as it is in the world's interest to acknowledge the Church as a historical reality, and to recognize her good influence, so the Church herself knows how richly she has profited by the history and development of humanity.

Thanks to the experience of past ages, the progress of the sciences, and the treasures hidden in the various forms of human culture, the nature of man himself is more clearly revealed and new roads to truth are opened. These benefits profit the Church, too, for from the beginning of her history, she has learned to express the message of Christ with the help of the ideas and terminology of various peoples, and has tried to clarify it with the wisdom of philosophers, too.

Her purpose has been to adapt the gospel to the grasp of all as well as to the needs of the learned, insofar as such was appropriate. Indeed, this accommodated preaching of the revealed Word ought to remain the law of all evangelization. For thus each nation develops the ability to express Christ's message in its own way. At the same time, a living exchange is fostered between the Church and the diverse cultures of people.[101]

To promote such an exchange, the Church requires special help, particularly in our day, when things are changing very rapidly and the ways of thinking are exceedingly various. She must rely on those who live in the world, are versed in different institutions and specialties, and grasp their innermost significance in the eyes of both believers and unbelievers. With the help of the Holy Spirit, it is the task of the entire People of God, especially pastors and theologians, to hear, distinguish, and interpret the many voices of our age, and to judge them in the light of the divine Word. In this way, revealed truth can always be more deeply penetrated, better understood, and set forth to greater advantage.

Since the Church has a visible and social structure as a sign of her unity in Christ, she can and ought to be enriched by the development of human social life. The reason is not that the constitution given her by Christ is defective, but so that she may understand it more penetratingly, express it better, and adjust it more successfully to our times.

She gratefully understands that in her community life, no less than in her individual sons, she receives a variety of helps from men of every rank and condition. For whoever promotes the human community at the family level, culturally, in its economic, social, and political dimensions, both nationally and internationally, such a one, according to God's design, is contributing greatly to the Church community as well, to the extent that it depends on things outside itself. Indeed, the Church admits that she has greatly profited and still profits from the antagonism of those who oppose or persecute her.[102]

Christ, the Alpha and the Omega

45. While helping the world and receiving many benefits from it, the Church has a single intention: that God's kingdom may come, and that the salvation of the whole human race may come to pass. For every benefit which the People of God during its earthly pilgrimage can offer to the human family stems from the fact that the Church is "the universal sacrament of salvation,"[103] simultaneously manifesting and exercising the mystery of God's love for man.

For God's Word, by whom all things were made, was himself made flesh so that as perfect man he might save all men and sum up all things in himself. The Lord is the goal of human history, the focal point of the longings of history and of civilization, the center of the human race, the joy of every heart, and the answer to all its yearnings.[104] He it is whom the Father raised from the dead, lifted on high, and stationed at his right hand, making him Judge of the living and the dead. Enlivened and united in his Spirit, we journey toward the consummation of human history, one which fully accords with the counsel of God's love: "To reestablish all things in Christ, both those in the heavens and those on the earth" (Eph. 1:10).

The Lord himself speaks: "Behold, I come quickly and my reward is with me, to render to each one according to his works. I am the Alpha and the Omega, the first and the last, the beginning and the end" (Rev. 22:12–13).

PART II: SOME PROBLEMS OF SPECIAL URGENCY

Preface

46. This Council has set forth the dignity of the human person and the work which men have been destined to undertake throughout the world both as individuals and as members of society. There are a number of particularly urgent needs characterizing the present age, needs which go to the roots of the human race. To a consideration of these in the light of the gospel and of human experience, the Council would now direct the attention of all.

Of the many subjects arousing universal concern today, it may be helpful to concentrate on these: marriage and the family, human culture, life in its economic, social, and political dimensions, the bonds between the family of nations, and peace. On each of these may there shine the radiant ideals proclaimed by Christ. By these ideals may Christians be led, and all mankind enlightened, as they search for answers to questions of such complexity.

CHAPTER 1: FOSTERING THE NOBILITY OF MARRIAGE AND THE FAMILY

Marriage and Family in the Modern World

47. The well-being of the individual person and of human and Christian society is intimately linked with the healthy condition of that community produced by marriage and family. Hence Christians and all men who behold this community in high esteem sincerely rejoice in the various ways by which men today find help in fostering this community of love and perfecting its life, and by which spouses and parents are assisted in their lofty calling. Those who rejoice in such aids look for additional benefits from them and labor to bring them about.

Yet the excellence of this institution is not everywhere reflected with equal brilliance. For polygamy, the plague of divorce, so-called free love, and other disfigurements have an obscuring effect. In addition, married love is too often profaned by excessive self-love, the worship of pleasure, and illicit practices against human generation. Moreover, serious disturbances are caused in families by modern economic conditions, by influences at once social and psychological, and by the demands of civil society. Finally, in certain parts of the world problems resulting from population growth are generating concern.

All these situations have produced anxious consciences. Yet, the power and strength of the institution of marriage and family can also be seen in the fact that time and again, despite the difficulties produced, the profound changes in modern society reveal the true character of this institution in one way or another.

Therefore, by presenting certain key points of Church doctrine in a clearer light, this Council wishes to offer guidance and support to those Christians and other men who are trying to keep sacred and to foster the natural dignity of the married state and its superlative value.

The Sanctity of Marriage and the Family

48. The intimate partnership of married life and love has been established by the Creator and qualified by his laws. It is rooted in the conjugal covenant of irrevocable personal consent. Hence, by that human act whereby spouses mutually bestow and accept each other, a relationship arises which by divine will and in the eyes of society too is a lasting one. For the good of the spouses and their offspring as well as of society, the existence of this sacred bond no longer depends on human decisions alone.

For God himself is the author of matrimony, endowed as it is with various benefits and purposes.[105] All of these have a very decisive bearing on the continuation of the human race, on the personal development and eternal destiny of the individual members of a family, and on the dignity, stability, peace, and prosperity of the family itself and of human society as a whole. By their very nature, the institution of matrimony itself and conjugal love are ordained for the procreation and education of children, and find in them their ultimate crown.

Thus a man and a woman, who by the marriage covenant of conjugal love "are no longer two, but one flesh" (Mt. 19:6), render mutual help and service to each other through an intimate union of their persons and of their actions. Through this union they experience the meaning of their oneness and attain to it with growing perfection day by day. As a mutual gift of two persons, this intimate union, as well as the good of the children, imposes total fidelity on the spouses and argues for an unbreakable oneness between them.[106]

Christ the Lord abundantly blessed this many faceted love, welling up as it does from the foundation of divine love and structured as it is on the model of his union with the Church. For as God of old made himself present[107] to his people through a covenant of love and fidelity, so now the Savior of men and the Spouse[108] of the Church comes into the lives of married Christians through the sacrament of matrimony. He abides with them thereafter so that, just as he loved the Church and handed himself over on her behalf,[109] the spouses may love each other with perpetual fidelity through mutual self-bestowal.

Authentic married love is caught up into divine love and is governed and enriched by Christ's redeeming power and the saving activity of the Church.

Thus this love can lead the spouses to God with powerful effect and can aid and strengthen them in the sublime office of being a father or a mother.[110]

For this reason, Christian spouses have a special sacrament by which they are fortified and receive a kind of consecration in the duties and dignity of their state.[111] By virtue of this sacrament, as spouses fulfill their conjugal and family obligations, they are penetrated with the spirit of Christ. This spirit suffuses their whole lives with faith, hope, and charity. Thus they increasingly advance their own perfection, as well as their mutual sanctification, and hence contribute jointly to the glory of God.

As a result, with their parents leading the way by example and family prayer, children and indeed everyone gathered around the family hearth will find a readier path to human maturity, salvation, and holiness. Graced with the dignity and office of fatherhood and motherhood, parents will energetically acquit themselves of a duty which devolves primarily on them, namely education, and especially religious education.

As living members of the family, children contribute in their own way to making their parents holy. For they will respond to the kindness of their parents with sentiments of gratitude, with love and trust. They will stand by them as children should when hardships overtake their parents and old age brings its loneliness. Widowhood, accepted bravely as a continuation of the marriage vocation, will be esteemed by all.[112] Families will share their spiritual riches generously with other families too. Thus the Christian family, which springs from marriage as a reflection of the loving covenant uniting Christ with the Church,[113] and as a participation in that covenant, will manifest to all men the Savior's living presence in the world, and the genuine nature of the Church. This the family will do by the mutual love of the spouses, by their generous fruitfulness, their solidarity and faithfulness, and by the loving way in which all members of the family work together.

Conjugal Love

49. The biblical Word of God several times urges the betrothed and the married to nourish and develop their wedlock by pure conjugal love and undivided affection.[114] Many men of our own age also highly regard true love between husband and wife as it manifests itself in a variety of ways depending on the worthy customs of various peoples and times.

This love is an eminently human one since it is directed from one person to another through an affection of the will. It involves the good of the whole person. Therefore it can enrich the expressions of body and mind with a unique dignity, ennobling these expressions as special ingredients and signs of the friendship distinctive of marriage. This love the Lord has judged worthy of special gifts, healing, perfecting, and exalting gifts of grace and of charity.

Such love, merging the human with the divine, leads the spouses to a free and mutual gift of themselves, a gift proving itself by gentle affection and by deed. Such love pervades the whole of their lives.[115] Indeed, by its generous activity it grows better and grows greater. Therefore it far excels mere erotic inclination, which, selfishly pursued, soon enough fades wretchedly away.

This love is uniquely expressed and perfected through the marital act. The actions within marriage by which the couple are united intimately and chastely are noble and worthy ones. Expressed in a manner which is truly human, these actions signify and promote that mutual self-giving by which spouses enrich each other with a joyful and a thankful will.

Sealed by mutual faithfulness and hallowed above all by Christ's sacrament, this love remains steadfastly true in body and in mind, in bright days or dark. It will never be profaned by adultery or divorce. Firmly established by the Lord, the unity of marriage will radiate from the equal personal dignity of wife and husband, a dignity acknowledged by mutual and total love.

The steady fulfillment of the duties of this Christian vocation demands notable virtue. For this reason, strengthened by grace for holiness of life, the couple will painstakingly cultivate and pray for constancy of love, largeheartedness, and the spirit of sacrifice.

Authentic conjugal love will be more highly prized, and wholesome public opinion created regarding it, if Christian couples give outstanding witness to faithfulness and harmony in the same love, and to their concern for educating their children; also, if they do their part in bringing about the needed cultural, psychological, and social renewal on behalf of marriage and the family.

Especially in the heart of their own families, young people should be aptly and seasonably instructed about the dignity, duty, and expression of married love. Trained thus in the cultivation of chastity, they will be able at a suitable age to enter a marriage of their own after an honorable courtship.

The Fruitfulness of Marriage

50. Marriage and conjugal love are by their nature ordained toward the begetting and educating of children. Children are really the supreme gift of marriage and contribute very substantially to the welfare of their parents. The God himself who said, "It is not good for man to be alone" (Gen. 2:18) and "who made man from the beginning male and female" (Mt. 19:4), wished to share with man a certain special participation in his own creative work. Thus he blessed male and female, saying: "Increase and multiply" (Gen. 1:28).

Hence, while not making the other purposes of matrimony of less account, the true practice of conjugal love, and the whole meaning of the family life which results from it, have this aim: that the couple be ready with stout hearts to cooperate with the love of the Creator and the Savior, who through them will enlarge and enrich his own family day by day.

Parents should regard as their proper mission the task of transmitting human life and educating those to whom it has been transmitted. They should realize that they are thereby cooperators with the love of God the Creator, and are, so to speak, the interpreters of that love. Thus they will fulfill their task with human and Christian responsibility. With docile reverence toward God, they will come to the right decision by common counsel and effort.

They will thoughtfully take into account both their own welfare and that of their children, those already born and those which may be foreseen. For this accounting they will reckon with both the material and the spiritual conditions of the times as well as of their state in life. Finally, they will consult the interests of the family group, of temporal society, and of the Church herself.

The parents themselves should ultimately make this judgment, in the sight of God. But in their manner of acting, spouses should be aware that they cannot proceed arbitrarily. They must always be governed according to a conscience dutifully conformed to the divine law itself, and should be submissive toward the Church's teaching office, which authentically interprets that law in the light of the gospel. That divine law reveals and protects the integral meaning of conjugal love, and impels it toward a truly human fulfillment.

Thus, trusting in divine Providence and refining the spirit of sacrifice,[116] married Christians glorify the Creator and strive toward fulfillment in Christ when, with a generous human and Christian sense of responsibility, they acquit themselves of the duty to procreate. Among the couples who fulfill their God-given task in this way, those merit special mention who with wise and common deliberation, and with a gallant heart, undertake to bring up suitably even a relatively large family.[117]

Marriage to be sure is not instituted solely for procreation. Rather, its very nature as an unbreakable compact between persons, and the welfare of the children, both demand that the mutual love of the spouses, too, be embodied in a rightly ordered manner, that it grow and ripen. Therefore, marriage persists as a whole manner and communion of life, and maintains its value and indissolubility, even when offspring are lacking—despite, rather often, the very intense desire of the couple.

Harmonizing Conjugal Love with Respect for Human Life

51. This Council realizes that certain modern conditions often keep couples from arranging their married lives harmoniously, and that they find themselves in circumstances where at least temporarily the size of their families should not be increased. As a result, the faithful exercise of love and the full intimacy of their lives are hard to maintain. But where the intimacy of married life is broken off, it is not rare for its faithfulness to be imperiled and its quality of fruitfulness ruined. For then the upbringing of the children and the courage to accept new ones are both endangered.

To these problems there are those who presume to offer dishonorable solutions. Indeed, they do not recoil from the taking of life. But the Church issues the reminder that a true contradiction cannot exist between the divine laws pertaining to the transmission of life and those pertaining to the fostering of authentic conjugal love.

For God, the Lord of life, has conferred on men the surpassing ministry of safeguarding life—a ministry which must be fulfilled in a manner which is worthy of man. Therefore from the moment of its conception life must be guarded with the greatest care, while abortion and infanticide are unspeakable crimes. The sexual characteristics of man and the human faculty of reproduction wonderfully exceed the dispositions of lower forms of life. Hence the acts themselves which are proper to conjugal love and which are exercised in accord with genuine human dignity must be honored with great reverence.

Therefore when there is question of harmonizing conjugal love with the responsible transmission of life, the moral aspect of any procedure does not depend solely on sincere intentions or on an evaluation of motives. It must be determined by objective standards. These, based on the nature of the human person and his acts, preserve the full sense of mutual self-giving and human procreation in the context of true love. Such a goal cannot be achieved unless the virtue of conjugal chastity is sincerely practiced. Relying on these principles, sons of the Church may not undertake methods of regulating procreation which are found blameworthy by the teaching authority of the Church in its unfolding of the divine law.[118]

Everyone should be persuaded that human life and the task of transmitting it are not realities bound up with this world alone. Hence they cannot be measured or perceived only in terms of it, but always have a bearing on the eternal destiny of men.

All Must Promote the Good Estate of Marriage and the Family

52. The family is a kind of school of deeper humanity. But if it is to achieve the full flowering of its life and mission, it needs the kindly communion of minds and the joint deliberation of spouses, as well as the painstaking cooperation of parents in the education of their children. The active presence of the father is highly beneficial to their formation. The children, especially the younger among them, need the care of their mother at home. This domestic role of hers must be safely preserved, though the legitimate social progress of women should not be underrated on that account.

Children should be so educated that as adults they can, with a mature sense of responsibility, follow their vocation, including a religious one, and choose their state of life. If they marry, they can thereby establish their family in favorable moral, social, and economic conditions. Parents or guardians should by prudent advice provide guidance to their young with respect to founding a family, and the young ought to listen gladly. At the same time no pressure, direct or indirect, should be put on the young to make them enter marriage or choose a specific partner.

Thus the family is the foundation of society. In it the various generations come together and help one another to grow wiser and to harmonize personal rights with the other requirements of social life. All those, therefore, who exercise influence over communities and social groups should work efficiently for the welfare of marriage and the family.

Public authority should regard it as a sacred duty to recognize, protect, and promote their authentic nature, to shield public morality, and to favor the prosperity of domestic life. The right of parents to beget and educate their children in the bosom of the family must be safeguarded. Children, too, who unhappily lack the blessing of a family should be protected by prudent legislation and various undertakings, and provided with the help they need.

Redeeming the present time[119] and distinguishing eternal realities from their changing expressions, Christians should actively promote the values of marriage and the family, both by the example of their own lives and by cooperation with other men of good will. Thus when difficulties arise, Christians will provide, on behalf of family life, those necessities and helps which are suitably modern. To this end, the Christian instincts of the faithful, the upright moral conscience of men, and the wisdom and experience of persons versed in the sacred sciences will have much to contribute.

Those, too, who are skilled in other sciences, notably the medical, biological, social, and psychological, can considerably advance the welfare of marriage and the family, along with peace of conscience, if by pooling their efforts they labor to explain more thoroughly the various conditions favoring a proper regulation of births.

It devolves on priests duly trained about family matters to nurture the vocation of spouses by a variety of pastoral means, by preaching God's Word, by liturgical worship, and by other spiritual aids to conjugal and family life; to sustain them sympathetically and patiently in difficulties, and to make them courageous through love. Thus families which are truly noble will be formed.

Various organizations, especially family associations, should try by their programs of instruction and action to strengthen young people and spouses themselves, particularly those recently wed, and to train them for family, social, and apostolic life.

Finally, let the spouses themselves, made to the image of the living God and enjoying the authentic dignity of persons, be joined to one another[120] in equal affection, harmony of mind, and the work of mutual sanctification. Thus they will follow Christ who is the principle of life.[121] Thus, too, by the joys and sacrifices of their vocation and through their faithful love, married people will become witnesses of the mystery of that love which the Lord revealed to the world by his dying and his rising up to life again.[122]

Chapter 2: The Proper Development of Culture

Introduction

53. It is a fact bearing on the very person of man that he can come to an authentic and full humanity only through culture, that is, through the cultiva-

tion of natural goods and values. Wherever human life is involved, therefore, nature and culture are quite intimately connected.

The word "culture" in its general sense indicates all those factors by which man refines and unfolds his manifold spiritual and bodily qualities. It means his effort to bring the world itself under his control by his knowledge and his labor. It includes the fact that by improving customs and institutions he renders social life more human both within the family and in the civic community. Finally, it is a feature of culture that throughout the course of time man expresses, communicates, and conserves in his works great spiritual experiences and desires, so that these may be of advantage to the progress of many, even of the whole human family.

Hence it follows that human culture necessarily has a historical and social aspect and that the word "culture" often takes on a sociological and ethnological sense. It is in this sense that we speak of a plurality of cultures.

Various conditions of community living, as well as various patterns for organizing the goods of life, arise from diverse ways of using things, of laboring, of expressing oneself, of practicing religion, of forming customs, of establishing laws and juridical institutions, of advancing the arts and sciences, and of promoting beauty. Thus the customs handed down to it form for each human community its proper patrimony. Thus, too, is fashioned the specific historical environment which enfolds the men of every nation and age and from which they draw the values which permit them to promote human and civic culture.

SECTION 1: THE CIRCUMSTANCES OF CULTURE IN THE WORLD TODAY

New Forms of Living

54. The living conditions of modern man have been so profoundly changed in their social and cultural dimensions, that we can speak of a new age in human history.[123] Fresh avenues are open, therefore, for the refinement and the wider diffusion of culture. These avenues have been paved by the enormous growth of natural, human, and social sciences, by progress in technology, and by advances in the development and organization of the means by which men communicate with one another.

Hence the culture of today possesses particular characteristics. For example, the so-called exact sciences sharpen critical judgment to a very fine edge. Recent psychological research explains human activity more profoundly. Historical studies make a signal contribution to bringing men to see things in their changeable and evolutionary aspects. Customs and usages are becoming increasingly uniform. Industrialization, urbanization, and other causes of community living create new forms of culture (mass culture), from which arise new ways of thinking, acting, and making use of leisure. The growth of communication between the various nations and social groups opens more widely to all the treasures of different cultures.

Man the Author of Culture

55. In every group or nation, there is an ever-increasing number of men and women who are conscious that they themselves are the artisans and the authors of the culture of their community. Throughout the world there is a similar growth in the combined sense of independence and responsibility. Such a development is of paramount importance for the spiritual and moral maturity of the human race. This truth grows clearer if we consider how the world is becoming unified and how we have the duty to build a better world based upon truth and justice. Thus we are witnesses of the birth of a new humanism, one in which man is defined first of all by his responsibility toward his brothers and toward history.

Problems and Duties

56. In these conditions, it is no wonder that, feeling his responsibility for the progress of culture, man nourishes higher hopes but also looks anxiously upon many contradictions which he will have to resolve:

What must be done to prevent the increased exchanges between cultures, which ought to lead to a true and fruitful dialogue between groups and nations, from disturbing the life of communities, destroying ancestral wisdom, or jeopardizing the uniqueness of each people?

How can the vitality and growth of a new culture be fostered without the loss of living fidelity to the heritage of tradition? This question is especially urgent when a culture resulting from the enormous scientific and technological progress must be harmonized with an education nourished by classical studies as adapted to various traditions.

As special branches of knowledge continue to shoot out so rapidly, how can the necessary synthesis of them be worked out, and how can men preserve the ability to contemplate and to wonder, from which wisdom comes?

What can be done to make all men on earth share in cultural values, when the culture of the more sophisticated grows ever more refined and complex?

Finally, how is the independence which culture claims for itself to be recognized as legitimate without the promotion of a humanism which is merely earth-bound, and even contrary to religion itself?

In the thick of these tensions, human culture must evolve today in such a way that it can develop the whole human person harmoniously and at the same time assist men in those duties which all men, especially Christians, are called to fulfill in the fraternal unity of the one human family.

SECTION 2: SOME PRINCIPLES OF PROPER CULTURAL DEVELOPMENT

Faith and Culture

57. Christians, on pilgrimage toward the heavenly city, should seek and savor the things which are above.[124] This duty in no way decreases, but rather

increases, the weight of their obligation to work with all men in constructing a more human world. In fact, the mystery of the Christian faith furnishes them with excellent incentives and helps toward discharging this duty more energetically and especially toward uncovering the full meaning of this activity, a meaning which gives human culture its eminent place in the integral vocation of man.

For when, by the work of his hands or with the aid of technology, man develops the earth so that it can bear fruit and become a dwelling worthy of the whole human family, and when he consciously takes part in the life of social groups, he carries out the design of God. Manifested at the beginning of time, the divine plan is that man should subdue[125] the earth, bring creation to perfection, and develop himself. When a man so acts he simultaneously obeys the great Christian commandment that he place himself at the service of his brother men.

Furthermore, when a man applies himself to the various disciplines of philosophy, of history, and of mathematical and natural science, and when he cultivates the arts, he can do very much to elevate the human family to a more sublime understanding of truth, goodness, and beauty, and to the formation of judgments which embody universal values. Thus mankind can be more clearly enlightened by that marvelous Wisdom which was with God from all eternity, arranging all things with him, playing upon the earth, delighting in the sons of men.[126]

In this way, the human spirit grows increasingly free of its bondage to creatures and can be more easily drawn to the worship and contemplation of the Creator. Moreover, under the impulse of grace, man is disposed to acknowledge the Word of God. Before he became flesh in order to save all things and to sum them up in himself, "He was in the world" already as "the true light that enlightens every man" (John 1:9–10).[127]

No doubt today's progress in science and technology can foster a certain exclusive emphasis on observable data, and an agnosticism about everything else. For the methods of investigation which these sciences use can be wrongly considered as the supreme rule for discovering the whole truth. By virtue of their methods, however, these sciences cannot penetrate to the intimate meaning of things. Yet the danger exists that man, confiding too much in modern discoveries, may even think that he is sufficient unto himself and no longer seek any higher realities.

These unfortunate results, however, do not necessarily follow from the culture of today, nor should they lead us into the temptation of not acknowledging its positive values. For among its values are these: scientific study and strict fidelity toward truth in scientific research, the necessity of working together with others in technical groups, a sense of international solidarity, an ever clearer awareness of the responsibility of experts to aid men and even to protect them, the desire to make the conditions of life more favorable for all, especially for those who are deprived of the opportunity to exercise responsibility or who are culturally poor.

All of these values can provide some preparation for the acceptance of the message of the gospel—a preparation which can be animated with divine love by him who came to save the world.

The Many Links between the Gospel and Culture

58. There are many links between the message of salvation and human culture. For God, revealing himself to his people to the extent of a full manifestation of himself in his Incarnate Son, has spoken according to the culture proper to different ages.

Living in various circumstances during the course of time, the Church, too, has used in her preaching the discoveries of different cultures to spread and explain the message of Christ to all nations, to probe it and more deeply understand it and to give it better expression in liturgical celebrations and in the life of the diversified community of the faithful.

But at the same time, the Church, sent to all peoples of every time and place, is not bound exclusively and indissolubly to any race or nation, nor to any particular way of life or any customary pattern of living, ancient or recent. Faithful to her own tradition and at the same time conscious of her universal mission, she can enter into communion with various cultural modes, to her own enrichment and theirs too.

The good news of Christ constantly renews the life and culture of fallen man. It combats and removes the errors and evils resulting from sinful allurements which are a perpetual threat. It never ceases to purify and elevate the morality of peoples. By riches coming from above, it makes fruitful, as it were from within, the spiritual qualities and gifts of every people and of every age. It strengthens, perfects, and restores[128] them in Christ. Thus by the very fulfillment of her own mission[129] the Church stimulates and advances human and civic culture. By her action, even in its liturgical form, she leads men toward interior liberty.

Harmony between the Forms of Culture

59. For the aforementioned reasons, the Church recalls to the mind of all that culture must be made to bear on the integral perfection of the human person, and on the good of the community and the whole of society. Therefore the human spirit must be cultivated in such a way that there results a growth in its ability to wonder, to understand, to contemplate, to make personal judgments, and to develop a religious, moral, and social sense.

Because it flows immediately from man's spiritual and social nature, culture has constant need of a just freedom if it is to develop. It also needs the legitimate possibility of exercising its independence according to its own principles. Rightly, therefore, it demands respect and enjoys a certain inviolability, at least as long as the rights of the individual and of the community, whether particular or universal, are preserved within the context of the common good.

This sacred synod, therefore, recalling the teaching of the First Vatican Council, declares that there are "two orders of knowledge" which are distinct, namely, faith and reason. It declares that the Church does not indeed forbid that "when the human arts and sciences are practiced they use their own principles and their proper method, each in its own domain." Hence, "acknowledging this just liberty," this sacred synod affirms the legitimate autonomy of human culture and especially of the sciences.[130]

All these considerations demand too, that, within the limits of morality and the general welfare, a man be free to search for the truth, voice his mind, and publicize it; that he be free to practice any art he chooses; and finally that he have appropriate access to information about public affairs.[131]

It is not the function of public authority to determine what the proper nature of forms of human culture should be. It should rather foster the conditions and the means which are capable of promoting cultural life among all citizens and even within the minorities of a nation.[132] Hence in this matter men must insist above all else that culture be not diverted from its own purpose made to serve political or economic interests.

SECTION 3: SOME ESPECIALLY URGENT DUTIES OF CHRISTIANS WITH REGARD TO CULTURE

Recognizing and Implementing the Right to Culture

60. The possibility now exists of liberating most men from the misery of ignorance. Hence it is a duty most befitting our times that men, especially Christians, should work strenuously on behalf of certain decisions which must be made in the economic and political fields, both nationally and internationally. By these decisions universal recognition and implementation should be given to the right of all men to a human and civic culture favorable to personal dignity and free from any discrimination on the grounds of race, sex, nationality, religious or social conditions.

Therefore it is necessary to provide every man with a sufficient abundance of cultural benefits, especially those which constitute so-called basic culture. Otherwise, because of illiteracy and a lack of responsible activity, very many will be prevented from collaborating in a truly human manner for the sake of the common good.

Efforts must be made to see that men who are capable of higher studies can pursue them. In this way, as far as possible, they can be prepared to undertake in society those duties, offices, and services which are in harmony with their natural aptitude and with the competence they will have acquired.[133] Thus all the individuals and the social groups comprising a given people will be able to attain the full development of their culture, a development in accord with their qualities and traditions.

Energetic efforts must also be expended to make everyone conscious of his right to culture and of the duty he has to develop himself culturally and to assist others. For existing conditions of life and of work sometimes thwart the cultural strivings of men and destroy in them the desire for self-improvement. This is especially true of country people and laborers. They need to be provided with working conditions which will not block their human development but rather favor it.

Women are now employed in almost every area of life. It is appropriate that they should be able to assume their full proper role in accordance with their own nature. Everyone should acknowledge and favor the proper and necessary participation of women in cultural life.

Cultural Education

61. Today it is more difficult than ever for a synthesis to be formed of the various branches of knowledge and the arts. For while the mass and the diversity of cultural factors are increasing, there is a decline in the individual man's ability to grasp and unify these elements. Thus the ideal of "the universal man" is disappearing more and more. Nevertheless, it remains each man's duty to preserve a view of the whole human person, a view in which the values of intellect, will, conscience, and fraternity are preeminent. These values are all rooted in God the Creator and have been wonderfully restored and elevated in Christ.

The family is, as it were, the primary mother and nurse of this attitude. There, in an atmosphere of love, children can more easily learn the true structure of reality. There, too, tested forms of human culture impress themselves upon the mind of the developing adolescent in a kind of automatic way.

Opportunities for the same kind of education can also be found in modern society, thanks especially to the increased circulation of books and to the new means of cultural and social communication. All such opportunities can foster a universal culture.

The widespread reduction in working hours, for instance, brings increasing advantages to numerous people. May these leisure hours be properly used for relaxation of spirit and the strengthening of mental and bodily health. Such benefits are available through spontaneous study and activity and through travel, which refines human qualities and enriches men with mutual understanding. These benefits are obtainable too from physical exercise and sports events, which can help to preserve emotional balance, even at the community level, and to establish fraternal relations among men of all conditions, nations, and races.

Hence let Christians work together to animate the cultural expressions and group activities characteristic of our times with a human and a Christian spirit.

All these benefits, however, cannot educate men to a full self-development unless at the same time deep thought is given to what culture and science mean in terms of the human person.

Harmony between Culture and Christian Formation

62. Although the Church has contributed much to the development of culture, experience shows that, because of circumstances, it is sometimes difficult to harmonize culture with Christian teaching.

These difficulties do not necessarily harm the life of faith. Indeed they can stimulate the mind to a more accurate and penetrating grasp of the faith. For recent studies and findings of science, history, and philosophy raise new questions which influence life and demand new theological investigations.

Furthermore, while adhering to the methods and requirements proper to theology, theologians are invited to seek continually for more suitable ways of communicating doctrine to the men of their times. For the deposit of faith or revealed truths are one thing; the manner in which they are formulated without violence to their meaning and significance is another.[134]

In pastoral care, appropriate use must be made not only of theological principles, but also of the findings of the secular sciences, especially of psychology and sociology. Thus the faithful can be brought to live the faith in a more thorough and mature way.

Literature and the arts are also, in their own way, of great importance to the life of the Church. For they strive to probe the unique nature of man, his problems, and his experiences as he struggles to know and perfect both himself and the world. They are preoccupied with revealing man's place in history and in the world, with illustrating his miseries and joys, his needs and strengths, and with foreshadowing a better life for him. Thus they are able to elevate human life as it is expressed in manifold forms, depending on time and place.

Efforts must therefore be made so that those who practice these arts can feel that the Church gives recognition to them in their activities, and so that, enjoying an orderly freedom, they can establish smoother relations with the Christian community. Let the Church also acknowledge new forms of art which are adapted to our age and are in keeping with the characteristics of various nations and regions. Adjusted in their mode of expression and conformed to liturgical requirements, they may be introduced into the sanctuary when they raise the mind to God.[135]

In this way the knowledge of God can be better revealed. Also, the preaching of the gospel can become clearer to man's mind and show its relevance to the conditions of human life.

May the faithful, therefore, live in very close union with the men of their time. Let them strive to understand perfectly their way of thinking and feeling, as expressed in their culture. Let them blend modern science and its theories and the understanding of the most recent discoveries with Christian morality and doctrine. Thus their religious practice and morality can keep pace with their scientific knowledge and with an ever-advancing technology. Thus too they will be able to test and interpret all things in a truly Christian spirit.

Through a sharing of resources and points of view, let those who teach in seminaries, colleges, and universities try to collaborate with men well versed in the other sciences. Theological inquiry should seek a profound understanding of revealed truth without neglecting close contact with its own times. As a result, it will be able to help those men skilled in various fields of knowledge to gain a better understanding of the faith.

This common effort will very greatly aid in the formation of priests. It will enable them to present to our contemporaries the doctrine of the Church concerning God, man, and the world in a manner better suited to them, with the result that they will receive it more willingly.[136] Furthermore, it is to be hoped that many laymen will receive an appropriate formation in the sacred sciences, and that some will develop and deepen these studies by their own labors. In order that such persons may fulfill their proper function, let it be recognized that all the faithful, clerical and lay, possess a lawful freedom of inquiry and of thought, and the freedom to express their minds humbly and courageously about those matters in which they enjoy competence.[137]

Chapter 3: Socioeconomic Life

Some Aspects of Economic Life

63. In the socioeconomic realm, too, the dignity and total vocation of the human person must be honored and advanced along with the welfare of society as a whole. For man is the source, the center, and the purpose of all socioeconomic life.

As in other areas of social life, modern economy is marked by man's increasing domination over nature, by closer and more intense relationships between citizens, groups, and countries and by their mutual dependence, and by more frequent intervention on the part of government. At the same time progress in the methods of production and in the exchange of goods and services has made the economy an apt instrument for meeting the intensified needs of the human family more successfully.

Reasons for anxiety, however, are not lacking. Many people, especially in economically advanced areas, seem to be hypnotized, as it were, by economics, so that almost their entire personal and social life is permeated with a certain economic outlook. These people can be found both in nations which favor a collective economy as well as in others.

Again, we are at a moment in history when the development of economic life could diminish social inequalities if that development were guided and coordinated in a reasonable and human way. Yet all too often it serves only to intensify the inequalities. In some places it even results in a decline in the social status of the weak and in contempt for the poor.

While an enormous mass of people still lacks the absolute necessities of life, some, even in less advanced countries, live sumptuously or squander wealth. Luxury and misery rub shoulders. While the few enjoy very great freedom of choice, the many are deprived of almost all possibility of acting on their own initiative and responsibility, and often subsist in living and working conditions unworthy of human beings.

A similar lack of economic and social balance is to be noted between agriculture, industry, and the services, and also between different parts of one and the same country. The contrast between the economically more advanced countries and other countries is becoming more serious day by day, and the very peace of the world can be jeopardized in consequence.

Our contemporaries are coming to feel these inequalities with an ever-sharper awareness. For they are thoroughly convinced that the wider technical and economic potential which the modern world enjoys can and should correct this unhappy state of affairs. Hence, numerous reforms are needed at the socioeconomic level, along with universal changes in ideas and attitudes.

Now in this area the Church maintains certain principles of justice and equity as they apply to individuals, societies, and international relations. In the course of the centuries and with the light of the gospel she has worked out these principles as right reason demanded. In modern times especially, the Church has enlarged upon them. This sacred Council wishes to reinforce these principles according to the circumstances of the times and to set forth certain guidelines, primarily with regard to the requirements of economic development.[138]

SECTION 1: ECONOMIC DEVELOPMENT

In the Service of Man

64. Today, more than ever before, progress in the production of agricultural and industrial goods and in the rendering of services is rightly aimed at making provision for the growth of a people and at meeting the rising expectations of the human race. Therefore, technical progress must be fostered, along with a spirit of initiative, an eagerness to create and expand enterprises, the adaptation of methods of production—in a word, all the elements making for such development.

The fundamental purpose of this productivity must not be the mere multiplication of products. It must not be profit or domination. Rather, it must be the service of man, and indeed of the whole man, viewed in terms of his material needs and the demands of his intellectual, moral, spiritual, and religious life. And when we say man, we mean every man whatsoever and every group of men, of whatever race and from whatever part of the world. Consequently, economic activity is to be carried out according to its own methods and laws but within the limits of morality,[139] so that God's plan for mankind can be realized.[140]

Under Man's Control

65. Economic development must be kept under the control of mankind. It must not be left to the sole judgment of a few men or groups possessing excessive economic power, or of the political community alone, or of certain especially powerful nations. It is proper, on the contrary, that at every level the largest possible number of people have an active share in directing that development. When it is a question of international developments, all nations should so participate. It is also necessary for the spontaneous activities of individuals and of independent groups to be coordinated with the efforts of pub-

lic authorities. These activities and these efforts should be aptly and harmoniously interwoven.

Growth must not be allowed merely to follow a kind of automatic course resulting from the economic activity of individuals. Nor must it be entrusted solely to the authority of government. Hence, theories which obstruct the necessary reforms in the name of a false liberty must be branded as erroneous. The same is true of those theories which subordinate the basic rights of individual persons and groups to the collective organization of production.[141]

Citizens, for their part, should remember that they have the right and the duty, which must be recognized by civil authority, to contribute according to their ability to the true progress of their own community. Especially in underdeveloped areas, where all resources must be put to urgent use, those men gravely endanger the public good who allow their resources to remain unproductive or who deprive their community of the material and spiritual aid it needs. The personal right of migration, however, is not to be impugned.

Removing Huge Differences

66. If the demands of justice and equity are to be satisfied, vigorous efforts must be made, without violence to the rights of persons or to the natural characteristics of each country, to remove as quickly as possible the immense economic inequalities which now exist. In many cases, these are worsening and are connected with individual and group discrimination.

In many areas, too, farmers experience special difficulties in raising products or in selling them. In such cases, country people must be helped to increase and to market what they produce, to make the necessary advances and changes, and to obtain a fair return. Otherwise, as too often happens, they will remain in the condition of lower-class citizens. Let farmers, especially young ones, skillfully apply themselves to perfecting their professional competence. Without it, no agricultural progress can take place.[142]

Justice and equity likewise require that the mobility which is necessary in a developing economy be regulated in such a way as to keep the life of individuals and their families from becoming insecure and precarious. Hence, when workers come from another country or district and contribute by their labor to the economic advancement of a nation or region, all discrimination with respect to wages and working conditions must be carefully avoided.

The local people, moreover, especially public authorities, should all treat them not as mere tools of production but as persons, and must help them to arrange for their families to live with them and to provide themselves with decent living quarters. The native should also see that these workers are introduced into the social life of the country or region which receives them. Employment opportunities, however, should be created in their own areas as far as possible.

In those economic affairs which are today subject to change, as in the new forms of industrial society in which automation, for example, is advancing, care must be taken that sufficient and suitable work can be obtained, along with appropriate technical and professional formation. The livelihood and the human dignity of those especially who are in particularly difficult circumstances because of illness or old age should be safeguarded.

SECTION 2: CERTAIN PRINCIPLES GOVERNING SOCIOECONOMIC LIFE AS A WHOLE

Labor and Leisure

67. Human labor which is expended in the production and exchange of goods or in the performance of economic services is superior to the other elements of economic life. For the latter have only the nature of tools.

Whether it is engaged in independently or paid for by someone else, this labor comes immediately from the person. In a sense, the person stamps the things of nature with his seal and subdues them to his will. It is ordinarily by his labor that a man supports himself and his family, is joined to his fellow men and serves them, and is enabled to exercise genuine charity and be a partner in the work of bringing God's creation to perfection. Indeed, we hold that by offering his labor to God a man becomes associated with the redemptive work itself of Jesus Christ, who conferred an eminent dignity on labor when at Nazareth he worked with his own hands.

From all these considerations there arise every man's duty to labor faithfully and also his right to work. It is the duty of society, moreover, according to the circumstances prevailing in it, and in keeping with its proper role, to help its citizens find opportunities for adequate employment. Finally, payment for labor must be such as to furnish a man with the means to cultivate his own material, social, cultural, and spiritual life worthily, and that of his dependents. What this payment should be will vary according to each man's assignment and productivity, the conditions of his place of employment, and the common good.[143]

Since economic activity is generally exercised through the combined labors of human beings, any way of organizing and directing that activity which would be detrimental to any worker would be wrong and inhuman. It too often happens, however, even in our day, that in one way or another workers are made slaves of their work. This situation can by no means be justified by so-called economic laws. The entire process of productive work, therefore, must be adapted to the needs of the person and to the requirements of his life, above all his domestic life. Such is especially the case with respect to mothers of families, but due consideration must be given to every person's sex and age.

The opportunity should also be afforded to workers to develop their own abilities and personalities through the work they perform. Though they should apply their time and energy to their employment with a due sense of responsibility, all workers should also enjoy sufficient rest and leisure to cultivate their family, cultural, social, and religious life. They should also have the opportunity to develop on their own the resources and potentialities to which, perhaps, their professional work gives but little scope.

Economic Participation and Conflict

68. In economic enterprises it is persons who work together, that is, free and independent human beings created to the image of God. Therefore the active participation of everyone in the running of an enterprise should be promoted.[144] This participation should be exercised in appropriately determined ways. It should take into account each person's function, whether it be one of ownership, hiring, management, or labor. It should provide for the necessary unity of operations.

However, decisions concerning economic and social conditions, on which the future of the workers and their children depends, are rather often made not within the enterprise itself but by institutions on a higher level. Hence the workers themselves should have a share also in controlling these institutions, either in person or through freely elected delegates.

Among the basic rights of the human person must be counted the right of freely founding labor unions. These unions should be truly able to represent the workers and to contribute to the proper arrangement of economic life. Another such right is that of taking part freely in the activity of these unions without risk of reprisal. Through this sort of orderly participation, joined with an ongoing formation in economic and social matters, all will grow day by day in the awareness of their own function and responsibility. Thus they will be brought to feel that according to their own proper capacities and aptitudes they are associates in the whole task of economic and social development and in the attainment of the universal common good.

When, however, socioeconomic disputes arise, efforts must be made to come to a peaceful settlement. Recourse must always be had above all to sincere discussion between the parties. Even in present-day circumstances, however, the strike can still be a necessary, though ultimate, means for the defense of the workers' own rights and the fulfillment of their just demands. As soon as possible, however, ways should be sought to resume negotiations and the discussion of reconciliation.

The Common Purpose of Created Things

69. God intended the earth and all that it contains for the use of every human being and people. Thus, as all men follow justice and unite in charity, created good should abound for them on a reasonable basis.[145] Whatever the forms of ownership may be, as adapted to the legitimate institutions of people according to diverse and changeable circumstances, attention must always be paid to the universal purpose for which created goods are meant. In using them, therefore, a man should regard his lawful possessions not merely as his own but also as common property in the sense that they should accrue to the benefit of not only himself but of others.[146]

For the rest, the right to have a share of earthly goods sufficient for oneself and one's family belongs to everyone. The Fathers and Doctors of the Church held this view, teaching that men are obliged to come to the relief of the poor, and to do so not merely out of their superfluous goods.[147] If a person is in extreme necessity, he has the right to take from the riches of others what he himself needs.[148] Since there are so many people in this world afflicted with hunger, this sacred Council urges all, both individuals and governments, to remember the saying of the Fathers: "Feed the man dying of hunger, because if you have not fed him you have killed him."[149] According to their ability, let all individuals and governments undertake a genuine sharing of their goods. Let them use these goods especially to provide individuals and nations with the means for helping and developing themselves.

In economically less advanced societies, it is not rare for the communal purpose of earthly goods to be partially satisfied through the customs and traditions proper to a community. By such means the absolute essentials are furnished to each member. If, however, customs cannot answer the new needs of this age, an effort must be made to avoid regarding them as altogether unchangeable. At the same time, rash action should not be taken against worthy customs which, provided that they are suitably adapted to present-day circumstances, do not cease to be very useful.

Similarly, in highly developed nations a body of social institutions dealing with insurance and security can, for its part, make the common purpose of earthly goods effective. Family and social services, especially those which provide for culture and education, should be further promoted. Still, care must be taken lest, as a result of all these provisions, the citizenry fall into a kind of sluggishness toward society, and reject the burdens of office and of public service.

Distribution and Money

70. The distribution of goods should be directed toward providing employment and sufficient income for the people of today and of the future. Whether individuals, groups, or public authorities make the decisions concerning this distribution and the planning of the economy, they are bound to keep these objectives in mind. They must realize their serious obligation of seeing to it that provision is made for the necessities of a decent life on the part of individuals and of the whole community. They must also look out for the future and establish a proper balance between the needs of present-day consumption, both individual and collective, and the necessity of distributing goods on behalf of the coming generation. They should also bear constantly in mind the urgent needs of underdeveloped countries and regions. In financial transactions they should beware of hurting the welfare of their own country or of other countries. Care should also be taken lest the economically weak countries unjustly suffer loss from a change in the value of money.

Ownership and Property

71. Ownership and other forms of private control over material goods contribute to the expression of personality. Moreover, they furnish men with an occasion for exercising their role in society and in the economy. Hence it is very important to facilitate the access of both individuals and communities to some control over material goods.

Private ownership or some other kind of dominion over material goods provides everyone with a wholly necessary area of independence, and should be regarded as an extension of human freedom. Finally since it adds incentives for carrying on one's function and duty, it constitutes a kind of prerequisite for civil liberties.[150]

The forms of such dominion or ownership are varied today and are becoming increasingly diversified. They all remain a source of security not to be underestimated, even in the face of the public funds, rights, and services provided by society. This is true not only of material goods but also of intangible goods, such as professional skills.

The right of private control, however, is not opposed to the right inherent in various forms of public ownership. Still, goods can be transferred to the public domain only by the competent authority, according to the demands and within the limits of the common good, and with fair compensation. It is a further right of public authority to guard against any misuse of private property which injures the common good.[151]

By its very nature, private property has a social quality deriving from the law of the communal purpose of earthly goods.[152] If this social quality is overlooked, property often becomes an occasion of greed and of serious disturbances. Thus, to those who attack the concept of private property, a pretext is given for calling the right itself into question.

In many underdeveloped areas there are large or even gigantic rural estates which are only moderately cultivated or lie completely idle for the sake of profit. At the same time the majority of the people are either without land or have only very small holdings, and there is evident and urgent need to increase land productivity.

It is not rare for those who are hired to work for the landowners, or who till a portion of the land as tenants, to receive a wage or income unworthy of human beings, to lack decent housing, and to be exploited by middlemen. Deprived of all security, they live under such personal servitude that almost every opportunity for acting on their own initiative and responsibility is denied to them, and all advancement in human culture and all sharing in social and political life are ruled out.

Depending on circumstances, therefore, reforms must be instituted if income is to grow, working conditions improve, job security increase, and an incentive to working on one's own initiative be provided. Indeed, insufficiently cultivated estates should be distributed to those who can make these lands fruitful. In this case, the necessary ways and means, especially educational aids and the right facilities for cooperative organization, must be supplied. Still, whenever the common good requires expropriation, compensation must be reckoned in equity after all the circumstances have been weighed.

Economics and Christ's Kingdom

72. Christians who take an active part in modern socioeconomic development and defend justice and charity should be convinced that they can make a great contribution to the prosperity of mankind and the peace of the world. Whether they do so as individuals or in association, let their example be a shining one. After acquiring whatever skills and experience are absolutely necessary, they should in faithfulness to Christ and his gospel observe the right order of values in their earthly activities. Thus their whole lives, both individual and social, will be permeated with the spirit of the beatitudes, notably with the spirit of poverty.

Whoever in obedience to Christ seeks first the kingdom of God will as a consequence receive a stronger and purer love for helping all his brothers and for perfecting the work of justice under the inspiration of charity.[153]

Chapter 4: The Life of the Political Community

Modern Politics

73. Our times have witnessed profound changes too in the institutions of peoples and in the ways that peoples are joined together. These changes are resulting from the cultural, economic, and social evolution of these same peoples. The changes are having a great impact on the life of the political community, especially with regard to universal rights and duties both in the exercise of civil liberty and in the attainment of the common good, and with regard to the regulation of the relations of citizens among themselves, and with public authority.

From a keener awareness of human dignity there arises in many parts of the world a desire to establish a political-juridical order in which personal rights can gain better protection. These include the rights of free assembly, of common action, of expressing personal opinions, and of professing a religion both privately and publicly. For the protection of personal rights is a necessary condition for the active participation of citizens, whether as individuals or collectively, in the life and government of the state.

Among numerous people, cultural, economic, and social progress has been accompanied by the desire to assume a larger role in organizing the life of the political community. In many consciences there is a growing intent that the rights of national minorities be honored while at the same time these minorities honor their duties toward the political community. In addition men are learning more every day to respect the opinions and religious beliefs of others. At the same time a broader spirit of cooperation is taking hold. Thus all citizens, and not just a privileged few, are actually able to enjoy personal rights.

Men are voicing disapproval of any kind of government which blocks civil or religious liberty, multiplies the victims of ambition and political crimes, and wrenches the exercise of authority from pursuing the common good to serving the advantage of a certain faction or of the rulers themselves. There are some such governments holding power in the world.

No better way exists for attaining a truly human political life than by fostering an inner sense of justice, benevolence, and service for the common good, and by strengthening basic beliefs about the true nature of the political community, and about the proper exercise and limits of public authority.

Nature and Goal of Politics

74. Individuals, families, and various groups which compose the civic community are aware of their own insufficiency in the matter of establishing a fully human condition of life. They see the need for that wider community in which each would daily contribute his energies toward the ever better attainment of the common good.[154] It is for this reason that they set up the political community in its manifold expressions.

Hence the political community exists for that common good in which the community finds its full justification and meaning, and from which it derives its pristine and proper right. Now, the common good embraces the sum of those conditions of social life by which individuals, families, and groups can achieve their own fulfillment in a relatively thorough and ready way.[155]

Many different people go to make up the political community, and these can lawfully incline toward diverse ways of doing things. Now, if the political community is not to be torn to pieces as each man follows his own viewpoint, authority is needed. This authority must dispose the energies of the whole citizenry toward the common good, not mechanically or despotically, but primarily as a moral force which depends on freedom and the conscientious discharge of the burdens of any office which has been undertaken.

It is therefore obvious that the political community and public authority are based on human nature and hence belong to an order of things divinely foreordained. At the same time the choice of government and the method of selecting leaders are left to the free will of citizens.[156]

It also follows that political authority, whether in the community as such or in institutions representing the state, must always be exercised within the limits of morality and on behalf of the dynamically conceived common good, according to a juridical order enjoying legal status. When such is the case citizens are conscience-bound to obey.[157] This fact clearly reveals the responsibility, dignity, and importance of those who govern.

Where public authority oversteps its competence and oppresses the people, these people should nevertheless obey to the extent that the objective common good demands. Still it is lawful for them to defend their own rights and those of their fellow citizens against any abuse of this authority, provided that in so doing they observe the limits imposed by natural law and the gospel.

The practical ways in which the political community structures itself and regulates public authority can vary according to the particular character of a people and its historical development. But these methods should always serve to mold men who are civilized, peace-loving, and well disposed toward all—to the advantage of the whole human family.

Political Participation

75. It is in full accord with human nature that juridical-political structures should, with ever better success and without any discrimination, afford all their citizens the chance to participate freely and actively in establishing the constitutional bases of a political community, governing the state, determining the scope and purpose of various institutions, and choosing leaders.[158] Hence let all citizens be mindful of their simultaneous right and duty to vote freely in the interest of advancing the common good. The Church regards as worthy of praise and consideration the work of those who, as a service to others, dedicate themselves to the welfare of the state and undertake the burdens of this task.

If conscientious cooperation between citizens is to achieve its happy effect in the normal course of public affairs, a positive system of law is required. In it should be established a division of governmental roles and institutions and, at the same time, an effective and independent system for the protection of rights. Let the rights of all persons, families, and associations, along with the exercise of those rights, be recognized, honored, and fostered.[159] The same holds for those duties which bind all citizens. Among the latter should be remembered that of furnishing the commonwealth with the material and spiritual services required for the common good.

Authorities must beware of hindering family, social, or cultural groups, as well as intermediate bodies and institutions. They must not deprive them of their own lawful and effective activity, but should rather strive to promote them willingly and in an orderly fashion. For their part, citizens both as individuals and in association should be on guard against granting government too much authority and inappropriately seeking from it excessive conveniences and advantages, with a consequent weakening of the sense of responsibility on the part of individuals, families, and social groups.

Because of the increased complexity of modern circumstances, government is more often required to intervene in social and economic affairs, by way of bringing about conditions more likely to help citizens and groups freely attain to complete human fulfillment with greater effect. The proper relationship between socialization[160] on the one hand and personal independence and development on the other can be variously interpreted according to the locales in question and the degree of progress achieved by a given people.

When the exercise of rights is temporarily curtailed on behalf of the common good, it should be restored as quickly as possible after the emergency passes. In any case it harms humanity when government takes on totalitarian or dictatorial forms injurious to the rights of persons or social groups.

Citizens should develop a generous and loyal devotion to their country, but without any narrowing of mind. In other words, they must always look simultaneously to the welfare of the whole human family, which is tied together by the manifold bonds linking races, peoples, and nations.

Let all Christians appreciate their special and personal vocation in the political community. This vocation requires that they give conspicuous example of devotion to the sense of duty and of service to the advancement of the common good. Thus they can also show in practice how authority is to be harmonized with freedom, personal initiative with consideration for the bonds uniting the whole social body, and necessary unity with beneficial diversity.

Christians should recognize that various legitimate though conflicting views can be held concerning the regulation of temporal affairs. They should respect their fellow citizens when they promote such views honorably even by group action. Political parties should foster whatever they judge necessary for the common good. But they should never prefer their own advantage over this same common good.

Civic and political education is today supremely necessary for the people, especially young people. Such education should be painstakingly provided, so that all citizens can make their contribution to the political community. Let those who are suited for it, or can become so, prepare themselves for the difficult but most honorable art of politics.[161] Let them work to exercise this art without thought of personal convenience and without benefit of bribery. Prudently and honorably let them fight against injustice and oppression, the arbitrary rule of one man or one party, and lack of tolerance. Let them devote themselves to the welfare of all sincerely and fairly, indeed with charity and political courage.

Politics and the Church

76. It is highly important, especially in pluralistic societies, that a proper view exist of the relation between the political community and the Church. Thus the faithful will be able to make a clear distinction between what a Christian conscience leads them to do in their own name as citizens, whether as individuals or in association, and what they do in the name of the Church and in union with her shepherds.

The role and competence of the Church being what it is, she must in no way be confused with the political community, nor bound to any political system. For she is at once a sign and a safeguard of the transcendence of the human person.

In their proper spheres, the political community and the Church are mutually independent and self-governing. Yet, by a different title, each serves the personal and social vocation of the same human beings. This service can be more effectively rendered for the good of all, if each works better for wholesome mutual cooperation, depending on the circumstances of time and place. For man is not restricted to the temporal sphere. While living in history he fully maintains his eternal vocation.

The Church, founded on the Redeemer's love, contributes to the wider application of justice and charity within and between nations. By preaching the truth of the gospel and shedding light on all areas of human activity through her teaching and the example of the faithful, she shows respect for the political freedom and responsibility of citizens and fosters these values.

The apostles, their successors, and those who assist these successors have been sent to announce to men Christ, the Savior of the world. Hence in the exercise of their apostolate they must depend on the power of God, who very often reveals the might of the gospel through the weakness of its witnesses. For those who dedicate themselves to the ministry of God's Word should use means and helps proper to the gospel. In many respects these differ from the supports of the earthly city.

There are, indeed, close links between earthly affairs and those aspects of man's condition which transcend this world. The Church herself employs the things of time to the degree that her own proper mission demands. Still she does not lodge her hope in privileges conferred by civil authority. Indeed, she stands ready to renounce the exercise of certain legitimately acquired rights if it becomes clear that their use raises doubt about the sincerity of her witness or that new conditions of life demand some other arrangement.

But it is always and everywhere legitimate for her to preach the faith with true freedom, to teach her social doctrine, and to discharge her duty among men without hindrance. She also has the right to pass moral judgments, even on matters touching the political order, whenever basic personal rights or the salvation of souls make such judgments necessary. In so doing, she may use only those helps which accord with the gospel and with the general welfare as it changes according to time and circumstance.

Holding faithfully to the gospel and exercising her mission in the world, the Church consolidates peace among men, to God's glory.[162] For it is her task to uncover, cherish, and ennoble[163] all that is true, good, and beautiful in the human community.

Chapter 5: The Fostering of Peace and the Promotion of a Community of Nations

Introduction

77. In our generation, when men continue to be afflicted by acute hardships and anxieties arising from ongoing wars or the threat of them, the whole human family has reached an hour of supreme crisis in its advance toward maturity. Moving gradually together and everywhere more conscious already of its oneness, this family cannot accomplish its task of constructing for all men everywhere a world more genuinely human unless each person devotes himself with renewed determination to the reality of peace. Thus it happens that the gospel message, which is in harmony with the loftier strivings and aspirations of the human race, takes on a new luster in our days as it declares

that the artisans of peace are blessed, "for they shall be called children of God" (Matt. 5:9).

Consequently, as it points out the authentic and most noble meaning of peace and condemns the frightfulness of war, this Council fervently desires to summon Christians to cooperate with all men in making secure among themselves a peace based on justice and love, and in setting up agencies of peace. This Christians should do with the help of Christ, the Author of peace.

The Nature of Peace

78. Peace is not merely the absence of war. Nor can it be reduced solely to the maintenance of a balance of power between enemies. Nor is it brought about by dictatorship. Instead, it is rightly and appropriately called "an enterprise of justice" (Isa. 32:7). Peace results from that harmony built into human society by its divine Founder, and actualized by men as they thirst after ever greater justice.

The common good of men is in its basic sense determined by the eternal law. Still the concrete demands of this common good are constantly changing as time goes on. Hence peace is never attained once and for all, but must be built up ceaselessly. Moreover, since the human will is unsteady and wounded by sin, the achievement of peace requires that everyone constantly master his passions and that lawful authority keep vigilant.

But such is not enough. This peace cannot be obtained on earth unless personal values are safeguarded and men freely and trustingly share with one another the riches of their inner spirits and their talents. A firm determination to respect other men and peoples and their dignity, as well as the studied practice of brotherhood, are absolutely necessary for the establishment of peace. Hence peace is likewise the fruit of love, which goes beyond what justice can provide.

That earthly peace which arises from love of neighbor symbolizes and results from the peace of Christ, who comes forth from God the Father. For by his cross the Incarnate Son, the Prince of Peace, reconciled all men with God. By thus restoring the unity of all men in one people and one body, he slew hatred in his own flesh.[164] After being lifted on high by his resurrection, he poured the Spirit of love into the hearts of men.

For this reason, all Christians are urgently summoned "to practice the truth in love" (Eph. 4:15) and to join with all true peacemakers in pleading for peace and bringing it about.

Motivated by this same spirit, we cannot fail to praise those who renounce the use of violence in the vindication of their rights and who resort to methods of defense which are otherwise available to weaker parties too, provided that this can be done without injury to the rights and duties of others or of the community itself.

Insofar as men are sinful, the threat of war hangs over them, and hang over them it will until the return of Christ. But to the extent that men vanquish sin by a union of love, they will vanquish violence as well, and make these words come true: "They shall beat their swords into plowshares and their spears into pruning hooks; one nation shall not raise the sword against another, nor shall they train for war again" (Isa. 2:4).

SECTION 1: THE AVOIDANCE OF WAR

Curbing the Savagery of War

79. In spite of the fact that recent wars have wrought physical and moral havoc on our world, conflicts still produce their devastating effect day by day somewhere in the world. Indeed, now that every kind of weapon produced by modern science is used in war, the fierce character of warfare threatens to lead the combatants to a savagery far surpassing that of the past. Furthermore, the complexity of the modern world and the intricacy of international relations allow guerrilla warfare to be drawn out by new methods of deceit and subversion. In many cases the use of terrorism is regarded as a new way to wage war.

Contemplating this melancholy state of humanity, the Council wishes to recall first of all the permanent binding force of universal natural law and its all-embracing principles. Man's conscience itself gives ever more emphatic voice to these principles. Therefore, actions which deliberately conflict with these same principles, as well as orders commanding such actions, are criminal. Blind obedience cannot excuse those who yield to them. Among such must first be counted those actions designed for the methodical extermination of an entire people, nation, or ethnic minority. These actions must be vehemently condemned as horrendous crimes. The courage of those who openly and fearlessly resist men who issue such commands merits supreme commendation.

On the subject of war, quite a large number of nations have subscribed to various international agreements aimed at making military activity and its consequences less inhuman. Such are conventions concerning the handling of wounded or captured soldiers, and various similar agreements. Agreements of this sort must be honored. Indeed they should be improved upon so that they can better and more workably lead to restraining the frightfulness of war.

All men, especially government officials and experts in these matters, are bound to do everything they can to effect these improvements. Moreover, it seems right that laws make humane provisions for the case of those who for reasons of conscience refuse to bear arms, provided, however, that they accept some other form of service to the human community.

Certainly, war has not been rooted out of human affairs. As long as the danger of war remains and there is no competent and sufficiently powerful authority at the international level, governments cannot be denied the right to legitimate defense once every means of peaceful settlement has been exhausted. Therefore, government authorities and others who share public responsibility have the duty to protect the welfare of the people entrusted to their care and to conduct such grave matters soberly.

But it is one thing to undertake military action for the just defense of the people, and something else again to seek the subjugation of other nations. Nor does the possession of war potential make every military or political use of it lawful. Neither does the mere fact that war has unhappily begun mean that all is fair between the warring parties.

Those who are pledged to the service of their country as members of its armed forces should regard themselves as agents of security and freedom on behalf of their people. As long as they fulfill this role properly, they are making a genuine contribution to the establishment of peace.

Total War

80. The horror and perversity of war are immensely magnified by the multiplication of scientific weapons. For acts of war involving these weapons can inflict massive and indiscriminate destruction far exceeding the bounds of legitimate defense. Indeed, if the kind of instruments which can now be found in the armories of the great nations were to be employed to their fullest, an almost total and altogether reciprocal slaughter of each side by the other would follow, not to mention the widespread devastation which would take place in the world and the deadly aftereffects which would be spawned by the use of such weapons.

All these considerations compel us to undertake an evaluation of war with an entirely new attitude.[165] The men of our time must realize that they will have to give a somber reckoning for their deeds of war. For the course of the future will depend largely on the decisions they make today.

With these truths in mind, this most holy synod makes its own the condemnations of total war already pronounced by recent popes,[166] and issues the following declaration:

Any act of war aimed indiscriminately at the destruction of entire cities or of extensive areas along with their population is a crime against God and man himself. It merits unequivocal and unhesitating condemnation.

The unique hazard of modern warfare consists in this: it provides those who possess modern scientific weapons with a kind of occasion for perpetrating just such abominations. Moreover, through a certain inexorable chain of events, it can urge men on to the most atrocious decisions. That such in fact may never happen in the future, the bishops of the whole world, in unity assembled, beg all men, especially government officials and military leaders, to give unremitting thought to the awesome responsibility which is theirs before God and the entire human race.

The Arms Race

81. Scientific weapons, to be sure, are not amassed solely for use in war. The defensive strength of any nation is considered to be dependent upon its

capacity for immediate retaliation against an adversary. Hence this accumulation of arms, which increases each year, also serves, in a way heretofore unknown, as a deterrent to possible enemy attack. Many regard this state of affairs as the most effective way by which peace of a sort can be maintained between nations at the present time.

Whatever be the case with this method of deterrence, men should be convinced that the arms race in which so many countries are engaged is not a safe way to preserve a steady peace. Nor is the so-called balance resulting from this race a sure and authentic peace. Rather than being eliminated thereby, the causes of war threaten to grow gradually stronger.

While extravagant sums are being spent for the furnishing of ever new weapons, an adequate remedy cannot be provided for the multiple miseries afflicting the whole modern world. Disagreements between nations are not really and radically healed. On the contrary other parts of the world are infected with them. New approaches initiated by reformed attitudes must be adopted to remove this trap and to restore genuine peace by emancipating the world from its crushing anxiety.

Therefore, it must be said again: the arms race is an utterly treacherous trap for humanity, and one which injures the poor to an intolerable degree. It is much to be feared that if this race persists, it will eventually spawn all the lethal ruin whose path it is now making ready.

Warned by the calamities which the human race has made possible, let us make use of the interlude granted us from above and in which we rejoice. In greater awareness of our own responsibility let us find means for resolving our disputes in a manner more worthy of man. Divine Providence urgently demands of us that we free ourselves from the age-old slavery of war. But if we refuse to make this effort, we do not know where the evil road we have ventured upon will lead us.

The Total Banning of War, and International Action for Avoiding War

82. It is our clear duty, then, to strain every muscle as we work for the time when all war can be completely outlawed by international consent. This goal undoubtedly requires the establishment of some universal public authority acknowledged as such by all, and endowed with effective power to safeguard, on the behalf of all, security, regard for justice, and respect for rights.

But before this hoped-for authority can be set up, the highest existing international centers must devote themselves vigorously to the pursuit of better means for obtaining common security. Peace must be born of mutual trust between nations rather than imposed on them through fear of one another's weapons. Hence everyone must labor to put an end at last to the arms race, and to make a true beginning of disarmament, not indeed a unilateral disarmament, but one proceeding at an equal pace according to agreement, and backed up by authentic and workable safeguards.[167]

In the meantime, efforts which have already been made and are still under way to eliminate the danger of war are not to be underrated. On the contrary, support should be given to the good will of the very many leaders who work hard to do away with war, which they abominate. Though burdened by the enormous preoccupations of their high office, these men are nonetheless motivated by the very grave peacemaking task to which they are bound, even if they cannot ignore the complexity of matters as they stand.

We should fervently ask God to give these men the strength to go forward perseveringly and to follow through courageously on this work of building peace with vigor. It is a work of supreme love for mankind. Today it most certainly demands that these leaders extend their thoughts and their spirit beyond the confines of their own nation, that they put aside national selfishness and ambition to dominate other nations, and that they nourish a profound reverence for the whole of humanity, which is already making its way so laboriously toward greater unity.

The problems of peace and of disarmament have already been the subject of extensive, strenuous, and relentless examination. Together with international meetings dealing with these problems, such studies should be regarded as the first steps toward solving these serious questions. They should be promoted with even greater urgency in the hope that they will yield practical results in the future.

Nevertheless, men should take heed not to entrust themselves only to the efforts of others, while remaining careless about their own attitudes. For government officials, who must simultaneously guarantee the good of their own people and promote the universal good, depend on public opinion and feeling to the greatest possible extent. It does them no good to work at building peace so long as feelings of hostility, contempt, and distrust, as well as racial hatred and unbending ideologies, continue to divide men and place them in opposing camps.

Hence arises a surpassing need for renewed education of attitudes and for new inspiration in the area of public opinion. Those who are dedicated to the work of education, particularly of the young, or who mold public opinion, should regard as their most weighty task the effort to instruct all in fresh sentiments of peace. Indeed, every one of us should have a change of heart as we regard the entire world and those tasks which we can perform in unison for the betterment of our race.

But we should not let false hope deceive us. For enmities and hatred must be put away and firm, honest agreements concerning world peace reached in the future. Otherwise, for all its marvelous knowledge, humanity, which is already in the middle of a grave crisis, will perhaps be brought to that mournful hour in which it will experience no peace other than the dreadful peace of death.

But, while we say this, the Church of Christ takes her stand in the midst of the anxiety of this age, and does not cease to hope with the utmost confidence. She intends to propose to our age over and over again, in season and out of season, this apostolic message: "Behold, now is the acceptable time" for a change of heart; "behold, now is the day of salvation!"[168]

SECTION 2: BUILDING UP THE INTERNATIONAL COMMUNITY

The Causes and Cures of Discord

83. If peace is to be established, the primary requisite is to eradicate the causes of dissension between men. Wars thrive on these, especially on injustice. Many of these causes stem from excessive economic inequalities and from excessive slowness in applying the needed remedies. Other causes spring from a quest for power and from contempt for personal rights. If we are looking for deeper explanations, we can find them in human jealousy, distrust, pride, and other egotistic passions.

Man cannot tolerate so many breakdowns in right order. What results is that the world is ceaselessly infected with arguments between men and acts of violence, even when war is not raging. Moreover, these same evils are found in relationships between nations. Hence, if such evils are to be overcome or prevented, and violence kept from becoming unbridled, it is altogether necessary that international institutions cooperate to a better and surer extent and that they be coordinated. Also, unwearying efforts must be made to create agencies for the promotion of peace.

The Community of Nations and International Organizations

84. Today the bonds of mutual dependence become increasingly close between all citizens and all the peoples of the world. The universal common good needs to be intelligently pursued and more effectively achieved. Hence it is now necessary for the family of nations to create for themselves an order which corresponds to modern obligations, particularly with reference to those numerous regions still laboring under intolerable need.

For the attainment of these goals, agencies of the international community should do their part to provide for the various necessities of men. In the field of social life this means food, health, education, and employment. In certain situations which can obtain anywhere, it means the general need to promote the growth of developing nations, to attend to the hardships of refugees scattered throughout the world, or to assist migrants and their families.

The international agencies, both universal and regional, which already exist assuredly deserve well of the human race. These stand forth as the first attempts to lay international foundations under the whole human community for the solving of the critical problems of our age, the promotion of global progress, and the prevention of any kind of war. The Church rejoices at the spirit of true fraternity flourishing between Christians and non-Christians in all these areas. This spirit strives to see that ever more intense efforts are made for the relief of the world's enormous miseries.

International Cooperation at the Economic Level

85. The modern interconnection between men also demands the establishment of greater international cooperation in the economic field. For although nearly all peoples have gained their independence, it is still far from true that they are free from excessive inequalities and from every form of undue dependence, or that they have put behind them danger of serious internal difficulties.

The development of any nation depends on human and financial assistance. Through education and professional formation, the citizens of each nation should be prepared to shoulder the various offices of economic and social life. Such preparation needs the help of foreign experts. When they render assistance these experts should do so not in a lordly fashion, but as helpers and coworkers.

The developing nations will be unable to procure the necessary material assistance unless the practices of the modern business world undergo a profound change. Additional help should be offered by advanced nations, in the form of either grants or investments. These offers should be made generously and without avarice. They should be accepted honorably.

If an economic order is to be created which is genuine and universal, there must be an abolition of excessive desire for profit, nationalistic pretensions, the lust for political domination, militaristic thinking, and intrigues designed to spread and impose ideologies.

Proposals are made in favor of numerous economic and social systems. It is to be hoped that experts in such affairs will find common bases for a healthy world trade. This hope will be more readily realized if individuals put aside their personal prejudices and show that they are prepared to undertake sincere discussions.

Some Useful Norms

86. The following norms would seem to be appropriate for this cooperation:

a) Developing nations should strongly desire to seek the complete human fulfillment of their citizens as the explicit and fixed goal of progress. Let them be mindful that progress begins and develops primarily from the efforts and endowments of the people themselves. Hence, instead of depending solely on outside help, they should rely chiefly on the full unfolding of their own resources and the cultivation of their own qualities and tradition. Those who have greater influence on others should be outstanding in this respect.

b) As for the advanced nations, they have a very heavy obligation to help the developing peoples in the discharge of the aforementioned responsibilities. If this worldwide collaboration is to be established, certain psychological and material adjustments will be needed among the advanced nations and should be brought about.

Thus these nations should carefully consider the welfare of weaker and poorer nations when negotiating with them. For such nations need for their own livelihood the income derived from the sale of domestic products.

c) The international community should see to the coordination and stimulation of economic growth. These objectives must be pursued in such a way, however, that the resources organized for this purpose can be shared as effectively and justly as possible. This same community should regulate economic relations throughout the world so that they can unfold in a way which is fair. In so doing, however, the community should honor the principle of subsidiarity.

Let adequate organizations be established for fostering and harmonizing international trade, especially with respect to the less advanced countries, and for repairing the deficiencies caused by an excessive disproportion in the power possessed by various nations. Such regulatory activity, combined with technical, cultural, and financial help, ought to afford the needed assistance to nations striving for progress, enabling them to achieve economic growth expeditiously.

d) In many instances there exists a pressing need to reform economic and social structures. But nations must beware of technical solutions immaturely proposed, especially those which offer men material advantages while militating against his spiritual nature and development. For, "Not by bread alone does man live, but by every word that comes forth from the mouth of God" (Mt. 4:4). Each branch of the human family possesses in itself and in its worthier traditions some part of the spiritual treasure entrusted by God to humanity, even though many do not know the source of this treasure.

International Cooperation in the Matter of Population

87. International cooperation becomes supremely necessary with respect to those peoples who, in addition to many other problems, are today often enough burdened in a special way with the difficulties stemming from a rapid population growth. There is an urgent need for all nations, especially the richer ones, to cooperate fully and intensely in an exploration as to how there can be prepared and distributed to the human community whatever is required for the livelihood and proper training of men. Some peoples, indeed, would greatly better their conditions of life if they could be duly trained to abandon ancient methods of farming in favor of modern techniques. With necessary prudence they should adapt these techniques to their own situations. In addition they need to establish a better social order and regulate the distribution of land with greater fairness.

Within the limits of their own competence, government officials have rights and duties with regard to the population problems of their own nation, for instance, in the matter of social legislation as it affects families, of migration to cities, of information relative to the condition and needs of the nation. Since the minds of men are so powerfully disturbed about this problem, the Council also desires that, especially in universities, Catholic experts in all these aspects should skillfully pursue their studies and projects and give them an ever wider scope.

Many people assert that it is absolutely necessary for population growth to be radically reduced everywhere or at least in certain nations. They say this must be done by every possible means and by every kind of government intervention. Hence this Council exhorts all to beware against solutions contradicting the moral law, solutions which have been promoted publicly or privately, and sometimes actually imposed.

For in view of the inalienable human right to marry and beget children, the question of how many children should be born belongs to the honest judgment of parents. The question can in no way be committed to the decision of government. Now since the judgment of the parents supposes a rightly formed conscience, it is highly important that everyone be given the opportunity to practice upright and truly human responsibility. This responsibility respects the divine law and takes account of circumstances and the times. It requires that educational and social conditions in various places be changed for the better, and especially that religious instruction or at least full moral training be provided.

Human beings should also be judiciously informed of scientific advances in the exploration of methods by which spouses can be helped in arranging the number of their children. The reliability of these methods should be adequately proven and their harmony with the moral order should be clear.

The Duty of Christians to Provide Support

88. Christians should collaborate willingly and wholeheartedly in establishing an international order involving genuine respect for all freedoms and amicable brotherhood between all men. This objective is all the more pressing since the greater part of the world is still suffering from so much poverty that it is as if Christ himself were crying out in these poor to beg the charity of the disciples.

Some nations with a majority of citizens who are counted as Christians have an abundance of this world's goods, while others are deprived of the necessities of life and are tormented with hunger, disease, and every kind of misery. This situation must not be allowed to continue, to the scandal of humanity. For the spirit of poverty and of charity are the glory and authentication of the Church of Christ.

Christians, especially young people, are to be praised and supported, therefore, when they volunteer their services to help other men and nations. Indeed, it is the duty of the whole People of God, following the word and example of the bishops, to do their utmost to alleviate the sufferings of the modern age. As was the ancient custom in the Church, they should meet this obligation out of the substance of their goods, and not only out of what is superfluous.

Without being inflexible and completely uniform, the collection and distribution of aid should be conducted in an orderly fashion in dioceses, nations, and throughout the entire world. (Wherever it seems appropriate, this activity of Catholics should be carried on in unison with other Christian brothers.) For the spirit of charity does not forbid but rather requires that charitable activity be exercised in a provident and orderly manner. Therefore, it is essential for those who intend to dedicate themselves to the service of the developing nations to be properly trained in suitable institutions.

Effective Presence of the Church on the International Scene

89. In pursuit of her divine mission, the Church preaches the gospel to all men and dispenses the treasures of grace. Thus, by imparting knowledge of the divine and natural law, she everywhere contributes to strengthening peace and to placing brotherly relations between individuals and peoples on solid ground. Therefore, to encourage and stimulate cooperation among men, the Church must be thoroughly present in the midst of the community of nations. She must achieve such a presence both through her public institutions and through the full and sincere collaboration of all Christians, a collaboration motivated solely by the desire to be of service to all.

This goal will come about more effectively if the faithful themselves, conscious of their responsibility as men and as Christians, strive to stir up in their own area of influence a willingness to cooperate readily with the international community. In both religious and civic education, special care must be given to the proper formation of youth in this respect.

The Role of Christians in International Institutions

90. An outstanding form of international activity on the part of Christians undoubtedly consists in the cooperative effort which, as individuals and in groups, they make to institutes established for the encouragement of cooperation among nations. The same is true of their efforts to establish such agencies. There are also various international Catholic associations which can serve in many ways to construct a peaceful and fraternal community of nations. These deserve to be strengthened by an increase in the number of well-qualified associates and in the needed resources. Let them be fortified too by a suitable coordination of their energies. For today effective action as well as the need for dialogue demand joint projects.

Moreover, such associations contribute much to the development of a universal outlook—something certainly appropriate for Catholics. They also help to form an awareness of genuine universal solidarity and responsibility.

Finally, this Council desires that by way of fulfilling their role properly in the international community, Catholics should seek to cooperate actively and in a positive manner both with their separated brothers, who together with them profess the gospel of love, and with all men thirsting for true peace.

In view of the immense hardships which still afflict the majority of men today, the Council regards it as most opportune that some agency of the universal Church be set up for the worldwide promotion of justice for the poor and of Christ's kind of love for them. The role of such an organization will be to stimulate the Catholic community to foster progress in needy regions, and social justice on the international scene.

CONCLUSION

The Role of Individual Believers and Dioceses

91. Drawn from the treasures of Church teaching, the proposals of this sacred synod look to the assistance of every man of our time, whether he believes in God, or does not explicitly recognize Him. Their purpose is to help men gain a sharper insight into their full destiny, so that they can fashion the world more to man's surpassing dignity, search for a brotherhood which is universal and more deeply rooted, and meet the urgencies of our age with a gallant and unified effort born of love.

Undeniably this conciliar program is but a general one in several of its parts—and deliberately so, given the immense variety of situations and forms of human culture in the world. Indeed, while it presents teaching already accepted in the Church, the program will have to be further pursued and amplified, since it often deals with matters in a constant state of development. Still, we have relied on the Word of God and the spirit of the gospel. Hence we entertain the hope that many of our proposals will be able to bring substantial benefit to everyone, especially after they have been adapted to individual nations and mentalities by the faithful, under the guidance of their pastors.

Dialogue between All Men

92. By virtue of her mission to shed on the whole world the radiance of the gospel message, and to unify under one Spirit all men of whatever nation, race, or culture, the Church stands forth as a sign of that brotherliness which allows honest dialogue and invigorates it.

Such a mission requires in the first place that we foster within the Church herself mutual esteem, reverence, and harmony, through the full recognition of lawful diversity. Thus all those who compose the one People of God, both pastors and the general faithful, can engage in dialogue with ever-abounding fruitfulness. For the bonds which unite the faithful are mightier than anything which divides them. Hence, let there be unity in what is necessary, freedom in what is unsettled, and charity in any case.

Our hearts embrace also those brothers and communities not yet living with us in full communion. To them we are linked nonetheless by our profession of the Father and the Son and the Holy Spirit, and by the bond of charity. We are mindful that the unity of Christians is today awaited and desired by many, too, who do not believe in Christ. For the further it advances toward truth and love under the powerful impulse of the Holy Spirit, the more this unity will be a harbinger of unity and peace for the world at large.

Therefore, by common effort and in ways which are today increasingly appropriate for seeking this splendid goal effectively, let us take pains to pattern ourselves after the gospel more exactly every day, and thus work as brothers in rendering service to the human family. For in Christ Jesus this family is called into the family of the sons of God.

We also turn our thoughts to all who acknowledge God, and who preserve in their traditions precious elements of religion and humanity. We want frank conversation to compel us all to receive the inspirations of the Spirit faithfully and to measure up to them energetically.

For our part, the desire for such dialogue, which can lead to truth through love alone, excludes no one, though an appropriate measure of prudence must undoubtedly be exercised. We include those who cultivate beautiful qualities of the human spirit, but do not yet acknowledge the Source of these qualities.

We include those who oppress the Church and harass her in manifold ways. Since God the Father is the origin and purpose of all men, we are all called to be brothers. Therefore, if we have been summoned to the same destiny, which is both human and divine, we can and we should work together without violence and deceit in order to build up the world in genuine peace.

Building Up the World and Fulfilling Its Purpose

93. Mindful of the Lord's saying: "By this will all men know that you are my disciples, if you have love for one another" (John 13:35), Christians cannot yearn for anything more ardently than to serve the men of the modern world ever more generously and effectively. Therefore, holding faithfully to the gospel and benefiting from its resources, and united with every man who loves and practices justice, Christians have shouldered a gigantic task demanding fulfillment in this world. Concerning this task they must give a reckoning to him who will judge every man on the last day.

Not everyone who cries, "Lord, Lord," will enter into the kingdom of heaven, but those who do the Father's will and take a strong grip on the work at hand. Now, the Father wills that in all men we recognize Christ our brother and love him effectively in word and in deed. By thus giving witness to the truth, we will share with others the mystery of the heavenly Father's love. As a consequence, men throughout the world will be aroused to a lively hope—the gift of the Holy Spirit—that they will finally be caught up in peace and utter happiness in that fatherland radiant with the splendor of the Lord.

"Now, to him who is able to accomplish all things in a measure far beyond what we ask or conceive, in keeping with the power that is at work in us—to him be glory in the Church and in Christ Jesus down through all the ages of time without end. Amen" (Eph. 3:20–21).

Each and every one of the things set forth in this Pastoral Constitution has won the consent of the Fathers of this most sacred Council. We too, by the apostolic authority conferred on us by Christ, join with the venerable Fathers in approving, decreeing, and establishing these things in the Holy Spirit, and we direct that what has thus been enacted in synod be published to God's glory.

Rome, at St. Peter's, December 7, 1965
I, Paul, Bishop of the Catholic Church

NOTES

1. The pastoral constitution *De Ecclesia in Mundo Huius Temporis* is made up of two parts; yet it constitutes an organic unity.

By way of explanation: the constitution is called "pastoral" because, while resting on doctrinal principles, it seeks to express the relation of the Church to the world and modern mankind. The result is that, on the one hand, a pastoral slant is present in the first part, and, on the other hand, a doctrinal slant is present in the second part.

In the first part, the Church develops her teaching on man, on the world which is the enveloping context of man's existence, and on man's relations to his fellow men. In part two, the Church gives closer consideration to various aspects of modern life and human society; special consideration is given to those questions and problems which, in this general area, seem to have a greater urgency in our day. As a result, in part two the subject matter which is viewed in the light of doctrinal principles is made up of diverse elements. Some elements have a permanent value; others, only a transitory one.

Consequently, the Constitution must be interpreted according to the general norms of theological interpretation. Interpreters must bear in mind—especially in part two—the changeable circumstances which the subject matter, by its very nature, involves.

2. Cf. Jn. 18:37; Mt. 10:28; Mk. 10:45.
3. Cf. Rom. 7:14ff.
4. Cf. 2 Cor. 5:15.
5. Cf. Acts 4:12.
6. Cf. Heb. 13:8.
7. Cf. Col. 1:15.
8. Cf. Gen. 1:26; Wis. 2:23.
9. Cf. Eccl. (Sir.) 17:3–10.
10. Cf. Rom. 1:21–25.
11. Cf. Jn. 8:34.
12. Cf. Dan. 3:57–90.
13. Cf. 1 Cor. 6:13–20.
14. Cf. 1 Kg. 16:7; Jer. 17:10.
15. Cf. Eccl. (Sir.) 17:7–8.
16. Cf. Rom. 2:15–16.
17. Cf. Pius XII, radio address on the correct formation of a Christian conscience in the young, Mar. 23, 1952: AAS (1952), p. 271.
18. Cf. Mt. 22:37–40; Gal. 5:14.
19. Cf. Eccl. (Sir.) 15:14.
20. Cf. 2 Cor. 5:10.
21. Cf. Wis. 1:13; 2:23–24; Rom. 5:21; 6:23; Jas. 1:15.
22. Cf. 1 Cor. 15:56–57.

23. Cf. Pius XI, encyclical letter *Divini Redemptoris*, March 19, 1937: AAS 29 (1937), pp. 65–106; Pius XII, encyclical letter *Ad Apostolorum Principis*, June 29, 1958: AAS 50 (1958), pp. 601–14; John XXIII, encyclical letter *Mater et Magistra*, May 15, 1961: AAS 35 (1961), pp. 451–53; Paul VI, encyclical letter *Ecclesiam Suam*, Aug. 6, 1964: AAS 56 (1964), pp. 651–653.

24. Cf. Second Vatican Council, dogmatic constitution *Lumen Gentium*, Chap. 1, Art. 8: AAS 57 (1965), p. 12.

25. Cf. Phil. 1:27.

26. St. Augustine, *Confessions* I, 1: PL 32, 661.

27. Cf. Rom. 5:14. Cf. Tertullian, *De carnis resurrectione* 6: "The shape that the slime of the earth was given was intended with a view to Christ, the future man.": p. 2, 282; CSEL 47, p. 33, 1.12–13.

28. Cf. 2 Cor. 4:4.

29. Cf. Second Council of Constantinople, can. 7: "The divine Word was not changed into a human nature, nor was a human nature absorbed by the Word." Denz. 219 (428). Cf. also Third Council of Constantinople: "For just as his most holy and immaculate human nature, though deified, was not destroyed (*Theotheisa ouk anerethe*), but rather remained in its proper state and mode of being": Denz. 291 (556). Cf. Council of Chalcedon: "to be acknowledged in two natures, without confusion, change; division, or separation." Denz. 148 (302).

30. Cf. Third Council of Constantinople: "and so his human will, though deified, is not destroyed": Denz. 291 (556).

31. Cf. Heb. 4:15.

32. Cf. 2 Cor. 5:18–19; Col. 1:20–22.

33. Cf. 1 Pet. 2:21; Mt. 16:24; Lk. 14:27.

34. Cf. Rom. 8:29; Col. 3:10–14.

35. Cf. Rom. 8:1–11.

36. Cf. 2 Cor. 4:14.

37. Cf. Phil. 3:19; Rom. 8:17.

38. Cf. Second Vatican Council dogmatic constitution *Lumen Gentium*, Chap. 11, Art. 16: AAS 5 (1965), p. 20.

39. Cf. Rom. 8:32.

40. Cf. the Byzantine Easter Liturgy.

41. Cf. Rom. 8:15 and Gal. 4:6; cf. also Jn. 1:22 and Jn. 3:1–2.

42. Cf. John XXIII, encyclical letter *Mater et Magistra*, May 15, 1961: AAS 53 (1961), pp. 401–64, and encyclical letter *Pacem in Terris*, Apr. 11, 1963: AAS 55 (1963), pp. 257–304; Paul VI, encyclical letter *Ecclesiam Suam*, Aug. 6, 1964: AAS 54 (1964), pp. 609–59.

43. Cf. Lk. 17:33.

44. Cf. St. Thomas, 1 Ethica Lect. 1.

45. Cf. John XXIII, encyclical letter *Mater et Magistra*: AAS 53 (1961), p. 418. Cf. also Pius XI, encyclical letter *Quadragesimo Anno*: AAS 23 (1931), pp. 222ff.

46. Cf. John XXIII, encyclical letter *Mater et Magistra*: AAS 53 (1961).
47. Cf. Mk. 2:27.
48. Cf. John XXIII, encyclical letter *Pacem in Terris*: AAS 55 (1963), p. 266.
49. Cf. Jas. 2:15–16.
50. Cf. Lk. 16:18–31.
51. Cf. John XXIII, encyclical letter *Pacem in Terris*: AAS 55 (1963), pp. 299, 300.
52. Cf. Lk. 6:37–38; Mt. 7:1–2; Rom. 2:1–11; 14:10; 14:10–12.
53. Cf. Mt. 5:43–47.
54. Cf. dogmatic constitution *Lumen Gentium*, Chap. II, Art. 9: AAS 57 (1965), pp. 12–13.
55. Cf. Ex. 24:1–8.
56. Cf. Gen. 1:26–27; 9:3; Wis. 9:3.
57. Cf. Ps. 8:7 and 10.
58. Cf. John XXIII, encyclical letter *Pacem in Terris*: AAS 55 (1963), p. 297.
59. Cf. *Message to All Mankind* sent by the Fathers at the beginning of the Second Vatican Council, Oct. 20, 1962: AAS 54 (1962), p. 823.
60. Cf. Paul VI, address to the diplomatic corps, Jan. 7, 1965: AAS 57 (1965), p. 232.
61. Cf. First Vatican Council, *Dogmatic Constitution on the Catholic Faith*, Chap. 111: Denz. 1785–1786 (3004–3005).
62. Cf. Msgr. Pio Paschini, *Vita e opere di Galileo Galilei*, 2 volumes, Vatican Press (1964).
63. Cf. Mt. 24:13; 13:24–30 and 36–43.
64. Cf. 2 Cor. 6:10.
65. Cf. Jn. 1:3 and 14.
66. Cf. Eph. 1:10.
67. Cf. Jn. 3:16; Rom. 5:8.
68. Cf. Acts 2:36; Mt. 28:18.
69. Cf. Rom. 15:16.
70. Cf. Acts 1:7.
71. Cf. 1 Cor. 7:31; Irenaeus, *Adversus haereses*, V, 36, PG, VIII, 1221.
72. Cf. 2 Cor. 5:2; 2 Pet. 3:13.
73. Cf. 1 Cor. 2:9; Apoc. 21:4–5.
74. Cf. 1 Cor. 15:42 and 53.
75. Cf. 1 Cor. 13:8; 3:14.
76. Cf. Rom. 8:19–21.
77. Cf. Lk. 9:25.
78. Cf. Pius XI, encyclical letter *Quadragesimo Anno*: AAS 23 (1931), p. 207.
79. Preface of the Feast of Christ the King.
80. Cf. Paul VI, encyclical letter *Ecclesiam Suam*, III: AAS 56 (1964), pp. 637–59.

81. Cf. Tit. 3:4: "love of mankind."

82. Cf. Eph. 1:3; 5:6, 13–14, 23.

83. Second Vatican Council, dogmatic constitution *Lumen Gentium*, Chap. I, Art. 8: AAS 57 (1965), p. 12.

84. Ibid., Chap. II, Art. 9: AAS 57 (1965), p. 14; cf. Art. 8: AAS loc. cit., p. 11.

85. Ibid., Chap. I, Art. 8: AAS 57 (1965), p. 11.

86. Cf. ibid., Chap. IV, Art. 38: AAS 57 (1965), p. 43 with note 120.

87. Cf. Rom. 8:14–17.

88. Cf. Mt. 22:39.

89. Dogmatic constitution *Lumen Gentium*, Chap. II, Art. 9: AAS 57 (1956), pp. 12–14.

90. Cf. Pius XII, Address to the International Union of Institutes of Archeology, History and History of Art, Mar. 9, 1956: AAS 48 (1965), p. 212: "Its divine Founder, Jesus Christ, has not given it any mandate or fixed any end of the cultural order. The goal which Christ assigns to it is strictly religious. . . . The Church must lead men to God, in order that they may be given over to him without reserve. . . . The Church can never lose sight of the strictly religious, supernatural goal. The meaning of all its activities, down to the last canon of its code, can only cooperate directly or indirectly in this goal."

91. Dogmatic constitution *Lumen Gentium*, Chap. 1, Art. 1: AAS 57 (1965), p. 5.

92. Cf. Heb. 13:14.

93. Cf. 2 Th. 3:6–13; Eph. 4:28.

94. Cf. Is. 58:1–12.

95. Cf. Mt. 23:3–23; Mt. 7:10–13.

96. Cf. John XXIII, encyclical letter *Mater et Magistra*, IV: AAS 53 (1961), pp. 456–57; cf. 1: AAS loc. cit., pp. 407, 410–11.

97. Cf. dogmatic constitution *Lumen Gentium*, Chap. III, Art. 28: AAS 57 (1965), p. 35.

98. Ibid., Art. 28: AAS loc. cit., pp. 35–36.

99. Cf. St. Ambrose, *De virginitate*, Chap. VIII, Art. 48: ML 16, 278.

100. Cf. dogmatic constitution *Lumen Gentium*, Chap. II, Art. 15: AAS 57 (1965), p. 20.

101. Cf. dogmatic constitution *Lumen Gentium*, Chap. II, Art. 13: AAS 57 (1965), p. 17.

102. Cf. Justin, *Dialogus cum Tryphone*, Chap. 100; MG 6, 729 (ed. Otto), 1897, pp. 391–93: ". . . but the greater the number of persecutions which are inflicted upon us, so much the greater the number of other men who become devout believers through the name of Jesus." Cf. *Tertullian Apologeticus*, Chap. L, 13: "Every time you mow us down like grass, we increase in number: the blood of Christians is a seed!" Cf. dogmatic constitution *Lumen Gentium*, Chap. II, Art. 9: AAS 57 (1965), p. 14.

103. Cf. dogmatic constitution *Lumen Gentium*, Chap. II, Art. 15: AAS 57 (1965), p. 20.

104. Cf. Paul VI, address given on Feb. 3, 1965.

105. Cf. St. Augustine, *De bono Coniugii*: PL 40, 375–76 and 394; Thomas Aquinas, *Summa Theologica*, Suppl. Quaest. 49, Art. 3 ad 1; *Decretum pro Armenis*: Denz.-Schoen. 1327; Pius XI, encyclical letter *Casti Connubii*: AAS 22 (1930), pp. 547–48; Denz.-Schoen.

106. Cf. Pius XI, encyclical letter *Casti Connubii*: AAS 22 (1930), pp. 546–47; Denz.-Schoen. 3706.

107. Cf. Hos. 2; Jer. 3:6–13; Ezek. 16 and 23; Is. 54.

108. Cf. Mt. 9:15; Mk. 2:19–20; Lk. 5:34–35; Jn. 3:29; cf. also 2 Cor. 11:2; Eph. 5:27; Apoc. 19:7–8; 21:2 and 9.

109. Cf. Eph. 5:25.

110. Cf. Second Vatican Council, dogmatic constitution *Lumen Gentium*: MS 57 (1965), pp. 15–16, 40–41, 47.

111. Pius XI, encyclical letter *Casti Connubii*: AAS 22 (1930), p. 583.

112. Cf. 1 Tim. 5:3.

113. Cf. Eph. 5:32.

114. Cf. Gen. 2:22–24; Pr. 5:15–20; 31:10–31; Tob. 8:4–8; Cant. 1:2–3; 1:16; 4:16; 5:1; 7:8–14; 1 Cor. 7:3–6; Eph. 5:25–33.

115. Cf. Pius XI, encyclical letter *Casti Connubii*: AAS 22 (1930), p. 547 and 548; Denz.-Schoen. 3707.

116. Cf. 1 Cor. 7:5.

117. Cf. Pius XII, Address *Tra le viste*, Jan. 20, 1958: AAS 50 (1958), p. 91.

118. Cf. Pius XI, encyclical letter *Casti Connubii*: AAS 22 (1930), Denz.-Schoen. 3716–3718; Pius XII, *Allocutio Conventui Unionis Italicae inter Obstetrics*, Oct. 29, 1951: AAS 43 (1951), pp. 835–54; Paul VI, address to a group of cardinals, June 23, 1964: AAS 56 (1964), pp. 581–89. Certain questions which need further and more careful investigation have been handed over, at the command of the supreme pontiff, to a commission for the study of population, family, and births, in order that, after it fulfills its function, the supreme pontiff may pass judgment. With the doctrine of the magisterium in this state, this holy synod does not intend to propose immediately concrete solutions. (In the Latin text this is footnote 14 of Chap. I, in Part 2 of the document.—Ed.)

119. Cf. Eph. 5:16; Col. 4:5.

120. Cf. *Sacramentarium Gregorianum*: PL 78, 262.

121. Cf. Rom. 5:15 and 18; 6:5–11; Gal. 2:20.

122. Cf. Eph. 5:25–27.

123. Cf. introductory statement of this Constitution, Art. 4ff.

124. Cf. Col. 3:1–2.

125. Cf. Gen. 1:28.

126. Cf. Pr. 8:30–31.

127. Cf. St. Irenaeus, *Adversus haereses*: III, II, 8 (ed. Sagnard, p. 200; cf. ibid., 16, 6: pp. 290–92; 21, 10–22: pp. 370–72; 22, 3: p. 378, etc.).

128. Cf. Eph. 1:10.

129. Cf. the words of Pius XI to Father M. D. Roland-Gosselin: "It is necessary never to lose sight of the fact that the objective of the Church is to evangelize, not to civilize. If it civilizes, it is for the sake of evangelization" (Semaines sociales de France, Versailles, 6, pp. 461–62).

130. First Vatican Council, *Constitution on the Catholic Faith*: Denz. 1795, 1799 (3015, 3019). Cf. Pius XI, encyclical letter *Quadragesimo Anno*: AAS 23 (1931), p. 190.

131. Cf. John XXIII, encyclical letter *Pacem in Terris*: AAS 55 (1963), p. 260.

132. Cf. John XXIII, encyclical letter *Pacem in Terris*: AAS 55 (1963), p. 283; Pius XII, radio address, Dec. 24, 1941: AAS 34 (1942), pp. 16–17.

133. John XXIII, encyclical letter *Pacem in Terris*: AAS 55 (1963), p. 260.

134. Cf. John XXIII, speech delivered on Oct. 11, 1962, at the beginning of the Council: AAS 54 (1962), p. 792.

135. Cf. *Constitution on the Sacred Liturgy*, Art. 123, AAS 56 (1964), p. 131; Paul VI, discourse to the artists of Rome: AAS 56 (1964), pp. 439–42.

136. Cf. Second Vatican Council, *Decree on Priestly Formation and Declaration on Christian Education*.

137. Cf. dogmatic constitution *Lumen Gentium*, Chap. IV, Art. 37: AAS 57 (1965), pp. 42–43.

138. Cf. Pius XII, address on Mar. 23, 1952: AAS 44 (1952), p. 273; John XXIII, allocution to the Catholic Association of Italian Workers, May 1, 1959: AAS 51 (1959), p. 358.

139. Cf. Pius XI, encyclical letter *Quadragesimo Anno*: AAS 23 (1931), pp. 190ff; Pius XII, address of Mar. 23, 1952: AAS 44 (1952), pp. 276ff; John XXIII encyclical letter *Mater et Magistra*: AAS 53 (1961), p. 450; Vatican Council II, Decree *Inter Mirifica* (On the Instruments of Social Communication), Chapter I, Art. 6: AAS 56 (1964), p. 147.

140. Cf. Mt. 16:26; Lk. 16:1–31; Col. 3:17.

141. Cf. Leo XIII, encyclical letter *Libertas, in Acta Leonis XIII*; t. VIII, pp. 220ff; Pius XI, encyclical letter *Quadragesimo Anno*: AAS 23 (1931), pp. 191ff; Pius XI, encyclical letter *Divini Redemptoris*: AAS 29 (1937), pp. 65ff; Pius XII, Christmas message, 1941: AAS 34 (1942), pp. 10ff; John XXIII, encyclical letter *Mater et Magistra*: AAS 53 (1961), pp. 401–464.

142. In reference to agricultural problems cf. especially John XXIII, encyclical letter *Mater et Magistra*: AAS 53 (1961), pp. 341ff.

143. Cf. Leo XIII, encyclical letter *Rerum Novarum*: AAS 23 (1890–91), pp. 649, 662; Pius XI, encyclical letter *Quadragesimo Anno*: AAS 23 (1931), pp. 200–201; Pius XI, encyclical letter *Divini Redemptoria*: AAS 29 (1937), p. 92; Pius XII, radio address on Christmas Eve, 1942: AAS 35 (1943), p. 20; Pius XII, allocution of June 13, 1943: AAS 35, p. 172; Pius XII, radio address

to the workers of Spain, Mar. 11, 1951: AAS 43 (1951), p. 215; John XXIII, encyclical letter *Mater et Magistra*: AAS 53 (1961), p. 419.

144. Cf. John XXIII, encyclical letter *Mater et Magistra*: AAS 53 (1961), pp. 408, 424, 427; however, the word "curatione" has been taken from the Latin text of the encyclical letter *Quadragesimo Anno*: AAS 23 (1931), p. 199. Under the aspect of the evolution of the question cf. also: Pius XII, allocution of June 3, 1950; AAS 42 (1950), pp. 485–88; Paul VI, allocution of June 8, 1964: AAS 56 (1964), pp. 574–79.

145. Cf. Pius XII, encyclical *Sertum Laetitiae*: AAS 31 (1939), p. 642; John XXIII, consistorial allocution: AAS 52 (1960), pp. 5–11; John XXIII, encyclical letter *Mater et Magistra*: AAS 53 (1961), p. 411.

146. Thomas Aquinas, *Summa Theologica*: II-II q. 32, a. 5 ad 2; ibid. q. 66, a. 2; cf. explanation in Leo XIII, encyclical letter *Rerum Novarum*: AAS 23 (1890–91), p. 671; cf. also Pius XII allocution of June 1, 1941: AAS 33 (1941), p. 199; Pius XII, Christmas radio address, 1954: AAS 47 (1955), p. 27.

147. Cf. St. Basil, *Hom. in illud Lucae "Destruam horrea mea,"* Art. 2 (PG 31, 263); Lactantius, *Divinarum institutionum*, lib. *V. On Justice* (PL 6, 565 B): St. Augustine, *In Ioann*. Ev. Tr. 50 Art. 6 (PL 35, 1760); St. Augustine, *Enarratio in Ps. CXLVII*, (PL 37, 192); St. Gregory the Great, *Homiliae in Ev*., hom. 20 (PL 76, 1165); St. Gregory the Great, *Regulae Pastoralis liber*, pars III, c. 21 (PL 77, 87); St. Bonaventure, in III Sent. d. 33, dub 1 (ed. Quacracchi III, 728); St. Bonaventure, In IV Sent. d. 15, p. 11 a. 2. q. 1 (ed. cit. IV, 371b); q. de superfluo (ms. Assisi, Bibl. Comun. 186, ff 112a–113a); St. Albert the Great, in III Sent., d. 33, a. 3, sol. 1 (ed. Borgnet XXVIII, 611); Id In IV Sent. d. 15, a. 16 (ed. cit. XXIX, 494–497). As for the determination of what is superfluous in our day and age, cf. John XXIII, radio-television message of Sept. 11, 1962: AAS 54 (1962), p. 682: "The obligation of every man, the urgent obligation of the Christian man, is to reckon what is superfluous by the measure of the needs of others, and to see to it that the administration and the distribution of created goods serve the common good."

148. In that case, the old principle holds true: "In extreme necessity all goods are common, that is, all goods are to be shared." On the other hand, for the order, extension, and manner by which the principle is applied in the proposed text, besides the modern authors cf. Thomas Aquinas, *Summa Theologica* II-II, q. 66, a. 7. Obviously, for the correct application of the principle, all the conditions that are morally required must be met.

149. Cf. Gratian, *Decretum*, C. 21 dist. LXXXVI (ed. Friedberg I, 302). This axiom is also found already in PL 54, 591 A (cf. in Antonianum 27 [1952], 349–366).

150. Cf. Leo XIII, encyclical letter *Rerum Novarum*: AAS 23 (1890–91), pp. 643–46; Pius XI, encyclical letter *Quadragesimo Anno*: AAS 23 (1931), p. 191; Pius XII, radio message of June 1, 1941: AAS 33 (1941), p. 199; Pius XII, radio message on Christmas Eve, 1942: AAS 35 (1943), p. 17; Pius XII,

radio message of Sept. 1, 1944: AAS 36 (1944), p. 253; John XXIII, encyclical letter *Mater et Magistra*: AAS 53 (1961), pp. 428–429.

151. Cf. Pius XI, encyclical letter *Quadragesimo Anno*: AAS 23 (1931), p. 214; John XXIII, encyclical letter *Mater et Magistra*: AAS 53 (1961), p. 429.

152. Cf. Pius XII, radio message of Pentecost, 1941: AAS 44 (1941), p. 199; John XXIII, encyclical letter *Mater et Magistra*: AAS 53 (1961), p. 430.

153. For the right use of goods according to the doctrine of the New Testament, cf. Lk. 3:11; 10:30ff; 11:41; 1 Pet. 5:3; Mk. 8:36; 12:39–41; Jas. 5:1–6; 1 Tim. 6:8; Eph. 4:28; 2 Cor. 8:13; 1 John 3:17.

154. Cf. John XXIII, encyclical letter *Mater et Magistra*: AAS 53 (1961), p. 417.

155. Cf. John XXIII, ibid.

156. Cf. Rom. 13:1–5.

157. Cf. Rom. 13:5.

158. Cf. Pius XII, radio message, Dec. 24, 1942: AAS 35 (1943), pp. 9–24; Dec. 24, 1944: AAS 37 (1945), pp. 11–17; John XXIII, encyclical letter *Pacem in Terris*: AAS 55 (1963), pp. 263, 271, 277, and 278.

159. Cf. Pius XII, radio message of June 7, 1941: AAS 33 (1941), p. 200; John XXIII, encyclical letter *Pacem in Terris*: l.c., pp. 273 and 274.

160. Cf. John XXIII, encyclical letter *Mater et Magistra*: AAS 53 (1961), p. 416.

161. Pius XI, allocution *Ai dirigenti della Federazione Universitaria Cattolica*: Discorsi di Pio XI (ed. Bertetto), Turin, vol. 1 (1960), p. 743.

162. Cf. Lk. 2:14.

163. Cf. Second Vatican Council, dogmatic constitution *Lumen Gentium*, Art. 13: AAS 57 (1965), p. 17.

164. Cf. Eph. 2:16; Col. 1:20–22.

165. Cf. John XXIII, encyclical letter *Pacem in Terris*, Apr. 11, 1963: AAS 55 (1963), p. 291: "Therefore in this age of ours which prides itself on its atomic power, it is irrational to believe that war is still an apt means of vindicating violated rights."

166. Cf. Pius XII, allocution of Sept. 30, 1954: AAS 46 (1954), p. 589; radio message of Dec. 24, 1954: AAS 47 (1955), pp. 15ff; John XXIII, encyclical letter *Pacem in Terris*: AAS 55 (1963), pp. 286–91; Paul VI, allocution to the United Nations, Oct. 4, 1965.

167. Cf. John XXIII, encyclical letter *Pacem in Terris* where reduction of arms is mentioned: AAS 55 (1963), p. 287.

168. Cf. 2 Cor. 2:6.

Populorum Progressio: *On the Development of Peoples* *(Paul VI, 1967)*

INTRODUCTION

The choice of Giovanni Cardinal Montini of Milan as the successor to John XXIII was almost a foregone conclusion. He had enjoyed many marks of papal favor and played an important role in the first session of the Second Vatican Council. Ascending to the papacy in the wake of the tremendous reforms sweeping the church, Paul VI was to need all the skills of conciliation and compromise acquired in his long diplomatic career. Fully committed to the success of the Council, he was equally determined to maintain the power and dignity of the papal office, a set of loyalties which would cause him much anguish in the years ahead.

Populorum Progressio, written in 1967, placed the social question in its worldwide context. Paul VI offered an economic interpretation of the sources of war and argued for economic justice as the surest road to peace. The pope rejected unequivocally many of the basic precepts for capitalism, including unrestricted private property, the profit motive, and reliance on free trade in a world economy. He emphasized the right in justice of the poorer nations to the aid of the wealthier nations and suggested quite explicitly that, in an extreme situation, the poor retain the right to a violent solution to their problems.

A major theme is Paul's vision of development, which takes place on an individual level and is oriented to a transcendent humanism, growth always open to further maturity. Development is also social because each individual is part of a larger whole. True and integral development includes the acquisition of knowledge, culture, and the necessities of life; the desire for cooperation and peace, with a corresponding recognition of human dignity; the recognition of supreme values and the destiny of the person; and the acceptance of faith, which opens individuals to union with God.

Other agenda of the encyclical included the recognition of the social dimension of property, an equitable distribution of the world's resources, and trade, a new area of attention. Here Paul focused on the problems of neocolonialism.

While many agreed with the pope's description of the problems and even shared his sense of urgency, such people often also felt helpless in trying to address these issues. As with so many other dimensions of post-conciliar Catholicism, new windows had been opened, new demands made, but the exact direction the church and the world should follow was unclear. Poised in delicate balance between the church's role in the developed world and its moral commitment to freedom, justice, and peace, Pope Paul VI attempted to provide leadership for the present with a sense of continuity with the past. It was a most difficult task.

POPULORUM PROGRESSIO

ENCYCLICAL LETTER
OF HIS HOLINESS,

POPE PAUL VI

To the Bishops, Priests
Religious, the Faithful,
and to All Men of Good Will

1. The development of peoples has the Church's close attention, particularly the development of those peoples who are striving to escape from hunger, misery, endemic diseases, and ignorance; of those who are looking for a wider share in the benefits of civilization and a more active improvement of their human qualities; of those who are aiming purposefully at their complete fulfillment. Following on the Second Vatican Ecumenical Council a renewed consciousness of the demands of the Gospel makes it her duty to put herself at the service of all, to help them grasp their serious problem in all its dimensions, and to convince them that solidarity in action at this turning point in human history is a matter of urgency.

2. Our predecessors in their great encyclicals, Leo XIII in *Rerum Novarum,*[1] Pius XI in *Quadragesimo Anno*[2] and John XXIII in *Mater et Magistra*[3] and *Pacem in Terris*[4]—not to mention the messages of Pius XII[5] to the world—did not fail in the duty of their office of shedding the light of the Gospel on the social questions of their times.

3. Today the principal fact that we must all recognize is that the social question has become worldwide. John XXIII stated this in unambiguous terms[6] and the Council echoed him in its *Pastoral Constitution on the Church in the Modern World.*[7] This teaching is important and its application urgent. Today the peoples in hunger are making a dramatic appeal to the peoples blessed with abundance. The Church shudders at this cry of anguish and calls each one to give a loving response of charity to this brother's cry for help.

4. Before we became pope, two journeys, to Latin America in 1960 and to Africa in 1962, brought us into direct contact with the acute problems pressing on continents full of life and hope. Then on becoming father of all we made further journeys, to the Holy Land and India, and were able to see and virtually touch the very serious difficulties besetting peoples of long-standing civilizations who are at grips with the problem of development. While the Second Vatican Ecumenical Council was being held in Rome, providential circumstances permitted us to address in person the General Assembly of the

United Nations, and we pleaded the cause of poor peoples before this distinguished body.

5. Then quite recently, in our desire to carry out the wishes of the Council and give specific expression to the Holy See's contribution to this great cause of peoples in development, we considered it our duty to set up a pontifical commission in the Church's central administration, charged with "bringing to the whole of God's People the full knowledge of the part expected of them at the present time, so as to further the progress of poorer peoples, to encourage social justice among nations, to offer to less developed nations the means whereby they can further their own progress";[8] its name, which is also its program, is *Justice and Peace*. We think that this can and should bring together men of good will with our Catholic sons and our Christian brothers. So it is to all that we address this solemn appeal for concrete action toward man's complete development and the development of all mankind.

PART I: FOR MAN'S COMPLETE DEVELOPMENT

1. THE DATA OF THE PROBLEM

6. Freedom from misery; the greater assurance of finding subsistence, health, and fixed employment; an increased share of responsibility without oppression of any kind and in security from situations that do violence to their dignity as men; better education—in brief, to seek to do more, know more and have more in order to be more: that is what men aspire to now when a greater number of them are condemned to live in conditions that make this lawful desire illusory. Besides, peoples who have recently gained national independence experience the need to add to this political freedom a fitting autonomous growth, social as well as economic, in order to assure their citizens of a full human enhancement and to take their rightful place with other nations.

7. Though insufficient for the immensity and urgency of the task, the means inherited from the past are not lacking. It must certainly be recognized that colonizing powers have often furthered their own interests, power, or glory, and that their departure has sometimes left a precarious economy, bound up for instance with the production of one kind of crop whose market prices are subject to sudden and considerable variation. Yet while recognizing the damage done by a certain type of colonialism and its consequences, one must at the same time acknowledge the qualities and achievement of colonizers who brought their science and technical knowledge and left beneficial results of their presence in so many underprivileged regions. The structures established by them persist, however incomplete they may be; they diminished ignorance and sickness, brought the benefits of communications and improved living conditions.

8. Yet once this is admitted, it remains only too true that the resultant situation is manifestly inadequate for facing the hard reality of modern econom-

ics. Left to itself it works rather to widen the differences in the world's levels of life, not to diminish them: rich peoples enjoy rapid growth whereas the poor develop slowly. The imbalance is on the increase: some produce a surplus of foodstuffs, others cruelly lack them and see their exports made uncertain.

9. At the same time social conflicts have taken on world dimensions. The acute disquiet which has taken hold of the poor classes in countries that are becoming industrialized is now embracing those whose economy is almost exclusively agrarian: farming people, too, are becoming aware of their "undeserved hardship."[9] There is also the scandal of glaring inequalities not merely in the enjoyment of possessions but even more in the exercise of power. While a small restricted group enjoys a refined civilization in certain regions, the remainder of the population, poor and scattered, is "deprived of nearly all possibility of personal initiative and of responsibility, and often times even its living and working conditions are unworthy of the human person."[10]

10. Furthermore, the conflict between traditional civilizations and the new elements of industrial civilization break down structures which do not adapt themselves to new conditions. Their framework, sometimes rigid, was the indispensable prop to personal and family life; older people remain attached to it, the young escape from it, as from a useless barrier, to turn eagerly to new forms of life in society. The conflict of the generations is made more serious by a tragic dilemma: whether to retain ancestral institutions and convictions and renounce progress, or to admit techniques and civilizations from outside and reject along with the traditions of the past all their human richness. In effect, the moral, spiritual, and religious supports of the past too often give way without securing in return any guarantee of a place in the new world.

11. In this confusion the temptation becomes stronger to risk being swept away toward types of messianism which give promises but create illusions. The resulting dangers are patent: violent popular reactions, agitation toward insurrection, and a drifting toward totalitarian ideologies. Such are the data of the problem. Its seriousness is evident to all.

2. THE CHURCH AND DEVELOPMENT

12. True to the teaching and example of her divine Founder, who cited the preaching of the Gospel to the poor as a sign of his mission,[11] the Church has never failed to foster the human progress of the nations to which she brings faith in Christ. Her missionaries have built, not only churches, but also hostels and hospitals, schools and universities. Teaching the local populations the means of deriving the best advantages from their natural resources, missionaries have often protected them from the greed of foreigners. Without doubt their work, inasmuch as it was human, was not perfect, and sometimes the announcement of the authentic Gospel message was infiltrated by many ways of thinking and acting which were characteristic of their home country.

But the missionaries were also able to develop and foster local institutions. In many a region they were among the pioneers in material progress as well as in cultural advancement. Let it suffice to recall the example of Father Charles de Foucauld, whose charity earned him the title "Universal Brother," and who edited an invaluable dictionary of the Touareg language. We ought to pay tribute to these pioneers who have been too often forgotten, but who were urged on by the love of Christ, just as we honor their imitators and successors who today still continue to put themselves at the generous and unselfish service of those to whom they announce the Gospel.

13. However, local and individual undertakings are no longer enough. The present situation of the world demands concerted action based on a clear vision of all economic, social, cultural, and spiritual aspects. Experienced in human affairs, the Church, without attempting to interfere in any way in the politics of States, "seeks but a solitary goal: to carry forward the work of Christ himself under the lead of the befriending Spirit. And Christ entered this world to give witness to the truth, to rescue and not to sit in judgment, to serve and not to be served."[12] Founded to establish on earth the kingdom of heaven and not to conquer any earthly power, the Church clearly states that the two realms are distinct, just as the two powers, ecclesiastical and civil, are supreme, each in its own domain.[13] But, since the Church lives in history, she ought to "scrutinize the signs of the times and interpret them in the light of the Gospel."[14] Sharing the noblest aspirations of men and suffering when she sees them not satisfied, she wishes to help them attain their full flowering, and that is why she offers men what she possesses as her characteristic attribute: a global vision of man and of the human race.

Christian Vision of Development

14. Development cannot be limited to mere economic growth. In order to be authentic, it must be complete: integral, that is, it has to promote the good of every man and of the whole man. As an eminent specialist has very rightly and emphatically declared: "We do not believe in separating the economic from the human, nor development from the civilizations in which it exists. What we hold important is man, each man and each group of men, and we even include the whole of humanity."[15]

15. In the design of God, every man is called upon to develop and fulfill himself, for every life is a vocation. At birth, everyone is granted, in germ, a set of aptitudes and qualities for him to bring to fruition. Their coming to maturity, which will be the result of education received from the environment and personal efforts, will allow each man to direct himself toward the destiny intended for him by his Creator. Endowed with intelligence and freedom, he is responsible for his fulfillment as he is for his salvation. He is aided, or sometimes impeded, by those who educate him and those with whom he lives, but each one remains, whatever be these influences affecting him, the principal agent of his own success or failure. By the unaided effort of his own

intelligence and his will, each man can grow in humanity, can enhance his personal worth, can become more a person.

16. However, this self-fulfillment is not something optional. Just as the whole of creation is ordained to its Creator, so spiritual beings should of their own accord orient their lives to God, the first truth and the supreme good. Thus it is that human fulfillment constitutes, as it were, a summary of our duties. But there is much more: this harmonious enrichment of nature by personal and responsible effort is ordered to a further perfection. By reason of his union with Christ, the source of life, man attains to new fulfillment of himself, to a transcendent humanism which gives him his greatest possible perfection: this is the highest goal of personal development.

17. But each man is a member of society. He is part of the whole of mankind. It is not just certain individuals, but all men who are called to this fullness of development. Civilizations are born, develop and die. But humanity is advancing along the path of history like the waves of a rising tide encroaching gradually on the shore. We have inherited from past generations, and we have benefitted from the work of our contemporaries: for this reason we have obligations toward all, and we cannot refuse to interest ourselves in those who will come after us to enlarge the human family. The reality of human solidarity, which is a benefit for us, also imposes a duty.

18. This personal and communal development would be threatened if the true scale of values were undermined. The desire for necessities is legitimate, and work undertaken to obtain them is a duty: If any man will not work, neither let him eat.[16] But the acquiring of temporal goods can lead to greed, to the insatiable desire for more, and can make increased power a tempting objective. Individuals, families, and nations can be overcome by avarice, be they poor or rich, and all can fall victim to a stifling materialism.

19. Increased possession is not the ultimate goal of nations nor of individuals. All growth is ambivalent. It is essential if man is to develop as a man, but in a way it imprisons man if he considers it the supreme good, and it restricts his vision. Then we see hearts harden and minds close, and men no longer gather together in friendship but out of self-interest, which soon leads to opposition and disunity. The exclusive pursuit of possessions thus becomes an obstacle to individual fulfillment and to man's true greatness. Both for nations and for individual men, avarice is the most evident form of moral underdevelopment.

20. If further development calls for the work of more and more technicians, even more necessary is the deep thought and reflection of wise men in search of a new humanism which will enable modern man to find himself anew by embracing the higher values of love and friendship, of prayer and contemplation.[17] This is what will permit the fullness of authentic development, a development which is for each and all the transition from less human conditions to those which are more human.

21. Less human conditions: the lack of material necessities for those who are without the minimum essential for life, the moral deficiencies of those

who are mutilated by selfishness. Less human conditions: oppressive social structures, whether due to the abuses of ownership or to the abuses of power, to the exploitation of workers or to unjust transactions. Conditions that are more human: the passage from misery toward the possession of necessities, victory over social scourges, the growth of knowledge, the acquisition of culture. Additional conditions that are more human: increased esteem for the dignity of others, the turning toward the spirit of poverty,[18] cooperation for the common good, the will and desire for peace. Conditions that are still more human: the acknowledgment by man of supreme values, and of God their source and their finality. Conditions that, finally and above all, are more human: faith, a gift of God accepted by the good will of man, and unity in the charity of Christ, who calls us all to share as sons in the life of the living God, the Father of all men.

3. ACTION TO BE UNDERTAKEN

The Universal Purpose of Created Things

22. "Fill the earth and subdue it";[19] the Bible, from the first page on, teaches us that the whole of creation is for man, that it is his responsibility to develop it by intelligent effort and by means of his labor to perfect it, so to speak, for his use. If the world is made to furnish each individual with the means of livelihood and the instruments for his growth and progress, each man has therefore the right to find in the world what is necessary for himself. The recent Council reminded us of this: "God intended the earth and all that it contains for the use of every human being and people. Thus, as all men follow justice and unite in charity, created goods should abound for them on a reasonable basis."[20] All other rights whatsoever, including those of property and of free commerce, are to be subordinated to this principle. They should not hinder but on the contrary favor its application. It is a grave and urgent social duty to redirect them to their primary finality.

23. "If someone who has the riches of this world sees his brother in need and closes his heart to him, how does the love of God abide in him?"[21] It is well-known how strong were the words used by the Fathers of the Church to describe the proper attitude of persons who possess anything toward persons in need. To quote Saint Ambrose: "You are not making a gift of your possessions to the poor person. You are handing over to him what is his. For what has been given in common for the use of all, you have arrogated to yourself. The world is given to all, and not only to the rich."[22] That is, private property does not constitute for anyone an absolute and unconditioned right. No one is justified in keeping for his exclusive use what he does not need, when others lack necessities. In a word, "according to the traditional doctrine as found in the Fathers of the Church and the great theologians, the right to property must never be exercised to the detriment of the common good." If there should arise a conflict "between acquired private rights and primary community exigen-

cies," it is the responsibility of public authorities "to look for a solution, with the active participation of individuals and social groups."[23]

24. If certain landed estates impede the general prosperity because they are extensive, unused, or poorly used, or because they bring hardship to peoples or are detrimental to the interests of the country, the common good sometimes demands their expropriation. While giving a clear statement on this,[24] the Council recalled no less clearly that the available revenue is not to be used in accordance with mere whim, and that no place must be given to selfish speculation. Consequently it is unacceptable that citizens with abundant incomes from the resources and activity of their country should transfer a considerable part of this income abroad purely for their own advantage, without care for the manifest wrong they inflict on their country by doing this.[25]

Industrialization

25. The introduction of industry is a necessity for economic growth and human progress; it is also a sign of development and contributes to it. By persistent work and use of his intelligence man gradually wrests nature's secrets from her and finds a better application for her riches. As his self-mastery increases, he develops a taste for research and discovery, an ability to take a calculated risk, boldness in enterprises, generosity in what he does, and a sense of responsibility.

26. But it is unfortunate that on these new conditions of society a system has been constructed which considers profit as the key motive for economic progress, competition as the supreme law of economics, and private ownership of the means of production as an absolute right that has no limits and carries no corresponding social obligation. This unchecked liberalism leads to dictatorship rightly denounced by Pius XI as producing "the international imperialism of money."[26] One cannot condemn such abuses too strongly by solemnly recalling once again that the economy is at the service of man.[27] But if it is true that a type of capitalism has been the source of excessive suffering, injustices, and fratricidal conflicts whose effects still persist, it would also be wrong to attribute to industrialization itself evils that belong to the woeful system which accompanied it. On the contrary one must recognize in all justice the irreplaceable contribution made by the organization of labor and of industry to what development has accomplished.

27. Similarly with work: while it can sometimes be given exaggerated significance, it is for all something willed and blessed by God. Man created to his image "must cooperate with his Creator in the perfecting of creation and communicate to the earth the spiritual imprint he himself has received."[28] God, who has endowed man with intelligence, imagination, and sensitivity, has also given him the means of completing his work in a certain way: whether he be artist or craftsman, engaged in management, industry or agriculture, everyone who works is a creator. Bent over a material that resists his efforts, a man by his work gives his imprint to it, acquiring, as he does so, perseverance,

skill, and a spirit of invention. Further, when work is done in common, when hope, hardship, ambition, and joy are shared, it brings together and firmly unites the wills, minds, and hearts of men; in its accomplishment, men find themselves to be brothers.[29]

28. Work of course can have contrary effects, for it promises money, pleasure, and power, invites some to selfishness, others to revolt; it also develops professional awareness, sense of duty and charity to one's neighbor. When it is more scientific and better organized, there is a risk of its dehumanizing those who perform it, by making them its servants, for work is human only if it remains intelligent and free. John XXIII gave a reminder of the urgency of giving everyone who works his proper dignity by making him a true sharer in the work he does with others: "every effort should be made that the enterprise become a community of persons in the dealings, activities and standing of all its members."[30] Man's labor means much more still for the Christian: the mission of sharing in the creation of the supernatural world[31] which remains incomplete until we all come to build up together that perfect man of whom St. Paul speaks "who realizes the fullness of Christ."[32]

Urgency of the Task to Be Done

29. We must make haste: too many are suffering, and the distance is growing that separates the progress of some and the stagnation, not to say the regression, of others. Yet the work required should advance smoothly if there is not to be the risk of losing indispensable equilibrium. A hasty agrarian reform can fail. Industrialization if introduced suddenly can displace structures still necessary, and produce hardships in society which would be a setback in terms of human values.

30. There are certainly situations whose injustice cries to heaven. When whole populations destitute of necessities live in a state of dependence barring them from all initiative and responsibility, and all opportunity to advance culturally and share in social and political life, recourse to violence, as a means to right these wrongs to human dignity, is a grave temptation.

31. We know, however, that a revolutionary uprising—save where there is manifest, long-standing tyranny which would do great damage to fundamental personal rights and dangerous harm to the common good of the country—produces new injustices, throws more elements out of balance and brings on new disasters. A real evil should not be fought against at the cost of greater misery.

32. We want to be clearly understood: the present situation must be faced with courage and the injustices linked with it must be fought against and overcome. Development demands bold transformations, innovations that go deep. Urgent reforms should be undertaken without delay. It is for each one to take his share in them with generosity, particularly those whose education, position and opportunities afford them wide scope for action. May they show an example, and give of their own possessions as several of our brothers in the epis-

copacy have done.[33] In so doing they will live up to men's expectations and be faithful to the Spirit of God, since it is "the ferment of the Gospel which has aroused and continues to arouse in man's heart the irresistible requirements of his dignity."[34]

Programs and Planning

33. Individual initiative alone and the mere free play of competition could never assure successful development. One must avoid the risk of increasing still more the wealth of the rich and the dominion of the strong, while leaving the poor in their misery and adding to the servitude of the oppressed. Hence programs are necessary in order "to encourage, stimulate, coordinate, supplement and integrate"[35] the activity of individuals and of intermediary bodies. It pertains to the public authorities to choose, even to lay down the objectives to be pursued, the ends to be achieved, and the means for attaining these, and it is for them to stimulate all the forces engaged in this common activity. But let them take care to associate private initiative and intermediary bodies with this work. They will thus avoid the danger of complete collectivization or of arbitrary planning, which, by denying liberty, would prevent the exercise of the fundamental rights of the human person.

34. This is true since every program, made to increase production, has, in the last analysis, no other raison d'etre than the service of man. Such programs should reduce inequalities, fight discriminations, free man from various types of servitude, and enable him to be the instrument of his spiritual growth. To speak of development is in effect to show as much concern for social progress as for economic growth. It is not sufficient to increase overall wealth for it to be distributed equitably. It is not sufficient to promote technology to render the world a more human place in which to live. The mistakes of their predecessors should warn those on the road to development of the dangers to be avoided in this field. Tomorrow's technocracy can beget evils no less redoubtable than those due to the liberalism of yesterday. Economics and technology have no meaning except from man whom they should serve. And man is only truly man in as far as, master of his own acts and judge of their worth, he is author of his own advancement, in keeping with nature which was given to him by his Creator and whose possibilities and exigencies he himself freely assumes.

35. It can even be affirmed that economic growth depends in the very first place upon social progress: thus basic education is the primary object of any plan of development. Indeed hunger for education is no less debasing than hunger for food: an illiterate is a person with an undernourished mind. To be able to read and write, to acquire a professional formation, means to recover confidence in oneself and to discover that one can progress along with the others. As we said in our message to the UNESCO Congress held in 1965 at Teheran, for man literacy is "a fundamental factor of social integration, as well as of personal enrichment, and for society it is a privileged instrument of economic progress and of development."[36] We also rejoice at the good work

accomplished in this field by private initiative, by the public authorities, and by international organizations: these are the primary agents of development, because they render man capable of acting for himself.

36. But man finds his true identity only in his social milieu, where the family plays a fundamental role. The family's influence may have been excessive to the detriment of the fundamental rights of the individual. The long-standing social frameworks, often too rigid and badly organized, existing in developing countries, are, nevertheless, still necessary for a time, yet progressively relaxing their excessive hold on the population. But the natural family, monogamous and stable, such as the divine plan conceived it[37] and as Christianity sanctified it, must remain the place where "the various generations come together and help one another to grow wiser and to harmonize personal rights with the other requirements to social life."[38]

37. It is true that too frequently an accelerated demographic increase adds its own difficulties to the problems of development: the size of the population increases more rapidly than available resources, and things are found to have reached apparently an impasse. From that moment the temptation is great to check the demographic increase by means of radical measures. It is certain that public authorities can intervene, within the limit of their competence, by favoring the availability of appropriate information and by adopting suitable measures, provided that these are in conformity with the moral law and that they respect the rightful freedom of married couples. Where the inalienable right to marriage and procreation is lacking, human dignity has ceased to exist. Finally, it is for the parents to decide, with full knowledge of the matter, on the number of their children, taking into account their responsibilities toward God, themselves, the children they have already brought into the world, and the community to which they belong. In all this they must follow the demands of their own conscience enlightened by God's law authentically interpreted, and sustained by confidence in him.[39]

38. In the task of development, man, who finds his life's primary environment in the family, is often aided by professional organizations. If it is their objective to promote the interests of their members, their responsibility is also great with regard to the educative task which at the same time they can and ought to accomplish. By means of the information they provide and the formation they propose, they can do much to give to all a sense of the common good and of the consequent obligations that fall upon each person.

39. All social action involves a doctrine. The Christian cannot admit that which is based upon a materialistic and atheistic philosophy, which respects neither the religious orientation of life to its final end, nor human freedom and dignity. But, provided that these values are safeguarded, a pluralism of professional organizations and trade unions is admissible, and from certain points of view useful, if thereby liberty is protected and emulation stimulated. And we most willingly pay homage to all those who labor in them to give unselfish service to their brothers.

40. In addition to professional organizations, there are also institutions which are at work. Their role is no less important for the success of development. "The future of the world stands in peril," the Council gravely affirms, "unless wiser men are forthcoming." And it adds: "many nations, poorer in economic goods, are quite rich in wisdom and able to offer noteworthy advantages to others."[40] Rich or poor, each country possesses a civilization handed down by its ancestors: institutions called for by life in this world, and higher manifestations of the life of the spirit, manifestations of an artistic, intellectual, and religious character. When the latter possess true human values, it would be grave error to sacrifice them to the former. A people that would act in this way would thereby lose the best of its patrimony; in order to live, it would be sacrificing its reasons for living. Christ's teaching also applies to people: "What does it profit a man to gain the whole world if he suffers the loss of his soul?"[41]

41. Less well off peoples can never be sufficiently on their guard against this temptation which comes to them from wealthy nations. For these nations all too often set an example of success in a highly technical and culturally developed civilization; they also provide the model for a way of acting that is principally aimed at the conquest of material prosperity. Not that material prosperity of itself precludes the activity of the human spirit. On the contrary, the human spirit, "increasingly free of its bondage to creatures, can be more easily drawn to the worship and contemplation of the Creator."[42] However, "modern civilization itself often complicates the approach to God, not for any essential reason, but because it is excessively engrossed in earthly affairs."[43] Developing nations must know how to discriminate among those things that are held out to them; they must be able to assess critically, and eliminate those deceptive goods which would only bring about a lowering of the human ideal, and to accept those values that are sound and beneficial, in order to develop them alongside their own, in accordance with their own genius.

42. What must be aimed at is complete humanism.[44] And what is that if not the fully rounded development of the whole man and of all men? A humanism closed in on itself, and not open to the values of the spirit and to God who is their source, could achieve apparent success. True, man can organize the world apart from God, but "without God man can organize it in the end only to man's detriment. An isolated humanism is an inhuman humanism."[45] There is no true humanism but that which is open to the Absolute and is conscious of a vocation which gives human life its true meaning. Far from being the ultimate measure of all things, man can only realize himself by reaching beyond himself. As Pascal has said so well: "Man infinitely surpasses man."[46]

PART II: THE DEVELOPMENT OF THE HUMAN RACE IN THE SPIRIT OF SOLIDARITY

43. There can be no progress toward the complete development of man without the simultaneous development of all humanity in the spirit of

solidarity. As we said at Bombay: "Man must meet man, nation meet nation, as brothers and sisters, as children of God. In this mutual understanding and friendship, in this sacred communion, we must also begin to work together to build the common future of the human race."[47] We also suggested a search for concrete and practical ways of organization and cooperation, so that all available resources be pooled and thus a true communion among all nations be achieved.

44. This duty is the concern especially of better-off nations. Their obligations stem from a brotherhood that is at once human and supernatural, and take on a threefold aspect: the duty of human solidarity—the aid that the rich nations must give to developing countries; the duty of social justice—the rectification of inequitable trade relations between powerful nations and weak nations; the duty of universal charity—the effort to bring about a world that is more human toward all men, where all will be able to give and receive, without one group making progress at the expense of the other. The question is urgent, for on it depends the future of the civilization of the world.

1. AID FOR THE WEAK

45. "If a brother or a sister be naked," says Saint James, "if they lack their daily nourishment, and one of you says to them: 'Go in peace, be warmed and be filled,' without giving them what is necessary for the body, what good does it do?"[48] Today no one can be ignorant any longer of the fact that in whole continents countless men and women are ravaged by hunger, countless numbers of children are undernourished, so that many of them die in infancy, while the physical growth and mental development of many others are retarded and as a result whole regions are condemned to the most depressing despondency.

46. Anguished appeals have already been sounded in the past: that of John XXIII was warmly received.[49] We ourselves repeated it in our Christmas message of 1963,[50] and again in 1966 on behalf of India.[51] The campaign against hunger being carried on by the Food and Agriculture Organization (FAO) and encouraged by the Holy See has been generously supported. Our *Caritas Internationalis* is at work everywhere, and many Catholics, at the urging of our brothers in the episcopacy, contribute generously of their means and spend themselves without counting the cost in assisting those who are in want, continually widening the circle of those they look upon as neighbors.

47. But neither all this nor the private and public funds that have been invested, nor the gifts and loans that have been made, can suffice. It is not just a matter of eliminating hunger, or even of reducing poverty. The struggle against destitution, though urgent and necessary, is not enough. It is a question, rather, of building a world where every man, no matter what his race, religion, or nationality, can live a fully human life, freed from servitude imposed on him by other men or by natural forces over which he has not suf-

ficient control; a world where freedom is not an empty word and where the poor man Lazarus can sit down at the same table with the rich man.[52] This demands great generosity, much sacrifice, and unceasing effort on the part of the rich man. Let each one examine his conscience, a conscience that conveys a new message for our times. Is he prepared to support out of his own pocket works and undertakings organized in favor of the most destitute? Is he ready to pay higher taxes so that the public authorities can intensify their efforts in favor of development? Is he ready to pay a higher price for imported goods so that the producer may be more justly rewarded? Or to leave this country, if necessary and if he is young, in order to assist in this development of the young nations?

48. The same duty of solidarity that rests on individuals exists also for nations: "Advanced nations have a very heavy obligation to help the developing peoples."[53] It is necessary to put this teaching of the Council into effect. Although it is normal that a nation should be the first to benefit from the gifts that Providence has bestowed on it as the fruit of the labors of its people, still no country can claim on that account to keep its wealth for itself alone. Every nation must produce more and better quality goods to give to all its inhabitants a truly human standard of living, and also to contribute to the common development of the human race. Given the increasing needs of the underdeveloped countries, it should be considered quite normal for an advanced country to devote a part of its production to meet their needs, and to train teachers, engineers, technicians, and scholars prepared to put their knowledge and their skill at the disposal of less fortunate peoples.

49. We must repeat once more that the superfluous wealth of rich countries should be placed at the service of poor nations. The rule, which up to now held good for the benefit of those nearest to us, must today be applied to all the needy of this world. Besides, the rich will be the first to benefit as a result. Otherwise their continued greed will certainly call down upon them the judgment of God and the wrath of the poor, with consequences no one can foretell. If today's flourishing civilizations remain selfishly wrapped up in themselves, they could easily place their highest values in jeopardy, sacrificing their will to be great to the desire to possess more. To them we could apply also the parable of the rich man whose fields yielded an abundant harvest and who did not know where to store his harvest: "God said to him: 'Fool, this night do they demand your soul of you.' "[54]

50. In order to be fully effective, these efforts ought not remain scattered or isolated, much less be in competition for reasons of power or prestige: the present situation calls for concerted planning. A planned program is of course better and more effective than occasional aid left to individual good will. It presupposes, as we said above, careful study, the selection of ends, and the choice of means, as well as a reorganization of efforts to meet the needs of the present and the demands of the foreseeable future. More important, a concerted plan has advantages that go beyond the field of economic growth and

social progress; for in addition it gives significance and value to the work undertaken. While shaping the world it sets a higher value on man.

51. But it is necessary to go still further. At Bombay we called for the establishment of a great *World Fund*, to be made up of part of the money spent on arms, to relieve the most destitute of this world.[55] What is true of the immediate struggle against want holds good also when there is a question of development. Only worldwide collaboration, of which a common fund would be both means and symbol, will succeed in overcoming vain rivalries and in establishing a fruitful and peaceful exchange between peoples.

52. There is certainly no need to do away with bilateral and multilateral agreements: they allow ties of dependence and feelings of betterness, left over from the era of colonialism, to yield place to the happier relationship of friendship, based on a footing of constitutional and political equality. However, if they were to be fitted into the framework of worldwide collaboration, they would be beyond all suspicion, and as a result there would be less distrust on the part of the receiving nations. These would have less cause for fearing that, under the cloak of financial aid or technical assistance, there lurk certain manifestations of what has come to be called neocolonialism, in the form of political pressures and economic suzerainty aimed at maintaining or acquiring complete dominance.

53. Besides, who does not see that such a fund would make it easier to take measures to prevent certain wasteful expenditures, the result of fear or pride? When so many people are hungry, when so many families suffer from destitution, when so many remain steeped in ignorance, when so many schools, hospitals, and homes worthy of the name remain to be built, all public or private squandering of wealth, all expenditure prompted by motives of national or personal ostentation, every exhausting armaments race, becomes an intolerable scandal. We are conscious of our duty to denounce it. Would that those in authority listened to our words before it is too late!

54. This means that it is absolutely necessary to create among all peoples that dialogue for whose establishment we expressed our hope in our first encyclical, *Ecclesiam Suam*.[56] This dialogue between those who contribute wealth and those who benefit from it will provide the possibility of making an assessment of the contribution necessary, not only drawn up in terms of the generosity and the available wealth of the donor nations, but also conditioned by the real needs of the receiving countries and the use to which the financial assistance can be put. Developing countries will thus no longer risk being overwhelmed by debts whose repayment swallows up the greater part of their gains. Rates of interest and time for repayment of the loan could be so arranged as not to be too great a burden on either party, taking into account free gifts, interest-free or low-interest loans, and the time needed for liquidating the debts. Guarantees could be given to those who provide the capital that it will be put to use according to an agreed plan and with a reasonable measure of efficiency, since there is no question of encouraging parasites or the indolent. And the receiving countries could demand that there be no interfer-

ence in their political life or subversion of their social structures. As sovereign states they have the right to conduct their own affairs, to decide on their policies, and to move freely toward the kind of society they choose. What must be brought about, therefore, is a system of cooperation freely undertaken, an effective and mutual sharing, carried out with equal dignity on either side, for the construction of a more human world.

55. The task might seem impossible in those regions where the cares of day-to-day survival fill the entire existence of families incapable of planning the kind of work which would open the way to a future that is less desperate. These, however, are the men and women who must be helped, who must be persuaded to work for their own betterment and endeavor to acquire gradually the means to that end. This common task will not succeed without concerted, constant, and courageous efforts. But let everyone be convinced of this: the very life of poor nations, civil peace in developing countries, and world peace itself are at stake.

2. EQUITY IN TRADE RELATIONS

56. The efforts which are being made to assist developing nations on a financial and technical basis, though considerable, would be illusory if their benefits were to be partially nullified as a consequence of the trade relations existing between rich and poor countries. The confidence of these latter would be severely shaken if they had the impression that what was being given them with one hand was being taken away with the other.

57. Of course, highly industrialized nations export for the most part manufactured goods, while countries with less developed economics have only food, fibers, and other raw materials to sell. As a result of technical progress the value of manufactured goods is rapidly increasing and they can always find an adequate market. On the other hand, raw materials produced by underdeveloped countries are subject to wide and sudden fluctuations in price, a state of affairs far removed from the progressively increasing value of industrial products. As a result, nations whose industrialization is limited are faced with serious difficulties when they have to rely on their exports to balance their economy and to carry out their plans for development. The poor nations remain ever poor while the rich ones become still richer.

58. In other words, the rule of free trade, taken by itself, is no longer able to govern international relations. Its advantages are certainly evident when the parties involved are not affected by any excessive inequalities of economic power: it is an incentive to progress and a reward for effort. That is why industrially developed countries see in it a law of justice. But the situation is no longer the same when economic conditions differ too widely from country to country: prices which are "freely" set in the market can produce unfair results. One must recognize that it is the fundamental principle of liberalism, as the rule for commercial exchange, which is questioned here.

59. The teaching of Leo XIII in *Rerum Novarum* is always valid: if the positions of the contracting parties are too unequal, the consent of the parties does not suffice to guarantee the justice of their contract, and the rule of free agreement remains subservient to the demands of the natural law.[57] What was true of the just wage for the individual is also true of international contracts: an economy of exchange can no longer be based solely on the law of free competition, a law which, in its turn, too often creates an economic dictatorship. Freedom of trade is fair only if it is subject to the demands of social justice.

60. Moreover, this has been understood by the developed nations themselves, which are striving, by means of appropriate measures, to reestablish within their own economies a balance, which competition, if left to itself, tends to compromise. Thus it happens that these nations often support their agriculture at the price of sacrifices imposed on economically more favored sectors. Similarly, to maintain the commercial relations which are developing among themselves, especially within a common market, the financial, fiscal, and social policy of these nations tries to restore comparable opportunities to competing industries which are not equally prospering.

61. In this area one cannot employ two systems of weights and measures. What holds for a national economy or among developed countries is valid also in commercial relations between rich nations and poor nations. Without abolishing the competitive market, it should be kept within the limits which make it just and moral, and therefore human. In trade between developed and underdeveloped economies, conditions are too disparate and the degrees of genuine freedom available too unequal. In order that international trade be human and moral, social justice requires that it restore to the participants a certain equality of opportunity. This equality is a long-term objective, but to reach it, we must begin now to create true equality in discussions and negotiations. Here again international agreements on a rather wide scale would be helpful: they would establish general norms for regulating certain prices, for guaranteeing certain types of production, for supporting certain new industries. Who is there who does not see that such a common effort aimed at increased justice in business relations between peoples would bestow on developing nations positive assistance, the effects of which would be not only immediate but lasting?

62. Among still other obstacles which are opposed to the formation of a world which is more just and which is better organized toward a universal solidarity, we wish to speak of nationalism and racism. It is only natural that communities which have recently reached their political independence should be jealous of a national unity which is still fragile, and that they should strive to protect it. Likewise, it is to be expected that nations endowed with an ancient culture should be proud of the patrimony which their history has bequeathed to them. But these legitimate feelings should be ennobled by that universal charity which embraces the entire human family. Nationalism isolates people from their true good. It would be especially harmful where the weakness of national economies demands rather the pooling of efforts, of knowledge, and

of funds, in order to implement programs of development and to increase commercial and cultural exchange.

63. Racism is not the exclusive lot of young nations, where sometimes it hides beneath the rivalries of clans and political parties, with heavy losses for justice and at the risk of civil war. During the colonial period it often flared up between the colonists and the indigenous population, and stood in the way of mutually profitable understanding, often giving rise to bitterness in the wake of genuine injustices. It is still an obstacle to collaboration among disadvantaged nations and a cause of division and hatred within countries whenever individuals and families see the inviolable rights of the human person held in scorn, as they themselves are unjustly subjected to a regime of discrimination because of their race or their color.

64. We are deeply distressed by such a situation which is laden with threats for the future. We are, nonetheless, hopeful: a more deeply felt need for collaboration, a heightened sense of unity will finally triumph over misunderstandings and selfishness. We hope that the countries whose development is less advanced will be able to take advantage of their proximity in order to organize among themselves, on a broadened territorial basis, areas for concerted development: to draw up programs in common, to coordinate investments, to distribute the means of production, and to organize trade. We hope also that multilateral and international bodies, by means of the reorganization which is required, will discover the ways that will allow peoples which are still underdeveloped to break through the barriers which seem to enclose them and to discover for themselves, in full fidelity to their own proper genius, the means for their social and human progress.

65. Such is the goal we must attain. World unity, ever more effective, should allow all peoples to become the artisans of their destiny. The past has too often been characterized by relationships of violence between nations; may the day dawn when international relations will be marked with the stamp of mutual respect and friendship, of interdependence in collaboration, the betterment of all seen as the responsibility of each individual. The younger or weaker nations ask to assume their active part in the construction of a better world, one which shows deeper respect for the rights and the vocation of the individual. This is a legitimate appeal; everyone should hear it and respond to it.

3. UNIVERSAL CHARITY

66. The world is sick. Its illness consists less in the unproductive monopolization of resources by a small number of men than in the lack of brotherhood among individuals and peoples.

67. We cannot insist too much on the duty of welcoming others—a duty springing from human solidarity and Christian charity—which is incumbent both on the families and the cultural organizations of the host countries.

Centers of welcome and hostels must be multiplied, especially for youth. This must be done first to protect them from loneliness, the feeling of abandonment, and distress, which undermine all moral resistance. This is also necessary to protect them from the unhealthy situation in which they find themselves, forced as they are to compare the extreme poverty of their homeland with the luxury and waste which often surround them. It should be done also to protect them against the subversive teachings and temptations to aggression which assail them, as they recall so much "unmerited misery."[58] Finally, and above all, this hospitality should aim to provide them, in the warm atmosphere of a brotherly welcome, with the example of wholesome living, an esteem for genuine and effective Christian charity, an esteem for spiritual values.

68. It is painful to think of the numerous young people who come to more advanced countries to receive the science, the competence, and the culture which will make them more qualified to serve their homeland, and who certainly acquire there a formation of high quality, but who often lose the esteem for the spiritual values which often were to be found, as a precious patrimony, in the civilizations where they had grown up.

69. The same welcome is due to emigrant workers, who live in conditions which are often inhuman, and who economize on what they earn in order to send a little relief to their family living in misery in their native land.

70. Our second recommendation is for those whose business calls them to countries recently opened to industrialization: industrialists, merchants, leaders or representatives of larger enterprises. It happens that they are not lacking in social sensitivity in their own country; why then do they return to the inhuman principles of individualism when they operate in less-developed countries? Their advantaged situation should on the contrary move them to become the initiators of social progress and of human advancement in the area where their business calls them. Their very sense of organization should suggest to them the means for making intelligent use of the labor of the indigenous population, of forming qualified workers, of training engineers and staffs, of giving scope to their initiative, of introducing them progressively into higher positions, thus preparing them to share, in the near future, in the responsibilities of management. At least let justice always rule the relations between superiors and their subordinates. Let standard contracts with reciprocal obligations govern these relationships. Finally, let no one, whatever his status, be subjected unjustly to the arbitrariness of others.

71. We are happy that experts are being sent in larger and larger numbers on development missions by institutions, whether international or bilateral, or by private organizations: "they ought not conduct themselves in a lordly fashion, but as helpers and co-workers."[59] A people quickly perceives whether those who come to help them do so with or without affection, whether they come merely to apply their techniques or to recognize in man his full value.

Their message is in danger of being rejected if it is not presented in the context of brotherly love.

72. Hence, necessary technical competence must be accompanied by authentic signs of disinterested love. Freed of all nationalistic pride and of every appearance of racism, experts should learn how to work in close collaboration with all. They realize that their competence does not confer on them a superiority in every field. The civilization which formed them contains, without doubt, elements of universal humanism, but it is not the only civilization nor does it enjoy a monopoly of valuable elements. Moreover it cannot be imported without undergoing adaptations. The men on these missions will be intent on discovering, along with its history, the component elements of the cultural riches of the country receiving them. Mutual understanding will be established which will enrich both cultures.

73. Between civilizations, as between persons, sincere dialogue indeed creates brotherhood. The work of development will draw nations together in the attainment of goals pursued with a common effort if all, from governments and their representatives to the last expert, are inspired by brotherly love and moved by the sincere desire to build a civilization founded on world solidarity. A dialogue based on man, and not on commodities or technical skills, will then begin. It will be fruitful if it brings to the peoples who benefit from it the means of self-betterment and spiritual growth, if the technicians act as educators, and if the instruction imparted is characterized by so lofty a spiritual and moral tone that it guarantees not merely economic, but human development. When aid programs have been terminated, the relationships thus established will endure. Who does not see of what importance they will be for the peace of the world?

74. Many young people have already responded with warmth and enthusiasm to the appeal of Pius XII for lay missionaries.[60] Many also are those who have spontaneously put themselves at the disposition of official or private organizations which are collaborating with developing nations. We are pleased to learn that in certain nations "military service" can be partially accomplished by doing "social service," a "service pure and simple." We bless these undertakings and the good will which inspires them. May all those who wish to belong to Christ hear his appeal: "I was hungry and you gave me to eat, thirsty and you gave me to drink, a stranger and you took me in, naked and you clothed me, sick and you visited me, a prisoner and you came to see me."[61] No one can remain indifferent to the lot of his brothers who are still buried in wretchedness, and victims of insecurity, slaves of ignorance. Like the heart of Christ, the heart of the Christian must sympathize with this misery: "I have pity on this multitude."[62]

75. The prayer of all ought to rise with fervor to the Almighty. Having become aware of such great misfortunes, the human race will apply itself with intelligence and steadfastness to abolish them. This prayer should be matched by the resolute commitment of each individual—according to the measure of his strength and possibilities—to the struggle against underdevelopment. May individuals, social groups, and nations join hands in brotherly

fashion, the strong aiding the weak to grow, exerting all their competence, enthusiasm, and disinterested love. More than any other, the individual who is animated by true charity labors skillfully to discover the causes of misery, to find the means to combat it, to overcome it resolutely. A creator of peace, he "will follow his path, lighting the lamps of joy and playing their brilliance and loveliness on the hearts of men across the surface of the globe, leading them to recognize, across all frontiers, the faces of their brothers, the faces of their friends."[63]

4. DEVELOPMENT IS THE NEW NAME FOR PEACE

76. Excessive economic, social, and cultural inequalities among peoples arouse tensions and conflicts, and are a danger to peace. As we said to the Fathers of the Council when we returned from our journey of peace to the United Nations: "The condition of the peoples in process of development ought to be the object of our consideration; or better: our charity for the poor in the world—and there are multitudes of them—must become more considerate, more active, more generous."[64] To wage war on misery and to struggle against injustice is to promote, along with improved conditions, the human and spiritual progress of all men, and therefore the common good of humanity. Peace cannot be limited to a mere absence of war, the result of an ever precarious balance of forces. No, peace is something that is built up day after day, in the pursuit of an order intended by God, which implies a more perfect form of justice among men.[65]

77. The peoples themselves have the prime responsibility to work for their own development. But they will not bring this about in isolation. Regional agreements among weak nations for mutual support, understandings of wider scope entered into for their help, more far-reaching agreements to establish programs for closer cooperation among groups of nations—these are the milestones on the road to development that leads to peace.

78. This international collaboration on a worldwide scale requires institutions that will prepare, coordinate and direct it, until finally there is established an order of justice which is universally recognized. With all our heart, we encourage these organizations which have undertaken this collaboration for the development of the peoples of the world, and our wish is that they grow in prestige and authority. "Your vocation," as we said to the representatives of the United Nations in New York, "is to bring not some people but all peoples to treat each other as brothers. . . . Who does not see the necessity of thus establishing progressively a world authority, capable of acting effectively in the juridical and political sectors?"[66]

79. Some would consider such hopes utopian. It may be that these persons are not realistic enough, and that they have not perceived the dynamism of a world which desires to live more fraternally—a world which, in spite of its ignorance, its mistakes, and even its sins, its relapses into barbarism, and its

wanderings far from the road of salvation, is, even unawares, taking slow but sure steps toward its Creator. This road toward a greater humanity requires effort and sacrifice; but suffering itself, accepted for the love of our brethren, favors the progress of the entire human family. Christians know that union with the sacrifice of our Savior contributes to the building up of the body of Christ in its plentitude: the assembled people of God.[67]

80. We are all united in this progress toward God. We have desired to remind all men how crucial is the present moment, how urgent the work to be done. The hour for action has now sounded. At stake are the survival of so many innocent children and, for so many families overcome by misery, the access to conditions fit for human beings; at stake are the peace of the world and the future of civilization. It is time for all men and all peoples to face up to their responsibilities.

A FINAL APPEAL

81. First, we appeal to all our sons. In countries undergoing development no less than in others, the laymen should take up as their own proper task the renewal of the temporal order. If the role of the hierarchy is to teach and to interpret authentically the norms of morality to be followed in this matter, it belongs to the laymen, without waiting passively for orders and directives, to take the initiative freely and to infuse a Christian spirit into the mentality, customs, laws, and structures of the community in which they live.[68] Changes are necessary, basic reforms are indispensable: the laymen should strive resolutely to permeate them with the spirit of the Gospel. We ask our Catholic sons who belong to the more favored nations to bring their talents and give their active participation to organizations, be they of an official or private nature, civil or religious, which are working to overcome the difficulties of the developing nations. They will certainly desire to be in the first ranks of those who collaborate to establish as fact and reality an international morality based on justice and equity.

82. We are sure that all Christians, our brethren, will wish to expand their common cooperative effort in order to help mankind vanquish selfishness, pride, and rivalries, to overcome ambitions and injustices, to open up to all the road to a more human life, where each man will be loved and helped as his brother, as his neighbor. And, still deeply impressed by the memory of our unforgettable encounter in Bombay with our non-Christian brethren, we invite them anew to work with all their heart and their intelligence toward this goal, that all the children of men may lead a life worthy of the children of God.

83. Finally, we turn to all men of good will who believe that the way to peace lies in the area of development. Delegates to international organizations, government officials, gentlemen of the press, educators: all of you, each in your own way, are the builders of a new world. We entreat almighty God to enlighten your minds and strengthen your determination to alert public

opinion and to involve the peoples of the world. Educators, it is your task to awaken in persons, from their earliest years, a love for the peoples who live in misery. Gentlemen of the press, it is up to you to place before our eyes the story of the efforts exerted to promote mutual assistance among peoples, as well as the spectacle of the miseries which men tend to forget in order to quiet their consciences. Thus at least the wealthy will know that the poor stand outside their doors waiting to receive some leftovers from their banquets.

84. Government officials, it is your concern to mobilize your peoples to form a more effective world solidarity, and above all to make them accept the necessary taxes on their luxuries and their wasteful expenditures, in order to bring about development and to save the peace. Delegates to international organizations, it depends on you to see that the dangerous and futile rivalry of powers should give place to collaboration which is friendly, peaceful, and free of vested interests, in order to achieve a responsible development of mankind, in which all men will have an opportunity to find their fulfillment.

85. If it is true that the world is in trouble because of the lack of thinking, then we call upon men of reflection and learning, Catholics, Christians, those who hold God in honor, who thirst for an absolute, for justice, and for truth; we call upon all men of good will. Following Christ, we make bold to ask you earnestly: "Seek and you shall find,"[69] open the paths which lead to mutual assistance among peoples, to a deepening of human knowledge, to an enlargement of heart, to a more brotherly way of living with a truly universal human society.

86. All of you who have heard the appeal of suffering peoples, all of you who are working to answer their cries, you are the apostles of a development which is good and genuine, which is not wealth that is self-centered and sought for its own sake, but rather an economy which is put at the service of man, the bread which is daily distributed to all, as source of brotherhood and a sign of Providence.

87. With a full heart we bless you, and we appeal to all men of good will to join you in a spirit of brotherhood. For if the new name for peace is development, who would not wish to labor for it with all his powers? Yes, we ask you, all of you, to heed our cry of anguish, in the name of the Lord.

From the Vatican, on the Feast of Easter, the twenty-sixth day of March in the year one thousand nine hundred and sixty-seven.

PAUL VI

NOTES

1. Cf. *Acta Leonis XIII*, t. XI (1892), pp. 97–148.
2. Cf. AAS 23 (1931), pp. 177–228.
3. Cf. AAS 53 (1961), pp. 401–64.
4. Cf. AAS 55 (1963), pp. 257–304.

5. Cf. in particular the Radio Message of June 1, 1941, for the fiftieth anniversary of *Rerum Novarum*, in AAS 33 (1941), pp. 195–205; Christmas Radio Message of 1942, in AAS 35 (1943), pp. 9–24; Address to a group of workers on the anniversary of *Rerum Novarum*, May 14, 1953, in AAS 45 (1953), pp. 402–8.

6. Cf. Encyclical *Mater et Magistra*, May 15, 1961, AAS 53 (1961), p. 440.

7. *Gaudium et Spes*, 63–72: AAS 58 (1966), pp. 1084–94.

8. Motu Proprio *Catholicam Christi Ecclesiam*, Jan. 6, 1967, AAS 59 (1967), p. 27.

9. Encyclical *Rerum Novarum*, May 15, 1891: *Acta Leonis XIII*, t. XI (1892), p. 98.

10. *Gaudium et Spes*, 63.

11. Cf. Lk. 7:22.

12. *Gaudium et Spes*, 63.

13. Cf. Encyclical *Immortale Dei*, Nov. 1, 1885: *Acta Leonis XIII*, t. V (1885), p. 127.

14. *Gaudium et Spes*, 4.

15. L.J. Lebret, O.P., *Dynamique concrète du développement*, Paris: Economic et Humanisme, Les Editions Ouvrières, 1961, p. 28.

16. 2 Thess. 3:10.

17. Cf., for example, J. Maritain, *Les conditions spirituelles du progrès et de la paix*, in *Rencontre des cultures à l'UNESCO sous le signe du Concile oecuménique Vatican II*, Paris: Mame, 1966, p. 66.

18. Cf. Mt. 5:3.

19. Gen. 1:28.

20. *Gaudium et Spes*, 69.

21. 1 Jn. 3:17.

22. *De Nabuthe*, c. 12, n. 53 (P.L. 14, 747). Cf. J.-R. Palanque, *Saint Ambroise et l'empire romain*, Paris: de Boccard, 1933, pp. 336f.

23. Letter to the 52d Session of the French Social Weeks (Brest, 1965), in *L'homme et la révolution urbaine*, Lyons Chronique sociale, 1965, pp. 8 and 9. Cf. *L'Osservatore Romano*, July 10, 1965, *Documentation catholique*, t. 62, Paris, 1965, col. 1365.

24. *Gaudium et Spes*, 71.

25. Cf. ibid., 65.

26. Encyclical *Quadragesimo Anno*, May 15, 1931, AAS 23 (1931), p. 212.

27. Cf., for example, Colin Clark, *The Conditions of Economic Progress*, 3rd ed., London: Macmillan and Co., and New York: St. Martin's Press, 1960, pp. 3–6.

28. Letter to the 51st Session of the French Social Weeks (Lyons, 1964), in *Le travail et les travailleurs dans la societé contemporaine*, Lyons, Chronique sociale, 1965, p. 6. Cf. *L'Osservatore Romano*, July 10, 1964; *Documentation catholique*, t. 61, Paris, 64, col. 931.

29. Cf., for example, M.-D. Chenu, O.P., *Pour une théologie du travail*, Paris: Editions du Seuil, 1955, Eng. tr.: *The Theology of Work: An Exploration*, Dublin: Gill and Son, 1963.

30. *Mater et Magistra*, AAS 53 (1961), p. 423.

31. Cf., for example, O. von Nell-Breuning, S.J., *Wirtschaft und Gesellschaft*, t. 1: *Grundfragen*, Freiburg: Herder, 1956, pp. 83–84.

32. Eph. 4:13.

33. Cf., for example, Bishop Manue Larrain Errázuriz of Talca, Chile, President of CELAM, *Lettre pastorale sur le développement et la paix*, Paris: Pax Christi, 1965.

34. *Gaudium et Spes*, 26.

35. *Mater et Magistra*, AAS 53 (1961), p. 414.

36. *L'Osservatore Romano*, Sept. 11, 1965, *Documentation catholique*, t. 62, Paris, 1965, col. 1674–75.

37. Mt. 19:16.

38. *Gaudium et Spes*, 52.

39. Cf. ibid., 50–51 and note 14; and 87.

40. Ibid., 15.

41. Mt. 16:26.

42. *Gaudium et Spes*, 57.

43. Ibid., 19.

44. Cf., for example, J. Maritain, *L'humanisme intégral*, Paris: Aubier, 1936. Eng. tr.: *True Humanism*, London: Geoffrey Bles; and New York: Charles Scribner's Sons, 1938.

45. H. de Lubac, S.J., *Le drame de l'humanisme athée*, Paris: Spes, 1945, p. 10. Eng. tr. *The Drama of Atheistic Humanism*, London: Sheed and Ward, 1949, p. vii.

46. Blaise Pascal, *Pensées*, ed. Brunschvicg, n. 434. Cf. M. Zundel, *L'homme passe l'homme*, Le Caire, Editions du lien, 1944.

47. Address to the Representatives of non-Christian Religions, Dec. 3, 1964, AAS 57 (1965), p. 132.

48. Jas. 2:15–16.

49. Cf. *Mater et Magistra*, AAS 53 (1961), pp. 440f.

50. Cf. AAS 56 (1964), pp. 57–58.

51. Cf. *Encicliche e Discorsi di Paolo VI*, vol. IX, Roma, ed. Paoline, 1966, pp. 132–36, *Documentation catholique*, t. 43, Paris, 1966, col. 403–6.

52. Cf. Lk. 16:19–31.

53. *Gaudium et Spes*, 86.

54. Lk. 12:20.

55. Message to the world, entrusted to journalists on Dec. 4, 1964. Cf. AAS 57 (1965), p. 135.

56. Cf. AAS 56 (1964), pp. 639f.

57. Cf. *Acta Leonis XIII*, t. XI (1892), p. 131.

58. Cf. ibid., p. 98.

59. *Gaudium et Spes*, 85.

60. Cf. Encyclical *Fidei Donum*, Apr. 21, 1957, AAS 49 (1957), p. 246.

61. Mt. 25:35–36.

62. Mk. 8:2.

63. Address of John XXIII upon Reception of the Balzan Prize for Peace, May 10, 1963, AAS 55 (1963), p. 455.

64. AAS 57 (1965), p. 89.

65. Cf. Encyclical *Pacem in Terris*, Apr. 11, 1963, AAS 55 (1963), p. 301.

66. AAS 57 (1965), p. 880.

67. Cf. Eph. 4:12; *Lumen Gentium*, 13.

68. Cf. *Apostolicam Actuositatem*, 7, 13 and 24.

69. Lk. 11:9.

Octogesima Adveniens:
A Call to Action
on the Eightieth Anniversary
of Rerum Novarum
(Paul VI, 1971)

INTRODUCTION

Timed to coincide with the eightieth anniversary of *Rerum Novarum* and the tenth anniversary of *Mater et Magistra*, this encyclical, published in 1971, was addressed directly to Catholics, urging them to incorporate more seriously the new sense of Christian responsibility in the world into all phases of their lives. *Octogesima Adveniens* emphasized that action for justice was a personal responsibility of every Christian, that this responsibility rested on Christian organizations and institutions, that it involved both the effort to bear witness to the principles of justice in personal and community life and acting to give those principles life in society.

Pope Paul recognized that Christian communities had to analyze the situation proper to their own country in the light of the gospel and to draw principles of reflection, norms of judgment, and directives of action both from the gospel and the church's message. Most important, because situations differed from country to country, no universal program could be prescribed and local churches had to develop their own program of social justice.

Urbanization is a new theme in this encyclical. Paul VI sees individuals facing a new loneliness as a result of the anonymity, poverty, indifference, waste, and overconsumption often found in cities. These situations lend themselves easily to new forms of exploitation and domination.

Another new issue is the environment. Given rapid technological advances and the resources needed to keep pace with this development, severe questions about the future capacity of the earth to support the human race came to the fore. Thus the pope calls for a new sense of responsibility for the environment, which must support all of the inhabitants of the earth.

While recognizing and, indeed, voicing a high level of suspicion about the various ideologies that support many political programs, this letter recognizes the urgency of contemporary problems and argues strongly that Christians are called to action and participation in the social and political processes of the countries in which they live. This new call to action recognizes that Christians must become involved in social reforms as part of their mission as Christians. Although such a mission raises difficult political and practical problems, such difficulties do not absolve Christians of their duties. Rather, the urgency of the situation heightens the social responsibility of the Christian.

OCTOGESIMA ADVENIENS

A CALL TO ACTION
APOSTOLIC LETTER OF HIS HOLINESS

POPE PAUL VI

To Cardinal Maurice Roy,
President of the Council of the Laity
and of the Pontifical Commission
Justice and Peace,
on the Occasion
of the Eightieth Anniversary of
the Encyclical Rerum Novarum

Venerable Brother,

1. The eightieth anniversary of the publication of the encyclical *Rerum Novarum*, the message of which continues to inspire action for social justice, prompts us to take up again and to extend the teaching of our predecessors, in response to the new needs of a changing world. The Church, in fact, travels forward with humanity and shares its lot in the setting of history. At the same time that she announces to men the Good News of God's love and of salvation in Christ, she clarifies their activity in the light of the Gospel and in this way helps them to correspond to God's plan of love and to realize the fullness of their aspirations.

Universal Appeal for More Justice

2. It is with confidence that we see the Spirit of the Lord pursuing his work in the hearts of men and in every place gathering together Christian communities conscious of their responsibilities in society. On all the continents, among all races, nations, and cultures, and under all conditions the Lord continues to raise up authentic apostles of the Gospel.

We have had the opportunity to meet these people, to admire them and to give them our encouragement in the course of our recent journeys. We have gone into the crowds and have heard their appeals, cries of distress, and at the same time cries of hope. Under these circumstances we have seen in a new perspective the grave problems of our time. These problems of course are particular to each part of the world, but at the same time they are common to all mankind, which is questioning itself about its future and about the tendency and the meaning of the changes taking place. Flagrant inequalities exist in the economic, cultural, and political development of the nations: while some regions are heavily industrialized, others are still at the agricultural stage; while some countries enjoy prosperity, others are struggling against starvation; while some peoples have a high standard of culture, others are still engaged in eliminating illiteracy. From all sides there rises a yearning for more justice and a desire for a better guaranteed peace in mutual respect among individuals and peoples.

Diversity of Situations

3. There is of course a wide diversity among the situations in which Christians—willingly or unwillingly—find themselves according to regions, sociopolitical systems, and cultures. In some places they are reduced to silence, regarded with suspicion, and as it were kept on the fringe of society, enclosed without freedom in a totalitarian system. In other places they are a weak minority whose voice makes itself heard with difficulty. In some other nations, where the Church sees her place recognized, sometimes officially so, she too finds herself subjected to the repercussions of the crisis which is unsettling society; some of her members are tempted by radical and violent solutions from which they believe that they can expect a happier outcome. While some people, unaware of present injustices, strive to prolong the existing situation, others allow themselves to be beguiled by revolutionary ideologies which promise them, not without delusion, a definitively better world.

4. In the face of such widely varying situations it is difficult for us to utter a unified message and to put forward a solution which has universal validity. Such is not our ambition, nor is it our mission. It is up to the Christian communities to analyze with objectivity the situation which is proper to their own country, to shed on it the light of the Gospel's unalterable words and to draw principles of reflection, norms of judgment and directives for action from the social teaching of the Church. This social teaching has been worked out in the course of history and notably, in this industrial era, since the historic date of the message of Pope Leo XIII on "the condition of the workers," and it is an honor and joy for us to celebrate today the anniversary of that message. It is up to these Christian communities, with the help of the Holy Spirit, in communion with the bishops who hold responsibility and in dialogue with other Christian brethren and all men of good will, to discern the options and commitments which are called for in order to bring about the social, political, and economic changes seen in many cases to be urgently needed. In this search for the changes which should be promoted, Christians must first of all renew their confidence in the forcefulness and special character of the demands made by the Gospel. The Gospel is not out-of-date because it was proclaimed, written and lived in a different sociocultural context. Its inspiration, enriched by the living experience of Christian tradition over the centuries, remains ever new for converting men and for advancing the life of society. It is not however to

be utilized for the profit of particular temporal options, to the neglect of its universal and eternal message.[1]

Specific Message of the Church

5. Amid the disturbances and uncertainties of the present hour, the Church has a specific message to proclaim and a support to give to men in their efforts to take in hand and give direction to their future. Since the period in which the encyclical *Rerum Novarum* denounced in a forceful and imperative manner the scandal of the condition of the workers in the nascent industrial society, historical evolution has led to an awareness of other dimensions and other applications of social justice. The encyclicals *Quadragesimo Anno*[2] and *Mater et Magistra*[3] already noted this fact. The recent Council for its part took care to point them out, in particular in the Pastoral Constitution *Gaudium et Spes*. We ourself have already continued these lines of thought in our encyclical *Populorum Progressio*. "Today," we said, "the principal fact that we must all recognize is that the social question has become worldwide."[4] "A renewed consciousness of the demands of the Gospel makes it the Church's duty to put herself at the service of all, to help them grasp their serious problem in all its dimensions, and to convince them that solidarity in action at this turning point in human history is a matter of urgency."[5]

6. It will moreover be for the forthcoming synod of bishops itself to study more closely and to examine in greater detail the Church's mission in the face of grave issues raised today by the question of justice in the world. But the anniversary of *Rerum Novarum*, venerable brother, gives us the opportunity today to confide our preoccupations and thoughts in the face of this problem to you as president of the Pontifical Commission Justice and Peace and of the Council of Laity. In this way it is also our wish to offer these bodies of the Holy See our encouragement in their ecclesial activity in the service of men.

Extent of Present-day Changes

7. In so doing, our purpose—without however forgetting the permanent problems already dealt with by our predecessors—is to draw attention to a number of questions. These are questions which because of their urgency, extent, and complexity must in the years to come take first place among the preoccupations of Christians, so that with other men the latter may dedicate themselves to solving the new difficulties which put the very future of man in jeopardy. It is necessary to situate the problems created by the modern economy in the wider context of a new civilization. These problems include human conditions of production, fairness in the exchange of goods and in the division of wealth, the significance of the increased needs of consumption, and the sharing of responsibility. In the present changes, which are so profound and so rapid, each day man discovers himself anew, and he questions himself about the meaning of his own being and of his collective survival. Reluctant to gather the lessons of a past that he considers over and done with and too

different from the present, man nevertheless needs to have light shed upon his future—a future which he perceives to be as uncertain as it is changing—by permanent eternal truths. These are truths which are certainly greater than man but, if he so wills, he can himself find their traces.[6]

NEW SOCIAL PROBLEMS

Urbanization

8. A major phenomenon draws our attention, as much in the industrialized countries as in those which are developing: urbanization.

After long centuries, agrarian civilization is weakening. Is sufficient attention being devoted to the arrangement and improvement of the life of the country people, whose inferior and at times miserable economic situation provokes the flight to the unhappy crowded conditions of the city outskirts, where neither employment nor housing awaits them?

This unceasing flight from the land, industrial growth, continual demographic expansion, and the attraction of urban centers bring about concentrations of population, the extent of which is difficult to imagine, for people are already speaking in terms of a "megalopolis" grouping together tens of millions of persons. Of course there exist medium-sized towns, the dimension of which ensures a better balance in the population. While being able to offer employment to those that progress in agriculture makes available, they permit an adjustment of the human environment which better avoids the proletarianism and crowding of the great built-up areas.

9. The inordinate growth of these centers accompanies industrial expansion, without being identified with it. Based on technological research and the transformation of nature, industrialization constantly goes forward, giving proof of incessant creativity. While certain enterprises develop and are concentrated, others die or change their location. Thus new social problems are created: professional or regional unemployment, redeployment and mobility of persons, permanent adaptation of workers, and disparity of conditions in the different branches of industry. Unlimited competition utilizing the modern means of publicity incessantly launches new products and tries to attract the consumer, while earlier industrial installations which are still capable of functioning become useless. While very large areas of the population are unable to satisfy their primary needs, superfluous needs are ingeniously created. It can thus rightly be asked if, in spite of all his conquests, man is not turning back against himself the results of his activity. Having rationally endeavored to control nature,[7] is he not now becoming the slave of the objects which he makes?

Christians in the City

10. Is not the rise of an urban civilization which accompanies the advance of industrial civilization a true challenge to the wisdom of man, to his capacity for organization and to his farseeing imagination? Within industrial society

urbanization upsets both the ways of life and the habitual structures of existence: the family, the neighborhood, and the very framework of the Christian community. Man is experiencing a new loneliness; it is not in the face of a hostile nature which it has taken him centuries to subdue, but in an anonymous crowd which surrounds him and in which he feels himself a stranger. Urbanization, undoubtedly an irreversible stage in the development of human societies, confronts man with difficult problems. How is he to master its growth, regulate its organization, and successfully accomplish its animation for the good of all?

In this disordered growth, new proletariats are born. They install themselves in the heart of the cities sometimes abandoned by the rich; they dwell on the outskirts—which become a belt of misery besieging in a still-silent protest with luxury which blatantly cries out from centers of consumption and waste. Instead of favoring fraternal encounter and mutual aid, the city fosters discrimination and also indifference. It lends itself to new forms of exploitation and of domination whereby some people in speculating on the needs of others derive inadmissible profits. Behind the facades, much misery is hidden, unsuspected even by the closest neighbors; other forms of misery spread where human dignity founders: delinquency, criminality, abuse of drugs, and eroticism.

11. It is in fact the weakest who are the victims of dehumanizing living conditions, degrading for conscience and harmful for the family institution. The promiscuity of working people's housing makes a minimum of intimacy impossible; young couples waiting in vain for a decent dwelling at a price they can afford are demoralized and their union can thereby even be endangered; youth escape from a home which is too confined and seek in the street compensations and companionships which cannot be supervised. It is the grave duty of those responsible to strive to control this process and to give it direction.

There is an urgent need to remake at the level of the street, of the neighborhood, or of the great agglomerative dwellings the social fabric whereby man may be able to develop the needs of his personality. Centers of special interest and of culture must be created or developed at the community and parish levels with different forms of associations, recreational centers, and spiritual and community gatherings where the individual can escape from isolation and form anew fraternal relationships.

12. To build up the city, the place where men and their expanded communities exist, to create new modes of neighborliness and relationships, to perceive an original application of social justice and to undertake responsibility for this collective future, which is foreseen as difficult, is a task in which Christians must share. To those who are heaped up in an urban promiscuity which becomes intolerable it is necessary to bring a message of hope. This can be done by brotherhood which is lived and by concrete justice. Let Christians, conscious of this new responsibility, not lose heart in view of the vast

and faceless society; let them recall Jonah who traversed Niniveh, the great city, to proclaim therein the good news of God's mercy and was upheld in his weakness by the sole strength of the word of almighty God. In the Bible, the city is in fact often the place of sin and pride—the pride of man who feels secure enough to be able to build his life without God and even to affirm that he is powerful against God. But there is also the example of Jerusalem, the Holy City, the place where God is encountered, the promise of the city which comes from on high.[8]

Youth

13. Urban life and industrial change bring strongly to light questions which until now were poorly grasped. What place, for example, in this world being brought to birth, should be given to youth? Everywhere dialogue is proving to be difficult between youth, with its aspirations, renewal, and also insecurity for the future, and the adult generations. It is obvious to all that here we have a source of serious conflicts, division, and opting out, even within the family, and a questioning of modes of authority, education for freedom, and the handing on of values and beliefs, which strikes at the deep roots of society.

The Role of Women

Similarly, in many countries a charter for women which would put an end to an actual discrimination and would establish relationships of equality in rights and of respect for their dignity is the object of study and at times of lively demands. We do not have in mind that false equality which would deny the distinctions laid down by the Creator himself and which would be in contradiction with woman's proper role, which is of such capital importance, at the heart of the family as well as within society. Developments in legislation should on the contrary be directed to protecting her proper vocation and at the same time recognizing her independence as a person, and her equal rights to participate in cultural, economic, social, and political life.

Workers

14. As the Church solemnly reaffirmed in the recent Council, "the beginning, the subject, and the goal of all social institutions is and must be the human person."[9] Every man has the right to work, to a chance to develop his qualities and his personality in the exercise of his profession, to equitable remuneration which will enable him and his family "to lead a worthy life on the material, social, cultural, and spiritual level,"[10] and to assistance in case of need arising from sickness or age.

Although for the defense of these rights democratic societies accept today the principle of labor union rights, they are not always open to their exercise. The important role of union organizations must be admitted: their object is the representation of the various categories of workers, their lawful collaboration in the economic advance of society, and the development of the sense of their responsibility for the realization of the common good. Their activity, however, is not without its difficulties. Here and there the temptation can arise of profiting from a position of force to impose, particularly by strikes—the right to which as a final means of defense remains certainly recognized—conditions which are too burdensome for the overall economy and for the social body, or to desire to obtain in this way demands of a directly political nature. When it is a question of public services, required for the life of an entire nation, it is necessary to be able to assess the limit beyond which the harm caused to society becomes inadmissible.

Victims of Changes

15. In short, progress has already been made in introducing, in the area of human relationships, greater justice and greater sharing of responsibilities. But in this immense field much remains to be done. Further reflection, research and experimentation must be actively pursued, unless one is to be late in meeting the legitimate aspirations of the workers—aspirations which are being increasingly asserted according as their education, their consciousness of their dignity and the strength of their organizations increase.

Egoism and domination are permanent temptations for men. Likewise an ever finer discernment is needed, in order to strike at the roots of newly arising situations of injustice and to establish progressively a justice which will be less and less imperfect. In industrial change, which demands speedy and constant adaptation, those who will find themselves injured will be more numerous and at a greater disadvantage from the point of view of making their voices heard. The Church directs her attention to these new "poor"—the handicapped and the maladjusted, the old, different groups of those on the fringe of society, and so on—in order to recognize them, help them, defend their place and dignity in a society hardened by competition and the attraction of success.

Discrimination

16. Among the victims of situations of injustice—unfortunately no new phenomenon—must be placed those who are discriminated against, in law or in fact, on account of their race, origin, color, culture, sex, or religion.

Racial discrimination possesses at the moment a character of very great relevance by reason of the tension which it stirs up both within certain countries and on the international level. Men rightly consider unjustifiable and reject as inadmissible the tendency to maintain or introduce legislation or behavior systematically inspired by racialist prejudice. The members of mankind share the same basic rights and duties, as well as the same supernatural destiny. Within a country which belongs to each one, all should be equal before the law, find equal admittance to economic, cultural, civic, and social life, and benefit from a fair sharing of the nation's riches.

Right to Emigrate

17. We are thinking also of the precarious situation of a great number of emigrant workers whose condition as foreigners makes it all the more difficult for them to make any sort of social vindication, in spite of their real participation in the economic effort of the country that receives them. It is urgently necessary for people to go beyond a narrowly nationalist attitude in their regard and to give them a charter which will assure them a right to emigrate, favor their integration, facilitate their professional advancement, and give them access to decent housing where, if such is the case, their families can join them.[11]

Linked to this category are the people who, to find work, or to escape a disaster or a hostile climate, leave their regions and find themselves without roots among other people.

It is everyone's duty, but especially that of Christians,[12] to work with energy for the establishment of universal brotherhood, the indispensable basis for authentic justice and the condition for enduring peace: "We cannot in truthfulness call upon that God who is the Father of all if we refuse to act in a brotherly way toward certain men, created to God's image. A man's relationship with God the Father and his relationship with his brother men are so linked together that scripture says: 'He who does not love does not know God' (John 4:8)."[13]

Creating Employment

18. With demographic growth, which is particularly pronounced in the young nations, the number of those failing to find work and driven to misery or parasitism will grow in the coming years unless the conscience of man rouses itself and gives rise to a general movement of solidarity through an effective policy of investment and or organization of production and trade, as well as of education. We know the attention given to these problems within international organizations, and it is our lively wish that their members will not delay bringing their actions into line with their declarations.

It is disquieting in this regard to note a kind of fatalism which is gaining a hold even on people in positions of responsibility. This feeling sometimes leads to Malthusian solutions inculcated by active propaganda for contraception and abortion. In this critical situation, it must on the contrary be affirmed that the family, without which no society can stand, has a right to the assistance which will assure it of the conditions for a healthy development. "It is certain," we said in our encyclical *Populorum Progressio*, "that public authorities can intervene, within the limit of their competence, by favoring the availability of appropriate information and by adopting suitable measures, provided that these be in conformity with the moral law and that they respect the rightful freedom of married couples. Where the inalienable right to marriage and procreation is lacking, human dignity has ceased to exist."[14]

19. In no other age has the appeal to the imagination of society been so explicit. To this should be devoted enterprises of invention and capital as important as those invested for armaments or technological achievements. If man lets himself rush ahead without foreseeing in good time the emergence of new social problems, they will become too grave for a peaceful solution to be hoped for.

Media of Social Communication

20. Among the major changes of our times, we do not wish to forget to emphasize the growing role being assumed by the media of social communication and their influence on the transformation of mentalities, of knowledge, of organizations, and of society itself. Certainly they have many positive aspects. Thanks to them news from the entire world reaches us practically in an instant, establishing contacts which supersede distances and creating elements of unity among all men. A greater spread of education and culture is becoming possible. Nevertheless, by their very action the media of social communication are reaching the point of representing as it were a new power. One cannot but ask about those who really hold this power, the aims that they pursue and the means they use, and finally, about the effect of their activity on the exercise of individual liberty, both in the political and ideological spheres and in social, economic, and cultural life. The men who hold this power have a grave moral responsibility with respect to the truth of the information that they spread, the needs and the reactions that they generate, and the values which they put forward. In the case of television, moreover, what is coming into being is an original mode of knowledge and a new civilization: that of the image.

Naturally, the public authorities cannot ignore the growing power and influence of the media of social communication and the advantages and risks which their use involves for the civic community and for its development and real perfecting.

Consequently they are called upon to perform their own positive function for the common good by encouraging every constructive expression, by supporting individual citizens and groups in defending the fundamental values of the person and of human society, and also by taking suitable steps to prevent the spread of what would harm the common heritage of values on which orderly civil progress is based.[15]

The Environment

21. While the horizon of man is thus being modified according to the images that are chosen for him, another transformation is making itself felt, one which is the dramatic and unexpected consequence of human activity. Man is suddenly becoming aware that by an ill-considered exploitation of nature he risks destroying it and becoming in his turn the victim of this degradation. Not only is the material environment becoming a permanent menace—

pollution and refuse, new illnesses and absolute destructive capacity—but the human framework is no longer under man's control, thus creating an environment for tomorrow which may well be intolerable. This is a wide-ranging social problem which concerns the entire human family.

The Christian must turn to these new perceptions in order to take on responsibility, together with the rest of men, for a destiny which from now on is shared by all.

FUNDAMENTAL ASPIRATIONS AND CURRENTS OF IDEAS

22. While scientific and technological progress continues to overturn man's surroundings, his patterns of knowledge, work, consumption, and relationships, two aspirations persistently make themselves felt in these new contexts, and they grow stronger to the extent that he becomes better informed and better educated: the aspiration to equality and the aspiration to participation, two forms of man's dignity and freedom.

Advantages and Limitations of Juridical Recognition

23. Through this statement of the rights of man and the seeking for international agreements for the application of these rights, progress has been made toward inscribing these two aspirations in deeds and structures.[16] Nevertheless various forms of discrimination continually reappear—ethnic, cultural, religious, political, and so on. In fact, human rights are still too often disregarded, if not scoffed at, or else they receive only formal recognition. In many cases legislation does not keep up with real situations. Legislation is necessary, but it is not sufficient for setting up true relationships of justice and equality. In teaching us charity, the Gospel instructs us in the preferential respect due to the poor and the special situation they have in society: the more fortunate should renounce some of their rights so as to place their goods more generously at the service of others. If, beyond legal rules, there is really no deeper feeling of respect for and service to others, then even equality before the law can serve as an alibi for flagrant discrimination, continued exploitation, and actual contempt. Without a renewed education in solidarity, an overemphasis on equality can give rise to an individualism in which each one claims his own rights without wishing to be answerable for the common good.

In this field, everyone sees the highly important contribution of the Christian spirit, which moreover answers man's yearning to be loved. "Love for man, the prime value of the earthly order," ensures the conditions for peace, both social peace and international peace, by affirming our universal brotherhood.[17]

The Political Society

24. The two aspirations, to equality and to participation, seek to promote a democratic type of society. Various models are proposed, some are tried out, none of them gives complete satisfaction, and the search goes on between

ideological and pragmatic tendencies. The Christian has the duty to take part in this search and in the organization and life of political society. As a social being, man builds his destiny within a series of particular groupings which demand, as their completion and as a necessary condition for their development, a vaster society, one of a universal character, the political society. All particular activity must be placed within that wider society, and thereby it takes on the dimension of the common good.[18]

This indicates the importance of education for life in society, in which there are called to mind, not only information on each one's rights, but also their necessary correlative: the recognition of the duties of each one in regard to others. The sense and practice of duty are themselves conditioned by self-mastery and by the acceptance of responsibility and of the limits placed upon the freedom of the individual or of the group.

25. Political activity—need one remark that we are dealing primarily with an activity, not an ideology?—should be the projection of a plan of society which is consistent in its concrete means and in its inspiration, and which springs from a complete conception of man's vocation and of its differing social expressions. It is not for the State or even for political parties, which would be closed unto themselves, to try to impose an ideology by means that would lead to a dictatorship over minds, the worst kind of all. It is for cultural and religious groupings, in the freedom of acceptance which they presume, to develop in the social body, disinterestedly and in their own ways, those ultimate convictions on the nature, origin, and end of man and society.

In this field, it is well to keep in mind the principle proclaimed at the Second Vatican Council: "The truth cannot impose itself except by virtue of its own truth, and it makes its entrance into the mind at once quietly and with power."[19]

Ideologies and Human Liberty

26. Therefore the Christian who wishes to live his faith in a political activity which he thinks of as service cannot without contradicting himself adhere to ideological systems which radically or substantially go against his faith and his concept of man. He cannot adhere to the Marxist ideology, to its atheistic materialism, to its dialectic of violence and to the way it absorbs individual freedom in the collectivity, at the same time denying all transcendence to man and his personal and collective history; nor can he adhere to the liberal ideology which believes it exalts individual freedom by withdrawing it from every limitation, by stimulating it through exclusive seeking of interest and power, and by considering social solidarities as more or less automatic consequences of individual initiatives, not as an aim and a major criterion of the value of the social organization.

27. Is there need to stress the possible ambiguity of every social ideology? Sometimes it leads political or social activity to be simply the application of an abstract, purely theoretical idea; at other times it is thought which

becomes a mere instrument at the service of activity as a simple means of a strategy. In both cases is it not man that risks finding himself alienated? The Christian faith is above and is sometimes opposed to the ideologies, in that it recognizes God, who is transcendent and the Creator, and who, through all the levels of creation, calls on man as endowed with responsibility and freedom.

28. There would also be the danger of giving adherence to an ideology which does not rest on a true and organic doctrine, to take refuge in it as a final and sufficient explanation of everything, and thus to build a new idol, accepting, at times without being aware of doing so, its totalitarian and coercive character. And people imagine they find in it a justification for their activity, even violent activity, and an adequate response to a generous desire to serve. The desire remains but it allows itself to be consumed by an ideology which, even if it suggests certain paths to man's liberation, ends up by making him a slave.

29. It has been possible today to speak of a retreat of ideologies. In this respect the present time may be favorable for an openness to the concrete transcendence of Christianity. It may also be a more accentuated sliding toward a new positivism: universalized technology as the dominant form of activity, as the overwhelming pattern of existence, even as a language, without the question of its meaning being really asked.

Historical Movements

30. But outside of this positivism which reduces man to a single dimension even if it is an important one today and by so doing mutilates him, the Christian encounters in his activity concrete historical movements sprung from ideologies and in part distinct from them. Our venerated predecessor Pope John XXIII in *Pacem in Terris* already showed that it is possible to make a distinction: "Neither can false philosophical teachings regarding the nature, origin, and destiny of the universe and of man be identified with historical movements that have economic, social, cultural, or political ends, not even when these movements have originated from those teachings and have drawn and still draw inspiration therefrom. Because the teachings, once they are drawn up and defined, remain always the same, while the movements, being concerned with historical situations in constant evolution, cannot but be influenced by these latter and cannot avoid, therefore, being subject to changes, even of a profound nature. Besides, who can deny that those movements, insofar as they conform to the dictates of right reason and are interpreters of the lawful aspirations of the human person, contain elements that are positive and deserving of approval?"[20]

Attraction of Socialist Currents

31. Some Christians are today attracted by socialist currents and their various developments. They try to recognize therein a certain number of aspirations which they carry within themselves in the name of their faith. They feel

that they are part of that historical current and wish to play a part within it. Now this historical current takes on, under the same name, different forms according to different continents and cultures, even if it drew its inspiration, and still does in many cases, from ideologies incompatible with faith. Careful judgment is called for. Too often Christians attracted by socialism tend to idealize it in terms which, apart from anything else, are very general: a will for justice, solidarity and equality. They refuse to recognize the limitations of the historical socialist movements, which remain conditioned by the ideologies from which they originated. Distinctions must be made to guide concrete choices between the various levels of expression of socialism: a generous aspiration and a seeking for a more just society, historical movements with a political organization and aim, and an ideology which claims to give a complete and self-sufficient picture of man. Nevertheless, these distinctions must not lead one to consider such levels as completely separate and independent. The concrete link which, according to circumstances, exists between them must be clearly marked out. This insight will enable Christians to see the degree of commitment possible along these lines, while safeguarding the values, especially those of liberty, responsibility, and openness to the spiritual, which guarantee the integral development of man.

Historical Evolution of Marxism

32. Other Christians even ask whether a historical development of Marxism might not authorize certain concrete rapprochements. They note in fact a certain splintering of Marxism, which until now showed itself to be a unitary ideology which explained in atheistic terms the whole of man and the world since it did not go outside their development process. Apart from the ideological confrontation officially separating the various champions of Marxism-Leninism in their individual interpretations of the thought of its founders, and apart from the open opposition between the political systems which make use of its name today, some people lay down distinctions between Marxism's various levels of expression.

33. For some, Marxism remains essentially the active practice of class struggle. Experiencing the ever present and continually renewed force of the relationships of domination and exploitation among men, they reduce Marxism to no more than a struggle—at times with no other purpose—to be pursued and even stirred up in permanent fashion. For others, it is first and foremost the collective exercise of political and economic power under the direction of a single party, which would be the whole expression and guarantee of the welfare of all, and would deprive individuals and other groups of any possibility of initiative and choice. At a third level, Marxism, whether in power or not, is viewed as a socialist ideology based on historical materialism and the denial of everything transcendent. At other times, finally, it presents itself in a more attenuated form, one also more attractive to the modern mind: as a scientific activity, as a rigorous method of examining social and

political reality, and as the rational link, tested by history, between theoretical knowledge and the practice of revolutionary transformation. Although this type of analysis gives a privileged position to certain aspects of reality to the detriment of the rest, and interprets them in the light of its ideology, it nevertheless furnishes some people not only with a working tool but also a certitude preliminary to action: the claim to decipher in a scientific manner the mainsprings of the evolution of society.

34. While, through the concrete existing form of Marxism, one can distinguish these various aspects and the questions they pose for the reflection and activity of Christians, it would be illusory and dangerous to reach a point of forgetting the intimate link which radically binds them together, to accept the elements of Marxist analysis without recognizing their relationships with ideology, and to enter into the practice of class struggle and its Marxist interpretation, while failing to note the kind of totalitarian and violent society to which this process leads.

The Liberal Ideology

35. On another side, we are witnessing a renewal of the liberal ideology. This current asserts itself both in the name of economic efficiency, and for the defense of the individual against the increasingly overwhelming hold of organizations, and as a reaction against the totalitarian tendencies of political powers. Certainly, personal initiative must be maintained and developed. But do not Christians who take this path tend to idealize liberalism in their turn, making it a proclamation in favor of freedom? They would like a new model, more adapted to present-day conditions, while easily forgetting that at the very root of philosophical liberalism is an erroneous affirmation of the autonomy of the individual in his activity, his motivation, and the exercise of his liberty. Hence, the liberal ideology likewise calls for careful discernment on their part.

Christian Discernment

36. In this renewed encounter of the various ideologies, the Christian will draw from the sources of his faith and the Church's teaching the necessary principles and suitable criteria to avoid permitting himself to be first attracted by and then imprisoned within a system whose limitations and totalitarianism may well become evident to him too late, if he does not perceive them in their roots. Going beyond every system, without however failing to commit himself concretely to serving his brothers, he will assert, in the very midst of his options, the specific character of the Christian contribution for a positive transformation of society.[21]

Rebirth of Utopias

37. Today, moreover, the weaknesses of the ideologies are better perceived through the concrete systems in which they are trying to affirm themselves. Bureaucratic socialism, technocratic capitalism, and authoritarian democracy

are showing how difficult it is to solve the great human problem of living together in justice and equality. How in fact could they escape the materialism, egoism, or constraint which inevitably go with them? This is the source of a protest which is springing up more or less everywhere, as a sign of a deep-seated sickness, while at the same time we are witnessing the rebirth of what it is agreed to call "utopias." These claim to resolve the political problem of modern societies better than the ideologies. It would be dangerous to disregard this. The appeal to a utopia is often a convenient excuse for those who wish to escape from concrete tasks in order to take refuge in an imaginary world. To live in a hypothetical future is a facile alibi for rejecting immediate responsibilities. But it must clearly be recognized that this kind of criticism of existing society often provokes the forward-looking imagination both to perceive in the present the disregarded possibility hidden within it, and to direct itself toward a fresh future; it thus sustains social dynamism by the confidence that it gives to the inventive powers of the human mind and heart; and, if it refuses no overture, it can also meet the Christian appeal. The Spirit of the Lord, who animates man renewed in Christ, continually breaks down the horizons within which his understanding likes to find security and the limits to which his activity would willingly restrict itself; there dwells within him a power which urges him to go beyond every system and every ideology. At the heart of the world there dwells the mystery of man discovering himself to be God's son in the course of a historical and psychological process in which constraint and freedom as well as the weight of sin and the breath of the Spirit alternate and struggle for the upper hand.

The dynamism of Christian faith here triumphs over the narrow calculations of egoism. Animated by the power of the Spirit of Jesus Christ, the Savior of mankind, and upheld by hope, the Christian involves himself in the building up of the human city, one that is to be peaceful, just, and fraternal and acceptable as an offering to God.[22] In fact, "the expectation of a new earth must not weaken but rather stimulate our concern for cultivating this one. For here grows the body of a new human family, a body which even now is able to give some kind of foreshadowing of the new age."[23]

The Questioning of the Human Sciences

38. In this world dominated by scientific and technological change, which threatens to drag it toward a new positivism, another more fundamental doubt is raised. Having subdued nature by using his reason, man now finds that he himself is as it were imprisoned within his own rationality; he in turn becomes the object of science. The "human sciences" are today enjoying a significant flowering. On the one hand they are subjecting to critical and radical examination the hitherto accepted knowledge about man, on the grounds that this knowledge seems either too empirical or too theoretical. On the other hand, methodological necessity and ideological presuppositions too often lead the human sciences to isolate, in the various situations, certain aspects of man, and

yet to give these an explanation which claims to be complete or at least an interpretation which is meant to be all-embracing from a purely quantitative or phenomenological point of view. This scientific reduction betrays a dangerous presumption. To give a privileged position in this way to such an aspect of analysis is to mutilate man and, under the pretext of a scientific procedure, to make it impossible to understand man in his totality.

39. One must be no less attentive to the action which the human sciences can instigate, giving rise to the elaboration of models of society to be subsequently imposed on men as scientifically tested types of behavior. Man can then become the object of manipulations directing his desires and needs and modifying his behavior and even his system of values. There is no doubt that there exists here a grave danger for the societies of tomorrow and for man himself. For even if all agree to build a new society at the service of men, it is still essential to know what sort of man is in question.

40. Suspicion of the human sciences affects the Christian more than others, but it does not find him disarmed. For, as we ourself wrote in *Populorum Progressio*, it is here that there is found the specific contribution of the Church to civilizations: "Sharing the noblest aspirations of men and suffering when she sees them not satisfied, she wishes to help them attain their full flowering, and that is why she offers men what she possesses as her characteristic attribute: a global vision of man and of the human race."[24] Should the Church in its turn contest the proceedings of the human sciences, and condemn their pretensions? As in the case of the natural sciences, the Church has confidence in this research also and urges Christians to play an active part in it.[25] Prompted by the same scientific demands and the desire to know man better, but at the same time enlightened by their faith, Christians who devote themselves to the human sciences will begin a dialogue between the Church and this new field of discovery, a dialogue which promises to be fruitful. Of course, each individual scientific discipline will be able, in its own particular sphere, to grasp only a partial—yet true—aspect of man; the complete picture and the full meaning will escape it. But within these limits the human sciences give promise of a positive function that the Church willingly recognizes. They can even widen the horizons of human liberty to a greater extent than the conditioning circumstances perceived enable one to foresee. They could thus assist Christian social morality, which no doubt will see its field restricted when it comes to suggesting certain models of society, while its function of making a critical judgment and taking an overall view will be strengthened by its showing the relative character of the behavior and values presented by such and such a society as definitive and inherent in the very nature of man. These sciences are a condition at once indispensable and inadequate for a better discovery of what is human. They are a language which becomes more and more complex, yet one that deepens rather than solves the mystery of the heart of man; nor does it provide the complete and definitive answer to the desire which springs from his innermost being.

Ambiguous Nature of Progress

41. This better knowledge of man makes it possible to pass a better critical judgment upon and to elucidate a fundamental notion that remains at the basis of modern societies as their motive, their measure, and their goal: namely, progress. Since the nineteenth century, western societies and, as a result, many others have put their hopes in ceaselessly renewed and indefinite progress. They saw this progress as man's effort to free himself in face of the demands of nature and of social constraints; progress was the condition for and the yardstick of human freedom. Progress, spread by the modern media of information and by the demand for wider knowledge and greater consumption, has become an omnipresent ideology. Yet a doubt arises today regarding both its value and its result. What is the meaning of this never-ending, breathless pursuit of a progress that always eludes one just when one believes one has conquered it sufficiently in order to enjoy it in peace? If it is not attained, it leaves one dissatisfied. Without doubt, there has been just condemnation of the limits and even the misdeeds of a merely quantitative economic growth; there is a desire to attain objectives of a qualitative order also. The quality and the truth of human relations, the degree of participation and of responsibility, are no less significant and important for the future of society than the quantity and variety of the goods produced and consumed.

Overcoming the temptation to wish to measure everything in terms of efficiency and of trade, and in terms of the interplay of forces and interests, man today wishes to replace these quantitative criteria with the intensity of communication, the spread of knowledge and culture, mutual service and a combining of efforts for a common task. Is not genuine progress to be found in the development of moral consciousness, which will lead man to exercise a wider solidarity and to open himself freely to others and to God? For a Christian, progress necessarily comes up against the eschatological mystery of death. The death of Christ and his resurrection and the outpouring of the Spirit of the Lord help man to place his freedom, in creativity and gratitude, within the context of the truth of all progress and the only hope which does not deceive.[26]

CHRISTIANS FACE TO FACE WITH THESE NEW PROBLEMS

Dynamism of the Church's Social Teaching

42. In the face of so many new questions the Church makes an effort to reflect in order to give an answer, in its own sphere, to men's expectations. If today the problems seem original in their breadth and their urgency, is man without the means of solving them? It is with all its dynamism that the social teaching of the Church accompanies men in their search. If it does not intervene to authenticate a given structure or to propose a ready-made model, it does not thereby limit itself to recalling general principles. It develops through reflection applied to the changing situations of this world, under the driving

force of the Gospel as the source of renewal when its message is accepted in its totality and with all its demands. It also develops with the sensitivity proper to the Church which is characterized by a disinterested will to serve and by attention to the poorest.

Finally, it draws upon its rich experience of many centuries which enables it, while continuing its permanent preoccupations, to undertake the daring and creative innovations which the present state of the world requires.

For Greater Justice

43. There is a need to establish a greater justice in the sharing of goods, both within national communities and on the international level. In international exchanges there is a need to go beyond relationships based on force, in order to arrive at agreements reached with the good of all in mind. Relationships based on force have never in fact established justice in a true and lasting manner, even if at certain times the alteration of positions can often make it possible to find easier conditions for dialogue. The use of force moreover leads to the setting in motion of opposing forces, and from this springs a climate of struggle which opens the way to situations of extreme violence and to abuses.[27]

But, as we have often stated, the most important duty in the realm of justice is to allow each country to promote its own development, within the framework of a cooperation free from any spirit of domination, whether economic or political. The complexity of the problems raised is certainly great, in the present intertwining of mutual dependences. Thus it is necessary to have the courage to undertake a revision of the relationships between nations, whether it is a question of the international division of production, the structure of exchanges, the control of profits, the monetary system—without forgetting the actions of human solidarity—to question the models of growth of the rich nations and change people's outlooks, so that they may realize the prior call of international duty, and to renew international organizations so that they may increase in effectiveness.

44. Under the driving force of new systems of production, national frontiers are breaking down, and we can see new economic powers emerging, the multinational enterprises, which by the concentration and flexibility of their means can conduct autonomous strategies which are largely independent of the national political powers and therefore not subject to control from the point of view of the common good. By extending their activities, these private organizations can lead to a new and abusive form of economic domination on the social, cultural, and even political level. The excessive concentration of means and powers that Pope Pius XI already condemned on the fortieth anniversary of *Rerum Novarum* is taking on a new and very real image.

Change of Attitudes and Structures

45. Today men yearn to free themselves from need and dependence. But this liberation starts with the interior freedom that men must find again with

regard to their goods and their powers; they will never reach it except through a transcendent love for man, and, in consequence, through a genuine readiness to serve. Otherwise, as one can see only too clearly, the most revolutionary ideologies lead only to a change of masters; once installed in power in their turn, these new masters surround themselves with privileges, limit freedoms and allow other forms of injustice to become established.

Thus many people are reaching the point of questioning the very model of society. The ambition of many nations, in the competition that sets them in opposition and which carries them along, is to attain technological, economic, and military power. This ambition then stands in the way of setting up structures in which the rhythm of progress would be regulated with a view to greater justice, instead of accentuating inequalities and living in a climate of distrust and struggle which would unceasingly compromise peace.

Christian Meaning of Political Activity

46. Is it not here that there appears a radical limitation to economics? Economic activity is necessary and, if it is at the service of man, it can be "a source of brotherhood and a sign of Providence."[28] It is the occasion of concrete exchanges between men, of rights recognized, of services rendered, and of dignity affirmed in work. Though it is often a field of confrontation and domination, it can give rise to dialogue and foster cooperation. Yet it runs the risk of taking up too much strength and freedom.[29] This is why the need is felt to pass from economics to politics. It is true that in the term "politics" many confusions are possible and must be clarified, but each man feels that in the social and economic field, both national and international, the ultimate decision rests with political power.

Political power, which is the natural and necessary link for ensuring the cohesion of the social body, must have as its aim the achievement of the common good. While respecting the legitimate liberties of individuals, families, and subsidiary groups, it acts in such a way as to create, effectively and for the well-being of all, the conditions required for attaining man's true and complete good, including his spiritual end. It acts within the limits of its competence, which can vary from people to people and from country to country. It always intervenes with care for justice and with devotion to the common good, for which it holds final responsibility. It does not, for all that, deprive individuals and intermediary bodies of the field of activity and responsibility which are proper to them and which lead them to collaborate in the attainment of this common good. In fact, "the true aim of all social activity should be to help individual members of the social body, but never to destroy or absorb them."[30] According to the vocation proper to it, the political power must know how to stand aside from particular interests in order to view its responsibility with regard to the good of all men, even going beyond national limits. To take politics seriously at its different levels—local, regional, national, and worldwide—is to affirm the duty of man, of every man, to recognize the concrete reality and the value of the freedom of choice that is offered to him to seek to bring about both the good of the city and of the nation and of mankind. Politics are a demanding manner—but not the only one—of living the Christian commitment to the service of others. Without of course solving every problem, it endeavors to apply solutions to the relationships men have with one another. The domain of politics is wide and comprehensive, but it is not exclusive. An attitude of encroachment which would tend to set up politics as an absolute value would bring serious danger. While recognizing the autonomy of the reality of politics, Christians who are invited to take up political activity should try to make their choices consistent with the Gospel and, in the framework of a legitimate plurality, to give both personal and collective witness to the seriousness of their faith by effective and disinterested service of men.

Sharing in Responsibility

47. The passing to the political dimension also expressed a demand made by the man of today: a greater sharing in responsibility and in decision-making. This legitimate aspiration becomes more evident as the cultural level rises, as the sense of freedom develops and as man becomes more aware of how, in a world facing an uncertain future, the choices of today already condition the life of tomorrow. In *Mater et Magistra*[31] Pope John XXIII stressed how much the admittance to responsibility is a basic demand of man's nature, a concrete exercise of his freedom and a path to his development, and he showed how, in economic life and particularly in enterprise, this sharing in responsibilities should be ensured.[32] Today the field is wider, and extends to the social and political sphere in which a reasonable sharing in responsibility and in decisions must be established and strengthened. Admittedly, it is true that the choices proposed for a decision are more and more complex; the considerations that must be borne in mind are numerous, and the foreseeing of the consequences involves risk, even if new sciences strive to enlighten freedom at these important moments. However, although limits are sometimes called for, these obstacles must not slow down the giving of wider participation in working out decisions, making choices and putting them into practice. In order to counterbalance increasing technocracy, modern forms of democracy must be devised, not only making it possible for each man to become informed and to express himself, but also by involving him in a shared responsibility.

Thus human groups will gradually begin to share and to live as communities. Thus freedom, which too often asserts itself as a claim for autonomy by opposing the freedom of others, will develop in its deepest human reality: to involve itself and to spend itself in building up active and lived solidarity. But, for the Christian, it is by losing himself in God who sets him free that man finds true freedom, renewed in the death and resurrection of the Lord.

CALL TO ACTION

Need to Become Involved in Action

48. In the social sphere, the Church has always wished to assume a double function: first to enlighten minds in order to assist them to discover the truth and to find the right path to follow amid the different teachings that call for their attention; and secondly to take part in action and to spread, with a real care for service and effectiveness, the energies of the Gospel. Is it not in order to be faithful to this desire that the Church has sent on an apostolic mission among the workers priests who, by sharing fully the condition of the worker, are at that level the witnesses to the Church's solicitude and seeking?

It is to all Christians that we address a fresh and insistent call to action. In our encyclical on the development of peoples we urged that all should set themselves to the task: "Laymen should take up as their own proper task the renewal of the temporal order. If the role of the hierarchy is to teach and to interpret authentically the norms of morality to be followed in this matter, it belongs to the laity, without waiting passively for orders and directives, to take the initiative freely and to infuse a Christian spirit into the mentality, customs, laws, and structures of the community in which they live."[33] Let each one examine himself, to see what he has done up to now, and what he ought to do. It is not enough to recall principles, state intentions, point to crying injustices, and utter prophetic denunciations; these words will lack real weight unless they are accompanied for each individual by a livelier awareness of personal responsibility and by effective action. It is too easy to throw back on others responsibility for injustices, if at the same time one does not realize how each one shares in it personally, and how personal conversion is needed first. This basic humility will rid action of all inflexibility and sectarianism; it will also avoid discouragement in the face of a task which seems limitless in size. The Christian's hope comes primarily from the fact that he knows that the Lord is working with us in the world, continuing in his body which is the Church—and, through the Church, in the whole of mankind—the redemption which was accomplished on the cross and which burst forth in victory on the morning of the resurrection.[34] This hope springs also from the fact that the Christian knows that other men are at work, to undertake actions of justice and peace working for the same ends. For beneath an outward appearance of indifference, in the heart of every man there is a will to live in brotherhood and a thirst for justice and peace, which is to be expanded.

49. Thus, amid the diversity of situations, functions, and organizations, each one must determine, in his conscience, the actions which he is called to share in. Surrounded by various currents into which, beside legitimate aspirations, there insinuate themselves more ambiguous tendencies, the Christian must make a wise and vigilant choice and avoid involving himself in collaboration without conditions and contrary to the principles of a true humanism,

even in the name of a genuinely felt solidarity. If in fact he wishes to play a specific part as a Christian in accordance with his faith—a part that unbelievers themselves expect of him—he must take care in the midst of his active commitment to clarify his motives and to rise above the objectives aimed at, by taking a more all-embracing view which will avoid the danger of selfish particularism and oppressive totalitarianism.

Pluralism of Options

50. In concrete situations, and taking account of solidarity in each person's life, one must recognize a legitimate variety of possible options. The same Christian faith can lead to different commitments.[35] The Church invites all Christians to take up a double task of inspiring and of innovating, in order to make structures evolve, so as to adapt them to the real needs of today. From Christians who at first sight seem to be in opposition, as a result of starting from differing options, she asks an effort at mutual understanding of the other's positions and motives; a loyal examination of one's behavior and its correctness will suggest to each one an attitude of more profound charity which, while recognizing the differences, believes nonetheless in the possibility of convergence and unity. "The bonds which unite the faithful are mightier than anything which divides them."[36]

It is true that many people, in the midst of modern structures and conditioning circumstances, are determined by their habits of thought and their functions, even apart from the safeguarding of material interests. Others feel so deeply the solidarity of classes and cultures that they reach the point of sharing without reserve all the judgments and options of their surroundings.[37] Each one will take great care to examine himself and to bring about that true freedom according to Christ which makes one receptive to the universal in the very midst of the most particular conditions.

51. It is in this regard too that Christian organizations, under their different forms, have a responsibility for collective action. Without putting themselves in the place of the institutions of civil society, they have to express, in their own way and rising above their particular nature, the concrete demands of the Christian faith for a just, and consequently necessary, transformation of society.[38]

Today more than ever the Word of God will be unable to be proclaimed and heard unless it is accompanied by the witness of the power of the Holy Spirit, working within the action of Christians in the service of their brothers, at the points in which their existence and their future are at stake.

52. In expressing these reflections to you, venerable brother, we are of course aware that we have not dealt with all the social problems that today face the man of faith and men of good will. Our recent declarations—to which has been added your message of a short time ago on the occasion of the launching of the Second Development Decade—particularly concerning the duties of the community of nations in the serious question of the integral and

concerted development of man, are still fresh in people's minds. We address these present reflections to you with the aim of offering to the Council of the Laity and the Pontifical Commission Justice and Peace some fresh contributions, as well as an encouragement, for the pursuit of their task of "awakening the People of God to a full understanding of its role at the present time" and of "promoting the apostolate on the international level."[39]

It is with these sentiments, venerable brother, that we impart to you our apostolic blessing.

From the Vatican, May 14, 1971.

PAUL VI

NOTES

1. *Gaudium et Spes*, 10: AAS 58 (1966), p. 1033.
2. AAS 23 (1931), pp. 209ff.
3. AAS 53 (1961), p. 429.
4. 3, AAS 59 (1967), p. 258.
5. Ibid., 1: p. 257.
6. Cf. 2 Cor. 4:17.
7. *Populorum Progressio*, 25: AAS 59 (1967), pp. 269–70.
8. Cf. Rev. 3:12; 21:2.
9. *Gaudium et Spes*, 25: AAS 58 (1966), p. 1045.
10. Ibid., 67: p. 1089.
11. *Populorum Progressio*, 69: AAS 59 (1967), pp. 290–91.
12. Cf. Matt. 25:35.
13. *Nostra Aetate*, 5: AAS 58 (1966), p. 743.
14. 37, AAS 59 (1967), p. 276.
15. *Inter Mirifica*, 12: AAS 56 (1964), p. 149.
16. Cf. *Pacem in Terris*: AAS 55 (1963), pp. 261ff.
17. Cf. Message for the World Day of Peace, 1971: AAS 63 (1971), pp. 5–9.
18. Cf. *Gaudium et Spes*, 74: AAS 58 (1966), pp. 1095–1096.
19. *Dignitatis Humanae*, 1: AAS 58 (1966), p. 930.
20. AAS 55 (1963), p. 300.
21. Cf. *Gaudium et Spes*, 11: AAS 58 (1966), p. 1033.
22. Cf. Rom. 15:16.
23. *Gaudium et Spes*, 39: AAS 58 (1966), p. 1057.
24. 13: *Populorum Progressio*, AAS 59 (1967), p. 264.
25. Cf. *Gaudium et Spes*, 36: AAS 58 (1966), p. 1054.
26. Cf. Rom. 5:5.
27. *Populorum Progressio*, 56ff: AAS 59 (1967), pp. 285ff.
28. Ibid., 86: p. 299.
29. *Gaudium et Spes*, 63: AAS 58 (1966), p. 1085.

30. *Quadragesimo Anno*: AAS 23 (1931), p. 203; cf. *Mater et Magistra*: AAS 53 (1961), pp. 414, 428; *Gaudium et Spes*, 74–76: AAS 58 (1966), pp. 1095–1100.

31. AAS 53 (1961), pp. 420–22.

32. *Gaudium et Spes*, 68, 75: AAS 58 (1966), pp. 89–1090, 1097.

33. 81: AAS 59 (1967), pp. 296–97.

34. Cf. Matt. 28:30; Phil. 2:3–11.

35. *Gaudium et Spes*, 43: AAS 58 (1966), p. 1061.

36. Ibid., 92: p. 1113.

37. Cf. 1 Thess. 5:21.

38. *Lumen Gentium*, 31: AAS 57 (1965), pp. 37–38; *Apostolicam Actuositatem* 5: AAS 58 (1966), p. 842.

39. *Catholicam Christi Ecclesiam*, AAS 59 (1967), pp. 27 and 26.

Justice in the World (Synod of Bishops, 1971)

INTRODUCTION

As a way of implementing the Second Vatican Council, Paul VI announced the regular convening of synods of bishops. The 1971 synod dealt with two major questions: the priesthood, and justice in the world. While much of the media debate focused on questions of internal discipline with respect to the priesthood, the more substantive heritage of this synod was its contributions to the question of justice. The synod produced a strong, positive document sanctioned by papal and episcopal approval, which was available to give powerful support to those in all nations working to bring the church into a more active, vigilant, and pastoral relationship to the problems of world justice and peace.

Beginning by recognizing the structures of injustice in the world, the bishops focused on the necessity of structural change that incorporates the principle of justice into human relations. Additionally, the bishops made it clear that the church must stand with the poor and oppressed if it is to be faithful to this gospel mandate.

The most quoted statement of the document continues to serve as the foundation for the church's social justice mission: "Action on behalf of justice and participation in the transformation of the world fully appear to us as a constitutive dimension of the preaching of the Gospel" (Introduction). Thus concern for justice must be a part of all phases of Christian life; it provides a critical antidote to an exclusively otherworldly Christianity.

The synod addressed several of the critical questions of the day: technology, the arms race, nationalism, racial and class divisions, education, and the concentration of the world's wealth in the hands of a few. It grounded its evaluation of these problems in an incarnational theology which affirms that the relation of individuals with their neighbors is intimately bound up with their relation to God.

Although there is some pessimism in this document, and although the synod speaks in prophetic terms of the injustice present in our world, it concluded with a note of hope. This hope is based on the Christian vision that creation is groaning in the act of giving birth as it waits for the glory of God to be revealed. The bishops are encouraged by the efforts of individuals to lessen injustice, to lead lives of nonviolence, and to share in love and justice the goods of the earth. Such acts of love of neighbor make God present to the world and offer the hope of renewal.

JUSTICE IN THE WORLD

SYNOD OF BISHOPS
1971

INTRODUCTION

Gathered from the whole world, in communion with all who believe in Christ and with the entire human family, and opening our hearts to the Spirit who is making the whole of creation new, we have questioned ourselves about the mission of the People of God to further justice in the world.

Scrutinizing the "signs of the times" and seeking to detect the meaning of emerging history, while at the same time sharing the aspirations and questionings of all those who want to build a more human world, we have listened to the Word of God that we might be converted to the fulfilling of the divine plan for the salvation of the world.

Even though it is not for us to elaborate a very profound analysis of the situation of the world, we have nevertheless been able to perceive the serious injustices which are building around the world of men a network of domination, oppression, and abuses which stifle freedom and which keep the greater part of humanity from sharing in the building up and enjoyment of a more just and more fraternal world.

At the same time we have noted the inmost stirring moving the world in its depths. There are facts constituting a contribution to the furthering of justice. In associations of men and among peoples themselves there is arising a new awareness which shakes them out of any fatalistic resignation and which spurs them on to liberate themselves and to be responsible for their own destiny. Movements among men are seen which express hope in a better world and a will to change whatever has become intolerable.

Listening to the cry of those who suffer violence and are oppressed by unjust systems and structures, and hearing the appeal of a world that by its perversity contradicts the plan of its Creator, we have shared our awareness of the Church's vocation to be present in the heart of the world by proclaiming the Good News to the poor, freedom to the oppressed, and joy to the afflicted. The hopes and forces which are moving the world in its very foundations are not foreign to the dynamism of the Gospel, which through the power of the Holy Spirit frees men from personal sin and from its consequences in social life.

The uncertainty of history and the painful convergences in the ascending path of the human community direct us to sacred history; there God has revealed himself to us, and made known to us, as it is brought progressively to realization, his plan of liberation and salvation which is once and for all fulfilled in the Paschal Mystery of Christ. Action on behalf of justice and participation in the transformation of the world fully appear to us as a constitutive dimension of the preaching of the Gospel, or, in other words, of the Church's mission for the redemption of the human race and its liberation from every oppressive situation.

CHAPTER 1: JUSTICE AND WORLD SOCIETY

Crisis of Universal Solidarity

The world in which the Church lives and acts is held captive by a tremendous paradox. Never before have the forces working for bringing about a unified world society appeared so powerful and dynamic; they are rooted in the awareness of the full basic equality as well as of the human dignity of all. Since men are members of the same human family, they are indissolubly linked with one another in the one destiny of the whole world, in the responsibility for which they all share.

The new technological possibilities are based upon the unity of science, on the global and simultaneous character of communications, and on the birth of an absolutely interdependent economic world. Moreover, men are beginning to grasp a new and more radical dimension of unity; for they perceive that their resources, as well as the precious treasures of air and water—without which there cannot be life—and the small delicate biosphere of the whole complex of all life on earth, are not infinite, but on the contrary must be saved and preserved as a unique patrimony belonging to all mankind.

The paradox lies in the fact that within this perspective of unity the forces of division and antagonism seem today to be increasing in strength. Ancient divisions between nations and empires, between races and classes, today possess new technological instruments of destruction. The arms race is a threat to man's highest good, which is life; it makes poor peoples and individuals yet more miserable, while making richer those already powerful; it creates a continuous danger of conflagration, and in the case of nuclear arms, it threatens to destroy all life from the face of the earth. At the same time new divisions are being born to separate man from his neighbor. Unless combatted and overcome by social and political action, the influence of the new industrial and technological order favors the concentration of wealth, power and decision-making in the hands of a small public or private controlling group. Economic injustice and lack of social participation keep a man from attaining his basic human and civil rights.

In the last twenty-five years a hope has spread through the human race that economic growth would bring about such a quantity of goods that it would be possible to feed the hungry at least with the crumbs falling from the table, but this has proved a vain hope in underdeveloped areas and in pockets of poverty in wealthier areas, because of the rapid growth of population and of the labor force, because of rural stagnation and the lack of agrarian reform, and because of the massive migratory flow to the cities, where the industries, even though endowed with huge sums of money, nevertheless provide so few jobs that not infrequently one worker in four is left unemployed. These stifling oppressions constantly give rise to great numbers of "marginal" persons, ill-fed, inhumanly housed, illiterate, and deprived of political power as well as of the suitable means of acquiring responsibility and moral dignity.

Furthermore, such is the demand for resources and energy by the richer nations, whether capitalist or socialist, and such are the effects of dumping by them in the atmosphere and the sea that irreparable damage would be done to the essential elements of life on earth, such as air and water, if their high rates of consumption and pollution, which are constantly on the increase, were extended to the whole of mankind.

The strong drive toward global unity, the unequal distribution which places decisions concerning three quarters of income, investment and trade in the hands of one third of the human race, namely the more highly developed part, the insufficiency of a merely economic progress, and the new recognition of the material limits of the biosphere—all this makes us aware of the fact that in today's world new modes of understanding human dignity are arising.

The Right to Development

In the face of international systems of domination, the bringing about of justice depends more and more on the determined will for development.

In the developing nations and in the so-called socialist world, that determined will asserts itself especially in a struggle for forms of claiming one's rights and self-expression, a struggle caused by the evolution of the economic system itself.

This aspiring to justice asserts itself in advancing beyond the threshold at which begins a consciousness of enhancement of personal worth[1] with regard both to the whole man and the whole of mankind. This is expressed in an awareness of the right to development. The right to development must be seen as a dynamic interpenetration of all those fundamental human rights upon which the aspirations of individuals and nations are based.

This desire, however, will not satisfy the expectations of our time if it ignores the objective obstacles which social structures place in the way of conversion of hearts, or even of the realization of the ideal of charity. It demands on the contrary that the general condition of being marginal in society be overcome, so that an end will be put to the systematic barriers and vicious circles which oppose the collective advance toward enjoyment of adequate remuneration of the factors of production, and which strengthen the situation of discrimination with regard to access to opportunities and collective services from which a great part of the people are now excluded. If the developing nations and regions do not attain liberation through development, there is a real danger that the conditions of life created especially by colonial domination may evolve into a new form of colonialism in which the developing nations will be the victims of the interplay of international economic forces. That right to development is above all a right to hope according to the concrete measure of contemporary humanity. To respond to such a hope, the concept of evolution must be purified of those myths and false convictions which have up to now gone with a thought-pattern subject to a kind of deterministic and automatic notion of progress.

By taking their future into their own hands through a determined will for progress, the developing peoples—even if they do not achieve the final goal—will authentically manifest their own personalization. And in order that they may cope with the unequal relationships within the present world complex, a certain responsible nationalism gives them the impetus needed to acquire an identity of their own. From this basic self-determination can come attempts at putting together new political groupings allowing full development to these peoples; there can also come measures necessary for overcoming the inertia which could render fruitless such an effort—as in some cases population pressure; there can also come new sacrifices which the growth of planning demands of a generation which wants to build its own future.

On the other hand, it is impossible to conceive true progress without recognizing the necessity—within the political system chosen—of a development composed both of economic growth and participation; and the necessity too of an increase in wealth implying as well social progress by the entire community as it overcomes regional imbalance and islands of prosperity. Participation constitutes a right which is to be applied both in the economic and in the social and political field.

While we again affirm the right of people to keep their own identity, we see ever more clearly that the fight against a modernization destructive of the proper characteristics of nations remains quite ineffective as long as it appeals only to sacred historical customs and venerable ways of life. If modernization is accepted with the intention that it serve the good of the nation, men will be able to create a culture which will constitute a true heritage of their own in the manner of a true social memory, one which is active and formative of authentic creative personality in the assembly of nations.

Voiceless Injustices

We see in the world a set of injustices which constitute the nucleus of today's problems and whose solution requires the undertaking of tasks and functions in every sector of society, and even on the level of the global society toward which we are speeding in this last quarter of the twentieth century. Therefore we must be prepared to take on new functions and new duties in every sector of world society, if justice is really to be put into practice. Our action is to be directed above all at those men and nations which because of various forms of oppression and because of the present character of our society are silent, indeed voiceless, victims of injustice.

Take, for example, the case of migrants. They are often forced to leave their own country to find work, but frequently find the doors closed in their faces because of discriminatory attitudes, or, if they can enter, they are often obliged to lead an insecure life or are treated in an inhuman manner. The same is true of groups that are less well off on the social ladder such as workers and especially farm workers who play a very great part in the process of development.

To be especially lamented is the condition of so many millions of refugees, and of every group of people suffering persecution—sometimes in institutionalized form—for racial or ethnic origin or on tribal grounds. This persecution on tribal grounds can at times take on the characteristics of genocide.

In many areas justice is seriously injured with regard to people who are suffering persecution for their faith, or who are in many ways being ceaselessly subjected by political parties and public authorities to an action of oppressive atheization, or who are deprived of religious liberty either by being kept from honoring God in public worship, or by being prevented from publicly teaching and spreading their faith, or by being prohibited from conducting their temporal affairs according to the principles of their religion.

Justice is also being violated by forms of oppression, both old and new, springing from restriction of the rights of individuals. This is occurring both in the form of repression by the political power and of violence on the part of private reaction, and can reach the extreme of affecting the basic conditions of personal integrity. There are well-known cases of torture, especially of political prisoners, who besides are frequently denied due process or who are subjected to arbitrary procedures in their trial. Nor can we pass over the prisoners of war who even after the Geneva Convention are being treated in an inhuman manner.

The fight against legalized abortion and against the imposition of contraceptives and the pressures exerted against war are significant forms of defending the right to life.

Furthermore, contemporary consciousness demands truth in the communications system, including the right to the image offered by the media and the opportunity to correct its manipulation. It must be stressed that the right, especially that of children and the young, to education and to morally correct conditions of life and communications media is once again being threatened in our days. The activity of families in social life is rarely and insufficiently recognized by State institutions. Nor should we forget the growing number of persons who are often abandoned by their families and by the community: the old, orphans, the sick, and all kinds of people who are rejected.

The Need for Dialogue

To obtain true unity of purpose, as is demanded by the world society of men, a mediatory role is essential to overcome day by day the opposition, obstacles, and ingrained privileges which are to be met within the advance toward a more human society.

But effective mediation involves the creation of a lasting atmosphere of dialogue. A contribution to the progressive realization of this can be made by men unhampered by geopolitical, ideological, or socioeconomic conditions or by the generation gap. To restore the meaning of life by adherence to authentic values, the participation and witness of the rising generation of youth is as necessary as communication among peoples.

CHAPTER 2: THE GOSPEL MESSAGE AND THE MISSION OF THE CHURCH

In the face of the present-day situation of the world, marked as it is by the grave sin of injustice, we recognize both our responsibility and our inability to overcome it by our strength. Such a situation urges us to listen with a humble and open heart to the word of God, as he shows us new paths toward action in the cause of justice in the world.

The Saving Justice of God through Christ

In the Old Testament God reveals himself to us as the liberator of the oppressed and the defender of the poor, demanding from man faith in him and justice toward man's neighbor. It is only in the observance of the duties of justice that God is truly recognized as the liberator of the oppressed.

By his action and teaching Christ united in an indivisible way the relationship of man to God and the relationship of man to other men. Christ lived his life in the world as a total giving of himself to God for the salvation and liberation of men. In his preaching he proclaimed the fatherhood of God toward all men and the intervention of God's justice on behalf of the needy and the oppressed (Lk. 6:21–23). In this way he identified himself with his "least brethren," as he stated: "As you did it to one of the least of my brethren, you did it to me" (Matt. 25:40).

From the beginning the Church has lived and understood the death and resurrection of Christ as a call by God to conversion in the faith of Christ and in fraternal love, perfected in mutual help even to the point of a voluntary sharing of material goods.

Faith in Christ, the Son of God and the Redeemer, and love of neighbor constitute a fundamental theme of the writers of the New Testament. According to St. Paul, the whole of the Christian life is summed up in faith effecting that love and service of neighbor which involve the fulfillment of the demands of justice. The Christian lives under the interior law of liberty, which is a permanent call to man to turn away from self-sufficiency to confidence in God and from concern for self to a sincere love of neighbor. Thus takes place his genuine liberation and the gift of himself for the freedom of others.

According to the Christian message, therefore, man's relationship to his neighbor is bound up with his relationship to God; his response to the love of

God, saving us through Christ, is shown to be effective in his love and service of men. Christian love of neighbor and justice cannot be separated. For love implies an absolute demand for justice, namely a recognition of the dignity and rights of one's neighbor. Justice attains its inner fullness only in love. Because every man is truly a visible image of the invisible God and a brother of Christ, the Christian finds in every man God himself and God's absolute demand for justice and love.

The present situation of the world, seen in the light of faith, calls us back to the very essence of the Christian message, creating in us a deep awareness of its true meaning and of its urgent demands. The mission of preaching the Gospel dictates at the present time that we should dedicate ourselves to the liberation of man even in his present existence in this world. For unless the Christian message of love and justice shows its effectiveness through action in the cause of justice in the world, it will only with difficulty gain credibility with the men of our times.

The Mission of the Church, Hierarchy and Christians

The Church has received from Christ the mission of preaching the Gospel message, which contains a call to man to turn away from sin to the love of the Father, universal brotherhood, and a consequent demand for justice in the world. This is the reason why the Church has the right, indeed the duty, to proclaim justice on the social, national, and international level, and to denounce instances of injustice, when the fundamental rights of man and his very salvation demand it. The Church, indeed, is not alone responsible for justice in the world; however, she has a proper and specific responsibility which is identified with her mission of giving witness before the world of the need for love and justice contained in the Gospel message, a witness to be carried out in Church institutions themselves and in the lives of Christians.

Of itself it does not belong to the Church, insofar as she is a religious and hierarchical community, to offer concrete solutions in the social, economic, and political spheres for justice in the world. Her mission involves defending and promoting the dignity and fundamental rights of the human person.

The members of the Church, as members of society, have the same right and duty to promote the common good as do other citizens. Christians ought to fulfill their temporal obligations with fidelity and competence. They should act as a leaven in the world, in their family, professional, social, cultural and political life. They must accept their responsibilities in this entire area under the influence of the Gospel and the teaching of the Church. In this way they testify to the power of the Holy Spirit through their action in the service of men in those things which are decisive for the existence and the future of humanity. While in such activities they generally act on their own initiative without involving the responsibility of the ecclesiastical hierarchy, in a sense they do involve the responsibility of the Church whose members they are.

CHAPTER 3: THE PRACTICE OF JUSTICE

The Church's Witness

Many Christians are drawn to give authentic witness on behalf of justice by various modes of action for justice, action inspired by love in accordance with the grace which they have received from God. For some of them, this action finds its place in the sphere of social and political conflicts in which Christians bear witness to the Gospel by pointing out that in history there are sources of progress other than conflict, namely love and right. This priority of love in history draws other Christians to prefer the way of nonviolent action and work in the area of public opinion.

While the Church is bound to give witness to justice, she recognizes that everyone who ventures to speak to people about justice must first be just in their eyes. Hence we must undertake an examination of the modes of acting and of the possessions and lifestyle found within the Church herself.

Within the Church rights must be preserved. No one should be deprived of his ordinary rights because he is associated with the Church in one way or another. Those who serve the Church by their labor, including priests and religious, should receive a sufficient livelihood and enjoy that social security which is customary in their region. Lay people should be given fair wages and a system for promotion. We reiterate the recommendations that lay people should exercise more important functions with regard to Church property and should share in its administration.

We also urge that women should have their own share of responsibility and participation in the community life of society and likewise of the Church.

We propose that this matter be subjected to a serious study employing adequate means: for instance, a mixed commission of men and women, religious and lay people, of differing situations and competence.

The Church recognizes everyone's right to suitable freedom of expression and thought. This includes the right of everyone to be heard in a spirit of dialogue which preserves a legitimate diversity within the Church.

The form of judicial procedure should give the accused the right to know his accusers and also the right to a proper defense. To be complete, justice should include speed in its procedure. This is especially necessary in marriage cases.

Finally, the members of the Church should have some share in the drawing up of decisions, in accordance with the rules given by the Second Vatican Ecumenical Council and the Holy See, for instance with regard to the setting up of councils at all levels.

In regard to temporal possessions, whatever be their use, it must never happen that the evangelical witness which the Church is required to give becomes ambiguous. The preservation of certain positions of privilege must constantly be submitted to the test of this principle. Although in general it is difficult to draw a line between what is needed for right use and what is demanded by prophetic witness, we must certainly keep firmly to this principle:

our faith demands of us a certain sparingness in use, and the Church is obliged to live and administer its own goods in such a way that the Gospel is proclaimed to the poor. If instead the Church appears to be among the rich and the powerful of this world its credibility is diminished.

Our examination of conscience now comes to the lifestyle of all: bishops, priests, religious, and lay people. In the case of needy peoples it must be asked whether belonging to the Church places people on a rich island within an ambient of poverty. In societies enjoying a higher level of consumer spending, it must be asked whether our lifestyle exemplifies that sparingness with regard to consumption which we preach to others as necessary in order that so many millions of hungry people throughout the world may be fed.

Educating to Justice

Christians' specific contribution to justice is the day-to-day life of the individual believer acting like the leaven of the Gospel in his family, his school, his work, and his social and civic life. Included with this are the perspectives and meaning which the faithful can give to human effort. Accordingly, educational method must be such as to teach men to live their lives in its entire reality and in accord with the evangelical principles of personal and social morality which are expressed in the vital Christian witness of one's life.

The obstacles to the progress which we wish for ourselves and for mankind are obvious. The method of education very frequently still in use today encourages narrow individualism. Part of the human family lives immersed in a mentality which exalts possessions. The school and the communications media, which are often obstructed by the established order, allow the formation only of the man desired by that order, that is to say, man in its image, not a new man but a copy of man as he is.

But education demands a renewal of heart, a renewal based on the recognition of sin in its individual and social manifestations. It will also inculcate a truly and entirely human way of life in justice, love, and simplicity. It will likewise awaken a critical sense, which will lead us to reflect on the society in which we live and on its values; it will make men ready to renounce these values when they cease to promote justice for all men. In the developing countries, the principal aim of this education for justice consists in an attempt to awaken consciences to a knowledge of the concrete situation and in a call to secure a total improvement; by these means the transformation of the world has already begun.

Since this education makes men decidedly more human, it will help them to be no longer the object of manipulation by communications media or political forces. It will instead enable them to take in hand their own destinies and bring about communities which are truly human.

Accordingly, this education is deservedly called a continuing education, for it concerns every person and every age. It is also a practical education: it comes through action, participation, and vital contact with the reality of injustice.

Education for justice is imparted first in the family. We are well-aware that not only Church institutions but also other schools, trade unions, and political parties are collaborating in this.

The content of this education necessarily involves respect for the person and for his dignity. Since it is world justice which is in question here, the unity of the human family within which, according to God's plan, a human being is born must first of all be seriously affirmed. Christians find a sign of this solidarity in the fact that all human beings are destined to become in Christ sharers in the divine nature.

The basic principles whereby the influence of the Gospel has made itself felt in contemporary social life are to be found in the body of teaching set out in a gradual and timely way from the encyclical *Rerum Novarum* to the letter *Octogesima Adveniens*. As never before, the Church has, through the Second Vatican Council's constitution *Gaudium et Spes*, better understood the situation in the modern world, in which the Christian works out his salvation by deeds of justice. *Pacem in Terris* gave us an authentic charter of human rights. In *Mater et Magistra* international justice begins to take first place; it finds more elaborate expression in *Populorum Progressio*, in the form of a true and suitable treatise on the right to development, and in *Octogesima Adveniens* is found a summary of guidelines for political action.

Like the Apostle Paul, we insist, welcome or unwelcome, that the Word of God should be present in the center of human situations. Our interventions are intended to be an expression of that faith which is today binding on our lives and on the lives of the faithful. We all desire that these interventions should always be in conformity with circumstances of place and time. Our mission demands that we should courageously denounce injustice, with charity, prudence, and firmness, in sincere dialogue with all parties concerned. We know that our denunciations can secure assent to the extent that they are an expression of our lives and are manifested in continuous action.

The liturgy, which we preside over and which is the heart of the Church's life, can greatly serve education for justice. For it is a thanksgiving to the Father in Christ, which through its communitarian form places before our eyes the bonds of our brotherhood and again and again reminds us of the Church's mission. The liturgy of the word, catechesis, and the celebration of the sacraments have the power to help us to discover the teaching of the prophets, the Lord, and the apostles on the subject of justice. The preparation for baptism is the beginning of the formation of the Christian conscience. The practice of penance should emphasize the social dimension of sin and of the sacrament. Finally, the Eucharist forms the community and places it at the service of men.

Cooperation between Local Churches

That the Church may really be the sign of that solidarity which the family of nations desires, it should show in its own life greater cooperation between the Churches of rich and poor regions through spiritual communion and division of human and material resources. The present generous arrangements for assistance between Churches could be made more effective by real coordination (Sacred Congregation for the Evangelization of Peoples and the Pontifical Council "Cor Unum"), through their overall view in regard to the common administration of the gifts of God, and through fraternal solidarity, which would always encourage autonomy and responsibility on the part of the beneficiaries in the determination of criteria and the choice of concrete programs and their realization.

This planning must in no way be restricted to economic programs; it should instead stimulate activities capable of developing that human and spiritual formation which will serve as the leaven needed for the integral development of the human being.

Ecumenical Collaboration

Well aware of what has already been done in this field, together with the Second Vatican Ecumenical Council we very highly commend cooperation with our separated Christian brethren for the promotion of justice in the world, for bringing about development of peoples and for establishing peace. This cooperation concerns first and foremost activities for securing human dignity and man's fundamental rights, especially the right to religious liberty. This is the source of our common efforts against discrimination on the grounds of differences of religion, race and color, culture, and the like. Collaboration extends also to the study of the teaching of the Gospel insofar as it is the source of inspiration for all Christian activity. Let the Secretariat for Promoting Christian Unity and the Pontifical Commission Justice and Peace devote themselves in common counsel to developing effectively this ecumenical collaboration.

In the same spirit we likewise commend collaboration with all believers in God in the fostering of social justice, peace, and freedom; indeed we commend collaboration also with those who, even though they do not recognize the Author of the world, nevertheless, in their esteem for human values, seek justice sincerely and by honorable means.

International Action

Since the synod is of a universal character, it is dealing with those questions of justice which directly concern the entire human family. Hence, recognizing the importance of international cooperation for social and economic development, we praise above all else the inestimable work which has been done among the poorer peoples by the local Churches, the missionaries and the organizations supporting them; and we intend to foster those initiatives and institutions which are working for peace, international justice and the development of man. We therefore urge Catholics to consider well the following propositions:

1. Let recognition be given to the fact that international order is rooted in the inalienable rights and dignity of the human being. Let the United Nations

Declaration of Human Rights be ratified by all governments who have not yet adhered to it, and let it be fully observed by all.

2. Let the United Nations—which because of its unique purpose should promote participation by all nations—and international organizations be supported insofar as they are the beginning of a system capable of restraining the armaments race, discouraging trade in weapons, securing disarmament and settling conflicts by peaceful methods of legal action, arbitration, and international police action. It is absolutely necessary that international conflicts should not be settled by war, but that other methods better befitting human nature should be found. Let a strategy of nonviolence be fostered also, and let conscientious objection be recognized and regulated by law in each nation.

3. Let the aims of the Second Development Decade be fostered. These include the transfer of a precise percentage of the annual income of the richer countries to the developing nations, fairer prices for raw materials, the opening of the markets of the richer nations and, in some fields, preferential treatment for exports of manufactured goods from the developing nations. These aims represent first guidelines for a graduated taxation of income as well as for an economic and social plan for the entire world. We grieve whenever richer nations turn their backs on this ideal goal of worldwide sharing and responsibility. We hope that no such weakening of international solidarity will take away their force from the trade discussions being prepared by the United Nations Conference on Trade and Development (UNCTAD).

4. The concentration of power which consists in almost total domination of economics, research, investment, freight charges, sea transport, and securities should be progressively balanced by institutional arrangements for strengthening power and opportunities with regard to responsible decision by the developing nations and by full and equal participation in international organizations concerned with development. Their recent de facto exclusion from discussions on world trade and also the monetary arrangements which vitally affect their destiny are an example of lack of power which is inadmissible in a just and responsible world order.

5. Although we recognize that international agencies can be perfected and strengthened, as can any human instrument, we stress also the importance of the specialized agencies of the United Nations, in particular those directly concerned with the immediate and more acute questions of world poverty in the field of agrarian reform and agricultural development, health, education, employment, housing, and rapidly increasing urbanization. We feel we must point out in a special way the need for some fund to provide sufficient food and protein for the real mental and physical development of children. In the face of the population explosion we repeat the words by which Pope Paul VI defined the functions of public authority in his encyclical *Populorum Progressio*: "There is no doubt that public authorities can intervene, within the limit of their competence, by favoring the availability of appropriate information and by adopting suitable measures, provided that these be in con-

formity with the moral law and that they absolutely respect the rightful freedom of married couples."[2]

6. Let governments continue with their individual contributions to a development fund, but let them also look for a way whereby most of their endeavors may follow multilateral channels, fully preserving the responsibility of the developing nations, which must be associated in decision-making concerning priorities and investments.

7. We consider that we must also stress the new worldwide preoccupation which will be dealt with for the first time in the conference on the human environment to be held in Stockholm in June 1972. It is impossible to see what right the richer nations have to keep up their claim to increase their own material demands, if the consequence is either that others remain in misery or that the danger of destroying the very physical foundations of life on earth is precipitated. Those who are already rich are bound to accept a less material way of life, with less waste, in order to avoid the destruction of the heritage which they are obliged by absolute justice to share with all other members of the human race.

8. In order that the right to development may be fulfilled by action:

a) people should not be hindered from attaining development in accordance with their own culture;

b) through mutual cooperation, all peoples should be able to become the principal architects of their own economic and social development;

c) every people, as active and responsible members of human society, should be able to cooperate for the attainment of the common good on an equal footing with other peoples.

Recommendations of the Synod

The examination of conscience which we have made together, regarding the Church's involvement in action for justice, will remain ineffective if it is not given flesh in the life of our local Churches at all their levels. We also ask the episcopal conferences to continue to pursue the perspectives which we have had in view during the days of this meeting and to put our recommendations into practice, for instance by setting up centers of social and theological research.

We also ask that there be recommended to the Pontifical Commission for Justice and Peace, the Council of the Secretariat of the Synod and to competent authorities, the description, consideration, and deeper study of the wishes and desires of our assembly, and that these bodies should bring to a successful conclusion what we have begun.

CHAPTER 4: A WORD OF HOPE

The power of the Spirit, who raised Christ from the dead, is continuously at work in the world. Through the generous sons and daughters of the Church likewise, the People of God is present in the midst of the poor and of those who suffer oppression and persecution; it lives in its own flesh and its own heart the passion of Christ and bears witness to his resurrection.

The entire creation has been groaning till now in an act of giving birth, as it waits for the glory of the children of God to be revealed (cf. Rom. 8:22). Let Christians therefore be convinced that they will yet find the fruits of their own nature and effort cleansed of all impurities in the new earth which God is now preparing for them, and in which there will be the kingdom of justice and love, a kingdom which will be fully perfected when the Lord will come himself.

Hope in the coming kingdom is already beginning to take root in the hearts of men. The radical transformation of the world in the Paschal Mystery of the Lord gives full meaning to the efforts of men, and in particular of the young, to lessen injustice, violence, and hatred and to advance all together in justice, freedom, brotherhood, and love.

At the same time as it proclaims the Gospel of the Lord, its Redeemer and Savior, the Church calls on all, especially the poor, the oppressed and the afflicted, to cooperate with God to bring about liberation from every sin and to build a world which will reach the fullness of creation only when it becomes the work of man for man.

NOTES

1. Cf. Paul VI, *Populorum Progressio*, 15; AAS 59, 1967, p. 265.
2. Paul VI, *Populorum Progressio*, 37; AAS 59, 1967, p. 276.

Evangelii Nuntiandi: Evangelization in the Modern World (Paul VI, 1975)

INTRODUCTION

This Apostolic Exhortation, published in 1975, focused on the theme of making the church of the twentieth century better fitted for proclaiming the gospel; according to Paul, it is only in the gospel that modern people can find answers to their questions as well as the energy required for continued commitment to human liberation and the achievement of solidarity.

Evangelization is the transformation of humanity from within and making it new through the influence of the church. It is the conversion of "both the personal and collective consciences of people, the activities in which they engage, and the lives and concrete milieux which are theirs."

While grounded and motivated by a vision of the coming kingdom, evangelization also contains a clear message about human rights and duties; family life; life in society; international life; and peace, justice, development, and liberation. Thus one cannot, in Paul's vision, proclaim the command of love without simultaneously promoting justice and peace and the authentic advancement of people. This does not reduce the mission of evangelization to a secular project, but rather fulfills the deepest plan of creation and implements the evangelical order of charity. The liberation of people on all levels coheres with the Christian struggle for liberation to achieve the universal plan of salvation.

Special notice was taken here of ecclesial base communities (*communautés de base*) and their role in evangelization. Paul recognized their positive role but also set forth guidelines so that they maintain their relation with the larger church.

The pope also noted the special role of the laity in evangelizing their world of politics, society, and economics, as well as that of culture, science, the arts, and the mass media. Here the laity are to reveal the transcendent dimension of human life, which is often disregarded.

Finally, the task of evangelization is to spring from and promote a spirit of unity within the church as well as within the whole Christian community. Thus those involved in evangelization must reverence the truth, especially that first truth which is God. This evangelical truth is the basis for our liberation and peace of heart.

This Apostolic Exhortation summarized well the theses initiated by John XXIII, the Vatican Council, and the 1974 Synod of Bishops. It also presented many of Paul's concerns, present in previous encyclicals and to be further developed in later writings and speeches.

EVANGELII NUNTIANDI

APOSTOLIC EXHORTATION
EVANGELII NUNTIANDI
OF HIS HOLINESS

POPE PAUL VI

To the Episcopate, to the Clergy
and to All the Faithful
of the Entire World

ON EVANGELIZATION
IN THE MODERN WORLD

Venerable Brothers
and Dear Sons and Daughters,
Health and the Apostolic Blessing

SPECIAL COMMITMENT TO EVANGELIZATION

1. There is no doubt that the effort to proclaim the Gospel to the people of today, who are buoyed up by hope but at the same time often oppressed by fear and distress, is a service rendered to the Christian community and also to the whole of humanity.

For this reason the duty of confirming the brethren—a duty which with the office of being the Successor of Peter[1] we have received from the Lord, and which is for us a "daily preoccupation,"[2] a program of life and action, and a fundamental commitment of our Pontificate—seems to us all the more noble and necessary when it is a matter of encouraging our brethren in their mission as evangelizers, in order that, in this time of uncertainty and confusion, they may accomplish this task with ever increasing love, zeal and joy.

On the Occasion of Three Events

2. This is precisely what we wish to do here, at the end of this Holy Year during which the Church, "striving to proclaim the Gospel to all people,"[3] has had the single aim of fulfilling her duty of being the messenger of the Good News of Jesus Christ—the Good News proclaimed through two fundamental commands: "Put on the new self"[4] and "Be reconciled to God."[5]

We wish to do so on this tenth anniversary of the closing of the Second Vatican Council, the objectives of which are definitively summed up in this single theme: to make the Church of the twentieth century ever better fitted for proclaiming the Gospel to the people of the twentieth century.

We wish to do so one year after the Third General Assembly of the Synod of Bishops, which, as is well known, was devoted to evangelization; and we do so all the more willingly because it has been asked of us by the Synod Fathers themselves. In fact, at the end of that memorable Assembly, the Fathers decided to remit to the Pastor of the universal Church, with great trust and simplicity, the fruits of all their labors, stating that they awaited from him a fresh forward impulse, capable of creating within a Church still more firmly rooted in the undying power and strength of Pentecost a new period of evangelization.[6]

Theme Frequently Emphasized in the Course of Our Pontificate

3. We have stressed the importance of this theme of evangelization on many occasions, well before the Synod took place. On 22 June 1973 we said to the Sacred College of Cardinals: "The conditions of the society in which we live oblige all of us therefore to revise methods, to seek by every means to study how we can bring the Christian message to modern man. For it is only in the Christian message that modern man can find the answer to his questions and the energy for his commitment of human solidarity."[7] And we added that in order to give a valid answer to the demands of the Council which call for our attention, it is absolutely necessary for us to take into account a heritage of faith that the Church has the duty of preserving in its untouchable purity, and of presenting it to the people of our time, in a way that is as understandable and persuasive as possible.

In the Line of the 1974 Synod

4. This fidelity both to a message whose servants we are and to the people to whom we must transmit it living and intact is the central axis of evangelization. It poses three burning questions, which the 1974 Synod kept constantly in mind:

–In our day, what has happened to that hidden energy of the Good News, which is able to have a powerful effect on man's conscience?

–To what extent and in what way is that evangelical force capable of really transforming the people of this century?

–What methods should be followed in order that the power of the Gospel may have its effect?

Basically, these inquiries make explicit the fundamental question that the Church is asking herself today and which may be expressed in the following terms: after the Council and thanks to the Council, which was a time given her by God, at this turning point of history, does the Church or does she not find herself better equipped to proclaim the Gospel and to put it into people's hearts with conviction, freedom of spirit and effectiveness?

Invitation to Meditation

5. We can all see the urgency of giving a loyal, humble and courageous answer to this question, and of acting accordingly.

In our "anxiety for all the Churches,"[8] we would like to help our brethren and sons and daughters to reply to these inquiries. Our words come from the wealth of the Synod and are meant to be a meditation on evangelization. May they succeed in inviting the whole People of God assembled in the Church to make the same meditation; and may they give a fresh impulse to everyone, especially those "who are assiduous in preaching and teaching,"[9] so that each one of them may follow "a straight course in the message of the truth,"[10] and may work as a preacher of the Gospel and acquit himself perfectly of his ministry.

Such an exhortation seems to us to be of capital importance, for the presentation of the Gospel message is not an optional contribution for the Church. It is the duty incumbent on her by the command of the Lord Jesus, so that people can believe and be saved. This message is indeed necessary. It is unique. It cannot be replaced. It does not permit either indifference, syncretism or accommodation. It is a question of people's salvation. It is the beauty of the Revelation that it represents. It brings with it a wisdom that is not of this world. It is able to stir up by itself faith—faith that rests on the power of God.[11] It is truth. It merits having the apostle consecrate to it all his time and all his energies, and to sacrifice for it, if necessary, his own life.

1. FROM CHRIST THE EVANGELIZER TO THE EVANGELIZING CHURCH

Witness and Mission of Jesus

6. The witness that the Lord gives of himself and that Saint Luke gathered together in his Gospel—"I must proclaim the Good News of the kingdom of God"[12]—without doubt has enormous consequences, for it sums up the whole mission of Jesus: "That is what I was sent to do."[13] These words take on their full significance if one links them with the previous verses, in which Christ has just applied to himself the words of the Prophet Isaiah: "The Spirit of the Lord has been given to me, for he has anointed me. He has sent me to bring the good news to the poor."[14]

Going from town to town, preaching to the poorest—and frequently the most receptive—the joyful news of the fulfillment of the promises and of the Covenant offered by God is the mission for which Jesus declares that he is sent by the Father. And all the aspects of his mystery—the Incarnation itself, his miracles, his teaching, the gathering together of the disciples, the sending out of the Twelve, the Cross and the Resurrection, the permanence of his presence in the midst of his own—were components of his evangelizing activity.

Jesus, the First Evangelizer

7. During the Synod, the Bishops very frequently referred to this truth: Jesus himself, the Good News of God,[15] was the very first and the greatest evangelizer; he was so through and through: to perfection and to the point of the sacrifice of his earthly life.

To evangelize: what meaning did this imperative have for Christ? It is certainly not easy to express in a complete synthesis the meaning, the content and the modes of evangelization as Jesus conceived it and put it into practice. In any case the attempt to make such a synthesis will never end. Let it suffice for us to recall a few essential aspects.

Proclamation of the Kingdom of God

8. As an evangelizer, Christ first of all proclaims a kingdom, the Kingdom of God; and this is so important that, by comparison, everything else becomes "the rest," which is "given in addition."[16] Only the Kingdom therefore is absolute, and it makes everything else relative. The Lord will delight in describing in many ways the happiness of belonging to this Kingdom (a paradoxical happiness which is made up of things that the world rejects),[17] the demands of the Kingdom and its Magna Charta,[18] the heralds of the Kingdom,[19] its mysteries,[20] its children,[21] the vigilance and fidelity demanded of whoever awaits its definitive coming.[22]

Proclamation of Liberating Salvation

9. As the kernel and center of his Good News, Christ proclaims salvation, this great gift of God which is liberation from everything that oppresses man but which is above all liberation from sin and the Evil One, in the joy of knowing God and being known by him, of seeing him, and of being given over to him. All of this is begun during the life of Christ and definitively accomplished by his death and Resurrection. But it must be patiently carried on during the course of history, in order to be realized fully on the day of the final coming of Christ, whose date is known to no one except the Father.[23]

At the Price of Crucifying Effort

10. This Kingdom and this salvation, which are the key words of Jesus Christ's evangelization, are available to every human being as grace and mercy, and yet at the same time each individual must gain them by force—they belong to the violent, says the Lord,[24] through toil and suffering, through a life lived according to the Gospel, through abnegation and the Cross, through the spirit of the beatitudes. But above all each individual gains them through a total interior renewal which the Gospel calls metanoia; it is a radical conversion, a profound change of mind and heart.[25]

Tireless Preaching

11. Christ accomplished this proclamation of the Kingdom of God through the untiring preaching of a word which, it will be said, has no equal elsewhere: "Here is a teaching that is new, and with authority behind it."[26] And he won the approval of all, and they were astonished by the gracious words that came from his lips."[27] "There has never been anybody who has spoken like him."[28] His words reveal the secret of God, his plan and his promise, and thereby change the heart of man and his destiny.

With Evangelical Signs

12. But Christ also carries out this proclamation by innumerable signs, which amaze the crowds and at the same time draw them to him in order to see him, listen to him and allow themselves to be transformed by him: the sick are cured, water is changed into wine, bread is multiplied, the dead come back to life. And among all these signs there is the one to which he attaches great importance: the humble and the poor are evangelized, become his disciples and gather together "in his name" in the great community of those who believe in him. For this Jesus who declared, "I must preach the Good News of the Kingdom of God,"[29] is the same Jesus of whom John the Evangelist said that he had come and was to die "to gather together in unity the scattered children of God."[30] Thus he accomplishes his revelation, completing it and confirming it by the entire revelation that he makes of himself, by words and deeds, by signs and miracles, and more especially by his death, by his Resurrection and by the sending of the Spirit of Truth.[31]

For an Evangelized and Evangelizing Community

13. Those who sincerely accept the Good News, through the power of this acceptance and of shared faith, therefore gather together in Jesus' name in order to seek together the Kingdom, build it up and live it. They make up a community which is in its turn evangelizing. The command to the Twelve to go out and proclaim the Good News is also valid for all Christians, though in a different way. It is precisely for this reason that Peter calls Christians "a people set apart to sing the praises of God,"[32] those marvelous things that each one was able to hear in his own language.[33] Moreover, the Good News of the Kingdom which is coming and which has begun is meant for all people of all times. Those who have received the Good News and who have been gathered by it into the community of salvation can and must communicate and spread it.

Evangelization: Vocation Proper to the Church

14. The Church knows this. She has a vivid awareness of the fact that the Savior's words, "I must proclaim the Good News of the kingdom of God,"[34] apply in all truth to herself. She willingly adds with Saint Paul: "Not that I boast of preaching the gospel, since it is a duty that has been laid on me; I should be punished if I did not preach it!"[35] It is with joy and consolation that

at the end of the great Assembly of 1974 we heard these illuminating words: "We wish to confirm once more that the task of evangelizing all people constitutes the essential mission of the Church."[36] It is a task and mission which the vast and profound changes of present-day society make all the more urgent. Evangelizing is in fact the grace and vocation proper to the Church, her deepest identity. She exists in order to evangelize, that is to say in order to preach and teach, to be the channel of the gift of grace, to reconcile sinners with God, and to perpetuate Christ's sacrifice in the Mass, which is the memorial of his death and glorious Resurrection.

Reciprocal Links between the Church and Evangelization

15. Anyone who re-reads in the New Testament the origins of the Church follows her history step by step and watches her live and act, sees that she is linked to evangelization in her most intimate being:

–The Church is born of the evangelizing activity of Jesus and the Twelve. She is the normal, desired, most immediate and most visible fruit of this activity: "Go, therefore, make disciples of all the nations."[37] Now, "they accepted what he said and were baptized. That very day about three thousand were added to their number. . . . Day by day the Lord added to their community those destined to be saved."[38]

–Having been born consequently out of being sent, the Church in her turn is sent by Jesus. The Church remains in the world when the Lord of glory returns to the Father. She remains as a sign—simultaneously obscure and luminous—of a new presence of Jesus, of his departure and of his permanent presence. She prolongs and continues him. And it is above all his mission and his condition of being an evangelizer that she is called upon to continue.[39] For the Christian community is never closed in upon itself. The intimate life of this community—the life of listening to the Word and the Apostles' teaching, charity lived in a fraternal way, the sharing of bread[40]—this intimate life only acquires its full meaning when it becomes a witness, when it evokes admiration and conversion, and when it becomes the preaching and proclamation of the Good News. Thus it is the whole Church that receives the mission to evangelize, and the work of each individual member is important for the whole.

–The Church is an evangelizer, but she begins by being evangelized herself. She is the community of believers, the community of hope lived and communicated, the community of brotherly love; and she needs to listen unceasingly to what she must believe, to her reasons for hoping, to the new commandment of love. She is the People of God immersed in the world, and often tempted by idols, and she always needs to hear the proclamation of the "mighty works of God"[41] which converted her to the Lord; she always needs to be called together afresh by him and reunited. In brief, this means that she has a constant need of being evangelized, if she wishes to retain freshness, vigor and strength in order to proclaim the Gospel. The Second Vatican

Council recalled[42] and the 1974 Synod vigorously took up again this theme of the Church which is evangelized by constant conversion and renewal, in order to evangelize the world with credibility.

–The Church is the depositary of the Good News to be proclaimed. The promises of the New Alliance in Jesus Christ, the teaching of the Lord and the Apostles, the Word of life, the sources of grace and of God's loving kindness, the path of salvation—all these things have been entrusted to her. It is the content of the Gospel, and therefore of evangelization, that she preserves as a precious living heritage, not in order to keep it hidden but to communicate it.

–Having been sent and evangelized, the Church herself sends out evangelizers. She puts on their lips the saving Word, she explains to them the message of which she herself is the depositary, she gives them the mandate which she herself has received and she sends them out to preach. To preach not their own selves or their personal ideas,[43] but a Gospel of which neither she nor they are the absolute masters and owners, to dispose of it as they wish, but a Gospel of which they are the ministers, in order to pass it on with complete fidelity.

The Church, Inseparable from Christ

16. There is thus a profound link between Christ, the Church and evangelization. During the period of the Church that we are living in, it is she who has the task of evangelizing. This mandate is not accomplished without her, and still less against her.

It is certainly fitting to recall this fact at a moment like the present one when it happens that not without sorrow we can hear people—whom we wish to believe are well-intentioned but who are certainly misguided in their attitude—continually claiming to love Christ but without the Church, to listen to Christ but not the Church, to belong to Christ but outside the Church. The absurdity of this dichotomy is clearly evident in this phrase of the Gospel: "Anyone who rejects you rejects me."[44] And how can one wish to love Christ without loving the Church, if the finest witness to Christ is that of Saint Paul: "Christ loved the Church and sacrificed himself for her?"[45]

2. WHAT IS EVANGELIZATION?

Complexity of Evangelizing Action

17. In the Church's evangelizing activity there are of course certain elements and aspects to be specially insisted on. Some of them are so important that there will be a tendency simply to identify them with evangelization. Thus it has been possible to define evangelization in terms of proclaiming Christ to those who do not know him, of preaching, of catechesis, of conferring Baptism and the other Sacraments.

Any partial and fragmentary definition which attempts to render the reality of evangelization in all its richness, complexity and dynamism does so only at the risk of impoverishing it and even of distorting it. It is impossible to grasp the concept of evangelization unless one tries to keep in view all its essential elements.

These elements were strongly emphasized at the last Synod, and are still the subject of frequent study, as a result of the Synod's work. We rejoice in the fact that these elements basically follow the lines of those transmitted to us by the Second Vatican Council, especially in *Lumen Gentium*, *Gaudium et Spes* and *Ad Gentes*.

Renewal of Humanity

18. For the Church, evangelizing means bringing the Good News into all the strata of humanity, and through its influence transforming humanity from within and making it new: "Now I am making the whole of creation new."[46] But there is no new humanity if there are not first of all new persons renewed by Baptism[47] and by lives lived according to the Gospel.[48] The purpose of evangelization is therefore precisely this interior change, and if it had to be expressed in one sentence the best way of stating it would be to say that the Church evangelizes when she seeks to convert,[49] solely through the divine power of the Message she proclaims, both the personal and collective consciences of people, the activities in which they engage, and the lives and concrete milieux which are theirs.

And of the Strata of Humanity

19. Strata of humanity which are transformed: for the Church it is a question not only of preaching the Gospel in ever wider geographic areas or to ever greater numbers of people, but also of affecting and as it were upsetting, through the power of the Gospel, mankind's criteria of judgment, determining values, points of interest, lines of thought, sources of inspiration and models of life, which are in contrast with the Word of God and the plan of salvation.

Evangelization of Cultures

20. All this could be expressed in the following words: what matters is to evangelize man's culture and cultures (not in a purely decorative way as it were by applying a thin veneer, but in a vital way, in depth and right to their very roots), in the wide and rich sense which these terms have in *Gaudium et Spes*,[50] always taking the person as one's starting point and always coming back to the relationships of people among themselves and with God.

The Gospel, and therefore evangelization, are certainly not identical with culture, and they are independent in regard to all cultures. Nevertheless, the Kingdom which the Gospel proclaims is lived by men who are profoundly linked to a culture, and the building up of the Kingdom cannot avoid borrowing the elements of human culture or cultures. Though independent of cultures, the Gospel and evangelization are not necessarily incompatible with them; rather they are capable of permeating them all without becoming subject to any one of them.

The split between the Gospel and culture is without a doubt the drama of our time, just as it was of other times. Therefore every effort must be made to ensure a full evangelization of culture, or more correctly of cultures. They have to be regenerated by an encounter with the Gospel. But this encounter will not take place if the Gospel is not proclaimed.

Primary Importance of Witness of Life

21. Above all the Gospel must be proclaimed by witness. Take a Christian or a handful of Christians who, in the midst of their own community, show their capacity for understanding and acceptance, their sharing of life and destiny with other people, their solidarity with the efforts of all for whatever is noble and good. Let us suppose that, in addition, they radiate in an altogether simple and unaffected way their faith in values that go beyond current values, and their hope in something that is not seen and that one would not dare to imagine. Through this wordless witness these Christians stir up irresistible questions in the hearts of those who see how they live: Why are they like this? Why do they live in this way? What or who is it that inspires them? Why are they in our midst? Such a witness is already a silent proclamation of the Good News and a very powerful and effective one. Here we have an initial act of evangelization. The above questions will perhaps be the first that many non-Christians will ask, whether they are people to whom Christ has never been proclaimed, or baptized people who do not practice, or people who live as nominal Christians but according to principles that are in no way Christian, or people who are seeking, and not without suffering, something or someone whom they sense but cannot name. Other questions will arise, deeper and more demanding ones, questions evoked by this witness which involves presence, sharing, solidarity, and which is an essential element, and generally the first one, in evangelization.[51]

All Christians are called to this witness, and in this way they can be real evangelizers. We are thinking especially of the responsibility incumbent on immigrants in the country that receives them.

Need of Explicit Proclamation

22. Nevertheless this always remains insufficient, because even the finest witness will prove ineffective in the long run if it is not explained, justified—what Peter called always having "your answer ready for people who ask you the reason for the hope that you all have"[52]—and made explicit by a clear and unequivocal proclamation of the Lord Jesus. The Good News proclaimed by the witness of life sooner or later has to be proclaimed by the word of life. There is no true evangelization if the name, the teaching, the life, the promises, the Kingdom and the mystery of Jesus of Nazareth, the Son of God, are not proclaimed. The history of the Church, from the discourse of Peter on the morning of Pentecost onwards, has been intermingled and identified with the history of this proclamation. At every new phase of human history, the

Church, constantly gripped by the desire to evangelize, has but one preoccupation: whom to send to proclaim the mystery of Jesus? In what way is this mystery to be proclaimed? How can one ensure that it will resound and reach all those who should hear it? This proclamation—kerygma, preaching or catechesis—occupies such an important place in evangelization that it has often become synonymous with it; and yet it is only one aspect of evangelization.

For a Vital and Community Acceptance

23. In fact the proclamation only reaches full development when it is listened to, accepted and assimilated, and when it arouses a genuine adherence in the one who has thus received it. An adherence to the truths which the Lord in his mercy has revealed; still more, an adherence to a program of life—a life henceforth transformed—which he proposes. In a word, adherence to the Kingdom, that is to say the "new world," to the new state of things, to the new manner of being, of living, of living in community, which the Gospel inaugurates. Such an adherence, which cannot remain abstract and unincarnated, reveals itself concretely by a visible entry into a community of believers. Thus those whose life has been transformed enter a community which is itself a sign of transformation, a sign of newness of life: it is the Church, the visible sacrament of salvation.[53] But entry into the ecclesial community will in its turn be expressed through many other signs which prolong and unfold the sign of the Church. In the dynamism of evangelization, a person who accepts the Church as the Word which saves[54] normally translates it into the following sacramental acts: adherence to the Church and acceptance of the Sacraments, which manifest and support this adherence through the grace which they confer.

Involving a New Apostolate

24. Finally, the person who has been evangelized goes on to evangelize others. Here lies the test of truth, the touchstone of evangelization: it is unthinkable that a person should accept the Word and give himself to the Kingdom without becoming a person who bears witness to it and proclaims it in his turn.

To complete these considerations on the meaning of evangelization, a final observation must be made, one which we consider will help to clarify the reflections that follow.

Evangelization, as we have said, is a complex process made up of varied elements: the renewal of humanity, witness, explicit proclamation, inner adherence, entry into the community, acceptance of signs, apostolic initiative. These elements may appear to be contradictory, indeed mutually exclusive. In fact they are complementary and mutually enriching. Each one must always be seen in relationship with the others. The value of the last Synod was to have constantly invited us to relate these elements rather than to place them in opposition one to the other, in order to reach a full understanding of the Church's evangelizing activity.

It is this global vision which we now wish to outline, by examining the content of evangelization and the methods of evangelizing and by clarifying to whom the Gospel message is addressed and who today is responsible for it.

3. THE CONTENT OF EVANGELIZATION

Essential Content and Secondary Elements

25. In the message which the Church proclaims there are certainly many secondary elements. Their presentation depends greatly on changing circumstances. They themselves also change. But there is the essential content, the living substance, which cannot be modified or ignored without seriously diluting the nature of evangelization itself.

Witness Given to the Father's Love

26. It is not superfluous to recall the following points: to evangelize is first of all to bear witness, in a simple and direct way, to God revealed by Jesus Christ, in the Holy Spirit; to bear witness that in his Son God has loved the world—that in his Incarnate Word he has given being to all things and has called men to eternal life. Perhaps this attestation of God will be for many people the unknown God[55] whom they adore without giving him a name, or whom they seek by a secret call of the heart when they experience the emptiness of all idols. But it is fully evangelizing in manifesting the fact that for man the Creator is not an anonymous and remote power; he is the Father: ". . . that we should be called children of God; and so we are."[56] And thus we are one another's brothers and sisters in God.

At the Center of the Message: Salvation in Jesus Christ

27. Evangelization will also always contain—as the foundation, center and at the same time summit of its dynamism—a clear proclamation that, in Jesus Christ, the Son of God made man, who died and rose from the dead, salvation is offered to all men, as a gift of God's grace and mercy.[57] And not an immanent salvation, meeting material or even spiritual needs, restricted to the framework of temporal existence and completely identified with temporal desires, hopes, affairs and struggles, but a salvation which exceeds all these limits in order to reach fulfillment in a communion with the one and only divine Absolute: a transcendent and eschatological salvation, which indeed has its beginning in this life but which is fulfilled in eternity.

Under the Sign of Hope

28. Consequently evangelization cannot but include the prophetic proclamation of a hereafter, man's profound and definitive calling, in both continuity and discontinuity with the present situation: beyond time and history,

beyond the transient reality of this world, and beyond the things of this world, of which a hidden dimension will one day be revealed—beyond man himself, whose true destiny is not restricted to his temporal aspect but will be revealed in the future life.[58] Evangelization therefore also includes the preaching of hope in the promises made by God in the new Covenant in Jesus Christ, the preaching of God's love for us and of our love for God; the preaching of brotherly love for all men—the capacity of giving and forgiving, of self-denial, of helping one's brother and sister—which, springing from the love of God, is the kernel of the Gospel; the preaching of the mystery of evil and of the active search for good. The preaching likewise—and this is always urgent—of the search for God himself through prayer which is principally that of adoration and thanksgiving, but also through communion with the visible sign of the encounter with God which is the Church of Jesus Christ; and this communion in its turn is expressed by the application of those other signs of Christ living and acting in the Church which are the Sacraments. To live the Sacraments in this way, bringing their celebration to a true fullness, is not, as some would claim, to impede or to accept a distortion of evangelization: it is rather to complete it. For in its totality, evangelization—over and above the preaching of a message—consists in the implantation of the Church, which does not exist without the driving force which is the sacramental life culminating in the Eucharist.[59]

Message Touching Life as a Whole

29. But evangelization would not be complete if it did not take account of the unceasing interplay of the Gospel and of man's concrete life, both personal and social. This is why evangelization involves an explicit message, adapted to the different situations constantly being realized, about the rights and duties of every human being, about family life without which personal growth and development is hardly possible,[60] about life in society, about international life, peace, justice and development—a message especially energetic today about liberation.

A Message of Liberation

30. It is well known in what terms numerous Bishops from all the continents spoke of this at the last Synod, especially the Bishops from the Third World, with a pastoral accent resonant with the voice of the millions of sons and daughters of the Church who make up those peoples. Peoples, as we know, engaged with all their energy in the effort and struggle to overcome everything which condemns them to remain on the margin of life: famine, chronic disease, illiteracy, poverty, injustices in international relations and especially in commercial exchanges, situations of economic and cultural neo-colonialism sometimes as cruel as the old political colonialism. The Church, as the Bishops repeated, has the duty to proclaim the liberation of millions of human beings, many of whom are her own children—the duty of assisting

the birth of this liberation, of giving witness to it, of ensuring that it is complete. This is not foreign to evangelization.

Necessarily Linked to Human Advancement

31. Between evangelization and human advancement—development and liberation—there are in fact profound links. These include links of an anthropological order, because the man who is to be evangelized is not an abstract being but is subject to social and economic questions. They also include links in the theological order, since one cannot dissociate the plan of creation from the plan of Redemption. The latter plan touches the very concrete situations of injustice to be combatted and of justice to be restored. They include links of the eminently evangelical order, which is that of charity: how in fact can one proclaim the new commandment without promoting in justice and in peace the true, authentic advancement of man? We ourself have taken care to point this out, by recalling that it is impossible to accept "that in evangelization one could or should ignore the importance of the problems so much discussed today, concerning justice, liberation, development and peace in the world. This would be to forget the lesson which comes to us from the Gospel concerning love of our neighbor who is suffering and in need."[61]

The same voices which during the Synod touched on this burning theme with zeal, intelligence and courage have, to our great joy, furnished the enlightening principles for a proper understanding of the importance and profound meaning of liberation, such as it was proclaimed and achieved by Jesus of Nazareth and such as it is preached by the Church.

Without Reduction or Ambiguity

32. We must not ignore the fact that many, even generous Christians who are sensitive to the dramatic questions involved in the problem of liberation, in their wish to commit the Church to the liberation effort are frequently tempted to reduce her mission to the dimensions of a simply temporal project. They would reduce her aims to a man-centered goal; the salvation of which she is the messenger would be reduced to material well-being. Her activity, forgetful of all spiritual and religious preoccupation, would become initiatives of the political or social order. But if this were so, the Church would lose her fundamental meaning. Her message of liberation would no longer have any originality and would easily be open to monopolization and manipulation by ideological systems and political parties. She would have no more authority to proclaim freedom as in the name of God. This is why we have wished to emphasize, in the same address at the opening of the Synod, "the need to restate clearly the specifically religious finality of evangelization. This latter would lose its reason for existence if it were to diverge from the religious axis that guides it: the Kingdom of God, before anything else, in its fully theological meaning. . . ."[62]

Evangelical Liberation

33. With regard to the liberation which evangelization proclaims and strives to put into practice one should rather say this:

–it cannot be contained in the simple and restricted dimension of economics, politics, social or cultural life; it must envisage the whole man, in all his aspects, right up to and including his openness to the absolute, even the divine Absolute;

–it is therefore attached to a certain concept of man, to a view of man which it can never sacrifice to the needs of any strategy, practice or short-term efficiency.

Centered on the Kingdom of God

34. Hence, when preaching liberation and associating herself with those who are working and suffering for it, the Church is certainly not willing to restrict her mission only to the religious field and dissociate herself from man's temporal problems. Nevertheless she reaffirms the primacy of her spiritual vocation and refuses to replace the proclamation of the Kingdom by the proclamation of forms of human liberation; she even states that her contribution to liberation is incomplete if she neglects to proclaim salvation in Jesus Christ.

On an Evangelical Concept of Man

35. The Church links human liberation and salvation in Jesus Christ, but she never identifies them, because she knows through revelation, historical experience and the reflection of faith that not every notion of liberation is necessarily consistent and compatible with an evangelical vision of man, of things and of events; she knows too that in order that God's Kingdom should come it is not enough to establish liberation and to create well-being and development.

And what is more, the Church has the firm conviction that all temporal liberation, all political liberation—even if it endeavors to find its justification in such or such a page of the Old or New Testament, even if it claims for its ideological postulates and its norms of action theological data and conclusions, even if it pretends to be today's theology—carries within itself the germ of its own negation and fails to reach the ideal that it proposes for itself, whenever its profound motives are not those of justice in charity, whenever its zeal lacks a truly spiritual dimension and whenever its final goal is not salvation and happiness in God.

Involving a Necessary Conversion

36. The Church considers it to be undoubtedly important to build up structures which are more human, more just, more respectful of the rights of the person and less oppressive and less enslaving, but she is conscious that the best structures and the most idealized systems soon become inhuman if

the inhuman inclinations of the human heart are not made wholesome, if those who live in these structures or who rule them do not undergo a conversion of heart and of outlook.

Excluding Violence

37. The Church cannot accept violence, especially the force of arms—which is uncontrollable once it is let loose—and indiscriminate death as the path to liberation, because she knows that violence always provokes violence and irresistibly engenders new forms of oppression and enslavement which are often harder to bear than those from which they claimed to bring freedom. We said this clearly during our journey in Colombia: "We exhort you not to place your trust in violence and revolution: that is contrary to the Christian spirit, and it can also delay instead of advancing that social uplifting to which you lawfully aspire."[63] "We must say and reaffirm that violence is not in accord with the Gospel, that it is not Christian; and that sudden or violent changes of structures would be deceitful, ineffective of themselves, and certainly not in conformity with the dignity of the people."[64]

Specific Contribution of the Church

38. Having said this, we rejoice that the Church is becoming ever more conscious of the proper manner and strictly evangelical means that she possesses in order to collaborate in the liberation of many. And what is she doing? She is trying more and more to encourage large numbers of Christians to devote themselves to the liberation of men. She is providing these Christian "liberators" with the inspiration of faith, the motivation of fraternal love, a social teaching which the true Christian cannot ignore and which he must make the foundation of his wisdom and of his experience in order to translate it concretely into forms of action, participation and commitment. All this must characterize the spirit of a committed Christian, without confusion with tactical attitudes or with the service of a political system. The Church strives always to insert the Christian struggle for liberation into the universal plan of salvation which she herself proclaims.

What we have just recalled comes out more than once in the Synod debates. In fact we devoted to this theme a few clarifying words in our address to the Fathers at the end of the Assembly.[65]

It is to be hoped that all these considerations will help to remove the ambiguity which the word "liberation" very often takes on in ideologies, political systems or groups. The liberation which evangelization proclaims and prepares is the one which Christ himself announced and gave to man by his sacrifice.

Religious Liberty

39. The necessity of ensuring fundamental human rights cannot be separated from this just liberation which is bound up with evangelization and

which endeavors to secure structures safeguarding human freedoms. Among these fundamental human rights, religious liberty occupies a place of primary importance. We recently spoke of the relevance of this matter, emphasizing "how many Christians still today, because they are Christians, because they are Catholics, live oppressed by systematic persecution! The drama of fidelity to Christ and of the freedom of religion continues, even if it is disguised by categorical declarations in favor of the rights of the person and of life in society!"[66]

4. THE METHODS OF EVANGELIZATION

Search for Suitable Means

40. The obvious importance of the content of evangelization must not overshadow the importance of the ways and means.

This question of "how to evangelize" is permanently relevant, because the methods of evangelizing vary according to the different circumstances of time, place and culture, and because they thereby present a certain challenge to our capacity for discovery and adaptation.

On us particularly, the pastors of the Church, rests the responsibility for reshaping with boldness and wisdom, but in complete fidelity to the content of evangelization, the means that are most suitable and effective for communicating the Gospel message to the men and women of our times.

Let it suffice, in this meditation, to mention a number of methods which, for one reason or another, have a fundamental importance.

The Witness of Life

41. Without repeating everything that we have already mentioned, it is appropriate first of all to emphasize the following point: for the Church, the first means of evangelization is the witness of an authentically Christian life, given over to God in a communion that nothing should destroy and at the same time given to one's neighbor with limitless zeal. As we said recently to a group of lay people, "Modern man listens more willingly to witnesses than to teachers, and if he does listen to teachers, it is because they are witnesses."[67] Saint Peter expressed this well when he held up the example of a reverent and chaste life that wins over even without a word those who refuse to obey the word.[68] It is therefore primarily by her conduct and by her life that the Church will evangelize the world, in other words, by her living witness of fidelity to the Lord Jesus—the witness of poverty and detachment, of freedom in the face of the powers of this world, in short, the witness of sanctity.

A Living Preaching

42. Secondly, it is not superfluous to emphasize the importance and necessity of preaching. "And how are they to believe in him of whom they have

never heard? And how are they to hear without a preacher? . . . So faith comes from what is heard and what is heard comes by the preaching of Christ."[69] This law once laid down by the Apostle Paul maintains its full force today.

Preaching, the verbal proclamation of a message, is indeed always indispensable. We are well aware that modern man is sated by talk; he is obviously often tired of listening and, what is worse, impervious to words. We are also aware that many psychologists and sociologists express the view that modern man has passed beyond the civilization of the word, which is now ineffective and useless, and that today he lives in the civilization of the image. These facts should certainly impel us to employ, for the purpose of transmitting the Gospel message, the modern means which this civilization has produced. Very positive efforts have in fact already been made in this sphere. We cannot but praise them and encourage their further development. The fatigue produced these days by so much empty talk and the relevance of many other forms of communication must not however diminish the permanent power of the word, or cause a loss of confidence in it. The word remains ever relevant, especially when it is the bearer of the power of God.[70] This is why Saint Paul's axiom, "Faith comes from what is heard,"[71] also retains its relevance: it is the word that is heard which leads to belief.

Liturgy of the Word

43. This evangelizing preaching takes on many forms, and zeal will inspire the reshaping of them almost indefinitely. In fact there are innumerable events in life and human situations which offer the opportunity for a discreet but incisive statement of what the Lord has to say in this or that particular circumstance. It suffices to have true spiritual sensitivity for reading God's message in events. But at a time when the liturgy renewed by the Council has given greatly increased value to the Liturgy of the Word, it would be a mistake not to see in the homily an important and very adaptable instrument of evangelization. Of course it is necessary to know and put to good use the exigencies and the possibilities of the homily, so that it can acquire all its pastoral effectiveness. But above all it is necessary to be convinced of this and to devote oneself to it with love. This preaching, inserted in a unique way into the Eucharistic celebration, from which it receives special force and vigor, certainly has a particular role in evangelization, to the extent that it expresses the profound faith of the sacred minister and is impregnated with love. The faithful assembled as a Paschal Church, celebrating the feast of the Lord present in their midst, expect much from this preaching, and will greatly benefit from it provided that it is simple, clear, direct, well-adapted, profoundly dependent on Gospel teaching and faithful to the Magisterium, animated by a balanced apostolic ardor coming from its own characteristic nature, full of hope, fostering belief, and productive of peace and unity. Many parochial or other communities live and are held together thanks to the Sunday homily, when it possesses these qualities.

Let us add that, thanks to the same liturgical renewal, the Eucharistic celebration is not the only appropriate moment for the homily. The homily has a place and must not be neglected in the celebration of all the Sacraments, at paraliturgies, and in assemblies of the faithful. It will always be a privileged occasion for communicating the Word of the Lord.

Catechetics

44. A means of evangelization that must not be neglected is that of catechetical instruction. The intelligence, especially that of children and young people, needs to learn through systematic religious instruction the fundamental teachings, the living content of the truth which God has wished to convey to us and which the Church has sought to express in an ever richer fashion during the course of her long history. No one will deny that this instruction must be given to form patterns of Christian living and not to remain only notional. Truly the effort for evangelization will profit greatly—at the level of catechetical instruction given at church, in the schools, where this is possible, and in every case in Christian homes—if those giving catechetical instruction have suitable texts, updated with wisdom and competence, under the authority of the Bishops. The methods must be adapted to the age, culture and aptitude of the persons concerned; they must seek always to fix in the memory, intelligence and heart the essential truths that must impregnate all of life. It is necessary above all to prepare good instructors—parochial catechists, teachers, parents—who are desirous of perfecting themselves in this superior art, which is indispensable and requires religious instruction. Moreover, without neglecting in any way the training of children, one sees that present conditions render ever more urgent catechetical instruction, under the form of the catechumenate, for innumerable young people and adults who, touched by grace, discover little by little the face of Christ and feel the need of giving themselves to him.

Utilization of the Mass Media

45. Our century is characterized by the mass media or means of social communication, and the first proclamation, catechesis or the further deepening of faith cannot do without these means, as we have already emphasized.

When they are put at the service of the Gospel, they are capable of increasing almost indefinitely the area in which the Word of God is heard; they enable the Good News to reach millions of people. The Church would feel guilty before the Lord if she did not utilize these powerful means that human skill is daily rendering more perfect. It is through them that she proclaims "from the housetops"[72] the message of which she is the depositary. In them she finds a modern and effective version of the pulpit. Thanks to them she succeeds in speaking to the multitudes.

Nevertheless the use of the means of social communication for evangelization presents a challenge: through them the evangelical message should reach vast numbers of people, but with the capacity of piercing the conscience of each individual, of implanting itself in his heart as though he were the only person being addressed, with all his most individual and personal qualities, and evoke an entirely personal adherence and commitment.

Indispensable Personal Contact

46. For this reason, side-by-side with the collective proclamation of the Gospel, the other form of transmission, the person-to-person one, remains valid and important. The Lord often used it (for example with Nicodemus, Zacchaeus, the Samaritan woman, Simon the Pharisee), and so did the Apostles. In the long run, is there any other way of handing on the Gospel than by transmitting to another person one's personal experience of faith? It must not happen that the pressing need to proclaim the Good News to the multitudes should cause us to forget this form of proclamation whereby an individual's personal conscience is reached and touched by an entirely unique word that he receives from someone else. We can never sufficiently praise those priests who through the Sacrament of Penance or through pastoral dialogue show their readiness to guide people in the ways of the Gospel, to support them in their efforts, to raise them up if they have fallen, and always to assist them with discernment and availability.

Role of the Sacraments

47. Yet, one can never sufficiently stress the fact that evangelization does not consist only of the preaching and teaching of a doctrine. For evangelization must touch life: the natural life to which it gives a new meaning, thanks to the evangelical perspectives that it reveals; and the supernatural life, which is not the negation but the purification and elevation of the natural life.

This supernatural life finds its living expression in the seven Sacraments and in the admirable radiation of grace and holiness which they possess.

Evangelization thus exercises its full capacity when it achieves the most intimate relationship, or better still a permanent and unbroken intercommunication, between the Word and the Sacraments. In a certain sense it is a mistake to make a contrast between evangelization and sacramentalization, as is sometimes done. It is indeed true that a certain way of administering the Sacraments, without the solid support of catechesis regarding these same Sacraments and a global catechesis, could end up by depriving them of their effectiveness to a great extent. The role of evangelization is precisely to educate people in the faith in such a way as to lead each individual Christian to live the Sacraments as true Sacraments of faith—and not to receive them passively or to undergo them.

Popular Piety

48. Here we touch upon an aspect of evangelization which cannot leave us insensitive. We wish to speak about what today is often called popular religiosity.

One finds among the people particular expressions of the search for God and for faith, both in the regions where the Church has been established for centuries and where she is in the course of becoming established. These expressions were for a long time regarded as less pure and were sometimes despised, but today they are almost everywhere being rediscovered. During the last Synod the Bishops studied their significance with remarkable pastoral realism and zeal.

Popular religiosity of course certainly has its limits. It is often subject to penetration by many distortions of religion and even superstitions. It frequently remains at the level of forms of worship not involving a true acceptance by faith. It can even lead to the creation of sects and endanger the true ecclesial community.

But if it is well oriented, above all by a pedagogy of evangelization, it is rich in values. It manifests a thirst for God which only the simple and poor can know. It makes people capable of generosity and sacrifice even to the point of heroism, when it is a question of manifesting belief. It involves an acute awareness of profound attributes of God: fatherhood, providence, loving and constant presence. It engenders interior attitudes rarely observed to the same degree elsewhere: patience, the sense of the Cross in daily life, detachment, openness to others, devotion. By reason of these aspects, we readily call it "popular piety," that is, religion of the people, rather than religiosity.

Pastoral charity must dictate to all those whom the Lord has placed as leaders of the ecclesial communities the proper attitude in regard to this reality, which is at the same time so rich and so vulnerable. Above all one must be sensitive to it, know how to perceive its interior dimensions and undeniable values, be ready to help it to overcome its risks of deviation. When it is well oriented, this popular religiosity can be more and more for multitudes of our people a true encounter with God in Jesus Christ.

5. THE BENEFICIARIES OF EVANGELIZATION

Addressed to Everyone

49. Jesus' last words in Saint Mark's Gospel confer on the evangelization which the Lord entrusts to his Apostles a limitless universality: "Go out to the whole world; proclaim the Good News to all creation."[73]

The Twelve and the first generation of Christians understood well the lesson of this text and other similar ones; they made them into a program of action. Even persecution, by scattering the Apostles, helped to spread the Word and to establish the Church in ever more distant regions. The admission of Paul to the rank of the Apostles and his charism as the preacher to the pagans (the non-Jews) of Jesus' coming underlined this universality still more.

Despite All the Obstacles

50. In the course of twenty centuries of history, the generations of Christians have periodically faced various obstacles to this universal mission. On the one hand, on the part of the evangelizers themselves, there has been the temptation for various reasons to narrow down the field of their missionary activity. On the other hand, there has been the often humanly insurmountable resistance of the people being addressed by the evangelizer. Furthermore, we must note with sadness that the evangelizing work of the Church is strongly opposed, if not prevented, by certain public powers. Even in our own day it happens that preachers of God's Word are deprived of their rights, persecuted, threatened or eliminated solely for preaching Jesus Christ and his Gospel. But we are confident that despite these painful trials the activity of these apostles will never meet final failure in any part of the world.

Despite such adversities the Church constantly renews her deepest inspiration, that which comes to her directly from the Lord: To the whole world! To all creation! Right to the ends of the earth! She did this once more at the last Synod, as an appeal not to imprison the proclamation of the Gospel by limiting it to one sector of mankind or to one class of people or to a single type of civilization. Some examples are revealing.

First Proclamation to Those Who Are Far Off

51. To reveal Jesus Christ and his Gospel to those who do not know them has been, ever since the morning of Pentecost, the fundamental program which the Church has taken on as received from her Founder. The whole of the New Testament, and in a special way the Acts of the Apostles, bears witness to a privileged and in a sense exemplary moment of this missionary effort which will subsequently leave its mark on the whole history of the Church.

She carries out this first proclamation of Jesus Christ by a complex and diversified activity which is sometimes termed "pre-evangelization" but which is already evangelization in a true sense, although at its initial and still incomplete stage. An almost indefinite range of means can be used for this purpose: explicit preaching, of course, but also art, the scientific approach, philosophical research and legitimate recourse to the sentiments of the human heart.

Renewed Proclamation to a Dechristianized World

52. This first proclamation is addressed especially to those who have never heard the Good News of Jesus, or to children. But, as a result of the frequent situations of dechristianization in our day, it also proves equally necessary for innumerable people who have been baptized but who live quite outside Christian life, for simple people who have a certain faith but an imperfect knowledge of the foundations of that faith, for intellectuals who feel the need to know Jesus Christ in a light different from the instruction they received as children, and for many others.

Non-Christian Religions

53. This first proclamation is also addressed to the immense sections of mankind who practice non-Christian religions. The Church respects and esteems these non-Christian religions because they are the living expression of the soul of vast groups of people. They carry within them the echo of thousands of years of searching for God, a quest which is incomplete but often made with great sincerity and righteousness of heart. They possess an impressive patrimony of deeply religious texts. They have taught generations of people how to pray. They are all impregnated with innumerable "seeds of the Word"[74] and can constitute a true "preparation for the Gospel,"[75] to quote a felicitous term used by the Second Vatican Council and borrowed from Eusebius of Caesarea.

Such a situation certainly raises complex and delicate questions that must be studied in the light of Christian Tradition and the Church's Magisterium, in order to offer to the missionaries of today and of tomorrow new horizons in their contacts with non-Christian religions. We wish to point out, above all today, that neither respect and esteem for these religions nor the complexity of the questions raised is an invitation to the Church to withhold from these non-Christians the proclamation of Jesus Christ. On the contrary the Church holds that these multitudes have the right to know the riches of the mystery of Christ[76]—riches in which we believe that the whole of humanity can find, in unsuspected fullness, everything that it is gropingly searching for concerning God, man and his destiny, life and death, and truth. Even in the face of natural religious expressions most worthy of esteem, the Church finds support in the fact that the religion of Jesus, which she proclaims through evangelization, objectively places man in relation with the plan of God, with his living presence and with his action; she thus causes an encounter with the mystery of divine paternity that bends over toward humanity. In other words, our religion effectively establishes with God an authentic and living relationship which the other religions do not succeed in doing, even though they have, as it were, their arms stretched out toward heaven.

This is why the Church keeps her missionary spirit alive, and even wishes to intensify it in the moment of history in which we are living. She feels responsible before entire peoples. She has no rest so long as she has not done her best to proclaim the Good News of Jesus the Savior. She is always preparing new generations of apostles. Let us state this fact with joy at a time when there are not lacking those who think and even say that ardor and the apostolic spirit are exhausted, and that the time of the missions is now past. The Synod has replied that the missionary proclamation never ceases and that the Church will always be striving for the fulfillment of this proclamation.

Support for the Faith of Believers

54. Nevertheless the Church does not feel dispensed from paying unflagging attention also to those who have received the faith and who have been

in contact with the Gospel often for generations. Thus she seeks to deepen, consolidate, nourish and make ever more mature the faith of those who are already called the faithful or believers, in order that they may be so still more.

This faith is nearly always today exposed to secularism, even to militant atheism. It is a faith exposed to trials and threats, and even more, a faith besieged and actively opposed. It runs the risk of perishing from suffocation or starvation if it is not fed and sustained each day. To evangelize must therefore very often be to give this necessary food and sustenance to the faith of believers, especially through a catechesis full of Gospel vitality and in a language suited to people and circumstances.

The Church also has a lively solicitude for the Christians who are not in full communion with her. While preparing with them the unity willed by Christ, and precisely in order to realize unity in truth, she has the consciousness that she would be gravely lacking in her duty if she did not give witness before them of the fullness of the revelation whose deposit she guards.

Non-believers

55. Also significant is the preoccupation of the last Synod in regard to two spheres which are very different from one another but which at the same time are very close by reason of the challenge which they make to evangelization, each in its own way.

The first sphere is the one which can be called the increase of unbelief in the modern world. The Synod endeavored to describe this modern world: how many currents of thought, values and countervalues, latent aspirations or seeds of destruction, old convictions which disappear and new convictions which arise are covered by this generic name!

From the spiritual point of view, the modern world seems to be for ever immersed in what a modern author has termed "the drama of atheistic humanism."[77]

On the one hand one is forced to note in the very heart of this contemporary world the phenomenon which is becoming almost its most striking characteristic: secularism. We are not speaking of secularization, which is the effort, in itself just and legitimate and in no way incompatible with faith or religion, to discover in creation, in each thing or each happening in the universe, the laws which regulate them with a certain autonomy, but with the inner conviction that the Creator has placed these laws there. The last Council has in this sense affirmed the legitimate autonomy of culture and particularly of the sciences.[78] Here we are thinking of a true secularism: a concept of the world according to which the latter is self-explanatory, without any need for recourse to God, who thus becomes superfluous and an encumbrance. This sort of secularism, in order to recognize the power of man, therefore ends up by doing without God and even by denying him.

New forms of atheism seem to flow from it: a man-centered atheism, no longer abstract and metaphysical but pragmatic, systematic and militant. Hand in hand with this atheistic secularism, we are daily faced, under the most diverse forms, with a consumer society, the pursuit of pleasure set up as the supreme value, a desire for power and domination, and discrimination of every kind: the inhuman tendencies of this "humanism."

In this same modern world, on the other hand, and this is a paradox, one cannot deny the existence of real stepping-stones to Christianity, and of evangelical values at least in the form of a sense of emptiness or nostalgia. It would not be an exaggeration to say that there exists a powerful and tragic appeal to be evangelized.

The Non-practicing

56. The second sphere is that of those who do not practice. Today there is a very large number of baptized people who for the most part have not formally renounced their Baptism but who are entirely indifferent to it and not living in accordance with it. The phenomenon of the non-practicing is a very ancient one in the history of Christianity; it is the result of a natural weakness, a profound inconsistency which we unfortunately bear deep within us. Today however it shows certain new characteristics. It is often the result of the uprooting typical of our time. It also springs from the fact that Christians live in close proximity with non-believers and constantly experience the effects of unbelief. Furthermore, the non-practicing Christians of today, more so than those of previous periods, seek to explain and justify their position in the name of an interior religion, of personal independence or authenticity.

Thus we have atheists and unbelievers on the one side and those who do not practice on the other, and both groups put up a considerable resistance to evangelization. The resistance of the former takes the form of a certain refusal and an inability to grasp the new order of things, the new meaning of the world, of life and of history; such is not possible if one does not start from a divine absolute. The resistance of the second group takes the form of inertia and the slightly hostile attitude of the person who feels that he is one of the family, who claims to know it all and to have tried it all and who no longer believes it.

Atheistic secularism and the absence of religious practice are found among adults and among the young, among the leaders of society and among the ordinary people, at all levels of education, and in both the old Churches and the young ones. The Church's evangelizing action cannot ignore these two worlds, nor must it come to a standstill when faced with them; it must constantly seek the proper means and language for presenting, or re-presenting, to them God's revelation and faith in Jesus Christ.

Proclamation to the Multitudes

57. Like Christ during the time of his preaching, like the Twelve on the morning of Pentecost, the Church too sees before her an immense multitude of people who need the Gospel and have a right to it, for God "wants everyone to be saved and reach full knowledge of the truth."[79]

The Church is deeply aware of her duty to preach salvation to all. Knowing that the Gospel message is not reserved to a small group of the initiated, the privileged or the elect but is destined for everyone, she shares Christ's anguish at the sight of the wandering and exhausted crowds "like sheep without a shepherd" and she often repeats his words: "I feel sorry for all these people."[80] But the Church is also conscious of the fact that, if the preaching of the Gospel is to be effective, she must address her message to the heart of the multitudes, to communities of the faithful whose action can and must reach others.

***Ecclesial* Communautés de Base**

58. The last Synod devoted considerable attention to these "small communities," or *communautés de base*, because they are often talked about in the Church today. What are they, and why should they be the special beneficiaries of evangelization and at the same time evangelizers themselves?

According to the various statements heard in the Synod, such communities flourish more or less throughout the Church. They differ greatly among themselves, both within the same region and even more so from one region to another.

In some regions they appear and develop, almost without exception, within the Church, having solidarity with her life, being nourished by her teaching and united with her pastors. In these cases, they spring from the need to live the Church's life more intensely, or from the desire and quest for a more human dimension such as larger ecclesial communities can only offer with difficulty, especially in the big modern cities which lend themselves both to life in the mass and to anonymity. Such communities can quite simply be in their own way an extension on the spiritual and religious level—worship, deepening of faith, fraternal charity, prayer, contact with pastors—of the small sociological community such as the village, etc. Or again their aim may be to bring together, for the purpose of listening to and meditating on the Word, for the Sacraments and the bond of the agape, groups of people who are linked by age, culture, civil state or social situation: married couples, young people, professional people, etc., people who already happen to be united in the struggle for justice, brotherly aid to the poor, human advancement. In still other cases they bring Christians together in places where the shortage of priests does not favor the normal life of a parish community. This is all presupposed within communities constituted by the Church, especially individual Churches and parishes.

In other regions, on the other hand, *communautés de base* come together in a spirit of bitter criticism of the Church, which they are quick to stigmatize as "institutional" and to which they set themselves up in opposition as charismatic communities, free from structures and inspired only by the Gospel. Thus their obvious characteristic is an attitude of fault-finding and of rejection with regard to the Church's outward manifestations: her hierarchy, her signs. They are radically opposed to the Church. By following these lines their main inspiration very quickly becomes ideological, and it rarely happens that they do not quickly fall victim to some political option or current of thought, and then to a system, even a party, with all the attendant risks of becoming its instrument.

The difference is already notable: the communities which by their spirit of opposition cut themselves off from the Church, and whose unity they wound, can well be called *communautés de base*, but in this case it is a strictly sociological name. They could not, without a misuse of terms, be called ecclesial *communautés de base*, even if, while being hostile to the hierarchy, they claim to remain within the unity of the Church. This name belongs to the other groups, those which come together within the Church in order to unite themselves to the Church and to cause the Church to grow.

These latter communities will be a place of evangelization, for the benefit of the bigger communities, especially the individual Churches. And, as we said at the end of the last Synod, they will be a hope for the universal Church to the extent:

–that they seek their nourishment in the Word of God and do not allow themselves to be ensnared by political polarization or fashionable ideologies, which are ready to exploit their immense human potential;

–that they avoid the ever present temptation of systematic protest and a hypercritical attitude, under the pretext of authenticity and a spirit of collaboration;

–that they remain firmly attached to the local Church in which they are inserted, and to the universal Church, thus avoiding the very real danger of becoming isolated within themselves, then of believing themselves to be the only authentic Church of Christ, and hence of condemning the other ecclesial communities;

–that they maintain a sincere communion with the pastors whom the Lord gives to his Church, and with the Magisterium which the Spirit of Christ has entrusted to these pastors;

–that they never look on themselves as the sole beneficiaries or sole agents of evangelization—or even the only depositories of the Gospel—but, being aware that the Church is much more vast and diversified, accept the fact that this Church becomes incarnate in other ways than through themselves;

–that they constantly grow in missionary consciousness, fervor, commitment and zeal;

–that they show themselves to be universal in all things and never sectarian.

On these conditions, which are certainly demanding but also uplifting, the ecclesial *communautés de base* will correspond to their most fundamental vocation: as hearers of the Gospel which is proclaimed to them and privileged beneficiaries of evangelization, they will soon become proclaimers of the Gospel themselves.

6. THE WORKERS FOR EVANGELIZATION

The Church: Missionary in Her Entirety

59. If people proclaim in the world the Gospel of salvation, they do so by the command of, in the name of and with the grace of Christ the Saviour. "They will never have a preacher unless one is sent,"[81] wrote he who was without doubt one of the greatest evangelizers. No one can do it without having been sent.

But who then has the mission of evangelizing?

The Second Vatican Council gave a clear reply to this question: it is upon the Church that "there rests, by divine mandate, the duty of going out into the whole world and preaching the gospel to every creature."[82] And in another text: ". . . the whole Church is missionary, and the work of evangelization is a basic duty of the People of God."[83]

We have already mentioned this intimate connection between the Church and evangelization. While the Church is proclaiming the Kingdom of God and building it up, she is establishing herself in the midst of the world as the sign and instrument of this Kingdom which is and which is to come. The Council repeats the following expression of Saint Augustine on the missionary activity of the Twelve: "They preached the word of truth and brought forth Churches."[84]

An Ecclesial Act

60. The observation that the Church has been sent out and given a mandate to evangelize the world should awaken in us two convictions.

The first is this: evangelization is for no one an individual and isolated act; it is one that is deeply ecclesial. When the most obscure preacher, catechist or pastor in the most distant land preaches the Gospel, gathers his little community together or administers a Sacrament, even alone, he is carrying out an ecclesial act, and his action is certainly attached to the evangelizing activity of the whole Church by institutional relationships, but also by profound invisible links in the order of grace. This presupposes that he acts not in virtue of a mission which he attributes to himself or by a personal inspiration, but in union with the mission of the Church and in her name.

From this flows the second conviction: if each individual evangelizes in the name of the Church, who herself does so by virtue of a mandate from the Lord, no evangelizer is the absolute master of his evangelizing action, with a discretionary power to carry it out in accordance with individualistic criteria and perspectives; he acts in communion with the Church and her pastors.

We have remarked that the Church is entirely and completely evangelizing. This means that, in the whole world and in each part of the world where she is present, the Church feels responsible for the task of spreading the Gospel.

The Perspective of the Universal Church

61. Brothers and sons and daughters, at this stage of our reflection, we wish to pause with you at a question which is particularly important at the present time. In the celebration of the liturgy, in their witness before judges and executioners and in their apologetical texts, the first Christians readily expressed their deep faith in the Church by describing her as being spread throughout the universe. They were fully conscious of belonging to a large community which neither space nor time can limit: "From the just Abel right to the last of the elect,"[85] "indeed to the ends of the earth,"[86] "to the end of time."[87]

This is how the Lord wanted his Church to be: universal, a great tree whose branches shelter the birds of the air,[88] a net which catches fish of every kind[89] or which Peter drew in filled with one hundred and fifty-three big fish,[90] a flock which a single shepherd pastures.[91] A universal Church without boundaries or frontiers except, alas, those of the heart and mind of sinful man.

The Perspective of the Individual Church

62. Nevertheless this universal Church is in practice incarnate in the individual Churches made up of such or such an actual part of mankind, speaking such and such a language, heirs of a cultural patrimony, of a vision of the world, of an historical past, of a particular human substratum. Receptivity to the wealth of the individual Church corresponds to a special sensitivity of modern man.

Let us be very careful not to conceive of the universal Church as the sum, or, if one can say so, the more or less anomalous federation of essentially different individual Churches. In the mind of the Lord the Church is universal by vocation and mission, but when she puts down her roots in a variety of cultural, social and human terrains, she takes on different external expressions and appearances in each part of the world.

Thus each individual Church that would voluntarily cut itself off from the universal Church would lose its relationship to God's plan and would be impoverished in its ecclesial dimension. But, at the same time, a Church *toto orbe diffusa* would become an abstraction if she did not take body and life precisely through the individual Churches. Only continual attention to these two poles of the Church will enable us to perceive the richness of this relationship between the universal Church and the individual Churches.

Adaptation and Fidelity in Expression

63. The individual Churches, intimately built up not only of people but also of aspirations, of riches and limitations, of ways of praying, of loving, of looking at life and the world which distinguish this or that human gathering, have the task of assimilating the essence of the Gospel message and of transposing it, without the slightest betrayal of its essential truth, into the language that these particular people understand, then of proclaiming it in this language.

The transposition has to be done with the discernment, seriousness, respect and competence which the matter calls for in the field of liturgical expression,[92] and in the areas of catechesis, theological formulation, secondary ecclesial structures, and ministries. And the word "language" should be understood here less in the semantic or literary sense than in the sense which one may call anthropological and cultural.

The question is undoubtedly a delicate one. Evangelization loses much of its force and effectiveness if it does not take into consideration the actual people to whom it is addressed, if it does not use their language, their signs and symbols, if it does not answer the questions they ask, and if it does not have an impact on their concrete life. But on the other hand evangelization risks losing its power and disappearing altogether if one empties or adulterates its content under the pretext of translating it; if, in other words, one sacrifices this reality and destroys the unity without which there is no universality, out of a wish to adapt a universal reality to a local situation. Now, only a Church which preserves the awareness of her universality and shows that she is in fact universal is capable of having a message which can be heard by all, regardless of regional frontiers.

Legitimate attention to individual Churches cannot fail to enrich the Church. Such attention is indispensable and urgent. It responds to the very deep aspirations of peoples and human communities to find their own identity ever more clearly.

Openness to the Universal Church

64. But this enrichment requires that the individual Churches should keep their profound openness toward the universal Church. It is quite remarkable, moreover, that the most simple Christians, the ones who are most faithful to the Gospel and most open to the true meaning of the Church, have a completely spontaneous sensitivity to this universal dimension. They instinctively and very strongly feel the need for it, they easily recognize themselves in such a dimension. They feel with it and suffer very deeply within themselves when, in the name of theories which they do not understand, they are forced to accept a Church deprived of this universality, a regionalist Church, with no horizon.

As history in fact shows, whenever an individual Church has cut itself off from the universal Church and from its living and visible center—sometimes with the best of intentions, with theological, sociological, political or pastoral arguments, or even in the desire for a certain freedom of movement or action—it has escaped only with great difficulty (if indeed it has escaped) from two equally serious dangers. The first danger is that of a withering isolationism, and then, before long, of a crumbling away, with each of its cells breaking away from it just as it itself has broken away from the central nucleus. The second danger is that of losing its freedom when, being cut off from the center and from the other Churches which gave it strength and energy, it finds itself all alone and a prey to the most varied forces of enslavery and exploitation.

The more an individual Church is attached to the universal Church by solid bonds of communion, in charity and loyalty, in receptiveness to the Magisterium of Peter, in the unity of the *lex orandi* which is also the *lex credendi*, in the desire for unity with all the other Churches which make up the whole—the more such a Church will be capable of translating the treasure of faith into the legitimate variety of expressions of the profession of faith, of prayer and worship, of Christian life and conduct and of the spiritual influence on the people among which it dwells. The more will it also be truly evangelizing, that is to say capable of drawing upon the universal patrimony in order to enable its own people to profit from it, and capable too of communicating to the universal Church the experience and the life of this people, for the benefit of all.

The Unchangeable Deposit of Faith

65. It was precisely in this sense that at the end of the last Synod we spoke clear words full of paternal affection, insisting on the role of Peter's Successor as a visible, living and dynamic principle of the unity between the Churches and thus of the universality of the one Church.[93] We also insisted on the grave responsibility incumbent upon us, but which we share with our Brothers in the Episcopate, of preserving unaltered the content of the Catholic faith which the Lord entrusted to the Apostles. While being translated into all expressions, this content must be neither impaired nor mutilated. While being clothed with the outward forms proper to each people, and made explicit by theological expression which takes account of differing cultural, social and even racial milieux, it must remain the content of the Catholic faith just exactly as the ecclesial Magisterium has received it and transmits it.

Differing Tasks

66. The whole Church therefore is called upon to evangelize, and yet within her we have different evangelizing tasks to accomplish. This diversity of services in the unity of the same mission makes up the richness and beauty of evangelization. We shall briefly recall these tasks.

First, we would point out in the pages of the Gospel the insistence with which the Lord entrusts to the Apostles the task of proclaiming the Word. He chose them,[94] trained them during several years of intimate company,[95] constituted[96] and sent them out[97] as authorized witnesses and teachers of the message of salvation. And the Twelve in their turn sent out their successors who, in the apostolic line, continue to preach the Good News.

The Successor of Peter

67. The Successor of Peter is thus, by the will of Christ, entrusted with the pre-eminent ministry of teaching the revealed truth. The New Testament often

shows Peter "filled with the Holy Spirit" speaking in the name of all.[98] It is precisely for this reason that Saint Leo the Great describes him as he who has merited the primacy of the apostolate.[99] This is also why the voice of the Church shows the Pope "at the highest point—*in apice, in specula*—of the apostolate."[100] The Second Vatican Council wished to reaffirm this when it declared that "Christ's mandate to preach the Gospel to every creature (cf. Mk 16:15) primarily and immediately concerns the Bishops with Peter and under Peter."[101]

The full, supreme and universal power[102] which Christ gives to his Vicar for the pastoral government of his Church is thus specially exercised by the Pope in the activity of preaching and causing to be preached the Good News of salvation.

Bishops and Priests

68. In union with the Successor of Peter, the Bishops, who are successors of the Apostles, receive through the power of their episcopal ordination the authority to teach the revealed truth in the Church. They are teachers of the faith.

Associated with the Bishops in the ministry of evangelization and responsible by a special title are those who through priestly ordination "act in the person of Christ."[103] They are educators of the People of God in the faith and preachers, while at the same time being ministers of the Eucharist and of the other Sacraments.

We pastors are therefore invited to take note of this duty, more than any other members of the Church. What identifies our priestly service, gives a profound unity to the thousand and one tasks which claim our attention day by day and throughout our lives, and confers a distinct character on our activities, is this aim, ever present in all our action: to proclaim the Gospel of God.[104]

A mark of our identity which no doubts ought to encroach upon and no objection eclipse is this: as pastors, we have been chosen by the mercy of the Supreme Pastor,[105] in spite of our inadequacy, to proclaim with authority the Word of God, to assemble the scattered People of God, to feed this People with the signs of the action of Christ which are the Sacraments, to set this People on the road to salvation, to maintain it in that unity of which we are, at different levels, active and living instruments, and unceasingly to keep this community gathered around Christ faithful to its deepest vocation. And when we do all these things, within our human limits and by the grace of God, it is a work of evangelization that we are carrying out. This includes ourself as Pastor of the universal Church, our Brother Bishops at the head of the individual Churches, priests and deacons united with their Bishops and whose assistants they are, by a communion which has its source in the Sacrament of Orders and in the charity of the Church.

Religious

69. Religious, for their part, find in their consecrated life a privileged means of effective evangelization. At the deepest level of their being they are

caught up in the dynamism of the Church's life, which is thirsty for the divine Absolute and called to holiness. It is to this holiness that they bear witness. They embody the Church in her desire to give herself completely to the radical demands of the beatitudes. By their lives they are a sign of total availability to God, the Church and the brethren.

As such they have a special importance in the context of the witness which, as we have said, is of prime importance in evangelization. At the same time as being a challenge to the world and to the Church herself, this silent witness of poverty and abnegation, of purity and sincerity, of self-sacrifice in obedience, can become an eloquent witness capable of touching also non-Christians who have good will and are sensitive to certain values.

In this perspective one perceives the role played in evangelization by religious men and women consecrated to prayer, silence, penance and sacrifice. Other religious, in great numbers, give themselves directly to the proclamation of Christ. Their missionary activity depends clearly on the hierarchy and must be coordinated with the pastoral plan which the latter adopts. But who does not see the immense contribution that these religious have brought and continue to bring to evangelization? Thanks to their consecration they are eminently willing and free to leave everything and to go and proclaim the Gospel even to the ends of the earth. They are enterprising and their apostolate is often marked by an originality, by a genius that demands admiration. They are generous: often they are found at the outposts of the mission, and they take the greatest of risks for their health and their very lives. Truly the Church owes them much.

The Laity

70. Lay people, whose particular vocation places them in the midst of the world and in charge of the most varied temporal tasks, must for this very reason exercise a very special form of evangelization.

Their primary and immediate task is not to establish and develop the ecclesial community—this is the specific role of the pastors—but to put to use every Christian and evangelical possibility latent but already present and active in the affairs of the world. Their own field of evangelizing activity is the vast and complicated world of politics, society and economics, but also the world of culture, of the sciences and the arts, of international life, of the mass media. It also includes other realities which are open to evangelization, such as human love, the family, the education of children and adolescents, professional work, suffering. The more Gospel-inspired lay people there are engaged in these realities, clearly involved in them, competent to promote them and conscious that they must exercise to the full their Christian powers which are often buried and suffocated, the more these realities will be at the service of the Kingdom of God and therefore of salvation in Jesus Christ, without in any way losing or sacrificing their human content but rather pointing to a transcendent dimension which is often disregarded.

The Family

71. One cannot fail to stress the evangelizing action of the family in the evangelizing apostolate of the laity.

At different moments in the Church's history and also in the Second Vatican Council, the family has well deserved the beautiful name of "domestic Church."[106] This means that there should be found in every Christian family the various aspects of the entire Church. Furthermore, the family, like the Church, ought to be a place where the Gospel is transmitted and from which the Gospel radiates.

In a family which is conscious of this mission, all the members evangelize and are evangelized. The parents not only communicate the Gospel to their children, but from their children they can themselves receive the same Gospel as deeply lived by them.

And such a family becomes the evangelizer of many other families, and of the neighborhood of which it forms part. Families resulting from a mixed marriage also have the duty of proclaiming Christ to the children in the fullness of the consequences of a common Baptism; they have moreover the difficult task of becoming builders of unity.

Young People

72. Circumstances invite us to make special mention of the young. Their increasing number and growing presence in society and likewise the problems assailing them should awaken in everyone the desire to offer them with zeal and intelligence the Gospel ideal as something to be known and lived. And on the other hand, young people who are well trained in faith and prayer must become more and more the apostles of youth. The Church counts greatly on their contribution, and we ourself have often manifested our full confidence in them.

Diversified Ministries

73. Hence the active presence of the laity in the temporal realities takes on all its importance. One cannot, however, neglect or forget the other dimension: the laity can also feel themselves called, or be called, to work with their pastors in the service of the ecclesial community, for its growth and life, by exercising a great variety of ministries according to the grace and charisms which the Lord is pleased to give them.

We cannot but experience a great inner joy when we see so many pastors, religious and lay people, fired with their mission to evangelize, seeking ever more suitable ways of proclaiming the Gospel effectively. We encourage the openness which the Church is showing today in this direction and with this solicitude. It is an openness to meditation first of all, and then to ecclesial ministries capable of renewing and strengthening the evangelizing vigor of the Church.

It is certain that, side-by-side with the ordained ministries, whereby certain people are appointed pastors and consecrate themselves in a special way to the service of the community, the Church recognizes the place of non-ordained ministries which are able to offer a particular service to the Church.

A glance at the origins of the Church is very illuminating, and gives the benefit of an early experience in the matter of ministries. It was an experience which was all the more valuable in that it enabled the Church to consolidate herself and to grow and spread. Attention to the sources however has to be complemented by attention to the present needs of mankind and of the Church. To drink at these ever inspiring sources without sacrificing anything of their values, and at the same time to know how to adapt oneself to the demands and needs of today—these are the criteria which will make it possible to seek wisely and to discover the ministries which the Church needs and which many of her members will gladly embrace for the sake of ensuring greater vitality in the ecclesial community. These ministries will have a real pastoral value to the extent that they are established with absolute respect for unity and adhering to the directives of the pastors, who are the ones who are responsible for the Church's unity and the builders thereof.

These ministries, apparently new but closely tied up with the Church's living experience down the centuries—such as catechists, directors of prayer and chant, Christians devoted to the service of God's Word or to assisting their brethren in need, the heads of small communities, or other persons charged with the responsibility of apostolic movements—these ministries are valuable for the establishment, life, and growth of the Church, and for her capacity to influence her surroundings and to reach those who are remote from her. We owe also our special esteem to all the lay people who accept to consecrate a part of their time, their energies, and sometimes their entire lives, to the service of the missions.

A serious preparation is needed for all workers for evangelization. Such preparation is all the more necessary for those who devote themselves to the ministry of the Word. Being animated by the conviction, ceaselessly deepened, of the greatness and riches of the Word of God, those who have the mission of transmitting it must give the maximum attention to the dignity, precision and adaptation of their language. Everyone knows that the art of speaking takes on today a very great importance. How would preachers and catechists be able to neglect this?

We earnestly desire that in each individual Church the Bishops should be vigilant concerning the adequate formation of all the ministers of the Word. This serious preparation will increase in them the indispensable assurance and also the enthusiasm to proclaim today Jesus Christ.

7. THE SPIRIT OF EVANGELIZATION

Pressing Appeal

74. We would not wish to end this encounter with our beloved brethren and sons and daughters without a pressing appeal concerning the interior attitudes which must animate those who work for evangelization.

In the name of the Lord Jesus Christ, and in the name of the Apostles Peter and Paul, we wish to exhort all those who, thanks to the charisms of the Holy Spirit and to the mandate of the Church, are true evangelizers, to be worthy of this vocation, to exercise it without the reticence of doubt or fear, and not to neglect the conditions that will make this evangelization not only possible but also active and fruitful. These, among many others, are the fundamental conditions which we consider it important to emphasize.

Under the Action of the Holy Spirit

75. Evangelization will never be possible without the action of the Holy Spirit. The Spirit descends on Jesus of Nazareth at the moment of his baptism when the voice of the Father—"This is my beloved Son with whom I am well pleased"[107]—manifests in an external way the election of Jesus and his mission. Jesus is "led by the Spirit" to experience in the desert the decisive combat and the supreme test before beginning this mission.[108] It is "in the power of the Spirit"[109] that he returns to Galilee and begins his preaching at Nazareth, applying to himself the passage of Isaiah: "The Spirit of the Lord is upon me." And he proclaims: "Today this Scripture has been fulfilled."[110] To the disciples whom he was about to send forth he says, breathing on them: "Receive the Holy Spirit."[111]

In fact, it is only after the coming of the Holy Spirit on the day of Pentecost that the Apostles depart to all the ends of the earth in order to begin the great work of the Church's evangelization. Peter explains this event as the fulfillment of the prophecy of Joel: "I will pour out my Spirit."[112] Peter is filled with the Holy Spirit so that he can speak to the people about Jesus, the Son of God.[113] Paul too is filled with the Holy Spirit[114] before dedicating himself to his apostolic ministry, as is Stephen when he is chosen for the ministry of service and later on for the witness of blood.[115] The Spirit, who causes Peter, Paul and the Twelve to speak, and who inspires the words that they are to utter, also comes down "on those who heard the word."[116] It is in the "consolation of the Holy Spirit" that the Church increases.[117] The Holy Spirit is the soul of the Church. It is he who explains to the faithful the deep meaning of the teaching of Jesus and of his mystery. It is the Holy Spirit who, today just as at the beginning of the Church, acts in every evangelizer who allows himself to be possessed and led by him. The Holy Spirit places on his lips the words which he could not find by himself, and at the same time the Holy Spirit predisposes the soul of the hearer to be open and receptive to the Good News and to the Kingdom being proclaimed.

Techniques of evangelization are good, but even the most advanced ones could not replace the gentle action of the Spirit. The most perfect preparation of the evangelizer has no effect without the Holy Spirit. Without the Holy Spirit the most convincing dialectic has no power over the heart of man. Without him the most highly developed sehemas resting on a sociological or psychological basis are quickly seen to be quite valueless.

We live in the Church at a privileged moment of the Spirit. Everywhere people are trying to know him better, as the Scripture reveals him. They are happy to place themselves under his inspiration. They are gathering about him; they want to let themselves be led by him. Now if the Spirit of God has a preeminent place in the whole life of the Church, it is in her evangelizing mission that he is most active. It is not by chance that the great inauguration of evangelization took place on the morning of Pentecost, under the inspiration of the Spirit.

It must be said that the Holy Spirit is the principal agent of evangelization: it is he who impels each individual to proclaim the Gospel, and it is he who in the depths of consciences causes the word of salvation to be accepted and understood.[118] But it can equally be said that he is the goal of evangelization: he alone stirs up the new creation, the new humanity of which evangelization is to be the result, with that unity in variety which evangelization wishes to achieve within the Christian community. Through the Holy Spirit the Gospel penetrates to the heart of the world, for it is he who causes people to discern the signs of the times—signs willed by God—which evangelization reveals and puts to use within history.

The Bishops' Synod of 1974, which insisted strongly on the place of the Holy Spirit in evangelization, also expressed the desire that pastors and theologians—and we would also say the faithful marked by the seal of the Spirit by Baptism—should study more thoroughly the nature and manner of the Holy Spirit's action in evangelization today. This is our desire too, and we exhort all evangelizers, whoever they may be, to pray without ceasing to the Holy Spirit with faith and fervor and to let themselves prudently be guided by him as the decisive inspirer of their plans, their initiatives and their evangelizing activity.

Authentic Witnesses of Life

76. Let us now consider the very persons of the evangelizers.

It is often said nowadays that the present century thirsts for authenticity. Especially in regard to young people it is said that they have a horror of the artificial or false and that they are searching above all for truth and honesty.

These "signs of the times" should find us vigilant. Either tacitly or aloud—but always forcefully—we are being asked: Do you really believe what you are proclaiming? Do you live what you believe? Do you really preach what you live? The witness of life has become more than ever an essential condition for real effectiveness in preaching. Precisely because of this we are, to a certain extent, responsible for the progress of the Gospel that we proclaim.

"What is the state of the Church ten years after the Council?" we asked at the beginning of this meditation. Is she firmly established in the midst of the world and yet free and independent enough to call for the world's attention? Does she testify to solidarity with people and at the same time to the divine Absolute? Is she more ardent in contemplation and adoration and more zealous in missionary, charitable and liberating action? Is she ever more committed to the effort to search for the restoration of the complete unity of Christians, a unity that makes more effective the common witness, "so that the world may believe"?[119] We are all responsible for the answers that could be given to these questions.

We therefore address our exhortation to our brethren in the Episcopate, placed by the Holy Spirit to govern the Church.[120] We exhort the priests and deacons, the Bishops' collaborators in assembling the People of God and in animating spiritually the local communities. We exhort the religious, witnesses of a Church called to holiness and hence themselves invited to a life that bears testimony to the beatitudes of the Gospel. We exhort the laity: Christian families, youth, adults, all those who exercise a trade or profession, leaders, without forgetting the poor who are often rich in faith and hope—all lay people who are conscious of their evangelizing role in the service of their Church or in the midst of society and the world. We say to all of them: our evangelizing zeal must spring from true holiness of life, and, as the Second Vatican Council suggests, preaching must in its turn make the preacher grow in holiness, which is nourished by prayer and above all by love for the Eucharist.[121]

The world which, paradoxically, despite innumerable signs of the denial of God, is nevertheless searching for him in unexpected ways and painfully experiencing the need of him—the world is calling for evangelizers to speak to it of a God whom the evangelists themselves should know and be familiar with as if they could see the invisible.[122] The world calls for and expects from us simplicity of life, the spirit of prayer, charity toward all, especially toward the lowly and the poor, obedience and humility, detachment and self-sacrifice. Without this mark of holiness, our word will have difficulty in touching the heart of modern man. It risks being vain and sterile.

The Search for Unity

77. The power of evangelization will find itself considerably diminished if those who proclaim the Gospel are divided among themselves in all sorts of ways. Is this not perhaps one of the great sicknesses of evangelization today? Indeed, if the Gospel that we proclaim is seen to be rent by doctrinal disputes, ideological polarizations or mutual condemnations among Christians, at the mercy of the latters' differing views on Christ and the Church and even because of their different concepts of society and human institutions, how can those to whom we address our preaching fail to be disturbed, disoriented, even scandalized?

The Lord's spiritual testament tells us that unity among his followers is not only the proof that we are his but also the proof that he is sent by the Father. It is the test of the credibility of Christians and of Christ himself. As evangelizers, we must offer Christ's faithful not the image of people divided and separated by unedifying quarrels, but the image of people who are mature in faith and capable of finding a meeting point beyond the real tensions, thanks to a shared, sincere and disinterested search for truth. Yes, the destiny of evangelization is certainly bound up with the witness of unity given by the Church. This is a source of responsibility and also of comfort.

At this point we wish to emphasize the sign of unity among all Christians as the way and instrument of evangelization. The division among Christians is a serious reality which impedes the very work of Christ. The Second Vatican Council states clearly and emphatically that this division "damages the most holy cause of preaching the Gospel to all men, and it impedes many from embracing the faith."[123] For this reason, in proclaiming the Holy Year we considered it necessary to recall to all the faithful of the Catholic world that "before all men can be brought together and restored to the grace of God our Father, communion must be reestablished between those who by faith have acknowledged and accepted Jesus Christ as the Lord of mercy who sets men free and unites them in the Spirit of love and truth.[124] And it is with a strong feeling of Christian hope that we look to the efforts being made in the Christian world for this restoration of the full unity willed by Christ. Saint Paul assures us that "hope does not disappoint us."[125] While we still work to obtain full unity from the Lord, we wish to see prayer intensified. Moreover we make our own the desire of the Fathers of the Third General Assembly of the Synod of Bishops, for a collaboration marked by greater commitment with the Christian brethren with whom we are not yet united in perfect unity, taking as a basis the foundation of Baptism and the patrimony of faith which is common to us. By doing this we can already give a greater common witness to Christ before the world in the very work of evangelization. Christ's command urges us to do this; the duty of preaching and of giving witness to the Gospel requires this.

Servants of the Truth

78. The Gospel entrusted to us is also the word of truth. A truth which liberates[126] and which alone gives peace of heart is what people are looking for when we proclaim the Good News to them. The truth about God, about man and his mysterious destiny, about the world; the difficult truth that we seek in the Word of God and of which, we repeat, we are neither the masters nor the owners, but the depositaries, the heralds and the servants.

Every evangelizer is expected to have a reverence for truth, especially since the truth that he studies and communicates is none other than revealed truth and hence, more than any other, a sharing in the first truth which is God himself. The preacher of the Gospel will therefore be a person who even at the price of personal renunciation and suffering always seeks the truth that he must transmit to others. He never betrays or hides truth out of a desire to please men, in order to astonish or to shock, nor for the sake of originality or a desire to make an impression. He does not refuse truth. He does not obscure revealed truth by being too idle to search for it, or for the sake of his own comfort, or out of fear. He does not neglect to study it. He series it generously, without making it serve him.

We are the pastors of the faithful people, and our pastoral service impels us to preserve, defend, and to communicate the truth regardless of the sacrifices that this involves. So many eminent and holy pastors have left us the example of this love of truth. In many cases it was an heroic love. The God of truth expects us to be the vigilant defenders and devoted preachers of truth.

Men of learning—whether you be theologians, exegetes or historians—the work of evangelization needs your tireless work of research, and also care and tact in transmitting the truth to which your studies lead you but which is always greater than the heart of men, being the very truth of God.

Parents and teachers, your task—and the many conflicts of the present day do not make it an easy one—is to help your children and your students to discover truth, including religious and spiritual truth.

Animated by Love

79. The work of evangelization presupposes in the evangelizer an ever increasing love for those whom he is evangelizing. That model evangelizer, the Apostle Paul, wrote these words to the Thessalonians, and they are a program for us all: "With such yearning love we chose to impart to you not only the gospel of God but our very selves, so dear had you become to us."[127] What is this love? It is much more than that of a teacher; it is the love of a father; and again, it is the love of a mother.[128] It is this love that the Lord expects from every preacher of the Gospel, from every builder of the Church. A sign of love will be the concern to give the truth and to bring people into unity. Another sign of love will be a devotion to the proclamation of Jesus Christ, without reservation or turning back. Let us add some other signs of this love.

The first is respect for the religious and spiritual situation of those being evangelized. Respect for their tempo and pace; no one has the right to force them excessively. Respect for their conscience and convictions, which are not to be treated in a harsh manner.

Another sign of this love is concern not to wound the other person, especially if he or she is weak in faith,[129] with statements that may be clear for those who are already initiated but which for the faithful can be a source of bewilderment and scandal, like a wound in the soul.

Yet another sign of love will be the effort to transmit to Christians, not doubts and uncertainties born of an erudition poorly assimilated but certainties that are solid because they are anchored in the Word of God. The faithful need these certainties for their Christian life; they have a right to them, as children of God who abandon themselves entirely into his arms and to the exigencies of love.

With the Fervor of the Saints

80. Our appeal here is inspired by the fervor of the greatest preachers and evangelizers, whose lives were devoted to the apostolate. Among these we are glad to point out those whom we have proposed to the veneration of the

faithful during the course of the Holy Year. They have known how to overcome many obstacles to evangelization.

Such obstacles are also present today, and we shall limit ourself to mentioning the lack of fervor. It is all the more serious because it comes from within. It is manifested in fatigue, disenchantment, compromise, lack of interest and above all lack of joy and hope. We exhort all those who have the task of evangelizing, by whatever title and at whatever level, always to nourish spiritual fervor.[130]

This fervor demands first of all that we should know how to put aside the excuses which would impede evangelization. The most insidious of these excuses are certainly the ones which people claim to find support for in such and such a teaching of the Council.

Thus one too frequently hears it said, in various terms, that to impose a truth, be it that of the Gospel, or to impose a way, be it that of salvation, cannot but be a violation of religious liberty. Besides, it is added, why proclaim the Gospel when the whole world is saved by uprightness of heart? We know likewise that the world and history are filled with "seeds of the Word"; is it not therefore an illusion to claim to bring the Gospel where it already exists in the seeds that the Lord himself has sown?

Anyone who takes the trouble to study in the Council's documents the questions upon which these excuses draw too superficially will find quite a different view.

It would certainly be an error to impose something on the consciences of our brethren. But to propose to their consciences the truth of the Gospel and salvation in Jesus Christ, with complete clarity and with a total respect for the free options which it presents—"without coercion, or dishonorable or unworthy pressure"[131]—far from being an attack on religious liberty is fully to respect that liberty, which is offered the choice of a way that even non-believers consider noble and uplifting. Is it then a crime against others' freedom to proclaim with joy a Good News which one has come to know through the Lord's mercy?[132] And why should only falsehood and error, debasement and pornography have the right to be put before people and often unfortunately imposed on them by the destructive propaganda of the mass media, by the tolerance of legislation, the timidity of the good and the impudence of the wicked? The respectful presentation of Christ and his Kingdom is more than the evangelizer's right; it is his duty. It is likewise the right of his fellowmen to receive from him the proclamation of the Good News of salvation. God can accomplish this salvation in whomsoever he wishes by ways which he alone knows.[133] And yet, if his Son came, it was precisely in order to reveal to us, by his word and by his life, the ordinary paths of salvation. And he has commanded us to transmit this revelation to others with his own authority. It would be useful if every Christian and every evangelizer were to pray about the following thought: men can gain salvation also in other ways, by God's mercy, even though we do not preach the Gospel to them; but as for us, can we gain salvation if through negligence or fear or shame—what Saint Paul called "blushing for the Gospel"[134]—or as a result of false ideas we fail to preach it? For that would be to betray the call of God, who wishes the seed to bear fruit through the voice of the ministers of the Gospel; and it will depend on us whether this grows into trees and produces its full fruit.

Let us therefore preserve our fervor of spirit. Let us preserve the delightful and comforting joy of evangelizing, even when it is in tears that we must sow. May it mean for us—as it did for John the Baptist, for Peter and Paul, for the other Apostles and for a multitude of splendid evangelizers all through the Church's history—an interior enthusiasm that nobody and nothing can quench. May it be the great joy of our consecrated lives. And may the world of our time, which is searching, sometimes with anguish, sometimes with hope, be enabled to receive the Good News not from evangelizers who are dejected, discouraged, impatient or anxious, but from ministers of the Gospel whose lives glow with fervor, who have first received the joy of Christ, and who are willing to risk their lives so that the Kingdom may be proclaimed and the Church established in the midst of the world.

CONCLUSION

Heritage of the Holy Year

81. This then, brothers and sons and daughters, is our heartfelt plea. It echoes the voice of our brethren assembled for the Third General Assembly of the Synod of Bishops. This is the task we have wished to give you at the close of a Holy Year which has enabled us to see better than ever the needs and the appeals of a multitude of brethren, both Christians and non-Christians, who await from the Church the Word of salvation.

May the light of the Holy Year, which has shone in the local Churches and in Rome for millions of consciences reconciled with God, continue to shine in the same way after the Jubilee through a program of pastoral action with evangelization as its basic feature, for these years which mark the eve of a new century, the eve also of the third millennium of Christianity.

Mary, Star of Evangelization

82. This is the desire that we rejoice to entrust to the hands and the heart of the Immaculate Blessed Virgin Mary, on this day which is especially consecrated to her and which is also the tenth anniversary of the close of the Second Vatican Council. On the morning of Pentecost she watched over with her prayer the beginning of evangelization prompted by the Holy Spirit: may she be the Star of the evangelization ever renewed which the Church, docile to her Lord's command, must promote and accomplish, especially in these times which are difficult but full of hope!

In the name of Christ we bless you, your communities, your families, all those who are dear to you, in the words which Paul addressed to the Philippians:

"I give thanks to my God every time I think of you—which is constantly, in every prayer I utter—rejoicing, as I plead on your behalf, at the way you have all continually helped to promote the gospel . . . I hold all of you dear—you who . . . are sharers of my gracious lot . . . to defend the solid grounds on which the gospel rests. God himself can testify how much I long for each of you with the affection of Christ Jesus!"[135]

Given in Rome, at Saint Peter's, on the Solemnity of the Immaculate Conception of the Blessed Virgin Mary, December 8, 1975, the thirteenth year of our Pontificate.

PAUL VI

NOTES

1. Cf. Lk. 22:32.
2. 2 Cor. 11:28.
3. Cf. Second Vatican Ecumenical Council, Decree on the Church's Missionary Activity *Ad Gentes*, 1: AAS 58 (1966), p. 947.
4. Cf. Eph. 4:24; 2:15; Col. 3:10; Gal. 3:27; Rom. 13:4; 2 Cor. 5:17.
5. 2 Cor. 5:20.
6. Cf. Paul VI, Address for the closing of the Third General Assembly of the Synod of Bishops (October 26, 1974): AAS 66 (1974), pp. 634–635, 637.
7. Paul VI, Address to the College of Cardinals (June 22, 1973): AAS 65 (1973), p. 383.
8. 2 Cor. 11:38.
9. 1 Tim. 5:17.
10. 2 Tim. 2:15.
11. Cf. 1 Cor. 2:5.
12. Lk. 4:43.
13. Ibid.
14. Lk. 4:18; cf. Is. 61:1.
15. Cf. Mk. 1:1; Rom. 1:1–3.
16. Cf. Mt. 6:33.
17. Cf. Mt. 5:3–12.
18. Mt. 5–7.
19. Cf. Mt. 10.
20. Cf. Mt. 13.
21. Cf. Mt. 18.
22. Cf. Mt. 24–25.
23. Cf. Mt. 24:36; Acts 1:7; 1 Thess. 5:1–2.
24. Cf. Mt. 11:32; Lk. 16:16.
25. Cf. Mt. 4:17.
26. Mk. 1:27.
27. Lk. 4:22.

28. Jn. 7:46.

29. Lk. 4:43.

30. Jn. 11:2.

31. Cf. Second Vatican Ecumenical Council, Dogmatic Constitution on Divine Revelation *Dei Verbum*, 4: AAS 58 (1966), pp. 818–819.

32. 1 Pt. 2:9.

33. Cf. Acts 2:11.

34. Lk. 4:43.

35. 1 Cor. 9:16.

36. "Declaration of the Synod Fathers," 4: *L'Osservatore Romano* (October 27, 1974), p. 6.

37. Mt. 28:19.

38. Acts 2:41, 47.

39. Cf. Second Vatican Ecumenical Council, Dogmatic Constitution on the Church *Lumen Gentium*, 8: AAS 57 (1965), p. 11; Decree on the Church's Missionary Activity *Ad Gentes*, 5: AAS 58 (1966), pp. 951–952.

40. Cf. Acts 2:42–46; 4:32–35; 5:12–36.

41. Cf. Acts 2:11; 1 Pt. 2:9.

42. Cf. Decree on the Church's Missionary Activity *Ad Gentes*, 5, 11–2: AAS 58 (1966), pp. 951–952, 959–961.

43. Cf. 2 Cor. 4:5; Saint Augustine, *Sermo XLVI, De Pastoribus: CCL XLI*, pp. 529–530.

44. Lk. 10:6; cf. Saint Cyprian, *De Unitate Ecclesiae*, 14: PL 4, 527; Saint Augustine, *Enarrat. 88, Sermo*, 2, 14: PL 37, 114: Saint John Chrysostom, *Hom. de capto Eutropio*, 6: PG 52, 402.

45. Eph. 5:25.

46. Rev. 21:5, cf. 2 Cor. 5:17; Gal. 6:15.

47. Cf. Rom. 6:4.

48. Cf. Eph. 4:23–24; Col. 3:9–10.

49. Cf. Rom. 1:16; 1 Cor. 1:18, 2:4.

50. Cf. 53: AAS 58 (1966), p. 1073.

51. Cf. Tertullian *Apologeticum*, 39: CCL, 1, pp. 150–153; Minucius Felix, *Octavius* 9 and 31: CSLP, Turin 1963s, pp. 11–33, 47–48.

52. 1 Pt. 3:15.

53. Cf. Second Vatican Ecumenical Council, Dogmatic Constitution on the Church *Lumen Gentium*, 1, 9, 48: AAS 57 (1965), pp. 5, 12–14, 53–54, Pastoral Constitution on the Church in the Modern World *Gaudium et Spes*, 42, 45: AAS 58 (1966), pp. 1060–1061, 1065–1066; Decree on the Church's Missionary Activity *Ad Gentes*, 1, 5: AAS 58 (1966), pp. 947, 951–952.

54. Cf. Rom. 1:16; 1 Cor. 1:18.

55. Cf. Acts 17:22–23.

56. 1 Jn. 3:1; cf. Rom. 8:14–17.

57. Cf. Eph. 2:8; Rom. 1:16. Cf. Sacred Congregation for the Doctrine of the Faith, *Declaratio ad fidem tuendam in mysteria Incarnationis et SS. Trini-*

tatis e quibusdam recentibus erroribus (February 21, 1972): AAS 64 (1972), pp. 237–241.

58. Cf. 1 Jn. 3:2; Rom. 8:29; Phil. 3:20–21. Cf. Second Vatican Ecumenical Council, Dogmatic Constitution on the Church *Lumen Gentium*, 48–51: AAS 57 (1965), pp. 53–58.

59. Cf. Sacred Congregation for the Doctrine of the Faith, *Declaratio circa Catholicam Doctrinam de Ecclesia contra non-nullos errores hodiernos tuendam* (June 24, 1973): AAS 65 (1973), pp. 396–408.

60. Cf. Second Vatican Ecumenical Council, Pastoral Constitution on the Church in the Modern World *Gaudium et Spes*, 47–52: AAS 58 (1966), pp. 106–107; Paul VI, Encyclical Letter *Humanae Vitae*: AAS 60 (1968), pp. 481–503.

61. Paul VI, Address for the opening of the Third General Assembly of the Synod of Bishops (September 27, 1974): AAS 66 (1974), p. 562.

62. Ibid.

63. Paul VI, Address to the Campesinos of Colombia (August 23, 1958): AAS 60 (1968), p. 623.

64. Paul VI, Address for the "Day of Development" at Bogotá (August 23, 1968): AAS 60 (1968), p. 627; cf. Saint Augustine, *Epistola 229*, 2: *PL* 33, 1020.

65. Paul VI, Address for the closing of the Third General Assembly of the Synod of Bishops (October 26, 1974): AAS 66 (1974), p. 637.

66. Address given on October 15, 1975: *L'Ossservatore Romano* (October 17, 1975).

67. Pope Paul VI, Address to the Members of the *Consilium de Laicis* (October 2, 1974): AAS 66 (1974), p. 568.

68. Cf. 1 Pt. 3:1.

69. Rom. 10:4, 17.

70. Cf. 1 Cor. 2:1–5.

71. Rom. 10:17.

72. Cf. Mt. 10:27; Lk. 12:3.

73. Mk. 16:15.

74. Cf. Saint Justin, *I Apol.* 46, 1–4: *PG 6, I Apol.* 7 (8) 1–4; 10, 1–3; 13, 3–4; *Florilegium Patristicum* II, Bonn 1911[2], pp. 81, 125, 129, 133; Clement of Alexandria, *Stromata* I, 19, 91; 94: *S. Ch.* pp. 117–118; 119–120; Second Vatican Ecumenical Council, Decree on the Church's Missionary Activity *Ad Gentes*, 11: AAS 58 (1966), p. 960; cf. Dogmatic Constitution on the Church *Lumen Gentium*, 17: AAS 57 (1965), p. 21.

75. Eusebius of Caesarea, *Praeparatio Evangelica* I, 1: PG 21, 26–28; cf. Second Vatican Ecumenical Council, Dogmatic Constitution on the Church *Lumen Gentium*, 16: AAS 57 (1965), p. 20.

76. Cf. Eph. 3:8.

77. Cf. Henri de Lubac, *Le drame de l'humanisme athée*, ed. Spes, Paris, 1945.

78. Cf. Pastoral Constitution on the Church in the Modern World *Gaudium et Spes*, 59: AAS 58 (1966), p. 1083.

79. 1 Tim. 2:4.

80. Mt. 9:36; 15:32.

81. Rom. 10:15.

82. Declaration on Religious Liberty *Dignitatis Humanae*, 13: AAS 58 (1966), p. 939; cf. Dogmatic Constitution on the Church *Lumen Gentium*, 5: AAS 57 (1965), pp. 7–8; Decree on the Church's Missionary Activity *Ad Gentes*, 1: AAS 58 (1966), p. 947.

83. Decree on the Church's Missionary Activity *Ad Gentes*, 35: AAS 58 (1966), p. 983.

84. Saint Augustine, *Enarratio* in *Ps 44:23 CCL* XXVIII, p. 510. Cf. Decree on the Church's Missionary Activity *Ad Gentes*, 1: AAS 58 (1966), p. 947.

85. Saint Gregory the Great, *Homil. in Evangelia* 19, 1: PL 76, 1154.

86. Acts 1:8; cf. *Didache* 9, 1: Funk, *Patres Apostolici*, 1, 22.

87. Mt. 28:20.

88. Cf. Mt. 12:2.

89. Cf. Mt. 13:7.

90. Cf. Jn. 21:11.

91. Cf. Jn. 10:1–16.

92. Cf. Second Vatican Ecumenical Council, Constitution on the Sacred Liturgy *Sacrosanctum Concilium*, 37–38: AAS 56 (1964), p. 110; cf. also the liturgical books and other documents subsequently issued by the Holy See for the putting into practice of the liturgical reform desired by the same Council.

93. Paul VI, Address for the closing of the Third General Assembly of the Synod of Bishops (October 26, 1974): AAS 66 (1974), p. 636.

94. Cf. Jn. 15:16; Mk. 3:13–19; Lk. 6:13–16.

95. Cf. Acts 1:21–22.

96. Cf. Mk. 3:14.

97. Cf. Mk. 3:14–15; Lk. 9:2.

98. Acts 4:8; cf. 2:14; 3:12.

99. Cf. St. Leo the Great, *Sermo* 69, 3; *Sermo* 70, 1–3; *Sermo* 94, 3; *Sermo* 95, 2: S.C. 200, pp. 50–52; 58–66; 258–260; 268.

100. Cf. First Ecumenical Council of Lyons, Constitution *Ad apostolicae dignitatis*: *Conciliorum Oecumenicorum Decreta*, ed. *Istituto per le Scienze Religiose*, Bologna 1973, p. 278; Ecumenical Council of Vienne, Constitution *Ad providam Christi*, ed. cit., p. 343; Fifth Lateran Ecumenical Council, Constitution *In apostolici culminis*, ed. cit., p. 608; Constitution *Postquam ad universalis*, ed. cit., p. 609; Constitution *Supernae dispositionis,* ed. cit., p. 614; Constitution *Divina disponente clementia,* ed. cit., p. 638.

101. Decree on the Church's Missionary Activity *Ad Gentes*, 38: AAS 58 (1966), p. 985.

102. Cf. Second Vatican Ecumenical Council, Dogmatic Constitution on the Church *Lumen Gentium*, 22: AAS 57 (1965), p. 26.

103. Cf. Second Vatican Ecumenical Council, Dogmatic Constitution on the Church *Lumen Gentium*, 10, 37: AAS 57 (1965), pp. 14, 43; Decree on the Church's Missionary Activity *Ad Gentes*, 39: AAS 58 (1966), p. 986: Decree on the Ministry and Life of Priests *Presbyterorum Ordinis*, 2, 12, 13: AAS 58 (1966), pp. 992, 1010, 1011.

104. Cf. 1 Thess. 2:9.

105. Cf. 1 Pt. 5:4.

106. Dogmatic Constitution on the Church *Lumen Gentium*, 11: AAS 57 (1965), p. 16; Decree on the Apostolate of the Laity *Apostolicam Actuositatem*, 11: AAS 58 (1966), p. 848; Saint John Chrysostom, *In Genesim Serm.* VI, 2; VII, 1: *PG* 54, 607–68.

107. Mt. 3:17.

108. Mt. 4:1.

109. Lk. 4:14.

110. Lk. 4:18, 21; cf. Is. 61:1.

111. Jn. 20:22.

112. Acts 2:17.

113. Cf. Acts 4:8.

114. Cf. Acts 9:17.

115. Cf. Acts 6:5; 10:55.

116. Acts 10:44.

117. Acts 9:31.

118. Cf. Second Vatican Ecumenical Council, Decree on the Church's Missionary Activity *Ad Gentes*, 4: AAS 58 (1966), pp. 950–951.

119. Jn. 17:21.

120. Cf. Acts 20:28.

121. Cf. Decree on the Ministry and Life of Priests *Presbyterorum Orinis*, 13: AAS 58 (1966), p. 1011.

122. Cf. Heb. 11:37.

123. Decree on the Church's Missionary Activity *Ad Gentes*, 6: AAS 58 (1966), pp. 954–955; cf. Decree on Ecumenism *Unitatis Redintegratio*, 1: AAS 57 (1965), pp. 90–91.

124. Bull *Apostolorum Limina*, VII: AAS 66 (1974), p. 305.

125. Rom. 5:5.

126. Cf. Jn. 8:32.

127. Thess. 2:8; cf. Phil. 1:8.

128. Cf. 1 Thess. 2:7–11; 1 Cor. 4:15; Gal. 4:19.

129. Cf. 1 Cor. 8:9–13; Rom. 14:15.

130. Cf. Rom. 12:1.

131. Cf. Second Vatican Ecumenical Council, Declaration on Religious Liberty *Dignitatis Humanae*, 4: AAS 58 (1966), p. 933.

132. Cf. ibid., 9–14: *loc. cit.*, pp. 935–940.

133. Cf. Second Vatican Ecumenical Council, Decree on the Church's Missionary Activity *Ad Gentes*, 7: AAS 58 (1966), p. 955.

134. Cf. Rom. 1:16.

135. Phil. 1:3–4, 7–8.

PART IV

THE SOCIAL TEACHING OF JOHN PAUL II AND BENEDICT XVI

INTRODUCTION

John Paul II, as the first non-Italian pope in centuries, immediately received considerable public attention. Interest was heightened by his leadership in Poland, where his election added fuel to an already volatile conflict between the Communist government and an unexpected organization of popular forces, Solidarity. Because the new pope continued Paul VI's tradition of traveling, many were able to experience the power of his personality as he took his message in person to the entire world.

Yet in spite of his obvious personal popularity, controversy and occasional confusion surrounded his papacy. Although he expressly prohibited priests and religious from participating directly in political affairs, John Paul himself did not hesitate to immerse himself in Polish politics, directly through negotiations and indirectly by leading nationalistic songs from the Episcopal palace. He was a strong advocate of justice and human rights, speaking forcefully on behalf of the poor. Yet he seemed wedded to aspects of the status quo, especially within the church, was hesitant about promoting structural reform, and at times seemed to hope that liberation could be achieved by the conversion of the rich and powerful. His commitment to doctrinal and moral orthodoxy, centrally exercised hierarchical authority and limits on the role of women, caused considerable disaffection. While many saw this as a positive and long overdue step to restore order among pastoral leaders, others saw the loss of many post-conciliar gains, especially with respect to episcopal collegiality, shared responsibility, and affirmation of the laity. Thus Pope John Paul II set in motion several sometimes contrary currents.

Additionally, John Paul was extremely prolific, following Pius XII's example of delivering at least a speech a day, each international tour might result in five or six new major addresses. And while many of these were repeated, it was extremely difficult to keep up with the pope as he expanded his vision through his presentations. Here we will focus on those encyclicals that set forth his development of Catholic Social Teaching.

First, however, it is well to review two of his earlier letters, which presented his often original Christian humanism.

Redemptor Hominis, issued on March 1979, set the tone and provided a background for much of the pope's subsequent thought. At the heart of the encyclical was a deep and thorough theological anthropology. This defines Christ as the full measure of the human, arguing that the human being can plumb his or her full depth as a person only through contemplation of the person of Christ. In Christ, the fullness of the possibilities of the human are revealed and we have the model of who we might become. For John Paul, the dignity of the person is an integral part of the proclamation of the gospel, and the church must stand committed to protecting true human freedom (no. 12). The church is a "sign and safeguard of the transcendence of the human person" (no. 13). Additionally, and even more important, the human being in the concrete circumstances of his or her life is the "primary route that the Church must travel in fulfilling her mission: *he is the primary and fundamental way for the Church*" (no. 14). In its care for the human, the church must be firmly located in history, in culture, and attentive to the nuances of the human, not in the abstract but in the concrete. The church understands the human in the light of its fulfillment as revealed in the mystery of Christ, proclaimed and protected by the church. Indeed, such concern is an "essential, unbreakably united element of her mission." This phrasing is reminiscent of the 1971 Synod of Bishops' statement that such concerns for justice are a constitutive element of the church's mission, but John Paul broadens justice by locating human life in culture, which embodies politics and society.

Thus the pope's concern for culture, based on this theological anthropology, is a means of entering further into human history, not of escaping from it. The point of reference is transcendent, but the human lives in history, a history men and women are making, and the church is a historical actor, engaged and responsible.

The pope, then, looks to the signs of the times to see where the church should focus its activity of protecting the human. He centers his attention on the fear of our times: the threat that technological development is beyond our capacity to restrain or direct, the fear that our products may destroy us, the fear that we ourselves may be out of control. He sees that progress may not actually be progress, because it is not truly serving the human. Additionally, he points to the continuing problems with the world economy and the environment as particular places where attention needs to be focused so that humans can once again achieve their true dignity, freedom, and self-mastery. Thus, in *Redemptor Hominis*, John Paul laid a solid theological foundation for responding to the signs of the times. This vision firmly inserts the church into the world, but since the fullness of the vision of the human is rooted in Christ, it also has a transcendent standard for evaluating various responses to the problems of a culture or country.

The second major encyclical, *Dives in Misericordia*, issued on November 30, 1980, continued many of the themes of *Redemptor Hominis* but cast them in a new light. For example, John Paul reiterated his negative reading of many signs of the times, focusing on the dangers from nuclear weapons, social discord, and the primacy of things over people (nos. 10 and 11). But he put them in a new context: mercy as the transforming virtue that will reveal humans to themselves and permit a personal healing not always effected by strict justice.

The center of the encyclical is the development and analysis of the theme of mercy from the perspective of the Jewish and Christian scriptures. John Paul II shows how mercy is linked to justice in the themes of creation, and how it characterizes the reality of God by the reconciling act of forgiveness. Then the pope turns to the parable of the prodigal son to develop a further aspect of mercy. The pope argues that it was through the son's experience of self-degradation that he began to realize what he had lost: his dignity. And it is this realization that leads him to return to his father. The father, for his part, recognizes what has been returned to his son, his dignity. The joy of reunion is the joy of the mutually appreciated return of human dignity. Such appreciation of the dignity of the person is what keeps expressions of mercy from degrading the person, primarily by establishing the community of a relationship.

Additionally, John Paul describes how mercy and love complement justice and keep it from becoming formal and legalistic. Justice focuses on "objective and extrinsic goods while love and mercy bring it about that the people meet one another in that value which is man himself, with the dignity that is proper to him" (no. 14). Mercy serves, therefore, as the bond that unifies persons and establishes reciprocity between them based on their dignity and mutual love. Mercy leads justice beyond an external restoration of rights to the experience of reconciliation and thus makes people one. Human solidarity, our mutual dependence on one another, thus grounds our particular, specific concerns for justice and locates liberation in a global and communal context, recalling the earlier papal theme of social justice as concern for the common good.

Thus, by proclaiming mercy the church seeks to recognize the dignity of all persons, especially by placing them in a context in which reconciliation and love serve as the foundation for a relation of forgiveness on the basis of which justice will be served. This attitude, the pope argues, will soften the edges of justice and instill a gentler quality in society, which can work to transform our primary approaches to one another. These themes must be kept in mind when reading the sometimes complex, dense texts that follow.

On 2 April 2005, the 27-year reign of John Paul II ended with his death after a lengthy illness. For several years the world watched as John Paul II gradually deteriorated as he suffered the effects of what was eventually acknowledged as Parkinson's Disease. While on the one hand, his own life was a daily example of suffering borne courageously and offered as an example of the dignity of the person radiant even under adversity, on the other hand his increasing disability and incapacities raised serious questions about who was in charge of the church as well as the policy of lifetime appointment.

While the bureaucracy of the church ensured that for the most part life went on as usual, nonetheless important issues continued to face the church and appointments to various positions needed to be made. Additionally for many years the pope's health condition was either not discussed or clear signs of illness denied or ignored. During the Pope's last years, these issues were finally acknowledged as he underwent a series of hospitalizations and various health crises.

One clear legacy of John Paul II was his wonderful example of the acceptance of his illness and his offering of his life as an illustration of how to live a life of dignity under such circumstances. Clearly another part of his legacy is the massive legacy of social teaching he left the church, part of which is presented here. But another part of his legacy, as yet unaddressed, is the way his illness was managed as well as how to make provision for such health issues in the future. In times past, toward the end of one's life one got sick and died rather rapidly. Now various interventions can ensure that one's life is prolonged even with a serious illness. This is a new problem for the church and one that must be faced.

On 19 April 2005, the 78-year-old Joseph Cardinal Ratzinger was elected pope and took the name Benedict XVI. In a way his election was not too surprising as he had been Prefect of the Congregation for the Doctrine for the Faith for 27 years, the Dean of the College of Cardinals, and for many years had worked closely with John Paul II. Prior to his ecclesiastical career, curial work, and election to the papacy, Ratzinger served as a peritus to Cardinal Frings of Cologne during Vatican II and had a distinguished academic career, teaching at the Universities of Bonn, Muenster, Tuebingen, and Regensburg. His own theological vision developed within the Augustinian tradition and the theology of St. Bonaventure on whose theology of history he wrote his *Habilitationsschrift.*

Emerging from both an academic background and the Vatican bureaucracy, it is not surprising that Benedict XVI presented a less public and charismatic figure than his predecessor. Yet he maintains a strong public schedule and has made several international trips. Additionally Benedict maintains a strong literary output with many lectures, addresses, books and encyclicals.

Benedict's first encyclical was *Deus Caritas Est*, published on December 25, 2005. In this encyclical Benedict offers a vision of Christian love. This first section of the encyclical is a rich biblical, philosophical, and theological reflection on the nature of love. Here he notes that love is not to be understood as an intoxicant, but rather as the path for a journey of self-liberation (para. 6). Additionally Benedict argues that there is no radical separation between eros and agape for if there were, this separation would mean that the Christian would be totally removed from this world and its concerns (para. 7). Finally, the pope recognizes that while God is the source of all being, God is more properly understood as a lover, and the supreme manifestation of this love is Christ's offering of himself for all upon the cross (para. 10).

The second major section of the encyclical is a reflection on the inseparability of the love of God and the love of neighbor. He says: "As a community, the Church must practise love. Love thus needs to be organized if it is to be an ordered service to the community. The awareness of this responsibility has had a constitutive relevance in the Church from the beginning . . ." (para. 20) Thus Benedict argues that two facts about the church flow from this. First, "The Church's deepest nature is expressed in her three-fold responsibility: of proclaiming the word of God (*kerygma-martyria*), celebrating the sacraments (*leitourgia*), and exercising the ministry of charity (*diakonia*)" (para. 25). Second, "The Church is God's family in the world. In this family no one ought to go without the necessities of life. Yet at the same time *caritas-agape* extends beyond the frontiers of the Church" (para. 25).

The relation between charity and justice is important and Benedict sets this out clearly in two positions. "The just ordering of society and the State is a central responsibility of politics" and "Love—*caritas*—will always prove necessary, even in the most just society. There is no ordering of the State so just that it can eliminate the need for a service of love" (para. 28). The critical point made by the pope is that if one focuses exclusively on justice, then one is also in danger of reducing humanity to the material realm alone. In this the church has an indirect role, that of "purification of reason and to the reawakening of those moral forces without which just structures are neither established nor prove effective in the long run" (para. 29). And the direct duty of helping to establish this just social order is proper to the laity: "The mission of the lay faithful is therefore to configure social life correctly, respecting its legitimate autonomy and cooperating with other citizens according to their respective competences and fulfilling their own responsibility" (para. 29).

Thus the church is to live out its mission of love by responding to the specific needs of individuals, but while doing this remaining free of politics and ideology as it fulfills its mission, and by not proselytizing (para. 31). In this way the church will respect individuals while at the same time expressing its love for all people as it seeks to directly and indirectly help establish a social order that truly mirrors the love of God for all.

Benedict's second encyclical was *Spe Salvi* published on November 30, 2007. This encyclical is a lengthy philosophical, theological, and anthropological reflection on the question: for what may we hope? In his usual academic but also personal style, Benedict leads us through a very existential question of the reality of hope in our lives and the shape that it can give both to one's own life and to the life of society. Thus one of the critical subthemes of this encyclical is the social dimension of hope. Yet while this social aspect in never absent, the encyclical as a whole is much more scriptural and theological than either his first or third encyclicals. It is really an engagement with the question of how we can live our lives, how we can seek fulfillment, and how we may remain engaged in life. Thus for the pope, hope has both an informative and performative dimension (para. 4). And as well, hope itself can bring a certain ambiguity toward life itself.

> In some way we want life itself, true life, untouched even by death; yet at the same time we do not know the thing towards which we feel driven. We cannot stop reaching out for it, and yet we know that all we can experience or accomplish is not what we yearn for. This unknown "thing" is the true "hope" which drives us, and at the same time the fact that it is unknown is the cause of all forms of despair and also of all efforts, whether positive or destructive, directed towards worldly authenticity and human authenticity (para. 12).

Yet within this we also experience hope as social particularly since "'redemption' appears as the reestablishment of unity, in which we come together once more in a union that begins to take shape in the world community of believers" (para. 14). And this hope also serves as a living response to the critiques of Christianity offered by the Enlightenment and Marxism. While recognizing that Christianity itself must be subject to critique, nonetheless structures and structural reform alone cannot guarantee the moral well being of the world and the kingdom of God will not be definitively established on this earth. Thus the pope can say: "When someone has the experience of a great love in his life, this is a moment of 'redemption' which gives a new meaning to his life. But soon he will also realize that the love bestowed upon him cannot by itself resolve the question of his life. It is a love that remains fragile. It can be destroyed by death. The human being needs unconditional love" (para. 26).

With these reflections as a kind of prologue, Benedict then both poses an ethical question and provides a theological foundation for the answer.

> Hence, while we must always be committed to the improvement of the world, tomorrow's better world cannot be the proper and sufficient content of our hope. And in this regard the question always arises: when is the world "better"? What makes it good? By what standard are we to judge its goodness? What are the paths that lead to this "goodness"? (para. 30).
>
> Let us say once again: we need the greater and lesser hopes that keep us going day by day. But these are not enough without the great hope, which must surpass everything else. This great hope can only be God, who encompasses the whole of reality and who can bestow upon us what we, by ourselves, cannot attain. The fact that it comes to us as a gift is actually part of hope. God is the foundation of hope: not any god, but the God who has a human face and who has loved us to the end, each one of us and humanity in its entirety (para. 31).

The encyclical concludes with a reflection on the problem of evil and its relation to hope and justice. Benedict gives a very personal statement:

> I am convinced that the question of justice constitutes the essential argument, or on any case the strongest argument, in favor of faith in eternal life. The purely individual need for a fulfillment that is denied to us in this life, for an everlasting love that we await, is certainly an important motive for believing that man was made for eternity; but only in connection with the impossibility that the injustice of history should be the final word does the necessity for Christ's return and for new life become fully convincing (para. 43).

The pope brings this encyclical to a close by again uniting the theme of hope as related to personal salvation and the salvation of others. And this link is made through the pursuit of justice. "As Christians we should never limit ourselves to asking: how can I save myself? We should also ask: what can I do in order that others may be saved and that for them too the star of hope may rise? Then I will have done my utmost for my own personal salvation as well" (para. 48).

We are still early into the pontificate of Benedict XVI but already in his various speeches, international travels, and encyclicals, he has brought to the world a voice that has considered deeply the questions of our day and the message of love, hope and justice that Christianity can bring to our troubled world.

Laborem Exercens: On Human Work (John Paul II, 1981)

INTRODUCTION

Laborem Exercens, published on September 14, 1981, commemorates the ninetieth anniversary of *Rerum Novarum* by setting forth a philosophy and theology of work in the contemporary context.

This analysis is grounded in the book of Genesis and focuses on the themes of subduing the earth, having dominion over the earth, and being responsible for the earth. John Paul distinguishes between objective work—the agricultural means, industrial processes, or microprocessing by which humans subdue the earth—and subjective work—the human capacity to act in a "planned and rational way, capable of deciding about himself and with a tendency to self-realization" (no. 6). Work emerges from those who are expressing their nature and provides the grounding for the dignity of work. This analysis gives the pope the basis for concluding that work is for the person, not the person for work.

A second discussion is the distinction between labor and capital, made concrete by discussions of the exploitation of labor—treating workers as a means of production, and setting the lowest possible wage. For John Paul the conflict between labor and capital is not a class struggle, as Marx would have it, but the exploitation of labor. Because the conflict is moral, not exclusively ideological or political, the pope can reject the concept of an inevitable and perhaps violent class struggle. Additionally, since both property and capital are earned through labor, John Paul thinks this will provide a way for cooperation between these two groups.

Reflecting the distinction between objective and subjective work, John Paul proposes the principle of the priority of labor over capital: "Labor is a primary efficient cause, while capital, the whole collection of means of production, remains a mere instrument or instrumental cause" (no. 12). Capital is both work and a collection of things, based as it is on natural resources, money, and technologies. Because it is instrumental, capital must always be subject to labor. This serves as a basis for his argument against economism—the evaluation of labor only in accordance with its economic purpose—and materialism—the primacy and superiority of the material over the personal.

Four traditional rights of labor are then defended by the pope: suitable employment for all those capable of it; just remuneration for the work done; the organization of the labor process to respect the requirements of the person and his or her life; and the right to form unions. These rights are discussed within the context of the direct and indirect employer. The direct employer is the specific individual with whom the worker enters into a contract; the indirect employer sets the context in which the worker contracts with the direct employer. Any issues of wage justice or health care benefits, for example, must be established with respect to public policy, markets, and various structures of interdependence as well as with respect to a specific employer.

Finally, the pope identifies three values labor brings: through work humans transform nature and personally fulfill themselves; work provides a basis for family life and the resources it needs; and through work persons affirm their membership in a nation and participate in attaining the common good. By working, human beings achieve a deeper realization of their personhood through a deeper participation in community and the common good.

LABOREM EXERCENS

Venerable Brothers
and Dear Sons and Daughters,
Greetings and the Apostolic Blessing

Through work man must earn his daily bread[1] and contribute to the continual advance of science and technology and, above all, to elevating unceasingly the cultural and moral level of the society within which he lives in community with those who belong to the same family. And work means any activity by man, whether manual or intellectual, whatever its nature or circumstances; it means any human activity that can and must be recognized as work, in the midst of all the many activities of which man is capable and to which he is predisposed by his very nature, by virtue of humanity itself. Man is made to be in the visible universe an image and likeness of God himself,[2] and he is placed in it in order to subdue the earth.[3] From the beginning therefore he is called to work. Work is one of the characteristics that distinguishes man from the rest of creatures, whose activity for sustaining their lives cannot be called work. Only man is capable of work, and only man works, at the same time by work occupying his existence on earth. Thus work bears a particular mark of man and of humanity, the mark of a person operating within a community of persons. And this mark decides its interior characteristics; in a sense it constitutes its very nature.

1. INTRODUCTION

Human Work on the Ninetieth Anniversary of **Rerum Novarum**

1. Since May 15 of the present year was the ninetieth anniversary of the publication by the great pope of the "social question," Leo XIII, of the decisively important encyclical which begins with the words *Rerum Novarum*, I wish to devote this document to human work and, even more, to man in the vast context of the reality of work. As I said in the encyclical *Redemptor Hominis*, published at the beginning of my service in the See of St. Peter in Rome, man "is the primary and fundamental way for the church,"[4] precisely because of the inscrutable mystery of redemption in Christ; and so it is necessary to return constantly to this way and to follow it ever anew in the various aspects in which it shows us all the wealth and at the same time all the toil of human existence on earth.

Work is one of these aspects, a perennial and fundamental one, one that is always relevant and constantly demands renewed attention and decisive witness. Because fresh questions and problems are always arising, there are always fresh hopes, but also fresh fears and threats connected with this basic dimension of human existence: Man's life is built up every day from work, from work it derives its specific dignity, but at the same time work contains the unceasing measure of human toil and suffering and also of the harm and injustice which penetrate deeply into social life within individual nations and on the international level. While it is true that man eats the bread produced by the work of his hands[5]—and this means not only the daily bread by which his body keeps alive but also the bread of science and progress, civilization and culture—it is also a perennial truth that he eats this bread by "the sweat of his face,"[6] that is to say, not only by personal effort and toil, but also in the midst of many tensions, conflicts and crises, which in relationship with the reality of work disturb the life of individual societies and also of all humanity.

We are celebrating the ninetieth anniversary of the encyclical *Rerum Novarum* on the eve of new developments in technological, economic, and political conditions which, according to many experts, will influence the world of work and production no less than the industrial revolution of the last century. There are many factors of a general nature: the widespread introduction of automation into many spheres of production, the increase in the cost of energy and raw materials, the growing realization that the heritage of nature is limited and that it is being intolerably polluted, and the emergence on the political scene of peoples who, after centuries of subjection, are demanding their rightful place among the nations and in international decision-making. These new conditions and demands will require a reordering and adjustment of the structures of the modern economy and of the distribution of work. Unfortunately, for millions of skilled workers these changes may perhaps mean unemployment, at least for a time, or the need for retraining. They will very probably involve a reduction or a less rapid increase in material well-being for the more developed countries. But they can also bring relief and hope to the millions who today live in conditions of shameful and unworthy poverty.

It is not for the church to analyze scientifically the consequences that these changes may have on human society. But the church considers it her task always to call attention to the dignity and rights of those who work, to condemn situations in which that dignity and those rights are violated, and to help to guide the above-mentioned changes so as to ensure authentic progress by man and society.

In the Organic Development of the Church's Social Action and Teaching

2. It is certainly true that work as a human issue is at the very center of the "social question" to which, for almost a hundred years since the publication of the above-mentioned encyclical, the church's teaching and the many undertakings connected with her apostolic mission have been especially

directed. The present reflections on work are not intended to follow a different line, but rather to be in organic connection with the whole tradition of this teaching and activity. At the same time, however, I am making them, according to the indication in the Gospel, in order to bring out from the heritage of the Gospel "what is new and what is old."[7] Certainly work is part of "what is old"—as old as man and his life on earth. Nevertheless, the general situation of man in the modern world, studied and analyzed in its various aspects of geography, culture, and civilization, calls for the discovery of the new meanings of human work. It likewise calls for the formulation of the new tasks that in this sector face each individual, the family, each country, the whole human race, and finally the church herself.

During the years that separate us from the publication of the encyclical *Rerum Novarum*, the social question has not ceased to engage the church's attention. Evidence of this are the many documents of the magisterium issued by the popes and by the Second Vatican Council, pronouncements by individual episcopates, and the activity of the various centers of thought and of practical apostolic initiatives, both on the international level and at the level of the local churches. It is difficult to list here in detail all the manifestations of the commitment of the church and of Christians in the social question for they are too numerous. As a result of the council, the main coordinating center in this field is the Pontifical Commission for Justice and Peace, which has corresponding bodies within the individual bishops' conferences. The name of this institution is very significant. It indicates that the social question must be dealt with in its whole complex dimension. Commitment to justice must be closely linked with commitment to peace in the modern world. This twofold commitment is certainly supported by the painful experience of the two great world wars which in the course of the last ninety years have convulsed many European countries and, at least partially, countries in other continents. It is supported, especially since the World War II, by the permanent threat of a nuclear war and the prospect of the terrible self-destruction that emerges from it.

If we follow the main line of development of the documents of the supreme magisterium of the church, we find in them an explicit confirmation of precisely such a statement of the question. The key position, as regards the question of world peace, is that of John XXIII's encyclical *Pacem in Terris*. However, if one studies the development of the question of social justice, one cannot fail to note that, whereas during the period between *Rerum Novarum* and Pius XI's *Quadragesimo Anno* the church's teaching concentrates mainly on the just solution of the "labor question" within individual nations, in the next period the church's teaching widens its horizon to take in the whole world. The disproportionate distribution of wealth and poverty and the existence of some countries and continents that are developed and of others that are not call for a leveling out and for a search for ways to ensure just development for all. This is the direction of the teaching in John XXIII's encyclical *Mater et Magistra*, in the pastoral constitution *Gaudium et Spes* of the Second Vatican Council and in Paul VI's encyclical *Populorum Progressio.*

This trend of development of the church's teaching and commitment in the social question exactly corresponds to the objective recognition of the state of affairs. While in the past the "class" question was especially highlighted as the center of this issue, in more recent times it is the "world" question that is emphasized. Thus, not only the sphere of class is taken into consideration, but also the world sphere of inequality and injustice and, as a consequence, not only the class dimension, but also the world dimension of the tasks involved in the path toward the achievement of justice in the modern world. A complete analysis of the situation of the world today shows in an even deeper and fuller way the meaning of the previous analysis of social injustices; and it is the meaning that must be given today to efforts to build justice on earth, not concealing thereby unjust structures, but demanding that they be examined and transformed on a more universal scale.

The Question of Work, the Key to the Social Question

3. In the midst of all these processes—those of the diagnosis of objective social reality and also those of the church's teaching in the sphere of the complex and many-sided social question—the question of human work naturally appears many times. This issue is, in a way, a constant factor both of social life and of the church's teaching. Furthermore, in this teaching attention to the question goes back much further than the last ninety years. In fact the church's social teaching finds its source in sacred scripture, beginning with the book of Genesis and especially in the Gospel and the writings of the apostles. From the beginning it was part of the church's teaching, her concept of man and life in society, and especially the social morality which she worked out according to the needs of the different ages. This traditional patrimony was then inherited and developed by the teaching of the popes on the modern "social question," beginning with the encyclical *Rerum Novarum*. In this context, study of the question of work, as we have seen, has continually been brought up to date while maintaining that Christian basis of truth which can be called ageless.

While in the present document we return to this question once more—without however any intention of touching on all the topics that concern it—this is not merely in order to gather together and repeat what is already contained in the church's teaching. It is rather in order to highlight—perhaps more than has been done before—the fact that human work is a key, probably the essential key, to the whole social question, if we try to see that question really from the point of view of man's good. And if the solution—or rather the gradual solution—of the social question, which keeps coming up and becomes ever more complex, must be sought in the direction of "making life more human,"[8] then the key, namely human work, acquires fundamental and decisive importance.

2. WORK AND MAN

In the Book of Genesis

4. The church is convinced that work is a fundamental dimension of man's existence on earth. She is confirmed in this conviction by considering the whole heritage of the many sciences devoted to man: anthropology, paleontology, history, sociology, psychology, and so on; they all seem to bear witness to this reality in an irrefutable way. But the source of the church's conviction is above all the revealed word of God, and therefore what is a conviction of the intellect is also a conviction of faith. The reason is that the church—and it is worthwhile stating it at this point—believes in man: she thinks of man and addresses herself to him not only in the light of historical experience, not only with the aid of the many methods of scientific knowledge, but in the first place in the light of the revealed word of the living God. Relating herself to man, she seeks to express the eternal designs and transcendent destiny which the living God, the Creator and Redeemer, has linked with him.

The church finds in the very first pages of the book of Genesis the source of her conviction that work is a fundamental dimension of human existence on earth. An analysis of these texts makes us aware that they express—sometimes in an archaic way of manifesting thought—the fundamental truths about man, in the context of the mystery of creation itself. These truths are decisive for man from the very beginning, and at the same time they trace out the main lines of his earthly existence, both in the state of original justice and also after the breaking, caused by sin, of the Creator's original covenant with creation in man. When man, who had been created "in the image of God . . . male and female,"[9] hears the words: "Be fruitful and multiply, and fill the earth and subdue it,"[10] even though these words do not refer directly and explicitly to work, beyond any doubt they indirectly indicate it as an activity for man to carry out in the world. Indeed, they show its very deepest essence. Man is the image of God partly through the mandate received from his creator to subdue, to dominate, the earth. In carrying out this mandate, man, every human being, reflects the very action of the creator of the universe.

Work understood as a "transitive" activity, that is to say, an activity beginning in the human subject and directed toward an external object, presupposes a specific dominion by man over "the earth," and in its turn it confirms and develops this dominion. It is clear that the term "the earth" of which the biblical text speaks is to be understood in the first place as that fragment of the visible universe that man inhabits. By extension, however, it can be understood as the whole of the visible world insofar as it comes within the range of man's influence and of his striving to satisfy his needs. The expression "subdue the earth" has an immense range. It means all the resources that the earth (and indirectly the visible world) contains and which, through the conscious activity of man, can be discovered and used for his ends. And so these words, placed at the beginning of the Bible, never cease to be relevant. They embrace equally the past ages of civilization and economy, as also the whole of modern reality and future phases of development, which are perhaps already to some extent beginning to take shape, though for the most part they are still almost unknown to man and hidden from him.

While people sometimes speak of periods of "acceleration" in the economic life and civilization of humanity or of individual nations, linking these periods to the progress of science and technology and especially to discoveries which are decisive for social and economic life, at the same time it can be said that none of these phenomena of "acceleration" exceeds the essential consent of what was said in that most ancient of biblical texts. As man, through his work, becomes more and more the master of the earth, and as he confirms his dominion over the visible world, again through his work, he nevertheless remains in every case and at every phase of this process within the Creator's original ordering. And this ordering remains necessarily and indissolubly linked with the fact that man was created, as male and female, "in the image of God." This process is, at the same time, universal: It embraces all human beings, every generation, every phase of economic and cultural development, and at the same time it is a process that takes place within each human being, in each conscious human subject. Each and every individual is at the same time embraced by it. Each and every individual, to the proper extent and in an incalculable number of ways, takes part in the giant process whereby man "subdues the earth" through his work.

Work in the Objective Sense: Technology

5. This universality and, at the same time, this multiplicity of the process of "subduing the earth" throw light upon human work, because man's dominion over the earth is achieved in and by means of work. There thus emerges the meaning of work in an objective sense, which finds expression in the various epochs of culture and civilization. Man dominates the earth by the very fact of domesticating animals, rearing them and obtaining from them the food and clothing he needs, and by the fact of being able to extract various natural resources from the earth and the seas. But man "subdues the earth" much more when he begins to cultivate it and then to transform its products, adapting them to his own use. Thus agriculture constitutes through human work a primary field of economic activity and an indispensable factor of production. Industry in its turn will always consist in linking the earth's riches—whether nature's living resources, or the products of agriculture, or the mineral or chemical resources—with man's work, whether physical or intellectual. This is also in a sense true in the sphere of what are called service industries and also in the sphere of research, pure or applied.

In industry and agriculture man's work has today in many cases ceased to be mainly manual, for the toil of human hands and muscles is aided by more and more highly perfected machinery. Not only in industry but also in agriculture we are witnessing the transformations made possible by the gradual development of science and technology. Historically speaking this, taken as a whole, has caused great changes in civilization, from the beginning of the "industrial era" to the successive phases of development through new technologies, such as the electronics and the microprocessor technology in recent years.

While it may seem that in the industrial process it is the machine that "works" and man merely supervises it, making it function and keeping it going in various ways, it is also true that for this reason industrial development provides grounds for reproposing in new ways the question of human work. Both the original industrialization that gave rise to what is called the worker question and the subsequent industrial and post-industrial changes show in an eloquent manner that, even in the age of ever more mechanized "work," the proper subject of work continues to be man.

The development of industry and of the various sectors connected with it, even the most modern electronics technology, especially in the fields of miniaturization, communications, and telecommunications, and so forth, shows how vast is the role of technology, that ally of work that human thought has produced in the interaction between the subject and object of work (in the widest sense of the word). Understood in this case not as a capacity or aptitude for work, but rather as a whole set of instruments which man uses in his work, technology is undoubtedly man's ally. It facilitates his work, perfects, accelerates, and augments it. It leads to an increase in the quantity of things produced by work and in many cases improves their quality. However it is also a fact that in some instances technology can cease to be man's ally and become almost his enemy, as when the mechanization of work "supplants" him, taking away all personal satisfaction and the incentive to creativity and responsibility, when it deprives many workers of their previous employment or when, through exalting the machine, it reduces man to the status of its slave.

If the biblical words "subdue the earth" addressed to man from the very beginning are understood in the context of the whole modern age, industrial and post-industrial, then they undoubtedly include also a relationship with technology, with the world of machinery which is the fruit of the work of the human intellect and a historical confirmation of man's dominion over nature.

The recent stage of human history, especially that of certain societies, brings a correct affirmation of technology as a basic coefficient of economic progress; but at the same time this affirmation has been accompanied by and continues to be accompanied by essential questions concerning human work in relationship to its subject, which is man. These questions are particularly charged with content and tension of an ethical and social character. They therefore constitute a continual challenge for institutions of many kinds, for states and governments, for systems and international organizations; they also constitute a challenge for the church.

Work in the Subjective Sense: Man as the Subject of Work

6. In order to continue our analysis of work, an analysis linked with the word of the Bible telling man that he is to subdue the earth, we must concentrate our attention on work in the subjective sense, much more than we did on the objective significance, barely touching upon the vast range of problems known intimately and in detail to scholars in various fields and also, according to their specializations, to those who work. If the words of the book of Genesis to which we refer in this analysis of ours speak of work in the objective sense in an indirect way, they also speak only indirectly of the subject of work; but what they say is very eloquent and is full of great significance.

Man has to subdue the earth and dominate it, because as the "image of God" he is a person, that is to say, a subjective being capable of acting in a planned and rational way, capable of deciding about himself and with a tendency to self-realization. As a person, man is therefore the subject of work. As a person he works, he performs various actions belonging to the work process; independently of their objective content, these actions must all serve to realize his humanity, to fulfill the calling to be a person that is his by reason of his very humanity. The principal truths concerning this theme were recently recalled by the Second Vatican Council in the constitution *Gaudium et Spes*, especially in Chapter 1, which is devoted to man's calling.

And so this "dominion" spoken of in the biblical text being meditated upon here refers not only to the objective dimension of work, but at the same time introduces us to an understanding of its subjective dimension. Understood as a process whereby man and the human race subdue the earth, work corresponds to this basic biblical concept only when throughout the process man manifests himself and confirms himself as the one who "dominates." This dominion, in a certain sense, refers to the subjective dimension even more than to the objective one: This dimension conditions the very ethical nature of work. In fact there is no doubt that human work has an ethical value of its own, which clearly and directly remains linked to the fact that the one who carries it out is a person, a conscious and free subject, that is to say, a subject that decides about himself.

This truth, which in a sense constitutes the fundamental and perennial heart of Christian teaching on human work, has had and continues to have primary significance for the formulation of the important social problems characterizing whole ages.

The ancient world introduced its own typical differentiation of people into classes according to the type of work done. Work which demanded from the worker the exercise of physical strength, the work of muscles and hands, was considered unworthy of free men and was therefore given to slaves. By broadening certain aspects that already belonged to the Old Testament, Christianity brought about a fundamental change of ideas in this field, taking the whole content of the gospel message as its point of departure, especially the fact

that the one who, while being God, became like us in all things,[11] devoted most of the years of his life on earth to manual work at the carpenter's bench. This circumstance constitutes in itself the most eloquent "gospel of work," showing that the basis for determining the value of human work is not primarily the kind of work being done, but the fact that the one who is doing it is a person. The sources of the dignity of work are to be sought primarily in the subjective dimension, not in the objective one.

Such a concept practically does away with the very basis of the ancient differentiation of people into classes according to the kind of work done. This does not mean that from the objective point of view human work cannot and must not be rated and qualified in any way. It only means that the primary basis of the value of work is man himself, who is its subject. This leads immediately to a very important conclusion of an ethical nature: However true it may be that man is destined for work and called to it, in the first place work is "for man" and not man "for work." Through this conclusion one rightly comes to recognize the pre-eminence of the subjective meaning of work over the objective one. Given this way of understanding things and presupposing that different sorts of work that people do can have greater or lesser objective value, let us try nevertheless to show that each sort is judged above all by the measure of the dignity of the subject of work, that is to say, the person, the individual who carries it out. On the other hand, independent of the work that every man does, and presupposing that this work constitutes a purpose—at times a very demanding one—of his activity, this purpose does not possess a definite meaning in itself. In fact, in the final analysis it is always man who is the purpose of the work, whatever work it is that is done by man—even if the common scale of values rates it as the merest "service," as the most monotonous, even the most alienating work.

A Threat to the Right Order of Values

7. It is precisely these fundamental affirmations about work that always emerged from the wealth of Christian truth, especially from the very message of the "gospel of work," thus creating the basis for a new way of thinking, judging, and acting. In the modern period, from the beginning of the industrial age, the Christian truth about work had to oppose the various trends of materialistic and economistic thought.

For certain supporters of such ideas, work was understood and treated as a sort of "merchandise" that the worker—especially the industrial worker—sells to the employer, who at the same time is the possessor of the capital, that is to say, of all the working tools and means that make production possible. This way of looking at work was widespread especially in the first half of the nineteenth century. Since then explicit expressions of this sort have almost disappeared and have given way to more human ways of thinking about work and evaluating it. The interaction between the worker and the tools and means of production has given rise to the development of various forms of capitalism—

parallel with various forms of collectivism—into which other socioeconomic elements have entered as a consequence of new concrete circumstances, of the activity of workers' associations and public authorities, and of the emergence of large transnational enterprises. Nevertheless, the danger of treating work as a special kind of "merchandise" or as an impersonal "force" needed for production (the expression "work force" is in fact in common use) always exists, especially when the whole way of looking at the question of economics is marked by the premises of materialistic economism.

A systematic opportunity for thinking and evaluating in this way, and in a certain sense a stimulus for doing so, is provided by the quickening process of the development of a one-sidedly materialistic civilization, which gives prime importance to the objective dimension of work, while the subjective dimension—everything in direct or indirect relationship with the subject of work—remains on a secondary level. In all cases of this sort, in every social situation of this type, there is a confusion or even a reversal of the order laid down from the beginning by the words of the book of Genesis: Man is treated as an instrument of production,[12] whereas he—he alone, independent of the work he does—ought to be treated as the effective subject of work and its true maker and creator. Precisely this reversal of order, whatever the program or name under which it occurs, should rightly be called "capitalism"—in the sense more fully explained below. Everybody knows that capitalism has a definite historical meaning as a system, an economic and social system, opposed to "socialism" or "communism." But in the light of the analysis of the fundamental reality of the whole economic process—first and foremost of the production structure that work is—it should be recognized that the error of early capitalism can be repeated wherever man is in a way treated on the same level as the whole complex of the material means of production, as an instrument and not in accordance with the true dignity of his work—that is to say, where he is not treated as subject and maker, and for this very reason as the true purpose of the whole process of production.

This explains why the analysis of human work in the light of the words concerning man's "dominion" over the earth goes to the very heart of the ethical and social question. This concept should also find a central place in the whole sphere of social and economic policy, both within individual countries and in the wider field of international and intercontinental relationships, particularly with reference to the tensions making themselves felt in the world not only between East and West but also between North and South. Both John XXIII in the encyclical *Mater et Magistra* and Paul VI in the encyclical *Populorum Progressio* gave special attention to these dimensions of the modern ethical and social question.

Worker Solidarity

8. When dealing with human work in the fundamental dimension of its subject, that is to say, the human person doing the work, one must make at

least a summary evaluation of developments during the ninety years since *Rerum Novarum* in relation to the subjective dimension of work. Although the subject of work is always the same, that is to say man, nevertheless wide-ranging changes take place in the objective aspect. While one can say that, by reason of its subject, work is one single thing (one and unrepeatable every time), yet when one takes into consideration its objective directions, one is forced to admit that there exist many works, many different sorts of work. The development of human civilization brings continual enrichment in this field. But at the same time, one cannot fail to note that in the process of this development not only do new forms of work appear but also others disappear. Even if one accepts that on the whole this is a normal phenomenon, it must still be seen whether certain ethically and socially dangerous irregularities creep in and to what extent.

It was precisely one such wide-ranging anomaly that gave rise in the last century to what has been called "the worker question," sometimes described as "the proletariat question." This question and the problems connected with it gave rise to a just social reaction and caused the impetuous emergence of a great burst of solidarity between workers, first and foremost industrial workers. The call to solidarity and common action addressed to the workers—especially to those engaged in narrowly specialized, monotonous, and depersonalized work in industrial plants, when the machine tends to dominate man—was important and eloquent from the point of view of social ethics. It was the reaction against the degradation of man as the subject of work and against the unheard of accompanying exploitation in the field of wages, working conditions and social security for the worker. This reaction united the working world in a community marked by great solidarity.

Following the lines laid down by the encyclical *Rerum Novarum* and many later documents of the church's magisterium, it must be frankly recognized that the reaction against the system of injustice and harm that cried to heaven for vengeance[13] and that weighed heavily upon workers in that period of rapid industrialization was justified from the point of view of social morality. This state of affairs was favored by the liberal socio-political system, which in accordance with its "economistic" premises, strengthened and safeguarded economic initiative by the possessors of capital alone, but did not pay sufficient attention to the rights of the workers, on the grounds that human work is solely an instrument of production, and that capital is the basis, efficient factor, and purpose of production.

From that time, worker solidarity, together with a clearer and more committed realization by others of workers' rights, has in many cases brought about profound changes. Various forms of neo-capitalism or collectivism have developed. Various new systems have been thought out. Workers can often share in running businesses and in controlling their productivity, and in fact do so. Through appropriate associations they exercise influence over conditions of work and pay, and also over social legislation. But at the same time

various ideological or power systems and new relationships which have arisen at various levels of society have allowed flagrant injustices to persist or have created new ones. On the world level, the development of civilization and of communications has made possible a more complete diagnosis of the living and working conditions of man globally, but it has also revealed other forms of injustice much more extensive than those which in the last century stimulated unity between workers for particular solidarity in the working world. This is true in countries which have completed a certain process of industrial revolution. It is also true in countries where the main working milieu continues to be agriculture or other similar occupations.

Movements of solidarity in the sphere of work—a solidarity that must never mean being closed to dialogue and collaboration with others—can be necessary also with reference to the condition of social groups that were not previously included in such movements, but which in changing social systems and conditions of living are undergoing what is in effect "proletarianization" or which actually already find themselves in a "proletariat" situation, one which, even if not yet given that name, in fact deserves it. This can be true of certain categories or groups of the working "intelligentsia," especially when ever wider access to education and an ever increasing number of people with degrees or diplomas in the fields of their cultural preparation are accompanied by a drop in demand for their labor. This unemployment of intellectuals occurs or increases when the education available is not oriented toward the types of employment or service required by the true needs of society, or when there is less demand for work which requires education, at least professional education, than for manual labor, or when it is less well paid. Of course, education in itself is always valuable and an important enrichment of the human person; but in spite of that, "proletarianization" processes remain possible.

For this reason there must be continued study of the subject of work and of the subject's living conditions. In order to achieve social justice in the various parts of the world, in the various countries and in the relationships between them, there is a need for ever new movements of solidarity of the workers and with the workers. This solidarity must be present whenever it is called for by the social degrading of the subject of work, by exploitation of the workers and by the growing areas of poverty and even hunger. The church is firmly committed to this cause for she considers it her mission, her service, a proof of her fidelity to Christ, so that she can truly be the "church of the poor." And the "poor" appear under various forms; they appear in various places and at various times; in many cases they appear as a result of the violation of the dignity of human work: either because the opportunities for human work are limited as a result of the scourge of unemployment or because a low value is put on work and the rights that flow from it, especially the right to a just wage and to the personal security of the worker and his or her family.

Work and Personal Dignity

9. Remaining within the context of man as the subject of work, it is now appropriate to touch upon, at least in a summary way, certain problems that more closely define the dignity of human work in that they make it possible to characterize more fully its specific moral value. In doing this we must always keep in mind the biblical calling to "subdue the earth,"[14] in which is expressed the will of the Creator that work should enable man to achieve that "dominion" in the visible world that is proper to him.

God's fundamental and original intention with regard to man, whom he created in his image and after his likeness,[15] was not withdrawn or canceled out even when man, having broken the original covenant with God, heard the words: "In the sweat of your face you shall eat bread."[16] These words refer to the sometimes heavy toil that from then onward has accompanied human work; but they do not alter the fact that work is the means whereby man achieves that "dominion" which is proper to him over the visible world, by "subjecting" the earth. Toil is something that is universally known, for it is universally experienced. It is familiar, to those doing physical work under sometimes exceptionally laborious conditions. It is familiar not only to agricultural workers, who spend long days working the land, which sometimes "bears thorns and thistles,"[17] but also to those who work in mines and quarries, to steelworkers at their blast furnaces, to those who work in builders' yards and in construction work, often in danger of injury or death. It is also familiar to those at an intellectual workbench; to scientists; to those who bear the burden of grave responsibility for decisions that will have a vast impact on society. It is familiar to doctors and nurses, who spend days and nights at their patients' bedside. It is familiar to women, who sometimes without proper recognition on the part of society and even of their own families bear the daily burden and responsibility for their homes and the upbringing of their children. It is familiar to all workers and, since work is a universal calling, it is familiar to everyone.

And yet in spite of all this toil—perhaps, in a sense, because of it—work is a good thing for man. Even though it bears the mark of a *bonum arduum*, in the terminology of St. Thomas,[18] this does not take away the fact that, as such, it is a good thing for man. It is not only good in the sense that it is useful or something to enjoy; it is also good as being something worthy, that is to say, something that corresponds to man's dignity, that expresses this dignity and increases it. If one wishes to define more clearly the ethical meaning of work, it is this truth that one must particularly keep in mind. Work is a good thing for man—a good thing for his humanity—because through work man not only transforms nature, adapting it to his own needs, but he also achieves fulfillment as a human being and indeed in a sense becomes "more a human being."

Without this consideration it is impossible to understand the meaning of the virtue of industriousness, and more particularly it is impossible to understand why industriousness should be a virtue: For virtue, as a moral habit, is some-

thing whereby man becomes good as man.[19] This fact in no way alters our justifiable anxiety that in work, whereby matter gains in nobility, man himself should not experience a lowering of his own dignity.[20] Again, it is well-known that it is possible to use work in various ways against man, that it is possible to punish man with the system of forced labor in concentration camps, that work can be made into a means for oppressing man, and that in various ways it is possible to exploit human labor, that is to say, the workers. All this pleads in favor of the moral obligation to link industriousness as a virtue with the social order of work, which will enable man to become in work "more a human being" and not be degraded by it not only because of the wearing out of his physical strength (which, at least up to a certain point, is inevitable), but especially through damage to the dignity and subjectivity that are proper to him.

Work and Society: Family and Nation

10. Having thus confirmed the personal dimension of human work, we must go on to the second sphere of values which is necessarily linked to work. Work constitutes a foundation for the formation of family life, which is a natural right and something that man is called to. These two spheres of values—one linked to work and the other consequent on the family nature of human life—must be properly united and must properly permeate each other. In a way, work is a condition for making it possible to found a family, since the family requires the means of subsistence which man normally gains through work. Work and industriousness also influence the whole process of education in the family, for the very reason that everyone "becomes a human being" through, among other things, work, and becoming a human being is precisely the main purpose of the whole process of education. Obviously, two aspects of work in a sense come into play here: the one making family life and its upkeep possible, and the other making possible the achievement of the purposes of the family, especially education. Nevertheless, these two aspects of work are linked to one another and are mutually complementary in various points.

It must be remembered and affirmed that the family constitutes one of the most important terms of reference for shaping the social and ethical order of human work. The teaching of the church has always devoted special attention to this question, and in the present document we shall have to return to it. In fact, the family is simultaneously a community made possible by work and the first school of work, within the home, for every person.

The third sphere of values that emerges from this point of view—that of the subject of work—concerns the great society to which man belongs on the basis of particular cultural and historical links. This society—even when it has not yet taken on the mature form of a nation—is not only the great "educator" of every man, even though an indirect one (because each individual absorbs within the family the contents and values that go to make up the culture of a given nation); it is also a great historical and social incarnation of the work of all generations. All of this brings it about that man combines his deepest

human identity with membership of a nation, and intends his work also to increase the common good developed together with his compatriots, thus realizing that in this way work serves to add to the heritage of the whole human family, of all the people living in the world.

These three spheres are always important for human work in its subjective dimension. And this dimension, that is to say, the concrete reality of the worker, takes precedence over the objective dimension. In the subjective dimension there is realized, first of all, that "dominion" over the world of nature to which man is called from the beginning according to the words of the book of Genesis. The very process of "subduing the earth," that is to say work, is marked in the course of history and especially in recent centuries by an immense development of technological means. This is an advantageous and positive phenomenon, on condition that the objective dimension of work does not gain the upper hand over the subjective dimension, depriving man of his dignity and inalienable rights or reducing them.

3. CONFLICT BETWEEN LABOR AND CAPITAL IN THE PRESENT PHASE OF HISTORY

Dimensions of the Conflict

11. The sketch of the basic problems of work outlined above draws inspiration from the texts at the beginning of the Bible and in a sense forms the very framework of the church's teaching, which has remained unchanged throughout the centuries within the context of different historical experiences. However, the experiences preceding and following the publication of the encyclical *Rerum Novarum* form a background that endows that teaching with particular expressiveness and the eloquence of living relevance. In this analysis, work is seen as a great reality with a fundamental influence on the shaping in a human way of the world that the Creator has entrusted to man; it is a reality closely linked with man as the subject of work and with man's rational activity. In the normal course of events this reality fills human life and strongly affects its value and meaning. Even when it is accompanied by toil and effort, work is still something good, and so man develops through love for work. This entirely positive and creative, educational and meritorious character of man's work must be the basis for the judgments and decisions being made today in its regard in spheres that include human rights, as is evidenced by the international declarations on work and the many labor codes prepared either by the competent legislative institutions in the various countries or by organizations devoting their social, or scientific and social, activity to the problems of work. One organization fostering such initiatives on the international level is the International Labor Organization, the oldest specialized agency of the United Nations.

In the following part of these considerations I intend to return in greater detail to these important questions, recalling at least the basic elements of the

church's teaching on the matter. I must however first touch on a very important field of questions in which her teaching has taken shape in this latest period, the one marked and in a sense symbolized by the publication of the encyclical *Rerum Novarum*.

Throughout this period, which is by no means yet over, the issue of work has of course been posed on the basis of the great conflict that in the age of and together with industrial development emerged between "capital" and "labor," that is to say between the small but highly influential group of entrepreneurs, owners or holders of the means of production, and the broader multitude of people who lacked these means and who shared in the process of production solely by their labor. The conflict originated in the fact that the workers put their powers at the disposal of the entrepreneurs and these, following the principle of maximum profit, tried to establish the lowest possible wages for the work done by the employees. In addition there were other elements of exploitation connected with the lack of safety at work and of safeguards regarding the health and living conditions of the workers and their families.

This conflict, interpreted by some as a socioeconomic class conflict, found expression in the ideological conflict between liberalism, understood as the ideology of capitalism, and Marxism, understood as the ideology of scientific socialism and communism, which professes to act as the spokesman for the working class and the worldwide proletariat. Thus the real conflict between labor and capital was transformed into a systematic class struggle conducted not only by ideological means, but also and chiefly by political means. We are familiar with the history of this conflict and with the demands of both sides. The Marxist program, based on the philosophy of Marx and Engels, sees in class struggle the only way to eliminate class injustice in society and to eliminate the classes themselves. Putting this program into practice presupposes the collectivization of the means of production so that through the transfer of these means from private hands to the collectivity, human labor will be preserved from exploitation.

This is the goal of the struggle carried on by political as well as ideological means. In accordance with the principle of "the dictatorship of the proletariat," the groups that as political parties follow the guidance of Marxist ideology aim by the use of various kinds of influence, including revolutionary pressure, to win a monopoly of power in each society in order to introduce the collectivist system into it by eliminating private ownership of the means of production. According to the principal ideologists and leaders of this broad international movement, the purpose of this program of action is to achieve the social revolution and to introduce socialism and finally the communist system throughout the world.

As we touch on this extremely important field of issues, which constitutes not only a theory but a whole fabric of socioeconomic, political and international life in our age, we cannot go into the details, nor is this necessary, for they are known both from the vast literature on the subject and by experience.

Instead we must leave the context of these issues and go back to the fundamental issue of human work, which is the main subject of the considerations in this document. It is clear indeed that this issue, which is of such importance for man—it constitutes one of the fundamental dimensions of his earthly existence and of his vocation—can also be explained only by taking into account the full context of the contemporary situation.

The Priority of Labor

12. The structure of the present-day situation is deeply marked by many conflicts caused by man, and the technological means produced by human work play a primary role in it. We should also consider here the prospect of worldwide catastrophe in the case of a nuclear war, which would have almost unimaginable possibilities of destruction. In view of this situation we must first of all recall a principle that has always been taught by the church: the principle of the priority of labor over capital. This principle directly concerns the process of production: In this process labor is always a primary efficient cause, while capital, the whole collection of means of production, remains a mere instrument or instrumental cause. This principle is an evident truth that emerges from the whole of man's historical experience.

When we read in the first chapter of the Bible that man is to subdue the earth, we know that these words refer to all the resources contained in the visible world and placed at man's disposal. However, these resources can serve man only through work. From the beginning there is also linked with work the question of ownership, for the only means that man has for causing the resources hidden in nature to serve himself and others is his work. And to be able through his work to make these resources bear fruit, man takes over ownership of small parts of the various riches of nature: those beneath the ground, those in the sea, on land or in space. He takes over all these things by making them his workbench. He takes them over through work and for work.

The same principle applies in the successive phases of this process, in which the first phase always remains the relationship of man with the resources and riches of nature. The whole of the effort to acquire knowledge with the aim of discovering these riches and specifying the various ways in which they can be used by man and for man teaches us that everything that comes from man throughout the whole process of economic production, whether labor or the whole collection of means of production and the technology connected with these means (meaning the capability to use them in work), presupposes these riches and resources of the visible world, riches and resources that man finds and does not create. In a sense man finds them already prepared, ready for him to discover them and to use them correctly in the productive process. In every phase of the development of his work, man comes up against the leading role of the gift made by "nature," that is to say, in the final analysis, by the Creator. At the beginning of man's work is the mystery of creation. This affirmation, already indicated as my starting point,

is the guiding thread of this document and will be further developed in the last part of these reflections.

Further consideration of this question should confirm our conviction of the priority of human labor over what in the course of time we have grown accustomed to calling capital. Since the concept of capital includes not only the natural resources placed at man's disposal, but also the whole collection of means by which man appropriates natural resources and transforms them in accordance with his needs (and thus in a sense humanizes them), it must immediately be noted that all these means are the result of the historical heritage of human labor. All the means of production, from the most primitive to the ultramodern ones—it is man that has gradually developed them: man's experience and intellect. In this way there have appeared not only the simplest instruments for cultivating the earth, but also through adequate progress in science and technology, the more modern and complex ones: machines, factories, laboratories, and computers. Thus everything that is at the service of work, everything that in the present state of technology constitutes its ever more highly perfected "instrument," is the result of work.

This gigantic and powerful instrument—the whole collection of means of production that in a sense are considered synonymous with "capital"—is the result of work and bears the signs of human labor. At the present stage of technological advance, when man, who is the subject of work, wishes to make use of this collection of modern instruments, the means of production, he must first assimilate cognitively the result of the work of the people who invented those instruments, who planned them, built them and perfected them, and who continue to do so. Capacity for work—that is to say, for sharing efficiently in the modern production process—demands greater and greater preparation and, before all else, proper training. Obviously it remains clear that every human being sharing in the production process, even if he or she is only doing the kind of work for which no special training or qualifications are required, is the real efficient subject in this production process, while the whole collection of instruments, no matter how perfect they may be in themselves, is only a mere instrument subordinate to human labor.

This truth, which is part of the abiding heritage of the church's teaching, must always be emphasized with reference to the question of the labor system and with regard to the whole socioeconomic system. We must emphasize and give prominence to the primacy of man in the production process, the primacy of man over things. Everything contained in the concept of capital in the strict sense is only a collection of things. Man, as the subject of work and independent of the work he does—man alone is a person. This truth has important and decisive consequences.

Economism and Materialism

13. In the light of the above truth we see clearly, first of all, that capital cannot be separated from labor; in no way can labor be opposed to capital or

capital to labor, and still less can the actual people behind these concepts be opposed to each other, as will be explained later. A labor system can be right, in the sense of being in conformity with the very essence of the issue and in the sense of being intrinsically true and also morally legitimate, if in its very basis it overcomes the opposition between labor and capital through an effort at being shaped in accordance with the principle put forward above: the principle of the substantial and real priority of labor, of the subjectivity of human labor and its effective participation in the whole production process, independent of the nature of the services provided by the worker.

Opposition between labor and capital does not spring from the structure of the production process or from the structure of the economic process. In general the latter process demonstrates that labor and what we are accustomed to call capital are intermingled; it shows that they are inseparably linked. Working at any workbench, whether a relatively primitive or an ultramodern one, a man can easily see that through his work he enters into two inheritances: the inheritance of what is given to the whole of humanity in the resources of nature and the inheritance of what others have already developed on the basis of those resources, primarily by developing technology, that is to say, by producing a whole collection of increasingly perfect instruments for work. In working, man also "enters into the labor of others."[21] Guided both by our intelligence and by the faith that draws light from the word of God, we have no difficulty in accepting this image of the sphere and process of man's labor. It is a consistent image, one that is humanistic as well as theological. In it man is the master of the creatures placed at his disposal in the visible world. If some dependence is discovered in the work process, it is dependence of the Giver of all the resources of creation and also on other human beings, those to whose work and initiative we owe the perfected and increased possibilities of our own work. All that we can say of everything in the production process which constitutes a whole collection of "things," the instruments, the capital, is that it conditions man's work; we cannot assert that it constitutes as it were an impersonal "subject" putting man and man's work into a position of dependence.

This consistent image, in which the principle of the primacy of person over things is strictly preserved, was broken up in human thought, sometimes after a long period of incubation in practical living. The break occurred in such a way that labor was separated from capital and set in opposition to it, and capital was set in opposition to labor, as though they were two impersonal forces, two production factors juxtaposed in the same "economistic" perspective. This way of stating the issue contained a fundamental error, what we can call the error of economism, that of considering human labor solely according to its economic purpose. This fundamental error of thought can and must be called an error of materialism, in that economism directly or indirectly includes a conviction of the primacy and superiority of the material and directly or indirectly places the spiritual and the personal (man's activity,

moral values and such matters) in a position of subordination to material reality. This is still not theoretical materialism in the full sense of the term, but it is certainly practical materialism, a materialism judged capable of satisfying man's needs not so much on the grounds of premises derived from materialist theory as on the grounds of a particular way of evaluating things and so on the grounds of a certain hierarchy of goods based on the greater immediate attractiveness of what is material.

The error of thinking in the categories of economism went hand in hand with the formation of a materialist philosophy, as this philosophy developed from the most elementary and common phase (also called common materialism, because it professes to reduce spiritual reality to a superfluous phenomenon) to the phase of what is called dialectical materialism. However, within the framework of the present consideration, it seems that economism had a decisive importance for the fundamental issue of human work, in particular for the separation of labor and capital and for setting them up in opposition as two production factors viewed in the above-mentioned economistic perspective; and it seems that economism influenced this non-humanistic way of stating the issue before the materialist philosophical system did. Nevertheless it is obvious that materialism, including its dialectical form, is incapable of providing sufficient and definitive bases for thinking about human work, in order that the primacy of man over the capital instrument, the primacy of the person over things, may find in it adequate and irrefutable confirmation and support. In dialectical materialism too man is not first and foremost the subject of work and the efficient cause of the production process, but continues to be understood and treated, in dependence on what is material, as a kind of "resultant" of the economic or production relations prevailing at a given period.

Obviously the antinomy between labor and capital under consideration here—the antinomy in which labor was separated from capital and set up in opposition to it, in a certain sense on the ontic level as if it were just an element like any other in the economic process—did not originate merely in the philosophy and economic theories of the eighteenth century; rather it originated in the whole of the economic and social practice of that time, the time of the birth and rapid development of industrialization, in which what was mainly seen was the possibility of vastly increasing material wealth, the means, while the end, that is to say man, who should be served by the means, was ignored. It was this practical error that struck a blow first and foremost against human labor, against the workingman, and caused the ethically just social reaction already spoken of above. The same error, which is now part of history and which was connected with the period of primitive capitalism and liberalism, can nevertheless be repeated in other circumstances of time and place if people's thinking starts from the same theoretical or practical premises. The only chance there seems to be for radically overcoming this error is through adequate changes both in theory and in practice, changes in

line with the definite conviction of the primacy of the person over things and of human labor over capital as a whole collection of means of production.

Work and Ownership

14. The historical process briefly presented here has certainly gone beyond its initial phase, but it is still taking place and indeed is spreading in the relationships between nations and continents. It needs to be specified further from another point of view. It is obvious that when we speak of opposition between labor and capital, we are not dealing only with abstract concepts or "impersonal forces" operating in economic production. Behind both concepts there are people, living, actual people: On the one side are those who do the work without being the owners of the means of production, and on the other side those who act as entrepreneurs and who own these means or represent the owners. Thus the issue of ownership or property enters from the beginning into the whole of this difficult historical process. The encyclical *Rerum Novarum*, which has the social question as its theme, stresses this issue also, recalling and confirming the church's teaching on ownership, on the right to private property even when it is a question of the means of production. The encyclical *Mater et Magistra* did the same.

The above principle, as it was then stated and as it is still taught by the church, diverges radically from the program of collectivism as proclaimed by Marxism and put into practice in various countries in the decades following the time of Leo XIII's encyclical. At the same time it differs from the program of capitalism practiced by liberalism and by the political systems inspired by it. In the latter case, the difference consists in the way the right to ownership or property is understood. Christian tradition has never upheld this right as absolute and untouchable. On the contrary, it has always understood this right within the broader context of the right common to all to use the goods of the whole of creation: The right to private property is subordinated to the right to common use, to the fact that goods are meant for everyone.

Furthermore, in the church's teaching, ownership has never been understood in a way that could constitute grounds for social conflict in labor. As mentioned above, property is acquired first of all through work in order that it may serve work. This concerns in a special way ownership of the means of production. Isolating these means as a separate property in order to set it up in the form of "capital" in opposition to "labor"—and even to practice exploitation of labor—is contrary to the very nature of these means and their possession. They cannot be possessed against labor, they cannot even be possessed for possession's sake, because the only legitimate title to their possession—whether in the form of private ownership or in the form of public or collective ownership—is that they should serve labor and thus by serving labor that they should make possible the achievement of the first principle of this order, namely the universal destination of goods and the right to common use of them. From this point of view, therefore, in consideration of human labor and

of common access to the goods meant for man, one cannot exclude the socialization, in suitable conditions, of certain means of production. In the course of the decades since the publication of the encyclical *Rerum Novarum*, the church's teaching has always recalled all these principles, going back to the arguments formulated in a much older tradition, for example, the well-known arguments of the *Summa Theologiae* of St. Thomas Aquinas.[22]

In the present document, which has human work as its main theme, it is right to confirm all the effort with which the church's teaching has striven and continues to strive always to ensure the priority of work and thereby man's character as a subject in social life and especially in the dynamic structure of the whole economic process. From this point of view the position of "rigid" capitalism continues to remain unacceptable, namely the position that defends the exclusive right to private ownership of the means of production as an untouchable "dogma" of economic life. The principle of respect for work demands that this right should undergo a constructive revision both in theory and in practice. If it is true that capital, as the whole of the means of production, is at the same time the product of the work of generations, it is equally true that capital is being unceasingly created through the work done with the help of all these means of production, and these means can be seen as a great workbench at which the present generation of workers is working day after day. Obviously we are dealing here with different kinds of work, not only so-called manual labor, but also the many forms of intellectual work, including white-collar work and management.

In the light of the above, the many proposals put forward by experts in Catholic social teaching and by the highest magisterium of the church take on special significance:[23] proposals for joint ownership of the means of work, sharing by the workers in the management and/or profits of businesses, so-called shareholding by labor, etc. Whether these various proposals can or cannot be applied concretely, it is clear that recognition of the proper position of labor and the worker in the production process demands various adaptations in the sphere of the right to ownership of the means of production. This is so not only in view of older situations but also, first and foremost, in view of the whole of the situation and the problems in the second half of the present century with regard to the so-called Third World and the various new independent countries that have arisen, especially in Africa but elsewhere as well, in place of the colonial territories of the past.

Therefore, while the position of "rigid" capitalism must undergo continual revision in order to be reformed from the point of view of human rights, both human rights in the widest sense and those linked with man's work, it must be stated that from the same point of view these many deeply desired reforms cannot be achieved by an a priori elimination of private ownership of the means of production. For it must be noted that merely taking these means of production (capital) out of the hands of their private owners is not enough to ensure their satisfactory socialization. They cease to be the property of a certain

social group, namely the private owners, and become the property of organized society, coming under the administration and direct control of another group of people, namely those who, though not owning them, from the fact of exercising power in society manage them on the level of the whole national or the local economy.

This group in authority may carry out its task satisfactorily from the point of view of the priority of labor; but it may also carry it out badly by claiming for itself a monopoly of the administration and disposal of the means of production and not refraining even from offending basic human rights. Thus, merely converting the means of production into state property in the collectivist systems is by no means equivalent to "socializing" that property. We can speak of socializing only when the subject character of society is ensured, that is to say, when on the basis of his work each person is fully entitled to consider himself a part-owner of the great workbench at which he is working with everyone else. A way toward that goal could be found by associating labor with the ownership of capital, as far as possible, and by producing a wide range of intermediate bodies with economic, social and cultural purposes; they would be bodies enjoying real autonomy with regard to the public powers, pursuing their specific aims in honest collaboration with each other and in subordination to the demands of the common good, and they would be living communities both in form and in substance in the sense that the members of each body would be looked upon and treated as persons and encouraged to take an active part in the life of the body.[24]

The "Personalist" Argument

15. Thus the principle of the priority of labor over capital is a postulate of the order of social morality. It has key importance both in the system built on the principle of private ownership of the means of production and also in the systems in which private ownership of these means has been limited even in a radical way. Labor is in a sense inseparable from capital; in no way does it accept the antinomy, that is to say, the separation and opposition with regard to the means of production that has weighed upon human life in recent centuries as a result of merely economic premises. When man works, using all the means of production, he also wishes the fruit of this work to be used by himself and others, and he wishes to be able to take part in the very work process as a sharer in responsibility and creativity at the workbench to which he applies himself.

From this spring certain specific rights of workers, corresponding to the obligation of work. They will be discussed later. But here it must be emphasized in general terms that the person who works desires not only due remuneration for his work; he also wishes that within the production process provision be made for him to be able to know that in his work, even on something that is owned in common, he is working "for himself." This awareness is extinguished within him in a system of excessive bureaucratic centralization,

which makes the worker feel that he is just a cog in a huge machine moved from above, that he is for more reasons than one a mere production instrument rather than a true subject of work with an initiative of his own. The church's teaching has always expressed the strong and deep conviction that man's work concerns not only the economy but also, and especially, personal values. The economic system itself and the production process benefit precisely when these personal values are fully respected. In the mind of St. Thomas Aquinas,[25] this is the principal reason in favor of private ownership of the means of production. While we accept that for certain well-founded reasons exceptions can be made to the principle of private ownership—in our own time we even see that the system of "socialized ownership" has been introduced—nevertheless the personalist argument still holds good both on the level of principles and on the practical level. If it is to be rational and fruitful, any socialization of the means of production must take this argument into consideration. Every effort must be made to ensure that in this kind of system also the human person can preserve his awareness of working "for himself." If this is not done, incalculable damage is inevitably done throughout the economic process, not only economic damage but first and foremost damage to man.

4. RIGHTS OF WORKERS

Within the Broad Context of Human Rights

16. While work, in all its many senses, is an obligation, that is to say a duty, it is also a source of rights on the part of the worker. These rights must be examined in the broad context of human rights as a whole, which are connatural with man and many of which are proclaimed by various international organizations and increasingly guaranteed by the individual states for their citizens. Respect for this broad range of human rights constitutes the fundamental condition for peace in the modern world: peace both within individual countries and societies and in international relations, the church's magisterium has several times noted, especially since the encyclical *Pacem in Terris*. The human rights that flow from work are part of the broader context of those fundamental rights of the person.

However, within this context they have a specific character corresponding to the specific nature of human work as outlined above. It is in keeping with this character that we must view them. Work is, as has been said, an obligation, that is to say, a duty, on the part of man. This is true in all the many meanings of the word. Man must work both because the Creator has commanded it and because of his own humanity, which requires work in order to be maintained and developed. Man must work out of regard for others, especially his own family, but also for the society he belongs to, the country of which he is a child and the whole human family of which he is a member, since he is the heir to the work of generations and at the same time a sharer in building the future of those who will come after him in the succession of

history. All this constitutes the moral obligation of work, understood in its wide sense. When we have to consider the moral rights corresponding to this obligation of every person with regard to work, we must always keep before our eyes the whole vast range of points of reference in which the labor of every working subject is manifested.

For when we speak of the obligation of work and of the rights of the worker that correspond to this obligation, we think in the first place of the relationship between the employer, direct or indirect, and the worker.

The distinction between the direct and the indirect employer is seen to be very important when one considers both the way in which labor is actually organized and the possibility of the formation of just or unjust relationships in the field of labor.

Since the direct employer is the person or institution with whom the worker enters directly into a work contract in accordance with definite conditions, we must understand as the indirect employer many different factors, other than the direct employer, that exercise a determining influence on the shaping both of the work contract and, consequently, of just or unjust relationships in the field of human labor.

Direct and Indirect Employer

17. The concept of indirect employer includes both persons and institutions of various kinds and also collective labor contracts and the principles of conduct which are laid down by these persons and institutions and which determine the whole socioeconomic system or are its result. The concept of "indirect employer" thus refers to many different elements. The responsibility of the indirect employer differs from that of the direct employer—the term itself indicates that the responsibility is less direct—but it remains a true responsibility: The indirect employer substantially determines one or other facet of the labor relationship, thus conditioning the conduct of the direct employer when the latter determines in concrete terms the actual work contract and labor relations. This is not to absolve the direct employer from his own responsibility, but only to draw attention to the whole network of influences that condition his conduct. When it is a question of establishing an ethically correct labor policy, all these influences must be kept in mind. A policy is correct when the objective rights of the worker are fully respected.

The concept of indirect employer is applicable to every society and in the first place to the state. For it is the state that must conduct a just labor policy. However, it is common knowledge that in the present system of economic relations in the world there are numerous links between individual states, links that find expression, for instance, in the import and export process, that is to say, in the mutual exchange of economic goods, whether raw materials, semimanufactured goods or finished industrial products. These links also create mutual dependence, and as a result it would be difficult to speak in the case

of any state, even the economically most powerful, of complete self-sufficiency or autarky.

Such a system of mutual dependence is in itself normal. However it can easily become an occasion for various forms of exploitation or injustice and as a result influence the labor policy of individual states; and finally it can influence the individual worker who is the proper subject of labor. For instance the highly industrialized countries, and even more the businesses that direct on a large scale the means of industrial production (the companies referred to as multinational or transnational), fix the highest possible prices for their products, while trying at the same time to fix the lowest possible prices for raw materials or semimanufactured goods. This is one of the causes of an ever increasing disproportion between national incomes. The gap between most of the richest countries and the poorest ones is not diminishing or being stabilized, but is increasing more and more to the detriment, obviously, of the poor countries. Evidently this must have an effect on local labor policy and on the worker's situation in the economically disadvantaged societies. Finding himself in a system thus conditioned, the direct employer fixes working conditions below the objective requirements of the workers, especially if he himself wishes to obtain the highest possible profits from the business which he runs (or from the businesses which he runs, in the case of a situation of "socialized" ownership of the means of production).

It is easy to see that this framework of forms of dependence linked with the concept of the indirect employer is enormously extensive and complicated. It is determined, in a sense, by all the elements that are decisive for economic life within a given society and state, but also by much wider links and forms of dependence. The attainment of the worker's rights cannot however be doomed to be merely a result of economic systems which on a larger or smaller scale are guided chiefly by the criterion of maximum profit. On the contrary, it is respect for the objective rights of the worker—every kind of worker: manual or intellectual, industrial or agricultural, etc.—that must constitute the adequate and fundamental criterion for shaping the whole economy, both on the level of the individual society and state and within the whole of the world economic policy and of the systems of international relationships that derive from it.

Influence in this direction should be exercised by all the international organizations whose concern it is, beginning with the United Nations. It appears that the International Labor Organization and the Food and Agriculture Organization of the United Nations and other bodies too have fresh contributions to offer on this point in particular. Within the individual states there are ministries or public departments and also various social institutions set up for this purpose. All of this effectively indicates the importance of the indirect employer—as has been said above—in achieving full respect for the worker's rights, since the rights of the human person are the key element in the whole of the social moral order.

The Employment Issue

18. When we consider the rights of workers in relation to the "indirect employer," that is to say, all the agents at the national and international level that are responsible for the whole orientation of labor policy, we must first direct our attention to a fundamental issue: the question of finding work or, in other words, the issue of suitable employment for all who are capable of it. The opposite of a just and right situation in this field is unemployment, that is to say, the lack of work for those who are capable of it. It can be a question of general unemployment or of unemployment in certain sectors of work. The role of the agents included under the title of indirect employer is to act against unemployment, which in all cases is an evil and which, when it reaches a certain level, can become a real social disaster. It is particularly painful when it especially affects young people, who after appropriate cultural, technical and professional preparation fail to find work and see their sincere wish to work and their readiness to take on their own responsibility for the economic and social development of the community sadly frustrated. The obligation to provide unemployment benefits, that is to say, the duty to make suitable grants indispensable for the subsistence of unemployed workers and their families, is a duty springing from the fundamental principle of the moral order in this sphere, namely the principle of the common use of goods or, to put it in another and still simpler way, the right to life and subsistence.

In order to meet the danger of unemployment and to ensure employment for all, the agents defined here as "indirect employer" must make provision for overall planning with regard to the different kinds of work by which not only the economic life, but also the cultural life of a given society is shaped; they must also give attention to organizing that work in a correct and rational way. In the final analysis this overall concern weighs on the shoulders of the state, but it cannot mean one-sided centralization by the public authorities. Instead, what is in question is a just and rational coordination, within the framework of which the initiative of individuals, free groups and local work centers and complexes must be safeguarded, keeping in mind what has been said above with regard to the subject character of human labor.

The fact of the mutual dependence of societies and states and the need to collaborate in various areas mean that, while preserving the sovereign rights of each society and state in the field of planning and organizing labor in its own society, action in this important area must also be taken in the dimension of international collaboration by means of the necessary treaties and agreements. Here too the criterion for these pacts and agreements must more and more be the criterion of human work considered as a fundamental right of all human beings, work which gives similar rights to all those who work in such a way that the living standard of the workers in the different societies will less and less show those disturbing differences which are unjust and are apt to provoke even violent reactions. The international organizations have an enormous part to play in this area. They must let themselves be guided by an

exact diagnosis of the complex situations and of the influence exercised by natural, historical, civil and other such circumstances. They must also be more highly operative with regard to plans for action jointly decided on, that is to say, they must be more effective in carrying them out.

In this direction, it is possible to actuate a plan for universal and proportionate progress by all in accordance with the guidelines of Paul VI's encyclical *Populorum Progressio*. It must be stressed that the constitutive element in this progress and also the most adequate way to verify it in a spirit of justice and peace, which the church proclaims and for which she does not cease to pray to the Father of all individuals and of all peoples, is the continual reappraisal of man's work, both in the aspect of its objective finality and in the aspect of the dignity of the subject of all work, that is to say, man. The progress in question must be made through man and for man and it must produce its fruit in man. A test of this progress will be the increasingly mature recognition of the purpose of work and increasingly universal respect for the rights inherent in work in conformity with the dignity of man, the subject of work.

Rational planning and the proper organization of human labor in keeping with individual societies and states should also facilitate the discovery of the right proportions between the different kinds of employment: work on the land, in industry, in the various services, white-collar work and scientific or artistic work, in accordance with the capacities of individuals and for the common good of each society and of the whole of mankind. The organization of human life in accordance with the many possibilities of labor should be matched by a suitable system of instruction and education aimed first of all at developing mature human beings, but also aimed at preparing people specifically for assuming to good advantage an appropriate place in the vast and socially differentiated world of work.

As we view the whole human family throughout the world, we cannot fail to be struck by a disconcerting fact of immense proportions: the fact that while conspicuous natural resources remain unused there are huge numbers of people who are unemployed or underemployed and countless multitudes of people suffering from hunger. This is a fact that without any doubt demonstrates that both within the individual political communities and in their relationships on the continental and world levels there is something wrong with the organization of work and employment, precisely at the most critical and socially most important points.

Wages and Other Social Benefits

19. After outlining the important role that concern for providing employment for all workers plays in safeguarding respect for the inalienable rights of man in view of his work, it is worthwhile to take a closer look at these rights, which in the final analysis are formed within the relationship between worker and direct employer. All that has been said above on the subject of the indirect employer is aimed at defining these relationships more exactly, by

showing the many forms of conditioning within which these relationships are indirectly formed. This consideration does not however have a purely descriptive purpose; it is not a brief treatise on economics or politics. It is a matter of highlighting the deontological and moral aspect. The key problem of social ethics in this case is that of just remuneration for work done. In the context of the present there is no more important way for securing a just relationship between the worker and the employer than that constituted by remuneration for work. Whether the work is done in a system of private ownership of the means of production or in a system where ownership has undergone a certain "socialization," the relationship between the employer (first and foremost the direct employer) and the worker is resolved on the basis of the wage, that is, through just remuneration of the work done.

It should also be noted that the justice of a socioeconomic system and, in each case, its just functioning, deserve in the final analysis to be evaluated by the way in which man's work is properly remunerated in the system. Here we return once more to the first principle of the whole ethical and social order, namely the principle of the common use of goods. In every system, regardless of the fundamental relationships within it between capital and labor, wages, that is to say remuneration for work, are still a practical means whereby the vast majority of people can have access to those goods which are intended for common use: both the goods of nature and manufactured goods. Both kinds of goods become accessible to the worker through the wage which he receives as remuneration for his work. Hence in every case a just wage is the concrete means of verifying the justice of the whole socioeconomic system and, in any case, of checking that it is functioning justly. It is not the only means of checking, but it is a particularly important one and in a sense the key means.

This means of checking concerns above all the family. Just remuneration for the work of an adult who is responsible for a family means remuneration which will suffice for establishing and properly maintaining a family and for providing security for its future. Such remuneration can be given either through what is called a family wage—that is, a single salary given to the head of the family for his work, sufficient for the needs of the family without the spouse having to take up gainful employment outside the home—or through other social measures such as family allowances or grants to mothers devoting themselves exclusively to their families. These grants should correspond to the actual needs, that is, to the number of dependents for as long as they are not in a position to assume proper responsibility for their own lives.

Experience confirms that there must be a social re-evaluation of the mother's role, of the toil connected with it and of the need that children have for care, love and affection in order that they may develop into responsible, morally and religiously mature and psychologically stable persons. It will redound to the credit of society to make it possible for a mother—without inhibiting her freedom, without psychological or practical discrimination,

and without penalizing her as compared with other women—to devote herself to taking care of her children and educating them in accordance with their needs, which vary with age. Having to abandon these tasks in order to take up paid work outside the home is wrong from the point of view of the good of society and of the family when it contradicts or hinders these primary goals of the mission of a mother.[26]

In this context it should be emphasized that on a more general level the whole labor process must be organized and adapted in such a way as to respect the requirements of the person and his or her forms of life, above all life in the home, taking into account the individual's age and sex. It is a fact that in many societies women work in nearly every sector of life. But it is fitting that they should be able to fulfill their tasks in accordance with their own nature, without being discriminated against and without being excluded from jobs for which they are capable, but also without lack of respect for their family aspirations and for their specific role in contributing, together with men, to the good of society. The true advancement of women requires that labor should be structured in such a way that women do not have to pay for their advancement by abandoning what is specific to them and at the expense of the family, in which women as mothers have an irreplaceable role.

Besides wages, various social benefits intended to ensure the life and health of workers and their families play a part here. The expenses involved in health care, especially in the case of accidents at work, demand that medical assistance should be easily available for workers and that as far as possible it should be cheap or even free of charge. Another sector regarding benefits is the sector associated with the right to rest. In the first place this involves a regular weekly rest comprising at least Sunday and also a longer period of rest, namely the holiday or vacation taken once a year or possibly in several shorter periods during the year. A third sector concerns the right to a pension and to insurance for old age and in case of accidents at work. Within the sphere of these principal rights there develops a whole system of particular rights which, together with remuneration for work, determine the correct relationship between worker and employer. Among these rights there should never be overlooked the right to a working environment and to manufacturing processes which are not harmful to the workers' physical health or to their moral integrity.

Importance of Unions

20. All these rights, together with the need for the workers themselves to secure them, give rise to yet another right: the right of association, that is, to form associations for the purpose of defending the vital interests of those employed in the various professions. These associations are called labor or trade unions. The vital interests of the workers are to a certain extent common for all of them; at the same time, however, each type of work, each profession, has its own specific character which should find a particular reflection in these organizations.

In a sense, unions go back to the medieval guilds of artisans, insofar as those organizations brought together people belonging to the same craft and thus on the basis of their work. However, unions differ from the guilds on this essential point: The modern unions grew up from the struggle of the workers—workers in general but especially the industrial workers—to protect their just rights vis-à-vis the entrepreneurs and the owners of the means of production. Their task is to defend the existential interests of workers in all sectors in which their rights are concerned. The experience of history teaches that organizations of this type are an indispensable element of social life, especially in modern industrialized societies. Obviously this does not mean that only industrial workers can set up associations of this type. Representatives of every profession can use them to ensure their own rights. Thus there are unions of agricultural workers and of white-collar workers; there are also employers' associations. All, as has been said above, are further divided into groups or subgroups according to particular professional specializations.

Catholic social teaching does not hold that unions are no more than a reflection of the "class" structure of society and that they are a mouthpiece for a class struggle which inevitably governs social life. They are indeed a mouthpiece for the struggle for social justice, for the just rights of working people in accordance with their individual professions. However, this struggle should be seen as a normal endeavor "for" the just good: In the present case, for the good which corresponds to the needs and merits of working people associated by profession; but it is not a struggle "against" others. Even if in controversial questions the struggle takes on a character of opposition toward others, this is because it aims at the good of social justice, not for the sake of "struggle" or in order to eliminate the opponent. It is characteristic of work that it first and foremost unites people. In this consists its social power: the power to build a community. In the final analysis, both those who work and those who manage the means of production or who own them must in some way be united in this community. In the light of this fundamental structure of all work—in the light of the fact that, in the final analysis, labor and capital are indispensable components of the process of production in any social system—it is clear that even if it is because of their work needs that people unite to secure their rights, their union remains a constructive factor of social order and solidarity, and it is impossible to ignore it.

Just efforts to secure the rights of workers who are united by the same profession should always take into account the limitations imposed by the general economic situation of the country. Union demands cannot be turned into a kind of group or class "egoism," although they can and should also aim at correcting—with a view to the common good of the whole of society—everything defective in the system of ownership of the means of production or in the way these are managed. Social and socioeconomic life is certainly like a system of "connected vessels," and every social activity directed toward safeguarding the rights of particular groups should adapt itself to this system.

In this sense, union activity undoubtedly enters the field of politics, understood as prudent concern for the common good. However, the role of unions is not to "play politics" in the sense that the expression is commonly understood today. Unions do not have the character of political parties struggling for power; they should not be subjected to the decision of political parties or have too close links with them. In fact, in such a situation they easily lose contact with their specific role, which is to secure the just rights of workers within the framework of the common good of the whole of society; instead they become an instrument used for other purposes.

Speaking of the protection of the just rights of workers according to their individual professions, we must of course always keep in mind that which determines the subjective character of work in each profession, but at the same time, indeed before all else, we must keep in mind that which conditions the specific dignity of the subject of the work. The activity of union organizations opens up many possibilities in this respect, including their efforts to instruct and educate the workers and to foster their self-education. Praise is due to the work of the schools, what are known as workers' or people's universities and the training programs and courses which have developed and are still developing this field of activity. It is always to be hoped that, thanks to the work of their unions, workers will not only have more, but above all be more: in other words that they will realize their humanity more fully in every respect.

One method used by unions in pursuing the just rights of their members is the strike or work stoppage, as a kind of ultimatum to the competent bodies, especially the employers. This method is recognized by Catholic social teaching as legitimate in the proper conditions and within just limits.

In this connection workers should be assured the right to strike, without being subjected to personal penal sanctions for taking part in a strike. While admitting that it is a legitimate means, we must at the same time emphasize that a strike remains, in a sense, an extreme means. It must not be abused; it must not be abused especially for "political" purposes.

Furthermore, it must never be forgotten that, when essential community services are in question, they must in every case be ensured, if necessary by means of appropriate legislation. Abuse of the strike weapon can lead to the paralysis of the whole of socioeconomic life, and this is contrary to the requirements of the common good of society, which also corresponds to the properly understood nature of work itself.

Dignity of Agricultural Work

21. All that has been said thus far on the dignity of work, on the objective and subjective dimensions of human work, can be directly applied to the question of agricultural work and to the situation of the person who cultivates the earth by toiling in the fields.

This is a vast sector of work on our planet, a sector not restricted to one or other continent, nor limited to the societies which have already attained a

certain level of development and progress. The world of agriculture, which provides society with the goods it needs for its daily sustenance, is of fundamental importance.

The conditions of the rural population and of agricultural work vary from place to place, and the social position of agricultural workers differs from country to country. This depends not only on the level of development of agricultural technology but also, and perhaps more, on the recognition of the just rights of agricultural workers and, finally, on the level of awareness regarding the social ethics of work.

Agricultural work involves considerable difficulties, including unremitting and sometimes exhausting physical effort and a lack of appreciation on the part of society, to the point of making agricultural people feel that they are social outcasts and speeding up the phenomenon of their mass exodus from the countryside to the cities and unfortunately to still more dehumanizing living conditions. Added to this are the lack of adequate professional training and of proper equipment, the spread of a certain individualism, and also objectively unjust situations. In certain developing countries, millions of people are forced to cultivate the land belonging to others and are exploited by the big landowners, without any hope of ever being able to gain possession of even a small piece of land of their own. There is a lack of forms of legal protection for the agricultural workers themselves and for their families in case of old age, sickness or unemployment. Long days of hard physical work are paid miserably. Land which could be cultivated is left abandoned by the owners. Legal titles to possession of a small portion of land that someone has personally cultivated for years are disregarded or left defenseless against the "land hunger" of more powerful individuals or groups. But even in the economically developed countries, where scientific research, technological achievements, and state policy have brought agriculture to a very advanced level, the right to work can be infringed when the farmworkers are denied the possibility of sharing in decisions concerning their services, or when they are denied the right to free association with a view to their just advancement socially, culturally, and economically.

In many situations radical and urgent changes are therefore needed in order to restore to agriculture—and to rural people—their just value as the basis for a healthy economy, within the social community's development as a whole. Thus it is necessary to proclaim and promote the dignity of work, of all work but especially of agricultural work, in which man so eloquently "subdues" the earth he has received as a gift from God and affirms his "dominion" in the visible world.

The Disabled Person and Work

22. Recently, national communities and international organizations have turned their attention to another question connected with work, one full of implications: the question of disabled people. They too are fully human sub-

jects with corresponding innate, sacred, and inviolable rights, and, in spite of the limitations and sufferings affecting their bodies and faculties, they point up more clearly the dignity and greatness of man. Since disabled people are subjects with all their rights, they should be helped to participate in the life of society in all its aspects and at all the levels accessible to their capacities. The disabled person is one of us and participates fully in the same humanity that we possess. It would be radically unworthy of man, and a denial of our common humanity, to admit to the life of the community, and thus admit to work, only those who are fully functional. To do so would be to practice a serious form of discrimination, that of the strong and healthy against the weak and sick. Work in the objective sense should be subordinated, in this circumstance too, to the dignity of man, to the subject of work and not to economic advantage.

The various bodies involved in the world of labor, both the direct and the indirect employer, should therefore, by means of effective and appropriate measures, foster the right of disabled people to professional training and work, so that they can be given a productive activity suited to them. Many practical problems arise at this point, as well as legal and economic ones; but the community, that is to say, the public authorities, associations and intermediate groups, business enterprises, and the disabled themselves should pool their ideas and resources so as to attain this goal that must not be shirked: that disabled people may be offered work according to their capabilities, for this is demanded by their dignity as persons and as subjects of work. Each community will be able to set up suitable structures for finding or creating jobs for such people both in the usual public or private enterprises, by offering them ordinary or suitably adapted jobs, and in what are called "protected" enterprises and surroundings.

Careful attention must be devoted to the physical and psychological working conditions of disabled people—as for all workers—to their just remuneration, to the possibility of their promotion, and to the elimination of various obstacles. Without hiding the fact that this is a complex and difficult task, it is to be hoped that a correct concept of labor in the subjective sense will produce a situation which will make it possible for disabled people to feel that they are not cut off from the working world or dependent upon society, but that they are full-scale subjects of work, useful, respected for their human dignity and called to contribute to the progress and welfare of their families and of the community according to their particular capacities.

Work and the Emigration Question

23. Finally, we must say at least a few words on the subject of emigration in search of work. This is an age-old phenomenon which nevertheless continues to be repeated and is still today very widespread as a result of the complexities of modern life.

Man has the right to leave his native land for various motives—and also the right to return—in order to seek better conditions of life in another country.

This fact is certainly not without difficulties of various kinds. Above all it generally constitutes a loss for the country which is left behind. It is the departure of a person who is also a member of a great community united by history, tradition, and culture; and that person must begin life in the midst of another society united by a different culture and very often by a different language. In this case, it is the loss of a subject of work, whose efforts of mind and body could contribute to the common good of his own country, but these efforts, this contribution, are instead offered to another society which in a sense has less right to them than the person's country of origin.

Nevertheless, even if emigration is in some aspects an evil, in certain circumstances it is, as the phrase goes, a necessary evil. Everything should be done—and certainly much is being done to this end—to prevent this material evil from causing greater moral harm; indeed every possible effort should be made to ensure that it may bring benefit to the emigrant's personal, family, and social life, both for the country to which he goes and the country which he leaves. In this area much depends on just legislation, in particular with regard to the rights of workers. It is obvious that the question of just legislation enters into the context of the present considerations, especially from the point of view of these rights.

The most important thing is that the person working away from his native land, whether as a permanent emigrant or as a seasonal worker, should not be placed at a disadvantage in comparison with the other workers in that society in the matter of working rights. Emigration in search of work must in no way become an opportunity for financial or social exploitation. As regards the work relationship, the same criteria should be applied to immigrant workers as to all other workers in the society concerned. The value of work should be measured by the same standard and not according to the difference in nationality, religion, or race. For even greater reason the situation of constraint in which the emigrant may find himself should not be exploited. All these circumstances should categorically give way, after special qualifications have of course been taken into consideration, to the fundamental value of work, which is bound up with the dignity of the human person. Once more the fundamental principle must be repeated: the hierarchy of values and the profound meaning of work itself require that capital should be at the service of labor and not labor at the service of capital.

5. ELEMENTS FOR A SPIRITUALITY OF WORK

A Particular Task for the Church

24. It is right to devote the last part of these reflections about human work, on the occasion of the ninetieth anniversary of the encyclical *Rerum Novarum*, to the spirituality of work in the Christian sense. Since work in its subjective aspect is always a personal action, an "actus personae," it follows that the whole person, body and spirit, participates in it, whether it is manual or intel-

lectual work. It is also to the whole person that the word of the living God is directed, the evangelical message of salvation, in which we find many points which concern human work and which throw particular light on it.

These points need to be properly assimilated: an inner effort on the part of the human spirit, guided by faith, hope and charity, is needed in order that through these points the work of the individual human being may be given the meaning which it has in the eyes of God and by means of which work enters into the salvation process on a par with the other ordinary yet particularly important components of its texture.

The church considers it her duty to speak out on work from the viewpoint of its human value and of the moral order to which it belongs, and she sees this as one of her important tasks within the service that she renders to the evangelical message as a whole.

At the same time she sees it as her particular duty to form a spirituality of work which will help all people to come closer, through work, to God, the Creator and Redeemer, to participate in his salvific plan for man and the world and to deepen their friendship with Christ in their lives by accepting, through faith, a living participation in his threefold mission as priest, prophet, and king as the Second Vatican Council so eloquently teaches.

Work as a Sharing in the Activity of the Creator

25. As the Second Vatican Council says, ". . . throughout the course of the centuries, men have labored to better the circumstances of their lives through a monumental amount of individual and collective effort. To believers, this point is settled: Considered in itself, such human activity accords with God's will. For man, created to God's image, received a mandate to subject to himself the earth and all that it contains, and to govern the world with justice and holiness; a mandate to relate himself and the totality of things to him who was to be acknowledged as the Lord and creator of all. Thus, by the subjection of all things to man, the name of God would be wonderful in all the earth."[27]

The word of God's revelation is profoundly marked by the fundamental truth that man, created in the image of God, shares by his work in the activity of the creator and that, within the limits of his own human capabilities, man in a sense continues to develop that activity, and perfects it as he advances further and further in the discovery of the resources and values contained in the whole of creation. We find this truth at the very beginning of sacred scripture, in the book of Genesis, where the creation activity itself is presented in the form of "work" done by God during "six days,"[28] "resting" on the seventh day.[29] Besides, the last book of sacred scripture echoes the same respect for what God has done through his creative "work" when it proclaims: "Great and wonderful are your deeds, O Lord God the Almighty"[30]; this is similar to the book of Genesis, which concludes the description of each day of creation with the statement: "And God saw that it was good."[31]

This description of creation, which we find in the very first chapter of the book of Genesis, is also in a sense the first "gospel of work." For it shows what the dignity of work consists of: It teaches that man ought to imitate God, his creator, in working, because man alone has the unique characteristic of likeness to God. Man ought to imitate God both in working and also in resting, since God himself wished to present his own creative activity under the form of work and rest.

This activity by God in the world always continues, as the words of Christ attest: "My father is working still . . ."[32]; he works with creative power by sustaining in existence the world that he called into being from nothing, and he works with salvific power in the hearts of those whom from the beginning he has destined for "rest"[33] in union with himself in his "father's house."[34]

Therefore man's work too not only requires a rest every "seventh day,"[35] but also cannot consist in the mere exercise of human strength in external action; it must leave room for man to prepare himself, by becoming more and more what in the will of God he ought to be, for the "rest" that the Lord reserves for his servants and friends.[36]

Awareness that man's work is a participation in God's activity ought to permeate, as the Council teaches, even "the most ordinary everyday activities. For, while providing the substance of life for themselves and their families, men and women are performing their activities in a way which appropriately benefits society. They can justly consider that by their labor they are unfolding the Creator's work, consulting the advantages of their brothers and sisters, and contributing by their personal industry to the realization in history of the divine plan."[37]

This Christian spirituality of work should be a heritage shared by all. Especially in the modern age, the spirituality of work should show the maturity called for by the tensions and restlessness of mind and heart.

"Far from thinking that works produced by man's own talent and energy are in opposition to God's power, and that the rational creature exists as a kind of rival to the Creator, Christians are convinced that the triumphs of the human race are a sign of God's greatness and the flowering of his own mysterious design. For the greater man's power becomes, the farther his individual and community responsibility extends. . . . People are not deterred by the Christian message from building up the world, or impelled to neglect the welfare of their fellows. They are, rather, more stringently bound to do these very things."[38]

The knowledge that by means of work man shares in the work of creation constitutes the most profound motive for undertaking it in various sectors. "The faithful, therefore," we read in the constitution *Lumen Gentium*, "must learn the deepest meaning and the value of all creation, and its orientation to the praise of God. Even by their secular activity they must assist one another to live holier lives.

"In this way the world will be permeated by the spirit of Christ and more effectively achieve its purpose in justice, charity, and peace. . . . Therefore,

by their competence in secular fields and by their personal activity, elevated from within by the grace of Christ, let them work vigorously so that by human labor, technical skill, and civil culture, created goods may be perfected according to the design of the Creator and the light of his word."[39]

Christ, The Man of Work

26. The truth that by means of work man participates in the activity of God himself, his Creator, was given particular prominence by Jesus Christ—the Jesus at whom many of his first listeners in Nazareth "were astonished, saying, 'Where did this man get all this? What is the wisdom given to him? . . . Is not this the carpenter?' "[40]

For Jesus not only proclaimed but first and foremost fulfilled by his deeds the "Gospel," the word of eternal wisdom, that had been entrusted to him. Therefore, this was also "the gospel of work," because he who proclaimed it was himself a man of work, a craftsman like Joseph of Nazareth.[41] And if we do not find in his words a special command to work—but rather on one occasion a prohibition against too much anxiety about work and life[42]—at the same time the eloquence of the life of Christ is unequivocal: He belongs to the "working world," he has appreciation and respect for human work. It can indeed be said that he looks with love upon human work and the different forms that it takes, seeing in each one of these forms a particular facet of man's likeness with God, the Creator and Father. Is it not he who says: "My Father is the vinedresser,"[43] and in various ways puts into his teaching the fundamental truth about work which is already expressed in the whole tradition of the Old Testament, beginning with the book of Genesis?

The books of the Old Testament contain many references to human work and to the individual professions exercised by man: for example, the doctor,[44] the pharmacist,[45] the craftsman or artist,[46] the blacksmith[47]—we could apply these words to today's foundry workers—the potter,[48] the farmer,[49] the scholar,[50] the sailor,[51] the builder,[52] the musician,[53] the shepherd,[54] and the fisherman.[55]

The words of praise for the work of women are well-known.[56] In his parables on the kingdom of God, Jesus Christ constantly refers to human work: that of the shepherd,[57] the farmer,[58] the doctor,[59] the sower,[60] the householder,[61] the servant,[62] the steward,[63] the fisherman,[64] the merchant,[65] the laborer.[66] He also speaks of the various forms of women's work.[67] He compares the apostolate to the manual work of harvesters[68] or fishermen.[69] He refers to the work of scholars too.[70]

This teaching of Christ on work, based on the example of his life during his years in Nazareth, finds a particularly lively echo in the teaching of the Apostle Paul. Paul boasts of working at his trade (he was probably a tentmaker),[71] and thanks to that work he was able even as an apostle to earn his own bread.[72]

"With toil and labor we worked night and day, that we might not burden any of you."[73] Hence his instructions, in the form of exhortation and command,

on the subject of work: "Now such persons we command and exhort in the Lord Jesus Christ to do their work in quietness and to earn their own living," he writes to the Thessalonians.[74] In fact, noting that some "are living in idleness . . . not doing any work,"[75] the apostle does not hesitate to say in the same context: "If any one will not work, let him not eat."[76] In another passage he encourages his readers: "Whatever your task, work heartily, as serving the Lord and not men, knowing that from the Lord you will receive the inheritance as your reward."[77]

The teachings of the apostle of the Gentiles obviously have key importance for the morality and spirituality of human work. They are an important complement to the great though discreet gospel of work that we find in the life and parables of Christ, in what Jesus "did and taught."[78]

On the basis of these illuminations emanating from the source himself, the church has always proclaimed what we find expressed in modern terms in the teaching of the Second Vatican Council: "Just as human activity proceeds from man, so it is ordered toward man. For when a man works he not only alters things and society, he develops himself as well. He learns much, he cultivates his resources, he goes outside of himself and beyond himself. Rightly understood, this kind of growth is of greater value than any external riches which can be garnered. . . . Hence, the norm of human activity is this: that in accord with the divine plan and will it should harmonize with the genuine good of the human race, and allow people as individuals and as members of society to pursue their total vocation and fulfill it."[79]

Such a vision of the values of human work, or in other words such a spirituality of work, fully explains what we read in the same section of the Council's pastoral constitution with regard to the right meaning of progress: "A person is more precious for what he is than for what he has. Similarly, all that people do to obtain greater justice, wider brotherhood, and a more humane ordering of social relationships has greater worth than technical advances. For these advances can supply the material for human progress, but of themselves alone they can never actually bring it about."[80]

This teaching on the question of progress and development—a subject that dominates present-day thought—can be understood only as the fruit of a tested spirituality of human work; and it is only on the basis of such a spirituality that it can be realized and put into practice. This is the teaching, and also the program, that has its roots in "the gospel of work."

Human Work in the Light of the Cross and the Resurrection of Christ

27. There is yet another aspect of human work, an essential dimension of it, that is profoundly imbued with the spirituality based on the Gospel. All work, whether manual or intellectual, is inevitably linked with toil. The book of Genesis expresses it in a truly penetrating manner: The original blessing of work contained in the very mystery of creation and connected with man's elevation as the image of God is contrasted with the curse that sin brought with it:

"Cursed is the ground because of you; in toil you shall eat of it all the days of your life."[81] This toil connected with work marks the way of human life on earth and constitutes an announcement of death: "In the sweat of your face you shall eat bread till you return to the ground, for out of it you were taken."[82] Almost as an echo of these words, the author of one of the wisdom books says: "Then I considered all that my hands had done and the toil I had spent in doing it."[83] There is no one on earth who could not apply these words to himself.

In a sense, the final word of the Gospel on this matter as on others is found in the Paschal Mystery of Jesus Christ. It is here that we must seek an answer to these problems so important for the spirituality of human work. The Paschal Mystery contains the cross of Christ and his obedience unto death, which the Apostle contrasts with the disobedience which from the beginning has burdened man's history on earth.[84] It also contains the elevation of Christ, who by means of death on a cross returns to his disciples in the resurrection with the power of the Holy Spirit.

Sweat and toil, which work necessarily involves in the present condition of the human race, present the Christian and everyone who is called to follow Christ with the possibility of sharing lovingly in the work that Christ came to do.[85] This work of salvation came about through suffering and death on a cross. By enduring the toil of work in union with Christ crucified for us, man in a way collaborates with the son of God for the redemption of humanity. He shows himself a true disciple of Christ by carrying the cross in his turn every day[86] in the activity that he is called upon to perform.

Christ, "undergoing death itself for all of us sinners, taught us by example that we too must shoulder that cross which the world and the flesh inflict upon those who pursue peace and justice"; but also, at the same time, "appointed Lord by his resurrection and given all authority in heaven and on earth, Christ is now at work in people's hearts through the power of his Spirit. . . . He animates, purifies and strengthens those noble longings too by which the human family strives to make its life more human and to render the whole earth submissive to this goal."[87]

The Christian finds in human work a small part of the cross of Christ and accepts it in the same spirit of redemption in which Christ accepted his cross for us. In work, thanks to the light that penetrates us from the resurrection of Christ, we always find a glimmer of new life, of the new good, as if it were an announcement of "the new heavens and the new earth"[88] in which man and the world participate precisely through the toil that goes with work. Through toil—and never without it. On the one hand, this confirms the indispensability of the cross in the spirituality of human work; on the other hand, the cross which this toil constitutes reveals a new good springing from work itself, from work understood in depth and in all its aspects and never apart from work.

Is this new good—the fruit of human work—already a small part of that "new earth" where justice dwells?[89] If it is true that the many forms of toil that

go with man's work are a small part of the cross of Christ, what is the relationship of this new good to the resurrection of Christ? The council seeks to reply to this question also, drawing light from the very sources of the revealed word: "Therefore, while we are warned that it profits a man nothing if he gains the whole world and loses himself (cf. Luke 9:25), the expectation of a new earth must not weaken but rather stimulate our concern for cultivating this one. For here grows the body of a new human family, a body which even now is able to give some kind of foreshadowing of the new age. Earthly progress must be carefully distinguished from the growth of Christ's kingdom. Nevertheless, to the extent that the former can contribute to the better ordering of human society, it is of vital concern to the kingdom of God."[90]

In these present reflections devoted to human work we have tried to emphasize everything that seemed essential to it, since it is through man's labor that not only "the fruits of our activity" but also "human dignity, brotherhood and freedom" must increase on earth.[91] Let the Christian who listens to the word of the living God, uniting work with prayer, know the place that his work has not only in earthly progress but also in the development of the kingdom of God, to which we are all called through the power of the Holy Spirit and through the word of the Gospel.

In concluding these reactions, I gladly impart the apostolic blessing to all of you, venerable brothers and beloved sons and daughters.

I prepared this document for publication on last May 15, on the ninetieth anniversary of the encyclical *Rerum Novarum*, but it is only after my stay in the hospital that I have been able to revise it definitively.

Given at Castelgandolfo, on the 14th day of September, the Feast of the Triumph of the Cross, in the year 1981, the third of the Pontificate.

JOHN PAUL II

NOTES

1. Cf. Ps. 127(128):2; cf. also Gen. 3:17–19; Prov. 10:22; Exod. 1:8–14; Jer. 22:13.
2. Cf. Gen. 1:26.
3. Cf. Gen. 1:28.
4. Encycl. *Redemptor Hominis*, 14: AAS 71 (1979), p. 284.
5. Cf. Ps. 127(128):2.
6. Gen. 3:19.
7. Cf. Matt. 13:52.
8. Second Vatican Ecumenical Council, *Pastoral Constitution on the Church in the Modern World, Gaudium et Spes*, 38: AAS 58 (1966), p. 1055.
9. Gen. 1:27.
10. Gen. 1:28.
11. Cf. Heb. 2:17; Phil. 2:5–8.

12. Cf. Pope Pius XI, Encycl. *Quadragesimo Anno*: AAS 23 (1931), p. 221.
13. Deut. 24:15; James 5:4; and also Gen. 4:10.
14. Cf. Gen. 1:28.
15. Cf. Gen. 1:26–27.
16. Gen. 3:19.
17. Heb. 6:8; cf. Gen. 3:18.
18. Cf. Thomas Aquinas, *Summa Theologiae*, I-II, q. 40, a. 1, c.; I-II, q. 34, a. 2, ad 1.
19. Ibid.
20. Cf. Pope Pius XI, Encycl. *Quadragesimo Anno*: AAS 23 (1931), pp. 221–22.
21. Cf. John 4:38.
22. On the right to property see Thomas Aquinas, *Summa Theologiae*, I-II, q. 66, arts. 2 and 6; *De Regimine Principum*, book 1, chapters 15 and 17. On the social function of property see *Summa Theologiae*, II-II, q. 134, art. 1, ad 3.
23. Cf. Pope Pius XI, Encycl. *Quadragesimo Anno*: AAS 23 (1931), p. 199; Second Vatican Council, *Pastoral Constitution on the Church in the Modern World, Gaudium et Spes*, 68: AAS 58 (1966), pp. 1089–1090.
24. Cf. Pope John XXIII, Encycl. *Mater et Magistra:* AAS 53 (1961), p. 419.
25. Cf. Thomas Aquinas *Summa Theologiae*, II-II, q. 65, a. 2.
26. Second Vatican Ecumenical Council, *Pastoral Constitution on the Church in the Modern World, Gaudium et Spes*, 67: AAS 58 (1966), p. 1089.
27. Second Vatican Ecumenical Council, *Pastoral Constitution on the Church in the Modern World, Gaudium et Spes*, 34: AAS 58 (1966), pp. 1052–1053.
28. Cf. Gen. 2:2; Exod. 20:8, 11; Deut. 5:12–14.
29. Cf. Gen. 2:3.
30. Rev. 15:3.
31. Gen. 1:4, 10, 12, 18, 21, 25, 31.
32. John 5:17.
33. Cf. Heb. 4:1, 9–10.
34. John 14:2.
35. Cf. Deut. 5:12–14; Exod. 20:8–12.
36. Cf. Matt. 25:21.
37. Second Vatican Ecumenical Council, *Pastoral Constitution on the Church in the Modern World, Gaudium et Spes*, 34: AAS 58 (1966), pp. 1052–1053.
38. Ibid.
39. Second Vatican Ecumenical Council, *Dogmatic Constitution on the Church, Lumen Gentium*, 36: AAS 57 (1965), p. 41.
40. Mark 6:1–3.
41. Cf. Matt. 13:55.
42. Cf. Matt. 6:25–34.

43. John 15:1.
44. Cf. Sir. 38:1–3.
45. Cf. Sir. 38:4–8.
46. Cf. Exod. 31:1–5; Sir. 38:29–30.
47. Cf. Gen. 4:22; Isa. 44:12.
48. Cf. Jer. 18:3–4; Sir. 38:29–30.
49. Cf. Gen. 9:20; Is. 5:1–2.
50. Cf. Eccles. 12:9–12; Sir. 39:1–8.
51. Cf. Ps. 107(108):23–30; Wis. 14:2–3a.
52. Cf. Gen. 11:3; 2 Kings 12:12–13, 22:5–6.
53. Cf. Gen. 4:21.
54. Cf. Gen. 4:2, 37:3; Exod. 3:1; 1 Sam. 16:11; *et passim.*
55. Ezek. 47:10.
56. Cf. Prov. 31:15–27.
57. E.g. John 10:1–16.
58. Cf. Mark 12:1–12.
59. Cf. Luke 4:23.
60. Cf. Mark 4:1–9.
61. Cf. Matt. 13:52.
62. Cf. Matt. 24:45; Luke 12:42–48.
63. Cf. Luke 16:1–8.
64. Cf. Matt. 13:4, 7–50.
65. Cf. Matt. 13:45–46.
66. Cf. Matt. 20:1–6.
67. Cf. Matt. 13:33; Luke 15:8–9.
68. Cf. Matt. 9:37; John 4:35–38.
69. Cf. Matt. 4:19.
70. Cf. Matt. 13:52.
71. Cf. Acts 18:3.
72. Cf. Acts 20:34–35.
73. 2 Thess. 3:8. Saint Paul recognizes that missionaries have a right to their keep: 1 Cor. 9:6–14; Gal. 6:6; 2 Thess. 3:9; cf. Luke 10:7.
74. 2 Thess. 3:12.
75. 2 Thess. 3:11.
76. 2 Thess. 3:10.
77. Col. 3:23–24.
78. Cf. Acts 1:1.
79. Second Vatican Ecumenical Council, *Pastoral Constitution on the Church in the Modern World, Gaudium et Spes*, 35: AAS 58 (1966), p. 1053.
80. Ibid.
81. Gen. 3:17.
82. Gen. 3:19.
83. Eccles. 2:11.
84. Cf. Rom. 5:19.

85. Cf. John 17:4.

86. Cf. Luke 9:23.

87. Second Vatican Ecumenical Council, *Pastoral Constitution on the Church in the Modern World, Gaudium et Spes*, 38: AAS 58 (1966), pp. 1055–1056.

88. Cf. 2 Pet. 3:13; Rev. 21:1.

89. Cf. 2 Pet. 3:13.

90. Second Vatican Ecumenical Council, *Pastoral Constitution on the Church in the Modern World, Gaudium et Spes*, 39: AAS 58 (1966), p. 1057.

91. Ibid.

Sollicitudo Rei Socialis: *On Social Concern* *(John Paul II, 1987)*

INTRODUCTION

This encyclical was issued in December 1987 to commemorate the twentieth anniversary of *Populorum Progressio*. The encyclical reviews international relations and establishes the theme of solidarity as a central one for the pope. The encyclical has six major parts: an introduction; a celebration of *Populorum Progressio*, focusing particularly on the concept of development; a survey of the contemporary world, which highlights what the pope views as significant failures; a presentation of authentic human development; a theological interpretation of modern problems; and a concluding section, which offers several guidelines.

Much blame for the lack of development is laid at the door of the East-West blocs. The Eastern bloc is characterized as a system of Marxist collectivism and the Western as based on liberal capitalism; both are combined with industrialization. From the pope's perspective, both have caused significant international problems: the stagnation of developing countries, unacceptably exaggerated concerns of security, arms trade, and the arms race.

One remedy for these problems, especially as a means of criticizing the excesses of East-West ideologies, is to focus on authentic human development: the transcendence of the human being; a vocation to work, which is the ultimate grounding of development; and a framework of freedom and solidarity based on the dignity of the human person. The "solidarity which we propose is the path to peace and at the same time to development" (no. 39). Solidarity is a fruit of interdependence, which demands "the abandonment of the politics of blocs, the sacrifice of all forms of economic, military or political imperialism, and the transformation of mutual distrust into collaboration" (no. 39). The positive outcome is the development of a vision of a global common good based on a recognition of moral interdependence.

Several guidelines provide the structure for John Paul's vision. First is the preferential option for the poor, which applies not only to the internal life of the church but also to its social responsibilities. Second is the recognition that private property carries a "social mortgage," which means that "it has an intrinsically social function based upon and justified precisely by the principle

of the universal destination of goods" (no. 42). Third is the affirmation of religious and economic freedom, as well as the recognition of human rights through the rule of law. Finally, the pope affirms the necessity of developing nations taking responsibility for their own destiny by setting their own agenda, thus participating in the growing interdependence of the world.

Such a vision will not be easy to implement, especially given the past history of various blocs as well as the power of ideologies. Yet the vision of solidarity leading to interdependence gives a new standard, one that may perhaps lead people and governments to self-examination and to a shift in orientation.

SOLLICITUDO REI SOCIALIS

ENCYCLICAL LETTER
SOLLICITUDO REI SOCIALIS
OF THE SUPREME PONTIFF

JOHN PAUL II

To the Bishops
Priests
Religious Families
Sons and Daughters of the Church
and All People of Good Will

FOR THE TWENTIETH ANNIVERSARY OF
POPULORUM PROGRESSIO

Venerable Brothers
and Dear Sons and Daughters,
Health and the Apostolic Blessing

1. INTRODUCTION

1. The social concern of the Church, directed toward an authentic development of man and society which would respect and promote all the dimensions of the human person, has always expressed itself in the most varied ways. In recent years, one of the special means of intervention has been the magisterium of the Roman pontiffs which, beginning with the encyclical *Rerum Novarum* of Leo XIII as a point of reference,[1] has frequently dealt with the question and has sometimes made the dates of publication of the various social documents coincide with the anniversaries of that first document.[2]

The popes have not failed to throw fresh light by means of those messages upon new aspects of the social doctrine of the Church. As a result, this doctrine, beginning with the outstanding contribution of Leo XIII and enriched by the successive contributions of the magisterium, has now become an updated doctrinal "corpus." It builds up gradually, as the Church, in the fullness of the word revealed by Christ Jesus[3] and with the assistance of the Holy Spirit (cf. John 14:16, 26; 16:13–15), reads events as they unfold in the course of history. She thus seeks to lead people to respond, with the support also of rational

reflection and the human sciences, to their vocation as responsible builders of earthly society.

2. Part of this large body of social teaching is the distinguished encyclical *Populorum Progressio*,[4] which my esteemed predecessor Paul VI published on March 26, 1967.

The enduring relevance of this encyclical is easily recognized if we note the series of commemorations which took place during 1987 in various forms and in many parts of the ecclesiastical and civil world. For this same purpose, the Pontifical Commission *Iustitia et Pax* sent a circular letter to the synods of the Oriental Catholic Churches and to the Episcopal Conferences, asking for ideas and suggestions on the best way to celebrate the encyclical's anniversary, to enrich its teachings and, if need be, to update them. At the time of the twentieth anniversary, the same commission organized a solemn commemoration in which I myself took part and gave the concluding address.[5] And now, also taking into account the replies to the above-mentioned circular letter, I consider it appropriate, at the close of the year 1987, to devote an encyclical to the theme of *Populorum Progressio*.

3. In this way I wish principally to achieve *two objectives* of no little importance: on the one hand, to pay homage to this historic document of Paul VI and to its teaching; on the other hand, following in the footsteps of my esteemed predecessors in the See of Peter, to reaffirm the *continuity* of the social doctrine as well as its constant *renewal*. In effect, continuity and renewal are a proof of the *perennial value* of the teaching of the Church.

This twofold dimension is typical of her teaching in the social sphere. On the one hand it is *constant*, for it remains identical in its fundamental inspiration, in its "principles of reflection," in its "criteria of judgment," in its basic "directives for action,"[6] and above all in its vital link with the Gospel of the Lord. On the other hand, it is ever *new*, because it is subject to the necessary and opportune adaptations suggested by the changes in historical conditions and by the unceasing flow of the events which are the setting of the life of people and society.

4. I am convinced that the teachings of the encyclical *Populorum Progressio*, addressed to the people and the society of the '60s, retain all their force as an *appeal to conscience* today in the last part of the '80s, in an effort to trace the major lines of the present world always within the context of the aim and inspiration of the "development of peoples," which are still very far from being exhausted. I therefore propose to extend the impact of that message by bringing it to bear, with its possible applications, upon the present historical moment, which is no less dramatic than that of twenty years ago.

As we well know, time maintains a constant and unchanging rhythm. Today however we have the impression that it is passing *ever more quickly*, especially by reason of the multiplication and complexity of the phenomena in the midst of which we live. Consequently, the *configuration of the world* in the course of the last twenty years, while preserving certain funda-

mental constants, has undergone notable changes and presents some totally new aspects.

The present period of time, on the eve of the third Christian millennium, is characterized by a widespread expectancy, rather like a new "Advent,"[7] which to some extent touches everyone. It offers an opportunity to study the teachings of the encyclical in greater detail and to see their possible future developments.

The aim of the present *reflection* is to emphasize, through a theological investigation of the present world, the need for a fuller and more nuanced concept of development, according to the suggestions contained in the encyclical. Its aim is also to indicate some ways of putting it into effect.

2. ORIGINALITY OF THE ENCYCLICAL *POPULORUM PROGRESSIO*

5. As soon as it appeared, the document of Pope Paul VI captured the attention of public opinion by reason of its *originality*. In a concrete manner and with great clarity, it was possible to identify the above mentioned characteristics of *continuity* and *renewal* within the Church's social doctrine. The intention of rediscovering numerous aspects of this teaching, through a careful rereading of the encyclical, will therefore constitute the main thread of the present reflections.

But first I wish to say a few words about the *date* of publication: the year 1967. The very fact that Pope Paul VI chose to publish a *social encyclical* in that year invites us to consider the document in relationship to the Second Vatican Ecumenical Council, which had ended on December 8, 1965.

6. We should see something more in this than simple chronological *proximity*. The encyclical *Populorum Progressio* presents itself, in a certain way, as *a document which applies the teachings of the Council*. It not only makes continual reference to the texts of the Council,[8] but it also flows from the same concern of the Church which inspired the whole effort of the Council—and in a particular way the Pastoral Constitution *Gaudium et Spes*—to coordinate and develop a number of themes of her social teaching.

We can therefore affirm that the encyclical *Populorum Progressio* is a kind of response to the *Council's appeal* with which the Constitution *Gaudium et Spes* begins: "The joys and the hopes, the griefs and the anxieties of the people of this age, especially those who are poor or in any way afflicted, these too are the joys and hopes, the griefs and anxieties of the followers of Christ. Indeed, nothing genuinely human fails to raise an echo in their hearts."[9] These words express the *fundamental motive* inspiring the great document of the Council, which begins by noting the situation of *poverty* and of *underdevelopment* in which millions of human beings live.

This *poverty* and *underdevelopment* are, under another name, the "griefs and the anxieties" of today, of "especially those who are poor." Before this vast panorama of pain and suffering, the Council wished to suggest horizons

of joy and hope. The encyclical of Paul VI has the same purpose, in full fidelity to the inspiration of the Council.

7. There is also the *theme* of the encyclical which, in keeping with the great tradition of the Church's social teaching, takes up again in a direct manner the *new exposition* and *rich synthesis* which the Council produced, notably in the Constitution *Gaudium et Spes*.

With regard to the content and themes once again set forth by the encyclical, the following should be emphasized: the awareness of the duty of the Church, as "an expert in humanity," "to scrutinize the signs of the times and to interpret them in the light of the Gospel"[10]; the awareness, equally profound, of her mission of "service," a mission distinct from the function of the State, even when she is concerned with people's concrete situation[11]; the reference to the notorious inequalities in the situations of those same people[12]; the confirmation of the Council's teaching, a faithful echo of the centuries-old tradition of the Church regarding the "universal purpose of goods"[13]; the appreciation of the culture and the technological civilization which contribute to human liberation,[14] without failing to recognize their limits[15]; finally, on the specific theme of development, which is precisely the theme of the encyclical, the insistence on the "most serious duty" incumbent on the more developed nations "to help the developing countries."[16] The same idea of the development proposed by the encyclical flows directly from the approach which the pastoral constitution takes to this problem.[17]

These and other explicit references to the pastoral constitution lead one to conclude that the encyclical presents itself as an *application* of the Council's teaching in social matters to the specific problem of the *development* and the *underdevelopment of peoples*.

8. This brief analysis helps us to appreciate better the *originality* of the encyclical, which can be stated in *three* points.

The *first* is constituted by the *very fact* of a document, issued by the highest authority of the Catholic Church and addressed both to the Church herself and "to all people of good will,"[18] on a matter which at first sight is solely *economic* and *social*: the *development* of peoples. The term "development" is taken from the vocabulary of the social and economic sciences. From this point of view, the encyclical *Populorum Progressio* follows directly in the line of the encyclical *Rerum Novarum*, which deals with the "condition of the workers."[19] Considered superficially, both themes could seem extraneous to the legitimate concern of the Church seen as a *religious institution*—and "development" even more so than the "condition of the workers."

In continuity with the encyclical of Leo XIII, it must be recognized that the document of Paul VI possesses the merit of having emphasized the *ethical* and *cultural character* of the problems connected with development, and likewise the legitimacy and necessity of the Church's intervention in this field.

In addition, the social doctrine of the Church has once more demonstrated its character as an *application* of the word of God to people's lives and the

life of society, as well as to the earthly realities connected with them, offering "principles for reflection," "criteria of judgment," and "directives for action."[20] Here, in the document of Paul VI, one finds these three elements with a prevalently practical orientation, that is, directed toward *moral conduct.*

In consequence, when the Church concerns herself with the "development of peoples," she cannot be accused of going outside her own specific field of competence and, still less, outside the mandate received from the Lord.

9. The *second* point of *originality* of *Populorum Progressio* is shown by the *breadth of outlook* open to what is commonly called the "social question."

In fact, the encyclical *Mater et Magistra* of Pope John XXIII had already entered into this wider outlook,[21] and the Council had echoed the same in the Constitution *Gaudium et Spes.*[22] However, the social teaching of the Church had not yet reached the point of affirming with such clarity that the social question has acquired a worldwide dimension,[23] nor had this affirmation and the accompanying analysis yet been made into a "directive for action," as Paul VI did in his encyclical.

Such an explicit taking up of a position offers a *great wealth* of content, which it is appropriate to point out.

In the first place a *possible misunderstanding* has to be eliminated. Recognition that the "social question" has assumed a worldwide dimension does not at all mean that it has lost its *incisiveness* or its national and local importance. On the contrary, it means that the problems in industrial enterprises or in the workers' and union movements of a particular country or region are not to be considered as isolated cases with no connection. On the contrary they depend more and more on the influence of factors beyond regional boundaries and national frontiers.

Unfortunately, from the economic point of view, the developing countries are much more numerous than the developed ones; the multitudes of human beings who lack the goods and services offered by development are *much more numerous* than those who possess them.

We are therefore faced with a serious problem of *unequal distribution* of the means of subsistence originally meant for everybody, and thus also an unequal distribution of the benefits deriving from them. And this happens not through the *fault* of the needy people, and even less through a sort of *inevitability* dependent on natural conditions or circumstances as a whole.

The encyclical of Paul VI, in declaring that the social question has acquired worldwide dimensions, first of all points out a *moral fact*, one which has its foundation in an objective analysis of reality. In the words of the encyclical itself, "each one must be conscious" of this fact,[24] precisely because it directly concerns the conscience, which is the source of moral decisions.

In this framework, the *originality* of the encyclical consists not so much in the affirmation, historical in character, of the universality of the social question, but rather in the *moral evaluation* of this reality. Therefore political leaders, and citizens of rich countries considered as individuals, especially if they

are Christians, have *the moral obligation*, according to the degree of each one's responsibility, to *take into consideration*, in personal decisions and decisions of government, this relationship of universality, this interdependence which exists between their conduct and the poverty and underdevelopment of so many millions of people. Pope Paul's encyclical translates more succinctly the moral obligation as the "duty of solidarity"[25]; and this affirmation, even though many situations have changed in the world, has the same force and validity today as when it was written.

On the other hand, without departing from the lines of this moral vision, the *originality* of the encyclical also consists in the basic insight that the *very concept* of development, if considered in the perspective of universal interdependence, changes notably. True development *cannot* consist in the simple accumulation of wealth and in the greater availability of goods and services, if this is gained at the expense of the development of the masses, and without due consideration for the social, cultural and spiritual dimensions of the human being.[26]

10. As a *third point*, the encyclical provides a very original contribution to the social doctrine of the Church in its totality and to the very concept of development. This originality is recognizable in a phrase of the document's concluding paragraph, which can be considered as its summary, as well as its historic label: "Development is the new name for peace."[27]

In fact, if the social question has acquired a worldwide dimension, this is because *the demand for justice* can only be satisfied on that level. To ignore this demand could encourage the temptation among the victims of injustice to respond with violence, as happens at the origin of many wars. Peoples excluded from the fair distribution of the goods originally destined for all could ask themselves: why not respond with violence to those who first treat us with violence? And if the situation is examined in the light of the division of the world into ideological blocs—a division already existing in 1967—and in the light of the subsequent economic and political repercussions and dependencies, the danger is seen to be much greater.

The first consideration of the striking content of the encyclical's historic phrase may be supplemented by a second consideration to which the document itself alludes[28]: how can one justify the fact that *huge sums of money*, which could and should be used for increasing the development of peoples, are instead utilized for the enrichment of individuals or groups, or assigned to the increase of stockpiles of weapons, both in developed countries and in the developing ones, thereby upsetting the real priorities? This is even more serious given the difficulties which often hinder the direct transfer of capital set aside for helping needy countries. If "development is the new name for peace," war and military preparations are the major enemy of the integral development of peoples.

In the light of this expression of Pope Paul VI, we are thus invited to re-examine the *concept of development*. This of course is not limited to merely

satisfying material necessities through an increase of goods, while ignoring the sufferings of the many and making the selfishness of individuals and nations the principal motivation. As the Letter of St. James pointedly reminds us: "What causes wars, and what causes fightings among you? Is it not your passions that are at war in your members? You desire and do not have" (James 4:1–2).

On the contrary, in a different world, ruled by concern for the *common good* of all humanity, or by concern for the "spiritual and human development of all" instead of by the quest for individual profit, peace would be *possible* as the result of a "more perfect justice among people."[29]

Also this new element of the encyclical has a *permanent and contemporary value*, in view of the modern attitude which is so sensitive to the close link between respect for justice and the establishment of real peace.

3. SURVEY OF THE CONTEMPORARY WORLD

11. In its own time *the fundamental teaching* of the encyclical *Populorum Progressio* received great acclaim for its novel character. The social context in which we live today cannot be said to be completely *identical* to that of twenty years ago. For this reason, I now wish to conduct a brief review of some of the characteristics of today's world, in order to develop the teaching of Paul VI's encyclical, once again from the point of view of the "development of peoples."

12. The *first fact* to note is that the *hopes for development*, at that time so lively, today appear very far from being realized.

In this regard, the encyclical had no illusions. Its language, grave and at times dramatic, limited itself to stressing the seriousness of the situation and to bringing before the conscience of all the urgent obligation of contributing to its solution. In those years there was a *certain* widespread *optimism* about the possibility of overcoming, without excessive efforts, the economic backwardness of the poorer peoples, of providing them with infrastructures and assisting them in the process of industrialization.

In that historical context, over and above the efforts of each country, the United Nations Organization promoted consecutively *two decades of development*.[30] In fact, some measures, bilateral and multilateral, were taken with the aim of helping many nations, some of which had already been independent for some time, and others—the majority—being States just born from the process of decolonization. For her part, the Church felt the duty to deepen her understanding of the problems posed by the new situation, in the hope of supporting these efforts with her religious and human inspiration, in order to give them a "soul" and an effective impulse.

13. It cannot be said that these various religious, human, economic and technical initiatives have been in vain, for they have succeeded in achieving certain results. But in general, taking into account the various factors, one

cannot deny that the present situation of the world, from the point of view of development, offers a *rather negative* impression.

For this reason, I wish to call attention to a number of *general indicators*, without excluding other specific ones. Without going into an analysis of figures and statistics, it is sufficient to face squarely the reality of an *innumerable multitude of people*—children, adults and the elderly—in other words, real and unique human persons, who are suffering under the intolerable burden of poverty. There are many millions who are deprived of hope due to the fact that, in many parts of the world, their situation has noticeably worsened. Before these tragedies of total indigence and need, in which so many of *our brothers and sisters* are living, it is the Lord Jesus himself who comes to question us (cf. Matt. 25:31–46).

14. The first *negative observation* to make is the persistence and often the widening of the *gap* between the areas of the so-called developed North and the developing South. This geographical terminology is only indicative, since one cannot ignore the fact that the frontiers of wealth and poverty intersect within the societies themselves, whether developed or developing. In fact, just as social inequalities down to the level of poverty exist in rich countries, so, in parallel fashion, in the less developed countries one often sees manifestations of selfishness and a flaunting of wealth which is as disconcerting as it is scandalous.

The abundance of goods and services available in some parts of the world, particularly in the developed North, is matched in the South by an unacceptable delay, and it is precisely in this geopolitical area that the major part of the human race lives.

Looking at all the various sectors—the production and distribution of foodstuffs, hygiene, health and housing, availability of drinking water, working conditions (especially for women), life expectancy, and other economic and social indicators—the general picture is a disappointing one, both considered in itself and in relation to the corresponding data of the more developed countries. The word *gap* returns spontaneously to mind.

Perhaps this is not the appropriate word for indicating the true reality, since it could give the impression of a *stationary* phenomenon. This is not the case. The *pace of progress* in the developed and developing countries in recent years has differed, and this serves to widen the distances. Thus the developing countries, especially the poorest of them, find themselves in a situation of very serious delay.

We must also add the *differences of culture* and *value systems* between the various population groups, differences which do not always match the degree of *economic development*, but which help to create distances. These are elements and aspects which render *the social question much more complex*, precisely because this question has assumed a universal dimension.

As we observe the various parts of the world separated by this widening gap, and note that each of these parts seems to follow its own path with its own

achievements, we can understand the current usage which speaks of different worlds within our *one world*: the First World, the Second World, the Third World, and at times the Fourth World.[31] Such expressions, which obviously do not claim to classify exhaustively all countries, are significant: they are a sign of a widespread sense that the *unity of the world*, that is, *the unity of the human race*, is seriously compromised. Such phraseology, beyond its more or less objective value, undoubtedly conceals a *moral content*, before which the Church, which is a "sacrament or sign and instrument . . . of the unity of the whole human race,"[32] cannot remain indifferent.

15. However, the picture just given would be incomplete if one failed to add to the "economic and social indices" of underdevelopment other indices which are equally negative and indeed even more disturbing, beginning with the cultural level. These are *illiteracy*, the difficulty or impossibility of obtaining *higher education*, the inability to share in the *building of one's own nation*, the *various forms of exploitation* and of economic, social, political and even religious *oppression* of the individual and his or her rights, *discrimination of every type*, especially the exceptionally odious form based on difference of race. If some of these scourges are noted with regret in areas of the more developed North, they are undoubtedly more frequent, more lasting and more difficult to root out in the developing and less advanced countries.

It should be noted that in today's world, among other rights, *the right of economic initiative* is often suppressed. Yet it is a right which is important not only for the individual but also for the common good. Experience shows us that the denial of this right, or its limitation in the name of an alleged "equality" of everyone in society, diminishes, or in practice absolutely destroys the spirit of initiative, that is to say *the creative subjectivity of the citizen*. As a consequence, there arises, not so much a true equality as a "leveling down." In the place of creative initiative there appears passivity, dependence and submission to the bureaucratic apparatus which, as the only "ordering" and "decision-making" body—if not also the "owner"—of the entire totality of goods and the means of production, puts everyone in a position of almost absolute dependence, which is similar to the traditional dependence of the worker-proletarian in capitalism. This provokes a sense of frustration or desperation and predisposes people to opt out of national life, impelling many to emigrate and also favoring a form of "psychological" emigration.

Such a situation has its consequences also from the point of view of the "rights of the individual nations." In fact, it often happens that a nation is deprived of its subjectivity, that is to say the "sovereignty" which is its right, in its economic, political-social and in a certain way cultural significance, since in a national community all these dimensions of life are bound together.

It must also be restated that no social group, for example a political party, has the right to usurp the role of sole leader, since this brings about the destruction of the true subjectivity of society of the individual citizens, as happens in every form of totalitarianism. In this situation the individual and the

people become "objects," in spite of all declarations to the contrary and verbal assurances.

We should add here that in today's world there are many other *forms of poverty*. For are there not certain privations or deprivations which deserve this name? The denial or the limitation of human rights—as for example the right to religious freedom, the right to share in the building of society, the freedom to organize and to form unions, or to take initiatives in economic matters—do these not impoverish the human person as much as, if not more than, the deprivation of material goods? And is development which does not take into account the full affirmation of these rights really development on the human level?

In brief, modern underdevelopment is not only economic but also cultural, political and simply human, as was indicated twenty years ago by the encyclical *Populorum Progressio*. Hence at this point we have to ask ourselves if the sad reality of today might not be, at least in part, the result of a *too narrow idea* of development, that is, a mainly economic one.

16. It should be noted that in spite of the praiseworthy efforts made in the last two decades by the more developed or developing nations and the international organizations to find a way out of the situation, or at least to remedy some of its symptoms, the conditions have become *notably worse*.

Responsibility for this deterioration is due to various causes. Notable among them are undoubtedly grave instances of omissions on the part of the developing nations themselves, and especially on the part of those holding economic and political power. Nor can we pretend not to see the responsibility of the developed nations, which have not always, at least in due measure, felt the duty to help countries separated from the affluent world to which they themselves belong.

Moreover, one must denounce the existence of economic, financial, and social *mechanisms* which, although they are manipulated by people, often function almost automatically, thus accentuating the situation of wealth for some and poverty for the rest. These mechanisms, which are maneuvered directly or indirectly by the more developed countries, by their very functioning favor the interests of the people manipulating them. But in the end they suffocate or condition the economies of the less developed countries. Later on these mechanisms will have to be subjected to a careful analysis under the ethical-moral aspect.

Populorum Progressio already foresaw the possibility that under such systems the wealth of the rich would increase and the poverty of the poor would remain.[33] A proof of this forecast has been the appearance of the so-called Fourth World.

17. However much society worldwide shows signs of fragmentation, expressed in the conventional names First, Second, Third, and even Fourth World, their *interdependence* remains close. When this interdependence is separated from its ethical requirements, it has *disastrous consequences* for

the weakest. Indeed, as a result of a sort of internal dynamic and under the impulse of mechanisms which can only be called perverse, this *interdependence* triggers *negative effects* even in the rich countries. It is precisely within these countries that one encounters, though on a lesser scale, the *more specific manifestations* of underdevelopment. Thus it should be obvious that development either becomes shared in *common* by every part of the world or it undergoes a *process of regression* even in zones marked by constant progress. This tells us a great deal about the nature of *authentic* development: either *all* the nations of the world participate, or it will not be true development.

Among the *specific signs* of underdevelopment which increasingly affect the developed countries also, there are two in particular that reveal a tragic situation. The *first* is the *housing crisis*. During this International Year of the Homeless proclaimed by the United Nations, attention is focused on the millions of human beings lacking adequate housing or with no housing at all, in order to awaken everyone's conscience and to find a solution to this serious problem with its negative consequences for the individual, the family, and society.[34]

The lack of housing is being experienced *universally* and is due in large measure to the growing phenomenon of urbanization.[35] Even the most highly developed peoples present the sad spectacle of individuals and families literally struggling to survive, without a *roof* over their heads or with a roof *so inadequate* as to constitute no roof at all.

The lack of housing, an extremely serious problem in itself, should be seen as a sign and summing-up of a whole series of shortcomings: economic, social, cultural or simply human in nature. Given the extent of the problem, we should need little convincing of how far we are from an authentic development of peoples.

18. *Another indicator* common to the vast majority of nations is the phenomenon of *unemployment* and *underemployment*.

Everyone recognizes the *reality* and *growing seriousness* of this problem in the industrialized countries.[36] While it is alarming in the developing countries, with their high rate of population growth and their large numbers of young people, in the countries of high economic development the *sources of work* seem to be shrinking, and thus the opportunities for employment are decreasing rather than increasing.

This phenomenon too, with its series of negative consequences for individuals and for society, ranging from humiliation to the loss of that self-respect which every man and woman should have, prompts us to question seriously the type of development which has been followed over the past twenty years. Here the words of the encyclical *Laborem Exercens* are extremely appropriate: "It must be stressed that the constitutive element in the *progress* and also the most adequate *way to verify it* in a spirit of justice and peace, which the Church proclaims and for which she does not cease to pray . . . is *the continual reappraisal of man's work*, both in the aspect of its objective finality and in the aspect of the

dignity of the subject of all work, that is to say, man." On the other hand, "we cannot fail to be struck by *a disconcerting fact* of immense proportions: the fact that . . . there are huge numbers of people who are unemployed . . . a fact that without any doubt demonstrates that both within the individual political communities and in their relationships on the continental and world level there is something wrong with the organization of work and employment, precisely at the most critical and socially most important points."[37]

This second phenomenon, like the previous one, because it is *universal* in character and tends to *proliferate*, is a very telling negative sign of the state and the quality of the development of peoples which we see today.

19. A *third phenomenon*, likewise characteristic of the most recent period, even though it is not met with everywhere, is without doubt equally indicative of the *interdependence* between developed and less developed countries. It is the question of the *international debt*, concerning which the Pontifical Commission *Iustitia et Pax* has issued a document.[38]

At this point one cannot ignore the *close connection* between a problem of this kind—the growing seriousness of which was already foreseen in *Populorum Progressio*[39]—and the question of the development of peoples.

The reason which prompted the developing peoples to accept the offer of abundantly available capital was the hope of being able to invest it in development projects. Thus the availability of capital and the fact of accepting it as a loan can be considered a contribution to development, something desirable and legitimate in itself, even though perhaps imprudent and occasionally hasty.

Circumstances have changed, both within the debtor nations and in the international financial market; the instrument chosen to make a contribution to development has turned into a *counterproductive mechanism*. This is because the debtor nations, in order to service their debt, find themselves obliged to export the capital needed for improving or at least maintaining their standard of living. It is also because, for the same reason, they are unable to obtain new and equally essential financing.

Through this mechanism, the means intended for the development of peoples has turned into a *brake* upon development instead, and indeed in some cases has even *aggravated underdevelopment*.

As the recent document of the Pontifical Commission *Iustitia et Pax* states,[40] these observations should make us reflect on the *ethical character* of the interdependence of peoples. And along similar lines, they should make us reflect on the requirements and conditions, equally inspired by ethical principles, for cooperation in development.

20. If at this point we examine the *reasons* for this serious delay in the process of development, a delay which has occurred contrary to the indications of the encyclical *Populorum Progressio*, which had raised such great hopes, our attention is especially drawn to the *political* causes of today's situation.

Faced with a combination of factors which are undoubtedly complex, we cannot hope to achieve a comprehensive analysis here. However, we cannot

ignore a striking fact about the *political picture* since the Second World War, a fact which has considerable impact on the forward movement of the development of peoples.

I am referring to the *existence of two opposing blocs*, commonly known as the East and the West. The reason for this description is not purely political but is also, as the expression goes, *geopolitical*. Each of the two blocs tends to assimilate or gather around it other countries or groups of countries, to different degrees of adherence or participation.

The opposition is first of all *political*, inasmuch as each bloc identifies itself with a system of organizing society and exercising power which presents itself as an alternative to the other. The political opposition, in turn, takes its origin from a deeper opposition which is *ideological* in nature.

In the West there exists a system which is historically inspired by the principles of the *liberal capitalism* which developed with industrialization during the last century. In the East there exists a system inspired by the *Marxist collectivism* which sprang from an interpretation of the condition of the proletarian classes made in the light of a particular reading of history. Each of the two ideologies, on the basis of two very different visions of man and of his freedom and social role, has proposed and still promotes, on the economic level, antithetical forms of the organization of labor and of the structures of ownership, especially with regard to the so-called means of production.

It was inevitable that by developing antagonistic systems and centers of power, each with its own forms of propaganda and indoctrination, the *ideological opposition* should evolve into a growing *military opposition* and give rise to two blocs of armed forces, each suspicious and fearful of the other's domination.

International relations, in turn, could not fail to feel the effects of this "logic of blocs" and of the respective "spheres of influence." The tension between the two blocs which began at the end of the Second World War has dominated the whole of the subsequent forty years. Sometimes it has taken the form of "*cold war*," sometimes of "*wars by proxy*," through the manipulation of local conflicts, and sometimes it has kept people's minds in suspense and anguish by the threat of an *open and total war*.

Although at the present time this danger seems to have receded, yet without completely disappearing, and even though an initial agreement has been reached on the destruction of one type of nuclear weapon, the existence and opposition of the blocs continue to be a real and worrying fact which still colors the world picture.

21. This happens with particularly negative effects in international relations which concern the developing countries. For as we know the tension *between East and West* is not in itself an opposition between two different *levels* of development but rather between two *concepts* of the development of individuals and peoples, both concepts being imperfect and in need of radical correction. This opposition is transferred to the developing countries

themselves, and thus helps to widen the gap already existing on the economic level between *North and South* and which results from the distance between the two *worlds*: the more developed one and the less developed one.

This is one of the reasons why the Church's social doctrine adopts a critical attitude toward both liberal capitalism and Marxist collectivism. For from the point of view of development the question naturally arises: in what way and to what extent are these two systems capable of changes and updatings such as to favor or promote a true and integral development of individuals and peoples in modern society? In fact, these changes and updatings are urgent and essential for the cause of a development common to all.

Countries which have recently achieved independence, and which are trying to establish a cultural and political identity of their own, and need effective and impartial aid from all the richer and more developed countries, find themselves involved in, and sometimes overwhelmed by, ideological conflicts, which inevitably create internal divisions, to the extent in some cases of provoking full civil war. This is also because investments and aid for development are often diverted from their proper purpose and in opposition to the interests of the countries which ought to benefit from them. Many of these countries are becoming more and more aware of the danger of falling victim to a form of neocolonialism and are trying to escape from it. It is this awareness which in spite of difficulties, uncertainties and at times contradictions gave rise to the *International Movement of Non-Aligned Nations*, which, in its positive aspect, would like to affirm in an effective way the right of every people to its own identity, independence and security, as well as the right to share, on a basis of equality and solidarity, in the goods intended for all.

22. In the light of these considerations, we easily arrive at a clearer picture of the last twenty years and a better understanding of the conflicts in the northern hemisphere, namely between East and West, as an important cause of the retardation or stagnation of the South.

The developing countries, instead of becoming *autonomous nations* concerned with their own progress toward a just sharing in the goods and services meant for all, become parts of a machine, cogs on a gigantic wheel. This is often true also in the field of social communications, which, being run by centers mostly in the northern hemisphere, do not always give due consideration to the priorities and problems of such countries or respect their cultural make-up. They frequently impose a distorted vision of life and of man and thus fail to respond to the demands of true development.

Each of the two *blocs* harbors in its own way a tendency toward *imperialism*, as it is usually called, or towards forms of neocolonialism: an easy temptation to which they frequently succumb, as history, including recent history, teaches.

It is this abnormal situation, the result of a war and of an unacceptably exaggerated concern *for security*, which deadens the impulse toward united cooperation by all for the common good of the human race, to the detriment

especially of peaceful peoples who are impeded from their rightful access to the goods meant for all.

Seen in this way, the present division of the world is a *direct obstacle* to the real transformation of the conditions of underdevelopment in the developing and less advanced countries. However, peoples do not always resign themselves to their fate. Furthermore, the very needs of an economy stifled by military expenditure and by bureaucracy and intrinsic inefficiency now seem to favor processes which might mitigate the existing opposition and make it easier to begin a fruitful dialogue and genuine collaboration for peace.

23. The statement in the encyclical *Populorum Progressio* that the resources and investments devoted to arms production ought to be used to alleviate the misery of impoverished peoples[41] makes more urgent the appeal to overcome the opposition between the two blocs.

Today, the reality is that these resources are used to enable each of the two blocs to overtake the other and thus guarantee its own security. Nations which historically, economically and politically have the possibility of playing a leadership role are prevented by this fundamentally flawed distortion from adequately fulfilling their duty of solidarity for the benefit of peoples which aspire to full development.

It is timely to mention—and it is no exaggeration—that a leadership role among nations can only be justified by the possibility and willingness to contribute widely and generously to the common good.

If a nation were to succumb more or less deliberately to the temptation to close in upon itself and failed to meet the responsibilities following from its superior position in the community of nations, *it would fall seriously short* of its clear ethical duty. This is readily apparent in the circumstances of history, where believers discern the dispositions of Divine Providence, ready to make use of the nations for the realization of its plans, so as to render "vain the designs of the peoples" (cf. Ps. 33/32:10).

When the West gives the impression of abandoning itself to forms of growing and selfish isolation, and the East in its turn seems to ignore for questionable reasons its duty to cooperate in the task of alleviating human misery, then we are up against not only a betrayal of humanity's legitimate expectations—a betrayal that is a harbinger of unforeseeable consequences—but also a real desertion of a moral obligation.

24. If arms production is a serious disorder in the present world with regard to true human needs and the employment of the means capable of satisfying those needs, *the arms trade* is equally to blame. Indeed, with reference to the latter it must be added that the *moral judgment is even more severe*. As we all know, this is a trade without frontiers, capable of crossing even the barriers of the blocs. It knows how to overcome the division between East and West, and above all the one between North and South, to the point—and this is more serious—of pushing its way into the *different sections* which make up the southern hemisphere. We are thus confronted with a strange phe-

nomenon: while economic aid and development plans meet with the obstacle of insuperable ideological barriers, and with tariff and trader barriers, *arms* of whatever origin circulate with almost total freedom all over the world. And as the recent document of the Pontifical Commission *Iustitia et Pax* on the international debt points out,[42] everyone knows that in certain cases the capital lent by the developed world has been used in the underdeveloped world to buy weapons.

If to all this we add the *tremendous* and universally acknowledged *danger* represented by *atomic weapons* stockpiled on an incredible scale, the logical conclusion seems to be this: in today's world, including the world of economics, the prevailing picture is one destined to lead us more quickly *toward death* rather than one of concern for *true development* which would lead all towards a "more human" life, as envisaged by the encyclical *Populorum Progressio*.[43]

The consequences of this state of affairs are to be seen in the festering of a *wound* which typifies and reveals the imbalances and conflicts of the modern world: *the millions of refugees* whom war, natural calamities, persecution, and discrimination of every kind have deprived of home, employment, family, and homeland. The tragedy of these multitudes is reflected in the hopeless faces of men, women, and children who can no longer find a home in a divided and inhospitable world.

Nor may we close our eyes to another painful wound in today's world: the phenomenon of *terrorism*, understood as the intention to kill people and destroy property indiscriminately, and to create a climate of terror and insecurity, often including the taking of hostages. Even when some ideology or the desire to create a better society is adduced as the motivation for this inhuman behavior, acts of terrorism are never justifiable. Even less so when, as happens today, such decisions and such actions, which at times lead to real massacres, and to the abduction of innocent people who have nothing to do with the conflicts, claim to have a propaganda purpose for furthering a cause. It is still worse when they are an end in themselves, so that murder is committed merely for the sake of killing. In the face of such horror and suffering, the words I spoke some years ago are still true, and I wish to repeat them again: "What Christianity forbids is to seek solutions . . . by the ways of hatred, by the murdering of defenseless people, by the methods of terrorism."[44]

25. At this point something must be said about the *demographic problem* and the way it is spoken of today, following what Paul VI said in his encyclical[45] and what I myself stated at length in the apostolic exhortation *Familiaris Consortio*.[46]

One cannot deny the existence, especially in the southern hemisphere, of a demographic problem which creates difficulties for development. One must immediately add that in the northern hemisphere the nature of this problem is reversed: here, the cause for concern is the *drop in the birthrate*, with repercussions on the aging of the population, unable even to renew itself biologically. In itself, this is a phenomenon capable of hindering development. Just as

it is incorrect to say that such difficulties stem solely from demographic growth, neither is it proved that *all* demographic growth is incompatible with orderly development.

On the other hand, it is very alarming to see governments in many countries launching *systematic campaigns* against birth, contrary not only to the cultural and religious identity of the countries themselves but also contrary to the nature of true development. It often happens that these campaigns are the result of pressure and financing coming from abroad, and in some cases they are made a condition for the granting of financial and economic aid and assistance. In any event, there is an *absolute lack of respect* for the freedom of choice of the parties involved, men and women often subjected to intolerable pressures, including economic ones, in order to force them to submit to this new form of oppression. It is the poorest populations which suffer such mistreatment, and this sometimes leads to a tendency toward a form of racism, or the promotion of certain equally racist forms of eugenics.

This fact too, which deserves the most forceful condemnation, is a *sign* of an erroneous and perverse *idea* of true human development.

26. This mainly negative overview of the *actual situation* of development in the contemporary world would be incomplete without a mention of the coexistence of *positive aspects*.

The *first* positive note is the *full awareness* among large numbers of men and women of their own dignity and of that of every human being. This awareness is expressed, for example, in the more *lively concern* that *human rights should be respected*, and in the more vigorous rejection of their violation. One sign of this is the number of recently established private associations, some worldwide in membership, almost all of them devoted to monitoring with great care and commendable objectivity what is happening *internationally* in this sensitive field.

At this level one must acknowledge the *influence* exercised by the *Declaration of Human Rights*, promulgated some forty years ago by the United Nations Organization. Its very existence and gradual acceptance by the international community are signs of a growing awareness. The same is to be said, still in the field of human rights, of other juridical instruments issued by the United Nations Organization or other international organizations.[47]

The awareness under discussion applies not only to *individuals* but also to *nations* and *peoples*, which, as entities having a specific cultural identity, are particularly sensitive to the preservation, free exercise, and promotion of their precious heritage.

At the same time, in a world divided and beset by every type of conflict, the *conviction* is growing of a radical *interdependence* and consequently of the need for a solidarity which will take up interdependence and transfer it to the moral plane. Today perhaps more than in the past, people are realizing that they are linked together by a *common destiny*, which is to be constructed together, if catastrophe for all is to be avoided. From the depth of anguish, fear

and escapist phenomena like drugs, *typical of the contemporary world*, the idea is slowly emerging that the good to which we are all called and the happiness to which we aspire cannot be obtained without an *effort and commitment on the part of all*, nobody excluded, and the consequent renouncing of personal selfishness.

Also to be mentioned here, as a sign of *respect for life*—despite all the temptations to destroy it by abortion and euthanasia—is a *concomitant concern* for peace, together with an awareness that peace is *indivisible*. It is either *for all* or *for none*. It demands an ever greater degree of rigorous respect for *justice* and consequently a fair distribution of the results of true development.[48]

Among today's *positive signs* we must also mention a greater realization of the limits of available resources, and of the need to respect the integrity and the cycles of nature and to take them into account when planning for development, rather than sacrificing them to certain demagogic ideas about the latter. Today this is called *ecological concern*.

It is also right to acknowledge the generous commitment of statesmen, politicians, economists, trade unionists, people of science, and international officials—many of them inspired by religious faith—who at no small personal sacrifice try to resolve the world's ills and who give of themselves in every way so as to ensure that an ever increasing number of people may enjoy the benefits of peace and a quality of life worthy of the name.

The great *international organizations*, and a number of the regional organizations, *contribute* to this *in no small measure*. Their united efforts make possible more effective action.

It is also through these contributions that some third-world countries, despite the burden of many negative factors, have succeeded in reaching a *certain self-sufficiency in food*, or a degree of industrialization which makes it possible to survive with dignity and to guarantee sources of employment for the active population.

Thus, *all is not negative* in the contemporary world, nor would it be, for the heavenly Father's providence lovingly watches over even our daily cares (cf. Matt. 6:25–32; 10:23–31; Luke 12:6–7, 22–30). Indeed, the positive values which we have mentioned testify to a new moral concern, particularly with respect to the great human problems such as development and peace.

This fact prompts me to turn my thoughts to the *true nature* of the development of peoples, along the lines of the encyclical which we are commemorating, and as a mark of respect for its teaching.

4. AUTHENTIC HUMAN DEVELOPMENT

27. The examination which the encyclical invites us to make of the contemporary world leads us to note in the first place that development *is not* a straightforward process, *as it were automatic* and *in itself limitless*, as though,

given certain conditions, the human race were able to progress rapidly toward an undefined perfection of some kind.[49]

Such an idea—linked to a notion of "progress" with philosophical connotations deriving from the Enlightenment, rather than to the notion of "development"[50] which is used in a specifically economic and social sense—now seems to be seriously called into doubt, particularly since the tragic experience of the two world wars, the planned and partly achieved destruction of whole peoples, and the looming atomic peril. A naive *mechanistic optimism* has been replaced by a well-founded anxiety for the fate of humanity.

28. At the same time, however, the "economic" concept itself, linked to the word development, has entered into crisis. In fact there is better understanding today that the *mere accumulation* of goods and services, even for the benefit of the majority, is not enough for the realization of human happiness. Nor, in consequence, does the availability of the many *real benefits* provided in recent times by science and technology, including the computer sciences, bring freedom from every form of slavery. On the contrary, the experience of recent years shows that unless all the considerable body of resources and potential at man's disposal is guided by a *moral understanding* and by an orientation toward the true good of the human race, it easily turns against man to oppress him.

A *disconcerting conclusion* about the most recent period should serve to enlighten us: side-by-side with the miseries of underdevelopment, themselves unacceptable, we find ourselves up against a form of *superdevelopment*, equally inadmissible, because like the former it is contrary to what is good and to true happiness. This superdevelopment, which consists in an *excessive* availability of every kind of material goods for the benefit of certain social groups, easily makes people slaves of "possession" and of immediate gratification, with no other horizon than the multiplication or continual replacement of the things already owned with others still better. This is the so-called civilization of "consumption" or "consumerism," which involves so much "throwing-away" and "waste." An object already owned but now superseded by something better is discarded, with no thought of its possible lasting value in itself, nor of some other human being who is poorer.

All of us experience firsthand the sad effects of this blind submission to pure consumerism: in the first place a crass materialism, and at the same time a *radical dissatisfaction*, because one quickly learns—unless one is shielded from the flood of publicity and the ceaseless and tempting offers of products—that the more one possesses the more one wants, while deeper aspirations remain unsatisfied and perhaps even stifled.

The encyclical of Pope Paul VI pointed out the difference, so often emphasized today, between "having" and "being,"[51] which had been expressed earlier in precise words by the Second Vatican Council.[52] To "have" objects and goods does not in itself perfect the human subject, unless it contributes to the maturing and enrichment of that subject's "being," that is to say unless it contributes to the realization of the human vocation as such.

Of course, the difference between "being" and "having," the danger inherent in a mere multiplication or replacement of things possessed compared to the value of "being," need not turn into a *contradiction*. One of the greatest injustices in the contemporary world consists precisely in this: that the ones who possess much are relatively *few* and those who possess almost nothing are *many*. It is the injustice of the poor distribution of the goods and services originally intended for all.

This then is the picture: there are some people—the few who possess much—who do not really succeed in "being" because, through a reversal of the hierarchy of values, they are hindered by the cult of "having"; and there are others—the many who have little or nothing—who do not succeed in realizing their basic human vocation because they are deprived of essential goods.

The evil does not consist in "having" as such, but in possessing without regard for the *quality* and the *ordered hierarchy* of the goods one has. *Quality and hierarchy* arise from the subordination of goods and their availability to man's "being" and his true vocation.

This shows that although *development* has a *necessary economic dimension*, since it must supply the greatest possible number of the world's inhabitants with an availability of goods essential for them "to be," it is not limited to that dimension. If it is limited to this, then it turns against those whom it is meant to benefit.

The characteristics of full development, one which is "more human" and able to sustain itself at the level of the true vocation of men and women without denying economic requirements, were described by Paul VI.[53]

29. Development which is not only economic must be measured and oriented according to the reality and vocation of man seen in his totality, namely, according to his *interior dimension*. There is no doubt that he needs created goods and the products of industry, which is constantly being enriched by scientific and technological progress. And the ever greater availability of material goods not only meets needs but also opens new horizons. The danger of the misuse of material goods and the appearance of artificial needs should in no way hinder the regard we have for the new goods and resources placed at our disposal and the use we make of them. On the contrary, we must see them as a gift from God and as a response to the human vocation, which is fully realized in Christ.

However, in trying to achieve true development we must never lose sight of that *dimension* which is in the *specific nature* of man, who has been created by God in his image and likeness (cf. Gen. 1:26). It is a bodily and a spiritual nature, symbolized in the second creation account by the two elements: the *earth*, from which God forms man's body, and the *breath of life* which he breathes into man's nostrils (cf. Gen. 2:7).

Thus man comes to have a certain affinity with other creatures: he is called to use them, and to be involved with them. As the Genesis account says (cf. Gen. 2:15), he is placed in the garden with the duty of cultivating and watching

over it, being superior to the other creatures placed by God under his dominion (cf. Gen. 1:25–26). But at the same time man must remain subject to the will of God, who imposes limits upon his use and dominion over things (cf. Gen. 2:16–17), just as he promises him immortality (cf. Gen. 2:9; Wis. 2:23). Thus man, being the image of God, has a true affinity with him too.

On the basis of this teaching, development cannot consist only in the use, dominion over and *indiscriminate* possession of created things and the products of human industry, but rather in *subordinating* the possession, dominion, and use to man's divine likeness and to his vocation to immortality. This is the *transcendent reality* of the human being, a reality which is seen to be shared from the beginning by a couple, a man and a woman (cf. Gen. 1:27), and is therefore fundamentally social.

30. According to sacred scripture therefore, the notion of development is not only "lay" or "profane," but it is also seen to be, while having a socioeconomic dimension of its own, the *modern expression* of an essential dimension of man's vocation.

The fact is that man was not created, so to speak, immobile and static. The first portrayal of him, as given in the Bible, certainly presents him as a *creature* and *image*, *defined* in his deepest reality by the *origin* and *affinity* that constitute him. But all this plants within the human being—man and woman—the *seed* and the *requirement* of a special task to be accomplished by each individually and by them as a couple. The task is "to have dominion" over the other created beings, "to cultivate the garden." This is to be accomplished within the framework of *obedience* to the divine law and therefore with respect for the image received, the image which is the clear foundation of the power of dominion recognized as belonging to man as the means to his perfection (cf. Gen. 1:26–30; 2:15–16; Wis. 9:2–3).

When man disobeys God and refuses to submit to his rule, nature rebels against him and no longer recognizes him as its "master," for he has tarnished the divine image in himself. The claim to ownership and use of created things remains still valid, but after sin its exercise becomes difficult and full of suffering (cf. Gen. 3:17–19).

In fact, the following chapter of Genesis shows us that the descendants of Cain build "a city," engage in sheep farming, practice the arts (music) and technical skills (metallurgy); while at the same time people began to "call upon the name of the Lord" (cf. Gen. 4:17–26).

The story of the human race described by sacred scripture is, even after the fall into sin, a story of *constant achievements*, which, although always called into question and threatened by sin, are nonetheless repeated, increased and extended in response to the divine vocation given from the beginning to man and woman (cf. Gen. 1:26–28) and inscribed in the image which they received.

It is logical to conclude, at least on the part of those who believe in the word of God, that today's "development" is to be seen as a moment in the story

which began at creation, a story which is constantly endangered by reason of infidelity to the Creator's will, and especially by the temptation to idolatry. But this "development" fundamentally corresponds to the first premise. Anyone wishing to renounce the *difficult yet noble task* of improving the lot of man in his totality, and of all people, with the excuse that the struggle is difficult and that constant effort is required, or simply because of the experience of defeat and the need to begin again, that person would be betraying the will of God the Creator. In this regard, in the encyclical *Laborem Exercens* I referred to man's vocation to work, in order to emphasize the idea that it is always man who is the protagonist of development.[54]

Indeed, the Lord Jesus himself, in the parable of the talents, emphasizes the severe treatment given to the man who dared to hide the gift received: "You wicked and slothful servant! You knew that I reap where I have not sowed and gather where I have not winnowed? . . . So take the talent from him, and give it to him who has the ten talents" (Matt. 25:26–28). It falls to us, who receive the gifts of God in order to make them fruitful, to "sow" and "reap." If we do not, even what we have will be taken away from us.

A deeper study of these harsh words will make us commit ourselves more resolutely to the *duty*, which is urgent for everyone today, to work together for the full development of others: "development of the whole human being and of all people."[55]

31. *Faith in Christ the Redeemer*, while it illuminates from within the nature of development, also guides us in the task of collaboration. In the Letter of St. Paul to the Colossians, we read that Christ is "the first-born of all creation," and that "all things were created through him" and for him (Col. 1:15–16). In fact, "all things hold together in him," since "in him all the fullness of God was pleased to dwell, and through him to reconcile to himself all things" (v. 20).

A part of this divine plan, which begins from eternity in Christ, the perfect "image" of the Father, and which culminates in him, "the first-born from the dead" (v. 18), *is our own history*, marked by our personal and collective effort to raise up the human condition and to overcome the obstacles which are continually arising along our way. It thus prepares us to share in the fullness which "dwells in the Lord" and which he communicates "to his body, which is the Church" (v. 18; cf. Eph. 1:22–23). At the same time sin, which is always attempting to trap us and which jeopardizes our human achievements, is conquered and redeemed by the "reconciliation" accomplished by Christ (cf. Col. 1:20).

Here the perspectives widen. The dream of "unlimited progress" reappears, radically transformed by the *new outlook* created by Christian faith, assuring us that progress is possible only because God the Father has decided from the beginning to make man a sharer of his glory in Jesus Christ risen from the dead, in whom "we have redemption through his blood . . . the forgiveness of our trespasses" (Eph. 1:7). In him God wished to conquer sin and

make it serve our greater good,[56] which infinitely surpasses what progress could achieve.

We can say therefore—as we struggle amidst the obscurities and deficiencies of *underdevelopment* and *superdevelopment*—that one day this corruptible body will put on incorruptibility, this mortal body immortality (cf. 1 Cor. 15:54), when the Lord "delivers the kingdom to God the Father" (v. 24) and all the works and actions that are worthy of man will be redeemed.

Furthermore, the concept of faith makes quite clear the reasons which impel the *Church* to concern herself with the problems of development, to consider them a *duty of her pastoral ministry*, and to urge all to think about the nature and characteristics of authentic human development. Through her commitment she desires, on the one hand, to place herself at the service of the divine plan which is meant to order all things to the fullness which dwells in Christ (cf. Col. 1:19) and which he communicated to his body; and on the other hand she desires to respond to her fundamental vocation of being a "sacrament," that is to say "a sign and instrument of intimate union with God and of the unity of the whole human race."[57]

Some Fathers of the Church were inspired by this idea to develop in original ways a concept of the *meaning of history* and of *human work*, directed toward a goal which surpasses this meaning and which is always defined by its relationship to the work of Christ. In other words, one can find in the teaching of the Fathers an *optimistic vision* of history and work, that is to say of the *perennial value* of authentic human achievements, inasmuch as they are redeemed by Christ and destined for the promised kingdom.[58]

Thus, part of the *teaching* and most ancient *practice* of the Church is her conviction that she is obliged by her vocation—she herself, her ministers and each of her members—to relieve the misery of the suffering, both far and near, not only out of her "abundance" but also out of her "necessities." Faced by cases of need, one cannot ignore them in favor of superfluous church ornaments and costly furnishings for divine worship; on the contrary it could be obligatory to sell these goods in order to provide food, drink, clothing and shelter for those who lack these things.[59] As has been already noted, here we are shown a "*hierarchy of values*"—in the framework of the right to property—between "having" and "being," especially when the "having" of a few can be to the detriment of the "being" of many others.

In his encyclical Pope Paul VI stands in the line of this teaching, taking his inspiration from the pastoral constitution *Gaudium et Spes*.[60] For my own part, I wish to insist once more on the seriousness and urgency of that teaching, and I ask the Lord to give all Christians the strength to put it faithfully into practice.

32. The obligation to commit oneself to the development of peoples is not just an *individual* duty, and still less an *individualistic* one, as if it were possible to achieve this development through the isolated efforts of each individual. It is an imperative which obliges *each and every* man and woman, as well

as societies and nations. In particular, it obliges the Catholic Church and the other churches and ecclesial communities, with which we are completely willing to collaborate in this field. In this sense, just as we Catholics invite our Christian brethren to share in our initiatives, so too we declare that we are ready to collaborate in theirs, and we welcome the invitations presented to us. In this pursuit of integral human development we can also do much with the members of other religions, as in fact is being done in various places.

Collaboration in the development of the whole person and of every human being is in fact a duty of *all towards all*, and must be shared by the four parts of the world: East and West, North and South; or, as we say today, by the different "worlds." If, on the contrary, people try to achieve it in only one part, or in only one world, they do so at the expense of the others; and, precisely because the others are ignored, their own development becomes exaggerated and misdirected.

Peoples or *nations* too have a right to their own full development, which while including—as already said—the economic and social aspects, should also include individual cultural identity and openness to the transcendent. Not even the need for development can be used as an excuse for imposing on others one's own way of life or own religious belief.

33. Nor would a type of development which did not respect and promote *human rights*—personal and social, economic and political, including the *rights of nations and peoples*—be really *worthy of man*.

Today, perhaps more than in the past, the *intrinsic contradiction* of a development limited *only* to its economic element is seen more clearly. Such development easily subjects the human person and his deepest needs to the demands of economic planning and selfish profit.

The *intrinsic connection* between authentic development and respect for human rights once again reveals the *moral* character of development: the true elevation of man, in conformity with the natural and historical vocation of each individual, is not attained *only* by exploiting the abundance of goods and services, or by having available perfect infrastructures.

When individuals and communities do not see a rigorous respect for the moral, cultural, and spiritual requirements, based on the dignity of the person and on the proper identity of each community, beginning with the family and religious societies, then all the rest—availability of goods, abundance of technical resources applied to daily life, a certain level of material well-being—will prove unsatisfying and in the end contemptible. The Lord clearly says this in the Gospel, when he calls the attention of all to the true hierarchy of values: "For what will it profit a man, if he gains the whole world and forfeits his life?" (Matt. 16:26).

True development, in keeping with the *specific* needs of the human being—man or woman, child, adult or old person—implies, especially for those who actively share in this process and are responsible for it, a lively *awareness* of the *value* of the rights of all and of each person. It likewise implies a lively

awareness of the need to respect the right of every individual to the full use of the benefits offered by science and technology.

On the *internal level* of every nation, respect for all rights takes on great importance, especially: the right to life at every stage of its existence; the rights of the family, as the basic social community, or "cell of society"; justice in employment relationships; the rights inherent in the life of the political community as such; the rights based on the *transcendent vocation* of the human being, beginning with the right of freedom to profess and practice one's own religious belief.

On the *international level*, that is, the level of relations between States or, in present-day usage, between the different "worlds," there must be complete *respect* for the identity of each people, with its own historical and cultural characteristics. It is likewise essential, as the encyclical *Populorum Progressio* already asked, to recognize each people's equal right "to be seated at the table of the common banquet,"[61] instead of lying outside the door like Lazarus, while "the dogs come and lick his sores" (cf. Luke 16:21). Both peoples and individuals must enjoy the *fundamental equality*[62] which is the basis, for example, of the Charter of the United Nations Organization: the equality which is the basis of the right of all to share in the process of full development.

In order to be genuine, development must be achieved within the framework of *solidarity* and *freedom*, without ever sacrificing either of them under whatever pretext. The moral character of development and its necessary promotion are emphasized when the most rigorous respect is given to all the demands deriving from the order of *truth* and *good* proper to the human person. Furthermore the Christian who is taught to see that man is the image of God, called to share in the truth and the good which is *God himself*, does not understand a commitment to development and its application which excludes regard and respect for the unique dignity of this "image." In other words, true development must be based on *love of God and neighbor*, and must help to promote the relationships between individuals and society. This is the "civilization of love" of which Paul VI often spoke.

34. Nor can the moral character of development exclude respect *for the beings which constitute* the natural world, which the ancient Greeks—alluding precisely to the *order* which distinguishes it—called the "cosmos." Such realities also demand respect, by virtue of a threefold consideration which it is useful to reflect upon carefully.

The *first* consideration is the appropriateness of acquiring a *growing awareness* of the fact that one cannot use with impunity the different categories of beings, whether living or inanimate—animals, plants, the natural elements—simply as one wishes, according to one's own economic needs. On the contrary, one must take into account *the nature of each being* and of its *mutual connection* in an ordered system, which is precisely the "cosmos."

The *second consideration* is based on the realization—which is perhaps more urgent—that *natural resources* are limited; some are not, as it is said,

renewable. Using them as if they were inexhaustible, with *absolute dominion*, seriously endangers their availability not only for the present generation but above all for generations to come.

The *third consideration* refers directly to the consequences of a certain type of development on the *quality of life* in the industrialized zones. We all know that the direct or indirect result of industrialization is, ever more frequently, the pollution of the environment, with serious consequences for the health of the population.

Once again it is evident that development, the planning which governs it, and the way in which resources are used must include respect for moral demands. One of the latter undoubtedly imposes limits on the use of the natural world. The dominion granted to man by the Creator is not an absolute power, nor can one speak of a freedom to "use and misuse," or to dispose of things as one pleases. The limitation imposed from the beginning by the Creator himself and expressed symbolically by the prohibition not to "eat of the fruit of the tree" (cf. Gen. 2:16–17) shows clearly enough that, when it comes to the natural world, we are subject not only to biological laws but also to moral ones, which cannot be violated with impunity.

A true concept of development cannot ignore the use of the elements of nature, the renewability of resources and the consequences of haphazard industrialization—three considerations which alert our consciences to the *moral dimension* of development.[63]

5. A THEOLOGICAL READING OF MODERN PROBLEMS

35. Precisely because of the essentially moral character of development, it is clear that the *obstacles* to development likewise have a moral character. If in the years since the publication of Pope Paul's encyclical there has been no development—or very little, irregular, or even contradictory development—the reasons are not only economic. As has already been said, political motives also enter in. For the decisions which either accelerate or slow down the development of peoples are really political in character. In order to overcome the misguided mechanisms mentioned earlier and to replace them with new ones which will be more just and in conformity with the common good of humanity, an effective political will is needed. Unfortunately, after analyzing the situation we have to conclude that this political will has been insufficient.

In a document of a pastoral nature such as this, an analysis limited exclusively to the economic and political causes of underdevelopment (and, *mutatis mutandis*, of so-called superdevelopment) would be incomplete. It is therefore necessary to single out the *moral causes* which, with respect to the behavior of *individuals* considered as *responsible persons*, interfere in such a way as to slow down the course of development and hinder its full achievement.

Similarly, when the scientific and technical resources are available which, with the necessary concrete political decisions, ought to help lead peoples to

true development, the main obstacles to development will be overcome only by means of *essentially moral decisions*. For believers, and especially for Christians, these decisions will take their inspiration from the principles of faith, with the help of divine grace.

36. It is important to note therefore that a world which is divided into blocs, sustained by rigid ideologies, and in which instead of interdependence and solidarity different forms of imperialism hold sway, can only be a world subject to structures of sin. The sum total of the negative factors working against a true awareness of the universal *common good*, and the need to further it, gives the impression of creating, in persons and institutions, an obstacle which is difficult to overcome.[64]

If the present situation can be attributed to difficulties of various kinds, it is not out of place to speak of "structures of sin," which, as I stated in my apostolic exhortation *Reconciliatio et Paenitentia*, are rooted in personal sin, and thus always linked to the *concrete acts* of individuals who introduce these structures, consolidate them and make them difficult to remove.[65] And thus they grow stronger, spread, and become the source of other sins, and so influence people's behavior.

"Sin" and "structures of sin" are categories which are seldom applied to the situation of the contemporary world. However, one cannot easily gain a profound understanding of the reality that confronts us unless we give a name to the root of the evils which afflict us.

One can certainly speak of "selfishness" and of "shortsightedness," of "mistaken political calculations" and "imprudent economic decisions." And in each of these evaluations one hears an echo of an ethical and moral nature. Man's condition is such that a more profound analysis of individuals' actions and omissions cannot be achieved without implying, in one way or another, judgments or references of an ethical nature.

This evaluation is in itself *positive*, especially if it is completely consistent and if it is based on faith in God and on his law, which commands what is good and forbids evil.

In this consists the difference between sociopolitical analysis and formal reference to "sin" and the "structures of sin." According to this latter viewpoint, there enter in the will of the triune God, his plan for humanity, his justice and his mercy. The God who is *rich in mercy, the Redeemer of man, the Lord and giver of life*, requires from people clear-cut attitudes which express themselves also in actions or omissions toward one's neighbor. We have here a reference to the "second tablet" of the Ten Commandments (cf. Exod. 20:12–17; Deut. 5:16–21). Not to observe these is to offend God and hurt one's neighbor, and to introduce into the world influences and obstacles which go far beyond the actions and brief life span of an individual. This also involves interference in the process of the development of peoples, the delay or slowness of which must be judged also in this light.

37. This *general analysis*, which is religious in nature, can be supplemented by *a number of particular considerations* to demonstrate that among the actions and attitudes opposed to the will of God, the good of neighbor and the "structures" created by them, two are very typical: on the one hand, the *all-consuming desire for profit*, and on the other, *the thirst for power*, with the intention of imposing one's will upon others. In order to characterize better each of these attitudes, one can add the expression: "at any price." In other words, we are faced with the *absolutizing* of human attitudes with all its possible consequences.

Since these attitudes can exist independently of each other, they can be separated; however in today's world both are *indissolubly united*, with one or the other predominating.

Obviously, not only individuals fall victim to this double attitude of sin; nations and blocs can do so too. And this favors even more the introduction of the "structures of sin" of which I have spoken. If certain forms of modern "imperialism" were considered in the light of these moral criteria, we would see that hidden behind certain decisions, apparently inspired only by economics or politics, are real forms of idolatry: of money, ideology, class, technology.

I have wished to introduce this type of analysis above all in order to point out the true *nature* of the evil which faces us with respect to the development of peoples: it is a question of a *moral evil*, the fruit of *many sins* which lead to "structures of sin." To diagnose the evil in this way is to identify precisely, on the level of human conduct, *the path to be followed* in order *to overcome it*.

38. This path is *long and complex*, and what is more it is constantly threatened because of the intrinsic frailty of human resolutions and achievements, and because of the *mutability* of very unpredictable and external circumstances. Nevertheless, one must have the courage to set out on this path, and, where some steps have been taken or a part of the journey made, the courage to go on to the end.

In the context of these reflections, the decision to set out or to continue the journey involves, above all, a *moral* value which men and women of faith recognize as a demand of God's will, the only true foundation of an absolutely binding ethic.

One would hope that also men and women without an explicit faith would be convinced that the obstacles to integral development are not only economic but rest on *more profound attitudes* which human beings can make into absolute values. Thus one would hope that all those who, to some degree or other, are responsible for ensuring a "more human life" for their fellow human beings, whether or not they are inspired by a religious faith, will become fully aware of the urgent need to *change* the *spiritual attitudes* which define each individual's relationship with self, with neighbor, with even the remotest human communities, and with nature itself; and all of this in view of higher values such as the *common good* or, to quote the felicitous expression of the

encyclical *Populorum Progressio*, the full development "of the whole individual and of all people."[66]

For *Christians*, as for all who recognize the precise theological meaning of the word *sin*, a change of behavior or mentality or mode of existence is called "conversion," to use the language of the Bible (cf. Mark 13:3, 5; Isa. 30:15). This conversion specifically entails a relationship to God, to the sin committed, to its consequences and hence to one's neighbor, either an individual or a community. It is God, in "whose hands are the hearts of the powerful"[67] and the hearts of all, who according to his own promise and by the power of his Spirit can transform "hearts of stone" into "hearts of flesh" (cf. Ezek. 36:26).

On the path toward the desired conversion, toward the overcoming of the moral obstacles to development, it is already possible to point to the *positive* and *moral value* of the growing awareness of *interdependence* among individuals and nations. The fact that men and women in various parts of the world feel personally affected by the injustices and violations of human rights committed in distant countries, countries which perhaps they will never visit, is a further sign of a reality transformed into *awareness*, thus acquiring a *moral* connotation.

It is above all a question of *interdependence*, sensed as a *system determining* relationships in the contemporary world, in its economic, cultural, political, and religious elements, and accepted as a *moral category*. When interdependence becomes recognized in this way, the correlative response as a moral and social attitude, as a "virtue," is *solidarity*. This then is not a feeling of vague compassion or shallow distress at the misfortunes of so many people, both near and far. On the contrary, it is *a firm and persevering determination* to commit oneself to the *common good*; that is to say to the good of all and of each individual, because we are *all* really responsible *for all*. This determination is based on the *solid* conviction that what is hindering full development is that desire for profit and that thirst for power already mentioned. These attitudes and "structures of sin" are only conquered—presupposing the help of divine grace—by a *diametrically opposed attitude*: a commitment to the good of one's neighbor with the readiness, in the gospel sense, to "lose oneself" for the sake of the other instead of exploiting him, and to "serve him" instead of oppressing him for one's own advantage (cf. Matt. 10:40–42; 20:25; Mark 10:42–45; Luke 22:25–27).

39. The exercise of solidarity *within each society* is valid when its members recognize one another as persons. Those who are more influential, because they have a greater share of goods and common services, should feel *responsible* for the weaker and be ready to share with them all they possess. Those who are weaker, for their part, in the same spirit of *solidarity*, should not adopt a purely *passive* attitude or one that is *destructive* of the social fabric, but, while claiming their legitimate rights, should do what they can for the good of all. The intermediate groups, in their turn, should not selfishly insist on their particular interests, but respect the interests of others.

Positive signs in the contemporary world are the *growing awareness* of the solidarity of the poor among themselves, their *efforts to support one another*, and their *public demonstrations* on the social scene which, without recourse to violence, present their own needs and rights in the face of the inefficiency or corruption of the public authorities. By virtue of her own evangelical duty the Church feels called to take her stand beside the poor, to discern the justice of their requests, and to help satisfy them, without losing sight of the good of groups in the context of the common good.

The same criterion is applied by analogy in international relationships. Interdependence must be transformed into *solidarity*, based upon the principle that the goods of creation *are meant for all*. That which human industry produces through the processing of raw materials, with the contribution of work, must serve equally for the good of all.

Surmounting every type of *imperialism* and determination to preserve their *own hegemony*, the stronger and richer nations must have a sense of moral *responsibility* for the other nations, so that a *real international system* may be established which will rest on the foundation of the *equality* of all peoples and on the necessary respect for their legitimate differences. The economically weaker countries, or those still at subsistence level, must be enabled, with the assistance of other peoples and of the international community, to make a contribution of their own to the common good with their treasures of *humanity* and *culture*, which otherwise would be lost for ever.

Solidarity helps us to see the "other"—whether a *person, people, or nation*—not just as some kind of instrument, with a work capacity and physical strength to be exploited at low cost and then discarded when no longer useful, but as our "neighbor," a "helper" (cf. Gen. 2:18–20), to be made a sharer, on a par with ourselves, in the banquet of life to which all are equally invited by God. Hence the importance of reawakening the *religious awareness* of individuals and peoples.

Thus the exploitation, oppression, and annihilation of others are excluded. These facts, in the present division of the world into opposing blocs, combine to produce the *danger of war* and an excessive preoccupation with personal security, often to the detriment of the autonomy, freedom of decision, and even the territorial integrity of the weaker nations situated within the so-called "areas of influence" or "safety belts."

The "structures of sin" and the sins which they produce are likewise radically opposed to *peace and development*, for development, in the familiar expression of Pope Paul's encyclical, is "the new name for peace."[68]

In this way, the solidarity which we propose is the *path to peace and at the same time to development*. For world peace is inconceivable unless the world's leaders come to recognize that *interdependence* in itself demands the abandonment of the politics of blocs, the sacrifice of all forms of economic, military, or political imperialism, and the transformation of mutual distrust into *collaboration*. This is precisely the *act proper* to solidarity among individuals and nations.

The motto of the pontificate of my esteemed predecessor Pius XII was *Opus iustitiae pax*, "Peace as the fruit of justice." Today one could say, with the same exactness and the same power of biblical inspiration (cf. Isa. 32:17; James 3:18): *Opus solidaritatis pax*, "Peace as the fruit of solidarity."

The goal of peace, so desired by everyone, will certainly be achieved through the putting into effect of social and international justice, but also through the practice of the virtues which favor togetherness, and which teach us to live in unity, so as to build in unity, by giving and receiving, a new society and a better world.

40. *Solidarity* is undoubtedly a *Christian virtue*. In what has been said so far it has been possible to identify many points of contact between solidarity and *charity*, which is the distinguishing mark of Christ's disciples (cf. John 13:35).

In the light of faith, solidarity seeks to go beyond itself, to take on the *specifically Christian* dimension of total gratuity, forgiveness and reconciliation. One's neighbor is then not only a human being with his or her own rights and a fundamental equality with everyone else, but becomes the *living image* of God the Father, redeemed by the blood of Jesus Christ and placed under the permanent action of the Holy Spirit. One's neighbor must therefore be loved, even if an enemy, with the same love with which the Lord loves him or her; and for that person's sake one must be ready for sacrifice, even the ultimate one: to lay down one's life for the brethren (cf. 1 John 3:16).

At that point, awareness of the common fatherhood of God, of the brotherhood of all in Christ—"children in the Son"—and of the presence and life-giving action of the Holy Spirit will bring to our vision of the world *a new criterion* for interpreting it. Beyond human and natural bonds, already so close and strong, there is discerned in the light of faith a new *model* of the *unity* of the human race, which must ultimately inspire our *solidarity*. This supreme *model of unity*, which is a reflection of the intimate life of God, one God in three Persons, is what we Christians mean by the word *communion*. This specifically Christian communion, jealously preserved, extended and enriched with the Lord's help, is the *soul* of the Church's vocation to be a "sacrament," in the sense already indicated.

Solidarity therefore must play its part in the realization of this divine plan, both on the level of individuals and on the level of national and international society. The "evil mechanisms" and "structures of sin" of which we have spoken can be overcome only through the exercise of the human and Christian solidarity to which the Church calls us and which she tirelessly promotes. Only in this way can such positive energies be fully released for the benefit of development and peace.

Many of the Church's canonized saints offer a *wonderful witness* of such solidarity and can serve as examples in the present difficult circumstances. Among them I wish to recall St. Peter Claver and his service to the slaves at

Cartagena de Indias, and St. Maximilian Maria Kolbe, who offered his life in place of a prisoner unknown to him in the concentration camp at Auschwitz.

6. SOME PARTICULAR GUIDELINES

41. The Church does not have *technical solutions* to offer for the problem of underdevelopment as such, as Pope Paul VI already affirmed in his encyclical.[69] For the Church does not propose economic and political systems or programs, nor does she show preference for one or the other, provided that human dignity is properly respected and promoted, and provided she herself is allowed the room she needs to exercise her ministry in the world.

But the Church is an "expert in humanity,"[70] and this leads her necessarily to extend her religious mission to the various fields in which men and women expend their efforts in search of the always relative happiness which is possible in this world, in line with their dignity as persons.

Following the examples of my predecessors, I must repeat that whatever affects the dignity of individuals and peoples, such as authentic development, cannot be reduced to a "technical" problem. If reduced in this way, development would be emptied of its true content, and this would be an act of *betrayal* of the individuals and peoples whom development is meant to serve.

This is why the Church has *something to say* today, just as twenty years ago, and also in the future, about the nature, conditions, requirements, and aims of authentic development, and also about the obstacles which stand in its way. In doing so the Church fulfills her mission to *evangelize*, for she offers her *first* contribution to the solution of the urgent problem of development when she proclaims the truth about Christ, about herself and about man, applying this truth to a concrete situation.[71]

As her *instrument* for reaching this goal, the Church uses her *social doctrine*. In today's difficult situation, *a more exact awareness and a wider diffusion* of the "set of principles for reflection, criteria for judgment, and directives for action" proposed by the Church's teaching[72] would be of great help in promoting both the correct definition of the problems being faced and the best solution to them.

It will thus be seen at once that the questions facing us are above all moral questions; and that neither the analysis of the problem of development as such nor the means to overcome the present difficulties can ignore this essential dimension.

The Church's social doctrine is *not* a "third way" between *liberal capitalism* and *Marxist collectivism*, nor even a possible alternative to other solutions less radically opposed to one another: rather, it constitutes a *category of its own*. Nor is it an *ideology*, but rather the *accurate formulation* of the results of a careful reflection on the complex realities of human existence, in society and in the international order, in the light of faith and of the church's tradition. Its

main aim is to *interpret* these realities, determining their conformity with or divergence from the lines of the Gospel teaching on man and his vocation, a vocation which is at once earthly and transcendent; its aim is thus to *guide* Christian behavior. It therefore belongs to the field, not of *ideology*, but of *theology* and particularly of moral theology.

The teaching and spreading of her social doctrine are part of the Church's evangelizing mission. And since it is a doctrine aimed at guiding *people's behavior*, it consequently gives rise to a "commitment to justice," according to each individual's role, vocation and circumstances.

The *condemnation* of evils and injustices is also part of that *ministry of evangelization* in the social field which is an aspect of the Church's *prophetic role*. But it should be made clear that *proclamation* is always more important than *condemnation*, and the latter cannot ignore the former, which gives it true solidity and the force of higher motivation.

42. Today more than in the past, the Church's social doctrine must be open to an *international outlook*, in line with the Second Vatican Council,[73] the most recent encyclicals,[74] and particularly in line with the encyclical which we are commemorating.[75] It will not be superfluous therefore to reexamine and further clarify in this light the characteristic themes and guidelines dealt with by the magisterium in recent years.

Here I would like to indicate one of them: the *option* or *love of preference* for the poor. This is an option, or a *special form* of primacy in the exercise of Christian charity, to which the whole tradition of the Church bears witness. It affects the life of each Christian inasmuch as he or she seeks to imitate the life of Christ, but it applies equally to our *social responsibilities* and hence to our manner of living, and to the logical decisions to be made concerning the ownership and use of goods.

Today, furthermore, given the worldwide dimension which the social question has assumed,[76] this love of preference for the poor, and the decisions which it inspires in us, cannot but embrace the immense multitudes of the hungry, the needy, the homeless, those without medical care and, above all, those without hope of a better future. It is impossible not to take account of the existence of these realities. To ignore them would mean becoming like the "rich man" who pretended not to know the beggar Lazarus lying at his gate (cf. Luke 16:19–31).[77]

Our *daily life* as well as our decisions in the political and economic fields must be marked by these realities. Likewise the *leaders* of nations and the heads of *international bodies*, while they are obliged always to keep in mind the true human dimension as a priority in their development plans, should not forget to give precedence to the phenomenon of growing poverty. Unfortunately, instead of becoming fewer the poor are becoming more numerous, not only in less developed countries but—and this seems no less scandalous—in the more developed ones too.

It is necessary to state once more the characteristic principle of Christian social doctrine: the goods of this world are *originally meant for all.*[78] The right to private property is *valid and necessary*, but it does not nullify the value of this principle. Private property, in fact, is under a "social mortgage,"[79] which means that it has an intrinsically social function, based upon and justified precisely by the principle of the universal destination of goods. Likewise, in this concern for the poor, one must not overlook that *special form of poverty* which consists in being deprived of fundamental human rights, in particular the right to religious freedom and also the right to freedom of economic initiative.

43. The motivating concern for the poor—who are, in the very meaningful term, "the Lord's poor"[80]—must be translated at all levels into concrete actions, until it decisively attains a series of necessary reforms. Each local situation will show what reforms are most urgent and how they can be achieved. But those demanded by the situation of international imbalance, as already described, must not be forgotten.

In this respect I wish to mention specifically: the *reform of the international trade system*, which is mortgaged to protectionism and increasing bilateralism; the *reform of the world monetary and financial system*, today recognized as inadequate; the *question of technological exchanges* and their proper use; the *need* for a *review of the structure of the existing international organizations*, in the framework of an international juridical order.

The *international trade system* today frequently discriminates against the products of the young industries of the developing countries and discourages the producers of raw materials. There exists, too, a kind of *international division of labor*, whereby the low-cost products of certain countries which lack effective labor laws or which are too weak to apply them are sold in other parts of the world at considerable profit for the companies engaged in this form of production, which knows no frontiers.

The *world monetary and financial system* is marked by an excessive fluctuation of exchange rates and interest rates, to the detriment of the balance of payments and the debt situation of the poorer countries.

Forms of technology and their transfer constitute today one of the major problems of international exchange and of the grave damage deriving therefrom. There are quite frequent cases of developing countries being denied needed forms of technology or sent useless ones.

In the opinion of many, the *international organizations* seem to be at a stage of their existence when their operating methods, operating costs, and effectiveness need careful review and possible correction. Obviously, such a delicate process cannot be put into effect without the collaboration of all. This presupposes the overcoming of political rivalries and the renouncing of all desire to manipulate these organizations, which exist solely for *the common good*.

The existing institutions and organizations have worked well for the benefit of peoples. Nevertheless, humanity today is in a new and more difficult phase of

its genuine development. It needs a *greater degree of international ordering*, at the service of the societies, economies and cultures of the whole world.

44. Development demands above all a spirit of initiative on the part of the countries which need it.[81] Each of them must act in accordance with its own responsibilities, *not expecting everything* from the more favored countries, and acting in collaboration with others in the same situation. Each must discover and use to the best advantage its *own area of freedom*. Each must make itself capable of initiatives responding to its own needs as a society. Each must likewise realize its true needs, as well as the rights and duties which oblige it to respond to them. The development of peoples begins and is most appropriately accomplished in the dedication of each people to its own development, in collaboration with others.

It is important then that as far as possible *the developing nations themselves* should favor the *self-affirmation* of each citizen, through access to a wider culture and a free flow of information. Whatever promotes *literacy* and the *basic education* which completes and deepens it is a direct contribution to true development, as the encyclical *Populorum Progressio* proposed.[82] These goals are still far from being reached in so many parts of the world.

In order to take this path, *the nations themselves* will have to identify their own *priorities* and clearly recognize their own needs, according to the particular conditions of their people, their geographical setting and their cultural traditions.

Some nations will have to increase *food production*, in order to have always available what is needed for subsistence and daily life. In the modern world—where starvation claims so many victims, especially among the very young—there are examples of not particularly developed nations which have nevertheless achieved the goal of *food self-sufficiency* and have even become food exporters.

Other nations need to reform certain unjust structures, and in particular their *political institutions*, in order to replace corrupt, dictatorial, and authoritarian forms of government by *democratic* and *participatory* ones. This is a process which we hope will spread and grow stronger. For the "health" of a political community—as expressed in the free and responsible participation of all citizens in public affairs, in the rule of the law and in respect for the promotion of human rights—is the *necessary condition and sure guarantee* of the development of "the whole individual and of all people."

45. None of what has been said can be achieved *without the collaboration of all*—especially the international community—in the framework of a *solidarity* which includes everyone, beginning with the most neglected. But the developing nations themselves have the duty to practice *solidarity among themselves* and with the neediest countries of the world.

It is desirable, for example, that nations of the *same geographical area* should establish *forms of cooperation* which will make them less dependent on more powerful producers; they should open their frontiers to the products

of the area; they should examine how their products might complement one another; they should combine in order to set up those services which each one separately is incapable of providing; they should extend cooperation to the monetary and financial sector.

Interdependence is already a reality in many of these countries. To acknowledge it, in such a way as to make it more operative, represents an alternative to excessive dependence on richer and more powerful nations, as part of the hoped-for development, without opposing anyone, but discovering and making best use of the country's *own potential*. The developing countries belonging to one geographical area, especially those included in the term "South," can and ought to set up *new regional organizations* inspired by criteria of *equality, freedom and participation* in the comity of nations—as is already happening with promising results.

An essential condition for global *solidarity* is autonomy and free self-determination, also within associations such as those indicated. But at the same time solidarity demands a readiness to accept the sacrifices necessary for the good of the whole world community.

7. CONCLUSION

46. Peoples and individuals aspire to be free: their search for full development signals their desire to overcome the many obstacles preventing them from enjoying a "more human life."

Recently, in the period following the publication of the encyclical *Populorum Progressio*, a new way of confronting the problems of poverty and underdevelopment has spread in some areas of the world, especially in Latin America. This approach makes *liberation* the fundamental category and the first principle of action. The positive values, as well as the deviations and risks of deviation, which are damaging to the faith and are connected with this form of theological reflection and method, have been appropriately pointed out by the Church's magisterium.[83]

It is fitting to add that the aspiration to freedom from all forms of slavery affecting the individual and society is something *noble* and *legitimate*. This in fact is the purpose of development, or rather liberation and development, taking into account the intimate connection between the two.

Development which is merely economic is incapable of setting man free; on the contrary, it will end by enslaving him further. Development that does not include the *cultural, transcendent and religious dimensions* of man and society, to the extent that it does not recognize the existence of such dimensions and does not endeavor to direct its goals and priorities toward the same, is *even less* conducive to authentic liberation. Human beings are totally free only when they are completely *themselves*, in the fullness of their rights and duties. The same can be said about society as a whole.

The principal obstacle to be overcome on the way to authentic liberation is *sin* and the *structures* produced by sin as it multiplies and spreads.[84]

The freedom with which Christ has set us free (cf. Gal. 5:1) encourages us to become the *servants* of all. Thus the process of *development* and *liberation* takes concrete shape in the exercise of *solidarity*, that is to say in the love and service of neighbor, especially of the poorest: "For where truth and love are missing, the process of liberation results in the death of a freedom which will have lost all support."[85]

47. In the context of the *sad experiences* of recent years and of the *mainly negative picture* of the present moment, the Church must strongly affirm the *possibility* of overcoming the obstacles which, by excess or by defect, stand in the way of development. And she must affirm her confidence in a *true liberation*. Ultimately, this confidence and this possibility are based on the *Church's awareness* of the divine promise guaranteeing that our present history does not remain closed in upon itself but is open to the kingdom of God.

The Church has *confidence also in man*, though she knows the evil of which he is capable. For she well knows that—in spite of the heritage of sin, and the sin which each one is capable of committing—there exist in the human person sufficient qualities and energies, a fundamental "goodness" (cf. Gen. 1:31), because he is the image of the Creator, placed under the redemptive influence of Christ, who "united himself in some fashion with every man,"[86] and because the efficacious action of the Holy Spirit "fills the earth" (Wis. 1:7).

There is no justification then for despair or pessimism or inertia. Though it be with sorrow, it must be said that just as one may sin through selfishness and the desire for excessive profit and power, *one may also be found wanting* with regard to the urgent needs of multitudes of human beings submerged in conditions of underdevelopment, through *fear*, *indecision*, and, basically, through *cowardice*. We are *all* called, indeed *obliged*, to face the tremendous challenge of the last decade of the second millennium, also because the present dangers threaten everyone: a world economic crisis, a war without frontiers, without winners or losers. In the face of such a threat, the distinction between rich individuals and countries and poor individuals and countries *will have little value*, except that a greater responsibility rests on those who have more and can do more.

This is not however the *sole motive or even the most important one*. At stake is the *dignity of the human person*, whose *defense* and *promotion* have been entrusted to us by the Creator, and to whom the men and women at every moment of history are strictly and responsibly *in debt*. As many people are already more or less clearly aware, the present situation *does not seem to correspond to* this dignity. *Every individual* is called upon to play his or her part in this *peaceful* campaign, a campaign to be conducted by *peaceful* means, in order to secure *development in peace*, in order to safeguard nature itself and the world about us. The Church too feels profoundly involved in this enterprise, and she hopes for its ultimate success.

Consequently, following the example of Pope Paul VI with his encyclical *Populorum Progressio*,[87] I wish *to appeal* with simplicity and humility to *everyone*, to all men and women without exception. I wish to ask them to be convinced of the seriousness of the present moment and of each one's individual responsibility, and to implement—by the way they live as individuals and as families, by the use of their resources, by their civic activity, by contributing to economic and political decisions, and by personal commitment to national and international undertakings—the *measures* inspired by solidarity and love of preference for the poor. This is what is demanded by the present moment and above all by the very dignity of the human person, the indestructible image of God the Creator, which is *identical* in each one of us.

In this commitment, the sons and daughters of the Church must serve as examples and guides, for they are called upon, in conformity with the program announced by Jesus himself in the synagogue at Nazareth, to "preach good news to the poor . . . to proclaim release to the captives and recovering of sight to the blind, to set at liberty those who are oppressed, to proclaim the acceptable year of the Lord" (Luke 4:18–19). It is appropriate to emphasize the *preeminent role* that belongs to the *laity*, both men and women, as was reaffirmed in the recent assembly of the synod. It is their task to animate temporal realities with Christian commitment, by which they show that they are witnesses and agents of peace and justice.

I wish to address especially those who, through the sacrament of baptism and the profession of the same creed, *share* a *real*, though imperfect, *communion* with us. I am certain that the concern expressed in this encyclical as well as the motives inspiring it *will be familiar to them*, for these motives are inspired by the Gospel of Jesus Christ. We can find here a new invitation *to bear witness together* to our *common convictions* concerning the dignity of man, created by God, redeemed by Christ, made holy by the Spirit, and called upon in this world to live a life in conformity with this dignity.

I likewise address this appeal to the Jewish people, who share with us the inheritance of Abraham, "our father in faith" (cf. Rom. 4:11f.)[88] and the tradition of the Old Testament, as well as to the Muslims who, like us, believe in a just and merciful God. And I extend it to all the followers of *the world's great religions*.

The meeting held last October 27 in Assisi, the city of St. Francis, in order to pray for and commit ourselves to *peace*—each one in fidelity to his own religious profession—showed how much peace and, as its necessary condition, the development of the whole person and of all peoples, are also a *matter of religion*, and how the full achievement of both the one and the other depends on our *fidelity* to our vocation as men and women of faith. For it depends, above all, *on God*.

48. The Church well knows that *no temporal achievement* is to be identified with the kingdom of God, but that all such achievements simply *reflect* and in a sense *anticipate* the glory of the kingdom, the kingdom which we

await at the end of history, when the Lord will come again. But that expectation can never be an excuse for lack of concern for people in their concrete personal situations and in their social, national, and international life, since the former is conditioned by the latter, especially today.

However imperfect and temporary are all the things that can and ought to be done through the combined efforts of everyone and through divine grace, at a given moment of history, in order to make people's lives "more human," nothing will be *lost* or *will have been in vain.* This is the teaching of the Second Vatican Council, in an enlightening passage of the pastoral constitution *Gaudium et Spes*: "When we have spread on earth the fruits of our nature and our enterprise—human dignity, fraternal communion, and freedom—according to the command of the Lord and in his Spirit, we will find them once again, cleansed this time from the stain of sin, illumined and transfigured, when Christ presents to his Father an eternal and universal kingdom . . . here on earth that kingdom is already present in mystery."[89]

The kingdom of God becomes *present* above all in the celebration of the *sacrament of the Eucharist*, which is the Lord's sacrifice. In that celebration the fruits of the earth and the work of human hands—the bread and wine—are transformed mysteriously, but really and substantially, through the power of the Holy Spirit and the words of the minister, *into the body and blood* of the Lord Jesus Christ, the Son of God and Son of Mary, through whom the *kingdom of the Father* has been made present in our midst.

The goods of this world and the work of our hands—the bread and wine—serve for the coming of the *definitive kingdom*, since the Lord, through his Spirit, takes them up into himself in order to offer himself to the Father and to offer us with himself in the renewal of his one sacrifice, which anticipates God's kingdom and proclaims its final coming.

Thus the Lord *unites us with himself* through the Eucharist—sacrament and sacrifice—and he *unites us with himself and with one another* by a bond stronger than any natural union; and thus united, *he sends us* into the whole world to bear witness, through faith and works, to God's love, preparing the coming of his kingdom and anticipating it, though in the obscurity of the present time.

All of us who take part in the Eucharist are called to discover, through this sacrament, the profound *meaning* of our actions in the world in favor of development and peace; and to receive from it the strength to commit ourselves ever more generously, following the example of Christ, who in this sacrament lays down his life for his friends (cf. John 15:13). Our personal commitment, like Christ's and in union with his, will not be in vain but certainly fruitful.

49. I have called the current *Marian* Year in order that the Catholic faithful may look more and more to Mary, who goes before us on the pilgrimage of faith[90] and with maternal care intercedes for us before her Son, our Redeemer. I wish to *entrust to her* and to *her intercession* this *difficult moment* of the modern world, and the efforts that are being made and will be made, often

with great suffering, in order to contribute to the true development of peoples proposed and proclaimed by my predecessor Paul VI.

In keeping with Christian piety through the ages, we present to the blessed Virgin difficult individual situations, so that she may place them before her Son, asking that he *alleviate and change* them. But we also present to her *social situations* and *the international crisis* itself, in their worrying aspects of poverty, unemployment, shortage of food, the arms race, contempt for human rights, and situations or dangers of conflict, partial or total. In a filial spirit we wish to place all this before her "eyes of mercy," repeating once more with faith and hope the ancient antiphon: "Holy Mother of God, despise not our petitions in our necessities, but deliver us always from all dangers, O glorious and blessed Virgin."

Mary most holy, our Mother and Queen, is the one who turns to her Son and says: "They have no more wine" (John 2:3). She is also the one who praises God the Father, because "he has put down the mighty from their thrones and exalted those of low degree; he has filled the hungry with good things, and the rich he has sent empty away" (Luke 1:52–53). Her maternal concern extends to the *personal* and *social* aspects of people's life on earth.[91]

Before the most blessed Trinity, I entrust to Mary all that I have written in this encyclical, and I invite all to reflect and actively commit themselves to promoting the true development of peoples, as the prayer of the Mass for this intention states so well: "Father, you have given all peoples one common origin, and your will is to gather them as one family in yourself. Fill the hearts of all with the fire of your love, and the desire to ensure justice for all their brothers and sisters. By sharing the good things you give us, may we secure justice and equality for every human being, an end to all division and a human society built on love and peace."[92]

This, in conclusion, is what I ask in the name of all my brothers and sisters, to whom I send a special blessing as a sign of greeting and good wishes.

Given in Rome, at St. Peter's, on December 30 of the year 1987, the tenth of my Pontificate.

JOHN PAUL II

NOTES

1. Leo XIII, Encyclical *Rerum Novarum* (May 15, 1891): *Leonis XIII*, P.M. Acta XI (Rome, 1892), pp. 97–144.

2. Pius XI, encyclical *Quadragesimo Anno* (May 15, 1931): *Acta Apostolicae Sedis* 23 (1931), pp. 177–228; John XXIII, encyclical *Mater et Magistra* (May 15, 1961): AAS 53 (1961), pp. 401–64; Paul VI, apostolic letter *Octogesima Adveniens* (May 14, 1971): AAS 63 (1971), pp. 401–41; John Paul II, encyclical *Laborem Exercens* (Sept. 14, 1981): AAS 73 (1981), pp. 577–647. Also, Pius XII, radio message (June 1, 1941): AAS 33 (1941), pp. 195–205.

3. Cf. Second Vatican Ecumenical Council, *Dogmatic Constitution on Divine Revelation, Dei Verbum*, 4.

4. Paul VI, encyclical *Populorum Progressio* (March 26, 1967): AAS 59 (1967), pp. 257–99.

5. Cf. *L'Osservatore Romano*, May 25, 1987.

6. Cf. Congregation for the Doctrine of the Faith, *Instruction on Christian Freedom and Liberation, Libertatis Conscientia* (March 22, 1986), 72: AAS 79 (1987), p. 586; *Octogesima Adveniens*, 4.

7. Cf. encyclical *Redemptoris Mater* (March 25, 1987), 3: AAS 79 (1987), pp. 363f.; Homily at the Mass of Jan. 1, 1987: *L'Osservatore Romano*, Jan. 2, 1987.

8. The encyclical *Populorum Progressio* cites the documents of the Second Vatican Council nineteen times, and sixteen of the references are to the *Pastoral Constitution on the Church in the Modern World, Gaudium et Spes*.

9. *Gaudium et Spes*, 1.

10. Ibid., 4; cf. *Populorum Progressio*, 13.

11. Cf. *Gaudium et Spes*, 3; *Populorum Progressio*, 13.

12. Cf. *Gaudium et Spes*, 63; *Populorum Progressio*, 9.

13. Cf. *Gaudium et Spes*, 69; *Populorum Progressio*, 22.

14. Cf. *Gaudium et Spes*, 57; *Populorum Progressio*, 41.

15. Cf. *Gaudium et Spes*, 19; *Populorum Progressio*, 41.

16. Cf. *Gaudium et Spes*, 86; *Populorum Progressio*, 48.

17. Cf. *Gaudium et Spes*, 69; *Populorum Progressio*, 14–21.

18. Cf. the inscription of the encyclical *Populorum Progressio*.

19. The encyclical *Rerum Novarum* of Leo XIII has as its principal subject "the condition of the workers."

20. *Libertatis Conscientia*, 72; *Octogesima Adveniens*, 4.

21. Cf. *Mater et Magistra*, 53.

22. *Gaudium et Spes*, 63.

23. Cf. *Populorum Progressio*, 3, 9.

24. Cf. ibid., 3.

25. Ibid., 48.

26. Cf. ibid., 14: "Development cannot be limited to mere economic growth. In order to be authentic, it must be complete: integral, that is, it has to promote the good of every man and of the whole man."

27. Ibid., 87.

28. Cf. ibid., 53.

29. Cf. ibid., 76.

30. The decades referred to are the years 1960–1970 and 1970–1980; the present decade is the third (1980–1990).

31. The expression "Fourth World" is used not for the so-called less advanced countries, but also and especially for the bands of great or extreme poverty in countries of medium and high income.

32. Second Vatican Council, *Dogmatic Constitution on the Church, Lumen Gentium*, 1.

33. *Populorum Progressio*, 33.

34. It should be noted that the Holy See associated itself with the celebration of this international year with a special document issued by the Pontifical Justice and Peace Commission titled: *What Have You Done to Your Homeless Brother?* (Dec. 27, 1987).

35. Cf. *Octogesima Adveniens*, 8–9.

36. A recent U.N. publication titled *World Economic Survey 1987* provides the most recent data (cf. pp. 8–9). The percentage of unemployed in the developed countries with a market economy jumped from 3 percent of the work force in 1970 to 8 percent in 1986. It now amounts to twenty-nine million people.

37. *Laborem Exercens*, 18.

38. *At the Service of the Human Community: An Ethical Approach to the International Debt Question* (Dec. 27, 1986).

39. *Populorum Progressio*, 54: "Developing countries will thus no longer risk being overwhelmed by debts whose repayment swallows up the greater part of their gains. Rates of interest and time for repayment of the loan could be so arranged as not to be too great a burden on either party, taking into account free gifts, interest-free or low-interest loans, and the time needed for liquidating the debts."

40. Cf. "presentation" of the document *At the Service of the Human Community: An Ethical Approach to the International Debt Question* (Dec. 27, 1986).

41. Cf. *Populorum Progressio*, 53.

42. *At the Service of the Human Community*, III, 2, 1.

43. Cf. *Populorum Progressio*, 20–21.

44. Address at Drogheda, Ireland (Sept. 29, 1979), 5 AAS, 71 (1979), II, p. 1079.

45. Cf. *Populorum Progressio*, 37.

46. Cf. apostolic exhortation *Familiaris Consortio* (Nov. 22, 1981), especially in no. 20: AAS 74 (1982), pp. 115–17.

47. Cf. *Human Rights: Collection of International Instruments*, United Nations, New York, 1983; John Paul II, encyclical *Redemptor Hominis* (March 4, 1979), 17: AAS 71 (1979), p. 296.

48. Cf. *Gaudium et Spes*, 78; *Populorum Progressio*, 76: "To wage war on misery and to struggle against injustice is to promote, along with improved conditions, the human and spiritual progress of all men, and therefore the common good of humanity . . . Peace is something that is built up day after day, in the pursuit of an order intended by God, which implies a more perfect form of justice among men."

49. Cf. *Familiaris Consortio*, 6: "History is not simply a fixed progression toward what is better, but rather an event of freedom, and even a struggle between freedoms."

50. For this reason the word *development* was used in the encyclical rather than the word *progress*, but with an attempt to give the word *development* its fullest meaning.

51. *Populorum Progressio*, 19: "Increased possession is not the ultimate goal of nations or of individuals. All growth is ambivalent. . . . The exclusive pursuit of possessions thus becomes an obstacle to individual fulfillment and to man's true greatness. . . . Both for nations and for individual men, avarice is the most evident form of moral underdevelopment"; cf. also *Octogesima Adveniens*, 9.

52. Cf. *Gaudium et Spes*, 35; Paul VI, Address to the Diplomatic Corps (Jan. 7, 1965): AAS 57 (1965), p. 232.

53. Cf. *Populorum Progressio*, 20–21.

54. Cf. *Laborem Exercens*, 4; *Populorum Progressio*, 15.

55. Ibid., 42.

56. Cf. Easter Proclamation, Roman Missal (1975): "O happy fault, O necessary sin of Adam, which gained for us so great a Redeemer!"

57. *Lumen Gentium*, 1.

58. Cf. for example, St. Basil the Great, *Regulae Fusius Tractatae, Interrogatio* XXXVII, 1–2: PG 31, 1009–1012; Theodoret of Cyr, *De Providentia, Oratio* VII: PG 83, 665–86; St. Augustine, *De Civitate Dei*, XIX, 17: CCL 48, 683–85.

59. Cf. for example, St. John Chrysostom, *In Evang. S Matthaei, hom.* 50, 3–4: PG 58, 508–10; St. Ambrose, *De Officiis Ministrorum*, lib. II, XXVIII, 136–40: PL 16, 139–41; St. Possidius, *Vita S. Augustini Episcopi*, XXIV: PL 32, 53f.

60. *Populorum Progressio*, 23: "'If someone who has the riches of this world sees his brother in need and closes his heart to him, how does the love of God abide in him?' (1 John 3:17). It is well-known how strong were the words used by the Fathers of the Church to describe the proper attitude of persons who possess anything toward persons in need." In the previous number, the pope had cited no. 69 of the Pastoral Constitution, *Gaudium et Spes* of the Second Vatican Council.

61. Cf. *Populorum Progressio*, 47: "A world where freedom is not an empty word and where the poor man Lazarus can sit down at the same table with the rich man."

62. Cf. ibid.: "It is a question, rather, of building a world where every man, no matter what his race, religion, or nationality, can live a fully human life, freed from servitude imposed on him by other men"; cf. also *Gaudium et Spes*, 29. Such *fundamental equality* is one of the basic reasons why the church has always been opposed to every form of racism.

63. Cf. Homily at Val Visdende (July 12, 1987), 5: *L'Osservatore Romano*, July 13–14, 1987; *Octogesima Adveniens*, 21.

64. Cf. *Gaudium et Spes*, 25.

65. Apostolic exhortation *Reconciliatio et Paentientia* (Dec. 2, 1984), 16: "Whenever the Church speaks of *situations* of sin or when she condemns as

social sins certain situations or the collective behavior of certain social groups, big or small, or even of whole nations and blocs of nations, she knows and she proclaims that such cases of *social sin* are the result of the accumulation and concentration of many *personal sins*. It is a case of the very personal sins of those who cause or support evil or who exploit it; of those who are in a position to avoid, eliminate or at least limit certain social evils but who fail to do so out of laziness, fear, or the conspiracy of silence, through secret complicity or indifference; of those who take refuge in the supposed impossibility of changing the world, and also of those who sidestep the effort and sacrifice required, producing specious reasons of a higher order. The real responsibility, then, lies with individuals. A situation—or likewise an institution, a structure, society itself—is not in itself the subject of moral acts. Hence a situation cannot in itself be good or bad": AAS 77 (1985), p. 217.

66. *Populorum Progressio*, 42.

67. Cf. Liturgy of the Hours, Wednesday of the Third Week of Ordinary Time, Vespers.

68. *Populorum Progressio*, 87.

69. Cf. ibid., 13, 81.

70. Cf. ibid., 13.

71. Cf. Address at the opening of the Third General Conference of the Latin American Bishops (Jan. 28, 1979): AAS 71 (1979), pp. 189–96.

72. *Libertatis Conscientia*, 72; *Octogesima Adveniens*, 4.

73. *Gaudium et Spes*, 83–90: "Building Up the International Community."

74. Cf. *Mater et Magistra; Pacem in Terris*, Part 4; *Octogesima Adveniens*, 2–4.

75. *Populorum Progressio*, 3, 9.

76. Ibid., 3.

77. Ibid., 47; *Libertatis Conscientia*, 68.

78. Cf. *Gaudium et Spes*, 69; *Populorum Progressio*, 22; *Libertatis Conscientia*, 90; St. Thomas Aquinas, *Summa Theologiae*, IIa, IIae, q. 66, art. 2.

79. Cf. Address at the opening of the Third General Conference of the Latin American Bishops *ad limina* address to a group of Polish bishops (Dec. 17, 1987), 6: *L'Osservatore Romano*, Dec. 18, 1987.

80. Because the Lord wished to identify himself with them (Matt. 25:31–46) and takes special care of them (cf. Ps. 12:6; Luke 1:52f.).

81. *Populorum Progressio*, 55: "These are the men and women that need to be helped, that need to be convinced to take into their own hands their development, gradually acquiring the means"; cf. *Gaudium et Spes*, 86.

82. *Populorum Progressio*, 35: "Basic education is the first objective of a plan of development."

83. Cf. *Libertatis Conscientia*, Introduction.

84. *Reconciliatio et Paenitentia*, 15; *Libertatis Conscientia*, 38, 42.

85. *Libertatis Conscientia*, 24.

86. *Gaudium et Spes*, 22; *Redemptor Hominis*, 8.

87. *Populorum Progressio*, 5. "We believe that all men of good will, together with our Catholic sons and daughters and our Christian brethren, can and should agree on this program"; cf. also 81–83, 87.

88. Cf. Second Vatican Council, *Declaration on the Relationship of the Church to Non-Christian Religions, Nostra Aetate*, 4.

89. *Gaudium et Spes*, 39.

90. Cf. *Lumen Gentium*, 58; *Redemptoris Mater*, 5–6.

91. Cf. Paul VI, apostolic exhortation *Marialis Cultus* (Feb. 2, 1974), 37: AAS 66 (1974), pp. 148f; John Paul II, Homily at the Shrine of Our Lady of Zapopan, Mexico (Jan. 30, 1979), 4: AAS 71 (1979), p. 230.

92. Collect of the Mass "For the Development of Peoples"; Roman Missal, 1975, p. 820.

Centesimus Annus: *On the Hundredth Anniversary of* *Rerum Novarum* *(John Paul II, 1991)*

INTRODUCTION

To celebrate the hundredth anniversary of *Rerum Novarum*, Pope John Paul II promulgated *Centesimus Annus* to look back, look around, and look to the future. Using *Rerum Novarum* as a frame of reference, John Paul provides us with a comprehensive overview of the key points of Catholic social teaching as well as an application of them to specific issues.

The encyclical is divided into six major chapters which review the key teachings of *Rerum Novarum*, presents the new issues for discussion, examines the events of the momentous year 1989, provides a contemporary discussion of private property, analyzes issues in the relation between the state and culture, and concludes by presenting his view of Christian anthropology as the ground for the church's social mission.

Highlighted as key themes in *Rerum Novarum* and thematically discussed in the body of *Centesimus Annus* are the themes of the restoration of peace between social classes, the right to private property, just wages, the question of rights, and the relation between the citizen and state. Of particular importance throughout *Centesimus Annus* is the theme of restoring or establishing harmony between various social groups. This has been a dominant theme of John's pontificate and it shows up as a central feature of this encyclical.

Chapter 2 argues that the continuing problems of workers and the poor come from the errors of socialism and an atheistic vision of life. Socialism subordinates the good of the individual to that of society and eliminates the "concept of the person as an autonomous subject of moral decision" (13). Atheism deprives the human of his or her transcendent dignity which allows utilitarian, but ultimately inadequate, solutions to human problems. The chapter concludes by commenting on specific problems of our day, particularly working conditions and the arms race.

Chapter 3 celebrated the breakdown of the Communist regimes in Central and Eastern Europe and the weakening of oppressive regimes in Africa, Asia, and Latin America. But while celebrating the collapse of Marxism, the pope also recognizes the presence of accumulated individual, social, and regional

injustices over the last several decades and calls for steps to be taken to resolve these peacefully.

Chapter 4 examines the concept of private property. While standing with *Rerum Novarum*'s assertion of the right to private property, John Paul also recognizes that this is not an absolute right and that property has a social function. Additionally he also recognizes, but unfortunately does not develop, a new form of property: "the possession of know-how, technology and skill" (32).

Several other issues are discussed in this critical chapter. First is the problem of underdevelopment in the Third World in which John Paul notes that many of the problems raised by *Rerum Novarum* still are present and need resolution. Second, the problem of the deteriorating ecology is discussed, both on an environmental as well as a cultural level. Finally, issues of economic development are discussed. Recognizing the legitimacy of profit and that "the free market is the most efficient instrument for utilizing resources and effectively responding to needs" (35), the pope does not give a carte blanche to capitalism. He argues that many human needs find no place in the market and justice requires their resolution. He also critiques heavily the consumerist society and its impact on the poor.

In chapter 5 John Paul argues against the totalitarian state on the grounds of its denial of transcendent human dignity. The church values, he says, the values of the democratic system, but only insofar as it recognizes and implements appropriate human values. The role of the church with respect to culture is to promote "those aspects of human behavior which favor a true culture of peace" (51).

The pope concludes *Centesimus Annus* with a presentation of Christian anthropology which grounds the church's social vision and mission on the basis of a transcendent human dignity. Additionally "the social message of the Gospel must not be considered a theory, but above all else a basis and a motivation for action" (55). Only through such action for justice will the vision of *Rerum Novarum*, now interpreted contemporarily through *Centesimus Annus*, be implemented.

CENTESIMUS ANNUS

ON THE HUNDREDTH ANNIVERSARY
OF *RERUM NOVARUM*
ENCYCLICAL LETTER
MAY 1, 1991

Addressed by the Supreme Pontiff John Paul II to His Venerable Brothers in the Episcopate, the Priests and Deacons, Families of Men and Women Religious, All the Christian Faithful and All Men and Women of Good Will

POPE JOHN PAUL II

Venerable Brothers,
Beloved Sons and Daughters,
Health and the Apostolic Blessing

INTRODUCTION

1. The centenary of the promulgation of the encyclical which begins with the words "*rerum novarum*,"[1] by my predecessor of venerable memory Pope Leo XIII, is an occasion of great importance for the present history of the church and for my own Pontificate. It is an Encyclical that has the distinction of having been commemorated by solemn papal documents from its fortieth anniversary to its ninetieth. It may be said that its path through history has been marked by other documents which paid tribute to it and applied it to the circumstances of the day.[2]

In doing likewise for the hundredth anniversary, in response to requests from many bishops, church institutions, and study centers, as well as business leaders and workers, both individually and as members of associations, I wish first and foremost to satisfy the debt of gratitude which the whole church owes to this great pope and his "immortal document."[3] I also mean to show that the vital energies rising from that root have not been spent with the passing of the years, but rather have increased even more. This is evident from the various initiatives which have preceded, and which are to accompany and follow the celebration, initiatives promoted by episcopal conferences, by international agencies, universities and academic institutes, by professional associations, and by other institutions and individuals in many parts of the world.

2. The present encyclical is part of these celebrations, which are meant to thank God—the origin of "every good endowment and every perfect gift" (James 1:17)—for having used a document published a century ago by the See of Peter to achieve so much good and to radiate so much light in the church and in the world. Although the commemoration at hand is meant to honor *Rerum Novarum*, it also honors those encyclicals and other documents of my predecessors which have helped to make Pope Leo's encyclical present and alive in history, thus constituting what would come to be called the church's "social doctrine," "social teaching," or even "social magisterium."

The validity of this teaching has already been pointed out in two encyclicals published during my Pontificate: *Laborem Exercens* on human work, and *Sollicitudo Rei Socialis* on current problems regarding the development of individuals and peoples.[4]

3. I now wish to propose a "re-reading" of Pope Leo's encyclical by issuing an invitation to "look back" at the text itself in order to discover anew the richness of the fundamental principles which it formulated for dealing with the question of the condition of workers. But this is also an invitation to "look around" at the "new things" which surround us and in which we find ourselves caught up, very different from the "new things" which characterized the final decade of the last century. Finally, it is an invitation to "look to the future" at a time when we can already glimpse the third millennium of the Christian era, so filled with uncertainties but also with promises—uncertainties and promises which appeal to our imagination and creativity, and which reawaken our responsibility, as disciples of the "one teacher" (cf. Matt. 23:8), to show the way, to proclaim the truth and to communicate the life which is Christ (cf. John 14:6).

A re-reading of this kind will not only confirm the permanent value of such teaching, but will also manifest the true meaning of the church's tradition which, being ever living and vital, builds upon the foundation laid by our fathers in the faith, and particularly upon what "the Apostles passed down to the church"[5] in the name of Jesus Christ, who is her irreplaceable foundation (cf. 1 Cor. 3:11).

It was out of an awareness of his mission as the successor of Peter that Pope Leo XIII proposed to speak out, and Peter's successor today is moved by that same awareness. Like Pope Leo and the popes before and after him, I take my inspiration from the Gospel image of "the scribe who has been trained for the kingdom of heaven," whom the Lord compares to "a householder who brings out of his treasure what is new and what is old" (Matt. 13:52). The treasure is the great outpouring of the church's tradition, which contains "what is old"—received and passed on from the very beginning—and which enables us to interpret the "new things" in the midst of which the life of the church and the world unfolds.

Among the things which become "old" as a result of being incorporated into tradition, and which offer opportunities and material for enriching both

tradition and the life of faith, there is the fruitful activity of many millions of people, who, spurred on by the social magisterium, have sought to make that teaching the inspiration for their involvement in the world. Acting either as individuals or joined together in various groups, associations and organizations, these people represent a great movement for the defense of the human person and the safeguarding of human dignity. Amid changing historical circumstances, this movement has contributed to the building up of a more just society or at least to the curbing of injustice.

The present encyclical seeks to show the fruitfulness of the principles enunciated by Leo XIII, which belong to the church's doctrinal patrimony and, as such, involve the exercise of her teaching authority. But pastoral solicitude also prompts me to propose an analysis of some events of recent history. It goes without saying that part of the responsibility of pastors is to give careful consideration to current events in order to discern the new requirements of evangelization. However, such an analysis is not meant to pass definitive judgments since this does not fall per se within the magisterium's specific domain.

1. CHARACTERISTICS OF *RERUM NOVARUM*

4. Toward the end of the last century the church found herself facing a historical process which had already been taking place for some time, but which was by then reaching a critical point. The determining factor in this process was a combination of radical changes which had taken place in the political, economic, and social fields, and in the areas of science and technology, to say nothing of the wide influence of the prevailing ideologies. In the sphere of politics, the result of these changes was a new conception of society and of the state, and consequently of authority itself. A traditional society was passing away and another was beginning to be formed—one which brought the hope of new freedoms but also the threat of new forms of injustice and servitude.

In the sphere of economics, in which scientific discoveries and their practical application come together, new structures for the production of consumer goods had progressively taken shape. A new form of property had appeared—capital; and a new form of labor—labor for wages, characterized by high rates of production which lacked due regard for sex, age, or family situation, and were determined solely by efficiency, with a view to increasing profits.

In this way labor became a commodity to be freely bought and sold on the market, its price determined by the law of supply and demand, without taking into account the bare minimum required for the support of the individual and his family. Moreover, the worker was not even sure of being able to sell "his own commodity," continually threatened as he was by unemployment, which, in the absence of any kind of social security, meant the specter of death by starvation.

The result of this transformation was a society "divided into two classes, separated by a deep chasm."[6] This situation was linked to the marked change taking place in the political order already mentioned. Thus the prevailing political theory of the time sought to promote total economic freedom by appropriate laws, or, conversely, by a deliberate lack of any intervention. At the same time, another conception of property and economic life was beginning to appear in an organized and often violent form, one which implied a new political and social structure.

At the height of this clash, when people finally began to realize fully the very grave injustice of social realities in many places and the danger of a revolution fanned by ideals which were then called "socialist," Pope Leo XIII intervened with a document which dealt in a systematic way with the "condition of the workers." The encyclical had been preceded by others devoted to teachings of a political character; still others would appear later.[7] Here, particular mention must be made of the encyclical *Libertas Praestantissimum*, which called attention to the essential bond between human freedom and truth, so that freedom which refused to be bound to the truth would fall into arbitrariness and end up submitting itself to the vilest of passions, to the point of self-destruction. Indeed, what is the origin of all the evils to which *Rerum Novarum* wished to respond, if not a kind of freedom which, in the area of economic and social activity, cuts itself off from the truth about man?

The pope also drew inspiration from the teaching of his predecessors, as well as from the many documents issued by bishops, from scientific studies promoted by members of the laity, from the work of Catholic movements and associations, and from the church's practical achievements in the social field during the second half of the nineteenth century.

5. The "new things" to which the pope devoted his attention were anything but positive. The first paragraph of the encyclical describes in strong terms the "new things" (*rerum novarum*) which gave it its name: "That the spirit of revolutionary change which has long been disturbing the nations of the world should have passed beyond the sphere of politics and made its influence felt in the related sphere of practical economics is not surprising. Progress in industry, the development of new trades, the changing relationship between employers and workers, the enormous wealth of few as opposed to the poverty of the many, the increasing self-reliance of the workers and their closer association with each other, as well as a notable decline in morality: all these elements have led to the conflict now taking place."[8]

The pope and the church with him were confronted, as was the civil community, by a society which was torn by a conflict all the more harsh and inhumane because it knew no rule or regulation. It was the conflict between capital and labor, or—as the encyclical puts it—the worker question. It is precisely about this conflict, in the very pointed terms in which it then appeared, that the pope did not hesitate to speak.

Here we find the first reflection for our time, as suggested by the encyclical. In the face of a conflict which set man against man, almost as if they were "wolves," a conflict between the extremes of mere physical survival on the one side and opulence on the other, the pope did not hesitate to intervene by virtue of his "apostolic office,"[9] that is, on the basis of the mission received from Jesus Christ himself to "feed his lambs and tend his sheep" (cf. John 21:15–17), and to "bind and loose" on earth for the kingdom of heaven (cf. Matt. 16:19). The pope's intention was certainly to restore peace, and the present-day reader cannot fail to note his severe condemnation, in no uncertain terms, of the class struggle.[10] However, the pope was very much aware that peace is built on the foundation of justice: what was essential to the encyclical was precisely its proclamation of the fundamental conditions for justice in the economic and social situation of the time.[11]

In this way, Pope Leo XIII, in the footsteps of his predecessors, created a lasting paradigm for the church. The church, in fact, has something to say about specific human situations, both individual and communal, national and international. She formulates a genuine doctrine for these situations, a corpus which enables her to analyze social realities, to make judgments about them and to indicate directions to be taken for the just resolution of the problems involved.

In Pope Leo XIII's time such a concept of the church's right and duty was far from being commonly admitted. Indeed, a two-fold approach prevailed: one directed to this world and this life, to which faith ought to remain extraneous; the other directed toward a purely otherworldly salvation, which neither enlightens nor directs existence on earth. The pope's approach in publishing *Rerum Novarum* gave the church "citizenship status" as it were, amid the changing realities of public life, and this standing would be more fully confirmed later on. In effect, to teach and to spread her social doctrine pertains to the church's evangelizing mission and is an essential part of the Christian message, since this doctrine points out the direct consequences of that message in the life of society and situates daily work and struggles for justice in the context of bearing witness to Christ the Saviour. This doctrine is likewise a source of unity and peace in dealing with the conflicts which inevitably arise in social and economic life. Thus it is possible to meet these new situations without degrading the human person's transcendent dignity, either in oneself or in one's adversaries, and to direct those situations toward just solutions.

Today, at a distance of a hundred years, the validity of this approach affords me the opportunity to contribute to the development of Christian social doctrine. The "new evangelization," which the modern world urgently needs and which I have emphasized many times, must include among its essential elements a proclamation of the church's social doctrine. As in the days of Pope Leo XIII, this doctrine is still suitable for indicating the right way to respond to the great challenges of today, when ideologies are being increasingly discredited. Now, as then, we need to repeat that there can be no genuine solution

of the "social question" apart from the Gospel, and that the "new things" can find in the Gospel the context for their correct understanding and the proper moral perspective for judgment on them.

6. With the intention of shedding light on the conflict which had arisen between capital and labor, Pope Leo XIII affirmed the fundamental rights of workers. Indeed, the key to reading the encyclical is the dignity of the worker as such, and, for the same reason, the dignity of work, which is defined as follows: "to exert oneself for the sake of procuring what is necessary for the various purposes of life, and first of all for self-preservation."[12] The pope describes work as "personal, inasmuch as the energy expended is bound up with the personality and is the exclusive property of him who acts, and, furthermore, was given to him for his advantage."[13] Work thus belongs to the vocation of every person; indeed, man expresses and fulfills himself by working. At the same time, work has a "social" dimension through its intimate relationship not only to the family, but also to the common good, since "it may truly be said that it is only by the labor of working-men that states grow rich."[14] These are themes that I have taken up and developed in my encyclical *Laborem Exercens*.[15]

Another important principle is undoubtedly that of the right to "private property."[16] The amount of space devoted to this subject in the encyclical shows the importance attached to it. The pope is well aware that private property is not an absolute value, nor does he fail to proclaim the necessary complementary principles, such as the universal destination of the earth's goods.[17]

On the other hand, it is certainly true that the type of private property which Leo XIII mainly considers is land ownership.[18] But this does not mean that the reasons adduced to safeguard private property or to affirm the right to possess the things necessary for one's personal development and the development of one's family, whatever the concrete form which that right may assume, are not still valid today. This is something which must be affirmed once more in the face of the change we are witnessing in systems formerly dominated by collective ownership of the means of production, as well as in the face of the increasing instances of poverty or, more precisely, of hindrances to private ownership in many parts of the world, including those where systems predominate which are based on an affirmation of the right to private property. As a result of these changes and of the persistence of poverty, a deeper analysis of the problem is called for, an analysis which will be developed later in this document.

7. In close connection with the right to private property, Pope Leo XIII's encyclical also affirms other rights as inalienable and proper to the human person. Prominent among these, because of the space which the pope devotes to it and the importance which he attaches to it, is the "natural human right" to form private associations. This means above all the right to establish professional associations of employers and workers, or of workers alone.[19] Here we find the reason for the church's defense and approval of the establishment of

what are commonly called trade unions: certainly not because of ideological prejudices or in order to surrender to a class mentality, but because the right of association is a natural right of the human being, which therefore precedes his or her incorporation into political society. Indeed, the formation of unions "cannot . . . be prohibited by the state," because "the state is bound to protect natural rights, not to destroy them; and if it forbids its citizens to form associations, it contradicts the very principle of its own existence."[20]

Together with this right, which—it must be stressed—the pope explicitly acknowledges as belonging to workers, or, using his own language, to "the working class," the encyclical affirms just as clearly the right to the "limitation of working hours," the right to legitimate rest and the right of children and women[21] to be treated differently with regard to the type and duration of work.

If we keep in mind what history tells us about the practices permitted or at least not excluded by law regarding the way in which workers were employed, without any guarantees as to working hours or the hygienic conditions of the workplace, or even regarding the age and sex of apprentices, we can appreciate the pope's severe statement: "It is neither just nor human so to grind men down with excessive labor as to stupefy their minds and wear out their bodies." And referring to the "contract" aimed at putting into effect "labor relations" of this sort, he affirms with greater precision, that "in all agreements between employers and workers there is always the condition expressed or understood" that proper rest be allowed, proportionate to "the wear and tear of one's strength." He then concludes: "To agree in any other sense would be against what is right and just."[22]

8. The pope immediately adds another right which the worker has as a person. This is the right to a "just wage," which cannot be left to the "free consent of the parties, so that the employer, having paid what was agreed upon, has done his part and seemingly is not called upon to do anything beyond."[23] It was said at the time that the state does not have the power to intervene in the terms of these contracts, except to ensure the fulfillment of what had been explicitly agreed upon. This concept of relations between employers and employees, purely pragmatic and inspired by a thoroughgoing individualism, is severely censured in the encyclical as contrary to the twofold nature of work as a personal and necessary reality. For if work as something personal belongs to the sphere of the individual's free use of his own abilities and energy, as something necessary it is governed by the grave obligation of every individual to ensure "the presentation of life." "It necessarily follows," the pope concludes, "that every individual has a natural right to procure what is required to live; and the poor can procure that in no other way than by what they can earn through their work."[24]

A workman's wages should be sufficient to enable him to support himself, his wife and his children. "If through necessity or fear of a worse evil the workman accepts harder conditions because an employer or contractor will afford no better, he is made the victim of force and injustice."[25]

Would that these words, written at a time when what has been called "unbridled capitalism" was pressing forward, should not have to be repeated today with the same severity. Unfortunately, even today one finds instances of contracts between employers and employees which lack reference to the most elementary justice regarding the employment of children or women, working hours, the hygienic condition of the workplace and fair pay; and this is the case despite the international declarations and conventions on the subject[26] and the internal laws of states. The pope attributed to the "public authority" the "strict duty" of providing properly for the welfare of the workers, because a failure to do so violates justice; indeed, he did not hesitate to speak of "distributive justice."[27]

9. To these rights Pope Leo XIII adds another right regarding the condition of the working class, one which I wish to mention because of its importance: namely, the right to discharge freely one's religious duties. The pope wished to proclaim this right within the context of the other rights and duties of workers, notwithstanding the general opinion, even in his day, that such questions pertained exclusively to an individual's private life. He affirms the need for Sunday rest so that people may turn their thoughts to heavenly things and to the worship which they owe to Almighty God.[28] No one can take away this human right, which is based on a commandment; in the words of the pope: "no man may with impunity violate that human dignity which God himself treats with great reverence," and consequently, the state must guarantee to the worker the exercise of this freedom.[29]

It would not be mistaken to see in this clear statement a springboard for the principle of the right to religious freedom, which was to become the subject of many solemn international declarations and conventions,[30] as well as of the Second Vatican Council's well-known declaration and of my own repeated teachings.[31] In this regard, one may ask whether existing laws and the practice of industrialized societies effectively ensure in our own day the exercise of this basic right to Sunday rest.

10. Another important aspect, which has many applications to our own day, is the concept of the relationship between the state and its citizens. *Rerum Novarum* criticizes two social and economic systems: socialism and liberalism. The opening section, in which the right to private property is reaffirmed, is devoted to socialism. Liberalism is not the subject of a special section, but it is worth noting that criticisms of it are raised in the treatment of the duties of the state.[32] The state cannot limit itself to "favoring one portion of the citizens," namely the rich and prosperous, nor can it "neglect the other," which clearly represents the majority of society. Otherwise, there would be a violation of that law of justice which ordains that every person should receive his due. "When there is question of defending the rights of individuals, the defenseless and the poor have a claim to special consideration. The richer class has many ways of shielding itself, and stands less in need of help from the state; whereas the mass of the poor have no resources of their own to fall back on, and must chiefly

depend on the assistance of the state. It is for this reason that wage-earners, since they mostly belong to the latter class, should be specially cared for and protected by the Government."[33]

These passages are relevant today, especially in the face of the new forms of poverty in the world, and also because they are affirmations which do not depend on a specific notion of the state or on a particular political theory. Leo XIII is repeating an elementary principle of sound political organization, namely, the more that individuals are defenseless within a given society, the more they require the care and concern of others, and in particular the intervention of governmental authority.

In this way what we nowadays call the principle of solidarity, the validity of which both in the internal order of each nation and in the international order I have discussed in the encyclical *Sollicitudo Rei Socialis*,[34] is clearly seen to be one of the fundamental principles of the Christian view of social and political organization. This principle is frequently stated by Pope Leo XIII, who uses the term *friendship*, a concept already found in Greek philosophy. Pope Pius XI refers to it with the equally meaningful term *social charity*. Pope Paul VI, expanding the concept to cover the many modern aspects of the social question, speaks of a *civilization of love*.[35]

11. Re-reading the encyclical in the light of contemporary realities enables us to appreciate the church's constant concern for and dedication to categories of people who are especially beloved to the Lord Jesus. The contents of the text is an excellent testimony to the continuity within the church of the so-called "preferential option for the poor," an option which I defined as a "special form of primacy in the exercise of Christian charity."[36] Pope Leo's encyclical on the "condition of the workers" is thus an encyclical on the poor and on the terrible conditions to which the new and often violent process of industrialization had reduced great multitudes of people. Today, in many parts of the world, similar processes of economic, social and political transformation are creating the same evils.

If Pope Leo XIII calls upon the state to remedy the condition of the poor in accordance with justice, he does so because of his timely awareness that the state has the duty of watching over the common good and of ensuring that every sector of social life, not excluding the economic one, contributes to achieving that good, while respecting the rightful autonomy of each sector. This should not however lead us to think that Pope Leo expected the state to solve every social problem. On the contrary, he frequently insists on necessary limits to the state's intervention and on its instrumental character, inasmuch as the individual, the family and society are prior to the state, and inasmuch as the state exists in order to protect their rights and not stifle them.[37]

The relevance of these reflections for our own day is inescapable. It will be useful to return later to this important subject of the limits inherent in the nature of the state. For now, the points which have been emphasized (certainly not the only ones in the encyclical) are situated in continuity with the church's

social teaching, and in the light of a sound view of private property, work, the economic process, the reality of the state and, above all, of man himself. Other themes will be mentioned later when we examine certain aspects of the contemporary situation. From this point forward it will be necessary to keep in mind that the main thread and, in a certain sense, the guiding principle of Pope Leo's encyclical, and of all of the church's social doctrine, is a correct view of the human person and of his unique value, inasmuch as "man . . . is the only creature on earth which God willed for itself."[38] God has imprinted his own image and likeness on man (cf. Gen. 1:26), conferring upon him an incomparable dignity, as the encyclical frequently insists. In effect, beyond the rights which man acquires by his own work, there exist rights which do not correspond to any work he performs, but which flow from his essential dignity as a person.

2. TOWARD THE "NEW THINGS" OF TODAY

12. The commemoration of *Rerum Novarum* would be incomplete unless reference were also made to the situation of the world today. The document lends itself to such a reference, because the historical picture and the prognosis which it suggests have proved to be surprisingly accurate in the light of what has happened since then.

This is especially confirmed by the events which took place near the end of 1989 and at the beginning of 1990. These events, and the radical transformations which followed, can only be explained by the preceding situations which, to a certain extent, crystallized or institutionalized Leo XIII's predictions and the increasingly disturbing signs noted by his successors. Pope Leo foresaw the negative consequences—political, social and economic—of the social order proposed by "socialism," which at that time was still only a social philosophy and not yet a fully structured movement. It may seem surprising that "socialism" appeared at the beginning of the pope's critique of solutions to the "question of the working class" at a time when "socialism" was not yet in the form of a strong and powerful state, with all the resources which that implies, as was later to happen. However, he correctly judged the danger posed to the masses by the attractive presentation of this simple and radical solution to the "question of the working class" of the time—all the more so when one considers the terrible situation of injustice in which the working classes of the recently industrialized nations found themselves.

Two things must be emphasized here: first, the great clarity in perceiving, in all its harshness, the actual condition of the working class—men, women and children; secondly, equal clarity in recognizing the evil of a solution which, by appearing to reverse the positions of the poor and the rich, was in reality detrimental to the very people whom it was meant to help. The remedy would prove worse than the sickness. By defining the nature of the social-

ism of his day as the suppression of private property, Leo XIII arrived at the crux of the problem.

His words deserve to be re-read attentively: "To remedy these wrongs (the unjust distribution of wealth and the poverty of the workers), the Socialists encourage the poor man's envy of the rich and strive to do away with private property, contending that individual possessions should become the common property of all . . .; but their contentions are so clearly powerless to end the controversy that, were they carried into effect, the working man himself would be among the first to suffer. They are moreover emphatically unjust, for they would rob the lawful possessor, distort the functions of the state, and create utter confusion in the community."[39] The evils caused by the setting up of this type of socialism as a state system—what would later be called "Real Socialism"—could not be better expressed.

13. Continuing our reflections, and referring also to what has been said in the encyclicals *Laborem Exercens* and *Sollicitudo Rei Socialis*, we have to add that the fundamental error of socialism is anthropological in nature. Socialism considers the individual person simply as an element, a molecule within the social organism, so that the good of the individual is completely subordinated to the functioning of the socioeconomic mechanism. Socialism likewise maintains that the good of the individual can be realized without reference to his free choice, to the unique and exclusive responsibility which he exercises in the face of good or evil. Man is thus reduced to a series of social relationships, and the concept of the person as the autonomous subject of moral decision disappears, the very subject whose decisions build the social order. From this mistaken conception of the person there arise both a distortion of law, which defines the sphere of the exercise of freedom, and an opposition to private property. A person who is deprived of something he can call his own and of the possibility of earning a living through his own initiative, comes to depend on the social machine and on those who control it. This makes it much more difficult for him to recognize his dignity as a person, and hinders progress toward the building up of an authentic human community.

In contrast, from the Christian vision of the human person there necessarily follows a correct picture of society. According to *Rerum Novarum* and the whole social doctrine of the church, the social nature of man is not completely fulfilled in the state, but is realized in various intermediary groups, beginning with the family and including economic, social, political and cultural groups which stem from human nature itself and have their own autonomy, always with a view to the common good. This is what I have called the "subjectivity" of society which, together with the subjectivity of the individual, was cancelled out by "Real Socialism."[40]

If we then inquire as to the source of this mistaken concept of the nature of the person and the "subjectivity" of society, we must reply that its first cause is atheism. It is by responding to the call of God contained in the being of things that man becomes aware of his transcendent dignity. Every individual must give

this response, which constitutes the apex of his humanity, and no social mechanism or collective subject can substitute for it. The denial of God deprives the person of his foundation, and consequently leads to a reorganization of the social order without reference to the person's dignity and responsibility.

The atheism of which we are speaking is also closely connected with the rationalism of the Enlightenment, which views human and social reality in a mechanistic way. Thus there is a denial of the supreme insight concerning man's true greatness, his transcendence in respect to earthly realities, the contradiction in his heart between the desire for the fullness of what is good and his own inability to attain it and, above all, the need for salvation which results from this situation.

14. From the same atheistic source, socialism also derives its choice of the means of action condemned in *Rerum Novarum*, namely, class struggle. The pope does not, of course, intend to condemn every possible form of social conflict. The church is well aware that in the course of history conflicts of interest between different social groups inevitably arise, and that in the face of such conflicts Christians must often take a position, honestly and decisively. The encyclical *Laborem Exercens* moreover clearly recognized the positive role of conflict when it takes the form of a "struggle for social justice";[41] *Quadragesimo Anno* had already stated that "if the class struggle abstains from enmities and mutual hatred, it gradually changes into an honest discussion of differences founded on a desire for justice."[42]

However, what is condemned in class struggle is the idea that conflict is not restrained by ethical or juridical considerations, or by respect for the dignity of others (and consequently of oneself); a reasonable compromise is thus excluded, and what is pursued is not the general good of society, but a partisan interest which replaces the common good and sets out to destroy whatever stands in its way. In a word, it is a question of transferring to the sphere of internal conflict between social groups the doctrine of "total war," which the militarism and imperialism of that time brought to bear on international relations. As a result of this doctrine, the search for a proper balance between the interests of the various nations was replaced by attempts to impose the absolute domination of one's own side through the destruction of the other side's capacity to resist, using every possible means, not excluding the use of lies, terror tactics against citizens, and weapons of utter destruction (which precisely in those years were beginning to be designed). Therefore class struggle in the Marxist sense and militarism have the same root, namely, atheism and contempt for the human person, which place the principle of force above that of reason and law.

15. *Rerum Novarum* is opposed to state control of the means of production, which would reduce every citizen to being a "cog" in the state machine. It is no less forceful in criticizing a concept of the state which completely excludes the economic sector from the state's range of interest and action. There is

certainly a legitimate sphere of autonomy in economic life which the state should not enter. The state, however, has the task of determining the juridical framework within which economic affairs are to be conducted, and thus of safeguarding the prerequisites of a free economy, which presumes a certain equality between the parties, such that one party would not be so powerful as practically to reduce the other to subservience.[43]

In this regard, *Rerum Novarum* points the way to just reforms which can restore dignity to work as the free activity of man. These reforms imply that society and the state will both assume responsibility, especially for protecting the worker from the nightmare of unemployment. Historically, this has happened in two converging ways: either through economic policies aimed at ensuring balanced growth and full employment, or through unemployment insurance and re-training programs capable of ensuring a smooth transfer of workers from crisis sectors to those in expansion.

Furthermore, society and the state must ensure wage levels adequate for the maintenance of the worker and his family, including a certain amount for savings. This requires a continuous effort to improve workers' training and capability so that their work will be more skilled and productive, as well as careful controls and adequate legislative measures to block shameful forms of exploitation, especially to the disadvantage of the most vulnerable workers, of immigrants and of those on the margins of society. The role of trade unions in negotiating minimum salaries and working conditions is decisive in this area.

Finally, "humane" working hours and adequate free time need to be guaranteed, as well as the right to express one's own personality at the workplace without suffering any affront to one's conscience or personal dignity. This is the place to mention once more the role of trade unions, not only in negotiating contracts, but also as "places" where workers can express themselves. They serve the development of an authentic culture of work and help workers to share in a fully human way in the life of their place of employment.[44]

The state must contribute to the achievement of these goals both directly and indirectly. Indirectly and according to the principle of subsidiarity by creating favorable conditions for the free exercise of economic activity, which will lead to abundant opportunities for employment and sources of wealth. Directly and according to the principle of solidarity, by defending the weakest, by placing certain limits on the autonomy of the parties who determine working conditions, and by ensuring in every case the necessary minimum support for the unemployed worker.[45]

The encyclical and the related social teaching of the church had far-reaching influence in the years bridging the nineteenth and twentieth centuries. This influence is evident in the numerous reforms which were introduced in the areas of social security, pensions, health insurance and compensation in the case of accidents, within the framework of greater respect for the rights of workers.[46]

16. These reforms were carried out in part by states, but in the struggle to achieve them the role of the workers' movement was an important one. This movement, which began as a response of moral conscience to unjust and harmful situations, conducted a widespread campaign for reform, far removed from vague ideology and closer to the daily needs of workers. In this context its efforts were often joined to those of Christians in order to improve workers' living conditions. Later on, this movement was dominated to a certain extent by the Marxist ideology against which *Rerum Novarum* had spoken.

These same reforms were also partly the result of an open process by which society organized itself through the establishment of effective instruments of solidarity, which were capable of sustaining an economic growth more respectful of the values of the person. Here we should remember the numerous efforts to which Christians made a notable contribution in establishing producers', consumers' and credit cooperatives, in promoting general education and professional training, in experimenting with various forms of participation in the life of the workplace and in the life of society in general.

Thus, as we look at the past, there is good reason to thank God that the great encyclical was not without an echo in human hearts and indeed led to a generous response on the practical level. Still, we must acknowledge that its prophetic message was not fully accepted by people at the time. Precisely for this reason there ensued some very serious tragedies.

17. Reading the encyclical within the context of Pope Leo's whole magisterium,[47] we see how it points essentially to the socioeconomic consequences of an error which has even greater implications. As has been mentioned, this error consists in an understanding of human freedom which detaches it from obedience to the truth, and consequently from the duty to respect the rights of others. The essence of freedom then becomes self-love carried to the point of contempt for God and neighbor, a self-love which leads to an unbridled affirmation of self-interest and which refuses to be limited by any demand of justice.[48]

This very error had extreme consequences in the tragic series of wars which ravaged Europe and the world between 1914 and 1945. Some of these resulted from militarism and exaggerated nationalism, and from related forms of totalitarianism; some derived from the class struggle; still others were civil wars or wars of an ideological nature. Without the terrible burden of hatred and resentment which had built up as a result of so many injustices both on the international level and within individual states, such cruel wars would not have been possible, in which great nations invested their energies and in which there was no hesitation to violate the most sacred human rights, with the extermination of entire peoples and social groups being planned and carried out. Here we recall the Jewish people in particular, whose terrible fate has become a symbol of the aberration of which man is capable when he turns against God.

However, it is only when hatred and injustice are sanctioned and organized by the ideologies based on them, rather than on the truth about man, that

they take possession of entire nations and drive them to act.[49] *Rerum Novarum* opposed ideologies of hatred and showed how violence and resentment could be overcome by justice. May the memory of those terrible events guide the actions of everyone, particularly the leaders of nations in our own time, when other forms of injustice are fuelling new hatreds and when new ideologies which exalt violence are appearing on the horizon.

18. While it is true that since 1945 weapons have been silent on the European continent, it must be remembered that true peace is never simply the result of military victory, but rather implies both the removal of the causes of war and genuine reconciliation between peoples. For many years there has been in Europe and the world a situation of non-war rather than genuine peace. Half of the continent fell under the domination of a communist dictatorship, while the other half organized itself in defense against this threat. Many peoples lost the ability to control their own destiny and were enclosed within the suffocating boundaries of an empire in which efforts were made to destroy their historical memory and the centuries-old roots of their culture. As a result of this violent division of Europe, enormous masses of people were compelled to leave their homeland or were forcibly deported.

An insane arms race swallowed up the resources needed for the development of national economies and for assistance to the less developed nations. Scientific and technological progress, which should have contributed to man's well-being, was transformed into an instrument of war: science and technology were directed to the production of ever more efficient and destructive weapons. Meanwhile, an ideology, a perversion of authentic philosophy, was called upon to provide doctrinal justification for the new war. And this war was not simply expected and prepared for, but was actually fought with enormous bloodshed in various parts of the world. The logic of power blocs or empires, denounced in various church documents and recently in the encyclical *Sollicitudo Rei Socialis*,[50] led to a situation in which controversies and disagreements among Third World countries were systematically aggravated and exploited in order to create difficulties for the adversary.

Extremist groups, seeking to resolve such controversies through the use of arms, found ready political and military support and were equipped and trained for war; those who tried to find peaceful and humane solutions, with respect for the legitimate interests of all parties, remained isolated and often fell victim to their opponents. In addition, the precariousness of the peace which followed the Second World War was one of the principal causes of the militarization of many Third World countries and the fratricidal conflicts which afflicted them, as well as of the spread of terrorism and of increasingly barbaric means of political and military conflict. Moreover, the whole world was oppressed by the threat of an atomic war capable of leading to the extinction of humanity. Science used for military purposes had placed this decisive instrument at the disposal of hatred, strengthened by ideology. But if war can end without winners or losers in a suicide of humanity, then we must repudiate

the logic which leads to it: the idea that the effort to destroy the enemy, confrontation and war itself are factors of progress and historical advancement.[51] When the need for this repudiation is understood, the concepts of "total war" and "class struggle" must necessarily be called into question.

19. At the end of the Second World War, however, such a development was still being formed in people's consciences. What received attention was the spread of communist totalitarianism over more than half of Europe and over other parts of the world. The war, which should have re-established freedom and restored the right of nations, ended without having attained these goals. Indeed, in a way, for many peoples, especially those which had suffered most during the war, it openly contradicted these goals. It may be said that the situation which arose has evoked different responses.

Following the destruction caused by the war, we see in some countries and under certain aspects a positive effort to rebuild a democratic society inspired by social justice, so as to deprive communism of the revolutionary potential represented by masses of people subjected to exploitation and oppression. In general, such attempts endeavor to preserve free market mechanisms, ensuring, by means of a stable currency and the harmony of social relations, the conditions for steady and healthy economic growth in which people through their own work can build a better future for themselves and their families. At the same time, these attempts try to avoid making market mechanisms the only point of reference for social life, and they tend to subject them to public control which upholds the principle of the common destination of material goods. In this context, an abundance of work opportunities, a solid system of social security and professional training, the freedom to join trade unions and the effective action of unions, the assistance provided in cases of unemployment, the opportunities for democratic participation in the life of society—all these are meant to deliver work from the mere condition of a "commodity," and to guarantee its dignity.

Then there are the other social forces and ideological movements which oppose Marxism by setting up systems of "national security," aimed at controlling the whole of society in a systematic way, in order to make Marxist infiltration impossible. By emphasizing and increasing the power of the state, they wish to protect their people from communism, but in doing so they run the grave risk of destroying the freedom and values of the person, the very things for whose sake it is necessary to oppose communism.

Another kind of response, practical in nature, is represented by the affluent society or the consumer society. It seeks to defeat Marxism on the level of pure materialism by showing how a free market society can achieve a greater satisfaction of material human needs than communism, while equally excluding spiritual values. In reality, while on the one hand it is true that this social model shows the failure of Marxism to contribute to a humane and better society, on the other hand, insofar as it denies an autonomous existence and value to morality, law, culture and religion, it agrees with Marxism, in the sense that it totally reduces man to the sphere of economics and the satisfaction of material needs.

20. During the same period a widespread process of "decolonization" occurred, by which many countries gained or regained their independence and the right freely to determine their own destiny. With the formal re-acquisition of state sovereignty, however, these countries often find themselves merely at the beginning of the journey toward the construction of genuine independence. Decisive sectors of the economy still remain de facto in the hands of large foreign companies which are unwilling to commit themselves to the long-term development of the host country. Political life itself is controlled by foreign powers, while within the national boundaries there are tribal groups not yet amalgamated into a genuine national community. Also lacking is a class of competent professional people capable of running the state apparatus in an honest and just way, nor are there qualified personnel for managing the economy in an efficient and responsible manner.

Given this situation, many think that Marxism can offer a sort of shortcut for building up the nation and the state; thus many variants of socialism emerge with specific national characteristics. Legitimate demands for national recovery, forms of nationalism and also of militarism, principles drawn from ancient popular traditions (which are sometimes in harmony with Christian social doctrine) and Marxist-Leninist concepts and ideas—all these mingle in the many ideologies which take shape in ways that differ from case to case.

21. Lastly, it should be remembered that after the Second World War, and in reaction to its horrors, there arose a more lively sense of human rights, which found recognition in a number of international documents[52] and, one might say, in the drawing up of a new "right of nations," to which the Holy See has constantly contributed. The focal point of this evolution has been the United Nations Organization. Not only has there been a development in awareness of the rights of individuals, but also in awareness of the rights of nations, as well as a clearer realization of the need to act in order to remedy the grave imbalances that exist between the various geographical areas of the world. In a certain sense, these imbalances have shifted the center of the social question from the national to the international level.[53]

While noting this process with satisfaction, nevertheless one cannot ignore the fact that the overall balance of the various policies of aid for development has not always been positive. The United Nations, moreover, has not yet succeeded in establishing, as alternatives to war, effective means for the resolution of international conflicts. This seems to be the most urgent problem which the international community has yet to resolve.

3. THE YEAR 1989

22. It is on the basis of the world situation just described, and already elaborated in the encyclical *Sollicitudo Rei Socialis*, that the unexpected and promising significance of the events of recent years can be understood. Although

they certainly reached their climax in 1989 in the countries of Central and Eastern Europe, they embrace a longer period of time and a wider geographical area. In the course of the 80s, certain dictatorial and oppressive regimes fell one by one in some countries of Latin America and also of Africa and Asia. In other cases there began a difficult but productive transition toward more participatory and more just political structures. An important, even decisive, contribution was made by the church's commitment to defend and promote human rights. In situations strongly influenced by ideology, in which polarization obscured the awareness of a human dignity common to all, the church affirmed clearly and forcefully that every individual—whatever his or her personal convictions—bears the image of God and therefore deserves respect. Often, the vast majority of people identified themselves with this kind of affirmation, and this led to a search for forms of protest and for political solutions more respectful of the dignity of the person.

From this historical process new forms of democracy have emerged which offer a hope for change in fragile political and social structures weighed down by a painful series of injustices and resentments, as well as by a heavily damaged economy and serious social conflicts. Together with the whole church, I thank God for the often heroic witness borne in such difficult circumstances by many pastors, entire Christian communities, individual members of the faithful, and other people of good will; at the same time I pray that he will sustain the efforts being made by everyone to build a better future. This is, in fact, a responsibility which falls not only to the citizens of the countries in question, but to all Christians and people of good will. It is a question of showing that the complex problems faced by those peoples can be resolved through dialogue and solidarity, rather than by a struggle to destroy the enemy through war.

23. Among the many factors involved in the fall of oppressive regimes, some deserve special mention. Certainly, the decisive factor which gave rise to the changes was the violation of the rights of workers. It cannot be forgotten that the fundamental crisis of systems claiming to express the rule and indeed the dictatorship of the working class began with the great upheavals which took place in Poland in the name of solidarity. It was the throng of working people which foreswore the ideology which presumed to speak in their name. On the basis of a hard, lived experience of work and of oppression, it was they who recovered and, in a sense, rediscovered the content and principles of the church's social doctrine.

Also worthy of emphasis is the fact that the fall of this kind of "bloc" or empire was accomplished almost everywhere by means of peaceful protest, using only the weapons of truth and justice. While Marxism held that only by exacerbating social conflicts was it possible to resolve them through violent confrontation, the protests which led to the collapse of Marxism tenaciously insisted on trying every avenue of negotiation, dialogue, and witness to the truth, appealing to the conscience of the adversary and seeking to reawaken in him a sense of shared human dignity.

It seemed that the European order resulting from the Second World War and sanctioned by the Yalta Agreements could only be overturned by another war. Instead, it has been overcome by the non-violent commitment of people who, while always refusing to yield to the force of power, succeeded time after time in finding effective ways of bearing witness to the truth. This disarmed the adversary, since violence always needs to justify itself through deceit, and to appear, however falsely, to be defending a right or responding to a threat posed by others.[54] Once again I thank God for having sustained people's hearts amid difficult trials, and I pray that this example will prevail in other places and other circumstances. May people learn to fight for justice without violence, renouncing class struggle in their internal dispute and war in international ones.

24. The second factor in the crisis was certainly the inefficiency of the economic system, which is not to be considered simply as a technical problem, but rather a consequence of the violation of the human rights to private initiative, to ownership of property and to freedom in the economic sector. To this must be added the cultural and national dimension: it is not possible to understand man on the basis of economics alone, nor to define him simply on the basis of class membership. Man is understood in a more complete way when he is situated within the sphere of culture through his language, history, and the position he takes toward the fundamental events of life, such as birth, love, work and death. At the heart of every culture lies the attitude man takes to the greatest mystery: the mystery of God. Different cultures are basically different ways of facing the question of the meaning of personal existence. When this question is eliminated, the culture and moral life of nations are corrupted. For this reason the struggle to defend work was spontaneously linked to the struggle for culture and for national rights.

But the true cause of the new developments was the spiritual void brought about by atheism, which deprived the younger generations of a sense of direction and in many cases led them, in the irrepressible search for personal identity and for the meaning of life, to rediscover the religious roots of their national cultures, and to rediscover the person of Christ himself as the existentially adequate response to the desire in every human heart for goodness, truth and life. This search was supported by the witness of those who, in difficult circumstances and under persecution, remained faithful to God. Marxism had promised to uproot the need for God from the human heart, but the results have shown that it is not possible to succeed in this without throwing the heart into turmoil.

25. The events of 1989 are an example of the success of willingness to negotiate and of the Gospel spirit in the face of an adversary determined not to be bound by moral principles. These events are a warning to those who, in the name of political realism, wish to banish law and morality from the political arena. Undoubtedly, the struggle which led to the changes of 1989 called for clarity, moderation, suffering and sacrifice. In a certain sense, it was a

struggle born of prayer, and it would have been unthinkable without immense trust in God, the Lord of history, who carries the human heart in his hands. It is by uniting his own sufferings for the sake of truth and freedom to the sufferings of Christ on the Cross that man is able to accomplish the miracle of peace and is in a position to discern the often narrow path between the cowardice which gives in to evil and the violence which, under the illusion of fighting evil, only makes it worse.

Nevertheless, it cannot be forgotten that the manner in which the individual exercises his freedom is conditioned in innumerable ways. While these certainly have an influence on freedom, they do not determine it; they make the exercise of freedom more difficult or less difficult, but they cannot destroy it. Not only is it wrong from the ethical point of view to disregard human nature, which is made for freedom, but in practice it is impossible to do so. Where society is so organized as to reduce arbitrarily or even suppress the sphere in which freedom is legitimately exercised, the result is that the life of society becomes progressively disorganized and goes into decline.

Moreover, man, who was created for freedom, bears within himself the wound of original sin, which constantly draws him toward evil and puts him in need of redemption. Not only is this doctrine an integral part of Christian revelation; it also has great hermeneutical value insofar as it helps one to understand human reality. Man tends toward good, but he is also capable of evil. He can transcend his immediate interest and still remain bound to it. The social order will be all the more stable, the more it takes this fact into account and does not place in opposition personal interest and the interests of society as a whole, but rather seeks ways to bring them into fruitful harmony. In fact, where self-interest is violently suppressed, it is replaced by a burdensome system of bureaucratic control which dries up the wellsprings of initiative and creativity. When people think they possess the secret of a perfect social organization which makes evil impossible, they also think that they can use any means, including violence and deceit, in order to bring that organization into being. Politics then becomes a "secular religion" which operates under the illusion of creating paradise in this world. But no political society—which possesses its own autonomy and laws[55]—can ever be confused with the kingdom of God. The Gospel parable of the seeds among the wheat (cf. Matt. 13:24–30; 36–43) teaches that it is for God alone to separate the subjects of the kingdom from the subjects of the Evil One, and that this judgment will take place at the end of time. By presuming to anticipate judgment here and now, man puts himself in the place of God and sets himself against the patience of God.

Through Christ's sacrifice on the cross, the victory of the kingdom of God has been achieved once and for all. Nevertheless, the Christian life involves a struggle against temptation and the forces of evil. Only at the end of history will the Lord return in glory for the final judgment (cf. Matt. 25:21) with the establishment of a new heaven and a new earth (cf. 2 Pet. 3:13; Rev. 21:1); but

as long as time lasts the struggle between good and evil continues even in the human heart itself.

What sacred Scripture teaches us about the prospects of the kingdom of God is not without consequences for the life of temporal societies, which, as the adjective indicates, belong to the realm of time, with all that this implies of imperfection and impermanence. The kingdom of God, being in the world without being of the world, throws light on the order of human society, while the power of grace penetrates that order and gives it life. In this way the requirements of a society worthy of man are better perceived, deviations are corrected, the courage to work for what is good is reinforced. In union with all people of good will, Christians, especially the laity, are called to this task of imbuing human realities with the Gospel.[56]

26. The events of 1989 took place principally in the countries of Eastern and Central Europe. However, they have worldwide importance because they have positive and negative consequences which concern the whole human family. These consequences are not mechanistic or fatalistic in character, but rather are opportunities for human freedom to cooperate with the merciful plan of God who acts within history.

The first consequence was an encounter in some countries between the church and the workers' movement, which came about as a result of an ethical and explicitly Christian reaction against a widespread situation of injustice. For about a century the workers' movement had fallen in part under the dominance of Marxism, in the conviction that the working class, in order to struggle effectively against oppression, had to appropriate its economic and materialistic theories.

In the crisis of Marxism, the natural dictates of the consciences of workers have re-emerged in a demand for justice and a recognition of the dignity of work, in conformity with the social doctrine of the church.[57] The worker movement is part of a more general movement among workers and other people of good will for the liberation of the human person and for the affirmation of human rights. It is a movement which today has spread to many countries, and which, far from opposing the Catholic church, looks to her with interest.

The crisis of Marxism does not rid the world of the situations of injustice and oppression which Marxism itself exploited and on which it fed. To those who are searching today for a new and authentic theory and praxis of liberation, the church offers not only her social doctrine and, in general, her teaching about the human person redeemed in Christ, but also her concrete commitment and material assistance in the struggle against marginalization and suffering.

In the recent past, the sincere desire to be on the side of the oppressed and not to be cut off from the course of history has led many believers to seek in various ways an impossible compromise between Marxism and Christianity. Moving beyond all that was short-lived in these attempts, present circumstances are leading to a reaffirmation of the positive value of an authentic

theology of integral human liberation.[58] Considered from this point of view, the events of 1989 are proving to be important also for the countries of the Third World, which are searching for their own path to development, just as they were important for the countries of Central and Eastern Europe.

27. The second consequence concerns peoples of Europe themselves. Many individual, social, regional and national injustices were committed during and prior to the years in which communism dominated; much hatred and ill will have accumulated. There is a real danger that these will re-explode after the collapse of dictatorship, provoking serious conflicts and casualties should there be a lessening of the moral commitment and conscious striving to bear witness to truth which were the inspiration for past effort. It is to be hoped that hatred and violence will not triumph in people's hearts, especially among those who are struggling for justice, and that all people will grow in the spirit of peace and forgiveness.

What is needed are concrete steps to create or consolidate international structures capable of intervening through appropriate arbitration in conflicts which arise between nations, so that each nation can uphold its own rights and reach a just agreement and peaceful settlement vis-à-vis the rights of others. This is especially needed for the nations of Europe, which are closely united in a bond of common culture and an age-old history. A great effort is needed to rebuild morally and economically the countries which have abandoned communism. For a long time the most elementary economic relationships were distorted, and basic virtues of economic life, such as truthfulness, trustworthiness and hard work were denigrated. A patient material and moral reconstruction is needed, even as people, exhausted by longstanding privation, are asking their governments for tangible and immediate results in the form of material benefits and an adequate fulfillment of their legitimate aspirations.

The fall of Marxism has naturally had a great impact on the division of the planet into worlds which are closed to one another and in jealous competition. It has further highlighted the reality of interdependence among peoples, as well as the fact that human work, by its nature, is meant to unite peoples, not divide them. Peace and prosperity, in fact, are goods which belong to the whole human race: it is not possible to enjoy them in a proper and lasting way if they are achieved and maintained at the cost of other peoples and nations, by violating their rights or excluding them from the sources of well-being.

28. In a sense, for some countries of Europe the real post-war period is just beginning. The radical re-ordering of economic systems, hitherto collectivized, entails problems and sacrifices comparable to those which the countries of Western Europe had to face in order to rebuild after the Second World War. It is right that in the present difficulties the formerly communist countries should be aided by the united effort of other nations. Obviously they themselves must be the primary agents of their own development, but they must also be given a reasonable opportunity to accomplish this goal, something that cannot happen without the help of other countries. Moreover, their

present condition, marked by difficulties and shortages, is the result of a historical process in which the formerly communist countries were often objects and not subjects. Thus they find themselves in the present situation not as a result of free choice or mistakes which were made, but as a consequence of tragic historical events which were violently imposed on them, and which prevented them from following the path of economic and social development.

Assistance from other countries, especially the countries of Europe which were part of that history and which bear responsibility for it, represents a debt in justice. But it also corresponds to the interest and welfare of Europe as a whole, since Europe cannot live in peace if the various conflicts which have arisen as a result of the past are to become more acute because of a situation of economic disorder, spiritual dissatisfaction and desperation.

This need, however, must not lead to a slackening of efforts to sustain and assist the countries of the Third World, which often suffer even more serious conditions of poverty and want.[59] What is called for is a special effort to mobilize resources, which are not lacking in the world as a whole, for the purpose of economic growth and common development, redefining the priorities and hierarchies of values on the basis of which economic and political choices are made. Enormous resources can be made available by disarming the huge military machines which were constructed for the conflict between East and West. These resources could become even more abundant if, in place of war, reliable procedures for the resolution of conflicts could be set up, with the resulting spread of the principle of arms control and arms reduction, also in the countries of the Third World, through the adoption of appropriate measures against the arms trade.[60] But it will be necessary above all to abandon a mentality in which the poor—as individuals and as peoples—are considered a burden, as irksome intruders trying to consume what others have produced. The poor ask for the right to share in enjoying material goods and to make good use of their capacity for work, thus creating a world that is more just and prosperous for all. The advancement of the poor constitutes a great opportunity for the moral, cultural and even economic growth of all humanity.

29. Finally, development must not be understood solely in economic terms, but in a way that is fully human.[61] It is not only a question of raising all peoples to the level currently enjoyed by the richest countries, but rather of building up a more decent life through united labor, of concretely enhancing every individual's dignity and creativity, as well as his capacity to respond to his personal vocation, and thus to God's call. The apex of development is the exercise of the right and duty to seek God, to know him and to live in accordance with that knowledge.[62] In the totalitarian and authoritarian regimes, the principle that force predominates over reason was carried to the extreme. Man was compelled to submit to a conception of reality imposed on him by coercion, and not reached by virtue of his own reason and the exercise of his own freedom. This principle must be overturned and total recognition must be given to the right of the human conscience, which is bound only

to the truth, both natural and revealed. The recognition of these rights represents the primary foundation of every authentically free political order.[63] It is important to reaffirm this latter principle for several reasons:

a) because the old forms of totalitarianism and authoritarianism are not yet completely vanquished; indeed there is a risk that they will regain their strength. This demands renewed efforts of cooperation and solidarity between all countries.

b) because in the developed countries there is sometimes an excessive promotion of purely utilitarian values, with an appeal to the appetites and inclinations toward immediate gratification, making it difficult to recognize and respect hierarchy of the true values of human existence.

c) because in some countries new forms of religious fundamentalism are emerging which covertly, or even openly, deny to citizens of faiths other than that of the majority the full exercise of their civil and religious rights, preventing them from taking part in the cultural process, and restricting both the church's right to preach the Gospel and the rights of those who hear this preaching to accept it and to be converted to Christ. No authentic progress is possible without respect for the natural and fundamental right to know the truth and live according to that truth. The exercise and development of this right includes the right to discover and freely to accept Jesus Christ, who is man's true good.[64]

4. PRIVATE PROPERTY AND THE UNIVERSAL DESTINATION OF MATERIAL GOODS

30. In *Rerum Novarum*, Leo XIII strongly affirmed the natural character of the right to private property, using various arguments against the socialism of his time.[65] This right, which is fundamental for the autonomy and development of the person, has always been defended by the church up to our own day. At the same time, the church teaches that the possession of material goods is not an absolute right, and that its limits are inscribed in its very nature as a human right.

While the pope proclaimed the right to private ownership, he affirmed with equal clarity that the "use" of goods, while marked by freedom, is subordinated to their original common destination as created goods, as well as to the will of Jesus Christ as expressed in the Gospel. Pope Leo wrote: "those whom fortune favors are admonished . . . that they should tremble at the warnings of Jesus Christ . . . and that a most strict account must be given to the Supreme Judge for the use of all they possess"; and quoting Saint Thomas Aquinas, he added: "But if the question be asked, how must one's possessions be used? the church replies without hesitation that man should not consider his material possessions as his own, but as common to all . . .," because "above the laws and judgments of men stands the law, the judgment of Christ."[66]

The successors of Leo XIII have repeated this twofold affirmation: the necessity and therefore the legitimacy of private ownership, as well as the limits which are imposed on it.[67] The Second Vatican Council likewise clearly restated the traditional doctrine in words which bear repeating: "In making use of the exterior things we lawfully possess, we ought to regard them not just as our own but also as common, in the sense that they can profit not only the owners but others too"; and a little later we read: "Private property or some ownership of external goods affords each person the scope needed for personal and family autonomy, and should be regarded as an extension of human freedom. . . . Of its nature private property also has a social function which is based on the law of the common purpose of goods."[68] I have returned to this same doctrine, first in my address to the Third Conference of the Latin American Bishops at Puebla, and later in the encyclicals *Laborem Exercens* and *Sollicitudo Rei Socialis*.[69]

31. Re-reading this teaching on the right to property and the common destination of material wealth as it applies to the present time, the question can be raised concerning the origin of the material goods which sustain human life, satisfy people's needs and are an object of their rights.

The original source of all that is good is the very act of God, who created both the earth and man, and who gave the earth to man so that he might have dominion over it by his work and enjoy its fruits (Gen. 1:28). God gave the earth to the whole human race for the sustenance of all its members, without excluding or favoring anyone. This is the foundation of the universal destination of the earth's goods. The earth, by reason of its fruitfulness and its capacity to satisfy human needs, is God's first gift for the sustenance of human life. But the earth does not yield its fruits without a particular human response to God's gift, that is to say, without work. It is through work that man, using his intelligence and exercising his freedom, succeeds in dominating the earth and making it a fitting home. In this way, he makes part of the earth his own, precisely the part which he has acquired through work; this is the origin of individual property. Obviously, he also has the responsibility not to hinder others from having their own part of God's gift; indeed, he must cooperate with others so that together all can dominate the earth.

In history, these two factors—work and the land—are to be found at the beginning of every human society. However, they do not always stand in the same relationship to each other. At one time the natural fruitfulness of the earth appeared to be, and was in fact, the primary factor of wealth, while work was, as it were, the help and support for this fruitfulness. In our time, the role of human work is becoming increasingly important as the productive factor both of non-material and of material wealth. Moreover, it is becoming clearer how a person's work is naturally interrelated with the work of others. More than ever, work is work with others and work for others: it is a matter of doing something for someone else. Work becomes ever more fruitful and productive to the extent that people become more knowledgeable

of the productive potentialities of the earth and more profoundly cognizant of the needs of those for whom their work is done.

32. In our time, in particular, there exists another form of ownership which is becoming no less important than land: the possession of know-how, technology and skill. The wealth of the industrialized nations is based much more on this kind of ownership than on natural resources. Mention has just been made of the fact that people work with each other, sharing in a "community of work" which embraces ever widening circles. A person who produces something other than for his own use generally does so in order that others may use it after they have paid a just price, mutually agreed upon through free bargaining. It is precisely the ability to foresee both the needs of others and the combinations of productive factors most adapted to satisfying those needs that constitutes another important source of wealth in modern society. Besides, many goods cannot be adequately produced through the world of an isolated individual; they require the cooperation of many people in working toward a common goal. Organizing such a productive effort, planning its duration in time, making sure that it corresponds in a positive way to the demands which it must satisfy, and taking the necessary risks—all this too is a source of wealth in today's society. In this way, the role of disciplined and creative human work and, as an essential part of that work, initiative and entrepreneurial ability becomes increasingly evident and decisive.[70]

This process, which throws practical light on truth about the person which Christianity has constantly affirmed, should be viewed carefully and favorably. Indeed, besides the earth, man's principal resource is man himself. His intelligence enables him to discover the earth's productive potential and the many different ways in which human needs can be satisfied. It is his disciplined work in close collaboration with others that makes possible the creation of ever more extensive working communities which can be relied upon to transform man's natural and human environments. Important virtues are involved in this process, such as diligence, industriousness, prudence in undertaking reasonable risks, reliability and fidelity in interpersonal relationships, as well as courage in carrying out decisions which are difficult and painful but necessary, both for the overall working of a business and in meeting possible setbacks.

The modern business economy has positive aspects. Its basis is human freedom exercised in the economic field, just as it is exercised in many other fields. Economic activity is indeed but one sector in a great variety of human activities, and like every other sector, it includes the right to freedom, as well as the duty of making responsible use of freedom. But it is important to note that there are specific differences between the trends of modern society and those of the past, even the recent past. Whereas at one time the decisive factor of production was the land, and later capital—understood as a total complex of the instruments of production—today the decisive factor is increasingly man himself, that is, his knowledge, especially his scientific knowledge, his capacity for

interrelated and compact organization, as well as his ability to perceive the needs of others and to satisfy them.

33. However, the risks and problems connected with this kind of process should be pointed out. The fact is that many people, perhaps the majority today, do not have the means which would enable them to take their place in an effective and humanly dignified way within a productive system in which work is truly central. They have no possibility of acquiring the basic knowledge which would enable them to express their creativity and develop their potential. They have no way of entering the network of knowledge and intercommunication which would enable them to see their qualities appreciated and utilized. Thus, if not actually exploited, they are to a great extent marginalized; economic development takes place over their heads, so to speak, when it does not actually reduce the already narrow scope of their old subsistence economies. They are unable to compete against the goods which are produced in ways which are new and which properly respond to needs, needs which they had previously been accustomed to meeting through traditional forms of organization. Allured by the dazzle of an opulence which is beyond their reach, and at the same time driven by necessity, these people crowd the cities of the Third World where they are often without cultural roots, and where they are exposed to situations of violent uncertainty, without the possibility of becoming integrated. Their dignity is not acknowledged in any real way, and sometimes there are even attempts to eliminate them from history through coercive forms of demographic control which are contrary to human dignity.

Many other people, while not completely marginalized, live in situations in which the struggle for a bare minimum is uppermost. These are situations in which the rules of the earliest period of capitalism still flourish in conditions of "ruthlessness in no way inferior to the darkest moments of the first phase of industrialization. In other cases the land is still the central element in the economic process, but those who cultivate it are excluded from ownership and are reduced to a state of quasi-servitude."[71] In these cases, it is still possible today, as in the days of *Rerum Novarum*, to speak of inhuman exploitation. In spite of the great changes which have taken place in the more advanced societies, the human inadequacies of capitalism and the resulting domination of things over people are far from disappearing. In fact, for the poor, to the lack of material goods has been added a lack of knowledge and training which prevents them from escaping their state of humiliating subjection.

Unfortunately, the great majority of people in the Third World still live in such conditions. It would be a mistake, however, to understand this "world" in purely geographic terms. In some regions and in some social sectors of that world, development programs have been set up which are centered on the use not so much of the material resources available but of the "human resources." Even in recent years it was thought that the poorest countries would develop by isolating themselves from the world market and by depending only on their own resources. Recent experience has shown that countries which did this

have suffered stagnation and recession, while the countries which experienced development were those which succeeded in taking part in the general interrelated economic activities at the international level. It seems therefore that the chief problem is that of gaining fair access to the international market, based not on the unilateral principle of the exploitation of the natural resources of these countries but on the proper use of human resources.[72]

However, aspects typical of the Third World also appear in developed countries, where the constant transformation of the methods of production and consumption devalues certain acquired skills and professional expertise, and thus requires a continual effort of re-training and updating. Those who fail to keep up with the times can easily be marginalized, as can the elderly, the young people who are incapable of finding their place in the life of society and, in general, those who are weakest or part of the so-called Fourth World. The situation of women too is far from easy in these conditions.

34. It would appear that, on the level of individual nations and of international relations, the free market is the most efficient instrument for utilizing resources and effectively responding to needs. But this is true only for those needs which are "solvent," insofar as they are endowed with purchasing power, and for those resources which are "marketable," insofar as they are capable of obtaining a satisfactory price. But there are many human needs which find no place on the market. It is a strict duty of justice and truth not to allow fundamental human needs to remain unsatisfied, and not to allow those burdened by such needs to perish. It is also necessary to help these needy people to acquire expertise, to enter the circle of exchange, and to develop their skills in order to make the best use of their capacities and resources. Even prior to the logic of a fair exchange of goods and the forms of justice appropriate to it, there exists something which is due to man because he is man, by reason of his lofty dignity. Inseparable from that required "something" is the possibility to survive and, at the same time, to make an active contribution to the common good of humanity.

In Third World context, certain objectives stated by *Rerum Novarum* remain valid, and, in some cases, still constitute a goal yet to be reached, if man's work and his very being are not to be reduced to the level of a mere commodity. These objectives include a sufficient wage for the support of the family, social insurance for old age and unemployment, and adequate protection for the conditions of employment.

35. Here we find a wide range of opportunities for commitment and effort in the name of justice on the part of trade unions and other workers' organizations. These defend workers' rights and protect their interests as persons, while fulfilling a vital cultural role, so as to enable workers to participate more fully and honorably in the life of their nation and to assist them along the path of development.

In this sense, it is right to speak of a struggle against an economic system, if the latter is understood as a method of upholding the absolute predominance

of capital, the possession of the means of production and of the land, in contrast to the free and personal nature of human work.[73] In the struggle against such a system, what is being proposed as an alternative is not the socialist system, which in fact turns out to be state capitalism, but rather a society of free work, of enterprise and of participation. Such a society is not directed against the market, but demands that the market be appropriately controlled by the forces of society and by the state, so as to guarantee that the basic needs of the whole of society are satisfied.

The church acknowledges the legitimate role of profit as an indication that a business is functioning well. When a firm makes a profit, this means that productive factors have been properly employed and corresponding human needs have been duly satisfied. But profitability is not the only indicator of a firm's condition. It is possible for the financial accounts to be in order, and yet for the people—who make up the firm's most valuable asset—to be humiliated and their dignity offended. Besides being morally inadmissible, this will eventually have negative repercussions on the firm's economic efficiency. In fact, the purpose of a business firm is not simply to make a profit, but is to be found in its very existence as a community of persons who in various ways are endeavoring to satisfy their basic needs, and who form a particular group at the service of the whole of society. Profit is a regulator of the life of a business, but it is not the only one; other human and moral factors must also be considered which, in the long term, are at least equally important for the life of a business.

We have seen that it is unacceptable to say that the defeat of so-called "Real Socialism" leaves capitalism as the only model of economic organization. It is necessary to break down the barriers and monopolies which leave so many countries on the margins of development, and to provide all individuals and nations with the basic conditions which will enable them to share in development. This goal calls for programmed and responsible efforts on the part of the entire international community. Stronger nations must offer weaker ones opportunities for taking their place in international life, and the latter must learn how to use these opportunities by making the necessary efforts and sacrifices and by ensuring political and economic stability, the certainty of better prospects for the future, the improvement of workers' skills, and the training of competent business leaders who are conscious of their responsibilities.[74]

At present, the positive efforts which have been made along these lines are being affected by the still largely unsolved problem of the foreign debt of the poorer countries. The principle that debts must be paid is certainly just. However, it is not right to demand or expect payment when the effect would be the imposition of political choices leading to hunger and despair for entire peoples. It cannot be expected that the debts which have been contracted should be paid at the price of unbearable sacrifices. In such cases it is necessary to find—as in fact is partly happening—ways to lighten, defer or even

cancel the debt, compatible with the fundamental right of peoples to subsistence and progress.

36. It would now be helpful to direct our attention to the specific problems and threats emerging within the more advanced economies and which are related to their particular characteristics. In earlier stages of development, man always lived under the weight of necessity. His needs were few and were determined, to a degree, by the objective structures of his physical makeup. Economic activity was directed toward satisfying these needs. It is clear that today the problem is not only one of supplying people with a sufficient quantity of goods, but also of responding to a demand for quality: the quality of the goods to be produced and consumed, the quality of the services to be enjoyed, the quality of the environment and of life in general.

To call for an existence which is qualitatively more satisfying is of itself legitimate, but one cannot fail to draw attention to the new responsibilities and dangers connected with this phase of history. The manner in which new needs arise and are defined is always marked by a more or less appropriate concept of man and of his true good. A given culture reveals its overall understanding of life through the choices it makes in production and consumption. It is here that the phenomenon of consumerism arises. In singling out new needs and new means to meet them, one must be guided by a comprehensive picture of man which respects all the dimensions of his being and which subordinates his material and instinctive dimensions to his interior and spiritual ones. If, on the contrary, a direct appeal is made to his instincts—while ignoring in various ways the reality of the person as intelligent and free—then consumer attitudes and lifestyles can be created which are objectively improper and often damaging to his physical and spiritual health. Of itself, an economic system does not possess criteria for correctly distinguishing new and higher forms of satisfying human needs from artificial new needs which hinder the formation of a mature personality. Thus a great deal of educational and cultural work is urgently needed, including the education of consumers in the responsible use of their power of choice, the formation of a strong sense of responsibility among producers and among people in the mass media in particular, as well as the necessary intervention by public authorities.

A striking example of artificial consumption contrary to the health and dignity of the human person, and certainly not easy to control, is the use of drugs. Widespread drug use is a sign of a serious malfunction in the social system; it also implies a materialistic and, in a certain sense, destructive "reading" of human needs. In this way the innovative capacity of a free economy is brought to a one-sided and inadequate conclusion. Drugs, as well as pornography and other forms of consumerism which exploit the frailty of the weak, tend to fill the resulting spiritual void.

It is not wrong to want to live better; what is wrong is a style of life which is presumed to be better when it is directed toward "having" rather than "being," and which wants to have more, not in order to be more but in order

to spend life in enjoyment as an end in itself.[75] It is therefore necessary to create lifestyles in which the quest for truth, beauty, goodness and communion with others for the sake of common growth are the factors which determine consumer choices, savings and investments. In this regard, it is not a matter of the duty of charity alone, that is, the duty to give from one's "abundance," and sometimes even out of one's needs, in order to provide what is essential for the life of a poor person. I am referring to the fact that even the decision to invest in one place rather than another, in one productive sector rather than another, is always a moral and cultural choice. Given the utter necessity of certain economic conditions and of political stability, the decision to invest, that is, to offer people an opportunity to make good use of their own labor, is also determined by an attitude of human sympathy and trust in Providence, which reveal the human quality of the person making such decisions.

37. Equally worrying is the ecological question which accompanies the problem of consumerism and which is closely connected to it. In his desire to have and to enjoy rather than to be and to grow, man consumes the resources of the earth and his own life in an excessive and disordered way. At the root of the senseless destruction of the natural environment lies an anthropological error, which unfortunately is widespread in our day. Man, who discovers his capacity to transform and in a certain sense create the world through his own work, forgets that this is always based on God's prior and original gift of the things that are. Man thinks that he can make arbitrary use of the earth, subjecting it without restraint to his will, as though it did not have its own requisites and a prior God-given purpose, which man can indeed develop but must not betray. Instead of carrying out his role as a cooperator with God in the work of creation, man sets himself up in place of God and thus ends up provoking a rebellion on the part of nature, which is more tyrannized than governed by him.[76]

In all this, one notes first the poverty or narrowness of man's outlook, motivated as he is by a desire to possess things rather than to relate them to the truth, and lacking that disinterested, unselfish and aesthetic attitude that is born of wonder in the presence of being and of the beauty which enables one to see in visible things the message of the invisible God who created them. In this regard, humanity today must be conscious of its duties and obligations toward future generations.

38. In addition to the irrational destruction of the natural environment, we must also mention the more serious destruction of the human environment, something which is by no means receiving the attention it deserves. Although people are rightly worried—though much less than they should be—about preserving the natural habitats of the various animal species threatened with extinction, because they realize that each of these species makes its particular contribution to the balance of nature in general, too little effort is made to safeguard the moral conditions for an authentic "human ecology."

Not only has God given the earth to man, who must use it with respect for the original good purpose for which it was given to him, but man too is God's

gift to man. He must therefore respect the natural and moral structure with which he has been endowed. In this context, mention should be made of the serious problems of modern urbanization, of the need for urban planning which is concerned with how people are to live, and of the attention which should be given to a "social ecology" of work.

Man receives from God his essential dignity and with it the capacity to transcend every social order so as to move toward truth and goodness. But he is also conditioned by the social structure in which he lives, by the education he has received and by his environment. These elements can either help or hinder his living in accordance with the truth. The decisions which create a human environment can give rise to specific structures of sin which impede the full realization of those who are in any way oppressed by them. To destroy such structures and replace them with more authentic forms of living in community is a task which demands courage and patience.[77]

39. The first and fundamental structure for "human ecology" is the family, in which man receives his first formative ideas about truth and goodness, and learns what it means to love and to be loved, and thus what it actually means to be a person. Here we mean the family founded on marriage, in which the mutual gift of self by husband and wife creates an environment in which children can be born and develop their potentialities, become aware of their dignity and prepare to face their unique and individual destiny. But it often happens that people are discouraged from creating the proper conditions for human reproduction and are led to consider themselves and their lives as a series of sensations to be experienced rather than as a work to be accomplished. The result is a lack of freedom, which causes a person to reject a commitment to enter into a stable relationship with another person and to bring children into the world, or which leads people to consider children as one of the many "things" which an individual can have or not have, according to taste, and which compete with other possibilities.

It is necessary to go back to seeing the family as the sanctuary of life. The family is indeed sacred: it is the place in which life—the gift of God—can be properly welcomed and protected against the many attacks to which it is exposed, and can develop in accordance with what constitutes authentic human growth. In the face of the so-called culture of death, the family is the heart of the culture of life.

Human ingenuity seems to be directed more toward limiting, suppressing or destroying the sources of life including recourse to abortion, which unfortunately is so widespread in the world—than toward defending and opening up the possibilities of life. The encyclical *Sollicitudo Rei Socialis* denounced systematic anti-childbearing campaigns which, on the basis of a distorted view of the demographic problem and in a climate of "absolute lack of respect for the freedom of choice of the parties involved," often subject them "to intolerable pressures . . . in order to force them to submit to this new form of oppression."[78] These policies are extending their field of action by the use of new

techniques, to the point of poisoning the lives of millions of defenseless human beings, as if in a form of "chemical warfare."

These criticisms are directed not so much against an economic system as against an ethical and cultural system. The economy in fact is only one aspect and one dimension of the whole of human activity. If economic life is absolutized, if the production and consumption of goods become the center of social life and society's only value, not subject to any other value, the reason is to be found not so much in the economic system itself as in the fact that the entire sociocultural system, by ignoring the ethical and religious dimension, has been weakened, and ends by limiting itself to the production of goods and services alone.[79]

All of this can be summed up by repeating once more that economic freedom is only one element of human freedom. When it becomes autonomous, when man is seen more as a producer or consumer of goods than as a subject who produces and consumes in order to live, then economic freedom loses its necessary relationship to the human person and ends up by alienating and oppressing him.[80]

40. It is the task of the state to provide for the defense and preservation of common goods such as the natural and human environments, which cannot be safeguarded simply by market forces. Just as in the time of primitive capitalism the state had the duty of defending the basic rights of workers, so now, with the new capitalism, the state and all of society have the duty of defending those collective goods which, among others, constitute the essential framework for the legitimate pursuit of personal goals on the part of each individual.

Here we find a new limit on the market: there are collective and qualitative needs which cannot be satisfied by market mechanisms. There are important human needs which escape its logic. There are goods which by their very nature cannot and must not be bought or sold. Certainly the mechanisms of the market offer secure advantages: they help to utilize resources better; they promote the exchange of products; above all they give central place to the person's desires and preferences, which, in a contract, meet the desires and preferences of another person. Nevertheless, these mechanisms carry the risk of an "idolatry" of the market, an idolatry which ignores the existence of goods which by their nature are not and cannot be mere commodities.

41. Marxism criticized capitalist bourgeois societies, blaming them for the commercialization and alienation of human existence. This rebuke is of course based on a mistaken and inadequate idea of alienation, derived solely from the sphere of relationships of production and ownership, that is, giving them a materialistic foundation and moreover denying the legitimacy and positive value of market relationships even in their own sphere. Marxism thus ends up by affirming that only in a collective society can alienation be eliminated. However, the historical experience of socialist countries has sadly demonstrated that collectivism does not do away with alienation but rather increases it, adding to it a lack of basic necessities and economic inefficiency.

The historical experience of the West, for its part, shows that even if the Marxist analysis and its foundation of alienation are false, nevertheless alienation—and the loss of the authentic meaning of life—is a reality in Western societies too. This happens in consumerism, when people are ensnared in a web of false and superficial gratifications rather than being helped to experience their personhood in an authentic and concrete way. Alienation is found also in work, when it is organized so as to ensure maximum returns and profits with no concern whether the worker, through his own labor, grows or diminishes as a person, either through increased sharing in a genuinely supportive community or through increased isolation in a maze of relationships marked by destructive competitiveness and estrangement, in which he is considered only a means and not an end.

The concept of alienation needs to be led back to the Christian vision of reality, by recognizing in alienation a reversal of means and ends. When man does not recognize in himself and in others the value and grandeur of the human person, he effectively deprives himself of the possibility of benefitting from his humanity and of entering into that relationship of solidarity and communion with others for which God created him. Indeed, it is through the free gift of self that man truly finds himself.[81] This gift is made possible by the human person's essential "capacity for transcendence." Man cannot give himself to a purely human plan for reality, to an abstract ideal or to a false utopia. As a person, he can give himself to another person or to other persons, and ultimately to God, who is the author of his being and who alone can fully accept his gift.[82] A man is alienated if he refuses to transcend himself and to live the experience of self-giving and of the formation of an authentic human community oriented toward his final destiny, which is God. A society is alienated if its forms of social organization, production and consumption make it more difficult to offer this gift of self and to establish this solidarity between people.

Exploitation, at least in the forms analyzed and described by Karl Marx, has been overcome in Western society. Alienation, however, has not been overcome as it exists in various forms of exploitation, when people use one another, and when they seek an ever more refined satisfaction of their individual and secondary needs, while ignoring the principal and authentic needs which ought to regulate the manner of satisfying the other ones too.[83] A person who is concerned solely or primarily with possessing and enjoying, who is no longer able to control his instincts and passions, or to subordinate them by obedience to the truth, cannot be free: obedience to the truth about God and man is the first condition of freedom, making it possible for a person to order his needs and desires and to choose the means of satisfying them according to a correct scale of values, so that the ownership of things may become an occasion of growth for him. This growth can be hindered as a result of manipulation by the means of mass communication, which impose fashions and trends of opinion through carefully orchestrated repetition, without it being

possible to subject to critical scrutiny the premises on which these fashions and trends are based.

42. Returning now to the initial question: can it perhaps be said that, after the failure of communism, capitalism is the victorious social system, and that capitalism should be the goal of the countries now making efforts to rebuild their economy and society? Is this the model which ought to be proposed to the countries of the Third World which are searching for the path to true economic and civil progress?

The answer is obviously complex. If by *capitalism* is meant an economic system which recognizes the fundamental and positive role of business, the market, private property and the resulting responsibility for the means of production, as well as free human creativity in the economic sector, then the answer is certainly in the affirmative, even though it would perhaps be more appropriate to speak of a *business economy*, *market economy* or simply *free economy*. But if by capitalism is meant a system in which freedom in the economic sector is not circumscribed within a strong juridical framework which places it at the service of human freedom in its totality, and which sees it as a particular aspect of that freedom, the core of which is ethical and religious, then the reply is certainly negative.

The Marxist solution has failed, but the realities of marginalization and exploitation remain in the world, especially the Third World, as does the reality of human alienation, especially in the more advanced countries. Against these phenomena the church strongly raises her voice. Vast multitudes are still living in conditions of great material and moral poverty. The collapse of the communist system in so many countries certainly removes an obstacle to facing these problems in an appropriate and realistic way, but it is not enough to bring about their solution. Indeed, there is a risk that a radical capitalistic ideology could spread which refuses even to consider these problems, in the a priori belief that any attempt to solve them is doomed to failure, and which blindly entrusts their solution to the free development of market forces.

43. The church has no models to present; models that are real and truly effective can only arise within the framework of different historical situations, through the efforts of all those who responsibly confront concrete problems in all their social, economic, political and cultural aspects, as these interact with one another.[84] For such a task the church offers her social teaching as an indispensable and ideal orientation, a teaching which, as already mentioned, recognizes the positive value of the market and of enterprise, but which at the same time points out that these need to be oriented toward the common good. This teaching also recognizes the legitimacy of workers' efforts to obtain full respect for their dignity and to gain broader areas of participation in the life of industrial enterprises so that, while cooperating with others and under the direction of others, they can in a certain sense "work for themselves"[85] through the exercise of their intelligence and freedom.

The integral development of the human person through work does not impede but rather promotes the greater productivity and efficiency of work itself, even though it may weaken consolidated power structures. A business cannot be considered only as a "society of capital goods"; it is also a "society of persons" in which people participate in different ways and with specific responsibilities, whether they supply the necessary capital for the company's activities or take part in such activities through their labor. To achieve these goals there is still need for a broad associated workers' movement, directed toward the liberation and promotion of the whole person.

In the light of today's "new things," we have reread the relationship between individual or private property and the universal destination of material wealth. Man fulfills himself by using his intelligence and freedom. In so doing he utilizes the things of this world as objects and instruments and makes them his own. The foundation of the right to private initiative and ownership is to be found in this activity. By means of his work man commits himself, not only for his own sake but also for others and with others. Each person collaborates in the work of others and for their good. Man works in order to provide for the needs of his family, his community, his nation, and ultimately all humanity.[86] Moreover, he collaborates in the work of his fellow employees, as well as in the work of suppliers and in the customers' use of goods, in a progressively expanding chain of solidarity. Ownership of the means of production, whether in industry or agriculture, is just and legitimate if it serves useful work. It becomes illegitimate, however, when it is not utilized or when it serves to impede the work of others, in an effort to gain a profit which is not the result of the overall expansion of work and the wealth of society, but rather is the result of curbing them or of illicit exploitation, speculation or the breaking of solidarity among working people.[87] Ownership of this kind has no justification, and represents an abuse in the sight of God and man.

The obligation to earn one's bread by the sweat of one's brow also presumes the right to do so. A society in which this right is systematically denied, in which economic policies do not allow workers to reach satisfactory levels of employment, cannot be justified from an ethical point of view, nor can that society attain social peace.[88] Just as the person fully realizes himself in the free gift of self, so too ownership morally justifies itself in the creation, at the proper time and in the proper way, of opportunities for work and human growth for all.

5. STATE AND CULTURE

44. Pope Leo XIII was aware of the need for a sound theory of the state in order to ensure the normal development of man's spiritual and temporal activities, both of which are indispensable.[89] For this reason, in one passage of *Rerum Novarum* he presents the organization of society according to the three powers—legislative, executive and judicial—something which at the time

represented a novelty in church teaching.[90] Such an ordering reflects a realistic vision of man's social nature, which calls for legislation capable of protecting the freedom of all. To that end, it is preferable that each power be balanced by other powers and by other spheres of responsibility which keep it within proper bounds. This is the principle of the "rule of law," in which the law is sovereign, and not the arbitrary will of individuals.

In modern times, this concept has been opposed by totalitarianism, which, in its Marxist-Leninist form, maintains that some people, by virtue of a deeper knowledge of the laws of the development of society, or through membership of a particular class or through contact with the deeper sources of the collective consciousness, are exempt from error and can therefore arrogate to themselves the exercise of absolute power. It must be added that totalitarianism arises out of a denial of truth in the objective sense. If there is no transcendent truth, in obedience to which man achieves his full identity, then there is no sure principle for guaranteeing just relations between people. Their self-interest as a class, group or nation would inevitably set them in opposition to one another. If one does not acknowledge transcendent truth, then the force of power takes over, and each person tends to make full use of the means at his disposal in order to impose his own interests or his own opinion, with no regard for the rights of others. People are then respected only to the extent that they can be exploited for selfish ends. Thus, the root of modern totalitarianism is to be found in the denial of the transcendent dignity of the human person who, as the visible image of the invisible God, is therefore by his very nature the subject of rights which no one may violate—no individual, group, class, nation or state. Not even the majority of a social body may violate these rights, by going against the minority, by isolating, oppressing, or exploiting it, or by attempting to annihilate it.[91]

45. The culture and praxis of totalitarianism also involve a rejection of the church. The state or the party which claims to be able to lead history toward perfect goodness, and which sets itself above all values, cannot tolerate the affirmation of an objective criterion of good and evil beyond the will of those in power, since such a criterion, in given circumstances, could be used to judge their actions. This explains why totalitarianism attempts to destroy the church, or at least to reduce her to submission, making her an instrument of its own ideological apparatus.[92]

Furthermore, the totalitarian state tends to absorb within itself the nation, society, the family, religious groups and individuals themselves. In defending her own freedom, the church is also defending the human person, who must obey God rather than men (cf. Acts 5:29), as well as defending the family, the various social organizations and nations—all of which enjoy their own spheres of autonomy and sovereignty.

46. The church values the democratic system inasmuch as it ensures the participation of citizens in making political choices, guarantees to the governed the possibility both of electing and holding accountable those who govern

them, and of replacing them through peaceful means when appropriate.[93] Thus she cannot encourage the formation of narrow ruling groups which usurp the power of the state for individual interests or for ideological ends.

Authentic democracy is possible only in a state ruled by law, and on the basis of a correct conception of the human person. It requires that the necessary conditions be present for the advancement both of the individual through education and formation in true ideals, and of the "subjectivity" of society through the creation of structures of participation and shared responsibility. Nowadays there is a tendency to claim that agnosticism and skeptical relativism are the philosophy and the basic attitude which correspond to democratic forms of political life. Those who are convinced that they know the truth and firmly adhere to it are considered unreliable from a democratic point of view, since they do not accept that truth is determined by the majority, or that it is subject to variation according to different political trends. It must be observed in this regard that if there is no ultimate truth to guide and direct political activity, then ideas and convictions can easily be manipulated for reasons of power. As history demonstrates, a democracy without values easily turns into open or thinly disguised totalitarianism.

Nor does the church close her eyes to the danger of fanaticism or fundamentalism among those who, in the name of an ideology which purports to be scientific or religious, claim the right to impose on others their own concept of what is true and good. Christian truth is not of this kind. Since it is not an ideology, the Christian faith does not presume to imprison changing sociopolitical realities in a rigid schema, and it recognizes that human life is realized in history in conditions that are diverse and imperfect. Furthermore, in constantly reaffirming the transcendent dignity of the person, the church's method is always that of respect for freedom.[94]

But freedom attains its full development only by accepting the truth. In a world without truth, freedom loses its foundation and man is exposed to the violence of passion and to manipulation, both open and hidden. The Christian upholds freedom and serves it, constantly offering to others the truth which he has known (cf. John 8:31–32), in accordance with the missionary nature of his vocation. While paying heed to every fragment of truth which he encounters in the life experience and in the culture of individuals and of nations, he will not fail to affirm in dialogue with others all that his faith and the correct use of reason have enabled him to understand.[95]

47. Following the collapse of communist totalitarianism and of many other totalitarian and "national security" regimes, today we are witnessing a predominance, not without signs of opposition, of the democratic ideal, together with lively attention to and concern for human rights. But for this very reason it is necessary for peoples in the process of reforming their systems to give democracy an authentic and solid foundation through the explicit recognition of those rights.[96] Among the most important of these rights, mention must be made of the right to life, an integral part of which is the right of the child to

develop in the mother's womb from the moment of conception; the right to live in a united family and in a moral environment conducive to the growth of the child's personality; the right to develop one's intelligence and freedom in seeking and knowing the truth; the right to share in the work which makes wise use of the earth's material resources, and to derive from that work the means to support oneself and one's dependents; and the right freely to establish a family, to have and to rear children through the responsible exercise of one's sexuality. In a certain sense, the source and synthesis of these rights is religious freedom, understood as the right to live in the truth of one's faith and in conformity with one's transcendent dignity as a person.[97]

Even in countries with democratic forms of government, these rights are not always fully respected. Here we are referring not only to the scandal of abortion, but also to different aspects of a crisis within democracies themselves, which seem at times to have lost the ability to make decisions aimed at the common good. Certain demands which arise within society are sometimes not examined in accordance with criteria of justice and morality, but rather on the basis of the electoral or financial power of the groups promoting them. With time, such distortions of political conduct create distrust and apathy, with a subsequent decline in the political participation and civic spirit of the general population, which feel abused and disillusioned. As a result, there is a growing inability to situate particular interest within the framework of a coherent vision of the common good. The latter is not simply the sum total of particular interests; rather it involves an assessment and integration of those interests on the basis of a balanced hierarchy of values; ultimately it demands a correct understanding of the dignity and the rights of the person.[98]

The church respects the legitimate autonomy of the democratic order and is not entitled to express preferences for this or that institutional or constitutional solution. Her contribution to the political order is precisely her vision of the dignity of the person revealed in all its fullness in the mystery of the Incarnate Word.[99]

48. These general observations also apply to the role of the state in the economic sector. Economic activity, especially the activity of a market economy, cannot be conducted in an institutional, juridical or political vacuum. On the contrary, it presupposes sure guarantees of individual freedom and private property, as well as stable currency and efficient public services. Hence the principal task of the state is to guarantee this security, so that those who work and produce can enjoy the fruits of their labors and thus feel encouraged to work efficiently and honestly. The absence of stability, together with the corruption of public officials and the spread of improper sources of growing rich and of easy profits deriving from illegal or purely speculative activities, constitutes one of the chief obstacles to development and to the economic order.

Another task of the state is that of overseeing and directing the exercise of human rights in the economic sector. However, primary responsibility in this area belongs not to the state but to individuals and to the various groups and

associations which make up society. The state could not directly ensure the right to work for all its citizens unless it controlled every aspect of economic life and restricted the free initiative of individuals. This does not mean, however, that the state has no competence in this domain, as was claimed by those who argued against any rules in the economic sphere. Rather, the state has a duty to sustain business activities by creating conditions which will ensure job opportunities, by stimulating those activities where they are lacking or by supporting them in moments of crisis.

The state has the further right to intervene when particular monopolies create delays or obstacles to development. In addition to the tasks of harmonizing and guiding development, in exceptional circumstances the state can also exercise a substitute function, when social sectors or business systems are too weak or are just getting under way, and are not equal to the task at hand. Such supplementary interventions, which are justified by urgent reasons touching the common good, must be as brief as possible, so as to avoid removing permanently from society and business systems the functions which are properly theirs, and so as to avoid enlarging excessively the sphere of state intervention to the detriment of both economic and civil freedom.

In recent years the range of such intervention has vastly expanded, to the point of creating a new type of state, the so-called "welfare state." This has happened in some countries in order to respond better to many needs and demands, by remedying forms of poverty and deprivation unworthy of the human person. However, excesses and abuses, especially in recent years, have provoked very harsh criticisms of the welfare state, dubbed the "social assistance state." Malfunctions and defects in the social assistance state are the result of an inadequate understanding of the tasks proper to the state. Here again the principle of subsidiarity must be respected: a community of a higher order should not interfere in the internal life of a community of a lower order, depriving the latter of its functions, but rather should support it in case of need and help to coordinate its activity with the activities of the rest of society, always with a view to the common good.[100]

By intervening directly and depriving society of its responsibility, the social assistance state leads to a loss of human energies and an inordinate increase of public agencies, which are dominated more by bureaucratic ways of thinking than by concern for serving their clients, and which are accompanied by an enormous increase in spending. In fact, it would appear that needs are best understood and satisfied by people who are closest to them and who act as neighbors to those in need. It should be added that certain kinds of demands often call for a response which is not simply material but which is capable of perceiving the deeper human need. One thinks of the condition of refugees, immigrants, the elderly, the sick, and all those in circumstances which call for assistance, such as drug abusers: all these people can be helped effectively only by those who offer them genuine fraternal support, in addition to the necessary care.

49. Faithful to the mission received from Christ her Founder, the church has always been present and active among the needy, offering them material assistance in ways that neither humiliate nor reduce them to mere objects of assistance, but which help them to escape their precarious situation by promoting their dignity as persons. With heartfelt gratitude to God it must be pointed out that active charity has never ceased to be practiced in the church; indeed, today it is showing a manifold and gratifying increase. In this regard, special mention must be made of volunteer work, which the church favors and promotes by urging everyone to cooperate in supporting and encouraging its undertakings.

In order to overcome today's widespread individualistic mentality, what is required is a concrete commitment to solidarity and charity, beginning in the family with the mutual support of husband and wife and the care which the different generations give to one another. In this sense the family too can be called a community of work and solidarity. It can happen, however, that when a family does decide to live up fully to its vocation, it finds itself without the necessary support from the state and without sufficient resources. It is urgent therefore to promote not only family policies, but also those social policies which have the family as their principle object, policies which assist the family by providing adequate resources and efficient means of support, both for bringing up children and for looking after the elderly, so as to avoid distancing the latter from the family unit and in order to strengthen relations between generations.[101]

Apart from the family, other intermediate communities exercise primary functions and give life to specific networks of solidarity. These develop as real communities of persons and strengthen the social fabric, preventing society from becoming an anonymous and impersonal mass, as unfortunately often happens today. It is in interrelationships on many levels that a person lives, and that society becomes more "personalized." The individual today is often suffocated between two poles represented by the state and the marketplace. At times it seems as though he exists only as a producer and consumer of goods, or as an object of state administration. People lose sight of the fact that life in society has neither the market nor the state as its final purpose, since life itself has a unique value which the state and the market must serve. Man remains above all a being who seeks the truth and strives to live in that truth, deepening his understanding of it through a dialogue which involves past and future generations.[102]

50. From this open search for truth, which is renewed in every generation, the culture of a nation derives its character. Indeed, the heritage of values which has been received and handed down is always challenged by the young. To challenge does not necessarily mean to destroy or reject a priori, but above all to put these values to the test in one's own life, and through this existential verification to make them more real, relevant and personal, distinguishing the valid elements in the tradition from false and erroneous

ones, or from obsolete forms which can be usefully replaced by others more suited to the times.

In this context, it is appropriate to recall that evangelization too plays a role in the culture of the various nations, sustaining culture in its progress toward the truth, and assisting in the work of its purification and enrichment.[103] However, when a culture becomes inward looking, and tries to perpetuate obsolete ways of living by rejecting any exchange or debate with regard to the truth about man, then it becomes sterile and is heading for decadence.

51. All human activity takes place within a culture and interacts with culture. For an adequate formation of a culture, the involvement of the whole man is required, whereby he exercises his creativity, intelligence, and knowledge of the world and of people. Furthermore, he displays his capacity for self-control, personal sacrifice, solidarity and readiness to promote the common good. Thus the first and most important task is accomplished within man's heart. The way in which he is involved in building his own future depends on the understanding he has of himself and of his own destiny. It is on this level that the church's specific and decisive contribution to true culture is to be found. The church promotes those aspects of human behavior which favor a true culture of peace, as opposed to models in which the individual is lost in the crowd, in which the role of his initiative and freedom is neglected, and in which his greatness is posited in the arts of conflict and war. The church renders this service to human society by preaching the truth about the creation of the world, which God has placed in human hands so that people may make it fruitful and more perfect through their work; and by preaching the truth about the Redemption, whereby the Son of God has saved mankind and at the same time has united all people, making them responsible for one another. Sacred Scripture continually speaks to us of an active commitment to our neighbor and demands of us a shared responsibility for all of humanity.

This duty is not limited to one's own family, nation or state, but extends progressively to all mankind, since no one can consider himself extraneous or indifferent to the lot of another member of the human family. No one can say that he is not responsible for the well-being of his brother or sister (cf. Gen. 4:9; Luke 10:29–37; Matt. 25:31–46). Attentive and pressing concern for one's neighbor in a moment of need—made easier today because of the new means of communication which have brought people closer together—is especially important with regard to the search for ways to resolve international conflicts other than by war. It is not hard to see that the terrifying power of the means of destruction—to which even medium- and small-sized countries have access—and the ever closer links between the peoples of the whole world make it very difficult or practically impossible to limit the consequences of a conflict.

52. Pope Benedict XV and his Successors clearly understood this danger.[104] I myself, on the occasion of the recent tragic war in the Persian Gulf, repeated the cry: "Never again war!" No, never again war, which destroys the lives of innocent people, teaches how to kill, throws into upheaval even the lives of

those who do the killing and leaves behind a trail of resentment and hatred, thus making it all the more difficult to find a just solution of the very problems which provoked the war. Just as the time has finally come when in individual states a system of private vendetta and reprisal has given way to the rule of law, so too a similar step forward is now urgently needed in the international community. Furthermore, it must not be forgotten that at the root of war there are usually real and serious grievances: injustices suffered, legitimate aspirations frustrated, poverty, and the exploitation of multitudes of desperate people who see no real possibility of improving their lot by peaceful means.

For this reason, another name for peace is development.[105] Just as there is a collective responsibility for avoiding war, so too there is a collective responsibility for promoting development. Just as within individual societies it is possible and right to organize a solid economy which will direct the functioning of the market to the common good, so too there is a similar need for adequate interventions on the international level. For this to happen, a great effort must be made to enhance mutual understanding and knowledge, and to increase the sensitivity of consciences. This is the culture which is hoped for, one which fosters trust in the human potential of the poor, and consequently in their ability to improve their condition through work or to make a positive contribution to economic prosperity. But to accomplish this, the poor—be they individuals or nations—need to be provided with realistic opportunities. Creating such conditions calls for a concerted worldwide effort to promote development, an effort which also involves sacrificing the positions of income and of power enjoyed by the more developed economies.[106]

This may mean making important changes in established lifestyles, in order to limit the waste of environmental and human resources, thus enabling every individual, and all the peoples of the earth to have a sufficient share of those resources. In addition, the new material and spiritual resources must be utilized which are the result of the work and culture of peoples who today are on the margins of the international community, so as to obtain an overall human enrichment of the family of nations.

6. MAN IS THE WAY OF THE CHURCH

53. Faced with the poverty of the working class, Pope Leo XIII wrote: "We approach this subject with confidence, and in the exercise of the rights which manifestly pertain to us. . . . By keeping silence we would seem to neglect the duty incumbent on us."[107] During the last hundred years the church has repeatedly expressed her thinking, while closely following the continuing development of the social question. She has certainly not done this in order to recover former privileges or to impose her own vision. Her sole purpose has been care and responsibility for man, who has been entrusted to her by Christ himself: for this man, whom, as the Second Vatican Council recalls, is the only

creature on earth which God willed for its own sake, and for which God has his plan, that is, a share in eternal salvation. We are not dealing here with man in the "abstract," but with the real, "concrete," "historical" man. We are dealing with each individual, since each one is included in the mystery of Redemption, and through this mystery Christ has united himself with each one for ever.[108] It follows that the church cannot abandon man, and that "this man is the primary route that the church must travel in fulfilling her mission . . . the way traced out by Christ himself, the way that leads invariably through the mystery of the incarnation and the redemption."[109]

This, and this alone, is the principle which inspires the church's social doctrine. The church has gradually developed that doctrine in a systematic way, above all in the century that has followed the date we are commemorating, precisely because the horizon of the church's whole wealth of doctrine is man in his concrete reality as sinful and righteous.

54. Today, the church's social doctrine focuses especially on man as he is involved in a complex network of relationships within modern societies. The human sciences and philosophy are helpful for interpreting man's central place within society and for enabling him to understand himself better as a "social being." However, man's true identity is only fully revealed to him through faith, and it is precisely from faith that the church's social teaching begins. While drawing upon all the contributions made by the sciences and philosophy, her social teaching is aimed at helping man on the path of salvation.

The encyclical *Rerum Novarum* can be read as a valid contribution to socioeconomic analysis at the end of the nineteenth century, but its specific value derives from the fact that it is a document of the magisterium and is fully a part of the church's evangelizing mission, together with many other documents of this nature. Thus the church's social teaching is itself a valid instrument of evangelization. As such, it proclaims God and his mystery of salvation in Christ to every human being, and for that very reason reveals man to himself. In this light, and only in this light, does it concern itself with everything else: the human rights of the individual, and in particular of the "working class," the family and education, the duties of the state, the ordering of national and international society, economic life, culture, war and peace, and respect for life from the moment of conception until death.

55. The church receives "the meaning of man" from divine revelation. "In order to know man, authentic man, man in his fullness, one must know God," said Pope Paul VI, and he went on to quote Saint Catherine of Siena, who, in prayer, expressed the same idea: "In your nature, O eternal Godhead, I shall know my own nature."[110]

Christian anthropology therefore is really a chapter of theology, and for this reason, the church's social doctrine, by its concern for man and by its interest in him and in the way he conducts himself in the world, "belongs to the field . . . of theology and particularly of moral theology."[111] The theological dimension is needed both for interpreting and solving present-day problems in

human society. It is worth noting that this is true in contrast both to the "atheistic" solution, which deprives man of one of his basic dimensions, namely the spiritual one, and to permissive and consumerist solutions, which under various pretexts seek to convince man that he is free from every law and from God himself, thus imprisoning him within a selfishness which ultimately harms both him and others.

When the church proclaims God's salvation to man, when she offers and communicates the life of God through the sacraments, when she gives direction to human life through the commandments of love of God and neighbor, she contributes to the enrichment of human dignity. But just as the church can never abandon her religious and transcendent mission on behalf of man, so too she is aware that today her activity meets with particular difficulties and obstacles. That is why she devotes herself with ever new energies and methods to an evangelization which promotes the whole human being. Even on the eve of the third millennium she continues to be "a sign and safeguard of the transcendence of the human person,"[112] as indeed she has always sought to be from the beginning of her existence, walking together with man through history. The Encyclical *Rerum Novarum* itself is a significant sign of this.

56. On the hundredth anniversary of that encyclical I wish to thank all those who have devoted themselves to studying, expounding and making better known Christian social teaching. To this end, the cooperation of the local churches is indispensable, and I would hope that the present anniversary will be a source of fresh enthusiasm for studying, spreading and applying that teaching in various contexts.

In particular, I wish this teaching to be made known and applied in the countries which, following the collapse of "Real Socialism," are experiencing a serious lack of direction in the work of rebuilding. The Western countries, in turn, run the risk of seeing this collapse as a one-sided victory of their own economic system, and thereby failing to make necessary corrections in that system. Meanwhile, the countries of the Third World are experiencing more than ever the tragedy of underdevelopment, which is becoming more serious with each passing day.

After formulating principles and guidelines for the solution of the worker question, Pope Leo XIII made this incisive statement: "Everyone should put his hand to the work which falls to his share, and that at once and straightway, lest the evil which is already so great become through delay absolutely beyond remedy," and he added, "in regard to the church, her cooperation will never be found lacking."[113]

57. As far as the church is concerned, the social message of the Gospel must not be considered a theory, but above all else a basis and a motivation for action. Inspired by this message, some of the first Christians distributed their goods to the poor, bearing witness to the fact that, despite different social origins, it was possible for people to live together in peace and harmony. Through the power of the Gospel, down the centuries monks tilled the land,

men and women religious founded hospitals and shelters for the poor, confraternities as well as individual men and women of all states of life devoted themselves to the needy and to those on the margins of society, convinced as they were that Christ's words "as you did it to one of the least of these my brethren, you did it to me" (Matt. 25:40) were not intended to remain a pious wish, but were meant to become a concrete life commitment.

Today more than ever, the church is aware that her social message will gain credibility more immediately from the witness of actions than as a result of its internal logic and consistency. This awareness is also a source of her preferential option for the poor, which is never exclusive or discriminatory toward other groups. This option is not limited to material poverty, since it is well known that there are many other forms of poverty, especially in modern society—not only economic but cultural and spiritual poverty as well. The church's love for the poor, which is essential for her and a part of her constant tradition, impels her to give attention to a world in which poverty is threatening to assume massive proportions in spite of technological and economic progress. In the countries of the West, different forms of poverty are being experienced by groups which live on the margins of society, by the elderly and the sick, by the victims of consumerism, and even more immediately by so many refugees and migrants. In the developing countries, tragic crises loom on the horizon unless internationally coordinated measures are taken before it is too late.

58. Love for others, and in the first place love for the poor, in whom the church sees Christ himself, is made concrete in the promotion of justice. Justice will never be fully attained unless people see in the poor person, who is asking for help in order to survive, not an annoyance or a burden, but an opportunity for showing kindness and a chance for greater enrichment. Only such an awareness can give the courage needed to face the risk and the change involved in every authentic attempt to come to the aid of another. It is not merely a matter of "giving from one's surplus," but of helping entire peoples which are presently excluded or marginalized to enter into the sphere of economic and human development. For this to happen, it is not enough to draw on the surplus goods which in fact our world abundantly produces; it requires above all a change of lifestyles, of models of production and consumption, and of the established structures of power which today govern societies. Nor is it a matter of eliminating instruments of social organization which have proved useful, but rather of orienting them according to an adequate notion of the common good in relation to the whole human family. Today we are facing the so-called "globalization" of the economy, a phenomenon which is not to be dismissed, since it can create unusual opportunities for greater prosperity. There is a growing feeling, however, that this increasing internationalization of the economy ought to be accompanied by effective international agencies which will oversee and direct the economy to the common good, something that an individual state, even if it were the most powerful on earth, would not

be in a position to do. In order to achieve this result, it is necessary that there be increased coordination among the more powerful countries, and that in international agencies the interests of the whole human family be equally represented. It is also necessary that in evaluating the consequences of their decisions, these agencies always give sufficient consideration to peoples and countries which have little weight in the international market, but which are burdened by the most acute and desperate needs, and are thus more dependent on support for their development. Much remains to be done in this area.

59. Therefore, in order that the demands of justice may be met, and attempts to achieve this goal may succeed, what is needed is the gift of grace, a gift which comes from God. Grace, in cooperation with human freedom, constitutes that mysterious presence of God in history which is Providence.

The newness which is experienced in following Christ demands to be communicated to other people in their concrete difficulties, struggles, problems and challenges, so that these can then be illuminated and made more human in the light of faith. Faith not only helps people to find solutions; it makes even situations of suffering humanly bearable, so that in these situations people will not become lost or forget their dignity and vocation.

In addition, the church's social teaching has an important interdisciplinary dimension. In order better to incarnate the one truth about man in different and constantly changing social, economic and political contexts, this teaching enters into dialogue with the various disciplines concerned with man. It assimilates what these disciplines have to contribute, and helps them to open themselves to a broader horizon, aimed at serving the individual person who is acknowledged and loved in the fullness of his or her vocation.

Parallel with the interdisciplinary aspect, mention should also be made of the practical and as it were experiential dimension of this teaching, which is to be found at the crossroads where Christian life and conscience come into contact with the real world. This teaching is seen in the efforts of individuals, families, people involved in cultural and social life, as well as politicians and statesmen to give it a concrete form and application in history.

60. In proclaiming the principles for a solution of the worker question, Pope Leo XIII wrote: "This most serious question demands the attention and the efforts of others."[114] He was convinced that the grave problems caused by industrial society could be solved only by cooperation between all forces. This affirmation has become a permanent element of the church's social teaching, and also explains why Pope John XXIII addressed his Encyclical on peace to "all people of good will."

Pope Leo, however, acknowledged with sorrow that the ideologies of his time, especially liberalism and Marxism, rejected such cooperation. Since then, many things have changed, especially in recent years. The world today is ever more aware that solving serious national and international problems is not just a matter of economic production or of juridical or social organization, but also calls for specific ethical and religious values, as well as changes of

mentality, behavior and structures. The church feels a particular responsibility to offer this contribution and, as I have written in the encyclical *Sollicitudo Rei Socialis*, there is a reasonable hope that the many people who profess no religion will also contribute to providing the social question with the necessary ethical foundation.[115]

In that same encyclical I also addressed an appeal to the Christian churches and to all the great world religions, inviting them to offer the unanimous witness of our common convictions regarding the dignity of man, created by God.[116] In fact I am convinced that the various religions now and in the future, will have a preeminent role in preserving peace and in building a society worthy of man.

Indeed, openness to dialogue and to cooperation is required of all people of good will, and in particular of individuals and groups with specific responsibilities in the areas of politics, economics and social life, at both the national and international levels.

61. At the beginning of industrialized society, it was "a yoke little better than that of slavery itself" which led my predecessor to speak out in defense of man. Over the past hundred years the church has remained faithful to this duty. Indeed, she intervened in the turbulent period of class struggle after the First World War in order to defend man from economic exploitation and from the tyranny of the totalitarian systems. After the Second World War, she put the dignity of the person at the center of her social messages, insisting that material goods were meant for all, and that the social order ought to be free of oppression and based on a spirit of cooperation and solidarity. The church has constantly repeated that the person and society need not only material goods but spiritual and religious values as well. Furthermore, as she has become more aware of the fact that too many people live, not in the prosperity of the Western world, but in the poverty of the developing countries amid conditions which are still "a yoke little better than that of slavery itself," she has felt and continues to feel obliged to denounce this fact with absolute clarity and frankness, although she knows that her call will not always win favor with everyone.

One hundred years after the publication of *Rerum Novarum*, the church finds herself still facing "new things" and new challenges. The centenary celebration should therefore confirm the commitment of all people of good will and of believers in particular.

62. The present encyclical has looked at the past, but above all it is directed to the future. Like *Rerum Novarum*, it comes almost at the threshold of a new century, and its intention, with God's help, is to prepare for that moment.

In every age the true and perennial "newness of things" comes from the infinite power of God, who says: "Behold, I make all things new" (Rev. 21:5). These words refer to the fulfillment of history, when Christ "delivers the Kingdom to God the Father . . . that God may be everything to everyone" (1 Cor. 15:24, 28). But the Christian well knows that the newness which we await in

its fullness at the Lord's second coming has been present since the creation of the world, and in a special way since the time when God became man in Jesus Christ and brought about a "new creation" with him and through him (2 Cor. 5:17; Gal. 6:15).

In concluding this encyclical I again give thanks to Almighty God, who has granted his church the light and strength to accompany humanity on its earthly journey toward its eternal destiny. In the third millennium too, the church will be faithful in making man's way her own knowing that she does not walk alone, but with Christ her Lord. It is Christ who made man's way his own, and who guides him, even when he is unaware of it.

Mary, the mother of the Redeemer, constantly remained beside Christ in his journey toward the human family and in its midst, and she goes before the church on the pilgrimage of faith. May her maternal intercession accompany humanity toward the next millennium, in fidelity to him who "is the same yesterday and today and for ever" (cf. Heb. 13:8), Jesus Christ our Lord, in whose name I cordially impart my blessing to all.

Given in Rome, at Saint Peter's, on 1 May, the Memorial of Saint Joseph the Worker, in the year 1991, the thirteenth of my Pontificate.

JOHN PAUL II

NOTES

1. Leo XIII, encyclical *Rerum Novarum* (May 15, 1891): *Leonis XIII P.M. Acta*, XI, Rome 1892, 97–144.

2. Pius XI, encyclical *Quadragesimo Anno* (May 15, 1931): *Acta Apostolicae Sedis* 23 (1931), pp. 177–228; Pius XII, radio message of June 1, 1941: AAS 33 (1941), pp. 195–205; John XXIII, encyclical *Mater et Magistra* (May 15, 1961): AAS 53 (1961), 401–464; Paul VI, apostolic letter *Octogesima Adveniens* (May 14, 1971): AAS 63 (1971), pp. 401–41.

3. Cf. *Quadragesimo Anno*, III.

4. Encyclical *Laborem Exercens* (Sept. 14, 1981): AAS 73 (1981), pp. 577–647; encyclical *Sollicitudo Rei Socialis* (Dec. 30, 1987): AAS 80 (1988), 513–86.

5. Cf. St. Irenaeus, *Adversus Haereses*, I, 10, 1; III, 4, 1: PG 7, 549f; S. Ch. 264, pp. 154f; 211, 44–46.

6. *Rerum Novarum*, p. 132.

7. Cf., e.g., Leo XIII, encyclical *Arcanum Divinae Sapientiae* (Feb. 10, 1880): *Leonis XIII P.M. Acta*, II, Rome 1882, pp. 10–40; encyclical *Diuturnum Illud* (June 29, 1881): ibid., pp. 269–87; encyclical *Libertas Praestantissimum* (June 20, 1888): *Leonis XIII P.M. Acta*, VIII, Rome 1889, pp. 212–246; encyclical *Graves de communi* (Jan. 18, 1901): *Leonis XIII P.M. Acta*, XXI, Rome 1902, pp. 3–20.

8. *Rerum Novarum*, p. 97.

9. Ibid., p. 98.

10. Cf. ibid., pp. 109f.

11. Cf. ibid., description of working conditions; p. 44: anti-Christian workers' associations, pp. 101, 136f.

12. Ibid., p. 130; cf. also pp. 114f.

13. Ibid., p. 130.

14. Ibid., p. 123.

15. Cf. *Laborem Exercens*, 1, 2, 6.

16. Cf. *Rerum Novarum*, pp. 99–107.

17. Cf. ibid., pp. 102f.

18. Cf. ibid., pp. 101–104.

19. Cf. ibid., pp. 134f; 137f.

20. Ibid., p. 135.

21. Cf. ibid., pp. 128–129.

22. Ibid., p. 129.

23. Ibid.

24. Ibid., pp. 130f.

25. Ibid., p. 131.

26. Cf. Universal Declaration of Human Rights.

27. Cf. *Rerum Novarum*, pp. 121–123.

28. Cf. ibid., p. 127.

29. Ibid., pp. 126f.

30. Cf. Universal Declaration of Human Rights; Declaration on the elimination of every form of intolerance and discrimination based on religion or convictions.

31. Second Vatican Council, Declaration on Religious Liberty *Dignitatis Humanae*; John Paul II, letter to heads of state (Sept. 1, 1980): AAS 72 (1980), pp. 1252–1260; message for the 1988 World Day of Peace (Jan. 1, 1988): AAS 80 (1988), pp. 278–286.

32. *Rerum Novarum*, pp. 99–105; 130f; 135.

33. Ibid., p. 125.

34. Cf. *Sollicitudo Rei Socialis*, 38–40; cf. also *Mater et Magistra*, p. 407.

35. Cf. *Rerum Novarum*, pp. 114–116; *Quadragesimo Anno*, III; Paul VI, homily for the closing of the Holy Year (Dec. 25, 1975): AAS 68 (1976), p. 145; message for the 1977 World Day of Peace (Jan. 1, 1977): AAS 68 (1976), p. 709.

36. *Sollicitudo Rei Socialis*, 42.

37. Cf. *Rerum Novarum*, pp. 101f; 104f; 130f; 136.

38. Second Vatican Council, Pastoral Constitution on the Church in the Modern World *Gaudium et Spes*, 24.

39. *Rerum Novarum*, p. 99.

40. Cf. *Sollicitudo Rei Socialis*, 15, 28.

41. Cf. *Laborem Exercens*, 11–15.

42. *Quadragesimo Anno*, III, 113.

43. Cf. *Rerum Novarum*, pp. 121–125.

44. Cf. *Laborem Exercens*, 20; discourse to the International Labor Organization in Geneva (June 15, 1982): *Insegnamenti* V/2 (1982), pp. 2250–2266; Paul VI, discourse to the ILO (June 10, 1969): AAS 61 (1969), pp. 491–502.

45. Cf. *Laborem Exercens*, 8.

46. *Quadragesimo Anno*, 14.

47. Cf. *Arcanum Divinae Sapientiae*; *Diuturnum Illud*; encyclical *Immortale Dei* (Nov. 1, 1885); *Leonis XIII P.M. Acta*, V, Rome 1886, pp. 118–150; encyclical *Sapientiae Christianae* (Jan. 10, 1890): *Leonis XIII P.M. Acta*, X, Rome 1891, pp. 10–41; encyclical *Quod Apostolici Muneris* (Dec. 28, 1878): *Leonis XIII P.M. Acta*, I, Rome 1881, pp. 170–183; *Libertas Praestantissimum*.

48. Cf. *Libertas Praestantissimum*, 10.

49. Cf. message for the 1980 World Day of Peace: AAS 71 (1979), pp. 1572–1580.

50. Cf. *Sollicitudo Rei Socialis*, 20.

51. Cf. John XXIII, encyclical *Pacem in Terris* (April 11, 1963), III: AAS 55 (1963), pp. 286–289.

52. Cf. Universal Declaration of Human Rights, issued in 1948; *Pacem in Terris*, IV; Final Act of the Conference on Cooperation and Security in Europe, Helsinki, 1975.

53. Cf. Paul VI, encyclical *Populorum Progressio* (March 26, 1967), 61–65: AAS 59 (1967), pp. 287–289.

54. Cf. message for the 1980 World Day of Peace, pp. 1572–1580.

55. Cf. *Gaudium et Spes*, 36, 39.

56. Cf. Apostolic exhortation *Christifideles Laici* (Dec. 30, 1988), 32–44: AAS 81 (1989), 431–481.

57. Cf. *Laborem Exercens*, 20.

58. Cf. Congregation for the Doctrine of the Faith, Instruction on Christian Freedom and Liberation *Libertatis Conscientia* (March 22, 1986): AAS 79 (1987), pp. 554–599.

59. Cf. discourse at the Headquarters of the ECWA on the 10th anniversary of the "Appeal for the Sahel" (Ouagadougou, Burkina Faso, Jan. 29, 1990): AAS 82 (1990), pp. 816–821.

60. Cf. *Pacem in Terris*, III.

61. Cf. *Sollicitudo Rei Socialis*, 27–28; *Populorum Progressio*, 43–44.

62. Cf. *Sollicitudo Rei Socialis*, 29–31.

63. Cf. Helsinki Final Act and Vienna Accord; *Libertas Praestantissimum*, 5.

64. Cf. encyclical *Redemptoris Missio* (Dec. 7, 1990), 7: *L'Osservatore Romano*, Jan. 23, 1991.

65. Cf. *Rerum Novarum*, pp. 99–107; 131–133.

66. Ibid., pp. 111–113f.

67. Cf. *Quadragesimo Anno*, II; Pius XII, radio message on June 1, 1941, p. 199; *Mater et Magistra*, pp. 428–429; *Populorum Progressio*, 22–24.

68. *Gaudium et Spes*, 69, 71.

69. Cf. discourse to Latin American bishops at Puebla (Jan. 28, 1979), III, 4: AAS 71 (1979), pp. 199–201; *Laborem Exercens*, 14; *Sollicitudo Rei Socialis*, 42.

70. Cf. *Sollicitudo Rei Socialis*, 15.

71. Cf. *Laborem Exercens*, 21.

72. Cf. *Populorum Progressio*, 33–42.

73. Cf. *Laborem Exercens*, 7.

74. Cf. ibid., 8.

75. Cf. *Gaudium et Spes*, 35; *Populorum Progressio*, 19.

76. Cf. *Sollicitudo Rei Socialis*, 34; message for the 1990 World Day of Peace: AAS 82 (1990), pp. 147–156.

77. Cf. apostolic exhortation *Reconciliatio et Poenitentia* (Dec. 2, 1984), 16: AAS 77 (1985), pp. 213–217; *Quadragesimo Anno*, III.

78. *Sollicitudo Rei Socialis*, 25.

79. Cf. ibid., 34.

80. Cf. encyclical *Redemptor Hominis* (March 4, 1979), 15: AAS 71 (1979), pp. 286–289.

81. Cf. *Gaudium et Spes*, 24.

82. Cf. ibid., 41.

83. Cf. ibid., 26.

84. Cf. ibid., 36; *Octogesima Adveniens*, 2–5.

85. Cf. *Laborem Exercens*, 15.

86. Cf. ibid., 10.

87. Ibid., 14.

88. Cf. ibid., 18.

89. Cf. *Rerum Novarum*, pp. 126–128.

90. Ibid., pp. 121f.

91. Cf. *Libertas Praestantissimum*, pp. 224–226.

92. Cf. *Gaudium et Spes*, 76.

93. Cf. ibid., 29; Pius XII, Christmas radio message on Dec. 24, 1944: AAS 37 (1945), pp. 10–20.

94. Cf. *Dignitatis Humanae*.

95. Cf. *Redemptoris Missio*, 11.

96. Cf. *Redemptor Hominis*, 17.

97. Cf. message for the 1988 World Day of Peace, pp. 1572–1580; message for the 1991 World Day of Peace: *L'Osservatore Romano*, Dec. 19, 1990; *Dignitatis Humanae*, 1–2.

98. *Gaudium et Spes*, 26.

99. Cf. ibid., 22.

100. *Quadragesimo Anno*, I.

101. Cf. apostolic exhortation *Familiaris Consortio* (Nov. 22, 1981), 45: AAS 74 (1982), pp. 136f.

102. Cf. discourse to UNESCO (June 2, 1980): AAS 72 (1980), pp. 735–752.

103. Cf. *Redemptoris Missio*, 39, 52.

104. Cf. Benedict XV, exhortation *Ubi Primum* (Sept. 8, 1914): AAS 6 (1914), pp. 501f.; Pius XI, radio message to the Catholic faithful and to the entire world (Sept. 29, 1938): AAS 30 (1938), pp. 309f.; Pius XII, radio message to the entire world (Aug. 24, 1939): AAS 31 (1939), pp. 333–335; *Pacem in Terris*, III; Paul VI, discourse at the United Nations (Oct. 4, 1965): AAS 57 (1965), pp. 877–885.

105. Cf. *Populorum Progressio*, 76–77.

106. Cf. *Familiaris Consortio*, 48.

107. *Rerum Novarum*, p. 107.

108. Cf. *Redemptor Hominis*, 13.

109. Ibid., 14.

110. Paul VI, homily at the final public session of the Second Vatican Council (Dec. 7, 1965): AAS 58 (1966), p. 58.

111. *Sollicitudo Rei Socialis*, 41.

112. *Gaudium et Spes*, 76; cf. *Redemptor Hominis*, 13.

113. *Rerum Novarum*, p. 143.

114. Ibid., p. 107.

115. Cf. *Sollicitudo Rei Socialis*, 38.

116. Ibid., 47.

Caritas in Veritate: *On Integral Human Development in Charity and Truth* *(Benedict XVI, 2009)*

INTRODUCTION

Benedict XVI's third encyclical *Caritas in Veritate* continues the themes of love and hope developed in his previous encyclicals, *Deus Caritus Est* (2005) and *Spe Salvi* (2007) but focuses this time on the centrality of love in relation to truth. These encyclicals are typically characterized by the presentation of a theological framework in which the various themes of the encyclical are imbedded. Of interest in this encyclical are three major themes related to Franciscan theology, particularly that of St. Bonaventure. Prof. Joseph Ratzinger wrote his *Habilitationsschrift* on the theology of history in Bonaventure, and his theology provides an interesting perspective on this encyclical. First is the affirmation of all creation as a gift from the loving and generous God. This theme runs throughout the encyclical. Second, Bonaventure affirms that God has given us two books, that of Scripture and that of creation, in which we can learn of the Creator. This is affirmed by Benedict XVI, particularly in the section on ecology. Finally, the pope discusses the centrality of relationality for both understanding our relation to God and one another. For Bonaventure this is yet another image of the Trinity in our lives and also a source for learning how to live with one another. These themes culminate in the pope's affirming: "on the other hand, economic, social and political development, if it is to be authentically human, needs to make room for the *principle of gratuitousness* as an expression of fraternity" (34). As one reads the encyclical, one can note a different style and content from past ones; the theology of Bonaventure provides one reason for this.

The encyclical highlights themes from Paul VI's encyclical *Progressio Populorum* (1967). Benedict notes how Pope John Paul II also celebrated this in his encyclical *Sollicitudo Rei Socialis* (1987) and now he also wants to commemorate and reflect on themes in that encyclical. Here Benedict notes that seeking the common good "*is a requirement of justice and charity*" (7). This involves both being solicitous for all and developing the institutions that properly structure society for the benefit of all. Benedict also repeats the traditional

teaching that the church has no technical solutions for various problems nor does it seek to interfere in political issues. Rather the Church has a mission to truth and seeks to guarantee human freedom. The pope stresses two main themes of *Progressio*: The first is that "*the whole Church, in all her being and acting—when she proclaims, when she celebrates, when she performs works of charity—is engaged in promoting integral human development*." The second truth is that *authentic human development concerns the whole of the person in every single dimension*" (11). This led Paul VI to focus on the central role that charity has in full human development. For material and economic progress alone do not ultimately fulfill humans and may indeed lead to a lack of community; rather we have a transcendent vocation to live in community in the fullness of charity.

A variety of other themes emerge throughout this encyclical. The pope emphasizes that there are not "two typologies of social doctrine, one pre-conciliar and one post-conciliar, differing from one another: on the contrary, there is *a single teaching, consistent and at the same time ever new*. . . ." Coherence does not mean a closed system: on the contrary, it means dynamic faithfulness to a light received" (12). In this way Benedict hopes to close an ongoing debate within Catholic circles, though given the continual quotations from John Paul II in this encyclical and the continuing effects of John Paul II's attempts to shape Vatican II to his philosophical perspectives, such a discussion will probably continue. Also Benedict devotes considerable time to the current economic system. He highlights the value of a market economy with its moral foundation of personal responsibility. But the weak are not to be taken advantage of and market regulation is required to protect the marginalized. In connection with this, Benedict highlights the necessity of labor unions to defend the rights of workers and secure their well being.

The encyclical also focuses on a variety of life issues: procreation, bioethics, and the environment. In a phrase containing echoes of Bonaventure's understanding of nature, Benedict says nature is "a wondrous work of the Creator containing a 'grammar' which sets forth ends and criteria for its wise use, not its reckless exploitation" (48). How this grammar is to be discovered and used to read nature offers a suggestion of a more dynamic reading of traditional natural law and could serve as the basis for a much needed dialogue with scientists.

How this encyclical will help resolve debates on social justice, the economy, bioethics, the environment and the relation of various life issues remains to be seen. Benedict clearly indicates critical topics to be addressed, provides a framework for discussion, and reminds us that "Only if we are aware of our calling, as individuals and as a community, to be part of God's family as his sons and daughters, will we be able to generate a new vision and muster new energy in the service of a truly integral humanism" (78).

CARITAS IN VERITATE

ENCYCLICAL LETTER
CARITAS IN VERITATE
OF THE SUPREME PONTIFF

BENEDICT XVI

To the Bishops
Priests and Deacons
Men and Women Religious
the Lay Faithful
and All People of Good Will

ON INTEGRAL HUMAN DEVELOPMENT
IN CHARITY AND TRUTH

INTRODUCTION

1. Charity in truth, to which Jesus Christ bore witness by his earthly life and especially by his death and resurrection, is the principal driving force behind the authentic development of every person and of all humanity. Love—*caritas*—is an extraordinary force which leads people to opt for courageous and generous engagement in the field of justice and peace. It is a force that has its origin in God, Eternal Love and Absolute Truth. Each person finds his good by adherence to God's plan for him, in order to realize it fully: in this plan, he finds his truth, and through adherence to this truth he becomes free (cf. Jn. 8:32). To defend the truth, to articulate it with humility and conviction, and to bear witness to it in life are therefore exacting and indispensable forms of charity. Charity, in fact, "rejoices in the truth" (1 Cor. 13:6). All people feel the interior impulse to love authentically: love and truth never abandon them completely, because these are the vocation planted by God in the heart and mind of every human person. The search for love and truth is purified and liberated by Jesus Christ from the impoverishment that our humanity brings to it, and he reveals to us in all its fullness the initiative of love and the plan for true life that God has prepared for us. In Christ, *charity in truth* becomes the Face of his Person, a vocation for us to love our brothers and sisters in the truth of his plan. Indeed, he himself is the Truth (cf. Jn. 14:6).

2. Charity is at the heart of the Church's social doctrine. Every responsibility and every commitment spelt out by that doctrine is derived from charity which, according to the teaching of Jesus, is the synthesis of the entire Law (cf. Mt. 22:36–40). It gives real substance to the personal relationship with God and with neighbour; it is the principle not only of micro-relationships (with friends, with family members or within small groups) but also of macro-relationships (social, economic and political ones). For the Church, instructed by the Gospel, charity is everything because, as Saint John teaches (cf. 1 Jn. 4:8, 16) and as I recalled in my first Encyclical Letter, "God is love" (*Deus Caritas Est*): *everything has its origin in God's love, everything is shaped by it, everything is directed towards it*. Love is God's greatest gift to humanity, it is his promise and our hope.

I am aware of the ways in which charity has been and continues to be misconstrued and emptied of meaning, with the consequent risk of being misinterpreted, detached from ethical living and, in any event, undervalued. In the social, juridical, cultural, political and economic fields—the contexts, in other words, that are most exposed to this danger—it is easily dismissed as irrelevant for interpreting and giving direction to moral responsibility. Hence the need to link charity with truth not only in the sequence, pointed out by Saint Paul, of *veritas in caritate* (Eph. 4:15), but also in the inverse and complementary sequence of *caritas in veritate*. Truth needs to be sought, found and expressed within the "economy" of charity, but charity in its turn needs to be understood, confirmed and practised in the light of truth. In this way, not only do we do a service to charity enlightened by truth, but we also help give credibility to truth, demonstrating its persuasive and authenticating power in the practical setting of social living. This is a matter of no small account today, in a social and cultural context which relativizes truth, often paying little heed to it and showing increasing reluctance to acknowledge its existence.

3. Through this close link with truth, charity can be recognized as an authentic expression of humanity and as an element of fundamental importance in human relations, including those of a public nature. *Only in truth does charity shine forth*, only in truth can charity be authentically lived. Truth is the light that gives meaning and value to charity. That light is both the light of reason and the light of faith, through which the intellect attains to the natural and supernatural truth of charity: it grasps its meaning as gift, acceptance, and communion. Without truth, charity degenerates into sentimentality. Love becomes an empty shell, to be filled in an arbitrary way. In a culture without truth, this is the fatal risk facing love. It falls prey to contingent subjective emotions and opinions, the word "love" is abused and distorted, to the point where it comes to mean the opposite. Truth frees charity from the constraints of an emotionalism that deprives it of relational and social content, and of a fideism that deprives it of human and universal breathing-space. In the truth, charity reflects the personal yet public dimension of faith in the God of the Bible, who is both *Agápe* and *Lógos*: Charity and Truth, Love and Word.

4. Because it is filled with truth, charity can be understood in the abundance of its values, it can be shared and communicated. *Truth*, in fact, is *lógos* which creates *diá-logos*, and hence communication and communion. Truth, by enabling men and women to let go of their subjective opinions and impressions, allows them to move beyond cultural and historical limitations and to come together in the assessment of the value and substance of things. Truth opens and unites our minds in the *lógos* of love: this is the Christian proclamation and testimony of charity. In the present social and cultural context, where there is a widespread tendency to relativize truth, practising charity in truth helps people to understand that adhering to the values of Christianity is not merely useful but essential for building a good society and for true integral human development. A Christianity of charity without truth would be more or less interchangeable with a pool of good sentiments, helpful for social cohesion, but of little relevance. In other words, there would no longer be any real place for God in the world. Without truth, charity is confined to a narrow field devoid of relations. It is excluded from the plans and processes of promoting human development of universal range, in dialogue between knowledge and praxis.

5. Charity is love received and given. It is "grace" (*cháris*). Its source is the wellspring of the Father's love for the Son, in the Holy Spirit. Love comes down to us from the Son. It is creative love, through which we have our being; it is redemptive love, through which we are recreated. Love is revealed and made present by Christ (cf. Jn. 13:1) and "poured into our hearts through the Holy Spirit" (Rom. 5:5). As the objects of God's love, men and women become subjects of charity, they are called to make themselves instruments of grace, so as to pour forth God's charity and to weave networks of charity.

This dynamic of charity received and given is what gives rise to the Church's social teaching, which is *caritas in veritate in re sociali*: the proclamation of the truth of Christ's love in society. This doctrine is a service to charity, but its locus is truth. Truth preserves and expresses charity's power to liberate in the ever-changing events of history. It is at the same time the truth of faith and of reason, both in the distinction and also in the convergence of those two cognitive fields. Development, social well-being, the search for a satisfactory solution to the grave socio-economic problems besetting humanity, all need this truth. What they need even more is that this truth should be loved and demonstrated. Without truth, without trust and love for what is true, there is no social conscience and responsibility, and social action ends up serving private interests and the logic of power, resulting in social fragmentation, especially in a globalized society at difficult times like the present.

6. "*Caritas in veritate*" is the principle around which the Church's social doctrine turns, a principle that takes on practical form in the criteria that govern moral action. I would like to consider two of these in particular, of special relevance to the commitment to development in an increasingly globalized society: *justice and the common good.*

First of all, justice. *Ubi societas, ibi ius*: every society draws up its own system of justice. *Charity goes beyond justice*, because to love is to give, to offer what is "mine" to the other; but it never lacks justice, which prompts us to give the other what is "his," what is due to him by reason of his being or his acting. I cannot "give" what is mine to the other, without first giving him what pertains to him in justice. If we love others with charity, then first of all we are just towards them. Not only is justice not extraneous to charity, not only is it not an alternative or parallel path to charity: justice is inseparable from charity,[1] and intrinsic to it. Justice is the primary way of charity or, in Paul VI's words, "the minimum measure" of it,[2] an integral part of the love "in deed and in truth" (1 Jn. 3:18), to which Saint John exhorts us. On the one hand, charity demands justice: recognition and respect for the legitimate rights of individuals and peoples. It strives to build the *earthly city* according to law and justice. On the other hand, charity transcends justice and completes it in the logic of giving and forgiving.[3] The *earthly city* is promoted not merely by relationships of rights and duties, but to an even greater and more fundamental extent by relationships of gratuitousness, mercy and communion. Charity always manifests God's love in human relationships as well, it gives theological and salvific value to all commitment for justice in the world.

7. Another important consideration is the common good. To love someone is to desire that person's good and to take effective steps to secure it. Besides the good of the individual, there is a good that is linked to living in society: the common good. It is the good of "all of us," made up of individuals, families and intermediate groups who together constitute society.[4] It is a good that is sought not for its own sake, but for the people who belong to the social community and who can only really and effectively pursue their good within it. To desire the *common good* and strive towards it *is a requirement of justice and charity*. To take a stand for the common good is on the one hand to be solicitous for, and on the other hand to avail oneself of, that complex of institutions that give structure to the life of society, juridically, civilly, politically and culturally, making it the *pólis*, or "city." The more we strive to secure a common good corresponding to the real needs of our neighbours, the more effectively we love them. Every Christian is called to practise this charity, in a manner corresponding to his vocation and according to the degree of influence he wields in the *pólis*. This is the institutional path—we might also call it the political path—of charity, no less excellent and effective than the kind of charity which encounters the neighbour directly, outside the institutional mediation of the *pólis*. When animated by charity, commitment to the common good has greater worth than a merely secular and political stand would have. Like all commitment to justice, it has a place within the testimony of divine charity that paves the way for eternity through temporal action. Man's earthly activity, when inspired and sustained by charity, contributes to the building of the universal *city of God*, which is the goal of the history of the human family. In an increasingly globalized society, the common good and the effort to

obtain it cannot fail to assume the dimensions of the whole human family, that is to say, the community of peoples and nations,[5] in such a way as to shape the *earthly city* in unity and peace, rendering it to some degree an anticipation and a prefiguration of the undivided *city of God*.

8. In 1967, when he issued the Encyclical *Populorum Progressio*, my venerable predecessor Pope Paul VI illuminated the great theme of the development of peoples with the splendour of truth and the gentle light of Christ's charity. He taught that life in Christ is the first and principal factor of development[6] and he entrusted us with the task of travelling the path of development with all our heart and all our intelligence,[7] that is to say with the ardour of charity and the wisdom of truth. It is the primordial truth of God's love, grace bestowed upon us, that opens our lives to gift and makes it possible to hope for a "development of the whole man and of all men,"[8] to hope for progress "from less human conditions to those which are more human,"[9] obtained by overcoming the difficulties that are inevitably encountered along the way.

At a distance of over forty years from the Encyclical's publication, I intend to pay tribute and to honour the memory of the great Pope Paul VI, revisiting his teachings on *integral human development* and taking my place within the path that they marked out, so as to apply them to the present moment. This continual application to contemporary circumstances began with the Encyclical *Sollicitudo Rei Socialis*, with which the Servant of God Pope John Paul II chose to mark the twentieth anniversary of the publication of *Populorum Progressio*. Until that time, only *Rerum Novarum* had been commemorated in this way. Now that a further twenty years have passed, I express my conviction that *Populorum Progressio* deserves to be considered "the *Rerum Novarum* of the present age," shedding light upon humanity's journey towards unity.

9. Love in truth—*caritas in veritate*—is a great challenge for the Church in a world that is becoming progressively and pervasively globalized. The risk for our time is that the *de facto* interdependence of people and nations is not matched by ethical interaction of consciences and minds that would give rise to truly human development. Only in *charity, illumined by the light of reason and faith*, is it possible to pursue development goals that possess a more humane and humanizing value. The sharing of goods and resources, from which authentic development proceeds, is not guaranteed by merely technical progress and relationships of utility, but by the potential of love that overcomes evil with good (cf. Rom. 12:21), opening up the path towards reciprocity of consciences and liberties.

The Church does not have technical solutions to offer[10] and does not claim "to interfere in any way in the politics of States."[11] She does, however, have a mission of truth to accomplish, in every time and circumstance, for a society that is attuned to man, to his dignity, to his vocation. Without truth, it is easy to fall into an empiricist and sceptical view of life, incapable of rising to the level of praxis because of a lack of interest in grasping the values—

sometimes even the meanings—with which to judge and direct it. Fidelity to man requires *fidelity to the truth*, which alone is the *guarantee of freedom* (cf. Jn. 8:32) and of *the possibility of integral human development*. For this reason the Church searches for truth, proclaims it tirelessly and recognizes it wherever it is manifested. This mission of truth is something that the Church can never renounce. Her social doctrine is a particular dimension of this proclamation: it is a service to the truth which sets us free. Open to the truth, from whichever branch of knowledge it comes, the Church's social doctrine receives it, assembles into a unity the fragments in which it is often found, and mediates it within the constantly changing life-patterns of the society of peoples and nations.[12]

CHAPTER ONE

THE MESSAGE OF *POPULORUM PROGRESSIO*

10. A fresh reading of *Populorum Progressio*, more than forty years after its publication, invites us to remain faithful to its message of charity and truth, viewed within the overall context of Paul VI's specific magisterium and, more generally, within the tradition of the Church's social doctrine. Moreover, an evaluation is needed of the different terms in which the problem of development is presented today, as compared with forty years ago. The correct viewpoint, then, is that of the *Tradition of the apostolic faith*,[13] a patrimony both ancient and new, outside of which *Populorum Progressio* would be a document without roots—and issues concerning development would be reduced to merely sociological data.

11. The publication of *Populorum Progressio* occurred immediately after the conclusion of the Second Vatican Ecumenical Council, and in its opening paragraphs it clearly indicates its close connection with the Council.[14] Twenty years later, in *Sollicitudo Rei Socialis*, John Paul II, in his turn, emphasized the earlier Encyclical's fruitful relationship with the Council, and especially with the Pastoral Constitution *Gaudium et Spes*.[15] I too wish to recall here the importance of the Second Vatican Council for Paul VI's Encyclical and for the whole of the subsequent social Magisterium of the Popes. The Council probed more deeply what had always belonged to the truth of the faith, namely that the Church, being at God's service, is at the service of the world in terms of love and truth. Paul VI set out from this vision in order to convey two important truths. The first is that *the whole Church, in all her being and acting—when she proclaims, when she celebrates, when she performs works of charity—is engaged in promoting integral human development*. She has a public role over and above her charitable and educational activities: all the energy she brings to the advancement of humanity and of universal fraternity is manifested when she is able to operate in a climate of freedom. In not a few cases,

that freedom is impeded by prohibitions and persecutions, or it is limited when the Church's public presence is reduced to her charitable activities alone. The second truth is that *authentic human development concerns the whole of the person in every single dimension.*[16] Without the perspective of eternal life, human progress in this world is denied breathing-space. Enclosed within history, it runs the risk of being reduced to the mere accumulation of wealth; humanity thus loses the courage to be at the service of higher goods, at the service of the great and disinterested initiatives called forth by universal charity. Man does not develop through his own powers, nor can development simply be handed to him. In the course of history, it was often maintained that the creation of institutions was sufficient to guarantee the fulfilment of humanity's right to development. Unfortunately, too much confidence was placed in those institutions, as if they were able to deliver the desired objective automatically. In reality, institutions by themselves are not enough, because integral human development is primarily a vocation, and therefore it involves a free assumption of responsibility in solidarity on the part of everyone. Moreover, such development requires a transcendent vision of the person, it needs God: without him, development is either denied, or entrusted exclusively to man, who falls into the trap of thinking he can bring about his own salvation, and ends up promoting a dehumanized form of development. Only through an encounter with God are we able to see in the other something more than just another creature,[17] to recognize the divine image in the other, thus truly coming to discover him or her and to mature in a love that "becomes concern and care for the other."[18]

12. The link between *Populorum Progressio* and the Second Vatican Council does not mean that Paul VI's social magisterium marked a break with that of previous Popes, because the Council constitutes a deeper exploration of this magisterium within the continuity of the Church's life.[19] In this sense, clarity is not served by certain abstract subdivisions of the Church's social doctrine, which apply categories to Papal social teaching that are extraneous to it. It is not a case of two typologies of social doctrine, one pre-conciliar and one post-conciliar, differing from one another: on the contrary, there is *a single teaching, consistent and at the same time ever new.*[20] It is one thing to draw attention to the particular characteristics of one Encyclical or another, of the teaching of one Pope or another, but quite another to lose sight of the coherence of the overall doctrinal *corpus.*[21] Coherence does not mean a closed system: on the contrary, it means dynamic faithfulness to a light received. The Church's social doctrine illuminates with an unchanging light the new problems that are constantly emerging.[22] This safeguards the permanent and historical character of the doctrinal "patrimony"[23] which, with its specific characteristics, is part and parcel of the Church's ever-living Tradition.[24] Social doctrine is built on the foundation handed on by the Apostles to the Fathers of the Church, and then received and further explored by the great Christian doctors. This doctrine points definitively to the New Man, to the

"last Adam [who] became a life-giving spirit" (1 Cor. 15:45), the principle of the charity that "never ends" (1 Cor. 13:8). It is attested by the saints and by those who gave their lives for Christ our Saviour in the field of justice and peace. It is an expression of the prophetic task of the Supreme Pontiffs to give apostolic guidance to the Church of Christ and to discern the new demands of evangelization. For these reasons, *Populorum Progressio*, situated within the great current of Tradition, can still speak to us today.

13. In addition to its important link with the entirety of the Church's social doctrine, *Populorum Progressio* is *closely connected to the overall magisterium of Paul VI*, especially his social magisterium. His was certainly a social teaching of great importance: he underlined the indispensable importance of the Gospel for building a society according to freedom and justice, in the ideal and historical perspective of a civilization animated by love. Paul VI clearly understood that the social question had become worldwide[25] and he grasped the interconnection between the impetus towards the unification of humanity and the Christian ideal of a single family of peoples in solidarity and fraternity. *In the notion of development, understood in human and Christian terms, he identified the heart of the Christian social message*, and he proposed Christian charity as the principal force at the service of development. Motivated by the wish to make Christ's love fully visible to contemporary men and women, Paul VI addressed important ethical questions robustly, without yielding to the cultural weaknesses of his time.

14. In his Apostolic Letter *Octogesima Adveniens* of 1971, Paul VI reflected on the meaning of politics, and the *danger constituted by utopian and ideological visions* that place its ethical and human dimensions in jeopardy. These are matters closely connected with development. Unfortunately the negative ideologies continue to flourish. Paul VI had already warned against the technocratic ideology so prevalent today,[26] fully aware of the great danger of entrusting the entire process of development to technology alone, because in that way it would lack direction. Technology, viewed in itself, is ambivalent. If on the one hand, some today would be inclined to entrust the entire process of development to technology, on the other hand we are witnessing an upsurge of ideologies that deny *in toto* the very value of development, viewing it as radically anti-human and merely a source of degradation. This leads to a rejection, not only of the distorted and unjust way in which progress is sometimes directed, but also of scientific discoveries themselves, which, if well used, could serve as an opportunity of growth for all. The idea of a world without development indicates a lack of trust in man and in God. It is therefore a serious mistake to undervalue human capacity to exercise control over the deviations of development or to overlook the fact that man is constitutionally oriented towards "being more." Idealizing technical progress, or contemplating the utopia of a return to humanity's original natural state, are two contrasting ways of detaching progress from its moral evaluation and hence from our responsibility.

15. Two further documents by Paul VI without any direct link to social doctrine—the Encyclical *Humanae Vitae* (25 July 1968) and the Apostolic Exhortation *Evangelii Nuntiandi* (8 December 1975)—are highly important for delineating the *fully human meaning of the development that the Church proposes*. It is therefore helpful to consider these texts too in relation to *Populorum Progressio*.

The Encyclical *Humanae Vitae* emphasizes both the unitive and the procreative meaning of sexuality, thereby locating at the foundation of society the married couple, man and woman, who accept one another mutually, in distinction and in complementarity: a couple, therefore, that is open to life.[27] This is not a question of purely individual morality: *Humanae Vitae* indicates the *strong links between life ethics and social ethics*, ushering in a new area of magisterial teaching that has gradually been articulated in a series of documents, most recently John Paul II's Encyclical *Evangelium Vitae*.[28] The Church forcefully maintains this link between life ethics and social ethics, fully aware that "a society lacks solid foundations when, on the one hand, it asserts values such as the dignity of the person, justice and peace, but then, on the other hand, radically acts to the contrary by allowing or tolerating a variety of ways in which human life is devalued and violated, especially where it is weak or marginalized."[29]

The Apostolic Exhortation *Evangelii Nuntiandi*, for its part, is very closely linked with development, given that, in Paul VI's words, "evangelization would not be complete if it did not take account of the unceasing interplay of the Gospel and of man's concrete life, both personal and social."[30] "Between evangelization and human advancement—development and liberation—there are in fact profound links":[31] on the basis of this insight, Paul VI clearly presented the relationship between the proclamation of Christ and the advancement of the individual in society. *Testimony to Christ's charity, through works of justice, peace and development, is part and parcel of evangelization*, because Jesus Christ, who loves us, is concerned with the whole person. These important teachings form the basis for the missionary aspect[32] of the Church's social doctrine, which is an essential element of evangelization.[33] The Church's social doctrine proclaims and bears witness to faith. It is an instrument and an indispensable setting for formation in faith.

16. In *Populorum Progressio*, Paul VI taught that progress, in its origin and essence, is first and foremost a *vocation*: "in the design of God, every man is called upon to develop and fulfil himself, for every life is a vocation."[34] This is what gives legitimacy to the Church's involvement in the whole question of development. If development were concerned with merely technical aspects of human life, and not with the meaning of man's pilgrimage through history in company with his fellow human beings, nor with identifying the goal of that journey, then the Church would not be entitled to speak on it. Paul VI, like Leo XIII before him in *Rerum Novarum*,[35] knew that he was carrying out a duty

proper to his office by shedding the light of the Gospel on the social questions of his time.[36]

To regard *development as a vocation* is to recognize, on the one hand, that it derives from a transcendent call, and on the other hand that it is incapable, on its own, of supplying its ultimate meaning. Not without reason the word "vocation" is also found in another passage of the Encyclical, where we read: "There is no true humanism but that which is open to the Absolute, and is conscious of a vocation which gives human life its true meaning."[37] This vision of development is at the heart of *Populorum Progressio*, and it lies behind all Paul VI's reflections on freedom, on truth and on charity in development. It is also the principal reason why that Encyclical is still timely in our day.

17. A vocation is a call that requires a free and responsible answer. *Integral human development presupposes the responsible freedom* of the individual and of peoples: no structure can guarantee this development over and above human responsibility. The "types of messianism which give promises but create illusions"[38] always build their case on a denial of the transcendent dimension of development, in the conviction that it lies entirely at their disposal. This false security becomes a weakness, because it involves reducing man to subservience, to a mere means for development, while the humility of those who accept a vocation is transformed into true autonomy, because it sets them free. Paul VI was in no doubt that obstacles and forms of conditioning hold up development, but he was also certain that "each one remains, whatever be these influences affecting him, the principal agent of his own success or failure."[39] This freedom concerns the type of development we are considering, but it also affects situations of underdevelopment which are not due to chance or historical necessity, but are attributable to human responsibility. This is why "the peoples in hunger are making a dramatic appeal to the peoples blessed with abundance."[40] This too is a vocation, a call addressed by free subjects to other free subjects in favour of an assumption of shared responsibility. Paul VI had a keen sense of the importance of economic structures and institutions, but he had an equally clear sense of their nature as instruments of human freedom. Only when it is free can development be integrally human; only in a climate of responsible freedom can it grow in a satisfactory manner.

18. Besides requiring freedom, *integral human development as a vocation also demands respect for its truth.* The vocation to progress drives us to "do more, know more and have more in order to be more."[41] But herein lies the problem: what does it mean "to be more"? Paul VI answers the question by indicating the essential quality of "authentic" development: it must be "integral, that is, it has to promote the good of every man and of the whole man."[42] Amid the various competing anthropological visions put forward in today's society, even more so than in Paul VI's time, the Christian vision has the particular characteristic of asserting and justifying the unconditional value of the human person and the meaning of his growth. The Christian vocation to

development helps to promote the advancement of all men and of the whole man. As Paul VI wrote: "What we hold important is man, each man and each group of men, and we even include the whole of humanity."[43] In promoting development, the Christian faith does not rely on privilege or positions of power, nor even on the merits of Christians (even though these existed and continue to exist alongside their natural limitations),[44] but only on Christ, to whom every authentic vocation to integral human development must be directed. *The Gospel is fundamental for development*, because in the Gospel, Christ, "in the very revelation of the mystery of the Father and of his love, fully reveals humanity to itself."[45] Taught by her Lord, the Church examines the signs of the times and interprets them, offering the world "what she possesses as her characteristic attribute: a global vision of man and of the human race."[46] Precisely because God gives a resounding "yes" to man,[47] man cannot fail to open himself to the divine vocation to pursue his own development. The truth of development consists in its completeness: if it does not involve the whole man and every man, it is not true development. This is the central message of *Populorum Progressio*, valid for today and for all time. Integral human development on the natural plane, as a response to a vocation from God the Creator,[48] demands self-fulfilment in a "transcendent humanism which gives [to man] his greatest possible perfection: this is the highest goal of personal development."[49] The Christian vocation to this development therefore applies to both the natural plane and the supernatural plane; which is why, "when God is eclipsed, our ability to recognize the natural order, purpose and the 'good' begins to wane."[50]

19. Finally, the vision of development as a vocation brings with it the *central place of charity within that development*. Paul VI, in his Encyclical Letter *Populorum Progressio*, pointed out that the causes of underdevelopment are not primarily of the material order. He invited us to search for them in other dimensions of the human person: first of all, in the will, which often neglects the duties of solidarity; secondly in thinking, which does not always give proper direction to the will. Hence, in the pursuit of development, there is a need for "the deep thought and reflection of wise men in search of a new humanism which will enable modern man to find himself anew."[51] But that is not all. Underdevelopment has an even more important cause than lack of deep thought: it is "the lack of brotherhood among individuals and peoples."[52] Will it ever be possible to obtain this brotherhood by human effort alone? As society becomes ever more globalized, it makes us neighbours but does not make us brothers. Reason, by itself, is capable of grasping the equality between men and of giving stability to their civic coexistence, but it cannot establish fraternity. This originates in a transcendent vocation from God the Father, who loved us first, teaching us through the Son what fraternal charity is. Paul VI, presenting the various levels in the process of human development, placed at the summit, after mentioning faith, "unity in the charity of Christ who calls us all to share as sons in the life of the living God, the Father of all."[53]

20. These perspectives, which *Populorum Progressio* opens up, remain fundamental for giving breathing-space and direction to our commitment for the development of peoples. Moreover, *Populorum Progressio* repeatedly underlines the *urgent need for reform*,[54] and in the face of great problems of injustice in the development of peoples, it calls for courageous action to be taken without delay. This *urgency is also a consequence of charity in truth.* It is Christ's charity that drives us on: "*caritas Christi urget nos*" (2 Cor. 5:14). The urgency is inscribed not only in things, it is not derived solely from the rapid succession of events and problems, but also from the very matter that is at stake: the establishment of authentic fraternity.

The importance of this goal is such as to demand our openness to understand it in depth and to mobilize ourselves at the level of the "heart", so as to ensure that current economic and social processes evolve towards fully human outcomes.

CHAPTER TWO

HUMAN DEVELOPMENT IN OUR TIME

21. Paul VI had an *articulated vision of development.* He understood the term to indicate the goal of rescuing peoples, first and foremost, from hunger, deprivation, endemic diseases and illiteracy. From the economic point of view, this meant their active participation, on equal terms, in the international economic process; from the social point of view, it meant their evolution into educated societies marked by solidarity; from the political point of view, it meant the consolidation of democratic regimes capable of ensuring freedom and peace. After so many years, as we observe with concern the developments and perspectives of the succession of crises that afflict the world today, *we ask to what extent Paul VI's expectations have been fulfilled* by the model of development adopted in recent decades. We recognize, therefore, that the Church had good reason to be concerned about the capacity of a purely technological society to set realistic goals and to make good use of the instruments at its disposal. Profit is useful if it serves as a means towards an end that provides a sense both of how to produce it and how to make good use of it. Once profit becomes the exclusive goal, if it is produced by improper means and without the common good as its ultimate end, it risks destroying wealth and creating poverty. The economic development that Paul VI hoped to see was meant to produce real growth, of benefit to everyone and genuinely sustainable. It is true that growth has taken place, and it continues to be a positive factor that has lifted billions of people out of misery—recently it has given many countries the possibility of becoming effective players in international politics. Yet it must be acknowledged that this same economic growth has been and continues to be weighed down by *malfunctions and*

dramatic problems, highlighted even further by the current crisis. This presents us with choices that cannot be postponed concerning nothing less than the destiny of man, who, moreover, cannot prescind from his nature. The technical forces in play, the global interrelations, the damaging effects on the real economy of badly managed and largely speculative financial dealing, large-scale migration of peoples, often provoked by some particular circumstance and then given insufficient attention, the unregulated exploitation of the earth's resources: all this leads us today to reflect on the measures that would be necessary to provide a solution to problems that are not only new in comparison to those addressed by Pope Paul VI, but also, and above all, of decisive impact upon the present and future good of humanity. The different aspects of the crisis, its solutions, and any new development that the future may bring, are increasingly interconnected, they imply one another, they require new efforts of holistic understanding and a *new humanistic synthesis*. The complexity and gravity of the present economic situation rightly cause us concern, but we must adopt a realistic attitude as we take up with confidence and hope the new responsibilities to which we are called by the prospect of a world in need of profound cultural renewal, a world that needs to rediscover fundamental values on which to build a better future. The current crisis obliges us to re-plan our journey, to set ourselves new rules and to discover new forms of commitment, to build on positive experiences and to reject negative ones. The crisis thus becomes *an opportunity for discernment, in which to shape a new vision for the future*. In this spirit, with confidence rather than resignation, it is appropriate to address the difficulties of the present time.

22. Today the picture of development has *many overlapping layers*. The actors and the causes in both underdevelopment and development are manifold, the faults and the merits are differentiated. This fact should prompt us to liberate ourselves from ideologies, which often oversimplify reality in artificial ways, and it should lead us to examine objectively the full human dimension of the problems. As John Paul II has already observed, the demarcation line between rich and poor countries is no longer as clear as it was at the time of *Populorum Progressio*.[55] *The world's wealth is growing in absolute terms, but inequalities are on the increase*. In rich countries, new sectors of society are succumbing to poverty and new forms of poverty are emerging. In poorer areas some groups enjoy a sort of "superdevelopment" of a wasteful and consumerist kind which forms an unacceptable contrast with the ongoing situations of dehumanizing deprivation. "The scandal of glaring inequalities"[56] continues. Corruption and illegality are unfortunately evident in the conduct of the economic and political class in rich countries, both old and new, as well as in poor ones. Among those who sometimes fail to respect the human rights of workers are large multinational companies as well as local producers. International aid has often been diverted from its proper ends, through irresponsible actions both within the chain of donors and within that of the beneficiaries. Similarly, in the context of immaterial or cul-

tural causes of development and underdevelopment, we find these same patterns of responsibility reproduced. On the part of rich countries there is excessive zeal for protecting knowledge through an unduly rigid assertion of the right to intellectual property, especially in the field of health care. At the same time, in some poor countries, cultural models and social norms of behaviour persist which hinder the process of development.

23. Many areas of the globe today have evolved considerably, albeit in problematical and disparate ways, thereby taking their place among the great powers destined to play important roles in the future. Yet it should be stressed that *progress of a merely economic and technological kind is insufficient.* Development needs above all to be true and integral. The mere fact of emerging from economic backwardness, though positive in itself, does not resolve the complex issues of human advancement, neither for the countries that are spearheading such progress, nor for those that are already economically developed, nor even for those that are still poor, which can suffer not just through old forms of exploitation, but also from the negative consequences of a growth that is marked by irregularities and imbalances.

After the collapse of the economic and political systems of the Communist countries of Eastern Europe and the end of the so-called *opposing blocs*, a complete re-examination of development was needed. Pope John Paul II called for it, when in 1987 he pointed to the existence of these blocs as one of the principal causes of underdevelopment,[57] inasmuch as politics withdrew resources from the economy and from the culture, and ideology inhibited freedom. Moreover, in 1991, after the events of 1989, he asked that, in view of the ending of the blocs, there should be a comprehensive new plan for development, not only in those countries, but also in the West and in those parts of the world that were in the process of evolving.[58] This has been achieved only in part, and it is still a real duty that needs to be discharged, perhaps by means of the choices that are necessary to overcome current economic problems.

24. The world that Paul VI had before him—even though society had already evolved to such an extent that he could speak of social issues in global terms—was still far less integrated than today's world. Economic activity and the political process were both largely conducted within the same geographical area, and could therefore feed off one another. Production took place predominantly within national boundaries, and financial investments had somewhat limited circulation outside the country, so that the politics of many States could still determine the priorities of the economy and to some degree govern its performance using the instruments at their disposal. Hence *Populorum Progressio* assigned a central, albeit not exclusive, role to "public authorities."[59]

In our own day, the State finds itself having to address the limitations to its sovereignty imposed by the new context of international trade and finance, which is characterized by increasing mobility both of financial capital and

means of production, material and immaterial. This new context has altered the political power of States.

Today, as we take to heart the lessons of the current economic crisis, which sees the State's *public authorities* directly involved in correcting errors and malfunctions, it seems more realistic to *re-evaluate their role* and their powers, which need to be prudently reviewed and remodelled so as to enable them, perhaps through new forms of engagement, to address the challenges of today's world. Once the role of public authorities has been more clearly defined, one could foresee an increase in the new forms of political participation, nationally and internationally, that have come about through the activity of organizations operating in civil society; in this way it is to be hoped that the citizens' interest and participation in the *res publica* will become more deeply rooted.

25. From the social point of view, systems of protection and welfare, already present in many countries in Paul VI's day, are finding it hard and could find it even harder in the future to pursue their goals of true social justice in today's profoundly changed environment. The global market has stimulated first and foremost, on the part of rich countries, a search for areas in which to outsource production at low cost with a view to reducing the prices of many goods, increasing purchasing power and thus accelerating the rate of development in terms of greater availability of consumer goods for the domestic market. Consequently, the market has prompted new forms of competition between States as they seek to attract foreign businesses to set up production centres, by means of a variety of instruments, including favourable fiscal regimes and deregulation of the labour market. These processes have led to a *downsizing of social security systems* as the price to be paid for seeking greater competitive advantage in the global market, with consequent grave danger for the rights of workers, for fundamental human rights and for the solidarity associated with the traditional forms of the social State. Systems of social security can lose the capacity to carry out their task, both in emerging countries and in those that were among the earliest to develop, as well as in poor countries. Here budgetary policies, with cuts in social spending often made under pressure from international financial institutions, can leave citizens powerless in the face of old and new risks; such powerlessness is increased by the lack of effective protection on the part of workers' associations. Through the combination of social and economic change, *trade union organizations* experience greater difficulty in carrying out their task of representing the interests of workers, partly because Governments, for reasons of economic utility, often limit the freedom or the negotiating capacity of labour unions. Hence traditional networks of solidarity have more and more obstacles to overcome. The repeated calls issued within the Church's social doctrine, beginning with *Rerum Novarum*,[60] for the promotion of workers' associations that can defend their rights must therefore be honoured today even more than in the past, as a prompt and far-sighted response to the urgent need for new forms of cooperation at the international level, as well as the local level.

The *mobility of labour*, associated with a climate of deregulation, is an important phenomenon with certain positive aspects, because it can stimulate wealth production and cultural exchange. Nevertheless, uncertainty over working conditions caused by mobility and deregulation, when it becomes endemic, tends to create new forms of psychological instability, giving rise to difficulty in forging coherent life-plans, including that of marriage. This leads to situations of human decline, to say nothing of the waste of social resources. In comparison with the casualties of industrial society in the past, unemployment today provokes new forms of economic marginalization, and the current crisis can only make this situation worse. Being out of work or dependent on public or private assistance for a prolonged period undermines the freedom and creativity of the person and his family and social relationships, causing great psychological and spiritual suffering. I would like to remind everyone, especially governments engaged in boosting the world's economic and social assets, that the *primary capital to be safeguarded and valued is man, the human person in his or her integrity*: "Man is the source, the focus and the aim of all economic and social life."[61]

26. On the cultural plane, compared with Paul VI's day, the difference is even more marked. At that time cultures were relatively well defined and had greater opportunity to defend themselves against attempts to merge them into one. Today the possibilities of *interaction between cultures* have increased significantly, giving rise to new openings for intercultural dialogue: a dialogue that, if it is to be effective, has to set out from a deep-seated knowledge of the specific identity of the various dialogue partners. Let it not be forgotten that the increased commercialization of cultural exchange today leads to a twofold danger. First, one may observe a *cultural eclecticism* that is often assumed uncritically: cultures are simply placed alongside one another and viewed as substantially equivalent and interchangeable. This easily yields to a relativism that does not serve true intercultural dialogue; on the social plane, cultural relativism has the effect that cultural groups coexist side by side, but remain separate, with no authentic dialogue and therefore with no true integration. Secondly, the opposite danger exists, that of *cultural levelling* and indiscriminate acceptance of types of conduct and life-styles. In this way one loses sight of the profound significance of the culture of different nations, of the traditions of the various peoples, by which the individual defines himself in relation to life's fundamental questions.[62] What eclecticism and cultural levelling have in common is the separation of culture from human nature. Thus, cultures can no longer define themselves within a nature that transcends them,[63] and man ends up being reduced to a mere cultural statistic. When this happens, humanity runs new risks of enslavement and manipulation.

27. Life in many poor countries is still extremely insecure as a consequence of food shortages, and the situation could become worse: *hunger* still reaps enormous numbers of victims among those who, like Lazarus, are not

permitted to take their place at the rich man's table, contrary to the hopes expressed by Paul VI.[64] *Feed the hungry* (cf. Mt. 25:35, 37, 42) is an ethical imperative for the universal Church, as she responds to the teachings of her Founder, the Lord Jesus, concerning solidarity and the sharing of goods. Moreover, the elimination of world hunger has also, in the global era, become a requirement for safeguarding the peace and stability of the planet. Hunger is not so much dependent on lack of material things as on shortage of social resources, the most important of which are institutional. What is missing, in other words, is a network of economic institutions capable of guaranteeing regular access to sufficient food and water for nutritional needs, and also capable of addressing the primary needs and necessities ensuing from genuine food crises, whether due to natural causes or political irresponsibility, nationally and internationally. The problem of food insecurity needs to be addressed within a long-term perspective, eliminating the structural causes that give rise to it and promoting the agricultural development of poorer countries. This can be done by investing in rural infrastructures, irrigation systems, transport, organization of markets, and in the development and dissemination of agricultural technology that can make the best use of the human, natural and socio-economic resources that are more readily available at the local level, while guaranteeing their sustainability over the long term as well. All this needs to be accomplished with the involvement of local communities in choices and decisions that affect the use of agricultural land. In this perspective, it could be useful to consider the new possibilities that are opening up through proper use of traditional as well as innovative farming techniques, always assuming that these have been judged, after sufficient testing, to be appropriate, respectful of the environment and attentive to the needs of the most deprived peoples. At the same time, the question of equitable agrarian reform in developing countries should not be ignored. The right to food, like the right to water, has an important place within the pursuit of other rights, beginning with the fundamental right to life. It is therefore necessary to cultivate a public conscience that considers *food and access to water as universal rights of all human beings, without distinction or discrimination.*[65] It is important, moreover, to emphasize that solidarity with poor countries in the process of development can point towards a solution of the current global crisis, as politicians and directors of international institutions have begun to sense in recent times. Through support for economically poor countries by means of financial plans inspired by solidarity—so that these countries can take steps to satisfy their own citizens' demand for consumer goods and for development—not only can true economic growth be generated, but a contribution can be made towards sustaining the productive capacities of rich countries that risk being compromised by the crisis.

28. One of the most striking aspects of development in the present day is the important question of *respect for life*, which cannot in any way be detached from questions concerning the development of peoples. It is an

aspect which has acquired increasing prominence in recent times, obliging us to broaden our concept of poverty[66] and underdevelopment to include questions connected with the acceptance of life, especially in cases where it is impeded in a variety of ways.

Not only does the situation of poverty still provoke high rates of infant mortality in many regions, but some parts of the world still experience practices of demographic control, on the part of governments that often promote contraception and even go so far as to impose abortion. In economically developed countries, legislation contrary to life is very widespread, and it has already shaped moral attitudes and praxis, contributing to the spread of an anti-birth mentality; frequent attempts are made to export this mentality to other States as if it were a form of cultural progress.

Some non-governmental Organizations work actively to spread abortion, at times promoting the practice of sterilization in poor countries, in some cases not even informing the women concerned. Moreover, there is reason to suspect that development aid is sometimes linked to specific health-care policies which *de facto* involve the imposition of strong birth control measures. Further grounds for concern are laws permitting euthanasia as well as pressure from lobby groups, nationally and internationally, in favour of its juridical recognition.

Openness to life is at the centre of true development. When a society moves towards the denial or suppression of life, it ends up no longer finding the necessary motivation and energy to strive for man's true good. If personal and social sensitivity towards the acceptance of a new life is lost, then other forms of acceptance that are valuable for society also wither away.[67] The acceptance of life strengthens moral fibre and makes people capable of mutual help. By cultivating openness to life, wealthy peoples can better understand the needs of poor ones, they can avoid employing huge economic and intellectual resources to satisfy the selfish desires of their own citizens, and instead, they can promote virtuous action within the perspective of production that is morally sound and marked by solidarity, respecting the fundamental right to life of every people and every individual.

29. There is another aspect of modern life that is very closely connected to development: the denial of the *right to religious freedom.* I am not referring simply to the struggles and conflicts that continue to be fought in the world for religious motives, even if at times the religious motive is merely a cover for other reasons, such as the desire for domination and wealth. Today, in fact, people frequently kill in the holy name of God, as both my predecessor John Paul II and I myself have often publicly acknowledged and lamented.[68] Violence puts the brakes on authentic development and impedes the evolution of peoples towards greater socio-economic and spiritual well-being. This applies especially to terrorism motivated by fundamentalism,[69] which generates grief, destruction and death, obstructs dialogue between nations and diverts extensive resources from their peaceful and civil uses.

Yet it should be added that, as well as religious fanaticism that in some contexts impedes the exercise of the right to religious freedom, so too the deliberate promotion of religious indifference or practical atheism on the part of many countries obstructs the requirements for the development of peoples, depriving them of spiritual and human resources. *God is the guarantor of man's true development*, inasmuch as, having created him in his image, he also establishes the transcendent dignity of men and women and feeds their innate yearning to "be more." Man is not a lost atom in a random universe:[70] he is God's creature, whom God chose to endow with an immortal soul and whom he has always loved. If man were merely the fruit of either chance or necessity, or if he had to lower his aspirations to the limited horizon of the world in which he lives, if all reality were merely history and culture, and man did not possess a nature destined to transcend itself in a supernatural life, then one could speak of growth, or evolution, but not development. When the State promotes, teaches, or actually imposes forms of practical atheism, it deprives its citizens of the moral and spiritual strength that is indispensable for attaining integral human development and it impedes them from moving forward with renewed dynamism as they strive to offer a more generous human response to divine love.[71] In the context of cultural, commercial or political relations, it also sometimes happens that economically developed or emerging countries export this reductive vision of the person and his destiny to poor countries. This is the damage that "superdevelopment"[72] causes to authentic development when it is accompanied by "moral underdevelopment."[73]

30. In this context, the theme of integral human development takes on an even broader range of meanings: the correlation between its multiple elements requires a commitment to *foster the interaction of the different levels of human knowledge* in order to promote the authentic development of peoples. Often it is thought that development, or the socio-economic measures that go with it, merely require to be implemented through joint action. This joint action, however, needs to be given direction, because "all social action involves a doctrine."[74] In view of the complexity of the issues, it is obvious that the various disciplines have to work together through an orderly interdisciplinary exchange. Charity does not exclude knowledge, but rather requires, promotes, and animates it from within. Knowledge is never purely the work of the intellect. It can certainly be reduced to calculation and experiment, but if it aspires to be wisdom capable of directing man in the light of his first beginnings and his final ends, it must be "seasoned" with the "salt" of charity. Deeds without knowledge are blind, and knowledge without love is sterile. Indeed, "the individual who is animated by true charity labours skilfully to discover the causes of misery, to find the means to combat it, to overcome it resolutely."[75] Faced with the phenomena that lie before us, charity in truth requires first of all that we know and understand, acknowledging and respecting the specific competence of every level of knowledge. Charity is not an added extra, like an appendix to work

already concluded in each of the various disciplines: it engages them in dialogue from the very beginning. The demands of love do not contradict those of reason. Human knowledge is insufficient and the conclusions of science cannot indicate by themselves the path towards integral human development. There is always a need to push further ahead: this is what is required by charity in truth.[76] Going beyond, however, never means prescinding from the conclusions of reason, nor contradicting its results. Intelligence and love are not in separate compartments: *love is rich in intelligence and intelligence is full of love.*

31. This means that moral evaluation and scientific research must go hand in hand, and that charity must animate them in a harmonious interdisciplinary whole, marked by unity and distinction. The Church's social doctrine, which has "*an important interdisciplinary dimension*,"[77] can exercise, in this perspective, a function of extraordinary effectiveness. It allows faith, theology, metaphysics and science to come together in a collaborative effort in the service of humanity. It is here above all that the Church's social doctrine displays its dimension of wisdom. Paul VI had seen clearly that among the causes of underdevelopment there is a lack of wisdom and reflection, a lack of thinking capable of formulating a guiding synthesis[78], for which "a clear vision of all economic, social, cultural and spiritual aspects"[79] is required. The excessive segmentation of knowledge,[80] the rejection of metaphysics by the human sciences,[81] the difficulties encountered by dialogue between science and theology are damaging not only to the development of knowledge, but also to the development of peoples, because these things make it harder to see the integral good of man in its various dimensions. The "broadening [of] our concept of reason and its application"[82] is indispensable if we are to succeed in adequately weighing all the elements involved in the question of development and in the solution of socio-economic problems.

32. The significant new elements in the picture of the development of peoples today in many cases demand *new solutions*. These need to be found together, respecting the laws proper to each element and in the light of an integral vision of man, reflecting the different aspects of the human person, contemplated through a lens purified by charity. Remarkable convergences and possible solutions will then come to light, without any fundamental component of human life being obscured.

The dignity of the individual and the demands of justice require, particularly today, that economic choices do not cause disparities in wealth to increase in an excessive and morally unacceptable manner,[83] and that we continue to *prioritize the goal of access to steady employment* for everyone. All things considered, this is also required by "economic logic." Through the systemic increase of social inequality, both within a single country and between the populations of different countries (i.e. the massive increase in relative poverty), not only does social cohesion suffer, thereby placing democracy at risk, but so too does the economy, through the progressive erosion of "social

capital": the network of relationships of trust, dependability, and respect for rules, all of which are indispensable for any form of civil coexistence.

Economic science tells us that structural insecurity generates anti-productive attitudes wasteful of human resources, inasmuch as workers tend to adapt passively to automatic mechanisms, rather than to release creativity. On this point too, there is a convergence between economic science and moral evaluation. *Human costs always include economic costs*, and economic dysfunctions always involve human costs.

It should be remembered that the reduction of cultures to the technological dimension, even if it favours short-term profits, in the long term impedes reciprocal enrichment and the dynamics of cooperation. It is important to distinguish between short- and long-term economic or sociological considerations. Lowering the level of protection accorded to the rights of workers, or abandoning mechanisms of wealth redistribution in order to increase the country's international competitiveness, hinder the achievement of lasting development. Moreover, the human consequences of current tendencies towards a short-term economy—sometimes very short-term—need to be carefully evaluated. This requires *further and deeper reflection on the meaning of the economy and its goals*,[84] as well as a profound and far-sighted revision of the current model of development, so as to correct its dysfunctions and deviations. This is demanded, in any case, by the earth's state of ecological health; above all it is required by the cultural and moral crisis of man, the symptoms of which have been evident for some time all over the world.

33. More than forty years after *Populorum Progressio*, its basic theme, namely progress, *remains an open question*, made all the more acute and urgent by the current economic and financial crisis. If some areas of the globe, with a history of poverty, have experienced remarkable changes in terms of their economic growth and their share in world production, other zones are still living in a situation of deprivation comparable to that which existed at the time of Paul VI, and in some cases one can even speak of a deterioration. It is significant that some of the causes of this situation were identified in *Populorum Progressio*, such as the high tariffs imposed by economically developed countries, which still make it difficult for the products of poor countries to gain a foothold in the markets of rich countries. Other causes, however, mentioned only in passing in the Encyclical, have since emerged with greater clarity. A case in point would be the evaluation of the process of decolonization, then at its height. Paul VI hoped to see the journey towards autonomy unfold freely and in peace. More than forty years later, we must acknowledge how difficult this journey has been, both because of new forms of colonialism and continued dependence on old and new foreign powers, and because of grave irresponsibility within the very countries that have achieved independence.

The principal new feature has been the *explosion of worldwide interdependence*, commonly known as globalization. Paul VI had partially foreseen

it, but the ferocious pace at which it has evolved could not have been anticipated. Originating within economically developed countries, this process by its nature has spread to include all economies. It has been the principal driving force behind the emergence from underdevelopment of whole regions, and in itself it represents a great opportunity. Nevertheless, without the guidance of charity in truth, this global force could cause unprecedented damage and create new divisions within the human family. Hence charity and truth confront us with an altogether new and creative challenge, one that is certainly vast and complex. It is about *broadening the scope of reason and making it capable of knowing and directing these powerful new forces*, animating them within the perspective of that "civilization of love" whose seed God has planted in every people, in every culture.

CHAPTER THREE

FRATERNITY, ECONOMIC DEVELOPMENT AND CIVIL SOCIETY

34. *Charity in truth* places man before the astonishing experience of gift. Gratuitousness is present in our lives in many different forms, which often go unrecognized because of a purely consumerist and utilitarian view of life. The human being is made for gift, which expresses and makes present his transcendent dimension. Sometimes modern man is wrongly convinced that he is the sole author of himself, his life and society. This is a presumption that follows from being selfishly closed in upon himself, and it is a consequence—to express it in faith terms—of *original sin*. The Church's wisdom has always pointed to the presence of original sin in social conditions and in the structure of society: "Ignorance of the fact that man has a wounded nature inclined to evil gives rise to serious errors in the areas of education, politics, social action and morals."[85] In the list of areas where the pernicious effects of sin are evident, the economy has been included for some time now. We have a clear proof of this at the present time. The conviction that man is self-sufficient and can successfully eliminate the evil present in history by his own action alone has led him to confuse happiness and salvation with immanent forms of material prosperity and social action. Then, the conviction that the economy must be autonomous, that it must be shielded from "influences" of a moral character, has led man to abuse the economic process in a thoroughly destructive way. In the long term, these convictions have led to economic, social and political systems that trample upon personal and social freedom, and are therefore unable to deliver the justice that they promise. As I said in my Encyclical Letter *Spe Salvi*, history is thereby deprived of *Christian hope*,[86] deprived of a powerful social resource at the service of integral human development, sought in freedom and in justice. Hope encourages reason and gives it the strength to direct the will.[87] It is already present in faith, indeed it is called forth by faith. Charity in truth feeds on hope and, at the same time, manifests

it. As the absolutely gratuitous gift of God, hope bursts into our lives as something not due to us, something that transcends every law of justice. Gift by its nature goes beyond merit, its rule is that of superabundance. It takes first place in our souls as a sign of God's presence in us, a sign of what he expects from us. Truth—which is itself gift, in the same way as charity—is greater than we are, as Saint Augustine teaches.[88] Likewise the truth of ourselves, of our personal conscience, is first of all *given* to us. In every cognitive process, truth is not something that we produce, it is always found, or better, received. Truth, like love, "is neither planned nor willed, but somehow imposes itself upon human beings."[89]

Because it is a gift received by everyone, charity in truth is a force that builds community, it brings all people together without imposing barriers or limits. The human community that we build by ourselves can never, purely by its own strength, be a fully fraternal community, nor can it overcome every division and become a truly universal community. The unity of the human race, a fraternal communion transcending every barrier, is called into being by the word of God-who-is-Love. In addressing this key question, we must make it clear, on the one hand, that the logic of gift does not exclude justice, nor does it merely sit alongside it as a second element added from without; on the other hand, economic, social and political development, if it is to be authentically human, needs to make room for the *principle of gratuitousness* as an expression of fraternity.

35. In a climate of mutual trust, the *market* is the economic institution that permits encounter between persons, inasmuch as they are economic subjects who make use of contracts to regulate their relations as they exchange goods and services of equivalent value between them, in order to satisfy their needs and desires. The market is subject to the principles of so-called *commutative justice*, which regulates the relations of giving and receiving between parties to a transaction. But the social doctrine of the Church has unceasingly highlighted the importance of *distributive justice* and *social justice* for the market economy, not only because it belongs within a broader social and political context, but also because of the wider network of relations within which it operates. In fact, if the market is governed solely by the principle of the equivalence in value of exchanged goods, it cannot produce the social cohesion that it requires in order to function well. *Without internal forms of solidarity and mutual trust, the market cannot completely fulfil its proper economic function.* And today it is this trust which has ceased to exist, and the loss of trust is a grave loss. It was timely when Paul VI in *Populorum Progressio* insisted that the economic system itself would benefit from the wide-ranging practice of justice, inasmuch as the first to gain from the development of poor countries would be rich ones.[90] According to the Pope, it was not just a matter of correcting dysfunctions through assistance. The poor are not to be considered a "burden,"[91] but a resource, even from the purely economic point of view. It is nevertheless erroneous to hold that the market economy has an inbuilt need for

a quota of poverty and underdevelopment in order to function at its best. It is in the interests of the market to promote emancipation, but in order to do so effectively, it cannot rely only on itself, because it is not able to produce by itself something that lies outside its competence. It must draw its moral energies from other subjects that are capable of generating them.

36. Economic activity cannot solve all social problems through the simple application of *commercial logic*. This needs to be *directed towards the pursuit of the common good*, for which the political community in particular must also take responsibility. Therefore, it must be borne in mind that grave imbalances are produced when economic action, conceived merely as an engine for wealth creation, is detached from political action, conceived as a means for pursuing justice through redistribution.

The Church has always held that economic action is not to be regarded as something opposed to society. In and of itself, the market is not, and must not become, the place where the strong subdue the weak. Society does not have to protect itself from the market, as if the development of the latter were *ipso facto* to entail the death of authentically human relations. Admittedly, the market can be a negative force, not because it is so by nature, but because a certain ideology can make it so. It must be remembered that the market does not exist in the pure state. It is shaped by the cultural configurations which define it and give it direction. Economy and finance, as instruments, can be used badly when those at the helm are motivated by purely selfish ends. Instruments that are good in themselves can thereby be transformed into harmful ones. But it is man's darkened reason that produces these consequences, not the instrument *per se*. Therefore it is not the instrument that must be called to account, but individuals, their moral conscience and their personal and social responsibility.

The Church's social doctrine holds that authentically human social relationships of friendship, solidarity and reciprocity can also be conducted within economic activity, and not only outside it or "after" it. The economic sphere is neither ethically neutral, nor inherently inhuman and opposed to society. It is part and parcel of human activity and precisely because it is human, it must be structured and governed in an ethical manner.

The great challenge before us, accentuated by the problems of development in this global era and made even more urgent by the economic and financial crisis, is to demonstrate, in thinking and behaviour, not only that traditional principles of social ethics like transparency, honesty and responsibility cannot be ignored or attenuated, but also that in *commercial relationships* the *principle of gratuitousness* and the logic of gift as an expression of fraternity can and must *find their place within normal economic activity*. This is a human demand at the present time, but it is also demanded by economic logic. It is a demand both of charity and of truth.

37. The Church's social doctrine has always maintained that *justice must be applied to every phase of economic activity*, because this is always concerned

with man and his needs. Locating resources, financing, production, consumption and all the other phases in the economic cycle inevitably have moral implications. *Thus every economic decision has a moral consequence*. The social sciences and the direction taken by the contemporary economy point to the same conclusion. Perhaps at one time it was conceivable that first the creation of wealth could be entrusted to the economy, and then the task of distributing it could be assigned to politics. Today that would be more difficult, given that economic activity is no longer circumscribed within territorial limits, while the authority of governments continues to be principally local. Hence the canons of justice must be respected from the outset, as the economic process unfolds, and not just afterwards or incidentally. Space also needs to be created within the market for economic activity carried out by subjects who freely choose to act according to principles other than those of pure profit, without sacrificing the production of economic value in the process. The many economic entities that draw their origin from religious and lay initiatives demonstrate that this is concretely possible.

In the global era, the economy is influenced by competitive models tied to cultures that differ greatly among themselves. The different forms of economic enterprise to which they give rise find their main point of encounter in commutative justice. *Economic life* undoubtedly requires *contracts*, in order to regulate relations of exchange between goods of equivalent value. But it also needs *just laws* and *forms of redistribution* governed by politics, and what is more, it needs works redolent of the *spirit of gift*. The economy in the global era seems to privilege the former logic, that of contractual exchange, but directly or indirectly it also demonstrates its need for the other two: political logic, and the logic of the unconditional gift.

38. My predecessor John Paul II drew attention to this question in *Centesimus Annus*, when he spoke of the need for a system with three subjects: the *market*, the *State* and *civil society*.[92] He saw civil society as the most natural setting for an *economy of gratuitousness* and fraternity, but did not mean to deny it a place in the other two settings. Today we can say that economic life must be understood as a multi-layered phenomenon: in every one of these layers, to varying degrees and in ways specifically suited to each, the aspect of fraternal reciprocity must be present. In the global era, economic activity cannot prescind from gratuitousness, which fosters and disseminates solidarity and responsibility for justice and the common good among the different economic players. It is clearly a specific and profound form of economic democracy. Solidarity is first and foremost a sense of responsibility on the part of everyone with regard to everyone,[93] and it cannot therefore be merely delegated to the State. While in the past it was possible to argue that justice had to come first and gratuitousness could follow afterwards, as a complement, today it is clear that without gratuitousness, there can be no justice in the first place. What is needed, therefore, is a market that permits the free operation, in conditions of equal opportunity, of enterprises in pursuit of different

institutional ends. Alongside profit-oriented private enterprise and the various types of public enterprise, there must be room for commercial entities based on mutualist principles and pursuing social ends to take root and express themselves. It is from their reciprocal encounter in the marketplace that one may expect hybrid forms of commercial behaviour to emerge, and hence an attentiveness to ways of *civilizing the economy*. Charity in truth, in this case, requires that shape and structure be given to those types of economic initiative which, without rejecting profit, aim at a higher goal than the mere logic of the exchange of equivalents, of profit as an end in itself.

39. Paul VI in *Populorum Progressio* called for the creation of *a model of market economy capable of including within its range all peoples and not just the better off*. He called for efforts to build a more human world for all, a world in which "all will be able to give and receive, without one group making progress at the expense of the other."[94] In this way he was applying on a global scale the insights and aspirations contained in *Rerum Novarum*, written when, as a result of the Industrial Revolution, the idea was first proposed—somewhat ahead of its time—that the civil order, for its self-regulation, also needed intervention from the State for purposes of redistribution. Not only is this vision threatened today by the way in which markets and societies are opening up, but it is evidently insufficient to satisfy the demands of a fully humane economy. What the Church's social doctrine has always sustained, on the basis of its vision of man and society, is corroborated today by the dynamics of globalization.

When both the logic of the market and the logic of the State come to an agreement that each will continue to exercise a monopoly over its respective area of influence, in the long term much is lost: solidarity in relations between citizens, participation and adherence, actions of gratuitousness, all of which stand in contrast with *giving in order to acquire* (the logic of exchange) and *giving through duty* (the logic of public obligation, imposed by State law). In order to defeat underdevelopment, action is required not only on improving exchange-based transactions and implanting public welfare structures, but above all on gradually *increasing openness, in a world context, to forms of economic activity marked by quotas of gratuitousness and communion*. The exclusively binary model of market-plus-State is corrosive of society, while economic forms based on solidarity, which find their natural home in civil society without being restricted to it, build up society. The market of gratuitousness does not exist, and attitudes of gratuitousness cannot be established by law. Yet both the market and politics need individuals who are open to reciprocal gift.

40. Today's international economic scene, marked by grave deviations and failures, requires a *profoundly new way of understanding business enterprise*. Old models are disappearing, but promising new ones are taking shape on the horizon. Without doubt, one of the greatest risks for businesses is that they are almost exclusively answerable to their investors, thereby limiting their

social value. Owing to their growth in scale and the need for more and more capital, it is becoming increasingly rare for business enterprises to be in the hands of a stable director who feels responsible in the long term, not just the short term, for the life and the results of his company, and it is becoming increasingly rare for businesses to depend on a single territory. Moreover, the so-called outsourcing of production can weaken the company's sense of responsibility towards the stakeholders—namely the workers, the suppliers, the consumers, the natural environment and broader society—in favour of the shareholders, who are not tied to a specific geographical area and who therefore enjoy extraordinary mobility. Today's international capital market offers great freedom of action. Yet there is also increasing awareness of the need for greater *social responsibility* on the part of business. Even if the ethical considerations that currently inform debate on the social responsibility of the corporate world are not all acceptable from the perspective of the Church's social doctrine, there is nevertheless a growing conviction that *business management cannot concern itself only with the interests of the proprietors, but must also assume responsibility for all the other stakeholders who contribute to the life of the business*: the workers, the clients, the suppliers of various elements of production, the community of reference. In recent years a new cosmopolitan class of *managers* has emerged, who are often answerable only to the shareholders generally consisting of anonymous funds which *de facto* determine their remuneration. By contrast, though, many far-sighted managers today are becoming increasingly aware of the profound links between their enterprise and the territory or territories in which it operates. Paul VI invited people to give serious attention to the damage that can be caused to one's home country by the transfer abroad of capital purely for personal advantage.[95] John Paul II taught that *investment always has moral, as well as economic significance*.[96] All this—it should be stressed—is still valid today, despite the fact that the capital market has been significantly liberalized, and modern technological thinking can suggest that investment is merely a technical act, not a human and ethical one. There is no reason to deny that a certain amount of capital can do good, if invested abroad rather than at home. Yet the requirements of justice must be safeguarded, with due consideration for the way in which the capital was generated and the harm to individuals that will result if it is not used where it was produced.[97] What should be avoided is a speculative *use of financial resources* that yields to the temptation of seeking only short-term profit, without regard for the long-term sustainability of the enterprise, its benefit to the real economy and attention to the advancement, in suitable and appropriate ways, of further economic initiatives in countries in need of development. It is true that the export of investments and skills can benefit the populations of the receiving country. Labour and technical knowledge are a universal good. Yet it is not right to export these things merely for the sake of obtaining advantageous conditions, or worse, for purposes of exploitation, without making a real contribution to local society by

helping to bring about a robust productive and social system, an essential factor for stable development.

41. In the context of this discussion, it is helpful to observe that *business enterprise* involves a *wide range of values*, becoming wider all the time. The continuing hegemony of the binary model of market-plus-State has accustomed us to think only in terms of the private business leader of a capitalistic bent on the one hand, and the State director on the other. In reality, business has to be understood in an articulated way. There are a number of reasons, of a meta-economic kind, for saying this. Business activity has a human significance, prior to its professional one.[98] It is present in all work, understood as a personal action, an "*actus personae*,"[99] which is why every worker should have the chance to make his contribution knowing that in some way "he is working 'for himself.' "[100] With good reason, Paul VI taught that "everyone who works is a creator."[101] It is in response to the needs and the dignity of the worker, as well as the needs of society, that there exist various types of business enterprise, over and above the simple distinction between "private" and "public." Each of them requires and expresses a specific business capacity. In order to construct an economy that will soon be in a position to serve the national and global common good, it is appropriate to take account of this broader significance of business activity. It favours cross-fertilization between different types of business activity, with shifting of competences from the "non-profit" world to the "profit" world and vice versa, from the public world to that of civil society, from advanced economies to developing countries.

Political authority also involves a *wide range of values*, which must not be overlooked in the process of constructing a new order of economic productivity, socially responsible and human in scale. As well as cultivating differentiated forms of business activity on the global plane, we must also promote a dispersed political authority, effective on different levels. The integrated economy of the present day does not make the role of States redundant, but rather it commits governments to greater collaboration with one another. Both wisdom and prudence suggest not being too precipitous in declaring the demise of the State. In terms of the resolution of the current crisis, the State's role seems destined to grow, as it regains many of its competences. In some nations, moreover, the construction or reconstruction of the State remains a key factor in their development. The focus of *international aid*, within a solidarity-based plan to resolve today's economic problems, should rather be on consolidating constitutional, juridical and administrative systems in countries that do not yet fully enjoy these goods. Alongside economic aid, there needs to be aid directed towards reinforcing the guarantees proper to the *State of law*: a system of public order and effective imprisonment that respects human rights, truly democratic institutions. The State does not need to have identical characteristics everywhere: the support aimed at strengthening weak constitutional systems can easily be accompanied by the development of other political players, of a cultural, social, territorial or religious

nature, alongside the State. The articulation of political authority at the local, national and international levels is one of the best ways of giving direction to the process of economic globalization. It is also the way to ensure that it does not actually undermine the foundations of democracy.

42. Sometimes *globalization* is viewed in fatalistic terms, as if the dynamics involved were the product of anonymous impersonal forces or structures independent of the human will.[102] In this regard it is useful to remember that while globalization should certainly be understood as a socio-economic process, this is not its only dimension. Underneath the more visible process, humanity itself is becoming increasingly interconnected; it is made up of individuals and peoples to whom this process should offer benefits and development,[103] as they assume their respective responsibilities, singly and collectively. The breaking-down of borders is not simply a material fact: it is also a cultural event both in its causes and its effects. If globalization is viewed from a deterministic standpoint, the criteria with which to evaluate and direct it are lost. As a human reality, it is the product of diverse cultural tendencies, which need to be subjected to a process of discernment. The truth of globalization as a process and its fundamental ethical criterion are given by the unity of the human family and its development towards what is good. Hence a sustained commitment is needed so as to *promote a person-based and community-oriented cultural process of world-wide integration that is open to transcendence*.

Despite some of its structural elements, which should neither be denied nor exaggerated, "globalization, *a priori*, is neither good nor bad. It will be what people make of it."[104] We should not be its victims, but rather its protagonists, acting in the light of reason, guided by charity and truth. Blind opposition would be a mistaken and prejudiced attitude, incapable of recognizing the positive aspects of the process, with the consequent risk of missing the chance to take advantage of its many opportunities for development. The processes of globalization, suitably understood and directed, open up the unprecedented possibility of large-scale redistribution of wealth on a world-wide scale; if badly directed, however, they can lead to an increase in poverty and inequality, and could even trigger a global crisis. It is necessary to *correct the malfunctions*, some of them serious, that cause new divisions between peoples and within peoples, and also to ensure that the redistribution of wealth does not come about through the redistribution or increase of poverty: a real danger if the present situation were to be badly managed. For a long time it was thought that poor peoples should remain at a fixed stage of development, and should be content to receive assistance from the philanthropy of developed peoples. Paul VI strongly opposed this mentality in *Populorum Progressio*. Today the material resources available for rescuing these peoples from poverty are potentially greater than before, but they have ended up largely in the hands of people from developed countries, who have benefited more from the liberalization that has occurred in the mobility of capital and

labour. The world-wide diffusion of forms of prosperity should not therefore be held up by projects that are self-centred, protectionist or at the service of private interests. Indeed the involvement of emerging or developing countries allows us to manage the crisis better today. The transition inherent in the process of globalization presents great difficulties and dangers that can only be overcome if we are able to appropriate the underlying anthropological and ethical spirit that drives globalization towards the humanizing goal of solidarity. Unfortunately this spirit is often overwhelmed or suppressed by ethical and cultural considerations of an individualistic and utilitarian nature. Globalization is a multifaceted and complex phenomenon which must be grasped in the diversity and unity of all its different dimensions, including the theological dimension. In this way it will be possible to experience and to *steer the globalization of humanity in relational terms, in terms of communion and the sharing of goods*.

CHAPTER FOUR

THE DEVELOPMENT OF PEOPLE, RIGHTS AND DUTIES, THE ENVIRONMENT

43. "The reality of human solidarity, which is a benefit for us, also imposes a duty."[105] Many people today would claim that they owe nothing to anyone, except to themselves. They are concerned only with their rights, and they often have great difficulty in taking responsibility for their own and other people's integral development. Hence it is important to call for a renewed reflection on how *rights presuppose duties, if they are not to become mere licence.*[106] Nowadays we are witnessing a grave inconsistency. On the one hand, appeals are made to alleged rights, arbitrary and non-essential in nature, accompanied by the demand that they be recognized and promoted by public structures, while, on the other hand, elementary and basic rights remain unacknowledged and are violated in much of the world.[107] A link has often been noted between claims to a "right to excess," and even to transgression and vice, within affluent societies, and the lack of food, drinkable water, basic instruction and elementary health care in areas of the underdeveloped world and on the outskirts of large metropolitan centres. The link consists in this: individual rights, when detached from a framework of duties which grants them their full meaning, can run wild, leading to an escalation of demands which is effectively unlimited and indiscriminate. An overemphasis on rights leads to a disregard for duties. Duties set a limit on rights because they point to the anthropological and ethical framework of which rights are a part, in this way ensuring that they do not become licence. Duties thereby reinforce rights and call for their defence and promotion as a task to be undertaken in the service of the common good. Otherwise, if the only basis of human rights is to be found in the deliberations

of an assembly of citizens, those rights can be changed at any time, and so the duty to respect and pursue them fades from the common consciousness. Governments and international bodies can then lose sight of the objectivity and "inviolability" of rights. When this happens, the authentic development of peoples is endangered.[108] Such a way of thinking and acting compromises the authority of international bodies, especially in the eyes of those countries most in need of development. Indeed, the latter demand that the international community take up the duty of helping them to be "artisans of their own destiny,"[109] that is, to take up duties of their own. *The sharing of reciprocal duties is a more powerful incentive to action than the mere assertion of rights.*

44. The notion of rights and duties in development must also take account of the problems associated with *population growth*. This is a very important aspect of authentic development, since it concerns the inalienable values of life and the family.[110] To consider population increase as the primary cause of underdevelopment is mistaken, even from an economic point of view. Suffice it to consider, on the one hand, the significant reduction in infant mortality and the rise in average life expectancy found in economically developed countries, and on the other hand, the signs of crisis observable in societies that are registering an alarming decline in their birth rate. Due attention must obviously be given to responsible procreation, which among other things has a positive contribution to make to integral human development. The Church, in her concern for man's authentic development, urges him to have full respect for human values in the exercise of his sexuality. It cannot be reduced merely to pleasure or entertainment, nor can sex education be reduced to technical instruction aimed solely at protecting the interested parties from possible disease or the "risk" of procreation. This would be to impoverish and disregard the deeper meaning of sexuality, a meaning which needs to be acknowledged and responsibly appropriated not only by individuals but also by the community. It is irresponsible to view sexuality merely as a source of pleasure, and likewise to regulate it through strategies of mandatory birth control. In either case materialistic ideas and policies are at work, and individuals are ultimately subjected to various forms of violence. Against such policies, there is a need to defend the primary competence of the family in the area of sexuality,[111] as opposed to the State and its restrictive policies, and to ensure that parents are suitably prepared to undertake their responsibilities.

Morally responsible openness to life represents a rich social and economic resource. Populous nations have been able to emerge from poverty thanks not least to the size of their population and the talents of their people. On the other hand, formerly prosperous nations are presently passing through a phase of uncertainty and in some cases decline, precisely because of their falling birth rates; this has become a crucial problem for highly affluent societies. The decline in births, falling at times beneath the so-called "replacement level," also puts a strain on social welfare systems, increases their cost, eats into savings and hence the financial resources needed for investment, reduces the

availability of qualified labourers, and narrows the "brain pool" upon which nations can draw for their needs. Furthermore, smaller and at times miniscule families run the risk of impoverishing social relations, and failing to ensure effective forms of solidarity. These situations are symptomatic of scant confidence in the future and moral weariness. It is thus becoming a social and even economic necessity once more to hold up to future generations the beauty of marriage and the family, and the fact that these institutions correspond to the deepest needs and dignity of the person. In view of this, States are called to *enact policies promoting the centrality and the integrity of the family* founded on marriage between a man and a woman, the primary vital cell of society,[112] and to assume responsibility for its economic and fiscal needs, while respecting its essentially relational character.

45. Striving to meet the deepest moral needs of the person also has important and beneficial repercussions at the level of economics. *The economy needs ethics in order to function correctly*—not any ethics whatsoever, but an ethics which is people-centred. Today we hear much talk of ethics in the world of economy, finance and business. Research centres and seminars in business ethics are on the rise; the system of ethical certification is spreading throughout the developed world as part of the movement of ideas associated with the responsibilities of business towards society. Banks are proposing "ethical" accounts and investment funds. "Ethical financing" is being developed, especially through micro-credit and, more generally, microfinance. These processes are praiseworthy and deserve much support. Their positive effects are also being felt in the less developed areas of the world. It would be advisable, however, to develop a sound criterion of discernment, since the adjective "ethical" can be abused. When the word is used generically, it can lend itself to any number of interpretations, even to the point where it includes decisions and choices contrary to justice and authentic human welfare.

Much in fact depends on the underlying system of morality. On this subject the Church's social doctrine can make a specific contribution, since it is based on man's creation "in the image of God" (Gen 1:27), a datum which gives rise to the inviolable dignity of the human person and the transcendent value of natural moral norms. When business ethics prescinds from these two pillars, it inevitably risks losing its distinctive nature and it falls prey to forms of exploitation; more specifically, it risks becoming subservient to existing economic and financial systems rather than correcting their dysfunctional aspects. Among other things, it risks being used to justify the financing of projects that are in reality unethical. The word "ethical," then, should not be used to make ideological distinctions, as if to suggest that initiatives not formally so designated would not be ethical. Efforts are needed—and it is essential to say this—not only to create "ethical" sectors or segments of the economy or the world of finance, but to ensure that the whole economy—the whole of finance—is ethical, not merely by virtue of an external label, but by its respect

for requirements intrinsic to its very nature. The Church's social teaching is quite clear on the subject, recalling that the economy, in all its branches, constitutes a sector of human activity.[113]

46. When we consider the issues involved in the *relationship between business and ethics*, as well as the evolution currently taking place in methods of production, it would appear that the traditionally valid distinction between profit-based companies and non-profit organizations can no longer do full justice to reality, or offer practical direction for the future. In recent decades a broad intermediate area has emerged between the two types of enterprise. It is made up of traditional companies which nonetheless subscribe to social aid agreements in support of underdeveloped countries, charitable foundations associated with individual companies, groups of companies oriented towards social welfare, and the diversified world of the so-called "civil economy" and the "economy of communion." This is not merely a matter of a "third sector," but of a broad new composite reality embracing the private and public spheres, one which does not exclude profit, but instead considers it a means for achieving human and social ends. Whether such companies distribute dividends or not, whether their juridical structure corresponds to one or other of the established forms, becomes secondary in relation to their willingness to view profit as a means of achieving the goal of a more humane market and society. It is to be hoped that these new kinds of enterprise will succeed in finding a suitable juridical and fiscal structure in every country. Without prejudice to the importance and the economic and social benefits of the more traditional forms of business, they steer the system towards a clearer and more complete assumption of duties on the part of economic subjects. And not only that. *The very plurality of institutional forms of business gives rise to a market which is not only more civilized but also more competitive.*

47. The strengthening of different types of businesses, especially those capable of viewing profit as a means for achieving the goal of a more humane market and society, must also be pursued in those countries that are excluded or marginalized from the influential circles of the global economy. In these countries it is very important to move ahead with projects based on subsidiarity, suitably planned and managed, aimed at affirming rights yet also providing for the assumption of corresponding responsibilities. In *development programmes*, the principle of the *centrality of the human person*, as the subject primarily responsible for development, must be preserved. The principal concern must be to improve the actual living conditions of the people in a given region, thus enabling them to carry out those duties which their poverty does not presently allow them to fulfil. Social concern must never be an abstract attitude. Development programmes, if they are to be adapted to individual situations, need to be flexible; and the people who benefit from them ought to be directly involved in their planning and implementation. The criteria to be applied should aspire towards incremental development in a context of

solidarity—with careful monitoring of results—inasmuch as there are no universally valid solutions. Much depends on the way programmes are managed in practice. "The peoples themselves have the prime responsibility to work for their own development. But they will not bring this about in isolation."[114] These words of Paul VI are all the more timely nowadays, as our world becomes progressively more integrated. The dynamics of inclusion are hardly automatic. Solutions need to be carefully designed to correspond to people's concrete lives, based on a prudential evaluation of each situation. Alongside macro-projects, there is a place for micro-projects, and above all there is need for the active mobilization of all the subjects of civil society, both juridical and physical persons.

International cooperation requires people who can be part of the process of economic and human development through the solidarity of their presence, supervision, training and respect. From this standpoint, international organizations might question the actual effectiveness of their bureaucratic and administrative machinery, which is often excessively costly. At times it happens that those who receive aid become subordinate to the aid-givers, and the poor serve to perpetuate expensive bureaucracies which consume an excessively high percentage of funds intended for development. Hence it is to be hoped that all international agencies and non-governmental organizations will commit themselves to complete transparency, informing donors and the public of the percentage of their income allocated to programmes of cooperation, the actual content of those programmes and, finally, the detailed expenditure of the institution itself.

48. Today the subject of development is also closely related to the duties arising from *our relationship to the natural environment*. The environment is God's gift to everyone, and in our use of it we have a responsibility towards the poor, towards future generations and towards humanity as a whole. When nature, including the human being, is viewed as the result of mere chance or evolutionary determinism, our sense of responsibility wanes. In nature, the believer recognizes the wonderful result of God's creative activity, which we may use responsibly to satisfy our legitimate needs, material or otherwise, while respecting the intrinsic balance of creation. If this vision is lost, we end up either considering nature an untouchable taboo or, on the contrary, abusing it. Neither attitude is consonant with the Christian vision of nature as the fruit of God's creation.

Nature expresses a design of love and truth. It is prior to us, and it has been given to us by God as the setting for our life. Nature speaks to us of the Creator (cf. Rom. 1:20) and his love for humanity. It is destined to be "recapitulated" in Christ at the end of time (cf. Eph. 1:9–10; Col. 1:19–20). Thus it too is a "vocation."[115] Nature is at our disposal not as "a heap of scattered refuse,"[116] but as a gift of the Creator who has given it an inbuilt order, enabling man to draw from it the principles needed in order "to till it and keep it" (Gen. 2:15). But it should also be stressed that it is contrary to authentic

development to view nature as something more important than the human person. This position leads to attitudes of neo-paganism or a new pantheism—human salvation cannot come from nature alone, understood in a purely naturalistic sense. This having been said, it is also necessary to reject the opposite position, which aims at total technical dominion over nature, because the natural environment is more than raw material to be manipulated at our pleasure; it is a wondrous work of the Creator containing a "grammar" which sets forth ends and criteria for its wise use, not its reckless exploitation. Today much harm is done to development precisely as a result of these distorted notions. Reducing nature merely to a collection of contingent data ends up doing violence to the environment and even encouraging activity that fails to respect human nature itself. Our nature, constituted not only by matter but also by spirit, and as such, endowed with transcendent meaning and aspirations, is also normative for culture. Human beings interpret and shape the natural environment through culture, which in turn is given direction by the responsible use of freedom, in accordance with the dictates of the moral law. Consequently, projects for integral human development cannot ignore coming generations, but need to be *marked by solidarity and inter-generational justice*, while taking into account a variety of contexts: ecological, juridical, economic, political and cultural.[117]

49. Questions linked to the care and preservation of the environment today need to give due consideration to *the energy problem*. The fact that some States, power groups and companies hoard non-renewable energy resources represents a grave obstacle to development in poor countries. Those countries lack the economic means either to gain access to existing sources of non-renewable energy or to finance research into new alternatives. The stockpiling of natural resources, which in many cases are found in the poor countries themselves, gives rise to exploitation and frequent conflicts between and within nations. These conflicts are often fought on the soil of those same countries, with a heavy toll of death, destruction and further decay. The international community has an urgent duty to find institutional means of regulating the exploitation of non-renewable resources, involving poor countries in the process, in order to plan together for the future.

On this front too, there is a *pressing moral need for renewed solidarity*, especially in relationships between developing countries and those that are highly industrialized.[118] The technologically advanced societies can and must lower their domestic energy consumption, either through an evolution in manufacturing methods or through greater ecological sensitivity among their citizens. It should be added that at present it is possible to achieve improved energy efficiency while at the same time encouraging research into alternative forms of energy. What is also needed, though, is a worldwide redistribution of energy resources, so that countries lacking those resources can have access to them. The fate of those countries cannot be left in the hands of whoever is first to claim the spoils, or whoever is able to prevail over the rest. Here we are

dealing with major issues; if they are to be faced adequately, then everyone must responsibly recognize the impact they will have on future generations, particularly on the many young people in the poorer nations, who "ask to assume their active part in the construction of a better world."[119]

50. This responsibility is a global one, for it is concerned not just with energy but with the whole of creation, which must not be bequeathed to future generations depleted of its resources. Human beings legitimately exercise a *responsible stewardship over nature*, in order to protect it, to enjoy its fruits and to cultivate it in new ways, with the assistance of advanced technologies, so that it can worthily accommodate and feed the world's population. On this earth there is room for everyone: here the entire human family must find the resources to live with dignity, through the help of nature itself—God's gift to his children—and through hard work and creativity. At the same time we must recognize our grave duty to hand the earth on to future generations in such a condition that they too can worthily inhabit it and continue to cultivate it. This means being committed to making joint decisions "after pondering responsibly the road to be taken, decisions aimed at strengthening that *covenant between human beings and the environment*, which should mirror the creative love of God, from whom we come and towards whom we are journeying."[120] Let us hope that the international community and individual governments will succeed in countering harmful ways of treating the environment. It is likewise incumbent upon the competent authorities to make every effort to ensure that the economic and social costs of using up shared environmental resources are recognized with transparency and fully borne by those who incur them, not by other peoples or future generations: the protection of the environment, of resources and of the climate obliges all international leaders to act jointly and to show a readiness to work in good faith, respecting the law and promoting solidarity with the weakest regions of the planet.[121] One of the greatest challenges facing the economy is to achieve the most efficient use—not abuse—of natural resources, based on a realization that the notion of "efficiency" is not value-free.

51. *The way humanity treats the environment influences the way it treats itself, and vice versa.* This invites contemporary society to a serious review of its life-style, which, in many parts of the world, is prone to hedonism and consumerism, regardless of their harmful consequences.[122] What is needed is an effective shift in mentality which can lead to the adoption of *new life-styles* "in which the quest for truth, beauty, goodness and communion with others for the sake of common growth are the factors which determine consumer choices, savings and investments."[123] Every violation of solidarity and civic friendship harms the environment, just as environmental deterioration in turn upsets relations in society. Nature, especially in our time, is so integrated into the dynamics of society and culture that by now it hardly constitutes an independent variable. Desertification and the decline in productivity in some agricultural areas are also the result of impoverishment and underdevelopment

among their inhabitants. When incentives are offered for their economic and cultural development, nature itself is protected. Moreover, how many natural resources are squandered by wars! Peace in and among peoples would also provide greater protection for nature. The hoarding of resources, especially water, can generate serious conflicts among the peoples involved. Peaceful agreement about the use of resources can protect nature and, at the same time, the well-being of the societies concerned.

The Church has a responsibility towards creation and she must assert this responsibility in the public sphere. In so doing, she must defend not only earth, water and air as gifts of creation that belong to everyone. She must above all protect mankind from self-destruction. There is need for what might be called a human ecology, correctly understood. The deterioration of nature is in fact closely connected to the culture that shapes human coexistence: *when "human ecology"*[124] *is respected within society, environmental ecology also benefits.* Just as human virtues are interrelated, such that the weakening of one places others at risk, so the ecological system is based on respect for a plan that affects both the health of society and its good relationship with nature.

In order to protect nature, it is not enough to intervene with economic incentives or deterrents; not even an apposite education is sufficient. These are important steps, but *the decisive issue is the overall moral tenor of society.* If there is a lack of respect for the right to life and to a natural death, if human conception, gestation and birth are made artificial, if human embryos are sacrificed to research, the conscience of society ends up losing the concept of human ecology and, along with it, that of environmental ecology. It is contradictory to insist that future generations respect the natural environment when our educational systems and laws do not help them to respect themselves. The book of nature is one and indivisible: it takes in not only the environment but also life, sexuality, marriage, the family, social relations: in a word, integral human development. Our duties towards the environment are linked to our duties towards the human person, considered in himself and in relation to others. It would be wrong to uphold one set of duties while trampling on the other. Herein lies a grave contradiction in our mentality and practice today: one which demeans the person, disrupts the environment and damages society.

52. Truth, and the love which it reveals, cannot be produced: they can only be received as a gift. Their ultimate source is not, and cannot be, mankind, but only God, who is himself Truth and Love. This principle is extremely important for society and for development, since neither can be a purely human product; the vocation to development on the part of individuals and peoples is not based simply on human choice, but is an intrinsic part of a plan that is prior to us and constitutes for all of us a duty to be freely accepted. That which is prior to us and constitutes us—subsistent Love and Truth—shows us what goodness is, and in what our true happiness consists. *It shows us the road to true development.*

CHAPTER FIVE

THE COOPERATION OF THE HUMAN FAMILY

53. One of the deepest forms of poverty a person can experience is isolation. If we look closely at other kinds of poverty, including material forms, we see that they are born from isolation, from not being loved or from difficulties in being able to love. Poverty is often produced by a rejection of God's love, by man's basic and tragic tendency to close in on himself, thinking himself to be self-sufficient or merely an insignificant and ephemeral fact, a "stranger" in a random universe. Man is alienated when he is alone, when he is detached from reality, when he stops thinking and believing in a foundation.[125] All of humanity is alienated when too much trust is placed in merely human projects, ideologies and false utopias.[126] Today humanity appears much more interactive than in the past: this shared sense of being close to one another must be transformed into true communion. *The development of peoples depends, above all, on a recognition that the human race is a single family* working together in true communion, not simply a group of subjects who happen to live side by side.[127]

Pope Paul VI noted that "the world is in trouble because of the lack of thinking."[128] He was making an observation, but also expressing a wish: a new trajectory of thinking is needed in order to arrive at a better understanding of the implications of our being one family; interaction among the peoples of the world calls us to embark upon this new trajectory, so that integration can signify solidarity[129] rather than marginalization. Thinking of this kind requires a *deeper critical evaluation of the category of relation*. This is a task that cannot be undertaken by the social sciences alone, insofar as the contribution of disciplines such as metaphysics and theology is needed if man's transcendent dignity is to be properly understood.

As a spiritual being, the human creature is defined through interpersonal relations. The more authentically he or she lives these relations, the more his or her own personal identity matures. It is not by isolation that man establishes his worth, but by placing himself in relation with others and with God. Hence these relations take on fundamental importance. The same holds true for peoples as well. A metaphysical understanding of the relations between persons is therefore of great benefit for their development. In this regard, reason finds inspiration and direction in Christian revelation, according to which the human community does not absorb the individual, annihilating his autonomy, as happens in the various forms of totalitarianism, but rather values him all the more because the relation between individual and community is a relation between one totality and another.[130] Just as a family does not submerge the identities of its individual members, just as the Church rejoices in each "new creation" (Gal. 6:15; 2 Cor. 5:17) incorporated by Baptism into her living Body, so too the unity of the human family does not submerge the identities of

individuals, peoples and cultures, but makes them more transparent to each other and links them more closely in their legitimate diversity.

54. The theme of development can be identified with the inclusion-in-relation of all individuals and peoples within the one community of the human family, built in solidarity on the basis of the fundamental values of justice and peace. This perspective is illuminated in a striking way by the relationship between the Persons of the Trinity within the one divine Substance. The Trinity is absolute unity insofar as the three divine Persons are pure relationality. The reciprocal transparency among the divine Persons is total and the bond between each of them complete, since they constitute a unique and absolute unity. God desires to incorporate us into this reality of communion as well: "that they may be one even as we are one" (Jn. 17:22). The Church is a sign and instrument of this unity.[131] Relationships between human beings throughout history cannot but be enriched by reference to this divine model. In particular, *in the light of the revealed mystery of the Trinity*, we understand that true openness does not mean loss of individual identity but profound interpenetration. This also emerges from the common human experiences of love and truth. Just as the sacramental love of spouses unites them spiritually in "one flesh" (Gen. 2:24; Mt. 19:5; Eph. 5:31) and makes out of the two a real and relational unity, so in an analogous way truth unites spirits and causes them to think in unison, attracting them as a unity to itself.

55. The Christian revelation of the unity of the human race presupposes a *metaphysical interpretation of the "humanum" in which relationality is an essential element*. Other cultures and religions teach brotherhood and peace and are therefore of enormous importance to integral human development. Some religious and cultural attitudes, however, do not fully embrace the principle of love and truth and therefore end up retarding or even obstructing authentic human development. There are certain religious cultures in the world today that do not oblige men and women to live in communion but rather cut them off from one other in a search for individual well-being, limited to the gratification of psychological desires. Furthermore, a certain proliferation of different religious "paths," attracting small groups or even single individuals, together with religious syncretism, can give rise to separation and disengagement. One possible negative effect of the process of globalization is the tendency to favour this kind of syncretism[132] by encouraging forms of "religion" that, instead of bringing people together, alienate them from one another and distance them from reality. At the same time, some religious and cultural traditions persist which ossify society in rigid social groupings, in magical beliefs that fail to respect the dignity of the person, and in attitudes of subjugation to occult powers. In these contexts, love and truth have difficulty asserting themselves, and authentic development is impeded.

For this reason, while it may be true that development needs the religions and cultures of different peoples, it is equally true that adequate discernment is needed. Religious freedom does not mean religious indifferentism, nor does

it imply that all religions are equal.[133] Discernment is needed regarding the contribution of cultures and religions, especially on the part of those who wield political power, if the social community is to be built up in a spirit of respect for the common good. Such discernment has to be based on the criterion of charity and truth. Since the development of persons and peoples is at stake, this discernment will have to take account of the need for emancipation and inclusivity, in the context of a truly universal human community. "The whole man and all men" is also the criterion for evaluating cultures and religions. Christianity, the religion of the "God who has a human face,"[134] contains this very criterion within itself.

56. The Christian religion and other religions can offer their contribution to development *only if God has a place in the public realm*, specifically in regard to its cultural, social, economic, and particularly its political dimensions. The Church's social doctrine came into being in order to claim "citizenship status" for the Christian religion.[135] Denying the right to profess one's religion in public and the right to bring the truths of faith to bear upon public life has negative consequences for true development. The exclusion of religion from the public square—and, at the other extreme, religious fundamentalism—hinders an encounter between persons and their collaboration for the progress of humanity. Public life is sapped of its motivation and politics takes on a domineering and aggressive character. Human rights risk being ignored either because they are robbed of their transcendent foundation or because personal freedom is not acknowledged. Secularism and fundamentalism exclude the possibility of fruitful dialogue and effective cooperation between reason and religious faith. *Reason always stands in need of being purified by faith*: this also holds true for political reason, which must not consider itself omnipotent. For its part, *religion always needs to be purified by reason* in order to show its authentically human face. Any breach in this dialogue comes only at an enormous price to human development.

57. Fruitful dialogue between faith and reason cannot but render the work of charity more effective within society, and it constitutes the most appropriate framework for promoting *fraternal collaboration between believers and non-believers* in their shared commitment to working for justice and the peace of the human family. In the Pastoral Constitution *Gaudium et Spes*, the Council fathers asserted that "believers and unbelievers agree almost unanimously that all things on earth should be ordered towards man as to their centre and summit."[136] For believers, the world derives neither from blind chance nor from strict necessity, but from God's plan. This is what gives rise to the duty of believers to unite their efforts with those of all men and women of good will, with the followers of other religions and with non-believers, so that this world of ours may effectively correspond to the divine plan: living as a family under the Creator's watchful eye. A particular manifestation of charity and a guiding criterion for fraternal cooperation between believers and non-believers is undoubtedly the *principle of subsidiarity*,[137] an expression of

inalienable human freedom. Subsidiarity is first and foremost a form of assistance to the human person via the autonomy of intermediate bodies. Such assistance is offered when individuals or groups are unable to accomplish something on their own, and it is always designed to achieve their emancipation, because it fosters freedom and participation through assumption of responsibility. Subsidiarity respects personal dignity by recognizing in the person a subject who is always capable of giving something to others. By considering reciprocity as the heart of what it is to be a human being, subsidiarity is the most effective antidote against any form of all-encompassing welfare state. It is able to take account both of the manifold articulation of plans—and therefore of the plurality of subjects—as well as the coordination of those plans. Hence the principle of subsidiarity is particularly well-suited to managing globalization and directing it towards authentic human development. In order not to produce a dangerous universal power of a tyrannical nature, *the governance of globalization must be marked by subsidiarity*, articulated into several layers and involving different levels that can work together. Globalization certainly requires authority, insofar as it poses the problem of a global common good that needs to be pursued. This authority, however, must be organized in a subsidiary and stratified way,[138] if it is not to infringe upon freedom and if it is to yield effective results in practice.

58. *The principle of subsidiarity must remain closely linked to the principle of solidarity and vice versa*, since the former without the latter gives way to social privatism, while the latter without the former gives way to paternalist social assistance that is demeaning to those in need. This general rule must also be taken broadly into consideration when addressing issues concerning *international development aid*. Such aid, whatever the donors' intentions, can sometimes lock people into a state of dependence and even foster situations of localized oppression and exploitation in the receiving country. Economic aid, in order to be true to its purpose, must not pursue secondary objectives. It must be distributed with the involvement not only of the governments of receiving countries, but also local economic agents and the bearers of culture within civil society, including local Churches. Aid programmes must increasingly acquire the characteristics of participation and completion from the grass roots. Indeed, the most valuable resources in countries receiving development aid are human resources: herein lies the real capital that needs to accumulate in order to guarantee a truly autonomous future for the poorest countries. It should also be remembered that, in the economic sphere, the principal form of assistance needed by developing countries is that of allowing and encouraging the gradual penetration of their products into international markets, thus making it possible for these countries to participate fully in international economic life. Too often in the past, aid has served to create only fringe markets for the products of these donor countries. This was often due to a lack of genuine demand for the products in question: it is therefore necessary to help such countries improve their products and adapt them

more effectively to existing demand. Furthermore, there are those who fear the effects of competition through the importation of products—normally agricultural products—from economically poor countries. Nevertheless, it should be remembered that for such countries, the possibility of marketing their products is very often what guarantees their survival in both the short and long term. Just and equitable international trade in agricultural goods can be beneficial to everyone, both to suppliers and to customers. For this reason, not only is commercial orientation needed for production of this kind, but also the establishment of international trade regulations to support it and stronger financing for development in order to increase the productivity of these economies.

59. *Cooperation for development* must not be concerned exclusively with the economic dimension: it offers a wonderful *opportunity for encounter between cultures and peoples*. If the parties to cooperation on the side of economically developed countries—as occasionally happens—fail to take account of their own or others' cultural identity, or the human values that shape it, they cannot enter into meaningful dialogue with the citizens of poor countries. If the latter, in their turn, are uncritically and indiscriminately open to every cultural proposal, they will not be in a position to assume responsibility for their own authentic development.[139] Technologically advanced societies must not confuse their own technological development with a presumed cultural superiority, but must rather rediscover within themselves the oft-forgotten virtues which made it possible for them to flourish throughout their history. Evolving societies must remain faithful to all that is truly human in their traditions, avoiding the temptation to overlay them automatically with the mechanisms of a globalized technological civilization. In all cultures there are examples of ethical convergence, some isolated, some interrelated, as an expression of the one human nature, willed by the Creator; the tradition of ethical wisdom knows this as the natural law.[140] This universal moral law provides a sound basis for all cultural, religious and political dialogue, and it ensures that the multi-faceted pluralism of cultural diversity does not detach itself from the common quest for truth, goodness and God. Thus adherence to the law etched on human hearts is the precondition for all constructive social cooperation. Every culture has burdens from which it must be freed and shadows from which it must emerge. The Christian faith, by becoming incarnate in cultures and at the same time transcending them, can help them grow in universal brotherhood and solidarity, for the advancement of global and community development.

60. In the search for solutions to the current economic crisis, *development aid for poor countries must be considered a valid means of creating wealth for all*. What aid programme is there that can hold out such significant growth prospects—even from the point of view of the world economy—as the support of populations that are still in the initial or early phases of economic development? From this perspective, more economically developed nations should

do all they can to allocate larger portions of their gross domestic product to development aid, thus respecting the obligations that the international community has undertaken in this regard. One way of doing so is by reviewing their internal social assistance and welfare policies, applying the principle of subsidiarity and creating better integrated welfare systems, with the active participation of private individuals and civil society. In this way, it is actually possible to improve social services and welfare programmes, and at the same time to save resources—by eliminating waste and rejecting fraudulent claims—which could then be allocated to international solidarity. A more devolved and organic system of social solidarity, less bureaucratic but no less coordinated, would make it possible to harness much dormant energy, for the benefit of solidarity between peoples.

One possible approach to development aid would be to apply effectively what is known as fiscal subsidiarity, allowing citizens to decide how to allocate a portion of the taxes they pay to the State. Provided it does not degenerate into the promotion of special interests, this can help to stimulate forms of welfare solidarity from below, with obvious benefits in the area of solidarity for development as well.

61. Greater solidarity at the international level is seen especially in the ongoing promotion—even in the midst of economic crisis—of *greater access to education*, which is at the same time an essential precondition for effective international cooperation. The term "education" refers not only to classroom teaching and vocational training—both of which are important factors in development—but to the complete formation of the person. In this regard, there is a problem that should be highlighted: in order to educate, it is necessary to know the nature of the human person, to know who he or she is. The increasing prominence of a relativistic understanding of that nature presents serious problems for education, especially moral education, jeopardizing its universal extension. Yielding to this kind of relativism makes everyone poorer and has a negative impact on the effectiveness of aid to the most needy populations, who lack not only economic and technical means, but also educational methods and resources to assist people in realizing their full human potential.

An illustration of the significance of this problem is offered by the phenomenon of *international tourism*,[141] which can be a major factor in economic development and cultural growth, but can also become an occasion for exploitation and moral degradation. The current situation offers unique opportunities for the economic aspects of development—that is to say the flow of money and the emergence of a significant amount of local enterprise—to be combined with the cultural aspects, chief among which is education. In many cases this is what happens, but in other cases international tourism has a negative educational impact both for the tourist and the local populace. The latter are often exposed to immoral or even perverted forms of conduct, as in

the case of so-called sex tourism, to which many human beings are sacrificed even at a tender age. It is sad to note that this activity often takes place with the support of local governments, with silence from those in the tourists' countries of origin, and with the complicity of many of the tour operators. Even in less extreme cases, international tourism often follows a consumerist and hedonistic pattern, as a form of escapism planned in a manner typical of the countries of origin, and therefore not conducive to authentic encounter between persons and cultures. We need, therefore, to develop a different type of tourism that has the ability to promote genuine mutual understanding, without taking away from the element of rest and healthy recreation. Tourism of this type needs to increase, partly through closer coordination with the experience gained from international cooperation and enterprise for development.

62. Another aspect of integral human development that is worthy of attention is the phenomenon of *migration.* This is a striking phenomenon because of the sheer numbers of people involved, the social, economic, political, cultural and religious problems it raises, and the dramatic challenges it poses to nations and the international community. We can say that we are facing a social phenomenon of epoch-making proportions that requires bold, forward-looking policies of international cooperation if it is to be handled effectively. Such policies should set out from close collaboration between the migrants' countries of origin and their countries of destination; it should be accompanied by adequate international norms able to coordinate different legislative systems with a view to safeguarding the needs and rights of individual migrants and their families, and at the same time, those of the host countries. No country can be expected to address today's problems of migration by itself. We are all witnesses of the burden of suffering, the dislocation and the aspirations that accompany the flow of migrants. The phenomenon, as everyone knows, is difficult to manage; but there is no doubt that foreign workers, despite any difficulties concerning integration, make a significant contribution to the economic development of the host country through their labour, besides that which they make to their country of origin through the money they send home. Obviously, these labourers cannot be considered as a commodity or a mere workforce. They must not, therefore, be treated like any other factor of production. Every migrant is a human person who, as such, possesses fundamental, inalienable rights that must be respected by everyone and in every circumstance.[142]

63. No consideration of the problems associated with development could fail to highlight the direct link between *poverty and unemployment.* In many cases, poverty results from a *violation of the dignity of human work*, either because work opportunities are limited (through unemployment or underemployment), or "because a low value is put on work and the rights that flow from it, especially the right to a just wage and to the personal security of the worker and his or her family."[143] For this reason, on 1 May 2000 on the occasion of the Jubilee of Workers, my venerable predecessor Pope John Paul II

issued an appeal for "a global coalition in favour of 'decent work,' "[144] supporting the strategy of the International Labour Organization. In this way, he gave a strong moral impetus to this objective, seeing it as an aspiration of families in every country of the world. What is meant by the word "decent" in regard to work? It means work that expresses the essential dignity of every man and woman in the context of their particular society: work that is freely chosen, effectively associating workers, both men and women, with the development of their community; work that enables the worker to be respected and free from any form of discrimination; work that makes it possible for families to meet their needs and provide schooling for their children, without the children themselves being forced into labour; work that permits the workers to organize themselves freely, and to make their voices heard; work that leaves enough room for rediscovering one's roots at a personal, familial and spiritual level; work that guarantees those who have retired a decent standard of living.

64. While reflecting on the theme of work, it is appropriate to recall how important it is that *labour unions*—which have always been encouraged and supported by the Church—should be open to the new perspectives that are emerging in the world of work. Looking to wider concerns than the specific category of labour for which they were formed, union organizations are called to address some of the new questions arising in our society: I am thinking, for example, of the complex of issues that social scientists describe in terms of a conflict between worker and consumer. Without necessarily endorsing the thesis that the central focus on the worker has given way to a central focus on the consumer, this would still appear to constitute new ground for unions to explore creatively. The global context in which work takes place also demands that national labour unions, which tend to limit themselves to defending the interests of their registered members, should turn their attention to those outside their membership, and in particular to workers in developing countries where social rights are often violated. The protection of these workers, partly achieved through appropriate initiatives aimed at their countries of origin, will enable trade unions to demonstrate the authentic ethical and cultural motivations that made it possible for them, in a different social and labour context, to play a decisive role in development. The Church's traditional teaching makes a valid distinction between the respective roles and functions of trade unions and politics. This distinction allows unions to identify civil society as the proper setting for their necessary activity of defending and promoting labour, especially on behalf of exploited and unrepresented workers, whose woeful condition is often ignored by the distracted eye of society.

65. *Finance*, therefore—through the renewed structures and operating methods that have to be designed after its misuse, which wreaked such havoc on the real economy—now needs to go back to being an *instrument directed towards improved wealth creation and development*. Insofar as they are instru-

ments, the entire economy and finance, not just certain sectors, must be used in an ethical way so as to create suitable conditions for human development and for the development of peoples. It is certainly useful, and in some circumstances imperative, to launch financial initiatives in which the humanitarian dimension predominates. However, this must not obscure the fact that the entire financial system has to be aimed at sustaining true development. Above all, the intention to do good must not be considered incompatible with the effective capacity to produce goods. Financiers must rediscover the genuinely ethical foundation of their activity, so as not to abuse the sophisticated instruments which can serve to betray the interests of savers. Right intention, transparency, and the search for positive results are mutually compatible and must never be detached from one another. If love is wise, it can find ways of working in accordance with provident and just expediency, as is illustrated in a significant way by much of the experience of credit unions.

Both the regulation of the financial sector, so as to safeguard weaker parties and discourage scandalous speculation, and experimentation with new forms of finance, designed to support development projects, are positive experiences that should be further explored and encouraged, highlighting *the responsibility of the investor*. Furthermore, the *experience of micro-finance*, which has its roots in the thinking and activity of the civil humanists—I am thinking especially of the birth of pawnbroking—should be strengthened and fine-tuned. This is all the more necessary in these days when financial difficulties can become severe for many of the more vulnerable sectors of the population, who should be protected from the risk of usury and from despair. The weakest members of society should be helped to defend themselves against usury, just as poor peoples should be helped to derive real benefit from micro-credit, in order to discourage the exploitation that is possible in these two areas. Since rich countries are also experiencing new forms of poverty, micro-finance can give practical assistance by launching new initiatives and opening up new sectors for the benefit of the weaker elements in society, even at a time of general economic downturn.

66. Global interconnectedness has led to the emergence of a new political power, that of *consumers and their associations*. This is a phenomenon that needs to be further explored, as it contains positive elements to be encouraged as well as excesses to be avoided. It is good for people to realize that purchasing is always a moral—and not simply economic—act. Hence *the consumer has a specific social responsibility*, which goes hand-in-hand with the social responsibility of the enterprise. Consumers should be continually educated[145] regarding their daily role, which can be exercised with respect for moral principles without diminishing the intrinsic economic rationality of the act of purchasing. In the retail industry, particularly at times like the present when purchasing power has diminished and people must live more frugally, it is necessary to explore other paths: for example, forms of cooperative purchasing like the consumer cooperatives that have been in operation since

the nineteenth century, partly through the initiative of Catholics. In addition, it can be helpful to promote new ways of marketing products from deprived areas of the world, so as to guarantee their producers a decent return. However, certain conditions need to be met: the market should be genuinely transparent; the producers, as well as increasing their profit margins, should also receive improved formation in professional skills and technology; and finally, trade of this kind must not become hostage to partisan ideologies. A more incisive role for consumers, as long as they themselves are not manipulated by associations that do not truly represent them, is a desirable element for building economic democracy.

67. In the face of the unrelenting growth of global interdependence, there is a strongly felt need, even in the midst of a global recession, for a reform of the *United Nations Organization*, and likewise of *economic institutions and international finance*, so that the concept of the family of nations can acquire real teeth. One also senses the urgent need to find innovative ways of implementing the principle of the *responsibility to protect*[146] *and of giving poorer nations an effective voice in shared decision-making. This seems necessary in order to arrive at a political, juridical and economic order which can increase and give direction to international cooperation for the development of all peoples in solidarity. To manage the global economy; to revive economies hit by the crisis; to avoid any deterioration of the present crisis and the greater imbalances that would result; to bring about integral and timely disarmament, food security and peace; to guarantee the protection of the environment and to regulate migration: for all this, there is urgent need of a true world political authority*, as my predecessor Blessed John XXIII indicated some years ago. Such an authority would need to be regulated by law, to observe consistently the principles of subsidiarity and solidarity, to seek to establish the common good,[147] and *to make a commitment to securing authentic integral human development inspired by the values of charity in truth.* Furthermore, such an authority would need to be universally recognized and to be vested with the effective power to ensure security for all, regard for justice, and respect for rights.[148] Obviously it would have to have the authority to ensure compliance with its decisions from all parties, and also with the coordinated measures adopted in various international forums. Without this, despite the great progress accomplished in various sectors, international law would risk being conditioned by the balance of power among the strongest nations. The integral development of peoples and international cooperation require the establishment of a greater degree of international ordering, marked by subsidiarity, for the management of globalization.[149] They also require the construction of a social order that at last conforms to the moral order, to the interconnection between moral and social spheres, and to the link between politics and the economic and civil spheres, as envisaged by the Charter of the United Nations.

CHAPTER SIX

THE DEVELOPMENT OF PEOPLES AND TECHNOLOGY

68. The development of peoples is intimately linked to the development of individuals. The human person by nature is actively involved in his own development. The development in question is not simply the result of natural mechanisms, since as everybody knows, we are all capable of making free and responsible choices. Nor is it merely at the mercy of our caprice, since we all know that we are a gift, not something self-generated. Our freedom is profoundly shaped by our being, and by its limits. No one shapes his own conscience arbitrarily, but we all build our own "I" on the basis of a "self" which is given to us. Not only are other persons outside our control, but each one of us is outside his or her own control. *A person's development is compromised, if he claims to be solely responsible for producing what he becomes.* By analogy, the development of peoples goes awry if humanity thinks it can re-create itself through the "wonders" of technology, just as economic development is exposed as a destructive sham if it relies on the "wonders" of finance in order to sustain unnatural and consumerist growth. In the face of such Promethean presumption, we must fortify our love for a freedom that is not merely arbitrary, but is rendered truly human by acknowledgment of the good that underlies it. To this end, man needs to look inside himself in order to recognize the fundamental norms of the natural moral law which God has written on our hearts.

69. The challenge of development today is closely linked to *technological progress*, with its astounding applications in the field of biology. Technology—it is worth emphasizing—is a profoundly human reality, linked to the autonomy and freedom of man. In technology we express and confirm the hegemony of the spirit over matter. "The human spirit, 'increasingly free of its bondage to creatures, can be more easily drawn to the worship and contemplation of the Creator.' "[150] Technology enables us to exercise dominion over matter, to reduce risks, to save labour, to improve our conditions of life. It touches the heart of the vocation of human labour: in technology, seen as the product of his genius, man recognizes himself and forges his own humanity. Technology is the objective side of human action[151] whose origin and *raison d'etre* is found in the subjective element: the worker himself. For this reason, technology is never merely technology. It reveals man and his aspirations towards development, it expresses the inner tension that impels him gradually to overcome material limitations. *Technology, in this sense, is a response to God's command to till and to keep the land* (cf. Gen. 2:15) that he has entrusted to humanity, and it must serve to reinforce the covenant between human beings and the environment, a covenant that should mirror God's creative love.

70. Technological development can give rise to the idea that technology is self-sufficient when too much attention is given to the "*how*" questions, and not enough to the many "*why*" questions underlying human activity. For this reason technology can appear ambivalent. Produced through human creativity as a tool of personal freedom, technology can be understood as a manifestation of absolute freedom, the freedom that seeks to prescind from the limits inherent in things. The process of globalization could replace ideologies with technology,[152] allowing the latter to become an ideological power that threatens to confine us within an *a priori* that holds us back from encountering being and truth. Were that to happen, we would all know, evaluate and make decisions about our life situations from within a technocratic cultural perspective to which we would belong structurally, without ever being able to discover a meaning that is not of our own making. The "technical" worldview that follows from this vision is now so dominant that truth has come to be seen as coinciding with the possible. But when the sole criterion of truth is efficiency and utility, development is automatically denied. True development does not consist primarily in "doing." The key to development is a mind capable of thinking in technological terms and grasping the fully human meaning of human activities, within the context of the holistic meaning of the individual's being. Even when we work through satellites or through remote electronic impulses, our actions always remain human, an expression of our responsible freedom. Technology is highly attractive because it draws us out of our physical limitations and broadens our horizon. *But human freedom is authentic only when it responds to the fascination of technology with decisions that are the fruit of moral responsibility.* Hence the pressing need for formation in an ethically responsible use of technology. Moving beyond the fascination that technology exerts, we must reappropriate the true meaning of freedom, which is not an intoxication with total autonomy, but a response to the call of being, beginning with our own personal being.

71. This deviation from solid humanistic principles that a technical mindset can produce is seen today in certain technological applications in the fields of development and peace. Often the development of peoples is considered a matter of financial engineering, the freeing up of markets, the removal of tariffs, investment in production, and institutional reforms—in other words, a purely technical matter. All these factors are of great importance, but we have to ask why technical choices made thus far have yielded rather mixed results. We need to think hard about the cause. Development will never be fully guaranteed through automatic or impersonal forces, whether they derive from the market or from international politics. *Development is impossible without upright men and women, without financiers and politicians whose consciences are finely attuned to the requirements of the common good.* Both professional competence and moral consistency are necessary. When technology is allowed to take over, the result is confusion between ends and means, such that the sole criterion for action in business is thought to be the maximization of profit, in

politics the consolidation of power, and in science the findings of research. Often, underneath the intricacies of economic, financial and political interconnections, there remain misunderstandings, hardships and injustice. The flow of technological know-how increases, but it is those in possession of it who benefit, while the situation on the ground for the peoples who live in its shadow remains unchanged: for them there is little chance of emancipation.

72. Even peace can run the risk of being considered a technical product, merely the outcome of agreements between governments or of initiatives aimed at ensuring effective economic aid. It is true that *peace-building* requires the constant interplay of diplomatic contacts, economic, technological and cultural exchanges, agreements on common projects, as well as joint strategies to curb the threat of military conflict and to root out the underlying causes of terrorism. Nevertheless, if such efforts are to have lasting effects, they must be based on values rooted in the truth of human life. That is, the voice of the peoples affected must be heard and their situation must be taken into consideration, if their expectations are to be correctly interpreted. One must align oneself, so to speak, with the unsung efforts of so many individuals deeply committed to bringing peoples together and to facilitating development on the basis of love and mutual understanding. Among them are members of the Christian faithful, involved in the great task of upholding the fully human dimension of development and peace.

73. Linked to technological development is the increasingly pervasive presence of the *means of social communications*. It is almost impossible today to imagine the life of the human family without them. For better or for worse, they are so integral a part of life today that it seems quite absurd to maintain that they are neutral—and hence unaffected by any moral considerations concerning people. Often such views, stressing the strictly technical nature of the media, effectively support their subordination to economic interests intent on dominating the market and, not least, to attempts to impose cultural models that serve ideological and political agendas. Given the media's fundamental importance in engineering changes in attitude towards reality and the human person, we must reflect carefully on their influence, especially in regard to the ethical-cultural dimension of globalization and the development of peoples in solidarity. Mirroring what is required for an ethical approach to globalization and development, so too the *meaning and purpose of the media must be sought within an anthropological perspective*. This means that they can have a *civilizing effect* not only when, thanks to technological development, they increase the possibilities of communicating information, but above all when they are geared towards a vision of the person and the common good that reflects truly universal values. Just because social communications increase the possibilities of interconnection and the dissemination of ideas, it does not follow that they promote freedom or internationalize development and democracy for all. To achieve goals of this kind, they need to focus on promoting the dignity of persons and peoples, they need

to be clearly inspired by charity and placed at the service of truth, of the good, and of natural and supernatural fraternity. In fact, human freedom is intrinsically linked with these higher values. The media can make an important contribution towards the growth in communion of the human family and the *ethos* of society when they are used to promote universal participation in the common search for what is just.

74. A particularly crucial battleground in today's cultural struggle between the supremacy of technology and human moral responsibility is the field of *bioethics*, where the very possibility of integral human development is radically called into question. In this most delicate and critical area, the fundamental question asserts itself force-fully: is man the product of his own labours or does he depend on God? Scientific discoveries in this field and the possibilities of technological intervention seem so advanced as to force a choice between two types of reasoning: reason open to transcendence or reason closed within immanence. We are presented with a clear *either/or*. Yet the rationality of a self-centered use of technology proves to be irrational because it implies a decisive rejection of meaning and value. It is no coincidence that closing the door to transcendence brings one up short against a difficulty: how could being emerge from nothing, how could intelligence be born from chance?[153] Faced with these dramatic questions, reason and faith can come to each other's assistance. Only together will they save man. *Entranced by an exclusive reliance on technology, reason without faith is doomed to flounder in an illusion of its own omnipotence. Faith without reason risks being cut off from everyday life.*[154]

75. Paul VI had already recognized and drawn attention to the global dimension of the social question.[155] Following his lead, we need to affirm today that *the social question has become a radically anthropological question*, in the sense that it concerns not just how life is conceived but also how it is manipulated, as bio-technology places it increasingly under man's control. *In vitro* fertilization, embryo research, the possibility of manufacturing clones and human hybrids: all this is now emerging and being promoted in today's highly disillusioned culture, which believes it has mastered every mystery, because the origin of life is now within our grasp. Here we see the clearest expression of technology's supremacy. In this type of culture, the conscience is simply invited to take note of technological possibilities. Yet we must not underestimate the disturbing scenarios that threaten our future, or the powerful new instruments that the "culture of death" has at its disposal. To the tragic and widespread scourge of abortion we may well have to add in the future—indeed it is already surreptiously present—the systematic eugenic programming of births. At the other end of the spectrum, a pro-euthanasia mindset is making inroads as an equally damaging assertion of control over life that under certain circumstances is deemed no longer worth living. Underlying these scenarios are cultural viewpoints that deny human dignity. These practices in turn foster a materialistic and mechanistic under-

standing of human life. Who could measure the negative effects of this kind of mentality for development? How can we be surprised by the indifference shown towards situations of human degradation, when such indifference extends even to our attitude towards what is and is not human? What is astonishing is the arbitrary and selective determination of what to put forward today as worthy of respect. Insignificant matters are considered shocking, yet unprecedented injustices seem to be widely tolerated. While the poor of the world continue knocking on the doors of the rich, the world of affluence runs the risk of no longer hearing those knocks, on account of a conscience that can no longer distinguish what is human. God reveals man to himself; reason and faith work hand in hand to demonstrate to us what is good, provided we want to see it; the natural law, in which creative Reason shines forth, reveals our greatness, but also our wretchedness insofar as we fail to recognize the call to moral truth.

76. One aspect of the contemporary technological mindset is the tendency to consider the problems and emotions of the interior life from a purely psychological point of view, even to the point of neurological reductionism. In this way man's interiority is emptied of its meaning and gradually our awareness of the human soul's ontological depths, as probed by the saints, is lost. *The question of development is closely bound up with our understanding of the human soul*, insofar as we often reduce the self to the psyche and confuse the soul's health with emotional well-being. These over-simplifications stem from a profound failure to understand the spiritual life, and they obscure the fact that the development of individuals and peoples depends partly on the resolution of problems of a spiritual nature. *Development must include not just material growth but also spiritual growth*, since the human person is a "unity of body and soul,"[156] born of God's creative love and destined for eternal life. The human being develops when he grows in the spirit, when his soul comes to know itself and the truths that God has implanted deep within, when he enters into dialogue with himself and his Creator. When he is far away from God, man is unsettled and ill at ease. Social and psychological alienation and the many neuroses that afflict affluent societies are attributable in part to spiritual factors. A prosperous society, highly developed in material terms but weighing heavily on the soul, is not of itself conducive to authentic development. The new forms of slavery to drugs and the lack of hope into which so many people fall can be explained not only in sociological and psychological terms but also in essentially spiritual terms. The emptiness in which the soul feels abandoned, despite the availability of countless therapies for body and psyche, leads to suffering. *There cannot be holistic development and universal common good unless people's spiritual and moral welfare is taken into account*, considered in their totality as body and soul.

77. The supremacy of technology tends to prevent people from recognizing anything that cannot be explained in terms of matter alone. Yet everyone experiences the many immaterial and spiritual dimensions of life.

Knowing is not simply a material act, since the object that is known always conceals something beyond the empirical datum. All our knowledge, even the most simple, is always a minor miracle, since it can never be fully explained by the material instruments that we apply to it. In every truth there is something more than we would have expected, in the love that we receive there is always an element that surprises us. We should never cease to marvel at these things. In all knowledge and in every act of love the human soul experiences something "over and above," which seems very much like a gift that we receive, or a height to which we are raised. The development of individuals and peoples is likewise located on a height, if we consider *the spiritual dimension* that must be present if such development is to be authentic. It requires new eyes and a new heart, capable of *rising above a materialistic vision of human events*, capable of glimpsing in development the "beyond" that technology cannot give. By following this path, it is possible to pursue the integral human development that takes its direction from the driving force of charity in truth.

CONCLUSION

78. Without God man neither knows which way to go, nor even understands who he is. In the face of the enormous problems surrounding the development of peoples, which almost make us yield to discouragement, we find solace in the sayings of our Lord Jesus Christ, who teaches us: "Apart from me you can do nothing" (Jn. 15:5) and then encourages us: "I am with you always, to the close of the age" (Mt. 28:20). As we contemplate the vast amount of work to be done, we are sustained by our faith that God is present alongside those who come together in his name to work for justice. Paul VI recalled in *Populorum Progressio* that man cannot bring about his own progress unaided, because by himself he cannot establish an authentic humanism. Only if we are aware of our calling, as individuals and as a community, to be part of God's family as his sons and daughters, will we be able to generate a new vision and muster new energy in the service of a truly integral humanism. The greatest service to development, then, is a Christian humanism[157] that enkindles charity and takes its lead from truth, accepting both as a lasting gift from God. Openness to God makes us open towards our brothers and sisters and towards an understanding of life as a joyful task to be accomplished in a spirit of solidarity. On the other hand, ideological rejection of God and an atheism of indifference, oblivious to the Creator and at risk of becoming equally oblivious to human values, constitute some of the chief obstacles to development today. *A humanism which excludes God is an inhuman humanism.* Only a humanism open to the Absolute can guide us in the promotion and building of forms of social and civic life—structures, institutions, culture and *ethos*—without

exposing us to the risk of becoming ensnared by the fashions of the moment. Awareness of God's undying love sustains us in our laborious and stimulating work for justice and the development of peoples, amid successes and failures, in the ceaseless pursuit of a just ordering of human affairs. *God's love calls us to move beyond the limited and the ephemeral, it gives us the courage to continue seeking and working for the benefit of all*, even if this cannot be achieved immediately and if what we are able to achieve, alongside political authorities and those working in the field of economics, is always less than we might wish.[158] God gives us the strength to fight and to suffer for love of the common good, because he is our All, our greatest hope.

79. *Development needs Christians with their arms raised towards God* in prayer, Christians moved by the knowledge that truth-filled love, *caritas in veritate*, from which authentic development proceeds, is not produced by us, but given to us. For this reason, even in the most difficult and complex times, besides recognizing what is happening, we must above all else turn to God's love. Development requires attention to the spiritual life, a serious consideration of the experiences of trust in God, spiritual fellowship in Christ, reliance upon God's providence and mercy, love and forgiveness, self-denial, acceptance of others, justice and peace. All this is essential if "hearts of stone" are to be transformed into "hearts of flesh" (Ezek. 36:26), rendering life on earth "divine" and thus more worthy of humanity. All this is *of man*, because man is the subject of his own existence; and at the same time it is *of God*, because God is at the beginning and end of all that is good, all that leads to salvation: "the world or life or death or the present or the future, all are yours; and you are Christ's; and Christ is God's" (1 Cor. 3:22–23). Christians long for the entire human family to call upon God as "Our Father!" In union with the only-begotten Son, may all people learn to pray to the Father and to ask him, in the words that Jesus himself taught us, for the grace to glorify him by living according to his will, to receive the daily bread that we need, to be understanding and generous towards our debtors, not to be tempted beyond our limits, and to be delivered from evil (cf. Mt. 6:9–13).

At the conclusion of the *Pauline Year*, I gladly express this hope in the Apostle's own words, taken from the *Letter to the Romans*: "Let love be genuine; hate what is evil, hold fast to what is good; love one another with brotherly affection; outdo one another in showing honour" (Rom. 12:9–10). May the Virgin Mary—proclaimed *Mater Ecclesiae* by Paul VI and honoured by Christians as *Speculum Iustitiae* and *Regina Pacis*—protect us and obtain for us, through her heavenly intercession, the strength, hope and joy necessary to continue to dedicate ourselves with generosity to the task of bringing about the "*development of the whole man and of all men.*"[159]

Given in Rome, at Saint Peter's, on 29 June, the Solemnity of the Holy Apostles Peter and Paul, in the year 2009, the fifth of my Pontificate.

BENEDICTUS PP. XVI

NOTES

1. Cf. Paul VI, Encyclical Letter *Populorum Progressio* (26 March 1967), 22: AAS 59 (1967), 268; Second Vatican Ecumenical Council, Pastoral Constitution on the Church in the Modern World *Gaudium et Spes*, 69.

2. *Address for the Day of Development* (23 August 1968): AAS 60 (1968), 626–627.

3. Cf. John Paul II, *Message for the 2002 World Day of Peace:* AAS 94 (2002), 132–140.

4. Cf. Second Vatican Ecumenical Council, Pastoral Constitution on the Church in the Modern World *Gaudium et Spes*, 26.

5. Cf. John XXIII, Encyclical Letter *Pacem in Terris* (11 April 1963): AAS 55 (1963), 268–270.

6. Cf. no. 16: loc. cit., 265.

7. Cf. ibid., 82: loc. cit., 297.

8. Ibid., 42: loc. cit., 278.

9. Ibid., 20: loc. cit., 267.

10. Cf. Second Vatican Ecumenical Council, Pastoral Constitution on the Church in the Modern World *Gaudium et Spes*, 36; Paul VI, Apostolic Letter *Octogesima Adveniens* (14 May 1971), 4: AAS 63 (1971), 403–404; John Paul II, Encyclical Letter *Centesimus Annus* (1 May 1991), 43: AAS 83 (1991), 847.

11. Paul VI, Encyclical Letter *Populorum Progressio*, 13: loc. cit., 263–264.

12. Cf. Pontifical Council for Justice and Peace, *Compendium of the Social Doctrine of the Church*, 76.

13. Cf. Benedict XVI, *Address at the Inauguration of the Fifth General Conference of the Bishops of Latin America and the Caribbean* (Aparecida, 13 May 2007).

14. Cf. nos. 3-5: loc. cit., 258–260.

15. Cf. John Paul II, Encyclical Letter *Sollicitudo Rei Socialis* (30 December 1987), 6–7: AAS 80 (1988), 517–519.

16. Cf. Paul VI, Encyclical Letter *Populorum Progressio*, 14: loc. cit., 264.

17. Cf. Benedict XVI, Encyclical Letter *Deus Caritas Est* (25 December 2005), 18: AAS 98 (2006), 232.

18. Ibid., 6: loc. cit., 222.

19. Cf. Benedict XVI, *Christmas Address to the Roman Curia*, 22 December 2005.

20. Cf. John Paul II, Encyclical Letter *Sollicitudo Rei Socialis*, 3: loc. cit., 515.

21. Cf. ibid., 1: loc. cit., 513–514.

22. Cf. ibid., 3: loc. cit., 515.

23. Cf. John Paul II, Encyclical Letter *Laborem Exercens* (14 September 1981), 3: AAS 73 (1981), 583–584.

24. Cf. John Paul II, Encyclical Letter *Centesimus Annus*, 3: loc. cit., 794–796.

25. Cf. Encyclical Letter *Populorum Progressio*, 3: loc. cit., 258.

26. Cf. ibid., 34: loc. cit., 274.

27. Cf. nos. 8-9: AAS 60 (1968), 485–487; Benedict XVI, *Address to the participants at the International Congress promoted by the Pontifical Lateran University on the fortieth anniversary of Paul VI's Encyclical "Humanae Vitae,"* 10 May 2008.

28. Cf. Encyclical Letter *Evangelium Vitae* (25 March 1995), 93: AAS 87 (1995), 507–508.

29. Ibid., 101: loc. cit., 516–518.

30. No. 29: AAS 68 (1976), 25.

31. Ibid., 31: loc. cit., 26.

32. Cf. John Paul II, Encyclical Letter *Sollicitudo Rei Socialis*, 41: loc. cit., 570–572.

33. Cf. ibid.; Id., Encyclical Letter *Centesimus Annus*, 5, 54: loc. cit., 799, 859–860.

34. No. 15: loc. cit., 265.

35. Cf. ibid., 2: loc. cit., 258; Leo XIII, Encyclical Letter *Rerum Novarum* (15 May 1891): *Leonis XIII P.M. Acta*, XI, Romae 1892, 97–144; John Paul II, Encyclical Letter *Sollicitudo Rei Socialis*, 8: loc. cit., 519-520; Id., Encyclical Letter *Centesimus Annus*, 5: loc. cit., 799.

36. Cf. Encyclical Letter *Populorum Progressio*, 2, 13: loc. cit., 258, 263–264.

37. Ibid., 42: loc. cit., 278.

38. Ibid., 11: loc. cit., 262; cf. John Paul II, Encyclical Letter *Centesimus Annus*, 25: loc. cit., 822–824.

39. Encyclical Letter *Populorum Progressio*, 15: loc. cit., 265.

40. Ibid., 3: loc. cit., 258.

41. Ibid., 6: loc. cit., 260.

42. Ibid., 14: loc. cit., 264.

43. Ibid.; cf. John Paul II, Encyclical Letter *Centesimus Annus*, 53–62: loc. cit., 859–867; Id., Encyclical Letter *Redemptor Hominis* (4 March 1979), 13–14: AAS 71 (1979), 282–286.

44. Cf. Paul VI, Encyclical Letter *Populorum Progressio*, 12: loc. cit., 262–263.

45. Second Vatican Ecumenical Council, Pastoral Constitution on the Church in the Modern World *Gaudium et Spes*, 22.

46. Paul VI, Encyclical Letter *Populorum Progressio*, 13: loc. cit., 263–264.

47. Cf. Benedict XVI, *Address to the Participants in the Fourth National Congress of the Church in Italy*, Verona, 19 October 2006.

48. Cf. Paul VI, Encyclical Letter *Populorum Progressio*, 16: loc. cit., 265.

49. Ibid.

50. Benedict XVI, *Address to Young People at Barangaroo*, Sydney, 17 July 2008.

51. Paul VI, Encyclical Letter *Populorum Progressio*, 20: loc. cit., 267.

52. Ibid., 66: loc. cit., 289–290.

53. Ibid., 21: loc. cit., 267–268.

54. Cf. nos. 3, 29, 32: loc. cit., 258, 272, 273.

55. Cf. Encyclical Letter, *Sollicitudo Rei Socialis*, 28: loc. cit., 548–550.

56. Paul VI, Encyclical Letter *Populorum Progressio*, 9: loc. cit., 261–262.

57. Cf. Encyclical Letter *Sollicitudo Rei Socialis*, 20: loc. cit., 536–537.

58. Cf. John Paul II, Encyclical Letter *Centesimus Annus*, 22–29: loc. cit., 819–830.

59. Cf. nos. 23, 33: loc. cit., 268–269, 273–274.

60. Cf. loc. cit., 135.

61. Second Vatican Ecumenical Council, Pastoral Constitution on the Church in the Modern World *Gaudium et Spes*, 63.

62. Cf. John Paul II, Encyclical Letter *Centesimus Annus*, 24: loc. cit., 821–822.

63. Cf. John Paul II, Encyclical Letter *Veritatis Splendor* (6 August 1993), 33, 46, 51: AAS 85 (1993), 1160, 1169–1171, 1174–1175; Id., *Address to the Assembly of the United Nations*, 5 October 1995, 3.

64. Cf. Encyclical Letter *Populorum Progressio*, 47: loc. cit., 280–281; John Paul II, Encyclical Letter *Sollicitudo Rei Socialis*, 42: loc. cit., 572–574.

65. Cf. Benedict XVI, *Message for the 2007 World Food Day*: AAS 99 (2007), 933–935.

66. Cf. John Paul II, Encyclical Letter *Evangelium Vitae*, 18, 59, 63–64: loc. cit., 419–421, 467–468, 472–475.

67. Cf. Benedict XVI, *Message for the 2007 World Day of Peace*, 5.

68. Cf. John Paul II, *Message for the 2002 World Day of Peace*, 4–7, 12–15: AAS 94 (2002), 134–136, 138–140; Id., *Message for the 2004 World Day of Peace*, 8: AAS 96 (2004), 119; Id., *Message for the 2005 World Day of Peace*, 4: AAS 97 (2005), 177–178; Benedict XVI, *Message for the 2006 World Day of Peace*, 9–10: AAS 98 (2006), 60–61; Id., *Message for the 2007 World Day of Peace*, 5, 14: loc. cit., 778, 782–783.

69. Cf. John Paul II, *Message for the 2002 World Day of Peace*, 6: loc. cit., 135; Benedict XVI, *Message for the 2006 World Day of Peace*, 9–10: loc. cit., 60–61.

70. Cf. Benedict XVI, *Homily at Mass*, Islinger Feld, Regensburg,12 September 2006.

71. Cf. Benedict XVI, Encyclical Letter *Deus Caritas Est*, 1: loc. cit., 217–218.

72. John Paul II, Encyclical Letter *Sollicitudo Rei Socialis*, 28: loc. cit., 548–550.

73. Paul VI, Encyclical Letter *Populorum Progressio*, 19: loc. cit., 266–267.

74. Ibid., 39: loc. cit., 276–277.

75. Ibid., 75: loc. cit., 293–294.

76. Cf. Benedict XVI, Encyclical Letter *Deus Caritas Est*, 28: loc. cit., 238–240.

77. John Paul II, Encyclical Letter *Centesimus Annus*, 59: loc. cit., 864.

78. Cf. Encyclical Letter *Populorum Progressio*, 40, 85: loc. cit., 277, 298–299.

79. Ibid., 13: loc. cit., 263–264.

80. Cf. John Paul II, Encyclical Letter *Fides et Ratio* (14 September 1998), 85: AAS 91 (1999), 72–73.

81. Cf. ibid., 83: loc. cit., 70–71.

82. Benedict XVI, *Address at the University of Regensburg*, 12 September 2006.

83. Cf. Paul VI, Encyclical Letter *Populorum Progressio*, 33: loc. cit., 273–274.

84. Cf. John Paul II, *Message for the 2000 World Day of Peace*, 15: AAS 92 (2000), 366.

85. *Catechism of the Catholic Church*, 407; cf. John Paul II, Encyclical Letter *Centesimus Annus*, 25: loc. cit., 822–824.

86. Cf. no. 17: AAS 99 (2007), 1000.

87. Cf. ibid., 23: loc. cit., 1004–1005.

88. Saint Augustine expounds this teaching in detail in his dialogue on free will (*De libero arbitrio*, II, 3, 8ff.). He indicates the existence within the human soul of an "internal sense". This sense consists in an act that is fulfilled outside the normal functions of reason, an act that is not the result of reflection, but is almost instinctive, through which reason, realizing its transient and fallible nature, admits the existence of something eternal, higher than itself, something absolutely true and certain. The name that Saint Augustine gives to this interior truth is at times the name of God (*Confessions* X, 24, 35; XII, 25, 35; *De libero arbitrio* II, 3, 8), more often that of Christ (*De magistro* 11:38; *Confessions* VII, 18, 24; XI, 2, 4).

89. Benedict XVI, Encyclical Letter *Deus Caritas Est*, 3: loc. cit., 219.

90. Cf. no. 49: loc. cit., 281.

91. John Paul II, Encyclical Letter *Centesimus Annus*, 28: loc. cit., 827–828.

92. Cf. no. 35: loc. cit., 836–838.

93. Cf. John Paul II, Encyclical Letter *Sollicitudo Rei Socialis*, 38: loc. cit., 565–566.

94. No. 44: loc. cit., 279.

95. Cf. ibid., 24: loc. cit., 269.

96. Cf. Encyclical Letter *Centesimus Annus*, 36: loc. cit., 838–840.

97. Cf. Paul VI, Encyclical Letter *Populorum Progressio*, 24: loc. cit., 269.

98. Cf. John Paul II, Encyclical Letter *Centesimus Annus*, 32: loc. cit., 832–833; Paul VI, Encyclical Letter *Populorum Progressio*, 25: loc. cit., 269–270.

99. John Paul II, Encyclical Letter *Laborem Exercens*, 24: loc. cit., 637–638.

100. Ibid., 15: loc. cit., 616–618.

101. Encyclical Letter *Populorum Progressio*, 27: loc. cit., 271.

102. Cf. Congregation for the Doctrine of the Faith, Instruction on Christian Freedom and Liberation *Libertatis Conscientia* (22 March 1987), 74: AAS 79 (1987), 587.

103. Cf. John Paul II, Interview published in the Catholic daily newspaper *La Croix*, 20 August 1997.

104. John Paul II, *Address to the Pontifical Academy of Social Sciences*, 27 April 2001.

105. Paul VI, Encyclical Letter *Populorum Progressio*, 17: loc. cit., 265–266.

106. Cf. John Paul II, *Message for the 2003 World Day of Peace*, 5: AAS 95 (2003), 343.

107. Cf. ibid.

108. Cf. Benedict XVI, *Message for the 2007 World Day of Peace*, 13: loc. cit., 781–782.

109. Paul VI, Encyclical Letter *Populorum Progressio*, 65: loc. cit., 289.

110. Cf. ibid., 36–37: loc. cit., 275–276.

111. Cf. ibid., 37: loc. cit., 275–276.

112. Cf. Second Vatican Ecumenical Council, Decree on the Apostolate of Lay People *Apostolicam Actuositatem*, 11.

113. Cf. Paul VI, Encyclical Letter *Populorum Progressio*, 14: loc. cit., 264; John Paul II, Encyclical Letter *Centesimus Annus*, 32: loc. cit., 832–833.

114. Paul VI, Encyclical Letter *Populorum Progressio*, 77: loc. cit., 295.

115. John Paul II, *Message for the 1990 World Day of Peace*, 6: AAS 82 (1990), 150.

116. Heraclitus of Ephesus (Ephesus, c. 535 B.C.–c. 475 B.C.), Fragment 22B124, in H. Diels and W. Kranz, *Die Fragmente der Vorsokratiker*, Weidmann, Berlin, 1952, 6(th) ed.

117. Pontifical Council for Justice and Peace, *Compendium of the Social Doctrine of the Church*, 451–487.

118. Cf. John Paul II, *Message for the 1990 World Day of Peace*, 10: loc. cit., 152–153.

119. Paul VI, Encyclical Letter *Populorum Progressio*, 65: loc. cit., 289.

120. Benedict XVI, *Message for the 2008 World Day of Peace*, 7: AAS 100 (2008), 41.

121. Cf. Benedict XVI, *Address to the General Assembly of the United Nations Organization*, New York, 18 April 2008.

122. Cf. John Paul II, *Message for the 1990 World Day of Peace*, 13: loc. cit., 154–155.

123. John Paul II, Encyclical Letter *Centesimus Annus*, 36: loc. cit., 838–840.

124. Ibid., 38: loc. cit., 840–841; Benedict XVI, *Message for the 2007 World Day of Peace*, 8: loc. cit., 779.

125. Cf. John Paul II, Encyclical Letter *Centesimus Annus*, 41: loc. cit., 843–845.

126. Cf. ibid.

127. Cf. John Paul II, Encyclical Letter *Evangelium Vitae*, 20: loc. cit., 422–424.

128. Encyclical Letter *Populorum Progressio*, 85: loc. cit., 298–299.

129. Cf. John Paul II, *Message for the 1998 World Day of Peace*, 3: AAS 90 (1998), 150; *Address to the Members of the Vatican Foundation "Centesimus Annus—Pro Pontifice,"* 9 May 1998, 2; *Address to the Civil Authorities and Diplomatic Corps of Austria*, 20 June 1998, 8; *Message to the Catholic University of the Sacred Heart*, 5 May 2000, 6.

130. According to Saint Thomas *"ratio partis contrariatur rationi personae," In III Sent.*, d. 5, q. 3, a. 2; also *"Homo non ordinatur ad communitatem politicam secundum se totum et secundum omnia sua," Summa Theologiae* I-II, q. 21, a. 4, ad 3.

131. Cf. Second Vatican Ecumenical Council, Dogmatic Constitution on the Church *Lumen Gentium*, 1.

132. Cf. John Paul II, *Address to the Sixth Public Session of the Pontifical Academies of Theology and of Saint Thomas Aquinas*, 8 November 2001, 3.

133. Cf. Congregation for the Doctrine of the Faith, Declaration on the Unicity and Salvific Universality of Jesus Christ and the Church *Dominus Iesus* (6 August 2000), 22: AAS 92 (2000), 763–764; Id., *Doctrinal Note on some questions regarding the participation of Catholics in political life* (24 November 2002), 8: AAS 96 (2004), 369–370.

134. Benedict XVI, Encyclical Letter *Spe Salvi*, 31: loc. cit., 1010; *Address to the Participants in the Fourth National Congress of the Church in Italy*, Verona, 19 October 2006.

135. John Paul II, Encyclical Letter *Centesimus Annus*, 5: loc. cit., 798–800; Benedict XVI, *Address to the Participants in the Fourth National Congress of the Church in Italy*, Verona, 19 October 2006.

136. No. 12.

137. Cf. Pius XI, Encyclical Letter *Quadragesimo Anno* (15 May 1931): AAS 23 (1931), 203; John Paul II, Encyclical Letter *Centesimus Annus*, 48: loc. cit., 852–854; *Catechism of the Catholic Church*, 1883.

138. Cf. John XXIII, Encyclical Letter *Pacem in Terris,* loc. cit., 274.

139. Cf. Paul VI, Encyclical Letter *Populorum Progressio*, 10, 41: loc. cit., 262, 277–278.

140. Cf. Benedict XVI, *Address to Members of the International Theological Commission*, 5 October 2007; *Address to the Participants in the International Congress on Natural Moral Law*, 12 February 2007.

141. Cf. Benedict XVI, *Address to the Bishops of Thailand on their "Ad Limina" Visit*, 16 May 2008.

142. Cf. Pontifical Council for the Pastoral Care of Migrants and Itinerant People, Instruction *Erga Migrantes Caritas Christi* (3 May 2004): AAS 96 (2004), 762–822.

143. John Paul II, Encyclical Letter *Laborem Exercens*, 8: loc. cit., 594–598.

144. Jubilee of Workers, *Greeting after Mass*, 1 May 2000.

145. Cf. John Paul II, Encyclical Letter *Centesimus Annus*, 36: loc. cit., 838–840.

146. Cf. Benedict XVI, *Address to the Members of the General Assembly of the United Nations Organization*, New York, 18 April 2008.

147. Cf. John XXIII, Encyclical Letter *Pacem in Terris,* loc. cit., 293; Pontifical Council for Justice and Peace, *Compendium of the Social Doctrine of the Church*, 441.

148. Cf. Second Vatican Ecumenical Council, Pastoral Constitution on the Church in the Modern World *Gaudium et Spes*, 82.

149. Cf. John Paul II, Encyclical Letter *Sollicitudo Rei Socialis*, 43: loc. cit., 574–575.

150. Paul VI, Encyclical Letter *Populorum Progressio*, 41: loc. cit., 277–278; cf. Second Vatican Ecumenical Council, Pastoral Constitution on the Church in the Modern World *Gaudium et Spes*, 57.

151. Cf. John Paul II, Encyclical Letter *Laborem Exercens*, 5: loc. cit., 586–589.

152. Cf. Paul VI, Apostolic Letter *Octogesima Adveniens*, 29: loc. cit., 420.

153. Cf. Benedict XVI, *Address to the Participants in the Fourth National Congress of the Church in Italy*, Verona, 19 October 2006; Id., *Homily at Mass*, Islinger Feld, Regensburg, 12 September 2006.

154. Cf. Congregation for the Doctrine of the Faith, Instruction on certain bioethical questions *Dignitas Personae* (8 September 2008): AAS 100 (2008), 858–887.

155. Cf. Encyclical Letter *Populorum Progressio*, 3: loc. cit., 258.

156. Second Vatican Ecumenical Council, Pastoral Constitution on the Church in the Modern World *Gaudium et Spes*, 14.

157. Cf. Paul VI, Encyclical Letter *Populorum Progressio*, 42: loc. cit., 278.

158. Cf. Benedict XVI, Encyclical Letter *Spe Salvi*, 35: loc. cit., 1013–1014.

159. Paul VI, Encyclical Letter *Populorum Progressio*, 42: loc. cit., 278.

Part V

The U.S. Bishops and Catholic Social Teaching

INTRODUCTION

The American Catholic bishops began applying papal social teaching to American conditions with their 1919 program of social reconstruction. When public attention turned away from reform in the 1920s, the bishops turned their attention elsewhere as well. With the onset of the Great Depression in 1929, however, the bishops once again took up problems of economic and social justice, and commented regularly on the major issues of the New Deal years. When national priorities shifted after Pearl Harbor, those of the bishops did as well. In the postwar years unprecedented prosperity and rapid expansion of the Catholic population turned episcopal attention to parishes, schools, and charities; their public comments in those years centered on the Cold War, education, and family life. Only in 1963, when the civil rights movement was exploding across the country, did the bishops again systematically consider the moral aspects of domestic social and economic life. During the tumultuous decade that followed, they backed civil rights legislation, launched the Campaign for Human Development to provide seed money for grassroots efforts to overcome poverty, and supported a series of trade union organizing campaigns among Hispanic-Americans. In 1971 they publicly concluded that the American war in Vietnam could no longer be justified. In January 1973 the Supreme Court decriminalized abortion; the bishops condemned the action and urged a constitutional amendment to reverse the decision. Abortion, the arms race, and the continuing presence of domestic poverty all deeply concerned the hierarchy and led to its continued commitment to a public presence even after public opinion turned more conservative in the 1970s.

On abortion and world hunger, the bishops combined regular appeals to government and the public with pastoral plans designed to awaken deeper understanding and commitment within the church. Through their committees and staff the bishops regularly went on record on issues of both domestic and foreign policy. Beginning in 1972, they marked each election year with testimony on a range of issues before the platform committees of both major parties and with a public statement on "political responsibility" designed both to inform the public of the moral dimension of outstanding issues and to guide the conscience of Catholic voters. In each election individual bishops and occasionally the bishops' conference became involved in commenting on candidates; while avoiding endorsements, these comments invariably aroused widespread public controversy. Most controversial was the gap between the bishops' public pronouncements, which placed opposition to abortion as one important issue among several, and actions of individual bishops, which seemed to make abortion the single issue by which candidates should be evaluated. Most bishops, in theory at least, agreed with Joseph Cardinal Bernardin who, in a series of 1983 speeches, outlined a "seamless garment" of pro-life commitment that linked opposition to abortion, the arms race, capital punishment, and economic injustice.

The aggressive effort of the bishops to raise moral questions about national policy reached a peak in 1983, when they issued a major pastoral letter on nuclear arms, *The Challenge of Peace: God's Promise and Our Response.* Since the 1971 Vietnam statement the bishops had regularly examined the moral issues surrounding nuclear weapons. They were encouraged to do so by strong peace statements from the popes, by the persistent work of the Catholic peace movement, and by the presence of a small but growing number of bishops committed to nonviolence and all-out opposition to nuclear weapons. Bishop Thomas Gumbleton of Detroit led an active chapter of Pax Christi, while Archbishop Raymond Hunthausen of Seattle and Bishop Raymond Matthiessen of Amarillo, Texas, received nationwide publicity for strong statements favoring tax resistance and refusal of employment in the manufacture of nuclear hardware.

In 1979, when the SALT II Treaty was before the Congress, the bishops debated at length before deciding to endorse the treaty. In testimony before Congress, John Cardinal Krol of Philadelphia stated that their support was conditional on steps toward significant efforts at arms reduction. If this proved not to be the case, he warned, the bishops would be forced to reconsider their long-standing support for the possession and threatened use of the nuclear deterrent. When the treaty was withdrawn and President Carter began an intensified effort at arms escalation, the bishops decided to study the matter. A committee headed by Bernardin and including the pacifist Gumbleton and New York's John Cardinal O'Connor, a former Navy chaplain, began a full review of the moral issues surrounding the arms race. Their first draft became public and sparked a national debate within and beyond the church. The committee had consulted with a wide range of experts in preparing the draft, and now received advice from interested parties. The process of public dialogue, sometimes rather bitter, continued through the second and third drafts. The Reagan administration became involved, commenting publicly and sending high-ranking officials to meet with the bishops. Committee members were called to Rome to consult with the Vatican and with bishops from other NATO countries. At several stages the committee seemed to soften the document's surprisingly strong language, but many of those changes were rescinded by the body of bishops. The letter was finally approved for publication in November 1983.

While the Bernardin committee was completing its work on *The Challenge of Peace*, another committee, chaired by Archbishop Rembert Weakland of Milwaukee, had begun drafting a pastoral letter on the American economy. It originated in the felt need to provide a moral commentary on American economic life to balance a strong letter on Marxist communism issued in 1980. Impressed by the success of the Bernardin process of consultation, the economic committee also met with experts and submitted drafts for public consideration. Deliberately rejecting the idea of providing a moral commentary on capitalism or a systematic analysis of the American economy, the committee instead attempted to follow Paul VI's directive to apply Catholic social teaching to concrete problems within the United States. Poverty, employment, trade, and food and agriculture were examined in detail and evaluated in light of long-standing principles of Catholic social teaching, and proposals were made for reforms aimed particularly at improving conditions for the poor. In addition, the bishops proposed a new American experiment in economic democracy, arguing that outstanding economic issues needed to be addressed through new structures of cooperation among labor, management, and the general public, and between government and the private sector. The letter, finally completed in November 1986, was a bit less specific than the peace letter in its policy proposals, but more sharply critical of national values and practices.

Together, the two letters mark a significant development in American Catholicism. Both letters make very clear the need to incorporate justice and peace into every facet of the life of the church. They express a critical distance between the church and American society, as the church draws, from its own tradition, norms on the basis of which to assess national practice and determine its own responsibilities. At the same time, while valuing prophetic witness, the bishops take their stand within and not apart from American society, sharing responsibility for the problems that exist, avoiding for the most part judgmental and moralistic statements about their fellow citizens, and urging vigorous public efforts to clarify the moral dimensions of political and economic life and to move forward toward goals of equality, justice, security, and peace. Clearly the bishops wish to be, and wish their people to be, both faithful Christians and responsible citizens, and they recognize that achieving those two objectives can involve difficult choices. Saying no to nuclear war is one thing, the bishops note in the peace pastoral; translating that no into concrete personal and political choices is another, a more ambiguous and difficult task. Nevertheless, the effort to do so, to deal with questions not just from a church standpoint but from a public one as well, represents a significant contribution not only to American national life but also to a world church still learning to relate constructively to democratic ideals and structures. For the bishops the major task is to adhere consistently to the principles they have put forward and find ways to translate the teaching these letters contain into concrete programs within the church and apostolic movements in the larger society.

"Brothers and Sisters to Us," the U.S. Bishops' pastoral letter on racism, was issued in 1979. Reading this letter in 2010 brings awareness of how much progress has occurred: a more diverse hierarchy and priesthood, better integrated parishes, and the election of the first African-American President. But in many ways, the empirical content of this letter has changed very little. Much of what was written in 1979 unfortunately is still the case. The letter notes, for example, that while many external appearances have changed with respect to the removal of overt signs of racism and segregation and the promulgation of Civil Rights legislation, many of these changes simply cover over a latent racism at the core of our society. The letter highlights three areas where such signs of racism continue: first, segregated housing patterns; second, a disproportionate number of minorities in our prisons; third, attitudes that say too much has been given to minorities. These realities continue and in some instances are even exacerbated.

The bishops understand racism not only as a terrible social reality, but foremost as a sin, a sin with several tragic consequences. First, the sin of racism blots out the image of God and distorts how we see the other. The sin relegates minorities to an inferior personal and social status. Finally, it violates the human dignity present in each person by its implicit assumption of either the inferiority of others or an outright denial of their personhood. The bishops also note that this sin is not simply personal; it is also a social sin in that racist attitudes become imbedded in the fabric of our society and in our institutions.

The response to this is personal, ecclesial, and social. Personally each individual needs to examine his or her conscience to begin the process of identifying and weeding out our own racist attitudes and behaviors. The church needs to examine its own behavior to eliminate any vestiges of racism in its policies and institutions. Socially, we need to promote social justice that both rectifies evils done to others but also promotes the participation of all so that together we can achieve the common good.

Brothers and Sisters to Us (U.S. Catholic Bishops Pastoral Letter on Racism, 1979)

Racism is an evil which endures in our society and in our Church. Despite apparent advances and even significant changes in the last two decades, the reality of racism remains. In large part it is only external appearances which have changed.

In 1958 we spoke out against the blatant forms of racism that divided people through discriminatory laws and enforced segregation. We pointed out the moral evil that denied human persons their dignity as children of God and their God-given rights.[1] A decade later in a second pastoral letter we again underscored the continuing scandal of racism and called for decisive action to eradicate it from our society.[2]

We recognize and applaud the readiness of many Americans to make new strides forward in reducing and eliminating prejudice against minorities. We are convinced that the majority of Americans realize that racial discrimination is both unjust and unworthy of this nation.

We do not deny that changes have been made, that laws have been passed, that policies have been implemented. We do not deny that the ugly external features of racism which marred our society have in part been eliminated. But neither can it be denied that too often what has happened has been only a covering over, not a fundamental change. Today the sense of urgency has yielded to an apparent acceptance of the status quo. The climate of crisis engendered by demonstrations, protests, and confrontation has given way to a mood of indifference; and other issues occupy our attention.

In response to this mood, we wish to call attention to the persistent presence of racism and in particular to the relationship between racial and economic justice. Racism and economic oppression are distinct but interrelated forces which dehumanize our society. Movement toward authentic justice demands a simultaneous attack on both evils. Our economic structures are undergoing fundamental changes which threaten to intensify social inequalities in our nation. We are entering an era characterized by limited resources, restricted job markets and dwindling revenues. In this atmosphere, the poor and racial minorities are being asked to bear the heaviest burden of the new economic pressures.

This new economic crisis reveals an unresolved racism that permeates our society's structures and resides in the hearts of many among the majority.

Because it is less blatant, this subtle form of racism is in some respects even more dangerous—harder to combat and easier to ignore. Major segments of the population are being pushed to the margins of society in our nation. As economic pressures tighten, often those people who are black, Hispanic, Native American, and Asian—and always poor—slip further into the unending cycle of poverty, deprivation, ignorance, disease, and crime. Racial identity is for them an iron curtain barring the way to a decent life and livelihood. The economic pressures exacerbate racism, particularly where poor white people are competing with minorities for limited job opportunities. The Church must not be unmindful of these economic pressures. We must be sensitive to the unfortunate and unnecessary racial tension that results from this kind of economic need.

Mindful of its duty to be the advocate for whose who hunger and thirst for justice's sake, the Church cannot remain silent about the racial injustices in society and its own structures. Our concern over racism follows, as well, from our strong commitment to evangelization. Pope John Paul II has defined evangelization as bringing consciences, both individual and social, into conformity with the Gospel.[3] We would betray our commitment to evangelize ourselves and our society were we not to strongly voice our condemnation of attitudes and practices so contrary to the Gospel. Therefore, as the bishops of the United States, we once again address our pastoral reflections on racism to our brothers and sisters of all races.

We do this, conscious of the fact that racism is only one form of discrimination that infects our society. Such discrimination belies both our civil and religious traditions. The United States of America rests on a constitutional heritage that recognizes the equality, dignity, and inalienable rights of all its citizens. Further, we are heirs of a religious teaching which proclaims that all men and women, as children of God, are brothers and sisters. Every form of discrimination against individuals and groups—whether because of race, ethnicity, religion, gender, economic status, or national or cultural origin—is a serious injustice which has severely weakened our social fabric and deprived our country of the unique contributions of many of our citizens. While cognizant of these broader concerns, we wish to draw attention here to the particular form of discrimination that is based on race.

THE SIN OF RACISM

Racism is a sin: a sin that divides the human family, blots out the image of God among specific members of that family, and violates the fundamental human dignity of those called to be children of the same Father. Racism is the sin that says some human beings are inherently superior and others essentially inferior because of race. It is the sin that makes racial characteristics the determining factor for the exercise of human rights. It mocks the words of Jesus: "Treat others the way you would have them treat you."[4] Indeed, racism is more than a disregard for the words of Jesus; it is a denial of the truth of the dignity of each human being revealed by the mystery of the Incarnation.

In order to find the strength to overcome the evil of racism, we must look to Christ. In Christ Jesus "there does not exist among you Jew or Greek, slave or free, male or female. All are one in Christ Jesus."[5] As Pope John Paul II has said so clearly, "Our spirit is set in one direction, the only direction for our intellect, will and heart is toward Christ our Redeemer, toward Christ the Redeemer of [humanity.]"[6] It is in Christ, then, that the Church finds the central cause for its commitment to justice, and to the struggle for the human rights and dignity of all persons.

When we give in to our fears of the other because he or she is of a race different from ourselves, when we prejudge the motives of others precisely because they are of a different color, when we stereotype or ridicule the other because of racial characteristics and heritage, we fail to heed the command of the Prophet Amos: "Seek good and not evil, that you may live; then truly will the Lord . . . be with you as you claim! . . . Then let justice surge like water, and goodness like an unfailing stream."[7]

Today in our country men, women, and children are being denied opportunities for full participation and advancement in our society because of their race. The educational, legal, and financial systems, along with other structures and sectors of our society, impede people's progress and narrow their access because they are black, Hispanic, Native American, or Asian.

The structures of our society are subtly racist, for these structures reflect the values which society upholds. They are geared to the success of the majority and the failure of the minority. Members of both groups give unwitting approval by accepting things as they are. Perhaps no single individual is to blame. The sinfulness is often anonymous but nonetheless real. The sin is social in nature in that each of us, in varying degrees, is responsible. All of us in some measure are accomplices. As our recent pastoral letter on moral values states: "The absence of personal fault for an evil does not absolve one of all responsibility. We must seek to resist and undo injustices we have not caused, least we become bystanders who tacitly endorse evil and so share in guilt in it."[8]

RACISM IS A FACT

Because the courts have eliminated statutory racial discrimination and Congress has enacted civil rights legislation, and because some minority people have achieved some measure of success, many people believe that racism is no longer a problem in American life. The continuing existence of racism becomes apparent, however, when we look beneath the surface of our national life: as, for example, in the case of unemployment figures. In the second quarter of 1979, 4.9% of white Americans were unemployed; but for blacks the figure was 11.6%; for Hispanics, 8.3%; and for Native Americans on reservations, as high as 40%. The situation is even more disturbing when one realizes that 35% of black youth, 19.1% of Hispanic youth, and an estimated 60% of Native American youth are unemployed.[9] Quite simply, this means that an alarming proportion of tomorrow's adults are cut off from gainful employment—an essential prerequisite of responsible adulthood. These same youths presently suffer the crippling effects of a segregated educational system which in many cases fails to enlighten the mind and free the spirit, which too often inculcates a conviction of inferiority, and which frequently graduates persons who are ill-prepared and inadequately trained. In addition, racism raises its ugly head in the violence that frequently surrounds attempts to achieve racial balance in education and housing.

With respect to family life, we recognize that decades of denied access to opportunities have been for minority families a crushing burden. Racial discrimination has only exacerbated the harmful relationship between poverty and family instability.

Racism is only too apparent in housing patterns in our major cities and suburbs. Witness the deterioration of inner cities and the segregation of many suburban areas by means of unjust practices of social steering and blockbusting. Witness also the high proportion of Hispanics, blacks, and Indians on welfare and the fact that the median income of nonwhite families is only 63% of the average white family income. Moreover, the gap between the rich and the poor is widening, not decreasing.[10]

Racism is apparent when we note that the population in our prisons consists disproportionately of minorities; that violent crime is the daily companion of a life of poverty and deprivation; and that the victims of such crimes are also disproportionately nonwhite and poor. Racism is also apparent in the attitudes and behavior of some law enforcement officials and in the unequal availability of legal assistance.

Finally, racism is sometimes apparent in the growing sentiment that too much is being given to racial minorities by way of affirmative action programs or allocations to redress long-standing imbalances in minority representation and government-funded programs for the disadvantaged. At times, protestations claiming that all persons should be treated equally reflect the desire to maintain a status quo that favors one race and social group at the expense of the poor and the nonwhite.

Racism obscures the evils of the past and denies the burdens that history has placed upon the shoulders of our black, Hispanic, Native American, and Asian brothers and sisters. An honest look at the past makes plain the need for restitution wherever possible—makes evident the justice of restoration and redistribution.

A LOOK AT THE PAST

Racism has been part of the social fabric of America since its European colonization. Whether it be the tragic past of the Native Americans, the Mexicans, the Puerto Ricans, or the blacks, the story is one of slavery, peonage, economic exploitation, brutal repression, and cultural neglect. All have suffered indignity; most have been uprooted, defrauded or dispossessed of their lands; and none have escaped one or another form of collective degradation by a powerful majority. Our history is littered with the debris of broken promises and treaties, as well as lynchings and massacres that almost destroyed the Indians, humiliated the Hispanics, and crushed the blacks.

But despite this tragic history, the racial minorities of our country have survived and increased. Each racial group has sunk its roots deep in the soil of our culture, thus helping to give to the United States its unique character and its diverse coloration. The contribution of each racial minority is distinctive and rich; each is a source of internal strength for our nation. The history of all gives a witness to a truth absorbed by now into the collective consciousness of Americans: their struggle has been a pledge of liberty and a challenge to future greatness.

RACISM TODAY

Crude and blatant expressions of racist sentiment, though they occasionally exist, are today considered bad form. Yet racism itself persists in covert ways. Under the guise of other motives, it is manifest in the tendency to stereotype and marginalize whole segments of the population whose presence is perceived as a threat. It is manifest also in the indifference that replaces open hatred. The minority poor are seen as the dross of a post-industrial society—without skills, without motivation, without incentive. They are expendable. Many times the new face of racism is the computer print-out, the graph of profits and losses, the pink slip, the nameless statistic. Today's racism flourishes in the triumph of private concern over public responsibility, individual success over social commitment, and personal fulfillment over authentic compassion. Then too, we recognize that racism also exists in the attitude and behavior of some who are themselves members of minority groups. Christian ideals of justice must be brought to bear in both the private and the public sector in order that covert racism be eliminated wherever it exists.

The new forms of racism must be brought face-to-face with the figure of Christ. It is Christ's word that is the judgment on this world; it is Christ's cross that is the measure of our response; and it is Christ's face that is the composite of all persons but in a most significant way of today's poor, today's marginal people, today's minorities.

GOD'S JUDGMENT AND PROMISE

The Voice of Scripture

The Christian response to the challenges of our times is to be found in the Good News of Jesus. The words that signaled the start of His public ministry must be the watchword for every Christian response to injustice, "He unrolled the scroll and found the passage where it was written: The spirit of the Lord is upon me; therefore, he has anointed me. He has sent me to bring glad tidings to the poor, to proclaim liberty to captives, recovery of sight to the blind and release to prisoners, to announce a year of favor from the Lord. Rolling up the scroll he gave it back . . . and sat down. . . . 'Today this Scripture passage is fulfilled in your hearing.' "[11]

God's word proclaims the oneness of the human family—from the first words of Genesis, to the "Come, Lord Jesus" of the Book of Revelation. God's Word in Genesis announces that all men and women are created in God's image; not just *some* races and racial types, but *all* bear the imprint of the Creator and are enlivened by the breath of His one Spirit.

In proclaiming the liberation of Israel, God's word proclaims the liberation of all people from slavery. God's Word further proclaims that all people are accountable to and for each other. This is the message of that great parable of the Final Judgment: "When the Son of Man comes in his glory, escorted by all the angels of heaven . . . all the nations will be assembled before him. Then he will separate them into two groups. . . . The king will say to those on his right: 'Come. You have my Father's blessing! . . . For I was hungry and you gave me food, I was thirsty and you gave me drink. I was a stranger and you welcomed me. . . . I assure you, as often as you did it for one of my least brothers, you did it for me.' "[12]

God's word proclaims that the person "who listens to God's word but does not put it into practice is like a man who looks into a mirror at the face he was born with . . . then goes off and promptly forgets what he looked like."[13] We have forgotten that we "are strangers and aliens no longer. . . . [We] are fellow citizens of the saints and members of the household of God. [We] form a building which rises on the foundation of the apostles and prophets, with Christ Jesus himself as the capstone."[14]

The Voice of the Church

This is the mystery of our Church, that all men and women are brothers and sisters, all one in Christ, all bear the image of the Eternal God. The Church is truly universal, embracing all races, for it is "the visible sacrament of this saving unity."[15] The Church, moreover, follows the example of its founder and, "through its children, is one with [people] of every condition, but especially with the poor and the afflicted."[16]

This Church has a duty to proclaim the truth about the human being as disclosed in the truth about Jesus Christ. As our Holy Father Pope John Paul II has written: "On account of the mystery of the Redemption [every human being] is entrusted to the solicitude of the Church." The human being is "the primary and fundamental way for the Church."[17]

It is important to realize in the case of racism that what we are dealing with is a distortion at the very heart of human nature. The ultimate remedy against evils such as this will not come solely from human effort. What is needed is the recreation of the human being according to the image revealed in Jesus Christ. For He reveals in himself what each human being can and must become.

How great, therefore, is that sin of racism which weakens the Church's witness as the universal sign of unity among all peoples! How great the scandal given by racist Catholics who make the Body of Christ, the Church, a sign of racial oppression! Yet all too often the Church in our country has been for many a "white Church," a racist institution.

Each of us as Catholics must acknowledge a share in the mistakes and sins of the past. Many of us have been prisoners of fear and prejudice. We have preached the Gospel while closing our eyes to the racism it condemns. We have allowed conformity to social pressures to replace compliance with social justice.

But past mistakes must not hinder the Church's response to the challenges of the present. Worldwide, the Church today is not just European and American; it is also African, Asian, Indian, and Oceanic. It is western, eastern, northern, and southern, black and also brown, white and also red and yellow. In our country, one quarter of the Catholics are Spanish speaking. A million blacks make Catholicism one of the largest denominations among black Americans today. Among our nation's original inhabitants, the Native Americans, the Church's presence is increasingly becoming developed and expressed within the cultures of the various Native American tribes.

It is a fact that Catholic dioceses and religious communities across the country for years have committed selected personnel and substantial funds to relieve oppression and to correct injustices and have striven to bring the Gospel to the diverse racial groups in our land. The Church has sought to aid the poor and downtrodden, who for the most part are also the victims of racial oppression. But this relationship has been and remains two-sided and reciprocal; for the initiative of racial minorities, clinging to their Catholic faith, has helped the Church to grow, adapt, and become truly Catholic and remarkably diverse. Today in our own land the face of Catholicism is the face of all humanity—a face of many colors, a countenance of many cultural forms.

Yet more is needed. The prophetic voice of the Church, which is to be heard in every generation and even to the ends of the earth, must not be muted—especially not by the counterwitness of some of its own people. Let the Church speak out, not only in the assemblies of the bishops, but in every diocese and parish in the land, in every chapel and religious house, in every school, in every social service agency, and in every institution that bears the name Catholic. As Pope John Paul II has proclaimed, the Church must be aware of the threats to humanity and of all that opposes the endeavor to make life itself more human. The Church must strive to make every element of human life correspond to the true dignity of the human person.[18] And during his recent visit to this country, Pope John Paul II discussed the direct implications of this for the Church in the United States:

> "It will always remain one of the glorious achievements of this nation that, when people looked toward America, they received together with freedom also a chance for their own advancement. This tradition must be honored also today. The freedom that was gained must be ratified each day by the firm rejection of whatever wounds, weakens or dishonors human life. And so I appeal to all who love freedom and justice to give a chance to all in need, to the poor and the powerless. Break open the hopeless cycles of poverty and ignorance that are still the lot of too many of our brothers and sisters; the hopeless cycles of prejudices that linger on despite enormous progress toward effective equality in education and employment; the cycles of despair in which are imprisoned all those that lack decent food, shelter or employment. . . ."[19]

Therefore, let the Church proclaim to all that the sin of racism defiles the image of God and degrades the sacred dignity of humankind which has been revealed by the mystery of the Incarnation. Let all know that it is a terrible sin that mocks the cross of Christ and ridicules the Incarnation. For the brother and sister of our Brother Jesus Christ are brother and sister to us.

The Voice of the World

We find God's will for us not only in the word of Scripture and in the teaching of his Church but also in the issues and events of secular society. "The Church . . . recognizes that worthy elements are found in today's social movements, especially an evolution toward unity, a process of wholesome socialization and of association in civic and economic realms."[20] Thus spoke the Church in the Second Vatican Council. That same Council urged the Church, especially the laity, to work in the temporal sphere on behalf of justice and the unity of humankind.[21]

With this in mind, we pay special tribute to those who have struggled and struggle today for civil rights and economic justice in our own country. Nor do we overlook the United Nations' Universal Declaration of Human Rights which still speaks to the conscience of the entire world and the several international covenants which demand the elimination of discrimination based on race. None of these, unfortunately, have been ratified by our country, whereas we in America should have been the first to do so. All have a duty to heed the voice of God speaking in these documents.

OUR RESPONSE

Racism is not merely one sin among many; it is a radical evil that divides the human family and denies the new creation of a redeemed world. To struggle against it demands an equally radical transformation, in our own minds and hearts as well as in the structure of our society.

Conversion is the ever-present task of each Christian. In offering certain guidelines for this change of heart as it pertains to racism, we note that these are only first steps in what ought to be a continuing dialogue throughout the Catholic community and the nation at large. In this context we would urge that existing programs and plans, such as those dealing with family ministry, parish renewal, and evangelization, be used as vehicles for implementing the measures addressed here.

OUR PERSONAL LIVES

To the extent that racial bias affects our personal attitudes and judgments, to the extent that we allow another's race to influence our relationship and limit our openness, to the extent that we see yet close our hearts to our brothers and sisters in need,[22]—to that extent we are called to conversion and renewal in love and justice.

As individuals we should try to influence the attitudes of others by expressly rejecting racial stereotypes, racial slurs and racial jokes. We should influence the members of our families, especially our children, to be sensitive to the authentic human values and cultural contributions of each racial grouping in our country.

We should become more sensitive ourselves, and thereby sensitize our acquaintances by learning more about how social structures inhibit the economic, educational, and social advancement of the poor. We should make a personal commitment to join with others in political efforts to bring about justice for the victims of such deprivation.

OUR COMMUNITY CHURCH

The Church must be constantly attentive to the Lord's voice as He calls on His people daily not to harden their hearts.[23] We urge that on all levels the Catholic Church in the United States examine its conscience regarding attitudes and behavior towards blacks, Hispanics, Native Americans, and Asians. We urge consideration of the evil of racism as it exists in the local Church and reflection upon the means of combating it. We urge scrupulous attention at every level to insure that minority representation goes beyond mere tokenism and involves authentic sharing in responsibility and decision making.

We encourage Catholics to join hands with members of other religious groups in the spirit of ecumenism to achieve the common objectives of justice and peace. During the struggle for legal recognition of racial justice, an important chapter in American history was written as religious groups, Jewish, Protestant, and Catholic, joined in support of the civil rights movement which found much of its initiative and inspiration within the black Protestant Churches. This cooperation should continue to serve as a model for our times.

All too often in the very places where blacks, Hispanics, Native Americans, and Asians are numerous, the Church's officials and representatives, both clerical and lay, are predominantly white. Efforts to achieve racial balance in government, the media, the armed services, and other crucial areas of secular life should not only be supported but surpassed in the institutions and the programs of the Catholic Church.

Particular care should be taken to foster vocations among minority groups.[24] Training for the priesthood, the permanent diaconate, and religious life should not entail an abandonment of culture and traditions or a loss of racial identity but should seek ways in which such culture and traditions might contribute to that training. Special attention is required whenever it is necessary to correct racist attitudes or behaviors among seminary staff and seminarians. Seminary education ought to include an awareness of the history and the contributions of minorities as well as an appreciation of the enrichment of the liturgical expression, especially at the local parish level, which can be found in their respective cultures.

We affirm the teaching of Vatican II on the liturgy by noting that "the liturgy is the summit toward which the activity of the Church is directed."[25] The Church must "respect and foster the spiritual . . . gifts of the various races and peoples"[26] and encourage the incorporation of these gifts into the liturgy.

We see the value of fostering greater diversity of racial and minority group representation in the hierarchy. Furthermore, we call for the adoption of an effective affirmative action program in every diocese and religious institution.

We strongly urge that special attention be directed to the plight of undocumented workers and that every effort be made to remove the fear and prejudice of which they are victims.

We ask in particular that Catholic institutions such as schools, universities, social service agencies, and hospitals, where members of racial minorities are often employed in large numbers, review their policies to see that they faithfully conform to the Church's teaching on justice for workers and respect for their rights. We recommend that investment portfolios be examined in order to determine whether racist institutions and policies are inadvertently being supported; and that, wherever possible, the capital of religious groups be made available for new forms of alternative investment, such as cooperatives, land trusts, and housing for the poor. We further recommend that Catholic institutions avoid the services of agencies and industries which refuse to take affirmative action to achieve equal opportunity and that the Church itself always be a model as an equal opportunity employer.

We recommend that leadership training programs be established on the local level in order to encourage effective leadership among racial minorities on all levels of the Church, local as well as national.

In particular, we recommend the active spiritual and financial support of associations and institutions organized by Catholic blacks, Hispanics, Native Americans, and Asians within the Church for the promotion of ministry to and by their respective communities. There is also a need for more attention to finding ways in which minorities can work together across racial and cultural lines to avoid duplication and competition among themselves. There is also a need for cooperative efforts between racial minorities and other social action groups, such as labor and the women's movement.

Finally, we urgently recommend the continuation and expansion of Catholic schools in the inner cities and other disadvantaged areas. No other form of Christian ministry has been more widely acclaimed or desperately sought by leaders of various racial communities. For a century and a half the Church in the United States has been distinguished by its efforts to educate the poor and disadvantaged, many of whom are not of the Catholic faith. That tradition continues today in—among other places—Catholic schools, where so many blacks, Hispanics, Native Americans, and Asians receive a form of education and formation which constitutes a key to greater freedom and dignity. It would be tragic if today, in the face of acute need and even near despair, the Church, for centuries the teacher and the guardian of civilization, should withdraw from this work in our own society. No sacrifice can be so great, no price can be so high, no short-range goals can be so important as to warrant the lessening of our commitment to Catholic education in minority neighborhoods. More affluent parishes should be made aware of this need and of their opportunity to share resources with the poor and needy in a way that recognizes the dignity of both giver and receiver.

SOCIETY AT LARGE

Individuals move on many levels in our complex society: each of us is called to speak and act in many different settings. In each case may we speak and act according to our competence and as the Gospel bids us. With this as our prayer, we refrain from giving detailed answers to complex questions on which we ourselves have no special competence. Instead, we propose several guidelines of a general nature.

The difficulties of these new times demand a new vision and a renewed courage to transform our society and achieve justice for all. We must fight for the dual goals of racial and economic justice with determination and creativity. Domestically, justice demands that we strive for authentic full employment, recognizing the special need for employment of those who, whether men or women, carry the principal responsibility for support of a family. Justice also demands that we strive for decent working conditions, adequate income, housing, education, and health care for all. Government at the national and local levels must be held accountable by all citizens for the essential services which all are entitled to receive. The private sector should work with various racial communities to insure that they receive a just share of the profits they have helped to create.

Globally, we live in an interdependent community of nations, some rich, some poor. Some are high consumers of the world's resources; some eke out an existence on a near-starvation level. As it happens, most of the rich, consuming nations are white and Christian; most of the world's poor are of other races and religions.

Concerning our relationship to other nations, our Christian faith suggests several principles. First, racial difference should not interfere with our dealing justly and peacefully with all other nations. Secondly, those nations which possess more of the world's riches must, in justice, share with those who are in serious need. Finally, the private sector should be aware of its responsibility to promote racial justice, not subordination or exploitation, to promote genuine development in poor societies, not mere consumerism and materialism.

CONCLUSION

Our words here are an initial response to one of the major concerns which emerged during the consultation on social justice entitled "A Call to Action," which was part of the U.S. Catholic participation in the national bicentennial. The dialogue must continue among the Catholics of our country. We have proposed guidelines and principles and as the bishops of the Catholic Conference in the United States, we must give the leadership to this effort by a commitment of our time, of personnel and of significant financial resources. Others must develop the programs and plan operations. There must be no turning back along the road of justice, no sighing for bygone times of privilege, no nostalgia for simple solutions from another age. For we are children of the age to come, when the first shall be last and the last shall be first, when blessed are they who serve Christ the Lord in all His brothers and sisters, especially those who are poor and suffer injustice.

NOTES

1. *Discrimination and Christian Conscience*. National Catholic Welfare Conference, 1958.
2. *National Race Crisis*. National Conference of Catholic Bishops, 1968.
3. Pope John Paul II, Address at the Third General Assembly of the Latin American Bishops, Puebla, Mexico, January 28, 1979, p. 1.2.
4. Matthew 7:12.
5. Galatians 3:28.
6. *Redemptor Hominis*, 7. Pope John Paul II, 1979.
7. Amos 5:14, 24.
8. *To Live in Christ Jesus*, p. 25. National Conference of Catholic Bishops, 1976.

9. *Employment and Earnings*, Vol. 26, No. 10, Dept. of Labor, Bureau of Labor Statistics, October, 1979. Precise data on youth unemployment among Native Americans are not available. The 60% unemployment figure is an estimate by the U.S. Dept. of Labor.

10. *Widening Economic Gap*, National Urban League, Research Dept., 1979. See also "Consumer Income," Current Population Report, Series P60 #118, 1979.

11. Luke 4:17–21.

12. Matthew 25:31–40.

13. James 1:23–24.

14. Ephesians 2:19–20.

15. *Dogmatic Constitution on the Church*, 9.

16. *Decree on the Church's Missionary Activity*, 12.

17. *Redemptor Hominis*, 13, 14.

18. *Redemptor Hominis*, 14.

19. Homily at Battery Park, New York. Pope John Paul II, October, 1979.

20. *Pastoral Constitution on the Church in the Modern World*, 42.

21. *Pastoral Constitution on the Church in the Modern World*, 43.

22. I John 3:17.

23. Psalms 94:8.

24. Concern for vocations from minority groups and the preparation of priests to serve in a multi-cultural and multi-racial society has been previously expressed in *The Program for Priestly Formation*, which was developed and approved by the National Conference of Catholic Bishops, 1976.

25. *Constitution on the Sacred Liturgy*, 10.

26. *Constitution on the Sacred Liturgy*, 37.

The Challenge of Peace: God's Promise and Our Response (U.S. Catholic Bishops, 1983)

INTRODUCTION

1. "The whole human race faces a moment of supreme crisis in its advance toward maturity." Thus the Second Vatican Council opened its treatment of modern warfare.[1] Since the Council, the dynamic of the nuclear arms race has intensified. Apprehension about nuclear war is almost tangible and visible today. As Pope John Paul II said in his message to the United Nations concerning disarmament: "Currently, the fear and preoccupation of so many groups in various parts of the world reveals that people are more frightened about what would happen if irresponsible parties unleash some nuclear war."[2]

2. As bishops and pastors ministering in one of the major nuclear nations, we have encountered this terror in the minds and hearts of our people—indeed, we share it. We write this letter because we agree that the world is at a moment of crisis, the effects of which are evident in people's lives. It is not our intent to play on fears, however, but to speak words of hope and encouragement in time of fear. Faith does not insulate us from the challenges of life; rather, it intensifies our desire to help solve them precisely in light of the good news which has come to us in the person of Jesus, the Lord of history. From the resources of our faith, we wish to provide hope and strength to all who seek a world free of the nuclear threat. Hope sustains one's capacity to live with danger without being overwhelmed by it; hope is the will to struggle against obstacles even when they appear insuperable. Ultimately our hope rests in the God who gave us life, sustains the world by his power, and has called us to revere the lives of every person and all peoples.

3. The crisis of which we speak arises from this fact: nuclear war threatens the existence of our planet; this is a more menacing threat than any the world has known. It is neither tolerable nor necessary that human beings live under this threat. But removing it will require a major effort of intelligence, courage, and faith. As Pope John Paul II said at Hiroshima: "From now on it is only through a conscious choice and through a deliberate policy that humanity can survive."[3]

4. As Americans, citizens of the nation which was first to produce atomic weapons, which has been the only one to use them and which today is one of the handful of nations capable of decisively influencing the course of the

nuclear age, we have grave human, moral and political responsibilities to see that a "conscious choice" is made to save humanity. This letter is therefore both an invitation and a challenge to Catholics in the United States to join with others in shaping the conscious choices and deliberate policies required in this "moment of supreme crisis."

I. PEACE IN THE MODERN WORLD: RELIGIOUS PERSPECTIVES AND PRINCIPLES

5. The global threat of nuclear war is a central concern of the universal Church, as the words and deeds of recent popes and the Second Vatican Council vividly demonstrate. In this pastoral letter we speak as bishops of the universal Church, heirs of the religious and moral teaching on modern warfare of the last four decades. We also speak as bishops of the Church in the United States, who have both the obligation and the opportunity to share and interpret the moral and religious wisdom of the Catholic tradition by applying it to the problems of war and peace today.

6. The nuclear threat transcends religious, cultural, and national boundaries. To confront its danger requires all the resources reason and faith can muster. This letter is a contribution to a wider common effort, meant to call Catholics and all members of our political community to dialogue and specific decisions about this awesome question.

7. The Catholic tradition on war and peace is a long and complex one, reaching from the Sermon on the Mount to the statements of Pope John Paul II. Its development cannot be sketched in a straight line and it seldom gives a simple answer to complex questions. It speaks through many voices and has produced multiple forms of religious witness. As we locate ourselves in this tradition, seeking to draw from it and to develop it, the document which provides profound inspiration and guidance for us is the *Pastoral Constitution on the Church in the Modern World* of Vatican II, for it is based on doctrinal principles and addresses the relationship of the Church to the world with respect to the most urgent issues of our day.[4]

8. A rule of interpretation crucial for the *Pastoral Constitution* is equally important for this pastoral letter although the authority inherent in these two documents is quite distinct. Both documents use principles of Catholic moral teaching and apply them to specific contemporary issues. The bishops at Vatican II opened the *Pastoral Constitution* with the following guideline on how to relate principles to concrete issues:

> In the first part, the Church develops her teaching on man, on the world which is the enveloping context of man's existence, and on man's relations to his fellow men. In Part II, the Church gives closer consideration to various aspects of modern life and human society; special consideration is given to those questions and problems which, in this general area,

> seem to have a greater urgency in our day. As a result, in Part II the subject matter which is viewed in the light of doctrinal principles is made up of diverse elements. Some elements have a permanent value; others, only a transitory one. Consequently, the constitution must be interpreted according to the general norms of theological interpretation. Interpreters must bear in mind—especially in Part II—the changeable circumstances which the subject matter, by its very nature, involves.[5]

9. In this pastoral letter, too, we address many concrete questions concerning the arms race, contemporary warfare, weapons systems, and negotiating strategies. We do not intend that our treatment of each of these issues carry the same moral authority as our statement of universal moral principles and formal Church teaching. Indeed, we stress here at the beginning that not every statement in this letter has the same moral authority. At times we reassert universally binding moral principles (e.g., noncombatant immunity and proportionality). At still other times we reaffirm statements of recent popes and the teaching of Vatican II. Again, at other times we apply moral principles to specific cases.

10. When making applications of these principles, we realize—and we wish readers to recognize—that prudential judgments are involved based on specific circumstances which can change or which can be interpreted differently by people of good will (e.g., the treatment of "no first use"). However, the moral judgments that we make in specific cases, while not binding in conscience, are to be given serious attention and consideration by Catholics as they determine whether their moral judgments are consistent with the Gospel.

11. We shall do our best to indicate, stylistically and substantively, whenever we make such applications. We believe such specific judgments are an important part of this letter, but they should be interpreted in light of another passage from the *Pastoral Constitution*:

> Often enough the Christian view of things will itself suggest some specific solution in certain circumstances. Yet it happens rather frequently, and legitimately so, that with equal sincerity some of the faithful will disagree with others on a given matter. Even against the intention of their proponents, however, solutions proposed on one side or another may be easily confused by many people with the Gospel message. Hence it is necessary for people to remember that no one is allowed in the aforementioned situations to appropriate the Church's authority for his opinion. They should always try to enlighten one another through honest discussion, preserving mutual charity and caring above all for the common good.[6]

12. This passage acknowledges that, on some complex social questions, the Church expects a certain diversity of views even though all hold the same

universal moral principles. The experience of preparing this pastoral letter has shown us the range of strongly held opinion in the Catholic community on questions of war and peace. Obviously, as bishops we believe that such differences should be expressed within the framework of Catholic moral teaching. We urge mutual respect among different groups in the Church as they analyze this letter and the issues it addresses. Not only conviction and commitment are needed in the Church, but also civility and charity.

13. The *Pastoral Constitution* calls us to bring the light of the Gospel to bear upon "the signs of the times." Three signs of the times have particularly influenced the writing of this letter. The first, to quote Pope John Paul II at the United Nations, is that "the world wants peace, the world needs peace."[7] The second is the judgment of Vatican II about the arms race: "The arms race is one of the greatest curses on the human race and the harm it inflicts upon the poor is more than can be endured."[8] The third is the way in which the unique dangers and dynamics of the nuclear arms race present qualitatively new problems which must be addressed by fresh applications of traditional moral principles. In light of these three characteristics, we wish to examine Catholic teaching on peace and war.

14. The Catholic social tradition, as exemplified in the *Pastoral Constitution* and recent papal teachings, is a mix of biblical, theological, and philosophical elements which are brought to bear upon the concrete problems of the day. The biblical vision of the world, created and sustained by God, scarred by sin, redeemed in Christ and destined for the Kingdom, is at the heart of our religious heritage. This vision requires elaboration, explanation, and application in each age; the important task of theology is to penetrate ever more adequately the nature of the biblical vision of peace and relate it to a world not yet at peace. Consequently, the teaching about peace examines both how to construct a more peaceful world and how to assess the phenomenon of war.

15. At the center of the Church's teaching on peace and at the center of all Catholic social teaching are the transcendence of God and the dignity of the human person. The human person is the clearest reflection of God's presence in the world; all of the Church's work in pursuit of both justice and peace is designed to protect and promote the dignity of every person. For each person not only reflects God, but is the expression of God's creative work and the meaning of Christ's redemptive ministry. Christians approach the problem of war and peace with fear and reverence. God is the Lord of life, and so each human life is sacred; modern warfare threatens the obliteration of human life on a previously unimaginable scale. The sense of awe and "fear of the Lord" which former generations felt in approaching these issues weighs upon us with new urgency. In the words of the *Pastoral Constitution*:

> Men of this generation should realize that they will have to render an account of their warlike behavior; the destiny of generations to come depends largely on the decisions they make today.[9]

16. Catholic teaching on peace and war has had two purposes: to help Catholics form their consciences and to contribute to the public policy debate about the morality of war. These two purposes have led Catholic teaching to address two distinct but overlapping audiences. The first is the Catholic faithful, formed by the premises of the ©ospel and the principles of Catholic moral teaching. The second is the wider civil community, a more pluralistic audience, in which our brothers and sisters with whom we share the name Christian, Jews, Moslems, other religious communities, and all people of good will also make up our polity. Since Catholic teaching has traditionally sought to address both audiences, we intend to speak to both in this letter, recognizing that Catholics are also members of the wider political community.

17. The conviction, rooted in Catholic ecclesiology, that both the community of the faithful and the civil community should be addressed on peace and war has produced two complementary but distinct styles of teaching. The religious community shares a specific perspective of faith and can be called to live out its implications. The wider civil community, although it does not share the same vision of faith, is equally bound by certain key moral principles. For all men and women find in the depth of their consciences a law written on the human heart by God.[10] From this law reason draws moral norms. These norms do not exhaust the Gospel vision, but they speak to critical questions affecting the welfare of the human community, the role of states in international relations, and the limits of acceptable action by individuals and nations on issues of war and peace.

18. Examples of these two styles can be found in recent Catholic teaching. At times the emphasis is upon the problems and requirements for a just public policy (e.g., Pope John Paul II at the U.N. Special Session 1982); at other times the emphasis is on the specific role Christians should play (e.g., Pope John Paul II at Coventry, England, 1982). The same difference of emphasis and orientation can be found in Pope John XXIII's *Peace on Earth* and Vatican II's *Pastoral Constitution.*

19. As bishops we believe that the nature of Catholic moral teaching, the principles of Catholic ecclesiology, and the demands of our pastoral ministry require that this letter speak both to Catholics in a specific way and to the wider political community regarding public policy. Neither audience and neither mode of address can be neglected when the issue has the cosmic dimensions of the nuclear arms race.

20. We propose, therefore, to discuss both the religious vision of peace among peoples and nations and the problems associated with realizing this vision in a world of sovereign states, devoid of any central authority and divided by ideology, geography, and competing claims. We believe the religious vision has an objective basis and is capable of progressive realization. Christ is our peace, for He has "made us both one, and has broken down the dividing wall of hostility . . . that he might create in himself one new man in place of the two, so making peace, and might reconcile us both to God"

(Eph. 2:14–16). We also know that this peace will be achieved fully only in the Kingdom of God. The realization of the Kingdom, therefore, is a continuing work, progressively accomplished, precariously maintained, and needing constant effort to preserve the peace achieved and expand its scope in personal and political life.

21. Building peace within and among nations is the work of many individuals and institutions; it is the fruit of ideas and decisions taken in the political, cultural, economic, social, military, and legal sectors of life. We believe that the Church, as a community of faith and social institution, has a proper, necessary, and distinctive part to play in the pursuit of peace.

22. The distinctive contribution of the Church flows from her religious nature and ministry. The Church is called to be, in a unique way, the instrument of the Kingdom of God in history. Since peace is one of the signs of that Kingdom present in the world, the Church fulfills part of her essential mission by making the peace of the Kingdom more visible in our time.

23. Because peace, like the Kingdom of God itself, is both a divine gift and a human work, the Church should continually pray for the gift and share in the work. We are called to be a Church at the service of peace, precisely because peace is one manifestation of God's word and work in our midst. Recognition of the Church's responsibility to join with others in the work of peace is a major force behind the call today to develop a theology of peace. Much of the history of Catholic theology on war and peace has focused on limiting the resort to force in human affairs; this task is still necessary, and is reflected later in this Pastoral Letter, but it is not a sufficient response to Vatican II's challenge "to undertake a completely fresh reappraisal of war."[11]

24. A fresh reappraisal which includes a developed theology of peace will require contributions from several sectors of the Church's life: biblical studies, systematic and moral theology, ecclesiology, and the experience and insights of members of the Church who have struggled in various ways to make and keep the peace in this often violent age. This Pastoral Letter is more an invitation to continue the new appraisal of war and peace than a final synthesis of the results of such an appraisal. We have some sense of the characteristics of a theology of peace, but not a systematic statement of their relationships.

25. A theology of peace should ground the task of peacemaking solidly in the biblical vision of the Kingdom of God, then place it centrally in the ministry of the Church. It should specify the obstacles in the way of peace, as these are understood theologically and in the social and political sciences. It should both identify the specific contributions a community of faith can make to the work of peace and relate these to the wider work of peace pursued by other groups and institutions in society. Finally, a theology of peace must include a message of hope. The vision of hope must be available to all, but one source of its content should be found in a Church at the service of peace.

26. We offer now a first step toward a message of peace and hope. It consists of a sketch of the biblical conception of peace; a theological understanding of how peace can be pursued in a world marked by sin; a moral assessment of key issues facing us in the pursuit of peace today; and an assessment of the political and personal tasks required of all people of good will in this most crucial period of history.

A. Peace and the Kingdom

27. For us as believers, the sacred Scriptures provide the foundation for confronting war and peace today. Any use of Scripture in this area is conditioned by three factors. *First*, the term "peace" has been understood in different ways at various times and in various contexts. For example, peace can refer to an individual's sense of well-being or security, or it can mean the cessation of armed hostility, producing an atmosphere in which nations can relate to each other and settle conflicts without resorting to the use of arms. For men and women of faith, peace will imply a right relationship with God, which entails forgiveness, reconciliation, and union. Finally, the Scriptures point to eschatological peace, a final, full realization of God's salvation when all creation will be made whole. Among these various meanings, the last two predominate in the Scriptures and provide direction to the first two.

28. *Second*, the Scriptures as we have them today were written over a long period of time and reflect many varied historical situations, all different from our own. Our understanding of them is both complicated and enhanced by these differences, but not in any way obscured or diminished by them. *Third*, since the Scriptures speak primarily of God's intervention in history, they contain no specific treatise on war and peace. Peace and war must always be seen in light of God's intervention in human affairs and our response to that intervention. Both are elements within the ongoing revelation of God's will for creation.

29. Acknowledging this complexity, we still recognize in the Scriptures a unique source of revelation, a word of God which is addressed to us as surely as it has been to all preceding generations. We call upon the spirit of God who speaks in that word and in our hearts to aid us in our listening. The sacred texts have much to say to us about the ways in which God calls us to live in union with and in fidelity to the divine will. They provide us with direction for our lives and hold out to us an object of hope, a final promise, which guides and directs our actions here and now.

1. OLD TESTAMENT

30. War and peace are significant and highly complex elements within the multilayered accounts of the creation and development of God's people in the Old Testament.

a. War

31. Violence and war are very much present in the history of the people of God, particularly from the Exodus period to the monarchy. God is often seen as the one who leads the Hebrews in battle, protects them from their enemies, makes them victorious over other armies (see, for example, Dt. 1:30; 20:4; Jos. 2:24; Jgs. 3:28). The metaphor of warrior carried multifaceted connotations for a people who knew themselves to be smaller and weaker than the nations which surrounded them. It also enabled them to express their conviction about God's involvement in their lives and his desire for their growth and development. This metaphor provided the people with a sense of security; they had a God who would protect them even in the face of overwhelming obstacles. It was also a call to faith and to trust; the mighty God was to be obeyed and followed. No one can deny the presence of such images in the Old Testament nor their powerful influence upon the articulation of this people's understanding of the involvement of God in their history. The warrior God was highly significant during long periods of Israel's understanding of its faith. But this image was not the only image, and it was gradually transformed, particularly after the experience of the exile, when God was no longer identified with military victory and might. Other images and other understandings of God's activity became predominant in expressing the faith of God's people.

b. Peace

32. Several points must be taken into account in considering the image of peace in the Old Testament. First, all notions of peace must be understood in light of Israel's relation to God. Peace is always seen as a gift from God and as fruit of God's saving activity. Secondly, the individual's personal peace is not greatly stressed. The well-being and freedom from fear which result from God's love are viewed primarily as they pertain to the community and its unity and harmony. Furthermore, this unity and harmony extend to all of creation; true peace implied a restoration of the right order not just among peoples, but within all of creation. Third, while the images of war and the warrior God become less dominant as a more profound and complex understanding of God is presented in the texts, the images of peace and the demands upon the people for covenantal fidelity to true peace grow more urgent and more developed.

c. Peace and Fidelity to the Covenant

33. If Israel obeyed God's laws, God would dwell among them. "I will walk among you and will be your God and you shall be my people" (Lv. 26:12). God would strengthen the people against those who opposed them and would give peace in the land. The description of life in these circumstances witnesses to unity among peoples and creation, to freedom from fear and to security (Lv. 26:3–16). The right relationship between the people and God was grounded in and expressed by a covenantal union. The covenant bound the people to God in fidelity and obedience; God was also committed in the

covenant to be present with the people, to save them, to lead them to freedom. Peace is a special characteristic of this covenant; when the prophet Ezekiel looked to the establishment of the new, truer covenant, he declared that God would establish an everlasting covenant of peace with the people (Ezk. 37:26).

34. Living in covenantal fidelity with God had ramifications in the lives of the people. It was part of fidelity to care for the needy and helpless; a society living with fidelity was one marked by justice and integrity. Furthermore, covenantal fidelity demanded that Israel put its trust in God alone and look only to him for its security. When Israel tended to forget the obligations of the covenant, prophets arose to remind the people and call them to return to God. True peace is an image which they stressed.

35. Ezekiel, who promised a covenant of peace, condemned in no uncertain terms the false prophets who said there was peace in the land while idolatry and injustice continued (Ezk. 13:16). Jeremiah followed in this tradition and berated those who "healed the wounds of the people lightly" and proclaimed peace while injustice and infidelity prevailed (Jer. 6:14; 8:10–12). Jeremiah and Isaiah both condemned the leaders when, against true security, they depended upon their own strength or alliances with other nations rather than trusting in God (Is. 7:1–9; 30:14; Jer. 37:10). The lament of Isaiah 48:18 makes clear the connection between justice, fidelity to God's law, and peace; he cries out: "O that you had hearkened to my commandments! Then your peace would have been like a river, and your righteousness like the waves of the sea."

d. Hope for Eschatological Peace

36. Experience made it clear to the people of God that the covenant of peace and the fullness of salvation had not been realized in their midst. War and enmity were still present, injustices thrived, sin still manifested itself. These same experiences also convinced the people of God's fidelity to a covenant which they often neglected. Because of this fidelity, God's promise of a final salvation involving all peoples and all creation and of an ultimate reign of peace became an integral part of the hope of the Old Testament. In the midst of their failures and sin, God's people strove for greater fidelity to him and closer relationship with him; they did so because, believing in the future they had been promised, they directed their lives and energies toward an eschatological vision for which they longed. Peace is an integral component of that vision.

37. The final age, the Messianic time, is described as one in which the "Spirit is poured on us from on high." In this age, creation will be made whole, "justice will dwell in the wilderness," the effect of righteousness will be peace, and the people will "abide in a peaceful habitation and in secure dwellings and in quiet resting places" (Is. 32:15–20). There will be no need for instruments of war (Is. 2:4; Mi. 4:3),[12] God will speak directly to the people and "righteousness and peace will embrace each other" (Ps. 85:10–11). A

messiah will appear, a servant of God upon whom God has placed his spirit and who will faithfully bring forth justice to the nations: "He will not cry or lift up his voice, or make it heard in the street; a bruised reed he will not break and a dimly burning wick he will not quench; he will faithfully bring forth justice" (Is. 42:2–3).

38. The Old Testament provides us with the history of a people who portrayed their God as one who intervened in their lives, who protected them and led them to freedom, often as a mighty leader in battle. They also appear as a people who longed constantly for peace. Such peace was always seen as a result of God's gift which came about in fidelity to the covenantal union. Furthermore, in the midst of their unfulfilled longing, God's people clung tenaciously to hope in the promise of an eschatological time when, in the fullness of salvation, peace and justice would embrace and all creation would be secure from harm. The people looked for a messiah, one whose coming would signal the beginning of that time. In their waiting, they heard the prophets call them to love according to the covenantal vision, to repent, and to be ready for God's reign.

2. NEW TESTAMENT

39. As Christians we believe that Jesus is the messiah or Christ so long awaited. God's servant (Mt. 12:18–21), prophet and more than prophet (Jn. 4:19–26), the one in whom the fullness of God was pleased to dwell, through whom all things in heaven and on earth were reconciled to God, Jesus made peace by the blood of the cross (Col. 1:19–20). While the characteristics of the *shalom* of the Old Testament (gift from God, inclusive of all creation, grounded in salvation and covenantal fidelity, inextricably bound up with justice) are present in the New Testament traditions, all discussion of war and peace in the New Testament must be seen within the context of the unique revelation of God that is Jesus Christ and of the reign of God which Jesus proclaimed and inaugurated.

a. War

40. There is no notion of a warrior God who will lead the people in an historical victory over its enemies in the New Testament. The only war spoken of is found in apocalyptic images of the final moments, especially as they are depicted in the Book of Revelation. Here war stands as image of the eschatological struggle between God and Satan. It is a war in which the Lamb is victorious (Rv. 17:14).

41. Military images appear in terms of the preparedness which one must have for the coming trials (Lk. 14:31; 22:35–38). Swords appear in the New Testament as an image of division (Mt. 12:34; Heb. 4:12); they are present at the arrest of Jesus, and he rejects their use (Lk. 22:51 and parallel texts); weapons are transformed in Ephesians, when the Christians are urged to put on the whole

armor of God which includes the breastplate of righteousness, the helmet of salvation, the sword of the Spirit, "having shod your feet in the equipment of the Gospel of peace" (Eph. 6:10–17; cf. I Thes. 5:8–9). Soldiers, too, are present in the New Testament. They are at the crucifixion of Jesus, of course, but they are also recipients of the baptism of John, and one centurion receives the healing of his servant (Mt. 8:5–13 and parallel texts; cf. Jn. 4:46–53).

42. Jesus challenged everyone to recognize in him the presence of the reign of God and to give themselves over to that reign. Such a radical change of allegiance was difficult for many to accept and families found themselves divided, as if by a sword. Hence, the Gospels tell us that Jesus said he came not to bring peace but rather the sword (Mt. 10:34). The peace which Jesus did not bring was the false peace which the prophets had warned against. The sword which he did bring was that of the division caused by the word of God which, like a two-edged sword, "pierces to the division of soul and spirit, of joints and marrow, and discerns the thoughts and intentions of the heart" (Heb. 4:12).

43. All are invited into the reign of God. Faith in Jesus and trust in God's mercy are the criteria. Living in accord with the demands of the kingdom rather than those of one's specific profession is decisive.[13]

b. Jesus and Reign of God

44. Jesus proclaimed the reign of God in his words and made it present in his actions. His words begin with a call to conversion and a proclamation of the arrival of the Kingdom. "The time is fulfilled, and the Kingdom of God is at hand; repent, and believe in the Gospel" (Mk. 1:15; Mt. 4:17). The call to conversion was at the same time an invitation to enter God's reign. Jesus went beyond the prophets' cries for conversion when he declared that, in him, the reign of God had begun and was in fact among the people (Lk. 17:20–21; 12:32).

45. His words, especially as they are preserved for us in the Sermon on the Mount, describe a new reality in which God's power is manifested and the longing of the people is fulfilled. In God's reign the poor are given the kingdom, the mourners are comforted, the meek inherit the earth, those hungry for righteousness are satisfied, the merciful know mercy, the pure see God, the persecuted know the kingdom, and peacemakers are called the children of God (Mt. 5:3–10).

46. Jesus' words also depict for us the conduct of one who lives under God's reign. His words call for a new way of life which fulfills and goes beyond the law. One of the most striking characteristics of this new way is forgiveness. All who hear Jesus are repeatedly called to forgive one another, and to do so not just once, but many, many times (Mt. 6:14–15; Lk. 6:37; Mt. 18:21–22; Mk. 11:25; Lk. 11:4; 17:3–4). The forgiveness of God, which is the beginning of salvation, is manifested in communal forgiveness and mercy.

47. Jesus also described God's reign as one in which love is an active, life-giving, inclusive force. He called for a love which went beyond family ties and bonds of friendship to reach even those who were enemies (Mt. 5:44–48;

Lk. 6:27–28). Such a love does not seek revenge but rather is merciful in the face of threat and opposition (Mt. 5:39–42; Lk. 6:29–31). Disciples are to love one another as Jesus has loved them (Jn. 15:12).

48. The words of Jesus would remain an impossible, abstract ideal were it not for two things: the actions of Jesus and his gift of the spirit. In his actions, Jesus showed the way of living in God's reign; he manifested the forgiveness which he called for when he accepted all who came to him, forgave their sins, healed them, released them from the demons who possessed them. In doing these things, he made the tender mercy of God present in a world which knew violence, oppression, and injustice. Jesus pointed out the injustices of his time and opposed those who laid burdens upon the people or defiled true worship. He acted aggressively and dramatically at times, as when he cleansed the temple of those who had made God's house into a "den of robbers" (Mt. 21:12–17 and parallel texts; Jn. 3:13–25).

49. Most characteristic of Jesus' actions are those in which he showed his love. As he had commanded others, his love led him even to the giving of his own life to effect redemption. Jesus' message and his actions were dangerous ones in his time, and they led to his death—a cruel and viciously inflicted death, a criminal's death (Gal. 3:13). In all of his suffering, as in all of his life and ministry, Jesus refused to defend himself with force or with violence. He endured violence and cruelty so that God's love might be fully manifest and the world might be reconciled to the One from whom it had become estranged. Even at his death, Jesus cried out for forgiveness for those who were his executioners: "Father, forgive them . . ." (Lk. 23:34).

50. The resurrection of Jesus is the sign to the world that God indeed does reign, does give life in death, and that the love of God is stronger even than death (Rom. 8:36–39).

51. Only in light of this, the fullest demonstration of the power of God's reign, can Jesus' gift of peace—a peace which the world cannot give (Jn. 14:27)—be understood. Jesus gives that peace to his disciples, to those who had witnessed the helplessness of the crucifixion and the power of the resurrection (Jn. 20:19, 20, 26). The peace which he gives to them as he greets them as their risen Lord is the fullness of salvation. It is the reconciliation of the world and God (Rom. 5:1–2; Col. 1:20); the restoration of the unity and harmony of all creation which the Old Testament spoke of with such longing. Because the walls of hostility between God and humankind were broken down in the life and death of the true, perfect servant, union and well-being between God and the world were finally fully possible (Eph. 2:13–22; Gal. 3:28).

c. Jesus and the Community of Believers

52. As his first gift to his followers, the risen Jesus gave his gift of peace. This gift permeated the meetings between the risen Jesus and his followers (Jn. 20:19–29). So intense was that gift and so abiding was its power that the remembrance of that gift and the daily living of it became the hallmark of the

community of faith. Simultaneously, Jesus gave his spirit to those who followed him. These two personal and communal gifts are inseparable. In the spirit of Jesus the community of believers was enabled to recognize and to proclaim the savior of the world.

53. Gifted with Jesus' own spirit, they could recognize what God had done and know in their own lives the power of the One who creates from nothing. The early Christian communities knew that this power and the reconciliation and peace which marked it were not yet fully operative in their world. They struggled with external persecution and with interior sin, as do all people. But their experience of the spirit of God and their memory of the Christ who was with them nevertheless enabled them to look forward with unshakable confidence to the time when the fullness of God's reign would make itself known in the world. At the same time, they knew that they were called to be ministers of reconciliation (2 Cor. 5:19–20), people who would make the peace which God had established visible through the love and the unity within their own communities.

54. Jesus Christ, then, is our peace, and in his death-resurrection he gives God's peace to our world. In him God has indeed reconciled the world, made it one, and has manifested definitely that his will is this reconciliation, this unity between God and all peoples, and among the peoples themselves. The way to union has been opened, the covenant of peace established. The risen Lord's gift of peace is inextricably bound to the call to follow Jesus and to continue the proclamation of God's reign. Matthew's Gospel (Mt. 28:16–20; cf. Lk. 24:44–53) tells us that Jesus' last words to his disciples were a sending forth and a promise: "I shall be with you all days." In the continuing presence of Jesus, disciples of all ages find the courage to follow him. To follow Jesus Christ implies continual conversion in one's own life as one seeks to act in ways which are consonant with the justice, forgiveness, and love of God's reign. Discipleship reaches out to the ends of the earth and calls for reconciliation among all peoples so that God's purpose, "a plan for the fullness of time, to unite all things in him" (Eph. 1:10), will be fulfilled.

3. CONCLUSION

55. Even a brief examination of war and peace in the Scriptures makes it clear that they do not provide us with detailed answers to the specifics of the questions which we face today. They do not speak specifically of nuclear war or nuclear weapons, for these were beyond the imagination of the communities in which the Scriptures were formed. The sacred texts do, however, provide us with urgent direction when we look at today's concrete realities. The fullness of eschatological peace remains before us in hope and yet the gift of peace is already ours in the reconciliation effected in Jesus Christ. These two profoundly religious meanings of peace inform and influence all other meanings for Christians. Because we have been gifted with God's peace in the risen

Christ, we are called to our own peace and to the making of peace in our world. As disciples and as children of God, it is our task to seek for ways in which to make the forgiveness, justice and mercy and love of God visible in a world where violence and enmity are too often the norm. When we listen to God's word, we hear again and always the call to repentance and to belief: to repentance because although we are redeemed we continue to need redemption; to belief, because although the reign of God is near, it is still seeking its fullness.

B. Kingdom and History

56. The Christian understanding of history is hopeful and confident but also sober and realistic. "Christian optimism based on the glorious cross of Christ and the outpouring of the Holy Spirit is no excuse for self-deception. For Christians, peace on earth is always a challenge because of the presence of sin in man's heart."[14] Peace must be built on the basis of justice in a world where the personal and social consequences of sin are evident.

57. Christian hope about history is rooted in our belief in God as creator and sustainer of our existence and our conviction that the Kingdom of God will come in spite of sin, human weakness, and failure. It is precisely because sin is part of history that the realization of the peace of the kingdom is never permanent or total. This is the continuing refrain from the patristic period to Pope John Paul II:

> For it was sin and hatred that were an obstacle to peace with God and with others: He destroyed them by the offering of life on the cross; He reconciled in one body those who were hostile (cf. Eph. 2:16; Rom. 12:5). . . . Although Christians put all their best energies into preventing war or stopping it, they do not deceive themselves about their ability to cause peace to triumph, nor about the effect of their efforts to this end. They therefore concern themselves with all human initiatives in favor of peace and very often take part in them. But they regard them with realism and humility. One could almost say that they revitalize them in two senses: they relate them both to the self-deception of humanity and to God's saving plan.[15]

58. Christians are called to live the tension between the vision of the reign of God and its concrete realization in history. The tension is often described in terms of "already but not yet": i.e., we already live in the grace of the Kingdom, but it is not yet the completed Kingdom. Hence, we are a pilgrim people in a world marked by conflict and injustice. Christ's grace is at work in the world; his command of love and his call to reconciliation are not purely future ideals but call us to obedience today.

59. With Pope Paul VI and Pope John Paul II we are convinced that "peace is possible."[16] At the same time, experience convinces us that "in this world

a totally and permanently peaceful human society is unfortunately a utopia, and that ideologies that hold up that prospect as easily attainable are based on hopes that cannot be realized, whatever the reason behind them."[17]

60. This recognition—that peace is possible but never assured and that its possibility must be continually protected and preserved in the face of obstacles and attacks upon it—accounts in large measure for the complexity of Catholic teaching on warfare. In the Kingdom of God, peace and justice will be fully realized. Justice is always the foundation of peace. In history, efforts to pursue both peace and justice are at times in tension, and the struggle for justice may threaten certain forms of peace.

61. It is within this tension of kingdom and history that Catholic teaching has addressed the problem of war. Wars mark the fabric of human history, distort the life of nations today, and, in the form of nuclear weapons, threaten the destruction of the world as we know it and the civilization which has been patiently constructed over centuries. The causes of war are multiple and not easily identified. Christians will find in any violent situation the consequences of sin: not only sinful patterns of domination, oppression or aggression, but the conflict of values and interests which illustrate the limitations of a sinful world. The threat of nuclear war which affects the world today reflects such sinful patterns and conflicts.

62. In the "already but not yet" of Christian existence, members of the Church choose different paths to move toward the realization of the kingdom in history. As we examine both the positions open to individuals for forming their consciences on war and peace and the Catholic teaching on the obligation of the state to defend society, we draw extensively on the *Pastoral Constitution* for two reasons.

63. First, we find its treatment of the nature of peace and the avoidance of war compelling, for it represents the prayerful thinking of bishops of the entire world and calls vigorously for fresh new attitudes, while faithfully reflecting traditional Church teaching. Secondly, the Council fathers were familiar with more than the horrors of World Wars I and II. They saw conflicts continuing "to produce their devastating effect day by day somewhere in the world," the increasing ferocity of warfare made possible by modern scientific weapons, guerrilla warfare "drawn out by new methods of deceit and subversion," and terrorism regarded as a new way to wage war.[18] The same phenomena mark our day.

64. For similar reasons we draw heavily upon the popes of the nuclear age, from Pope Pius XII through Pope John Paul II. The teaching of popes and Councils must be incarnated by each local church in a manner understandable to its culture. This allows each local church to bring its unique insights and experience to bear on the issues shaping our world. From 1966 to the present, American bishops, individually and collectively, have issued numerous statements on the issues of peace and war, ranging from the Vietnam War to conscientious objection and the use of nuclear weapons. These statements reflect not only the concerns of the hierarchy but also the voices of our people who have increasingly

expressed to us their alarm over the threat of war. In this letter we wish to continue and develop the teaching on peace and war which we have previously made, and which reflects both the teaching of the universal Church and the insights and experience of the Catholic community of the United States.

65. It is significant that explicit treatment of war and peace is reserved for the final chapter of the *Pastoral Constitution.* Only after exploring the nature and destiny of the human person does the Council take up the nature of peace, which it sees not as an end in itself, but as an *indispensable condition* for the task "of constructing for all men everywhere a world more genuinely human."[19] An understanding of this task is crucial to understanding the Church's view of the moral choices open to us as Christians.

C. The Moral Choices for the Kingdom

66. In one of its most frequently quoted passages, the *Pastoral Constitution* declares that it is necessary "to undertake a completely fresh reappraisal of war."[20] The Council's teaching situates this call for a "fresh reappraisal" within the context of a broad analysis of the dignity of the human person and the state of the world today. If we lose sight of this broader discussion we cannot grasp the Council's wisdom. For the issue of war and peace confronts everyone with a basic question: what contributes to, and what impedes, the construction of a more genuinely human world? If we are to evaluate war with an entirely new attitude, we must be serious about approaching the human person with an entirely new attitude. The obligation for all of humanity to work toward universal respect for human rights and human dignity is a fundamental imperative of the social, economic, and political order.

67. It is clear, then, that to evaluate war with a new attitude, we must go far beyond an examination of weapons systems or military strategies. We must probe the meaning of the moral choices which are ours as Christians. In accord with the vision of Vatican II, we need to be sensitive to both the danger of war and the conditions of true freedom within which moral choices can be made.[21] Peace is the setting in which moral choice can be most effectively exercised. How can we move toward that peace which is indispensable for true human freedom? How do we define such peace?

1. THE NATURE OF PEACE

68. The Catholic tradition has always understood the meaning of peace in positive terms. Peace is both a gift of God and a human work. It must be constructed on the basis of central human values: truth, justice, freedom, and love. The *Pastoral Constitution* states the traditional conception of peace:

> Peace is not merely the absence of war. Nor can it be reduced solely to the maintenance of a balance of power between enemies. Nor is it

brought about by dictatorship. Instead, it is richly and appropriately called "an enterprise of justice" (Is. 32:17). Peace results from that harmony built into human society by its divine founder and actualized by men as they thirst after ever greater justice.[22]

69. Pope John Paul II has enhanced this positive conception of peace by relating it with new philosophical depth to the Church's teaching on human dignity and human rights. The relationship was articulated in his 1979 Address to the General Assembly of the United Nations and also in his "World Day of Peace Message 1982":

> Unconditional and effective respect for each one's unprescriptable and inalienable rights is the necessary condition in order that peace may reign in a society. Vis-à-vis these basic rights all others are in a way derivatory and secondary. In a society in which these rights are not protected, the very idea of universality is dead, as soon as a small group of individuals set up for their own exclusive advantage a principle of discrimination whereby the rights and even the lives of others are made dependent on the whim of the stronger.[23]

70. As we have already noted, however, the protection of human rights and the preservation of peace are tasks to be accomplished in a world marked by sin and conflict of various kinds. The Church's teaching on war and peace establishes a strong presumption against war which is binding on all; it then examines when this presumption may be overriden, precisely in the name of preserving the kind of peace which protects human dignity and human rights.

2. THE PRESUMPTION AGAINST WAR AND THE PRINCIPLE OF LEGITIMATE SELF-DEFENSE

71. Under the rubric, "curbing the savagery of war," the Council contemplates the "melancholy state of humanity." It looks at this world as it is, not simply as we would want it to be. The view is stark: ferocious new means of warfare threatening savagery surpassing that of the past, deceit, subversion, terrorism, genocide. This last crime, in particular, is vehemently condemned as horrendous, but all activities which deliberately conflict with the all-embracing principles of universal natural law, which is permanently binding, are criminal, as are all orders commanding such action. Supreme commendation is due the courage of those who openly and fearlessly resist those who issue such commands. All individuals, especially government officials and experts, are bound to honor and improve upon agreements which are "aimed at making military activity and its consequences less inhuman" and which "better and more workably lead to restraining the frightfulness of war."[24]

72. This remains a realistic appraisal of the world today. Later in this section the Council calls for us "to strain every muscle as we work for the time when all war can be completely outlawed by international consent." We are told, however, that this goal requires the establishment of some universally recognized public authority with effective power "to safeguard, on the behalf of all, security, regard for justice, and respect for rights."[25] *But what of the present?* The Council is exceedingly clear, as are the popes:

> Certainly, war has not been rooted out of human affairs. As long as the danger of war remains and there is no competent and sufficiently powerful authority at the international level, governments cannot be denied the right to legitimate defense once every means of peaceful settlement has been exhausted. Therefore, government authorities and others who share public responsibility have the duty to protect the welfare of the people entrusted to their care and to conduct such grave matters soberly.
>
> But it is one thing to undertake military action for the just defense of the people, and something else again to seek the subjugation of other nations. Nor does the possession of war potential make every military or political use of it lawful. Neither does the mere fact that war has unhappily begun mean that all is fair between the warring parties.[26]

73. The Christian has no choice but to defend peace, properly understood, against aggression. This is an inalienable obligation. It is the *how* of defending peace which offers moral options. We stress this principle again because we observe so much misunderstanding about both those who resist bearing arms and those who bear them. Great numbers from both traditions provide examples of exceptional courage, examples the world continues to need. Of the millions of men and women who have served with integrity in the armed forces, many have laid down their lives. Many others serve today throughout the world in the difficult and demanding task of helping to preserve that "peace of a sort" of which the Council speaks. We see many deeply sincere individuals who, far from being indifferent or apathetic to world evils, believe strongly in conscience that they are best defending true peace by refusing to bear arms. In some cases they are motivated by their understanding of the Gospel and the life and death of Jesus as forbidding all violence. In others, their motivation is simply to give personal example of Christian forbearance as a positive, constructive approach toward loving reconciliation with enemies. In still other cases, they propose or engage in "active nonviolence" as programmed resistance to thwart aggression, or to render ineffective any oppression attempted by force of arms. No government, and certainly no Christian, may simply assume that such individuals are mere pawns of conspiratorial forces or guilty of cowardice.

74. Catholic teaching sees these two distinct moral responses as having a complementary relationship, in the sense that both seek to serve the common

good. They differ in their perception of how the common good is to be defended most effectively, but both responses testify to the Christian conviction that peace must be pursued and rights defended within moral restraints and in the context of defining other basic human values.

75. In all of this discussion of distinct choices, of course, we are referring to options open to individuals. The Council and the popes have stated clearly that governments threatened by armed, unjust aggression must defend their people. This includes defense by armed force, if necessary, as a last resort. We shall discuss below the conditions and limits imposed on such defense. Even when speaking of individuals, however, the Council is careful to preserve the fundamental *right* of defense. Some choose not to vindicate their rights by armed force and adopt other methods of defense, but they do not lose the right of defense nor may they renounce their obligations to others. They are praised by the Council, as long as the rights and duties of others or of the community itself are not injured.

76. Pope Pius XII is especially strong in his conviction about the responsibility of the Christian to resist unjust aggression:

> *A people threatened with an unjust aggression, or already its victim, may not remain passively indifferent, if it would think and act as befits a Christian.* All the more does the solidarity of the family of nations forbid others to behave as mere spectators, in any attitude of apathetic neutrality. Who will ever measure the harm already caused in the past by such indifference to war of aggression, which is quite alien to the Christian instinct? How much more keenly has it brought any advantage in recompense? On the contrary, it has only reassured and encouraged the authors and fomentors of aggression, while it obliges the several peoples, left to themselves, to increase their armaments indefinitely . . . Among (the) goods (of humanity) some are of such importance for society, that it is perfectly lawful to defend them against unjust aggression. *Their defense is even an obligation for the nations as a whole, who have a duty not to abandon a nation that is attacked.*[27]

77. None of the above is to suggest, however, that armed force is the only defense against unjust aggression, regardless of circumstances. Well does the Council require that grave matters concerning the protection of peoples be conducted *soberly*. The Council fathers were well aware that in today's world, the "horror and perversity of war are immensely magnified by the multiplication of scientific weapons. For acts of war involving these weapons can inflict massive and indiscriminate destruction far exceeding the bounds of legitimate defense."[28] Hence, we are warned: "Men of our time must realize that they will have to give a somber reckoning for their deeds of war. For the course of the future will depend largely on the decisions they make today."[29] There must be serious and continuing study and efforts to develop pro-

grammed methods for both individuals and nations to defend against unjust aggression without using violence.

78. We believe work to develop nonviolent means of fending off aggression and resolving conflict best reflects the call of Jesus both to love and to justice. Indeed, each increase in the potential destructiveness of weapons and therefore of war serves to underline the rightness of the way that Jesus mandated to his followers. But, on the other hand, the fact of aggression, oppression and injustice in our world also serves to legitimate the resort to weapons and armed force in defense of justice. We must recognize the reality of the paradox we face as Christians living in the context of the world as it presently exists, we must continue to articulate our belief that love is possible and the only real hope for all human relations, and yet accept that force, even deadly force, is sometimes justified and that nations must provide for their defense. It is the mandate of Christians, in the face of this paradox, to strive to resolve it through an even greater commitment to Christ and his message. As Pope John Paul II said:

> Christians are aware that plans based on aggression, domination and the manipulation of others lurk in human hearts, and sometimes even secretly nourish human intentions, in spite of certain declarations or manifestations of a pacifist nature. For Christians know that in this world a totally and permanently peaceful human society is unfortunately a utopia, and that ideologies that hold up that prospect as easily attainable are based on hopes that cannot be realized, whatever the reason behind them. It is a question of a mistaken view of the human condition, a lack of application in considering the question as a whole; or it may be a case of evasion in order to calm fear, or in still other cases a matter of calculated self-interest. Christians are convinced, if only because they have learned from personal experience, that these deceptive hopes lead straight to the false peace of totalitarian regimes. But this realistic view in no way prevents Christians from working for peace; instead, it stirs up their ardor, for they also know that Christ's victory over deception, hate, and death gives those in love with peace a more decisive motive for action than what the most generous theories about man have to offer; Christ's victory likewise gives a hope more surely based than any hope held out by the most audacious dreams.
>
> This is why Christians, even as they strive to resist and prevent every form of warfare, have no hesitation in recalling that, in the name of an elementary requirement of justice, peoples have a right and even a duty to protect their existence and freedom by proportionate means against an unjust aggressor.[30]

79. In light of the framework of Catholic teaching on the nature of peace, the avoidance of war, and the state's right of legitimate defense, we can now spell out certain moral principles within the Catholic tradition which provide guidance for public policy and individual choice.

3. THE JUST-WAR CRITERIA

80. The moral theory of the "just-war" or "limited-war" doctrine begins with the presumption which binds all Christians: we should do no harm to our neighbors; how we treat our enemy is the key test of whether we love our neighbor; and the possibility of taking even one human life is a prospect we should consider in fear and trembling. How is it possible to move from these presumptions to the idea of a justifiable use of lethal force?

81. Historically and theologically the clearest answer to the question is found in St. Augustine. Augustine was impressed by the fact and the consequences of sin in history—the "not yet" dimension of the kingdom. In his view war was both the result of sin and a tragic remedy for sin in the life of political societies. War arose from disordered ambitions, but it could also be used, in some cases at least, to restrain evil and protect the innocent. The classic case which illustrated his view was the use of lethal force to prevent aggression against innocent victims. Faced with the fact of attack on the innocent, the presumption that we do no harm, even to our enemy, yielded to the command of love understood as the need to restrain an enemy who would injure the innocent.

82. The just-war argument has taken several forms in the history of Catholic theology, but this Augustinian insight is its central premise.[31] In the twentieth century, papal teaching has used the logic of Augustine and Aquinas[32] to articulate a right of self-defense for states in a decentralized international order and to state the criteria for exercising that right. The essential position was stated by Vatican II: "As long as the danger of war persists and there is no international authority with the necessary competence and power, governments cannot be denied the right of lawful self-defense, once all peace efforts have failed."[33] We have already indicated the centrality of this principle for understanding Catholic teaching about the state and its duties.

83. Just-war teaching has evolved, however, as an effort to prevent war; only if war cannot be rationally avoided, does the teaching then seek to restrict and reduce its horrors. It does this by establishing a set of rigorous conditions which must be met if the decision to go to war is to be morally permissible. Such a decision, especially today, requires extraordinarily strong reasons for overriding the presumption *in favor of peace* and *against* war. This is one significant reason why valid just-war teaching makes provision for conscientious dissent. It is presumed that all sane people prefer peace, never *want* to initiate war, and accept even the most justifiable defensive war only as a sad necessity. Only the most powerful reasons may be permitted to override such objection. In the words of Pope Pius XII:

> The Christian will for peace . . . is very careful to avoid recourse to the force of arms in the defense of rights which, however legitimate, do not offset the risk of kindling a blaze with all its spiritual and material consequences.[34]

84. The determination of *when* conditions exist which allow the resort to force in spite of the strong presumption against it is made in light of *jus ad bellum* criteria. The determination of *how* even a justified resort to force must be conducted is made in light of the *jus in bello* criteria. We shall briefly explore the meaning of both.[35]

Jus ad Bellum

85. Why and when recourse to war is permissible.

86. ***a) Just Cause:*** War is permissible only to confront "a real and certain danger," i.e., to protect innocent life, to preserve conditions necessary for decent human existence, and to basic human rights. As both Pope Pius XII and Pope John XXIII made clear, if war of retribution was ever justifiable, the risks of modern war negate such a claim today.

87. ***b) Competent Authority:*** In the Catholic tradition the right to use force has always been joined to the common good; war must be declared by those with responsibility for public order, not by private groups or individuals.

88. The requirement that a decision to go to war must be made by competent authority is particularly important in a democratic society. It needs detailed treatment here since it involves a broad spectrum of related issues. Some of the bitterest divisions of society in our own nation's history, for example, have been evoked over the question of whether or not a president of the United States has acted constitutionally and legally in involving our country in a *de facto* war, even if—indeed, especially if—war was never formally declared. Equally perplexing problems of conscience can be raised for individuals expected or legally required to go to war even though our duly elected representatives in Congress have, in fact, voted for war.

89. The criterion of competent authority is of further importance in a day when revolutionary war has become commonplace. Historically, the just-war tradition has been open to a "just revolution" position, recognizing that an oppressive government may lose its claim to legitimacy. Insufficient analytical attention has been given to the moral issues of revolutionary warfare. The mere possession of sufficient weaponry, for example, does not legitimize the initiation of war by "insurgents" against an established government, any more than the government's systematic oppression of its people can be carried out under the doctrine of "national security."

90. While the legitimacy of revolution in some circumstances cannot be denied, just-war teachings must be applied as rigorously to revolutionary-counterrevolutionary conflicts as to others. The issue of who constitutes competent authority and how such authority is exercised is essential.

91. When we consider in this letter the issues of conscientious objection (C.O.) and selective conscientious objection (S.C.O.), the issue of competent authority will arise again.

92. ***c) Comparative Justice:*** Questions concerning the *means* of waging war today, particularly in view of the destructive potential of weapons, have

tended to override questions concerning the comparative justice of the positions of respective adversaries or enemies. In essence: which side is sufficiently "right" in a dispute, and are the values at stake critical enough to override the presumption against war? The question in its most basic form is this: do the rights and values involved justify killing? For whatever the means used, war, by definition, involves violence, destruction, suffering, and death.

93. The category of comparative justice is destined to emphasize the presumption against war which stands at the beginning of just-war teaching. In a world of sovereign states recognizing neither a common moral authority nor a central political authority, comparative justice stresses that no state should act on the basis that it has "absolute justice" on its side. Every party to a conflict should acknowledge the limits of its "just cause" and the consequent requirement to use *only* limited means in pursuit of its objectives. Far from legitimizing a crusade mentality, comparative justice is designed to relativize absolute claims and to restrain the use of force even in a "justified" conflict.[36]

94. Given techniques of propaganda and the ease with which nations and individuals either assume or delude themselves into believing that God or right is clearly on their side, the test of comparative justice may be extremely difficult to apply. Clearly however, this is not the case in every instance of war. Blatant aggression from without and subversion from within are often enough readily identifiable by all reasonably fair-minded people.

95. ***d) Right Intention:*** Right intention is related to just cause—war can be legitimately intended only for the reasons set forth above as a just cause. During the conflict, right intention means pursuit of peace and reconciliation, including avoiding unnecessarily destructive acts or imposing unreasonable conditions (e.g., unconditional surrender).

96. ***e) Last Resort:*** For resort to war to be justified, all peaceful alternatives must have been exhausted. There are formidable problems in this requirement. No international organization currently in existence has exercised sufficient internationally recognized authority to be able either to mediate effectively in most cases or to prevent conflict by the intervention of United Nations or other peacekeeping forces. Furthermore, there is a tendency for nations or peoples which perceive conflict between or among other nations as advantageous to themselves to attempt to prevent a peaceful settlement rather than advance it.

97. We regret the apparent unwillingness of some to see in the United Nations organization the potential for world order which exists and to encourage its development. Pope Paul VI called the United Nations the last hope for peace. The loss of this hope cannot be allowed to happen. Pope John Paul II is again instructive on this point:

> I wish above all to repeat my confidence in you, the leaders and members of the International Organizations, and in you, the international officials! In the course of the last ten years, your organizations have too

> often been the object of attempts at manipulation on the part of nations wishing to exploit such bodies. However it remains true that the present multiplicity of violent clashes, divisions and blocks on which bilateral relations founder, offer the great International Organizations the opportunity to engage upon the qualitative change in their activities, even to reform on certain points their own structures in order to take into account new realities and to enjoy effective power.[37]

98. ***f) Probability of Success:*** This is a difficult criterion to apply, but its purpose is to prevent irrational resort to force or hopeless resistance when the outcome of either will clearly be disproportionate or futile. The determination includes a recognition that at times defense of key values, even against great odds, may be a "proportionate" witness.

99. ***g) Proportionality:*** In terms of the *jus ad bellum* criteria, proportionality means that the damage to be inflicted and the costs incurred by war must be proportionate to the good expected by taking up arms. Nor should judgments concerning proportionality be limited to the temporal order without regard to a spiritual dimension in terms of "damage," "cost," and "the good expected." In today's interdependent world even a local conflict can affect people everywhere; this is particularly the case when the nuclear powers are involved. Hence a nation cannot justly go to war today without considering the effect of its action on others and on the international community.

100. This principle of proportionality applies throughout the conduct of the war as well as to the decision to begin warfare. During the Vietnam war our bishops' conference ultimately concluded that the conflict had reached such a level of devastation to the adversary and damage to our own society that continuing it could not be justified.[38]

Jus in Bello

101. Even when the stringent conditions which justify resort to war are met, the conduct of war (i.e., strategy, tactics, and individual actions) remains subject to continuous scrutiny in light of two principles which have special significance today precisely because of the destructive capability of modern technological warfare. These principles are proportionality and discrimination. In discussing them here, we shall apply them to the question of *jus ad bellum* as well as *jus in bello*; for today it becomes increasingly difficult to make a decision to use any kind of armed force, however limited initially in intention and in the destructive power of the weapons employed, without facing at least the possibility of escalation to broader, or even total, war and to the use of weapons of horrendous destructive potential. This is especially the case when adversaries are "superpowers," as the Council clearly envisioned:

> Indeed, if the kind of weapons now stocked in the arsenals of the great powers were to be employed to the fullest, the result would be the almost

> complete reciprocal slaughter of one side by the other, not to speak of the widespread devastation that would follow in the world and the deadly after-effects resulting from the use of such weapons.[39]

102. It should not be thought, of course, that massive slaughter and destruction would result only from the extensive use of nuclear weapons. We recall with horror the carpet and incendiary bombings of World War II, the deaths of hundreds of thousands in various regions of the world through "conventional" arms, the unspeakable use of gas and other forms of chemical warfare, the destruction of homes and of crops, the utter suffering war has wrought during the centuries before and the decades since the use of the "atom bomb." Nevertheless, every honest person must recognize that, especially given the proliferation of modern scientific weapons, we now face possibilities which are appalling to contemplate. Today, as never before, we must ask not merely what *will* happen, but what *may* happen, especially if major powers embark on war. Pope John Paul II has repeatedly pleaded that world leaders confront this reality:

> [I]n view of the difference between classical warfare and nuclear or bacteriological war—a difference so to speak of nature—and in view of the scandal of the arms race seen against the background of the needs of the Third World, this right [of defense], which is very real in principle, only underlines the urgency of world society to equip itself with effective means of negotiation. In this way the nuclear terror that haunts our time can encourage us to enrich our common heritage with a very simple discovery that is within our reach, namely that war is the most barbarous and least effective way of resolving conflicts.[40]

103. The Pontifical Academy of Sciences reaffirmed the Holy Father's theme, in its November 1981 "Statement on the Consequences of Nuclear War." Then, in a meeting convoked by the Pontifical Academy, representatives of national academies of science from throughout the world issued a "Declaration on the Prevention of Nuclear War" which specified the meaning of Pope John Paul II's statement that modern warfare differs by nature from previous forms of war. The scientists said:

> Throughout its history humanity has been confronted with war, but since 1945 the nature of warfare has changed so profoundly that the future of the human race, of generations yet unborn, is imperiled. . . . For the first time it is possible to cause damage on such a catastrophic scale as to wipe out a large part of civilization and to endanger its very survival. The large-scale use of such weapons could trigger major and irreversible ecological and genetic changes whose limits cannot be predicted.[41]

And earlier, with such thoughts plainly in mind, the Council had made its own "the condemnation of total war already pronounced by recent popes."[42] This condemnation is demanded by the principles of proportionality and discrimination. Response to aggression must not exceed the nature of the aggression. To destroy civilization as we know it by waging a "total war" as today it *could* be waged would be a monstrously disproportionate response to aggression on the part of any nation.

104. Moreover, the lives of innocent persons may never be taken directly, regardless of the purpose alleged for doing so. To wage truly "total" war is by definition to take huge numbers of innocent lives. Just response to aggression must be discriminate; it must be directed against unjust aggressors, not against innocent people caught up in a war not of their making. The Council therefore issued its memorable declaration:

> Any act of war aimed indiscriminately at the destruction of entire cities or of extensive areas along with their population is a crime against God and man himself. It merits unequivocal and unhesitating condemnation.[43]

105. When confronting choices among specific military options, the question asked by proportionality is: once we take into account not only the military advantages that will be achieved by using this means but also all the harms reasonably expected to follow from using it, can its use still be justified? We know, of course, that no end can justify means evil in themselves, such as the executing of hostages or the targeting of noncombatants. Nonetheless, even if the means adopted is not evil in itself, it is necessary to take into account the probable harms that will result from using it and the justice of accepting those harms. It is of utmost importance, in assessing harms and the justice of accepting them, to think about the poor and the helpless, for they are usually the ones who have the least to gain and the most to lose when war's violence touches their lives.

106. In terms of the arms race, if the *real* end in view is legitimate defense against unjust aggression, and the means to this end are not evil in themselves, we must still examine the question of proportionality concerning attendant evils. Do the exorbitant costs, the general climate of insecurity generated, the possibility of accidental detonation of highly destructive weapons, the danger of error and miscalculation that could provoke retaliation and war—do such evils or others attendant upon and indirectly deriving from the arms race make the arms race itself a disproportionate response to aggression? Pope John Paul II is very clear in his insistence that the exercise of the right and duty of a people to protect their existence and freedom is contingent on the use of proportionate means.[44]

107. Finally, another set of questions concerns the interpretation of the principle of discrimination. The principle prohibits directly intended attacks on noncombatants and nonmilitary targets. It raises a series of questions about the term "intentional," the category of "noncombatant," and the meaning of "military."

108. These questions merit the debate occurring with increasing frequency today. We encourage such debate, for concise and definitive answers still appear to be wanting. Mobilization of forces in modern war includes not only the military, but to a significant degree the political, economic, and social sectors. It is not always easy to determine who is directly involved in a "war effort" or to what degree. Plainly, though, not even by the broadest definition can one rationally consider combatants entire classes of human beings such as schoolchildren, hospital patients, the elderly, the ill, the average industrial worker producing goods not directly related to military purposes, farmers, and many others. They may never be directly attacked.

109. Direct attacks on military targets involve similar complexities. Which targets are "military" ones and which are not? To what degree, for instance, does the use (by either revolutionaries or regular military forces) of a village or housing in a civilian populated area invite attack? What of a munitions factory in the heart of a city? Who is directly responsible for the deaths of noncombatants should the attack be carried out? To revert to the question raised earlier, how many deaths of noncombatants are "tolerable" as a result of indirect attacks—attacks directed against combat forces and military targets, which nevertheless kill noncombatants at the same time?

110. These two principles, in all their complexity, must be applied to the range of weapons—conventional, nuclear, biological, and chemical—with which nations are armed today.

4. THE VALUE OF NONVIOLENCE

111. Moved by the example of Jesus' life and by his teaching, some Christians have from the earliest days of the Church committed themselves to a nonviolent lifestyle.[45] Some understood the Gospel of Jesus to prohibit all killing. Some affirmed the use of prayer and other spiritual methods as means of responding to enmity and hostility.

112. In the middle of the second century, St. Justin proclaimed to his pagan readers that Isaiah's prophecy about turning swords into ploughshares and spears into sickles had been fulfilled as a consequence of Christ's coming:

> And we who delighted in war, in the slaughter of one another, and in every other kind of iniquity have in every part of the world converted our weapons into implements of peace—our swords into ploughshares, our spears into farmers' tools—and we cultivate piety, justice, brotherly charity, faith, and hope, which we derive from the Father through the crucified Savior. . . .[46]

113. Writing in the third century, St. Cyprian of Carthage struck a similar note when he indicated that the Christians of his day did not fight against their enemies. He himself regarded their conduct as proper:

> They do not even fight against those who are attacking since it is not granted to the innocent to kill even the aggressor, but promptly to deliver up their souls and blood that, since so much malice and cruelty are rampant in the world, they may more quickly withdraw from the malicious and the cruel.[47]

114. Some of the early Christian opposition to military service was a response to the idolatrous practices which prevailed in the Roman army. Another powerful motive was the fact that army service involved preparation for fighting and killing. We see this in the case of St. Martin of Tours during the fourth century, who renounced his soldierly profession with the explanation: "Hitherto I have served you as a soldier. Allow me now to become a soldier of God . . . I am a soldier of Christ. It is not lawful for me to fight."[48]

115. In the centuries between the fourth century and our own day, the theme of Christian nonviolence and Christian pacifism has echoed and re-echoed, sometimes more strongly, sometimes more faintly. One of the great nonviolent figures in those centuries was St. Francis of Assisi. Besides making personal efforts on behalf of reconciliation and peace, Francis stipulated that laypersons who became members of his Third Order were not "to take up lethal weapons, or bear them about, against anybody."

116. The vision of Christian nonviolence is not passive about injustice and the defense of the rights of others; it rather affirms and exemplifies what it means to resist injustice through nonviolent methods.

117. In the twentieth century, prescinding from the non-Christian witness of a Mahatma Gandhi and its worldwide impact, the nonviolent witness of such figures as Dorothy Day and Martin Luther King has had profound impact upon the life of the Church in the United States. The witness of numerous Christians who had preceded them over the centuries was affirmed in a remarkable way at the Second Vatican Council.

118. Two of the passages which were included in the final version of the *Pastoral Constitution* gave particular encouragement for Catholics in all walks of life to assess their attitudes toward war and military service in the light of Christian pacifism. In paragraph 79 the Council fathers called upon governments to enact laws protecting the rights of those who adopted the position of conscientious objection to all war: "Moreover, it seems right that laws make humane provisions for the case of those who for reasons of conscience refuse to bear arms, provided, however, that they accept some other form of service to the human community."[49] This was the first time a call for legal protection of conscientious objection had appeared in a document of such prominence. In addition to its own profound meaning this statement took on even more significance in the light of the praise that the Council fathers had given in the preceding section "to those who renounce the use of violence and the vindication of their rights."[50] In *Human Life in Our Day* (1968) we called for legislative provision to recognize selective conscientious objectors as well.[51]

119. As Catholic bishops it is incumbent upon us to stress to our own community and to the wider society the significance of this support for a pacifist option for individuals in the teaching of Vatican II and the reaffirmation that the popes have given to nonviolent witness since the time of the Council.

120. In the development of a theology of peace and the growth of the Christian pacifist position among Catholics, these words of the *Pastoral Constitution* have special significance: "All these factors force us to undertake a completely fresh reappraisal of war."[52] The Council fathers had reference to "the development of armaments by modern science (which) has immeasurably magnified the horrors and wickedness of war."[53] While the just-war teaching has clearly been in possession for the past 1,500 years of Catholic thought, the "new moment" in which we find ourselves sees the just-war teaching and nonviolence as distinct but interdependent methods of evaluating warfare. They diverge on some specific conclusions, but they share a common presumption against the use of force as a means of settling disputes.

121. Both find their roots in the Christian theological tradition; each contributes to the full moral vision we need in pursuit of a human peace. We believe the two perspectives support and complement one another, each preserving the other from distortion. Finally, in an age of technological warfare, analysis from the viewpoint of nonviolence and analysis from the viewpoint of the just-war teaching often converge and agree in their opposition to methods of warfare which are in fact indistinguishable from total warfare.

II. WAR AND PEACE IN THE MODERN WORLD: PROBLEMS AND PRINCIPLES

122. Both the just-war teaching and nonviolence are confronted with a unique challenge by nuclear warfare. This must be the starting point of any further moral reflection: nuclear weapons particularly and nuclear warfare as it is planned today, raise new moral questions. No previously conceived moral position escapes the fundamental confrontation posed by contemporary nuclear strategy. Many have noted the similarity of the statements made by eminent scientists and Vatican II's observation that we are forced today "to undertake a completely fresh reappraisal of war." The task before us is not simply to repeat what we have said before; it is first to consider anew whether and how our religious-moral tradition can assess, direct, contain, and, we hope, help to eliminate the threat posed to the human family by the nuclear arsenals of the world. Pope John Paul II captured the essence of the problem during his pilgrimage to Hiroshima:

> In the past it was possible to destroy a village, a town, a region, even a country. Now it is the whole planet that has come under threat.[54]

123. The Holy Father's observation illustrates why the moral problem is also a religious question of the most profound significance. In the nuclear arsenals of the United States or the Soviet Union alone, there exists a capacity to do something no other age could imagine: we can threaten the entire planet.[55] For people of faith this means we read the Book of Genesis with a new awareness; the moral issue at stake in nuclear war involves the meaning of sin in its most graphic dimensions. Every sinful act is a confrontation of the creature and the creator. Today the destructive potential of the nuclear powers threatens the human person, the civilization we have slowly constructed, and even the created order itself.

124. We live today, therefore, in the midst of a cosmic drama; we possess a power which should never be used, but which might be used if we do not reverse our direction. We live with nuclear weapons knowing we cannot afford to make one serious mistake. This fact dramatizes the precariousness of our position, politically, morally, and spiritually.

125. A prominent "sign of the times" today is a sharply increased awareness of the danger of the nuclear arms race. Such awareness has produced a public discussion about nuclear policy here and in other countries which is unprecedented in its scope and depth. What has been accepted for years with almost no question is now being subjected to the sharpest criticism. What previously had been defined as a safe and stable system of deterrence is today viewed with political and moral skepticism. Many forces are at work in this new evaluation, and we believe one of the crucial elements is the Gospel vision of peace which guides our work in this Pastoral Letter. The nuclear age has been the theater of our existence for almost four decades; today it is being evaluated with a new perspective. For many the leaven of the Gospel and the light of the Holy Spirit create the decisive dimension of this new perspective.

A. The New Moment

126. At the center of the new evaluation of the nuclear arms race is a recognition of two elements: the destructive potential of nuclear weapons, and the stringent choices which the nuclear age poses for both politics and morals.

127. The fateful passage into the nuclear age as a military reality began with the bombing of Nagasaki and Hiroshima, events described by Pope Paul VI as a "butchery of untold magnitude."[56] Since then, in spite of efforts at control and plans for disarmament (e.g., the Baruch Plan of 1946), the nuclear arsenals have escalated, particularly in the two superpowers. The qualitative superiority of these two states, however, should not overshadow the fact that four other countries possess nuclear capacity and a score of states are only steps away from becoming "nuclear nations."

128. This nuclear escalation has been opposed sporadically and selectively but never effectively. The race has continued in spite of carefully expressed doubts by analysts and other citizens and in the face of forcefully expressed

opposition by public rallies. Today the opposition to the arms race is no longer selective or sporadic, it is widespread and sustained. The danger and destructiveness of nuclear weapons are understood and resisted with new urgency and intensity. There is in the public debate today an endorsement of the position submitted by the Holy See at the United Nations in 1976: the arms race is to be condemned as a danger, an act of aggression against the poor, and a folly which does not provide the security it promises.[57]

129. Papal teaching has consistently addressed the folly and danger of the arms race; but the new perception of it which is now held by the general public is due in large measure to the work of scientists and physicians who have described for citizens the concrete human consequences of a nuclear war.[58]

130. In a striking demonstration of his personal and pastoral concern for preventing nuclear war, Pope John Paul II commissioned a study by the Pontifical Academy of Sciences which reinforced the findings of other scientific bodies. The Holy Father had the study transmitted by personal representative to the leaders of the United States, the Soviet Union, the United Kingdom, and France, and to the president of the General Assembly of the United Nations. One of its conclusions is especially pertinent to the public debate in the United States:

> Recent talk about winning or even surviving a nuclear war must reflect a failure to appreciate a medical reality: Any nuclear war would inevitably cause death, disease and suffering of pandemonic proportions and without the possibility of effective medical intervention. That reality leads to the same conclusion physicians have reached for life-threatening epidemics throughout history. Prevention is essential for control.[59]

131. This medical conclusion has a moral corollary. Traditionally, the Church's moral teaching sought first to prevent war and then to limit its consequences if it occurred. Today the possibilities for placing political and moral limits on nuclear war are so minimal that the moral task, like the medical, is prevention: as a people, we must refuse to legitimate the idea of nuclear war. Such a refusal will require not only new ideas and new vision, but what the Gospel calls conversion of the heart.

132. To say "no" to nuclear war is both a necessary and a complex task. We are moral teachers in a tradition which has always been prepared to relate moral principles to concrete problems. Particularly in this letter we could not be content with simply restating general moral principles or repeating well-known requirements about the ethics of war. We have had to examine, with the assistance of a broad spectrum of advisors of varying persuasions, the nature of existing and proposed weapons systems, the doctrines which govern their use, and the consequences of using them. We have consulted people who engage their lives in protest against the existing nuclear strategy

of the United States, and we have consulted others who have held or do hold responsibility for this strategy. It has been a sobering and perplexing experience. In light of the evidence which witnesses presented and in light of our study, reflection, and consultation, we must reject nuclear war. But we feel obliged to relate our judgment to the specific elements which comprise the nuclear problem.

133. Though certain that the dangerous and delicate nuclear relationship the superpowers now maintain should not exist, we understand how it came to exist. In a world of sovereign states, devoid of central authority and possessing the knowledge to produce nuclear weapons, many choices were made, some clearly objectionable, others well-intended with mixed results, which brought the world to its present dangerous situation.

134. We see with increasing clarity the political folly of a system which threatens mutual suicide, the psychological damage this does to ordinary people, especially the young, the economic distortion of priorities—billions readily spent for destructive instruments while pitched battles are waged daily in our legislatures over much smaller amounts for the homeless, the hungry, and the helpless here and abroad. But it is much less clear how we translate a "no" to nuclear war into the personal and public choices which can move us in a new direction, toward a national policy and an international system which more adequately reflect the values and vision of the Kingdom of God.

135. These tensions in our assessment of the politics and strategy of the nuclear age reflect the conflicting elements of the nuclear dilemma and the balance of terror which it has produced. We have said earlier in this letter that the fact of war reflects the existence of sin in the world. The nuclear threat and the danger it poses to human life and civilization exemplify in a qualitatively new way the perennial struggle of the political community to contain the use of force, particularly among states.

136. Precisely because of the destructive nature of nuclear weapons, strategies have been developed which previous generations would have found unintelligible. Today military preparations are undertaken on a vast and sophisticated scale, but the declared purpose is not to use the weapons produced. Threats are made which would be suicidal to implement. The key to security is no longer only military secrets, for in some instances security may best be served by informing one's adversary publicly what weapons one has and what plans exist for their use. The presumption of the nation-state system, that sovereignty implies an ability to protect a nation's territory and population, is precisely the presumption denied by the nuclear capacities of both superpowers. In a sense each is at the mercy of the other's perception of what strategy is "rational," what kind of damage is "unacceptable," how "convincing" one side's threat is to the other.

137. The political paradox of deterrence has also strained our moral conception. May a nation threaten what it may never do? May it possess what

it may never use? Who is involved in the threat each superpower makes: government officials? or military personnel? or the citizenry in whose defense the threat is made?

138. In brief, the danger of the situation is clear; but how to prevent the use of nuclear weapons, how to assess deterrence, and how to delineate moral responsibility in the nuclear age are less clearly seen or stated. Reflecting the complexity of the nuclear problem, our arguments in this pastoral must be detailed and nuanced; but our "no" to nuclear war must, in the end, be definitive and decisive.

B. Religious Leadership and the Public Debate

139. Because prevention of nuclear war appears, from several perspectives, to be not only the surest but only way to limit its destructive potential, we see our role as moral teachers precisely in terms of helping to form public opinion with a clear determination to resist resort to nuclear war as an instrument of national policy. If "prevention is the only cure," then there are diverse tasks to be performed in preventing what should never occur. As bishops we see a specific task defined for us in Pope John Paul II's "World Day of Peace Message 1982":

> Peace cannot be built by the power of rulers alone. Peace can be firmly constructed only if it corresponds to the resolute determination of all people of good will. Rulers must be supported and enlightened by a public opinion that encourages them or, where necessary, expresses disapproval.[60]

140. The pope's appeal to form public opinion is not an abstract task. Especially in a democracy, public opinion can passively acquiesce in policies and strategies or it can, through a series of measures, indicate the limits beyond which a government should not proceed. The "new moment" which exists in the public debate about nuclear weapons provides a creative opportunity and a moral imperative to examine the relationship between public opinion and public policy. We believe it is necessary, for the sake of prevention, to build a barrier against the concept of nuclear war as a viable strategy for defense. There should be a clear public resistance to the rhetoric of "winnable" nuclear wars, or unrealistic expectations of "surviving" nuclear exchanges, and strategies of "protracted nuclear war." We oppose such rhetoric.

141. We seek to encourage a public attitude which sets stringent limits on the kind of actions our own government and other governments will take on nuclear policy. We believe religious leaders have a task in concert with public officials, analysts, private organizations, and the media to set the limits beyond which our military policy should not move in word or action. Charting

a moral course in a complex public policy debate involves several steps. We will address four questions, offering our reflections on them as an invitation to a public moral dialogue:

1) the use of nuclear weapons;
2) the policy of deterrence in principle and in practice;
3) specific steps to reduce the danger of war;
4) long-term measures of policy and diplomacy.

C. The Use of Nuclear Weapons

142. Establishing moral guidelines in the nuclear debate means addressing first the question of the use of nuclear weapons. That question has several dimensions.

143. It is clear that those in the Church who interpret the Gospel teaching as forbidding all use of violence would oppose any use of nuclear weapons under any conditions. In a sense the existence of these weapons simply confirms and reinforces one of the initial insights of the nonviolent position, namely, that Christians should not use lethal force since the hope of using it selectively and restrictively is so often an illusion. Nuclear weapons seem to prove this point in a way heretofore unknown.

144. For the tradition which acknowledges some legitimate use of force, some important elements of contemporary nuclear strategies move beyond the limits of moral justification. A justifiable use of force must be both discriminatory and proportionate. Certain aspects of both U.S. and Soviet strategies fail both tests as we shall discuss below. The technical literature and the personal testimony of public officials who have been closely associated with U.S. nuclear strategy have both convinced us of the overwhelming probability that major nuclear exchange would have no limits.[61]

145. On the more complicated issue of "limited" nuclear war, we are aware of the extensive literature and discussion which this topic has generated.[62] As a general statement, it seems to us that public officials would be unable to refute the following conclusion of the study made by the Pontifical Academy of Sciences:

> Even a nuclear attack directed only at military facilities would be devastating to the country as a whole. This is because military facilities are widespread rather than concentrated at only a few points. Thus, many nuclear weapons would be exploded.
>
> Furthermore, the spread of radiation due to the natural winds and atmospheric mixing would kill vast numbers of people and contaminate large areas. The medical facilities of any nation would be inadequate to care for the survivors. An objective examination of the medical situation that would follow a nuclear war leads to but one conclusion: prevention is our only recourse.[63]

MORAL PRINCIPLES AND POLICY CHOICES

146. In light of these perspectives we address the questions more explicitly: (1) counterpopulation warfare; (2) initiation of nuclear war; and (3) limited nuclear war.

1. Counterpopulation Warfare

147. Under no circumstances may nuclear weapons or other instruments of mass slaughter be used for the purpose of destroying population centers or other predominantly civilian targets. Popes have repeatedly condemned "total war," which implies such use. For example, as early as 1954 Pope Pius XII condemned nuclear warfare "when it entirely escapes the control of man," and results in "the pure and simple annihilation of all human life within the radius of action."[64] The condemnation was repeated by the Second Vatican Council:

> Any act of war aimed indiscriminately at the destruction of entire cities or of extensive areas along with their population is a crime against God and man himself. It merits unequivocal and unhesitating condemnation.[65]

148. Retaliatory action whether nuclear or conventional which would indiscriminately take many wholly innocent lives, lives of people who are in no way responsible for reckless actions of their government, must also be condemned. This condemnation, in our judgment, applies even to the retaliatory use of weapons striking enemy cities after our own have already been struck. No Christian can rightfully carry out orders or policies deliberately aimed at killing noncombatants.[66]

149. We make this judgment at the beginning of our treatment of nuclear strategy precisely because the defense of the principle of noncombatant immunity is so important for an ethic of war and because the nuclear age has posed such extreme problems for the principle. Later in this letter we shall discuss specific aspects of U.S. policy in light of this principle and in light of recent U.S. policy statements stressing the determination not to target directly or strike directly against civilian populations. Our concern about protecting the moral value of noncombatant immunity, however, requires that we make a clear reassertion of the principle our first word on this matter.

2. The Initiation of Nuclear War

150. We do not perceive any situation in which the deliberate initiation of nuclear warfare, on however restricted a scale, can be morally justified. Non-nuclear attacks by another state must be resisted by other than nuclear means. Therefore, a serious moral obligation exists to develop non-nuclear defensive strategies as rapidly as possible.

151. A serious debate is under way on this issue.[67] It is cast in political terms, but it has a significant moral dimension. Some have argued that at the

very beginning of a war nuclear weapons might be used, only against military targets, perhaps in limited numbers. Indeed it has long been American and NATO policy that nuclear weapons, especially so-called tactical nuclear weapons, would likely be used if NATO forces in Europe seemed in danger of losing a conflict that until then had been restricted to conventional weapons. Large numbers of tactical nuclear weapons are now deployed in Europe by the NATO forces and about as many by the Soviet Union. Some are substantially smaller than the bomb used on Hiroshima, some are larger. Such weapons, if employed in great numbers, would totally devastate the densely populated countries of Western and Central Europe.

152. Whether under conditions of war in Europe, parts of Asia or the Middle East, or the exchange of strategic weapons directly between the United States and the Soviet Union, the difficulties of limiting the use of nuclear weapons are immense. A number of expert witnesses advise us that commanders operating under conditions of battle probably would not be able to exercise strict control; the number of weapons used would rapidly increase, the targets would be expanded beyond the military, and the level of civilian casualties would rise enormously.[68] No one can be certain that this escalation would not occur, even in the face of political efforts to keep such an exchange "limited." The chances of keeping use limited seem remote, and the consequences of escalation to mass destruction would be appalling. Former public officials have testified that it is improbable that any nuclear war could actually be kept limited. Their testimony and the consequences involved in this problem lead us to conclude that the danger of escalation is so great that it would be morally unjustifiable to initiate nuclear war in any form. The danger is rooted not only in the technology of our weapons systems but in the weakness and sinfulness of human communities. We find the moral responsibility of beginning nuclear war not justified by rational political objectives.

153. This judgment affirms that the willingness to initiate nuclear war entails a distinct, weighty moral responsibility; it involves transgressing a fragile barrier—political, psychological, and moral—which has been constructed since 1945. We express repeatedly in this letter our extreme skepticism about the prospects for controlling a nuclear exchange, however limited the first use might be. Precisely because of this skepticism, we judge resort to nuclear weapons to counter a conventional attack to be morally unjustifiable.[69] Consequently we seek to reinforce the barrier against any use of nuclear weapons. Our support of a "no first use" policy must be seen in this light.

154. At the same time we recognize the responsibility the United States has had and continues to have in assisting allied nations in their defense against either a conventional or a nuclear attack. Especially in the European theater, the deterrence of a *nuclear* attack may require nuclear weapons for a time, even though their possession and deployment must be subject to rigid restrictions.

155. The need to defend against a conventional attack in Europe imposes the political and moral burden of developing adequate, alternative modes of defense to prevent reliance on nuclear weapons. Even with the best coordinated effort—hardly likely in view of contemporary political division on this question—development of an alternative defense position will still take time.

156. In the interim, deterrence against a conventional attack relies upon two factors: the not inconsiderable conventional forces at the disposal of NATO and the recognition by a potential attacker that the outbreak of large-scale conventional war could escalate to the nuclear level through accident or miscalculation by either side. We are aware that NATO's refusal to adopt a "no first use" pledge is to some extent linked to the deterrent effect of this inherent ambiguity. Nonetheless, in light of the probable effects of initiating nuclear war, we urge NATO to move rapidly toward the adoption of a "no first use" policy, but doing so in tandem with development of an adequate alternative defense posture.

3. *Limited Nuclear War*

157. It would be possible to agree with our first two conclusions and still not be sure about retaliatory use of nuclear weapons in what is called a "limited exchange." The issue at stake is the *real* as opposed to the *theoretical* possibility of a "limited nuclear exchange."

158. We recognize that the policy debate on this question is inconclusive and that all participants are left with hypothetical projections about probable reactions in a nuclear exchange. While not trying to adjudicate the technical debate, we are aware of it and wish to raise a series of questions which challenge the actual meaning of "limited" in this discussion.

–Would leaders have sufficient information to know what is happening in a nuclear exchange?

–Would they be able under the conditions of stress, time pressures, and fragmentary information to make the extraordinarily precise decision needed to keep the exchange limited if this were technically possible?

–Would military commanders be able, in the midst of the destruction and confusion of a nuclear exchange, to maintain a policy of "discriminate targeting"? Can this be done in modern warfare, waged across great distances by aircraft and missiles?

–Given the accidents we know about in peacetime conditions, what assurances are there that computer errors could be avoided in the midst of a nuclear exchange?

–Would not the casualties, even in a war defined as limited by strategists, still run in the millions?

–How "limited" would be the long-term effects of radiation, famine, social fragmentation, and economic dislocation?

159. Unless these questions can be answered satisfactorily, we will continue to be highly skeptical about the real meaning of "limited." One of the cri-

teria of the just-war tradition is a reasonable hope of success in bringing about justice and peace. We must ask whether such a reasonable hope can exist once nuclear weapons have been exchanged. The burden of proof remains on those who assert that meaningful limitation is possible.

160. A nuclear response to either conventional or nuclear attack can cause destruction which goes far beyond "legitimate defense." Such use of nuclear weapons would not be justified.

161. In the face of this frightening and highly speculative debate on a matter involving millions of human lives, we believe the most effective contribution of moral judgment is to introduce perspectives by which we can assess the empirical debate. Moral perspective should be sensitive not only to the quantitative dimensions of a question but to its psychological, human, and religious characteristics as well. The issue of limited war is not simply the size of weapons contemplated or the strategies projected. The debate should include the psychological and political significance of crossing the boundary from the conventional to the nuclear arena in any form. To cross this divide is to enter a world where we have no experience of control, much testimony against its possibility, and therefore no moral justification for submitting the human community to this risk.[70] We therefore express our view that the first imperative is to prevent any use of nuclear weapons and our hope that leaders will resist the notion that nuclear conflict can be limited, contained, or won in any traditional sense.

D. Deterrence in Principle and Practice

162. The moral challenge posed by nuclear weapons is not exhausted by an analysis of their possible uses. Much of the political and moral debate of the nuclear age has concerned the strategy of deterrence. Deterrence is at the heart of the U.S.-Soviet relationship, currently the most dangerous dimension of the nuclear arms race.

1. The Concept and Development of Deterrence Policy

163. The concept of deterrence existed in military strategy long before the nuclear age, but it has taken on a new meaning and significance since 1945. Essentially, deterrence means "dissuasion of a potential adversary from initiating an attack or conflict, often by the threat of unacceptable retaliatory damage."[71] In the nuclear age, deterrence has become the centerpiece of both U.S. and Soviet policy. Both superpowers have for many years now been able to promise a retaliatory response which can inflict "unacceptable damage." A situation of stable deterrence depends on the ability of each side to deploy its retaliatory forces in ways that are not vulnerable to an attack (i.e., protected against a "first strike"); preserving stability requires a willingness by both sides to refrain from deploying weapons which appear to have a first strike capability.

164. This general definition of deterrence does not explain either the elements of a deterrence strategy or the evolution of deterrence policy since 1945. A detailed description of either of these subjects would require an extensive essay, using materials which can be found in abundance in the technical literature on the subject of deterrence.[72] Particularly significant is the relationship between "declaratory policy" (the public explanation of our strategic intentions and capabilities) and "action policy" (the actual planning and targeting policies to be followed in a nuclear attack).

165. The evolution of deterrence strategy has passed through several stages of declaratory policy. Using the U.S. case as an example, there is a significant difference between "massive retaliation" and "flexible response," and between "mutual assured destruction" and "countervailing strategy." It is also possible to distinguish between "counterforce" and "countervalue" targeting policies, and to contrast a posture of "minimum deterrence" with "extended deterrence." These terms are well known in the technical debate on nuclear policy; they are less well known and sometimes loosely used in the wider public debate. It is important to recognize that there has been substantial continuity in U.S. action policy in spite of real changes in declaratory policy.[73]

166. The recognition of these different elements in the deterrent and the evolution of policy means that moral assessment of deterrence requires a series of distinct judgments. They include: an analysis of *the factual character* of the deterrent (e.g., what is involved in targeting doctrine); analysis of the *historical development* of the policy (e.g., whether changes have occurred which are significant for moral analysis of the policy); the relationship of deterrence policy and other aspects of *U.S.-Soviet affairs*; and determination of the key *moral questions* involved in deterrence policy.

2. *The Moral Assessment of Deterrence*

167. The distinctively new dimensions of nuclear deterrence were recognized by policymakers and strategists only after much reflection. Similarly, the moral challenge posed by nuclear deterrence was grasped only after careful deliberation. The moral and political paradox posed by deterrence was concisely stated by Vatican II:

> Undoubtedly, armaments are not amassed merely for use in wartime. Since the defensive strength of any nation is thought to depend on its capacity for immediate retaliation, the stockpiling of arms which grows from year to year serves, in a way hitherto unthought of, as a deterrent to potential attackers. Many people look upon this as the most effective way known at the present time for maintaining some sort of peace among nations. Whatever one may think of this form of deterrent, people are convinced that the arms race, which quite a few countries have entered, is no infallible way of maintaining real peace and that the resulting so-called balance of power is no sure genuine path to achieving it.

> Rather than eliminate the causes of war, the arms race serves only to aggravate the position. As long as extravagant sums of money are poured into the development of new weapons, it is impossible to devote adequate aid in tackling the misery which prevails at the present day in the world. Instead of eradicating international conflict once and for all, the contagion is spreading to other parts of the world. New approaches, based on reformed attitudes, will have to be chosen in order to remove this stumbling block, to free the earth from its pressing anxieties, and give back to the world a genuine peace.[74]

168. Without making a specific moral judgment on deterrence, the Council clearly designated the elements of the arms race: the tension between "peace of a sort" preserved by deterrence and "genuine peace" required for a stable international life; the contradiction between what is spent for destructive capacity and what is needed for constructive development.

169. In the post-conciliar assessment of war and peace, and specifically of deterrence, different parties to the political-moral debate within the Church and in civil society have focused on one aspect or another of the problem. For some, the fact that nuclear weapons have not been used since 1945 means that deterrence has worked, and this fact satisfies the demands of both the political and the moral order. Others contest this assessment by highlighting the risk of failure involved in continued reliance on deterrence and pointing out how politically and morally catastrophic even a single failure would be. Still others note that the absence of nuclear war is not necessarily proof that the policy of deterrence has prevented it. Indeed, some would find in the policy of deterrence the driving force in the superpower arms race. Still other observers, many of them Catholic moralists, have stressed that deterrence may not morally include the intention of deliberately attacking civilian populations or noncombatants.

170. The statements of the NCCB/USCC over the past several years have both reflected and contributed to the wider moral debate on deterrence. In the NCCB pastoral letter, *To Live In Christ Jesus* (1976), we focused on the moral limits of declaratory policy while calling for stronger measures of arms control.[75] In 1979 John Cardinal Krol, speaking for the USCC in support of SALT II ratification, brought into focus the other element of the deterrence problem: the actual use of nuclear weapons may have been prevented (a moral good), but the risk of failure and the physical harm and moral evil resulting from possible nuclear war remained. "This explains," Cardinal Krol stated, "the Catholic dissatisfaction with nuclear deterrence and the urgency of the Catholic demand that the nuclear arms race be reversed. It is of the utmost importance that negotiations proceed to meaningful and continuing reductions in nuclear stockpiles, and eventually to the phasing out altogether of nuclear deterrence and the threat of mutual-assured destruction."[76]

171. These two texts, along with the conciliar statement, have influenced much of Catholic opinion expressed recently on the nuclear question.

172. In June 1982, Pope John Paul II provided new impetus and insight to the moral analysis with his statement to the United Nations Second Special Session on Disarmament. The pope first situated the problem of deterrence within the context of world politics. No power, he observes, will admit to wishing to start a war, but each distrusts others and considers it necessary to mount a strong defense against attack. He then discusses the notion of deterrence:

> Many even think that such preparations constitute the way—even the only way—to safeguard peace in some fashion or at least to impede to the utmost in an efficacious way the outbreak of wars, especially major conflicts which might lead to the ultimate holocaust of humanity and the destruction of the civilization that man has constructed so laboriously over the centuries.
>
> In this approach one can see the "philosophy" of peace which was proclaimed in the ancient Roman principle: *Si vis pacem, para bellum.* Put in modern terms, this "philosophy" has the label of "deterrence" and one can find it in various guises of the search for a "balance of forces" which sometimes has been called, and not without reason, the "balance of terror."[77]

173. Having offered this analysis of the general concept of deterrence, the Holy Father introduces his considerations on disarmament, especially, but not only, nuclear disarmament. Pope John Paul II makes this statement about the morality of deterrence:

> In current conditions "deterrence" based on balance, certainly not as an end in itself but as a step on the way toward a progressive disarmament, may still be judged morally acceptable. Nonetheless, in order to ensure peace, it is indispensable not to be satisfied with this minimum which is always susceptible to the real danger of explosion.[78]

174. In Pope John Paul II's assessment we perceive two dimensions of the contemporary dilemma of deterrence. One dimension is the danger of nuclear war, with its human and moral costs. The possession of nuclear weapons, the continuing quantitative growth of the arms race, and the danger of nuclear proliferation all point to the grave danger of basing "peace of a sort" on deterrence. The other dimension is the independence and freedom of nations and entire peoples, including the need to protect smaller nations from threats to their independence and integrity. Deterrence reflects the radical distrust which marks international politics, a condition identified as a major problem by Pope John XXIII in *Peace on Earth* and reaf-

firmed by Pope Paul VI and Pope John Paul II. Thus a balance of forces, preventing either side from achieving superiority, can be seen as a means of safeguarding both dimensions.

175. The moral duty today is to prevent nuclear war from ever occurring *and* to protect and preserve those key values of justice, freedom and independence which are necessary for personal dignity and national integrity. In reference to these issues, Pope John Paul II judges that deterrence may still be judged morally acceptable, "certainly not as an end in itself but as a step on the way toward a progressive disarmament."

176. On more than one occasion the Holy Father has demonstrated his awareness of the fragility and complexity of the deterrence relationship among nations. Speaking to UNESCO in June 1980, he said:

> Up to the present, we are told that nuclear arms are a force of dissuasion which have prevented the eruption of a major war. And that is probably true. Still, we must ask if it will always be this way.[79]

In a more recent and more specific assessment Pope John Paul II told an international meeting of scientists on August 23, 1982:

> You can more easily ascertain that the logic of nuclear deterrence cannot be considered a final goal or an appropriate and secure means for safeguarding international peace.[80]

177. Relating Pope John Paul's general statements to the specific policies of the U.S. deterrent requires both judgments of fact and an application of moral principles. In preparing this letter we have tried, through a number of sources, to determine as precisely as possible the factual character of U.S. deterrence strategy. Two questions have particularly concerned us: 1) the targeting doctrine and strategic plans for the use of the deterrent, particularly their impact on civilian casualties; and 2) the relationship of deterrence strategy and nuclear war-fighting capability to the likelihood that war will in fact be prevented.

MORAL PRINCIPLES AND POLICY CHOICES

178. Targeting doctrine raises significant moral questions because it is a significant determinant of what would occur if nuclear weapons were ever to be used. Although we acknowledge the need for deterrence, not all forms of deterrence are morally acceptable. There are moral limits to deterrence policy as well as to policy regarding use. Specifically, it is not morally acceptable to intend to kill the innocent as part of a strategy of deterring nuclear war. The question of whether U.S. policy involves an intention to strike civilian centers (directly targeting civilian populations) has been one of our factual concerns.

179. This complex question has always produced a variety of responses, official and unofficial in character. The NCCB Committee has received a series of statements of clarification of policy from U.S. government officials.[81] Essentially these statements declare that it is not U.S. strategic policy to target the Soviet civilian population as such or to use nuclear weapons deliberately for the purpose of destroying population centers. These statements respond, in principle at least, to one moral criterion for assessing deterrence policy: the immunity of noncombatants from direct attack either by conventional or nuclear weapons.

180. These statements do not address or resolve another very troublesome moral problem, namely, that an attack on military targets or militarily significant industrial targets could involve "indirect" (i.e., unintended) but massive civilian casualties. We are advised, for example, that the United States strategic nuclear targeting plan (SIOP—Single Integrated Operational Plan) has identified 60 "military" targets within the city of Moscow alone, and that 40,000 "military" targets for nuclear weapons have been identified in the whole of the Soviet Union.[82] It is important to recognize that Soviet policy is subject to the same moral judgment; attacks on several "industrial targets" or politically significant targets in the United States could produce massive civilian casualties. The number of civilians who would necessarily be killed by such strikes is horrendous.[83] This problem is unavoidable because of the way modern military facilities and production centers are so thoroughly interspersed with civilian living and working areas. It is aggravated if one side deliberately positions military targets in the midst of a civilian population. In our consultations, administration officials readily admitted that, while they hoped any nuclear exchange could be kept limited, they were prepared to retaliate in a massive way if necessary. They also agreed that once any substantial numbers of weapons were used, the civilian casualty levels would quickly become truly catastrophic, and that even with attacks limited to "military" targets, the number of deaths in a substantial exchange would be almost indistinguishable from what might occur if civilian centers had been deliberately and directly struck. These possibilities pose a different moral question and are to be judged by a different moral criterion: the principle of proportionality.

181. While any judgment of proportionality is always open to differing evaluations, there are actions which can be decisively judged to be disproportionate. A narrow adherence exclusively to the principle of noncombatant immunity as a criterion for policy is an inadequate moral posture for it ignores some evil and unacceptable consequences. Hence, we cannot be satisfied that the assertion of an intention not to strike civilians directly, or even the most honest effort to implement that intention, by itself constitutes a "moral policy" for the use of nuclear weapons.

182. The location of industrial or militarily significant economic targets within heavily populated areas or in those areas affected by radioactive fallout could well involve such massive civilian casualties that, in our judgment, such

a strike would be deemed morally disproportionate, even though not intentionally indiscriminate.

183. The problem is not simply one of producing highly accurate weapons that might minimize civilian casualties in any single explosion, but one of increasing the likelihood of escalation at a level where many, even "discriminating," weapons would cumulatively kill very large numbers of civilians. Those civilian deaths would occur both immediately and from the long-term effects of social and economic devastation.

184. A second issue of concern to us is the relationship of deterrence doctrine to war-fighting strategies. We are aware of the argument that war-fighting capabilities enhance the credibility of the deterrent, particularly the strategy of extended deterrence. But the development of such capabilities raises other strategic and moral questions. The relationship of war-fighting capabilities and targeting doctrine exemplifies the difficult choices in this area of policy. Targeting civilian populations would violate the principle of discrimination—one of the central moral principles of a Christian ethic of war. But "counterforce targeting," while preferable from the perspective of protecting civilians, is often joined with a declaratory policy which conveys the notion that nuclear war is subject to precise rational and moral limits. We have already expressed our severe doubts about such a concept. Furthermore, a purely counterforce strategy may seem to threaten the viability of other nations' retaliatory forces making deterrence unstable in a crisis and war more likely.

185. While we welcome any effort to protect civilian populations, we do not want to legitimize or encourage moves which extend deterrence beyond the specific objective of preventing the use of nuclear weapons or other actions which could lead directly to a nuclear exchange.

186. These considerations of concrete elements of nuclear deterrence policy, made in light of John Paul II's evaluation, but applying it through our own prudential judgments, lead us to a strictly conditioned moral acceptance of nuclear deterrence. We cannot consider it adequate as a long-term basis for peace.

187. This strictly conditioned judgment yields *criteria* for morally assessing the elements of deterrence strategy. Clearly, these criteria demonstrate that we cannot approve of every weapons system, strategic doctrine, or policy initiative advanced in the name of strengthening deterrence. On the contrary, these criteria require continual public scrutiny of what our government proposes to do with the deterrent.

188. *On the basis of these criteria we wish now to make some specific evaluations*:

1) If nuclear deterrence exists only to prevent the *use* of nuclear weapons by others, then proposals to go beyond this to planning for prolonged periods of repeated nuclear strikes and counter-strikes, or "prevailing" in nuclear war, are not acceptable. They encourage notions that nuclear war can be engaged in with tolerable human and moral consequences. Rather, we must continually say "no" to the idea of nuclear war.

2) If nuclear deterrence is our goal, "sufficiency" to deter is an adequate strategy; the quest for nuclear superiority must be rejected.

3) Nuclear deterrence should be used as a step on the way toward progressive disarmament. Each proposed addition to our strategic system or change in strategic doctrine must be assessed precisely in light of whether it will render steps toward "progressive disarmament" more or less likely.

189. Moreover, these criteria provide us with the means to make some judgments and recommendations about the recent direction of U.S. strategic policy. Progress toward a world freed of dependence on nuclear deterrence must be carefully carried out. But it must not be delayed. There is an urgent moral and political responsibility to use the "peace of a sort" we have as a framework to move toward authentic peace through nuclear arms control, reductions, and disarmament. Of primary importance in this process is the need to prevent the development and deployment of destabilizing weapons systems on either side; a second requirement is to insure that the more sophisticated command and control systems do not become mere hair triggers for automatic launch on warning; a third is the need to prevent the proliferation of nuclear weapons in the international system.

190. In light of these general judgments *we oppose* some specific proposals in respect to our present deterrence posture:

1) The addition of weapons which are likely to be vulnerable to attack, yet also possess a "prompt hard-target kill" capability that threatens to make the other side's retaliatory forces vulnerable. Such weapons may seem to be useful primarily in a first strike;[84] we resist such weapons for this reason and we oppose Soviet deployment of such weapons which generate fear of a first strike against U.S. forces.

2) The willingness to foster strategic planning which seeks a nuclear war-fighting capability that goes beyond the limited function of deterrence outlined in this letter.

3) Proposals which have the effect of lowering the nuclear threshold and blurring the difference between nuclear and conventional weapons.

191. In support of the concept of "sufficiency" as an adequate deterrent, and in light of the present size and composition of both the U.S. and Soviet strategic arsenals, *we recommend*:

1) Support for immediate, bilateral, verifiable agreements to halt the testing, production, and deployment of new nuclear weapons systems.[85]

2) Support for negotiated bilateral deep cuts in the arsenals of both superpowers, particularly those weapons systems which have destabilizing characteristics; U.S. proposals like those for START (Strategic Arms Reduction Talks) and INF (Intermediate-range Nuclear Forces) negotiations in Geneva are said to be designed to achieve deep cuts;[86] our hope is that they will be pursued in a manner which will realize these goals.

3) Support for early and successful conclusion of negotiations of a comprehensive test ban treaty.

4) Removal by all parties of short-range nuclear weapons which multiply dangers disproportionate to their deterrent value.

5) Removal by all parties of nuclear weapons from areas where they are likely to be overrun in the early stages of war, thus forcing rapid and uncontrollable decisions on their use.

6) Strengthening of command and control over nuclear weapons to prevent inadvertent and unauthorized use.

192. These judgments are meant to exemplify how a lack of unequivocal condemnation of deterrence is meant only to be an attempt to acknowledge the role attributed to deterrence, but not to support its extension beyond the limited purpose discussed above. Some have urged us to condemn all aspects of nuclear deterrence. This urging has been based on a variety of reasons, but has emphasized particularly the high and terrible risks that either deliberate use or accidental detonation of nuclear weapons could quickly escalate to something utterly disproportionate to any acceptable moral purpose. That determination requires highly technical judgments about hypothetical events. Although reasons exist which move some to condemn reliance on nuclear weapons for deterrence, we have not reached this conclusion for the reasons outlined in this letter.

193. Nevertheless, there must be no misunderstanding of our profound skepticism about the moral acceptability of any use of nuclear weapons. It is obvious that the use of any weapons which violate the principle of discrimination merits unequivocal condemnation. We are told that some weapons are designed for purely "counterforce" use against military forces and targets. The moral issue, however, is not resolved by the design of weapons or the planned intention for use; there are also consequences which must be assessed. It would be a perverted political policy or moral casuistry which tried to justify using a weapon which "indirectly" or "unintentionally" killed a million innocent people because they happened to live near a "militarily significant target."

194. Even the "indirect effects" of initiating nuclear war are sufficient to make it an unjustifiable moral risk in any form. It is not sufficient, for example, to contend that "our" side has plans for "limited" or "discriminate" use. Modern warfare is not readily contained by good intentions or technological designs. The psychological climate of the world is such that mention of the term "nuclear" generates uneasiness. Many contend that the use of one tactical nuclear weapon could produce panic, with completely unpredictable consequences. It is precisely this mix of political, psychological, and technological uncertainty which has moved us in this letter to reinforce with moral prohibitions and prescriptions the prevailing political barrier against resort to nuclear weapons. Our support for enhanced command and control facilities, for major reductions in strategic and tactical nuclear forces, and for a "no first use" policy (as set forth in this letter) is meant to be seen as a complement to our desire to draw a moral line against nuclear war.

195. Any claim by any government that it is pursuing a morally acceptable policy of deterrence must be scrutinized with the greatest care. We are prepared and eager to participate in our country in the ongoing public debate on moral grounds.

196. The need to rethink the deterrence policy of our nation, to make the revisions necessary to reduce the possibility of nuclear war, and to move toward a more stable system of national and international security will demand a substantial intellectual, political, and moral effort. It also will require, we believe, the willingness to open ourselves to the providential care, power and word of God, which call us to recognize our common humanity and the bonds of mutual responsibility which exist in the international community in spite of political differences and nuclear arsenals.

197. Indeed, we do acknowledge that there are many strong voices within our own episcopal ranks and within the wider Catholic community in the United States which challenge the strategy of deterrence as an adequate response to the arms race today. They highlight the historical evidence that deterrence has not, in fact, set in motion substantial processes of disarmament.

198. Moreover, these voices rightly raise the concern that even the conditional acceptance of nuclear deterrence as laid out in a letter such as this might be inappropriately used by some to reinforce the policy of arms buildup. In its stead, they call us to raise a prophetic challenge to the community of faith—a challenge which goes beyond nuclear deterrence, toward more resolute steps to actual bilateral disarmament and peacemaking. We recognize the intellectual ground on which the argument is built and the religious sensibility which gives it its strong force.

199. The dangers of the nuclear age and the enormous difficulties we face in moving toward a more adequate system of global security, stability, and justice require steps beyond our present conceptions of security and defense policy. In the following section we propose a series of steps aimed at a more adequate policy for preserving peace in a nuclear world.

III. THE PROMOTION OF PEACE: PROPOSALS AND POLICIES

200. In a world which is not yet the fulfillment of God's Kingdom, a world where both personal actions and social forces manifest the continuing influence of sin and disorder among us, consistent attention must be paid to preventing and limiting the violence of war. But this task, addressed extensively in the previous section of this letter, does not exhaust Catholic teaching on war and peace. A complementary theme, reflected in the Scriptures and the theology of the Church and significantly developed by papal teaching in this century, is the building of peace as the way to prevent war. This

traditional theme was vividly reasserted by Pope John Paul in his homily at Coventry Cathedral:

> Peace is not just the absence of war. It involves mutual respect and confidence between peoples and nations. It involves collaboration and binding agreements. Like a cathedral, peace must be constructed patiently and with unshakable faith.[87]

201. This positive conception of peacemaking profoundly influences many people in our time. At the beginning of this letter we affirmed the need for a more fully developed theology of peace. The basis of such a theology is found in the papal teaching of this century. In this section of our pastoral we wish to illustrate how the positive vision of peace contained in Catholic teaching provides direction for policy and personal choices.

A. Specific Steps to Reduce the Danger of War

202. The dangers of modern war are specific and visible; our teaching must be equally specific about the needs of peace. Effective arms control leading to mutual disarmament, ratification of pending treaties,[88] development of nonviolent alternatives, are but some of the recommendations we would place before the Catholic community and all men and women of good will. These should be part of a foreign policy which recognizes and respects the claims of citizens of every nation to the same inalienable rights we treasure, and seeks to ensure an international security based on the awareness that the creator has provided this world and all its resources for the sustenance and benefit of the entire human family. The truth that the globe is inhabited by a single family in which all have the same basic needs and all have a right to the goods of the earth is a fundamental principle of Catholic teaching which we believe to be of increasing importance today. In an interdependent world all need to affirm their common nature and destiny; such a perspective should inform our policy vision and negotiating posture in pursuit of peace today.

1. Accelerated Work for Arms Control, Reduction, and Disarmament

203. Despite serious efforts, starting with the Baruch plans and continuing through SALT I and SALT II, the results have been far too limited and partial to be commensurate with the risks of nuclear war. Yet efforts for negotiated control and reduction of arms must continue. In his 1982 address to the United Nations, Pope John Paul II left no doubt about the importance of these efforts:

> Today once again before you all I reaffirm my confidence in the power of true negotiations to arrive at just and equitable solutions.[89]

204. In this same spirit, we urge negotiations to halt the testing, production, and deployment of new nuclear weapons systems. Not only should steps be taken to end development and deployment, but the numbers of existing weapons must be reduced in a manner which lessens the danger of war.

205. Arms control and disarmament must be a process of verifiable agreements especially between two superpowers. While we do not advocate a policy of unilateral disarmament, we believe the urgent need for control of the arms race requires a willingness for each side to take some first steps. The United States has already taken a number of important independent initiatives to reduce some of the gravest dangers and to encourage a constructive Soviet response; additional initiatives are encouraged. By independent initiatives we mean carefully chosen limited steps which the United States could take for a defined period of time, seeking to elicit a comparable step from the Soviet Union. If an appropriate response is not forthcoming, the United States would no longer be bound by steps taken. Our country has previously taken calculated risks in favor of freedom and of human values; these have included independent steps taken to reduce some of the gravest dangers of nuclear war.[90] Certain risks are required today to help free the world from bondage to nuclear deterrence and the risk of nuclear war. Both sides, for example, have an interest in avoiding deployment of destabilizing weapons systems.

206. There is some history of successful independent initiatives which have beneficially influenced the arms race without a formal public agreement. In 1963 President Kennedy announced that the United States would unilaterally forgo further nuclear testing; the next month Soviet Premier Nikita Khrushchev proposed a limited test ban which eventually became the basis of the U.S.-Soviet partial test ban treaty. Subsequently, both superpowers removed about 10,000 troops from Central Europe and each announced a cut in production of nuclear material for weapons.

207. a) Negotiation on arms control agreements in isolation, without persistent and parallel efforts to reduce the political tensions which motivate the buildup of armaments, will not suffice. The United States should therefore have a continuing policy of maximum political engagement with governments of potential adversaries, providing for repeated, systematic discussion and negotiation of areas of friction. This policy should be carried out by a system of periodic, carefully prepared meetings at several levels of government, including summit meetings at regular intervals. Such channels of discussion are too important to be regarded by either of the major powers as a concession or an event made dependent on daily shifts in international developments.

208. b) The Nuclear Non-Proliferation Treaty of 1968 (NPT) acknowledged that the spread of nuclear weapons to hitherto non-nuclear states (horizontal proliferation) could hardly be prevented in the long run in the absence of serious efforts by the nuclear states to control and reduce their own nuclear arsenals (vertical proliferation). Article VI of the NPT pledged the super-

powers to serious efforts to control and to reduce their own nuclear arsenals; unfortunately, this promise has not been kept. Moreover, the multinational controls envisaged in the treaty seem to have been gradually relaxed by the states exporting fissionable materials for the production of energy. If these tendencies are not constrained, the treaty may eventually lose its symbolic and practical effectiveness. For this reason the United States should, in concert with other nuclear exporting states, seriously reexamine its policies and programs and make clear its determination to uphold the spirit as well as the letter of the treaty.

2. Continued Insistence on Efforts to Minimize the Risk of Any War

209. While it is right and proper that priority be given to reducing and ultimately eliminating the likelihood of nuclear war, this does not of itself remove the threat of other forms of warfare. Indeed, negotiated reduction in nuclear weapons available to the superpowers could conceivably increase the danger of non-nuclear wars.

210. a) Because of this we strongly support negotiations aimed at reducing and limiting conventional forces and at building confidence between possible adversaries, especially in regions of potential military confrontations. We urge that prohibitions outlawing the production and use of chemical and biological weapons be reaffirmed and observed. Arms control negotiations must take account of the possibility that conventional conflict could trigger the nuclear confrontation the world must avoid.

211. b) Unfortunately, as is the case with nuclear proliferation, we are witnessing a relaxation of restraints in the international commerce in conventional arms. Sales of increasingly sophisticated military aircraft, missiles, tanks, antitank weapons, antipersonnel bombs, and other systems by the major supplying countries (especially the Soviet Union, the United States, France, and Great Britain) have reached unprecedented levels.

212. Pope John Paul II took specific note of the problem in his U.N. address:

> The production and sale of conventional weapons throughout the world is a truly alarming and evidently growing phenomenon. . . . Moreover the traffic in these weapons seems to be developing at an increasing rate and seems to be directed most of all toward developing countries.[91]

213. It is a tragic fact that U.S. arms sales policies in the last decade have contributed significantly to the trend the Holy Father deplores. We call for a reversal of this course. The United States should renew earlier efforts to develop multilateral controls on arms exports, and should in this case also be willing to take carefully chosen independent initiatives to restrain the arms trade. Such steps would be particularly appropriate where the receiving government faces charges of gross and systematic human rights violations.[92]

214. c) Nations must accept a limited view of those interests justifying military force. True self-defense may include the protection of weaker states, but does not include seizing the possessions of others, or the domination of other states or peoples. We should remember the caution of Pope John Paul II: "In alleging the threat of a potential enemy, is it really not rather the intention to keep for itself a means of threat, in order to get the upper hand with the aid of one's own arsenal of destruction?"[93] Central to a moral theory of force is the principle that it must be a last resort taken only when *all* other means of redress have been exhausted. Equally important in the age of modern warfare is the recognition that the justifiable reasons for using force have been restricted to instances of self-defense or defense of others under attack.

3. The Relationship of Nuclear and Conventional Defenses

215. The strong position we have taken against the use of nuclear weapons, and particularly the stand against the initiation of nuclear war in any form, calls for further clarification of our view of the requirements for conventional defense.

216. Nuclear threats have often come to take the place of efforts to deter or defend against non-nuclear attack with weapons that are themselves non-nuclear, particularly in the NATO-Warsaw Pact confrontation. Many analysts conclude that, in the absence of nuclear deterrent threats, more troops and conventional (non-nuclear) weapons would be required to protect our allies. Rejection of some forms of nuclear deterrence could therefore conceivably require a willingness to pay higher costs to develop conventional forces. Leaders and peoples of other nations might also have to accept higher costs for their own defense, particularly in Western Europe, if the threat to use nuclear weapons first were withdrawn. We cannot judge the strength of these arguments in particular cases. It may well be that some strengthening of conventional defense would be a proportionate price to pay, if this will reduce the possibility of a nuclear war. We acknowledge this reluctantly, aware as we are of the vast amount of scarce resources expended annually on instruments of defense in a world filled with other urgent, unmet human needs.

217. It is not for us to settle the technical debate about policy and budgets. From the perspective of a developing theology of peace, however, we feel obliged to contribute a moral dimension to the discussion. We hope that a significant reduction in numbers of conventional arms and weaponry would go hand in hand with diminishing reliance on nuclear deterrence. The history of recent wars (even so-called "minor" or "limited" wars) has shown that conventional war can also become indiscriminate in conduct and disproportionate to any valid purpose. We do not want in any way to give encouragement to a notion of "making the world safe for conventional war," which introduces its own horrors.

218. Hence, we believe that any program directed at reducing reliance on nuclear weapons is not likely to succeed unless it includes measures to reduce

tensions, and to work for the balanced reduction of conventional forces. We believe that important possibilities exist which, if energetically pursued, would ensure against building up conventional forces as a concomitant of reductions in nuclear weapons. Examples are to be found in the ongoing negotiations for mutual balanced force reductions, the prospects for which are certainly not dim and would be enhanced by agreements on strategic weapons, and in the confidence-building measures still envisaged under the Helsinki agreement and review conference.

219. We must re-emphasize with all our being, nonetheless, that it is not only nuclear war that must be prevented, but war itself. Therefore, with Pope John Paul II we declare:

> Today, the scale and the horror of modern warfare—whether nuclear or not—makes it totally unacceptable as a means of settling differences between nations. War should belong to the tragic past, to history, it should find no place on humanity's agenda for the future.[94]

Reason and experience tell us that a continuing upward spiral, even in conventional arms, coupled with an unbridled increase in armed forces, instead of securing true peace will almost certainly be provocative of war.

4. *Civil Defense*

220. Attention must be given to existing programs for civil defense against nuclear attack, including blast and fall-out shelters and relocation plans. It is unclear in the public mind whether these are intended to offer significant protection against at least some forms of nuclear attack or are being put into place to enhance the credibility of the strategic deterrent forces by demonstrating an ability to survive attack. This confusion has led to public skepticism and even ridicule of the program and casts doubt on the credibility of the government. An independent commission of scientists, engineers, and weapons experts is needed to examine if these or any other plans offer a realistic prospect of survival for the nation's population or its cherished values, which a nuclear war would presumably be fought to preserve.

5. *Efforts to Develop Nonviolent Means of Conflict Resolution*

221. We affirm a nation's right to defend itself, its citizens, and its values. Security is the right of all, but that right, like everything else, must be subject to divine law and the limits defined by that law. We must find means of defending peoples that do not depend upon the threat of annihilation. Immoral means can never be justified by the end sought; no objective, however worthy of good in itself, can justify sinful acts or policies. Though our primary concern through this statement is war and the nuclear threat, these principles apply as well to all forms of violence, including insurgency, counterinsurgency, "destabilization," and the like.

222. a) The Second Vatican Council praised "those who renounce the use of violence in the vindication of their rights and who resort to methods of defense which are otherwise available to weaker parties provided that this can be done without injury to the rights and duties of others or of the community itself."[95] To make such renunciation effective and still defend what must be defended, the arts of diplomacy, negotiation, and compromise must be developed and fully exercised. Nonviolent means of resistance to evil deserve much more study and consideration than they have thus far received. There have been significant instances in which people have successfully resisted oppression without recourse to arms.[96] Nonviolence is not the way of the weak, the cowardly, or the impatient. Such movements have seldom gained headlines, even though they have left their mark on history. The heroic Danes who would not turn Jews over to the Nazis and the Norwegians who would not teach Nazi propaganda in schools serve as inspiring examples in the history of nonviolence.

223. Nonviolent resistance, like war, can take many forms depending upon the demands of a given situation. There is, for instance, organized popular defense instituted by government as part of its contingency planning. Citizens would be trained in the techniques of peaceable noncompliance and noncooperation as a means of hindering an invading force or nondemocratic government from imposing its will. Effective nonviolent resistance requires the united will of a people and may demand as much patience and sacrifice from those who practice it as is now demanded by war and preparation for war. It may not always succeed. Nevertheless, before the possibility is dismissed as impractical or unrealistic, we urge that it be measured against the almost certain effects of a major war.

224. b) Nonviolent resistance offers a common ground of agreement for those individuals who choose the option of Christian pacifism even to the point of accepting the need to die rather than to kill, and those who choose the option of lethal force allowed by the theology of just war. Nonviolent resistance makes clear that both are able to be committed to the same objective: defense of their country.

225. c) Popular defense would go beyond conflict resolution and compromise to a basic synthesis of beliefs and values. In its practice, the objective is not only to avoid causing harm or injury to another creature, but, more positively, to seek the good of the other. Blunting the aggression of an adversary or oppressor would not be enough. The goal is winning the other over, making the adversary a friend.

226. It is useful to point out that these principles are thoroughly compatible with—and to some extent derived from Christian teachings and must be part of any Christian theology of peace. Spiritual writers have helped trace the theory of nonviolence to its roots in Scripture and tradition and have illustrated its practice and success in their studies of the church fathers and the age of martyrs. Christ's own teachings and example provide a model way of life incorporating the truth, and a refusal to return evil for evil.

227. Nonviolent popular defense does not ensure that lives would not be lost. Nevertheless, once we recognize that the almost certain consequences of existing policies and strategies of war carry with them a very real threat to the future existence of humankind itself, practical reason as well as spiritual faith demand that it be given serious consideration as an alternative course of action.

228. d) Once again we declare that the only true defense for the world's population is the rejection of nuclear war and the conventional wars which could escalate into nuclear war. With Pope John Paul II, we call upon educational and research institutes to take a lead in conducting peace studies: "Scientific studies on war, its nature, causes, means, objectives, and risks have much to teach us on the conditions for peace . . ."[97] To achieve this end, we urge that funds equivalent to a designated percentage (even one-tenth of one percent) of current budgetary allotments for military purposes be set aside to support such peace research.

229. In 1981, the Commission on Proposals for the National Academy of Peace and Conflict Resolution recommended the establishment of the U.S. Academy of Peace, a recommendation nearly as old as this country's constitution. The commission found that "peace is a legitimate field of learning that encompasses rigorous, interdisciplinary research, education, and training directed toward peacemaking expertise."[98] We endorse the commission's recommendation and urge all citizens to support training in conflict resolution, nonviolent resistance, and programs devoted to service to peace and education for peace. Such an academy would not only provide a center for peace studies and activities, but also be a tangible evidence of our nation's sincerity in its often professed commitment to international peace and the abolition of war. We urge universities, particularly Catholic universities, in our country to develop programs for rigorous, interdisciplinary research, education, and training directed toward peacemaking expertise.

230. We, too, must be prepared to do our part to achieve these ends. We encourage churches and educational institutions, from primary schools to colleges and institutes of higher learning, to undertake similar programs at their own initiative. Every effort must be made to understand and evaluate the arms race, to encourage truly transnational perspectives on disarmament, and to explore new forms of international cooperation and exchange. No greater challenge or higher priority can be imagined than the development and perfection of a theology of peace suited to a civilization poised on the brink of self-destruction. It is our prayerful hope that this document will prove to be a starting point and inspiration for that endeavor.

6. The Role of Conscience

231. A dominant characteristic of the Second Vatican Council's evaluation of modern warfare was the stress it placed on the requirement for proper formation of conscience. Moral principles are effective restraints on power

only when policies reflect them and individuals practice them. The relationship of the authority of the state and the conscience of the individual on matters of war and peace takes a new urgency in the face of the destructive nature of modern war.

232. a) In this connection we reiterate the position we took in 1980. Catholic teaching does not question the right in principle of a government to require military service of its citizens provided the government shows it is necessary. A citizen may not casually disregard his country's conscientious decision to call its citizens to acts of "legitimate defense." Moreover, the role of Christian citizens in the armed forces is a service to the common good and an exercise of the virtue of patriotism, so long as they fulfill this role within defined moral norms.[99]

233. b) At the same time, no state may demand blind obedience. Our 1980 statement urged the government to present convincing reasons for draft registration, and opposed reinstitution of conscription itself except in the case of a national defense emergency. Moreover, it reiterated our support for conscientious objection in general and for selective conscientious objection to participation in a particular war, either because of the ends being pursued or the means being used. We called selective conscientious objection a moral conclusion which can be validly derived from the classical teaching of just-war principles. We continue to insist upon respect for and legislative protection of the rights of both classes of conscientious objectors. We also approve requiring alternative service to the community—not related to military needs—by such persons.

B. Shaping a Peaceful World

234. Preventing nuclear war is a moral imperative; but the avoidance of war, nuclear or conventional, is not a sufficient conception of international relations today. Nor does it exhaust the content of Catholic teaching. Both the political needs and the moral challenge of our time require a positive conception of peace, based on a vision of a just world order. Pope Paul VI summarized classical Catholic teaching in his encyclical, *The Development of Peoples*: "Peace cannot be limited to a mere absence of war, the result of an ever precarious balance of forces. No, peace is something built up day after day, in the pursuit of an order intended by God, which implies a more perfect form of justice among men and women."[100]

1. *World Order in Catholic Teaching*

235. This positive conception of peace sees it as the fruit of order; order, in turn, is shaped by the values of justice, truth, freedom and love. The basis of this teaching is found in sacred Scripture, St. Augustine and St. Thomas. It

has found contemporary expression and development in papal teaching of this century. The popes of the nuclear age, from Pius XII through John Paul II, have affirmed pursuit of international order as the way to banish the scourge of war from human affairs.[101]

236. The fundamental premise of world order in Catholic teaching is a theological truth: the unity of the human family—rooted in common creation, destined for the kingdom, and united by moral bonds of rights and duties. This basic truth about the unity of the human family pervades the entire teaching on war and peace: for the pacifist position it is one of the reasons why life cannot be taken, while for the just-war position, even in a justified conflict bonds of responsibility remain in spite of the conflict.

237. Catholic teaching recognizes that in modern history, at least since the Peace of Westphalia (1648), the international community has been governed by nation-states. Catholic moral theology, as expressed for example in chapters 2 and 3 of *Peace on Earth*, accords a real but relative moral value to sovereign states. The value is real because of the functions states fulfill as sources of order and authority in the political community; it is relative because boundaries of the sovereign state do not dissolve the deeper relationships of responsibility existing in the human community. Just as within nations the moral fabric of society is described in Catholic teaching in terms of reciprocal rights and duties—between individuals, and then between the individual and the state—so in the international community *Peace on Earth* defines the rights and duties which exist among states.[102]

238. In the past twenty years Catholic teaching has become increasingly specific about the content of these international rights and duties. In 1963, *Peace on Earth* sketched the political and legal order among states. In 1966, *The Development of Peoples* elaborated an order of economic rights and duties. In 1979, Pope John Paul II articulated the human rights basis of international relations in his "Address to the United Nations General Assembly."

239. These documents and others which build upon them, outlined a moral order of international relations, i.e., how the international community *should* be organized. At the same time this teaching has been sensitive to the actual pattern of relations prevailing among states. While not ignoring present geopolitical realities, one of the primary functions of Catholic teaching on world order has been to point the way toward a more integrated international system.

240. In analyzing this path toward world order, the category increasingly used in Catholic moral teaching (and, more recently, in the social sciences also) is the interdependence of the world today. The theological principle of unity has always affirmed a human interdependence; but today this bond is complemented by the growing political and economic interdependence of the world, manifested in a whole range of international issues.[103]

241. An important element missing from world order today is a properly constituted political authority with the capacity to shape our material

interdependence in the direction of moral interdependence. Pope John XXIII stated the case in the following way:

> Today the universal common good poses problems of world-wide dimensions, which cannot be adequately tackled or solved except by the efforts of public authority endowed with a wideness of powers, structure and means of the same proportions: that is, of public authority which is in a position to operate in an effective manner on a world-wide basis. The moral order itself, therefore, demands that such a form of public authority be established.[104]

242. Just as the nation-state was a step in the evolution of government at a time when expanding trade and new weapons technologies made the feudal system inadequate to manage conflicts and provide security, so we are now entering an era of new, global interdependencies requiring global systems of governance to manage the resulting conflicts and ensure our common security. Major global problems such as worldwide inflation, trade and payments deficits, competition over scarce resources, hunger, widespread unemployment, global environmental dangers, the growing power of transnational corporations, and the threat of international financial collapse, as well as the danger of world war resulting from these growing tensions cannot be remedied by a single nation-state approach. They shall require the concerted effort of the whole world community. As we shall indicate below, the United Nations should be particularly considered in this effort.

243. In the nuclear age, it is in the regulation of interstate conflicts and ultimately the replacement of military by negotiated solutions that the supreme importance and necessity of a moral as well as a political concept of the international common good can be grasped. The absence of adequate structures for addressing these issues places even greater responsibility on the policies of individual states. By a mix of political vision and moral wisdom, states are called to interpret the national interest in light of the larger global interest.

244. We are living in a global age with problems and conflicts on a global scale. Either we shall learn to resolve these problems together, or we shall destroy one another. Mutual security and survival require a new vision of the world as one interdependent planet. We have rights and duties not only within our diverse national communities but within the larger world community.

2. The Superpowers in a Disordered World

245. No relationship more dramatically demonstrates the fragile nature of order in international affairs today than that of the United States and the Soviet Union. These two sovereign states have avoided open war, nuclear or conventional, but they are divided by philosophy, ideology, and competing ambitions. Their competition is global in scope and involves everything from

comparing nuclear arsenals to printed propaganda. Both have been criticized in international meetings because of their policies in the nuclear arms race.[105]

246. In our 1980 pastoral letter on Marxism, we sought to portray the significant differences between Christian teaching and Marxism; at the same time we addressed the need for states with different political systems to live together in an interdependent world:

> The Church recognizes the depth and dimensions of the ideological differences that divide the human race, but the urgent practical need for cooperative efforts in the human interest overrules these differences. Hence Catholic teaching seeks to avoid exacerbating the ideological opposition and to focus upon the problems requiring common efforts across the ideological divide: keeping the peace and empowering the poor.[106]

247. We believe this passage reflects the teaching of *Peace on Earth*, the continuing call for dialogue of Pope Paul VI and the 1979 address of Pope John Paul II at the United Nations. We continue to stress this theme even while we recognize the difficulty of realizing its objectives.

248. The difficulties are particularly severe on the issue of the arms race. For most Americans, the danger of war is commonly defined primarily in terms of the threat of Soviet military expansionism and the consequent need to deter or defend against a Soviet military threat. Many assume that the existence of this threat is permanent and that nothing can be done about it except to build and maintain overwhelming or at least countervailing military power.[107]

249. The fact of a Soviet threat, as well as the existence of a Soviet imperial drive for hegemony, at least in regions of major strategic interest, cannot be denied. The history of the Cold War has produced varying interpretations of which side caused which conflict, but whatever the details of history illustrate, the plain fact is that the memories of Soviet policies in Eastern Europe and recent events in Afghanistan and Poland have left their mark in the American political debate. Many peoples are forcibly kept under communist domination despite their manifest wishes to be free. Soviet power is very great. Whether the Soviet Union's pursuit of military might is motivated primarily by defensive or aggressive aims might be debated, but the effect is nevertheless to leave profoundly insecure those who must live in the shadow of that might.

250. Americans need have no illusions about the Soviet system of repression and the lack of respect in that system for human rights, or about Soviet covert operations and pro-revolutionary activities. To be sure, our own system is not without flaws. Our government has sometimes supported repressive governments in the name of preserving freedom, has carried out repugnant covert operations of its own, and remains imperfect in its domestic record of

ensuring equal rights for all. At the same time, there is a difference. NATO is an alliance of democratic countries which have freely chosen their association; the Warsaw Pact is not.

251. To pretend that as a nation we have lived up to all our own ideals would be patently dishonest. To pretend that all evils in the world have been or are now being perpetrated by dictatorial regimes would be both dishonest and absurd. But having said this, and admitting our own faults, it is imperative that we confront reality. The facts simply do not support the invidious comparisons made at times, even in our own society, between our way of life, in which most basic human rights are at least recognized even if they are not always adequately supported, and those totalitarian and tyrannical regimes in which such rights are either denied or systematically suppressed. Insofar as this is true, however, it makes the promotion of human rights in our foreign policy, as well as our domestic policy, all the more important. It is the acid test of our commitment to our democratic values. In this light, any attempts to justify, for reasons of state, support for regimes that continue to violate human rights is all the more morally reprehensible in its hypocrisy.

252. A glory of the United States is the range of political freedoms its system permits us. We, as bishops, as Catholics, as citizens, exercise those freedoms in writing this letter, with its share of criticisms of our government. We have true freedom of religion, freedom of speech, and access to a free press. We could not exercise the same freedoms in contemporary Eastern Europe or in the Soviet Union. Free people must always pay a proportionate price and run some risks—responsibly—to preserve their freedom.

253. It is one thing to recognize that the people of the world do not want war. It is quite another thing to attribute the same good motives to regimes or political systems that have consistently demonstrated precisely the opposite in their behavior. There are political philosophies with understandings of morality so radically different from ours, that even negotiations proceed from different premises, although identical terminology may be used by both sides. This is no reason for not negotiating. It is a very good reason for not negotiating blindly or naively.

254. In this regard, Pope John Paul II offers some sober reminders concerning dialogue and peace:

> [O]ne must mention the tactical and deliberate lie, which misuses language, which has recourse to the most sophisticated techniques of propaganda, which deceives and distorts dialogue and incites to aggression . . . while certain parties are fostered by ideologies which, in spite of their declarations, are opposed to the dignity of the human person, ideologies which see in struggle the motive force of history, that see in force the source of rights, that see in the discernment of the enemy the ABC of politics, dialogue is fixed and sterile. Or, if it still exists, it is a superficial and falsified reality. It becomes very difficult, not to say

impossible, therefore. There follows almost a complete lack of communication between countries and blocs. Even the international institutions are paralyzed. And the setback to dialogue then runs the risk of serving the arms race. However, even in what can be considered as an impasse to the extent that individuals support such ideologies, the attempt to have a lucid dialogue seems still necessary in order to unblock the situation and to work for the possible establishment of peace on particular points. This is to be done by counting upon common sense, on the possibilities of danger for everyone and on the just aspirations to which the peoples themselves largely adhere.[108]

255. The cold realism of this text, combined with the conviction that political dialogue and negotiations must be pursued, in spite of obstacles, provides solid guidance for U.S.-Soviet relations. Acknowledging all the differences between the two philosophies and political systems, the irreducible truth is that objective mutual interests do exist between the superpowers. Proof of this concrete if limited convergence of interest can be found in some vitally important agreements on nuclear weapons which have already been negotiated in the areas of nuclear testing and nuclear explosions in space as well as the SALT I agreements.

256. The fact that the Soviet Union now possesses a huge arsenal of strategic weapons as threatening to us as ours may appear to them does not exclude the possibility of success in such negotiations. The conviction of many European observers that a *modus vivendi* (often summarized as "detente") is a practical possibility in political, economic, and scientific areas should not be lightly dismissed in our country.

257. Sensible and successful diplomacy, however, will demand that we avoid the trap of a form of anti-Sovietism which fails to grasp the central danger of a superpower rivalry in which both the U.S. and the U.S.S.R. are the players, and fails to recognize the common interest both states have in never using nuclear weapons. Some of those dangers and common interests would exist in any world where two great powers, even relatively benign ones, competed for power, influence, and security. The diplomatic requirement for addressing the U.S.-Soviet relationship is not romantic idealism about Soviet intentions and capabilities but solid realism which recognizes that everyone will lose in a nuclear exchange.

258. As bishops we are concerned with issues which go beyond diplomatic requirements. It is of some value to keep raising in the realm of the political debate truths which ground our involvement in the affairs of nations and peoples. Diplomatic dialogue usually sees the other as a potential or real adversary. Soviet behavior in some cases merits the adjective reprehensible, but the Soviet people and their leaders are human beings created in the image and likeness of God. To believe we are condemned in the future only to what has been the past of U.S.-Soviet relations is to underestimate both our human

potential for creative diplomacy and God's action in our midst which can open the way to changes we could barely imagine. We do not intend to foster illusory ideas that the road ahead in superpower relations will be devoid of tension or that peace will be easily achieved. But we do warn against that "hardness of hearts" which can close us or others to the changes needed to make the future different from the past.

3. Interdependence: From Fact to Policy

259. While the nuclear arms race focuses attention on the U.S.-Soviet relationship, it is neither politically wise nor morally justifiable to ignore the broader international context in which that relationship exists. Public attention, riveted on the big powers, often misses the plight of scores of countries and millions of people simply trying to survive. The interdependence of the world means a set of interrelated human questions. Important as keeping the peace in the nuclear age is, it does not solve or dissolve the other major problems of the day. Among these problems the pre-eminent issue is the continuing chasm in living standards between the industrialized world (East and West) and the developing world. To quote Pope John Paul II:

> So widespread is the phenomenon that it brings into question the financial, monetary, production and commercial mechanisms that, resting on various political pressures, support the world economy. These are proving incapable either of remedying the unjust social situations inherited from the past or of dealing with the urgent challenges and ethical demands of the present.[109]

260. The East-West competition, central as it is to world order and important as it is in the foreign policy debate, does not address this moral question which rivals the nuclear issue in its human significance. While the problem of the developing nations would itself require a pastoral letter, Catholic teaching has maintained an analysis of the problem which should be identified here. The analysis acknowledges internal causes of poverty, but also concentrates on the way the larger international economic structures affect the poor nations. These particularly involve trade, monetary, investment and aid policies.

261. Neither of the superpowers is conspicuous in these areas for initiatives designed to address "the absolute poverty" in which millions live today.[110]

262 From our perspective and experience as bishops, we believe there is a much greater potential for response to these questions in the minds and hearts of Americans than has been reflected in U.S. policy. As pastors who often appeal to our congregations for funds destined for international programs, we find good will and great generosity the prevailing characteristics. The spirit of generosity which shaped the Marshall Plan is still alive in the American public.

263. We must discover how to translate this personal sense of generosity and compassion into support for policies which would respond to papal teaching in international economic issues. It is precisely the need to expand our conception of international charity and relief to an understanding of the need for social justice in terms of trade, aid and monetary issues which was reflected in Pope John Paul II's call to American Catholics in Yankee Stadium:

> Within the framework of your national institutions and in cooperation with all your compatriots, you will also want to seek out the structural reasons which foster or cause the different forms of poverty in the world and in your own country, so that you can apply the proper remedies. You will not allow yourselves to be intimidated or discouraged by oversimplified explanations which are more ideological than scientific—explanations which try to account for a complex evil by some single cause. But neither will you recoil before the reforms—even profound ones—of attitudes and structures that may prove necessary in order to recreate over and over again the conditions needed by the disadvantaged if they are to have a fresh chance in the hard struggle of life. The poor of the United States and of the world are your brothers and sisters in Christ.[111]

264. The Pope's words highlight an intellectual, moral, and political challenge for the United States. Intellectually, there is a need to rethink the meaning of national interest in an interdependent world. Morally, there is a need to build upon the spirit of generosity present in the U.S. public, directing it toward a more systematic response to the major issues affecting the poor of the world. Politically, there is a need for U.S. policies which promote the profound structural reforms called for by recent papal teaching.

265. Precisely in the name of international order papal teaching has, by word and deed, sought to promote multilateral forms of cooperation toward the developing world. The U.S. capacity for leadership in multilateral institutions is very great. We urge much more vigorous and creative response to the needs of the developing countries by the United States in these institutions.

266. The significant role the United States could play is evident in the daily agenda facing these institutions. Proposals addressing the relationship of the industrialized and developing countries on a broad spectrum of issues, all in need of "profound reforms," are regularly discussed in the United Nations and other international organizations. Without U.S. participation, significant reform and substantial change in the direction of addressing the needs of the poor will not occur. Meeting these needs is an essential element for a peaceful world.

267. Papal teaching of the last four decades has not only supported international institutions in principle, it has supported the United Nations specifically. Pope Paul VI said to the U.N. General Assembly:

> The edifice which you have constructed must never fail; it must be perfected and made equal to the needs which world history will present. You mark a stage in the development of mankind for which retreat must never be admitted, but for which it is necessary that advance be made.[112]

268. It is entirely necessary to examine the United Nations carefully, to recognize its limitations and propose changes where needed. Nevertheless, in light of the continuing endorsement found in papal teaching, we urge that the United States adopt a stronger supportive leadership role with respect to the United Nations. The growing interdependence of the nations and peoples of the world, coupled with the extragovernmental presence of multinational corporations, requires new structures of cooperation. As one of the founders of and major financial contributors to the United Nations, the United States can, and should, assume a more positive and creative role in its life today.

269. It is in the context of the United Nations that the impact of the arms race on the prospects for economic development is highlighted. The numerous U.N. studies on the relationship of development and disarmament support the judgment of Vatican II cited earlier in this letter: "The arms race is one of the greatest curses on the human race and the harm it inflicts upon the poor is more than can be endured."[113]

270. We are aware that the precise relationship between disarmament and development is neither easily demonstrated nor easily reoriented. But the fact of a massive distortion of resources in the face of crying human need creates a moral question. In an interdependent world, the security of one nation is related to the security of all. When we consider how and what we pay for defense today, we need a broader view than the equation of arms with security.[114] The threats to the security and stability of an interdependent world are not all contained in missiles and bombers.

271. If the arms race in all its dimensions is not reversed, resources will not be available for the human needs so evident in many parts of the globe and in our own country as well. But we also know that making resources available is a first step; policies of wise use would also have to follow. Part of the process of thinking about the economics of disarmament includes the possibilities of conversion of defense industries to other purposes. Many say the possibilities are great if the political will is present. We say the political will to reorient resources to human needs and redirect industrial, scientific, and technological capacity to meet those needs is part of the challenge of the nuclear age. Those whose livelihood is dependent upon industries which can be reoriented should rightfully expect assistance in making the transition to new forms of employment. The economic dimension of the arms race is broader than we can assess here, but these issues we have raised are among the primary questions before the nation.[115]

272. An interdependent world requires an understanding that key policy questions today involve mutuality of interest. If the monetary and trading sys-

tems are not governed by sensitivity to mutual needs, they can be destroyed. If the protection of human rights and the promotion of human needs are left as orphans in the diplomatic arena, the stability we seek in increased armaments will eventually be threatened by rights denied and needs unmet in vast sectors of the globe. If future planning about conservation of and access to resources is relegated to a pure struggle of power, we shall simply guarantee conflict in the future.

273. The moral challenge of interdependence concerns shaping the relationships and rules of practice which will support our common need for security, welfare, and safety. The challenge tests our idea of human community, our policy analysis, and our political will. The need to prevent nuclear war is absolutely crucial, but even if this is achieved, there is much more to be done.

IV. THE PASTORAL CHALLENGE AND RESPONSE

A. The Church: A Community of Conscience, Prayer, and Penance

274. Pope John Paul II, in his first encyclical, recalled with gratitude the teaching of Pius XII on the Church. He then went on to say:

> Membership in that body has for its source a particular call, united with the saving action of grace. Therefore, if we wish to keep in mind this community of the People of God, which is so vast and so extremely differentiated, we must see first and foremost Christ saying in a way to each member of the community: "Follow Me." It is the community of the disciples, each of whom in a different way—at times very consciously and consistently, at other times not very consciously and very consistently—is following Christ. This shows also the deeply "personal" aspect and dimension of this society.[116]

275. In the following pages we should like to spell out some of the implications of being a community of Jesus' disciples in a time when our nation is so heavily armed with nuclear weapons and is engaged in a continuing development of new weapons together with strategies for their use.

276. It is clear today, perhaps more than in previous generations, that convinced Christians are a minority in nearly every country of the world—including nominally Christian and Catholic nations. In our own country we are coming to a fuller awareness that a response to the call of Jesus is both personal and demanding. As believers we can identify rather easily with the early Church as a company of witnesses engaged in a difficult mission. To be disciples of Jesus requires that we continually go beyond where we now are. To obey the call of Jesus means separating ourselves from all attachments and affiliation that could prevent us from hearing and following our authentic

vocation. To set out on the road to discipleship is to dispose oneself for a share in the cross (cf. Jn. 16:20). To be a Christian, according to the New Testament, is not simply to believe with one's mind, but also to become a doer of the word, a wayfarer with and a witness to Jesus. This means, of course, that we never expect complete success within history and that we must regard as normal even the path of persecution and the possibility of martyrdom.

277. We readily recognize that we live in a world that is becoming increasingly estranged from Christian values. In order to remain a Christian, one must take a resolute stand against many commonly accepted axioms of the world. To become true disciples, we must undergo a demanding course of induction into the adult Christian community. We must continually equip ourselves to profess the full faith of the Church in an increasingly secularized society. We must develop a sense of solidarity, cemented by relationships with mature and exemplary Christians who represent Christ and his way of life.

278. All of these comments about the meaning of being a disciple or a follower of Jesus today are especially relevant to the quest for genuine peace in our time.

B. Elements of a Pastoral Response

279. We recommend and endorse for the faithful some practical programs to meet the challenge to their faith in this area of grave concern.

1. Educational Programs and Formation of Conscience

280. Since war, especially the threat of nuclear war, is one of the central problems of our day, how we seek to solve it could determine the mode, and even the possibility, of life on earth. God made human beings stewards of the earth; we cannot escape this responsibility. Therefore we urge every diocese and parish to implement balanced and objective educational programs to help people at all age levels to understand better the issues of war and peace. Development and implementation of such programs must receive a high priority during the next several years. They must teach the full impact of our Christian faith. To accomplish this, this Pastoral Letter in its entirety, including its complexity, should be used as a guide and a framework for such programs, as they lead people to make moral decisions about the problems of war and peace, keeping in mind that the applications of principles in this Pastoral Letter do not carry the same moral authority as our statements of universal moral principles and formal Church teaching.

281. In developing educational programs, we must keep in mind that questions of war and peace have a profoundly moral dimension which responsible Christians cannot ignore. They are questions of life and death. True, they also have a political dimension because they are embedded in public policy. But the fact that they are also political is no excuse for denying the Church's obligation to provide its members with the help they need in forming their

consciences. We must learn together how to make correct and responsible moral judgments. We reject, therefore, criticism of the Church's concern with these issues on the ground that it "should not become involved in politics." We are called to move from discussion to witness and action.

282. At the same time, we recognize that the Church's teaching authority does not carry the same force when it deals with technical solutions involving particular means as it does when it speaks of principles or ends. People may agree in abhorring an injustice, for instance, yet sincerely disagree as to what practical approach will achieve justice. Religious groups are as entitled as others to their opinion in such cases, but they should not claim that their opinions are the only ones that people of good will may hold.

283. The Church's educational programs must explain clearly those principles or teachings about which there is little question. Those teachings, which seek to make explicit the Gospel call to peace and the tradition of the Church, should then be applied to concrete situations. They must indicate what the possible legitimate options are and what the consequences of those options may be. While this approach should be self-evident, it needs to be emphasized. Some people who have entered the public debate on nuclear warfare, at all points on the spectrum of opinion, appear not to understand or accept some of the clear teachings of the Church as contained in papal or conciliar documents. For example, some would place almost no limits on the use of nuclear weapons if they are needed for "self-defense." Some on the other side of the debate insist on conclusions which may be legitimate options but cannot be made obligatory on the basis of actual Church teaching.

2. True Peace Calls for "Reverence for Life"

284. All of the values we are promoting in this letter rest ultimately in the disarmament of the human heart and the conversion of the human spirit to God who alone can give authentic peace. Indeed, to have peace in our world, we must first have peace within ourselves. As Pope John Paul II reminded us in his 1982 World Day of Peace message, world peace will always elude us until peace becomes a reality for each of us personally. "It springs from the dynamism of free wills guided by reason towards the common good that is to be attained in truth, justice and love."[117] Interior peace becomes possible only when we have a conversion of spirit. We cannot have peace with hate in our hearts.

285. No society can live in peace with itself, or with the world, without a full awareness of the worth and dignity of every human person, and of the sacredness of all human life (Jas. 4:1–2). When we accept violence in any form as commonplace, our sensitivities become dulled. When we accept violence, war itself can be taken for granted. Violence has many faces: oppression of the poor, deprivation of basic human rights, economic exploitation, sexual exploitation and pornography, neglect or abuse of the aged and the helpless, and innumerable other acts of inhumanity. Abortion in particular blunts a

sense of the sacredness of human life. In a society where the innocent unborn are killed wantonly, how can we expect people to feel righteous revulsion at the act or threat of killing noncombatants in war?

286. We are well aware of the differences involved in the taking of human life in warfare and the taking of human life through abortion. As we have discussed throughout this document, even justifiable defense against aggression may result in the indirect or unintended loss of innocent human lives. This is tragic, but may conceivably be proportionate to the values defended. Nothing, however, can justify direct attack on innocent human life, in or out of warfare. Abortion is precisely such an attack.

287. We know that millions of men and women of good will, of all religious persuasions, join us in our commitment to try to reduce the horrors of war, and particularly to assure that nuclear weapons will never again be used, by any nation, anywhere, for any reason. Millions join us in our "no" to nuclear war, in the certainty that nuclear war would inevitably result in the killing of millions of innocent human beings, directly or indirectly. Yet many part ways with us in our efforts to reduce the horror of abortion and our "no" to war on innocent human life in the womb, killed not indirectly, but directly.

288. We must ask how long a nation willing to extend a constitutional guarantee to the "right" to kill defenseless human beings by abortion is likely to refrain from adopting strategic warfare policies deliberately designed to kill millions of defenseless human beings, if adopting them should come to seem "expedient." Since 1973, approximately 15 million abortions have been performed in the United States, symptoms of a kind of disease of the human spirit. And we now find ourselves seriously discussing the pros and cons of such questions as infanticide, euthanasia, and the involvement of physicians in carrying out the death penalty. Those who would celebrate such a national disaster can only have blinded themselves to its reality.

289. Pope Paul VI was resolutely clear: *If you wish peace, defend life.*[118] We plead with all who would work to end the scourge of war to begin by defending life at its most defenseless, the life of the unborn.

3. Prayer

290. A conversion of our hearts and minds will make it possible for us to enter into a closer communion with our Lord. We nourish that communion by personal and communal prayer, for it is in prayer that we encounter Jesus, who is our peace, and learn from him the way to peace.

291. In prayer we are renewed in faith and confirmed in our hope in God's promise.

292. The Lord's promise is that he is in our midst when we gather in prayer. Strengthened by this conviction, we beseech the risen Christ to fill the world with his peace. We call upon Mary, the first disciple and the Queen of Peace, to intercede for us and for the people of our time that we may walk in the way of peace. In this context, we encourage devotion to Our Lady of Peace.

293. As believers, we understand peace as a gift of God. This belief prompts us to pray constantly, personally and communally, particularly through the reading of Scripture and devotion to the rosary, especially in the family. Through these means and others, we seek the wisdom to begin the search for peace and the courage to sustain us as instruments of Christ's peace in the world.

294. The practice of contemplative prayer is especially valuable for advancing harmony and peace in the world. For this prayer rises, by divine grace, where there is total disarmament of the heart and unfolds in an experience of love which is the moving force of peace. Contemplation fosters a vision of the human family as united and interdependent in the mystery of God's love for all people. This silent, interior prayer bridges temporarily the "already" and "not yet," this world and God's Kingdom of peace.

295. The Mass in particular is a unique means of seeking God's help to create the conditions essential for true peace in ourselves and in the world. In the Eucharist we encounter the risen Lord, who gave us his peace. He shares with us the grace of the redemption, which helps us to preserve and nourish this precious gift. Nowhere is the Church's urgent plea for peace more evident in the liturgy than in the Communion Rite. After beginning this rite of the Mass with the Lord's Prayer, praying for reconciliation now and in the Kingdom to come, the community asks God to "grant us peace in our day," not just at some time in the distant future. Even before we are exhorted "to offer each other the sign of peace," the priest continues the Church's prayer for peace, recalling the Lord Jesus Christ's own legacy of peace:

> Lord Jesus Christ, you said to your apostles: I leave you peace, my peace I give you. Look not on our sins, but on the faith of your Church, and grant us the peace and unity of your kingdom.

Therefore, we encourage every Catholic to make the sign of peace at Mass an authentic sign of our reconciliation with God and with one another. This sign of peace is also a visible expression of our commitment to work for peace as a Christian community. We approach the table of the Lord only after having dedicated ourselves as a Christian community to peace and reconciliation. As an added sign of commitment, we suggest that there always be a petition for peace in the general intercessions at every eucharistic celebration.

296. We implore other Christians and everyone of good will to join us in this continuing prayer for peace, as we beseech God for peace within ourselves, in our families and community, in our nation, and in the world.

4. Penance

297. Prayer by itself is incomplete without penance. Penance directs us toward our goal of putting on the attitudes of Jesus himself. Because we are all capable of violence, we are never totally conformed to Christ and are always

in need of conversion. The twentieth century alone provides adequate evidence of our violence as individuals and as a nation. Thus, there is continual need for acts of penance and conversion. The worship of the Church, particularly through the sacrament of reconciliation and communal penance services, offers us multiple ways to make reparation for the violence in our own lives and in our world.

298. As a tangible sign of our need and desire to do penance we, for the cause of peace, commit ourselves to fast and abstinence on each Friday of the year. We call upon our people voluntarily to do penance on Friday by eating less food and by abstaining from meat. This return to a traditional practice of penance, once well observed in the U.S. Church, should be accompanied by works of charity and service toward our neighbors. Every Friday should be a day significantly devoted to prayer, penance, and almsgiving for peace.

299. It is to such forms of penance and conversion that the Scriptures summon us. In the words of the prophet Isaiah:

> Is not the sort of fast that pleases me, to break unjust fetters and undo the thongs of the yoke, to let the oppressed go free and break every yoke, to share your bread with the hungry, and shelter the homeless poor, to clothe the person you see to be naked and not turn from your own kin? Then will your light shine like the dawn and your wound be quickly healed over. If you do away with the yoke, the clenched fist, the wicked word, if you give your bread to the hungry and relief to the oppressed, your light will rise in the darkness, and your shadows become like noon (Is. 58:6–8; 10).

300. The present nuclear arms race has distracted us from the words of the prophets, has turned us from peacemaking, and has focused our attention on a nuclear buildup leading to annihilation. We are called to turn back from this evil of total destruction and turn instead in prayer and penance toward God, toward our neighbor, and toward the building of a peaceful world:

> I set before you life or death, a blessing or a curse. Choose life then, so that you and your descendants may live in the love of Yahweh your God, obeying His voice, clinging to Him; for in this your life consists, and on this depends your long stay in the land which Yahweh swore to your fathers Abraham, Isaac and Jacob, He would give them (Dt. 30:19–20).

C. Challenge and Hope

301. The arms race presents questions of conscience we may not evade. As American Catholics, we are called to express our loyalty to the deepest values we cherish: peace, justice, and security for the entire human family. National goals and policies must be measured against that standard.

302. We speak here in a specific way to the Catholic community. After the passage of nearly four decades and a concomitant growth in our understanding of the ever-growing horror of nuclear war, we must shape the climate of opinion which will make it possible for our country to express profound sorrow over the atomic bombing in 1945. Without that sorrow, there is no possibility of finding a way to repudiate future use of nuclear weapons or of conventional weapons in such military actions as would not fulfill just-war criteria.

303. ***To Priests, Deacons, Religious, and Pastoral Ministers:*** We recognize the unique role in the Church which belongs to priests and deacons by reason of the sacrament of holy orders and their unique responsibility in the community of believers. We also recognize the valued and indispensable role of men and women religious. To all of them and to all other pastoral ministers we stress that the cultivation of the Gospel vision of peace as a way of life for believers and as a leaven in society should be a major objective. As bishops, we are aware each day of our dependence upon your efforts. We are aware, too, that this letter and the new obligations it could present to the faithful may create difficulties for you in dealing with those you serve. We have confidence in your capacity and ability to convert these difficulties into an opportunity to give a fuller witness to our Lord and his message. This letter will be known by the faithful only as well as you know it, preach and teach it, and use it creatively.

304. ***To Educators:*** We have outlined in this letter Catholic teaching on war and peace, but this framework will become a living message only through your work in the Catholic community. To teach the ways of peace is not "to weaken the nation's will" but to be concerned for the nation's soul. We address theologians in a particular way, because we know that we have only begun the journey toward a theology of peace; without your specific contributions this desperately needed dimension of our faith will not be realized. Through your help we may provide new vision and wisdom for church and state.

305. We are confident that all the models of Catholic education which have served the Church and our country so well in so many ways will creatively rise to the challenge of peace.

306. ***To Parents:*** Your role, in our eyes, is unsurpassed by any other; the foundation of society is the family. We are conscious of the continuing sacrifices you make in the efforts to nurture the full human and spiritual growth of your children. Children hear the Gospel message first from your lips. Parents who consciously discuss issues of justice in the home and who strive to help children solve conflicts through nonviolent methods enable their children to grow up as peacemakers. We pledge our continuing pastoral support in the common objective we share of building a peaceful world for the future of children everywhere.

307. ***To Youth:*** Pope John Paul II singles you out in every country where he visits as the hope of the future; we agree with him. We call you to choose

your future work and professions carefully. How you spend the rest of your lives will determine, in large part, whether there will any longer be a world as we know it. We ask you to study carefully the teachings of the Church and the demands of the Gospel about war and peace. We encourage you to seek careful guidance as you reach conscientious decisions about your civic responsibilities in this age of nuclear military forces.

308. We speak to you, however, as people of faith. We share with you our deepest conviction that in the midst of the dangers and complexities of our time God is with us, working through us and sustaining us all in our efforts of building a world of peace with justice for each person.

309. ***To Men and Women in Military Service:*** Millions of you are Catholics serving in the armed forces. We recognize that you carry special responsibilities for the issues we have considered in this letter. Our perspective on your profession is that of Vatican II: "All those who enter the military service in loyalty to their country should look upon themselves as the custodians of the security and freedom of their fellow countrymen; and where they carry out their duty properly, they are contributing to the maintenance of peace."[119]

310. It is surely not our intention in writing this letter to create problems for Catholics in the armed forces. Every profession, however, has its specific moral questions and it is clear that the teaching on war and peace developed in this letter poses a special challenge and opportunity to those in the military profession. Our pastoral contact with Catholics in military service, either through our direct experience or through our priests, impresses us with the demanding moral standards we already see observed and the commitment to Catholic faith we find. We are convinced that the challenges of this letter will be faced conscientiously. The purpose of defense policy is to defend the peace; military professionals should understand their vocation this way. We believe they do, and we support this view.

311. We remind all in authority and in the chain of command that their training and field manuals have long prohibited, and still do prohibit, certain actions in the conduct of war, especially those actions which inflict harm on innocent civilians. The question is not whether certain measures are unlawful or forbidden in warfare, but which measures: to refuse to take such actions is not an act of cowardice or treason but one of courage and patriotism.

312. We address particularly those involved in the exercise of authority over others. We are aware of your responsibilities and impressed by the standard of personal and professional duty you uphold. We feel, therefore, that we can urge you to do everything you can to assure that every peaceful alternative is exhausted before war is even remotely considered. In developing battle plans and weapons systems, we urge you to try to ensure that these are designed to reduce violence, destruction, suffering, and death to a minimum, keeping in mind especially noncombatants and other innocent persons.

313. Those who train individuals for military duties must remember that the citizen does not lose his or her basic human rights by entrance into mili-

tary service. No one, for whatever reason, can justly treat a military person with less dignity and respect than that demanded for and deserved by every human person. One of the most difficult problems of war involves defending a free society without destroying the values that give it meaning and validity. Dehumanization of a nation's military personnel by dulling their sensibilities and generating hatred toward adversaries in an effort to increase their fighting effectiveness robs them of basic human rights and freedoms, degrading them as persons.

314. Attention must be given to the effects on military personnel themselves of the use of even legitimate means of conducting war. While attacking legitimate targets and wounding or killing opposed combat forces may be morally justified, what happens to military persons required to carry out these actions? Are they treated merely as instruments of war, insensitive as the weapons they use? With what moral or emotional experiences do they return from war and attempt to resume normal civilian lives? How does their experience affect society? How are they treated by society?

315. It is not only basic human rights of adversaries that must be respected, but those of our own forces as well. We re-emphasize, therefore, the obligation of responsible authorities to ensure appropriate training and education of combat forces and to provide appropriate support for those who have experienced combat. It is unconscionable to deprive those veterans of combat whose lives have been severely disrupted or traumatized by their combat experiences of proper psychological and other appropriate treatment and support.

316. Finally, we are grateful for the sacrifice so many in military service must make today and for the service offered in the past by veterans. We urge that those sacrifices be mitigated so far as possible by the provision of appropriate living and working conditions and adequate financial recompense. Military persons and their families must be provided continuing opportunity for full spiritual growth, the exercise of their religious faith, and a dignified mode of life.

317. We especially commend and encourage our priests in military service. In addition to the message already addressed to all priests and religious, we stress the special obligations and opportunities you face in direct pastoral service to the men and women of the armed forces. To complement a teaching document of this scope, we shall need the sensitive and wise pastoral guidance only you can provide. We promise our support in facing this challenge.

318. ***To Men and Women in Defense Industries:*** You also face specific questions, because the defense industry is directly involved in the development and production of the weapons of mass destruction which have concerned us in this letter. We do not presume or pretend that clear answers exist to many of the personal, professional and financial choices facing you in your varying responsibilities. In this letter we have ruled out certain uses of nuclear weapons, while also expressing conditional moral acceptance for deterrence.

All Catholics, at every level of defense industries, can and should use the moral principles of this letter to form their consciences. We realize that different judgments of conscience will face different people, and we recognize the possibility of diverse concrete judgments being made in this complex area. We seek as moral teachers and pastors to be available to all who confront these questions of personal and vocational choice. Those who in conscience decide that they should no longer be associated with defense activities should find support in the Catholic community. Those who remain in these industries or earn a profit from the weapons industry should find in the Church guidance and support for the ongoing evaluation of their work.

319. ***To Men and Women of Science:*** At Hiroshima Pope John Paul said: "Criticism of science and technology is sometimes so severe that it comes close to condemning science itself. On the contrary, science and technology are a wonderful product of a God-given human creativity, since they have provided us with wonderful possibilities and we all gratefully benefit from them. But we know that this potential is not a neutral one. It can be used either for man's progress or for his degradation."[120] We appreciate the efforts of scientists, some of whom first unlocked the secret of atomic power and others of whom have developed it in diverse ways, to turn the enormous power of science to the cause of peace.

320. Modern history is not lacking scientists who have looked back with deep remorse on the development of weapons to which they contributed, sometimes with the highest motivation, even believing that they were creating weapons that would render all other weapons obsolete and convince the world of the unthinkableness of war. Such efforts have ever proved illusory. Surely, equivalent dedication of scientific minds to reverse current trends, and to pursue concepts as bold and adventuresome in favor of peace as those which in the past have magnified the risks of war, could result in dramatic benefits for all of humanity. We particularly note in this regard the extensive efforts of public education undertaken by physicians and scientists on the medical consequences of nuclear war.

321. We do not, however, wish to limit our remarks to the physical sciences alone. Nor do we limit our remarks to physical scientists. In his address at the United Nations University in Hiroshima, Pope John Paul II warned about misuse of "the social sciences and the human behavioral sciences when they are utilized to manipulate people, to crush their minds, souls, dignity and freedom. . . ."[121] The positive role of social science in overcoming the dangers of the nuclear age is evident in this letter. We have been dependent upon the research and analysis of social scientists in our effort to apply the moral principles of the Catholic tradition to the concrete problems of our day. We encourage social scientists to continue this work of relating moral wisdom and political reality. We are in continuing need of your insights.

322. ***To Men and Women of the Media:*** We have directly felt our dependence upon you in writing this letter; all the problems we have confronted have

been analyzed daily in the media. As we have grappled with these issues, we have experienced some of the responsibility you bear for interpreting them. On the quality of your efforts depends in great measure the opportunity the general public will have for understanding this letter.

323. ***To Public Officials:*** Vatican II spoke forcefully of "the difficult yet noble art of politics."[122] No public issue is more difficult than avoiding war; no public task more noble than building a secure peace. Public officials in a democracy must both lead and listen; they are ultimately dependent upon a popular consensus to sustain policy. We urge you to lead with courage and to listen to the public debate with sensitivity.

324. Leadership in a nuclear world means examining with great care and objectivity every potential initiative toward world peace, regardless of how unpromising it might at first appear. One specific initiative which might be taken now would be the establishment of a task force including the public sector, industry, labor, economists and scientists with the mandate to consider the problems and challenges posed by nuclear disarmament to our economic well-being and industrial output. Listening includes being particularly attentive to the consciences of those who sincerely believe that they may not morally support warfare in general, a given war, or the exercise of a particular role within the armed forces. Public officials might well serve all of our fellow citizens by proposing and supporting legislation designed to give maximum protection to this precious freedom, true freedom of conscience.

325. In response to public officials who both lead and listen, we urge citizens to respect the vocation of public service. It is a role easily maligned but not easily fulfilled. Neither justice nor peace can be achieved with stability in the absence of courageous and creative public servants.

326. ***To Catholics as Citizens:*** All papal teaching on peace has stressed the crucial role of public opinion. Pope John Paul II specified the tasks before us: "There is no justification for not raising the question of the responsibility of each nation and each individual in the face of possible wars and of the nuclear threat."[123] In a democracy, the responsibility of the nation and that of its citizens coincide. Nuclear weapons pose especially acute questions of conscience for American Catholics. As citizens we wish to affirm our loyalty to our country and its ideals, yet we are also citizens of the world who must be faithful to the universal principles proclaimed by the Church. While some other countries also possess nuclear weapons, we may not forget that the United States was the first to build and to use them, Like the Soviet Union, this country now possesses so many weapons as to imperil the continuation of civilization. Americans share responsibility for the current situation, and cannot evade responsibility for trying to resolve it.

327. The virtue of patriotism means that as citizens we respect and honor our country, but our very love and loyalty make us examine carefully and regularly its role in world affairs, asking that it live up to its full potential as an agent of peace with justice for all people.

> Citizens must cultivate a generous and loyal spirit of patriotism, but without being narrow-minded. This means that they will always direct their attention to the good of the whole human family, united by the different ties which bind together races, people, and nations.[124]

328. In a pluralistic democracy like the United States, the Church has a unique opportunity, precisely because of the strong constitutional protection of both religious freedom and freedom of speech and the press, to help call attention to the moral dimensions of public issues. In a previous pastoral letter, *Human Life In Our Day*, we said: "In our democratic system, the fundamental right of political dissent cannot be denied, nor is rational debate on public policy decisions of government in the light of moral and political principles to be discouraged. It is the duty of the governed to analyze responsibly the concrete issues of public policy."[125] In fulfilling this role, the Church helps to create a community of conscience in the wider civil community. It does this in the first instance by teaching clearly within the Church the moral principles which bind and shape the Catholic conscience. The Church also fulfills a teaching role, however, in striving to share the moral wisdom of the Catholic tradition with the larger society.

329. In the wider public discussion, we look forward in a special way to cooperating with all other Christians with whom we share common traditions. We also treasure cooperative efforts with Jewish and Islamic communities, which possess a long and abiding concern for peace as a religious and human value. Finally, we reaffirm our desire to participate in a common public effort with all men and women of good will who seek to reverse the arms race and secure the peace of the world.

CONCLUSION

330. As we close this lengthy letter, we try to answer two key questions as directly as we can.

331. Why do we address these matters fraught with such complexity, controversy and passion? We speak as pastors, not politicians. We are teachers, not technicians. We cannot avoid our responsibility to lift up the moral dimensions of the choices before our world and nation. The nuclear age is an era of moral as well as physical danger. We are the first generation since Genesis with the power to virtually destroy God's creation. We cannot remain silent in the face of such danger. Why do we address these issues? We are simply trying to live up to the call of Jesus to be peacemakers in our own time and situation.

332. What are we saying? Fundamentally, we are saying that the decisions about nuclear weapons are among the most pressing moral questions of our age. While these decisions have obvious military and political aspects, they involve fundamental moral choices. In simple terms, we are saying that good ends (defending one's country, protecting freedom, etc.) cannot justify immoral

means (the use of weapons which kill indiscriminately and threaten whole societies). We fear that our world and nation are headed in the wrong direction. More weapons with greater destructive potential are produced every day. More and more nations are seeking to become nuclear powers. In our quest for more and more security, we fear we are actually becoming less and less secure.

333. In the words of our Holy Father, we need a "moral about-face." The whole world must summon the moral courage and technical means to say "no" to nuclear conflict; "no" to weapons of mass destruction; "no" to an arms race which robs the poor and the vulnerable; and "no" to the moral danger of a nuclear age which places before humankind indefensible choices of constant terror or surrender. Peacemaking is not an optional commitment. It is a requirement of our faith. We are called to be peacemakers, not by some movement of the moment, but by our Lord Jesus. The content and context of our peacemaking is set, not by some political agenda or ideological program, but by the teaching of his Church.

334. Thus far in this Pastoral Letter we have made suggestions we hope will be helpful in the present world crisis. Looking ahead to the long and productive future of humanity for which we all hope, we feel that a more all-inclusive and final solution is needed. We speak here of the truly effective international authority for which Pope John XXIII ardently longed in *Peace on Earth*,[126] and of which Pope Paul VI spoke to the United Nations on his visit there in 1965.[127] The hope for such a structure is not unrealistic, because the point has been reached where public opinion sees clearly that, with the massive weaponry of the present, war is no longer viable. There *is* a substitute for war. There is negotiation under the supervision of a global body realistically fashioned to do its job. It must be given the equipment to keep constant surveillance on the entire earth. Present technology makes this possible. It must have the authority, freely conferred upon it by all the nations, to investigate what seems to be preparations for war by any one of them. It must be empowered by all the nations to enforce its commands on every nation. It must be so constituted as to pose no threat to any nation's sovereignty. Obviously the creation of such a sophisticated instrumentality is a gigantic task, but is it hoping for too much to believe that the genius of humanity, aided by the grace and guidance of God, is able to accomplish it? To create it may take decades of unrelenting daily toil by the world's best minds and most devoted hearts, but it shall never come into existence unless we make a beginning now.

335. As we come to the end of our Pastoral Letter we boldly propose the beginning of this work. The evil of the proliferation of nuclear arms becomes more evident every day to all people. No one is exempt from their danger. If ridding the world of the weapons of war could be done easily, the whole human race would do it gladly tomorrow. Shall we shrink from the task because it is hard?

336. We turn to our own government and we beg it to propose to the United Nations that it begin this work immediately; that it create an international task

force for peace; that this task force, with membership open to every nation, meet daily through the years ahead with one sole agenda: the creation of a world that will one day be safe from war. Freed from the bondage of war that holds it captive in its threat, the world will at last be able to address its problems and to make genuine human progress, so that every day there may be more freedom, more food, and more opportunity for every human being who walks the face of the earth.

337. Let us have the courage to believe in the bright future and in a God who wills it for us—not a perfect world, but a better one. The perfect world, we Christians believe, is beyond the horizon, in an endless eternity where God will be all in all. But a better world is here for human hands and hearts and minds to make.

338. For the community of faith the risen Christ is the beginning and end of all things. For all things were created through him and all things will return to the Father through him.

339. It is our belief in the risen Christ which sustains us in confronting the awesome challenge of the nuclear arms race. Present in the beginning as the word of the Father, present in history as the word incarnate, and with us today in his word, sacraments, and spirit, He is the reason for our hope and faith. Respecting our freedom, He does not solve our problems but sustains us as we take responsibility for His work of creation and try to shape it in the ways of the Kingdom. We believe His grace will never fail us. We offer this letter to the Church and to all who can draw strength and wisdom from it in the conviction that we must not fail Him. We must subordinate the power of the nuclear age to human control and direct it to human benefit. As we do this we are conscious of God's continuing work among us, which will one day issue forth in the beautiful final Kingdom prophesied by the seer of the Book of Revelation:

> Then I saw a new heaven and a new earth; for the first heaven and the first earth had passed away and the sea was no more. And I saw the holy city, new Jerusalem, coming down out of heaven from God, prepared as a bride adorned for her husband; and I heard a great voice from the throne saying, "Behold, the dwelling of God is with men. He will dwell with them, and they shall be his people, and God himself will be with them, he will wipe away every tear from their eyes, and death shall be no more, neither shall there be mourning nor crying nor pain any more, for the former things have passed away." And he who sat upon the throne said, "Behold, I make all things new" (Rv. 21:1–5).

NOTES

1. Vatican II, *The Pastoral Constitution on the Church in the Modern World* (hereafter cited: *Pastoral Constitution*), 77. Papal and conciliar texts

will be referred to by title with paragraph number. Several collections of these texts exist although no single collection is comprehensive; see the following: *Peace and Disarmament: Documents of the World Council of Churches and the Roman Catholic Church* (Geneva and Rome: 1982) (hereafter cited: *Documents*, with page number); J. Gremillion, *The Gospel of Peace and Justice: Catholic Social Teaching Since Pope John* (Maryknoll, N.Y.: 1976); D.J. O'Brien and T.A. Shannon, eds., *Renewing the Earth: Catholic Documents on Peace, Justice and Liberation* (New York: 1977); A. Flannery, O.P., ed., *Vatican Council II: The Conciliar and Post Conciliar Documents* (Collegeville, Minn.: 1975); W. Abbot, ed., *The Documents of Vatican II* (New York: 1966). Both the Flannery and Abbot translations of the *Pastoral Constitution* are used in this letter.

2. John Paul II, "Message to the Second Special Session of the United Nations General Assembly Devoted to Disarmament" (June 1982) (hereafter cited: "Message U.N. Special Session 1982"), 7.

3. John Paul II, "Address to Scientists and Scholars," 4, *Origins* 10 (1981):621.

4. The *Pastoral Constitution* is made up of two parts; yet it constitutes an organic unity. By way of explanation: the constitution is called "pastoral" because, while resting on doctrinal principles, it seeks to express the relation of the Church to the world and modern mankind. The result is that, on the one hand, a pastoral slant is present in the first part and, on the other hand, a doctrinal slant is present in the second part. *Pastoral Constitution*, note 1 above.

5. Ibid.

6. Ibid., 13.

7. John Paul II, "Message U.N. Special Session 1982," 2.

8. *Pastoral Constitution*, 81.

9. Ibid., 80.

10. Ibid., 16.

11. Ibid., 80.

12. The exact opposite of this vision is presented in Joel 3:10 where the foreign nations are told that their weapons will do them no good in the face of God's coming wrath.

13. An omission in the New Testament is significant in this context. Scholars have made us aware of the presence of revolutionary groups in Israel during the time of Jesus. Barabbas, for example, was "among the rebels in prison who had committed murder in the insurrection" (Mk. 15:7). Although Jesus had come to proclaim and to bring about the true reign of God which often stood in opposition to the existing order, he makes no reference to nor does he join in any attempts such as those of the Zealots to overthrow authority by violent means. See M. Smith, "Zealots and Sicarii, Their Origins and Relations," *Harvard Theological Review* 64 (1971):1–19.

14. John Paul II, "World Day of Peace Message 1982," 12, *Origins* 11 (1982): 477.

15. Ibid., 11–12, pp. 477–78.

16. John Paul II, "Message U.N. Special Session 1982," 13, Pope Paul VI, "World Day of Peace Message 1973."

17. John Paul II, "World Day of Peace Message 1982," 12, cited, p. 478.

18. *Pastoral Constitution*, 79.

19. Ibid., 77.

20. Ibid., 80.

21. Ibid., 17.

22. Ibid., 78.

23. John Paul II, "World Day of Peace Message 1982," 9, cited. The *Pastoral Constitution* stresses that peace is not only the fruit of justice, but also love, which commits us to engage in "the studied practice of brotherhood" (no. 78).

24. *Pastoral Constitution*, 79.

25. Ibid., 82.

26. Ibid., 79.

27. Pius XII, "Christmas Message," 1948. The same theme is reiterated in Pius XII's "Message" of October 3, 1953: "The community of nations must reckon with unprincipled criminals who, in order to realize their ambitious plans, are not afraid to unleash total war. This is the reason why other countries if they wish to preserve their very existence and their most precious possessions, and unless they are prepared to accord free action to international criminals, have no alternative but to get ready for the day when they must defend themselves. *This right to be prepared for self-defense cannot be denied, even in these days, to any state.*"

28. *Pastoral Constitution*, 80.

29. Ibid.

30. John Paul II, "World Day of Peace Message 1982," 12, cited, p. 478.

31. Augustine called it a Manichaean heresy to assert that war is intrinsically evil and contrary to Christian charity, and stated: "War and conquest are a sad necessity in the eyes of men of principle, yet it would be still more unfortunate if wrongdoers should dominate just men" (*The City of God*, Book IV, C. 15).

Representative surveys of the history and theology of the just-war tradition include: F. H. Russell, *The Just War in the Middle Ages* (New York: 1975); P. Ramsey, *War and the Christian Conscience* (Durham, N.C.: 1961), *The Just War: Force and Political Responsibility* (New York: 1968); James T. Johnson, *Ideology, Reason and the Limitation of War* (Princeton: 1975), *Just-War Tradition and the Restraint of War: A Moral and Historical Inquiry* (Princeton: 1981); L. B. Walters, *Five Classic Just-War Theories* (Ph.D. Dissertation, Yale University, 1971); W. O'Brien, *War and/or Survival* (New York: 1969), *The Conduct of Just and Limited War* (New York: 1981); J. C. Murray, "Remarks on the Moral Problem of War," *Theological Studies* 20 (1959):40–61.

32. Aquinas treats the question of war in the *Summa Theologica*, II-IIae q. 40; also cf. II-IIae, q. 64.

33. *Pastoral Constitution*, 79.

34. Pius XII, "Christmas Message," 1948.

35. For an analysis of the content and relationship of these principles cf.: R. Potter, "The Moral Logic of War," *McCormick Quarterly* 23 (1970): 203–33; J. Childress, "Just War Criteria," in T. Shannon, ed., *War or Peace: The Search for New Answers* (New York: 1980).

36. James T. Johnson, *Ideology, Reason and the Limitation of War*, cited; W. O'Brien, *The Conduct of Just and Limited War*, cited, pp. 13–30; W. Vanderpol, *La doctrine scolastique du droit de guerre*, p. 387ff; J. C. Murray, "Theology and Modern Warfare," in W. J. Nagel, ed., *Morality and Modern Warfare*, p. 80ff.

37. John Paul II, "World Day of Peace Message 1983," 11.

38. National Conference of Catholic Bishops, *Resolution on Southeast Asia* (Washington, D.C: 1971).

39. *Pastoral Constitution*, 80.

40. John Paul II, "World Day of Peace Message 1982," 12, cited.

41. "Declaration on Prevention of Nuclear War" (Sept. 24, 1982).

42. *Pastoral Constitution*, 80.

43. Ibid.

44. John Paul II, "World Day of Peace Message 1982," 12, cited.

45. Representative authors in the tradition of Christian pacifism and nonviolence include: R. Bainton, *Christian Attitudes Toward War and Peace* (Abington: 1960), chs. 4, 5, 10; J. Yoder, *The Politics of Jesus* (Grand Rapids: 1972), *Nevertheless: Varieties of Religious Pacifism* (Scottsdale: 1971); T. Merton, *Faith and Violence: Christian Teaching and Christian Practice* (Notre Dame: 1968); G. Zahn, *War, Conscience and Dissent* (New York: 1967); E. Egan, "The Beatitudes: Works of Mercy and Pacifism," in T. Shannon, ed., *War or Peace: The Search for New Answers* (New York: 1980), pp. 169–187; J. Fahey, "The Catholic Church and the Arms Race," *Worldview* 22 (1979):38–41; J. Douglass, *The Nonviolent Cross: A Theology of Revolution and Peace* (New York: 1966).

46. Justin, *Dialogue with Trypho*, ch. 110; cf. also *The First Apology*, chs. 14, 39.

47. Cyprian, *Collected Letters*; Letters to Cornelius.

48. Sulpicius Severus, *The Life of Martin*, 4.3.

49. *Pastoral Constitution*, 79.

50. Ibid., 78.

51. United States Catholic Conference, *Human Life in Our Day* (Washington, D.C.: 1968), p. 44.

52. *Pastoral Constitution*, 80.

53. Ibid.

54. John Paul II, "Address to Scientists and Scholars," 4, cited, p. 621.

55. Cf. "Declaration on Prevention of Nuclear War."

56. Paul VI, "World Day of Peace Message 1976," in *Documents*, p. 198.

57. "Statement of the Holy See to the United Nations" (1976), in *The Church and the Arms Race*; Pax Christi-USA (New York: 1976), pp. 23–24.

58. R. Adams and S. Cullen. *The Final Epidemic: Physicians and Scientists on Nuclear War* (Chicago: 1981).

59. Pontifical Academy of Sciences, "Statement on the Consequences of the Use of Nuclear Weapons," in *Documents*, p. 241.

60. John Paul II, "World Day of Peace Message 1982," 6, cited, p. 476.

61. The following quotations are from public officials who have served at the highest policy levels in recent administrations of our government: "It is time to recognize that no one has ever succeeded in advancing any persuasive reason to believe that any use of nuclear weapons, even on the smallest scale, could reliably be expected to remain limited." M. Bundy, G. F. Kennan, R. S. McNamara and G. Smith, "Nuclear Weapons and the Atlantic Alliance," *Foreign Affairs* 60 (1982):757.

"From my experience in combat there is no way that [nuclear escalation] . . . can be controlled because of the lack of information, the pressure of time and the deadly results that are taking place on both sides of the battle line." Gen. A. S. Collins, Jr. (former deputy commander in chief of U.S. Army in Europe), "Theatre Nuclear Warfare: The Battlefield," in J. F. Reichart and S. R. Sturn, eds., *American Defense Policy*, 5th ed. (Baltimore: 1982), pp. 359–60.

"None of this potential flexibility changes my view that a full-scale thermonuclear exchange would be an unprecedented disaster for the Soviet Union as well as for the United States. Nor is it at all clear that an initial use of nuclear weapons—however selectively they might be targeted—could be kept from escalating to a full-scale thermonuclear exchange, especially if command-and-control centers were brought under attack. The odds are high, whether weapons were used against tactical or strategic targets, that control would be lost on both sides and the exchange would become unconstrained." Harold Brown, *Department of Defense Annual Report FY 1979* (Washington, D.C.: 1978).

Cf. also: *The Effects of Nuclear War* (Washington, D.C.: U.S. Government Printing Office, 1979).

62. For example, cf.: H. A. Kissinger, *Nuclear Weapons and Foreign Policy* (New York: 1957), *The Necessity for Choice* (New York: 1960); R. Osgood and R. Tucker, *Force, Order and Justice* (Baltimore: 1967); R. Aron, *The Great Debate: Theories of Nuclear Strategy* (New York: 1965); D. Ball, *Can Nuclear War Be Controlled?* Adelphi Paper 161 (London: 1981); M. Howard, "On Fighting a Nuclear War," *International Security* 5 (1981):3–17.

63. "Statement on the Consequences of the Use of Nuclear Weapons," cited, p. 243.

64. Pius XII, "Address to the VIII Congress of the World Medical Association," in *Documents*, p. 131.

65. *Pastoral Constitution*, 80.

66. Ibid.

67. M. Bundy, et al., "Nuclear Weapons," cited, K. Kaiser, G. Leber, A. Mertes, F. J. Schulze, "Nuclear Weapons and the Presentation of Peace," *Foreign Affairs* 60 (1982):1157–1170; cf. other responses to Bundy article in the same issue of *Foreign Affairs*.

68. Testimony given to the National Conference of Catholic Bishops Committee during preparation of this pastoral letter. The testimony is reflected in the quotes found in note 61.

69. Our conclusions and judgments in this area although based on careful study and reflection of the application of moral principles do not have, of course, the same force as the principles themselves and therefore allow for different opinions, as the Summary makes clear.

70. Undoubtedly aware of the long and detailed technical debate on limited war, Pope John Paul II highlighted the unacceptable moral risk of crossing the threshold to nuclear war in his "Angelus Message" of December 13, 1981: "I have, in fact, the deep conviction that, in the light of a nuclear war's effects, which can be scientifically foreseen as certain, the only choice that is morally and humanly valid is represented by the reduction of nuclear armaments, while waiting for their future complete elimination, carried out simultaneously by all the parties, by means of explicit agreements and with the commitment of accepting effective controls." In *Documents*, p. 240.

71. W. H. Kincade and J. D. Porro, *Negotiating Security: An Arms Control Reader* (Washington, D.C.: 1979).

72. Several surveys are available, for example cf.: J. H. Kahin, *Security in the Nuclear Age: Developing U.S. Strategic Policy* (Washington, D.C.: 1975); M. Mandelbaum, *The Nuclear Question: The United States and Nuclear Weapons 1946–1976* (Cambridge, England: 1979); S. Brodie, "Development of Nuclear Strategy," *International Security* 2 (1978):65–83.

73. The relationship of these two levels of policy is the burden of an article by D. Ball, "U.S. Strategic Forces: How Would They Be Used?" *International Security* 7 (1982/83):31–60.

74. *Pastoral Constitution*, 81.

75. United States Catholic Conference, *To Live in Christ Jesus* (Washington, D.C.: 1976), p. 34.

76. John Cardinal Krol, "Testimony on Salt II," *Origins* (1979):197.

77. John Paul II, "Message U.N. Special Session 1982," 3.

78. Ibid., 8.

79. John Paul II, "Address to UNESCO, 1980," 21.

80. John Paul II, "Letter to International Seminar on the World Implications of a Nuclear Conflict," August 23, 1982, text in *NC News Documentary*, August 24, 1982.

81. Particularly helpful was the letter of January 15, 1983, of Mr. William Clark, national security adviser, to Cardinal Bernardin. Mr. Clark stated: "For

moral, political, and military reasons, the United States does not target the Soviet civilian population as such. There is no deliberately opaque meaning conveyed in the last two words. We do not threaten the existence of Soviet civilization by threatening Soviet cities. Rather, we hold at risk the war-making capability of the Soviet Union—its armed forces, and the industrial capacity to sustain war. It would be irresponsible for us to issue policy statements which might suggest to the Soviets that it would be to their advantage to establish privileged sanctuaries within heavily populated areas, thus inducing them to locate much of their war-fighting capability within those urban sanctuaries." A reaffirmation of the administration's policy is also found in Secretary Weinberger's *Annual Report to the Congress* (Caspar Weinberger, *Annual Report to the Congress*, February 1, 1983, p. 55): "The Reagan Administration's policy is that under no circumstances may such weapons be used deliberately for the purpose of destroying populations." Also, the letter of Mr. Weinberger to Bishop O'Connor of February 9, 1983, has a similar statement.

82. S. Zuckerman, *Nuclear Illusion and Reality* (New York: 1982); D. Ball, cited, p. 36; T. Powers, "Choosing a Strategy for World War III," *The Atlantic Monthly*, November 1982, pp. 82–110.

83. Cf. the comments in Pontifical Academy of Sciences, "Statement on the Consequences of the Use of Nuclear Weapons," cited.

84. Several experts in strategic theory would place both the MX missile and Pershing II missiles in this category.

85. In each of the successive drafts of this letter we have tried to state a central moral imperative: that the arms race should be stopped and disarmament begun. The implementation of this imperative is open to a wide variety of approaches. Hence we have chosen our own language in this paragraph, not wanting either to be identified with one specific political initiative or to have our words used against specific political measures.

86. Cf. President Reagan's "Speech to the National Press Club" (November 18, 1981) and "Address at Eureka College" (May 9, 1982), Department of State, *Current Policy* no. 316 and 387.

87. John Paul II, "Homily at Bagington Airport," Coventry, 2, *Origins* 12 (1982):55.

88. The two treaties are the Threshold Test Ban Treaty signed July 3, 1974, and the Treaty on Nuclear Explosions for Peaceful Purposes (P.N.E.) signed May 28, 1976.

89. John Paul II, "Message to U.N. Special Session 1982," 8.

90. Mr. Weinberger's letter to Bishop O'Connor specifies actions taken on command and control facilities designed to reduce the chance of unauthorized firing of nuclear weapons.

91. John Paul II, "Message to U.N. Special Session 1982," 9. Cf. United States Catholic Conference, *At Issue 2: Arms Export Policies—Ethical Choices* (Washington, D.C.: 1978) for suggestions about controlling the conventional arms trade.

92. The International Security Act of 1976 provides for such human rights review.

93. John Paul II. "Address to the United Nations General Assembly," *Origins* 9 (1979): 268.

94. John Paul II. "Homily at Bagington Airport," Coventry, 2; cited, p. 55.

95. *Pastoral Constitution*, 78.

96. G. Sharp, *The Politics of Nonviolent Action* (Boston: 1973); R. Fisher and W. Ury, *Getting to Yes: Negotiating Agreement Without Giving In* (Boston: 1981).

97. John Paul II, "World Day of Peace Message 1982," 7, cited, p. 476.

98. *To Establish the United States Academy of Peace: Report of the Commission on Proposals for the National Academy of Peace and Conflict Resolution* (Washington, D.C.: 1981), pp. 119–120.

99. United States Catholic Conference, *Statement on Registration and Conscription for Military Service* (Washington, D.C.: 1980). Cf. also *Human Life in Our Day*, cited, pp. 42–45.

100. Paul VI, *The Development of Peoples* (1967), 76.

101. Cf. V. Yzermans, ed., *Major Addresses of Pius XII*, 2 Vols. (St. Paul: 1961) and J. Gremillion, *The Gospel of Peace and Justice*, cited.

102. Cf. John XXIII, *Peace on Earth* (1963), esp. 80–145.

103. A sampling of the policy problems and possibilities posed by interdependence can be found in: R. O. Keohane and J. S. Nye, Jr., *Power and Interdependence* (Boston: 1977); S. Hoffmann, *Primacy or World Order* (New York: 1978); The Overseas Development Council, *The U.S. and World Development* 1979; 1980; 1982 (Washington, D.C.).

104. John XXIII, *Peace on Earth* (1963), 137.

105. This has particularly been the case in the two U.N. Special Sessions on Disarmament, 1979, 1982.

106. United States Catholic Conference, *Marxist Communism* (Washington, D.C.: 1980), p. 19.

107. The debate on U.S.-Soviet relations is extensive; recent examples of it are found in: A. Ulam, "U.S.-Soviet Relations: Unhappy Coexistence," *America and the World, 1978; Foreign Affairs* 57 (1979):556–71; W. G. Hyland, "U.S.-Soviet Relations: The Long Road Back," *America and the World, 1981; Foreign Affairs* 60 (1982): 525–50; R. Legvold, "Containment Without Confrontation," *Foreign Policy* 40 (1980):74–98; S. Hoffmann, "Muscle and Brains," *Foreign Policy* 37 (1979–80):3–27; P. Hassner, "Moscow and The Western Alliance," *Problems of Communism* 30 (1981):37–54; S. Bialer, "The Harsh Decade: Soviet Policies in the 1980s," *Foreign Affairs* 59 (1981):999–1020; G. Kennan, *The Nuclear Delusion: Soviet-American Relations in the Atomic Age* (New York: 1982); N. Podhoretz, *The Present Danger* (New York: 1980); P. Nitze, "Strategy in the 1980s," *Foreign Affairs* 59 (1980):82–101; R. Strode and C. Gray, "The Imperial Dimension of Soviet Military Power," *Problems of Communism* 30 (1981):1–15; International Institute for Strategic Studies, *Prospects of Soviet Power in the 1980s*,

Parts I and II, Adelphi Papers 151 and 152 (London: 1979); S. S. Kaplan, ed., *Diplomacy of Power: Soviet Armed Forces as a Political Instrument* (Washington, D.C.: 1981); R. Barnet, *The Giants: Russia and America* (New York: 1977); M. McGuire, *Soviet Military Requirements* (The Brookings Institution: Washington, D.C., 1982); R. Tucker, "The Purposes of American Power," *Foreign Affairs* 59 (1980/81):241–74; A. Geyer, *The Idea of Disarmament: Rethinking the Unthinkable* (Washington, D.C.: 1982). For a review of Soviet adherence to treaties, cf.: "The SALT Syndrome Charges and Facts: Analysis of an 'Anti-SALT' Documentary," report prepared by U.S. government agencies (State, Defense, CIA, ACDA, and NSC), reprinted in *The Defense Monitor* 10, 8A, Center for Defense Information.

108. John Paul II, "World Day of Peace Message 1983," 7, cited.

109. John Paul II, "The Redeemer of Man," 16, *Origins* 8 (1980):635.

110. The phrase and its description are found in R. S. McNamara, *Report to the Board of Governors of the World Bank* 1978; cf. also 1979; 1980 (Washington, D.C.).

111. John Paul II, "Homily at Yankee Stadium," 4, *Origins* 9 (1979):311.

112. Paul VI, "Address to the General Assembly of the United Nations" (1965), 2.

113. *Pastoral Constitution*, 81.

114. Cf. Hoffman, cited; Independent Commission on Disarmament and Security Issues, *Common Security* (New York: 1982).

115. For an analysis of the policy problems of reallocating resources, cf.: Bruce M. Russett, *The Prisoners of Insecurity* (San Francisco: 1983). Cf.: *Common Security*, cited; Russett, cited; *U.N. Report on Disarmament and Development* (New York: 1982); United Nations, *The Relationship Between Disarmament and Development: A Summary*, Fact Sheet 21 (New York: 1982).

116. John Paul II, "The Redeemer of Man," 21, cited, p. 641. Much of the following reflects the content of A. Dulles, *A Church to Believe In: Discipleship and the Dynamics of Freedom* (New York: 1982), ch. 1.

117. John Paul II, "World Day of Peace Message 1982," 4, cited, p. 475.

118. Paul VI, "World Day of Peace Message 1977."

119. *Pastoral Constitution*, 79.

120. John Paul II, "Address to Scientists and Scholars," 3, cited, p. 621.

121. Ibid.

122. *Pastoral Constitution*, 75.

123. John Paul II, "Address at Hiroshima," 2, *Origins* 10 (1981):620.

124. *Pastoral Constitution*, 75.

125. *Human Life in Our Day*, cited, p. 41.

126. John XXIII, *Peace on Earth* (1963), 137.

127. Paul VI, "Address to the General Assembly of the United Nations," (1965), 2.

Economic Justice for All (U.S. Catholic Bishops, 1986)

Brothers and Sisters in Christ:

1. We are believers called to follow Our Lord Jesus Christ and proclaim his Gospel in the midst of a complex and powerful economy. This reality poses both opportunities and responsibilities for Catholics in the United States. Our faith calls us to measure this economy, not only by what it produces, but also by how it touches human life and whether it protects or undermines the dignity of the human person. Economic decisions have human consequences and moral content; they help or hurt people, strengthen or weaken family life, advance or diminish the quality of justice in our land.

2. This is why we have written *Economic Justice for All: A Pastoral Letter on Catholic Social Teaching and the U.S. Economy*. This letter is a personal invitation to Catholics to use the resources of our faith, the strength of our economy, and the opportunities of our democracy to shape a society that better protects the dignity and basic rights of our sisters and brothers, both in this land and around the world.

3. The pastoral letter has been a work of careful inquiry, wide consultation, and prayerful discernment. The letter has been greatly enriched by this process of listening and refinement. We offer this introductory pastoral message to Catholics in the United States seeking to live their faith in the marketplace—in homes, offices, factories, and schools; on farms and ranches; in boardrooms and union halls; in service agencies and legislative chambers. We seek to explain why we wrote the pastoral letter, to introduce its major themes, and to share our hopes for the dialogue and action it might generate.

Why We Write

4. We write to share our teaching, to raise questions, to challenge one another to live our faith in the world. We write as heirs of the biblical prophets who summon us "to do the right and to love goodness, and to walk humbly with your God" (Mi. 6:8). We write as followers of Jesus who told us in the Sermon on the Mount: "Blessed are the poor in spirit. . . . Blessed are the meek. . . . Blessed are they who hunger and thirst for righteousness. . . . You are the salt of the earth. . . . You are the light of the world" (Mt. 5:1–6, 13–14). These words challenge us not only as believers but also as consumers, citizens, workers, and owners. In the parable of the Last Judgment, Jesus said, "For I

was hungry and you gave me food, I was thirsty and you gave me drink. . . . As often as you did it for one of my least brothers, you did it for me" (Mt. 25:35–40). The challenge for us is to discover in our own place and time what it means to be "poor in spirit" and "the salt of the earth" and what it means to serve "the least among us" and to "hunger and thirst for righteousness."

5. Followers of Christ must avoid a tragic separation between faith and everyday life. They can neither shirk their earthly duties nor, as the Second Vatican Council declared, "immerse [them]selves in earthly activities as if these latter were utterly foreign to religion, and religion were nothing more than the fulfillment of acts of worship and the observance of a few moral obligations" (*Pastoral Constitution on the Church in the Modern World*, no. 43).

6. Economic life raises important social and moral questions for each of us and for society as a whole. Like family life, economic life is one of the chief areas where we live out our faith, love our neighbor, confront temptation, fulfill God's creative design, and achieve our holiness. Our economic activity in factory, field, office, or shop feeds our families—or feeds our anxieties. It exercises our talents—or wastes them. It raises our hopes—or crushes them. It brings us into cooperation with others—or sets us at odds. The Second Vatican Council instructs us "to preach the message of Christ in such a way that the light of the Gospel will shine on all activities of the faithful" (*Pastoral Constitution*, no. 43). In this case, we are trying to look at economic life through the eyes of faith, applying traditional church teaching to the U.S. economy.

7. In our letter, we write as pastors, not public officials. We speak as moral teachers, not economic technicians. We seek not to make some political or ideological point but to lift up the human and ethical dimensions of economic life, aspects too often neglected in public discussion. We bring to this task a dual heritage of Catholic social teaching and traditional American values.

8. As *Catholics*, we are heirs of a long tradition of thought and action on the moral dimensions of economic activity. The life and words of Jesus and the teaching of his Church call us to serve those in need and to work actively for social and economic justice. As a community of believers, we know that our faith is tested by the quality of justice among us, that we can best measure our life together by how the poor and the vulnerable are treated. This is not a new concern for us. It is as old as the Hebrew prophets, as compelling as the Sermon on the Mount, and as current as the powerful voice of Pope John Paul II defending the dignity of the human person.

9. As *Americans*, we are grateful for the gift of freedom and committed to the dream of "liberty and justice for all." This nation, blessed with extraordinary resources, has provided an unprecedented standard of living for millions of people. We are proud of the strength, productivity, and creativity of our economy, but we also remember those who have been left behind in our progress. We believe that we honor our history best by working for the day when all our sisters and brothers share adequately in the American dream.

10. As *bishops*, in proclaiming the Gospel for these times we also manage institutions, balance budgets, meet payrolls. In this we see the human face of our economy. We feel the hurts and hopes of our people. We feel the pain of our sisters and brothers who are poor, unemployed, homeless, living on the edge. The poor and vulnerable are on our doorsteps, in our parishes, in our service agencies, and in our shelters. We see too much hunger and injustice, too much suffering and despair, both in our own country and around the world.

11. As *pastors*, we also see the decency, generosity, and vulnerability of our people. We see the struggles of ordinary families to make ends meet and to provide a better future for their children. We know the desire of managers, professionals, and business people to shape what they do by what they believe. It is the faith, good will, and generosity of our people that gives us hope as we write this letter.

Principal Themes of the Pastoral Letter

12. The pastoral letter is not a blueprint for the American economy. It does not embrace any particular theory of how the economy works, nor does it attempt to resolve the disputes between different schools of economic thought. Instead, our letter turns to Scripture and to the social teachings of the Church. There, we discover what our economic life must serve, what standards it must meet. Let us examine some of these basic moral principles.

13. *Every economic decision and institution must be judged in light of whether it protects or undermines the dignity of the human person.* The pastoral letter begins with the human person. We believe the person is sacred—the clearest reflection of God among us. Human dignity comes from God, not from nationality, race, sex, economic status, or any human accomplishment. We judge any economic system by what it does *for* and *to* people and by how it permits all to *participate* in it. The economy should serve people, not the other way around.

14. *Human dignity can be realized and protected only in community.* In our teaching, the human person is not only sacred but also social. How we organize our society—in economics and politics, in law and policy—directly affects human dignity and the capacity of individuals to grow in community. The obligation to "love our neighbor" has an individual dimension, but it also requires a broader social commitment to the common good. We have many partial ways to measure and debate the health of our economy: gross national product, per capita income, stock market prices, and so forth. The Christian vision of economic life looks beyond them all and asks, Does economic life enhance or threaten our life together as a community?

15. *All people have a right to participate in the economic life of society.* Basic justice demands that people be assured a minimum level of participation in the economy. It is wrong for a person or group to be excluded unfairly or to be unable to participate or contribute to the economy. For

example, people who are both able and willing, but cannot get a job are deprived of the participation that is so vital to human development. For, it is through employment that most individuals and families meet their material needs, exercise their talents, and have an opportunity to contribute to the larger community. Such participation has a special significance in our tradition because we believe that it is a means by which we join in carrying forward God's creative activity.

16. *All members of society have a special obligation to the poor and vulnerable.* From the Scriptures and church teaching, we learn that the justice of a society is tested by the treatment of the poor. The justice that was the sign of God's covenant with Israel was measured by how the poor and unprotected—the widow, the orphan, and the stranger—were treated. The kingdom that Jesus proclaimed in his word and ministry excludes no one. Throughout Israel's history and in early Christianity, the poor are agents of God's transforming power. "The Spirit of the Lord is upon me, therefore he has anointed me. He has sent me to bring glad tidings to the poor" (Lk. 4:18). This was Jesus' first public utterance. Jesus takes the side of those most in need. In the Last Judgment, so dramatically described in St. Matthew's Gospel, we are told that we will be judged according to how we respond to the hungry, the thirsty, the naked, the stranger. As followers of Christ, we are challenged to make a fundamental "option for the poor"—to speak for the voiceless, to defend the defenseless, to assess life styles, policies, and social institutions in terms of their impact on the poor. This "option for the poor" does not mean pitting one group against another, but rather, strengthening the whole community by assisting those who are most vulnerable. As Christians, we are called to respond to the needs of *all* our brothers and sisters, but those with the greatest needs require the greatest response.

17. *Human rights are the minimum conditions for life in community.* In Catholic teaching, human rights include not only civil and political rights but also economic rights. As Pope John XXIII declared, "all people have a right to life, food, clothing, shelter, rest, medical care, education, and employment." This means that when people are without a chance to earn a living, and must go hungry and homeless, they are being denied basic rights. Society must ensure that these rights are protected. In this way, we will ensure that the minimum conditions of economic justice are met for all our sisters and brothers.

18. *Society as a whole, acting through public and private institutions, has the moral responsibility to enhance human dignity and protect human rights.* In addition to the clear responsibility of private institutions, government has an essential responsibility in this area. This does not mean that government has the primary or exclusive role, but it does have a positive moral responsibility in safeguarding human rights and ensuring that the minimum conditions of human dignity are met for all. In a democracy, government is a means by which we can act together to protect what is important to us and to promote our common values.

19. These six moral principles are not the only ones presented in the pastoral letter, but they give an overview of the moral vision that we are trying to share. This vision of economic life cannot exist in a vacuum; it must be translated into concrete measures. Our pastoral letter spells out some specific applications of Catholic moral principles. We call for a new national commitment to full employment. We say it is a social and moral scandal that one of every seven Americans is poor, and we call for concerted efforts to eradicate poverty. The fulfillment of the basic needs of the poor is of the highest priority. We urge that all economic policies be evaluated in light of their impact on the life and stability of the family. We support measures to halt the loss of family farms and to resist the growing concentration in the ownership of agricultural resources. We specify ways in which the United States can do far more to relieve the plight of poor nations and assist in their development. We also reaffirm church teaching on the rights of workers, collective bargaining, private property, subsidiarity, and equal opportunity.

20. We believe that the recommendations in our letter are reasonable and balanced. In analyzing the economy, we reject ideological extremes and start from the fact that ours is a "mixed" economy, the product of a long history of reform and adjustment. We know that some of our specific recommendations are controversial. As bishops, we do not claim to make these prudential judgments with the same kind of authority that marks our declarations of principle. But, we feel obliged to teach by example how Christians can undertake concrete analysis and make specific judgments on economic issues. The Church's teachings cannot be left at the level of appealing generalities.

21. In the pastoral letter, we suggest that the time has come for a "New American Experiment"—to implement economic rights, to broaden the sharing of economic power, and to make economic decisions more accountable to the common good. This experiment can create new structures of economic partnership and participation within firms at the regional level, for the whole nation, and across borders.

22. Of course, there are many aspects of the economy the letter does not touch, and there are basic questions it leaves to further exploration. There are also many specific points on which men and women of good will may disagree. We look for a fruitful exchange among differing viewpoints. We pray only that all will take to heart the urgency of our concerns; that together we will test our views by the Gospel and the Church's teaching; and that we will listen to other voices in a spirit of mutual respect and open dialogue.

A Call to Conversion and Action

23. We should not be surprised if we find Catholic social teaching to be demanding. The Gospel is demanding. We are always in need of conversion, of a change of heart. We are richly blessed, and as St. Paul assures us, we are destined for glory. Yet, it is also true that we are sinners; that we are not

always wise or loving or just; that, for all our amazing possibilities, we are incompletely born, wary of life, and hemmed in by fears and empty routines. We are unable to entrust ourselves fully to the living God, and so we seek substitute forms of security in material things, in power, in indifference, in popularity, in pleasure. The Scriptures warn us that these things can become forms of idolatry. We know that, at times, in order to remain truly a community of Jesus' disciples, we will have to say "no" to certain aspects in our culture, to certain trends and ways of acting that are opposed to a life of faith, love, and justice. Changes in our hearts lead naturally to a desire to change how we act. With what care, human kindness, and justice do I conduct myself at work? How will my economic decisions to buy, sell, invest, divest, hire, or fire serve human dignity and the common good? In what career can I best exercise my talents so as to fill the world with the Spirit of Christ? How do my economic choices contribute to the strength of my family and community, to the values of my children, to a sensitivity to those in need? In this consumer society, how can I develop a healthy detachment from things and avoid the temptation to assess who I am by what I have? How do I strike a balance between labor and leisure that enlarges my capacity for friendships, for family life, for community? What government policies should I support to attain the well-being of all, especially the poor and vulnerable?

24. The answers to such questions are not always clear—or easy to live out. But, conversion is a lifelong process. And, it is not undertaken alone. It occurs with the support of the whole believing community, through baptism, common prayer, and our daily efforts, large and small, on behalf of justice. As a Church, we must be people after God's own heart, bonded by the Spirit, sustaining one another in love, setting our hearts on God's Kingdom, committing ourselves to solidarity with those who suffer, working for peace and justice, acting as a sign of Christ's love and justice in the world. The Church cannot redeem the world from the deadening effects of sin and injustice unless it is working to remove sin and injustice in its own life and institutions. All of us must help the Church to practice in its own life what it preaches to others about economic justice and cooperation.

25. The challenge of this pastoral letter is not merely to think differently, but also to act differently. A renewal of economic life depends on the conscious choices and commitments of individual believers who practice their faith in the world. The road to holiness for most of us lies in our secular vocations. We need a spirituality that calls forth and supports lay initiative and witness not just in our churches but also in business, in the labor movement, in the professions, in education, and in public life. Our faith is not just a weekend obligation, a mystery to be celebrated around the altar on Sunday. It is a pervasive reality to be practiced every day in homes, offices, factories, schools, and businesses across our land. We cannot separate what we believe from how we act in the marketplace and the broader community, for this is where we make our primary contribution to the pursuit of economic justice.

26. We ask each of you to read the pastoral letter, to study it, to pray about it, and match it with your own experience. We ask you to join with us in service to those in need. Let us reach out personally to the hungry and the homeless, to the poor and the powerless, and to the troubled and the vulnerable. In serving them, we serve Christ. Our service efforts cannot substitute for just and compassionate public policies, but they can help us practice what we preach about human life and human dignity.

27. The pursuit of economic justice takes believers into the public arena, testing the policies of government by the principles of our teaching. We ask you to become more informed and active citizens, using your voices and votes to speak for the voiceless, to defend the poor and the vulnerable and to advance the common good. We are called to shape a constituency of conscience, measuring every policy by how it touches the least, the lost, and the left-out among us. This letter calls us to conversion and common action, to new forms of stewardship, service, and citizenship.

28. The completion of a letter such as this is but the beginning of a long process of education, discussion, and action. By faith and baptism, we are fashioned into new creatures, filled with the Holy Spirit and with a love that compels us to seek out a new profound relationship with God, with the human family, and with all created things. Jesus has entered our history as God's anointed son who announces the coming of God's Kingdom, a kingdom of justice and peace and freedom. And, what Jesus proclaims, he embodies in his actions. His ministry reveals that the reign of God is something more powerful than evil, injustice, and the hardness of hearts. Through his crucifixion and resurrection, he reveals that God's love is ultimately victorious over all suffering, all horror, all meaninglessness, and even over the mystery of death. Thus, we proclaim words of hope and assurance to all who suffer and are in need.

29. We believe that the Christian view of life, including economic life, can transform the lives of individuals, families, schools, and our whole culture. We believe that with your prayers, reflection, service, and action, our economy can be shaped so that human dignity prospers and the human person is served. This is the unfinished work of our nation. This is the challenge of our faith.

CHAPTER 1: THE CHURCH AND THE FUTURE OF THE U.S. ECONOMY

1. Every perspective on economic life that is human, moral, and Christian must be shaped by three questions: What does the economy do *for* people? What does it do *to* people? And how do people *participate* in it? The economy is a human reality: men and women working together to develop and care for the whole of God's creation. All this work must serve the material and spiritual well-being of people. It influences what people hope for themselves and

their loved ones. It affects the way they act together in society. It influences their very faith in God.[1]

2. The Second Vatican Council declared that "the joys and hopes, the griefs and anxieties of the people of this age, especially those who are poor or in any way afflicted, these too are the joys and hopes, the griefs and anxieties of the followers of Christ."[2] There are many signs of hope in U.S. economic life today:

- Many fathers and mothers skillfully balance the arduous responsibilities of work and family life. There are parents who pursue a purposeful and modest way of life and by their example encourage their children to follow a similar path. A large number of women and men, drawing on their religious tradition, recognize the challenging vocation of family life and child rearing in a culture that emphasizes material display and self-gratification.
- Conscientious business people seek new and more equitable ways to organize resources and the workplace. They face hard choices over expanding or retrenching, shifting investments, hiring or firing.
- Young people choosing their life's work ask whether success and security are compatible with service to others.
- Workers whose labor may be toilsome or repetitive try daily to ennoble their work with a spirit of solidarity and friendship.
- New immigrants brave dislocations while hoping for the opportunities realized by the millions who came before them.

3. These signs of hope are not the whole story. There have been failures—some of them massive and ugly:

- Poor and homeless people sleep in community shelters and in our church basements; the hungry line up in soup lines.
- Unemployment gnaws at the self-respect of both middle-aged persons who have lost jobs and the young who cannot find them.
- Hardworking men and women wonder if the system of enterprise that helped them yesterday might destroy their jobs and their communities tomorrow.
- Families confront major new challenges: dwindling social supports for family stability; economic pressures that force both parents of young children to work outside the home; a driven pace of life among the successful that can sap love and commitment; lack of hope among those who have less or nothing at all. Very different kinds of families bear different burdens of our economic system.
- Farmers face the loss of their land and way of life; young people find it difficult to choose farming as a vocation; farming communities are threatened; migrant farmworkers break their backs in serf-like conditions for disgracefully low wages.

4. *And beyond our own shores, the reality of 800 million people living in absolute poverty and 450 million malnourished or facing starvation casts an ominous shadow over all these hopes and problems at home.*

5. Anyone who sees all this will understand our concern as pastors and bishops. People shape the economy and in turn are shaped by it. Economic arrangements can be sources of fulfillment, of hope, of community—or of frustration, isolation, and even despair. They teach virtues—or vices—and day by day help mold our characters. They affect the quality of people's lives; at the extreme even determining whether people live or die. Serious economic choices go beyond purely technical issues to fundamental questions of value and human purpose.[3] We believe that in facing these questions the Christian religious and moral tradition can make an important contribution.

A. The U.S. Economy Today: Memory and Hope

6. The United States is among the most economically powerful nations on earth. In its short history the U.S. economy has grown to provide an unprecedented standard of living for most of its people. The nation has created productive work for millions of immigrants and enabled them to broaden their freedoms, improve their families' quality of life, and contribute to the building of a great nation. Those who came to this country from other lands often understood their new lives in the light of biblical faith. They thought of themselves as entering a promised land of political freedom and economic opportunity. The United States *is* a land of vast natural resources and fertile soil. It *has* encouraged citizens to undertake bold ventures. Through hard work, self-sacrifice, and cooperation, families have flourished; towns, cities, and a powerful nation have been created.

7. But we should recall this history with sober humility. The American experiment in social, political, and economic life has involved serious conflict and suffering. Our nation was born in the face of injustice to native Americans, and its independence was paid for with the blood of revolution. Slavery stained the commercial life of the land through its first two hundred and fifty years and was ended only by a violent civil war. The establishment of women's suffrage, the protection of industrial workers, the elimination of child labor, the response to the Great Depression of the 1930s, and the civil rights movement of the 1960s all involved a sustained struggle to transform the political and economic institutions of the nation.

8. The U.S. value system emphasizes economic freedom. It also recognizes that the market is limited by fundamental human rights. Some things are never to be bought or sold.[4] This conviction has prompted positive steps to modify the operation of the market when it harms vulnerable members of society. Labor unions help workers resist exploitation. Through their government, the people of the United States have provided support for education,

access to food, unemployment compensation, security in old age, and protection of the environment. The market system contributes to the success of the U.S. economy, but so do many efforts to forge economic institutions and public policies that enable *all* to share in the riches of the nation. The country's economy has been built through a creative struggle; entrepreneurs, business people, workers, unions, consumers, and government have all played essential roles.

9. The task of the United States today is as demanding as that faced by our forebears. Abraham Lincoln's words at Gettysburg are a reminder that complacency today would be a betrayal of our nation's history: "It is for us, the living, rather to be dedicated here to the unfinished work . . . they have thus far nobly advanced."[5] There is unfinished business in the American experiment in freedom and justice for all.

B. Urgent Problems of Today

10. The preeminent role of the United States in an increasingly interdependent global economy is a central sign of our times.[6] The United States is still the world's economic giant. Decisions made here have immediate effects in other countries; decisions made abroad have immediate consequences for steelworkers in Pittsburgh, oil company employees in Houston, and farmers in Iowa. U.S. economic growth is vitally dependent on resources from other countries and on their purchases of our goods and services. Many jobs in U.S. industry and agriculture depend on our ability to export manufactured goods and food.

11. In some industries the mobility of capital and technology makes wages the main variable in the cost of production. Overseas competitors with the same technology but with wage rates as low as one-tenth of ours put enormous pressure on U.S. firms to cut wages, relocate abroad, or close. U.S. workers and their communities should not be expected to bear these burdens alone.

12. All people on this globe share a common ecological environment that is under increasing pressure. Depletion of soil, water, and other natural resources endangers the future. Pollution of air and water threatens the delicate balance of the biosphere on which future generations will depend.[7] The resources of the earth have been created by God for the benefit of all, and we who are alive today hold them in trust. This is a challenge to develop a new ecological ethic that will help shape a future that is both just and sustainable.

13. In short, nations separated by geography, culture, and ideology are linked in a complex commercial, financial, technological, and environmental network. These links have two direct consequences. First, they create hope for a new form of community among all peoples, one built on dignity, solidarity, and justice. Second, this rising global awareness calls for greater attention to the stark inequities across countries in the standards of living and control of resources. We must not look at the welfare of U.S. citizens as the only good

to be sought. Nor may we overlook the disparities of power in the relationships between this nation and the developing countries. The United States is the major supplier of food to other countries, a major source of arms sales to developing nations, and a powerful influence in multilateral institutions such as the International Monetary Fund, the World Bank, and the United Nations. What Americans see as a growing interdependence is regarded by many in the less developed countries as a pattern of domination and dependence.

14. Within this larger international setting, there are also a number of challenges to the domestic economy that call for creativity and courage. The promise of the "American dream"—freedom for all persons to develop their God-given talents to the full—remains unfulfilled for millions in the United States today.

15. Several areas of U.S. economic life demand special attention. Unemployment is the most basic. Despite the large number of new jobs the U.S. economy has generated in the past decade, approximately 8 million people seeking work in this country are unable to find it, and many more are so discouraged they have stopped looking.[8] Over the past two decades the nation has come to tolerate an increasing level of unemployment. The 6 to 7 percent rate deemed acceptable today would have been intolerable twenty years ago. Among the unemployed are a disproportionate number of blacks, Hispanics, young people, or women who are the sole support of their families.[9] Some cities and states have many more unemployed persons than others as a result of economic forces that have little to do with people's desire to work. Unemployment is a tragedy no matter whom it strikes, but the tragedy is compounded by the unequal and unfair way it is distributed in our society.

16. Harsh poverty plagues our country despite its great wealth. More than 33 million Americans are poor; by any reasonable standard another 20 to 30 million are needy. Poverty is increasing in the United States, not decreasing.[10] For a people who believe in "progress," this should be cause for alarm. These burdens fall most heavily on blacks, Hispanics, and Native Americans. Even more disturbing is the large increase in the number of women and children living in poverty. Today children are the largest single group among the poor. This tragic fact seriously threatens the nation's future. That so many people are poor in a nation as rich as ours is a social and moral scandal that we cannot ignore.

17. Many working people and middle-class Americans live dangerously close to poverty. A rising number of families must rely on the wages of two or even three members just to get by. From 1968 to 1978 nearly a quarter of the U.S. population was in poverty part of the time and received welfare benefits in at least one year.[11] The loss of a job, illness, or the breakup of a marriage may be all it takes to push people into poverty.

18. The lack of a mutually supportive relation between family life and economic life is one of the most serious problems facing the United States today.[12] The economic and cultural strength of the nation is directly linked to

the stability and health of its families.[13] When families thrive, spouses contribute to the common good through their work at home, in the community, and in their jobs; and children develop a sense of their own worth and of their responsibility to serve others. When families are weak or break down entirely, the dignity of parents and children is threatened. High cultural and economic costs are inflicted on society at large.

19. The precarious economic situation of so many people and so many families calls for examination of U.S. economic arrangements. Christian conviction and the American promise of liberty and justice for all give the poor and the vulnerable a special claim on the nation's concern. They also challenge all members of the Church to help build a more just society.

20. The investment of human creativity and material resources in the production of the weapons of war makes these economic problems even more difficult to solve. Defense Department expenditures in the United States are almost $300 billion per year. The rivalry and mutual fear between superpowers divert into projects that threaten death, minds and money that could better human life. Developing countries engage in arms races they can ill afford, often with the encouragement of the superpowers. Some of the poorest countries of the world use scarce resources to buy planes, guns, and other weapons when they lack the food, education, and health care their people need. Defense policies must be evaluated and assessed in light of their real contribution to freedom, justice, and peace for the citizens of our own and other nations. We have developed a perspective on these multiple moral concerns in our 1983 pastoral letter, *The Challenge of Peace: God's Promise and Our Response*.[14] When weapons or strategies make questionable contributions to security, peace, and justice and will also be very expensive, spending priorities should be redirected to more pressing social needs.[15]

21. Many other social and economic challenges require careful analysis: the movement of many industries from the Snowbelt to the Sunbelt, the federal deficit and interest rates, corporate mergers and takeovers, the effects of new technologies such as robotics and information systems in U.S. industry, immigration policy, growing international traffic in drugs, and the trade imbalance. All of these issues do not provide a complete portrait of the economy. Rather they are symptoms of more fundamental currents shaping U.S. economic life today: the struggle to find meaning and value in human work, efforts to support individual freedom in the context of renewed social cooperation, the urgent need to create equitable forms of global interdependence in a world now marked by extreme inequality. These deeper currents are cultural and moral in content. They show that the long-range challenges facing the nation call for sustained reflection on the values that guide economic choices and are embodied in economic institutions. Such explicit reflection on the ethical content of economic choices and policies must become an integral part of the way Christians relate religious belief to the realities of everyday life. In this way, the "split between the faith which many profess and their daily lives,"[16] which

Vatican II counted among the more serious errors of the modern age, will begin to be bridged.

C. The Need for Moral Vision

22. Sustaining a common culture and a common commitment to moral values is not easy in our world. Modern economic life is based on a division of labor into specialized jobs and professions. Since the industrial revolution, people have had to define themselves and their work ever more narrowly to find a niche in the economy. The benefits of this are evident in the satisfaction many people derive from contributing their specialized skills to society. But the costs are social fragmentation, a decline in seeing how one's work serves the whole community, and an increased emphasis on personal goals and private interests.[17] This is vividly clear in discussions of economic justice. Here it is often difficult to find a common ground among people with different backgrounds and concerns. One of our chief hopes in writing this letter is to encourage and contribute to the development of this common ground.[18]

23. Strengthening common moral vision is essential if the economy is to serve all people more fairly. Many middle-class Americans feel themselves in the grip of economic demands and cultural pressures that go far beyond the individual family's capacity to cope. Without constructive guidance in making decisions with serious moral implications, men and women who hold positions of responsibility in corporations or government find their duties exacting a heavy price. We want these reflections to help them contribute to a more just economy.

24. The quality of the national discussion about our economic future will affect the poor most of all, in this country and throughout the world. The life and dignity of millions of men, women, and children hang in the balance. Decisions must be judged in light of what they do *for* the poor, what they do *to* the poor, and what they enable the poor to do *for themselves*. The fundamental moral criterion for all economic decisions, policies, and institutions is this: They must be at the service of *all people, especially the poor*.

25. This letter is based on a long tradition of Catholic social thought, rooted in the Bible and developed over the past century by the popes and the Second Vatican Council in response to modern economic conditions. This tradition insists that human dignity, realized in community with others and with the whole of God's creation, is the norm against which every social institution must be measured.[19]

26. This teaching has a rich history. It is also dynamic and growing.[20] Pope Paul VI insisted that all Christian communities have the responsibility "to analyze with objectivity the situation which is proper to their own country, to shed on it the light of the Gospel's unalterable words and to draw principles of reflection, norms of judgment, and directives for action from the social teaching of the Church."[21] Therefore, we build on the past work of our own

bishops' conference, including the 1919 *Program of Social Reconstruction* and other Pastoral Letters.[22] In addition many people from the Catholic, Protestant, and Jewish communities, in academic, business or political life, and from many different economic backgrounds have also provided guidance. We want to make the legacy of Christian social thought a living, growing resource that can inspire hope and help shape the future.

27. We write, then, first of all to provide guidance for members of our own Church as they seek to form their consciences about economic matters. No one may claim the name Christian and be comfortable in the face of the hunger, homelessness, insecurity, and injustice found in this country and the world. At the same time, we want to add our voice to the public debate about the directions in which the U.S. economy should be moving. We seek the cooperation and support of those who do not share our faith or tradition.

The common bond of humanity that links all persons is the source of our belief that the country can attain a renewed public moral vision. The questions are basic and the answers are often elusive; they challenge us to serious and sustained attention to economic justice.

CHAPTER 2: THE CHRISTIAN VISION OF ECONOMIC LIFE

28. The basis for all that the Church believes about the moral dimensions of economic life is its vision of the transcendent worth—the sacredness—of human beings. *The dignity of the human person, realized in community with others, is the criterion against which all aspects of economic life must be measured.*[1] All human beings, therefore, are ends to be served by the institutions that make up the economy, not means to be exploited for more narrowly defined goals. Human personhood must be respected with a reverence that is religious. When we deal with each other, we should do so with the sense of awe that arises in the presence of something holy and sacred. For that is what human beings are: we are created in the image of God (Gn. 1:27). Similarly, all economic institutions must support the bonds of community and solidarity that are essential to the dignity of persons. Wherever our economic arrangements fail to conform to the demands of human dignity lived in community, they must be questioned and transformed. These convictions have a biblical basis. They are also supported by a long tradition of theological and philosophical reflection and through the reasoned analysis of human experience by contemporary men and women.

29. In presenting the Christian moral vision, we turn first to the Scriptures for guidance. Though our comments are necessarily selective, we hope that pastors and other church members will become personally engaged with the biblical texts. The Scriptures contain many passages that speak directly of economic life. We must also attend to the Bible's deeper vision of God, of the purpose of creation, and of the dignity of human life in society. Along with

other churches and ecclesial communities who are "strengthened by the grace of Baptism and the hearing of God's Word," we strive to become faithful hearers and doers of the word.[2] We also claim the Hebrew Scriptures as common heritage with our Jewish brothers and sisters, and we join with them in the quest for an economic life worthy of the divine revelation we share.

A. Biblical Perspectives

30. The fundamental conviction of our faith is that human life is fulfilled in the knowledge and love of the living God in communion with others. The Sacred Scriptures offer guidance so that men and women may enter into full communion with God and with each other, and witness to God's saving acts. We discover there a God who is creator of heaven and earth, and of the human family. Though our first parents reject the God who created them, God does not abandon them, but from Abraham and Sarah forms a people of promise. When this people is enslaved in an alien land, God delivers them and makes a covenant with them in which they are summoned to be faithful to the *torah* or sacred teaching. The focal points of Israel's faith—creation, covenant, and community—provide a foundation for reflection on issues of economic and social justice.

1. CREATED IN GOD'S IMAGE

31. After the exile, when Israel combined its traditions into a written *torah*, it prefaced its history as a people with the story of the creation of all peoples and of the whole world by the same God who created them as a nation (Gn. 1–11). God is the creator of heaven and earth (Gn. 14:19–22; Is. 40:28; 45:18); creation proclaims God's glory (Ps. 89:6–12) and is "very good" (Gn. 1:31). Fruitful harvests, bountiful flocks, a loving family are God's blessings on those who heed God's word. Such is the joyful refrain that echoes throughout the Bible. One legacy of this theology of creation is the conviction that no dimension of human life lies beyond God's care and concern. God is present to creation, and creative engagement with God's handiwork is itself reverence for God.

32. At the summit of creation stands the creation of man and woman, made in God's image (Gn. 1:26–27). *As such every human being possesses an inalienable dignity that stamps human existence prior to any division into races or nations and prior to human labor and human achievement (Gn. 4–11).* Men and women are also to share in the creative activity of God. They are to be fruitful, to care for the earth (Gn. 2:15), and to have "dominion" over it (Gn. 1:28), which means they are "to govern the world in holiness and justice and to render judgment in integrity of heart" (Wis. 9:3). Creation is a gift; women and men are to be faithful stewards in caring for the earth. They can justly consider that by their labor they are unfolding the Creator's work.[3]

33. The narratives of Genesis 1–11 also portray the origin of the strife and suffering that mar the world. Though created to enjoy intimacy with God and the fruits of the earth, Adam and Eve disrupted God's design by trying to live independently of God through a denial of their status as creatures. They turned away from God and gave to God's creation the obedience due to God alone. For this reason the prime sin in so much of the biblical tradition is idolatry: service of the creature rather than of the creator (Rom. 1:25), and the attempt to overturn creation by making God in human likeness. The Bible castigates not only the worship of idols, but also manifestations of idolatry, such as the quest for unrestrained power and the desire for great wealth (Is. 40:12–20; 44:1–20; Wis. 13:1–14:31; Col. 3:5, "the greed that is idolatry"). The sin of our first parents had other consequences as well. Alienation from God pits brother against brother (Gn. 4:8–16), in a cycle of war and vengeance (Gn. 4:22–23). Sin and evil abound, and the primeval history culminates with another assault on the heavens, this time ending in a babble of tongues scattered over the face of the earth (Gn. 11:1–9). Sin simultaneously alienates human beings from God and shatters the solidarity of the human community. Yet this reign of sin is not the final word. The primeval history is followed by the call of Abraham, a man of faith, who was to be the bearer of the promise to many nations (Gn. 12:1–4). Throughout the Bible we find this struggle between sin and repentance. God's judgment on evil is followed by God's seeking out a sinful people.

34. The biblical vision of creation has provided one of the most enduring legacies of Church teaching. To stand before God as the creator is to respect God's creation, both the world of nature and of human history. *From the patristic period to the present, the Church has affirmed that misuse of the world's resources or appropriation of them by a minority of the world's population betrays the gift of creation since "whatever belongs to God belongs to all."*[4]

2. A PEOPLE OF THE COVENANT

35. When the people of Israel, our forerunners in faith, gathered in thanksgiving to renew their covenant (Jos. 24:1–15), they recalled the gracious deeds of God (Dt. 6:20–25; 26:5–11). When they lived as aliens in a strange land and experienced oppression and slavery, they cried out. The Lord, the God of their ancestors, heard their cries, knew their afflictions, and came to deliver them (Ex. 3:7–8). By leading them out of Egypt, God created a people that was to be the Lord's very own (Jer. 24:7; Hos. 2:25). They were to imitate God by treating the alien and the slave in their midst as God had treated them (Ex. 22:20–22; Jer. 34:8–14).

36. In the midst of this saving history stands the covenant at Sinai (Ex. 19–24). It begins with an account of what God has done for the people (Ex. 19:1–6; cf. Jos. 24:1–13) and includes from God's side a promise of steadfast love (*hesed*) and faithfulness (*'emeth*, Ex. 34:5–7). The people are summoned to

ratify this covenant by faithfully worshiping God alone and by directing their lives according to God's will, which was made explicit in Israel's great legal codes such as the Decalogue (Ex. 20:1–17) and the Book of the Covenant (Ex. 20:22–23:33). Far from being an arbitrary restriction on the life of the people, these codes made life in community possible.[5] The specific laws of the covenant protect human life and property, demand respect for parents and the spouses and children of one's neighbor, and manifest a special concern for the vulnerable members of the community: widows, orphans, the poor, and strangers in the land. Laws such as that for the Sabbath year when the land was left fallow (Ex. 23:11; Lv. 25:1–7) and for the year of release of debts (Dt. 15:1–11) summoned people to respect the land as God's gift and reminded Israel that as a people freed by God from bondage they were to be concerned for the poor and oppressed in their midst. Every fiftieth year a jubilee was to be proclaimed as a year of "liberty throughout the land" and property was to be restored to its original owners (Lv. 25:8–17, cf. Is. 61:12; Lk. 4:18–19).[6] The codes of Israel reflect the norms of the covenant: reciprocal responsibility, mercy, and truthfulness. They embody a life in freedom from oppression: worship of the One God, rejection of idolatry, mutual respect among people, care and protection for every member of the social body. Being free and being a co-responsible community are God's intentions for us.

37. When the people turn away from the living God to serve idols and no longer heed the commands of the covenant, God sends prophets to recall his saving deeds and to summon them to return to the one who betrothed them "in right and in justice, in love and in mercy" (Hos. 2:21). The substance of prophetic faith is proclaimed by Micah: "to do justice and to love kindness, and to walk humbly with your God" (Mi. 6:8, RSV). Biblical faith in general, and prophetic faith especially, insist that fidelity to the covenant joins obedience to God with reverence and concern for the neighbor. The biblical terms which best summarize this double dimension of Israel's faith are *sedaqah*, justice (also translated as righteousness), and *mishpat* (right judgment or justice embodied in a concrete act or deed). The biblical understanding of justice gives a fundamental perspective to our reflections on social and economic justice.[7]

38. God is described as a "God of justice" (Is. 30:18) who loves justice (Is. 61:8, cf. Pss. 11:7; 33:5; 37:28; 99:4) and delights in it (Jer. 9:23). God demands justice from the whole people (Dt. 16:20) and executes justice for the needy (Ps. 140:13). Central to the biblical presentation of justice is that the justice of a community is measured by its treatment of the powerless in society, most often described as the widow, the orphan, the poor, and the stranger (non-Israelite) in the land. The Law, the Prophets, and the Wisdom literature of the Old Testament all show deep concern for the proper treatment of such people.[8] What these groups of people have in common is their vulnerability and lack of power. They are often alone and have no protector or advocate. Therefore, it is God who hears their cries (Pss. 109:21; 113:7), and the king who is God's anointed is commanded to have special concern for them.

39. Justice has many nuances.[9] Fundamentally, it suggests a sense of what is right or of what should happen. For example, paths are just when they bring you to your destination (Gn. 24:48; Ps. 23:3), and laws are just when they create harmony within the community, as Isaiah says: "Justice will bring about peace; right will produce calm and security" (Is. 32:17). God is "just" by acting as God should, coming to the people's aid and summoning them to conversion when they stray. People are summoned to be "just," that is, to be in a proper relation to God, by observing God's laws which form them into a faithful community. Biblical justice is more comprehensive than subsequent philosophical definitions. It is not concerned with a strict definition of rights and duties, but with the rightness of the human condition before God and within society. Nor is justice opposed to love; rather, it is both a manifestation of love and a condition for love to grow.[10] Because God loves Israel, he rescues them from oppression and summons them to be a people that "does justice" and loves kindness. The quest for justice arises from loving gratitude for the saving acts of God and manifests itself in wholehearted love of God and neighbor.

40. These perspectives provide the foundation for a biblical vision of economic justice. Every human person is created as an image of God, and the denial of dignity to a person is a blot on this image. Creation is a gift to all men and women, not to be appropriated for the benefit of a few; its beauty is an object of joy and reverence. The same God who came to the aid of an oppressed people and formed them into a covenant community continues to hear the cries of the oppressed and to create communities which are responsive to God's word. God's love and life are present when people can live in a community of faith and hope. These cardinal points to the faith of Israel also furnish the religious context for understanding the saving action of God in the life and teaching of Jesus.

3. THE REIGN OF GOD AND JUSTICE

41. Jesus enters human history as God's anointed son who announces the nearness of the reign of God (Mk. 1:9–14). This proclamation summons us to acknowledge God as creator and covenant partner and challenges us to seek ways in which God's revelation of the dignity and destiny of all creation might become incarnate in history. It is not simply the promise of the future victory of God over sin and evil, but that this victory has already begun—in the life and teaching of Jesus.

42. What Jesus proclaims by word, he enacts in his ministry. He resists temptations of power and prestige, follows his Father's will, and teaches us to pray that it be accomplished on earth. He warns against attempts to "lay up treasures on earth" (Mt. 6:19) and exhorts his followers not to be anxious about material goods but rather to seek first God's reign and God's justice (Mt. 6:25–33). His mighty works symbolize that the reign of God is more powerful than evil, sickness, and the hardness of the human heart. He offers

God's loving mercy to sinners (Mk. 2:17), takes up the cause of those who suffered religious and social discrimination (Lk. 7:36–50; 15:1–2), and attacks the use of religion to avoid the demands of charity and justice (Mk. 7:9–13; Mt. 23:23).

43. When asked what was the greatest commandment, Jesus quoted the age-old Jewish affirmation of faith that God alone is One and to be loved with the whole heart, mind, and soul (Dt. 6:4–5) and immediately adds: "You shall love your neighbor as yourself" (Lv. 19:18; Mk. 12:28–34). This dual command of love that is at the basis of all Christian morality is illustrated in the Gospel of Luke by the parable of a Samaritan who interrupts his journey to come to the aid of a dying man (Lk. 10:29–37). Unlike the other wayfarers who look on the man and pass by, the Samaritan "was moved with compassion at the sight"; he stops, tends the wounded man, and takes him to a place of safety. In this parable compassion is the bridge between mere seeing and action; love is made real through effective action.[11]

44. Near the end of his life, Jesus offers a vivid picture of the last judgment (Mt. 25:31–46). All the nations of the world will be assembled and will be divided into those blessed who are welcomed into God's Kingdom or those cursed who are sent to eternal punishment. The blessed are those who fed the hungry, gave drink to the thirsty, welcomed the stranger, clothed the naked, and visited the sick and imprisoned; the cursed are those who neglected these works of mercy and love. Neither the blessed nor the cursed are astounded that they are judged by the Son of Man, nor that judgment is rendered according to works of charity. The shock comes when they find that in neglecting the poor, the outcast, and the oppressed, they were rejecting Jesus himself. Jesus who came as "Emmanuel" (God with us, Mt. 1:23) and who promises to be with his people until the end of the age (Mt. 28:20) is hidden in those most in need; to reject them is to reject God made manifest in history.

4. CALLED TO BE DISCIPLES IN COMMUNITY

45. Jesus summoned his first followers to a change of heart and to take on the yoke of God's reign (Mk. 1:14–15; Mt. 11:29). They are to be the nucleus of that community which will continue the work of proclaiming and building God's Kingdom through the centuries. As Jesus called the first disciples in the midst of their everyday occupations of fishing and tax collecting, so he again calls people in every age in the home, in the workplace, and in the marketplace.

46. The Church is, as Pope John Paul II reminded us, "a community of disciples" in which "we must see first and foremost Christ saying to each member of the community: follow me."[12] To be a Christian is to join with others in responding to this personal call and in learning the meaning of Christ's life. It is to be sustained by that loving intimacy with the Father that Jesus experienced in his work, in his prayer, and in his suffering.

47. Discipleship involves imitating the pattern of Jesus' life by openness to God's will in the service of others (Mk. 10:42–45). Disciples are also called to follow him on the way of the cross, and to heed his call that those who lose their lives for the sake of the Gospel will save them (Mk. 8:34–35). Jesus' death is an example of that greater love which lays down one's life for others (cf. Jn. 15:12–18). It is a model for those who suffer persecution for the sake of justice (Mt. 5:10). The death of Jesus was not the end of his power and presence, for he was raised up by the power of God. Nor did it mark the end of the disciples' union with him. After Jesus had appeared to them and when they received the gift of the Spirit (Acts 2:1–12), they became apostles of the good news to the ends of the earth. In the face of poverty and persecution they transformed human lives and formed communities which became signs of the power and presence of God. Sharing in this same resurrection faith, contemporary followers of Christ can face the struggles and challenges that await those who bring the Gospel vision to bear on our complex economic and social world.

5. POVERTY, RICHES, AND THE CHALLENGE OF DISCIPLESHIP

48. The pattern of Christian life as presented in the Gospel of Luke has special relevance today. In her *Magnificat*, Mary rejoices in a God who scatters the proud, brings down the mighty, and raises up the poor and lowly (Lk. 1:51–53). The first public utterance of Jesus is "The Spirit of the Lord is upon me, because he has anointed me to preach the good news to the poor" (Lk. 4:18; cf. Is. 61:1–2). Jesus adds to the blessing on the poor a warning, "Woe to you who are rich, for you have received your consolation" (Lk. 6:24). He warns his followers against greed and reliance on abundant possessions and underscores this by the parable of the man whose life is snatched away at the very moment he tries to secure his wealth (Lk. 12:13–21). In Luke alone, Jesus tells the parable of the rich man who does not see the poor and suffering Lazarus at his gate (Lk. 16:19–31). When the rich man finally "sees" Lazarus, it is from the place of torment and the opportunity for conversion has passed. Pope John Paul II has often recalled this parable to warn the prosperous not to be blind to the great poverty that exists beside great wealth.[13]

49. Jesus, especially in Luke, lives as a poor man, like the prophets takes the side of the poor, and warns of the dangers of wealth.[14] The terms used for poor, while primarily describing lack of material goods, also suggest dependence and powerlessness. The poor are also an exiled and oppressed people whom God will rescue (Is. 51:21–23) as well as a faithful remnant who take refuge in God (Zep. 3:12–13). Throughout the Bible, material poverty is a misfortune and a cause of sadness. A constant biblical refrain is that the poor must be cared for and protected and that when they are exploited, God hears their cries (Prv. 22:22–23). Conversely, even though the goods of the earth are to be enjoyed and people are to thank God for material blessings, wealth is a

constant danger. The rich are wise in their own eyes (Prv. 28:11), and are prone to apostasy and idolatry (Am. 5:413; Is. 2:6–8), as well as to violence and oppression (Jas. 2:6–7).[15] Since they are neither blinded by wealth nor make it into an idol, the poor can be open to God's presence; throughout Israel's history and in early Christianity the poor are agents of God's transforming power.

50. The poor are often related to the lowly (Mt. 5:3, 5) to whom God reveals what was hidden from the wise (Mt. 11:25–30). When Jesus calls the poor "blessed," he is not praising their condition of poverty, but their openness to God. When he states that the reign of God is theirs, he voices God's special concern for them, and promises that they are to be the beneficiaries of God's mercy and justice. When he summons disciples to leave all and follow him, he is calling them to share his own radical trust in the Father and his freedom from care and anxiety (cf. Mt. 6:25–34). The practice of evangelical poverty in the Church has always been a living witness to the power of that trust and to the joy that comes with that freedom.

51. Early Christianity saw the poor as an object of God's special love, but it neither canonized material poverty nor accepted deprivation as an inevitable fact of life. Though few early Christians possessed wealth or power (1 Cor. 1:26–28; Jas. 2:5), their communities had well-off members (Acts 16:14; 18:8). Jesus' concern for the poor was continued in different forms in the early Church. The early community at Jerusalem distributed its possessions so that "there was no needy person among them," and held "all things in common"—a phrase that suggests not only shared material possessions, but more fundamentally, friendship and mutual concern among all its members (Acts 4:32–34; 2:44). While recognizing the dangers of wealth, the early Church proposed the proper use of possessions to alleviate need and suffering, rather than universal dispossession. Beginning in the first century and throughout history, Christian communities have developed varied structures to support and sustain the weak and powerless in societies that were often brutally unconcerned about human suffering.

52. Such perspectives provide a basis today for what is called the "preferential option for the poor."[16] Though in the Gospels and in the New Testament as a whole the offer of salvation is extended to all peoples, Jesus takes the side of those most in need, physically and spiritually. The example of Jesus poses a number of challenges to the contemporary Church. It imposes a prophetic mandate to speak for those who have no one to speak for them, to be a defender of the defenseless, who in biblical terms are the poor. It also demands a compassionate vision that enables the Church to see things from the side of the poor and powerless and to assess lifestyle, policies, and social institutions in terms of their impact on the poor. It summons the Church also to be an instrument in assisting people to experience the liberating power of God in their own lives so that they may respond to the Gospel in freedom and in dignity. Finally, and most radically, it calls for an emptying of self, both individually

and corporately, that allows the Church to experience the power of God in the midst of poverty and powerlessness.

6. A COMMUNITY OF HOPE

53. The biblical vision of creation, covenant, and community, as well as the summons to discipleship, unfolds under the tension between promise and fulfillment. The whole Bible is spanned by the narratives of the first creation (Gn. 1–3) and the vision of a restored creation at the end of history (Rv. 21:1–4). Just as creation tells us that God's desire was one of wholeness and unity between God and the human family and within this family itself, the images of a new creation give hope that enmity and hatred will cease and justice and peace will reign (Is. 11:4–6; 25:1–8). Human life unfolds "between the times," the time of the first creation and that of a restored creation (Rom. 8:18–25). Although the ultimate realization of God's plan lies in the future, Christians in union with all people of good will are summoned to shape history in the image of God's creative design, and in response to the reign of God proclaimed and embodied by Jesus.

54. A Christian is a member of a new community, "God's own people" (1 Pt. 2:9–10), who, like the people of Exodus, owes its existence to the gracious gift of God and is summoned to respond to God's will made manifest in the life and teaching of Jesus. A Christian walks in the newness of life (Rom. 6:4), and is "a new creation; the old has passed away, the new has come" (2 Cor. 5:17). This new creation in Christ proclaims that God's creative love is constantly at work, offers sinners forgiveness, and reconciles a broken world. Our action on behalf of justice in our world proceeds from the conviction that, despite the power of injustice and violence, life has been fundamentally changed by the entry of the Word made flesh into human history.

55. Christian communities that commit themselves to solidarity with those suffering and to confrontation with those attitudes and ways of acting which institutionalize injustice, will themselves experience the power and presence of Christ. They will embody in their lives the values of the new creation while they labor under the old. The quest for economic and social justice will always combine hope and realism, and must be renewed by every generation. It involves diagnosing those situations that continue to alienate the world from God's creative love as well as presenting hopeful alternatives that arise from living in a renewed creation. This quest arises from faith and is sustained by hope as it seeks to speak to a broken world of God's justice and loving kindness.

7. A LIVING TRADITION

56. Our reflection on U.S. economic life today must be rooted in this biblical vision of the kingdom and discipleship, but it must also be shaped by

the rich and complex tradition of Catholic life and thought. Throughout its history, the Christian community has listened to the words of Scripture and sought to enact them in the midst of daily life in very different historical and cultural contexts.

57. In the first centuries, when Christians were a minority in a hostile society, they cared for one another through generous almsgiving. In the patristic era, the church fathers repeatedly stressed that the goods of the earth were created by God for the benefit of every person without exception, and that all have special duties toward those in need. The monasteries of the Middle Ages were centers of prayer, learning, and education. They contributed greatly to the cultural and economic life of the towns and cities that sprang up around them. In the twelfth century the new mendicant orders dedicated themselves to following Christ in poverty and to the proclamation of the good news to the poor.

58. These same religious communities also nurtured some of the greatest theologians of the Church's tradition, thinkers who synthesized the call of Christ with the philosophical learning of Greek, Roman, Jewish, and Arab worlds. Thomas Aquinas and the other scholastics devoted rigorous intellectual energy to clarifying the meaning of both personal virtue and justice in society. In more recent centuries Christians began to build a large network of hospitals, orphanages, and schools, to serve the poor and society at large. And beginning with Leo XIII's *Rerum Novarum*, down to the writings and speeches of John Paul II, the popes have more systematically addressed the rapid change of modern society in a series of social encyclicals. These teachings of modern popes and of the Second Vatican Council are especially significant for efforts to respond to the problems facing society today.[17]

59. We also have much to learn from the strong emphasis in Protestant traditions on the vocation of lay people in the world and from ecumenical efforts to develop an economic ethic that addresses newly emergent problems. And in a special way our fellow Catholics in developing countries have much to teach us about the Christian response to an ever more interdependent world.

60. Christians today are called by God to carry on this tradition through active love of neighbor, a love that responds to the special challenges of this moment in human history. The world is wounded by sin and injustice, in need of conversion and of the transformation that comes when persons enter more deeply into the mystery of the death and Resurrection of Christ. The concerns of this pastoral letter are not at all peripheral to the central mystery at the heart of the Church.[18] They are integral to the proclamation of the Gospel and part of the vocation of every Christian today.[19]

B. Ethical Norms for Economic Life

61. These biblical and theological themes shape the overall Christian perspective on economic ethics. This perspective is also subscribed to by many who do not share Christian religious convictions. Human understanding and

religious belief are complementary, not contradictory. For human beings are created in God's image, and their dignity is manifest in the ability to reason and understand, in their freedom to shape their own lives and the life of their communities, and in the capacity for love and friendship. In proposing ethical norms, therefore, we appeal both to Christians and to all in our pluralist society to show that respect and reverence owed to the dignity of every person. Intelligent reflection on the social and economic realities of today is also indispensable in the effort to respond to economic circumstances never envisioned in biblical times. Therefore, we now want to propose an ethical framework that can guide economic life today in ways that are both faithful to the Gospel and shaped by human experience and reason.

62. First we outline the *duties* all people have to each other and to the whole community: love of neighbor, the basic requirements of justice, and the special obligation to those who are poor or vulnerable. Corresponding to these duties are the *human rights* of every person; the obligation to protect the dignity of all demands respect for these rights. Finally these duties and rights entail several *priorities* that should guide the economic choices of individuals, communities, and the nation as a whole.

1. THE RESPONSIBILITIES OF SOCIAL LIVING

63. Human life is life in community. Catholic social teaching proposes several complementary perspectives that show how moral responsibilities and duties in the economic sphere are rooted in this call to community.

A. Love and Solidarity

64. *The commandments to love God with all one's heart and to love one's neighbor as oneself are the heart and soul of Christian morality.* Jesus offers himself as the model of this all-inclusive love: ". . . love one another as I have loved you" (Jn. 15:12). These commands point out the path toward true human fulfillment and happiness. They are not arbitrary restrictions on human freedom. Only active love of God and neighbor makes the fullness of community happen. Christians look forward in hope to a true communion among all persons with each other and with God. The Spirit of Christ labors in history to build up the bonds of solidarity among all persons until that day on which their union is brought to perfection in the Kingdom of God.[20] Indeed Christian theological reflection on the very reality of God as a trinitarian unity of persons—Father, Son, and Holy Spirit—shows that being a person means being united to other persons in mutual love.[21]

65. What the Bible and Christian tradition teach, human wisdom confirms. Centuries before Christ, the Greeks and Romans spoke of the human person as a "social animal" made for friendship, community, and public life. These insights show that human beings achieve self-realization not in isolation, but in interaction with others.[22]

66. The virtues of citizenship are an expression of Christian love more crucial in today's interdependent world than ever before. These virtues grow out of a lively sense of one's dependence on the commonweal and obligations to it. This civic commitment must also guide the economic institutions of society. In the absence of a vital sense of citizenship among the businesses, corporations, labor unions, and other groups that shape economic life, society as a whole is endangered. Solidarity is another name for this social friendship and civic commitment that make human moral and economic life possible.

67. The Christian tradition recognizes, of course, that the fullness of love and community will be achieved only when God's work in Christ comes to completion in the Kingdom of God. This kingdom has been inaugurated among us, but God's redeeming and transforming work is not yet complete. Within history, knowledge of how to achieve the goal of social unity is limited. Human sin continues to wound the lives of both individuals and larger social bodies and places obstacles in the path toward greater social solidarity. If efforts to protect human dignity are to be effective, they must take these limits on knowledge and love into account. Nevertheless, sober realism should not be confused with resigned or cynical pessimism. It is a challenge to develop a courageous hope that can sustain efforts that will sometimes be arduous and protracted.

B. Justice and Participation

68. Biblical justice is the goal we strive for. This rich biblical understanding portrays a just society as one marked by the fullness of love, compassion, holiness, and peace. On their path through history, however, sinful human beings need more specific guidance on how to move toward the realization of this great vision of God's Kingdom. This guidance is contained in the norms of basic or minimal justice. These norms state the *minimum* levels of mutual care and respect that all persons owe to each other in an imperfect world.[23] Catholic social teaching, like much philosophical reflection, distinguishes three dimensions of basic justice: commutative justice, distributive justice, and social justice.[24]

69. *Commutative justice calls for fundamental fairness in all agreements and exchanges between individuals or private social groups.* It demands respect for the equal human dignity of all persons in economic transactions, contracts, or promises. For example, workers owe their employers diligent work in exchange for their wages. Employers are obligated to treat their employees as persons, paying them fair wages in exchange for the work done and establishing conditions and patterns of work that are truly human.[25]

70. *Distributive justice requires that the allocation of income, wealth, and power in society be evaluated in light of its effects on persons whose basic material needs are unmet.* The Second Vatican Council stated: "The right to have a share of earthly goods sufficient for oneself and one's family belongs to everyone. The fathers and doctors of the Church held this view, teaching

that we are obliged to come to the relief of the poor and to do so not merely out of our superfluous goods."[26] Minimum material resources are an absolute necessity for human life. If persons are to be recognized as members of the human community, then the community has an obligation to help fulfill these basic needs unless an absolute scarcity of resources makes this strictly impossible. No such scarcity exists in the United States today.

71. Justice also has implications for the way the larger social, economic, and political institutions of society are organized. *Social justice implies that persons have an obligation to be active and productive participants in the life of society and that society has a duty to enable them to participate in this way.* This form of justice can also be called "contributive," for it stresses the duty of all who are able to help create the goods, services, and other nonmaterial or spiritual values necessary for the welfare of the whole community. In the words of Pius XI, "It is of the very essence of social justice to demand from each individual all that is necessary for the common good."[27] Productivity is essential if the community is to have the resources to serve the well-being of all. Productivity, however, cannot be measured solely by its output in goods and services. Patterns of production must also be measured in light of their impact on the fulfillment of basic needs, employment levels, patterns of discrimination, environmental quality, and sense of community.

72. The meaning of social justice also includes a duty to organize economic and social institutions so that people can contribute to society in ways that respect their freedom and the dignity of their labor. Work should enable the working person to become "more a human being," more capable of acting intelligently, freely, and in ways that lead to self-realization.[28]

73. Economic conditions that leave large numbers of able people unemployed, underemployed, or employed in dehumanizing conditions fail to meet the converging demands of these three forms of basic justice. Work with adequate pay for all who seek it is the primary means for achieving basic justice in our society. Discrimination in job opportunities or income levels on the basis of race, sex, or other arbitrary standards can never be justified.[29] It is a scandal that such discrimination continues in the United States today. Where the effects of past discrimination persist, society has the obligation to take positive steps to overcome the legacy of injustice. Judiciously administered affirmative action programs in education and employment can be important expressions of the drive for solidarity and participation that is at the heart of true justice. Social harm calls for social relief.

74. Basic justice also calls for the establishment of a floor of material well-being on which all can stand. This is a duty of the whole of society and it creates particular obligations for those with greater resources. This duty calls into question extreme inequalities of income and consumption when so many lack basic necessities. Catholic social teaching does not maintain that a flat, arithmetical equality of income and wealth is a demand of justice, but it does challenge economic arrangements that leave large numbers of people impoverished.

Further, it sees extreme inequality as a threat to the solidarity of the human community, for great disparities lead to deep social divisions and conflict.[30]

75. This means that all of us must examine our way of living in light of the needs of the poor. Christian faith and the norms of justice impose distinct limits on what we consume and how we view material goods. The great wealth of the United States can easily blind us to the poverty that exists in this nation and the destitution of hundreds of millions of people in other parts of the world. Americans are challenged today as never before to develop the inner freedom to resist the temptation constantly to seek more. Only in this way will the nation avoid what Paul VI called "the most evident form of moral underdevelopment," namely greed.[31]

76. These duties call not only for individual charitable giving but also for a more systematic approach by businesses, labor unions, and the many other groups that shape economic life—as well as government. The concentration of privilege that exists today results far more from institutional relationships that distribute power and wealth inequitably than from differences in talent or lack of desire to work. These institutional patterns must be examined and revised if we are to meet the demands of basic justice. For example, a system of taxation based on assessment according to ability to pay[32] is a prime necessity for the fulfillment of these social obligations.

C. Overcoming Marginalization and Powerlessness

77. These fundamental duties can be summarized this way: *Basic justice demands the establishment of minimum levels of participation in the life of the human community for all persons*. The ultimate injustice is for a person or group to be treated actively or abandoned passively as if they were nonmembers of the human race. To treat people this way is effectively to say that they simply do not count as human beings. This can take many forms, all of which can be described as varieties of marginalization, or exclusion from social life.[33] This exclusion can occur in the political sphere: restriction of free speech, concentration of power in the hands of a few, or outright repression by the state. It can also take economic forms that are equally harmful. Within the United States, individuals, families, and local communities fall victim to a downward cycle of poverty generated by economic forces they are powerless to influence. The poor, the disabled, and the unemployed too often are simply left behind. This pattern is even more severe beyond our borders in the least-developed countries. Whole nations are prevented from fully participating in the international economic order because they lack the power to change their disadvantaged position. Many people within the less developed countries are excluded from sharing in the meager resources available in their homelands by unjust elites and unjust governments. These patterns of exclusion are created by free human beings. In this sense they can be called forms of social sin.[34] Acquiescence in them or failure to correct them when it is possible to do so is a sinful dereliction of Christian duty.

78. Recent Catholic social thought regards the task of overcoming these patterns of exclusion and powerlessness as a most basic demand of justice. Stated positively, justice demands that social institutions be ordered in a way that guarantees all persons the ability to participate actively in the economic, political, and cultural life of society.[35] The level of participation may legitimately be greater for some persons than for others, but there is a basic level of access that must be made available for all. Such participation is an essential expression of the social nature of human beings and of their communitarian vocation.

2. HUMAN RIGHTS: THE MINIMUM CONDITIONS FOR LIFE IN COMMUNITY

79. Catholic social teaching spells out the basic demands of justice in greater detail in the human rights of every person. These fundamental rights are prerequisites for a dignified life in community. The Bible vigorously affirms the sacredness of every person as a creature formed in the image and likeness of God. The biblical emphasis on covenant and community also shows that human dignity can only be realized and protected in solidarity with others. In Catholic social thought, therefore, respect for human rights and a strong sense of both personal and community responsibility are linked, not opposed. Vatican II described the common good as "the sum of those conditions of social life which allow social groups and their individual members relatively thorough and ready access to their own fulfillment."[36] These conditions include the rights to fulfillment of material needs, a guarantee of fundamental freedoms, and the protection of relationships that are essential to participation in the life of society.[37] These rights are bestowed on human beings by God and grounded in the nature and dignity of human persons. They are not created by society. Indeed society has a duty to secure and protect them.[38]

80. The full range of human rights has been systematically outlined by John XXIII in his encyclical *Peace on Earth*. His discussion echoes the United Nations Universal Declaration of Human Rights and implies that internationally accepted human rights standards are strongly supported by Catholic teaching. These rights include the civil and political rights to freedom of speech, worship, and assembly. A number of human rights also concern human welfare and are of a specifically economic nature. First among these are the rights to life, food, clothing, shelter, rest, medical care, and basic education. These are indispensable to the protection of human dignity. In order to ensure these necessities, all persons have a right to earn a living, which for most people in our economy is through remunerative employment. All persons also have a right to security in the event of sickness, unemployment, and old age. Participation in the life of the community calls for the protection of this same right to employment, as well as the right to healthful working conditions, to wages, and other benefits sufficient to provide individuals and their families with a

standard of living in keeping with human dignity, and to the possibility of property ownership.[39] These fundamental personal rights—civil and political as well as social and economic—state the minimum conditions for social institutions that respect human dignity, social solidarity, and justice. They are all essential to human dignity and to the integral development of both individuals and society, and are thus moral issues.[40] Any denial of these rights harms persons and wounds the human community. Their serious and sustained denial violates individuals and destroys solidarity among persons.

81. Social and economic rights call for a mode of implementation different from that required to secure civil and political rights. Freedom of worship and of speech imply immunity from interference on the part of both other persons and the government. The rights to education, employment, and social security, for example, are empowerments that call for positive action by individuals and society at large.

82. However, both kinds of rights call for positive action to create social and political institutions that enable all persons to become active members of society. Civil and political rights allow persons to participate freely in the public life of the community, for example, through free speech, assembly, and the vote. In democratic countries these rights have been secured through a long and vigorous history of creating the institutions of constitutional government. In seeking to secure the full range of social and economic rights today, a similar effort to shape new economic arrangements will be necessary.

83. The first step in such an effort is the development of a new cultural consensus that the basic economic conditions of human welfare are essential to human dignity and are due persons by right. Second, the securing of these rights will make demands on *all* members of society, on all private sector institutions, and on government. A concerted effort on all levels in our society is needed to meet these basic demands of justice and solidarity. Indeed political democracy and a commitment to secure economic rights are mutually reinforcing.

84. Securing economic rights for all will be an arduous task. There are a number of precedents in U.S. history, however, which show that the work has already begun.[41] The country needs a serious dialogue about the appropriate levels of private and public sector involvement that are needed to move forward. There is certainly room for diversity of opinion in the Church and in U.S. society on *how* to protect the human dignity and economic rights of all our brothers and sisters.[42] In our view, however, there can be no legitimate disagreement on the basic moral objectives.

3. MORAL PRIORITIES FOR THE NATION

85. *The common good demands justice for all, the protection of the human rights of all.*[43] Making cultural and economic institutions more supportive of the freedom, power, and security of individuals and families must be a central, long-range objective for the nation. Every person has a duty to contribute to

building up the commonweal. All have a responsibility to develop their talents through education. Adults must contribute to society through their individual vocations and talents. Parents are called to guide their children to the maturity of Christian adulthood and responsible citizenship. Everyone has special duties toward the poor and the marginalized. Living up to these responsibilities, however, is often made difficult by the social and economic patterns of society. Schools and educational policies both public and private often serve the privileged exceedingly well, while the children of the poor are effectively abandoned as second-class citizens. Great stresses are created in family life by the way work is organized and scheduled, and by the social and cultural values communicated on TV. Many in the lower middle class are barely getting by and fear becoming victims of economic forces over which they have no control.

86. *The obligation to provide justice for all means that the poor have the single most urgent economic claim on the conscience of the nation.* Poverty can take many forms, spiritual as well as material. All people face struggles of the spirit as they ask deep questions about their purpose in life. Many have serious problems in marriage and family life at some time in their lives, and all of us face the certain reality of sickness and death. The Gospel of Christ proclaims that God's love is stronger than all these forms of diminishment. Material deprivation, however, seriously compounds such sufferings of the spirit and heart. To see a loved one sick is bad enough, but to have no possibility of obtaining health care is worse. To face family problems, such as the death of a spouse or a divorce, can be devastating, but to have these lead to the loss of one's home and end with living on the streets is something no one should have to endure in a country as rich as ours. In developing countries these human problems are even more greatly intensified by extreme material deprivation. This form of human suffering can be reduced if our own country, so rich in resources, chooses to increase its assistance.

87. As individuals and as a nation, therefore, we are called to make a fundamental "option for the poor."[44] The obligation to evaluate social and economic activity from the viewpoint of the poor and the powerless arises from the radical command to love one's neighbor as one's self. Those who are marginalized and whose rights are denied have privileged claims if society is to provide justice for *all*. This obligation is deeply rooted in Christian belief. As Paul VI stated:

> In teaching us charity, the Gospel instructs us in the preferential respect due the poor and the special situation they have in society: the more fortunate should renounce some of their rights so as to place their goods more generously at the service of others.[45]

John Paul II has described this special obligation to the poor as "a call to have a special openness with the small and the weak, those that suffer and weep, those that are humiliated and left on the margin of society, so as to help them win their dignity as human persons and children of God."[46]

88. The prime purpose of this special commitment to the poor is to enable them to become active participants in the life of society. It is to enable *all* persons to share in and contribute to the common good.[47] The "option for the poor," therefore, is not an adversarial slogan that pits one group or class against another. Rather it states that the deprivation and powerlessness of the poor wounds the whole community. The extent of their suffering is a measure of how far we are from being a true community of persons. These wounds will be healed only by greater solidarity with the poor and among the poor themselves.

89. In summary, the norms of love, basic justice, and human rights imply that personal decisions, social policies, and economic institutions should be governed by several key priorities. These priorities do not specify everything that must be considered in economic decision making. They do indicate the most fundamental and urgent objectives.

90. a. *The fulfillment of the basic needs of the poor is of the highest priority*. Personal decisions, policies of private and public bodies, and power relationships must all be evaluated by their effects on those who lack the minimum necessities of nutrition, housing, education, and health care. In particular, this principle recognizes that meeting fundamental human needs must come before the fulfillment of desires for luxury consumer goods, for profits not conducive to the common good, and for unnecessary military hardware.

91. b. *Increasing active participation in economic life by those who are presently excluded or vulnerable is a high social priority*. The human dignity of all is realized when people gain the power to work together to improve their lives, strengthen their families, and contribute to society. Basic justice calls for more than providing help to the poor and other vulnerable members of society. It recognizes the priority of policies and programs that support family life and enhance economic participation through employment and widespread ownership of property. It challenges privileged economic power in favor of the well-being of all. It points to the need to improve the present situation of those unjustly discriminated against in the past. And it has very important implications for both the domestic and the international distribution of power.

92. c. *The investment of wealth, talent, and human energy should be specially directed to benefit those who are poor or economically insecure*. Achieving a more just economy in the United States and the world depends in part on increasing economic resources and productivity. In addition, the ways these resources are invested and managed must be scrutinized in light of their effects on non-monetary values. Investment and management decisions have crucial moral dimensions: they create jobs or eliminate them; they can push vulnerable families over the edge into poverty or give them new hope for the future; they help or hinder the building of a more equitable society. Indeed they can have either positive or negative influence on the fairness of the global economy. Therefore, this priority presents a strong moral challenge to policies that put

large amounts of talent and capital into the production of luxury consumer goods and military technology while failing to invest sufficiently in education, health, the basic infrastructure of our society, and economic sectors that produce urgently needed jobs, goods, and services.

93. d. *Economic and social policies as well as the organization of the work world should be continually evaluated in light of their impact on the strength and stability of family life.* The long-range future of this nation is intimately linked with the well-being of families, for the family is the most basic form of human community.[48] Efficiency and competition in the marketplace must be moderated by greater concern for the way work schedules and compensation support or threaten the bonds between spouses and between parents and children. Health, education, and social service programs should be scrutinized in light of how well they ensure both individual dignity and family integrity.

94. These priorities are not policies. They are norms that should guide the economic choices of all and shape economic institutions. They can help the United States move forward to fulfill the duties of justice and protect economic rights. They were strongly affirmed as implications of Catholic social teaching by Pope John Paul II during his visit to Canada in 1984: "The needs of the poor take priority over the desires of the rich; the rights of workers over the maximization of profits; the preservation of the environment over uncontrolled industrial expansion; production to meet social needs over production for military purposes."[49] There will undoubtedly be disputes about the concrete applications of these priorities in our complex world. We do not seek to foreclose discussion about them. However, we believe that an effort to move in the direction they indicate is urgently needed.

95. The economic challenge of today has many parallels with the political challenge that confronted the founders of our nation. In order to create a new form of political democracy they were compelled to develop ways of thinking and political institutions that had never existed before. Their efforts were arduous and their goals imperfectly realized, but they launched an experiment in the protection of civil and political rights that has prospered through the efforts of those who came after them. *We believe the time has come for a similar experiment in securing economic rights: the creation of an order that guarantees the minimum conditions of human dignity in the economic sphere for every person.* By drawing on the resources of the Catholic moral-religious tradition, we hope to make a contribution through this letter to such a new "American Experiment": a new venture to secure economic justice for all.

C. Working for Greater Justice: Persons and Institutions

96. The economy of this nation has been built by the labor of human hands and minds. Its future will be forged by the ways persons direct all this work toward greater justice. The economy is not a machine that operates according

to its own inexorable laws, and persons are not mere objects tossed about by economic forces. Pope John Paul II has stated that "human work is a key, probably the essential key, to the whole social question."[50] The Pope's understanding of work includes virtually all forms of productive human activity: agriculture, entrepreneurship, industry, the care of children, the sustaining of family life, politics, medical care, and scientific research. Leisure, prayer, celebration, and the arts are also central to the realization of human dignity and to the development of a rich cultural life. It is in their daily work, however, that persons become the subjects and creators of the economic life of the nation.[51] Thus, it is primarily through their daily labor that people make their most important contributions to economic justice.

97. All work has a threefold moral significance. First, it is a principal way that people exercise the distinctive human capacity for self-expression and self-realization. Second, it is the ordinary way for human beings to fulfill their material needs. Finally, work enables people to contribute to the well-being of the larger community. Work is not only for one's self. It is for one's family, for the nation, and indeed for the benefit of the entire human family.[52]

98. These three moral concerns should be visible in the work of all, no matter what their role in the economy: blue collar workers, managers, homemakers, politicians, and others. They should also govern the activities of the many different, overlapping communities and institutions that make up society: families, neighborhoods, small businesses, giant corporations, trade unions, the various levels of government, international organizations, and a host of other human associations including communities of faith.

99. Catholic social teaching calls for respect for the full richness of social life. The need for vital contributions from different human associations—ranging in size from the family to government—has been classically expressed in Catholic social teaching in the "principle of subsidiarity":

> Just as it is gravely wrong to take from individuals what they can accomplish by their own initiative and industry and give it to the community, so also it is an injustice and at the same time a grave evil and disturbance of right order to assign to a greater and higher association what lesser and subordinate organizations can do. For every social activity ought of its very nature to furnish help *(subsidium)* to the members of the body social, and never destroy and absorb them.[53]

100. This principle guarantees institutional pluralism. It provides space for freedom, initiative, and creativity on the part of many social agents. At the same time, it insists that *all* these agents should work in ways that help build up the social body. Therefore, in all their activities these groups should be working in ways that express their distinctive capacities for action, that help meet human needs, and that make true contributions to the common good of the human community. The task of creating a more just U.S. economy is the

vocation of all and depends on strengthening the virtues of public service and responsible citizenship in personal life and on all levels of institutional life.[54]

101. Without attempting to describe the tasks of all the different groups that make up society, we want to point to the specific rights and duties of some of the persons and institutions whose work for justice will be particularly important to the future of the U.S. economy. These rights and duties are among the concrete implications of the principle of subsidiarity. Further implications will be discussed in Chapter IV of this letter.

1. WORKING PEOPLE AND LABOR UNIONS

102. Though John Paul II's understanding of work is a very inclusive one, it fully applies to those customarily called "workers" or "labor" in the United States. Labor has great dignity, so great that all who are able to work are obligated to do so. The duty to work derives both from God's command and from a responsibility to one's own humanity and to the common good.[55] The virtue of industriousness is also an expression of a person's dignity and solidarity with others. All working people are called to contribute to the common good by seeking excellence in production and service.

103. Because work is this important, people have a right to employment. In return for their labor, workers have a right to wages and other benefits sufficient to sustain life in dignity. As Pope Leo XIII stated, every working person has "the right of securing things to sustain life."[56] The way power is distributed in a free market economy frequently gives employers greater bargaining power than employees in the negotiation of labor contracts. Such unequal power may press workers into a choice between an inadequate wage and no wage at all. But justice, not charity, demands certain minimum guarantees. The provision of wages and other benefits sufficient to support a family in dignity is a basic necessity to prevent this exploitation of workers. The dignity of workers also requires adequate health care, security for old age or disability, unemployment compensation, healthful working conditions, weekly rest, periodic holidays for recreation and leisure, and reasonable security against arbitrary dismissal.[57] These provisions are all essential if workers are to be treated as persons rather than simply as a "factor of production."

104. The Church fully supports the right of workers to form unions or other associations to secure their rights to fair wages and working conditions. This is a specific application of the more general right to associate. In the words of Pope John Paul II, "The experience of history teaches that organizations of this type are an indispensable element of social life, especially in modern industrialized societies."[58] Unions may also legitimately resort to strikes where this is the only available means to the justice owed to workers.[59] No one may deny the right to organize without attacking human dignity itself. Therefore, we firmly oppose organized efforts, such as those regrettably now seen in this country, to break existing unions and prevent workers from organizing.

Migrant agricultural workers today are particularly in need of the protection, including the right to organize and bargain collectively. U.S. labor law reform is needed to meet these problems as well as to provide more timely and effective remedies for unfair labor practices.

105. Denial of the right to organize has been pursued ruthlessly in many countries beyond our borders. We vehemently oppose violations of the freedom to associate, wherever they occur, for they are an intolerable attack on social solidarity.

106. Along with the rights of workers and unions go a number of important responsibilities. Individual workers have obligations to their employers, and trade unions also have duties to society as a whole. Union management in particular carries a strong responsibility for the good name of the entire union movement. Workers must use their collective power to contribute to the well-being of the whole community and should avoid pressing demands whose fulfillment would damage the common good and the rights of more vulnerable members of society.[60] It should be noted, however, that wages paid to workers are but one of the factors affecting the competitiveness of industries. Thus, it is unfair to expect unions to make concessions if managers and shareholders do not make at least equal sacrifices.

107. Many U.S. unions have exercised leadership in the struggle for justice for minorities and women. Racial and sexual discrimination, however, have blotted the record of some unions. Organized labor has a responsibility to work positively toward eliminating the injustice this discrimination has caused.

108. Perhaps the greatest challenge facing U.S. workers and unions today is that of developing a new vision of their role in the U.S. economy of the future. The labor movement in the United States stands at a crucial moment. The dynamism of the unions that led to their rapid growth in the middle decades of this century has been replaced by a decrease in the percentage of U.S. workers who are organized. American workers are under heavy pressures today that threaten their jobs. The restrictions on the right to organize in many countries abroad make labor costs lower there, threaten American workers and their jobs, and lead to the exploitation of workers in these countries. In these difficult circumstances, guaranteeing the rights of U.S. workers calls for imaginative vision and creative new steps, not reactive or simply defensive strategies. For example, organized labor can play a very important role in helping to provide the education and training needed to help keep workers employable. Unions can also help both their own members and workers in developing countries by increasing their international efforts. A vital labor movement will be one that looks to the future with a deepened sense of global interdependence.

109. There are many signs that these challenges are being discussed by creative labor leaders today. Deeper and broader discussions of this sort are needed. This does not mean that only organized labor faces these new problems. All other sectors and institutions in the U.S. economy need similar

vision and imagination. Indeed new forms of cooperation among labor, management, government, and other social groups are essential, and will be discussed in Chapter IV of this letter.

2. OWNERS AND MANAGERS

110. The economy's success in fulfilling the demands of justice will depend on how its vast resources and wealth are managed. Property owners, managers, and investors of financial capital must all contribute to creating a more just society. Securing economic justice depends heavily on the leadership of men and women in business and on wise investment by private enterprises. Pope John Paul II has pointed out, "The degree of well-being which society today enjoys would be unthinkable without the dynamic figure of the business person, whose function consists of organizing human labor and the means of production so as to give rise to the goods and services necessary for the prosperity and progress of the community."[61] The freedom of entrepreneurship, business, and finance should be protected, but the accountability of this freedom to the common good and the norms of justice must be assured.

111. Persons in management face many hard choices each day, choices on which the well-being of many others depends. Commitment to the public good and not simply the private good of their firms is at the heart of what it means to call their work a vocation and not simply a career or a job. We believe that the norms and priorities discussed in this letter can be of help as they pursue their important tasks. The duties of individuals in the business world, however, do not exhaust the ethical dimensions of business and finance. The size of a firm or bank is in many cases an indicator of relative power. Large corporations and large financial institutions have considerable power to help shape economic institutions within the United States and throughout the world. With this power goes responsibility and the need for those who manage it to be held to moral and institutional accountability.

112. Business and finance have the duty to be faithful trustees of the resources at their disposal. No one can ever own capital resources absolutely or control their use without regard for others and society as a whole.[62] This applies first of all to land and natural resources. Short-term profits reaped at the cost of depletion of natural resources or the pollution of the environment violate this trust.

113. Resources created by human industry are also held in trust. Owners and managers have not created this capital on their own. They have benefited from the work of many others and from the local communities that support their endeavors.[63] They are accountable to these workers and communities when making decisions. For example, reinvestment in technological innovation is often crucial for the long-term viability of a firm. The use of financial resources solely in pursuit of short-term profits can stunt the production of needed goods and services; a broader vision of managerial responsibility is needed.

114. The Catholic tradition has long defended the right to private ownership of productive property.[64] This right is an important element in a just economic policy. It enlarges our capacity for creativity and initiative.[65] Small and medium-sized farms, businesses, and entrepreneurial enterprises are among the most creative and efficient sectors of our economy. They should be highly valued by the people of the United States, as are land ownership and home ownership. Widespread distribution of property can help avoid excessive concentration of economic and political power. For these reasons ownership should be made possible for a broad sector of our population.[66]

115. The common good may sometimes demand that the right to own be limited by public involvement in the planning or ownership of certain sectors of the economy. Support of private ownership does not mean that anyone has the right to unlimited accumulation of wealth. "Private property does not constitute for anyone an absolute or unconditioned right. No one is justified in keeping for his exclusive use what he does not need, when others lack necessities."[67] Pope John Paul II has referred to limits placed on ownership by the duty to serve the common good as a "social mortgage" on private property.[68] For example, these limits are the basis of society's exercise of eminent domain over privately owned land needed for roads or other essential public goods. The Church's teaching opposes collectivist and statist economic approaches. But it also rejects the notion that a free market automatically produces justice. Therefore, as Pope John Paul II has argued, "One cannot exclude the socialization, in suitable conditions, of certain means of production."[69] The determination of when such conditions exist must be made on a case by case basis in light of the demands of the common good.

116. United States business and financial enterprises can also help determine the justice or injustice of the world economy. They are not all-powerful, but their real power is unquestionable. Transnational corporations and financial institutions can make positive contributions to development and global solidarity. Pope John Paul II has pointed out, however, that the desire to maximize profits and reduce the cost of natural resources and labor has often tempted these transnational enterprises to behavior that increases inequality and decreases the stability of the international order.[70] By collaborating with those national governments that serve their citizens justly and with intergovernmental agencies, these corporations can contribute to overcoming the desperate plight of many persons throughout the world.

117. Business people, managers, investors, and financiers follow a vital Christian vocation when they act responsibly and seek the common good. We encourage and support a renewed sense of vocation in the business community. We also recognize that the way business people serve society is governed and limited by the incentives which flow from tax policies, the availability of credit, and other public policies.

118. Businesses have a right to an institutional framework that does not penalize enterprises that act responsibly. Governments must provide regula-

tions and a system of taxation which encourage firms to preserve the environment, employ disadvantaged workers, and create jobs in depressed areas. Managers and stockholders should not be torn between their responsibilities to their organizations and their responsibilities toward society as a whole.

3. CITIZENS AND GOVERNMENT

119. In addition to rights and duties related to specific roles in the economy, everyone has obligations based simply on membership in the social community. By fulfilling these duties, we create a true commonwealth. Volunteering time, talent, and money to work for greater justice is a fundamental expression of Christian love and social solidarity. All who have more than they need must come to the aid of the poor. People with professional or technical skills needed to enhance the lives of others have a duty to share them. And the poor have similar obligations: to work together as individuals and families to build up their communities by acts of social solidarity and justice. These voluntary efforts to overcome injustice are part of the Christian vocation.

120. Every citizen also has the responsibility to work to secure justice and human rights through an organized social response. In the words of Pius XI, "Charity will never be true charity unless it takes justice into account. . . . Let no one attempt with small gifts of charity to exempt himself from the great duties imposed by justice."[71] The guaranteeing of basic justice for all is not an optional expression of largesse but an inescapable duty for the whole of society.

121. The traditional distinction between society and the state in Catholic social teaching provides the basic framework for such organized public efforts. The Church opposes all statist and totalitarian approaches to socioeconomic questions. Social life is richer than governmental power can encompass. All groups that compose society have responsibilities to respond to the demands of justice. We have just outlined some of the duties of labor unions and business and financial enterprises. These must be supplemented by initiatives by local community groups, professional associations, educational institutions, churches, and synagogues. All the groups that give life to this society have important roles to play in the pursuit of economic justice.

122. For this reason, it is all the more significant that the teachings of the Church insist that *government has a moral function: protecting human rights and securing basic justice for all members of the commonwealth.*[72] Society as a whole and in all its diversity is responsible for building up the common good. But it is government's role to guarantee the minimum conditions that make this rich social activity possible, namely, human rights and justice.[73] This obligation also falls on individual citizens as they choose their representatives and participate in shaping public opinion.

123. More specifically, it is the responsibility of all citizens, acting through their government, to assist and empower the poor, the disadvantaged, the

handicapped, and the unemployed. Government should assume a positive role in generating employment and establishing fair labor practices, in guaranteeing the provision and maintenance of the economy's infrastructure, such as roads, bridges, harbors, public means of communication, and transport. It should regulate trade and commerce in the interest of fairness.[74] Government may levy the taxes necessary to meet these responsibilities, and citizens have a moral obligation to pay those taxes. The way society responds to the needs of the poor through its public policies is the litmus test of its justice or injustice. The political debate about these policies is the indispensable forum for dealing with the conflicts and tradeoffs that will always be present in the pursuit of a more just economy.

124. The primary norm for determining the scope and limits of governmental intervention is the "principle of subsidiarity" cited above. This principle states that, in order to protect basic justice, government should undertake only those initiatives which exceed the capacity of individuals or private groups acting independently. Government should not replace or destroy smaller communities and individual initiative. Rather it should help them to contribute more effectively to social well-being and supplement their activity when the demands of justice exceed their capacities. This does not mean, however, that the government that governs least governs best. Rather it defines good government intervention as that which truly "helps" other social groups contribute to the common good by directing, urging, restraining, and regulating economic activity as "the occasion requires and necessity demands."[75] This calls for cooperation and consensus-building among the diverse agents in our economic life, including government. The precise form of government involvement in this process cannot be determined in the abstract. It will depend on an assessment of specific needs and the most effective ways to address them.

D. Christian Hope and the Courage to Act

125. The Christian vision is based on the conviction that God has destined the human race and all creation for "a kingdom of truth and life, of holiness and grace, of justice, love, and peace."[76] This conviction gives Christians strong hope as they face the economic struggles of the world today. This hope is not a naive optimism that imagines that simple formulas for creating a fully just society are ready at hand. The Church's experience through history and in nations throughout the world today has made it wary of all ideologies that claim to have the final answer to humanity's problems.[77] Christian hope has a much stronger foundation than such ideologies, for it rests on the knowledge that God is at work in the world, "preparing a new dwelling place and a new earth where justice will abide."[78]

126. This hope stimulates and strengthens Christian efforts to create a more just economic order in spite of difficulties and setbacks.[79] Christian hope

is strong and resilient, for it is rooted in a faith that knows that the fullness of life comes to those who follow Christ in the way of the Cross. In pursuit of concrete solutions, all members of the Christian community are called to an ever finer discernment of the hurts and opportunities in the world around them, in order to respond to the most pressing needs and thus build up a more just society.[80] This is a communal task calling for dialogue, experimentation, and imagination. It also calls for deep faith and courageous love.

CHAPTER 3: SELECTED ECONOMIC POLICY ISSUES

127. We have outlined this moral vision as a guide to all who seek to be faithful to the Gospel in their daily economic decisions and as a challenge to transform the economic arrangements that shape our lives and our world. These arrangements embody and communicate social values and therefore have moral significance both in themselves and in their effects. Christians, like all people, must be concerned about how the concrete outcomes of their economic activity serve human dignity; they must assess the extent to which the structures and practices of the economy support or undermine their moral vision.

128. Such an assessment of economic practices, structures, and outcomes leads to a variety of conclusions. Some people argue that an unfettered free-market economy, where owners, workers, and consumers pursue their enlightened self-interest, provides the greatest possible liberty, material welfare, and equity. The policy implication of this view is to intervene in the economy as little as possible because it is such a delicate mechanism that any attempt to improve it is likely to have the opposite effect. Others argue that the capitalist system is inherently inequitable and therefore contradictory to the demands of Christian morality, for it is based on acquisitiveness, competition, and self-centered individualism. They assert that capitalism is fatally flawed and must be replaced by a radically different system that abolishes private property, the profit motive, and the free market.

129. Catholic social teaching has traditionally rejected these ideological extremes because they are likely to produce results contrary to human dignity and economic justice.[1] Starting with the assumption that the economy has been created by human beings and can be changed by them, the Church works for improvement in a variety of economic and political contexts; but it is not the Church's role to create or promote a specific new economic system. Rather, the Church must encourage all reforms that hold out hope of transforming our economic arrangements into a fuller systemic realization of the Christian moral vision. The Church must also stand ready to challenge practices and institutions that impede or carry us farther away from realizing this vision.

130. In short, the Church is not bound to any particular economic, political, or social system; it has lived with many forms of economic and social

organization and will continue to do so, evaluating each according to moral and ethical principles: What is the impact of the system on people? Does it support or threaten human dignity?

131. In this document we offer reflections on the particular reality that is the U.S. economy. In doing so we are aware of the need to address not only individual issues within the economy but also the larger question of the economic system itself. Our approach in analyzing the U.S. economy is pragmatic and evolutionary in nature. We live in a "mixed" economic system which is the product of a long history of reform and adjustment. It is in the spirit of this American pragmatic tradition of reform that we seek to continue the search for a more just economy. Our nation has many assets to employ in this quest—vast economic, technological, and human resources and a system of representative government through which we can all help shape economic decisions.

132. Although we have chosen in this chapter to focus primarily on some aspects of the economy where we think reforms are realistically possible, we also emphasize that Catholic social teaching bears directly on larger questions concerning the economic system itself and the values it expresses—questions that cannot be ignored in the Catholic vision of economic justice.[2] For example, does our economic system place more emphasis on maximizing profits than on meeting human needs and fostering human dignity? Does our economy distribute its benefits equitably or does it concentrate power and resources in the hands of a few? Does it promote excessive materialism and individualism? Does it adequately protect the environment and the nation's natural resources? Does it direct too many scarce resources to military purposes? These and other basic questions about the economy need to be scrutinized in light of the ethical norms we have outlined. We urge continuing exploration of these systemic questions in a more comprehensive way than this document permits.

133. We have selected the following subjects to address here: 1) employment, 2) poverty, 3) food and agriculture, and 4) the U.S. role in the global economy. These topics were chosen because of their relevance to both the economic "signs of the times" and the ethical norms of our tradition. Each exemplifies U.S. policies that are basic to the establishment of economic justice in the nation and the world, and each illustrates key moral principles and norms for action from Catholic social teaching. Our treatment of these issues does not constitute a comprehensive analysis of the U.S. economy. We emphasize that these are illustrative topics intended to exemplify the interaction of moral values and economic issues in our day, not to encompass all such values and issues. This document is not a technical blueprint for economic reform. Rather, it is an attempt to foster a serious moral analysis leading to a more just economy.

134. In focusing on some of the central economic issues and choices in American life in the light of moral principles, we are aware that the movement

from principle to policy is complex and difficult and that although moral values are essential in determining public policies, they do not dictate specific solutions. They must interact with empirical data, with historical, social, and political realities, and with competing demands on limited resources. The soundness of our prudential judgments depends not only on the moral force of our principles, but also on the accuracy of our information and the validity of our assumptions.

135. Our judgments and recommendations on specific economic issues, therefore, do not carry the same moral authority as our statements of universal moral principles and formal church teaching; the former are related to circumstances which can change or which can be interpreted differently by people of good will. We expect and welcome debate on our specific policy recommendations. Nevertheless, we want our statements on these matters to be given serious consideration by Catholics as they determine whether their own moral judgments are consistent with the Gospel and with Catholic social teaching. We believe that differences on complex economic questions should be expressed in a spirit of mutual respect and open dialogue.[3]

A. Employment

136. Full employment is the foundation of a just economy. The most urgent priority for domestic economic policy is the creation of new jobs with adequate pay and decent working conditions. We must make it possible as a nation for every one who is seeking a job to find employment within a reasonable amount of time. Our emphasis on this goal is based on the conviction that human work has a special dignity and is a key to achieving justice in society.[4]

137. Employment is a basic right, a right which protects the freedom of all to participate in the economic life of society. It is a right which flows from the principles of justice which we have outlined above. Corresponding to this right is the duty on the part of society to ensure that the right is protected. The importance of this right is evident in the fact that for most people employment is crucial to self-realization and essential to the fulfillment of material needs. Since so few in our economy own productive property, employment also forms the first line of defense against poverty. Jobs benefit society as well as workers, for they enable more people to contribute to the common good and to the productivity required for a healthy economy.

1. THE SCOPE AND EFFECTS OF UNEMPLOYMENT

138. Joblessness is becoming a more widespread and deep-seated problem in our nation. There are about 8 million people in the United States looking for a job who cannot find one. They represent about 7 percent of the labor force.[5] The official rate of unemployment does not include those who have given up

looking for work or those who are working part-time, but want to work full-time. When these categories are added, it becomes clear that about one-eighth of the workforce is directly affected by unemployment.[6] The severity of the unemployment problem is compounded by the fact that almost three-fourths of those who are unemployed receive no unemployment insurance benefits.[7]

139. In recent years there has been a steady trend toward higher and higher levels of unemployment, even in good times. Between 1950 and 1980 the annual unemployment rate exceeded current levels only during the recession years of 1975 and 1976. Periods of economic recovery during these three decades brought unemployment rates down to 3 and 4 percent. Since 1979, however, the rate has generally been above 7 percent.

140. Who are the unemployed? Blacks, Hispanics, Native Americans, young adults, female heads of households, and those who are inadequately educated are represented disproportionately among the ranks of the unemployed. The unemployment rate among minorities is almost twice as high as the rate among whites. For female heads of households the unemployment rate is over 10 percent. Among black teenagers, unemployment reaches the scandalous rate of more than one in three.[8]

141. The severe human costs of high unemployment levels become vividly clear when we examine the impact of joblessness on human lives and human dignity. It is a deep conviction of American culture that work is central to the freedom and well-being of people. The unemployed often come to feel they are worthless and without a productive role in society. Each day they are unemployed our society tells them: We don't need your talent. We don't need your initiative. We don't need *you*. Unemployment takes a terrible toll on the health and stability of both individuals and families. It gives rise to family quarrels, greater consumption of alcohol, child abuse, spouse abuse, divorce, and higher rates of infant mortality.[9] People who are unemployed often feel that society blames them for being unemployed. Very few people survive long periods of unemployment without some psychological damage even if they have sufficient funds to meet their needs.[10] At the extreme, the strains of job loss may drive individuals to suicide.[11]

142. In addition to the terrible waste of individual talent and creativity, unemployment also harms society at large. Jobless people pay little or no taxes, thus lowering the revenues for city, state, and the federal governments. At the same time, rising unemployment requires greater expenditures for unemployment compensation, food stamps, welfare, and other assistance. It is estimated that in 1986, for every one percentage point increase in the rate of unemployment, there will be roughly a $40 billion increase in the federal deficit.[12] The costs to society are also evident in the rise in crime associated with joblessness. The Federal Bureau of Prisons reports that increases in unemployment have been followed by increases in the prison population. Other studies have shown links between the rate of joblessness and the frequency of homicides, robberies, larcenies, narcotics arrests, and youth crimes.[13]

143. Our own experiences with the individuals, families, and communities that suffer the burdens of unemployment compel us to the conviction that as a nation we simply cannot afford to have millions of able-bodied men and women unemployed. We cannot afford the economic costs, the social dislocation, and the enormous human tragedies caused by unemployment. In the end, however, what we can least afford is the assault on human dignity that occurs when millions are left without adequate employment. Therefore, we cannot but conclude that current levels of unemployment are intolerable, and they impose on us a moral obligation to work for policies that will reduce joblessness.

2. UNEMPLOYMENT IN A CHANGING ECONOMY

144. The structure of the U.S. economy is undergoing a transformation that affects both the quantity and the quality of jobs in our nation. The size and makeup of the workforce, for example, have changed markedly in recent years. For a number of reasons, there are now more people in the labor market than ever before in our history. Population growth has pushed up the supply of potential workers. In addition, large numbers of women have entered the labor force not only in order to put their talents and education to greater use, but also out of economic necessity. Many families need two salaries if they are to live in a decently human fashion. Female-headed households often depend heavily on the mother's income to stay off the welfare rolls. Immigrants seeking a better existence in the United States have also added to the size of the labor force. These demographic changes, however, cannot fully explain the higher levels of unemployment.

145. Technological changes are also having dramatic impacts on the employment picture in the United States. Advancing technology brings many benefits, but it can also bring social and economic costs, including the downgrading and displacement of workers. High technology and advanced automation are changing the very face of our nation's industries and occupations. In the 1970s, about 90 percent of all new jobs were in service occupations. By 1990, service industries are expected to employ 72 percent of the labor force. Much of the job growth in the 1980s is expected to be in traditionally low-paying, high-turnover jobs such as sales, clerical, janitorial, and food service.[14] Too often these jobs do not have career ladders leading to higher skilled, higher paying jobs. Thus, the changing industrial and occupational mix in the U.S. economy could result in a shift toward lower paying and lower skilled jobs.

146. Increased competition in world markets is another factor influencing the rate of joblessness in our nation. Many other exporting nations have acquired and developed up-to-the-minute technology, enabling them to increase productivity dramatically. Combined with very low wages in many nations, this has allowed them to gain a larger share of the U.S. market to cut into U.S. export markets. At the same time many corporations have closed

plants in the United States and moved their capital, technology, and jobs to foreign affiliates.

147. Discrimination in employment is one of the causes for high rates of joblessness and low pay among racial minorities and women. Beyond the normal problems of locating a job, blacks, Hispanics, Native Americans, immigrants, and other minorities bear this added burden of discrimination. Discrimination against women is compounded by the lack of adequate child care services and by the unwillingness of many employers to provide flexible employment or extend fringe benefits to part-time employees.

148. High levels of defense spending also have an effect on the number of jobs in our economy. In our pastoral letter, *The Challenge of Peace*, we noted the serious economic distortions caused by the arms race and the disastrous effects that it has on society's ability to care for the poor and the needy. Employment is one area in which this interconnection is very evident. The hundreds of billions of dollars spent by our nation each year on the arms race create a massive drain on the U.S. economy as well as a very serious "brain drain." Such spending on the arms race means a net loss in the number of jobs created in the economy, because defense industries are less labor-intensive than other major sectors of the economy.[15] Moreover, nearly half of the American scientific and engineering force works in defense-related programs and over 60 percent of the entire federal research and development budget goes to the military.[16] We must ask whether our nation will ever be able to modernize our economy and achieve full employment if we continue to devote so much of our financial and human resources to defense-related activities.

149. These are some of the factors that have driven up the rate of unemployment in recent years. Although our economy has created more than 20 million new jobs since 1970,[17] there continues to be a chronic and growing job shortage. In the face of this challenge, our nation's economic institutions have failed to adapt adequately and rapidly enough. For example, failure to invest sufficiently in certain industries and regions, inadequate education and training for new workers, and insufficient mechanisms to assist workers displaced by new technology have added to the unemployment problem.

150. Generating an adequate number of jobs in our economy is a complex task in view of the changing and diverse nature of the problem. It involves numerous trade-offs and substantial costs. Nevertheless, it is not an impossible task. Achieving the goal of full employment may require major adjustments and creative strategies that go beyond the limits of existing policies and institutions, but it is a task we must undertake.

3. GUIDELINES FOR ACTION

151. We recommend that the nation make a major new commitment to achieve full employment. At present there is nominal endorsement of the full employment ideal, but no firm commitment to bringing it about. If every effort

were now being made to create the jobs required, one might argue that the situation today is the best we can do. But such is not the case. The country is doing far less than it might to generate employment.

152. Over the last decade, economists, policy makers, and the general public have shown greater willingness to tolerate unemployment levels of 6 to 7 percent or even more.[18] Although we recognize the complexities and trade-offs involved in reducing unemployment, we believe that 6 to 7 percent unemployment is neither inevitable nor acceptable. While a zero unemployment rate is clearly impossible in an economy where people are constantly entering the job market and others are changing jobs, appropriate policies and concerted private and public action can improve the situation considerably, if we have the will to do so. No economy can be considered truly healthy when so many millions of people are denied jobs by forces outside their control. The acceptance of present unemployment rates would have been unthinkable twenty years ago. It should be regarded as intolerable today.

153. We must first establish a consensus that everyone has a right to employment. Then the burden of securing full employment falls on all of us—policy makers, business, labor, and the general public—to create and implement the mechanisms to protect that right. We must work for the formation of a new national consensus and mobilize the necessary political will at all levels to make the goal of full employment a reality.

154. Expanding employment in our nation will require significant steps in both the private and public sectors, as well as joint action between them. Private initiative and entrepreneurship are essential to this task, for the private sector accounts for about 80 percent of the jobs in the United States, and most new jobs are being created there.[19] Thus, a viable strategy for employment generation must assume that a large part of the solution will be with private firms and small businesses. At the same time, it must be recognized that government has a prominent and indispensable role to play in addressing the problem of unemployment. The market alone will not automatically produce full employment. Therefore, the government must act to ensure that this goal is achieved by coordinating general economic policies, by job creation programs, and by other appropriate policy measures.

155. Effective action against unemployment will require a careful mix of general economic policies and targeted employment programs. Taken together, these policies and programs should have full employment as their number one goal.

a. General Economic Policies

156. The general or macroeconomic policies of the federal government are essential tools for encouraging the steady economic growth that produces more and better jobs in the economy. *We recommend that the fiscal and monetary policies of the nation—such as federal spending, tax, and interest rate policies—should be coordinated so as to achieve the goal of full employment.*

157. General economic policies that attempt to expand employment must also deal with the problem of inflation.[20] The risk of inflationary pressures resulting from such expansionary policies is very real. Our response to this risk, however, must not be to abandon the goal of full employment, but to develop effective policies that keep inflation under control.

158. While economic growth is an important and necessary condition for the reduction of unemployment, it is not sufficient in and of itself. In order to work for full employment and restrain inflation, it is also necessary to adopt more specific programs and policies targeted toward particular aspects of the unemployment problem.[21]

b. Targeted Employment Programs

159. (1) *We recommend expansion of job-training and apprenticeship programs in the private sector administered and supported jointly by business, labor unions, and government.* Any comprehensive employment strategy must include systematic means of developing the technical and professional skills needed for a dynamic and productive economy. Investment in a skilled work force is a prerequisite both for sustaining economic growth and achieving greater justice in the United States. The obligation to contribute to this investment falls on both the private and public sectors. Today business, labor, and government need to coordinate their efforts and pool their resources to promote a substantial increase in the number of apprenticeship programs and to expand on-the-job training programs. We recommend a national commitment to eradicate illiteracy and to provide people with the skills necessary to adapt to the changing demands of employment.

160. With the rapid pace of technological change, continuing education and training are even more important today than in the past. Businesses have a stake in providing it, for skilled workers are essential to increased productivity. Labor unions should support it, for their members are increasingly vulnerable to displacement and job loss unless they continue to develop their skills and their flexibility on the job. Local communities have a stake as well, for their economic well-being will suffer serious harm if local industries fail to develop and are forced to shut down.

161. The best medicine for the disease of plant-closings is prevention. Prevention depends not only on sustained capital investment to enhance productivity through advanced technology but also on the training and retraining of workers within the private sector. In circumstances where plants are forced to shut down, management, labor unions, and local communities must see to it that workers are not simply cast aside. Retraining programs will be even more urgently needed in these circumstances.

162. (2) *We recommend increased support for direct job creation programs targeted on the long-term unemployed and those with special needs.* Such programs can take the form of direct public service employment and also of public subsidies for employment in the private sector. Both approaches

would provide jobs for those with low skills less expensively and with less inflation than would general stimulation of the economy.[22] The cost of providing jobs must also be balanced against the savings realized by the government through decreased welfare and unemployment insurance expenditures and increased revenues from the taxes paid by the newly employed.

163. Government funds, if used effectively, can also stimulate private sector jobs for the long-term unemployed and for groups particularly hard to employ. Experiments need to be conducted on the precise ways such subsidies would most successfully attract business participation and ensure the generation of permanent jobs.

164. These job generation efforts should aim specifically at bringing marginalized persons into the labor force. They should produce a net increase in the number of jobs rather than displacing the burden of unemployment from one group of persons to another. They should also be aimed at long-term jobs and should include the necessary supportive services to assist the unemployed in finding and keeping jobs.

165. Jobs that are created should produce goods and services needed and valued by society. It is both good common sense and sound economics to create jobs directly for the purpose of meeting society's unmet needs. Across the nation, in every state and locality, there is ample evidence of social needs that are going unmet. Many of our parks and recreation facilities are in need of maintenance and repair. Many of the nation's bridges and highways are in disrepair. We have a desperate need for more low-income housing. Our educational systems, day-care services, senior citizen services, and other community programs need to be expanded. These and many other elements of our national life are areas of unmet need. At the same time, there are more than 8 million Americans looking for productive and useful work. Surely we have the capacity to match these needs by giving Americans who are anxious to work a chance for productive employment in jobs that are waiting to be done. The overriding moral value of enabling jobless persons to achieve a new sense of dignity and personal worth through employment also strongly recommends these programs.

166. These job creation efforts will require increased collaboration and fresh alliances between the private and public sectors at all levels. There are already a number of examples of how such efforts can be successful.[23] We believe that the potential of these kinds of partnerships has only begun to be tapped.

c. *Examining New Strategies*

167. In addition to the actions suggested above, we believe there is also a need for careful examination and experimentation with alternative approaches that might improve both the quantity and quality of jobs. More extensive use of job sharing, flex time, and a reduced work week are among the topics that should continue to be on the agenda of public discussion. Consideration

should also be given to the possibility of limiting or abolishing compulsory overtime work. Similarly, methods might be examined to discourage the overuse of part-time workers, who do not receive fringe benefits.[24] New strategies also need to be explored in the area of education and training for the hard-to-employ, displaced workers, the handicapped, and others with special needs. Particular attention is needed to achieve pay equity between men and women, as well as upgrading the pay scale and working conditions of traditionally low-paying jobs. The nation should renew its efforts to develop effective affirmative action policies that assist those who have been excluded by racial or sexual discrimination in the past. New strategies for improving job placement services at the national and local levels are also needed. Improving occupational safety is another important concern that deserves increased attention.

168. Much greater attention also needs to be devoted to the long-term task of converting some of the nation's military production to more peaceful and socially productive purposes. The nation needs to seek more effective ways to retool industries, to retrain workers, and to provide the necessary adjustment assistance for communities affected by this kind of economic conversion.

169. These are among the avenues that need to be explored in the search for just employment policies. A belief in the inherent dignity of human work and in the right to employment should motivate people in all sectors of society to carry on that search in new and creative ways.

B. Poverty

170. More than 33 million Americans—about one in every seven people in our nation—are poor by the government's official definition. The norms of human dignity and the preferential option for the poor compel us to confront this issue with a sense of urgency. Dealing with poverty is not a luxury to which our nation can attend when it finds the time and resources. Rather, it is a moral imperative of the highest priority.

171. Of particular concern is the fact that poverty has increased dramatically during the last decade. Since 1973 the poverty rate has increased by nearly a third. Although the recent recovery has brought a slight decline in the rate, it remains at a level that is higher than at almost any other time during the last two decades.[25]

172. As pastors we have seen firsthand the faces of poverty in our midst. Homeless people roam city streets in tattered clothing and sleep in doorways or on subway grates at night. Many of these are former mental patients released from state hospitals. Thousands stand in line at soup kitchens because they have no other way of feeding themselves. Millions of children are so poorly nourished that their physical and mental development are seriously harmed.[26] We have also seen the growing economic hardship and insecurity experienced by moderate-income Americans when they lose their jobs and their income due to forces beyond their control. These are alarming signs and

trends. They pose for our nation an urgent moral and human challenge: to fashion a society where no one goes without the basic material necessities required for human dignity and growth.

173. Poverty can be described and defined in many different ways. It can include spiritual as well as material poverty. Likewise, its meaning changes depending on the historical, social, and economic setting. Poverty in our time is different from the more severe deprivation experienced in earlier centuries in the U.S. or in Third World nations today. Our discussion of poverty in this chapter is set within the context of present-day American society. By poverty, we are referring here to the lack of sufficient material resources required for a decent life. We use the government's official definition of poverty, although we recognize its limits.[27]

1. CHARACTERISTICS OF POVERTY

174. Poverty is not an isolated problem existing solely among a small number of anonymous people in our central cities. Nor is it limited to a dependent underclass or to specific groups in the United States. It is a condition experienced at some time by many people in different walks of life and in different circumstances. Many poor people are working but at wages insufficient to lift them out of poverty.[28] Others are unable to work and therefore dependent on outside sources of support. Still others are on the edge of poverty; although not officially defined as poor, they are economically insecure and at risk of falling into poverty.

175. While many of the poor manage to escape from beneath the official poverty line, others remain poor for extended periods of time. Long-term poverty is concentrated among racial minorities and families headed by women. It is also more likely to be found in rural areas and in the South.[29] Of the long-term poor, most are either working at wages too low to bring them above the poverty line or are retired, disabled, or parents of preschool children. Generally they are not in a position to work more hours than they do now.[30]

a. Children in Poverty

176. Poverty strikes some groups more severely than others. Perhaps most distressing is the growing number of children who are poor. Today one in every four American children under the age of six, and one in every two black children under six, are poor. The number of children in poverty rose by four million over the decade between 1973 and 1983, with the result that there are now more poor children in the United States than at any time since 1965.[31] The problem is particularly severe among female-headed families, where more than half of all children are poor. Two-thirds of black children and nearly three-quarters of Hispanic children in such families are poor.

177. Very many poor families with children receive no government assistance, have no health insurance, and cannot pay medical bills. Less than half

are immunized against preventable diseases such as diphtheria and polio.[32] Poor children are disadvantaged even before birth; their mothers' lack of access to high quality prenatal care leaves them at much greater risk of premature birth, low birth weight, physical and mental impairment, and death before their first birthday.

b. Women and Poverty

178. The past twenty years have witnessed a dramatic increase in the number of women in poverty.[33] This includes women raising children alone as well as women with inadequate income following divorce, widowhood, or retirement. More than one-third of all female-headed families are poor. Among minority families headed by women the poverty rate is over 50 percent.[34]

179. Wage discrimination against women is a major factor behind these high rates of poverty. Many women are employed but remain poor because their wages are too low. Women who work outside their homes full-time and year-round earn only 61 percent of what men earn. Thus, being employed full-time is not by itself a remedy for poverty among women. Hundreds of thousands of women hold full-time jobs but are still poor. Sixty percent of all women work in only ten occupations, and most new jobs for women are in areas with low pay and limited chances of advancement. Many women suffer discrimination in wages, salaries, job classifications, promotions, and other areas.[35] As a result, they find themselves in jobs that have low status, little security, weak unionization, and few fringe benefits. Such discrimination is immoral and efforts must be made to overcome the effects of sexism in our society.

180. Women's responsibilities for childrearing are another important factor to be considered. Despite the many changes in marriage and family life in recent decades, women continue to have primary responsibility in this area. When marriages break up, mothers typically take custody of the children and bear the major financial responsibility for supporting them. Women often anticipate that they will leave the labor force to have and raise children, and often make job and career choices accordingly. In other cases they are not hired or promoted to higher paying jobs because of their childbearing responsibilities. In addition, most divorced or separated mothers do not get child support payments. In 1983, less than half of women raising children alone had been awarded child support, and of those, only half received the full amount to which they were entitled. Even fewer women (14 percent) are awarded alimony, and many older women are left in poverty after a lifetime of homemaking and childbearing.[36] Such women have great difficulty finding jobs and securing health insurance.

c. Racial Minorities and Poverty

181. Most poor people in our nation are white, but the rates of poverty in our nation are highest among those who have borne the brunt of racial prejudice and discrimination. For example, blacks are about three times more likely

to be poor than whites. While one out of every nine white Americans is poor, one of every three blacks and Native Americans and more than one of every four Hispanics are poor.[37] While some members of minority communities have successfully moved up the economic ladder, the overall picture indicates that black family income is only 55 percent of white family income, reflecting an income gap that is wider now than at any time in the last fifteen years.[38]

182. Despite the gains which have been made toward racial equality, prejudice and discrimination in our own time as well as the effects of past discrimination continue to exclude many members of racial minorities from the mainstream of American life. Discriminatory practices in labor markets, in educational systems, and in electoral politics create major obstacles for blacks, Hispanics, Native Americans, and other racial minorities in their struggle to improve their economic status.[39] Such discrimination is evidence of the continuing presence of racism in our midst. In our pastoral letter, *Brothers and Sisters to Us*, we have described this racism as a sin—"a sin that divides the human family, blots out the image of God among specific members of that family, and violates the fundamental human dignity of those called to be children of the same Father."[40]

2. ECONOMIC INEQUALITY

183. Important to our discussion of poverty in America is an understanding of the degree of economic inequality in our nation. Our economy is marked by a very uneven distribution of wealth and income. For example, it is estimated that 28 percent of the total net wealth is held by the richest 2 percent of families in the United States. The top 10 percent holds 57 percent of the net wealth.[41] If homes and other real estate are excluded, the concentration of ownership of financial wealth is even more glaring. In 1983, 54 percent of the total net financial assets were held by 2 percent of all families, those whose annual income is over $125,000. Eighty-six percent of these assets were held by the top 10 percent of all families.[42]

184. Although disparities in the distribution of income are less extreme, they are still striking. In 1984 the bottom 20 percent of American families received only 4.7 percent of the total income in the nation and the bottom 40 percent received only 15.7 percent, the lowest share on record in U.S. history. In contrast, the top one-fifth received 42.9 percent of the total income, the highest share since 1948.[43] These figures are only partial and very imperfect measures of the inequality in our society.[44] However, they do suggest that the degree of inequality is quite large. In comparison with other industrialized nations, the United States is among the more unequal in terms of income distribution.[45] Moreover, the gap between rich and poor in our nation has increased during the last decade.[46] These inequities are of particular concern because they reflect the uneven distribution of power in our society. They suggest that the level of participation in the political and social spheres is also very uneven.

185. Catholic social teaching does not require absolute equality in the distribution of income and wealth. Some degree of inequality not only is acceptable, but also may be considered desirable for economic and social reasons, such as the need for incentives and the provision of greater rewards for greater risks. However, unequal distribution should be evaluated in terms of several moral principles we have enunciated: the priority of meeting the basic needs of the poor and the importance of increasing the level of participation by all members of society in the economic life of the nation. These norms establish a strong presumption against extreme inequality of income and wealth as long as there are poor, hungry, and homeless people in our midst. They also suggest that extreme inequalities are detrimental to the development of social solidarity and community. In view of these norms we find the disparities of income and wealth in the United States to be unacceptable. Justice requires that all members of our society work for economic, political, and social reforms that will decrease these inequities.

3. GUIDELINES FOR ACTION

186. Our recommendations for dealing with poverty in the United States build upon several moral principles that were explored in chapter two of this letter. The themes of human dignity and the preferential option for the poor are at the heart of our approach; they compel us to confront the issue of poverty with a real sense of urgency.

187. The principle of social solidarity suggests that alleviating poverty will require fundamental changes in social and economic structures that perpetuate glaring inequalities and cut off millions of citizens from full participation in the economic and social life of the nation. The process of change should be one that draws together all citizens, whatever their economic status, into one community.

188. The principle of participation leads us to the conviction that the most appropriate and fundamental solutions to poverty will be those that enable people to take control of their own lives. For poverty is not merely the lack of adequate financial resources. It entails a more profound kind of deprivation, a denial of full participation in the economic, social, and political life of society and an inability to influence decisions that affect one's life. It means being powerless in a way that assaults not only one's pocketbook but also one's fundamental human dignity. Therefore, we should seek solutions that enable the poor to help themselves through such means as employment. Paternalistic programs which do too much *for* and too little *with* the poor are to be avoided.

189. The responsibility for alleviating the plight of the poor falls upon all members of society. As individuals, all citizens have a duty to assist the poor through acts of charity and personal commitment. But private charity and voluntary action are not sufficient. We also carry out our moral responsibility

to assist and empower the poor by working collectively through government to establish just and effective public policies.

190. Although the task of alleviating poverty is complex and demanding, we should be encouraged by examples of our nation's past successes in this area. Our history shows that we can reduce poverty. During the 1960s and early 1970s, the official poverty rate was cut in half, due not only to a healthy economy, but also to public policy decisions that improved the nation's income transfer programs. It is estimated, for example, that in the late 1970s federal benefit programs were lifting out of poverty about 70 percent of those who would have otherwise been poor.[47]

191. During the last twenty-five years, the Social Security Program has dramatically reduced poverty among the elderly.[48] In addition, in 1983 it lifted out of poverty almost 1.5 million children of retired, deceased, and disabled workers.[49] Medicare has enhanced the life expectancy and health status of elderly and disabled people, and Medicaid has reduced infant mortality and greatly improved access to health care for the poor.[50]

192. These and other successful social welfare programs are evidence of our nation's commitment to social justice and a decent life for everyone. They also indicate that we have the capacity to design programs that are effective and provide necessary assistance to the needy in a way that respects their dignity. Yet it is evident that not all social welfare programs have been successful. Some have been ill-designed, ineffective, and wasteful. No one has been more aware of this than the poor themselves, who have suffered the consequences. Where programs have failed, we should discard them, learn from our mistakes, and fashion a better alternative. Where programs have succeeded, we should acknowledge that fact and build on those successes. In every instance, we must summon a new creativity and commitment to eradicate poverty in our midst and to guarantee all Americans their right to share in the blessings of our land.

193. Before discussing directions for reform in public policy, we must speak frankly about misunderstandings and stereotypes of the poor. For example, a common misconception is that most of the poor are racial minorities. In fact, about two-thirds of the poor are white.[51] It is also frequently suggested that people stay on welfare for many years, do not work, could work if they wanted to, and have children who will be on welfare. In fact, reliable data show that these are not accurate descriptions of most people who are poor and on welfare. Over a decade people move on and off welfare, and less than 1 percent obtain these benefits for all ten years.[52] Nor is it true that the rolls of Aid to Families with Dependent Children (AFDC) are filled with able-bodied adults who could but will not work. The majority of AFDC recipients are young children and their mothers who must remain at home.[53] These mothers are also accused of having more children so that they can raise their allowances. The truth is that 70 percent of AFDC families have only one or two children and that there is little financial advantage in having another. In a given year, almost half of all families who receive AFDC include an adult

who has worked full- or part-time.[54] Research has consistently demonstrated that people who are poor have the same strong desire to work that characterizes the rest of the population.[55]

194. We ask everyone to refrain from actions, words, or attitudes that stigmatize the poor, that exaggerate the benefits received by the poor, and that inflate the amount of fraud in welfare payments.[56] These are symptoms of a punitive attitude towards the poor. The belief persists in this country that the poor are poor by choice or through laziness, that anyone can escape poverty by hard work, and that welfare programs make it easier for people to avoid work. Thus, public attitudes toward programs for the poor tend to differ sharply from attitudes about other benefits and programs. Some of the most generous subsidies for individuals and corporations are taken for granted and are not even called benefits but entitlements.[57] In contrast, programs for the poor are called handouts and receive a great deal of critical attention, even though they account for less than 10 percent of the federal budget.[58]

195. We now wish to propose several elements which we believe are necessary for a national strategy to deal with poverty. We offer this not as a comprehensive list but as an invitation for others to join the discussion and take up the task of fighting poverty.

196. a. *The first line of attack against poverty must be to build and sustain a healthy economy that provides employment opportunities at just wages for all adults who are able to work.* Poverty is intimately linked to the issue of employment. Millions are poor because they have lost their jobs or because their wages are too low. The persistent high levels of unemployment during the last decade are a major reason why poverty has increased in recent years.[59] Expanded employment especially in the private sector would promote human dignity, increase social solidarity, and promote self-reliance of the poor. It should also reduce the need for welfare programs and generate the income necessary to support those who remain in need and cannot work: elderly, disabled, and chronically ill people, and single parents of young children. It should also be recognized that the persistence of poverty harms the larger society because the depressed purchasing power of the poor contributes to the periodic cycles of stagnation in the economy.

197. In recent years the minimum wage has not been adjusted to keep pace with inflation. Its real value has declined by 24 percent since 1981. We believe Congress should raise the minimum wage in order to restore some of the purchasing power it has lost due to inflation.

198. While job creation and just wages are major elements of a national strategy against poverty, they are clearly not enough. Other more specific policies are necessary to remedy the institutional causes of poverty and to provide for those who cannot work.

199. b. *Vigorous action should be undertaken to remove barriers to full and equal employment for women and minorities.* Too many women and minorities are locked into jobs with low pay, poor working conditions, and

little opportunity for career advancement. So long as we tolerate a situation in which people can work full-time and still be below the poverty line—a situation common among those earning the minimum wage—too many will continue to be counted among the "working poor." Concerted efforts must be made through job training, affirmative action, and other means to assist those now prevented from obtaining more lucrative jobs. Action should also be taken to upgrade poorer paying jobs and to correct wage differentials that discriminate unjustly against women.

200. c. *Self-help efforts among the poor should be fostered by programs and policies in both the private and public sectors.* We believe that an effective way to attack poverty is through programs that are small in scale, locally based, and oriented toward empowering the poor to become self-sufficient. Corporations, private organizations, and the public sector can provide seed money, training and technical assistance, and organizational support for self-help projects in a wide variety of areas such as low-income housing, credit unions, worker cooperatives, legal assistance, and neighborhood and community organizations. Efforts that enable the poor to participate in the ownership and control of economic resources are especially important.

201. Poor people must be empowered to take charge of their own futures and become responsible for their own economic advancement. Personal motivation and initiative, combined with social reform, are necessary elements to assist individuals in escaping poverty. By taking advantage of opportunities for education, employment, and training, and by working together for change, the poor can help themselves to be full participants in our economic, social, and political life.

202. d. *The tax system should be continually evaluated in terms of its impact on the poor.* This evaluation should be guided by three principles. First, the tax system should raise adequate revenues to pay for the public needs of society, especially to meet the basic needs of the poor. Secondly, the tax system should be structured according to the principle of progressivity, so that those with relatively greater financial resources pay a higher rate of taxation. The inclusion of such a principle in tax policies is an important means of reducing the severe inequalities of income and wealth in the nation. Action should be taken to reduce or offset the fact that most sales taxes and payroll taxes place a disproportionate burden on those with lower incomes. Thirdly, families below the official poverty line should not be required to pay income taxes. Such families are, by definition, without sufficient resources to purchase the basic necessities of life. They should not be forced to bear the additional burden of paying income taxes.[60]

203. e. *All of society should make a much stronger commitment to education for the poor.* Any long-term solution to poverty in this country must pay serious attention to education, public and private, in school and out of school. Lack of adequate education, especially in the inner city setting, prevents many poor people from escaping poverty. In addition, illiteracy, a problem that

affects tens of millions of Americans, condemns many to joblessness or chronically low wages. Moreover, it excludes them in many ways from sharing in the political and spiritual life of the community.[61] Since poverty is fundamentally a problem of powerlessness and marginalization, the importance of education as a means of overcoming it cannot be overemphasized.

204. Working to improve education in our society is an investment in the future, an investment that should include both the public and private school systems. Our Catholic schools have the well-merited reputation of providing excellent education, especially for the poor. Catholic inner-city schools provide an otherwise unavailable educational alternative for many poor families. They provide one effective vehicle for disadvantaged students to lift themselves out of poverty. We commend the work of all those who make great sacrifices to maintain these inner-city schools. We pledge ourselves to continue the effort to make Catholic schools models of education for the poor.

205. We also wish to affirm our strong support for the public school system in the United States. There can be no substitute for quality education in public schools, for that is where the large majority of all students, including Catholic students, are educated. In Catholic social teaching, basic education is a fundamental human right.[62] In our society a strong public school system is essential if we are to protect that right and allow everyone to develop to their maximum ability. Therefore, we strongly endorse the recent calls for improvements in and support for public education, including improving the quality of teaching and enhancing the rewards for the teaching profession.[63] At all levels of education we need to improve the ability of our institutions to provide the personal and technical skills that are necessary for participation not only in today's labor market but also in contemporary society.

206. f. *Policies and programs at all levels should support the strength and stability of families, especially those adversely affected by the economy.* As a nation, we need to examine all aspects of economic life and assess their effects on families. Employment practices, health insurance policies, income security programs, tax policy, and service programs can either support or undermine the abilities of families to fulfill their roles in nurturing children and caring for infirm and dependent family members.

207. We affirm the principle enunciated by John Paul II that society's institutions and policies should be structured so that mothers of young children are not forced by economic necessity to leave their children for jobs outside the home.[64] The nation's social welfare and tax policies should support parents' decisions to care for their own children and should recognize the work of parents in the home because of its value for the family and for society.

208. For those children whose parents do work outside the home, there is a serious shortage of affordable, quality day care. Employers, governments, and private agencies need to improve both the availability and the quality of child care services. Likewise, families could be assisted by the establishment of parental leave policies that would assure job security for new parents.

209. The high rate of divorce and the alarming extent of teenage pregnancies in our nation are distressing signs of the breakdown of traditional family values. These destructive trends are present in all sectors of society: rich and poor; white, black, and brown; urban and rural. However, for the poor they tend to be more visible and to have more damaging economic consequences. These destructive trends must be countered by a revived sense of personal responsibility and commitment to family values.

210. g. *A thorough reform of the nation's welfare and income-support programs should be undertaken.* For millions of poor Americans the only economic safety net is the public welfare system. The programs that make up this system should serve the needs of the poor in a manner that respects their dignity and provides adequate support. In our judgment the present welfare system does not adequately meet these criteria.[65] We believe that several improvements can and should be made within the framework of existing welfare programs. However, in the long run, more far-reaching reforms that go beyond the present system will be necessary. Among the immediate improvements that could be made are the following:

211. (1) *Public assistance programs should be designed to assist recipients, wherever possible, to become self-sufficient through gainful employment.* Individuals should not be worse off economically when they get jobs than when they rely only on public assistance. Under current rules, people who give up welfare benefits to work in low-paying jobs soon lose their Medicaid benefits. To help recipients become self-sufficient and reduce dependency on welfare, public assistance programs should work in tandem with job creation programs that include provisions for training, counseling, placement, and child care. Jobs for recipients of public assistance should be fairly compensated so that workers receive the full benefits and status associated with gainful employment.

212. (2) *Welfare programs should provide recipients with adequate levels of support.* This support should cover basic needs in food, clothing, shelter, health care, and other essentials. At present only 4 percent of poor families with children receive enough cash welfare benefits to lift them out of poverty.[66] The combined benefits of AFDC and food stamps typically come to less than three-fourths of the official poverty level.[67] Those receiving public assistance should not face the prospect of hunger at the end of the month, homelessness, sending children to school in ragged clothing, or inadequate medical care.

213. (3) *National eligibility standards and a national minimum benefit level for public assistance programs should be established.* Currently welfare eligibility and benefits vary greatly among states. In 1985 a family of three with no earnings had a maximum AFDC benefit of $96 a month in Mississippi and $558 a month in Vermont.[68] To remedy these great disparities, which are far larger than the regional differences in the cost of living, and to assure a floor of benefits for all needy people, our nation should establish and

fund national minimum benefit levels and eligibility standards in cash assistance programs.[69] The benefits should also be indexed to reflect changes in the cost of living. These changes reflect standards that our nation has already put in place for aged and disabled people and veterans. Is it not possible to do the same for the children and their mothers who receive public assistance?

214. (4) *Welfare programs should be available to two-parent as well as single-parent families.* Most states now limit participation in AFDC to families headed by single parents, usually women.[70] The coverage of this program should be extended to two-parent families so that fathers who are unemployed or poorly paid do not have to leave home in order for their children to receive help. Such a change would be a significant step toward strengthening two-parent families who are poor.

4. CONCLUSION

215. The search for a more human and effective way to deal with poverty should not be limited to short-term reform measures. The agenda for public debate should also include serious discussion of more fundamental alternatives to the existing welfare system. We urge that proposals for a family allowance or a children's allowance be carefully examined as a possible vehicle for ensuring a floor of income support for all children and their families.[71] Special attention is needed to develop new efforts that are targeted on long-term poverty, which has proven to be least responsive to traditional social welfare programs. The "negative income tax" is another major policy proposal that deserves continued discussion.[72] These and other proposals should be part of a creative and ongoing effort to fashion a system of income support for the poor that protects their basic dignity and provides the necessary assistance in a just and effective manner.

C. Food and Agriculture

216. The fundamental test of an economy is its ability to meet the essential human needs of this generation and future generations in an equitable fashion. Food, water, and energy are essential to life; their abundance in the United States has tended to make us complacent. But these goods—the foundation of God's gift of life—are too crucial to be taken for granted. God reminded the people of Israel that "the land is mine; for you are strangers and guests with me" (Lv. 25:23, RSV). Our Christian faith calls us to contemplate God's creative and sustaining action and to measure our own collaboration with the Creator in using the earth's resources to meet human needs. While Catholic social teaching on the care of the environment and the management of natural resources is still in the process of development, a Christian moral perspective clearly gives weight and urgency to their use in meeting human needs.

217. No aspect of this concern is more pressing than the nation's food system. We are concerned that this food system may be in jeopardy as increasing numbers of farm bankruptcies and foreclosures result in increased concentration of land ownership.[73] We are likewise concerned about the increasing damage to natural resources resulting from many modern agricultural practices: the overconsumption of water, the depletion of topsoil, and the pollution of land and water. Finally, we are concerned about the stark reality of world hunger in spite of food surpluses. Our food production system is clearly in need of evaluation and reform.

1. U.S. AGRICULTURE—PAST AND PRESENT

218. The current crisis has to be assessed in the context of the vast diversity of U.S. crops and climates. For example, subsistence farming in Appalachia, where so much of the land is absentee-owned and where coal mining and timber production are the major economic interests, has little in common with family farm grain production in the central Midwest or ranching in the Great Plains. Likewise, large-scale irrigated fruit, vegetable, and cotton production in the central valley of California is very different from dairy farming in Wisconsin or tobacco and peanut production in the Southeast.

219. Two aspects of the complex history of U.S. land and food policy are particularly relevant. First, the United States entered this century with the ownership of productive land widely distributed. The Preemption Acts of the early nineteenth century and the Homestead Act of 1862 were an important part of that history. Wide distribution of ownership was reflected in the number and decentralization of farms in the United States, a trend that reached its peak in the 1930s. The U.S. farm system included nearly 7 million owner-operators in 1935.[74] By 1983 the number of U.S. farms had declined to 2.4 million, and only about 3 percent of the population were engaged in producing food.[75] Second, U.S. food policy has had a parallel goal of keeping the consumer cost of food low. As a result, Americans today spend less of their disposable income on food than people in any other industrialized country.[76]

220. These outcomes require scrutiny. First of all, the loss of farms and the exodus of farmers from the land have led to the loss of a valued way of life, the decline of many rural communities, and the increased concentration of land ownership. Secondly, while low food prices benefit consumers who are left with additional income to spend on other goods, these pricing policies put pressure on farmers to increase output and hold down costs. This has led them to replace human labor with cheaper energy, expand farm size to employ new technologies favoring larger-scale operations, neglect soil and water conservation, underpay farmworkers, and oppose farmworker unionization.[77]

221. Today nearly half of U.S. food production comes from the 4 percent of farms with over $200,000 in gross sales.[78] Many of these largest farms are no longer operated by families, but by managers hired by owners.[79] Nearly

three-quarters of all farms, accounting for only 13 percent of total farm sales, are comparatively small. They are often run by part-time farmers who derive most of their income from off-farm employment. The remaining 39 percent of sales comes from the 24 percent of farms grossing between $40,000 and $200,000. It is this group of farmers, located throughout the country and caught up in the long-term trend toward fewer and larger farms, who are at the center of the present farm crisis.

222. During the 1970s new markets for farm exports created additional opportunities for profit and accelerated the industrialization of agriculture, a process already stimulated by new petroleum-based, large-scale technologies that allowed farmers to cultivate many more acres. Federal tax policies and farm programs fostered this tendency by encouraging too much capital investment in agriculture and overemphasizing large-scale technologies.[80] The results were greater production, increases in the value of farmland, and heavy borrowing to finance expansion. In the 1980s, with export markets shrinking and commodity prices and land values declining, many farmers cannot repay their loans.

223. The situation has been aggravated by certain "external" factors: persistent high interest rates that make it difficult to repay or refinance loans, the heavy debt burden of food-deficient countries, the high value of the dollar, dramatically higher U.S. budget and trade deficits, and generally reduced international trade following the worldwide recession of the early 1980s. The United States is unlikely to recapture its former share of the world food and fiber trade, and it is not necessarily an appropriate goal to attempt to do so. Exports are not the solution to U.S. farm problems. Past emphasis on producing for overseas markets has contributed to the strain on our natural resource base and has also undermined the efforts of many less developed countries in attaining self-reliance in feeding their own people. In attempting to correct these abuses, however, we must not reduce our capability to help meet emergency food needs.

224. Some farmers face financial insolvency because of their own eagerness to take advantage of what appeared to be favorable investment opportunities. This was partly in response to the encouragement of public policy incentives and the advice of economists and financiers. Nevertheless, farmers should share some responsibility for their current plight.

225. Four other aspects of the current situation concern us: first, land ownership is becoming further concentrated as units now facing bankruptcy are added to existing farms and nonfarm corporations. Diversity of ownership and widespread participation are declining in this sector of the economy as they have in others. Since differing scales of operation and the investment of family labor have been important for American farm productivity, this increasing concentration of ownership in almost all sectors of agriculture points to an important change in that system.[81] Of particular concern is the growing phenomenon of "vertical integration" whereby companies gain con-

trol of two or three of the links in the food chain: as suppliers of farm inputs, landowners, and food processors. This increased concentration could also adversely affect food prices.

226. Second, diversity and richness in American society are lost as farm people leave the land and rural communities decay. It is not just a question of coping with additional unemployment and a need for retraining and relocation. It is also a matter of maintaining opportunities for employment and human development in a variety of economic sectors and cultural contexts.

227. Third, although the United States has set a world standard for food production, it has not done so without cost to our natural resource base.[82] On nearly one-quarter of our most productive cropland, topsoil erosion currently exceeds the rate at which it can be replaced by natural processes. Similarly, underground water supplies are being depleted in areas where food production depends on irrigation. Furthermore, chemical fertilizers, pesticides, and herbicides, considered now almost essential to today's agriculture, pollute the air, water, and soil, and pose countless health hazards. Finally, where the expansion of residential, industrial, and recreational areas makes it rewarding to do so, vast acreages of prime farmland, three million acres per year by some estimates, are converted to nonfarm use. The continuation of these practices, reflecting short-term investment interests or immediate income needs of farmers and other landowners, constitutes a danger to future food production because these practices are not sustainable.

228. Farm owners and farmworkers are the immediate stewards of the natural resources required to produce the food that is necessary to sustain life. These resources must be understood as gifts of a generous God. When they are seen in that light and when the human race is perceived as a single moral community, we gain a sense of the substantial responsibility we bear as a nation for the world food system. Meeting human needs today and in the future demands an increased sense of stewardship and conservation from owners, managers, and regulators of all resources, especially those required for the production of food.

229. Fourth, the situation of racial minorities in the U.S. food system is a matter of special pastoral concern. They are largely excluded from significant participation in the farm economy. Despite the agrarian heritage of so many Hispanics, for example, they operate only a minute fraction of America's farms.[83] Black-owned farms, at one time a significant resource for black participation in the economy, have been disappearing at a dramatic rate in recent years,[84] a trend that the U.S. Commission on Civil Rights has warned "can only serve to further diminish the stake of blacks in the social order and reinforce their skepticism regarding the concept of equality under the law."[85]

230. It is largely as hired farm laborers rather than farm owners that minorities participate in the farm economy. Along with many white farmworkers, they are, by and large, the poorest paid and least benefited of any laboring group in the country. Moreover, they are not as well protected by law

and public policy as other groups of workers; and their efforts to organize and bargain collectively have been systematically and vehemently resisted, usually by farmers themselves. Migratory field workers are particularly susceptible to exploitation. This is reflected not only in their characteristically low wages but also in the low standards of housing, health care, and education made available to these workers and their families.[86]

2. GUIDELINES FOR ACTION

231. We are convinced that current trends in the food sector are not in the best interests of the United States or of the global community. The decline in the number of moderate-sized farms, increased concentration of land ownership, and the mounting evidence of poor resource conservation raise serious questions of morality and public policy. As pastors, we cannot remain silent while thousands of farm families caught in the present crisis lose their homes, their land, and their way of life. We approach this situation, however, aware that it reflects longer-term conditions that carry consequences for the food system as a whole and for the resources essential for food production.

232. While much of the change needed must come from the cooperative efforts of farmers themselves, we strongly believe that there is an important role for public policy in the protection of dispersed ownership through family farms, as well as in the preservation of natural resources. We suggest three guidelines for both public policy and private efforts aimed at shaping the future of American agriculture.

233. *First, moderate-sized farms operated by families on a full-time basis should be preserved and their economic viability protected.* Similarly, small farms and part-time farming, particularly in areas close to cities, should be encouraged. As we have noted elsewhere in this pastoral letter,[87] there is genuine social and economic value in maintaining a wide distribution in the ownership of productive property. The democratization of decision making and control of the land resulting from wide distribution of farm ownership are protections against concentration of power and a consequent possible loss of responsiveness to public need in this crucial sector of the economy.[88] Moreover, when those who work in an enterprise also share in its ownership, their active commitment to the purpose of the endeavor and their participation in it are enhanced. Ownership provides incentives for diligence and is a source of an increased sense that the work being done is one's own. This is particularly significant in a sector as vital to human well-being as agriculture.

234. Furthermore, diversity in farm ownership tends to prevent excessive consumer dependence on business decisions that seek maximum return on invested capital, thereby making the food system overly susceptible to fluctuations in the capital markets. This is particularly relevant in the case of non-farm corporations that enter agriculture in search of high profits. If the return

drops substantially, or if it appears that better profits can be obtained by investing elsewhere, the corporation may cut back or even close down operations without regard to the impact on the community or on the food system in general. In similar circumstances full-time farmers, with a heavy personal investment in their farms and strong ties to the community, are likely to persevere in the hope of better times. Family farms also make significant economic and social contributions to the life of rural communities.[89] They support farm suppliers and other local merchants, and their farms support the tax base needed to pay for roads, schools, and other vital services.

235. This rural interdependence has value beyond the rural community itself. Both Catholic social teaching and the traditions of our country have emphasized the importance of maintaining the rich plurality of social institutions that enhances personal freedom and increases the opportunity for participation in community life. Movement toward a smaller number of very large farms employing wage workers would be a movement away from this institutional pluralism. By contributing to the vitality of rural communities, full-time residential farmers enrich the social and political life of the nation as a whole. Cities, too, benefit soundly and economically from a vibrant rural economy based on family farms. Because of out-migration of farm and rural people, too much of this enriching diversity has been lost already.

236. *Second, the opportunity to engage in farming should be protected as a valuable form of work.* At a time when unemployment in the country is already too high, any unnecessary increase in the number of unemployed people, however small, should be avoided. Farm unemployment leads to further rural unemployment as rural businesses lose their customers and close down. The loss of people from the land also entails the loss of expertise in farm and land management and creates a need for retraining and relocating another group of displaced workers.

237. Losing any job is painful, but losing one's farm and having to leave the land can be tragic. It often means the sacrifice of a family heritage and a way of life. Once farmers sell their land and their equipment, their move is practically irreversible. The costs of returning are so great that few who leave ever come back. Even the small current influx of people into agriculture attracted by lower land values will not balance this loss. Society should help those who would and could continue effectively in farming.

238. *Third, effective stewardship of our natural resources should be a central consideration in any measures regarding U.S. agriculture.* Such stewardship is a contribution to the common good that is difficult to assess in purely economic terms, because it involves the care of resources entrusted to us by our Creator for the benefit of all. Responsibility for the stewardship of these resources rests on society as a whole. Since farmers make their living from the use of this endowment, however, they bear a particular obligation to be caring stewards of soil and water. They fulfill this obligation by participating in soil and water conservation programs, using farm practices that

enhance the quality of the resources, and maintaining prime farmland in food production rather than letting it be converted to nonfarm uses.

3. POLICIES AND ACTIONS

239. The human suffering involved in the present situation and the long-term structural changes occurring in this sector call for responsible action by the whole society. A half-century of federal farm-price supports, subsidized credit, production-oriented research and extension services, and special tax policies for farmers have made the federal government a central factor in almost every aspect of American agriculture.[90] No redirection of current trends can occur without giving close attention to these programs.

240. A prime consideration in all agricultural trade and food assistance policies should be the contribution our nation can make to global food security. This means continuing and increasing food aid without depressing Third World markets or using food as a weapon in international politics. It also means not subsidizing exports in ways that lead to trade wars and instability in international food markets.

241. We offer the following suggestions for governmental action with regard to the farm and food sector of the economy.

242. a. The current crisis calls for special measures to assist otherwise viable family farms that are threatened with bankruptcy or foreclosure. Operators of such farms should have access to emergency credit, reduced rates of interest, and programs of debt restructuring. Rural lending institutions facing problems because of nonpayment or slow payment of large farm loans should also have access to temporary assistance. Farmers, their families, and their communities will gain immediately from these and other short-term measures aimed at keeping these people on the land.

243. b. Established federal farm programs, whose benefits now go disproportionately to the largest farmers,[91] should be reassessed for their long-term effects on the structure of agriculture. Income-support programs that help farmers according to the amount of food they produce or the number of acres they farm should be subject to limits that ensure a fair income to all farm families and should restrict participation to producers who genuinely need such income assistance. There should also be a strict ceiling on price-support payments which assist farmers in times of falling prices, so that benefits go to farms of moderate or small size. To succeed in redirecting the benefits of these programs while holding down costs to the public, consideration should be given to a broader application of mandatory production control programs.[92]

244. c. We favor reform of tax policies which now encourage the growth of large farms, attract investments into agriculture by non-farmers seeking tax shelters, and inequitably benefit large and well-financed farming operations.[93] Offsetting nonfarm income with farm "losses" has encouraged high-income investors to acquire farm assets with no intention of depending on

them for a living as family farmers must. The ability to depreciate capital equipment faster than its actual decline in value has benefited wealthy investors and farmers. Lower tax rates on capital gains have stimulated farm expansion and larger investments in energy-intensive equipment and technologies as substitutes for labor. Changes in estate tax laws have consistently favored the largest estates. All of these results have demonstrated that reassessment of these and similar tax provisions is needed.[94] We continue, moreover, to support a progressive land tax on farm acreage to discourage the accumulation of excessively large holdings.[95]

245. d. Although it is often assumed that farms must grow in size in order to make the most efficient and productive use of sophisticated and costly technologies, numerous studies have shown that medium-sized commercial farms achieve most of the technical cost efficiencies available in agriculture today. We, therefore, recommend that the research and extension resources of the federal government and the nation's land grant colleges and universities be redirected toward improving the productivity of small and medium-sized farms.[96]

246. e. Since soil and water conservation, like other efforts to protect the environment, are contributions to the good of the whole society, it is appropriate for the public to bear a share of the cost of these practices and to set standards for environmental protection. Government should, therefore, encourage farmers to adopt more conserving practices and distribute the costs of this conservation more broadly.

247. f. Justice demands that worker guarantees and protections such as minimum wages and benefits and unemployment compensation be extended to hired farmworkers on the same basis as all other workers. There is also an urgent need for additional farmworker housing, health care, and educational assistance.

4. SOLIDARITY IN THE FARM COMMUNITY

248. While there is much that government can and should do to change the direction of farm and food policy in this country, that change in direction also depends upon the cooperation and good will of farmers. The incentives in our farm system to take risks, to expand farm size, and to speculate in farmland values are great. Hence, farmers and ranchers must weigh these incentives against the values of family, rural community, care of the soil, and a food system responsive to long-term as well as short-term food needs of the nation and the world. The ever present temptation to individualism and greed must be countered by a determined movement toward solidarity in the farm community. Farmers should approach farming in a cooperative way, working with other farmers in the purchase of supplies and equipment and in the marketing of produce. It is not necessary for every farmer to be in competition against every other farmer. Such cooperation can be extended to the role farmers play

through their various general and community organizations in shaping and implementing governmental farm and food policies.[97] Likewise, it is possible to seek out and adopt technologies that reduce costs and enhance productivity without demanding increases in farm size. New technologies are not forced on farmers; they are chosen by farmers themselves.

249. Farmers also must end their opposition to farmworker unionization efforts. Farmworkers have a legitimate right to belong to unions of their choice and to bargain collectively for just wages and working conditions. In pursuing that right they are protecting the value of labor in agriculture, a protection that also applies to farmers who devote their own labor to their farm operations.

5. CONCLUSION

250. The U.S. food system is an integral part of the larger economy of the nation and the world. As such this integral role necessitates the cooperation of rural and urban interests in resolving the challenges and problems facing agriculture. The very nature of agricultural enterprise and the family farm traditions of this country have kept it a highly competitive sector with a widely dispersed ownership of the most fundamental input to production, the land. That competitive, diverse structure, proven to be a dependable source of nutritious and affordable food for this country and millions of people in other parts of the world, is now threatened. The food necessary for life, the land and water resources needed to produce that food, and the way of life of the people who make the land productive are at risk. Catholic social and ethical traditions attribute moral significance to each of these. Our response to the present situation should reflect a sensitivity to that moral significance, a determination that the United States will play its appropriate role in meeting global food needs, and a commitment to bequeath to future generations an enhanced natural environment and the same ready access to the necessities of life that most of us enjoy today. To farmers and farmworkers who are suffering because of the farm crisis, we promise our solidarity, prayers, counseling and the other spiritual resources of our Catholic faith.

D. The U.S. Economy and the Developing Nations: Complexity, Challenge, and Choices

1. THE COMPLEXITY OF ECONOMIC RELATIONS IN AN INTERDEPENDENT WORLD

251. The global economy is made up of national economies of industrialized countries of the North and the developing countries of the South, together with the network of economic relations that link them. It constitutes the framework in which the solidarity we seek on a national level finds its international expression. Traditional Catholic teaching on this global interdependence

emphasizes the dignity of the human person, the unity of the human family, the universally beneficial purpose of the goods of the earth, the need to pursue the international common good, as well as the good of each nation, and the imperative of distributive justice. The United States plays a leading role in the international economic system, and we are concerned that U.S. relations with all nations—Canada, Japan, European countries, and our other trading partners, as well as the socialist countries—reflect this teaching and be marked by fairness and mutual respect.

252. Nevertheless, without in the least discounting the importance of these linkages, our emphasis on the preferential option for the poor moves us to focus our attention mainly on U.S. relations with the Third World. Unless conscious steps are taken toward protecting human dignity and fostering human solidarity in these relationships, we can look forward to increased conflict and inequity, threatening the fragile economies of these relatively poor nations far more than our own relatively strong one. Moreover, equity requires, even as the fact of interdependence becomes more apparent, that the *quality* of interdependence be improved, in order to eliminate "the scandal of the shocking inequality between the rich and the poor"[98] in a world divided ever more sharply between them.

253. Developing countries, moreover, often perceive themselves more as *dependent* on the industrialized countries, especially the United States, because the international system itself, as well as the way the United States acts in it, subordinates them. The prices at which they must sell their commodity exports and purchase their food and manufactured imports, the rates of interest they must pay and the terms they must meet to borrow money, the standards of economic behavior of foreign investors, the amounts and conditions of external aid, etc., are essentially determined by the industrialized world. Moreover, their traditional cultures are increasingly susceptible to the aggressive cultural penetration of Northern (especially U.S.) advertising and media programing. The developing countries are junior partners at best.

254. The basic tenets of church teaching take on a new moral urgency as we deepen our understanding of how disadvantaged large numbers of people and nations are in this interdependent world. Half the world's people, nearly two and a half billion, live in countries where the annual per capita income is $400 or less.[99] At least 800 million people in those countries live in absolute poverty, "beneath any rational definition of human decency."[100] Nearly half a billion are chronically hungry, despite abundant harvests worldwide.[101] Fifteen out of every 100 children born in those countries die before the age of five, and millions of the survivors are physically or mentally stunted. No aggregate of individual examples could portray adequately the appalling inequities within those desperately poor countries and between them and our own. And their misery is not the inevitable result of the march of history or of the intrinsic nature of particular cultures, but of human decisions and human institutions.

255. On the international economic scene three main sets of actors warrant particular attention: individual nations, which retain great influence; multilateral institutions, which channel money, power, ideas, and influence; transnational corporations and banks, which have grown dramatically in number, size, scope, and strength since World War II.[102] In less identifiable ways trade unions, popular movements, private relief and development agencies, and regional groupings of nations also affect the global economy. The interplay among all of them sets the context for policy choices that determine whether genuine interdependence is promoted or the dependence of the disadvantaged is deepened.

256. In this arena, where fact and ethical challenges intersect, the moral task is to devise rules for the major actors that will move them toward a just international order. One of the most vexing problems is that of reconciling the transnational corporations' profit orientation with the common good that they, along with governments and their multilateral agencies, are supposed to serve.

257. The notion of interdependence erases the fading line between domestic and foreign policy. Many foreign policy decisions (for example, on trade, investment, and immigration) have direct and substantial impact on domestic constituencies in the United States. Similarly, many decisions thought of as domestic (for example, on farm policy, interest rates, the federal budget, or the deficit) have important consequences for other countries. This increasingly recognized link of domestic and foreign issues poses new empirical and moral questions for national policy.

2. THE CHALLENGE OF CATHOLIC SOCIAL TEACHING

258. Catholic teaching on the international economic order recognizes this complexity, but does not provide specific solutions. Rather, we seek to ensure that moral considerations are taken into account. All of the elements of the moral perspective we have outlined above have important implications for international relationships. (1) The demands of *Christian love* and *human solidarity* challenge all economic actors to choose community over chaos. They require a definition of political community that goes beyond national sovereignty to policies that recognize the moral bonds among all people. (2) *Basic justice* implies that all peoples are entitled to participate in the increasingly interdependent global economy in a way that ensures their freedom and dignity. When whole communities are effectively left out or excluded from equitable participation in the international order, basic justice is violated. We want a world that works fairly for all. (3) *Respect for human rights*, both political and economic, implies that international decisions, institutions, and policies must be shaped by values that are more than economic. The creation of a global order in which these rights are secure for all must be a prime objective for all relevant actors on the international stage. (4) *The special place of*

the poor in this moral perspective means that meeting the basic needs of the millions of deprived and hungry people in the world must be the number one objective of international policy.

259. These perspectives constitute a call for fundamental reform in the international economic order. Whether the problem is preventing war and building peace, or addressing the needs of the poor, Catholic teaching emphasizes not only the individual conscience, but also the political, legal, and economic structures through which policy is determined and issues are adjudicated.[103] We do not seek here to evaluate the various proposals for international economic reform or deal here with economic relations between the United States and other industrialized countries. We urge, as a basic and overriding consideration, that both empirical and moral evidence, especially the precarious situation of the developing countries, calls for the renewal of the dialogue between the industrialized countries of the North and the developing countries of the South, with the aim of reorganizing international economic relations to establish greater equity and help meet the basic human needs of the poor majority.[104]

260. *Here, as elsewhere, the preferential option for the poor is the central priority for policy choice.* It offers a unique perspective on foreign policy in whose light U.S. relationships, especially with developing countries, can be reassessed. Standard foreign policy analysis deals with calculations of power and definitions of national interest; but the poor are, by definition, not powerful. If we are to give appropriate weight to their concerns, their needs, and their interests, we have to go beyond economic gain or national security as a starting point for the policy dialogue. We want to stand with the poor everywhere, and we believe that relations between the U.S. and developing nations should be determined in the first place by a concern for basic human needs and respect for cultural traditions.

3. THE ROLE OF THE UNITED STATES IN THE GLOBAL ECONOMY: CONSTRUCTIVE CHOICES

261. As we noted in *The Challenge of Peace*, recent popes have strongly supported the United Nations as a crucial step forward in the development and organization of the human community; we share their regret that no political entity now exists with the responsibility and power to promote the global common good, and we urge the United States to support UN efforts to move in that direction. Building a just world economic order in the absence of such an authority demands that national governments promote public policies that increase the ability of poor nations and marginalized people to participate in the global economy. Because no other nation's economic power yet matches ours, we believe that this responsibility pertains especially to the United States; but it must be carried out in cooperation with other industrialized coun-

tries as in the case of halting the rise of the dollar. This is yet another evidence of the fact of interdependence. Joint action toward these goals not only promotes justice and reduces misery in the Third World, but also is in the interest of the United States and other industrialized nations.

262. Yet in recent years U.S. policy toward development in the Third World has become increasingly one of selective assistance based on an East-West assessment of North-South problems, at the expense of basic human needs and economic development. Such a view makes national security the central policy principle.[105] Developing countries have become largely testing grounds in the East-West struggle; they seem to have meaning or value mainly in terms of this larger geopolitical calculus. The result is that issues of human need and economic development take second place to the political-strategic argument. This tendency must be resisted.

263. Moreover, U.S. performance in North-South negotiations often casts us in the role of resisting developing-country proposals without advancing realistic ones of our own.[106] North-South dialogue is bound to be complex, protracted, and filled with symbolic and often unrealistic demands; but the situation has now reached the point where the rest of the world expects the United States to assume a reluctant, adversarial posture in such discussions. The U.S. approach to the developing countries needs urgently to be changed; a country as large, rich, and powerful as ours has a moral obligation to lead in helping to reduce poverty in the Third World.

264. We believe that U.S. policy toward the developing world should reflect our traditional regard for human rights and our concern for social progress. In economic policy, as we noted in our pastoral letter on nuclear war, the major international economic relationships of aid, trade, finance, and investment are interdependent among themselves and illustrate the range of interdependence issues facing U.S. policy. All three of the major economic actors are active in all these relationships. Each relationship offers us the possibility of substantial, positive movement toward increasing social justice in the developing world; in each, regrettably, we fall short. It is urgent that immediate steps be taken to correct these deficiencies.

265. ***a. Development Assistance:*** The official development assistance that the industrialized and the oil-producing countries provide the Third World in the form of grants, low-interest/long-term loans, commodities, and technical assistance is a significant contribution to their development. Although the annual share of U.S. gross national product (GNP) devoted to foreign aid is now less than one-tenth of that of the Marshall Plan, which helped rebuild devastated but advanced European economies, we remain the largest donor country. We still play a central role in these resource transfers, but we no longer set an example for other donors. We lag proportionately behind most other industrial nations in providing resources and seem to care less than before about development in the Third World. Our bilateral aid has become increasingly militarized and security-related and our contributions to multilat-

eral agencies have been reduced in recent years.[107] Not all of these changes are justifiable. The projects of the International Development Association, for example, seem worthy of support.

266. This is a grave distortion of the priority that development assistance should command. We are dismayed that the United States, once the pioneer in foreign aid, is almost last among the seventeen industrialized nations in the Organization for Economic Cooperation and Development (OECD) in percentage of GNP devoted to aid. Reduction of the U.S. contribution to multilateral development institutions is particularly regrettable, because these institutions are often better able than the bilateral agencies to focus on the poor and reduce dependency in developing countries.[108] This is also an area in which, in the past, our leadership and example have had great influence. A more affirmative U.S. role in these institutions, which we took the lead in creating, could improve their performance, send an encouraging signal of U.S. intentions, and help reopen the dialogue on the growing poverty and dependency of the Third World.

267. ***b. Trade:*** Trade continues to be a central component of international economic relations. It contributed in a major way to the rapid economic growth of many developing countries in the 1960s and 1970s and will probably continue to do so, though at a slower rate. The preferential option for the poor does not, by itself, yield a trade policy; but it does provide a frame of reference. In particular, an equitable trading system that will help the poor should allocate its benefits fairly and ensure that exports from developing countries receive fair prices reached by agreement among all trading partners. Developing nations have a right to receive a fair price for their raw materials that allows for a reasonable degree of profit.

268. Trade policy illustrates the conflicting pressures that interdependence can generate: claims of injustice from developing countries denied market access are countered by claims of injustice in the domestic economies of industrialized countries when jobs are threatened and incomes fall. Agricultural trade and a few industrial sectors present particularly acute examples of this.

269. We believe the ethical norms we have applied to domestic economic questions are equally valid here.[109] As in other economic matters, the basic questions are: Who benefits from the particular policy measure? How can any benefit or adverse impact be equitably shared? We need to examine, for example, the extent to which the success in the U.S. market of certain imports is derived from exploitative labor conditions in the exporting country, conditions that in some cases have attracted the investment in the first place. The United States should do all it can to ensure that the trading system treats the poorest segments of developing countries' societies fairly and does not lead to human rights violations. In particular the United States should seek effective special measures under the General Agreement on Tariffs and Trade (GATT)[110] to benefit the poorest countries.

270. At the same time, U.S. workers and their families hurt by the operation of the trading system must be helped through training and other measures to adjust to changes that advance development and decrease poverty in the Third World. This is a very serious, immediate, and intensifying problem. In our judgment, adjustment assistance programs in the United States have been poorly designed and administered, and inadequately funded. A society and an economy such as ours can better adjust to trade dislocations than can poverty-ridden developing countries.

271. ***c. Finance:*** Aid and trade policies alone, however enlightened, do not constitute a sufficient approach to the developing countries; they must also be looked at in conjunction with international finance and investment. The debtor-creditor relationship well exemplifies both the interdependence of the international economic order and its asymmetrical character, i.e., the *dependence* of the developing countries. The aggregate external debt of the developing countries now approaches $1 trillion,[111] more than one-third of their combined GNP; this total doubled between 1979 and 1984 and continues to rise. On average, the first 20 percent of export earnings goes to service that debt without significantly reducing the principal; in some countries debt service is nearly 100 percent of such earnings, leaving scant resources available for the countries' development programs.

272. The roots of this very complex debt crisis are both historic and systemic. *Historically*, the three major economic actors share the responsibility for the present difficulty because of decisions made and actions taken during the 1970s and 1980s. In 1972 the Soviet Union purchased the entire U.S. grain surplus, and grain prices trebled. Between 1973 and 1979, the Organization of Petroleum Exporting Countries raised the price of oil eightfold and thereafter deposited most of the profits in commercial banks in the North. In order to profit from the interest-rate spread on these deposits, the banks pushed larger and larger loans on eager Third World borrowers needing funds to purchase more and more expensive oil. A second doubling of oil prices in 1979 forced many of these countries to refinance their loans and borrow more money at escalating interest rates. A global recession beginning in 1979 caused the prices of Third World export commodities to fall and thus reduced the ability to meet the increasingly burdensome debt payments out of export earnings.

273. The global *system* of finance, development, and trade established by the Bretton Woods Conference in 1944—the World Bank, the International Monetary Fund (IMF), and the GATT—was created by the North to prevent a recurrence of the economic problems that were perceived to have led to World War II. Forty years later that system seems incapable, without basic changes, of helping the debtor countries—which had no part in its creation—manage their increasingly untenable debt situation effectively and equitably. The World Bank, largest of these institutions, has been engaged primarily in lending for specific projects rather than for general economic health. The IMF was intended to be a short-term lender that would help out with temporary

balance of payments, or cash-flow problems; but in the current situation it has come to the fore as a monitor of commercial financial transactions and an evaluator of debtors' creditworthiness—and therefore the key institution for resolving these problems. The GATT, which is not an institution, had been largely supplanted, as trade monitor for the developing countries, by UNCTAD[112] in which the latter have more confidence.

274. This crisis, however, goes beyond the system; it affects people. It afflicts and oppresses large numbers of people who are already severely disadvantaged. That is the scandal: it is the poorest people who suffer most from the austerity measures required when a country seeks the IMF "seal of approval" which establishes its creditworthiness for a commercial loan (or perhaps an external aid program). It is these same people who suffer most when commodity prices fall, when food cannot be imported or they cannot buy it, and when natural disasters occur. Our commitment to the preferential option for the poor does not permit us to remain silent in these circumstances. Ways must be found to meet the immediate emergency—moratorium on payments, conversion of some dollar-denominated debt into local-currency debt, creditors' accepting a share of the burden by partially writing down selected loans, capitalizing interest, or perhaps outright cancellation.

275. The poorest countries, especially those in sub-Saharan Africa which are least developed, most afflicted by hunger and malnutrition, and most vulnerable to commodity price declines, are in extremely perilous circumstances.[113] Although their aggregate debt of more than $100 billion (much of it owed to multilateral institutions), is about one-quarter that of Latin America, their collateral (oil, minerals, manufactures, grain, etc.) is much less adequate, their ability to service external debt much weaker, and the possibility of their rescheduling it very small. For low-income countries like these, the most useful immediate remedies are longer payment periods, lower interest rates, and modification of IMF adjustment requirements that exacerbate the already straitened circumstances of the poor.[114] Especially helpful for some African countries would be cancellation of debts owed to governments, a step already taken by some creditor nations.

276. Better-off debtor countries also need to be able to adjust their debts without penalizing the poor. Although the final policy decisions about the allocation of adjustment costs belong to the debtor government, internal equity considerations should be taken into account in determining the conditions of debt rescheduling and additional lending; for example, wage reductions should not be mandated, basic public services to the poor should not be cut, and measures should be required to reduce the flight of capital. Since this debt problem, like most others, is systemic, a case-by-case approach is not sufficient: lending policies and exchange-rate considerations are not only economic questions, but are thoroughly and intensely political.

277. Beyond all this, the growing external debt that has become the overarching economic problem of the Third World also requires systemic change

to provide immediate relief and to prevent recurrence. The Bretton Woods institutions do not adequately represent Third World debtors, and their policies are not dealing effectively with problems affecting those nations. These institutions need to be substantially reformed and their policies reviewed at the same time that the immediate problem of Third World debt is being dealt with. The United States should promote, support, and participate fully in such reforms and reviews. Such a role is not only morally right, but is in the economic interest of the United States; more than a third of this debt is owed to U.S. banks. The viability of the international banking system (and of those U.S. banks) depends in part on the ability of debtor countries to manage those debts. Stubborn insistence on full repayment could force them to default—which would lead to economic losses in the United States. In this connection, we should not overlook the impact of U.S. budget and trade deficits on interest rates. These high interest rates exacerbate the already difficult debt situation. They also attract capital away from investment in economic development in Third World countries.

278. ***d. Foreign Private Investment:*** Although direct private investment in the developing countries by U.S.-based transnational corporations has declined in recent years, it still amounts to about $60 billion and accounts for sizeable annual transfers. Such investment in developing countries should be increased, consistent with the host country's development goals and with benefits equitably distributed. Particular efforts should be made to encourage investments by medium-sized and small companies, as well as to joint ventures, which may be more appropriate to the developing country's situation. For the foreseeable future, however, private investment will probably not meet the infrastructural needs of the poorest countries—roads, transportation, communications, education, health, etc.—since these do not generally show profits and therefore do not attract private capital. Yet without this infrastructure, no real economic growth can take place.

279. Direct foreign investment, risky though it may be for both the investing corporation and the developing country, can provide needed capital, technology, and managerial expertise. Care must be taken lest such investment create or perpetuate dependency, harming especially those at the bottom of the economic ladder. Investments that sustain or worsen inequities in a developing country, that help to maintain oppressive elites in power, or that increase food dependency by encouraging cash cropping for export at the expense of local needs, should be discouraged. Foreign investors, attracted by low wage rates in less developed countries, should consider both the potential loss of jobs in the home country and the potential exploitation of workers in the host country.[115] Both the products and the technologies of the investing firms should be appropriate to the developing country, neither catering just to a small number of high-income consumers, nor establishing capital-intensive processes that displace labor, especially in the agricultural sector.[116]

280. Such inequitable results, however, are not necessary consequences of transnational corporate activity. Corporations can contribute to development by attracting and training high caliber managers and other personnel, by helping organize effective marketing systems, by generating additional capital, by introducing or reinforcing financial accountability, and by sharing the knowledge gained from their own research and development activities. Although the ability of the corporations to plan, operate, and communicate across national borders without concern for domestic considerations makes it harder for governments to direct their activities toward the common good, the effort should be made; the Christian ethic is incompatible with a primary or exclusive focus on maximization of profit. We strongly urge U.S. and international support of efforts to develop a code of conduct for foreign corporations that recognizes their quasi-public character and encourages both development and the equitable distribution of their benefits. Transnational corporations should be required to adopt such a code, and to conform their behavior to its provisions.

281. ***e. The World Food Problem—A Special Urgency:*** These four resource transfer channels—aid, trade, finance, and investment—intersect and overlap in all economic areas, but in none more clearly than in the international food system. The largest single segment of development assistance support goes to the agricultural sector and to food aid for short-term emergencies and vulnerable groups; food constitutes one of the most critical trade sectors; developing countries have borrowed extensively in the international capital markets to finance food imports; and a substantial portion of direct private investment flows into the agricultural sector.

282. The development of U.S. agriculture has moved the United States into a dominant position in the international food system. The best way to meet the responsibilities this dominance entails is to design and implement a U.S. food and agriculture policy that contributes to increased food security—that is, access by everyone to an adequate diet. A world with nearly half a billion hungry people is not one in which food security has been achieved. The problem of hunger has a special significance for those who read the Scriptures and profess the Christian faith. From the Lord's command to feed the hungry, to the Eucharist we celebrate as the Bread of Life, the fabric of our faith demands that we be creatively engaged in sharing the food that sustains life. There is no more basic human need. The Gospel imperative takes on new urgency in a world of abundant harvests where hundreds of millions of people face starvation. Relief and prevention of their hunger cannot be left to the arithmetic of the marketplace.[117]

283. The chronic hunger of those who live literally from day to day is one symptom of the underlying problem of poverty; relieving and preventing hunger is part of a larger, coordinated strategy to attack poverty itself. People must be enabled either to grow or to buy the food they need, without depending on an indefinite dole; there is no substitute for long-term agricultural and

food-system development in the nations now caught in the grip of hunger and starvation. Most authorities agree that the key to this development is the small farmers, most of whom are prevented from participating in the food system by the lack of a market incentive resulting from the poverty of the bulk of the populations and by the lack of access to productive agricultural inputs, especially land, resulting mainly from their own poverty. In these poor, food-deficit countries, no less than in our own, the small family farm deserves support and protection.

284. But recognizing the long-term problem does not dissolve the short-term obligation of the world's major food-exporting nation to provide food aid sufficient to meet the nutritional needs of poor people, and to provide it not simply to dispose of surpluses but in a way that does not discourage local food production. There can be no successful solution to the problem of hunger in the world without U.S. participation in a cooperative effort that simultaneously increases food aid and launches a long-term program to help develop food self-reliance in food-deficit developing countries.

285. Hunger is often seen as being linked with the problem of population growth, as effect to cause. While this relationship is sometimes presented in oversimplified fashion, we cannot fail to recognize that the earth's resources are finite and that population tends to grow rapidly. Whether the world can provide a truly human life for twice as many people or more as now live in it (many of whose lives are sadly deficient today) is a matter of urgent concern that cannot be ignored.[118]

286. Although we do not believe that people are poor and hungry primarily because they have large families, the Church fully supports the need for all to exercise responsible parenthood. Family size is heavily dependent on levels of economic development, education, respect for women, availability of health care, and the cultural traditions of communities. Therefore, in dealing with population growth we strongly favor efforts to address these social and economic concerns.

287. Population policies must be designed as part of an overall strategy of integral human development. They must respect the freedom of parents and avoid coercion. As Pope Paul VI has said concerning population policies: "It is true that too frequently an accelerated demographic increase adds its own difficulties to the problems of development: the size of the population increases more rapidly than available resources, and things are found to have reached apparently an impasse. From that moment the temptation is great to check the demographic increase by means of radical measures. It is certain that public authorities can intervene, within the limit of their competence, by favoring the availability of appropriate information and by adopting suitable measures, provided that these be in conformity with the moral law and that they respect the rightful freedom of married couples. Where the inalienable right to marriage and procreation is lacking, human dignity has ceased to exist."[119]

4. U.S. RESPONSIBILITY FOR REFORM IN THE INTERNATIONAL ECONOMIC SYSTEM

288. The United States cannot be the sole savior of the developing world, nor are Third World countries entirely innocent with respect to their own failures or totally helpless to achieve their own destinies. Many of these countries will need to initiate positive steps to promote and sustain development and economic growth—streamline bureaucracies, account for funds, plan reasonable programs, and take further steps toward empowering their people. Progress toward development will surely require them to take some tough remedial measures as well: prevent the flight of capital, reduce borrowing, modify price discrimination against rural areas, eliminate corruption in the use of funds and other resources, and curtail spending on inefficient public enterprises. The pervasive U.S. presence in many parts of our interdependent world, however, also creates a responsibility for us to increase the use of U.S. economic power—not just aid—in the service of human dignity and human rights, both political and economic.

289. In particular, as we noted in our earlier letter, *The Challenge of Peace*, the contrast between expenditures on armaments and on development reflects a shift in priorities from meeting human needs to promoting "national security" and represents a massive distortion of resource allocations. In 1982, for example, the military expenditures of the industrialized countries were seventeen times larger than their foreign assistance; in 1985 the United States alone budgeted more than twenty times as much for defense as for foreign assistance, and nearly two-thirds of the latter took the form of military assistance (including subsidized arms sales) or went to countries because of their perceived strategic value to the United States.[120] *Rather than promoting U.S. arms sales, especially to countries that cannot afford them, we should be campaigning for an international agreement to reduce this lethal trade.*

290. In short, the international economic order, like many aspects of our own economy, is in crisis; the gap between rich and poor countries and between rich and poor people within countries is widening. The United States represents the most powerful single factor in the international economic equation. But even as we speak of crisis, we see an opportunity for the United States to launch a worldwide campaign for justice and economic rights to match the still incomplete, but encouraging, political democracy we have achieved in the United States with so much pain and sacrifice.

291. To restructure the international order along lines of greater equity and participation and apply the preferential option for the poor to international economic activity will require sacrifices of at least the scope of those we have made over the years in building our own nation. We need to call again upon the qualities of leadership and vision that have marked our history when crucial choices were demanded. As Pope John Paul II said during his 1979 visit to the United States, "America, which in the past decades has demonstrated

goodness and generosity in providing food for the hungry of the world, will, I am sure, be able to match this generosity with an equally convincing contribution to the establishing of a world order that will create the necessary economic and trade conditions for a more just relationship between all the nations of the world."[121]

292. We share his conviction that most of the policy issues generally called economic are, at root, moral and therefore require the application of moral principles derived from the Scriptures and from the evolving social teaching of the Church and other traditions.[122] We also recognize that we are dealing here with sensitive international issues that cross national boundaries. Nevertheless, in order to pursue justice and peace on a global scale, *we call for a U.S. international economic policy designed to empower people everywhere and enable them to continue to develop a sense of their own worth, improve the quality of their lives, and ensure that the benefits of economic growth are shared equitably.*

E. Conclusion

293. None of the issues we have addressed in this chapter can be dealt with in isolation. They are interconnected, and their resolution requires difficult trade-offs among competing interests and values. The changing international economy, for example, greatly influences efforts to achieve full employment in the United States and to maintain a healthy farm sector. Similarly, as we have noted, policies and programs to reduce unemployment and poverty must not ignore a potential inflationary impact. These complexities and trade-offs are real and must be confronted, but they are not an excuse for inaction. They should not paralyze us in our search for a more just economy.

294. Many of the reforms we have suggested in this chapter would be expensive. At a time when the United States has large annual deficits some might consider these costs too high. But this discussion must be set in the context of how our resources are allocated and the immense human and social costs of failure to act on these pressing problems. We believe that the question of providing adequate revenues to meet the needs of our nation must be faced squarely and realistically. Reforms in the tax code which close loopholes and generate new revenues, for example, are among the steps that need to be examined in order to develop a federal budget that is both fiscally sound and socially responsible. The cost of meeting our social needs must also be weighed against the $300 billion a year allocated for military purposes. Although some of these expenditures are necessary for the defense of the nation, some elements of the military budget are both wasteful and dangerous for world peace.[123] Careful reductions should be made in these areas in order to free up funds for social and economic reforms. In the end, the question is not whether the United States can provide the necessary funds to meet our social needs, but whether we have the political will to do so.

CHAPTER 4: A NEW AMERICAN EXPERIMENT: PARTNERSHIP FOR THE PUBLIC GOOD

295. For over two hundred years the United States has been engaged in a bold experiment in democracy. The founders of the nation set out to establish justice, promote the general welfare, and secure the blessings of liberty for themselves and their posterity. Those who live in this land today are the beneficiaries of this great venture. Our review of some of the most pressing problems in economic life today shows, however, that this undertaking is not yet complete. Justice for all remains an aspiration; a fair share in the general welfare is denied to many. In addition to the particular policy recommendations made above, a long-term and more fundamental response is needed. This will call for an imaginative vision of the future that can help shape economic arrangements in creative new ways. We now want to propose some elements of such a vision and several innovations in economic structures that can contribute to making this vision a reality.

296. Completing the unfinished business of the American experiment will call for new forms of cooperation and partnership among those whose daily work is the source of the prosperity and justice of the nation. The United States prides itself on both its competitive sense of initiative and its spirit of teamwork. Today a greater spirit of partnership and teamwork is needed; competition alone will not do the job. It has too many negative consequences for family life, the economically vulnerable, and the environment. Only a renewed commitment by all to the common good can deal creatively with the realities of international interdependence and economic dislocations in the domestic economy. The virtues of good citizenship require a lively sense of participation in the commonwealth and of having obligations as well as rights within it.[1] The nation's economic health depends on strengthening these virtues among all its people, and on the development of institutional arrangements supportive of these virtues.[2]

297. The nation's founders took daring steps to create structures of participation, mutual accountability, and widely distributed power to ensure the political rights and freedoms of all. We believe that similar steps are needed today to expand economic participation, broaden the sharing of economic power, and make economic decisions more accountable to the common good. As noted above, the principle of subsidiarity states that the pursuit of economic justice must occur on all levels of society. It makes demands on communities as small as the family, as large as the global society and on all levels in between. There are a number of ways to enhance the cooperative participation of these many groups in the task of creating this future. Since there is no single innovation that will solve all problems, we recommend careful experimentation with several possibilities that hold considerable hope for increasing partnership and strengthening mutual responsibility for economic justice.

A. Cooperation within Firms and Industries

298. A new experiment in bringing democratic ideals to economic life calls for serious exploration of ways to develop new patterns of partnership among those working in individual firms and industries.[3] Every business, from the smallest to the largest, including farms and ranches, depends on many different persons and groups for its success: workers, managers, owners or shareholders, suppliers, customers, creditors, the local community, and the wider society. Each makes a contribution to the enterprise, and each has a stake in its growth or decline. Present structures of accountability, however, do not acknowledge all these contributions or protect these stakes. A major challenge in today's economy is the development of new institutional mechanisms for accountability that also preserve the flexibility needed to respond quickly to a rapidly changing business environment.[4]

299. New forms of partnership between workers and managers are one means for developing greater participation and accountability within firms.[5] Recent experience has shown that both labor and management suffer when the adversarial relationship between them becomes extreme. As Pope Leo XIII stated, "Each needs the other completely: capital cannot do without labor, nor labor without capital."[6] The organization of firms should reflect and enhance this mutual partnership. In particular, the development of work patterns for men and women that are more supportive of family life will benefit both employees and the enterprises they work for.

300. Workers in firms and on farms are especially in need of stronger institutional protection, for their jobs and livelihood are particularly vulnerable to the decisions of others in today's highly competitive labor market. Several arrangements are gaining increasing support in the United States: profit sharing by the workers in a firm; enabling employees to become company stockholders; granting employees greater participation in determining the conditions of work; cooperative ownership of the firm by all who work within it; and programs for enabling a much larger number of Americans, regardless of their employment status, to become shareholders in successful corporations. Initiatives of this sort can enhance productivity, increase the profitability of firms, provide greater job security and work satisfaction for employees, and reduce adversarial relations.[7] In our 1919 *Program of Social Reconstruction*, we observed "the full possibilities of increased production will not be realized so long as the majority of workers remain mere wage earners. The majority must somehow become owners, at least in part, of the instruments of production."[8] We believe this judgment remains generally valid today.

301. None of these approaches provides a panacea, and all have certain drawbacks. Nevertheless we believe that continued research and experimentation with these approaches will be of benefit. Catholic social teaching has endorsed on many occasions innovative methods for increasing worker

participation within firms.[9] The appropriateness of these methods will depend on the circumstances of the company or industry in question and on their effectiveness in actually increasing a genuinely cooperative approach to shaping decisions. The most highly publicized examples of such efforts have been in large firms facing serious financial crises. If increased participation and collaboration can help a firm avoid collapse, why should it not give added strength to healthy businesses? Cooperative ownership is particularly worthy of consideration in new entrepreneurial enterprises.[10]

302. Partnerships between labor and management are possible only when both groups possess real freedom and power to influence decisions. This means that unions ought to continue to play an important role in moving toward greater economic participation within firms and industries. Workers rightly reject calls for less adversarial relations when they are a smokescreen for demands that labor make all the concessions. For partnership to be genuine it must be a two-way street, with creative initiative and a willingness to cooperate on all sides.

303. When companies are considering plant closures or the movement of capital, it is patently unjust to deny workers any role in shaping the outcome of these difficult choices.[11] In the heavy manufacturing sector today, technological change and international competition can be the occasion of painful decisions leading to the loss of jobs or wage reductions. While such decisions may sometimes be necessary, a collaborative and mutually accountable model of industrial organization would mean that workers not be expected to carry all the burdens of an economy in transition. Management and investors must also accept their share of sacrifices, especially when management is thinking of closing a plant or transferring capital to a seemingly more lucrative or competitive activity. The capital at the disposal of management is in part the product of the labor of those who have toiled in the company over the years, including currently employed workers.[12] As a minimum, workers have a right to be informed in advance when such decisions are under consideration, a right to negotiate with management about possible alternatives, and a right to fair compensation and assistance with retraining and relocation expenses should these be necessary. Since even these minimal rights are jeopardized without collective negotiation, industrial cooperation requires a strong role for labor unions in our changing economy.

304. Labor unions themselves are challenged by the present economic environment to seek new ways of doing business. The purpose of unions is not simply to defend the existing wages and prerogatives of the fraction of workers who belong to them, but also to enable workers to make positive and creative contributions to the firm, the community, and the larger society in an organized and cooperative way.[13] Such contributions call for experiments with new directions in the U.S. labor movement.

305. The parts played by managers and shareholders in U.S. corporations also need careful examination. In U.S. law, the primary responsibility of man-

agers is to exercise prudent business judgment in the interest of a profitable return to investors. But morally this legal responsibility may be exercised only within the bounds of justice to employees, customers, suppliers, and the local community. Corporate mergers and hostile takeovers may bring greater benefits to shareholders, but they often lead to decreased concern for the well-being of local communities and make towns and cities more vulnerable to decisions made from afar.

306. Most shareholders today exercise relatively little power in corporate governance.[14] Although shareholders can and should vote on the selection of corporate directors and on investment questions and other policy matters, it appears that return on investment is the governing criterion in the relation between them and management. We do not believe this is an adequate rationale for shareholder decisions. The question of how to relate the rights and responsibilities of shareholders to those of the other people and communities affected by corporate decisions is complex and insufficiently understood. We, therefore, urge serious, long-term research and experimentation in this area. More effective ways of dealing with these questions are essential to enable firms to serve the common good.

B. Local and Regional Cooperation

307. The context within which U.S. firms do business has direct influence on their ability to contribute to the common good. Companies and indeed whole industries are not sole masters of their own fate. Increased cooperative efforts are needed to make local, regional, national, and international conditions more supportive of the pursuit of economic justice.

308. In the principle of subsidiarity, Catholic social teaching has long stressed the importance of small and intermediate-sized communities or institutions in exercising moral responsibility. These mediating structures link the individual to society as a whole in a way that gives people greater freedom and power to act.[15] Such groups include families, neighborhoods, church congregations, community organizations, civic and business associations, public interest and advocacy groups, community development corporations, and many other bodies. All these groups can play a crucial role in generating creative partnerships for the pursuit of the public good on the local and regional level.

309. The value of partnership is illustrated by considering how new jobs are created. The development of new businesses to serve the local community is key to revitalizing areas hit hard by unemployment.[16] The cities and regions in greatest need of these new jobs face serious obstacles in attracting enterprises that can provide them. Lack of financial resources, limited entrepreneurial skill, blighted and unsafe environments, and a deteriorating infrastructure create a vicious cycle that makes new investment in these areas more risky and therefore less likely.

310. Breaking out of this cycle will require a cooperative approach that draws on all the resources of the community.[17] Community development corporations can keep efforts focused on assisting those most in need. Existing business, labor, financial, and academic institutions can provide expertise in partnership with innovative entrepreneurs. New cooperative structures of local ownership will give the community or region an added stake in businesses and even more importantly give these businesses a greater stake in the community.[18] Government on the local, state, and national levels must play a significant role, especially through tax structures that encourage investment in hard hit areas and through funding aimed at conservation and basic infrastructure needs. Initiatives like these can contribute to a multilevel response to the needs of the community.

311. The Church itself can work as an effective partner on the local and regional level. First-hand knowledge of community needs and commitment to the protection of the dignity of all should put Church leaders in the forefront of efforts to encourage a community-wide cooperative strategy. Because churches include members from many different parts of the community, they can often serve as mediator between groups who might otherwise regard each other with suspicion. We urge local church groups to work creatively and in partnership with other private and public groups in responding to local and regional problems.

C. Partnership in the Development of National Policies

312. The causes of our national economic problems and their possible solutions are the subject of vigorous debate today. The discussion often turns on the role the national government has played in creating these problems and could play in remedying them. We want to point to several considerations that could help build new forms of effective citizenship and cooperation in shaping the economic life of our country.

313. First, while economic freedom and personal initiative are deservedly esteemed in our society, we have increasingly come to recognize the inescapably social and political nature of the economy. The market is always embedded in a specific social and political context. The tax system affects consumption, saving, and investment. National monetary policy, domestic and defense programs, protection of the environment and worker safety, and regulation of international trade all shape the economy as a whole. These policies influence domestic investment, unemployment rates, foreign exchange, and the health of the entire world economy.

314. The principle of subsidiarity calls for government intervention when small or intermediate groups in society are unable or unwilling to take the steps needed to promote basic justice. Pope John XXIII observed that the growth of more complex relations of interdependence among citizens has led to an increased role for government in modern societies.[19] This role is to work

in partnership with the many other groups in society, helping them fulfill their tasks and responsibilities more effectively, not replacing or destroying them. The challenge of today is to move beyond abstract disputes about whether more or less government intervention is needed, to consideration of creative ways of enabling government and private groups to work together effectively.

315. It is in this light that we understand Pope John Paul II's recommendation that "society make provision for overall planning" in the economic domain.[20] Planning must occur on various levels, with the government ensuring that basic justice is protected and also protecting the rights and freedoms of all other agents. In the Pope's words:

> In the final analysis this overall concern weighs on the shoulders of the state, but it cannot mean one-sided centralization by the public authorities. Instead what is in question is a just and rational coordination within the framework of which the initiative of individuals, free groups, and local work centers and complexes must be safeguarded.[21]

316. We are well aware that the mere mention of economic planning is likely to produce a strong negative reaction in U.S. society. It conjures up images of centralized planning boards, command economies, inefficient bureaucracies, and mountains of government paperwork. It is also clear that the meaning of "planning" is open to a wide variety of interpretations and takes very different forms in various nations.[22] The Pope's words should not be construed as an endorsement of a highly centralized form of economic planning, much less a totalitarian one. His call for a "just and rational coordination" of the endeavors of the many economic actors is a call to seek creative new partnership and forms of participation in shaping national policies.

317. There are already many forms of economic planning going on within the U.S. economy today. Individuals and families plan for their economic future. Management and labor unions regularly develop both long- and short-term plans. Towns, cities, and regions frequently have planning agencies concerned with their social and economic future. When state legislatures and the U.S. Congress vote on budgets or on almost any other bill that comes before them, they are engaged in a form of public planning. Catholic social teaching does not propose a single model for political and economic life by which these levels are to be institutionally related to each other. It does insist that reasonable coordination among the different parts of the body politic is an essential condition for achieving justice. This is a moral precondition of good citizenship that applies to both individual and institutional actors. In its absence no political structure can guarantee justice in society or the economy. Effective decisions in these matters will demand greater cooperation among all citizens. To encourage our fellow citizens to consider more carefully the appropriate balance of private and local initiative with national economic policy, we make several recommendations.

318. *First, in an advanced industrial economy like ours, all parts of society, including government, must cooperate in forming national economic policies.* Taxation, monetary policy, high levels of government spending, and many other forms of governmental regulation are here to stay. A modern economy without governmental interventions of the sort we have alluded to is inconceivable. These interventions, however, should help, not replace, the contributions of other economic actors and institutions and should direct them to the common good. The development of effective new forms of partnership between private and public agencies will be difficult in a situation as immensely complex as that of the United States in which various aspects of national policy seem to contradict one another.[23] On the theoretical level, achieving greater coordination will make demands on those with the technical competence to analyze the relationship among different parts of the economy. More practically, it will require the various subgroups within our society to sharpen their concern for the common good and moderate their efforts to protect their own short-term interests.

319. *Second, the impact of national economic policies on the poor and the vulnerable is the primary criterion for judging their moral value.* Throughout this letter we have stressed the special place of the poor and the vulnerable in any ethical analysis of the U.S. economy. National economic policies that contribute to building a true commonwealth should reflect this by standing firmly for the rights of those who fall through the cracks of our economy: the poor, the unemployed, the homeless, the displaced. Being a citizen of this land means sharing in the responsibility for shaping and implementing such policies.

320. *Third, the serious distortion of national economic priorities produced by massive national spending on defense must be remedied.* Clear-sighted consideration of the role of government shows that government and the economy are already closely intertwined through military research and defense contracts. Defense-related industries make up a major part of the U.S. economy and have intimate links with both the military and civilian government; they often depart from the competitive model of free-market capitalism. Moreover, the dedication of so much of the national budget to military purposes has been disastrous for the poor and vulnerable members of our own and other nations. The nation's spending priorities need to be revised in the interests of both justice and peace.[24]

321. We recognize that these proposals do not provide a detailed agenda. We are also aware that there is a tension between setting the goals for coherent policies and actually arriving at them by democratic means. But if we can increase the level of commitment to the common good and the virtues of citizenship in our nation, the ability to achieve these goals will greatly increase. It is these fundamental moral concerns that lead us as bishops to join the debate on national priorities.

D. Cooperation at the International Level

322. If our country is to guide its international economic relationships by policies that serve human dignity and justice, we must expand our understanding of the moral responsibility of citizens to serve the common good of the entire planet. Cooperation is not limited to the local, regional, or national level. Economic policy can no longer be governed by national goals alone. The fact that the "social question has become worldwide"[25] challenges us to broaden our horizons and enhance our collaboration and sense of solidarity on the global level. The cause of democracy is closely tied to the cause of economic justice. The unfinished business of the American experiment includes the formation of new international partnerships, especially with the developing countries, based on mutual respect, cooperation, and a dedication to fundamental justice.

323. The principle of subsidiarity calls for government to intervene in the economy when basic justice requires greater social coordination and regulation of economic actors and institutions. In global economic relations, however, no international institution provides this sort of coordination and regulation. The U.N. system, including the World Bank, the International Monetary Fund, and the General Agreement on Tariffs and Trade, does not possess the requisite authority. Pope John XXIII called this institutional weakness a "structural defect" in the organization of the human community. The structures of world order including economic ones, "no longer correspond to the objective requirements of the universal common good."[26]

324. Locked together in a world of limited material resources and a growing array of common problems, we help or hurt one another by the economic policies we choose. All the economic agents in our society, therefore, must consciously and deliberately attend to the good of the whole human family. We must all work to increase the effectiveness of international agencies in addressing global problems that cannot be handled through the actions of individual countries. In particular we repeat our plea made in *The Challenge of Peace* urging "that the United States adopt a stronger supportive leadership role with respect to the United Nations."[27] In the years following World War II, the United States took the lead in establishing multilateral bodies to deal with postwar economic problems. Unfortunately, in recent years this country has taken steps that have weakened rather than strengthened multilateral approaches. This is a shortsighted policy and should be reversed if the long-term interests of an interdependent globe are to be served.[28] In devising more effective arrangements for pursuing international economic justice, the overriding problem is how to get from where we are to where we ought to be. Progress toward that goal demands positive and often difficult action by corporations, banks, labor unions, governments, and other major actors on the international stage. But whatever the difficulty, the need to give priority to alleviating poverty in developing

countries is undeniable; and the cost of continued inaction can be counted in human lives lost or stunted, talents wasted, opportunities foregone, misery and suffering prolonged, and injustice condoned.

325. Self-restraint and self-criticism by all parties are necessary first steps toward strengthening the international structures to protect the common good. Otherwise, growing interdependence will lead to conflict and increased economic threats to human dignity. This is an important long-term challenge to the economic future of this country and its place in the emerging world economic community.

CHAPTER 5: A COMMITMENT TO THE FUTURE

326. Because Jesus' command to love our neighbor is universal, we hold that the life of each person on this globe is sacred. This commits us to bringing about a just economic order where all, without exception, will be treated with dignity and to working in collaboration with those who share this vision. The world is complex and this may often tempt us to seek simple and self-centered solutions; but as a community of disciples we are called to a new hope and to a new vision that we must live without fear and without oversimplification. Not only must we learn more about our moral responsibility for the larger economic issues that touch the daily life of each and every person on this planet, but we also want to help shape the Church as a model of social and economic justice. Thus, this chapter deals with the Christian vocation in the world today, the special challenges to the Church at this moment of history, ways in which the themes of this letter should be followed up, and a call to the kind of commitment that will be needed to reshape the future.

A. The Christian Vocation in the World Today

327. This letter has addressed many matters commonly regarded as secular, for example, employment rates, income levels, and international economic relationships. Yet, the affairs of the world, including economic ones, cannot be separated from the spiritual hunger of the human heart. We have presented the biblical vision of humanity and the Church's moral and religious tradition as a framework for asking the deeper questions about the meaning of economic life and for actively responding to them. But words alone are not enough. The Christian perspective on the meaning of economic life must transform the lives of individuals, families, in fact, our whole culture. The Gospel confers on each Christian the vocation to love God and neighbor in ways that bear fruit in the life of society. That vocation consists above all in a change of heart: a conversion expressed in praise of God and in concrete deeds of justice and service.

1. CONVERSION

328. The transformation of social structures begins with and is always accompanied by a conversion of the heart.[1] As disciples of Christ each of us is called to a deep personal conversion and to "action on behalf of justice and participation in the transformation of the world."[2] By faith and baptism we are fashioned into a "new creature"; we are filled with the Holy Spirit and a new love that compels us to seek out a new profound relationship with God, with the human family, and with all created things.[3] Renouncing self-centered desires, bearing one's daily cross, and imitating Christ's compassion, all involve a personal struggle to control greed and selfishness, a personal commitment to reverence one's own human dignity and the dignity of others by avoiding self-indulgence and those attachments that make us insensitive to the conditions of others and that erode social solidarity. Christ warned us against attachments to material things, against total self-reliance, against the idolatry of accumulating material goods and seeking safety in them. We must take these teachings seriously and in their light examine how each of us lives and acts toward others. But personal conversion is not gained once and for all. It is a process that goes on through our entire life. Conversion, moreover, takes place in the context of a larger faith community: through baptism into the Church, through common prayer, and through our activity with others on behalf of justice.

2. WORSHIP AND PRAYER

329. Challenging U.S. economic life with the Christian vision calls for a deeper awareness of the integral connection between worship and the world of work. Worship and common prayer are the wellsprings that give life to any reflection on economic problems and that continually call the participants to greater fidelity to discipleship. To worship and pray to the God of the universe is to acknowledge that the healing love of God extends to all persons and to every part of existence, including work, leisure, money, economic and political power and their use, and to all those practical policies that either lead to justice or impede it. Therefore, when Christians come together in prayer, they make a commitment to carry God's love into all these areas of life.

330. The unity of work and worship finds expression in a unique way in the Eucharist. As people of a new covenant, the faithful hear God's challenging word proclaimed to them—a message of hope to the poor and oppressed—and they call upon the Holy Spirit to unite all into one body of Christ. For the Eucharist to be a living promise of the fullness of God's Kingdom, the faithful must commit themselves to living as redeemed people with the same care and love for all people that Jesus showed. The body of Christ which worshipers receive in Communion is also a reminder of the reconciling

power of his death on the Cross. It empowers them to work to heal the brokenness of society and human relationships and to grow in a spirit of self-giving for others.

331. The liturgy teaches us to have grateful hearts: to thank God for the gift of life, the gift of this earth, and the gift of all people. It turns our hearts from self-seeking to a spirituality that sees the signs of true discipleship in our sharing of goods and working for justice. By uniting us in prayer with all the people of God, with the rich and the poor, with those near and dear, and with those in distant lands, liturgy challenges our way of living and refines our values. Together in the community of worship, we are encouraged to use the goods of this earth for the benefit of all. In worship and in deeds for justice, the Church becomes a "sacrament," a visible sign of that unity in justice and peace that God wills for the whole of humanity.[4]

3. CALL TO HOLINESS IN THE WORLD

332. Holiness is not limited to the sanctuary or to moments of private prayer; it is a call to direct our whole heart and life toward God and according to God's plan for this world. For the laity holiness is achieved in the midst of the world, in family, in community, in friendships, in work, in leisure, in citizenship. Through their competency and by their activity, lay men and women have the vocation to bring the light of the Gospel to economic affairs, "so that the world may be filled with the Spirit of Christ and may more effectively attain its destiny in justice, in love, and in peace."[5]

333. But as disciples of Christ we must constantly ask ourselves how deeply the biblical and ethical vision of justice and love permeates our thinking. How thoroughly does it influence our way of life? We may hide behind the complexity of the issues or dismiss the significance of our personal contribution; in fact, each one has a role to play, because every day each one makes economic decisions. Some, by reason of their work or their position in society, have a vocation to be involved in a more decisive way in those decisions that affect the economic well-being of others. They must be encouraged and sustained by all in their search for greater justice.

334. At times we will be called upon to say no to the cultural manifestations that emphasize values and aims that are selfish, wasteful, and opposed to the Scriptures. Together we must reflect on our personal and family decisions and curb unnecessary wants in order to meet the needs of others. There are many questions we must keep asking ourselves: Are we becoming ever more wasteful in a "throw-away" society? Are we able to distinguish between our true needs and those thrust on us by advertising and a society that values consumption more than saving? All of us could well ask ourselves whether as a Christian prophetic witness we are not called to adopt a simpler lifestyle, in the face of the excessive accumulation of material goods that characterizes an affluent society.

335. Husbands and wives, in particular, should weigh their needs carefully and establish a proper priority of values as they discuss the questions of both parents working outside the home and the responsibilities of raising children with proper care and attention. At times we will be called as individuals, as families, as parishes, as Church, to identify more closely with the poor in their struggle for participation and to close the gap of understanding between them and the affluent. By sharing the perspectives of those who are suffering, we can come to understand economic and social problems in a deeper way, thus leading us to seek more durable solutions.

336. In the workplace the laity are often called to make tough decisions with little information about the consequences that such decisions have on the economic lives of others. Such times call for collaborative dialogue together with prayerful reflection on Scripture and ethical norms. The same can be said of the need to elaborate policies that will reflect sound ethical principles and that can become a part of our political and social system. Since this is a part of the lay vocation and its call to holiness, the laity must seek to instill a moral and ethical dimension into the public debate on these issues and help enunciate the ethical questions that must be faced. To weigh political options according to criteria that go beyond efficiency and expediency requires prayer, reflection, and dialogue on all the ethical norms involved. Holiness for the laity will involve all the sacrifices needed to lead such a life of prayer and reflection within a worshiping and supporting faith community. In this way the laity will bridge the gap that so easily arises between the moral principles that guide the personal life of the Christian and the considerations that govern decisions in society in the political forum and in the marketplace.

4. LEISURE

337. Some of the difficulty in bringing Christian faith to economic life in the United States today results from the obstacles to establishing a balance of labor and leisure in daily life. Tedious and boring work leads some to look for fulfillment only during time off the job. Others have become "workaholics," people who work compulsively and without reflection on the deeper meaning of life and their actions. The quality and pace of work should be more human in scale enabling people to experience the dignity and value of their work and giving them time for other duties and obligations. This balance is vitally important for sustaining the social, political, educational, and cultural structures of society. The family, in particular, requires such balance. Without leisure there is too little time for nurturing marriages, for developing parent-child relationships, and for fulfilling commitments to other important groups: the extended family, the community of friends, the parish, the neighborhood, schools, and political organizations. Why is it one hears so little today about shortening the work week, especially if both parents are working?

Such a change would give them more time for each other, for their children, and for their other social and political responsibilities.

338. Leisure is connected to the whole of one's value system and influenced by the general culture one lives in. It can be trivialized into boredom and laziness, or end in nothing but a desire for greater consumption and waste. For disciples of Christ, the use of leisure may demand being countercultural. The Christian tradition sees in leisure, time to build family and societal relationships and an opportunity for communal prayer and worship, for relaxed contemplation and enjoyment of God's creation, and for the cultivation of the arts which help fill the human longing for wholeness. Most of all, we must be convinced that economic decisions affect our use of leisure and that such decisions are also to be based on moral and ethical considerations. In this area of leisure we must be on our guard against being swept along by a lack of cultural values and by the changing fads of an affluent society. In the creation narrative God worked six days to create the world and rested on the seventh (Gn. 2:1–4). We must take that image seriously and learn how to harmonize action and rest, work and leisure, so that both contribute to building up the person as well as the family and community.

B. Challenges to the Church

339. The Church is all the people of God, gathered in smaller faith communities, guided and served by a pope and a hierarchy of bishops, ministered to by priests, deacons, religious, and laity, through visible institutions and agencies. Church is, thus, primarily a communion of people bonded by the Spirit with Christ as their Head, sustaining one another in love, and acting as a sign or sacrament in the world. By its nature it is people called to a transcendent end; but, it is also a visible social institution functioning in this world. According to their calling, members participate in the mission and work of the Church and share, to varying degrees, the responsibility for its institutions and agencies.[6] At this moment in history, it is particularly important to emphasize the responsibilities of the whole Church for education and family life.

1. EDUCATION

340. We have already emphasized the commitment to quality education that is necessary if the poor are to take their rightful place in the economic structures of our society. We have called the Church to remember its own obligation in this regard and we have endorsed support for improvements in public education.

341. The educational mission of the Church is not only to the poor but to all its members. We reiterate our 1972 statement: "Through education, the Church seeks to prepare its members to proclaim the Good News and to

translate this proclamation into action. Since the Christian vocation is a call to transform oneself and society with God's help, the educational efforts of the Church must encompass the twin purposes of personal sanctification and social reform in the light of Christian values."[7] Through her educational mission the Church seeks: to integrate knowledge about this world with revelation about God; to understand God's relationship to the human race and its ultimate destiny in the Kingdom of God; to build up human communities of justice and peace; and to teach the value of all creation. By inculcating these values the educational system of the Church contributes to society and to social justice. Economic questions are, thus, seen as a part of a larger vision of the human person and the human family, the value of this created earth, and the duties and responsibilities that all have toward each other and toward this universe.

342. For these reasons the Church must incorporate into all levels of her educational system the teaching of social justice and the biblical and ethical principles that support it. We call on our universities, in particular, to make Catholic social teaching and the social encyclicals of the popes a part of their curriculum, especially for those whose vocation will call them to an active role in U.S. economic and political decision making. Faith and technological progress are not opposed one to another, but this progress must not be channeled and directed by greed, self-indulgence, or novelty for its own sake, but by values that respect human dignity and foster social solidarity.

343. The Church has always held that the first task and responsibility for education lies in the hands of parents: they have the right to choose freely the schools or other means necessary to educate their children in the faith.[8] The Church also has consistently held that public authorities must ensure that public subsidies for the education of children are allocated so that parents can freely choose to exercise this right without incurring unjust burdens. This parental right should not be taken from them. We call again for equitable sharing in public benefits for those parents who choose private and religious schools for their children. Such help should be available especially for low-income parents. Though many of these parents sacrifice a great deal for their children's education, others are effectively deprived of the possibility of exercising this right.

2. SUPPORTING THE FAMILY

344. Economic life has a profound effect on all social structures and particularly on the family. A breakdown of family life often brings with it hardship and poverty. Divorce, failure to provide support to mothers and children, abandonment of children, pregnancies out of wedlock, all contribute to the amount of poverty among us. Though these breakdowns of marriage and the family are more visible among the poor, they do not affect only that one segment of our society. In fact, one could argue that many of these breakdowns

come from the false values found among the more affluent—values which ultimately pervade the whole of society.

345. More studies are needed to probe the possible connections between affluence and family and marital breakdowns. The constant seeking for self-gratification and the exaggerated individualism of our age, spurred on by false values often seen in advertising and on television, contribute to the lack of firm commitment in marriage and to destructive notions of responsibility and personal growth.[9]

346. With good reason, the Church has traditionally held that the family is the basic building block of any society. In fighting against economic arrangements that weaken the family, the Church contributes to the well-being of society. The same must be said of the Church's teaching on responsible human sexuality and its relationship to marriage and family. Economic arrangements must support the family and promote its solidity.

3. THE CHURCH AS ECONOMIC ACTOR

347. Although all members of the Church are economic actors every day in their individual lives, they also play an economic role united together as Church. On the parish and diocesan level, through its agencies and institutions, the Church employs many people; it has investments; it has extensive properties for worship and mission. *All the moral principles that govern the just operation of any economic endeavor apply to the Church and its agencies and institutions; indeed the Church should be exemplary.* The Synod of Bishops in 1971 worded this challenge most aptly: "While the Church is bound to give witness to justice, she recognizes that anyone who ventures to speak to people about justice must first be just in their eyes. Hence, we must undertake an examination of the modes of acting and of the possessions and lifestyle found within the Church herself."[10]

348. Catholics in the United States can be justly proud of their accomplishments in building and maintaining churches and chapels, and an extensive system of schools, hospitals, and charitable institutions. Through sacrifices and personal labor our immigrant ancestors built these institutions. For many decades religious orders of women and men taught in our schools and worked in our hospitals with very little remuneration. Right now, we see the same spirit of generosity among the religious and lay people even as we seek to pay more adequate salaries.

349. We would be insincere were we to deny a need for renewal in the economic life of the Church itself and for renewed zeal on the part of the Church in examining its role in the larger context of reinforcing in U.S. society and culture those values that support economic justice.[11]

350. We select here five areas for special reflection: (1) wages and salaries, (2) rights of employees, (3) investments and property, (4) works of charity, and (5) working for economic justice.

351. We bishops commit ourselves to the principle that those who serve the Church—laity, clergy, and religious—should receive a sufficient livelihood and the social benefits provided by responsible employers in our nation. These obligations, however, cannot be met without the increased contributions of all the members of the Church. We call on all to recognize the responsibility to contribute monetarily to the support of those who carry out the public mission of the Church. Sacrificial giving or tithing by all the people of God would provide the funds necessary to pay these adequate salaries for religious and lay people; the lack of funds is the usual underlying cause for the lack of adequate salaries. The obligation to sustain the Church's institutions—education and health care, social service agencies, religious education programs, care of the elderly, youth ministry, and the like—falls on all the members of the community because of their baptism; the obligation is not just on the users or on those who staff them. Increased resources are also needed for the support of elderly members of religious communities. These dedicated women and men have not always asked for or received the stipends and pensions that would have assured their future. It would be a breach of our obligations to them to let them or their communities face retirement without adequate funds.

352. Many volunteers provide services to the Church and its mission which cannot be measured in dollars and cents. These services are important to the life and vitality of the Church in the United States and carry on a practice that has marked the history of the Church in this country since its founding. In this tradition, we ask young people to make themselves available for a year or more of voluntary service before beginning their training for more specific vocations in life; we also recommend expanding voluntary service roles for retired persons; we encourage those who have accepted this challenge.

353. All church institutions must also fully recognize the rights of employees to organize and bargain collectively with the institution through whatever association or organization they freely choose.[12] In the light of new creative models of collaboration between labor and management described earlier in this letter, we challenge our church institutions to adopt new fruitful modes of cooperation. Although the Church has its own nature and mission that must be respected and fostered, we are pleased that many who are not of our faith, but who share similar hopes and aspirations for the human family, work for us and with us in achieving this vision. In seeking greater justice in wages, we recognize the need to be alert particularly to the continuing discrimination against women throughout Church and society, especially reflected in both the inequities of salaries between women and men and in the concentration of women in jobs at the lower end of the wage scale.

354. Individual Christians who are shareholders and those responsible within church institutions that own stocks in U.S. corporations must see to it that the invested funds are used responsibly. Although it is a moral and legal fiduciary responsibility of the trustees to ensure an adequate return on investment for the support of the work of the Church, their stewardship embraces

broader moral concerns. As part-owners, they must cooperate in shaping the policies of those companies through dialogue with management, through votes at corporate meetings, through the introduction of resolutions, and through participation in investment decisions. We praise the efforts of dioceses and other religious and ecumenical bodies that work together toward these goals. We also praise efforts to develop alternative investment policies, especially those which support enterprises that promote economic development in depressed communities and which help the Church respond to local and regional needs.[13] When the decision to divest seems unavoidable, it should be done after prudent examination and with a clear explanation of the motives.

355. The use of church property demands special attention today. Changing demographic patterns have left many parishes and institutions with empty or partially used buildings. The decline in the number of religious who are teaching in the schools and the reduction in the number of clergy often result in large residences with few occupants. In this regard, the Church must be sensitive to the image the possession of such large facilities often projects, namely, that it is wealthy and extravagant in the use of its resources. This image can be overcome only by clear public accountability of its financial holdings, of its properties and the use, and of the services it renders to its members and to society at large. We support and encourage the creative use of these facilities by many parishes and dioceses to serve the needs of the poor.

356. The Church has a special call to be a servant of the poor, the sick, and the marginalized, thereby becoming a true sign of the Church's mission—a mission shared by every member of the Christian community. The Church now serves many such people through one of the largest private human services delivery systems in the country. The networks of agencies, institutions, and programs provide services to millions of persons of all faiths. Still we must be reminded that in our day our Christian concerns must increase and extend beyond our borders, because everyone in need is our neighbor. We must also be reminded that charity requires more than alleviating misery. It demands genuine love for the person in need. It should probe the meaning of suffering and provoke a response that seeks to remedy causes. True charity leads to advocacy.

357. Yet charity alone is not a corrective to all economic social ills. All citizens, working through various organizations of society and through government, bear the responsibility of caring for those who are in need. The Church, too, through all its members individually and through its agencies, must work to alleviate injustices that prevent some from participating fully in economic life. Our experience with the Campaign for Human Development confirms our judgment about the validity of self-help and empowerment of the poor. The campaign, which has received the positive support of American Catholics since it was launched in 1970, provides a model that we think sets a high standard for similar efforts. We bishops know of the many faithful in all walks of life who use their skills and their compassion to seek innovative ways

to carry out the goals we are proposing in this letter. As they do this, they *are* the Church acting for economic justice. At the same time, we hope they will join together with us and their priests to influence our society so that even more steps can be taken to alleviate injustices. Grassroots efforts by the poor themselves, helped by community support, are indispensable. The entire Christian community can learn much from the way our deprived brothers and sisters assist each other in their struggles.

358. In addition to being an economic actor, the Church is a significant cultural actor concerned about the deeper cultural roots of our economic problems. As we have proposed a new experiment in collaboration and participation in decision making by all those affected at all levels of U.S. society, so we also commit the Church to become a model of collaboration and participation.

C. The Road Ahead

359. The completion of a letter such as this one is but the beginning of a long process of education, discussion, and action; its contents must be brought to all members of the Church and of society.

360. In this respect we mentioned the twofold aim of this pastoral letter: to help Catholics form their consciences on the moral dimensions of economic decision making and to articulate a moral perspective in the general societal and political debate that surrounds these questions. These two purposes help us to reflect on the different ways the institutions and ministers of the Church can assist the laity in their vocation in the world. Renewed emphasis on Catholic social teaching in our schools, colleges, and universities; special seminars with corporate officials, union leaders, legislators, bankers, and the like; the organization of small groups composed of people from different ways of life to meditate together on the Gospel and ethical norms; speakers' bureaus; family programs; clearinghouses of available material; pulpit aids for priests; diocesan television and radio programs; research projects in our universities—all of these are appropriate means for continued discussion and action. Some of these are done best on the parish level, others by the state Catholic conferences, and others by the National Conference of Catholic Bishops. These same bodies can assist the laity in the many difficult decisions that deal with political options that affect economic decisions. Where many options are available, it must be the concern of all in such debates that we as Catholics do not become polarized. All must be challenged to show how the decisions they make and the policies they suggest flow from the ethical moral vision outlined here. As new problems arise, we hope through our continual reflection that we will be able to help refine Catholic social teaching and contribute to its further development.

361. We call upon our priests, in particular, to continue their study of these issues, so that they can proclaim the Gospel message in a way that not only challenges the faithful but also sustains and encourages their vocation in and

to the world. Priestly formation in our seminaries will also have to prepare candidates for this role.

362. We wish to emphasize the need to undertake research into many of the areas this document could not deal with in depth and to continue exploration of those we have dealt with. We encourage our Catholic universities, foundations, and other institutions to assist in these necessary projects. The following areas for further research are merely suggestive, not exhaustive: the impact of arms production and large military spending on the domestic economy and on culture; arms production and sales as they relate to Third World poverty; tax reforms to express the preferential option for the poor; the rights of women and minorities in the work force; the development of communications technology and its global influences; robotics, automation, and reduction of defense industries as they will affect employment; the economy and the stability of the family; legitimate profit versus greed; securing economic rights; environmental and ecological questions; future roles of labor and unions; international financial institutions and Third World debt; our national deficit; world food problems; "full employment" and its implementation; plant closings and dealing with the human costs of an evolving economy; cooperatives and new modes of sharing; welfare reform and national eligibility standards; income support systems; concentration of land ownership; assistance to Third World nations; migration and its effects; population policies and development; the effects of increased inequality of incomes in society.

D. Commitment to a Kingdom of Love and Justice

363. Confronted by this economic complexity and seeking clarity for the future, we can rightly ask ourselves one single question: How does our economic system affect the lives of people—*all* people? Part of the American dream has been to make this world a better place for people to live in; at this moment of history that dream must include everyone on this globe. Since we profess to be members of a "catholic" or universal Church, we all must raise our sights to a concern for the well-being of everyone in the world. Third World debt becomes our problem. Famine and starvation in sub-Saharan Africa become our concern. Rising military expenditures everywhere in the world become part of our fears for the future of this planet. We cannot be content if we see ecological neglect or the squandering of natural resources. In this letter we bishops have spoken often of economic interdependence; now is the moment when all of us must confront the reality of such economic bonding and its consequences and see it as a moment of grace—a *kairos*—that can unite all of us in a common community of the human family. We commit ourselves to this global vision.

364. We cannot be frightened by the magnitude and complexity of these problems. We must not be discouraged. In the midst of this struggle, it is inevitable that we become aware of greed, laziness, and envy. No utopia is

possible on this earth; but as believers in the redemptive love of God and as those who have experienced God's forgiving mercy, we know that God's providence is not and will not be lacking to us today.

365. The fulfillment of human needs, we know, is not the final purpose of the creation of the human person. We have been created to share in the divine life through a destiny that goes far beyond our human capabilities and before which we must in all humility stand in awe. Like Mary in proclaiming her *Magnificat*, we marvel at the wonders God has done for us, how God has raised up the poor and the lowly and promised great things for them in the Kingdom. God now asks of us sacrifices and reflection on our reverence for human dignity—in ourselves and in others—and on our service and discipleship, so that the divine goal for the human family and this earth can be fulfilled. Communion with God, sharing God's life, involves a mutual bonding with all on this globe. Jesus taught us to love God and one another and that the concept of neighbor is without limit. We know that we are called to be members of a new covenant of love. We have to move from our devotion to independence, through an understanding of interdependence, to a commitment to human solidarity. That challenge must find its realization in the kind of community we build among us. Love implies concern for all—especially the poor—and a continued search for those social and economic structures that permit everyone to share in a community that is a part of a redeemed creation (Rom. 8:21–23).

NOTES

Chapter 1

1. Vatican Council II, *The Pastoral Constitution on the Church in the Modern World*, 33. [Note: This pastoral letter frequently refers to documents of the Second Vatican Council, papal encyclicals, and other official teachings of the Roman Catholic Church. Most of these texts have been published by the United States Catholic Conference; many are available in collections, though no single collection is comprehensive.]

2. *Pastoral Constitution*, 1.

3. See ibid., 10, 42, 43; Congregation for the Doctrine of the Faith, *Instruction on Christian Freedom and Liberation* (Washington, D.C.: USCC, 1986), 34–36.

4. See Pope John Paul II, *On Human Work* (1981), 14; and Pope Paul VI, *Octogesima Adveniens* (1971), 35. See also Arthur Okun, *Equality and Efficiency: The Big Tradeoff* (Washington, D.C.: The Brookings Institution, 1975), ch. 1; Michael Walzer, *Spheres of Justice: A Defense of Pluralism and Equality* (New York: Basic Books, 1983), ch. 4; Jon P. Gunnermann, "Capitalism and Commutative Justice," paper presented at the 1985 meeting of the Society of Christian Ethics.

5. Abraham Lincoln, Address at Dedication of National Cemetery at Gettysburg, November 19, 1863.

6. Pope John XXIII, *Peace on Earth* (1963), 130–31.

7. Synod of Bishops, *Justice in the World* (1971), 8; Pope John Paul II, *Redeemer of Man* (1979), 15.

8. U.S. Department of Labor, Bureau of Labor Statistics, *The Employment Situation: August 1985* (September 1985), Table A-1.

9. Ibid.

10. U.S. Bureau of the Census, Current Population Reports, Series P-60, 145, *Money Income and Poverty Status of Families and Persons in the United States: 1983* (Washington, D.C.: U.S. Government Printing Office, 1984), 20.

11. Greg H. Duncan, *Years of Poverty, Years of Plenty: The Changing Economic Fortunes of American Workers and Their Families* (Ann Arbor, Mich.: Institute for Social Research, University of Michigan, 1984).

12. See Pope John Paul II, *Familiaris Consortio* (1981), 46.

13. *Pastoral Constitution*, 47.

14. National Conference of Catholic Bishops, *The Challenge of Peace: God's Promise and Our Response* (Washington, D.C.: USCC, 1983).

15. Cardinal Joseph L. Bernardin and Cardinal John J. O'Connor, Testimony before the House Foreign Relations Committee, June 26, 1984, *Origins* 14:10 (August 10, 1984): 157.

16. *Pastoral Constitution*, 43.

17. See, for example, Peter Berger, Brigitte Berger, and Hansfried Kellner, *The Homeless Mind: Modernization and Consciousness* (New York: Vintage, 1974).

18. For a recent study of the importance and difficulty of achieving such a common language and vision see Robert N. Bellah, Richard Madsen, William M. Sullivan, Ann Swidler, and Stephen M. Tipton, *Habits of the Heart: Individualism and Commitment in American Life* (Berkeley, Calif.: University of California Press, 1985). See also Martin E. Marty, *The Public Church* (New York: Crossroads, 1981).

19. Pope John XXIII, *Mater et Magistra* (1961), 219; *Pastoral Constitution*, 40.

20. Congregation for the Doctrine of the Faith, *Instruction on Certain Aspects of the Theology of Liberation* (Washington, D.C.: USCC, 1984); Pope Paul VI, *Octogesima Adveniens* (1971), 42.

21. *Octogesima Adveniens*, 4.

22. Administrative Committee of the National Catholic War Council, *Program of Social Reconstruction*, February 12, 1919. Other notable statements on the economy by our predecessors are *The Present Crisis*, April 25, 1933; *Statement on Church and Social Order*, February 4, 1940; *The Economy: Human Dimensions*, November 20, 1975. These and numerous other statements of the U.S. Catholic episcopate can be found in Hugh J. Nolan, ed., *Pas-*

toral Letters of the United States Catholic Bishops, 4 vols. (Washington, D.C.: USCC, 1984).

Chapter 2

1. *Mater et Magistra*, 219–20. See *Pastoral Constitution*, 63.

2. Vatican Council II, *Decree on Ecumenism*, 22–23.

3. C. Westermann, *Creation* (Philadelphia: Fortress Press, 1974); and B. Vawter, *On Genesis: A New Reading* (Garden City, N.Y.: Doubleday, 1977). See also *Pastoral Constitution*, 34.

4. St. Cyprian, *On Works and Almsgiving*, 25, trans. R. J. Deferrari, *St. Cyprian: Treatises*, 36 (New York: Fathers of the Church, 1958), 251. Original text in Migne, *Patrologia Latina*, vol. 4, 620. On the Patristic teaching, see C. Avila, *Ownership: Early Christian Teaching* (Maryknoll, N.Y.: Orbis Books, 1983). Collection of original texts and translations.

5. T. Ogletree, *The Use of the Bible in Christian Ethics* (Philadelphia: Fortress Press, 1983), 47–85.

6. Though scholars debate whether the Jubilee was a historical institution or an ideal, its images were continually evoked to stress God's sovereignty over the land and God's concern for the poor and the oppressed (e.g., Is. 61:1–2; Lk. 4:16–19). See R. North, *Sociology of the Biblical Jubilee* (Rome: Biblical Institute, 1954); S. Ringe, *Jesus, Liberation and the Biblical Jubilee: Images for Ethics and Christology* (Philadelphia: Fortress Press, 1985).

7. On justice, see J. R. Donahue, "Biblical Perspectives on Justice," in John C. Haughey, ed., *The Faith That Does Justice* (New York: Paulist Press, 1977), 68–112; and S. C. Mott, *Biblical Ethics and Social Change* (New York: Oxford University Press, 1982).

8. See Ex. 22:20–26; Dt. 15:1–11; Jb. 29:12–17; Pss. 69:34; 72:2,4,12–24; 82:3–4; Prv. 14:21,31; Is. 3:14–15; 10:2; Jer. 22:16; Zec. 7:9–10.

9. J. Pedersen, *Israel: Its Life and Culture*, vol. I-II (London: Oxford University Press, 1926), 337–40.

10. J. Alfaro, *Theology of Justice in the World* (Rome: Pontifical Commission on Justice and Peace, 1973), 40–41; E. McDonagh, *The Making of Disciples* (Wilmington, Del.: Michael Glazier, 1982), 119.

11. Pope John Paul II has drawn on this parable to exhort us to have a "compassionate heart" to those in need in his Apostolic Letter "On the Christian Meaning of Human Suffering" (*Salvifici Doloris*) (Washington, D.C.: USCC, 1984), 34–39.

12. *Redeemer of Man*, 21.

13. Address to Workers at Sao Paulo, 8, *Origins* 10:9 (July 31, 1980): 139; and Address at Yankee Stadium, *Origins* 9:19 (October 25, 1979): 311–312.

14. J. Dupont and A. George, eds., *La pauvreté évangelique* (Paris: Cerf, 1971); M. Hengel, *Property and Riches in the Early Church* (Philadelphia:

Fortress Press, 1974); L. Johnson, *Sharing Possessions: Mandate and Symbol of Faith* (Philadelphia: Fortress Press, 1981); D. L. Mealand, *Poverty and Expectation in the Gospels* (London: SPCK, 1980); W. Pilgrim, *Good News to the Poor: Wealth and Poverty in Luke-Acts* (Minneapolis: Augsburg, 1981); and W. Stegemann, *The Gospel and the Poor* (Philadelphia: Fortress Press, 1984).

15. See Am. 4:1–3; Jb. 20:19; Sir. 13:4–7; Jas. 2:6; 5:1–6; Rv. 18:11–19.

16. See paras. 85–91.

17. See Chapter 1 note 1 above.

18. Extraordinary Synod of Bishops (1985) *The Final Report*, II, A (Washington, D.C.: USCC, 1986).

19. Pope Paul VI, *On Evangelization in the Modern World*, 31.

20. Ibid., 24.

21. *Pastoral Constitution*, 32.

22. Ibid., 25.

23. See para. 39.

24. Josef Pieper, *The Four Cardinal Virtues* (Notre Dame, Ind.: University of Notre Dame Press, 1966), 43–116; David Hollenbach, "Modern Catholic Teachings Concerning Justice," in John C. Haughey, ed., *The Faith That Does Justice* (New York: Paulist Press, 1977), 207–231.

25. Jon P. Gunnemann, "Capitalism and Commutative Justice," presented at the 1985 meeting of the Society of Christian Ethics, forthcoming in *The Annual of the Society of Christian Ethics.*

26. *Pastoral Constitution*, 69.

27. Pope Pius XI, *Divini Redemptoris*, 51. See John A. Ryan, *Distributive Justice*, third edition (New York: Macmillan, 1942), 188. The term "social justice" has been used in several different but related ways in the Catholic ethical tradition. See William Ferree, "The Act of Social Justice," *Philosophical Studies*, vol. 72 (Washington, D.C.: The Catholic University of America Press, 1943).

28. *On Human Work*, 6, 9.

29. *Pastoral Constitution*, 29.

30. Ibid. See below, paras. 180–182.

31. Pope Paul VI, *On the Development of Peoples* (1967), 19.

32. *Mater et Magistra*, 132.

33. *Justice in the World*, 10, 16; and *Octogesima Adveniens*, 15.

34. *Pastoral Constitution*, 25; *Justice in the World*, 51; Pope John Paul II, *The Gift of the Redemption*, Apostolic Exhortation on Reconciliation and Penance (Washington, D.C.: USCC, 1984), 16; Congregation for the Doctrine of the Faith, *Instruction on Christian Freedom and Liberation*, 42, 74.

35. In the words of the 1971 Synod of Bishops: "Participation constitutes a right which is to be applied in the economic and in the social and political field," *Justice in the World*, 18.

36. *Pastoral Constitution*, 26.

37. Pope John Paul II, Address at the General Assembly of the United Nations (October 2, 1979), 13, 14.

38. See Pope Pius XII, 1941 Pentecost Address, in V. Yzermans, *The Major Addresses of Pope Pius XII*, vol. I (St. Paul: North Central, 1961), 32–33.

39. *Peace on Earth*, 8–27. See *On Human Work*, 18–19. *Peace on Earth* and other modern papal statements refer explicitly to the "right to work" as one of the fundamental economic rights. Because of the ambiguous meaning of the phrase in the United States, and also because the ordinary way people earn their living in our society is through paid employment, the NCCB has affirmed previously that the protection of human dignity demands that the right to useful employment be secured for all who are able and willing to work. See NCCB, *The Economy: Human Dimensions* (November 20, 1975), 5, in NCCB, *Justice in the Marketplace*, 470. See also Congregation for the Doctrine of the Faith, *Instruction on Christian Freedom and Liberation*, 85.

40. *The Development of Peoples*, 14.

41. Martha H. Good, "Freedom from Want: The Failure of United States Courts to Protect Subsistence Rights," *Human Rights Quarterly* 6 (1984): 335–365.

42. *Pastoral Constitution*, 43.

43. *Mater et Magistra*, 65.

44. On the recent use of this term see: Congregation for the Doctrine of the Faith, *Instruction on Christian Freedom and Liberation*, 46–50, 66–68; *Evangelization in Latin America's Present and Future*, Final Document of the Third General Conference of the Latin American Episcopate (Puebla, Mexico, January 27–February 13, 1979), esp. part VI, ch. 1, "A Preferential Option for the Poor," in J. Eagleson and P. Scharper, eds., *Puebla and Beyond* (Maryknoll: Orbis Books, 1979), 264–267; Donal Dorr, *Option for the Poor: A Hundred Years of Vatican Social Teaching* (Dublin: Gill and Macmillan/Maryknoll, N.Y.: Orbis Books, 1983).

45. *Octogesima Adveniens*, 23.

46. Address to Bishops of Brazil, 6, 9, *Origins* 10:9 (July 31, 1980): 135.

47. Pope John Paul II, Address to Workers at Sao Paulo, 4, *Origins* 10:9 (July 31, 1980): 138; Congregation for the Doctrine of the Faith, *Instruction on Christian Freedom and Liberation*, 66–68.

48. *Pastoral Constitution*, 47.

49. Address on Christian Unity in a Technological Age (Toronto, September 14, 1984) in *Origins* 14:16 (October 4, 1984): 248.

50. *On Human Work*, 3.

51. Ibid., 5, 6.

52. Ibid., 6, 10.

53. *Quadragesimo Anno*, 79. The meaning of this principle is not always accurately understood. For studies of its interpretation in Catholic teaching see: Calvez and Perrin in John F. Cronin, *Catholic Social Principles* (Milwaukee: Bruce, 1950), 328–342; Johannes Messner, "Freedom as a Principle of Social

Order: An Essay in the Substance of Subsidiary Function," *Modern Schoolman* 28 (1951): 97–110; Richard E. Mulcahy, "Subsidiarity," *New Catholic Encyclopedia* vol. 13 (New York: McGraw-Hill, 1966), 762; Franz H. Mueller, "The Principle of Subsidiarity in Christian Tradition," *American Catholic Sociological Review* 4 (October 1943): 144–157; Oswald von Nell-Breuning, "Zur Sozialreform, Erwagungen zum Subsidiaritatsprinzip," *Stimmen der Zeit* 157, Bd. 81 (1955–1956): 1–11; id., "Subsidiarity," *Sacramentum Mundi*, vol. 6 (New York: Herder and Herder, 1970), 6, 114–116; Arthur Fridolin Utz, *Formen und Grenzen des Subsidiaritatsprinzips* (Heidelberg: F. H. Kerle Verlag, 1956); id., "The Principle of Subsidiarity and Contemporary Natural Law," *Natural Law Forum* 3 (1958): 170–183; id., *Grundsatze der Sozialpolitik: Solidaritat und Subsidiaritat in der Alterversicherung* (Stuttgart: Sewald Verlag, 1969).

54. *Pastoral Constitution*, 31.

55. *On Human Work*, 16.

56. *Rerum Novarum*, 62; see also 9.

57. *On Human Work*, 19.

58. Ibid., 20.

59. Ibid.

60. Ibid.

61. Pope John Paul II, Address to Business Men and Economic Managers (Milan, May 22, 1983) in *L'Osservatore Romano*, weekly edition in English (June 20, 1983): 9:1.

62. Thomas Aquinas, *Summa Theologiae*, IIa, IIae, q. 66.

63. As Pope John Paul II has stated: "This gigantic and powerful instrument—the whole collection of the means of production that in a sense are considered synonymous with 'capital'—is the result of work and bears the signs of human labor." *On Human Work*, 12.

64. *Rerum Novarum*, 10, 15, 36.

65. *Mater et Magistra*, 109.

66. *Rerum Novarum*, 65, 66; *Mater et Magistra*, 115.

67. *On the Development of Peoples*, 23.

68. Pope John Paul II, Opening Address at the Puebla Conference, Puebla, Mexico (January 28, 1979), in John Eagleson and Philip Scharper, eds., *Puebla and Beyond*, 67.

69. *On Human Work*, 14.

70. Ibid., 17.

71. *Divini Redemptoris*, 49.

72. *Peace on Earth*, 60–62.

73. Vatican Council II, *Declaration on Religious Freedom (Dignitatis Humanae)*, 6. See John Courtney Murray, *The Problem of Religious Freedom*, Woodstock Papers, no. 7 (Westminster, Md.: Newman Press, 1965).

74. *Peace on Earth*, 63–64. *Quadragesimo Anno*, 80. In *Rerum Novarum* Pope Leo XIII set down the basic norm that determines when government

intervention is called for: "If, therefore, any injury has been done to or threatens either the common good or the interests of individual groups, which injury cannot in any other way be repaired or prevented, it is necessary for public authority to intervene." *Rerum Novarum*, 52. Pope John XXIII synthesized the Church's understanding of the function of governmental intervention this way: "The State, whose purpose is the realization of the common good in the temporal order, can by no means disregard the economic activity of its citizens. Indeed it should be present to promote in suitable manner the production of a sufficient supply of material goods, . . . contribute actively to the betterment of the living conditions of workers, . . . see to it that labor agreements are entered into according to the norms of justice and equity, and that in the environment of work the dignity of the human being is not violated either in body or spirit." *Mater et Magistra*, 20–21.

75. *Quadragesimo Anno*, 79.

76. Preface for the Feast of Christ the King, *The Sacramentary of the Roman Missal*.

77. *Octogesima Adveniens*, 26–35.

78. *Pastoral Constitution*, 39.

79. Ibid.

80. *Octogesima Adveniens*, 42.

Chapter 3

1. *Octogesima Adveniens*, 26, 41; and *On Human Work*, 7,13.

2. *Program of Social Reconstruction*, 33–40.

3. See *The Challenge of Peace: God's Promise and Our Response*, 9–10.

4. *On Human Work*, 3.

5. U.S. Department of Labor, Bureau of Labor Statistics, *The Employment Situation: April 1986* (May 1986).

6. Full Employment Action Council, *Employment in America: Illusory Recovery in a Decade of Decline* (Washington, D.C., February 1985), 19. Calculations based on data from the U.S. Department of Labor's Bureau of Labor Statistics.

7. U.S. Department of Labor, Bureau of Labor Statistics, *The Employment Situation: August 1985*; and U.S. Department of Labor, Employment and Training Administration, *Unemployment Insurance Claims*, Reference week of June 22, 1985.

8. *The Employment Situation: August 1985*.

9. Brenner, "Fetal, Infant and Maternal Mortality during Periods of Economic Instability," *International Journal of Health Services* (Summer 1973); P. H. Ellison, "Neurology of Hard Times," *Clinical Pediatrics* (March 1977); S. V. Kasl and S. Cobb, "Some Mental Health Consequences of Plant Closings and Job Loss," in L. Ferman and J. P. Gordus, eds., *Mental Health and the Economy* (Kalamazoo, Mich.: W. E. Upjohn Institute for Employment Research, 1979), 255–300; L. E. Kopolow and F. M. Ochberg, "Spinoff from

a Downward Swing," *Mental Health* 59 (Summer 1975); D. Shaw, "Unemployment Hurts More than the Pocketbook," *Today's Health* (March 1978).

10. Richard M. Cohn, *The Consequences of Unemployment on Evaluation of Self*, Doctoral dissertation, Department of Psychology (University of Michigan, 1977); John A. Garraty, *Unemployment in History: Economic Thought and Public Policy* (New York: Harper and Row, 1978); Harry Maurer, *Not Working: An Oral History of the Unemployed* (New York: Holt, Rinehart, and Winston, 1979).

11. M. Harvey Brenner, *Estimating the Social Cost of National Economic Policy* (U.S. Congress, Joint Economic Committee, 1976); see Brenner, *Mental Illness and the Economy* (Cambridge, Mass.: Harvard University Press, 1973).

12. Congressional Budget Office, *Economic and Budget Outlook: FY 1986–FY 1990* (Washington, D.C., February 1985), 75.

13. *Correlation of Unemployment and Federal Prison Population* (Washington, D.C.: U.S. Bureau of Prisons, March 1975); M. Yeager, "Unemployment and Imprisonment," *Journal of Criminal Law and Criminology* 70:4 (1979); Testimony of M. H. Brenner in *Unemployment and Crime* (U.S. Congress, House Hearings, 1977), 25.

14. Committee on the Evolution of the Work, AFL-CIO, *The Future of Work* (Washington, D.C.: AFL-CIO, 1983), 11.

15. Congressional Budget Office, *Defense Spending and the Economy* (Washington, D.C.: Government Printing Office, 1983). See also Michael Edelstein, *The Economic Impact of Military Spending* (New York: Council on Economic Priorities, 1977); and Robert De Grasse, Jr., *Military Expansion, Economic Decline* (New York: Council on Economic Priorities, 1983). See also U.S. Department of Labor, Bureau of Labor Statistics Report, "Structure of the U.S. Economy in 1980 and 1985" (Washington, D.C.: Government Printing Office, 1975); and Marion Anderson, *The Empty Pork Barrel* (Lansing, Mich.: Employment Research Associates, 1982).

16. U.S. Office of Management and Budget, *Historical Tables*, Budget of the United States Government Fiscal Year 1986 (Washington, D.C.: U.S. Government Printing Office, 1985), Table 10.2,10.2(3). See also, National Science Foundation Report, "Characteristics of Experienced Scientists and Engineers" (1978), Detailed Statistical Tables (Washington, D.C.: U.S. Government Printing Office, 1978).

17. "Statistical Supplement to International Comparison of Unemployment," Bureau of Labor Statistics (May 1984): 7. Unpublished.

18. Isabel V. Sawhill and Charles F. Stone state the prevailing view among economists this way: "High employment is usually defined as the rate of unemployment consistent with no additional inflation, a rate currently believed by many, but not all, economists to be in the neighborhood of 6 percent." "The Economy: The Key to Success," in John L. Palmer and Isabel V. Sawhill, eds., *The Reagan Record: An Assessment of America's Changing*

Domestic Priorities (Cambridge, Mass.: Bollinger, 1984), 72. See also Stanley Fischer and Rudiger Dornbusch, *Economics* (New York: McGraw-Hill, 1983), 731–743.

19. W. L. Birch, "Who Creates Jobs?" *The Public Interest* 65 (Fall 1981): 3–14.

20. Martin Neil Baily and Arthur M. Okun, eds., *The Battle Against Unemployment and Inflation*, third edition (New York: Norton, 1982); and Martin Neil Baily, "Labor Market Performance, Competition and Inflation," in Baily, ed., *Workers, Jobs and Inflation* (Washington, D.C.: The Brookings Institution, 1982). See also, Lawrence Klein, "Reducing Unemployment Without Inflation"; and James Tobin, "Unemployment, Poverty, and Economic Policy," testimony before the Subcommittee on Economic Stabilization, U.S. House of Representatives Committee on Banking, Finance and Urban Affairs (March 19, 1985), serial no. 99-5 (Washington, D.C.: U.S. Government Printing Office, 1985), 15–18, 31–33.

21. Tobin, "Unemployment, Poverty, and Economic Policy"; and Klein, "Reducing Unemployment Without Inflation."

22. Robert H. Haveman, "Toward Efficiency and Equity through Direct Job Creation," *Social Policy* 11:1 (May/June 1980): 48.

23. William H. McCarthy, *Reducing Urban Unemployment: What Works at the Local Level* (Washington, D.C.: National League of Cities, October 1985); William Schweke, "States that Take the Lead on a New Industrial Policy," in Betty G. Lall, ed., *Economic Dislocation and Job Loss* (New York: Cornell University, New York State School of Industrial and Labor Relations, 1985), 97–106; David Robinson, *Training and Jobs Programs in Action: Case Studies in Private Sector Initiatives for the Hard to Employ* (New York: Committee for Economic Development, 1978). See also ch. IV of this pastoral letter.

24. Rudy Oswald, "The Economy and Workers' Jobs, The Living Wage and a Voice," in John W. Houch and Oliver F. Williams, eds., *Catholic Social Teaching and the U.S. Economy: Working Papers for a Bishops' Pastoral* (Washington, D.C.: University Press of America, 1984), 77–89. On the subject of shortening the work week, Oswald points out that in the first 40 years of this century, the average work week fell from 60 hours to 40 hours. However, the standard work week has been unchanged now for almost 50 years.

25. U.S. Bureau of the Census, Current Population Reports, Series P-60, no. 149, *Money Income and Poverty Status of Families in the United States: 1984* (Washington, D.C.: U.S. Government Printing Office, 1985).

26. Massachusetts Department of Public Health, *Massachusetts Nutrition Survey* (Boston, Mass.: 1983).

27. There is considerable debate about the most suitable definition of poverty. Some argue that the government's official definition understates the number of the poor, and that a more adequate definition would indicate that as many as 50 million Americans are poor. For example, they note that the

poverty line has declined sharply as a percent of median family income—from 48% in 1959 to 35% in 1983. Others argue that the official indicators should be reduced by the amount of in-kind benefits received by the poor such as food stamps. By some calculations that would reduce the number counted as poor to about 12 million. We conclude that for present purposes the official government definition provides a suitable middle ground. That definition is based on a calculation that multiplies the cost of USDA's lowest cost food plan times three. The definition is adjusted for inflation each year.

Among other reasons for using the official definition is that it allows one to compare poverty figures over time. For additional readings on this topic see: L. Rainwater, *What Money Buys: Inequality and the Social Meanings of Income* (New York: Basic Books, 1975); id., *Persistent and Transitory Poverty: A New Look* (Cambridge, Mass.: Joint Center for Urban Studies, 1980); M. Orshansky, "How Poverty is Measured," *Monthly Labor Review* 92 (1969): 37–41; M. Anderson, *Welfare* (Stanford, Calif.: Hoover Institution Press, 1978); and Michael Harrington, *The New American Poverty* (New York: Holt, Rinehart, and Winston, 1984), 81–82.

28. Of those in poverty, 3 million work year-round and are still poor. Of the 22.2 million poor who are 15 years or over, more than 9 million work sometime during the year. Since 1979, the largest increases of poverty in absolute terms have been among those who work and are still poor. U.S. Bureau of the Census, *Money, Income and Poverty*.

29. U.S. Bureau of the Census, Current Population Reports, series P-60, no. 149,19. Blacks make up about 12% of the entire population but 62% of the long-term poor. Only 19% of the overall population live in families headed by women, but they make up 61% of the long-term poor. Twenty-eight percent of the nation's total population reside in nonmetropolitan areas, but 34% of the nation's poor live in these areas.

30. G. J. Duncan et al., *Years of Poverty, Years of Plenty: The Changing Economic Fortunes of American Workers and Their Families* (Ann Arbor, Mich.: Institute for Social Research, The University of Michigan, 1984). This book is based on the Panel Study of Income Dynamics, a survey of 5,000 American families conducted annually by the Survey Research Center of the University of Michigan. See G. J. Duncan and J. N. Morgan, *Five Thousand American Families—Patterns of Economic Progress*, vol. III (Ann Arbor: University of Michigan, 1975).

31. Congressional Research Service and Congressional Budget Office, *Children in Poverty* (Washington, D.C., May 22, 1985), 57. This recent study also indicates that children are now the largest age group in poverty. We are the first industrialized nation in the world in which children are the poorest age group. See Daniel Patrick Moynihan, *Family and Nation* (New York: Harcourt, Brace, Jovanovich, 1986), 112.

32. Children's Defense Fund, *American Children in Poverty* (Washington, D.C., 1984).

33. This trend has been commonly referred to as the "feminization of poverty." This term was coined by Dr. Diana Pierce in the *1980 Report to the President* of the National Advisory Council on Economic Opportunity to describe the dramatic increase in the proportion of the poor living in female-headed households.

34. U.S. Bureau of the Census, Technical Paper 55, *Estimates of Poverty Including the Value of Non-Cash Benefits: 1984* (Washington, D.C., August 1985), 5, 23.

35. Barbara Raskin and Heidi Hartmann, *Women's Work, Men's Work, Sex Segregation on the Job*, National Academy of Sciences (Washington, D.C.: National Academy Press, 1986), pp. 10–126.

36. U.S. Bureau of the Census, series P-23, no. 124, *Special Study Child Support and Alimony: 1981 Current Population Report* (Washington, D.C., 1981).

37. U.S. House of Representatives Subcommittee on Oversight and Public Assistance and Unemployment Compensation, Committee on Ways and Means, *Background Material on Poverty* (Washington, D.C., October, 1983). See also Committee on Ways and Means, U.S. House of Representatives, *Children in Poverty*, 3.

38. The National Urban League, *The Status of Black America 1984* (New York, January 1984).

39. Ibid.

40. NCCB, *Brothers and Sisters to Us*, Pastoral Letter on Racism in Our Day (Washington, D.C.: USCC, 1979).

41. Federal Reserve Board, "Survey of Consumer Finances, 1983: A Second Report," reprint from the *Federal Reserve Bulletin* (Washington, D.C., December 1984), 857–868. This survey defines net worth as the difference between gross assets and gross liabilities. The survey's estimates include all financial assets, equity in homes and other real property, as well as all financial liabilities such as consumer credit and other debts.

42. Ibid., 863–864.

43. U.S. Bureau of the Census, series P-60, no. 149, 11.

44. Income distribution figures give only a static picture of income shares. They do not reflect the significant movement of families into and out of different income categories over an extended period of time. See *Years of Poverty, Years of Plenty*, 13. It should also be noted that these figures reflect pre-tax incomes. However, since the national tax structure is proportional for a large segment of the population, it does not have a significant impact on the distribution of income. See Joseph Pechman, *Who Paid Taxes, 1966–85?* (Washington, D.C.: The Brookings Institution, 1985), 51.

45. Lars Osberg, *Economic Inequality in the United States* (New York: M. E. Sharpe, Inc., 1984), 24–28.

46. U.S. Bureau of the Census, series P-60, no. 149,11.

47. "Poverty in the United States: Where Do We Stand Now?" *Focus* (University of Wisconsin: Institute for Research on Poverty, Winter 1984). See also Danzinger and Gottschalk, "The Poverty of Losing Ground," *Challenge* 28:2 (May/June 1985). As these studies indicate, the slowing of the economy after 1969 tended to push more people into poverty, a trend that was offset to a great extent by the broadening of federal benefit programs. Likewise, the cutbacks in federal programs for the poor in recent years have contributed to the increase in poverty. For other analyses of the causes and cures of poverty see Charles Murray, *Losing Ground: American Social Policy 1950–1980* (New York: Basic Books, Inc., 1984); Ben J. Wattenberg, *The Good News Is the Bad News Is Wrong* (New York: Simon and Schuster, 1984); and Michael Harrington, *The New American Poverty* (New York: Holt, Rinehart, and Winston, 1984).

48. *Family and Nation*, 111–113.

49. Committee on Ways and Means, *Children In Poverty*. Calculation based on Tables 6-1 and 6-2, 180–181; and estimates of social insurance transfers on 221–222.

50. Paul Starr, *The Social Transformation of American Medicine* (New York: Basic Books, Inc., 1982), 373.

51. U.S. Bureau of the Census, series P-60, no. 149,11.

52. *Years of Poverty, Years of Plenty*, 13.

53. Center on Social Welfare Policy and Law, *Beyond the Myths: The Families Helped by the AFDC Program* (New York, 1985).

54. Ibid. This booklet cites Census Bureau data showing that in 1980 about 45% of those families who received AFDC also had earned income during that year, and that the average number of weeks worked during the year was 32.1.

55. Leonard Goodwin, *Causes and Cures of Welfare* (Lexington, Mass.: Lexington Books, 1983), ch. 1. See also Leonard Goodwin, "Can Workfare Work?" *Public Welfare* 39 (Fall 1981):19–25.

56. *Beyond the Myths*. With respect to error and fraud rates in AFDC, this booklet notes that erroneous payments in the AFDC program account for less than 10% of the benefits paid. No more than 8.1% of the families on AFDC received overpayments as a result of client error. In less than 4.5% of all AFDC cases nationally are questions of fraud raised. Moreover, in over 40% of these cases, a review of the facts indicated that there was insufficient evidence to support an allegation of fraud.

57. P. G. Peterson, "No More Free Lunch for the Middle Class," *New York Times Magazine* (January 17, 1982).

58. Interfaith Action for Economic Justice, *End Results: The Impact of Federal Policies Since 1980 on Low-Income Americans* (Washington, D.C.), 2.

59. "The Poverty of Losing Ground," 32–38.

60. The tax reform legislation of 1986 did a great deal to achieve this goal. It removed from the federal income tax rolls virtually all families below the official poverty line.

61. Jonathan Kozol, *Illiterate America* (New York: Anchor Press/ Doubleday, 1985).

62. *Peace on Earth*, 13.

63. These reports and studies include: E. Boyer, *High School: A Report on Secondary Education in America* (Princeton: Carnegie Foundation for the Advancement of Teaching, 1983); P. Cusick, *The American High School and the Egalitarian Ideal* (New York: Longman, 1983); J. L. Goodlad, *A Place Called School: Prospects for the Future* (New York: McGraw-Hill, 1983); The National Commission on Excellence in Education, *A Nation at Risk: The Imperative for Educational Reform* (Washington, D.C.: U.S. Department of Education, 1983); D. Ravitch, *The Troubled Crusade: American Education, 1945–1980* (New York: Basic Books, 1983); T. R. Sizer, *Horace's Compromise: The Dilemma of the American High School* (Boston: Houghton Mifflin, 1984); Task Force on Education for Economic Growth, *Action for Excellence: A Comprehensive Plan to Improve Our Nation's Schools* (Denver: Education Commission of the States, 1983); and The Twentieth Century Fund Task Force on Federal Elementary and Secondary Education Policy, *Making the Grade* (New York: Twentieth Century Fund, 1983). For a discussion of the issues raised in these reports see *Harvard Educational Review* 54:1 (February 1984):1–31.

64. The Vatican, *Charter of the Rights of the Family* (Washington, D.C.: USCC, 1983). See also *On Human Work*, 19; *Familiaris Consortio*, 23, 81; and "Christian Solidarity Leads to Action," in Address to Austrian Workers (Vienna, September 1983) in *Origins* 13:16 (September 29, 1983): 275.

65. H. R. Rodgers, Jr., *The Cost of Human Neglect: America's Welfare* (Armonk, N.Y.: M. E. Sharpe, Inc., 1982); C. T. Waxman, *The Stigma of Poverty*, second edition (New York: Pergamon Press, 1983), especially ch. 5; and S. A. Levitan and C. M. Johnson, *Beyond the Safety Net: Reviving the Promise of Opportunity in America* (Cambridge, Mass.: Ballinger, 1984).

66. Congressional Research Service, *Children in Poverty*.

67. U.S. House of Representatives Committee on Ways and Means, *Background Materials and Data on Programs Within the Jurisdiction of the Committee on Ways and Means* (Washington, D.C., February 22, 1985), 345–346.

68. Ibid., 347–348.

69. In 1982, similar recommendations were made by eight former Secretaries of Health, Education, and Welfare (now Health and Human Services). In a report called "Welfare Policy in the United States," they suggested a number of ways in which national minimal standards might be set and strongly urged the establishment of a floor for all states and territories.

70. Committee on Ways and Means, *Background Materials and Data on Programs*.

71. France adopted a "family" or "children's" allowance in 1932, followed by Italy in 1936, The Netherlands in 1939, the United Kingdom in

1945, and Sweden in 1947. Arnold Heidenheimer, Hugh Heclo, and Carolyn Teich Adams, *Comparative Public Policy: The Politics of Social Choice in Europe and America* (New York: St. Martin's Press, 1975), 189, 199. See also Robert Kuttner, *The Economic Illusion* (Boston: Houghton Mifflin Co., 1984), 243–246; and Joseph Piccione, *Help for Families on the Front Lines: The Theory and Practice of Family Allowances* (Washington, D.C.: The Free Congress Research and Education Foundation, 1983).

72. Milton Friedman, *Capitalism and Freedom* (University of Chicago Press, 1962), 190–195.

73. *The Current Financial Condition of Farmers and Farm Lenders*, Ag. Info. Bulletin no. 490 (Washington, D.C.: U.S. Department of Agriculture Economic Research Service, March 1985), viii–x.

74. Data on farms and farm population are drawn from *Agricultural Statistics*, annual reports of the U.S. Department of Agriculture, Washington, D.C.

75. Irma T. Elo and Calvin L. Beale, *Rural Development, Poverty, and Natural Resources* (Washington, D.C.: National Center for Food and Agricultural Policy, Resources for the Future, 1985).

76. *National Food Review*, USDA, no. 29 (Winter/Spring 1985). In 1984 Americans were spending 15.1% of their disposable income on food. This is an average figure. Many low-income people spent a good deal more and others much less.

77. Luther Tweeten, *Causes and Consequences of Structural Change in the Farming Industry* (Washington, D.C.: National Planning Association, 1984), 7.

78. *Economic Indicators of the Farm Sector: Income and Balance Sheet Statistics, 1983*, ECIFS 3-3 (Washington, D.C.: U.S. Department of Agriculture Economic Research Service, September 1984).

79. Marion Clawson, *Ownership Patterns of Natural Resources in America: Implications for Distribution of Wealth and Income* (Washington, D.C.: Resources for the Future, Summer 1983).

80. *Causes and Consequences*, 7; and *A Time to Choose: Summary Report on the Structure of Agriculture* (Washington, D.C.: U.S. Department of Agriculture, January 1981).

81. The nature of this transformation and its implications have been addressed previously by the USCC Committee on Social Development and World Peace in a February 1979 statement *The Family Farm* and again in May 1980 by the bishops of the Midwest in a joint pastoral letter *Strangers and Guests: Toward Community in the Heartland.*

82. *Soil Conservation in America: What Do We Have To Lose?* (Washington, D.C.: American Farmland Trust, 1984); E. Philip LeVeen, "Domestic Food Security and Increasing Competition for Water," in Lawrence Busch and William B. Lacey, eds., *Food Security in the United States* (Boulder, Colo.: Westview Press, 1984), 52. See also *America's Soil and Water: Conditions*

and Trends (Washington, D.C.: U.S. Department of Agriculture Soil Conservation Service, 1981).

83. *1982 Census of Agriculture.*

84. U.S. Commission on Civil Rights, *The Decline of Black Farming in America* (Washington, D.C.: U.S. Commission on Civil Rights, February 1982), esp. 65–69 regarding their property.

85. Ibid., 8.

86. U.S. Department of Labor, *Hearings Concerning Proposed Full Sanitation Standards*, document no. H-308 (Washington, D.C., 1984).

87. Ch. II, para. 112.

88. *A Time to Choose*, 148.

89. Luther Tweeten, "The Economics of Small Farms," *Science* 219 (March 4, 1983): 1041.

90. U.S. Department of Agriculture, *History of Agricultural Price-Support and Adjustment Programs, 1933–1984*, Ag. Info. Bulletin no. 485 (Washington, D.C.: U.S. Department of Agriculture Economic Research Service, December 1984).

91. *The Distribution of Benefits from the 1982 Federal Crop Programs* (Washington, D.C.: U.S. Senate Committee on the Budget, November 1984).

92. "The Great Debate on Mandatory Production Controls" in *Farm Policy Perspectives: Setting the Stage for 1985 Agricultural Legislation* (Washington, D.C.: U.S. Senate Committee on Agriculture, Nutrition, and Forestry, April 1984).

93. *A Time to Choose*, 91.

94. Richard Dunford, *The Effects of Federal Income Tax Policy on U.S. Agriculture* (Washington, D.C.: Subcommittee on Agriculture and Transportation of the Joint Economic Committee of the Congress of the United States, December 21, 1984).

95. This proposal was put forward thirteen years ago in *Where Shall the People Live?* A Special Message of the United States Catholic Bishops (Washington, D.C.: USCC, 1972).

96. Thomas E. Miller, et al., *Economies of Size in U.S. Field Crop Farming* (Washington, D.C.: U.S. Department of Agriculture Economic Research Service, July 1981).

97. See ch. IV.

98. *Instruction on Certain Aspects of the Theology of Liberation*, I:6. See also *Peace on Earth*, 13–131; and *On Human Work*, 11.

99. Overseas Development Council, *U.S. Policy and the Third World: Agenda 1985–1986.*

100. Robert S. McNamara, *Address to the Board of Governors of the World Bank* (Washington, D.C.: World Bank, September 30, 1980).

101. U.N. Food and Agricultural Organization, *Dimensions of Need*, E 9 (Rome, 1982). The U.N. World Food Council uses this figure consistently, most recently at its 11th annual meeting in Paris.

102. Joseph Greenwald and Kenneth Flamm, *The Global Factory* (Washington, D.C.: The Brookings Institution, 1985); see also Ronald Muller and Richard Barnet, *Global Reach* (New York: Simon and Schuster, 1974); Raymond Vernon, *The Economic and Political Consequences of Multinational Enterprise* (Cambridge, Mass.: Harvard University Press, 1972); the United Nations Center on Transnational Corporations maintains current data on these institutions.

103. *Peace on Earth*, 56–63.

104. *On the Development of Peoples*, 44, 58–63; quoted also by Pope John Paul II, *Origins* 14:16 (October 4, 1984): 247.

105. President's Commission on Security and Economic Assistance (Carlucci Commission), *A Report to the Secretary of State* (Washington, D.C., November 1983).

106. For example: After a dozen years of negotiations, during which nearly all of the issues were resolved to U.S. satisfaction, the United States refused to sign the Law of the Seas treaty; only the United States failed to support the U.N. infant formula resolution; the United States has not ratified the two U.N. Covenants on Human Rights, etc.

107. U.S. Agency for International Development, *Congressional Presentation, Fiscal Year 1986, Main Volume* (Washington, D.C., 1985).

108. The clients of the International Development Association, the "soft loan window" of the World Bank, are the poorest countries. The United States insisted upon—and obtained—a 25% reduction in IDA's current (seventh) replenishment. Taking inflation into account, this meant a 40% drop in real terms at exactly the moment when developing-country debt levels are punishingly high and the prices of their export commodities are almost at rock bottom.

109. See ch. II.

110. The GATT—third of the Bretton Woods "institutions" (with the World Bank and the IMF)—is in fact a treaty, monitored and supported by a secretariat located in Geneva, Switzerland. Periodic "rounds" of negotiations among its several score members, North and South, modify and extend its provisions and regulations.

111. Debt figures have been compiled from data published by the World Bank, the IMF, and the Bank for International Settlements.

112. The United Nations Conference on Trade and Development (UNCTAD) originated in Geneva in 1964 at a meeting convened by the U.N. to discuss trade, development, and related problems of low-income countries. It established a quadrennial meeting and created permanent machinery in the U.N. to deal with these problems. A Trade and Development Board (TDB), with standing committees, meets every two years; and there is a small secretariat to staff it. UNCTAD is viewed as representing the developing countries' continuing effort to have a larger voice in international decisions affecting trade and development and to secure more favorable terms of trade.

113. *U.S. Policy and the Third World*, Table B-5.

114. When the IMF helps a country adjust to balance-of-payments problems (e.g., by assisting in the rescheduling of its external debt), it negotiates certain conditions with the debtor country in order to improve its immediate financial position. In general, these require the borrowing country to earn and save more. The adjustments, usually referred to as "conditionality," tend to fall most heavily on the poor through reduction of government spending on consumer subsidies and public services, and often of wages.

115. North American Coalition for Human Rights in Korea, *Testimony before the U.S. Trade Representative*, June 24, 1985.

116. E. F. Schumacher, *Small Is Beautiful: Economics As If People Mattered* (New York: Harper and Row, 1973).

117. *On the Development of Peoples*, 44, 58–63.

118. Ibid., 37; *Pastoral Constitution*, 87.

119. *On the Development of Peoples*, 37.

120. Ruth Leger Sivard, *World Military and Social Expenditures 1983* (Washington, D.C.: World Priorities, 1983), 23.

121. Pontifical Commission Justitia et Pax, *The Social Teaching of John Paul II*, 6 (October 6, 1979).

122. *On the Development of Peoples*, 44, 58–63.

123. See "Testimony on U.S. Arms Control Policy," *Origins* 14:10 (August 9, 1984): 154ff.

Chapter 4

1. *Octogesima Adveniens*, 24.

2. For different analyses along these lines with quite different starting points see Martin Carnoy, Derek Shearer, and Russell Rumberger, *A New Social Contract* (New York: Harper and Row, 1983); Amatai Etzioni, *An Immodest Agenda: Reconstructing America before the Twenty-First Century* (New York: McGraw-Hill, 1983); Charles F. Lindblom, *Politics and Markets* (New York: Basic Books, 1977), esp. 346–48; George C. Lodge, *The New American Ideology* (New York: Alfred A. Knopf, 1975); Douglas Sturm, "Corporations, Constitutions, and Covenants," *Journal of the American Academy of Religion*, 41(1973): 331–55; Lester Thurow, *The Zero-Sum Society* (New York: Basic Books, 1980), esp. ch. 1; Roberto Mangabeira Unger, *Knowledge and Politics* (New York: Free Press, 1975); George F. Will, *Statecraft as Soulcraft: What Government Does* (New York: Simon and Schuster, 1982), esp. ch. 6.

3. *Pastoral Constitution*, 68. *See Mater et Magistra*, 75–77.

4. Charles W. Powers provided a helpful discussion of these matters in a paper presented at a conference on the first draft of this pastoral letter sponsored by the Harvard University Divinity School and the Institute for Policy Studies, Cambridge, Massachusetts, March 29–31, 1985.

5. See John Paul II, "The Role of Business in a Changing Workplace," 3, *Origins* 15 (February 6, 1986): 567.

6. *Rerum Novarum*, 28. For an analysis of the relevant papal teachings on institutions of collaboration and partnership, see John Cronin, *Catholic Social Principles: The Social Teaching of the Catholic Church Applied to American Economic Life* (Milwaukee: Bruce, 1950), ch. VII; Oswald von Nell-Breuning, *Reorganization of Social Economy: The Social Encyclical Developed and Explained*, trans. Bernard W. Dempsey (Milwaukee: Bruce, 1936), chs. X–XII; Jean-Yves Calvez and Jacques Perrin, *The Church and Social Justice*, trans. J. R. Kirwan (Chicago: Regnery, 1961), ch. XIX.

7. Michael Conte, Arnold S. Tannenbaum, and Donna McCulloch, *Employee Ownership*, Research Report Series, Institute for Social Research (Ann Arbor, Mich.: University of Michigan, 1981); Robert A. Dahl, *A Preface to Economic Democracy* (Berkeley: University of California Press, 1985); Harvard Business School, "The Mondragon Cooperative Movement," case study prepared by David P. Ellerman (Cambridge, Mass.: Harvard Business School, n.d.); Robert Jackall and Henry M. Levin, eds., *Worker Cooperatives in America* (Berkeley: University of California Press, 1984); Derek Jones and Jan Svejnar, eds., *Participatory and Self-Managed Firms: Evaluating Economic Performance* (Lexington, Mass.: D. C. Heath, 1982); Irving H. Siegel and Edgar Weinberg, *Labor-Management Cooperation: The American Experience* (Kalamazoo, Mich.: W. E. Upjohn Institute for Employment Research, 1982); Stuart M. Speiser, "Broadened Capital Ownership—The Solution to Major Domestic and International Problems," *Journal of Post Keynesian Economics VIII* (1985): 426–434; Jaroslav Vanek, ed., *Self-Management: Economic Liberation of Man* (London: Penguin, 1975); Martin L. Weitzman, *The Share Economy* (Cambridge, Mass.: Harvard University Press, 1984).

8. Program of Social Reconstruction in *Justice in the Marketplace*, 381.

9. *Mater et Magistra*, 32, 77, 85–103; *On Human Work*, 14.

10. For examples of worker-owned and operated enterprises supported by the Campaign for Human Development's revolving loan fund see CHD's *Annual Report* (Washington, D.C.: USCC).

11. *Quadragesimo Anno* states the basic norm on which this conclusion is based: "It is wholly false to ascribe to property alone or to labor alone whatever has been obtained through the combined effort of both, and it is wholly unjust for either, denying the efficacy of the other, to arrogate to itself whatever has been produced" (53).

12. *On Human Work*, 12.

13. Ibid., 20. This point was well made by John Cronin twenty-five years ago: "Even if most injustice and exploitation were removed, unions would still have a legitimate place. They are the normal voice of labor, necessary to organize social life for the common good. There is positive need for such organization today, quite independently of any social evils which may prevail. Order and harmony do not happen; they are the fruit of conscious and organized effort. While we may hope that the abuses which occasioned the rise of unions may disappear, it does not thereby follow that unions will have lost

their function. On the contrary, they will be freed from unpleasant, even though temporarily necessary, tasks and able to devote all their time and efforts to a better organization of social life." *Catholic Social Principles*, 418. See also AFL-CIO Committee on the Evolution of Work, *The Future of Work* (Washington, D.C.: AFL-CIO, 1983).

14. For a classic discussion of the relative power of managers and shareholders see A. A. Berle and Gardiner C. Means, *The Modern Corporation and Private Property* (New York: Macmillan, 1932).

15. Peter L. Berger and Richard John Neuhaus, *To Empower People: The Role of Mediating Structures in Public Policy* (Washington, D.C.: American Enterprise Institute, 1977).

16. United States Small Business Administration, *1978 Annual Report* (Washington, D.C.: Government Printing Office, 1979).

17. For recent discussion from a variety of perspectives see: Robert Friedman and William Schweke, eds., *Expanding the Opportunity to Produce: Revitalizing the American Economy through New Enterprise Development: A Policy Reader* (Washington, D.C.: Corporation for New Enterprise Development, 1981); Jack A. Meyer, ed., *Meeting Human Needs: Toward a New Public Philosophy* (Washington, D.C.: American Enterprise Institute, 1982); Committee for Economic Development, *Jobs for the Hard-to-Employ: New Directions for a Public-Private Partnership* (New York: Committee for Economic Development, 1978); Gar Alperovitz and Jeff Faux, *Rebuilding America: A Blueprint for the New Economy* (New York: Pantheon Books, 1984).

18. Christopher Mackin, *Strategies for Local Ownership and Control: A Policy Analysis* (Somerville, Mass.: Industrial Cooperative Association, 1983).

19. *Mater et Magistra*, 59, 62.

20. *On Human Work*, 18.

21. Ibid.

22. For examples and analysis of different meanings of economic planning see Naomi Caiden and Aaron Wildavsky, *Planning and Budgeting in Poor Countries* (New York: Wiley, 1974); Robert Dahl and Charles E. Lindblom, *Politics, Economics and Welfare: Planning and Politico-Economic Systems Resolved into Basic Social Processes* (Chicago: University of Chicago Press, 1976); Stephen S. Cohen, *Modern Capitalist Planning: The French Model* (Berkeley: University of California Press, 1977); Albert Waterston, *Development Planning: Lessons of Experience* (Baltimore: Johns Hopkins Press, 1965); *Rebuilding America*, chs. 14, 15.

23. For example, many students of recent policy point out that monetary policy on the one hand and fiscal policies governing taxation and government expenditures on the other have been at odds with each other, with larger public deficits and high interest rates as the outcome. See Alice M. Rivlin, ed., *Economic Choices 1984* (Washington, D.C.: The Brookings Institution, 1984), esp. ch. 2.

24. *The Challenge of Peace*, 270–271.

25. *On the Development of Peoples*, 3.

26. *Peace on Earth*, 134–135.

27. *The Challenge of Peace*, 268.

28. See Robert O. Keohane and Joseph S. Nye, Jr., "Two Cheers for Multilateralism," *Foreign Policy* 60 (Fall 1985):148–167.

Chapter 5

1. *Reconciliation and Penance*, 13.

2. *Justice in the World*, 6.

3. Medellin Documents: *Justice* (1968), 4.

4. *Dogmatic Constitution on the Church*, 1; *Pastoral Constitution*, 42, 45; *Constitution on the Liturgy*, 26; *Decree on the Church's Missionary Activity*, 5; *Liturgy and Social Justice*, ed. by Mark Searle (Collegeville, Minn.: Liturgical Press, 1980); National Conference of Catholic Bishops, *The Church at Prayer* (Washington, D.C.: USCC, 1983).

5. *Dogmatic Constitution on the Church*, 36.

6. *Justice in the World*, 41.

7. National Conference of Catholic Bishops, *To Teach as Jesus Did*, A Pastoral Message on Education (Washington, D.C.: USCC, 1972), 7.

8. Cf. Vatican Council II, *Declaration on Christian Education*, 3, 6. See also, *Charter of the Rights of the Family*, 5b; *Instruction on Christian Freedom and Liberation*, 94.

9. Pope John Paul II, *On the Family* (Washington, D.C.: USCC, 1981), 6. See also Robert N. Bellah, Richard Madsen, William M. Sullivan, Ann Swidler, Steven M. Tipton, *Habits of the Heart: Individualism and Commitment in American Life* (Berkeley: University of California Press, 1985); *The Family Today and Tomorrow: The Church Addresses Her Future* (Boston, Mass.: The Pope John Center, 1985).

10. *Justice in the World*, 40.

11. *Dogmatic Constitution on the Church*, 8.

12. National Conference of Catholic Bishops, *Health and Health Care* (Washington, D.C.: USCC, 1981), 50.

13. See ch. 4 of this pastoral letter.

Index